ENVIRONMENTAL ETHICS

ENVIRONMENTAL ETHICS

What Really Matters
What Really Works

David Schmidtz
Elizabeth Willott

New York   Oxford
OXFORD UNIVERSITY PRESS
2002

Oxford University Press

Oxford   New York
Athens   Auckland   Bangkok   Bogotá   Buenos Aires   Cape Town
Chennai   Dar es Salaam   Delhi   Florence   Hong Kong   Istanbul   Karachi
Kolkata   Kuala Lumpur   Madrid   Melbourne   Mexico City   Mumbai   Nairobi
Paris   São Paulo   Singapore   Taipei   Tokyo   Toronto   Warsaw

and associated companies in
Berlin   Ibadan

Published by Oxford University Press, Inc.
198 Madison Avenue, New York, New York 10016
http://www.oup-usa.org

Oxford is a registered trademark of Oxford University Press

Library of Congress Cataloging-in-Publication Data
Environmental ethics: what really matters, what really works / [edited by] David
Schmidtz, Elizabeth Willott.
     p. cm.
   ISBN-13 978-0-19-513909-9
     1. Environmental ethics.   I. Schmidtz, David. II. Willott, Elizabeth.
GE42.E585   2002
179′.1—dc21   2001021210

9 8 7 6 5

Printed in the United States of America
on acid-free paper

CONTENTS

II WHAT REALLY WORKS? ESSAYS ON HUMAN ECOLOGY

9 Human Population   265

10 What It Takes To Preserve Wilderness   284

11 Sustainable Use and Institutional Structure   330

12 Poverty as an Environmental Problem   373

Acknowledgments

We want to thank Elissa Morris at Oxford University Press for approaching us with the idea for this project. Elissa originally proposed that we write a text. As teachers, though, we use collections of articles rather than single-author texts, so we offered to produce the sort of collection that we use in our courses. Elissa countered that she was looking not simply for another collection but for something reflecting our own outlooks. We accepted the challenge, agreeing to incorporate quite a bit of our own material, and the result is what you have before you. For advice, assistance, and encouragement on various parts of this project, we wish to thank anonymous readers for Oxford University Press, and also Audie Alcorn, Jennifer Baker, Al Bergeson, Andrew Cohen, Liam Dalzell, Peter Danielson, Kirk Emerson, Joel Feinberg, Walter Grinder, Kristen Hessler, Robert Hood, Larry James, Avery Kolers, Mark LeBar, Andrew Light, Chris Maloney, Robert Miller, Cara Nine, Alastair Norcross, Tom Regan, Don Scherer, Bob Varady, Gary Varner, Clark Wolf, and Matt Zwolinski.

We thank David Benatar, Darrel Moellendorf, Michael Pendlebury, and above all, Kobus Krüger, for showing us Africa.

Finally, we want to thank all of the students who have taken our environmental courses over the years, for honestly wanting to know what matters, and what works.

Introduction
Why Environmental Ethics?

Elizabeth Willott and David Schmidtz

It is dawn. We have come to the mountains of eastern Arizona, seeking inspiration. We left our computer at the trailhead, in the van, having no need for such fancy technology on our hike. We do need our state-of-the-art boots, though, for the hike up the west side of Mount Baldy is seven miles; the hike down the east side is another twelve. We thank Mount Baldy for this glorious morning, but in fairness we also thank the van and all the other technological developments that make it possible for us to be here.

We live in a world of problems, but environmental ethics reminds us not only that these mountains need to be saved and that they can be, but that they are *worth* saving. Environmental ethics teaches us how to enjoy the world, not just how to fix it.

Not that we do not want to fix the world, of course, but fixing is a tricky, double-edged idea. On one hand, to "fix" is to repair or improve, and there is nothing wrong with that, in principle. On the other hand, to "fix" is to stabilize or set in place so as to prevent further change, as when we describe a mortgage rate or a lecture schedule as fixed. Therein lies a problem, for in that second sense, ecologies are not fixed, and cannot be. It is of the essence of an ecosystem that it is a thing in flux.

Of course, human nature being what it is, flux makes people nervous. Rightly or wrongly, we feel more secure when things are "fixed." So we want to "fix" our ecosystem, but we cannot. Not without turning it into something other than the ongoing process it is. Ecosystems evolve. Human society evolves. Something decays and is lost in the process. Always. And we, like generations before us and generations to come, will lament its passing. There probably has never been a generation that did not view its world as going to hell in one way or another. We are only human. Still, we are here. We are now. Shouldn't we enjoy it?

Or perhaps *enjoy* is too mild a word to describe what it is like to be among wind-hewn rocks, hearing the call of a crow, wondering for how many eons that call has echoed from that perch. Or stopping to count the growth rings in a fallen ponderosa pine and giving up at 150. Or stopping just short of Baldy's summit because it is marked as sacred ground by the Apache, wondering where the Apache were in 1492, wondering whether they already regarded this land as sacred when Columbus was still looking for a shorter route to India.

ENVIRONMENTAL ETHICS AS A BRANCH OF PHILOSOPHY

Throughout this book, we will avoid jargon as much as we can. There are, however, some basic terms you will need to know. The discipline of philosophy can be divided into fields. Typically it is divided into three. In the simplest terms: *metaphysics* is the study of the fundamental nature of reality; *epistemology* is the study of knowledge, and how we acquire it; *ethics* is the study of goodness and rightness—our reasons for acting in one way rather than another, or our reasons for trying to be one kind of person rather than another.

The study of ethics generally is guided by certain presuppositions. Among the main presuppositions are these. First, we are more or less rational beings, capable of understanding the world. Second, we can act on the basis of what we understand. Third, our actions can serve a purpose—we can make a difference.

Ethics itself can be divided into subfields. *Normative* ethics is the study of rightness in action, and goodness in states of affairs. *Descriptive* ethics is the study of opinions or beliefs about normative ethics. (Descriptive ethics often is considered to be a province of anthropology, not philosophy. The point of separating normative from descriptive ethics is to emphasize that seeking the truth about ethics is not the same as cataloguing opinions about ethics.) The third subfield, *metaethics,* studies the meanings and presuppositions of moral theories and moral language and asks what it would be like to justify a moral theory. In effect, then, where normative ethics is the enterprise of formulating theories about what is right and good, metaethics steps back to study normative ethics itself.

Within the subfield of normative ethics, we seek to formulate theories of the good, sometimes called theories of value. We also seek to formulate a theory of right action. When we try to apply the results of normative ethics—whether theory of the good or the right—we move into the realm of applied ethics. The primary areas within applied ethics currently are medical ethics, business ethics, and environmental ethics.[1] Lumping the three together is slightly misleading, though. Business and medicine are professions, typically studied in separate professional schools rather than in colleges of art and science; thus business ethics and medical ethics currently are forms of professional ethics in large measure (although this may change). In contrast, the environment is not a profession. There are no environmental schools in the way there are medical and business schools, and environmental ethics is not the study of ethical issues specific to any particular occupation. Environmental ethics is a way of applying normative ethics to a particular set of practical issues, but it also is a new way of doing normative ethics in general. Environmental ethics asks what we owe each other, and to ourselves, given our ecological context. It also asks what, if anything, we owe to nonhuman animals, to plants, to fragile geological wonders, to species, and even to ecosystems themselves. It asks what kind of life we should aspire to live, and what kind of world we should aspire to live in. It is the study of the value of human life, and the value of life in general. In short, part of the beauty of environmental ethics is that it not only *applies* normative ethics, it *encompasses* normative ethics.

One way to do philosophy is from the armchair, without facts. Would it be right to convert all the golf courses into marshland? To shut down all the factory farms? Is it wrong for Monsanto to develop and sell genetically engineered cotton seeds? Wrong for farmers to buy and plant genetically engineered seed, and eventually sell the harvest? Wrong for our colleagues in the agricultural sciences to advise cotton farmers on how to use the new seed while minimizing harmful environmental consequences? Wrong for you to support this whole system when you buy clothing made of genetically engineered cotton?

We could try to answer these questions by consulting our abstract theories, backed by intuitions, fears, and uninformed assumptions. When we do environmental ethics, though, it is hard to avoid the thought that doing environmental ethics without gathering pertinent facts is unethical. Accordingly, while this book necessarily is about abstract theory, it also explores the efforts of various authors to learn how the real world actually works. We hope you enjoy both parts, and we thank you for taking a look. In the following pages, we ask a lot of questions. Indeed, we have more questions than answers. (This is partly for pedagogical reasons, but also because the questions are too difficult to settle here, so far as we can see.) We hope you find our questions interesting, and we hope you enjoy the challenge of coming to your own conclusions.

THE LAST MAN

At a conference in 1973, Richard Sylvan (then known as Richard Routley) proposed a science fiction thought experiment that helped to launch environmental ethics as a branch of academic philosophy.[2] (This is the only science fiction example you will encounter in this book. In environmental ethics, there is no need to make up strange cases, for environmental issues permeate everyday life.) Routley's thought experiment came to be known as the "Last Man" argument.[3]

The thought experiment presents you with a situation something like this: You are the last human being. You shall soon die. When you are gone, the only life remaining will be plants, microbes, and invertebrates. For some reason, the following thought runs through your head: Before I die, it sure would be nice to destroy the last remaining redwood. Just for fun.

Sylvan's audience was left to ponder. What, if anything, would be *wrong* with destroying that redwood? Destroying it won't hurt anyone, so what's the problem? Environmental philosophers have been trying to answer that question ever since, and you will hear the question echoing through this book.[4]

How would you answer it?

INSTRUMENTAL AND INTRINSIC VALUE

Perhaps the most fundamental question in environmental ethics is: What should be our attitude toward nature? No environmental ethicist says we should regard nature as merely a repository of natural resources, but we are divided over what *kind* of respect nature commands, or what kind of value we should regard nature as having. We will outline major divisions, but first, a word of caution about definitions. As in almost any field, writers use terms in different ways, so please do not assume every author you read will use these terms in exactly the same way. When we define a term, we are trying to indicate, roughly speaking, how most people use the term. Also, we will keep the discussion as simple as we can, setting aside all but the most central issues. Be forewarned, though, that beneath the (relatively!) simple surface lies a nasty tangle of extremely difficult philosophical problems that many smart people have spent years trying to untangle, with only partial success.[5]

We can begin by noting that people value things like redwoods in more than one way. Clearly, many objects are useful as means to further ends. We consider them valuable as tools or instruments rather than as intrinsically valuable in their own right. In environmental ethics, we refer to this sort of usefulness as an object's *instrumental* value.

In contrast, an object has *noninstrumental* value when it has a value apart from any usefulness it may have as a means to further ends. If an object is good quite apart from what it is good for, it has noninstrumental value. The difference is a bit like the difference between an excellent paintbrush and an excellent painting. Compared to the brush, the painting has a different kind of value, not just a different amount. Likewise, even if we have no interest in that last redwood as a source of lumber, we might value it simply because it is the majestic living thing that it is. If we value the last redwood in that way, then we are seeing it as having a kind of goodness that is independent of what it is good *for*.[6] We are seeing it as more like the painting than like the paintbrush.

One of the main tasks in the field of environmental ethics is to be more precise about noninstrumental value, but achieving greater precision is not easy. People sometimes speak of an object's *intrinsic* value, and often they mean roughly what we have called noninstrumental value. For example, an art dealer might assess two paintings, and might say that while the first painting has a higher resale value under current market conditions, the second is actually the better painting when judged on its intrinsic merits. The painting has a kind of value simply because of its intrinsic beauty, independent of any usefulness it may have when used to raise money. In different words, we attach instrumental value to an object when we value what we can use it for, or exchange it for; we attach intrinsic value when we value what the object is, period.

Does that last redwood have intrinsic value?

VALUED OBJECTS AND VALUING SUBJECTS

One important conceptual issue, then, concerns the difference between instrumental and intrinsic value. One source of confusion here is that we are tempted to think of "intrinsic" as a synonym for "really important." Likewise, we are tempted to speak of instrumental values as "merely" instrumental, as if instrumental values were necessarily small. Both of these assumptions are false. A souvenir postcard from the Grand Canyon can have a small intrinsic value while a kidney transplant can have a large instrumental value.[7] The systematic difference between intrinsic and instrumental is not a matter of one being bigger than the other. The real difference is more subtle, a matter of the type (rather than the amount) of respect the different values command.

A second key conceptual issue concerns the relation between valued objects and valuing subjects. Saying an object is valued presupposes that some subject is doing the valuing. All valuing, it seems, is a relation between valued object and valuing subject. Instrumental value is one kind of relation; intrinsic value is another. An object has instrumental value to me when it is useful to me. It has intrinsic value to me when I value it in its own right, independently of what it is good for. Both are values to me, although not in the same way.

After the last person is gone, there will be no valuing subjects left, therefore no one to whom the last redwood can be useful, and therefore no possibility of the redwood having *instrumental* value. Must we say the same about the redwood's *intrinsic* value, since no one is left who can value the last redwood for its own sake? When no one is left to value it, does that mean it will have no value?

IS VALUE SUBJECTIVE?

Before we can answer these questions, we need to mention a third conceptual issue regarding the difference between objective and subjective value. To say valuing is a relation between valuing subject and valued object is not to say value is purely subjective (that is, purely a matter of opinion or preference, as opposed to being the kind of judgment that can be correct or incorrect). For example, when I say vitamin C has instrumental value to me, my judgment can be correct or incorrect. It can be objectively true that vitamin C serves the purpose I think it serves, thus objectively true that vitamin C has that kind of value to me. I choose whether to care about my health, to some degree, but given that I do in fact care, my valuing vitamin C is grounded in reality in a way it would not be if my beliefs about vitamin C were inaccurate.[8]

The objectivity of intrinsic values is less obvious. On one hand, it is objectively true that redwoods have the properties that inspire me to think of them as intrinsically valuable. They are alive, they truly are as old and as huge as I think they are, and so on. On the other hand, reasonable people can remain unconvinced that a redwood's aesthetic (intrinsic) value is as objective as vitamin C's nutritional (instrumental) value.

We said all valuing seems to be a relation between valued object and valuing subject. Sometimes, when we value an object, we seem to be *creating* the relationship. (When I decide to start collecting stamps, stamps suddenly have a value to me that they did not have before my decision.) Other times, we seem to be recognizing a preexisting relationship rather than creating one. The preexisting relationship consists of the fact that, given our nature and given the object's nature, we have reason to value the object even if we do not know it. Thus, ascorbic acid had value to us even before we discovered that it is an essential vitamin (i.e., vitamin C). Given what ascorbic acid is, and given what we are—we are beings who want to remain healthy and who need ascorbic acid to remain healthy—it is an objective fact that we have reason to value ascorbic acid. (Note, though, that this objective fact is a fact about a relation between ascorbic acid and us. Nothing is implied concerning whether ascorbic acid has value apart from that relation.)

What about the last redwood? Is it like ascorbic acid? Is it an objective fact that we have reason to value redwoods? Insofar as we have reason to value redwoods, is our reason something we discover, or something we create?

DOES VALUE PRESUPPOSE A VALUER?

Now suppose, when the last person is gone, nothing will be left that needs ascorbic acid. Will it continue to be an objective fact that ascorbic acid has value? No. Ascorbic acid has value to us here and now, but in a world without animals that need it, there is nothing to whom it could have value.

Again, what about that last redwood? Does it make sense to say the last redwood would command respect? In a world without sentient beings, whose respect would it command? Are redwoods the sort of thing that have value to us here and now, but would not have value in a mindless world?

To this last question, some theorists would answer yes, and would add that we should not find this troubling. What matters is whether the last redwood commands the last person's respect, which is independent of whether the tree will have intrinsic value after the last person is gone. (Analogously, it matters that we need ascorbic acid here and now. It does not matter that ascorbic acid would have no value in a world without animals that need it.) Others will say something is missing from this picture: the fact that redwoods have value, period. They will insist that the world would be a better place with that last redwood in it, regardless of whether anyone is left to appreciate it. But why insist on this? Practically speaking, what difference does it make?

There is no easy way to settle this debate. The problem, in part, is that we use the word *value* in more than one way. Sometimes, we use the word as a verb. We say, "I value redwoods." In that sense, value clearly presupposes a valuer—objects are valued only if valued by a valuing subject. Other times, we use the word as a noun, and then the relation between value and valuer is less clear. When I say, "Redwoods have value," that may simply be another way of saying, "I value redwoods." Or, I may be saying something different, such as, "I have *reason* to value redwoods." When I say redwoods are intrinsically valuable, I seem to be saying the latter. When I say the mindless planet would be a better place with that last redwood in it, I am saying I would have reason (and so would you) to value the last redwood. I cannot be saying the last redwood would be valued by beings on *that* planet, because in the thought experiment valuing subjects no longer exist on that planet. For the same reason, I cannot mean anything on that planet has *reason* to value the last redwood: The thought experiment stipulates that subjects capable of having reasons no longer exist. Presumably, what I really mean is, valuing subjects such as you and me, here and now, have reason to value redwoods (even when they have no instrumental value), and therefore, in the world we are imagining, we *would* have reason to value the last redwood.

Where does that leave us? We are in deep and treacherous philosophical waters here, but the upshot is twofold. First, when I tell you the last redwood has intrinsic value, I am not saying you or I or anyone else actually is there to respect it. But second, I am saying that if we *were* there, it *would* be true that we ought to respect it. When the last person is gone, there will be no perspective in that world from which the last redwood would have value, but it remains true that the last redwood would have value from my perspective, here and now. So if you ask me whether the last redwood would have value, you are asking me here and now for my perspective on the last redwood's value, and that is what I am giving you when I answer, yes, it would have value.

Suppose the last person is a painter. The last person might reason as follows: My paint-brushes have value because they are useful. After I am gone, there will be no one to use them. Therefore, they will no longer be useful. Therefore, they will no longer have in-strumental value. My paintings, though, are different. My paintings have value because they are beautiful. After I am gone, they will still be beautiful. (They are beautiful to me, and after I am gone, they will continue to be the kind of thing I *would* find beautiful if I were still around.) Therefore, won't they still have value even after I am gone? To an-swer yes is to see the paintings as having intrinsic value.[9]

If this still seems too abstract, then think about everyday analogs of the same problem. If I tell my insurance agent I want my children to be financially secure when I die, the agent does not say, "You're confused. The fact is, when you're dead, you're dead. You will no longer be a sentient valuing creature. Therefore, you won't care. So why not spend the money on something you care about?" If my agent said that, I should reply, "No, you're the one who is confused. I am not saying that after I die, it will matter to me *then* what happens to my children. What I'm saying is, it matters to me now. I am imagining a world in which I no longer exist, so when I say I value my children's financial security in that world, I'm not saying I value it from a perspective that exists in that world. I'm saying I value it from my perspective here and now. Here and now, I see my children's security as having a value that will survive my death. In other words, my attitude toward my children is that their value does not depend on my attitude. From my perspective, here and now, they are worthy of my love and respect, and they will continue to be worthy even after I am gone."

In a way, then, valuing does presuppose a valuer. *Intrinsic* valuing, though, presup-poses a special *kind* of valuer, namely a kind of valuer who can see the valued object as having value, period—who can see the object as worthy of respect in and of itself, quite apart from any usefulness it may have in producing, promoting, or securing other values.

MORAL STANDING

The fundamental question is, as we said earlier: What should be our attitude toward na-ture? In particular, many theorists have pondered whether it is possible for nonhumans to have the sort of moral standing that humans have. As we understand the term, a being has *moral standing* just in case it has a right to be treated with respect. Things with moral standing are things to whom (or to which) we can have obligations. We can have oblig-ations *regarding* a painting, but not *to* a painting. We ought to treat beautiful paintings with respect, but not because we have obligations to the paintings. We ought to respect them because they are beautiful (or because their owners have rights), not because they have rights.

What about plants, then? Does a redwood command respect in the way excellent paint-ings command respect? Or does it command respect in the way persons command re-spect? Is it enough for us to have obligations *regarding* redwoods, or must we think of ourselves as having obligations *to* them as well?

What is your view? If we destroyed that last redwood, just for fun, would it be like destroying a *person* for fun, or would it be more like destroying a *painting* for fun?

Perhaps we should seek an intermediate position. Could we argue that moral standing comes in degrees? There are serious thinkers who view moral standing as a switch with only two settings. The switch is on or off. You either respect an entity or not. Other thinkers, equally serious, see moral standing as coming in degrees. Trees have some standing; people have more. Fish have some standing; dolphins have more. Mice have some; chimpanzees have more. Accordingly, if it seems preposterous that a mouse could have the same moral standing as a chimpanzee, it might be possible to argue that a mouse has a lesser, yet still real, moral standing.

WHAT KINDS OF THINGS HAVE MORAL STANDING?

Anything we can put to use is a potential bearer of instrumental value. Equally clearly, anything we can value simply because of what it is, independently of what it can be used for, is a potential bearer of intrinsic value. Paintings can have intrinsic value. Plants can have intrinsic value. Persons can have intrinsic value. But being a bearer of value (even intrinsic value) is a long way from having moral standing.

Almost everyone agrees that persons have moral standing, although different theorists explain that standing in different ways. Quickly put, some would say what separates plants from paintings is that plants have *lives*. What separates animals from plants is that animals have *perspectives*. What separates humans from other animals is that humans have *principles*. Humans have a unique or virtually unique capacity for self-conscious moral agency. (Do all humans have this capacity, though? Do all nonhumans lack it?)

What is the connection between having the capacity for self-conscious moral agency and having moral standing? That capacity is the paradigmatic case of what most theorists consider sufficient for moral standing, but is it necessary?

Suppose we say that it is. Would that imply that only humans have moral standing? (Again, be forewarned: These are difficult issues on which consensus may never be achieved.) *Anthropocentrism* is the view that the answer is yes. *Nonanthropocentrism,* in contrast, is a view that at least some nonhuman life has moral standing, either because some nonhumans have a capacity for self-conscious moral agency, or because the capacity for self-conscious moral agency is not the only basis for moral standing. (*Weak* anthropocentrists stress that while only humans have a full-blown right to be treated with respect, various nonhumans ought to be treated with respect not because they have rights but because they have intrinsic value.)

Nonanthropocentrists say at least some nonhuman life has a full-blown right to be treated with respect, but they do not agree on which nonhuman life has such standing, or why. Animal liberationists such as Peter Singer and Tom Regan depart from anthropocentrism in one direction. Rejecting the view that self-aware moral agency is the only basis for claiming moral rights, animal liberationists say sentience—the ability to feel pain and pleasure—is a more properly inclusive basis. They extend the realm of moral standing to all sentient animals, adding that everything within that realm has equal standing.

Other thinkers would extend moral standing literally to all living things. Where animal liberationists accuse anthropocentrists of being "speciesists," animal liberationists are in turn accused of "sentientism" by *biocentrists* who see sentience as an arbitrary cutoff and who endorse an even more radically inclusive view that simply being alive is the proper basis for moral standing. Among biocentrists, Paul Taylor says not only that the realm of moral standing extends to all living things, but also that literally everything within that realm has equal standing. Gary Varner agrees that all living things have standing—they all command *some* respect—but denies that they all command *equal* respect. Thus, while Taylor and Varner are both biocentrists, only Taylor is a *species egalitarian.*

We have distinguished different varieties of anthropocentrism and nonanthropocentrism. We also can distinguish between individualism and holism. *Individualism* is the view that only individual living things can have moral standing. Gary Varner thus calls himself a biocentric individualist. Opposed to individualism is *holism,* the view that individual living things are not the only kind of thing that can have moral standing. Can species have moral standing? How about fragile ecosystems? Biocentric holists such as Aldo Leopold and Holmes Rolston III believe the most serious environmental issues concern not the suffering of individual animals, and certainly not respect for individual plants, but the preservation of species and whole ecosystems: in a word, the environment.[10] Clearly, holism and individualism are real options. Each should be taken seriously by those who seek to understand the world and their place in it. Likewise, anthropocentrism and nonanthropocentrism are real options. You may be more attracted to one perspective rather than another, but each captures key insights in its own way.

When we commit to one view or the other, we risk losing sight of what is valuable in opposing views.[11] We will be tempted deliberately to distort opposing views, reducing them to cartoon caricatures. For example, we could define anthropocentrism as the view that only humans have intrinsic value and that anything nonhuman must have merely instrumental value at best. But that would be a caricature, not a serious theory. No one should deny that a vast array of objects, including redwoods, are intrinsically valued. The genuine division between anthropocentrists, animal liberationists, and biocentrists, the issue that leaves us with serious thinkers on each side, is the question of whether (or which) nonhumans command respect in the same way (if not to the same degree) that self-aware moral agents do. If certain nonhumans do command respect, is it because certain nonhumans (dolphins, chimpanzees) *are* self-aware moral agents, or is it because self-aware moral agency is not necessary for moral standing?

We are human, of course, and therefore our values are human values. But that does not make us anthropocentrists, for anthropocentrism does not say merely that we are human. Instead, anthropocentrism is a theory about which *objects* have moral standing. In particular, it is the theory that nonhumans do not belong in that category. Should we be anthropocentrists? Perhaps, but the bare fact that we are human does not make us anthropocentrists. It does not commit us to thinking that only human beings have moral standing. We have a choice.

Whether we should be holists or individualists, and why, is an ongoing matter of hot debate. Whether we should be anthropocentric, or how far beyond humanity the realm of moral standing should extend, is likewise a matter of hot debate. However these debates are resolved, though, we should not lose sight of the fundamental practical fact that we have much to gain from cultivating a more biocentric appreciation of nature. Simply appreciating nature—appreciating it for its own sake, treating it with respect—is how most of us begin to develop an environmental ethic. We learn that we live—and learn how to live—in a world of things worth appreciating.

WHAT REALLY WORKS

At the same time, we must also learn that we live, and how to live, in a world of never-ending disagreement about what we owe to each other and to our environment. For better or worse, we are, in many ways, free to choose how to live, and for the most part we choose as individuals. No person or government is in any position simply to decide how "we" are going to act. As individuals, we must decide how to live in a world full of people deciding how to live, each coming to different conclusions. Therefore, after we come to our own conclusions about what really matters, we still have a long way to go before we figure out what really works. Each of us needs to learn how to live in peace—an environmentally friendly peace—with people who have come to different conclusions about what really matters.

NOTES

1. This may change. Agricultural and engineering ethics, for example, may now be emerging as separate fields.

2. Richard Routley, "Is There a Need for a New, an Environmental, Ethic?" *Proceedings of the XVth World Congress of Philosophy* 1 (1973): 205–10.

3. We use the name "Last Man" for historical reasons, but we otherwise follow current conventions on gender neutrality.

4. We thought it would be best to divide the book into sections, but the divisions are somewhat arbitrary. Different sections are not different conversations so much as different aspects of a single conversation. We hope you will notice many connections between the different sections.

5. Such difficulties are in no way unique to ethics. Equally smart people have spent equally many years trying to figure out, for example, how to understand such deceptively simple questions as what it means for a sentence to be true. (Consider the sentence, "This sentence is false." True or false? Such puzzles leave specialists doubting we will ever have a fully general account of when a sentence is true.)

6. Our discussion of these issues is indebted to many, but perhaps especially to Eugene C. Hargrove, *Foundations of Environmental Ethics* (Denton, TX: Environmental Ethics Books, 1989).

7. See David Schmidtz, "A Place for Cost-Benefit Analysis" (this volume), for further discussion.

8. For an especially good discussion of these issues, see Robert Elliott, "Intrinsic Value, Environmental Obligation, and Naturalness," *The Monist* 75 (1992): 138–60.

9. My paintbrushes will continue to be the kind of thing I would find useful if I were still around, too. But there is a difference. As we have imagined the case, the last man's view is that his paintings will be beautiful after he is gone, but his paintbrushes will no longer be useful.

10. The holists we have in mind here are biocentric holists. In addition to these and anthropocentric and biocentric individualists, it also is possible to define a fourth category consisting of anthropocentric holists: people who attribute moral standing to such things as races, ethnic groups,

or the whole human species, but not to anything nonhuman. Although some people outside of environmental ethics may endorse such a view, it has not been a live option within the field.

11. A century ago, scientists debated whether light was a particle or a wave. People on each side found evidence to support their view, and denounced evidence supporting the alternative view. Today we acknowledge that light has some (but only some) wavelike properties and some (but only some) particle-like properties. We speak of light as wavelike in one context and as particle-like in another. Each way of speaking has value up to a point, and each way of speaking has the potential to mislead if taken out of context.

Final thought: Students who are new to philosophy often are stunned by the difficulty of ethical theory. Expecting a simple recipe, and disappointed at being told there is no such thing, they jump to the conclusion that morality is just a matter of opinion. But that is the wrong conclusion. Think about the game of chess. Some chess players are better than others, and in a given circumstance some moves are better than others. Yet there is no simple formula that explains the difference. As in ethics, knowing what to do takes wisdom, experience, a certain amount of self-confidence, and also a certain amount of humility.

Part I

What Really Matters

Essays on Value in Nature

Chapter 1
The Dawn of Reverence

Questions for Reflection and Discussion

A Fierce Green Fire

1. Aldo Leopold recalls shooting a wolf and watching "a fierce green fire dying in her eyes." He speaks of seeing something new in those eyes, and of changing his mind about the wisdom of exterminating wolves.

What exactly did Leopold see in the wolf's eyes? What exactly was wrong with shooting it? Did Leopold regret causing the animal needless pain? Or was it something else?

2. What is the role of philosophical argument? Do Easterbrook and Leopold merely present us with facts? Or do they present us with something that goes beyond facts and arguments—a sense of the wonder of life, perhaps? Should we let ourselves be swayed by such things?

3. We grew up near a place called "Head-Smashed-In Buffalo Jump" in Southern Alberta. It is a Blackfoot name, translated into English. Before the Blackfoot acquired guns and horses from Europe, they hunted bison by stampeding whole herds over a cliff. Dukeminier and Krier warn against forming "an unduly romantic image of Native American culture prior to the arrival of 'civilization.' There is considerable evidence that some American Indian tribes, rather than being natural ecologists who lived in respectful harmony with the land, exploited the environment ruthlessly by overhunting and extensive burning of forests."[1] What, then, should we think of Lynn White's thesis that the historical roots of our ecological crisis lie in Christianity? What crisis does White have in mind? Is White saying that if not for Christianity, there would be no environmental crises of any kind, or is his thesis something more subtle?

NOTES

1. Jesse Dukeminier and James E. Krier. *Property,* 3d ed. (Boston: Little, Brown, 1993), 62.

A Moment on the Earth

Gregg Easterbrook

If you would know the power of life over matter, know these things.

The sea turtle hatchling, born in the warm sands of a Florida beach, immediately stumbles to the ocean and throws itself in. Unknowing of the world, unaided by any parent, sought as prey by crabs and birds and perhaps facing its greatest danger from the featureless harshness of the cold waters, the hatchling begins floating among sargassum seaweeds, seeking to orient itself in the currents it will use to navigate as far as Ascension Island, thousands of miles distant. Answering some unknowable summons of antiquity the hatchling crosses the ocean alone, accomplishing without any physical technology a feat men and women in boats with radios and radars and turbo diesels and freeze-dried foods and ring-laser gyros have died attempting to accomplish.

Near the end of a life lived on the western shores of Africa the sea turtle answers a second summons, to return to the sands of its birth. This time it cannot float but must swim against the prevailing current. In some haunting way the turtle recalls exactly what it sensed as a hatchling—the precise successions of currents, wave patterns, salinity changes, and polarity from magnetic north. This is necessary because the goal is to return exactly to the patch of sand on which the turtle first knew the light of the temporal world. North America alone will not do; Florida alone will not do; it must be the same beach, the same feel and smell in every way.

Perhaps the sea turtle is a mere genetic automaton, driven by deterministic amino acid encodings toward a moot goal dropped into its DNA by some past random happenstance that signifies nothing. Or perhaps this journey has meaning.

Perhaps the turtle is willing to swim the breadth of the very ocean in order to experience once again the sweet tastes that accompanied it awakening to life—the early sensations of youth being the sweetest a living thing can ask to know. Perhaps this allows the sea turtle to end its days having not just existed and processed carbohydrates and excreted nitrogen and grown senescent but lived, taken a small yet noble role in an enterprise that may eventually fill the whole of the cosmos with meaning. Perhaps the turtle is driven not by mindless helixes but by longing—the longing of life over matter, the most insistent force in all the firmament.

One rare exception in a world of numbing pointlessness? Consider other examples of the profundity of life.

The spotted salamander lives underground almost the entire year. One day in spring when the temperature is at least 42 degrees Fahrenheit and it has rained hard the previous night, every spotted salamander emerges for a night of sporting and mating. When the night ends the salamanders return beneath the ground for another year. The timing of the emergence is always flawless.

Birds want berries for food. Plants want birds to distribute their gene lines by eating berries, flying somewhere, then relieving themselves of a portion of the berries designed to be indigestible: the seeds. Why do berries turn red? As a signal to birds that they are ripe and the time has come to eat them.

Each fall the yellow pine chipmunk collects and buries seeds of the yellow pine and the bitterbrush, a staple browsing food of deer. Some seeds the chipmunk returns to consume; some seeds the chipmunk forgets about. Forgotten seeds bloom in spring, perpetuating the yellow pine and the bitterbrush, which in turn feed the deer. The seeds have not only been dispersed by the chipmunk, they have been planted.

When a bear hibernates, in some unknown way its body recycles calcium to prevent osteoporosis and reabsorbs urea to prevent bladder failure. Bears can even carry a pregnancy through hibernation, continuing to make the necessary hormones; though in all nonhibernating mammals including people, fasting ends hormone production and causes miscarriage.

The sluggish caterpillar myrmecophilous, an attractive target for wasps, has two nectary glands that secrete a potion ants seem to consider champagne. If myrmecophilous thumps a branch in distress over the presence of a wasp, any nearby ants will rush to defend the caterpillar.

In the tree canopies of the tropical rainforest, star-shaped plants called bromeliads catch precipitation to form puddles. The puddles provide the plants with water, so they need not shoot roots to the ground: they also serve as little ponds for hundreds of other life forms.

Female guppies that live in streams where there are no predators prefer flashy males with bright markings and large fins. Female guppies that live in streams with many predators prefer plain males. Thus under safe conditions female guppies choose genes for attractiveness, to help their offspring get on socially. Under dangerous conditions female guppies choose genes for camouflage, to help their offspring survive by going unnoticed.

The opossum is believed to have existed for at least 60 million years. That is to say the opossum, a delicate thing easily harmed, is far older than the Rocky Mountains, a seemingly indestructible mass of dense minerals hewn from Earth's very continental plates. The whale is thought to have existed at least 12 million years, after somehow evolving from a land animal similar in appearance to a cow. That is to say the whale, a fragile living thing, is far older than the present alignment of ocean currents in which it swims. The sandhill crane seems to have existed for at least nine million years, perhaps making migratory stops along the area of the North Platte River of Nebraska, a favored present-day calling point, much of that time. The North Platte itself is somewhere around 15,000 years old. That is to say the sandhill crane, a fragile living thing today called endangered, is far, far older than the river at which it calls.

The monarch butterfly, a mere insect, migrates as much as 2,500 miles. Monarch brains no larger than a few grains of sand contain the topographical information necessary to navigate from the northern United States to Mexico. Several generations of the butterflies—born, metamorphosed, flying, mating, dying—are required to complete the passage of a family line from summering grounds to wintering area. Just try to guess what forces lead to the development of metamorphic creatures such as the butterfly, which essentially require two separate sets of genetic inheritances favored by two entirely separate circumstances of natural selection.

These are but a few of many, many examples of the wonder and complexity of life. I choose them because they may be less familiar than others. And I choose these two from genus Homo.

In the sediments of a lake near the Greek city of Nikopolis has been found a flint axe that is at least 200,000 and perhaps 500,000 years old. This tells us humans were not just quizzical primates, but tool users with minds already struggling to comprehend the world, an unimaginable length of time ago by our way of thinking.

In 1991 in the Qafzeh Cave near Haifa, Israel, archaeologists found the bones of a young human female delicately interned, arms wrapped around the bones of a neonate—suggesting mother and infant buried together after both died during childbirth. The bones are at least 100,000 years old. This tells us human beings had already begun to develop spiritual awareness—were already struggling with the meaning of life and the tragedy of its loss—an unimaginable length of time ago by our way of thinking.

Thinking Like a Mountain

Aldo Leopold

A deep chesty bawl echoes from rimrock to rimrock, rolls down the mountain, and fades into the far blackness of the night. It is an outburst of wild defiant sorrow, and of contempt for all the adversities of the world.

Every living thing (and perhaps many a dead one as well) pays heed to that call. To the deer it is a reminder of the way of all flesh, to the pine a forecast of midnight scuffles and of blood upon the snow, to the coyote a promise of gleanings to come, to the cowman a threat of red ink at the bank, to the hunter a challenge of fang against bullet. Yet behind these obvious and immediate hopes and fears there lies a deeper meaning, known only to the mountain itself. Only the mountain has lived long enough to listen objectively to the howl of a wolf.

Those unable to decipher the hidden meaning know nevertheless that it is there, for it is felt in all wolf country, and distinguishes that country from all other land. It tingles in the spine of all who hear wolves by night, or who scan their tracks by day. Even without sight or sound of wolf, it is implicit in a hundred small events: the midnight whinny of a pack horse, the rattle of rolling rocks, the bound of a fleeing deer, the way shadows lie under the spruces. Only the ineducable tyro can fail to sense the presence or absence of wolves, or the fact that mountains have a secret opinion about them.

My own conviction on this score dates from the day I saw a wolf die. We were eating lunch on a high rimrock, at the foot of which a turbulent river elbowed its way. We saw what we thought was a doe fording the torrent, her breast awash in white water. When she climbed the bank toward us and shook out her tail, we realized our error: it was a wolf. A half-dozen others, evidently grown pups, sprang from the willows and all joined in a welcoming mêlée of wagging tails and playful maulings. What was literally a pile of wolves writhed and tumbled in the center of an open flat at the foot of our rimrock.

In those days we had never heard of passing up a chance to kill a wolf. In a second we were pumping lead into the pack, but with more excitement than accuracy: how to aim a steep downhill shot is always confusing. When our rifles were empty, the old wolf was down, and a pup was dragging a leg into impassable slide-rocks.

We reached the old wolf in time to watch a fierce green fire dying in her eyes. I realized then, and have known ever since, that there was something new to me in those eyes—something known only to her and to the mountain. I was young then, and full of trigger-itch; I thought that because fewer wolves meant more deer, that no wolves would mean hunters' paradise. But after seeing the green fire die, I sensed that neither the wolf nor the mountain agreed with such a view.

Since then I have lived to see state after state extirpate its wolves. I have watched the face of many a newly wolfless mountain, and seen the south-facing slopes wrinkle with a maze of new deer trails. I have seen every edible bush and seedling browsed, first to anaemic desuetude, and then to death. I have seen every edible tree defoliated to the height of a saddlehorn. Such a mountain looks as if someone had given God a new pruning shears, and forbidden Him all other exercise. In the end the starved bones of the hoped-for deer herd, dead of its own too-much, bleach with the bones of the dead sage, or molder under the high-lined junipers.

I now suspect that just as a deer herd lives in mortal fear of its wolves, so does a mountain live in mortal fear of its deer. And perhaps with better cause, for while a buck pulled down by wolves can be re-

Aldo Leopold, "Thinking Like a Mountain," in *A Sand County Almanac* (Oxford: Oxford University Press, 1981), 137–41. Reprinted with permission of the publisher.

placed in two or three years, a range pulled down by too many deer may fail of replacement in as many decades.

So also with cows. The cowman who cleans his range of wolves does not realize that he is taking over the wolf's job of trimming the herd to fit the range. He has not learned to think like a mountain. Hence we have dustbowls, and rivers washing the future into the sea.

We all strive for safety, prosperity, comfort, long life, and dullness. The deer strives with his supple legs, the cowman with trap and poison, the statesman with pen, the most of us with machines, votes, and dollars, but it all comes to the same thing: peace in our time. A measure of success in this is all well enough, and perhaps is a requisite to objective thinking, but too much safety seems to yield only danger in the long run. Perhaps this is behind Thoreau's dictum: In wildness is the salvation of the world. Perhaps this is the hidden meaning in the howl of the wolf, long known among mountains, but seldom perceived among men.

The Historical Roots of Our Ecological Crisis

Lynn White, Jr.

A conversation with Aldous Huxley not infrequently put one at the receiving end of an unforgettable monologue. About a year before his lamented death he was discoursing on a favorite topic: Man's unnatural treatment of nature and its sad results. To illustrate his point he told how, during the previous summer, he had returned to a little valley in England where he had spent many happy months as a child. Once it had been composed of delightful grassy glades; now it was becoming overgrown with unsightly brush because the rabbits that formerly kept such growth under control had largely succumbed to a disease, myxomatosis, that was deliberately introduced by the local farmers to reduce the rabbits' destruction of crops. Being something of a Philistine, I could be silent no longer, even in the interests of great rhetoric. I interrupted to point out that the rabbit itself had been brought as a domestic animal to England in 1176, presumably to improve the protein diet of the peasantry.

All forms of life modify their contexts. The most spectacular and benign instance is doubtless the coral polyp. By serving its own ends, it has created a vast undersea world favorable to thousands of other kinds of animals and plants. Ever since man became a numerous species he has affected his environment notably. The hypothesis that his fire-drive method of hunting created the world's great grasslands and helped to exterminate the monster mammals of the Pleistocene from much of the globe is plausible, if not proved. For 6 millennia at least, the banks of the lower Nile have been a human artifact rather than the swampy African jungle which nature, apart from man, would have made it. The Aswan Dam, flooding 5000 square miles, is only the latest stage in a long process. In many regions terracing or irrigation, overgrazing, the cutting of forests by Romans to build ships to fight Carthaginians or by Crusaders to solve the logistics problems of their expeditions, have profoundly changed some ecologies. Observa-

Lynn White, Jr., "Historical Roots of Our Ecological Crisis," *Science* 155 (1967): 1203–1207. Reprinted with permission of the American Association for the Advancement of Science.

tion that the French landscape falls into two basic types, the open fields of the north and the *bocage* of the south and west, inspired Marc Bloch to undertake his classic study of medieval agricultural methods. Quite unintentionally, changes in human ways often affect nonhuman nature. It has been noted, for example, that the advent of the automobile eliminated huge flocks of sparrows that once fed on the horse manure littering every street.

The history of ecologic change is still so rudimentary that we know little about what really happened, or what the results were. The extinction of the European aurochs as late as 1627 would seem to have been a simple case of overenthusiastic hunting. On more intricate matters it often is impossible to find solid information. For a thousand years or more the Frisians and Hollanders have been pushing back the North Sea, and the process is culminating in our own time in the reclamation of the Zuider Zee. What, if any, species of animals, birds, fish, shore life, or plants have died out in the process? In their epic combat with Neptune, have the Netherlanders overlooked ecological values in such a way that the quality of human life in the Netherlands has suffered? I cannot discover that the questions have ever been asked, much less answered.

People, then, have often been a dynamic element in their own environment, but in the present state of historical scholarship we usually do not know exactly when, where, or with what effects man-induced changes came. As we enter the last third of the 20th century, however, concern for the problem of ecologic backlash is mounting feverishly. Natural science, conceived as the effort to understand the nature of things, had flourished in several eras and among several peoples. Similarly there had been an age-old accumulation of technological skills, sometimes growing rapidly, sometimes slowly. But it was not until about four generations ago that Western Europe and North America arranged a marriage between science and technology, a union of the theoretical and the empirical approaches to our natural environment. The emergence in widespread practice of the Baconian creed that scientific knowledge means technological power over nature can scarcely

be dated before about 1850, save in the chemical industries, where it is anticipated in the 18th century. Its acceptance as a normal pattern of action may mark the greatest event in human history since the invention of agriculture, and perhaps in nonhuman terrestrial history as well.

Almost at once the new situation forced the crystallization of the novel concept of ecology; indeed, the word *ecology* first appeared in the English language in 1873. Today, less than a century later, the impact of our race upon the environment has so increased in force that it has changed in essence. When the first cannons were fired, in the early 14th century, they affected ecology by sending workers scrambling to the forests and mountains for more potash, sulfur, iron ore, and charcoal, with some resulting erosion and deforestation. Hydrogen bombs are of a different order: a war fought with them might alter the genetics of all life on this planet. By 1285 London had a smog problem arising from the burning of soft coal, but our present combustion of fossil fuels threatens to change the chemistry of the globe's atmosphere as a whole, with consequences which we are only beginning to guess. With the population explosion, the carcinoma of planless urbanism, the now geological deposits of sewage and garbage, surely no creature other than man has ever managed to foul its nest in such short order.

There are many calls to action, but specific proposals, however worthy as individual items, seem too partial, palliative, negative: ban the bomb, tear down the billboards, give the Hindus contraceptives and tell them to eat their sacred cows. The simplest solution to any suspect change is, of course, to stop it, or, better yet, to revert to a romanticized past: make those ugly gasoline stations look like Anne Hathaway's cottage or (in the Far West) like ghost-town saloons. The "wilderness area" mentality invariably advocates deep-freezing an ecology, whether San Gimignano or the High Sierra, as it was before the first Kleenex was dropped. But neither atavism nor prettification will cope with the ecologic crisis of our time.

What shall we do? No one yet knows. Unless we think about fundamentals, our specific measures may produce new backlashes more serious than those they are designed to remedy.

As a beginning we should try to clarify our thinking by looking, in some historical depth, at the presuppositions that underlie modern technology and science. Science was traditionally aristocratic, speculative, intellectual in intent; technology was lower-class, empirical, action-oriented. The quite sudden fusion of these two, towards the middle of the 19th century, is surely related to the slightly prior and contemporary democratic revolutions which, by reducing social barriers, tended to assert a functional unity of brain and hand. Our ecologic crisis is the product of an emerging, entirely novel, democratic culture. The issue is whether a democratized world can survive its own implications. Presumably we cannot unless we rethink our axioms.

THE WESTERN TRADITIONS OF TECHNOLOGY AND SCIENCE

One thing is so certain that it seems stupid to verbalize it: both modern technology and modern science are distinctively *Occidental*. Our technology has absorbed elements from all over the world, notably from China; yet everywhere today, whether in Japan or in Nigeria, successful technology is Western. Our science is the heir to all the sciences of the past, especially perhaps to the work of the great Islamic scientists of the Middle Ages, who so often outdid the ancient Greeks in skill and perspicacity: al-Razi in medicine, for example; or ibn-al-Haytham in optics; or Omar Khayyám in mathematics. Indeed, not a few works of such geniuses seem to have vanished in the original Arabic and to survive only in medieval Latin translations that helped to lay the foundations for later Western developments. Today, around the globe, all significant science is Western in style and method, whatever the pigmentation or language of the scientists.

A second pair of facts is less well recognized because they result from quite recent historical scholarship. The leadership of the West, both in technology and in science, is far older than the so-called

Scientific Revolution of the 17th century or the so-called Industrial Revolution of the 18th century. These terms are in fact outmoded and obscure the true nature of what they try to describe—significant stages in two long and separate developments. By A.D. 1000 at the latest—and perhaps, feebly, as much as 200 years earlier—the West began to apply water power to industrial processes other than milling grain. This was followed in the late 12th century by the harnessing of wind power. From simple beginnings but with remarkable consistency of style, the West rapidly expanded its skills in the development of power machinery, labor-saving devices, and automation. Those who doubt should contemplate that most monumental achievement in the history of automation: the weight-driven mechanical clock, which appeared in two forms in the early 14th century. Not in craftsmanship but in basic technological capacity, the Latin West of the later Middle Ages far outstripped its elaborate, sophisticated, and esthetically magnificent sister cultures, Byzantium and Islam. In 1444 a great Greek ecclesiastic, Bessarion, who had gone to Italy, wrote a letter to a prince in Greece. He is amazed by the superiority of Western ships, arms, textiles, glass. But above all he is astonished by the spectacle of waterwheels sawing timbers and pumping the bellows to blast furnaces. Clearly, he had seen nothing of the sort in the Near East.

By the end of the 15th century the technological superiority of Europe was such that its small, mutually hostile nations could spill out over all the rest of the world, conquering, looting, and colonizing. The symbol of this technological superiority is the fact that Portugal, one of the weakest states of the Occident, was able to become, and to remain for a century, mistress of the East Indies. And we must remember that the technology of Vasco da Gama and Albuquerque was built by pure empiricism, drawing remarkably little support or inspiration from science.

In the present-day vernacular of understanding, modern science is supposed to have begun in 1543, when both Copernicus and Vesalius published their great works. It is no derogation of their accomplishments, however, to point out that such structures as the *Fabrica* and the *De revolutionibus* do not appear overnight. The distinctive Western tradition of science, in fact, began in the late 11th century with a massive movement of translation of Arabic and Greek scientific works into Latin. A few notable books—Theophrastus, for example—escaped the West's avid new appetite for science, but within less than 200 years, effectively the entire corpus of Greek and Muslim science was available in Latin, and was being eagerly read and criticized in the new European universities. Out of criticism arose new observation, speculation, and increasing distrust of ancient authorities. By the late 13th century Europe had seized global scientific leadership from the faltering hands of Islam. It would be as absurd to deny the profound originality of Newton, Galileo, or Copernicus as to deny that of the 14th century scholastic scientists like Buridan or Oresme on whose work they built. Before the 11th century, science scarcely existed in the Latin West, even in Roman times. From the 11th century onward, the scientific sector of Occidental culture has increased in a steady crescendo.

Since both our technological and our scientific movements got their start, acquired their character, and achieved world dominance in the Middle Ages, it would seem that we cannot understand their nature or their present impact upon ecology without examining fundamental medieval assumptions and developments.

MEDIEVAL VIEW OF MAN AND NATURE

Until recently, agriculture has been the chief occupation even in "advanced" societies; hence, any change in methods of tillage has much importance. Early plows, drawn by two oxen, did not normally turn the sod but merely scratched it. Thus, cross-plowing was needed and fields tended to be squarish. In the fairly light soils and semi-arid climates of the Near East and Mediterranean, this worked well. But such a plow was inappropriate to the wet climate and often sticky soils of northern Europe. By the lat-

ter part of the 7th century after Christ, however, following obscure beginnings, certain northern peasants were using an entirely new kind of plow, equipped with a vertical knife to cut the line of the furrow, a horizontal share to slice under the sod, and a moldboard to turn it over. The friction of this plow with the soil was so great that it normally required not two but eight oxen. It attacked the land with such violence that cross-plowing was not needed, and fields tended to be shaped in long strips.

In the days of the scratch-plow, fields were distributed generally in units capable of supporting a single family. Subsistence farming was the presupposition. But no peasant owned eight oxen: to use the new and more efficient plow, peasants pooled their oxen to form large plow-teams, originally receiving (it would appear) plowed strips in proportion to their contribution. Thus, distribution of land was based no longer on the needs of a family but, rather, on the capacity of a power machine to till the earth. Man's relation to the soil was profoundly changed. Formerly man had been part of nature; now he was the exploiter of nature. Nowhere else in the world did farmers develop any analogous agricultural implement. Is it coincidence that modern technology, with its ruthlessness toward nature, has so largely been produced by descendants of these peasants of northern Europe?

This same exploitive attitude appears slightly before A.D. 830 in Western illustrated calendars. In older calendars the months were shown as passive personifications. The new Frankish calendars, which set the style for the Middle Ages, are very different: they show men coercing the world around them—plowing, harvesting, chopping trees, butchering pigs. Man and nature are two things, and man is master.

These novelties seem to be in harmony with larger intellectual patterns. What people do about their ecology depends on what they think about themselves in relation to things around them. Human ecology is deeply conditioned by beliefs about our nature and destiny—that is, by religion. To Western eyes this is very evident in, say, India or Ceylon. It is equally true of ourselves and of our medieval ancestors.

The victory of Christianity over paganism was the greatest psychic revolution in the history of our culture. It has become fashionable today to say that, for better or worse, we live in "the post-Christian age." Certainly the forms of our thinking and language have largely ceased to be Christian, but to my eye the substance often remains amazingly akin to that of the past. Our daily habits of action, for example, are dominated by an implicit faith in perpetual progress which was unknown either to Greco-Roman antiquity or to the Orient. It is rooted in, and is indefensible apart from, Judeo-Christian teleology. The fact that Communists share it merely helps to show what can be demonstrated on many other grounds: that Marxism, like Islam, is a Judeo-Christian heresy. We continue today to live, as we have lived for about 1700 years, very largely in a context of Christian axioms.

What did Christianity tell people about their relations with the environment?

While many of the world's mythologies provide stories of creation, Greco-Roman mythology was singularly incoherent in this respect. Like Aristotle, the intellectuals of the ancient West denied that the visible world had had a beginning. Indeed, the idea of a beginning was impossible in the framework of their cyclical notion of time. In sharp contrast, Christianity inherited from Judaism not only a concept of time as nonrepetitive and linear but also a striking story of creation. By gradual stages a loving and all-powerful God had created light and darkness, the heavenly bodies, the earth and all its plants, animals, birds, and fishes. Finally, God had created Adam and, as an after thought, Eve to keep man from being lonely. Man named all the animals, thus establishing his dominance over them. God planned all of this explicitly for man's benefit and rule: no item in the physical creation had any purpose save to serve man's purposes. And, although man's body is made of clay, he is not simply part of nature: he is made in God's image.

Especially in its Western form, Christianity is the most anthropocentric religion the world has seen. As early as the 2nd century both Tertullian and Saint Irenaeus of Lyons were insisting that when God shaped Adam he was foreshadowing the image of the incarnate Christ, the Second Adam. Man shares, in great measure, God's transcendence of nature. Christianity, in absolute contrast to ancient paganism and Asia's religions (except, perhaps, Zoroastrianism), not only established a dualism of man and nature but also insisted that it is God's will that man exploit nature for his proper ends.

At the level of the common people this worked out in an interesting way. In Antiquity every tree, every spring, every stream, every hill had its own *genius loci,* its guardian spirit. These spirits were accessible to men, but were very unlike men; centaurs, fauns, and mermaids show their ambivalence. Before one cut a tree, mined a mountain, or dammed a brook, it was important to placate the spirit in charge of that particular situation, and to keep it placated. By destroying pagan animism, Christianity made it possible to exploit nature in a mood of indifference to the feelings of natural objects.

It is often said that for animism the Church substituted the cult of saints. True; but the cult of saints is functionally quite different from animism. The saint is not *in* natural objects; he may have special shrines, but his citizenship is in heaven. Moreover, a saint is entirely a man; he can be approached in human terms. In addition to saints, Christianity of course also had angels and demons inherited from Judaism and perhaps, at one remove, from Zoroastrianism. But these were all as mobile as the saints themselves. The spirits *in* natural objects, which formerly had protected nature from man, evaporated. Man's effective monopoly on spirit in this world was confirmed, and the old inhibitions to the exploitation of nature crumbled.

When one speaks in such sweeping terms, a note of caution is in order. Christianity is a complex faith, and its consequences differ in differing contexts. What I have said may well apply to the medieval West, where in fact technology made spectacular advances. But the Greek East, a highly civilized realm of equal Christian devotion, seems to have produced no marked technological innovation after the late 7th century, when Greek fire was invented. The key to the contrast may perhaps be found in a difference in the tonality of piety and thought which students of comparative theology find between the Greek and the Latin Churches. The Greeks believed that sin was intellectual blindness, and that salvation was found in illumination, orthodoxy—that is, clear thinking. The Latins, on the other hand, felt that sin was moral evil, and that salvation was to be found in right conduct. Eastern theology has been intellectualist. Western theology has been voluntarist. The Greek saint contemplates; the Western saint acts. The implications of Christianity for the conquest of nature would emerge more easily in the Western atmosphere.

The Christian dogma of creation, which is found in the first clause of all the Creeds, has another meaning for our comprehension of today's ecologic crisis. By revelation, God had given man the Bible, the Book of Scripture. But since God had made nature, nature also must reveal the divine mentality. The religious study of nature for the better understanding of God was known as natural theology. In the early Church, and always in the Greek East, nature was conceived primarily as a symbolic system through which God speaks to men: the ant is a sermon to sluggards; rising flames are the symbol of the soul's aspiration. This view of nature was essentially artistic rather than scientific. While Byzantium preserved and copied great numbers of ancient Greek scientific texts, science as we conceive it could scarcely flourish in such an ambience.

However, in the Latin West by the early 13th century natural theology was following a very different bent. It was ceasing to be the decoding of the physical symbols of God's communication with man and was becoming the effort to understand God's mind by discovering how his creation operates. The rainbow was no longer simply a symbol of hope first sent to Noah after the Deluge: Robert Grosseteste, Friar Roger Bacon, and Theodoric of Freiberg produced startlingly sophisticated work on the optics of the rainbow, but they did it as a venture in religious understanding. From the 13th century onward, up to and including Leibniz and Newton, every major scientist, in effect, explained his motivations in religious terms. Indeed, if Galileo had not been so expert an amateur theologian he would have got into far less trouble: the professionals resented his intrusion. And Newton seems to have regarded himself more as a theologian than as a scientist. It was not until the late 18th century that the hypothesis of God became unnecessary to many scientists.

It is often hard for the historian to judge, when men explain why they are doing what they want to do, whether they are offering real reasons or merely culturally acceptable reasons. The consistency with which scientists during the long formative centuries of Western science said that the task and the reward of the scientist was "to think God's thoughts after him" leads one to believe that this was their real motivation. If so, then modern Western science was cast in a matrix of Christian theology. The dynamism of religious devotion, shaped by the Judeo-Christian dogma of creation, gave it impetus.

AN ALTERNATIVE CHRISTIAN VIEW

We would seem to be headed toward conclusions unpalatable to many Christians. Since both *science* and *technology* are blessed words in our contemporary vocabulary, some may be happy at the notions, first, that, viewed historically, modern science is an extrapolation of natural theology and, second, that modern technology is at least partly to be explained as an Occidental, voluntarist realization of the Christian dogma of man's transcendence of and rightful mastery over nature. But, as we now recognize, somewhat over a century ago science and technology—hitherto quite separate activities—joined to give mankind powers which, to judge by many of the ecologic effects, are out of control. If so, Christianity bears a huge burden of guilt.

I personally doubt that disastrous ecologic backlash can be avoided simply by applying to our problems more science and more technology. Our science and technology have grown out of Christian attitudes toward man's relation to nature which are almost universally held not only by Christians and neo-Christians but also by those who fondly regard themselves as post-Christians. Despite Copernicus, all the cosmos rotates around our little globe. Despite Darwin, we are *not*, in our hearts, part of the natural process. We are superior to nature, contemptuous of it, willing to use it for our slightest whim. The newly elected Governor of California, like myself a churchman but less troubled than I, spoke for the Christian tradition when he said (as is alleged), "when you've seen one redwood tree, you've seen them all." To a Christian a tree can be no more than a physical fact. The whole concept of the sacred grove is alien to Christianity and to the ethos of the West. For nearly 2 millennia Christian missionaries have been chopping down sacred groves, which are idolatrous because they assume spirit in nature.

What we do about ecology depends on our ideas of the man-nature relationship. More science and more technology are not going to get us out of the present ecologic crisis until we find a new religion, or rethink our old one. The beatniks, who are the basic revolutionaries of our time, show a sound instinct in their affinity for Zen Buddhism, which conceives of the man-nature relationship as very nearly the mirror image of the Christian view. Zen, however, is as deeply conditioned by Asian history as Christianity is by the experience of the West, and I am dubious of its viability among us.

Possibly we should ponder the greatest radical in Christian history since Christ: Saint Francis of Assisi. The prime miracle of Saint Francis is the fact that he did not end at the stake, as many of his left-wing followers did. He was so clearly heretical that a General of the Franciscan Order, Saint Bonaventura, a great and perceptive Christian, tried to suppress the early accounts of Franciscanism. The key to an understanding of Francis is his belief in the virtue of humility—not merely for the individual but for man as a species. Francis tried to depose man from his monarchy over creation and set up a democracy of all God's creatures. With him the ant is no longer simply a homily for the lazy, flames a sign of the thrust of the soul toward union with God; now they are Brother Ant and Sister Fire, praising the

Creator in their own ways as Brother Man does in his.

Later commentators have said that Francis preached to the birds as a rebuke to men who would not listen. The records do not read so: he urged the little birds to praise God, and in spiritual ecstasy they flapped their wings and chirped rejoicing. Legends of saints, especially the Irish saints, had long told of their dealings with animals but always, I believe, to show their human dominance over creatures. With Francis it is different. The land around Gubbio in the Apennines was being ravaged by a fierce wolf. Saint Francis, says the legend, talked to the wolf and persuaded him of the error of his ways. The wolf repented, died in the odor of sanctity, and was buried in consecrated ground.

What Sir Steven Runciman calls "the Franciscan doctrine of the animal soul" was quickly stamped out. Quite possibly it was in part inspired, consciously or unconsciously, by the belief in reincarnation held by the Cathar heretics who at that time teemed in Italy and southern France, and who presumably had got it originally from India. It is significant that at just the same moment, about 1200, traces of metempsychosis are found also in western Judaism, in the Provençal *Cabbala*. But Francis held neither to transmigration of souls nor to pantheism. His view of nature and of man rested on a unique sort of pan-psychism of all things animate and inanimate, designed for the glorification of their transcendent Creator, who, in the ultimate gesture of cosmic humility, assumed flesh, lay helpless in a manger, and hung dying on a scaffold.

I am not suggesting that many contemporary Americans who are concerned about our ecologic crisis will be either able or willing to counsel with wolves or exhort birds. However, the present increasing disruption of the global environment is the product of a dynamic technology and science which were originating in the Western medieval world against which Saint Francis was rebelling in so original a way. Their growth cannot be understood historically apart from distinctive attitudes toward nature which are deeply grounded in Christian dogma.

The fact that most people do not think of these attitudes as Christian is irrelevant. No new set of basic values has been accepted in our society to displace those of Christianity. Hence we shall continue to have a worsening ecologic crisis until we reject the Christian axiom that nature has no reason for existence save to serve man.

The greatest spiritual revolutionary in Western history, Saint Francis, proposed what he thought was an alternative Christian view of nature and man's relation to it: he tried to substitute the idea of the equality of all creatures, including man, for the idea of man's limitless rule of creation. He failed. Both our present science and our present technology are so tinctured with orthodox Christian arrogance toward nature that no solution for our ecologic crisis can be expected from them alone. Since the roots of our trouble are so largely religious, the remedy must also be essentially religious, whether we call it that or not. We must rethink and refeel our nature and destiny. The profoundly religious, but heretical, sense of the primitive Franciscans for the spiritual autonomy of all parts of nature may point a direction. I propose Francis as a patron saint for ecologists.

Chapter 2
Animal Liberation and the Land Ethic

Questions for Reflection and Discussion

Practical Ethics

1. Peter Singer is probably today's most influential living philosopher. As Dale Jamieson observes, "While other philosophers have been more important in developing the discipline, none has changed more lives."[1] As Holmes Rolston III notes (in that same volume), "Few ethicists, indeed few persons responsible for the care and use of animals, are not more sensitive to animal welfare now than they were before the impact of Singer and his colleagues." In 1975, shampoos and cosmetics were tested by placing samples in rabbits' eyes. Today, the rabbit eye test is no longer legally required, and many manufacturers advertise "cruelty-free" products.

Was it wrong to use rabbits to test whether a new product is safe for humans? Why or why not? (If there were no alternative to using animals, if the only alternative to experimenting on animals would be, in effect, to experiment on human customers, would that make a difference?) If it was wrong to use animals, was it because animals have rights? Should we think of animals as having rights? Why or why not? If animals do not have rights, does that mean we can do whatever we want to them? Why or why not?

2. Although there is less cruelty to animals in laboratories today, other trends are more disturbing. In 1998, about 76,000 dogs and 25,000 cats were used in research. Is that a large number? To put it in perspective, between 2.4 million and 7.2 million unwanted cats and dogs were killed in American animal shelters in the same year, according to the Humane Society of America.[2] Yet to judge from media coverage, we seem more concerned about animals killed in laboratories. Should we be? At the animal shelter, we simply kill the animal. At the laboratory, we first use the animal as a mere means to human ends. Is that an important difference? If so, which is worse? Why?

3. Mark Sagoff says animal liberation and environmental ethics are a "bad marriage."[3] As noted, Holmes Rolston III praises Singer's efforts on behalf of animals. However, Rolston adds, Singer remains "blind to the still larger effort in environmental ethics to value

15

life at all its ranges and levels . . . Also, Singer has yet to count the vital processes, such as speciation, natural selection, and ecosystemic communities in which these individual organisms live" (*Singer and His Critics,* p. 249).

Consider a dilemma. We know today that natural predators play a key role in maintaining the balance of nature. Where does that leave human hunters? It depends. In North America, humans are what we call an *introduced* species, settling here perhaps 12,000 years ago. Thus, North American holists can advocate leaving natural predators to play their essential role in the ecosystem without at the same time favoring hunting by humans. In Africa, though, the situation is different. In Africa, humans are not an introduced species. Africa is where we evolved. Humans and their ancestors have been in Africa for five million years, roughly as long as the elephant. Humans and elephants coevolved. Elephants are what they are partly because of the system in which they evolved, a system in which human hunters played an integral role.[4]

So when do we interfere with nature? When we permit hunting, or when we forbid it? Rifles are unnatural, but in Africa, stopping the hunting is an equally unnatural intervention in an ancient ecological dance. When we stop people from hunting elephants, as we have done in Southern Africa in recent years, we are removing the system's keystone natural predator. The result is the same as anywhere else when we remove an ecosystem's keystone predator. Elephant populations are exploding, and sub-Saharan ecosystems are collapsing.

Should we try to stop Africans from hunting? What do you suppose Singer would advise? Would Rolston agree? Would you?

NOTES

1. Dale Jamieson, editor, *Singer and His Critics* (Oxford: Blackwell, 1999), p. 1.

2. Lynne Lamberg, "Researchers Urged to Tell Public How Animal Studies Benefit Human Health," *Journal of the American Medical Association* 282, no. 7 (1999): 619–21.

3. J. Baird Callicott has published a series of seminal papers on the tension between animal liberation and ecological ethics, beginning with "Animal Liberation: A Triangular Affair," *Environmental Ethics* 2 (1980): 311–38.

4. Until recently, humans have not had firearms, so it is reasonable to question how serious a predator humans could have been. Our introduction to the previous section noted that the Blackfoot in North America once hunted bison by stampeding whole herds over cliffs. Likewise, there were elephants in Spain four hundred thousand years ago. *Homo erectus* hunted them the same way the Blackfoot hunted bison here, stampeding them into swamps, according to Donald C. Johanson and Maitland A. Edey in *Lucy: The Beginnings of Humankind* (New York: Warner Books, 1981), 73–74.

All Animals Are Equal

Peter Singer

In recent years a number of oppressed groups have campaigned vigorously for equality. The classic instance is the Black Liberation movement, which demands an end to the prejudice and discrimination that has made blacks second-class citizens. The immediate appeal of the black liberation movement and its initial, if limited, success made it a model for other oppressed groups to follow. We became familiar with liberation movements for Spanish-Americans, gay people, and a variety of other minorities. When a majority group—women—began their campaign, some thought we had come to the end of the road. Discrimination on the basis of sex, it has been said, is the last universally accepted form of discrimination, practiced without secrecy or pretense even in those liberal circles that have long prided themselves on their freedom from prejudice against racial minorities.

One should always be wary of talking of "the last remaining form of discrimination." If we have learnt anything from the liberation movements, we should have learnt how difficult it is to be aware of latent prejudice in our attitudes to particular groups until this prejudice is forcefully pointed out.

A liberation movement demands an expansion of our moral horizons and an extension or reinterpretation of the basic moral principle of equality. Practices that were previously regarded as natural and inevitable come to be seen as the result of an unjustifiable prejudice. Who can say with confidence that all his or her attitudes and practices are beyond criticism? If we wish to avoid being numbered amongst the oppressors, we must be prepared to rethink even our most fundamental attitudes. We need to consider them from the point of view of those most disadvantaged by our attitudes, and the practices that follow from these attitudes. If we can make this unaccustomed mental switch we may discover a pattern in our attitudes and practices that consistently operates so as to benefit one group—usually the one to which we ourselves belong—at the expense of another. In this way we may come to see that there is a case for a new liberation movement. My aim is to advocate that we make this mental switch in respect of our attitudes and practices towards a very large group of beings: members of species other than our own—or, as we popularly though misleadingly call them, animals. In other words, I am urging that we extend to other species the basic principle of equality that most of us recognize should be extended to all members of our own species.

All this may sound a little far-fetched, more like a parody of other liberation movements than a serious objective. In fact, in the past the idea of "The Rights of Animals" really has been used to parody the case for women's rights. When Mary Wollstonecroft, a forerunner of later feminists, published her *Vindication of the Rights of Women* in 1792, her ideas were widely regarded as absurd, and they were satirized in an anonymous publication entitled *A Vindication of the Rights of Brutes*. The author of this satire (actually Thomas Taylor, a distinguished Cambridge philosopher) tried to refute Wollstonecroft's reasonings by showing that they could be carried one stage further. If sound when applied to women, why should the arguments not be applied to dogs, cats, and horses? They seemed to hold equally well for these "brutes"; yet to hold that brutes had rights was manifestly absurd; therefore the reasoning by which this conclusion had been reached must be unsound, and if unsound when applied to brutes, it must also be unsound when applied to women, since the very same arguments had been used in each case.

Peter Singer, "All Animals Are Equal," *Philosophical Exchange* 1 (1974): 103–16. Reprinted with permission of the author.

One way in which we might reply to this argument is by saying that the case for equality between men and women cannot validly be extended to nonhuman animals. Women have a right to vote, for instance, because they are just as capable of making rational decisions as men are; dogs, on the other hand, are incapable of understanding the significance of voting, so they cannot have the right to vote. There are many other obvious ways in which men and women resemble each other closely, while humans and other animals differ greatly. So, it might be said, men and women are similar beings, and should have equal rights, while humans and nonhumans are different and should not have equal rights.

The thought behind this reply to Taylor's analogy is correct up to a point, but it does not go far enough. There *are* important differences between humans and other animals, and these differences must give rise to *some* differences in the rights that each have. Recognizing this obvious fact, however, is no barrier to the case for extending the basic principle of equality to nonhuman animals. The differences that exist between men and women are equally undeniable, and the supporters of Women's Liberation are aware that these differences may give rise to different rights. Many feminists hold that women have the right to an abortion on request. It does not follow that since these same people are campaigning for equality between men and women they must support the right of men to have abortions too. Since a man cannot have an abortion, it is meaningless to talk of his right to have one. Since a pig can't vote, it is meaningless to talk of its right to vote. There is no reason why either Women's Liberation or Animal Liberation should get involved in such nonsense. The extension of the basic principle of equality from one group to another does not imply that we must treat both groups in exactly the same way, or grant exactly the same rights to both groups. Whether we should do so will depend on the nature of the members of the two groups. The basic principle of equality, I shall argue, is equality of consideration; and equal consideration for different beings may lead to different treatment and different rights.

So there is a different way of replying to Taylor's attempt to parody Wollstonecroft's arguments, a way which does not deny the differences between humans and nonhumans, but goes more deeply into the question of equality, and concludes by finding nothing absurd in the idea that the basic principle of equality applies to so called "brutes." I believe that we reach this conclusion if we examine the basis on which our opposition to discrimination on grounds of race or sex ultimately rests. We will then see that we would be on shaky ground if we were to demand equality for blacks, women, and other groups of oppressed humans while denying equal consideration to nonhumans.

When we say that all human beings, whatever their race, creed or sex, are equal, what is it that we are asserting? Those who wish to defend a hierarchical, inegalitarian society have often pointed out that by whatever test we choose, it simply is not true that all humans are equal. Like it or not, we must face the fact that humans come in different shapes and sizes; they come with differing moral capacities, differing intellectual abilities, differing amounts of benevolent feeling and sensitivity to the needs of others, differing abilities to communicate effectively, and differing capacities to experience pleasure and pain. In short, if the demand for equality were based on the actual equality of all human beings, we would have to stop demanding equality. It would be an unjustifiable demand.

Still, one might cling to the view that the demand for equality among human beings is based on the actual equality of the different races and sexes. Although humans differ as individuals in various ways, there are no differences between the races and sexes *as such*. From the mere fact that a person is black, or a woman, we cannot infer anything else about that person. This, it may be said, is what is wrong with racism and sexism. The white racist claims that whites are superior to blacks, but this is false—although there are differences between individuals, some blacks are superior to some whites in all of the capacities and abilities that could conceivably be relevant. The opponent of sexism would say the same:

a person's sex is no guide to his or her abilities, and this is why it is unjustifiable to discriminate on the basis of sex.

This is a possible line of objection to racial and sexual discrimination. It is not, however, the way that someone really concerned about equality would choose, because taking this line could, in some circumstances, force one to accept a most inegalitarian society. The fact that humans differ as individuals, rather than as races or sexes, is a valid reply to someone who defends a hierarchical society like, say, South Africa, in which all whites are superior in status to all blacks. The existence of individual variations that cut across the lines of race or sex, however, provides us with no defence at all against a more sophisticated opponent of equality, one who proposes that, say, the interests of those with I.Q. ratings above 100 be preferred to the interests of those with I.Q.s below 100. Would a hierarchical society of this sort really be so much better than one based on race or sex? I think not. But if we tie the moral principle of equality to the factual equality of the different races or sexes, taken as a whole, our opposition to racism and sexism does not provide us with any basis for objecting to this kind of inegalitarianism.

There is a second important reason why we ought not to base our opposition to racism and sexism on any kind of factual equality, even the limited kind which asserts that variations in capacities and abilities are spread evenly between the different races and sexes: we can have no absolute guarantee that these abilities and capacities really are distributed evenly, without regard to race or sex, among human beings. So far as actual abilities are concerned, there do seem to be certain measurable differences between both races and sexes. These differences do not, of course, appear in each case, but only when averages are taken. More important still, we do not yet know how much of these differences is really due to the different genetic endowments of the various races and sexes, and how much is due to environmental differences that are the result of past and continuing discrimination. Perhaps all of the important differences will eventually prove to be environmental

rather than genetic. Anyone opposed to racism and sexism will certainly hope that this will be so, for it will make the task of ending discrimination a lot easier; nevertheless it would be dangerous to rest the case against racism and sexism on the belief that all significant differences are environmental in origin. The opponent of, say, racism who takes this line will be unable to avoid conceding that if differences in ability did after all prove to have some genetic connection with race, racism would in some way be defensible.

It would be folly for the opponent of racism to stake his whole case on a dogmatic commitment to one particular outcome of a difficult scientific issue which is still a long way from being settled. While attempts to prove that differences in certain selected abilities between races and sexes are primarily genetic in origin have certainly not been conclusive, the same must be said of attempts to prove that these differences are largely the result of environment. At this stage of the investigation we cannot be certain which view is correct, however much we may hope it is the latter.

Fortunately, there is no need to pin the case for equality to one particular outcome of this scientific investigation. The appropriate response to those who claim to have found evidence of genetically-based differences in ability between the races or sexes is not to stick to the belief that the genetic explanation must be wrong, whatever evidence to the contrary may turn up: instead we should make it quite clear that the claim to equality does not depend on intelligence, moral capacity, physical strength, or similar matters of fact. Equality is a moral ideal, not a simple assertion of fact. There is no logically compelling reason for assuming that a factual difference in ability between two people justifies any difference in the amount of consideration we give to satisfying their needs and interests. The principle of the equality of human beings is not a description of an alleged actual equality among humans: it is a prescription of how we should treat humans.

Jeremy Bentham incorporated the essential basis of moral equality into his utilitarian system of ethics in the formula: "Each to count for one and none for more than one." In other words, the interests of every being affected by an action are to be taken into account and given the same weight as the like interests of any other being. A later utilitarian, Henry Sidgwick, put the point in this way: "The good of any one individual is of no more importance, from the point of view (if I may say so) of the Universe, than the good of any other."[1] More recently, the leading figures in contemporary moral philosophy have shown a great deal of agreement in specifying as a fundamental presupposition of their moral theories some similar requirement which operates so as to give everyone's interests equal consideration—although they cannot agree on how this requirement is best formulated.[2]

It is an implication of this principle of equality that our concern for others ought not to depend on what they are like, or what abilities they possess—although precisely what this concern requires us to do may vary according to the characteristics of those affected by what we do. It is on this basis that the case against racism and the case against sexism must both ultimately rest; and it is in accordance with this principle that speciesism is also to be condemned. If possessing a higher degree of intelligence does not entitle one human to use another for his own ends, how can it entitle humans to exploit non-humans?

Many philosophers have proposed the principle of equal consideration of interests, in some form or other, as a basic moral principle; but, as we shall see in more detail shortly, not many of them have recognized that this principle applies to members of other species as well as to our own. Bentham was one of the few who did realize this. In a forward-looking passage, written at a time when black slaves in British dominions were still being treated much as we now treat nonhuman animals, Bentham wrote:

> The day *may* come when the rest of the animal creation may acquire those rights which never could have been witholden from them but by the hand of tyranny. The French have already discovered that the blackness of the skin is no reason why a human being should be abandoned without redress to the caprice of a tormentor. It may one day come to be recognized that the number of the legs, the villosity of the skin, or the termination of the *os sacrum,* are reasons equally insufficient for abandoning a sensitive being to the same fate. What else is it that should trace the insuperable line? Is it the faculty of reason, or perhaps the faculty of discourse? But a full grown horse or dog is beyond comparison a more rational, as well as a more conversable animal, than an infant of a day, or a week, or even a month, old. But suppose they were otherwise, what would it avail? The question is not, Can they reason? nor Can they *talk?* but, *Can they suffer?*[3]

In this passage Bentham points to the capacity for suffering as the vital characteristic that gives a being the right to equal consideration. The capacity for suffering—or more strictly, for suffering and/or enjoyment or happiness—is not just another characteristic like the capacity for language, or for higher mathematics. Bentham is not saying that those who try to mark "the insuperable line" that determines whether the interests of a being should be considered happen to have selected the wrong characteristic. The capacity for suffering and enjoying things is a pre-requisite for having interests at all, a condition that must be satisfied before we can speak of interests in any meaningful way. It would be nonsense to say that it was not in the interests of a stone to be kicked along the road by a schoolboy. A stone does not have interests because it cannot suffer. Nothing that we can do to it could possibly make any difference to its welfare. A mouse, on the other hand, does have an interest in not being tormented, because it will suffer if it is.

If a being suffers, there can be no moral justification for refusing to take that suffering into consideration. No matter what the nature of the being, the principle of equality requires that its suffering be counted equally with the like suffering—in so far as rough comparisons can be made—of any other being. If a being is not capable of suffering, or of experiencing enjoyment or happiness, there is nothing to be taken into account. This is why the limit of sentience (using the term as a convenient, if not strictly accurate, shorthand for the capacity to suffer or experience enjoyment or happiness) is the only defensible boundary of concern for the interests of others. To mark this boundary by some characteristic like intelligence or rationality would be to mark it in an arbitrary way. Why not choose some other characteristic, like skin color?

The racist violates the principle of equality by giving greater weight to the interests of members of his own race, when there is a clash between their interests and the interests of those of another race. Similarly the speciesist allows the interests of his own species to override the greater interests of members of other species.[4] The pattern is the same in each case. Most human beings are speciesists. I shall now very briefly describe some of the practices that show this.

For the great majority of human beings, especially in urban, industrialized societies, the most direct form of contact with members of other species is at meal-times: we eat them. In doing so we treat them purely as means to our ends. We regard their life and well-being as subordinate to our taste for a particular kind of dish. I say "taste" deliberately—this is purely a matter of pleasing our palate. There can be no defence of eating flesh in terms of satisfying nutritional needs, since it has been established beyond doubt that we could satisfy our need for protein and other essential nutrients far more efficiently with a diet that replaced animal flesh by soy beans, or products derived from soy beans, and other high-protein vegetable products.[5]

It is not merely the act of killing that indicates what we are ready to do to other species in order to gratify our tastes. The suffering we inflict on the animals while they are alive is perhaps an even clearer indication of our speciesism than the fact that we are prepared to kill them. In order to have meat on the table at a price that people can afford, our society tolerates methods of meat production that confine sentient animals in cramped, unsuitable conditions for the entire durations of their lives. Animals are treated like machines that convert fodder into flesh, and any innovation that results in a higher "conversion ratio" is liable to be adopted. As one authority on the subject has said, "cruelty is acknowledged only when profitability ceases."[6] So hens are crowded four or five to a cage with a floor area of twenty inches by eighteen inches, or around the size of a single page of the *New York Times*. The cages have wire floors, since this reduces cleaning costs, though wire is unsuitable for the hens' feet; the floors slope, since this makes the eggs roll down for easy collection, although this makes it difficult for the hens to rest comfortably. In these conditions all the birds' natural instincts are thwarted: they cannot stretch their wings fully, walk freely, dust-bathe, scratch the ground, or build a nest. Although they have never known other conditions, observers have noticed that the birds vainly try to perform these actions. Frustrated at their inability to do so, they often develop what farmers call "vices," and peck each other to death. To prevent this, the beaks of young birds are often cut off.

This kind of treatment is not limited to poultry. Pigs are now also being reared in cages inside sheds. These animals are comparable to dogs in intelligence, and need a varied, stimulating environment if they are not to suffer from stress and boredom. Anyone who kept a dog in the way in which pigs are frequently kept would be liable to prosecution, in England at least, but because our interest in exploiting pigs is greater than our interest in exploiting dogs, we object to cruelty to dogs while consuming the produce of cruelty to pigs. Of the other animals, the condition of veal calves is perhaps worst of all, since these animals are so closely confined that they cannot even turn around or get up and lie down freely. In this way they do not develop unpalatable muscle. They are also made anaemic and kept short of roughage, to keep their flesh pale, since white veal fetches a higher price; as a result they develop a craving for iron and roughage, and have been observed to gnaw wood off the sides of their stalls, and lick greedily at any rusty hinge that is within reach.

Since, as I have said, none of these practices cater for anything more than our pleasures of taste, our practice of rearing and killing other animals in order to eat them is a clear instance of the sacrifice of the most important interests of other beings in order to satisfy trivial interests of our own. To avoid speciesism we must stop this practice, and each of us has a moral obligation to cease supporting the practice. Our custom is all the support that the meat-industry needs. The decision to cease giving it that support may be difficult, but it is no more difficult than it would have been for a white Southerner to go against the traditions of his society and free his slaves: if we do not change our dietary habits, how can we censure those slaveholders who would not change their own way of living?

The same form of discrimination may be observed in the widespread practice of experimenting on other species in order to see if certain substances are safe for human beings, or to test some psychological theory about the effect of severe punishment on learning, or to try out various new compounds just in case something turns up. People sometimes think that all this experimentation is for vital medical purposes, and so will reduce suffering overall. This comfortable belief is very wide of the mark. Drug companies test new shampoos and cosmetics that they are intending to put on the market by dropping them into the eyes of rabbits, held open by metal clips, in order to observe what damage results. Food additives, like artificial colorings and preservatives, are tested by what is known as the "LD$_{50}$"—a test designed to find the level of consumption at which 50% of a group of animals will die. In the process, nearly all of the animals are made very sick before some finally die, and others pull through. If the substance is relatively harmless, as it often is, huge doses have to be force-fed the animals, until in some cases sheer volume or concentration of the substance causes death.

Much of this pointless cruelty goes on in the universities. In many areas of science, non-human animals are regarded as an item of laboratory equipment, to be used and expended as desired. In psychology laboratories experimenters devise endless variations and repetitions of experiments that were of little value in the first place. To quote just one example, from the experimenter's own account in a psychology journal: at the University of Pennsylvania, Perrin S. Cohen hung six dogs in hammocks with electrodes taped to their hind feet. Elec-

tric shock of varying intensity was then administered through the electrodes. If the dog learnt to press its head against a panel on the left, the shock was turned off, but otherwise it remained on indefinitely. Three of the dogs, however, were required to wait periods varying from 2 to 7 seconds while being shocked before making the response that turned off the current. If they failed to wait, they received further shocks. Each dog was given from 26 to 46 "sessions" in the hammock, each session consisting of 80 "trials" or shocks, administered at intervals of one minute. The experimenter reported that the dogs, who were unable to move in the hammock, barked or bobbed their heads when the current was applied. The reported findings of the experiment were that there was a delay in the dogs' responses that increased proportionately to the time the dogs were required to endure the shock, but a gradual increase in the intensity of the shock had no systematic effect in the timing of the response. The experiment was funded by the National Institutes of Health, and the United States Public Health Service.[7]

In this example, and countless cases like it, the possible benefits to mankind are either non-existent or fantastically remote; while the certain losses to members of other species are very real. This is, again, a clear indication of speciesism.

In the past, argument about vivisection has often missed this point, because it has been put in absolutist terms: Would the abolitionist be prepared to let thousands die if they could be saved by experimenting on a single animal? The way to reply to this purely hypothetical question is to pose another: Would the experimenter be prepared to perform his experiment on an orphaned human infant, if that were the only way to save many lives? (I say "orphan" to avoid the complication of parental feelings, although in doing so I am being overfair to the experimenter, since the nonhuman subjects of experiments are not orphans.) If the experimenter is not prepared to use an orphaned human infant, then his readiness to use non-humans is simple discrimination, since adult apes, cats, mice and other mammals are more aware of what is happening to them, more self-directing and, so far as we can tell, at least as sensitive to pain, as any human infant. There seems to be no relevant characteristic that human infants possess that adult mammals do not have to the same or a higher degree. (Someone might try to argue that what makes it wrong to experiment on a human infant is that the infant will, in time and if left alone, develop into more than the nonhuman, but one would then, to be consistent, have to oppose abortion, since the fetus has the same potential as the infant—indeed, even contraception and abstinence might be wrong on this ground, since the egg and sperm, considered jointly, also have the same potential. In any case, this argument still gives us no reason for selecting a nonhuman, rather than a human with severe and irreversible brain damage, as the subject for our experiments.)

The experimenter, then, shows a bias in favor of his own species whenever he carries out an experiment on a nonhuman for a purpose that he would not think justified him in using a human being at an equal or lower level of sentience, awareness, ability to be self-directing, etc. No one familiar with the kind of results yielded by most experiments on animals can have the slightest doubt that if this bias were eliminated the number of experiments performed would be a minute fraction of the number performed today.

Experimenting on animals, and eating their flesh, are perhaps the two major forms of speciesism in our society. By comparison, the third and last form of speciesism is so minor as to be insignificant, but it is perhaps of some special interest to those for whom this article was written. I am referring to speciesism in contemporary philosophy.

Philosophy ought to question the basic assumptions of the age. Thinking through, critically and carefully, what most people take for granted is, I believe, the chief task of philosophy, and it is this task that makes philosophy a worthwhile activity. Regrettably, philosophy does not always live up to its historic role. Philosophers are human beings and they are subject to all the preconceptions of the society to which they belong. Sometimes they succeed in breaking free of the prevailing ideology: more often they become its most sophisticated defenders. So, in this case, philosophy as practiced in the universi-

ties today does not challenge anyone's preconceptions about our relations with other species. By their writings, those philosophers who tackle problems that touch upon the issue reveal that they make the same unquestioned assumptions as most other humans, and what they say tends to confirm the reader in his or her comfortable speciesist habits.

I could illustrate this claim by referring to the writings of philosophers in various fields—for instance, the attempts that have been made by those interested in rights to draw the boundary of the sphere of rights so that it runs parallel to the biological boundaries of the species *homo sapiens,* including infants and even mental defectives, but excluding those other beings of equal or greater capacity who are so useful to us at mealtimes and in our laboratories. I think it would be a more appropriate conclusion to this article, however, if I concentrated on the problem with which we have been centrally concerned, the problem of equality.

It is significant that the problem of equality, in moral and political philosophy, is invariably formulated in terms of human equality. The effect of this is that the question of the equality of other animals does not confront the philosopher, or student, as an issue itself—and this is already an indication of the failure of philosophy to challenge accepted beliefs. Still, philosophers have found it difficult to discuss the issue of human equality without raising, in a paragraph or two, the question of the status of other animals. The reason for this, which should be apparent from what I have said already, is that if humans are to be regarded as equal to one another, we need some sense of "equal" that does not require any actual, descriptive equality of capacities, talents or other qualities. If equality is to be related to any actual characteristics of humans, these characteristics must be some lowest common denominator, pitched so low that no human lacks them—but then the philosopher comes up against the catch that any such set of characteristics which covers *all* humans will not be possessed *only by humans*. In other words, it turns out that in the only sense in which we can truly say, as an assertion of fact, that all humans are equal, at least some members of other species are also equal—

equal, that is, to each other and to humans. If, on the other hand, we regard the statement "All humans are equal" in some non-factual way, perhaps as a prescription, then, as I have already argued, it is even more difficult to exclude non-humans from the sphere of equality.

This result is not what the egalitarian philosopher originally intended to assert. Instead of accepting the radical outcome to which their own reasonings naturally point, however, most philosophers try to reconcile their beliefs in human equality and animal inequality by arguments that can only be described as devious.

As a first example, I take William Frankena's well-known article "The Concept of Social Justice."[8] Frankena opposes the idea of basing justice on merit, because he sees that this could lead to highly inegalitarian results. Instead he proposes the principle that:

> . . . all men are to be treated as equals, not because they are equal, in any respect, but simply because they are human. They are human because they have emotions and desires, and are able to think, and hence are capable of enjoying a good life in a sense in which other animals are not.

But what is this capacity to enjoy the good life which all humans have, but no other animals? Other animals have emotions and desires, and appear to be capable of enjoying a good life. We may doubt that they can think—although the behavior of some apes, dolphins and even dogs suggests that some of them can—but what is the relevance of thinking? Frankena goes on to admit that by "the good life" he means "not so much the morally good life as the happy or satisfactory life," so thought would appear to be unnecessary for enjoying the good life; in fact to emphasize the need for thought would make difficulties for the egalitarian since only some people are capable of leading intellectually satisfying lives, or morally good lives. This makes it difficult to see what Frankena's principle of equality has to do with simply being *human*. Surely every sentient being is capable of leading a life that is happier or less mis-

erable than some alternative life, and hence has a claim to be taken into account. In this respect the distinction between humans and non-humans is not a sharp division, but rather a continuum along which we move gradually, and with overlaps between the species, from simple capacities for enjoyment and satisfaction, or pain and suffering, to more complex ones.

Faced with a situation in which they see a need for some basis for the moral gulf that is commonly thought to separate humans and animals, but finding no concrete difference that will do the job without undermining the equality of humans, philosophers tend to waffle. They resort to high-sounding phrases like "the intrinsic dignity of the human individual";[9] they talk of the "intrinsic worth of all men" as if men (humans?) had some worth that other beings did not,[10] or they say that humans, and only humans, are "ends in themselves," while "everything other than a person can only have value for a person."[11]

This idea of a distinctive human dignity and worth has a long history; it can be traced back directly to the Renaissance humanists, for instance to Pico della Mirandola's *Oration on the Dignity of Man*. Pico and other humanists based their estimate of human dignity on the idea that man possessed the central, pivotal position in the "Great Chain of Being" that led from the lowliest forms of matter to God himself; this view of the universe, in turn, goes back to both classical and Judeo-Christian doctrines. Contemporary philosophers have cast off these metaphysical and religious shackles and freely invoke the dignity of mankind without needing to justify the idea at all. Why should we not attribute "intrinsic dignity" or "intrinsic worth" to ourselves? Fellow-humans are unlikely to reject the accolades we so generously bestow on them, and those to whom we deny the honor are unable to object. Indeed, when one thinks only of humans, it can be very liberal, very progressive, to talk of the dignity of all human beings. In so doing, we implicitly condemn slavery, racism, and other violations of human rights. We admit that we ourselves are in some fundamental sense on a par with the poorest, most ignorant members of our own species. It is only when we think of humans as no more than a small sub-group of all the beings that inhabit our planet that we may realize that in elevating our own species we are at the same time lowering the relative status of all other species.

The truth is that the appeal to the intrinsic dignity of human beings appears to solve the egalitarian's problems only as long as it goes unchallenged. Once we ask *why* it should be that all humans—including infants, mental defectives, psychopaths, Hitler, Stalin and the rest—have some kind of dignity or worth that no elephant, pig, or chimpanzee can ever achieve, we see that this question is as difficult to answer as our original request for some relevant fact that justifies the inequality of humans and other animals. In fact, these two questions are really one: talk of intrinsic dignity or moral worth only takes the problem back one step, because any satisfactory defence of the claim that all and only humans have intrinsic dignity would need to refer to some relevant capacities or characteristics that all and only humans possess. Philosophers frequently introduce ideas of dignity, respect and worth at the point at which other reasons appear to be lacking, but this is hardly good enough. Fine phrases are the last resource of those who have run out of arguments.

In case there are those who still think it may be possible to find some relevant characteristic that distinguishes all humans from all members of other species, I shall refer again, before I conclude, to the existence of some humans who quite clearly are below the level of awareness, self-consciousness, intelligence, and sentience, of many nonhumans. I am thinking of humans with severe and irreparable brain damage, and also of infant humans. To avoid the complication of the relevance of a being's potential, however, I shall henceforth concentrate on permanently retarded humans.

Philosophers who set out to find a characteristic that will distinguish humans from other animals rarely take the course of abandoning these groups of humans by lumping them in with the other animals. It is easy to see why they do not. To take this line without re-thinking our attitudes to other animals would entail that we have the right to perform painful experiments on retarded humans for trivial reasons;

similarly it would follow that we had the right to rear and kill these humans for food. To most philosophers these consequences are as unacceptable as the view that we should stop treating nonhumans in this way.

Of course, when discussing the problem of equality it is possible to ignore the problem of mental defectives, or brush it aside as if somehow insignificant.[12] This is the easiest way out. What else remains? My final example of speciesism in contemporary philosophy has been selected to show what happens when a writer is prepared to face the question of human equality and animal equality without ignoring the existence of mental defectives, and without resorting to obscurantist mumbo-jumbo. Stanley Benn's clear and honest article "Egalitarianism and Equal Consideration of Interests"[13] fits this description.

Benn, after noting the usual "evident human inequalities," argues, correctly I think, for equality of consideration as the only possible basis for egalitarianism. Yet Benn, like other writers, is thinking only of "equal consideration of human interests." Benn is quite open in his defence of this restriction of equal consideration:

> . . . not to possess human shape *is* a disqualifying condition. However faithful or intelligent a dog may be, it would be a monstrous sentimentality to attribute to him interests that could be weighed in an equal balance with those of human beings . . . if, for instance, one had to decide between feeding a hungry baby or a hungry dog, anyone who chose the dog would generally be reckoned morally defective, unable to recognize a fundamental inequality of claims.
>
> This is what distinguishes our attitude to animals from our attitude to imbeciles. It would be odd to say that we ought to respect equally the dignity or personality of the imbecile and of the rational man . . . but there is nothing odd about saying that we should respect their interests equally, that is, that we should give to the interests of each the same serious consideration as claims to considerations necessary for some standard of well-being that we can recognize and endorse.

Benn's statement of the basis of the consideration we should have for imbeciles seems to me correct, but why should there be any fundamental inequality of claims between a dog and a human imbecile? Benn sees that if equal consideration depended on rationality, no reason could be given against using imbeciles for research purposes, as we now use dogs and guinea pigs. This will not do: "But of course we do distinguish imbeciles from animals in this regard," he says. That the common distinction is justifiable is something Benn does not question; his problem is how it is to be justified. The answer he gives is this:

> . . . we respect the interests of men and give them priority over dogs not *insofar* as they are rational, but because rationality is the human norm. We say it is *unfair* to exploit the deficiencies of the imbecile who falls short of the norm, just as it would be unfair, and not just ordinarily dishonest, to steal from a blind man. If we do not think in this way about dogs, it is because we do not see the irrationality of the dog as a deficiency or a handicap, but as normal for the species. The characteristics, therefore, that distinguish the normal man from the normal dog make it intelligible for us to talk of other men having interests and capacities, and therefore claims, of precisely the same kind as we make on our own behalf. But although these characteristics may provide the point of the distinction between men and other species, they are not in fact the qualifying conditions for membership, or the distinguishing criteria of the class of morally considerable persons; and this is precisely because a man does not become a member of a different species, with its own standards of normality, by reason of not possessing these characteristics.

The final sentence of this passage gives the argument away. An imbecile, Benn concedes, may have no characteristics superior to those of a dog; nevertheless this does not make the imbecile a member of "a different species" as the dog is. *Therefore* it would be "unfair" to use the imbecile for medical research as we use the dog. But why? That the imbecile is not rational is just the way things have

worked out, and the same is true of the dog—neither is any more responsible for their mental level. If it is unfair to take advantage of an isolated defect, why is it fair to take advantage of a more general limitation? I find it hard to see anything in this argument except a defence of preferring the interests of members of our own species because they are members of our own species. To those who think there might be more to it, I suggest the following mental exercise. Assume that it has been proven that there is a difference in the average, or normal, intelligence quotient for two different races, say whites and blacks. Then substitute the term "white" for every occurrence of "men" and "black" for every occurrence of "dog" in the passage quoted; and substitute "high I.Q." for "rationality" and when Benn talks of "imbeciles" replace this term by "dumb whites"— that is, whites who fall well below the normal white I.Q. score. Finally, change "species" to "race." Now re-read the passage. It has become a defence of a rigid, no-exceptions division between whites and blacks, based on I.Q. scores, *not withstanding an admitted overlap* between whites and blacks in this respect. The revised passage is, of course, outrageous, and this is not only because we have made fictitious assumptions in our substitutions. The point is that in the original passage Benn was defending a rigid division in the amount of consideration due to members of different species, despite admitted cases of overlap. If the original did not, at first reading strike us as being as outrageous as the revised version does, this is largely because although we are not racists ourselves, most of us are speciesists. Like the other articles, Benn's stands as a warning of the ease with which the best minds can fall victim to a prevailing ideology.

NOTES

1. *The Methods of Ethics* (7th Ed.), p. 382.
2. For example, R. M. Hare, *Freedom and Reason* (Oxford, 1963) and J. Rawls, *A Theory of Justice* (Harvard, 1972); for a brief account of the essential agreement on this issue between these and other positions, see R. M.

Hare, "Rules of War and Moral Reasoning," *Philosophy and Public Affairs,* 1:2 (1972).

3. *Introduction to the Principles of Morals and Legislation,* ch. XVII.

4. I owe the term "speciesism" to Dr. Richard Ryder.

5. In order to produce 1 lb. of protein in the form of beef or veal, we must feed 21 lbs. of protein to the animal. Other forms of livestock are slightly less inefficient, but the average ratio in the U.S. is still 1:8. It has been estimated that the amount of protein lost to humans in this way is equivalent to 90% of the annual world protein deficit. For a brief account, see Frances Moore Lappé, *Diet for a Small Planet* (New York: Friends of The Earth/Ballantine, 1971) pp. 4–11.

6. Ruth Harrison, *Animal Machines* (London: Stuart, 1964). For an account of farming conditions, see my *Animal Liberation* (New York Review Company, 1975).

7. *Journal of the Experimental Analysis of Behavior,* 13:1 (1970).

8. W. Frankena, "The Concept of Social Justice" in *Social Justice,* ed. R. Brandt (Englewood Cliffs; Prentice Hall, 1962), p. 19.

9. Frankena, "The Concept of Social Justice," p. 23.

10. H. A. Bedau, "Egalitarianism and the Idea of Equality" in *Nomos IX: Equality,* ed. J. R. Pennock and J. W. Chapman (New York: Chapman, 1967)

11. G. Vlastos, "Justice and Equality" in Brandt, *Social Justice,* p. 48.

12. For example, Bernard Williams, "The Idea of Equality," in *Philosophy, Politics and Society* (second series), ed. P. Laslett and W. Runciman (Oxford: Blackwell, 1962), p. 118; J. Rawls, *A Theory of Justice,* pp. 509–10.

13. Bedau, *Nomos IX: Equality.* The passages quoted start on p. 62.

The Land Ethic

Aldo Leopold

When God-like Odysseus returned from the wars in Troy, he hanged all on one rope a dozen slave-girls of his household whom he suspected of misbehavior during his absence.

This hanging involved no question of propriety. The girls were property. The disposal of property was then, as now, a matter of expediency, not of right and wrong.

Concepts of right and wrong were not lacking from Odysseus' Greece: witness the fidelity of his wife through the long years before at last his black-prowed galleys clove the wine-dark seas for home. The ethical structure of that day covered wives, but had not yet been extended to human chattels. During the three thousand years which have since elapsed, ethical criteria have been extended to many fields of conduct, with corresponding shrinkages in those judged by expediency only.

THE ETHICAL SEQUENCE

This extension of ethics, so far studied only by philosophers, is actually a process in ecological evolution. Its sequences may be described in ecological as well as in philosophical terms. An ethic, ecolog-

Aldo Leopold, "The Land Ethic," in *A Sand County Almanac* (Oxford: Oxford University Press, 1981), 237–65. Reprinted with permission of the publisher.

ically, is a limitation on freedom of action in the struggle for existence. An ethic, philosophically, is a differentiation of social from anti-social conduct. These are two definitions of one thing. The thing has its origin in the tendency of interdependent individuals or groups to evolve modes of co-operation. The ecologist calls these symbioses. Politics and economics are advanced symbioses in which the original free-for-all competition has been replaced, in part, by co-operative mechanisms with an ethical content.

The complexity of co-operative mechanisms has increased with population density, and with the efficiency of tools. It was simpler, for example, to define the anti-social uses of sticks and stones in the days of the mastodons than of bullets and billboards in the age of motors.

The first ethics dealt with the relation between individuals; the Mosaic Decalogue is an example. Later accretions dealt with the relation between the individual and society. The Golden Rule tries to integrate the individual to society; democracy to integrate social organization to the individual.

There is as yet no ethic dealing with man's relation to land and to the animals and plants which grow upon it. Land, like Odysseus' slave-girls, is still property. The land-relation is still strictly economic, entailing privileges but not obligations.

The extension of ethics to this third element in human environment is, if I read the evidence correctly, an evolutionary possibility and an ecological necessity. It is the third step in a sequence. The first two have already been taken. Individual thinkers since the days of Ezekiel and Isaiah have asserted that the despoliation of land is not only inexpedient but wrong. Society, however, has not yet affirmed their belief. I regard the present conservation movement as the embryo of such an affirmation.

An ethic may be regarded as a mode of guidance for meeting ecological situations so new or intricate, or involving such deferred reactions, that the path of social expediency is not discernible to the average individual. Animal instincts are modes of guidance for the individual in meeting such situations. Ethics are possibly a kind of community instinct in-the-making.

THE COMMUNITY CONCEPT

All ethics so far evolved rest upon a single premise: that the individual is a member of a community of interdependent parts. His instincts prompt him to compete for his place in the community, but his ethics prompt him also to co-operate (perhaps in order that there may be a place to compete for).

The land ethic simply enlarges the boundaries of the community to include soils, waters, plants, and animals, or collectively: the land.

This sounds simple: do we not already sing our love for and obligation to the land of the free and the home of the brave? Yes, but just what and whom do we love? Certainly not the soil, which we are sending helter-skelter downriver. Certainly not the waters, which we assume have no function except to turn turbines, float barges, and carry off sewage. Certainly not the plants, of which we exterminate whole communities without batting an eye. Certainly not the animals, of which we have already extirpated many of the largest and most beautiful species. A land ethic of course cannot prevent the alteration, management and use of these "resources," but it does affirm their right to continued existence, and, at least in spots their continued existence in a natural state.

In short, a land ethic changes the role of *Homo sapiens* from conqueror of the land-community to plain member and citizen of it. It implies respect for his fellow-members, and also respect for the community as such.

In human history, we have learned (I hope) that the conqueror role is eventually self-defeating. Why? Because it is implicit in such a role that the conqueror knows, *ex cathedra,* just what makes the community clock tick, and just what and who is valuable, and what and who is worthless, in community life. It always turns out that he knows neither, and this is why his conquests eventually defeat themselves. . . .

THE LAND PYRAMID

An ethic to supplement and guide the economic relation to land presupposes the existence of some mental image of land as a biotic mechanism. We can be ethical only in relation to something we can see, feel, understand, love, or otherwise have faith in.

The image commonly employed in conservation education is "the balance of nature." For reasons too lengthy to detail here, this figure of speech fails to describe accurately what little we know about the land mechanism. A much truer image is the one employed in ecology: the biotic pyramid. I shall first sketch the pyramid as a symbol of land, and later develop some of its implications in terms of land-use.

Plants absorb energy from the sun. This energy flows through a circuit called the biota, which may be represented by a pyramid consisting of layers. The bottom layer is the soil. A plant layer rests on the soil, an insect layer on the plants, a bird and rodent layer on the insects and so on up through various animal groups to the apex layer, which consists of the larger carnivores.

The species of a layer are alike not in where they came from, or in what they look like, but rather in what they eat. Each successive layer depends on those below it for food and often for other services, and each in turn furnishes food and services to those above. Proceeding upward, each successive layer decreases in numerical abundance. Thus, for every carnivore there are hundreds of his prey, thousands of their prey, millions of insects, uncountable plants. The pyramidal form of the system reflects this numerical progression from apex to base. Man shares an intermediate layer with the bears, raccoons, and squirrels which eat both meat and vegetables.

The lines of dependency for food and other services are called food chains. Thus soil-oak-deer-Indian is a chain that has now been largely converted to soil-corn-cow-farmer. Each species, including ourselves, is a link in many chains. The deer eats a hundred plants other than oak, and the cow a hundred plants other than corn. Both, then, are links in a hundred chains. The pyramid is a tangle of chains so complex as to seem disorderly, yet the stability of the system proves it to be a highly organized structure. Its functioning depends on the co-operation and competition of its diverse parts.

In the beginning, the pyramid of life was low and squat; the food chains short and simple. Evolution has added layer after layer, link after link. Man is one of thousands of accretions to the height and complexity of the pyramid. Science has given us many doubts, but it has given us at least one certainty: the trend of evolution is to elaborate and diversify the biota.

Land, then, is not merely soil; it is a fountain of energy flowing through a circuit of soils, plants, and animals. Food chains are the living channels which conduct energy upward; death and decay return it to the soil. The circuit is not closed; some energy is dissipated in decay, some is added by absorption from the air, some is stored in soils, peats, and long-lived forests; but it is a sustained circuit, like a slowly augmented revolving fund of life. There is always a net loss by downhill wash, but this is normally small and offset by the decay of rocks. It is deposited in the ocean and, in the course of geological time, raised to form new lands and new pyramids.

The velocity and character of the upward flow of energy depend on the complex structure of the plant and animal community, much as the upward flow of sap in a tree depends on its complex cellular organization. Without this complexity, normal circulation would presumably not occur. Structure means the characteristic numbers, as well as the characteristic kinds and functions, of the component species. This interdependence between the complex structure of the land and its smooth functioning as an energy unit is one of its basic attributes.

When a change occurs in one part of the circuit, many other parts must adjust themselves to it. Change does not necessarily obstruct or divert the flow of energy; evolution is a long series of self-induced changes, the net result of which has been to elaborate the flow mechanism and to lengthen the circuit. Evolutionary changes, however, are usually slow and local. Man's invention of tools has enabled him to make changes of unprecedented violence, rapidity, and scope.

One change is in the composition of floras and faunas. The larger predators are lopped off the apex of the pyramid; food chains, for the first time in history, become shorter rather than longer. Domesticated species from other lands are substituted for wild ones, and wild ones are moved to new habitats.

In this world-wide pooling of faunas and floras, some species get out of bounds as pests and diseases, others are extinguished. Such effects are seldom intended or foreseen; they represent unpredicted and often untraceable readjustments in the structure. Agricultural science is largely a race between the emergence of new pests and the emergence of new techniques for their control.

Another change touches the flow of energy through plants and animals and its return to the soil. Fertility is the ability of soil to receive, store, and release energy. Agriculture, by overdrafts on the soil, or by too radical a substitution of domestic for native species in the superstructure, may derange the channels of flow or deplete storage. Soils depleted of their storage, or of the organic matter which anchors it, wash away faster than they form. This is erosion.

Waters, like soil, are part of the energy circuit. Industry, by polluting waters or obstructing them with dams, may exclude the plants and animals necessary to keep energy in circulation.

Transportation brings about another basic change: the plants or animals grown in one region are now consumed and returned to the soil in another. Transportation taps the energy stored in rocks, and in the air, and uses it elsewhere; thus we fertilize the garden with nitrogen gleaned by the guano birds from the fishes of seas on the other side of the Equator. Thus the formerly localized and self-contained circuits are pooled on a world-wide scale.

The process of altering the pyramid for human occupation releases stored energy, and this often gives rise, during the pioneering period, to a deceptive exuberance of plant and animal life, both wild and tame. These releases of biotic capital tend to becloud or postpone the penalties of violence.

This thumbnail sketch of land as an energy circuit conveys three basic ideas:

(1) That land is not merely soil.
(2) That the native plants and animals kept the energy circuit open; others may or may not.

(3) That man-made changes are of a different order than evolutionary changes, and have effects more comprehensive than is intended or foreseen.

These ideas, collectively, raise two basic issues: Can the land adjust itself to the new order? Can the desired alterations be accomplished with less violence?

Biotas seem to differ in their capacity to sustain violent conversion. Western Europe, for example, carries a far different, pyramid than Caesar found there. Some large animals are lost; swampy forests have become meadows or plowland; many new plants and animals are introduced, some of which escape as pests; the remaining natives are greatly changed in distribution and abundance. Yet the soil is still there and, with the help of imported nutrients, still fertile; the waters flow normally; the new structure seems to function and to persist. There is no visible stoppage or derangement of the circuit.

Western Europe, then, has a resistant biota. Its inner processes are tough, elastic, resistant to strain. No matter how violent the alterations, the pyramid, so far, has developed some new modus vivendi which preserves its habitability for man, and for most of the other natives.

Japan seems to present another instance of radical conversion without disorganization.

Most other civilized regions, and some as yet barely touched by civilization, display various stages of disorganization, varying from initial symptoms to advanced wastage. In Asia Minor and North Africa diagnosis is confused by climatic changes, which may have been either the cause or the effect of advanced wastage. In the United States the degree of disorganization varies locally; it is worst in the Southwest, the Ozarks, and parts of the South, and least in New England and the Northwest. Better land-uses may still arrest it in the less advanced regions. In parts of Mexico, South America, South Africa, and Australia a violent and accelerating wastage is in progress, but I cannot assess the prospects.

This almost world-wide display of disorganization in the land seems to be similar to disease in an animal, except that it never culminates in complete disorganization or death. The land recovers, but at some reduced level of complexity, and with a reduced carrying capacity for people, plants, and animals. Many biotas currently regarded as "lands of opportunity" are in fact already subsisting on exploitative agriculture, i.e. they have already exceeded their sustained carrying capacity. Most of South America is overpopulated in this sense.

In arid regions we attempt to offset the process of wastage by reclamation, but it is only too evident that the prospective longevity of reclamation projects is often short. In our own West, the best of them may not last a century.

The combined evidence of history and ecology seems to support one general deduction: the less violent the man-made changes, the greater the probability of successful readjustment in the pyramid. Violence, in turn, varies with human population density; a dense population requires a more violent conversion. In this respect, North America has a better chance for permanence than Europe, if she can contrive to limit her density.

This deduction runs counter to our current philosophy, which assumes that because a small increase in density enriched human life, that an indefinite increase will enrich it indefinitely. Ecology knows of no density relationship that holds for indefinitely wide limits. All gains from density are subject to a law of diminishing returns.

Whatever may be the equation for men and land, it is improbable that we as yet know all its terms. Recent discoveries in mineral and vitamin nutrition reveal unsuspected dependencies in the up-circuit: incredibly minute quantities of certain substances determine the value of soils to plants, of plants to animals. What of the down-circuit? What of the vanishing species, the preservation of which we now regard as an esthetic luxury? They helped build the soil; in what unsuspected ways may they be essential to its maintenance? Professor Weaver proposes that we use prairie flowers to reflocculate the wasting soils of the dust bowl; who knows for what purpose cranes and condors, otters and grizzlies may some day be used? . . .

THE OUTLOOK

It is inconceivable to me that an ethical relation to land can exist without love, respect, and admiration for land, and a high regard for its value. By value, I of course mean something far broader than mere economic value; I mean value in the philosophical sense.

Perhaps the most serious obstacle impeding the evolution of a land ethic is the fact that our educational and economic system is headed away from, rather than toward, an intense consciousness of land. Your true modern is separated from the land by many middlemen, and by innumerable physical gadgets. He has no vital relation to it; to him it is the space between cities on which crops grow. Turn him loose for a day on the land, and if the spot does not happen to be a golf links or a "scenic" area, he is bored stiff. If crops could be raised by hydroponics instead of farming, it would suit him very well. Synthetic substitutes for wood, leather, wool, and other natural land products suit him better than the originals. In short, land is something he has "outgrown."

Almost equally serious as an obstacle to a land ethic is the attitude of the farmer for whom the land is still an adversary, or a taskmaster that keeps him in slavery. Theoretically, the mechanization of farming ought to cut the farmer's chains, but whether it really does is debatable.

One of the requisites for an ecological comprehension of land is an understanding of ecology, and this is by no means co-extensive with "education"; in fact, much higher education seems deliberately to avoid ecological concepts. An understanding of ecology does not necessarily originate in courses bearing ecological labels; it is quite as likely to be labeled geography, botany, agronomy, history, or economics. This is as it should be, but whatever the label, ecological training is scarce.

The case for a land ethic would appear hopeless but for the minority which is in obvious revolt against these "modern" trends.

The "key-log" which must be moved to release the evolutionary process for an ethic is simply this: quit thinking about decent land-use as solely an economic problem. Examine each question in terms of what is ethically and esthetically right, as well as what is economically expedient. A thing is right when it tends to preserve the integrity, stability, and beauty of the biotic community. It is wrong when it tends otherwise.

It of course goes without saying that economic feasibility limits the tether of what can or cannot be done for land. It always has and it always will. The fallacy the economic determinists have tied around our collective neck, and which we now need to cast off, is the belief that economics determines *all* land-use. This is simply not true. An innumerable host of actions and attitudes, comprising perhaps the bulk of all land relations, is determined by the land-users tastes and predilections, rather than by his purse. The bulk of all land relations hinges on investments of time, forethought, skill, and faith rather than on investments of cash. As a land-user thinketh, so is he.

I have purposely presented the land ethic as a product of social evolution because nothing so important as an ethic is ever "written." Only the most superficial student of history supposes that Moses wrote the Decalogue; it evolved in the minds of a thinking community, and Moses wrote a tentative summary of it for a "seminar." I say tentative because evolution never stops.

The evolution of a land ethic is an intellectual as well as emotional process. Conservation is paved with good intentions which prove to be futile, or even dangerous, because they are devoid of critical understanding either of the land, or of economic land-use. I think it is a truism that as the ethical frontier advances from the individual to the community, its intellectual content increases.

The mechanism of operation is the same for any ethic: social approbation for right actions; social disapproval for wrong actions.

By and large, our present problem is one of attitudes and implements. We are remodeling the Alhambra with a steam-shovel, and we are proud of our yardage. We shall hardly relinquish the shovel which after all has many good points, but we are in need of gentler and more objective criteria for its successful use.

WILDERNESS

Wilderness is the raw material out of which man has hammered the artifact called civilization.

Wilderness was never a homogeneous raw material. It was very diverse, and the resulting artifacts are very diverse. These differences in the end-product are known as cultures. The rich diversity of the world's cultures reflects a corresponding diversity in the wilds that gave them birth.

For the first time in the history of the human species, two changes are now impending. One is the exhaustion of wilderness in the more habitable portions of the globe. The other is the world-wide hybridization of cultures through modem transport and industrialization. Neither can be prevented, and perhaps should not be, but the question arises whether, by some slight amelioration of the impending changes, certain values can be preserved that would otherwise be lost.

To the laborer in the sweat of his labor, the raw stuff on his anvil is an adversary to be conquered. So was wilderness an adversary to the pioneer.

But to the laborer in repose, able for the moment to cast a philosophical eye on his world, that same raw stuff is something to be loved and cherished, because it gives definition and meaning to his life. This is a plea for the preservation of some tag-ends of wilderness, as museum pieces, for the edification of those who may one day wish to see, feel, or study the origins of their cultural inheritance. . . .

Values in and Duties to the Natural World

Holmes Rolston III

Environmental ethics stretches classical ethics to the breaking point. All ethics seeks an appropriate respect for life. But we do not need just a humanistic ethic applied to the environment as we have needed one for business, law, medicine, technology, international development, or nuclear disarmament. Respect for life does demand an ethic concerned about human welfare, an ethic like the others and now applied to the environment. But environmental ethics in a deeper sense stands on a frontier, as radically theoretical as it is applied. It alone asks whether there can be nonhuman objects of duty.

Neither theory nor practice elsewhere needs values outside of human subjects, but environmental ethics must be more biologically objective—nonanthropocentric. It challenges the separation of science and ethics, trying to reform a science that finds nature value-free and an ethics that assumes that only humans count morally. Environmental ethics seeks to escape relativism in ethics, to discover a way past culturally based ethics. However much our worldviews, ethics included, are embedded in our cultural heritages, and thereby theory-laden and value laden, all of us know that a natural world exists apart from human cultures. Humans interact with nature. Environmental ethics is the only ethics that breaks out of culture. It has to evaluate nature, both wild nature and the nature that mixes with culture, and to judge duty thereby. After accepting environmental ethics, you will no longer be the humanist you once were.

Environmental ethics requires risk. It explores poorly charted terrain, where one can easily get lost. One must hazard the kind of insight that first looks like foolishness. Some people approach environmental ethics with a smile—expecting chicken liberation and rights for rocks, misplaced concern for chipmunks and daisies. Elsewhere, they think, ethicists deal with sober concerns: medical ethics, busi-

ness ethics, justice in public affairs, questions of life and death and of peace and war. But the questions here are no less serious: The degradation of the environment poses as great a threat to life as nuclear war, and a more probable tragedy.

HIGHER ANIMALS

Logically and psychologically, the best and easiest breakthrough past the traditional boundaries of interhuman ethics is made when confronting higher animals. Animals defend their lives; they have a good of their own and suffer pains and pleasures like ourselves. Human moral concern should at least cross over into the domain of animal experience. . . .

Animals enjoy psychological lives, subjective experiences, the satisfaction of felt interests—intrinsic values that count morally when humans encounter them. But the pains, pleasures, interests, and welfare of individual animals are only one of the considerations in a more complex environmental ethics that cannot be reached by conferring rights on them or by a hedonist calculus, however far extended. We have to travel further into a more biologically based ethics.

ORGANISMS

If we are to respect all life, we have still another boundary to cross, from zoology to botany, from sentient to insentient life. In Yosemite National Park for almost a century humans entertained themselves by driving through a tunnel cut in a giant sequoia. Two decades ago the Wawona tree, weakened by the cut, blew down in a storm. People said, "Cut us another drive-through sequoia." The Yosemite environmen-

Holmes Rolston III, "Values in and Duties to the Natural World," in *Ecology, Economics, Ethics: The Broken Circle*, ed. F. Bormann and S. Kellert (New Haven: Yale University Press, 1991), 73–96. Reprinted with permission of the publisher.

tal ethic, deepening over the years, answered, "No. You ought not to mutilate majestic sequoias for amusement. Respect their life." Indeed, some ethicists count the value of redwoods so highly that they will spike redwoods, lest they be cut. In the Rawah Wilderness in alpine Colorado, old signs read, "Please leave the flowers for others to enjoy." When the signs rotted out, new signs urged a less humanist ethic: "Let the flowers live!"

But trees and flowers cannot care, so why should we? We are not considering animals that are close kin, nor can they suffer or experience anything. Plants are not valuers with preferences that can be satisfied or frustrated. It seems odd to assert that plants need our sympathy, odd to ask that we should consider their point of view. They have no subjective life, only objective life.

Perhaps the questions are wrong, because they are coming out of the old paradigm. We are at a critical divide. That is why I earlier warned that environmental ethicists who seek only to extend a humanistic ethic to mammalian cousins will get lost. Seeing no moral landmarks, those ethicists may turn back to more familiar terrain. Afraid of the naturalistic fallacy, they will say that people should enjoy letting flowers live or that it is silly to cut drive-through sequoias, that it is aesthetically more excellent for humans to appreciate both for what they are. But these ethically conservative reasons really do not understand what biological conservation is in the deepest sense.

It takes ethical courage to go on, to move past a hedonistic, humanistic logic to a bio-logic. Pains, pleasures, and psychological experience will further be useful categories, but—lest some think that from here on I as a philosopher become illogical and lose all ethical sense—let us orient ourselves by extending logical, propositional, cognitive, and normative categories into biology. Nothing matters to a tree, but much is vital to it. . . .

A vital ethic respects all life, not just animal pains and pleasures, much less just human preferences. The old signs in the Rawah Wilderness—"Please leave the flowers for others to enjoy"—were application signs using an old, ethically conservative, humanistic ethic. The new ones invite a change of reference frame—a wilder ethic that is more logical because it is more biological, a radical ethic that goes down to the roots of life, that really is conservative because it understands biological conservation at depths. What the injunction "Let the flowers live!" means is this: "Daisies, marsh marigolds, geraniums, and larkspurs are evaluative systems that conserve goods of their kind and, in the absence of evidence to the contrary, are good kinds. There are trails here by which you may enjoy these flowers. Is there any reason why your human interests should not also conserve these good kinds?" A drive-through sequoia causes no suffering; it is not cruel. But it is callous and insensitive to the wonder of life.

SPECIES

Sensitivity to the wonder of life, however, can sometimes make an environmental ethicist seem callous. On San Clemente Island, the U.S. Fish and Wildlife Service and the Natural Resource Office of the U.S. Navy planned to shoot two thousand feral goats to save three endangered plant species (*Malacothamnus clementinus, Castilleja grisea,* and *Delphinium kinkiense*), of which the surviving individuals numbered only a few dozen. After a protest, some goats were trapped and relocated. But trapping all of them was impossible, and many thousands were killed. In this instance, the survival of plant species was counted more than the lives of individual mammals; a few plants counted more than many thousands of goats.

Those who wish to restore rare species of big cats to the wild have asked about killing genetically inbred, inferior cats presently held in zoos, in order to make space available for the cats needed to reconstruct and maintain a population that is genetically more likely to survive upon release. All the Siberian tigers in zoos in North America are descendants of seven animals; if these tigers were replaced by others nearer to the wild type and with more genetic variability, the species might be saved in the wild. When we move to the level of species, sometimes we decide to kill individuals for the good of their kind.

Or we might now refuse to let nature take its course. [When a bison fell through the ice into a river in Yellowstone Park,] the Yellowstone ethicists let the bison drown, in spite of its suffering; [when three hundred bighorn sheep caught pinkeye, and were left blinded and starving,] they let the blinded bighorns die. But in the spring of 1984 a sow grizzly and her three cubs walked across the ice of Yellowstone Lake to Frank Island, two miles from shore. They stayed several days to feast on two elk carcasses, and the ice bridge melted. Soon afterward, they were starving on an island too small to support them. This time the Yellowstone ethicists promptly rescued the grizzlies and released them on the mainland, in order to protect an endangered species. They were not rescuing individual bears so much as saving the species.

Coloradans have declined to build the Two Forks Dam to supply urban Denver with water. Building the dam would require destroying a canyon and altering the Platte River flow, with many negative environmental consequences, including further endangering the whooping crane and endangering a butterfly, the Pawnee montane skipper. Elsewhere in the state, water development threatens several fish species, including the humpback chub, which requires the turbulent spring runoff stopped by dams. Environmental ethics doubts whether the good of humans who wish more water for development, both for industry and for bluegrass lawns, warrants endangering species of cranes, butterflies, and fish.

A species exists; a species ought to exist. An environmental ethics must make these assertions and move from biology to ethics with care. Species exist only instantiated in individuals, yet they are as real as individual plants or animals. The assertion that there are specific forms of life historically maintained in their environments over time seems as certain as anything else we believe about the empirical world. At times biologists revise the theories and taxa with which they map these forms, but species are not so much like lines of latitude and longitude as like mountains and rivers, phenomena objectively there to be mapped. The edges of these natural kinds will sometimes be fuzzy, to some extent discretionary. One species will slide into another over evolutionary time. But it does not follow from the fact that speciation is sometimes in progress that species are merely made up and not found as evolutionary lines with identity in time as well as space.

A consideration of species is revealing and challenging because it offers a biologically based counterexample to the focus on individuals—typically sentient and usually persons—so characteristic in classical ethics. In an evolutionary ecosystem, it is not mere individuality that counts; the species is also significant because it is a dynamic life-form maintained over time. The individual represents (re-presents) a species in each new generation. It is a token of a type, and the type is more important than the token. . . .

If, in this world of uncertain moral convictions, it makes any sense to assert that one ought not to kill individuals without justification, it makes more sense to assert that one ought not to superkill the species without superjustification. Several billion years' worth of creative toil, several million species of teeming life, have been handed over to the care of this late-coming species in which mind has flowered and morals have emerged. Ought not this sole moral species do something less self-interested than count all the produce of an evolutionary ecosystem as nothing but human resources? Such an attitude hardly seems biologically informed, much less ethically adequate. It is too provincial for intelligent humanity. Life on Earth is a many-splendored thing; extinction dims its luster. An ethics of respect for life is urgent at the level of species.

ECOSYSTEMS

A species is what it is where it is. No environmental ethics has found its way on Earth until it finds an ethic for the biotic communities in which all destinies are entwined. "A thing is right," urged Aldo Leopold (1968 [1949]), "when it tends to preserve the integrity, stability, and beauty of the biotic community. It is wrong when it tends otherwise." Again, we have two parts to the ethic: first, that ecosystems exist, both in the wild and in support of culture; second, that ecosystems ought to exist, both for what they are in themselves and as modified by culture. Again, we must move with care from the biological assertions to the ethical assertions.

Giant forest fires raged over Yellowstone National Park in the summer of 1988, consuming nearly a million acres despite the efforts of a thousand fire fighters. By far the largest ever known in the park, the fires seemed a disaster. But the Yellowstone land ethic enjoined: "Let nature take its course; let it burn." So the fires were not fought at first, but in midsummer, national authorities overrode that policy and ordered the fires put out. Even then, weeks later, fires continued to burn, partly because they were too big to control but partly too because Yellowstone personnel did not really want the fires put out. Despite the evident destruction of trees, shrubs, and wildlife, they believe that fires are a good thing—even when the elk and bison leave the park in search of food and are shot by hunters. Fires reset succession, release nutrients, recycle materials, and renew the biotic community. (Nearby, in the Teton Wilderness, a storm blew down fifteen thousand acres of trees, and some people proposed that the area be declassified from wilderness to allow commercial salvage of the timber. But a similar environmental ethic said, "No, let it rot.")

Aspen are important in the Yellowstone ecosystem. Although some aspen stands are climax and self-renewing, many are seral and give way to conifers. Aspen groves support many birds and much wildlife, especially beavers, whose activities maintain the riparian zones. Aspen are rejuvenated after fires, and the Yellowstone land ethic wants the aspen for their critical role in the biotic community. Elk browse the young aspen stems. To a degree this is a good thing, because it provides the elk with critical nitrogen, but in excess it is a bad thing. The elk have no predators, because the wolves are gone, and as a result the elk overpopulate. Excess elk also destroy the willows, and that destruction in turn destroys the beavers. So, in addition to letting fires burn, rejuvenating the aspen might require park managers to cull hundreds of elk—all for the sake of a healthy ecosystem.

The Yellowstone ethic wishes to restore wolves to the greater Yellowstone ecosystem. At the level of species, this change is desired because of what the wolf is in itself, but it is also desired because the greater Yellowstone ecosystem does not have its full integrity, stability, and beauty without this majestic animal at the top of the trophic pyramid. Restoring the wolf as a top predator would mean suffering and death for many elk, but that would be a good thing for the aspen and willows, the beavers, and the riparian habitat and would have mixed benefits for the bighorns and mule deer (the overpopulating elk consume their food, but the sheep and deer would also be consumed by the wolves). Restoration of wolves would be done over the protests of ranchers who worry about wolves eating their cattle; many of them also believe that the wolf is a bloodthirsty killer, a bad kind. Nevertheless, the Yellowstone ethic demands wolves, as it does fires, in appropriate respect for life in its ecosystem.

Letting nature take its ecosystemic course is why the Yellowstone ethic forbade rescuing the drowning bison but required rescuing the sow grizzly and her cubs, the latter case to insure that the big predators remain. After the bison drowned, coyotes, foxes, magpies, and ravens fed on the carcass. Later, even a grizzly bear fed on it. All this is a good thing because the system cycles on. On that account, rescuing the whales trapped in the winter ice seems less of a good thing, when we note that rescuers had to drive away polar bears that attempted to eat the dying whales.

Classical, humanistic ethics finds ecosystems to be unfamiliar territory. It is difficult to get the biology right and, superimposed on the biology, to get the ethics right. Fortunately, it is often evident that human welfare depends on ecosystemic support, and in this sense all our legislation about clean air, clean water, soil conservation, national and state forest policies, pollution controls, renewable resources, and so forth is concerned about ecosystem-level processes. Furthermore, humans find much of value in preserving wild ecosystems, and our wilderness and park system is impressive.

Still, a comprehensive environmental ethics needs the best, naturalistic reasons, as well as the good, humanistic ones, for respecting ecosystems. Ecosystems generate and support life, keep selection pressures high, enrich situated fitness, and allow congruent kinds to evolve in their places with sufficient containment. The ecologist finds that ecosystems are objectively satisfactory communities in the sense that organismic needs are sufficiently met for species to survive and flourish, and the critical ethicist finds (in a subjective judgment matching the objective process) that such ecosystems are satisfactory communities to which to attach duty. Our concern must be for the fundamental unit of survival. . . .

An ecosystem is a productive, projective system. Organisms defend only their selves, with individuals defending their continuing survival and with species increasing the numbers of kinds. But the evolutionary ecosystem spins a bigger story, limiting each kind, locking it into the welfare of others, promoting new arrivals, increasing kinds and the integration of kinds. Species increase their kind, but ecosystems increase kinds, superposing the latter increase onto the former. Ecosystems are selective systems, as surely as organisms are selective systems. The natural selection comes out of the system and is imposed on the individual. The individual is programmed to make more of its kind, but more is going on systemically than that; the system is making more kinds.

Communal processes—the competition between organisms, statistically probable interactions, plant and animal successions, speciation over historical time—generate an ever-richer community. Hence the evolutionary toil, elaborating and diversifying the biota, that once began with no species and results today in five million species, increasing over time the quality of lives in the upper rungs of the trophic pyramids. One-celled organisms evolved into many-celled, highly integrated organisms. Photosynthesis evolved and came to support locomotion—swimming, walking, running, flight. Stimulus-response mechanisms became complex instinctive acts. Warm-blooded animals followed cold-blooded ones. Complex nervous systems, conditioned behavior, and learning emerged. Sentience appeared—sight, hearing, smell, taste, pleasure, pain. Brains coupled with hands. Consciousness and self-consciousness arose. Culture was superposed on nature.

These developments do not take place in all ecosystems or at every level. Microbes, plants, and lower animals remain, good of their kinds and, serving continuing roles, good for other kinds. The understories remain occupied. As a result, the quantity of life and its diverse qualities continue—from protozoans to primates to people. There is a push-up, lock-up ratchet effect that conserves the upstrokes and the outreaches. The later we go in time, the more accelerated are the forms at the top of the trophic pyramids, the more elaborated are the multiple trophic pyramids of Earth. There are upward arrows over evolutionary time.

The system is a game with loaded dice, but the loading is a pro-life tendency, not mere stochastic process. Though there is no Nature in the singular, the system has a nature, a loading that pluralizes, putting natures into diverse kinds: $nature_1$, $nature_2$, $nature_3 \ldots nature_n$. It does so using random elements (in both organisms and communities), but this is a secret of its fertility, producing steadily intensified interdependencies and options. An ecosystem has no head, but it heads toward species diversification, support, and richness. Though not a superorganism, it is a kind of vital field.

Instrumental value uses something as a means to an end; intrinsic value is worthwhile in itself. No warbler eats insects to become food for a falcon; the warbler defends its own life as an end in itself and makes more warblers as it can. A life is defended intrinsically, without further contributory reference. But neither of these traditional terms is satisfactory at the level of the ecosystem. Though it has value *in* itself, the system does not have any value *for* itself. Though it is a value producer, it is not a value owner. We are no longer confronting instrumental value, as though the system were of value instrumentally as a fountain of life. Nor is the question one of intrinsic value, as though the system defended some unified form of life for itself. We have reached something for which we need a third term: systemic value. Duties arise in encounters with the system that projects and protects these member components in biotic community.

Ethical conservatives, in the humanistic sense, will say that ecosystems are of value only because they contribute to human experiences. But that mistakes the last chapter for the whole story, one fruit for the whole plant. Humans count enough to have the right to flourish in ecosystems, but not so much that they have the right to degrade or shut down ecosystems, not at least without a burden of proof that there is an overriding cultural gain. Those who have traveled partway into environmental ethics will say that ecosystems are of value because they contribute to animal experiences or to organismic life. But the really conservative, radical view sees that the stability, integrity, and beauty of biotic communities are what are most fundamentally to be conserved. In a comprehensive ethics of respect for life, we ought to set ethics at the level of ecosystems alongside classical, humanistic ethics.

Animal Liberation and Environmental Ethics: Bad Marriage, Quick Divorce

Mark Sagoff

I.

"The land ethic," Aldo Leopold wrote in *A Sand County Almanac*, "simply enlarges the boundaries of the community to include soils, waters, plants, and animals, or collectively, the land."[1] What kind of community does Leopold refer to? He might mean a *moral* community, for example, a group of individuals who respect each other's right to treatment as equals or who regard one another's interests with equal respect and concern. He may also mean an *ecological* community, that is, a community tied together by biological relationships in interdependent webs or systems of life.[2]

Let us suppose, for a moment, that Leopold has a *moral* community in mind; he would expand our *moral* boundaries to include not only human beings, but also soils, waters, plants and animals. Leopold's view, then, might not differ in principle from that of Christopher Stone, who has suggested that animals and even trees be given legal standing, so that their interests may be represented in court.[3] Stone sees the expansion of our moral consciousness in this way as part of a historical progress by which societies have recognized the equality of groups of oppressed people, notably blacks, women and children.[4] Laurence Tribe eloquently makes the same point:

> What is crucial to recognize is that the human capacity for empathy and identification is not static; the very process of recognizing rights in those higher vertebrates with whom we can already empathize could well pave the way for still further extensions as we move upward along the spiral of

Mark Sagoff, "Animal Liberation and Environmental Ethics: Bad Marriage, Quick Divorce," *Osgoode Hall Law Journal* 22 (1984): 297–307. Reprinted with permission of author.

moral evolution. It is not only the human liberation movements—involving first blacks, then women, and now children—that advance in waves of increased consciousness.[5]

Peter Singer, perhaps more than any other writer, has emphasized the analogy between human liberation movements (for example, abolitionism and sufferagism) and "animal liberation" or the "expansion of our moral horizons" to include members of other species in the "basic principle of equality."[6] Singer differs from Stone and Tribe, however, in two respects. First, he argues that the capacity of animals to suffer pain or to enjoy pleasure or happiness places people under a moral obligation which does not need to be enhanced by a doctrine about rights. Second, while Stone is willing to speak of the interests of his lawn in being watered,[7] Singer argues that "only a being with subjective experiences, such as the experience of pleasure or the experience of pain, can have interests in the full sense of the term."[8] A tree, as Singer explains, may be said to have an "interest" in being watered, but all this means is that it needs water to grow properly as an automobile needs oil to function properly.[9] Thus, Singer would not include rocks, trees, lakes, rivers or mountains in the moral community or the community of morally equal beings.

Singer's thesis, then, is not necessarily that animals have rights which we are to respect. Instead, he argues that they have utilities that ought to be treated on an equal basis with those of human beings. Whether Tribe and Stone argue a weaker or a different thesis depends upon the rights they believe animals and other natural things to have. They may believe that all animals have a right to be treated as equals, in effect, they may agree with Singer that the interests of *all* animals should receive equal respect and concern. On the other hand, Tribe, Stone or both may believe that animals have a right only to life or only to those very minimal and basic rights without which they could not conceivably enjoy any other right.[10] I will, for the moment, assume that Tribe and Stone agree that animals have basic rights, for example, a right to live or a right not to be killed for their meat. I will consider later the possibility that environmental law might protect the rights of animals without necessarily improving their welfare or protecting their lives.

Moral obligations to animals, to their well-being or to their rights, may arise in either of two ways. First, duties to non-human animals may be based on the principle that cruelty to animals is obnoxious, a principle nobody denies. Muckraking journalists (thank God for them) who depict the horrors which all too often occur in laboratories and on farms, appeal quite properly to the conviction and intuition that people should never inflict needless pain on animals and especially not for the sake of profit. When television documentaries or newspaper articles report the horrid ways in which domestic animals are often treated, the response is, as it should be, moral revulsion. This anger is directed at human responsibility for the callous, wanton and needless cruelty human beings inflict on domestic animals. It is not simply the pain but the way it is caused which justifies moral outrage.

Moral obligations, however, might rest instead on a stronger contention, which is that human beings are obliged to prevent and to relieve animal suffering however it is caused. Now, insofar as the animal equality or animal liberation movement makes a philosophically interesting claim, it insists on the stronger thesis, that there is an obligation to serve the interests, or at least to protect the lives, of *all* animals who suffer or are killed, whether on the farm or in the wild. Singer, for example, does not stop with the stultifying platitude that human beings ought not to be cruel to animals. No; he argues the controversial thesis that society has an obligation to prevent the killing of animals and even to relieve their suffering wherever, however, and as much as it is able, at a reasonable cost to itself.

II.

I began by supposing that Aldo Leopold viewed the community of nature as a *moral* community—one in which human beings, as members, have obligations to all other animals, presumably to minimize their pain. I suggested that Leopold, like Singer, may be committed to the idea that the natural environment should be preserved and protected only insofar as, and because, its protection satisfies the needs or promotes the welfare of individual animals and perhaps other living things. I believe, however, that this is plainly not Leopold's view. The principle of natural selection is not obviously a humanitarian principle; the predator-prey relation does not depend on moral empathy. Nature ruthlessly limits animal populations by doing violence to virtually every individual before it reaches maturity; these conditions respect animal equality only in the darkest sense. Yet these are precisely the ecological relationships which Leopold admires; they are the conditions which he would not interfere with, but protect. Apparently, Leopold does not think that an ecological system has to be an egalitarian moral system in order to deserve love and admiration. An ecological system has a beauty and an authenticity that demands respect—but plainly not on humanitarian grounds.

In a persuasive essay, J. Baird Callicott describes a number of differences between the ideas of Leopold and those of Singer—differences which suggest that Leopold's environmental ethic and Singer's humane utilitarianism lead in opposite directions. First, while Singer and other animal liberationists deplore the suffering of domestic animals, "Leopold manifests an attitude that can only be described as indifference."[11] Second, while Leopold expresses an urgent concern about the disappearance of species, Singer, consistently with his premises, is concerned with the welfare of individual animals, without special regard to their status as endangered species. Third, the preservation of wilderness, according to Leopold, provides "a means of perpetuating, in sport form, the more virile and primitive skills. . . ."[12] He had hunting in mind. Leopold recognized that since top predators are gone, hunters may serve an important ecological function. Leopold was himself an enthusiastic hunter and wrote unabashedly about his exploits pursuing game. The term "game" as applied to animals, Callicott wryly comments, "appears to be morally equivalent to referring to a sexually appealing young woman as a

'piece' or to a strong, young black man as a 'buck'— if animal rights, that is, are to be considered on par with women's rights and the rights of formerly enslaved races."[13]

Singer expresses disdain and chagrin at what he calls "environmentalist" organizations such as the Sierra Club and the Wildlife Fund, which actively support or refuse to oppose hunting. I can appreciate Singer's aversion to hunting, but why does he place the word "environmentalist" in shudder quotes when he refers to organizations like the Sierra Club? Environmentalist and conservationist organizations traditionally have been concerned with ecological, not humanitarian issues. They make no pretense of acting for the sake of individual animals; rather, they attempt to maintain the diversity, integrity, beauty and authenticity of the natural environment. These goals are ecological, not eleemosynary. Their goals are entirely consistent, then, with licensing hunters to shoot animals whose populations exceed the carrying capacity of their habitats. Perhaps hunting is immoral; if so, environmentalism is consistent with an immoral practice, but it is environmentalism without quotes nonetheless. The policies environmentalists recommend are informed by the concepts of population biology, not the concepts of animal equality. The S.P.C.A. does not set the agenda for the Sierra Club.

I do not in any way mean to support the practice of hunting; nor am I advocating environmentalism at this time. I merely want to point out that groups like the Sierra Club, the Wilderness Society and the World Wildlife Fund do not fail in their mission insofar as they devote themselves to causes other than the happiness or welfare of individual creatures; that never was their mission. These organizations, which promote a love and respect for the functioning of natural ecosystems, differ ideologically from organizations that make the suffering of animals their primary concern—groups like the Fund for Animals, the Animal Protection Institute, Friends of Animals, the American Humane Association, and various single issue groups such as Friends of the Sea Otter, Beaver Defenders, Friends of the Earthworm, and Worldwide Fair Play for Frogs.[14]

D. G. Ritchie, writing in 1916, posed a difficulty for those who argue that animals have rights or that we have obligations to them created simply by their capacity to suffer. If the suffering of animals creates a human obligation to mitigate it, is there not as much an obligation to prevent a cat from killing a mouse as to prevent a hunter from killing a deer? "Are we not to vindicate the rights of the persecuted prey of the stronger?" Ritchie asks. "Or is our declaration of the rights of every creeping thing to remain a mere hypocritical formula to gratify pug-loving sentimentalists?"[15]

If the animal liberation or animal equality movement is not to deteriorate into "a hypocritical formula to gratify pug-loving sentimentalists," it must insist, as Singer does, that moral obligations to animals are justified, in the first place, by their distress, and, in the second place, by human ability to relieve that distress. The liberationist must morally require society to relieve animal suffering wherever it can and at a lesser cost to itself, whether in the chicken coop or in the wild. Otherwise, the animal liberationist thesis becomes interchangeable with the platitude one learns along with how to tie shoestrings: people ought not to be cruel to animals. I do not deny that human beings are cruel to animals, that they ought not to be, that this cruelty should be stopped and that sermons to this effect are entirely appropriate and necessary. I deny only that these sermons have anything to do with environmentalism or provide a basis for an environmental ethic.

III.

In discussing the rights of human beings, Henry Shue describes two that are basic in the sense that "the enjoyment of them is essential to the enjoyment of all other rights."[16] These are the right to physical security and the right to minimum subsistence. These are positive, not merely negative rights. In other words, these rights require governments to provide security and subsistence, not merely to refrain from invading security and denying subsistence. These basic rights require society, where possible, to rescue individuals from starvation; this is more than the merely negative obligation not to cause starvation. No; if people have basic rights—and I have no doubt they

do—then society has a positive obligation to satisfy those rights. It is not enough for society simply to refrain from violating them.

This, surely, is true of the basic rights of animals as well, if we are to give the conception of "right" the same meaning for both people and animals. For example, to allow animals to be killed for food or to permit them to die of disease or starvation when it is within human power to prevent it, does not seem to balance fairly the interests of animals with those of human beings. To speak of the rights of animals, of treating them as equals, of liberating them, and at the same time to let nearly all of them perish unnecessarily in the most brutal and horrible ways is not to display humanity but hypocrisy in the extreme.

Where should society concentrate its efforts to provide for the basic welfare—the security and subsistence—of animals? Plainly, where animals most lack this security, when their basic rights, needs, or interests are most thwarted and where their suffering is most intense. Alas, this is in nature. Ever since Darwin, we have been aware that few organisms survive to reach sexual maturity; most are quickly annihilated in the struggle for existence. Consider as a rough but reasonable statement of the facts the following:

> All species reproduce in excess, way past the carrying capacity of their niche. In her lifetime a lioness might have 20 cubs; a pigeon, 150 chicks; a mouse, 1,000 kits; a trout, 20,000 fry, a tuna or cod, a million fry or more; an elm tree, several million seeds; and an oyster, perhaps a hundred million spat. If one assumes that the population of each of these species is, from generation to generation, roughly equal, then on the average only one offspring will survive to replace each parent. All the other thousands and millions will die, one way or another.[17]

The ways in which creatures in nature die are typically violent: predation, starvation, disease, parasitism, cold. The dying animal in the wild does not understand the vast ocean of misery into which it and billions of other animals are born only to drown. If the wild animal understood the conditions into which it is born, what would it think? It might reasonably prefer to be raised on a farm, where the chances of survival for a year or more would be good, and to escape from the wild, where they are negligible. Either way, the animal will be eaten: few die of old age. The path from birth to slaughter, however, is often longer and less painful in the barnyard than in the woods. Comparisons, sad as they are, must be made to recognize where a great opportunity lies to prevent or mitigate suffering. The misery of animals in nature—which humans can do much to relieve—makes every other form of suffering pale in comparison. Mother Nature is so cruel to her children she makes Frank Perdue look like a saint.

What is the practical course society should take once it climbs the spiral of moral evolution high enough to recognize its obligation to value the basic rights of animals equally with that of human beings? I do not know how animal liberationists, such as Singer, propose to relieve animal suffering in nature (where most of it occurs), but there are many ways to do so at little cost. Singer has suggested, with respect to pest control, that animals might be fed contraceptive chemicals rather than poisons.[18] It may not be beyond the reach of science to attempt a broad program of contraceptive care for animals in nature so that fewer will fall victim to an early and horrible death. The government is spending hundreds of millions of dollars to store millions of tons of grain. Why not lay out this food, laced with contraceptives, for wild creatures to feed upon? Farms which so overproduce for human needs might then satisfy the needs of animals. The day may come when entitlement programs which now extend only to human beings are offered to animals as well.

One may modestly propose the conversion of national wilderness areas, especially national parks, into farms in order to replace violent wild areas with more humane and managed environments. Starving deer in the woods might be adopted as pets. They might be fed in kennels; animals that once wandered the wilds in misery might get fat in feedlots instead. Birds that now kill earthworms may repair instead to birdhouses stocked with food, including textured soybean protein that looks and smells like worms. And to protect the brutes from cold, their dens could be heated, or shelters provided for the all too many who will otherwise freeze. The list of obligations is

long, but for that reason it is more, not less, compelling. The welfare of all animals is in human hands. Society must attend not solely to the needs of domestic animals, for they are in a privileged class, but to the needs of all animals, especially those which without help, would die miserably in the wild.

Now, whether you believe that this harangue is a *reductio* of Singer's position, and thus that it agrees in principle with Ritchie, or whether you think it should be taken seriously as an ideal is of no concern to me. I merely wish to point out that an environmentalist must take what I have said as a *reductio,* whereas an animal liberationist must regard it as stating a serious position, at least if the liberationist shares Singer's commitment to utilitarianism. Environmentalists cannot be animal liberationists. Animal liberationists cannot be environmentalists. The environmentalist would sacrifice the lives of individual creatures to preserve the authenticity, integrity and complexity of ecological systems. The liberationist—if the reduction of animal misery is taken seriously as a goal—must be willing, in principle, to sacrifice the authenticity, integrity and complexity of ecosystems to protect the rights, or guard the lives, of animals.

IV.

A defender of the rights of animals may answer that my argument applies only to someone like Singer who is strongly committed to a utilitarian ethic. Those who emphasize the rights of animals, however, need not argue that society should enter the interests of animals equitably into the felicific calculus on which policy is based. For example, Laurence Tribe appeals to the rights of animals not to broaden the class of wants to be included in a Benthamite calculus but to "move beyond wants" and thus to affirm duties "ultimately independent of a desire-satisfying conception."[19] Tribe writes:

To speak of "rights" rather than "wants," after all, is to acknowledge the possibility that want-maximizing or utility-maximizing actions will be ruled out in particular cases as inconsistent with a structure of agreed-upon obligations. It is Kant, not Bentham, whose thought suggests the first step toward making us "different persons from the manipulators and subjugators we are in danger of becoming."[20]

It is difficult to see how an appeal to rights helps society to "move beyond wants" or to affirm duties "ultimately independent of a desire-satisfying conception." Most writers in the Kantian tradition analyze rights as claims to something in which the claimant has an interest.[21] Thus, rights-theorists oppose utilitarianism not to go beyond wants but because they believe that some wants or interests are moral "trumps" over other wants and interests.[22] To say innocent people have a right not to be hanged for crimes they have not committed, even when hanging them would serve the general welfare, is to say that the interest of innocent people not to be hanged should outweigh the general interest in deterring crime. To take rights seriously, then, is simply to take some interests, or the general interest, more seriously than other interests for moral reasons. The appeal to rights simply is a variation on utilitarianism, in that it accepts the general framework of interests, but presupposes that there are certain interests that should not be traded off against others.[23]

A second problem with Tribe's reply is more damaging than the first. Only *individuals* may have rights, but environmentalists think in terms of protecting *collections, systems* and *communities*. Consider Aldo Leopold's oft-quoted remark: "A thing is right when it tends to preserve the integrity, stability, and beauty of the biotic community. It is wrong when it tends to do otherwise."[24] The obligation to preserve the "integrity, stability, and beauty of the biotic community," whatever those words mean, implies no duties whatever to individual animals in the community, except in the rare instance in which an individual is important to functioning of that community. For the most part, individual animals are completely expendable. An environmentalist is concerned only with maintaining a population. Accordingly, the moral obligation Leopold describes cannot be grounded in or derived from the rights of

individuals. Therefore, it has no basis in rights at all.[25]

Consider another example: the protection of endangered species. An individual whale may be said to have rights, but the species cannot; a whale does not suddenly have rights when its kind becomes endangered.[26] No; the moral obligation to preserve species is not an obligation to individual creatures. It cannot, then, be an obligation that rests on rights. This is not to say that there is no moral obligation with regard to endangered species, animals or the environment. It is only to say that moral obligations to nature cannot be enlightened or explained—one cannot even take the first step—by appealing to the rights of animals and other natural things.

V.

Garrett Hardin, in his "Foreword" to *Should Trees Have Standing?*, suggests that Stone's essay answers Leopold's call for a "new ethic to protect land and other natural amenities. . . ."[27] But as one reviewer has pointed out,

> Stone himself never refers to Leopold, and with good reason; he comes from a different place, and his proposal to grant rights to natural objects has emerged not from an ecological sensibility but as an extension of the philosophy of the humane movement.[28]

A humanitarian ethic—an appreciation not of nature, but of the welfare of animals—will not help us to understand or to justify an environmental ethic. It will not provide necessary or valid foundations for environmental law.

NOTES

1. Leopold, *A Sand County Almanac* (Oxford University Press, 1949) at 204.
2. For discussion, see Heffernan, *The Land Ethic: A Critical Appraisal,* Environmental Ethics 4 (1982): 235. Heffernan notes that "when Leopold talks of preserving the 'integrity, stability and beauty of the biotic commu-

nity' he is referring to preserving the characteristic structure of an ecosystem and its capacity to withstand change or stress." Leopold. *A Sand County Almanac* at 237.

3. Stone, *Should Trees Have Standing?* (Los Altos: Walter Kaufmann, 1974).

4. Stone, *Should Trees Have Standing?* at p. 44.

5. Tribe, "Ways Not to Think About Plastic Trees: New Foundations in Environmental Law," *Yale Law Journal* 83 (1973): 1315. See p. 1345

6. Singer, "All Animals Are Equal" *Philosophic Exchange* 1 (1974): 103.

7. Stone, *Should Trees Have Standing?* at 24.

8. Singer, "Not For Humans Only: The Place of Nonhumans in Environmental Issues," in *Ethics and the Problems of the Twenty-first Century,* ed. Goodpaster and Sayre (1979), p. 194.

9. Singer, "Not For Humans Only," p. 195.

10. For a discussion of basic rights, see Shue, *Basic Rights* (1980).

11. Callicott, *Animal Liberation: A Triangular Affair* (1980), Environmental Ethics 2 (1980): 311. See p. 315.

12. Leopold, *A Sand County Almanac,* p. 269.

13. Callicott, "Animal Liberation," p. 314–15.

14. Singer, "Not For Humans Only," p. 201.

15. Ritchie, *Natural Rights* (3rd ed., 1916), p. 107. For an excellent discussion of this passage, see Clark, "The Rights of Wild Things," *Inquiry* 22 (1979): 171.

16. Shue, *Basic Rights,* p. 18–29.

17. Hapgood, *Why Males Exist* (1979). See p. 34.

18. Singer, "Not For Humans Only," p. 198.

19. Tribe, "From Environmental Foundations to Constitutional Structures: Learning From Nature's Future," *Yale Law Journal* 84 (1974): 545. See pp. 551–52.

20. Tribe, "From Environmental Foundations," p. 552.

21. For discussion, see Feinberg, *Duties, Rights, and Claims* (1966). *American Philosophical Quarterly* 3 (1966): 137.

22. See Dworkin, "Liberalism," in *Public and Private Morality* (1978), ed. Stuart Hampshire. See pages 113–43. Rights "function as trump cards held by individuals." See p. 136.

23. Barry observes: "On the surface, rights theories stand in opposition to utilitarianism, for rights, whatever their foundation (or lack thereof), are supposed to trump claims that might be made on behalf of the general welfare. The point here is, however, that the whole notion of rights is simply a variation on utilitarianism in that it accepts the definition of the ethical problem as conterminous with the problem of conflicting interests, and replaces the felicific calculus (in which the interests are simply added) with one which does not permit certain interests to be traded off against others." Barry, "Self-government Revisited," *The Nature of Political Theory* (1983), ed. Miller and Siedentop. See p. 125; see generally pp. 121–54.

24. Leopold, *A Sand County Almanac,* p. 262.

25. For discussion of this point, see Katz, "Is There A Place For Animals in the Moral Consideration of Nature," *Ethics and Animals* 4 (1983): 74; Norton, "Environmental Ethics and Nonhuman Rights," (1982), *Environmental Ethics* 4 (1982): 17; Rodman, "The Liberation of Nature?" *Inquiry* 20 (1977): 83; Goodpaster, "On Being Morally Considerable" *Journal of Philosophy* 75 (1978): 308.

Tom Regan discusses this issue in *The Case for Animal Liberation* (1983). See p. 362.

Because paradigmatic rights-holders are individuals, and because the dominant thrust of contemporary environmental efforts (e.g., wilderness preservation) is to focus on the whole rather than on the part (i.e., the individual), there is an understandable reluctance on the part of environmentalists to "take rights seriously" or at least a reluctance to take them as seriously as the rights view contends we should. . . . A rights-based environmental ethic . . . ought not to be dismissed out of hand by environmentalists as being in principle antagonistic to the goals for which they work. It isn't. Were we to show proper respect for the rights of individuals who make up the biotic community, would not the *community* be preserved?

I believe this is an empirical question, the answer to which is "no." The environmentalist is concerned about preserving evolutionary processes; whether these processes, e.g., natural selection, have deep enough respect for the rights of individuals to be preserved on those grounds, is a question that might best be addressed by an evolutionary biologist.

26. Feinberg, "The Rights of Animals and Unborn Generations," in *Philosophy and the Environmental Crisis,* ed. Blackstone (1974), 43–end. See pp. 55–56.

27. Hardin, "Foreward," in Stone, *Should Trees Have Standing?* See p. xii.

28. Rodman, "The Liberation of Nature?" See p. 110.

Chapter 3
Extending the Realm of Rights

Questions for Reflection and Discussion

Natural Rights

1. Christopher Stone seems to argue that trees can have rights. Does his argument work just as well on behalf of rocks? Joel Feinberg says rocks cannot have rights. Why not? Do you agree?

2. If and when we decide that animals (or plants) have rights, we will have some issues to work out regarding what is involved in respecting such rights in practice. For example, if we believe a deer has a right to life, is it enough simply to avoid killing deer ourselves, or are we also committed to protecting each deer against whatever threatens its life? Are we obligated to protect them from carnivores? Are we obligated to protect them from human hunters but not from "natural" predators? Are we obligated to feed them when they cannot feed themselves? Is our obligation to interfere with nature, on behalf of deer, or to avoid interfering? (Is it clear what counts as interfering versus not interfering?)

Should Trees Have Standing? Toward Legal Rights for Natural Objects

Christopher D. Stone

Throughout legal history, each successive extension of rights to some new entity has been, theretofore, a bit unthinkable. We are inclined to suppose the rightlessness of rightless "things" to be a decree of Nature, not a legal convention acting in support of some status quo. It is thus that we defer considering the choices involved in all their moral, social, and economic dimensions. And so the United States Supreme Court could straightfacedly tell us in *Dred Scott* that Blacks had been denied the rights of citizenship "as a subordinate and inferior class of beings, who had been subjugated by the dominant race. . . ."[1] In the nineteenth century, the highest court in California explained that Chinese had not the right to testify against white men in criminal matters because they were "a race of people whom nature has marked as inferior, and who are incapable of progress or intellectual development beyond a certain point . . . between whom and ourselves nature has placed an impassable difference."[2] The popular conception of the Jew in the thirteenth century contributed to a law which treated them as "men *ferae naturae,* protected by a quasi-forest law. Like the roe and the deer, they form an order apart."[3] Recall, too, that it was not so long ago that the foetus was "like the roe and the deer." In an early suit attempting to establish a wrongful death action on behalf of a negligently killed foetus (now widely accepted practice), Holmes, then on the Massachusetts Supreme Court, seems to have thought it simply inconceivable "that a man might owe a civil duty and incur a conditional prospective liability in tort to one not yet in being."[4] The first woman in Wisconsin who thought she might have a right to practice law was told that she did not, in the following terms:

> The law of nature destines and qualifies the female sex for the bearing and nurture of the children of our race and for the custody of the homes of the world. . . . [A]ll life-long callings of women, inconsistent with these radical and sacred duties of their sex, as is the profession of the law, are departures from the order of nature; and when voluntary, treason against it. . . . The peculiar qualities of womanhood, its gentle graces, its quick sensibility, its tender susceptibility, its purity, its delicacy, its emotional impulses, its subordination of hard reason to sympathetic feeling, are surely not qualifications for forensic strife. Nature has tempered woman as little for the juridical conflicts of the court room, as for the physical conflicts of the battle field. . . .[5]

The fact is, that each time there is a movement to confer rights onto some new "entity," the proposal is bound to sound odd or frightening or laughable. This is partly because until the rightless thing receives its rights, we cannot see it as anything but a *thing* for the use of "us"—those who are holding rights at the time. In this vein, what is striking about the Wisconsin case above is that the court, for all its talk about women, so clearly was never able to see women as they are (and might become). All it could see was the popular "idealized" version of *an object it needed.* Such is the way the slave South looked upon the Black. There is something of a seamless web involved: there will be resistance to giving the thing "rights" until it can be seen and valued for it-

Christopher D. Stone, "Should Trees Have Standing?" *University of Southern California Law Review* 45 (1972): 450–501. Reprinted with permission of the publisher.

self; yet, it is hard to see it and value it for itself until we can bring ourselves to give it "rights"—which is almost inevitably going to sound inconceivable to a large group of people.

The reason for this little discourse on the unthinkable, the reader must know by now, if only from the title of the paper. I am quite seriously proposing that we give legal rights to forests, oceans, rivers, and other so-called "natural objects" in the environment—indeed, to the natural environment as a whole. . . .

TOWARD RIGHTS FOR THE ENVIRONMENT

Now, to say that the natural environment should have rights is not to say anything as silly as that no one should be allowed to cut down a tree. We say human beings have rights, but—at least as of the time of this writing—they can be executed. Corporations have rights, but they cannot plead the fifth amendment; *In re Gault* gave fifteen-year-olds certain rights in juvenile proceedings, but did not give them the right to vote. Thus, to say that the environment should have rights is not to say that it should have every right we can imagine, or even the same body of rights as human beings have. Nor is it to say that everything in the environment should have the same rights as every other thing in the environment. . . .

For a thing to be *a holder of legal rights,* something more is needed than that some authoritative body will review the actions and processes of those who threaten it. As I shall use the term, "holder of legal rights," each of three additional criteria must be satisfied. All three, one will observe, go towards making a thing *count* jurally—to have a legally recognized worth and dignity in its own right, and not merely to serve as a means to benefit "us" (whoever the contemporary group of rights-holders may be). They are, first, that the thing can institute legal actions *at its behest;* second, that in determining the granting of legal relief, the court must take *injury to it* into account; and, third, that relief must run to the *benefit of it.* . . .

THE RIGHTLESSNESS OF NATURAL OBJECTS AT COMMON LAW

Consider, for example, the common law's posture toward the pollution of a stream. True, courts have always been able, in some circumstances, to issue orders that will stop the pollution. . . . But the stream itself is fundamentally rightless, with implications that deserve careful reconsideration.

The first sense in which the stream is not a rights-holder has to do with standing. The stream itself has none. So far as the common law is concerned, there is in general no way to challenge the polluter's actions save at the behest of a lower riparian—another human being—able to show an invasion of *his* rights. . . .

The second sense in which the common law denies "rights" to natural objects has to do with the way in which the merits are decided in those cases in which someone is competent and willing to establish standing. At its more primitive levels, the system protected the "rights" of the property owning human with minimal weighting of any values. . . . Today we have come more and more to make balances—but only such as will adjust the economic best interests of identifiable humans. . . .

Thus, we find the highest court of Pennsylvania refusing to stop a coal company from discharging polluted mine water into a tributary of the Lackawana River because a plaintiff's "grievance is for a mere personal inconvenience; and . . . mere private personal inconveniences . . . must yield to the necessities of a great public industry, which although in the hands of a private corporation, subserves a great public interest."[6] The stream itself is lost sight of in "a quantitative compromise between two conflicting interests."[7]

The third way in which the common law makes natural objects rightless has to do with who is regarded as the beneficiary of a favorable judgment. Here, too, it makes a considerable difference that it is not the natural object that counts in its own right. To illustrate this point let me begin by observing that it makes perfectly good sense to speak of, and ascertain, the legal damage to a natural object, if only in the sense of "making it whole" with respect to the most obvious factors. The costs of making a forest whole, for example, would include the costs of reseeding, repairing watersheds, restocking wildlife—the sorts of costs the Forest Service undergoes after a fire. Making a polluted stream whole would include the costs of restocking with fish, water-fowl, and other animal and vegetable life, dredging, washing out impurities, establishing natural and/or artificial aerating agents, and so forth. Now, what is important to note is that, under our present system, even if a plaintiff riparian wins a water pollution suit for damages, no money goes to the benefit of the stream itself to repair *its* damages. . . .

None of the natural objects, whether held in common or situated on private land, has any of the three criteria of a rights-holder. They have no standing in their own right; their unique damages do not count in determining outcome; and they are not the beneficiaries of awards. In such a fashion, these objects have traditionally been regarded by the common law, and even by all but the most recent legislation, as objects for man to conquer and master and use—in such a way as the law once looked upon "man's" relationships to African Negroes. Even where special measures have been taken to conserve them, as by seasons on game and limits on timber cutting, the dominant motive has been to conserve them *for us*—for the greatest good of the greatest number of human beings. Conservationists, so far as I am aware, are generally reluctant to maintain otherwise. As the name implies, they want to conserve and guarantee *our* consumption and *our* enjoyment of these other living things. In their own right, natural objects have counted for little, in law as in popular movements.

As I mentioned at the outset, however, the rightlessness of the natural environment can and should change; it already shows some signs of doing so.

TOWARD HAVING STANDING IN ITS OWN RIGHT

It is not inevitable, nor is it wise, that natural objects should have no rights to seek redress in their own behalf. It is no answer to say that streams and forests cannot have standing because streams and forests cannot speak. Corporations cannot speak either; nor can states, estates, infants, incompetents, municipalities, or universities. Lawyers speak for them, as they customarily do for the ordinary citizen with legal problems. One ought, I think, to handle the legal problems of natural objects as one does the problems of legal incompetents—human beings who have become vegetable. If a human being shows signs of becoming senile and has affairs that he is de jure incompetent to manage, those concerned with his well being make such a showing to the court, and someone is designated by the court with the authority to manage the incompetent's affairs. . . .

On a parity of reasoning we should have a system in which, when a friend of a natural object perceives it to be endangered, he can apply to a court for the creation of a guardianship. . . .

The potential "friends" that such a statutory scheme would require will hardly be lacking. The Sierra Club, Environmental Defense Fund, Friends of the Earth, Natural Resources Defense Counsel, and the Izaak Walton League are just some of the many groups which have manifested unflagging dedication to the environment and which are becoming increasingly capable of marshalling the requisite technical experts and lawyers. If, for example, the Environmental Defense Fund should have reason to believe that some company's strip mining operations might be irreparably destroying the ecological balance of large tracts of land, it could, under this procedure, apply to the court in which the lands were situated to be appointed guardian. As guardian, it might be given rights of inspection (or visitation) to determine and bring to the court's attention a fuller finding on the land's condition. If there were indications that under the substantive law some redress might be available on the land's behalf, then the guardian would be entitled to raise the land's rights in the land's name, *i.e.,* without having to make the roundabout and often unavailing demonstration . . . that the "rights" of the club's members were being invaded. . . .

One reason for making the environment itself the beneficiary of a judgment is to prevent it from being "sold out" in a negotiation among private liti-

gants who agree not to enforce rights that have been established among themselves. Protection from this will be advanced by making the natural object a party to an injunctive settlement. Even more importantly, we should make it a beneficiary of money awards.
. . .

The idea of assessing damages as best we can and placing them in a trust fund is far more realistic than a hope that a total "freeze" can be put on the environmental status quo. Nature is a continuous theatre in which things and species (eventually man) are destined to enter and exit. In the meantime, co-existence of man and his environment means that each is going to have to compromise for the better of both. Some pollution of streams, for example, will probably be inevitable for some time. Instead of setting an unrealizable goal of enjoining absolutely the discharge of all such pollutants, the trust fund concept would (a) help assure that pollution would occur only in those instances where the social need for the pollutant's product (via his present method of production) was so high as to enable to poluter to cover all homocentric costs, plus some estimated costs to the environment per se, and (b) would be a corpus for preserving monies, if necessary, while the technology developed to a point where repairing the damaged portion of the environment was feasible. Such a fund might even finance the requisite research and development. . . .

A radical new conception of man's relationship to the rest of nature would not only be a step towards solving the material planetary problems; there are strong reasons for such a changed consciousness from the point of making us far better humans. If we only stop for a moment and look at the underlying human qualities that our present attitudes toward property and nature draw upon and reinforce, we have to be struck by how stultifying of our own personal growth and satisfaction they can become when they take rein of us. Hegel, in "justifying" private property, unwittingly reflects the tone and quality of some of the needs that are played upon:

A person has as his substantive end the right of putting his will into any and every thing and thereby making it his, because it has no such end in itself

and derives its destiny and soul from his will. This is the absolute right of appropriation which man has over all "things."[8]

What is it within us that gives us this need not just to satisfy basic biological wants, but to extend our wills over things, to objectify them, to make them ours, to manipulate them, to keep them at a psychic distance? Can it all be explained on "rational" bases? Should we not be suspect of such needs within us, cautious as to why we wish to gratify them? When I first read that passage of Hegel, I immediately thought not only of the emotional contrast with Spinoza, but of the passage in Carson McCullers' "A Tree, a Rock, a Cloud," in which an old derelict has collared a twelve-year-old boy in a streetcar cafe. The old man asks whether the boy knows "how love should be begun."

The old man leaned closer and whispered:

"A tree. A rock. A cloud."

"The weather was like this in Portland," he said. "At the time my science was begun. I meditated and I started very cautious. I would pick up something from the street and take it home with me. I bought a goldfish and I concentrated on the goldfish and I loved it. I graduated from one thing to another. Day by day I was getting this technique.

"For six years now I have gone around by myself and built up my science. And now I am a master. Son. I can love anything. No longer do I have to think about it even. I see a street full of people and a beautiful light comes in me. I watch a bird in the sky. Or I meet a traveler on the road. Everything, Son. And anybody. All stranger and all loved! Do you realize what a science like mine can mean?"[9]

To be able to get away from the view that Nature is a collection of useful senseless objects is, as McCullers' "madman" suggests, deeply involved in the development of our abilities to love—or, if that is putting it too strongly, to be able to reach a heightened awareness of our own, and others' capacities in their mutual interplay. To do so, we have to give up some psychic investment in our sense of separateness and specialness in the universe. And this, in turn, is hard giving indeed, because it involves us in a fight backwards, into earlier stages of civilization and childhood in which we had to trust (and perhaps fear) our environment, for we had not then the power to master it. Yet, in doing so, we—as persons—gradually free ourselves of needs for supportive illusions. Is not this one of the triumphs for "us" of our giving legal rights to (or acknowledging the legal rights of) the Blacks and women? . . .

The time may be on hand when these sentiments, and the early stirrings of the law, can be coalesced into a radical new theory or myth—felt as well as intellectualized—of man's relationships to the rest of nature. I do not mean "myth" in a demeaning sense of the term, but in the sense in which, at different times in history, our social "facts" and relationships have been comprehended and integrated by reference to the "myths" that we are co-signers of a social contract, that the Pope is God's agent, and that all men are created equal. Pantheism, Shinto, and Tao all have myths to offer. But they are all, each in its own fashion, quaint, primitive, and archaic. What is needed is a myth that can fit our growing body of knowledge of geophysics, biology, and the cosmos.

In this vein, I do not think it too remote that we may come to regard the Earth, as some have suggested, as one organism, of which Mankind is a functional part—the mind, perhaps: different from the rest of nature, but different as a man's brain is from his lungs.

NOTES

1. *Dred Scott v. Sanford,* 60 U.S. (19 How.) 396, 404–05 (1856).
2. *People v. Hall,* 4 Cal. 399, 405 (1854).
3. Schechter, "The Rightlessness of Mediaeval English Jewry," *Jewish Q. Rev.* 45 (1954) 121. See p. 135, quoting from M. Bateson, *Medieval England* (1904), p. 139.
4. *Dietrich v. Inhabitants of Northampton,* 138, Mass. 14, 16 (1884).
5. *In re Goddell,* 39 Wisc. 232, 245 (1875).
6. *Pennsylvania Coal Co. v. Sanderson,* 113 Pa. 126, 149, 6 A. 453, 459 (1886).
7. Hand, J. in *Smith v. Staso Milling Co.,* 18 F.2d 736, 738 (2d Cir. 1927) (emphasis added).
8. G. Hegel, *Hegel's Philosophy of Right,* (T. Knox transl., 1945). See p. 41.
9. C. McCullers, *The Ballad of the Sad Cafe and Other Stories,* (1958). See pp. 150–151.

The Rights of Animals

Joel Feinberg

Every philosophical paper must begin with an unproved assumption. Mine is the assumption that there will still be a world five hundred years from now, and that it will contain human beings who are very much like us. We have it within our power now, clearly, to affect the lives of these creatures for better or worse by contributing to the conservation or corruption of the environment in which they must live. I shall assume furthermore that it is psychologically possible for us to care about our remote de-

Joel Feinberg, "The Rights of Animals and Unborn Generations," originally published in *Philosophy and Environmental Crisis,* ed. by William Blackstone (Athens: University of Georgia Press, 1974), 43–68. Reprinted by permission of Jean Blackstone.

scendants, that many of us in fact do care, and indeed that we ought to care. My main concern then will be to show that it makes sense to speak of the rights of unborn generations against us, and that given the moral judgment that we ought to conserve our environmental inheritance for them, and its grounds, we might well say that future generations *do* have rights correlative to our present duties toward them. Protecting our environment now is also a matter of elementary prudence, and insofar as we do it for the next generation already here in the persons of our children, it is a matter of love. But from the perspective of our remote descendants it is basically a matter of justice, of respect for their rights. My main concern here will be to examine the concept of a right to better understand how that can be.

THE PROBLEM

To have a right is to have a claim[1] *to* something and *against* someone, the recognition of which is called for by legal rules or, in the case of moral rights, by the principles of an enlightened conscience. In the familiar cases of rights, the claimant is a competent adult human being, and the claimee is an officeholder in an institution or else a private individual, in either case, another competent adult human being. Normal adult human beings, then, are obviously the sorts of beings of whom rights can meaningfully be predicated. Everyone would agree to that, even extreme misanthropes who deny that anyone in fact has rights. On the other hand, it is absurd to say that rocks can have rights, not because rocks are morally inferior things unworthy of rights (that statement makes no sense either), but because rocks belong to a category of entities of whom rights cannot be meaningfully predicated. That is not to say that there are no circumstances in which we ought to treat rocks carefully, but only that the rocks themselves cannot validly claim good treatment from us. In between the clear cases of rocks and normal human beings, however, is a spectrum of less obvious cases, including some bewildering borderline ones. Is it meaningful or conceptually possible to ascribe rights to our dead

ancestors? to individual animals? to whole species of animals? to plants? to idiots and madmen? to fetuses? to generations yet unborn? Until we know how to settle these puzzling cases, we cannot claim fully to grasp the concept of a right, or to know the shape of its logical boundaries.

One way to approach these riddles is to turn one's attention first to the most familiar and unproblematic instances of rights, note their most salient characteristics, and then compare the borderline cases with them, measuring as closely as possible the points of similarity and difference. In the end, the way we classify the borderline cases may depend on whether we are more impressed with the similarities or the differences between them and the cases in which we have the most confidence.

It will be useful to consider the problem of individual animals first because their case is the one that has already been debated with the most thoroughness by philosophers so that the dialectic of claim and rejoinder has now unfolded to the point where disputants can get to the end game quickly and isolate the crucial point at issue. When we understand precisely what *is* at issue in the debate over animal rights, I think we will have the key to the solution of all the other riddles about rights.

INDIVIDUAL ANIMALS

Almost all modern writers agree that we ought to be kind to animals, but that is quite another thing from holding that animals can claim kind treatment from us as their due. Statutes making cruelty to animals a crime are now very common, and these, of course, impose legal duties on people not to mistreat animals; but that still leaves open the question whether the animals, as beneficiaries of those duties, possess rights correlative to them. We may very well have duties *regarding* animals that are not at the same time duties *to* animals, just as we may have duties regarding rocks, or buildings, or lawns, that are not duties *to* the rocks, buildings, or lawns. Some legal writers have taken the still more extreme position that animals themselves are not even the directly intended beneficiaries of statutes prohibiting cruelty to animals. During the nineteenth century, for example, it was commonly said that such statutes were designed to protect human beings by preventing the growth of cruel habits that could later threaten human beings with harm too. Prof. Louis B. Schwartz finds the rationale of the cruelty-to-animals prohibition in its protection of animal lovers from affronts to their sensibilities. "It is not the mistreated dog who is the ultimate object of concern," he writes. "Our concern is for the feelings of other human beings, a large proportion of whom, although accustomed to the slaughter of animals for food, readily identify themselves with a tortured dog or horse and respond with great sensitivity to its sufferings."[2] This seems to me to be factitious. How much more natural it is to say with John Chipman Gray that the true purpose of cruelty-to-animals statutes is "to preserve the dumb brutes from suffering."[3] The very people whose sensibilities are invoked in the alternative explanation, a group that no doubt now includes most of us, are precisely those who would insist that the protection belongs primarily to the animals themselves, not merely to their own tender feelings. Indeed, it would be difficult even to account for the existence of such feelings in the absence of a belief that the animals deserve the protection in their own right and for their own sakes.

Even if we allow, as I think we must, that animals are the intended direct beneficiaries of legislation forbidding cruelty to animals, it does not follow directly that animals have legal rights, and Gray himself, for one,[4] refused to draw this further inference. Animals cannot have rights, he thought, for the same reason they cannot have duties, namely, that they are not genuine "moral agents." Now, it is relatively easy to see why animals cannot have duties, and this matter is largely beyond controversy. Animals cannot be "reasoned with" or instructed in their responsibilities; they are inflexible and unadaptable to future contingencies; they are subject to fits of instinctive passion which they are incapable of repressing or controlling, postponing or sublimating. Hence, they cannot enter into contractual agreements, or make promises; they cannot be trusted; and they cannot

(except within very narrow limits and for purposes of conditioning) be blamed for what would be called "moral failures" in a human being. They are therefore incapable of being moral subjects, of acting rightly or wrongly in the moral sense, of having, discharging, or breeching duties and obligations.

But what is there about the intellectual incompetence of animals (which admittedly disqualifies them for duties) that makes them logically unsuitable for rights? The most common reply to this question is that animals are incapable of *claiming* rights on their own. They cannot make motion, on their own, to courts to have their claims recognized or enforced; they cannot initiate, on their own, any kind of legal proceedings; nor are they capable of even understanding when their rights are being violated, of distinguishing harm from wrongful injury, and responding with indignation and an outraged sense of justice instead of mere anger or fear.

No one can deny any of these allegations, but to the claim that they are the grounds for disqualification of rights of animals, philosophers on the other side of this controversy have made convincing rejoinders. It is simply not true, says W. D. Lamont,[5] that the ability to understand what a right is and the ability to set legal machinery in motion by one's own initiative are necessary for the possession of rights. If that were the case, then neither human idiots nor wee babies would have any legal rights at all. Yet it is manifest that both of these classes of intellectual incompetents have legal rights recognized and easily enforced by the courts. Children and idiots start legal proceedings, not on their own direct initiative, but rather through the actions of proxies or attorneys who are empowered to speak in their names. If there is no conceptual absurdity in this situation, why should there be in the case where a proxy makes a claim on behalf of an animal? People commonly enough make wills leaving money to trustees for the care of animals. Is it not natural to speak of the animal's right to his inheritance in cases of this kind? If a trustee embezzles money from the animal's account,[6] and a proxy speaking in the dumb brute's behalf presses the animal's claim, can he not be described as asserting the animal's *rights*? More exactly, the animal itself claims its rights through the vicarious actions of a human proxy speaking in its name and in its behalf. There appears to be no reason why we should require the animal to understand what is going on (so the argument concludes) as a condition for regarding it as a possessor of rights.

Some writers protest at this point that the legal relation between a principal and an agent cannot hold between animals and human beings. Between humans, the relation of agency can take two very different forms, depending upon the degree of discretion granted to the agent, and there is a continuum of combinations between the extremes. On the one hand, there is the agent who is the mere "mouthpiece" of his principal. He is a "tool" in much the same sense as is a typewriter or telephone; he simply transmits the instructions of his principal. Human beings could hardly be the agents or representatives of animals in this sense, since the dumb brutes could no more use human "tools" than mechanical ones. On the other hand, an agent may be some sort of expert hired to exercise his professional judgment on behalf of, and in the name of, the principal. He may be given, within some limited area of expertise, complete independence to act as he deems best, binding his principal to all the beneficial or detrimental consequences. This is the role played by trustees, lawyers, and ghost-writers. This type of representation requires that the agent have great skill, but makes little or no demand upon the principal, who may leave everything to the judgment of his agent. Hence, there appears, at first, to be no reason why an animal cannot be a totally passive principal in this second kind of agency relationship.

There are still some important dissimilarities, however. In the typical instance of representation by an agent, even of the second, highly discretionary kind, the agent is hired by a principal who enters into an agreement or contract with him; the principal tells his agent that within certain carefully specified boundaries "You may speak for me," subject always to the principal's approval, his right to give new directions, or to cancel the whole arrangement. No dog or cat could possibly do any of those things. Moreover, if it is the assigned task of the agent to defend

the principal's rights, the principal may often decide to release his claimee, or to waive his own rights, and instruct his agent accordingly. Again, no mute cow or horse can do that. But although the possibility of hiring, agreeing, contracting, approving, directing, canceling, releasing, waiving, and instructing is present in the typical (all-human) case of agency representation, there appears to be no reason of a logical or conceptual kind why that *must* be so, and indeed there are some special examples involving human principals where it is not in fact so. I have in mind legal rules, for example, that require that a defendant be represented at his trial by an attorney, and impose a state-appointed attorney upon reluctant defendants, or upon those tried *in* absentia, whether they like it or not. Moreover, small children and mentally deficient and deranged adults are commonly represented by trustees and attorneys, even though they are incapable of granting their own consent to the representation, or of entering into contracts, of giving directions, or waiving their rights. It may be that it is unwise to permit agents to represent principals without the latters' knowledge or consent. If so, then no one should ever be permitted to speak for an animal, at least in a legally binding way. But that is quite another thing than saying that such representation is logically incoherent or conceptually incongruous—the contention that is at issue.

H. J. McCloskey,[7] I believe, accepts the argument up to this point, but he presents a new and different reason for denying that animals can have legal rights. The ability to make claims, whether directly or through a representative, he implies, is essential to the possession of rights. Animals obviously cannot press their claims on their own, and so if they have rights, these rights must be assertable by agents. Animals, however, cannot be represented, McCloskey contends, and not for any of the reasons already discussed, but rather because representation, in the requisite sense, is always of interests, and animals (he says) are incapable of having interests.

Now, there is a very important insight expressed in the requirement that a being have interests if he is to be a logically proper subject of rights. This can be appreciated if we consider just why it is that mere things cannot have rights. Consider a very precious mere thing—a beautiful natural wilderness, or a complex and ornamental artifact, like the Taj Mahal. Such things ought to be cared for, because they would sink into decay if neglected, depriving some human beings, or perhaps even all human beings, of something of great value. Certain persons may even have as their own special job the care and protection of these valuable objects But we are not tempted in these cases to speak of "thing-rights" correlative to custodial duties, because, try as we might, we cannot think of mere things as possessing interests of their own. Some people may have a duty to preserve, maintain, or improve the Taj Mahal, but they can hardly have a duty to help or hurt it, benefit or aid it, succor or relieve it. Custodians may protect it for the sake of a nation's pride and art lovers' fancy; but they don't keep it in good repair for "its own sake," or for "its own true welfare," or "well-being." A mere thing, however valuable to others, has no good of its own. The explanation of that fact, I suspect, consists in the fact that mere things have no conative life: no conscious wishes, desires, and hopes; or urges and impulses; or unconscious drives, aims, and goals; or latent tendencies, direction of growth, and natural fulfilments. Interests must be compounded somehow out of conations; hence mere things have no interests. *A fortiori,* they have no interests to be protected by legal or moral rules. Without interests a creature can have no "good" of its own, the achievement of which can be its due. Mere things are not loci of value in their own right, but rather their value consists entirely in their being objects of other beings' interests.

So far McCloskey is on solid ground, but one can quarrel with his denial that any animals but humans have interests. I should think that the trustee of funds willed to a dog or cat is more than a mere custodian of the animal he protects. Rather his job is to look out for the interests of the animal and make sure no one denies it its due. The animal itself is the beneficiary of his dutiful services. Many of the higher animals at least have appetites, conative urges, and rudimentary purposes, the integrated satisfaction of which constitutes their welfare or good. We can, of course, with consistency treat animals as mere pests and deny that they have any rights; for most animals, especially those of the lower orders, we have no choice but to do so. But it seems to me, nevertheless, that in general, animals *are* among the sorts of beings of whom rights can meaningfully be predicated and denied.

Now, if a person agrees with the conclusion of the argument thus far, that animals are the sorts of beings that *can* have rights, and further, if he accepts the moral judgment that we ought to be kind to animals, only one further premise is needed to yield the conclusion that some animals do in fact have rights. We must now ask ourselves for whose sake ought we to treat (some) animals with consideration and humaneness? If we conceive our duty to be one of obedience to authority, or to one's own conscience merely, or one of consideration for tender human sensibilities only, then we might still deny that animals have rights, even though we admit that they are the kinds of beings that *can* have rights. But if we hold not only that we ought to treat animals humanely but also that we should do so for the animals' own sake, that such treatment is something we owe animals as their due, something that can be claimed for them, something the withholding of which would be an injustice and a wrong, and not merely a harm, then it follows that we do ascribe rights to animals. I suspect that the moral judgments most of us make about animals do pass these phenomenological tests, so that most of us do believe that animals have rights, but are reluctant to say so because of the conceptual confusions about the notion of a right that I have attempted to dispel above.

Now we can extract from our discussion of animal rights a crucial principle for tentative use in the resolution of the other riddles about the applicability of the concept of a right, namely, that the sorts of beings who *can* have rights are precisely those who have (or can have) interests. I have come to this tentative conclusion for two reasons: (1) because a right holder must be capable of being represented and it is impossible to represent a being that has no interests, and (2) because a right holder must be capable of being a beneficiary in his own person, and a being without interests is a being that is incapable of being harmed or benefitted, having no good or "sake" of its own. Thus, a being without interests has no "behalf" to act in, and no "sake" to act for. My strategy now will be to apply the "interest principle," as we can call it, to the other puzzles about rights, while being prepared to modify it where necessary (but as little as possible), in the hope of separating in a consistent and intuitively satisfactory fashion the beings who can have rights from those which cannot.

VEGETABLES

It is clear that we ought not to mistreat certain plants, and indeed there are rules and regulations imposing duties on persons not to misbehave in respect to certain members of the vegetable kingdom. It is forbidden, for example, to pick wildflowers in the mountainous tundra areas of national parks, or to endanger trees by starting fires in dry forest areas. Members of Congress introduce bills designed, as they say, to "protect" rare redwood trees from commercial pillage. Given this background, it is surprising that no one[8] speaks of plants as having rights. Plants, after all, are not "mere things"; they are vital objects with inherited biological propensities determining their natural growth. Moreover, we do say that certain conditions are "good" or "bad" for plants, thereby suggesting that plants, unlike rocks, are capable of having a "good." (This is a case, however, where "what we say" should not be taken seriously: we also say that certain kinds of paint are good or bad for the internal walls of a house, and this does not commit us to a conception of walls as beings possessed of a good or welfare of their own.) Finally, we are capable of feeling a kind of affection for particular plants, though we rarely personalize them, as we do in the case of animals, by giving them proper names.

Still, all are agreed that plants are not the kinds of beings that can have rights. Plants are never plausibly understood to be the direct intended beneficiaries of rules designed to "protect" them. We wish to keep redwood groves in existence for the sake of human beings who can enjoy their serene beauty, and for the sake of generations of human beings yet unborn. Trees are not the sorts of beings who have their "own sakes," despite the fact that they have biological propensities. Having no conscious wants or goals of their own, trees cannot know satisfaction or frustration, pleasure or pain. Hence, there is no possibility of kind or cruel treatment of trees. In these morally crucial respects, trees differ from the higher species of animals.

Yet trees are not mere things like rocks. They grow and develop according to the laws of their own nature. Aristotle and Aquinas both took trees to have their own "natural ends." Why then do I deny them the status of beings with interests of their own? The reason is that an interest, however the concept is finally to be analyzed, presupposes at least rudimentary cognitive equipment. Interests are compounded out of desires and aims, both of which presuppose something like *belief,* or cognitive awareness. A desiring creature may want X because he seeks anything that is ϕ, and X appears to be ϕ to him; or he may be seeking Y, and he believes, or expects, or hopes that X will be a means to Y. If he desires X in order to get Y, this implies that he believes that X will bring Y about, or at least that he has some sort of brute expectation that is a primitive correlate of belief. But what of the desire for ϕ (or for Y) itself? Perhaps a creature has such a "desire" as an ultimate set, as if he had come into existence all "wound up" to pursue ϕ-ness or Y-ness, and his not to reason why. Such a propensity, I think, would not qualify as a desire. Mere brute longings unmediated by beliefs—longings for one knows not what—might perhaps be a primitive form of consciousness (I don't want to beg that question) but they are altogether different from the sort of thing we mean by "desire," especially when we speak of human beings.

If some such account as the above is correct, we can never have any grounds for attributing a desire or a want to a creature known to be incapable even of rudimentary beliefs; and if desires or wants are the materials interests are made of, mindless creatures have no interests of their own. The law, therefore, cannot have as its intention the protection of their interests, so that "protective legislation" has to be understood as legislation protecting the interests human beings may have in them.

Plant life might nevertheless be thought at first to constitute a hard case for the interest principle for two reasons. In the first place, plants no less than animals are said to have needs of their own. To be sure, we can speak even of mere things as having needs too, but such talk misleads no one into thinking of the need as belonging, in the final analysis, to the "mere thing" itself. If we were so deceived we would not be thinking of the mere thing as a "mere thing" after all. We say, for example, that John Doe's walls need painting, or that Richard Roe's car needs a washing, but we direct our attitudes of sympathy or reproach (as the case may be) to John and Richard, not to their possessions. It would be otherwise, if we observed that some child is in need of a good meal. Our sympathy and concern in that case would be directed at the child himself as the true possessor of the need in question.

The needs of plants might well seem closer to the needs of animals than to the pseudoneeds of mere things. An owner may need a plant (say, for its commercial value or as a potential meal), but the plant itself, it might appear, needs nutrition or cultivation. Our confusion about this matter may stem from language. It is a commonplace that the word *need* is ambiguous. To say that A needs X may be to say either: (1) X is necessary to the achievement of one of A's goals, or to the performance of one of its functions, or (2) X is good for A; its lack would harm A or be injurious or detrimental to him (or it). The first sort of need-statement is value-neutral, implying no comment on the value of the goal or function in question; whereas the second kind of statement about needs commits its maker to a value judgment about what is good or bad for A in the long run, that is, about what is in A's interests. A being must have interests, therefore, to have needs in the second sense, but any kind of thing, vegetable or mineral, could have needs in the first sense. An automobile needs gas and oil to function, but it is no tragedy for it if it runs out—an empty tank does not hinder or retard its interests. Similarly, to say that a tree needs sun-

shine and water is to say that without them it cannot grow and survive; but unless the growth and survival of trees are matters of human concern, affecting human interests, practical or aesthetic, the needs of trees alone will not be the basis of any claim of what is "due" them in their own right. Plants may need things in order to discharge their functions, but their functions are assigned by human interests, not their own.

The second source of confusion derives from the fact that we commonly speak of plants as thriving and flourishing, or withering and languishing. One might be tempted to think of these states either as themselves consequences of the possession of interests so that even creatures without wants or beliefs can be said to have interests, or else as grounds independent of the possession of interests for the making of intelligible claims of rights. In either case, plants would be thought of as conceivable possessors of rights after all.

Consider what it means to speak of something as "flourishing." The verb *to flourish* apparently was applied originally and literally to plants only, and in its original sense it meant simply "to bear flowers: BLOSSOM"; but then by analogical extension of sense it came also to mean "to grow luxuriantly: increase, and enlarge," and then to "THRIVE" (generally), and finally, when extended to human beings, "to be prosperous," or to "increase in wealth, honor, comfort, happiness, or whatever is desirable."[9] Applied to human beings the term is, of course, a fixed metaphor. When a person flourishes, something happens to his interests analogous to what happens to a plant when it flowers, grows, and spreads. A person flourishes when his interests (whatever they may be) are progressing severally and collectively toward their harmonious fulfillment and spawning new interests along the way whose prospects are also good. To flourish is to glory in the advancement of one's interests, in short, to be happy.

Nothing is gained by twisting the botanical metaphor back from humans to plants. To speak of thriving human interests as if they were flowers is to speak naturally and well, and to mislead no one. But then to think of the flowers or plants as if they were interests (or the signs of interests) is to bring the metaphor back full circle for no good reason and in the teeth of our actual beliefs. Some of our talk about flourishing plants reveals quite clearly that the interests that thrive when plants flourish are human not "plant interests." For example, we sometimes make a flowering bush flourish by "frustrating" its own primary propensities. We pinch off dead flowers before seeds have formed, thus "encouraging" the plant to make new flowers in an effort to produce more seeds. It is not the plant's own natural propensity (to produce seeds) that is advanced, but rather the gardener's interest in the production of new flowers and the spectator's pleasure in aesthetic form, color, or scent. What we mean in such cases by saying that the plant flourishes is that our interest in the plant, not its own, is thriving. It is not always so clear that that is what we mean, for on other occasions there is a correspondence between our interests and the plant's natural propensities, a coinciding of what we want from nature and nature's own "intention." But the exceptions to this correspondence provide the clue to our real sense in speaking of a plant's good or "welfare." And even when there exists such a correspondence, it is often because we have actually remade the plant's nature so that our interests in it will flourish more "naturally" and effectively.

WHOLE SPECIES

The topic of whole species, whether of plants or animals, can be treated in much the same way as that of individual plants. A whole collection, as such, cannot have beliefs, expectations, wants, or desires, and can flourish or languish only in the human interest-related sense in which individual plants thrive and decay. Individual elephants can have interests, but the species elephant cannot. Even where individual elephants are not granted rights, human beings may have an interest—economic, scientific, or sentimental—in keeping the species from dying out, and *that* interest may be protected in various ways by law. But that is quite another matter from recognizing a right to survival belonging to the species itself. Still, the preservation of a whole species may quite properly seem to be a morally more important matter than the preservation of an individual animal. Individual animals can have rights but it is implausible to ascribe to them a right to life on the human model. Nor do we normally have duties to keep individual animals alive or even to abstain from killing them provided we do it humanely and nonwantonly in the promotion of legitimate human interests. On the other hand, we do have duties to protect threatened species, not duties to the species themselves as such, but rather duties to future human beings, duties derived from our housekeeping role as temporary inhabitants of this planet.

We commonly and very naturally speak of corporate entities, such as institutions, churches, and national states as having rights and duties, and an adequate analysis of the conditions for ownership of rights should account for that fact. A corporate entity, of course, is more than a mere collection of things that have some important traits in common. Unlike a biological species, an institution has a charter, or constitution, or bylaws, with rules defining offices and procedures, and it has human beings whose function it is to administer the rules and apply the procedures. When the institution has a duty to an outsider, there is always some determinant human being whose duty it is to do something for the outsider, and when the state, for example, has a right to collect taxes, there are always certain definite flesh and blood persons who have rights to demand tax money from other citizens. We have no reluctance to use the language of corporate rights and duties because we know that in the last analysis these are rights or duties of individual persons, acting in their "official capacities." And when individuals act in their official roles in accordance with valid empowering rules, their acts are imputable to the organization itself and become "acts of state." Thus, there is no need to posit any individual superperson named by the expression "the State" (or for that matter, "the company," "the club," or "the church".) Nor is there any reason to take the rights of corporate entities to be exceptions to the interest principle. The United States is not a superperson with wants and beliefs of its own, but it is a corporate entity with corporate interests that are, in turn, analyzable into the interests of its numerous flesh and blood members.

NOTES

1. I shall leave the concept of a claim unanalyzed here, but for a detailed discussion, see my "The Nature and Value of Rights," *Journal of Value Inquiry* 4 (Winter 1971): 263–277.

2. Louis B. Schwartz, "Morals, Offenses and the Model Penal Code," *Columbia Law Review* 63 (1963): 673.

3. John Chipman Gray, *The Nature and Sources of the Law,* 2d ed. (Boston: Beacon Press, 1963), p. 43.

4. And W. D. Ross for another. See *The Right and the Good* (Oxford: Clarendon Press, 1930), app. 1, pp. 48–56.

5. W. D. Lamont, *Principles of Moral Judgment* (Oxford: Clarendon Press, 1946), pp. 83–85.

6. H. J. McCloskey, "Rights," *Philosophical Quarterly* 15 (1965): 124.

7. McCloskey, "Rights," p. 124.

8. Outside of Samuel Butler's *Erewhon.*

9. Webster's Third New International Dictionary.

The Good of Trees

Robin Attfield

My title can be taken in at least two ways: as "the good of trees" as opposed to "the harm of trees" and as "the good of trees" in the sense of "the value of trees." It might also be taken in the sense of "the use of trees," particularly by those who hold that to speak strictly trees have no good of their own, and are good only for satisfying human interests; this view, however, I consider and reject in the course of Section I after a scrutiny of some writings of Professors Hare and Feinberg, who both seem to hold it. But even if trees have needs and a good of their own, they may still have no value of their own and may still be due no consideration in their own right: in Section II, I examine various proposed moral grounds for preserving trees without finding in them any basis for valuing trees beyond human and animal welfare. The resulting paradox, that trees have interests but no value of their own, is explored in Section III, in which I supply an argument and a thought experiment to show that trees can after all be of intrinsic value, even though we seldom need to take account of it in practice.

This essay is not in any way intended to derogate from arguments in support of belief in the rights of animals. Rather I hope it may contribute to the philosophy of intrinsic value and to the philosophy of ecology, and also throw light on the conceptual links between the notions of "purpose" and "interest," between "capacities" and "flourishing," between "diversity" and "good" and between "interests," "value" and "rights." My beliefs about the feelings of trees are unalarmingly traditional; indeed trees are discussed not for the sake of some Arboreal Liberation Campaign, but because they constitute an intriguing test case of several theories in meta-ethics and normative ethics, and because our attitudes to them are of considerable intrinsic interest.

I. HARM AND THE NEEDS OF TREES

There is a view held widely among philosophers that, if we speak strictly, the needs of trees and other plants depend wholly on the interests of humans, that

Robin Attfield, "The Good of Trees," in *Journal of Value Inquiry* 15 (1981): 35–54. Reprinted with permission of the publisher, Kluwer Academic Publishers.

plants can only be harmed when actual or possible human desires are frustrated, and that their harm consists precisely in this frustration. This view has been held not only by contemporary writers such as R. M. Hare[1] and Joel Feinberg;[2] there are some traces of it in the writings of Aquinas,[3] who represents as instruments creatures which, unlike rational agents, do not control their actions, instruments intended solely for the use of agents possessed of intellect; and a similar belief seems to have been held by the ancient Stoics.[4] I shall try to show this view to be a confused one, about which we need to get straight not only for the sake of trees but also so as to become clearer about harm and needs in general. (Some followers of Aquinas and of Kant hold a similar and in my opinion confused view about animals, but this view is contested by Feinberg, who argues in the same paper that some animals have interests and can have rights. While I agree with these conclusions of Feinberg, my own argument about the good of trees can be carried over so as to supplement his account of the interests of animals; for if the good of trees is partially or wholly independent of human interests, there can be little doubt that the same holds good of animals *a fortiori*.)

Hare expresses the basis of his position as follows: "To speak very crudely and inexactly, to say that some act would harm somebody is to say that it would prevent some interest of his being satisfied; and this, in turn, is to say that it would, or might in possible circumstances, prevent some desire of his being realized." This is crude and inexact because "might" lets in too much; nevertheless the conceptual link between "harm" and "interest" is left unqualified, while the link between "harm" and "desire" is presented thus: "I propose to assume for the sake of argument that there is some conceptual link between harm and frustration of prescriptions which are, will or would be assented to."

This dubious assumption leads Hare into a digression on its implications. If the foregoing is granted, Hare remarks, "only creatures which can assent to prescriptions can be harmed in the strict sense. This runs counter to our ordinary way of speaking." Indeed it does, as it yields the conclusions not only

that plants and animals cannot be harmed, but also that human embryos and infants cannot be harmed either. But Hare comes to the rescue, at least of plants and animals, by endorsing two analogical extensions of the notion of harm, "once established" for creatures which can assent to prescriptions. First, useful animals like horses and useful plants like apple trees can, like cars, be harmed when something is done to them which prevents their users from realizing their prescriptions. Second, even when there is no question of a user, we can speak analogically of the creature wanting things, and, as in the case of people, treat its goal-directed behavior as evidence of this (provided that we also pay attention to the dangers in the analogy)."

Talk of such desires is a "pardonable artificiality," but only if we extend the notion of wanting in this way can we reveal the origins of expressions like "good roots"; "the apple tree's good roots, if they are not good for helping it to produce the sort of apples that I want, must be good for helping it to grow into the kind of apple trees that it wants to be—i.e., to achieve the *telos* or end of apple trees by putting on as perfectly as possible their *eidos* or form. If we had not inherited a great deal of this teleological language, we should not speak of good roots in the case of trees not serving a human purpose."

In other words, harm always turns on the frustration of desires and good on their realization; so, where we talk of good and harm which are unaccompanied by desires, we must be pretending that desires really are present; that desires, so to speak, grow on trees. Our usage, though inherited, must be derivative, and only because of this is it pardonable; if we were strict and consistent non-animists we should not speak at all of the good or harm of useless plants; and what is unpardonable is to suppose that creatures lacking wants have a good of their own which has nothing to do with us.

It may seem unfair to put such emphasis on what Hare himself declares to be a digression; but his whole prescriptivist position over harm turns on it. For, as he himself says, these conclusions about animals and plants follow from his analysis of "harm," and so, by *modus tollens,* their falsity would by the same token imply the falsity of his prescriptivism. Hare has to maintain that our talk about harm to plants and animals is derivative, analogical and barely pardonable, lest we place it at the center of a naturalist theory on which the nature of harm depends on facts and necessary truths and not on prescriptions. Although I shall not defend such a theory here, the reader who cannot agree with Hare over plants will no doubt draw his or her own conclusions.

At all events Hare has to apply his theories to talk of the good of useless or userless trees. This being so, it is difficult to see how he can cope with much of the talk about trees to which Feinberg draws attention. Thus not only can trees grow, blossom and decay; they can thrive and wither, be endangered by fire and be protected from commercial pillage. Now what can thrive, reach maturity, be endangered and be protected, has, I contend, a good itself. How else could we know that it was thriving? Hare might claim that works of art could also be endangered and protected because of their beauty, which humans stand to enjoy, and might go on to claim that trees can only be endangered and protected in this particular sense; if so, he should hold that trees inaccessible to humans and the beauty of which humans do not stand to enjoy cannot be endangered. More plausibly he would fall back on his derivative notion of "harm," and grant that trees can be harmed in a sense beyond that in which statues can. They can be harmed because the realization of their quasi-aspirations can be imperiled.

But this is to suppose that people who talk of the thriving or endangering of forest trees must ground their talk in what most of them consider a childish and unsubstantiated belief, namely that trees have feelings and purposes, or are indwelt by forms or spirits with conative propensities; or, at best, it is to suppose that they would be willing to acknowledge their talk to be metaphorical, or poetic, or not capable of being taken seriously. Rather than such heroic and implausible suppositions, it would surely be preferable to grant that the good and harm of uncultivated species depend not on any prescriptions, desires, aspirations or wants, but on the capacities of their kind; that it is often open to us to harm them, but not to decide by prescriptions what shall count as their thriving, their decay or their degeneration. Talk of a tree's *eidos* or even of the *telos* it attains at its maturity may well have a place, but the place it has cannot turn on the tree's purposes, or on the belief that it has such.

Hare's remarks about the good of trees do seem to work better for the trees of the orchard, the garden and the plantation; such trees have been selectively bred so that their own fruition corresponds with human purposes. It may still not be the human purposes which make their fruitfulness or their shapeliness elements in their good; this will depend on which general theory of good and harm deserves acceptance. Nevertheless such trees can perhaps be harmed somewhat as Hare's first extension of the notion of harm suggests; their users' purposes can be frustrated if their inbred function is disrupted, somewhat as a car's inbuilt purpose can be nullified by wear and tear. Needless to say, they have a nature of their own in a way that cars do not; yet there is perhaps some analogy. It is rather over the trees, plants and animals of the wilderness that Hare's theory manifestly breaks down; but if these creatures have a good of their own, it is at least plausible that the same applies to domesticated and cultivated species too.

Feinberg, however, doubts whether trees do have a good of their own, or that they have needs beyond our purposes and the norms which as a result we supply for them. What impresses him is that no one (outside Samuel Butler's *Erewhon*) speaks of plants as having rights. He grants that "plants, after all, are not "mere things"; they are vital objects with inherited propensities determining their natural growth. Moreover we do say that certain conditions are "good" or "bad" for plants, thereby suggesting that plants, unlike rocks, are capable of having 'a good.'" But this talk is misleading: paint can be believed bad for the walls of a house in the absence of a belief that the walls have "a good or welfare of their own."

Feinberg's basic point is that trees do not have wants or goals, and hence cannot know satisfaction or frustration, pleasure or pain. As they cannot suffer, we cannot be cruel to them; and as they lack desire and cognition, they have no interests, and hence cannot be preserved for their own sakes. Rather when redwood groves are preserved it is for the sake of humans including generations unborn.

I grant Feinberg his premise, that plants lack beliefs and desires, and also, in a strict sense of the term "cruel," that we cannot be cruel to plants. Certainly we can show greater and lesser tenderness in their treatment: different forms of verge-cutting and hedge-cutting, for example, have very different effects on their survival and distribution, while overdoses of fertilizers and pesticides can cause them to wither prematurely. Nevertheless, although they can suffer disease and truncation, they cannot suffer agony or anguish, as perhaps a number of simpler animal species cannot either; and where it is impossible consciously to undergo either pain or the frustration of natural inclinations, cruelty is impossible too (except on the part of those who believe otherwise).

What I do not see, however, is that "desires or wants are the materials interests are made of" and hence that "mindless creatures have no interests of their own." In an earlier passage,[5] Feinberg holds that the explanation why mere things, such as the Taj Mahal or a beautiful natural wilderness, have no good of their own "consists in the fact that mere things have no conative life: no conscious wishes, desires and hopes; or urges and impulses; or unconscious drives, aims and goals; or latent tendencies, direction of growth and natural fulfillments (sic). Interests must be compounded somehow out of conations; hence mere things have no interests." And, if so, they have no value in their own right.

Now I have some doubt over classifying latent tendencies as conations; Feinberg's remarks about conations seem out of keeping with what they are intended to summarize. But of the two positions which might be attributed to him here, the fuller statement is preferable: latent tendencies, direction of growth and natural fulfilment do jointly seem, as Feinberg himself apparently suggests, sufficient conditions of having interests. This is not to endow machines or cities (if regarded as material objects) with interests,

as they lack natural fulfilment even when built according to a plan; nor are these conditions satisfied by things lacking inherited capacities, such as forests, swamps or even species (as opposed to their members), though the case of species will be considered again later. It does, however, imply, contrary to Feinberg's subsequent conclusions, that all individual animals and plants have interests. For all have latent tendencies at some time or other, all have a direction of growth, and all can flourish after their natural kind. There is no need to hold that trees have unconscious goals to reach the conclusion that trees have interests; indeed where nothing counts as a conscious goal it is hard to see how anything counts as an unconscious one either. The growth and thriving of trees does not need to be regarded as a kind of wanting, nor trees as possible objects of sympathy, for us to recognize that they too have a good of their own.

Feinberg, however, rejects this construction of our ordinary beliefs about plants. He grants that we talk of their needs, but holds that things only have needs of their own, as distinct from needs for the fulfilment of the goals of some extrinsic agent, when they have a good or interests of their own. Our talk of the needs of trees, however, he holds to resemble that of the needs of cars for oil and petrol: without sunshine and water they "cannot grow and survive; but unless the growth and survival of trees are matters of human concern, affecting human interests, practical or aesthetic, the needs of trees alone will not be the basis of any claim of what is "due" them in their own right. Plants may need things in order to discharge their functions, but their functions are assigned by human interests, not their own" (p. 54).

Feinberg's readers no doubt experience relief to hear that trees make no claims and have no rights; but this sentiment is really beside the point. Certainly Feinberg has by this stage advanced a theory relating interests and rights; but if both plants have no rights and the theory suggests a close connection between having rights and having interests, then that could as easily be a reason for rejecting or modifying the theory as for concluding that plants have no interests. At all events what is at stake is interests, not rights, and the real argument here has nothing to do with rights, but amounts to the claim that as trees only have needs where human interests require the growth or survival that the needs are necessary for, they have no needs, and hence no good, of their own.

This argument might seem more difficult to controvert than Hare's prescriptivist theory, since any need of a tree which I represent as having no benefit for humans is likely to be regarded as an object of at least my interest; and, even if the play on the meaning of "interest" is remarked, it will be held that objects of my investigative curiosity are also objects of my interests as a source of aesthetic enjoyment. Nevertheless the question which must be faced is whether trees would have needs if there were no humans, and indeed whether they had needs before humans first made their appearance. Once this question is put, the answer is obvious. Indeed Feinberg seems quite mistaken to hold that trees have no needs of their own. Trees had needs before people existed, and cannot be supposed to have lost them.

Feinberg does, however, present a reply to the view that talk of the thriving, flourishing, withering and languishing of trees shows them to have a good or interests of their own. His reply is of an etymological kind, slightly reminiscent of that of Hare over "harm." The original meaning of "flourish" was "blossom," but it was then extended to "grow luxuriantly, increase and enlarge" and to "thrive." Then it was further extended to persons; about this sense Feinberg says that "When a person flourishes, something happens to his interests analogous to what happens to a plant when it flowers, grows and spreads" (p. 54). (Is not more involved in a person flourishing than the progress of their "interests"?) Finally flourishing is represented as a conscious act or disposition in the claim that "To flourish is to glory in the advancement of one's interests, in short, to be happy" (p. 54), an account which seems not only to degrade happiness, but also to require attitudes not required by flourishing itself.

This etymological account prepares the way for the remark "Nothing is gained by twisting the botanical metaphor back from humans to plants." Feinberg does not expect the senses of "flourish" in the two cases to be telescoped, but he does fear that the re-application of the metaphor to its source will make people believe that plants have interests "in the teeth of our actual beliefs" (p. 55). In Feinberg's eyes, of course, the sense of flourishing tied to interests is also tied to consciousness: and he regards this sense as merely metaphorical, as if there were no common element in the flourishing of people, animals and trees, such as the fulfilment or development of natural propensities. I do not, of course, claim that "flourishing" is used univocally of different natural kinds; but as there does seem to be a common element, I do not see the justification for holding that it is not in the interest of plants to flourish. Truistically they are unaware of their interests; but even creatures with cognition are often unaware of theirs, whether they are flourishing or not.

Nevertheless Feinberg tries to defend his claims by contending that "Some of our talk about flourishing plants reveals quite clearly that the interests that thrive when plants flourish are human, not 'plant interests.'" Sometimes, admittedly, there is a coincidence between our interests and a plant's natural propensities; but there are exceptions, as when we frustrate the natural propensities of a plant by removing dead flowers before the seeds have formed to encourage new flowers, and still talk of its "flourishing"; and what we then mean "is that our interest in the plant, not its own, is thriving" (p. 55). Now plants bred to have large, colorful or exotic flowers do, when they flower, satisfy our interests, even though flowering is only a part of their flourishing as even a cultivated plant. It is probably the overlap between their nature and our purposes which allows us to call this condition "flourishing"; such talk does not however show that whether or not plants flourish turns on our interests rather than theirs. If it were our purpose to hang plastic lanterns on them, we could not claim that their bedecked condition was ipso facto one of flourishing; flourishing states have to be states in keeping with a plant's nature (which may, of course, be a cultivated nature).

The real exception, however, to the coincidence of plants' propensities and human interests is not the one which Feinberg believes he finds. What I have in mind is the common and garden experience of un-wanted flourishing. Not only do weeds flourish contrary to our interests; so do runaway hedges, trees the roots of which block drains and the shade of which annoys the neighbors, and luxuriant undergrowth which blocks our paths and by-ways; to say nothing of the stings and scratches of plants whose propensities include protection against predators. Often we have good reason to cut back such growth; yet, even as we curse it, we cannot usually deny that the plants are flourishing after their kind—and that in no ironical or animistic sense of "flourishing." But on Feinberg's theory we cannot cut back plants which in any proper sense flourish contrary to our interests, because they are conceptually impossible. Not so easily is paradise regained.

Underlying my criticisms of Hare and Feinberg there is, of course, the Aristotelian principle that the good life for a living organism turns on the fulfillment of its nature. This principle has recently been defended and applied to animals by Stephen Clark,[6] who concludes that it harms creatures to "deprive them, whether they were man or beast, of the proper fulfilment of their genetically programmed potentialities." Clark adds, by way of a reductio of his main opponents, the sound point that, if creatures' good is "defined by extrinsic teleology, by their use to man" then it must be held "that it is to a pig's benefit to be killed and eaten," and that it cannot flourish otherwise. But this is absurd. We should not deprive ourselves of a vocabulary in which to talk of creatures' good, or we shall not even be in a position to discuss whether or not we may disregard it.

The same principle can be restated as follows. Let the "essential" capacities of an x be capacities in the absence of which from most members of a species that species would not be the species of x's, and let "x" range over terms for living organisms. Then the flourishing of an x entails the development in it of the essential capacities of x's. I have elsewhere attempted to defend the application of this principle to humans;[7] but, as Clark says of Aristotle's similar argument, the objections which might be invoked against it over humans "do not begin to touch its application in the case of beasts." To this I should add,

"or to plants," besides, of course, endorsing his view that the objections to its application to humans are mistaken. But this agreement of Clark and myself about humans is not here at stake, except insofar as the general principle is. This principle is also a principle governing the nature of good and harm, and suggests the kind of theory of harm which I should adopt as against that of Hare. It also implies that trees can be harmed in their own right, and have a "sake" for which acts can be performed, and interests and needs of their own.

What it does not imply, however, is that trees are of value in their own right, have rights, or ought to be shown consideration. To issues like these I now turn, by considering the grounds for preserving trees. Whether the fact that trees have a good of their own is a reason for caring for them is, at this stage, an unanswered question.

II. GROUNDS FOR PRESERVING TREES

Many of the grounds for preserving trees are also, of course, grounds for preserving wild animals and areas of wilderness as well. Of these grounds almost certainly the most important group is associated with the interests of humans. Thus it is important to preserve trees, other wild creatures and their habitats for reasons of scientific research, to retain as wide a gene pool as possible for the sake of medicine and agriculture, and for recreation, retreat and the enjoyment of natural beauty. These grounds, and the extent of their application, are well discussed by John Passmore in *Man's Responsibility For Nature,*[8] and do not need to be discussed in detail here.

Passmore correctly remarks that such considerations will often be overridden by other human interests, and sets out upon a search for other grounds for preservation. This same difficulty has been noticed by Laurence H. Tribe, who observes that, if human interests only are taken into account, the replacement of natural trees by plastic ones would often be justified.[9] His solution is to suggest that forests and other natural objects of beauty such as cliffs might be recognized as having rights which could not easily be overridden. A difficulty here, however, would be the justification of such legal or moral rights, especially where the balance of advantage would favor their disregard. As Robert Nozick[10] urges in the related matter of the treatment of animals, to justify an absolute prohibition on the infliction of pain and suffering we should need a theory of "side constraints" on which the interests of the animal concerned could not be overridden on any ground: a theory of overriding moral rights. But such a theory, requiring as it does the sacrifice on occasion of basic human needs and even of human life in the interest of non-human animals, is so counter-intuitive that it is yet less likely to command acceptance than that of Tribe. Nevertheless our inclination to accept that constraints of some kind are required in the dealings of humans with animals suggests one lesson to be learned about the preservation of wildlife: for the interests of animals, once allowed to count for something, do constitute an additional ground for preserving the plants and the habitats on which they depend; and these interests will occasionally tilt the balance of advantage in favor of preservation.

Another writer who attempts to supplement the arguments from human interests in the cause of preservation, with their acknowledged shortcomings, is Mark Sagoff.[11] His view of the justification for preserving wildlife and wilderness is that they symbolically represent to us values which cannot be satisfactorily expressed without them, and that the loss of significant scenes and places diminishes ourselves. This view does perhaps explain a great part of our interest in nature, and also supplies an extra justification for preserving some tracts of it intact; but it is, of course, another justification drawn from human interests, and, like the counterpart justifications of science, recreation and retreat, is likely to be outweighed on occasion by people's interest in e.g. food, clothing and shelter.

In order further to assess grounds for the preservation of wildlife and wilderness which go beyond human interests we can conveniently return to Passmore's examination of our moral traditions in this same connection. The themes which he remarks concern the wrongness of causing unnecessary suffering to animals, of extirpating species and diversity, and of vandalism and wanton destruction, while he also touches on the tradition which commends reverence for life as such (and finds it wanting). As I have already acknowledged the moral relevance of animal interests to the preservation of trees, I shall concentrate on the other themes, to see if they require the interests of trees to figure among the grounds of morality.

One of the possible grounds for preserving both individual plants and species of plants is the desirability of diversity. The long history down from Plato's Timaeus of the principle that the more diverse a world is the better has been well traced by Lovejoy;[12] and in ecological connections it is an attractive principle, because of the important role played by even the humblest member of an ecosystem. But it is less easy to agree that diversity is desirable for its own sake, and that it is because of this that we are required where possible to preserve the manifold species of our planet. It is agreed on most sides that the enjoyment of sentient creatures is desirable for its own sake; and it is an important truth that delight and pleasure are usually fostered by the experience of diversities of sounds, colors, shapes and species, as well as by diversities of social traditions and individual personalities. So it may be that what makes diversity desirable is its enjoyment, together perhaps with the range of desirable activities which it facilitates.

To some, the above theory of the desirability of diversity may seem anthropocentric; in fact, as it takes into account the experiences and activities of non-human species, this impression would be illusory. Nevertheless it makes the diversity of plant species a matter of merely derivative value, at least unless the theory is supplemented in some way; and even if it is supplemented by pointing out the importance of diversity in ecosystems for their stability, the value of diversity remains derivative, depending on the interests of those creatures such as ourselves which benefit from ecological stability.

As this may all sound unsatisfactory, it should be tested. What we have to imagine is a world in which there are no conscious experiences and no activities (at least on the part of creatures); of this imaginary world we must then ask whether it would be any the worse if it became more uniform, e.g., by coming to lack objects of one particular form or composition. Such a thought-experiment may be barely possible until we imagine the agency which might carry out the deprivation. Yet this is the sort of question which it is appropriate to ask, rather than one about, say, whether the loss of one species of plant would impoverish the world. For there may be something intrinsically desirable about plant species not because of their diversity but because they are species of living organisms; and what is at stake is whether diversity is intrinsically desirable, whatever its domain.

The agency which we seem to need to imagine can be introduced by a variation on Richard Routley's "last man" example.[13] The last man knows, in my version of this example, that all life on this planet is about to be terminated by multilateral nuclear warfare. He is, indeed, himself the last surviving sentient organism, and knows that he too will die within a few minutes; but he also happens himself to be possessed of a workable missile capable of destroying all the planet's remaining resources of diamond. The gesture of doing so would certainly be futile, but for himself it has a symbolical significance; and the question with which he is faced, and which we can ask about his projected act, is whether it would do any harm or destroy anything of intrinsic value. If we set aside the possibility that the planet might some day be repopulated with sentient organisms, which would, it seems to me, make a difference, the answer is surely that there is nothing wrong with this act, morally indifferent as I should certainly recognize it to be. The world would not through his act be any the poorer. (Maybe the act deprives God and the company of heaven of the experience of diversity, and is on that ground objectionable; but if so the objection arises because of the loss of valuable experiences rather than because of the value of diversity itself.)

There seems, then, no reason for preferring a slightly more diverse inanimate world to a slightly less diverse one, unless its constituents are objects of someone's or something's experience. In other words, diversity is not intrinsically desirable. If then

there is something intrinsically undesirable in losses in the variety of living species, it will turn on their life and not on the loss to diversity as such.

It might here be suggested that it is rather the wrongness of vandalism which accounts for our objections to the elimination of species; indeed that his act was a piece of vandalism might be thought to show after all the wrongness of what was done by the "last man" of the recent example. Now certainly, as Passmore points out,[14] acts of destruction need justification; and certainly dispositions or policies involving the destruction of items of value for its own sake are strongly to be condemned. But even when policies and motives are bad (and this is not clearly true of the last man) the acts which stem from them are not always or necessarily wrong; and besides, vandalism is bad because of the harm habitually or usually done by vandals; so, if we are to hold that the elimination of a species is vandalism (which, I suspect, it often is) we need to show it to do harm or to be undesirable on some such more basic ground. The readiness of people to recognize vandalism may often curtail the need for further argument, as Pete Gunter reports about the tactics of some lumber companies opposed to the declaration of a National Park;[15] yet the recognition of vandalism entails the recognition of the unnecessary perpetration of evils, and it is these evils which constitute the basic objection to it. So we must continue to search for what of value is lost to the world when plants or their species are destroyed, to see whether such losses are all ultimately losses to sentient creatures or not.

The question now becomes whether the continuation of each living species is valuable in itself. Passmore tells us that according to Aquinas this is the attitude of God, who "in the case of every other species except man . . . cares nothing for the benefit of the individual but does watch over the species as a whole."[16] A partially similar view is taken by Feinberg about animal species: "the preservation of a whole species may quite properly seem to be a morally more important matter than the preservation of an individual animal."[17] But Feinberg grounds this duty in our duty to future humans, rather than to the species concerned as such. And this is one of the grounds for preservation, or rather one class of grounds, taken account of already.

One reason for concern for species is concern for their current members; and when Stephen Clark observes that "Our distress at the destruction of a living tree is not merely at our loss of pleasure in its beauty," he expresses a sentiment which many would echo. Yet concern for species is not the same as concern for the present individual members: it involves the belief that it is desirable that there be elms, etc., and if it is to be an independent ground, that it is intrinsically desirable. Once a species dies out, there will be no more individual members; so either if each life of that kind is valuable in its own right, or if at least it is valuable that there be lives of that kind, the occurrence is a tragedy regardless of the circumstances or consequences.

Now the other tradition discussed by Passmore, that which enjoins reverence for life, has sometimes maintained that each life of any kind is valuable in its own right, and valuable just because it is a life. But, as Jonathan Glover cogently argues,[18] the belief that "all life is sacred" needs drastic modification even when applied to humans: for some lives cease to be worth living, and some never were so; and, we might add, even if some lives which are not in general worth living still include some worthwhile activities and experiences, nevertheless there are some lives which no longer do, and some which never did. And when we turn to other species we find that a great many organisms lack even the capacity to flourish after their own kind, being genetically or accidentally stunted, or having entered the phase of natural decay.

Thus, even if we agree with Feinberg that (some) animals have (some) rights, we are not obliged to hold that every animal life, let alone every vegetable life, is intrinsically valuable. Indeed there is good reason not to hold this at all. Whatever our objections to the destruction of individual trees, it is not the mere fact of their being alive which can justify our reaction; for lives can lack any features which make them worthwhile to anyone or anything, including the creature the life of which is in question.

If so, the intrinsic undesirability of the elimination of a living species cannot turn on the intrinsic value of each and every species member. It could still, in theory, turn on the intrinsic value of there being lives of that kind; but it is hard to see why we should accept this belief, granted that there is nothing intrinsically valuable about diversity in itself. Certainly most species are vital for the continued existence of many others, and certainly we enjoy their variety and might reasonably feel diminished at the extinction of any single one. But this is to acknowledge the importance of each species to other species, not their intrinsic value. It could then be that the tragedy involved in the termination of a species depends on the diminution of the worthwhile activities of members of other species or on the baneful effects is has on such individuals; and these said individuals, to be capable of worthwhile activities, must at least be purposive in a way in which vegetables are not.

The modern understanding of the interdependence of species supplies additional reasons why, to avert harm to humans and animals, almost all species of living creatures should be preserved, together with some of their habitats. Nevertheless the above survey of the grounds for the preservation of wildlife and wilderness suggests that there are few if any grounds to be found beyond the welfare of humans and animals; for neither does mention of vandalism add to the list of basic grounds, nor is there anything intrinsically amiss in losses to diversity, in the extinction of species or in the curtailment of life rather than worthwhile life.

Moreover what is not intrinsically valuable can hardly be thought to have rights; for what has rights must be valuable in its own right. So apparently trees and plants lack rights, even though they are needed by humans many times over—and even though we should literally starve and suffocate without them.

III. THE VALUE AND RIGHTS OF TREES

The argument so far brings us to a paradox. Trees have needs and a good of their own, yet they have no intrinsic value and no rights of their own. Trees have interests, yet we have no obligation to protect those interests in themselves. And this is a position uncomfortably close to unreason; for, in other cases, what has interests of its own becomes ipso facto of moral concern, whereas in this case we are prepared to disregard a large set of interests and treat them as morally irrelevant.

Someone might at this point attempt to disavow the conclusion of Section I, and hold that, e.g., what has no purposes has no interests; but as we there saw, this would be entirely unreasonable. The more tentative conclusions of Section II, however, could more easily be re-examined. Thus it was never established that no tree is of intrinsic value, but only that, as not all lives are worth living, it could well be that the possible objects of moral concern are confined to the class of the agents of worthwhile activities (and potential activities), and thus that the lives of non-purposive organisms are of no moral significance in themselves. But the premise only shows that some plants are of no intrinsic value, and that not all life is sacred. It could, then, still be true that a full-grown oak is after all morally as important as the crows and the squirrels which shelter in it.

But trees, it will be said, not only lack activity and self-motion but also beliefs, desires and feelings. Squirrels merit moral consideration because they have capacities in some way like our own; trees do not because the similarities are vanishingly few. Granted that it is the capacities of humans which make them morally significant, this analogical argument must be accepted at least as to what it affirms about animals, and as to the commended priority of animals over plants. Yet are the similarities really negligible? Trees, like humans and squirrels, have capacities for nutrition and growth, for respiration and for self-protection; and it is capacities and propensities such as these which determine their interests. If then their interests are partially similar to interests of acknowledged moral relevance (i.e., to our own), can we disregard them totally?

One line of argument which might suggest that plants matter in their own right runs as follows. It is perhaps unimportant that species, regarded abstractly, should continue to have members, and perhaps not all the members matter either. But, regarded concretely as populations, species are often the units

which count, and are, at that, units which count a good deal: species such as "Grass" and the "Nitrogen-fixing Bacterium" are, as Clark[19] would have it, "ethically relevant individuals." And Clark is surely correct in claiming that they are "enormously more important to the world at large than any human individual." Members of species, it might be added, are often interdependent, while it is the species as a whole which maintains itself intact against external pressures and competition. Hence, it might be argued, sometimes whole species deserve consideration in their own right.

We should certainly be wary of rejecting all this on the wrong grounds. Thus Passmore concludes that species lack interests because they lack wants and purposes; but, as we have seen, wants and purposes are not necessary in this connection.[20] Indeed it may be that some simple organisms live in colonies which are like individual plants in having latent tendencies, direction of growth and natural fulfilments; and if so these colonies would have interests on the same basis as individual trees. But otherwise the waxing and waning of the populations of species are not, it seems to me, such that we can speak of the fulfilment of natural propensities which they have as species; so the interests which they have must simply be the resultants of the interests of their individual members, a reflection which holds good even of species with interdependent members. And this is as far as the argument about species regarded as populations gets us; for talk of the importance of a species to the world at large does not begin to show it to be of intrinsic value, rather than to be of consequential value.

Admittedly Clark also adduces the contention of Leopold that ecologically interdependent species owe each other consideration as members of a community. Leopold advocates a "land ethic," incorporating the whole terrestrial biotic community in the reference of the term "land." "All ethics so far evolved rest upon a single premise: that the individual is a member of a community of interdependent parts. . . . The land ethic simply enlarges the boundaries of the community to include soils, waters, plants, and animals, or collectively: the land."[21] There is here the suggestion that all interdependence entails mutual obligations. But, as Passmore observes,[22] this is not so. "In the only sense in which belonging to a community generates ethical obligation, they (sc. bacteria and men) do not belong to the same community." Passmore seems to weaken his point by requiring of members of a community that they recognize mutual obligations, a dubious claim which also begs the question against Leopold. But he is surely right that too little is shared and acknowledged by members of the biotic community for it to constitute the basis of obligations to all even on the part of those members to whom they can without absurdity be ascribed.

Is there even so a way of moving from the interests of humans, agreed to be of moral significance, and of sentient animals, increasingly recognized to matter in some degree, to the interests of non-sentient animals and plants, so that they too are taken into account? The makings of such an argument begin to appear in Jan Narveson's *Morality and Utility,* though I should emphasize that Narveson himself is concerned solely with people. What Narveson points out is, in effect, that every agent acknowledges that the satisfaction of his interests is intrinsically good. But if so, every agent must also acknowledge that the satisfaction of every other agent's individual interests is intrinsically good too, unless they can justify regarding others differently. Hence the satisfaction of everyone's interests must be of concern to every consistent moral agent.[23]

Not all the elements in this argument are of current relevance. Thus I do not need to tarry over what people will or will not acknowledge. The argument, regarded as concerned with the intrinsic value of the satisfaction of individual agents' interests, clearly requires us to justify any refusal to take interests into account. I do not begin to see how an adequate justification could be supplied over sentient animals; and even with regard to a refusal over trees it is not clear what the grounds of justification would be, though it is clear that grounds are needed.

One ground might be that trees are not sentient, and thus have radically different interests; if so, the reply is that they share with sentient organisms vegetative interests which are regarded as mattering in other cases; the physical well-being of organisms which have interests is not plausibly a matter of complete indifference, even in cases where the organisms cannot suffer pain or frustration. Another ground might be that trees are not agents, because they lack purposes; if so, the reply takes the form of a request why the interests of non-purposive organisms are not as intrinsically important as the similar interests of purposive organisms, or at least why they are not intrinsically important to some degree. If the answer to this request is that only agents can exercise sanctions, it is not of an appropriate character; if it is that only agents consciously experience frustration, it can be replied that in the case of animals the stunting of natural propensities comprises harm even when it is not understood or sensed as such by the animal affected, and if this harm is an evil, so plausibly is the stunting of organisms lacking sentience.

In all this I willingly grant that the differences in potential between different species are of the very greatest importance. Thus the goods and the harms open to most people because of their essential capacities vastly exceed those open to most animals, and similarly the blessings and sufferings made possible by capacities for purposiveness do indeed make the interests of non-purposive organisms count for less than those of purposive organisms and hence of agents. But this still does not show that the interests of trees count for nothing; and even if not all lives are worthwhile lives, it still might be that many or even most vegetable lives are worthwhile and of value in themselves. After all, we have still to account for the distress which at least some of us feel at the destruction of a living tree. So the issue of whether trees have an intrinsic value remains at least an open one.

To attempt to test the issue, I revert to a form of Routley's "last man" example closer to his original. So as to discount the value of trees for people and sentient animals, we imagine once again that people and sentient animals are one and all doomed to imminent and inevitable nuclear poisoning, and that this is known to the last surviving human. But this time we imagine him considering the symbolic protest of hewing down with an axe the last tree of its kind, a hitherto healthy elm which has survived the nuclear explosions and which could propagate its kind if left unassaulted. Nothing sentient is ever likely to evolve from its descendants; so the question which he faces, and we can ask about him, is whether there is anything wrong with chopping it down and whether the world would be the poorer for the loss of it. We must suppose further, of course, that he himself will not suffer if he does not cut down the tree; he has enough timber already for firewood and shelter for his own last hours.

This question may seem to raise a problem of method; for it is asked of circumstances about which some would say that we no longer know how to apply our ordinary concepts of value. It is unclear to me how they would claim to know this; I can only invite those who nevertheless make this claim to attend instead to more ordinary cases of the uprooting of healthy trees and our reaction to it. So long, however, as the last man retains his ordinary concepts of value and his capacity to apply them, the question would seem to be both conceptually proper and apposite; and, if so, the problem of method proves illusory.

Most people who face the question would, I believe, conclude that the world would be the poorer for this act of the "last man" and that it would be wrong. He would be unnecessarily destroying a living creature which could have renewed the stock of its own species. (I suspect that a similar reaction would be the typical one to more everyday uprootings, though of course the reasons for such a reaction would often in those cases be mixed ones. I also suspect that the reaction would seldom be different even if the interests of sentient creatures are discounted.) And if, without being swayed by the interests of sentient creatures, we share in these conclusions and reactions, we must also conclude that the interests of trees are of moral significance. Although they rarely come or should come foremost in ethical deliberation, they can and in principle should be considered.

There are, of course, in practice ample grounds for disregarding the interests of trees at most junctures. Human and/or animal interests are almost always at stake, and mere vegetation can be forgotten where those interests would be imperiled. The good of trees might outweigh some of our whims; but it does not outweigh our interests except where our interests depend on it. But this is not to make trees of no ethical relevance in themselves. Very slightly, they have interests mirroring ours; at very many removes they are our living kin. But interests do, it seems, supply reasons for consideration; and there is always the residual possibility of their interests being of greater significance than any others which are at stake.

Theoretically at least, the same applies to other plants, to non-sentient animals, and to those colonies of organisms which function as individuals; although just as among sentient animals so here too there are diversities in the degree of consideration due. There again, the overall grounds for preservation and careful treatment will be supplemented in respect of value to other organisms by enormously diverse amounts, but never more, I suspect, than in the case of trees.

All the same, my conclusion is not without practical significance. It implies among other things that some degree of respect is due to almost all life, even though the main ground for the preservation of natural kinds remains human interests; and it implies that, where natural trees could be replaced without aesthetic loss or other disadvantage to humans there are still reasons for not doing so. At the more theoretical level it suggests that nothing which has interests is to be viewed wholly instrumentally, and that things which have interests characteristically have some value in their own right. If trees have a good which is not our good, then they also constitute a good; if they have their own form of flourishing, they are thereby of value in themselves.

Do trees have rights? Only what is valuable in its own right has rights; but many trees do now seem valuable in their own right. Yet trees certainly do not have rights in Nozick's sense of there being "side-constraints" prohibiting various forms of treatment whatever the need or the benefits. At best, their interests have to be weighed with those of people and animals.

Need we, however, reject all forms of conceptual tie between interests and rights? The form of connection propounded by Feinberg is as follows. Creatures have rights if and only if they have interests, consideration is due to them, and it is due to them not for the sake of anything else but for their own sake.[24] Interests are necessary since what has rights must be capable of being represented and of being a beneficiary, having a welfare of its own. Feinberg believes, in the light of this condition, that trees lack rights; but, as we have seen, he is mistaken. Now no one would dispute that consideration is often due to trees where this just means that there are grounds for tending or preserving them; what is not usually accepted is that it is due to them for their own sake. If I am right and it is, then, granted Feinberg's conceptual connection of interests and rights, many trees have rights.

Such rights would, however, like all other rights be overridable from time to time; and the grounds for them, the intrinsic value of trees, would be so slender by comparison with the grounds of other rights as to be outweighed most of the time, so much so as to disappear into near oblivion. Yet if some trees have rights, then we should occasionally bear the fact in mind, or unsound theory will lead to misguidedness in action.

Alternatively someone who agrees that trees have interests and are of ethical relevance but cannot accept that they have rights might wish to reject or amend the conceptual tie delineated by Feinberg, such, perhaps, that only purposive or potentially purposive creatures can have rights. To such an amendment I should not object. Rights are not the sole ground of moral reasoning, and it does seem incongruous to represent the treatment of trees as a matter of justice. In any case the grounds for the ascription of rights in Feinberg's unamended sense to trees would remain, and we could show concern for their needs and interests without believing them to have rights. We could, I think, still talk of obligations to them, since if it is sometimes wrong to destroy them for no reason beyond themselves then it is on those occasions obligatory not to do so,[25] and indeed the obligation is due to nothing but the tree, if it is due to anything at all.

"And God said, 'Let the earth put forth vegetation, plants yielding seed, and fruit trees bearing fruit in which is their seed, each according to its kind, upon the earth.' And it was so. The earth brought forth vegetation, plants yielding seed according to their own kinds, and trees bearing fruit in which is their seed, each according to its kind. And God saw that it was good."[26] Of course, in Genesis 1 all creation is good; be that as it may, living creatures in any case, it would seem, characteristically have a value of their own.[27]

NOTES

1. R. M. Hare, *Essays on the Moral Concepts* (New York: Macmillan, 1972). See p. 98 and following.

2. Joel Feinberg, "The Rights of Animals and Unborn Generations," in *Philosophy and Environmental Crisis,* ed. William T. Blackstone (Athens: University of Georgia Press, 1974), pp. 43–68. See pp. 51–55.

3. "Summa Contra Gentiles," translated by the English Dominican Fathers, Benziger Brothers, 1928, ch. 112, quoted in *Animal Rights and Human Obligations,* ed. Tom Regan and Peter Singer (Englewood Cliffs, NJ: Prentice-Hall, 1976). See pp. 56–59.

4. See the discussion of the Stoic Balbus in Cicero's *De Natura Deorum* by John Passmore at p. 14 of *Man's Responsibility for Nature* (London: Duckworth, 1974)

5. Feinberg, "Rights of Animals and Unborn Generations." See pp. 49–50.

6. Stephen R.L. Clark, *The Moral Status of Animals* (Oxford: Clarendon Press, 1977). See pp. 57–58.

7. Robin Attfield, "On Being Human," *Inquiry,* 17 (1974): 175–92; also *A Theory of Value and Obligation,* chapters 3 to 5.

8. Passmore, *Man's Responsibility for Nature.* See pp. 101–10.

9. Laurence H. Tribe, "Ways Not to Think About Plastic Trees," *Yale Law Journal* 83 (1974): 1315–48.

10. Robert Nozick, *Anarchy, State and Utopia* (Oxford, Blackwell, 1974). See pp. 28–42.

11. Mark Sagoff, "On Preserving the Natural Environment," *Yale Law Journal* 84 (1974): 205–67.

12. A. O. Lovejoy, *The Great Chain of Being* (Harvard: Harvard University Press, 1936)

13. Richard Routley, "Is There a Need for a New, an Environmental Ethic?" in *Proceedings of The Fifteenth*

World Congress of Philosophy (Varna, 1973). See pp. 205–10.

14. Passmore, *Man's Responsibility for Nature*. See p. 124.

15. Pete A.Y. Gunter, "The Big Thicket," in Blackstone, *Philosophy and Environmental Crisis*: 117–37. See pp. 126–29.

16. Passmore, *Man's Responsibility for Nature*. See p. 117.

17. Feinberg, "Rights of Animals and Unborn Generations." See p. 56.

18. Jonathan Glover, *Causing Death and Saving Lives* (London: Penguin, 1977). See chapter 3.

19. Clark, *The Moral Status of Animals*. See p. 171.

20. Passmore, *Man's Responsibility for Nature*. See p. 55ff.

21. Aldo Leopold, *A Sand County Almanac* (New York: Oxford 1949). See p. 203ff, quoted by Clark at p. 164.

22. Passmore, *Man's Responsibility for Nature*. See p. 116.

23. Jan Narveson, *Morality and Utility* (Baltimore: Johns Hopkins Press, 1967) See pp. 271–75.

24. Feinberg effectively deals with the objection that right-holders must also be capable of making and of waiving claims on their own in "Rights of Animals and Unborn Generations." See pp. 46–49.

25. The claim that it is obligatory not to do what it is wrong to do and the criteria of obligation, wrongness and rightness are discussed more fully in Feinberg, "Supererogation and Double Standards," *Mind* 89: 481–99.

26. *Genesis,* ch. 1, vv. 11f., Revised Standard Version.

27. The current chapter first appeared in *Journal of Value Inquiry,* 15 (1981): 35–54. Also see Richard and Val Routley, "Against the Inevitability of Human Chauvinism" in *Ethics and Problems of the 21st Century,* ed. K. E. Goodpaster and K. M. Sayre. (Notre Dame and London: Notre Dame University Press, 1979). See pp. 36–59.

Duties Concerning Islands

Mary Midgley

Had Robinson Crusoe any duties on his island?

When I was a philosophy student, this used to be a familiar conundrum, which was supposed to pose a very simple question: namely, can you have duties to yourself? Mill, they correctly told us, said no.

> The term duty to oneself, when it means anything more than prudence, means self-respect or self-development and for none of these is anyone accountable to his fellow-creatures.[1]

Kant, on the other hand, said yes.

> Duties to ourselves are of primary importance and should have pride of place . . . nothing can be expected of a man who dishonours his own person.[2]

There is a serious disagreement here, not to be sneezed away just by saying—"it depends on what you mean by duty." Much bigger issues are involved. But quite how big has, I think, not yet been fully realised. To grasp this, I suggest that we rewrite a part of Crusoe's story, so as to bring in sight a different range of concerns, thus:

> *Sept. 19, 1685.* This day I set aside to devastate my island. My pinnace being now ready on the shore, and all things prepared for my departure, Friday's people also expecting me, and the wind blowing fresh away from my little harbour, I had in mind to see how all would burn. So then, setting sparks and powder craftily among certain dry spinneys which

Mary Midgley, "Duties Concerning Islands," *Encounter* 60 (1983): 36–43. Reprinted with permission of author.

I had chosen, I soon had it ablaze, nor was there left, by the next dawn, any green stick among the ruins. . . .

Now, work on the style how you will, you cannot make that into a convincing paragraph. Crusoe was not the most scrupulous of men, but he would have felt an invincible objection to this senseless destruction. So would the rest of us. Yet the language of our moral tradition has tended strongly, ever since the Enlightenment, to make that objection unstateable. All the terms which express that a claim is serious or binding—duty, right, law, morality, obligation, justice—have been deliberately narrowed in their use so as to apply only within the framework of contract, to describe only relations holding between free and rational agents. Since it has been decided a priori that rationality has no degrees and that cetaceans are not rational, it follows that, unless you take either religion or science fiction seriously, we can only have duties to humans, and sane, adult, fully responsible humans at that.

Now the morality we live by certainly does not accept this restriction. In common life we recognise many other duties as serious and binding, though of course not necessarily overriding. If philosophers want to call these something else instead of "duties," they must justify their move. We have here one of these clashes between the language of common morality (which is of course always to some extent confused and inarticulate) and an intellectual scheme which arose in the first place from a part of that morality, but has now taken off on its own and claims authority to correct other parts of its source.

There are always real difficulties here. As ordinary citizens we have to guard against dismissing such intellectual schemes too casually; we have to do justice to the point of them. But as philosophers, we have to resist the opposite temptation of taking the intellectual scheme as decisive, just because it is elegant and satisfying, or because the moral insight which is its starting-point is specially familiar to us. Today, this intellectualist bias is often expressed by calling the insights of common morality mere "intuitions." This is quite misleading, since it gives the

impression that they have been reached without thought, and that there is, by contrast, a scientific solution somewhere else to which they ought to bow as there might be if we were contrasting common-sense "intuitions" about the physical world with physics or astronomy. Even when they do not use that word, however, philosophers often manage to give the impression that whenever our moral views clash with any simple, convenient scheme, it is our *duty* to abandon them. Thus G. R. Grice:

> It is an inescapable consequence of the thesis presented in these pages that certain classes cannot have natural rights: animals, the human embryo, future generations, lunatics and children under the age of, say, ten. In the case of young children at least, my experience is that this consequence is found hard to accept. But it is a consequence of the theory; it is, I believe, true; and I think we should be willing to accept it. At first sight it seems a harsh conclusion, but it is not nearly so harsh as it appears. . . .
> (*Grounds of Moral Judgment*, 1967, pp. 146–47)

But it is in fact extremely harsh, since what he is saying is that the treatment of children ought not to be determined by their interests, but by the interests of the surrounding adults capable of contract, which of course can easily conflict with them.

In our own society, he explains, this does not actually make much difference, because parents here are so benevolent that they positively want to benefit their children; and accordingly here "the interests of children are reflected in the interests of their parents." But this, he adds, is just a contingent fact about us. "It is easy to imagine a society where this is not so," where, that is, parents are entirely exploitative. "In this circumstance, the morally correct treatment of children would no doubt be harsher than it is in our society. But the conclusion has to be accepted." Grice demands that we withdraw our objections to harshness, in deference to theoretical consistency. But "harsh" here does not mean just "brisk and bracing" like cold baths and a plain diet. (There might well be more of those where parents do feel bound to consider their children's interests.) It means unjust.

Our objection to unbridled parental selfishness is not a mere matter of tone or taste; it is a moral one. It therefore requires a moral answer, an explanation of the contrary value which the contrary theory expresses. Grice and those who argue like him take the ascetic, disapproving tone of people who have already displayed such a value, and who are met by a slovenly reluctance to rise to it. But they have not displayed that value. The ascetic tone cannot be justified merely by an appeal to consistency. An ethical theory which, when consistently followed through, has iniquitous consequences is a bad theory and must be changed. Certainly we can ask whether these consequences really are iniquitous; but this question must be handled seriously. We cannot directly conclude that the consequences cease to stink the moment they are seen to follow from our theory.

The theoretical model which has spread blight in this area is, of course, that of social contract, to fit which the whole cluster of essential moral terms which I mentioned—right, duty, justice, and the rest—has been progressively narrowed. This model shows human society as a spread of standard social atoms, originally distinct and independent, each of which combines with others only at its own choice and in its own private interest. This model is drawn from physics, and from 17th-century physics at that, where the ultimate particles of matter were conceived as hard, impenetrable, homogeneous little billiard-balls, with no hooks or internal structure. To see how such atoms could combine at all was very hard. Physics, accordingly, moved on from this notion to one which treats atoms and other particles as complex items, describable mainly in terms of forces, and those the same kind of forces which operate outside them. It has abandoned the notion of ultimate, solitary, independent individuals.

Social contract theory, however, retains it. On this physical—or archaeophysical—model, all significant moral relations between individuals are the symmetrical ones expressed by contract. If, on the other hand, we use a biological or "organic" model, we can talk also of a variety of asymmetrical relations found within a whole. Leaves relate not only to other leaves, but to fruit, twigs, branches, and the whole tree. People appear not only as individuals, but as members of their groups, families, tribes, species, ecosystems and biosphere, and have moral relations, as parts, to these various wholes.

The choice between these two ways of thinking is not, of course, a simple once-for-all affair. Different models are useful for different purposes. We can, however, reasonably point out, first, that the old physical pattern makes all attempts to explain combination extremely difficult. Second, that since human beings actually are living creatures, not crystals or galaxies, it is reasonable to expect that biological ways of thinking will be useful in understanding them.

In its own sphere, the social contract model has of course been of enormous value. Where we deal with clashes of interest between free and rational agents already in existence, and particularly where we want to disentangle a few of them from some larger group which really does not suit them, it is indispensable. And for certain political purposes during the last three centuries these clashes have been vitally important. An obsession with contractual thinking and a conviction that it is a cure-all are therefore understandable. But the trouble with such obsessions is that they distort the whole shape of thought and language in a way which makes them self-perpetuating, and constantly extends their empire. Terms come to be defined in a way which leaves only certain moral views expressible. This can happen without any clear intention on the part of those propagating them, and even contrary to their occasional declarations, simply from mental inertia.

Thus, John Rawls, having devoted most of his long book to his very subtle and exhaustive contractual view of justice, remarks without any special emphasis near the end that,

We should recall here the limits of a theory of justice. Not only are many aspects of morality left aside, but no account can be given of right conduct in regard to animals and the rest of nature. (*A Theory of Justice,* p. 512)

He concedes that these are serious matters.

Certainly it is wrong to be cruel to animals and the destruction of a whole species can be a great evil. The capacity for feelings of pleasure and pain and for the forms of life of which animals are capable clearly impose duties of compassion and humanity in their case.

All this is important, he says, and it calls for a wider metaphysical enquiry, but it is not his subject. Earlier in the same passage he touches on the question of permanently irrational human beings, and remarks that it "may present a difficulty. I cannot examine this problem here, but I assume that the account of equality would not be materially affected."

Won't it though? It is a strange project to examine a single virtue—justice—without at least sketching in one's view of the vast background of general morality which determines its shape and meaning, including, of course, such awkward and non-contractual virtues as "compassion and humanity." It isolates the duties which people owe each other *merely as thinkers* from those deeper and more general ones which they owe each other as beings who feel. It cannot, therefore, fail both to split man's nature and to isolate him from the rest of the creation to which he belongs. Such an account may not be *Hamlet* without the prince, but it is *Hamlet* with half the cast missing, and without the state of Denmark. More exactly, it is like a history of Poland which regards Russia, Germany, Europe, and the Roman Church as not part of its subject.

I am not attacking John Rawls' account on its own ground. I am simply pointing out what the history of ethics shows all too clearly—how much our thinking is shaped by what our sages *omit* to mention. The Greek philosophers never really raised the problem of slavery till towards the end of their epoch, and then few of them did so with conviction. This happened even though it lay right in the path of their enquiries into political justice and the value of the individual soul. Christianity did raise that problem, because its social background was different, and because the world was in the Christian era already in

turmoil, so that men were not presented with the narcotic of happy stability. But Christianity itself did not, until quite recently, raise the problem of the morality of punishment, and particularly of eternal punishment.

This failure to raise central questions was not in either case complete. One can find very intelligent and penetrating criticisms of slavery occurring from time to time in Greek writings—even in Aristotle's defence of that institution.[3] But they are mostly like Rawls's remark here. They conclude "this should be investigated some day." The same thing happens with Christian writings concerning punishment, except that the consideration "this is a great mystery" acts as an even more powerful paralytic to thought. Not much more powerful, however. Natural inertia, when it coincides with vested interest or the illusion of vested interest, is as strong as gravitation.

It is important that Rawls does not (like Grice) demand that we toe a line which would make certain important moral views impossible. Like Hume, who similarly excluded animals from justice, he simply leaves them out of his discussion. This move ought in principle to be harmless. But when it is combined with an intense concentration of discussion on contractual justice, and a corresponding neglect of compassion and humanity, it inevitably suggests that the excluded problems are relatively unimportant.

This suggestion is still more strongly conveyed by rulings which exclude the non-human world from rights, duties, and morality. Words like *rights* and *duties* are awkward because they do indeed have narrow senses approximating to the legal, but they also have much wider ones in which they cover the whole moral sphere. To say "They do not have rights" or "You do not have duties to them" conveys to any ordinary hearer a very simple message, namely, "They do not matter. . . ." This is an absolution, a removal of blame for ill-treatment of "them," whoever they may be.

To see how strong this informal, moral usage of "rights" is, we need only look at the history of that powerful notion, "the Rights of Man." These rights were not supposed to be ones conferred by law, since the whole point of appealing to them was to change laws so as to embody them. They were vague, but vast. They did not arise, as rights are often said to do, only within a community, since they were taken to apply in principle everywhere. The immense, and on the whole coherent, use which has been made of this idea by reforming movements shows plainly that the tension between the formal and the informal idea of *right* is part of the word's meaning, a fruitful connection of thought, not just a mistake. It is therefore hard to adopt effectively the compromise which some philosophers now favour, of saying that it is indeed wrong to treat animals in certain ways, but that we have no duties to them or that they have no rights.[4] "Animal rights" may be hard to formulate, as indeed are the rights of man. But "no rights" will not do.[5] The word may need to be dropped entirely.

The compromise is still harder with the word duty, which is rather more informal, and is more closely wedded to a private rather than political use. Where the realm of right and duty stops, there, to ordinary thinking, begins the realm of the optional. What is not a duty may be a matter of taste, style or feeling, of aesthetic sensibility, of habit and nostalgia, of etiquette and local custom; but it cannot be something which demands our attention whether we like it or not. When claims get into this area, they can scarcely be taken seriously.

This becomes clear when Kant tries to straddle the border. He says that we have no direct duties to animals, because they are not rational, but that we should treat them properly all the same because of "indirect duties" which are really duties to our own humanity.[6] This means that ill-treating them might lead us to ill-treat humans, and is also a sign of a bad or inhumane disposition. The whole issue thus becomes a contingent one of spiritual style or training, like contemplative exercises, intellectual practice, or indeed refined manners.[7] Some might need practice of this kind to make them kind to people; others might not and indeed might get on better without it. (Working off one's ill-temper on animals might make one treat people *better*.) But the question of cruelty to animals cannot be like this, because it is of the essence of such training exercises that they are internal. Anything that affects some other being is not just practice, it is real action. Anyone who refrained from cruelty *merely* from a wish not to sully his own character, without any direct consideration for the possible victims, would be frivolous and narcissistic.

A similar trivialisation follows where theorists admit duties of compassion and humanity to noncontractors, but deny duties of justice. Hume and Rawls, in making this move, do not explicitly subordinate these other duties, or say that they are less binding. But because they make the contract element so central to morality, this effect seems to follow. The priority of justice is expressed in such everyday proverbs as "Be just before you're generous." We are therefore rather easily persuaded to think that compassion, humanity, and so forth are perhaps emotional luxuries, to be indulged only after all debts are paid.

A moment's thought will show that this is wrong. Someone who receives simultaneously a request to pay a debt and another to comfort somebody bereaved or on their death-bed is not, as a matter of course, under obligation to pay the debt first. He has to look at circumstances on both sides; but in general we should probably expect the other duties to have priority. This is still more true if, on his way to pay the debt, he encounters a stranger in real straits, drowning or lying injured in the road. To give the debt priority, we probably need to think of his creditor as also being in serious trouble—which brings compassion and humanity in on both sides of the case.

What makes it so hard to give justice a different clientele from the other virtues—as Hume and Rawls do—is simply the fact that justice is such a pervading virtue. In general, all serious cases of cruelty, meanness, inhumanity, and the like are also cases of injustice. If we are told that a certain set of these cases does not involve injustice, our natural thought is that these cases must be *trivial*. Officially, Hume's and Rawls's restriction is not supposed to mean this.

What, however, is it supposed to mean? It is forty years since I first read David Hume's text, and I find his thought as obscure now as I did then. I well remember double-taking then, and going back over the paragraph for a point which I took it I must have missed. Can anyone see it?

> Were there [Hume says] a species of creature intermingled with men, which, though rational, were possessed of such inferior strength, both of body and mind, that they were incapable of all resistance, and could never, upon the highest provocation, make us feel the effects of their resentment; the necessary consequence, I think, is that we should be bound by the laws of humanity to give gentle usage to these creatures, but should not, properly speaking, lie under any restraint of justice with regard to them, nor could they possess any right or property, exclusive of such arbitrary lords. Our intercourse with them could not be called society, which supposes a degree of equality, but absolute command on one side and servile obedience on the other. This is plainly the situation of men with regard to animals. (*Enquiry Concerning the Principles of Morals,* para. 152)

I still think that the word justice, so defined, has lost its normal meaning. In ordinary life we think that duties of justice become *more* pressing, not less so, when we are dealing with the weak and inarticulate, who cannot argue back. It is the boundaries of prudence which depend on power, not those of justice.

Historically, Hume's position becomes more understandable when one sees its place in the development of social-contract thinking. The doubtful credit for confining justice to the human species seems to belong to Grotius, who finally managed to ditch the Roman notion of *ius naturale,* natural right or law common to all species. I cannot here discuss his remarkably unimpressive arguments for this.[8] The point I want to make here is simply the effect of these restrictive definitions of terms like justice on people's view of the sheer size of the problems raised by what falls outside them.

Writers who treat morality as primarily contractual tend to discuss non-contractual cases briefly, casually, and parenthetically, as though they were rather rare. (Rawls's comments on the problem of mental defectives are entirely typical here.) We have succeeded, they say, in laying most of the carpet; why are you making this fuss about those little wrinkles behind the sofa?

This treatment confirms a view, already suggested by certain aspects of contemporary politics in the United States, that those who fail to clock in as normal rational agents and make their contracts are just occasional exceptions, constituting one more "minority" group—worrying no doubt to the scrupulous, but not a central concern of any society. Let us, then, glance briefly at their scope, by roughly listing some cases which seem to involve us in non-contractual duties. (The order is purely provisional and the numbers are added just for convenience.)

Human Sector
1. *The dead*
2. *Posterity*
3. *Children*
4. *The senile*
5. *The temporarily insane*
6. *The permanently insane*
7. *Defectives, ranging down to "human vegetables"*
8. *Human embryos*

Animal Sector
9. *Sentient animals*
10. *Non-sentient animals*

Inanimate Sector
11. *Plants of all kinds*
12. *Artefacts, including works of art*
13. *Inanimate but structured objects—crystals, rivers, rocks etc.*

Comprehensive
14. *Unchosen human groups of all kinds, including families, villages, cities and the species*

15. *Unchosen multi-species groups, such as ecosystems, forests, and countries*
16. *The biosphere*

Miscellaneous
17. *Arts and sciences*
18. *Oneself*
19. *God*

No doubt I have missed a few, but that will do to go on with.

The point is this. If we look only at a few of these groupings, and without giving them full attention, it is easy to think that we can include one or two as honorary contracting members, by a slight stretch of our conceptual scheme, and find arguments for excluding the others from serious concern entirely. But if we keep our eye on the size of the range, this stops being plausible.

As far as sheer numbers go, this is no minority of the beings with whom we have to deal. We are a small minority of them. As far as importance goes, it is certainly possible to argue that some of these sorts of being should concern us more and others less; we need a priority system. But to build it, *moral* arguments are required. The various kinds of claims have to be understood and compared, not written off in advance. We cannot rule that those who, in our own and other cultures, suppose that there is a direct objection to injuring or destroying some of them, are always just confused, and mean only, in fact, that this item will be needed for rational human consumption.

The blank antithesis which Kant made between rational persons (having value) and mere things (having none) cannot serve us to map out this vast continuum. And the idea that, starting at some given point on this list, we have a general licence for destruction, is itself a moral view which would have to be justified.

Our culture differs from most others in the breadth of destructive licence which it does allow itself, and from the 17th century onwards, that licence has been greatly extended. Scruples about rapine have been continually dismissed as irrational, but it is not always clear what the rational principles are supposed to be with which they conflict. Western destructiveness has not in fact developed in response to a new set of disinterested intellectual principles, demonstrating the need for more people and less redwoods, but mainly as a by-product of greed and increasing commercial confidence.

Humanistic hostility to superstition has certainly played some part in the process, because respect for the non-human items on our list is often taken to be religious. But it does not have to be. Many scientists who are card-carrying atheists can still see the point of preserving the biosphere. So can the rest of us, religious or otherwise. It is the whole of which we are parts, and its other parts concern us for that reason.

But the language of rights is rather ill-suited for expressing this, because it has been developed mainly for the protection of people who, though oppressed, are in principle articulate. This makes it quite reasonable for theorists to say that rights belong only to those who understand them and can claim them. When confronted with the Human Sector of our list, these theorists can either dig themselves in like Grice and exclude the lot, or stretch the scheme like Rawls, by including the hypothetical rational choices which these honorary members *would* make if they were not unfortunately prevented.

Since many of these people seem less rational than many animals, zoophiles like Peter Singer have then a good case for calling this second device arbitrary and specious, and extending rights to the border of sentience.[9] Here, however, the meaning of the term does become thin, and when we reach the inanimate area, usage will scarcely cover it.[10] There may be a point in campaigning to extend usage. But to me it seems wiser on the whole not to waste energy on this verbal point, but instead to insist on the immense variety of kinds of being with which we have to deal. Once we grasp this, we ought not to be surprised that we are involved in many different kinds of claim or duty. The dictum that "rights and duties are correlative" is quite misleading, because the two words keep different company, and one may be narrowed without affecting the other.

What, then, about duties? I believe that this term can properly be used over the whole range. We have quite simply got many kinds of duties, including those to animals, to plants, and to the biosphere. But to speak in this way we must free the term once and for all from its restrictive contractual use, or irrelevant doubts will still haunt us. If we cannot do this, we shall have to exclude the word *duty,* along with *right* (as a noun) from all detailed discussion, using wider words like *wrong, right* (adjectival), and *ought* instead. This gymnastic would be possible but inconvenient.

The issue about duty becomes clear as soon as we look at the controversy from which I started, between Kant's and Mill's views on duties to oneself. What do we think about this? Are there duties of integrity, autonomy, self-knowledge, self-respect? It seems that there are.

Mill was right, of course, to point out that they are not duties *to* someone in the ordinary sense. The divided self is a metaphor. It is as natural and necessary a metaphor here as it is over, say, self-deception or self-control; but it certainly is not literal truth. The form of the requirement is different. Rights, for instance, certainly do not seem to come in here as they often would with duties to other persons; we shall scarcely say, "I have a right to my own respect." And the *kind* of things which we can owe ourselves are distinctive. It is not just chance who they are owed to. You cannot owe it to somebody else, as you can to yourself, to force him to act freely or with integrity. He owes that to himself; the rest of us can only remove outside difficulties.

As Kant justly said, our business is to promote our own perfection and the happiness of others; the perfection of others is an aim which belongs to them.[11] *Respect* indeed we owe both to ourselves and to others, but Kant may well be right to say that *self-respect* is really a different and deeper requirement, something without which all outward duties would become meaningless. (This may explain the paralysing effect of depression.)

Duties to oneself, in fact, are duties with a different *form.* They are far less close than outward duties to the literal model of debt, especially money debt. Money is a thing which can be owed in principle to anybody; it is the same whoever you owe it to; and if by chance you come to owe it to yourself, the debt vanishes. Not many of our duties are really of this impersonal kind; the attempt to commute other sorts of duty into money is a notorious form of evasion. Utilitarianism, however, wants to make all duties as homogeneous as possible, and that is the point of Mill's position. He views all our self-concerning motives as parts of the desire for happiness. Therefore he places all duty, indeed, all morality, in the outside world, as socially required restriction of that desire—an expression, that is, of other people's desire for happiness.

> We do not call anything wrong, unless we mean that a person ought to be punished in some way or another for doing it; if not by law, by the opinion of his fellow-creatures; if not by opinion, by the reproaches of his own conscience. This seems the real turning-point of the distinction between morality and simple expediency. It is a part of the notion of Duty in every one of its forms, that a person may rightly be compelled to fulfil it. Duty is a thing which may be *exacted* from a person, as one exacts a debt.[12]

But to make the notion of wrongness depend on punishment and public opinion in this way instead of the other way round is wild.

Mill never minded falling flat on his face from time to time in trying out a new notion for the public good. He did it for us here—and we should, I think, take proper advantage of his generosity, and accept the impossibility which he demonstrates. The concepts cannot be connected up this way round. Unless you think of certain facts as wrong, it makes no sense to talk of punishment. "Punishing" alcoholics with aversion therapy, or experimental rats with electric shocks, is not really punishing at all; it is just deterrence. This "punishment" will not make their previous actions wrong, nor has it anything to do with morality. The real point of morality returns into

Mill's scheme in the Trojan horse of "the reproaches of his own conscience." Why do they *matter*? Unless the conscience is talking sense—that is, on Utilitarian principles, unless it is delivering the judgment of society—it should surely be silenced? Mill, himself a man of enormous integrity and deeply concerned about autonomy, would never have agreed to silence it. But unless we do so, we shall have to complicate his scheme.

It may well be true that, in the last resort and at the deepest level, conscience and the desire for happiness converge. We do want to be honest. But in ordinary life and at the everyday level they can diverge amazingly. We do not want to be put out. What we know we ought to do is often most unwelcome to us, which is why we call it *duty*. And whole sections of that duty do not concern other people directly at all.

A good example is the situation in *Brave New World* where a few dissident citizens have grasped the possibility of a fuller and freer life. Nobody else wants this. Happiness is already assured. If there is a duty of change here, it must be first of all that of each to himself. True, they may feel bound also to help others to change, but hardly in a way which those others would exact. In fact, we may do better here by dropping the awkward second party altogether and saying that they all have a duty *of* living differently—one which will affect both themselves and others, but which does not require, as a debt does, a named person or people *to* whom it must be paid. Wider models like "the whole duty of man" may be more relevant.

This one example from my list will, I hope, be enough to explain the point. I cannot go through all of them, nor ought it to be necessary. Duties need not be quasi-contractual relations holding between symmetrical pairs of rational human agents. There are all kind of other obligations holding between asymmetrical pairs, or involving, as in this case, no outside beings at all.

To speak of duties *to* things in the inanimate and comprehensive sectors of my list is not necessarily to personify them superstitiously, or to indulge in chatter about "the secret life of plants."[13] It expresses merely that there are suitable and unsuitable ways of behaving in given situations. People have duties *as* farmers, parents, consumers, forest-dwellers, colonists, species members, ship-wrecked mariners, tourists, potential ancestors and actual descendants, etc. As such, it is the business of each not to forget his transitory and dependent position, the rich gifts which he has received, and the tiny part he plays in a vast, irreplaceable and fragile whole.

It is remarkable that we nowadays have to state this obvious truth as if it were new, and invent words like "ecological" to describe a whole vast class of duties. Most peoples are used to the idea. In stating it, and getting it back into the centre of our moral stage, we meet various difficulties, of which the most insidious is possibly the temptation to feed this issue as fuel to long-standing controversies about religion. Is concern for the nonhuman aspects of our biosphere necessarily superstitious and therefore to be resisted tooth and nail?

I have pointed out that it need not be religious at all. Certified rejectors of all known religions can share it. No doubt there is a wider sense in which any deep and impersonal concern can be called religious—one in which Marxism also is a religion. No doubt too all such deep concerns have their dangers, but certainly the complete absence of them has worse ones. Moreover, anyone wishing above all to avoid the religious dimension should consider that the intense individualism which has focused our attention exclusively on the social contract model is itself thoroughly mystical. It has glorified the individual human soul as an object having infinite and transcendent value, has hailed it as the only real creator, and has bestowed on it much of the panoply of God.

Nietzsche, who was responsible for much of this new theology,[14] took over from the old Thomistic theology which he plundered the assumption that all the rest of creation mattered only as a frame for man. This is not an impression which any disinterested observer would get from looking round at it, nor do we need it in order to take our destiny sufficiently seriously.

Robinson Crusoe then, I conclude, did have duties concerning his island, and with the caution just given we can reasonably call them duties *to* it.

They were not very exacting, and were mostly negative. They differed, of course, from those which a long-standing inhabitant of a country has. Here the language of *fatherland* and *motherland,* which is so widely employed, indicates rightly a duty of care and responsibility which can go very deep, and which long-settled people commonly do feel strongly. To insist that it is really only a duty to the exploiting human beings is not consistent with the emphasis often given to reverence for the actual trees, mountains, lakes, rivers, and the like which are found there. A decision to inhibit all this rich area of human love is a special manoeuvre for which reasons would need to be given, not a dispassionate analysis of existing duties and feelings.

What happens, however, when you are shipwrecked on an entirely strange island? As the history of colonisation shows, there is a tendency for people so placed to drop any reverence and become more exploitative. But it is not irresistible. Raiders who settle down can quite soon begin to feel at home, as the Vikings did in East Anglia, and can after a while become as possessive, proud, and protective towards their new land as old inhabitants. Crusoe from time to time shows this pride rather touchingly, and it would, I think, certainly have inhibited any moderate temptation such as that which I mentioned to have a good bonfire. What keeps him sane through his stay, however, is in fact his duty to God. If that had been absent, I should rather suppose that sanity would depend on a stronger and more positive attachment to the island itself and its creatures.

It is interesting, however, that Crusoe's story played its part in developing that same unrealistic, icy individualism which has gone so far towards making both sorts of attachment seem corrupt or impossible. Rousseau delighted in Defoe's *Robinson Crusoe,* and praised it as the only book fit to be given to a child, *not* because it showed a man in his true relation to animal and vegetable life, but because it was the bible of individualism.

The surest way to raise him [the child] above prejudice and to base his judgments on the true relations of things, is to put him in the place of a solitary man, and to judge all things as they would be judged by such a man in relation to their own utility. . . . So long as only bodily needs are recognised, man is self-sufficing . . . the child knows no other happiness but food and freedom! (*Emile,* Everyman ed., pp. 147–8)

That false atomic notion of human psychology—a prejudice above which nobody ever raised Rousseau—is the flaw in all social-contract thinking. If he were right, every member of the human race would need a separate island, and heaven knows what our ecological problems would be then.

Perhaps, after all, we had better count our blessings.

NOTES

1. J. S. Mill, *Essay on Liberty,* Ch. IV (Everyman ed.), p. 135.

2. Immanuel Kant, "Duties to Oneself," in *Lectures on Ethics* (tr. Infield, 1930), p. 118.

3. Aristotle, Politics I, 3–8, cf. *Nicomachean Ethics* VII, 11.

4. E.g. John Passmore, *Man's Responsibility for Nature* (1974). See pp. 116–117; H. J. McCloskey, "Rights," *Philosophical Quarterly* (No. 15), 1965.

5. Nor will it help for philosophers to say "it is not the case that they have rights." Such pompous locutions have either no meaning at all, or the obvious one.

6. Kant, "Duties Towards Animals and Spirits," *Lectures on Ethics,* p. 240.

7. A point well discussed by Stephen Clark, *The Moral Status of Animals* (1977). See pp. 12–13.

8. For details see John Rodman, "Animal Justice; The Counter-Revolution in Natural Right and Law," *Inquiry* 22 (Summer 1979): No. 1 and 2.

9. A case first made by Jeremy Bentham, *Introduction to the Principles of Morals and Legislation,* Ch. 17, and ably worked out by Peter Singer in *Animal Liberation* (1976), Chs. 1, 5 and 6.

10. It is worth noticing that long before this, when

dealing merely with "the Rights of Man," the term often seems obscure, because to list and specify these rights is so much harder than to shout for them. The phrase is probably more useful as a slogan, indicating a general direction, than as a detailed conceptual tool.

11. Kant, "Preface to the Metaphysical Elements of Ethics," *Introduction to Ethics,* Chs. 4 and 5.

12. J. S. Mill, *Utilitarianism* (Everyman ed.), Ch. 5, p. 45.

13. The book so titled, by Peter Tompkins and Christopher Bird (1973), claimed to show, by various experiments involving electrical apparatus, that plants can feel. Attempts to duplicate their experiments have, however, totally failed to produce any similar results. See A. W. Galson and C. L. Slayman, "The Not So Secret Life of Plants," *American Scientist* (No. 67 p. 337). It seems possible that the original results were due to a fault in the electrical apparatus.

The attempt shows, I think, one of the confusions which continually arise from insisting that all duties must be of the same form. We do not need to prove that plants are animals in order to have reason to spare them. This point is discussed by Marian Dawkins in her book *Animal Suffering* (Chapman and Hall, 1981), pp. 117–119.

14. See particularly *Thus Spake Zarathustra,* part 3, "Of Old and New Tables," and *The Joyful Wisdom* (otherwise called *The Gay Science*), p. 125 (the Madman's Speech). I have discussed this rather mysterious appointment of man to succeed God in a paper called "Creation and Originality," published in a volume of my essays called *Heart and Mind: The Varieties of Moral Experience* (Harvester Press, 1981).

Chapter 4
Species Equality and Respect for Nature

Questions for Reflection and Discussion

Where Do We Draw the Line?

1. We think all humans are equal, in some way. What does that really mean? We do not believe all humans should be paid the same wage, but what exactly do we believe? We think all humans command equal respect in some sense, but not in every sense. In the human context, then, equality turns out to be a complex notion with uncertain implications. Similarly, if we say all species are equal, we need not be saying all animals (and all plants, for that matter) have equal rights. We need not be saying they should be treated as if they were human. But then, what *do* we mean? What does Paul Taylor mean?

2. Today, in the temperate climates of Europe and North America, mosquitoes are primarily an irritant. In the tropics of Africa, Asia, and South America, mosquitoes are among the most dangerous animals you could ever have the misfortune to meet, for they transmit diseases that kill millions of human beings every year.

DDT is an inexpensive insecticide still used to control malaria-transmitting mosquitoes in many parts of the world. In the United States, we could afford to ban the use of DDT, and did so in 1972. We had alternatives. We put screens on our windows. We drained wetlands and eradicated mosquito habitat. In many countries, such measures are unaffordable. Do people in developing countries have the right to use DDT to save themselves from mosquito-transmitted diseases?

If or when they have an obligation not to use DDT, to whom or to what do they have this obligation? To consumers of their agricultural products? To the birds and fish that might be put at risk? To the mosquitoes themselves? To the malaria parasite?

Do you believe all species are equal? Where do we draw the line? If we want to agree with Paul Taylor that all living things are in some sense equal, do we really mean *every living thing?* If so, where does that leave us? Docs it imply that we have obligations to mosquitoes?

The Ethics of Respect for Nature

Paul W. Taylor

HUMAN-CENTERED AND LIFE-CENTERED SYSTEMS OF ENVIRONMENTAL ETHICS

In this paper I show how the taking of a certain ultimate moral attitude toward nature, which I call "respect for nature," has a central place in the foundations of a life-centered system of environmental ethics. I hold that a set of moral norms (both standards of character and rules of conduct) governing human treatment of the natural world is a rationally grounded set if and only if, first, commitment to those norms is a practical entailment of adopting the attitude of respect for nature as an ultimate moral attitude, and second, the adopting of that attitude on the part of all rational agents can itself be justified. When the basic characteristics of the attitude of respect for nature are made clear, it will be seen that a life-centered system of environmental ethics need not be holistic or organicist in its conception of the kinds of entities that are deemed the appropriate objects of moral concern and consideration. Nor does such a system require that the concepts of ecological homeostasis, equilibrium, and integrity provide us with normative principles from which could be derived (with the addition of factual knowledge) our obligations with regard to natural ecosystems. The "balance of nature" is not itself a moral norm, however important may be the role it plays in our general outlook on the natural world that underlies the attitude of respect for nature. I argue that finally it is the good (well-being, welfare) of individual organisms, considered as entities having inherent worth, that determines our moral relations with the Earth's wild communities of life.

In designating the theory to be set forth as life-centered, I intend to contrast it with all anthropocentric views. According to the latter, human actions affecting the natural environment and its nonhuman inhabitants are right (or wrong) by either of two criteria: they have consequences which are favorable (or unfavorable) to human well-being, or they are consistent (or inconsistent) with the system of norms that protect and implement human rights. From this human-centered standpoint it is to humans and only to humans that all duties are ultimately owed. We may have responsibilities *with regard to* the natural ecosystems and biotic communities of our planet, but these responsibilities are in every case based on the contingent fact that our treatment of those ecosystems and communities of life can further the realization of human values and/or human rights. We have no obligation to promote or protect the good of nonhuman living things, independently of this contingent fact.

A life-centered system of environmental ethics is opposed to human-centered ones precisely on this point. From the perspective of a life-centered theory, we have prima facie moral obligations that are owed to wild plants and animals themselves as members of the Earth's biotic community. We are morally bound (other things being equal) to protect or promote their good for *their* sake. Our duties to respect the integrity of natural ecosystems, to preserve endangered species, and to avoid environmental pollution stem from the fact that these are ways in which we can help make it possible for wild species populations to achieve and maintain a healthy existence in a natural state. Such obligations are due those living things out of recognition of their inherent worth.

Paul W. Taylor, "The Ethics of Respect for Nature," *Environmental Ethics* 3 (1981): 197–218. Reprinted with permission of the author and the journal.

They are entirely additional to and independent of the obligations we owe to our fellow humans. Although many of the actions that fulfill one set of obligations will also fulfill the other, two different grounds of obligation are involved. Their well-being, as well as human well-being, is something to be realized *as an end in itself.*

If we were to accept a life-centered theory of environmental ethics, a profound reordering of our moral universe would take place. We would begin to look at the whole of the Earth's biosphere in a new light. Our duties with respect to the "world" of nature would be seen as making prima facie claims upon us to be balanced against our duties with respect to the "world" of human civilization. We could no longer simply take the human point of view and consider the effects of our actions exclusively from the perspective of our own good.

THE GOOD OF A BEING AND THE CONCEPT OF INHERENT WORTH

What would justify acceptance of a life-centered system of ethical principles? In order to answer this it is first necessary to make clear the fundamental moral attitude that underlies and makes intelligible the commitment to live by such a system. It is then necessary to examine the considerations that would justify any rational agent's adopting that moral attitude.

Two concepts are essential to the taking of a moral attitude of the sort in question. A being which does not "have" these concepts, that is, which is unable to grasp their meaning and conditions of applicability, cannot be said to have the attitude as part of its moral outlook. These concepts are, first, that of the good (well-being, welfare) of a living thing, and second, the idea of an entity possessing inherent worth. I examine each concept in turn.

(1) Every organism, species population, and community of life has a good of its own which moral agents can intentionally further or damage by their actions. To say that an entity has a good of its own is simply to say that, without reference to any *other* entity, it can be benefited or harmed. One can act in its overall interest or contrary to its overall interest, and environmental conditions can be good for it (advantageous to it) or bad for it (disadvantageous to it). What is good for an entity is what "does it good" in the sense of enhancing or preserving its life and well-being. What is bad for an entity is something that is detrimental to its life and well-being.

We can think of the good of an individual nonhuman organism as consisting in the full development of its biological powers. Its good is realized to the extent that it is strong and healthy. It possesses whatever capacities it needs for successfully coping with its environment and so preserving its existence throughout the various stages of the normal life cycle of its species. The good of a population or community of such individuals consists in the population or community maintaining itself from generation to generation as a coherent system of genetically and ecologically related organisms whose average good is at an optimum level for the given environment. (Here *average good* means that the degree of realization of the good of *individual organisms* in the population or community is, on average, greater than it would be under any other ecologically functioning order of interrelations among those species populations in the given ecosystem.)

The idea of a being having a good of its own, as I understand it, does not entail that the being must have interests or take an interest in what affects its life for better or for worse. We can act in a being's interest or contrary to its interest without its being interested in what we are doing to it in the sense of wanting or not wanting us to do it. It may, indeed, be wholly unaware that favorable and unfavorable events are taking place in its life. I take it that trees, for example, have no knowledge or desires or feelings. Yet it is undoubtedly the case that trees can be harmed or benefited by our actions. We can crush their roots by running a bulldozer too close to them. We can see to it that they get adequate nourishment and moisture by fertilizing and watering the soil around them. Thus we can help or hinder them in the realization of their good. It is the good of trees themselves that is thereby affected. We can similarly act so as to further the good of an entire tree population of a certain species (say, all the redwood trees in a California valley) or the good of a whole community of plant life in a given wilderness area, just as we can do harm to such a population or community.

When construed in this way, the concept of a being's good is not coextensive with sentience or the capacity for feeling pain. William Frankena has argued for a general theory of environmental ethics in which the ground of a creature's being worthy of moral consideration is its sentience. I have offered some criticisms of this view elsewhere, but the full refutation of such a position, it seems to me, finally depends on the positive reasons for accepting a life-centered theory of the kind I am defending in this essay.[1]

It should be noted further that I am leaving open the question of whether machines—in particular, those which are not only goal directed, but also self-regulating—can properly be said to have a good of their own.[2] Since I am concerned only with human treatment of wild organisms, species populations, and communities of life as they occur in our planet's natural ecosystems, it is to those entities alone that the concept "having a good of its own" will here be applied. I am not denying that other living things, whose genetic origin and environmental conditions have been produced, controlled, and manipulated by humans for human ends, do have a good of their own in the same sense as do wild plants and animals. It is not my purpose in this essay, however, to set out or defend the principles that should guide our conduct with regard to their good. It is only insofar as their production and use by humans have good or ill effects upon natural ecosystems and their wild inhabitants that the ethics of respect for nature comes into play.

(2) The second concept essential to the moral attitude of respect for nature is the idea of inherent worth. We take that attitude toward wild living things (individuals, species populations, or whole biotic communities) when and only when we regard them as entities possessing inherent worth. Indeed, it is

only because they are conceived in this way that moral agents can think of themselves as having validly binding duties, obligations, and responsibilities that are *owed* to them as their *due*. I am not at this juncture arguing why they *should* be so regarded; I consider it at length below. But so regarding them is a presupposition of our taking the attitude of respect toward them and accordingly understanding ourselves as bearing certain moral relations to them. This can be shown as follows:

What does it mean to regard an entity that has a good of its own as possessing inherent worth? Two general principles are involved: the principle of moral consideration and the principle of intrinsic value.

According to the principle of moral consideration, wild living things are deserving of the concern and consideration of all moral agents simply in virtue of their being members of the Earth's community of life. From the moral point of view their good must be taken into account whenever it is affected for better or worse by the conduct of rational agents. This holds no matter what species the creature belongs to. The good of each is to be accorded some value and so acknowledged as having some weight in the deliberations of all rational agents. Of course, it may be necessary for such agents to act in ways contrary to the good of this or that particular organism or group of organisms in order to further the good of others, including the good of humans. But the principle of moral consideration prescribes that, with respect to each being an entity having its own good, every individual is deserving of consideration.

The principle of intrinsic value states that, regardless of what kind of entity it is in other respects, if it is a member of the Earth's community of life, the realization of its good is something *intrinsically* valuable. This means that its good is prima facie worthy of being preserved or promoted as an end in itself and for the sake of the entity whose good it is. Insofar as we regard any organism, species population, or life community as an entity having inherent worth, we believe that it must never be treated as if it were a mere object or thing whose entire value lies in being instrumental to the good of some other entity. The well-being of each is judged to have value in and of itself.

Combining these two principles, we can now define what it means for a living thing or group of living things to possess inherent worth. To say that it possesses inherent worth is to say that its good is deserving of the concern and consideration of all moral agents, and that the realization of its good has intrinsic value, to be pursued as an end in itself and for the sake of the entity whose good it is.

The duties owed to wild organisms, species populations, and communities of life in the Earth's natural ecosystems are grounded on their inherent worth. When rational, autonomous agents regard such entities as possessing inherent worth, they place intrinsic value on the realization of their good and so hold themselves responsible for performing actions that will have this effect and for refraining from actions having the contrary effect. . . .

THE JUSTIFIABILITY OF THE ATTITUDE OF RESPECT FOR NATURE

The attitude we take toward living things in the natural world depends on the way we look at them, on what kind of beings we conceive them to be, and on how we understand the relations we bear to them. Underlying and supporting our attitude is a certain belief system that constitutes a particular world view or outlook on nature and the place of human life in it. To give good reasons for adopting the attitude of respect for nature, then, we must first articulate the *belief system* which underlies and supports that attitude. If it appears that the belief system is internally coherent and well-ordered, and if, as far as we can now tell, it is consistent with all known scientific truths relevant to our knowledge of the object of the attitude (which in this case includes the whole set of the Earth's natural ecosystems and their communities of life), then there remains the task of indicating why scientifically informed and rational thinkers with a developed capacity of reality awareness can find it acceptable as a way of conceiving of the nat-

ural world and our place in it. To the extent we can do this we provide at least a reasonable argument for accepting the belief system and the ultimate moral attitude it supports.

I do not hold that such a belief system can be *proven* to be true, either inductively or deductively. As we shall see, not all of its components can be stated in the form of empirically verifiable propositions. Nor is its internal order governed by purely logical relationships. But the system as a whole, I contend, constitutes a coherent, unified, and rationally acceptable "picture" or "map" of a total world. By examining each of its main components and seeing how they fit together, we obtain a scientifically informed and well-ordered conception of nature and the place of humans in it.

This belief system underlying the attitude of respect for nature I call (for want of a better name) "the biocentric outlook on nature." Since it is not wholly analyzable into empirically confirmable assertions, it should not be thought of as simply a compendium of the biological sciences concerning our planet's ecosystems. It might best be described as a philosophical world view, to distinguish it from a scientific theory or explanatory system. However, one of its major tenets is the great lesson we have learned from the science of ecology: the interdependence of all living things in an organically unified order whose balance and stability are necessary conditions for the realization of the good of its constituent biotic communities. . . .

THE BIOCENTRIC OUTLOOK ON NATURE

The biocentric outlook on nature has four main components. (1) Humans are thought of as members of the Earth's community of life, holding that membership on the same terms as apply to all the nonhuman members. (2) The Earth's natural ecosystems as a totality are seen as a complex web of interconnected elements, with the sound biological functioning of each being dependent on the sound biological functioning of the others. (This is the component referred to above as the great lesson that the science of ecology has taught us.) (3) Each individual organism is conceived of as a teleological center of life, pursuing its own good in its own way. (4) Whether we are concerned with standards of merit or with the concept of inherent worth, the claim that humans by their very nature are superior to other species is a groundless claim and, in the light of elements (1), (2), and (3) above, must be rejected as nothing more than an irrational bias in our own favor.

The conjunction of these four ideas constitutes the biocentric outlook on nature. In the remainder of this paper I give a brief account of the first three components, followed by a more detailed analysis of the fourth. I then conclude by indicating how this outlook provides a way of justifying the attitude of respect for nature.

HUMANS AS MEMBERS OF THE EARTH'S COMMUNITY OF LIFE

We share with other species a common relationship to the Earth. In accepting the biocentric outlook we take the fact of our being an animal species to be a fundamental feature of our existence. We consider it an essential aspect of "the human condition." We do not deny the differences between ourselves and other species, but we keep in the forefront of our consciousness the fact that in relation to our planet's natural ecosystems we are but one species population among many. Thus we acknowledge our origin in the very same evolutionary process that gave rise to all other species and we recognize ourselves to be confronted with similar environmental challenges to those that confront them. The laws of genetics, of natural selection, and of adaptation apply equally to all of us as biological creatures. In this light we consider ourselves as one with them, not set apart from them. We, as well as they, must face certain basic conditions of existence that impose requirements on us for our survival and well-being. Each animal and plant is like us in having a good of its own. Although our human good (what is of true value in human life, including the exercise of individual autonomy in

choosing our own particular value systems) is not like the good of a nonhuman animal or plant, it can no more be realized than their good can without the biological necessities for survival and physical health.

When we look at ourselves from the evolutionary point of view we see that not only are we very recent arrivals on Earth, but that our emergence as a new species on the planet was originally an event of no particular importance to the entire scheme of things. The Earth was teeming with life long before we appeared. Putting the point metaphorically, we are relative newcomers, entering a home that has been the residence of others for hundreds of millions of years, a home that must now be shared by all of us together.

The comparative brevity of human life on Earth may be vividly depicted by imagining the geological time scale in spatial terms. Suppose we start with algae, which have been around for at least 600 million years. (The earliest protozoa actually predated this by several *billion* years.) If the time that algae have been here were represented by the length of a football field (300 feet), then the period during which sharks have been swimming in the world's oceans and spiders have been spinning their webs would occupy three quarters of the length of the field; reptiles would show up at about the center of the field; mammals would cover the last third of the field; hominids (mammals of the family *Hominidae*) the last two feet; and the species *Homo sapiens* the last six inches.

Whether this newcomer is able to survive as long as other species remains to be seen. But there is surely something presumptuous about the way humans look down on the "lower" animals, especially those that have become extinct. We consider the dinosaurs, for example, to be biological failures, though they existed on our planet for 65 million years. One writer has made the point with beautiful simplicity:

We sometimes speak of the dinosaurs as failures; there will be time enough for that judgment when we have lasted even for one tenth as long . . . .[3]

The possibility of the extinction of the human species, a possibility which starkly confronts us in the contemporary world, makes us aware of another respect in which we should not consider ourselves privileged beings in relation to other species. This is the fact that the well-being of humans is dependent upon the ecological soundness and health of many plant and animal communities, while their soundness and health does not in the least depend upon human well-being. Indeed, from their standpoint the very existence of humans is quite unnecessary. Every last man, woman, and child could disappear from the face of the Earth without any significant detrimental consequence for the good of wild animals and plants. On the contrary, many of them would be greatly benefited. The destruction of their habitats by human "developments" would cease. The poisoning and polluting of their environment would come to an end. The Earth's land, air, and water would no longer be subject to the degradation they are now undergoing as the result of large-scale technology and uncontrolled Population growth. Life communities in natural ecosystems would gradually return to their former healthy state. Tropical forests for example, would again be able to make their full contribution to a life-sustaining atmosphere for the whole planet. The rivers, lakes, and oceans of the world would (perhaps) eventually become clean again. Spilled oil, plastic trash, and even radioactive waste might finally, after many centuries, cease doing their terrible work. Ecosystems would return to their proper balance, suffering only the disruptions of natural events such as volcanic eruptions and glaciation. From these the community of life could recover, as it has so often done in the past. But the ecological disasters now perpetrated on it by humans—disasters from which it might never recover—these it would no longer have to endure.

If, then, the total, final, absolute extermination of our species (by our own hands?) should take place and if we should not carry all the others with us into oblivion, not only would the Earth's community of life continue to exist, but in all probability its well-being would be enhanced. Our presence, in short, is not needed. If we were to take the standpoint of the community and give voice to its true interest, the ending of our six-inch epoch would most likely be greeted with a hearty "Good riddance!"

THE NATURAL WORLD AS AN ORGANIC SYSTEM

To accept the biocentric outlook and regard ourselves and our place in the world from its perspective is to see the whole natural order of the Earth's biosphere as a complex but unified web of interconnected organisms, objects, and events. The ecological relationships between any community of living things and their environment form an organic whole of functionally interdependent parts. Each ecosystem is a small universe itself in which the interactions of its various species populations comprise an intricately woven network of cause-effect relations. Such dynamic but at the same time relatively stable structures as food chains, predator-prey relations, and plant succession in a forest are self-regulating, energy-recycling mechanisms that preserve the equilibrium of the whole.

As far as the well-being of wild animals and plants is concerned, this ecological equilibrium must not be destroyed. The same holds true of the well-being of humans. When one views the realm of nature from the perspective of the biocentric outlook, one never forgets that in the long run the integrity of the entire biosphere of our planet is essential to the realization of the good of its constituent communities of life, both human and nonhuman.

Although the importance of this idea cannot be overemphasized, it is by now so familiar and so widely acknowledged that I shall not further elaborate on it here. However, I do wish to point out that this "holistic" view of the Earth's ecological systems does not itself constitute a moral norm. It is a factual aspect of biological reality, to be understood as a set of causal connections in ordinary empirical terms. Its significance for humans is the same as its significance for nonhumans, namely, in setting basic conditions for the realization of the good of living things. Its ethical implications for our treatment of the natural environment lie entirely in the fact that our *knowledge* of these causal connections is an essential *means* to fulfilling the aims we set for ourselves in adopting the attitude of respect for nature. In addition, its theoretical implications for the ethics of respect for nature lie in the fact that it (along with the other elements of the biocentric outlook) makes the adopting of that attitude a rational and intelligible thing to do.

INDIVIDUAL ORGANISMS AS TELEOLOGICAL CENTERS OF LIFE

As our knowledge of living things increases, as we come to a deeper understanding of their life cycles, their interactions with other organisms, and the manifold ways in which they adjust to the environment, we become more fully aware of how each of them is carrying out its biological functions according to the laws of its species-specific nature. But besides this, our increasing knowledge and understanding also develop in us a sharpened awareness of the uniqueness of each individual organism. Scientists who have made careful studies of particular plants and animals, whether in the field or in laboratories, have often acquired a knowledge of their subjects as identifiable individuals. Close observation over extended periods of time has led them to an appreciation of the unique "personalities" of their subjects. Sometimes a scientist may come to take a special interest in a particular animal or plant, all the while remaining strictly objective in the gathering and recording of data. Nonscientists may likewise experience this development of interest when, as amateur naturalists, they make accurate observations over sustained periods of close acquaintance with an individual organism. As one becomes more and more familiar with the organism and its behavior, one becomes fully sensitive to the particular way it is living out its life cycle. One may become fascinated by it and even experience some involvement with its good and bad fortunes (that is, with the occurrence of environmental conditions favorable or unfavorable to the realization of its good). The organism

comes to mean something to one as a unique, irreplaceable individual. The final culmination of this process is the achievement of a genuine understanding of its point of view and, with that understanding, an ability to "take" that point of view. *Conceiving of it as a center of life, one is able to look at the world from its perspective.*

This development from objective knowledge to the recognition of individuality, and from the recognition of individuality to full awareness of an organism's standpoint, is a process of heightening our consciousness of what it means to be an individual living thing. We grasp the particularity of the organism as a teleological center of life, striving to preserve itself and to realize its own good in its own unique way.

It is to be noted that we need not be falsely anthropomorphizing when we conceive of individual plants and animals in this manner. Understanding them as teleological centers of life does not necessitate "reading into" them human characteristics. We need not, for example, consider them to have consciousness. Some of them may be aware of the world around them and others may not. Nor need we deny that different kinds and levels of awareness are exemplified when consciousness in some form is present. But conscious or not, all are equally teleological centers of life in the sense that each is a unified system of goal-oriented activities directed toward their preservation and well-being.

When considered from an ethical point of view, a teleological center of life is an entity whose "world" can be viewed from the perspective of *its* life. In looking at the world from that perspective we recognize objects and events occurring in its life as being beneficent, maleficent, or indifferent. The first are occurrences which increase its powers to preserve its existence and realize its good. The second decrease or destroy those powers. The third have neither of these effects on the entity. With regard to our human role as moral agents, we can conceive of a teleological center of life as a being whose standpoint we can take in making judgments about what events in the world are good or evil, desirable or undesirable. In making those judgments it is what promotes or protects the being's own good, not what benefits moral agents themselves, that sets the standard of evaluation. Such judgments can be made about anything that happens to the entity which is favorable or unfavorable in relation to its good. As was pointed out earlier, the entity itself need not have any (conscious) *interest* in what is happening to it for such judgments to be meaningful and true.

It is precisely judgments of this sort that we are disposed to make when we take the attitude of respect for nature. In adopting that attitude those judgments are given weight as reasons for action in our practical deliberation. They become morally relevant facts in the guidance of our conduct.

THE DENIAL OF HUMAN SUPERIORITY

This fourth component of the biocentric outlook on nature is the single most important idea in establishing the justifiability of the attitude of respect for nature. Its central role is due to the special relationship it bears to the first three components of the outlook. This relationship will be brought out after the concept of human superiority is examined and analyzed.[4]

In what sense are humans alleged to be superior to other animals? We are different from them in having certain capacities that they lack. But why should these capacities be a mark of superiority? From what point of view are they judged to be signs of superiority and what sense of superiority is meant? After all, various nonhuman species have capacities that humans lack. There is the speed of a cheetah, the vision of an eagle, the agility of a monkey. Why should not these be taken as signs of *their* superiority over humans?

One answer that comes immediately to mind is that these capacities are not as *valuable* as the human capacities that are claimed to make us superior. Such uniquely human characteristics as rational thought, aesthetic creativity, autonomy and self-determination, and moral freedom, it might be held, have a higher value than the capacities found in other species. Yet we must ask: valuable to whom, and on what grounds?

The human characteristics mentioned are all valuable to humans. They are essential to the preservation and enrichment of our civilization and culture. Clearly it is from the human standpoint that they are being judged to be desirable and good. It is not difficult here to recognize a begging of the question. Humans are claiming human superiority from a strictly human point of view, that is, from a point of view in which the good of humans is taken as the standard of judgment. All we need to do is to look at the capacities of nonhuman animals (or plants, for that matter) from the standpoint of *their* good to find a contrary judgment of superiority. The speed of the cheetah, for example, is a sign of its superiority to humans when considered from the standpoint of the good of its species. If it were as slow a runner as a human, it would not be able to survive. And so for all the other abilities of nonhumans which further their good but which are lacking in humans. In each case the claim to human superiority would be rejected from a nonhuman standpoint.

When superiority assertions are interpreted in this way, they are based on judgments of *merit*. To judge the merits of a person or an organism one must apply grading or ranking standards to it. (As I show below, this distinguishes judgments of merit from judgments of inherent worth.) Empirical investigation then determines whether it has the "good-making properties" (merits) in virtue of which it fulfills the standards being applied. In the case of humans, merits may be either moral or nonmoral. We can judge one person to be better than (superior to) another from the moral point of view by applying certain standards to their character and conduct. Similarly, we can appeal to nonmoral criteria in judging someone to be an excellent piano player, a fair cook, a poor tennis player, and so on. Different social purposes and roles are implicit in the making of such judgments, providing the frame of reference for the choice of standards by which the nonmoral merits of people are determined. Ultimately such purposes and roles stem from a society's way of life as a whole. Now a society's way of life may be thought of as the cultural form given to the realization of human values. Whether moral or nonmoral standards are being applied, then, all judgments of people's merits finally depend on human values. All are made from an exclusively human standpoint.

The question that naturally arises at this juncture is: why should standards that are based on human values be assumed to be the only valid criteria of merit and hence the only true signs of superiority? This question is especially pressing when humans are being judged superior in merit to nonhumans. It is true that a human being may be a better mathematician than a monkey, but the monkey may be a better tree climber than a human being. If we humans value mathematics more than tree climbing, that is because our conception of civilized life makes the development of mathematical ability more desirable than the ability to climb trees. But is it not unreasonable to judge nonhumans by the values of human civilization, rather than by values connected with what it is for a member of *that* species to live a good life? If all living things have a good of their own, it at least makes sense to judge the merits of nonhumans by standards derived from *their* good. To use only standards based on human values is already to commit oneself to holding that humans are superior to nonhumans, which is the point in question.

A further logical flaw arises in connection with the widely held conviction that humans are *morally* superior beings because they possess, while others lack, the capacities of a moral agent (free will, accountability, deliberation, judgment, practical reason). This view rests on a conceptual confusion. As far as moral standards are concerned, only beings that have the capacities of a moral agent can properly be judged to be *either* moral (morally good) *or* immoral (morally deficient). Moral standards are simply not applicable to beings that lack such capacities. Animals and plants cannot therefore be said to be morally inferior in merit to humans. Since the only beings that can have moral merits *or be deficient in such merits* are moral agents, it is conceptually incoherent to judge humans as superior to nonhumans on the ground that humans have moral capacities while nonhumans don't.

Up to this point I have been interpreting the claim that humans are superior to other living things as a grading or ranking judgment regarding their comparative merits. There is, however, another way of understanding the idea of human superiority. According to this interpretation, humans are superior to nonhumans not as regards their merits but as regards their inherent worth. Thus the claim of human superiority is to be understood as asserting that all humans, simply in virtue of their humanity, have *a greater inherent worth* than other living things.

The inherent worth of an entity does not depend on its merits.[5] To consider something as possessing inherent worth, we have seen, is to place intrinsic value on the realization of its good. This is done regardless of whatever particular merits it might have or might lack, as judged by a set of grading or ranking standards. In human affairs, we are all familiar with the principle that one's worth as a person does not vary with one's merits or lack of merits. The same can hold true of animals and plants. To regard such entities as possessing inherent worth entails disregarding their merits and deficiencies, whether they are being judged from a human standpoint or from the standpoint of their own species.

The idea of one entity having more merit than another, and so being superior to it in merit, makes perfectly good sense. Merit is a grading or ranking concept, and judgments of comparative merit are based on the different degrees to which things satisfy a given standard. But what can it mean to talk about one thing being superior to another in inherent worth? In order to get at what is being asserted in such a claim it is helpful first to look at the social origin of the concept of degrees of inherent worth.

The idea that humans can possess different degrees of inherent worth originated in societies having rigid class structures. Before the rise of modern democracies with their egalitarian outlook, one's membership in a hereditary class determined one's social status. People in the upper classes were looked up to, while those in the lower classes were looked down upon. In such a society one's social superiors and social inferiors were clearly defined and easily recognized.

Two aspects of these class-structured societies are especially relevant to the idea of degrees of inherent worth. First, those born into the upper classes were deemed more worthy of respect than those born into the lower orders. Second, the superior worth of upper class people had nothing to do with their merits nor did the inferior worth of those in the lower classes rest on their lack of merits. One's superiority or inferiority entirely derived from a social position one was born into. The modern concept of a meritocracy simply did not apply. One could not advance into a higher class by any sort of moral or nonmoral achievement. Similarly, an aristocrat held his title and all the privileges that went with it just because he was the eldest son of a titled nobleman. Unlike the bestowing of knighthood in contemporary Great Britain, one did not earn membership in the nobility by meritorious conduct.

We who live in modern democracies no longer believe in such hereditary social distinctions. Indeed, we would wholeheartedly condemn them on moral grounds as being fundamentally unjust. We have come to think of class systems as a paradigm of social injustice, it being a central principle of the democratic way of life that among humans there are no superiors and no inferiors. Thus we have rejected the whole conceptual framework in which people are judged to have different degrees of inherent worth. That idea is incompatible with our notion of human equality based on the doctrine that all humans, simply in virtue of their humanity, have the same inherent worth. (The belief in universal human rights is one form that this egalitarianism takes.)

The vast majority of people in modern democracies, however, do not maintain an egalitarian outlook when it comes to comparing human beings with other living things. Most people consider our own species to be superior to all other species and this superiority is understood to be a matter of inherent worth, not merit. There may exist thoroughly vicious and depraved humans who lack all merit. Yet because they are human they are thought to belong to a higher class of entities than any plant or animal. That one is born into the species *Homo sapiens* entitles one to have lordship over those who are one's inferiors,

namely, those born into other species. The parallel with hereditary social classes is very close. Implicit in this view is a hierarchical conception of nature according to which an organism has a position of superiority of inferiority in the Earth's community of life simply on the basis of its genetic background. The "lower" orders of life are looked down upon and it is considered perfectly proper that they serve the interests of those belonging to the highest order, namely humans. The intrinsic value we place on the well-being of our fellow humans reflects our recognition of their rightful position as our equals. No such intrinsic value is to be placed on the good of other animals, unless we choose to do so out of fondness or affection for them. But their well-being imposes no moral requirement on us. In this respect there is an absolute difference in moral status between ourselves and them.

This is the structure of concepts and beliefs that people are committed to insofar as they regard humans to be superior in inherent worth to all other species. I now wish to argue that this structure of concepts and beliefs is completely groundless. If we accept the first three components of the biocentric outlook and from that perspective look at the major philosophical traditions which have supported that structure, we find it to be at bottom nothing more than the expression of an irrational bias in our own favor. The philosophical traditions themselves rest on very questionable assumptions or else simply beg the question. I briefly consider three of the main traditions to substantiate the point. These are classical Greek humanism, Cartesian dualism, and the Judeo-Christian concept of the Great Chain of Being.

The inherent superiority of humans over other species was implicit in the Greek definition of man as a rational animal. Our animal nature was identified with "brute" desires that need the order and restraint of reason to rule them (just as reason is the special virtue of those who rule in the ideal state). Rationality was then seen to be the key to our superiority over animals. It enables us to live on a higher plane and endows us with a nobility and worth that other creatures lack. This familiar way of comparing humans with other species is deeply ingrained in our Western philosophical outlook. The point to consider here is that this view does not actually provide an argument *for* human superiority but rather makes explicit the framework of thought that is implicitly used by those who think of humans as inherently superior to nonhumans. The Greeks who held that humans, in virtue of their rational capacities, have a kind of worth greater than that of any nonrational being, never looked at rationality as but one capacity of living things among many others. But when we consider rationality from the standpoint of the first three elements of the ecological outlook, we see that its value lies in its importance for *human* life. Other creatures achieve their species-specific good without the need of rationality, although they often make use of capacities that human lack. So the humanistic outlook of classical Greek thought does not give us a neutral (nonquestion-begging) ground on which to construct a scale of degrees of inherent worth possessed by different species of living things.

The second tradition, centering on the Cartesian dualism of soul and body, also fails to justify the claim to human superiority. That superiority is supposed to derive from the fact that we have souls while animals do not. Animals are mere automata and lack the divine element that makes us spiritual beings. I won't go into the now familiar criticisms of this two-substance view. I only add the point that, even if humans are composed of an immaterial, unextended soul and a material, extended body, this in itself is not a reason to deem them of greater worth than entities that are only bodies. Why is a soul substance a thing that adds value to its possessor? Unless some theological reasoning is offered here (which many, including myself, would find unacceptable on epistemological grounds), no logical connection is evident. An immaterial something which thinks is better than a material something which does not think only if thinking itself has value, either intrinsically or instrumentally. Now it is intrinsically valuable to humans alone, who value it as an end in itself, and it is instrumentally valuable to those who benefit from it, namely humans.

For animals that neither enjoy thinking for its own sake nor need it for living the kind of life for which they are best adapted, it has no value. Even if "thinking" is broadened to include all forms of consciousness, there are still many living things that can do without it and yet live what is for their species a good life. The anthropocentricity underlying the claim to human superiority runs throughout Cartesian dualism.

A third major source of the idea of human superiority is the Judeo-Christian concept of the Great Chain of Being. Humans are superior to animals and plants because their Creator has given them a higher place on the chain. It begins with God at the top, and then moves to the angels, who are lower than God but higher than humans, then to humans, positioned between the angels and the beasts (partaking of the nature of both), and then on down to the lower levels occupied by nonhuman animals, plants, and finally inanimate objects. Humans, being "made in God's image," are inherently superior to animals and plants by virtue of their being closer (in their essential nature) to God.

The metaphysical and epistemological difficulties with this conception of a hierarchy of entities are, in my mind, insuperable. Without entering into this matter here, I only point out that if we are unwilling to accept the metaphysics of traditional Judaism and Christianity, we are again left without good reasons for holding to the claim of inherent human superiority.

The foregoing considerations (and others like them) leave us with but one ground for the assertion that a human being, regardless of merit, is a higher kind of entity than any other living thing. This is the mere fact of the genetic makeup of the species *Homo sapiens*. But this is surely irrational and arbitrary. Why should the arrangement of genes of a certain type be a mark of superior value, especially when this fact about an organism is taken by itself, unrelated to any other aspect of its life? We might just as well refer to any other genetic makeup as a ground of superior value. Clearly we are confronted here with a wholly arbitrary claim that can only be explained as an irrational bias in our own favor.

That the claim is nothing more than a deep-seated prejudice is brought home to us when we look at our relation to other species in the light of the first three elements of the biocentric outlook. Those elements taken conjointly give us a certain overall view of the natural world and of the place of humans in it. When we take this view we come to understand other living things, their environmental conditions, and their ecological relationships in such a way as to awake in us a deep sense of our kinship with them as fellow members of the Earth's community of life. Humans and nonhumans alike are viewed together as integral parts of one unified whole in which all living things are functionally interrelated. Finally, when our awareness focuses on the individual lives of plants and animals, each is seen to share with us the characteristic of being a teleological center of life striving to realize its own good in its own unique way.

As this entire belief system becomes part of the conceptual framework through which we understand and perceive the world, we come to see ourselves as bearing a certain moral relation to nonhuman forms of life. Our ethical role in nature takes on a new significance. We begin to look at other species as we look at ourselves, seeing them as beings which have a good they are striving to realize just as we have a good we are striving to realize. We accordingly develop the disposition to view the world from the standpoint of their good as well as from the standpoint of our own good. Now if the groundlessness of the claim that humans are inherently superior to other species were brought clearly before our minds, we would not remain intellectually neutral toward that claim but would reject it as being fundamentally at variance with our total world outlook. In the absence of any good reasons for holding it, the assertion of human superiority would then appear simply as the expression of an irrational and self-serving prejudice that favors one particular species over several million others.

Rejecting the notion of human superiority entails its positive counterpart: the doctrine of species impartiality. One who accepts that doctrine regards all living things as possessing inherent worth—the *same* inherent worth, since no one species has been shown to be either "higher" or "lower" than any other. Now we saw earlier that, insofar as one thinks of a living thing as possessing inherent worth, one considers it to be the appropriate object of the attitude of respect and believes that attitude to be the only fitting or suitable one for all moral agents to take toward it.

Here, then, is the key to understanding how the attitude of respect is rooted in the biocentric outlook of nature. The basic connection is made through the denial of human superiority. Once we reject the claim that humans are superior either in merit or in worth to other living things, we are ready to adopt the attitude of respect. The denial of human superiority is itself the result of taking the perspective on nature built into the first three elements of the biocentric outlook.

Now the first three elements of the biocentric outlook, it seems clear, would be found acceptable to any rational and scientifically informed thinker who is fully "open" to the reality of the lives of nonhuman organisms. Without denying our distinctively human characteristics, such a thinker can acknowledge the fundamental respects in which we are members of the Earth's community of life and in which the biological conditions necessary for the realization of our human values are inextricably linked with the whole system of nature. In addition, the conception of individual living things as teleological centers of life simply articulates how a scientifically informed thinker comes to understand them as the result of increasingly careful and detailed observations. Thus, the biocentric outlook recommends itself as an acceptable system of concepts and beliefs to anyone who is clear-minded, unbiased, and factually enlightened, and who has a developed capacity of reality awareness with regard to the lives of individual organisms. This, I submit, is as good a reason for making the moral commitment involved in adopting the attitude of respect for nature as any theory of environmental ethics could possibly have.

MORAL RIGHTS AND THE MATTER OF COMPETING CLAIMS

I have not asserted anywhere in the foregoing account that animals or plants have moral rights. This omission was deliberate. I do not think that the reference class of the concept, bearer of moral rights, should be extended to include nonhuman living things. My reasons for taking this position, however, go beyond the scope of this paper. I believe I have been able to accomplish many of the same ends which those who ascribe rights to animals or plants wish to accomplish. There is no reason, moreover, why plants and animals, including whole species populations and life communities, cannot be accorded *legal* rights under my theory. To grant them legal protection could be interpreted as giving them legal entitlement to be protected, and this, in fact, would be a means by which a society that subscribed to the ethics of respect for nature could give public recognition to their inherent worth.

There remains the problem of competing claims, even when wild plants and animals are not thought of as bearers of moral rights. If we accept the biocentric outlook and accordingly adopt the attitude of respect for nature as our ultimate moral attitude, how do we resolve conflicts that arise from our respect for persons in the domain of human ethics and our respect for nature in the domain of environmental ethics? This is a question that cannot adequately be dealt with here. My main purpose in this paper has been to try to establish a base point from which we can start working toward a solution to the problem. I have shown why we cannot just begin with an initial presumption in favor of the interests of our own species. It is after all within our power as moral beings to place limits on human population and technology with the deliberate intention of sharing the Earth's bounty with other species. That such sharing is an ideal difficult to realize even in an approximate way does not take away its claim to our deepest moral commitment.

NOTES

1. W. K. Frankena, "Ethics and the Environment," in *Ethics and Problems of the 21st Century*, ed. K. E. Goodpaster and K. M. Sayre (South Bend: University of Notre Dame Press, 1979), pp. 3–20. I critically examine Frankena's views in "Frankena on Environmental Ethics," *Monist*, 64 (July 1981), no. 3: 313–324.

2. In the light of considerations set forth in Daniel Dennett's *Brainstorms: Philosophical Essays on Mind and Psychology* (Montgomery, VT: Bradford Books, 1978), it is advisable to leave this question unsettled at this time. When machines are developed that function in the way our brains do, we may well come to deem them proper subjects of moral consideration.

3. Stephen R. L. Clark, *The Moral Status of Animals* (Oxford: Clarendon Press, 1977), p. 112.

4. My criticisms of the dogma of human superiority gain independent support from a carefully reasoned essay by R. and V. Routley showing the many logical weaknesses in arguments for human-centered theories of environmental ethics. R. and V. Routley, "Against the Inevitability of Human Chauvinism," in *Ethics and Problems of the 21st Century*, ed. K. E. Goodpaster and K. M. Sayre, (South Bend: University of Notre Dame Press, 1979), pp. 36–59.

5. For this way of distinguishing between merit and inherent worth, I am indebted to Gregory Vlastos, "Justice and Equality," in *Social Justice*, ed. R. Brandt (Englewood Cliffs, NJ: Prentice-Hall, 1962), pp. 31–72.

Are All Species Equal?

David Schmidtz

Species egalitarianism is the view that all living things have equal moral standing. To have moral standing is, at a minimum, to command respect, to be more than a mere thing. Is there reason to believe all living things have moral standing in even this most minimal sense? If so—that is, if all living things command respect—is there reason to believe they all command *equal* respect?

I will try to explain why members of other species command our respect but also why they do not command equal respect. The intuition that we should have respect for nature is part of what motivates people to embrace species egalitarianism, but we need not be species egalitarians to have respect for nature. I close by questioning whether species egalitarianism is even compatible with respect for nature.

RESPECT FOR NATURE

According to Paul Taylor, anthropocentrism "gives either exclusive or primary consideration to human interests above the good of other species."[1] The alternative to anthropocentrism is biocentrism, and it is biocentrism that, in Taylor's view, grounds species egalitarianism:

The beliefs that form the core of the biocentric outlook are four in number:

(a) The belief that humans are members of the Earth's Community of life in the same sense and on the same terms in which other living things are members of that community.
(b) The belief that the human species, along with all other species, are integral elements in a system of interdependence . . .

(c) The belief that all organisms are teleological centers of life in the sense that each is a unique individual pursuing its own good in its own way.
(d) The belief that humans are not inherently superior to other living beings.[2]

Taylor concludes, "Rejecting the notion of human superiority entails its positive counterpart: the doctrine of species impartiality. One who accepts that doctrine regards all living things as possessing inherent worth—the *same* inherent worth, since no one species has been shown to be either higher or lower than any other."[3]

Taylor does not say this is a valid argument, but he thinks that if we concede (a), (b), and (c), it would be unreasonable not to move to (d), and then to his egalitarian conclusion. Is he right? For those who accept Taylor's three premises (and who thus interpret those premises in terms innocuous enough to render them acceptable), there are two responses. First, we may go on to accept (d), following Taylor, but then still deny that there is any warrant for moving from there to Taylor's egalitarian conclusion. Having accepted that our form of life is not superior, we might choose instead to regard it as inferior. More plausibly, we might view our form of life as noncomparable. We simply do not have the same kind of value as nonhumans. The question of how we compare to nonhumans has a simple answer: we do not compare to them. We are not equal. We are not unequal. We are simply different.

Alternatively, we may reject (d) and say humans are indeed inherently superior but our superiority is a moot point. Whether we are inherently superior (that is, superior as a form of life) does not matter

David Schmidtz, "Are All Species Equal?" *Journal of Applied Philosophy* 15 (1998): 57–67. Reprinted by permission of the author and the Society for Applied Philosophy.

much. Even if we are superior, the fact remains that within the web of ecological interdependence mentioned in premises (a) and (b), it would be a mistake to ignore the needs and the telos of the other species referred to in premise (c). Thus, there are two ways of rejecting Taylor's argument for species egalitarianism. Each, on its face, is compatible with the respect for nature that motivates Taylor's egalitarianism in the first place.

These are preliminary worries, then, about Taylor's argument. Taylor's critics have been harsh, perhaps too harsh. After building on some criticisms while rejecting others, I explore some of our reasons to have respect for nature and ask whether they translate into reasons to be species egalitarians.

IS SPECIES EGALITARIANISM HYPOCRITICAL?

Paul Taylor is among the most intransigent of species egalitarians, yet he allows that human needs override the needs of nonhumans. In response, William C. French, for example, argues that species egalitarians cannot have it both ways. French perceives a contradiction between the egalitarian principles that Taylor officially endorses and the unofficial principles he offers as the real principles by which we should live. Having proclaimed that we are all equal, French asks, what licenses Taylor to say that, in cases of conflict, nonhuman interests can legitimately be sacrificed to vital human interests?[4]

Good question. Yet, somehow Taylor's alleged inconsistency is too obvious. Perhaps his position is not as blatantly inconsistent as it appears. Let me suggest how Taylor could respond. Suppose I find myself in a situation of mortal combat with an enemy soldier. If I kill my enemy to save my life, that does not entail that I regard my enemy as inherently inferior (i.e., as an inferior form of life). Likewise, if I kill a bear to save my life, that does not entail that I regard the bear as inherently inferior. Therefore, Taylor can, without hypocrisy, deny that species egalitarianism requires a radically self-effacing pacifism.

What, then, does species egalitarianism require? It requires us to avoid mortal combat whenever we can, not just with other humans but with living things in general. On this view, we ought to regret finding ourselves in kill-or-be-killed situations that we could have avoided. There is no point in regretting the fact that we must kill in order to eat, though, for there is no avoiding that. Species egalitarianism is compatible with our having a limited license to kill.

What seems far more problematic for species egalitarianism is that it seems to suggest that it makes no difference *what* we kill. Vegetarians typically think it is worse to kill a cow than to kill a carrot. Are they wrong? Yes they are, according to species egalitarianism. In this respect, species egalitarianism cannot be right. I believe we have reason to respect nature. However, we fail to give nature due respect if we say we should have no more respect for a cow than for a carrot.

IS SPECIES EGALITARIANISM ARBITRARY?

Suppose interspecies comparisons are possible. Suppose the capacities of different species, and whatever else gives living things moral standing, are commensurable. In that case, it could turn out that all living things are equal, but that would be quite a fluke.

Taylor says a being has intrinsic worth just in case it has a good of its own. And Taylor thinks even plants have a good of their own in the relevant sense. They seek their own good in their own way. As mentioned earlier, Taylor defines anthropocentrism as giving exclusive or primary consideration to human interests above the good of other species. So, when we acknowledge the ability to think as a valuable capacity, and acknowledge that some but not all living things possess this valuable capacity, are we giving exclusive or primary consideration to human interests? Probably not. Is there something wrong with noticing that there are valuable capacities that not all living things possess? Put it this way: if biocentrism involves resolving to ignore the fact that cognitive capacity is something we value—if biocentrism amounts to a resolution to value only those capacities that all living things share—then biocentrism is at least as arbitrary and question-begging as anthropocentrism.

It will not do to defend species egalitarianism by singling out a property that all living things possess, arguing that this property is morally important, then concluding that all living things are therefore of equal moral importance. The problem with this sort of argument is that, where there is one property that provides a basis for moral standing, there might be others. Other properties might be possessed by some but not all living things, and might provide bases for different kinds or degrees of moral standing.

Obviously, Taylor knows that not all living things have the ability to think, and he would not deny that the ability to think is a valuable capacity. What he would say, though, is that it begs the question to rank the ability to think as *more* valuable than the characteristic traits of plants and other animals. Taylor himself assumes that human rationality is on a par with, for example, a cheetah's foot-speed: no less valuable, but no more valuable either.[5] In this case, though, perhaps it is Taylor who begs the question. It hardly seems unreasonable to see the difference between the foot-speed of chimpanzees and cheetahs as a difference of degree, while seeing the difference between the intelligence of a chimpanzee and the intelligence of a carrot as a difference in kind. Chimpanzees are very smart. Carrots, in contrast, are not merely a lot less smart. Carrots are not smart at all. They do not even make it into the same category.

Anthropocentrists might argue, against Taylor, that the good associated with the ability to think is superior to the good associated with a tree's ability to grow and reproduce. Could they be wrong? Let us suppose they are wrong. For argument's sake, suppose the ability to grow and reproduce is *superior* to the ability to think. Wouldn't that mean *trees* are superior to *chimpanzees?* Absolutely not. It is not as if chimpanzees have one singular virtue, the ability to think, while trees have another singular virtue, the ability to grow and reproduce. Rather, both trees and chimpanzees share one virtue: the ability to grow and reproduce. They are both teleological centers of life, to use Taylor's phrase. But chimpanzees have a second virtue as well: the ability to think.

Of course, it is more complicated than this, for in fact both trees and chimpanzees have a long list of capacities. The crucial point, though, is this. Although both trees and chimpanzees are teleological centers of life, and although we can agree that this is valuable, and that trees and chimpanzees share equally in this particular value, we cannot conclude that trees and chimpanzees have equal value. We are entitled to conclude only that they are of equal value so far as being a teleological center of life is concerned.[6] From that, we may of course infer that *one* of the grounds of our moral standing (i.e., that we grow and reproduce) is something we share with all living things. Beyond that, nothing about equality even suggests itself. In particular, it begs no questions to notice that there are grounds for moral standing that humans do not share with all living things.

SPECIESISM AND SOCIAL POLICY

Peter Singer and others speak as if speciesism—the idea that some species are superior to others—is necessarily a kind of bias in favor of humans and against nonhuman animals. (Singer has no problem with being "biased" against plants.) This is a mistake. If we have more respect for chimpanzees than for mice, then we are speciesists, no matter what status we accord to human beings. But we *should* have more respect for chimpanzees than for mice, shouldn't we?

Suppose we take an interest in how chimpanzees rank compared to mice. Perhaps we wonder what we would do in an emergency where we could save a drowning chimpanzee or a drowning mouse but not both. More realistically, suppose we conclude we must do experiments involving animals (because, let's say, there is no other way to develop an effective treatment for an otherwise catastrophic disease), and now we have to choose which animals. Whichever we use, the animals we use will die. We decide to use mice. Then a species egalitarian says, "Why not use chimpanzees? They're all the same anyway, morally speaking, and you'll get more reliable data." If we believe all living things are equal, or even if we think only that all animals are equal, then why not use the chimpanzee?

In reality, chimpanzees are the wrong kind of animal to experiment on when researchers could get by with mice. To that extent, speciesism is closer to the moral truth than is species egalitarianism. Moreover, although in philosophy we tend to use science fiction examples, the situation just described is an everyday problem in the scientific community. Suppose researchers had to choose between harvesting the organs of a chimpanzee or a brain-damaged human baby. Peter Singer[7] says we cannot have it both ways. He argues that if the ability to think makes the difference, then the brain-damaged infant commands no more respect than a chimpanzee, and may indeed command less. Singer concludes that if we need to use one or the other in a painful and/or lethal medical experiment, and if it does not matter which one we use so far as the experiment is concerned, then we ought to use the brain-damaged child, not the chimpanzee.[8]

Does this seem obvious? It should not. Actually, it appears to be Singer who is trying to have it both ways. The mistake here is subtle, but it is, nevertheless, clearly a mistake. Singer does not reject speciesism so much as what he considers to be the wrong kind of speciesism. If we claimed the rightness of eating beef has to be settled individual cow by individual cow, it would be Singer who would insist that cows are the wrong *kind* of thing for us to be eating, and that we need a policy governing our exploitation of cows as a species. Yet, when Singer criticizes those who exalt the value of rationality, he says rationality is relevant to justification only at the individual level.

Some speciesists are impressed with humanity's characteristic rationality . They say this characteristic justifies respect for humanity, not merely for particular humans who exemplify human rationality. Other speciesists are more impressed with the ability to feel pain. They say this ability justifies respecting cows in general, not just those individual cows that have proven they can feel pain.

Singer is a speciesist of the latter kind. Singer has to agree that if most chimpanzees have morally important characteristics that most mice lack, we do not need to compare individual chimpanzees and mice on a case by case basis in order to have a moral justification for passing laws that stop researchers from using chimpanzees in their experiments when mice would do just as well. It is Singer who wants to insist that researchers cannot be allowed to decide on a case by case basis whether to use mice or chimpanzees or people in their experiments, when turnips would do just as well. Likewise, it is Singer who wants to insist individual consumers should not decide on a case by case basis whether to eat cows or turnips; they ought to quit eating cows, period. In the medical research policy area, what we actually do, and rightly so, is ignore Singer's point that some animals are smarter than some people, and instead formulate policy on the basis of characteristic features of the species. And if Singer objects to the policy we choose, it will not be because our policy is based on features of the species. His objection will be that we used the wrong feature. He will say the feature we ought to have used is the ability to feel pain.

Of course, some chimpanzees lack characteristic features in virtue of which chimpanzees command respect as a species, just as some humans lack characteristic features in virtue of which humans command respect as a species. It is equally obvious that some chimpanzees have cognitive capacities superior to the cognitive capacities of some humans. But when it comes to questions of practical policy, such as we face when trying to formulate policy regarding animal experimentation, whether every human being is superior in every respect to every chimpanzee is beside the point. The point is that we can, we do, and we must make policy decisions on the basis of our recognition that turnips, mice, chimpanzees, and humans are relevantly different types.

EQUALITY AND TRANSCENDENCE

Even if speciesists are right to see a nonarbitrary distinction between humans and other living things, though, the fact remains that claims of superiority do not easily translate into justifications of domination.[9] We can have reasons to treat nonhuman species with respect, regardless of whether we consider them to be on a moral par with *Homo sapiens.*

What kind of reasons do we have for treating members of other species with respect? We might have respect for chimpanzees or even mice on the grounds that they are sentient. Even mice have a rudimentary point of view and rudimentary hopes and dreams, and we might well respect them for that. But what about plants? Plants, unlike mice and chimpanzees, do not care what happens to them. It is literally true that they could not care less. So, why should we care? Is it even possible for us to have any good reason, other than a purely instrumental reason, to care what happens to plants?

When we are alone in a forest, wondering whether it would be fine to chop down a tree for fun, our perspective on what happens to the tree is, so far as we know, the only perspective there is. The tree does not have its own. Thus, explaining why we have reason to care about trees requires us to explain caring from our point of view, since that (we are supposing) is all there is. In that case, we do not have to satisfy *trees* that we are treating them properly; rather, we have to satisfy ourselves. So, again, can we have noninstrumental reasons for caring about trees—for treating them with respect?

One reason to care (not the only one) is that gratuitous destruction is a failure of self-respect. It is a repudiation of the kind of self-awareness and self-respect that we can achieve by repudiating wantonness. So far as I know, no one finds anything puzzling in the idea that we have reason to treat our lawns or living rooms with respect. Lawns and living rooms have instrumental value, but there is more to it than that. Most of us have the sense that taking reasonable care of our lawns and living rooms is somehow a matter of self-respect, not merely a matter of preserving their instrumental value. Do we have similar reasons to treat forests with respect? I think we do. There is an aesthetic involved, the repudiation of which would be a failure of self-respect. (Obviously, not everyone feels the same way about forests. Not everyone feels the same way about lawns

and living rooms, either. But the point here is to make sense of respect for nature, not to argue that respect for nature is in fact universal or that failing to respect nature is irrational.) If and when we identify with a Redwood, in the sense of being inspired by it, having respect for its size and age and so on, then as a psychological fact, we really do face questions about how we ought to treat it. If and when we come to see a Redwood in that light, subsequently turning our backs on it becomes a kind of self-effacement. The values we thereby fail to take seriously are *our* values, not the tree's.

So, I am saying the attitude we take toward gazelles (for example) raises issues of self-respect insofar as we see ourselves as relevantly like gazelles. Here is a different and complementary way of looking at the issue. Consider that lions owe nothing to gazelles. Therefore, if we owe it to gazelles not to hunt them, it must be because we are *unlike* lions, not (or not only) because we are *like* gazelles.

Unlike lions, we have a choice about whether to hunt gazelles, and we are capable of deliberating about that choice in a reflective way. We are capable of caring about the gazelle's pain, the gazelle's beauty, the gazelle's hopes and dreams (such as they are), and so forth. If we do care, then in a more or less literal way, something is wrong with us—we are less than fully human—if we cannot adjust our behavior in light of what we care about. And if we do not care, then we are missing something. For a human being, to lack a broad respect for living things and beautiful things and well-functioning things is to be stunted in a way.

Our coming to see members of other species as commanding respect is itself a way of transcending our animal natures. It is ennobling. It is part of our natures unthinkingly to see ourselves as superior, and to try to dominate accordingly; our capacity to see ourselves as equal is one of the things that makes us different. (It may be one of the things that makes us superior.)[10] Coming to see all living things as equal may not be the best way of transcending our animal natures—it does not work for me—but it is one way.

Another way of transcending our animal natures and expressing due respect for nature is simply to not bother to keep score. This latter way is, I think, better. It is more respectful of our own reflective natures. It does not dwell on rankings. It does not insist on seeing equality where a more reflective being simply would see what is there to be seen and would not shy away from respecting what is unique as well as what is common. Someone might say we need to rank animals as our equals so as to be fair, but that appears to be false. I can be fair to my friends without ranking them. Imagine a friend saying, "I disagree! In fact, failing to rank us is insulting! You have to rank us as equals!" What would be the point? Perhaps my friends are each other's equals (in some respect?). Let us assume they are. Even so, that hardly establishes any need to *rank* them as equal. For most purposes, it is better for them simply to be friends. Sometimes, respect is simply respect. It need not be based on a pecking order.

Children rank their friends. It is one of the things children do not yet understand about friendship. Sometimes, the idea of ranking things, even as equals, is a child's game. It is beneath us.

RESPECT FOR EVERYTHING

Thus, a broad respect for living or beautiful or well-functioning things need not translate into equal respect. It need not translate into universal respect, either. I can appreciate mosquitoes to a degree. Elizabeth Willott (co-editor of this volume and a biochemist who studies mosquito immune systems) even finds them beautiful, or so she says. My own appreciation, by contrast, is thin and grudging and purely intellectual. In neither degree nor kind is it anything like my appreciation for Elizabeth, or for human beings in general, or even for the rabbits I sometimes found eating my flowers in the morning when I lived in Ohio. Part of our responsibility as moral agents is to be somewhat choosy about what we respect and how we respect it. I can see why people shy away from openly accepting that responsibility, but they still have it.

We might suppose speciesism is as arbitrary as racism unless we can show that the differences are morally relevant. This is, to be sure, a popular sentiment among animal liberationists such as Peter Singer and Tom Regan. But are we really like racists when we think it is worse to kill a dolphin than to kill a tuna? The person who says there is a relevant similarity between speciesism and racism has the burden of proof: go ahead and identify the similarity. Is seeing moral significance in biological differences between chimpanzees and mice anything like seeing moral significance in biological differences between races? I think not.

Is it true that we need good reason to exclude plants and animals from the realm of things we regard as commanding respect? Or do we need reason to *in*clude them? Should we be trying to identify properties in virtue of which a thing forfeits presumptive (equal) moral standing? Or does it make more sense to be trying to identify properties in virtue of which a thing commands respect? The latter seems more natural to me, which suggests the burden of proof lies with those who claim we should have respect for all living things.

I would not say, though, that this burden is unbearable. One reason to have regard for other living things has to do with self-respect. (As I said earlier, when we mistreat a tree that we admire, the values we fail to respect are our values, not the tree's.) A second reason has to do with self-realization. (As I said, exercising our capacity for moral regard is a form of self-realization.) Finally, at least some species seem to share with human beings precisely those characteristics that lead us to see human life as especially worthy of esteem. For example, Lawrence Johnson describes experiments in which rhesus monkeys show extreme reluctance to obtain food by means that would subject monkeys in neighboring cages to electric shock.[11] He describes the case of Washoe, a chimpanzee who learned sign language. Anyone who has tried to learn a foreign language ought to be able to appreciate how astonishing an intellectual feat it is that an essentially nonlinguistic creature could learn a language—a language that is not merely foreign but the language of another species.[12]

However, although he believes Washoe has moral standing, Johnson does not believe that the moral standing of chimpanzees, and indeed of all living creatures, implies we must resolve never to kill.

Thus, Johnson (an Australian) supports killing introduced animal species (feral dogs, rabbits, and so forth) to protect Australia's native species, including native plant species.[13]

Is Johnson advocating a speciesist version of the Holocaust? Has he shown himself to be no better than a racist? I think not. Johnson is right to want to take drastic measures to protect Australia's natural flora, and the idea of respecting trees is intelligible. Certainly one thing I feel in the presence of Redwoods is something like a feeling of respect. But I doubt that what underlies Johnson's willingness to kill feral dogs is mere respect for Australia's native plants. I suspect his approval of such killings turns to some extent on needs and aesthetic sensibilities of human beings, not just interests of plants. For example, if the endangered native species happened to be a malaria-carrying mosquito, I doubt Johnson would advocate wiping out an exotic species of amphibian in order to protect the mosquitoes.

Aldo Leopold[14] urged us to see ourselves as plain citizens of, rather than conquerors of, the biotic community, but there are some species with whom we can never be fellow citizens. The rabbits eating my flowers in the back yard are neighbors, and I cherish their company, minor frictions notwithstanding. I feel no sense of community with mosquitoes, though, and not merely because they are not warm and fuzzy. Some mosquito species are so adapted to making human beings miserable that mortal combat is not accidental; rather, combat is a natural state. It is how such creatures live. I think it is fair to say human beings are not able to respond to malaria-carrying mosquitoes in a caring manner. At very least, most of us would think less of a person who did respond to them in a caring manner. We would regard the person's caring as a parody of respect for nature.

The conclusion that *all* living things have moral standing is unmotivated. For human beings, viewing apes as having moral standing is a form of self-respect. Viewing viruses as having moral standing is not. It is good to have a sense of how amazing living things are, but being able to marvel at living things is not the same as thinking all living things

have moral standing. Life as such commands respect only in the limited but important sense that for self-aware and reflective creatures who want to act in ways that make sense, deliberately killing something is an act that does not make sense unless we have good reason to do it. Destroying something for no good reason is (at best) the moral equivalent of vandalism.

THE HISTORY OF THE DEBATE

There is an odd project in the history of philosophy that equates what seem to be three distinct projects:

1. determining our essence;
2. specifying how we are different from all other species;
3. specifying what makes us morally important.

Equating these three projects has important ramifications. Suppose for the sake of argument that what makes us morally important is that we are capable of suffering. If what makes us morally important is necessarily the same property that constitutes our essence, then our essence is that we are capable of suffering. And if our essence necessarily is what makes us different from all other species, then we can deduce that dogs are not capable of suffering.

Likewise with rationality. If rationality is our essence, then rationality is what makes us morally important and also what makes us unique. Therefore, we can deduce that chimpanzees are not rational. Alternatively, if some other animal becomes rational, does that mean our essence will change? Is that why some people find Washoe, the talking chimpanzee, threatening?

The three projects, needless to say, should not be conflated in the way philosophy seems historically to have conflated them, but we can reject species equality without conflation. If we like, we can select a property with respect to which all living things are the same, then say that property confers moral standing, then say all living things have moral standing. To infer that all living things have the same standing, though, would be to ignore the possibility that there are other morally important properties with respect to which not all living things are equal.

There is room to wonder whether species egalitarianism is even compatible with respect for nature. Is it true we should have no more regard for dolphins than for tuna? Is it true that the moral standing of chimpanzees is no higher than that of mice? I worry that such claims are not only untrue, but also disrespectful. Dolphins and chimpanzees command more respect than species egalitarianism allows.

There is no denying that it demeans us to destroy living things we find beautiful or otherwise beneficial. What about living things in which we find neither beauty nor benefit? It is, upon reflection, obviously in our interest to enrich our lives by finding them beautiful or beneficial, if we can. By and large, we must agree with Leopold that it is too late for conquering the biotic community. Our task now is to find ways of fitting in. Species egalitarianism is one way of trying to understand how we fit in. In the end, it is not an acceptable way. Having respect for nature and being a species egalitarian are two different things.

NOTES

1. Paul W. Taylor, "In Defense of Biocentrism," *Environmental Ethics,* 5 (1983): 237–43, here p. 240.

2. Paul Taylor, *Respect for Nature* (Princeton: Princeton University Press, 1986) p. 99ff. See also Taylor "The Ethics of Respect for Nature," in this volume.

3. Taylor, "Ethics of Respect for Nature."

4. William C. French, "Against Biospherical Egalitarianism," *Environmental Ethics,* 17 (1995): 39–57, here pp. 44ff. See also James C. Anderson, "Species Equality and the Foundations of Moral Theory, *Environmental Values,* 2 (1993): 347–65, here p. 350.

5. Taylor, "Ethics of Respect for Nature."

6. For a similar critique of Taylor from an Aristotelian perspective, see Anderson, p. 348. See also Louis G. Lombardi, "Inherent Worth, Respect, and Rights, *Environmental Ethics,* 5 (1993): 257–70.

7. Peter Singer, *Animal Liberation,* 2nd edition (New York: Random House, 1990) pp. 1–23.

8. See also Lawrence Johnson, *A Morally Deep World* (New York: Cambridge Press, 1991) p. 52.

9. This is effectively argued by Anderson (p. 362).

10. Aldo Leopold has expressed a related thought. When the Cincinnati Zoo erected a monument to the passenger pigeon, Leopold wrote, "We have erected a monument to commemorate the funeral of a species. . . . For one species to mourn the death of another is a new thing under the sun. . . . In this fact, . . . lies objective evidence of our superiority over the beasts." Aldo Leopold, "On a Monument to the Pigeon," *A Sand County Almanac* (New York: Oxford University Press, 1966, first published in 1949) p. 116–17.

11. Johnson, p. 64n.

12. This is what I wrote in the original version of this article. I since have learned that families of lowland gorillas have their own fairly complicated language of hand signals, which leads me to suspect I may have been mistaken in describing chimpanzees as essentially nonlinguistic.

13. Johnson, p. 174.

14. Leopold, *A Sand County Almanac,* p. 240.

Chapter 5
Environmental Holism

Questions for Reflection and Discussion

Keeping Our Hands Clean

1. We were in Australia recently, and had the pleasure of attending a talk by Tom Regan defending animal rights. When Tom concluded, the audience applauded, but the first question was an all-out attack. "You say animals have rights," the questioner said, "but I can tell by looking at you that you are a hypocrite." That was all. The questioner sat down. The room was silent.

Finally, Tom said, "I never said I was perfect. I suppose when you say you can tell by looking that I'm a hypocrite, you're talking about my leather belt and my leather shoes and my woolen sports jacket." Tom continued. "I don't deny that I have blood on my hands. I could mention that the belt and shoes are actually vinyl, and the jacket is actually cotton. But how many animals were killed in the process of extracting the petroleum that went into making the vinyl? How many animals were killed in the process of growing and harvesting the cotton that went into the jacket? I have no idea. All I know is, I don't have clean hands. And all I can do from here is to minimize the killing as best I can."[1]

So Tom Regan has a problem. He has good intentions, but good intentions do not guarantee clean hands. How forgiving should Tom be of himself? How forgiving should Tom be of his fellow environmentalists, most of whom do not care nearly as much about animal suffering as does Tom?

What of holists whose top priority is the management of ecosystems, and who therefore would kill individual animals as a way of limiting herd size and thereby maintaining ecological balance? Is there any room for compromise?

2. Gary Varner argues (quite persuasively) that any organism has interests just in case it has biological needs. But then Varner also stipulates, as a matter of definition, that an organism has moral standing if and only if it has interests. So it appears to follow simply by definition that plants have moral standing. Where does that leave us? What does this conclusion tell us about how we ought to treat plants?

3. Deep Ecology (see Devall and Sessions) begins with Aldo Leopold's dictum that the Earth does not belong to us. Humans are plain citizens of the biotic community, not

lords and masters, and not police. A corollary of that dictum: Nature can take care of itself, if we let it. One of today's foremost deep ecologists, Lawrence Johnson, says, "It could just be that some things are none of our business. Moral philosophers sometimes seem to suggest that we must formulate a policy for every conceivable situation, a prescription for every ill.[2]" However, "Just as in purely human affairs, it is all too easy for us to think that we know what we are doing and that we are acting for the best, when actually we are making things worse. . . . Even if we could, in our wisdom, produce a greater balance of good by interfering, it may possibly be that some parties to a conflict have a right not to be subject to even our benevolent interference. . . . For our part, we might have a right not to be our brother's keeper on a full-time basis" (p. 222). Johnson concludes that, typically, "we are not called upon to police the biosphere" (p. 244).

What do you think? Is Johnson underestimating our ability to manage nature? Is he overestimating nature's ability to manage itself?

NOTES

1. When we showed this passage to Professor Regan, he asked us to add the following thought. "There is a morally relevant difference between supporting practices, like raising animals to eat or trapping them for their fur, whose very purpose involves killing animals, and being implicated in practices, like drilling for oil and growing cotton, that do not have the killing of animals as a defining purpose. So, yes, there is blood on my hands at the end of the day, just as there is blood on everyone's. My modest point is that where the blood comes from makes a difference."

2. Lawrence E. Johnson, *A Morally Deep World* (New York: Cambridge University Press, 1991) p. 221.

How to Worry About Endangered Species

Tom Regan

The rights view is a view about the moral rights of individuals. Species are not individuals, and the rights view does not recognize the moral rights of species to anything, including survival. What it recognizes is the prima facie right of individuals not to be harmed, and thus the prima facie right of individuals not to be killed. That an individual animal is among the last remaining members of a species confers no further right on that animal, and its right not to be harmed must be weighed equitably with the rights of any others who have this right. If, in a prevention situation, we had to choose between saving the last two members of an endangered species or saving another individual who belonged to a species that was plentiful but whose death would be a greater prima facie harm to that individual than the harm

Tom Regan, "How to Worry About Endangered Species," *The Case for Animal Rights* (Berkeley: University of California Press, 1983), 359–63. Reprinted with permission of the author and the publisher.

that death would be to the two, then the rights view requires that we save that individual. Moreover, numbers make no difference in such a case. If the choice were between saving the last thousand or million members of the species to which the two belong, that would make no moral difference. The aggregate of their lesser harms does not harm any individual in a way that is prima facie comparable to the harm that would be done to this solitary individual. Nor would aggregating the losses of other interested parties (e.g., human aesthetic or scientific interests) make any difference. The sum of these losses harms no individual in a way that is prima facie comparable to the harm that would be done to the single individual if we chose to override his right.

The rights view is not opposed to efforts to save endangered species. It only insists that we be clear about the reasons for doing so. On the rights view, the reason we ought to save the members of endangered species of animals is not because the species is endangered but because the individual animals have valid claims and thus rights against those who would destroy their natural habitat, for example, or who would make a living off their dead carcasses through poaching and traffic in exotic animals, practices that unjustifiably override the rights of these animals. But though the rights view must look with favor on any attempt to protect the rights of any animal, and so supports efforts to protect the members of endangered species, these very efforts, aimed specifically at protecting the members of species that are endangered, can foster a mentality that is antagonistic to the implications of the rights view. If people are encouraged to believe that the harm done to animals matters morally *only when* these animals belong to endangered species, then these same people will be encouraged to regard the harm done to *other* animals as morally acceptable. In this way people may be encouraged to believe that, for example, the trapping of plentiful animals raises no serious moral question, whereas the trapping of rare animals does. This is not what the rights view implies. The mere size of the relative population of the species to which a given animal belongs makes no moral difference to the grounds for attributing rights to that individual animal or to the basis for determining when that animal's rights may be justifiably overridden or protected.

Though said before, it bears repeating: *the rights view is not indifferent to efforts to save endangered species. It supports these efforts.* It supports them, however, not because these animals are few in number; primarily it supports them because they are equal in value to all who have inherent value, ourselves included, sharing with us the fundamental right to be treated with respect. Since they are not mere receptacles or renewable resources placed here for our use, the harm done to them as individuals cannot be justified merely by aggregating the disparate benefits derived by commercial developers, poachers, and other interested third parties. That is what makes the commercial exploitation of endangered species wrong, not that the species are endangered. On the rights view, the same principles apply to the moral assessment of rare or endangered animals as apply to those that are plentiful, and the same principles apply whether the animals in question are wild or domesticated.

The rights view does not deny, nor is it antagonistic to recognizing, the importance of human aesthetic, scientific, sacramental, and other interests in rare and endangered species or in wild animals generally. What it denies is that (1) the value of these animals is reducible to, or is interchangeable with, the aggregate satisfaction of these human interests, and that (2) the determination of how these animals should be treated, including whether they should be saved in preference to more plentiful animals, is to be fixed by the yardstick of such human interests, either taken individually or aggregatively. Both points cut both ways, concerning, as they do, both how animals may and how they may not be treated. In particular, any and all harm done to rare or endangered animals, done in the name of aggregated human interests, is wrong, according to the rights view, because it violates the individual animal's right to respectful treatment. With regard to wild animals, the general policy recommended by the rights view is: *let them be!* Since this will require increased human intervention in *human* practices that threaten rare or endangered species (e.g., halting the destruction of natural habitat and closer surveillance of poaching, with much stiffer fines and longer prison sentences), the rights view sanctions this intervention, assuming that those humans involved are treated with the respect they are due. Too little is not enough.

RIGHTS AND ENVIRONMENTAL ETHICS: AN ASIDE

The difficulties [of developing a rights-based environmental ethic] include reconciling the *individualistic* nature of moral rights with the more *holistic* view of nature emphasized by many of the leading environmental thinkers. Aldo Leopold is illustrative of this latter tendency. "A thing is right," he states, "when it tends to preserve the integrity, stability, and beauty of the biotic community. It is wrong when it tends otherwise."[1] The implications of this view include the clear prospect that the individual may be sacrificed for the greater biotic good, in the name of "the integrity, stability, and beauty of the biotic community." It is difficult to see how the notion of the rights of the individual could find a home within a view that, emotive connotations to one side, might be fairly dubbed "environmental fascism." To use Leopold's telling phrase, man is "*only* a member of the biotic team,"[2] and as such has the same moral standing as any other "member" of "the team." If, to take an extreme, fanciful but, it is hoped, not unfair example, the situation we faced was either to kill a rare wildflower or a (plentiful) human being, and if the wildflower, as a "team member," would contribute more to "the integrity, stability, and beauty of the biotic community" than the human, then presumably we would not be doing wrong if we killed the human and saved the wildflower. The rights view cannot abide this position, not because the rights view categorically denies that inanimate objects can have rights (more on this momentarily) but because it denies the propriety of deciding what should be done to individuals who have rights by appeal to aggregative considerations, including, therefore, computations about what will or will not maximally "contribute to the integrity, stability, and beauty of the biotic community." Individual rights are not to be outweighed by such considerations (which is not to say that they are never to be outweighed). Environmental fascism and the rights view are like oil and water: they don't mix.

The rights view does not deny the possibility that collections or systems of natural objects might have inherent value—that is, might have a kind of value that is not the same as, is not reducible to, and is incommensurate with any one individual's pleasures, preference-satisfactions, and the like, or with the sum of such goods for any number of individuals. The beauty of an undisturbed, ecologically balanced forest, for example, might be conceived to have value of this kind. The point is certainly arguable. What is far from certain is how moral rights could be meaningfully attributed to the *collection* of trees or the ecosystem. Since neither is an individual, it is unclear how the notion of moral rights can be meaningfully applied. Perhaps this difficulty can be surmounted. It is fair to say, however, that no one writing in this important area of ethics has yet done so.[3]

Because paradigmatic right-holders are individuals, and because the dominant thrust of contemporary environmental efforts (e.g., wilderness preservation) is to focus on the whole rather than on the part (i.e., the individual), there is an understandable reluctance on the part of environmentalists to "take rights seriously," or at least a reluctance to take them as seriously as the rights view contends we should. But this may be a case of environmentalists not seeing the forest for the trees—or, more accurately, of not seeing the trees for the forest. The implications of the successful development of a rights-based environmental ethic, one that made the case that individual inanimate natural objects (e.g., *this* redwood) have inherent value and a basic moral right to treatment respectful of that value, should be welcomed by environmentalists. If individual trees have inherent value, they have a kind of value that is not the same as, is not reducible to, and is incommensurate with the intrinsic values of the pleasures, preference-satisfactions, and the like, of others, and since the rights of the individual never are to be overridden merely on the grounds of aggregating such values for all those affected by the outcome, a rights-based environmental ethic would bar the door to those who would uproot wilderness in the name of "human progress," whether this progress be aggregated economic, educational, recreational, or other human interests. On the rights view, assuming this could be successfully extended to inanimate natural objects, our general policy regarding wilderness would be precisely what the preservationists want—namely, let it be! Before those who favor such preservation dismiss the rights view in favor of the holistic view more commonly voiced in environmental circles, they might think twice about the implications of the two. There is the danger that the baby will be thrown out with the bath water. A rights-based environmental ethic remains a live option, one that, though far from being established, merits continued explo-

ration. It ought not to be dismissed out of hand by environmentalists as being in principle antagonistic to the goals for which they work. It isn't. Were we to show proper respect for the rights of the individuals who make up the biotic community, would not the *community* be preserved? And is not that what the more holistic, systems-minded environmentalists want?

NOTES

1. Aldo Leopold, *A Sand County Almanac* (New York: Oxford University Press, 1949), p. 217.

2. Leopold, *A Sand County Almanac,* p. 209, emphasis added.

3. For further remarks on these matters, see my "What Sorts of Beings Can Have Rights?" and "The Nature and Possibility of an Environmental Ethic," both in Regan, *All That Dwell Therein.*

Biocentric Individualism

Gary Varner

INTRODUCTION

As a boy, I often wandered in the woods near my home in central Ohio. One August day, I dug up a maple seedling from the woods and planted it in one of my mother's flowerbeds beside the house. Within hours, the seedling was terribly wilted. Convinced that I had mortally wounded the plant, I felt a wave of guilt and, wishing to hasten what I believed to be its inevitable and imminent demise, I pulled it up, broke its small stalk repeatedly, and stuffed it in the trash. When my mother later explained that the plant was only in temporary shock from being transplanted

into full sun, I felt an even larger wave of guilt for having dispatched it unnecessarily.

Was I just a soft-headed lad? Even then, I did not think that the plant was conscious, and since childhood, I have not again tried to "euthanize" a doomed plant. I feel no guilt about weeding the garden, mowing the lawn, or driving over the plants which inevitably crowd the four wheel drive paths I gravitate towards while camping. Nevertheless, I now let "weeds" grow indiscriminately in my wooded backyard, I mow around the odd wildflower that pops up amid the Bermuda grass out front, and I sometimes swerve to avoid a plant when tracking solitude in my truck. I believe that insects are not conscious, that they are in the same category, morally speaking, as plants, yet I often carry cockroaches and wasps outside rather than kill them. I'll even pause while mowing to let a grasshopper jump to safety My relative diffidence regarding insects could just be erring on the side of caution. I believe that insects *probably* are not conscious, whereas I am *cock-sure* that plants are not; so when I do dispatch an insect, I make a point of crushing it quite thoroughly, including its head. Similarly, my current plant-regarding decisions are doubtless inspired in part by aesthetic judgments rather than concern for their non-conscious well-being. The wildflowers in my front yard are just more interesting to look at than a continuous stretch of Bermuda grass, and my unkempt backyard buffers me from my neighbors. Still, I believe it is better— *morally* better—that plants thrive rather than die, even if they do not benefit humans or other, conscious creatures. So if I was just soft-headed to feel bad about that maple seedling, then my gray matter hasn't quite firmed up yet.

But *am* I just soft-headed, or is there a rational case to be made for plants and other presumably nonconscious organisms? A few philosophers have thought so. The famous doctor and theologian, Albert Schweitzer, wrote:

> A man is truly ethical only when he obeys the compulsion to help all life which he is able to assist, and shrinks from injuring anything that lives. He does not ask how far this or that life deserves one's sympathy as being valuable, nor, beyond that, whether and to what degree it is capable of feeling. Life as such is sacred to him. He tears no leaf from a tree, plucks no flower, and takes care to crush no insect. If in summer he is working by lamplight, he prefers to keep the window shut and breathe a stuffy atmosphere rather than see one insect after another fall with singed wings upon his table.

> If he walks on the road after a shower and sees an earthworm which has strayed on it, . . . he lifts if from the deadly stone surface, and puts it on the grass. If he comes across an insect which has fallen into a puddle, he stops a moment in order to hold out a leaf or a stalk on which it can save itself. (Schweitzer 1955, p. 310)

And in the contemporary literature of environmental ethics, Paul Taylor's 1986 book, *Respect For Nature: A Theory of Environmental Ethics,* is a mustread for any serious student of the field. In it (and in a 1981 essay which is reproduced in this volume) Taylor argues that extending a Kantian ethic of respect to non-conscious individuals is plausible once one understands that organisms, "conscious or not, all are equally teleological centers of life in the sense that each is a unified system of goal-oriented activities directed toward their preservation and well-being," that each has a good of its own which is "prima facie worthy of being preserved or promoted as an end in itself and for the sake of the entity whose good it is" (Taylor 1981, pp. 210, 201 in original edition).

I call views like Schweitzer's and Taylor's *biocentric individualism,* because they attribute moral standing to all living things while denying that holistic entities like species or ecosystems have moral standing. Hence they are *bio*centric—rather than, say anthropocentric or sentientist—but they are still *individualist* views—rather than versions of holism.

Schweitzer's and Taylor's views differ in important ways. Perhaps most significantly, Schweitzer talks as if we incur guilt every time we harm a living thing, even when we do so to preserve human life. He writes:

> Whenever I in any way sacrifice or injure life, I am not within the sphere of the ethical, but I become guilty, whether it be egoistically guilty for the sake of maintaining my own existence or welfare, or unegoistically guilty for the sake of maintaining a greater number of other existences or their welfare. (Schweitzer 1955, p. 325).

In the '40s and '50s, Schweitzer was celebrated in the popular media for bringing modern hospital services to the heart of Africa. Yet he appears to have thought that he incurred guilt when he saved human lives by killing disease microbes, not to mention when he killed things to eat. By contrast, in his book, Taylor makes it clear that he believes we are justified in violating plants' (and some animals') most basic interests in a range of cases: certainly for the sake of surviving, but also for the sake of furthering non-basic, but culturally important, interests of humans. He does impose on this a requirement of "minimum wrong," that is, harming as few living things as possible in the process (Taylor 1986, p. 289), but Taylor, unlike Schweitzer, believes that we can prioritize interests in a way that justifies us in preserving our own lives and pursuing certain non-basic interests at the expense of plants' (and some animals') most basic interests.

I will return to this question of which interests take precedence in various cases of conflict later. That is certainly an important question for any biocentric individualist. After all, if you think that even disease microbes and radishes have moral standing, then you need an explanation of how your interests can override those of millions of plants and microbes which must be doomed in the course of living a full human life. Otherwise, you are left with Schweitzer's perpetual guilt. But if I wasn't just being a soft-headed lad when I regretted killing that maple seedling—if there is a rational case to be made for plants (and other non-conscious organisms) having moral standing—then the first question is: Why think this?

WHY THINK THAT PLANTS HAVE MORAL STANDING?

I have two basic arguments for the conclusion that they do. Before discussing these arguments, however, it is important to be more clear about what, specifically, is being asked.

As I use the terms, to say that an entity has moral standing is to say that it has interests, and to say that it has interests is to say that it has needs and/or desires, and that the satisfaction of those needs and/or desires creates intrinsic value. When I say that their satisfaction creates intrinsic value, I mean that it makes the world a better place, independent of the entity's relations to other things. As the introduction to this volume emphasizes, the term "intrinsic value" is a key one in environmental ethics, but it is also a very nuanced one. There certainly is a distinction to be drawn between valuing something because it is useful, and valuing it apart from its usefulness. One

way of expressing the biocentric individualist stance, then, would be to describe it as the view that moral agents ought to value plants' lives intrinsically rather than merely instrumentally. However, putting it this way suggests that plants' flourishing might not be a good thing if there were no conscious valuers around to consider it, and one of my arguments for biocentric individualism purports to show that plants' flourishing is a good thing independent of there being any conscious valuers around at all. So I define biocentric individualism in terms of plants having interests, the satisfaction of which creates intrinsic value as defined above, whether or not there are any conscious valuers around.

A second thing to be clear about is what I mean by "plants." For simplicity's sake, I will speak simply of "plants," but unless stated otherwise, what I mean by this is *all non-conscious organisms*. Later I will take up the question of which non-human animals lack consciousness. For now, suffice it to say that even after the taxonomic revisions of the 1970s, the animal kingdom includes a number of organisms that are poor candidates for consciousness, e.g. barnacles and sponges. Besides plants, the new taxonomy includes three whole kingdoms, the members of which are equally poor candidates. The fungi are just heterotrophic plants. Organisms in the new kingdoms monera and protista—single celled organisms like bacteria and amoebas (respectively)—were previously classified as animals. But in this essay, "plants" is a shorthand for all of these non-conscious organisms.

In summary, I assume the following definitions of these key terms:

Moral standing: An entity has moral standing if and only if it has interests.

Interests: An entity has interests if and only if the fulfillment of its needs and/or desires creates intrinsic value.

Intrinsic value: Intrinsic value is the value something has independently of its relationships to other things. If a thing has intrinsic value, then its existence (flourishing, etc.) makes the world a better place, independently of its value to anything else or any other entity's awareness of it.

Plants: Unless stated otherwise, "plants" refers to all non-conscious organisms, including (presumably) all members of the plant kingdom, but also all members of the kingdoms fungi, monera, and protista, as well as some members of the animal kingdom (to be specified later).

So the question is: Why think that all those "plants" have interests, the satisfaction of which creates intrinsic value, independently of any conscious organism's interest in them?

My first argument for this conclusion is developed in detail in my book, *In Nature's Interests?* (Varner 1998, chapter three). There I argue against the dominant, mental state theory of individual welfare (for short, the mental state theory). The dominant account of individual welfare in recent Western moral philosophy has identified what is in an individual's interests with what the individual actually desires, plus what the individual would desire if he or she were both adequately informed and impartial across phases of his or her life. This dominant account then identifies what is in an individual's *best* interests with the latter, with what he or she would desire under those idealized conditions. Formally:

The mental state theory of individual welfare: X is in an individual A's interests just in case:

1. A actually desires X, or
2. A would desire X if A were sufficiently informed and impartial across phases of his or her life; and
3. What is in A's *best* interests is defined in terms of clause (2).

Something like this theory is accepted by most contemporary moral and political philosophers.

My first argument for the moral standing of plants begins by pointing to an inadequacy of the mental state theory.

Argument 1: The mental state theory seems to provide an inadequate account of the interests of conscious individuals. If that is so, and if the way to fix it involves acknowledging that intrinsic value is created by the satisfaction of non-conscious, biologically based needs of such individuals, then it makes sense to attribute interests to plants. For although plants are incapable of having desires, they have biologically based needs just as do conscious individuals.

Here is an example that brings out the problem I see in the mental state theory:

Example 1: By the nineteenth century, British mariners were carrying citrus fruit on long sea voyages to prevent the debilitating disease of scurvy. It was not until this century that scientists discovered that we need about 10 milligrams of ascorbic acid a day, and that citrus fruits prevent scurvy because they contain large amounts of ascorbic acid.

To see how this raises a problem, consider what is meant by being "adequately informed" in the second clause of the mental state theory. Some authors limit "adequate information" to the best scientific knowledge of the day. But then it would be false that those mariners had any interest in getting 10 milligrams of ascorbic acid a day. This is because they did not in fact desire it (they did not even know it exists), and even having the best scientific knowledge of the day would not have led them to desire it because no one then knew about it. The problem is that it certainly seems wrong to say that getting 10 milligrams of ascorbic acid a day was not in their interests.

This problem is easily avoided by adding a clause about biologically based needs to our theory of individual welfare. Renamed appropriately, the theory would now be something like this:

The psycho-biological theory of individual welfare: X is in an individual A's interests just in case:

1. A actually desires X,
2. A would desire X if A were sufficiently informed and impartial across phases of his or her life; or
3. X serves some biologically based need of A.

In my book (Varner 1998, pp. 64–71), I give a detailed analysis of the complex notion of a biologically based need, arguing that these can be determined by examining the evolutionary history of an organism. Here, I think it unnecessary to revisit that analysis. Ascorbic acid clearly served a biologically based need of sailors before modern scientists discovered it. So, on this psycho-biological theory, it was in those sailors' interest to get enough of it, even though no one knew anything about ascorbic acid at the time.

Note that this new theory says nothing about what is in one's *best* interests. I replaced clause (3) in the mental state theory rather than adding another clause because identifying what is in one's best interests with what one would desire under ideal motivational and informational conditions—clause (2)—faces similar problems. Other things being equal, it seems that getting enough ascorbic acid was in those mariners' best interests, even though they would still not have desired it even under the best motivational and informational conditions. So even after adding a clause about biologically based needs, it would still be a mistake to identify what is in one's best interests with clause (2).

One limitation of the nineteenth-century mariners example is that being "sufficiently informed" can be analyzed other than in terms of having "the best scientific knowledge of the day." We could, for instance, analyze it in terms of having all the scientific knowledge that humans will ever or could ever accumulate. I believe there are other problems with this analysis (see Varner 1998, pp. 58–60), but it would solve the problem raised by the above example. However, here is another example that brings out the same kind of problem with the mental state theory, and where the alternative analysis of "sufficiently informed" doesn't help:

Example 2: Like many cat owners, I grapple with the question of whether and when to allow my cat, Nanci, to go outside. Cats find the outdoors endlessly fascinating, but they also encounter health risks outside, including exposure to feline leukemia virus (FeLV) and fleas (which Nanci happens to be allergic to).

I frankly do not know whether or not keeping Nanci indoors is in her best interests, all things considered. Nonetheless, it does seem clear that keeping her inside would serve some interests of hers, in at least some ways. For instance, it would prevent exposure to FeLV and fleas. Yet the mental state theory does not support this intuition because it is not clear that it even makes sense to talk about what an animal like Nanci would desire if she were "sufficiently informed and impartial across phases of her life." I assume that Nanci is congenitally incapable of understanding the relevant information about FeLV and fleas. So on the mental state theory, what are we to say about her going outside? It looks like we have to conclude that, whenever she in fact wants to go out, she has no interest whatsoever in staying inside, because clause (2) is irrelevant in her case. It just doesn't make sense, in the case of animals like Nanci, to talk about what they would desire were they "sufficiently informed" (let alone "impartial across phases of their lives"). What is in their interests is whatever they happen to desire at any moment in time. This is another counter-intuitive implication of the mental state theory, and one which the psycho-biological theory avoids. Although the psycho-biological theory as formulated above is silent on the issue of what is in an individual's best interests, it at least supports the intuition that Nanci has some interest in staying inside (because doing so would serve her biologically based needs by preventing exposure to FeLV and fleas), even if she now desires to go outside and no sense can be made of what an animal like her would desire under ideal epistemological and motivational conditions.

The examples of Nanci and the nineteenth-century mariners together illustrate a general problem for the mental state theory. The theory ties all of our interests to what we desire, either actually or under ideal epistemological and motivational conditions, but not all of our interests are tied in this way to our conscious desires and beliefs. Most (maybe even all) of our desires are tied to our beliefs about the world, because as our beliefs change, our desires change. For instance, suppose that I desire to marry Melody, primarily because I believe that she is a fine fiddler. When I find out that my belief about her is false, my desire to marry her will presumably be extinguished. Similarly, if I do not desire to marry Melinda only because I believe that she is a lousy fiddler, when I find out that she is actually a virtuoso, I will presumably form a desire to marry her. My interest in marrying each woman comes and goes with my beliefs about her. However, nothing I could possibly believe about the world, whether true or false, could change the fact that I need about 10 milligrams a day of ascorbic acid to stay healthy, and no matter how strongly I might desire it, I will never be able to make it true that going without ascorbic acid is in my interest. My interest in ascorbic acid is determined by a biological need that exists wholly independent of my beliefs and desires. This is a central advantage of the psycho-biological theory over the mental state theory. Some things are only in our interests if we happen to desire them or have certain beliefs about the world, but other things are in our interests no matter what we desire or believe, or what we would desire and believe under ideal conditions. We can refer to the former as preference interests and to the latter as biological interests. The mental state theory errs by identifying all of our interests with our preference interests. The psycho-biological theory acknowledges these, but also accounts for biological interests that are wholly independent of our preference interests.

That being said, my first argument for the moral standing of plants is now complete. The above examples are intended to illustrate how the dominant, mental state theory of individual welfare is flawed, because it ties all of individuals' interests to their actual or hypothetical desires. An obvious way to fix this problem is to hold that individuals also have biological interests in the fulfillment of their various

biologically based needs, whether they (like the nineteenth-century mariners) could only become aware of these needs under special circumstances, or they (like Nanci the cat) are congenitally incapable of desiring that those needs be fulfilled. But then, since plants too have biologically based needs, they too have interests, even though they are congenitally incapable of desiring anything at all.

I did not include my second argument for the view that plants have moral standing in my 1998 book because, frankly, I doubted that it would be persuasive to anyone not already essentially convinced. Nevertheless, I think that this second argument expresses very clearly the most basic value assumption of the biocentric individualist. It also ties in to famous thought experiments in ethical theory and environmental ethics, and so I include it here.

The argument is driven by a variant of a famous thought experiment that British philosopher G. E. Moore used to cast doubt on sentientism (the view that only sentient—that is conscious—organisms have moral standing). Moore discussed the classical utilitarians (Jeremy Bentham, John Stuart Mill, and Henry Sidgwick, who were all sentientists) at length and in particular responded to Sidgwick's claim that "No one would consider it rational to aim at the production of beauty in external nature, apart from any possible contemplation of it by human beings." Moore responded:

Well, I may say at once, that I, for one, do consider this rational; and let us see if I cannot get any one to agree with me. Consider what this admission really means. It entitles us to put the following case. Let us imagine one world exceedingly beautiful. Imagine it as beautiful as you can; put into it whatever on this earth you most admire—mountains, rivers, the sea; trees, and sunsets, stars and moon. Imagine these all combined in the most exquisite proportions, so that no one thing jars against another, but each contributes to increase the beauty of the whole. And then imagine the ugliest world you can possibly conceive. Imagine it simply one heap of filth, containing everything that is most disgusting to us, for whatever reason, and the whole, as far as may be, without one redeeming feature. Such a pair of worlds we are entitled to compare: they fall within Prof. Sidgwick's meaning, and the comparison is highly relevant to it. The only thing we are not entitled to imagine is that any human being ever has or ever, by any possibility, *can,* live in either, can ever see and enjoy the beauty of the one or hate the foulness of the other. Well, even so, supposing them quite apart from any possible contemplation by human beings; still, is it irrational to hold that it is better that the beautiful world should exist, than the one which is ugly? Would it not be well, in any case, to do what we could to produce it rather than the other? (Moore 1903, p. 83)

Moore thought we would agree with him in answering yes. But then, he continued:

If it be once admitted that the beautiful world *in itself* is better than the ugly, then it follows, that however many beings may enjoy it, and however much better their enjoyment may be than it is itself, yet its mere existence adds *something* to the goodness of the whole . . . (Moore 1903, pp. 83–85; emphases in original)

That is, Moore concluded, the mere existence of beauty adds intrinsic value to the world.

I have always been unsure what to think about Moore's thought experiment, so apparently I am of two minds when it comes to saying that the mere existence of beauty adds intrinsic value to the world. However, I have always felt certain about my answer to an analogous question. Suppose that instead of choosing between creating a beautiful world and an ugly world, the choice were between creating a world devoid of life and a world brimming with living things, neither of which would ever evolve conscious life or even be visited or known about by any conscious organisms. If, like me, you believe that it matters which world is produced and that it would be better to produce the world chock-full of non-conscious life, then you seem to be committed to biocentric individualism. For you appear to believe that life—even non-conscious life— has intrinsic value. To paraphrase Moore:

Argument 2: If we admit that a world of non-conscious living things is *in itself* better than a world devoid of all life, then it follows that however much better it is to be both conscious and alive, the mere existence of non-conscious life adds *something* to the goodness of the world.

Note that this contrasts with the "last man" thought experiment, as characterized in the introduction to this volume (where the last person on earth destroys a tree "just for fun"), in two important ways. First, in my variant of Moore's thought experiment, it is stipulated that there is no person on the scene at all. This is important because an anthropocentrist might try to explain the problem with the last man in terms of his action's effects on his own character. Second, and more importantly, in the "last man" case, the tree is said to be "the last remaining Redwood," but in my variant of Moore's thought experiment, nothing is said about the plants in question being rare. If we agree that it matters which of my worlds is produced, and that it would be better to produce the plant-filled world, then we seem to agree that the lives of even the most mundane plants add intrinsic value to the world.

JUST WHAT ARE PLANTS' INTERESTS WORTH?

The next question has to be: Just *how valuable* are the interests of plants, in relation to those of humans and other animals? Moral hierarchies are unpopular in many quarters. In particular, feminist philosophers often condemn hierarchical views of beings' relative moral significance for being instruments of patriarchal oppression (see, for instance, Karen Warren's contribution to this volume). But as a biocentric individualist, I feel forced to endorse one. Otherwise, how could I live with myself? I gleefully tear radishes from the garden for a snack, swatting mosquitoes all the while. I take antibiotics for a persistent sinus infection, and (at least when I'm not on antibiotics) I send countless intestinal bacteria on a deadly joyride into the city sewer system every morning. Unless I can give good reasons for thinking that my interests somehow trump those of microbes and plants (if not also animals), I am left with Albert Schweitzer's view, quoted above, that we "become guilty" whenever we "in any way sacrifice or injure life," even when fighting off disease organisms, eating, and defecating. In my book (Varner 1998, chapter four), I argue that a plausible assumption about what I call "hierarchically structured interests" does the trick, when coupled with empirical observations about certain broad categories of interests.

Here is what I mean by hierarchically structured interests:

Hierarchically structured interests: Two interests are hierarchically structured when the satisfaction of one requires the satisfaction of the other, but not vice-versa.

Certain types of interests clearly stand in this relationship to other types of interests. For example, satisfying my desire to succeed professionally requires the satisfaction of innumerable more particular desires across decades, but not vice-versa. It takes years to succeed professionally, and therefore I have to satisfy innumerable day-to-day desires to eat this or that in the course of completing that long-term project. But each particular desire to eat can be satisfied without satisfying my long-term desire to succeed professionally. So my desires to eat and to succeed professionally are hierarchically structured in the above sense.

Generally, what the contemporary American philosopher Bernard Williams calls "ground projects" and "categorical desires" stand in this relationship to day-to-day desires for particular things. Here is how Williams defines these terms:

Ground projects and categorical desires: A ground project is "a nexus of projects . . . which are closely related to [one's] existence and which to a significant degree give a meaning to [one's] life," and a categorical desire is one that answers the question "Why is life worth living?" (Williams 1981, pp. 13, 12; 1973, pp. 85–86)

A person's ground project normally is a nexus of categorical desires, and generally, a ground project requires decades to complete. There are, of course, exceptions. It is conceivable that a person might have literally only one categorical desire, a desire which he or she could satisfy in one fell swoop. Perhaps a young gymnast aiming at a gold medal in the Olympics is a realistic approximation of this, but notice that even in the case of the gymnast: (1) satisfying the desire for a gold medal requires years of training, and (2) we would probably think it unhealthy and abnormal if the gymnast had no other ground project, if there were no other, longer-term desires that made her life worth living beyond the Olympics. So a ground project normally involves a host of very long-term desires, which bear the above kind of hierarchical relationship with the individual's day-to-day desires for this or that specific thing.

Here is a plausible assumption about interests that are clearly hierarchically structured:

Assumption: Generally speaking, ensuring the satisfaction of interests from similar levels in similar hierarchies of different individuals creates similar amounts of value, and the dooming of interests from similar levels in similar hierarchies of different individuals creates similar levels of disvalue.

In stating the assumption in this way, I do not mean to imply that we can make very fine-tuned judgements about which interests are more valuable than others.[1] All I claim is that interests from certain very broad categories *generally* bear this relationship to interests from other very broad categories. In particular, I argue that the following two principles are reasonable in light of the assumption:

Principle P1 (the priority of desires principle): Generally speaking, the death of an entity that has desires is a worse thing than the death of an entity that does not.

Principle P2′ (the priority of ground projects principle): Generally speaking, the satisfaction of ground projects is more important than the satisfaction of non-categorical desires.

Since I introduced the above assumption by discussing human ground projects, let me begin with principle P2′.

I call it P2′, rather than just P2, because in my book I first introduce, and dismiss, this principle:

Principle P2 (the priority of *human* desires principle): The satisfaction of the desires of humans is more important than the satisfaction of the desires of animals.

Principle P2 would solve the problem under discussion in this section, but it is transparently speciesist. It says that humans' desires are more important than any other organisms' simply because they are desires of *humans*. Principle P2′ compares ground projects to non-categorical desires without asserting that humans' desires are more important than any other organisms'. If it turns out that some non-human animals have ground projects, then Principle P2′ applies equally to theirs. Which animals, if any, have ground projects is an empirical question, as is the question of whether all human beings do. Surely some human beings do not. For instance, anencephalic babies and the permanently comatose clearly do not, and perhaps others, like the most profoundly retarded, or those who have lost the will to live, do not. Regarding animals, my hunch is that very few if any non-human animals have ground projects, but maybe some do (perhaps some great apes or cetaceans). The crucial thing to note is that principle P2′ is not speciesist. It does not say that humans' interests are more important *because they are humans' interests*. Principle P2′ only says that ground projects, wherever they occur, generally have more value than non-categorical desires. P2′ leaves the question of which beings have ground projects open for empirical investigation; it does not stipulate that only humans have this especially valuable kind of interest.

So why think that ground projects are more valuable than non-categorical desires? The reason is that, as we saw above, ground projects normally stand in a hierarchical relationship to day-to-day desires for particular things; satisfying a ground project requires the satisfaction of innumerable day-to-day desires for particular things, but not vice-versa. So under the above assumption (that various interests within each type generally have similar amounts of value), satisfying a ground project generally creates more value than satisfying any such day-to-day desire.

I will discuss the implications of P2′ in the next section, along with those of P1. First, however, let me discuss the justification of P1. Notice that P1 does not assert that just any desire trumps any biological need or set thereof. Some day-to-day desires for particular things are incredibly trivial and it would be implausible to say that these trivial desires trump seemingly important biological interests like one's biological interest in good cardiovascular health. But all that principle P1 states is that "Generally speaking, the death of an entity that has desires is a worse thing than the death of an entity that does not." This is plausible under the assumption stated above, given the following general fact: maintenance of the capacity to form and satisfy desires requires the on-going satisfaction of the lion's share of one's biological needs. Certainly not every biological need of a conscious organism must be fulfilled for it to go on forming desires. In particular, the account I give in my book implies that the continued functioning of my vasa deferentia is in my biological interest (Varner 1998, p. 97), but obviously I would go on desiring sex (among other things) after a vasectomy. One of the deep challenges to my position (as Vermont philosopher Bill Throop has driven home to me in conversation) is deciding how to individuate interests. Do I have just one biological interest in the continued functioning of my whole cardiovascular system? One interest in the functioning of my heart and another in the functioning of my vascular system? Or do I have myriad interests, in the functioning of my various ventricles, veins, arteries, and so on? This is a difficult issue, but however it gets sorted out, it seems plausible to say that just as satisfying a ground project requires the satisfaction of innumerable day-to-day desires for particular things, maintaining the general capacity to form and satisfy desires requires the on-going satisfaction of the lion's share of one's biological needs. As a conscious process, maintenance of the capacity to form and satisfy desires presumably requires maintenance of myriad biological organs and subsystems, including, at the very least, the respiratory and cardiovascular systems, and most of the central nervous system. The argument for principle P1, then, is this: The only interests plants have in common with conscious organisms are biological interests. The ability to form and satisfy desires stands in a hierarchical relationship to such biological interests. But if interests of these two types generally have similar value, then conscious animals' lives have more value than plants' lives, because animals satisfy both types of interests in the course of their lives, whereas plants satisfy only one type.

The question posed in this section has not been answered precisely. My argument has not shown precisely how much the interests of plants are worth, relative to the interests of humans or other animals. For reasons given in my book (Varner 1998, pp. 80–88), I think it is impossible to give such a precise answer to this question. However, if principle P1 is indeed justified by the principle of inclusiveness (coupled with the assumption articulated above), then it is plausible to conclude that the *lives* of plants are, generally, less valuable than the *lives* of desiring creatures, including yours and mine. And that goes a long way towards showing that biocentric individualism is a practicable view, although most environmental philosophers have doubted that it is.

IS BIOCENTRIC INDIVIDUALISM PRACTICABLE?

One reason for doubt would be that before Paul Taylor, the only well-known biocentric individualist was Albert Schweitzer, and as we have seen, he said flatly that we are guilty for merely keeping ourselves alive

by eating and fighting disease. However, as the foregoing section shows, a biocentric individualist can reasonably endorse a hierarchy of interests and related principles showing why it is better that we do this than let ourselves perish. We can at least say that my view implies this rough hierarchy of value:

ground projects

non-categorical desires

biological interests

Principle P2′ states that the satisfaction of a ground project is better than (creates more value than) the satisfaction of any interest of the other two kinds. Thus killing an individual with a ground project robs the world of a special kind of value. According to principle P1, the lives of many non-human animals have more value than the lives of plants, because these conscious organisms have both biological interests and non-categorical desires, whereas plants have only biological interests. Thus killing an animal robs the world of more value than does killing a plant.

The second part of this value hierarchy focuses attention on questions about consciousness that were alluded to earlier: which animals are conscious, which ones have desires? These questions are related, but not equivalent. I assume that all "genuine" desires are conscious, or at least potentially conscious, just as pain is. However, the evidence for desires in non-human animals may not overlap the evidence for pain, because I also assume that desires require relatively sophisticated cognitive capacities, whereas the bare consciousness of pain may not. A detailed treatment of this issue is beyond the scope of this essay, but here is a summary of the conclusions I reach from the more detailed treatment in my book (Varner 1998, pp. 26–30). All normal, mature mammals and birds very probably *do* have desires, and there is a somewhat weaker case for saying that "herps" (reptiles and amphibians) do too. The case for saying that fish have desires is decisively weaker. However, the available evidence makes it very likely that all vertebrates, including fish, can feel pain. This is a curious result—it sounds odd to say that fish could feel pain without desiring an end to it—and so I suspect that as more kinds of scientific studies are available than I considered in my book, the evidence for pain and for desire in the animal kingdom will converge. However, for the sake of discussion here, I assume that although mammals and birds have desires, fish and invertebrates do not.[2]

We can now spell out more specifically the implications of the principles defended in the preceding section. Principle P1 tells us that it is better to kill desireless organisms than desiring ones. This addresses Schweitzer's hyperbolic guilt, because it shows that it would be worse for a human being to kill herself than it would be for her to kill any plant or microbe for the sake of good nutrition or fighting off disease. However, in light of the above discussion of consciousness, this does not imply that vegetarian diets are better, since most invertebrates apparently lack consciousness, and even fish may lack desires. Also, since it is possible to obtain animal byproducts like eggs and dairy foods from animals without killing them, a lacto-ovo diet might be perfectly respectful of animals' intrinsic value. (There are other ethical considerations, of course, as well as complicated issues in human nutrition. For an overview, see the essays in Comstock 1994.)

I also suspect that Principle P2′ can be used to make a case for the humane killing of animals who clearly have (non-categorical) desires. My reasoning is as follows. To the extent that hunting and slaughter-based animal agriculture play an important role in sustainable human communities, the value of protecting the background conditions for satisfying humans' ground projects would seem to support the necessary killing, at least if the animals live good lives and are killed humanely. Obviously, various animals, including mammals and birds, played a very large role in both paleolithic hunting-gathering societies and in the emergence of agriculture. Domesticated mammals continue to have a crucial role in sustainable agricultural systems in so-called "developing" nations, where they provide not only food but draft power and fertilizer. But at present it is still un-

clear to me just how much killing of animals might be necessary in utopian sustainable communities of the future.

In light of these implications of Principles P1 and P2′, the biocentric individualist stance hardly looks unlivable in the way Schweitzer's talk of perpetual guilt would suggest. There is a deeper reason that many environmental philosophers dismiss the biocentric individualist stance, however. They fear that it somehow devalues nature and thus, even if it is not literally an unlivable ethic, it is "inadequate" as an *environmental* ethic. This charge of "inadequacy" takes at least two distinct forms, and the biocentric individualist response to each must be different.

First, it is often claimed that individualist theories in general (that is, anthropocentrism and sentientism in addition to biocentric individualism) have implications that do not comport with the environmentalist agenda, which includes things like endangered species programs, the elimination of exotic species from natural areas, and the whole emphasis on preserving remaining natural areas. The heart of this claim is that because they focus on individuals, such theories get the wrong answers in a range of cases. For instance, environmentalists are keenly interested in preserving remaining natural areas, but, so this objection goes, biocentric individualism cannot justify this emphasis. For if we compare a woods and a cultivated field, or an old growth forest and a managed timber lot, they may look equally valuable from a biocentric individualist stance. Simply put, if only biological interests are at stake, then a cultivated area supporting thousands of thriving plants creates just as much value as a wild area that supports the same number of plants. Similarly, the biological interests of common plants seem no more valuable than the biological interests of rare plants.

This first version of the "inadequacy" charge misfires precisely because there *is* more at stake than the biological interests of the plants involved. Environmentalists commonly claim that in order to preserve the ecological context in which humans can live healthy, productive, and innovative lives into the indefinite future, we must stop the current trend of species extinctions and preserve most remaining wild areas. Characterizing the environmentalists' claim as a general need to safeguard background biological diversity in our environment, my response to the first version of the inadequacy charge is this. Principle P2′ attaches preeminent importance to safeguarding humans' ability to satisfy their ground projects. But if safeguarding this ability requires safeguarding background biological diversity in our environment, then doing so is of preeminent importance, at least instrumentally, in my view. That is, to the extent that environmentalists are correct that their practical agenda safeguards long-term human interests, any version of biocentric individualism which, like mine, attributes preeminent importance to certain interests of humans can probably endorse their agenda.

At this point it is important to note that two senses of the term "anthropocentric" are sometimes conflated in discussions of environmental ethics. In one sense of the term, a view is anthropocentric just in case it denies that non-human nature has any intrinsic value whatsoever. Obviously, biocentric individualism is not anthropocentric in this sense. But in another sense, a view is called anthropocentric if it gives pride of place to certain interests which only humans have. Schweitzer's version of biocentric individualism is not anthropocentric in this second sense, but because I doubt that any non-human animals have ground projects, mine is. For clarity's sake, I use the labels "valuational anthropocentrism" and "axiological anthropocentrism" to refer, respectively, to views that deny all intrinsic value to non-humans and to views that acknowledge the intrinsic value of some non-human beings but insist that only humans have certain preeminently important interests (Varner 1998, p. 121).

The other form of the "inadequacy" charge focuses on the fact that for the biocentric individualist, even if holistic entities like species and ecosystems have enormous value, this value is still only instrumental. Environmentalists, it is claimed, tend to think that such entities have intrinsic value rather than merely instrumental value, and thus environmentalists tend to think more like holists.

I think this version of the "inadequacy" charge misconstrues one of the central questions of environmental ethics. As environmental philosophers, we should not think of ourselves as focusing on the question: What do environmentalists *in fact* think has intrinsic value? Rather, we should be asking: What *should* we think has intrinsic value? Or, what do we *have good reasons* to think has intrinsic value? Defining an "adequate" environmental ethic as one that matches the pre-theoretic intuitions of self-professed environmentalists turns the discipline of environmental ethics into a kind of moral anthropology rather than a reasoned search for truth. In this essay, I have not developed a case against environmental holism, but the arguments of this section do show that biocentric individualism cannot be summarily dismissed as impracticable, either generally or in regard to environmental policy specifically.

CONCLUSION

My larger goal in this essay has been to show that one need not be soft-headed to think that it matters, morally speaking, how we treat plants. It would, in my judgment, be unreasonable to obsess on the microbes one's immune system is killing every day or on how one's dinner vegetables were dealt their death-blows, but it is not irrational to think that it is good to save the life of plants and non-conscious animals when one can. Good arguments can be given for thinking this, and someone who thinks this can consistently live a good human life.

And, of course, if it is reasonable to think that plants' lives have intrinsic value, then it was not irrational for me to feel at least a little bit guilty about killing that maple seedling unnecessarily.

SOURCES CITED

Comstock, Gary. "Might Morality Require Veganism?" Special issue of *Journal of Agricultural and Environmental Ethics* 7, no. 1 (1994).

Moore, G. E. *Principia Ethica*. London: Cambridge University Press, 1903.

Schweitzer, Albert. *The Philosophy of Civilization.* New York: Macmillan, 1955.

Taylor, Paul. "The Ethics of Respect for Nature." *Environmental Ethics* 3 (1981): 197–218.

Taylor, Paul. *Respect for Nature: A Theory of Environmental Ethics.* Princeton: Princeton University Press, 1986.

Varner, Gary E. *In Nature's Interests? Interests, Animal Rights, and Environmental Ethics.* New York: Oxford University Press, 1998.

Williams, Bernard. *Problems of the Self.* Cambridge: Cambridge University Press, 1973.

Williams, Bernard. *Moral Luck.* Cambridge: Cambridge University Press, 1981.

NOTES

1. Strictly speaking, my view is that the *satisfaction* of interests creates intrinsic value, but in this essay I speak interchangeably of "the value of various interests," "the value of various interests' satisfaction," and "the value created by the satisfaction of various interests."

2. The issue is further complicated by the phenomenon of convergent evolution—some invertebrates could have evolved coping strategies that most other invertebrates have not. In particular, cephalopods (octopus, squid, and cuttlefish) may have evolved consciousness of pain and cognitive capacities that other invertebrates lack but most or all vertebrates have.

Deep Ecology

Bill Devall and George Sessions

The term *deep ecology* was coined by Arne Naess in his 1973 article, "The Shallow and the Deep, Long-Range Ecology Movements."[1] Naess was attempting to describe the deeper, more spiritual approach to Nature exemplified in the writings of Aldo Leopold and Rachel Carson. He thought that this deeper approach resulted from a more sensitive openness to ourselves and nonhuman life around us. The essence of deep ecology is to keep asking more searching questions about human life, society, and Nature as in the Western philosophical tradition of Socrates. As examples of this deep questioning, Naess points out "that we ask why and how, where others do not. For instance, ecology as a science does not ask what kind of a society would be the best for maintaining a particular ecosystem—that is considered a question for value theory, for politics, for ethics." Thus deep ecology goes beyond the so-called factual scientific level to the level of self and Earth wisdom.

Deep ecology goes beyond a limited piecemeal shallow approach to environmental problems and attempts to articulate a comprehensive religious and philosophical worldview. The foundations of deep ecology are the basic intuitions and experiencing of ourselves and Nature which comprise ecological consciousness. Certain outlooks on politics and public policy flow naturally from this consciousness. And in the context of this book, we discuss the minority tradition as the type of community most conducive both to cultivating ecological consciousness and to asking the basic questions of values and ethics addressed in these pages.

Many of these questions are perennial philosophical and religious questions faced by humans in all cultures over the ages. What does it mean to be a

Bill Devall and George Sessions, *Deep Ecology* (Salt Lake: Peregrine Smith, 1985), 65–77. Reprinted with permission of the publisher, Gibbs Smith.

unique human individual? How can the individual self maintain and increase its uniqueness while also being an inseparable aspect of the whole system wherein there are no sharp breaks between self and the *other?* An ecological perspective, in this deeper sense, results in what Theodore Roszak calls "an awakening of wholes greater than the sum of their parts. In spirit, the discipline is contemplative and therapeutic."[2]

Ecological consciousness and deep ecology are in sharp contrast with the dominant worldview of technocratic-industrial societies which regards humans as isolated and fundamentally separate from the rest of Nature, as superior to, and in charge of, the rest of creation. But the view of humans as separate and superior to the rest of Nature is only part of larger cultural patterns. For thousands of years, Western culture has become increasingly obsessed with the idea of *dominance:* with dominance of humans over nonhuman Nature, masculine over the feminine, wealthy and powerful over the poor, with the dominance of the West over non-Western cultures. Deep ecological consciousness allows us to see through these erroneous and dangerous illusions.

For deep ecology, the study of our place in the Earth household includes the study of ourselves as part of the organic whole. Going beyond a narrowly materialist scientific understanding of reality, the spiritual and the material aspects of reality fuse together. While the leading intellectuals of the dominant worldview have tended to view religion as "just superstition," and have looked upon ancient spiritual practice and enlightenment, such as found in Zen Buddhism, as essentially subjective, the search for deep ecological consciousness is the search for a more objective consciousness and state of being through an active deep questioning and meditative process and way of life.

Many people have asked these deeper questions and cultivated ecological consciousness within the context of different spiritual traditions—Christianity, Taoism, Buddhism, and Native American rituals, for example. While differing greatly in other regards, many in these traditions agree with the basic principles of deep ecology.

Warwick Fox, an Australian philosopher, has succinctly expressed the central intuition of deep ecology: "It is the idea that we can make no firm ontological divide in the field of existence: That there is no bifurcation in reality between the human and the non-human realms . . . to the extent that we perceive boundaries, we fall short of deep ecological consciousness."[3]

From this most basic insight or characteristic of deep ecological consciousness, Arne Naess has developed two *ultimate norms* or intuitions which are themselves not derivable from other principles or intuitions. They are arrived at by the deep questioning process and reveal the importance of moving to the philosophical and religious level of wisdom. They cannot be validated, of course, by the methodology of modern science based on its usual mechanistic assumptions and its very narrow definition of data. These ultimate norms are *self-realization* and *biocentric equality.*

SELF-REALIZATION

In keeping with the spiritual traditions of many of the world's religions, the deep ecology norm of self-realization goes beyond the modern Western *self* which is defined as an isolated ego striving primarily for hedonistic gratification or for a narrow sense of individual salvation in this life or the next. This socially programmed sense of the narrow self or social self dislocates us, and leaves us prey to whatever fad or fashion is prevalent in our society or social reference group. We are thus robbed of beginning the search for our unique spiritual/biological personhood. Spiritual growth, or unfolding, begins when we cease to understand or see ourselves as isolated and narrow competing egos and begin to identify with other humans from our family and friends to, eventually, our species. But the deep ecology sense of self requires a further maturity and growth, an identification which goes beyond humanity to include the nonhuman world. We must see beyond our narrow contemporary cultural assumptions and values, and the conventional wisdom of our time and place, and this is best achieved by the meditative deep questioning process. Only in this way can we hope to attain full mature personhood and uniqueness.

A nurturing nondominating society can help in the "real work" of becoming a whole person. The "real work" can be summarized symbolically as the realization of "self-in-Self" where "Self" stands for organic wholeness. This process of the full unfolding of the self can also be summarized by the phrase, "No one is saved until we are all saved," where the phrase "one" includes not only me, an individual human, but all humans, whales, grizzly bears, whole rain forest ecosystems, mountains and rivers, the tiniest microbes in the soil, and so on.

BIOCENTRIC EQUALITY

The intuition of biocentric equality is that all things in the biosphere have an equal right to live and blossom and to reach their own individual forms of unfolding and self-realization within the larger Self-realization. This basic intuition is that all organisms and entities in the ecosphere, as parts of the interrelated whole, are equal in intrinsic worth. Naess suggests that biocentric equality as an intuition is true in principle, although in the process of living, all species use each other as food, shelter, etc. Mutual predation is a biological fact of life, and many of the world's religions have struggled with the spiritual implications of this. Some animal liberationists who attempt to side-step this problem by advocating vegetarianism are forced to say that the entire plant kingdom including rain forests have no right to their own existence. This evasion flies in the face of the basic intuition of equality.[4] Aldo Leopold expressed this intuition when he said humans are "plain citizens" of the biotic community, not lord and master over all other species.

Biocentric equality is intimately related to the all-inclusive Self-realization in the sense that if we harm the rest of Nature then we are harming ourselves. There are no boundaries and everything is interrelated. But insofar as we perceive things as individual organisms or entities, the insight draws us to respect all human and nonhuman individuals in their own right as parts of the whole without feeling the need to set up hierarchies of species with humans at the top.

The practical implications of this intuition or norm suggest that we should live with minimum rather than maximum impact on other species and on the Earth in general. Thus we see another as our guiding principle: "simple in means, rich in ends." . . .

A fuller discussion of the biocentric norm as it unfolds itself in practice begins with the realization that we, as individual humans, and as communities of humans, have vital needs which go beyond such basics as food, water, and shelter to include love, play, creative expression, intimate relationships with a particular landscape (or Nature taken in its entirety) as well as intimate relationships with other humans, and the vital need for spiritual growth, for becoming a mature human being.

Our vital material needs are probably more simple than many realize. In technocratic-industrial societies there is overwhelming propaganda and advertising which encourages false needs and destructive desires designed to foster increased production and consumption of goods. Most of this actually diverts us from facing reality in an objective way and from beginning the "real work" of spiritual growth and maturity.

Many people who do not see themselves as supporters of deep ecology nevertheless recognize an overriding vital human need for a healthy and high-quality natural environment for humans, if not for all life, with minimum intrusion of toxic waste, nuclear radiation from human enterprises, minimum acid rain and smog, and enough free flowing wilderness so humans can get in touch with their sources, the natural rhythms and the flow of time and place.

Drawing from the minority tradition and from the wisdom of many who have offered the insight of interconnectedness, we recognize that deep ecologists can offer suggestions for gaining maturity and encouraging the processes of harmony with Nature, but that there is no grand solution which is guaranteed to save us from ourselves.

The ultimate norms of deep ecology suggest a view of the nature of reality and our place as an individual (many in the one) in the larger scheme of things. They cannot be fully grasped intellectually but are ultimately experiential.

BASIC PRINCIPLES OF DEEP ECOLOGY

In April 1984, during the advent of spring and John Muir's birthday, George Sessions and Arne Naess summarized fifteen years of thinking on the principles of deep ecology while camping in Death Valley, California. In this great and special place, they articulated these principles in a literal, somewhat neutral way, hoping that they would be understood and accepted by persons coming from different philosophical and religious positions.

Readers are encouraged to elaborate their own versions of deep ecology, clarify key concepts and think through the consequences of acting from these principles.

Basic Principles

1. The well-being and flourishing of human and nonhuman Life on Earth have value in themselves (synonyms: intrinsic value, inherent value). These values are independent of the usefulness of the nonhuman world for human purposes.
2. Richness and diversity of life forms contribute to the realization of these values and are also values in themselves.
3. Humans have no right to reduce this richness and diversity except to satisfy *vital* needs.
4. The flourishing of human life and cultures is compatible with a substantial decrease of the human population. The flourishing of nonhuman life requires such a decrease.
5. Present human interference with the nonhuman world is excessive, and the situation is rapidly worsening.
6. Policies must therefore be changed. These policies affect basic economic, technological, and ideological structures. The resulting state

of affairs will be deeply different from the present.
7. The ideological change is mainly that of appreciating *life quality* (dwelling in situations of inherent value) rather than adhering to an increasingly higher standard of living. There will be a profound awareness of the difference between big and great.
8. Those who subscribe to the foregoing points have an obligation directly or indirectly to try to implement the necessary changes.

Naess and Sessions Provide Comments on the Basic Principles

RE (1)

This formulation refers to the biosphere, or more accurately, to the ecosphere as a whole. This includes individuals, species, populations, habitat, as well as human and nonhuman cultures. From our current knowledge of all-pervasive intimate relationships, this implies a fundamental deep concern and respect. Ecological processes of the planet should, on the whole, remain intact. "The world environment should remain 'natural' " (Gary Snyder).

The term "life" is used here in a more comprehensive nontechnical way to refer also to what biologists classify as "nonliving"; rivers (watersheds), landscapes, ecosystems. For supporters of deep ecology, slogans such as "Let the river live" illustrate this broader usage so common in most cultures.

Inherent value as used in (1) is common in deep ecology literature ("The presence of inherent value in a natural object is independent of any awareness, interest, or appreciation of it by a conscious being").[5]

RE (2)

More technically, this is a formulation concerning diversity and complexity. From an ecological standpoint, complexity and symbiosis are conditions for maximizing diversity. So-called simple, lower, or primitive species of plants and animals contribute essentially to the richness and diversity of life. They have value in themselves and are not merely steps toward the so-called higher or rational life forms. The second principle presupposes that life itself, as a process over evolutionary time, implies an increase of diversity and richness. The refusal to acknowledge that some life forms have greater or lesser intrinsic value than others (see points 1 and 2) runs counter to the formulations of some ecological philosophers and New Age writers.

Complexity, as referred to here, is different from complication. Urban life may be more complicated than life in a natural setting without being more complex in the sense of multifaceted quality.

RE (3)

The term "vital need" is left deliberately vague to allow for considerable latitude in judgment. Differences in climate and related factors, together with differences in the structures of societies as they now exist, need to be considered (for some Eskimos, snowmobiles are necessary today to satisfy vital needs).

People in the materially richest countries cannot be expected to reduce their excessive interference with the nonhuman world to a moderate level overnight. The stabilization and reduction of the human population will take time. Interim strategies need to be developed. But this in no way excuses the present complacency—the extreme seriousness of our current situation must first be realized. But the longer we wait the more drastic will be the measures needed. Until deep changes are made substantial decreases in richness and diversity are liable to occur: the rate of extinction of species will be ten to one hundred times greater than any other period of earth history.

RE (4)

The United Nations Fund for Population Activities in their State of World Population Report (1984) said that high human population growth rates (over 2.0 percent annum) in many developing countries "were diminishing the quality of life for many millions of people." During the decade 1974–1984, the world population grew by nearly 800 million—more than the size of India. "And we will be adding about one Bangladesh (population 93 million) per annum between now and the year 2000."

The report noted that "The growth rate of the human population has declined for the first time in human history. But at the same time, the number of people being added to the human population is bigger than at any time in history because the population base is larger."

Most of the nations in the developing world (including India and China) have as their official government policy the goal of reducing the rate of human population increase, but there are debates over the types of measures to take (contraception, abortion, etc.) consistent with human rights and feasibility.

The report concludes that if all governments set specific population targets as public policy to help alleviate poverty and advance the quality of life, the current situation could be improved.

As many ecologists have pointed out, it is also absolutely crucial to curb population growth in the so-called developed (i.e., overdeveloped) industrial societies. Given the tremendous rate of consumption and waste production of individuals in these societies, they represent a much greater threat and impact on the biosphere per capita than individuals in Second and Third World countries.

RE (5)

This formulation is mild. For a realistic assessment of the situation, see the unabbreviated version of the I.U.C.N.'s *World Conservation Strategy*. There are other works to be highly recommended, such as Gerald Barney's *Global 2000 Report to the President of the United States*.

The slogan of "noninterference" does not imply that humans should not modify some ecosystems as do other species. Humans have modified the earth and will probably continue to do so. At issue is the nature and extent of such interference.

The fight to preserve and extend areas of wilderness or near wilderness should continue and should focus on the general ecological functions of these areas (one such function: large wilderness areas are required in the biosphere to allow for continued evolutionary speciation of animals and plants). Most present designated wilderness areas and game preserves are not large enough to allow for such speciation.

RE (6)

Economic growth as conceived and implemented today by the industrial states is incompatible with (1)–(5). There is only a faint resemblance between ideal sustainable forms of economic growth and present policies of the industrial societies. And "sustainable" still means "sustainable in relation to humans."

Present ideology tends to value things because they are scarce and because they have a commodity value. There is prestige in vast consumption and waste (to mention only several relevant factors).

Whereas "self-determination," "local community," and "think globally, act locally," will remain key terms in the ecology of human societies, nevertheless the implementation of deep changes requires increasingly global action—action across borders.

Governments in Third World countries (with the exception of Costa Rica and a few others) are uninterested in deep ecological issues. When the governments of industrial societies try to promote ecological measures through Third World governments, practically nothing is accomplished (e.g., with problems of desertification). Given this situation, support for global action through non-governmental international organizations becomes increasingly important. Many of these organizations are able to act globally "from grassroots to grassroots," thus avoiding negative governmental interference.

Cultural diversity today requires advanced technology, that is, techniques that advance the basic goals of each culture. So-called soft, intermediate, and alternative technologies are steps in this direction.

RE (7)

Some economists criticize the term "quality of life" because it is supposed to be vague. But on closer inspection, what they consider to be vague is actually the nonquantitative nature of the term. One cannot quantify adequately what is important for the quality of life as discussed here, and there is no need to do so.

RE (8)

There is ample room for different opinions about priorities: what should be done first, what next? What is most urgent? What is clearly necessary as opposed to what is highly desirable but not absolutely pressing?

NOTES

1. Arne Naess, "The Shallow and The Deep, Long-Range Ecology Movements: A Summary," *Inquiry* 16 (Oslo, 1973), pp. 95–100.

2. Theodore Roszak, *Where the Wasteland Ends* (New York: Anchor, 1972).

3. Warwick Fox, "The Intuition of Deep Ecology" (Paper presented at the Ecology and Philosophy Conference, Australian National University, September, 1983). To appear in *The Ecologist* (England, Fall 1984).

4. Tom Regan, *The Case for Animal Rights* (New York: Random House, 1983). For excellent critiques of the animal rights movement, see John Rodman, "The Liberation of Nature?" *Inquiry* 20 (Oslo, 1977). J. Baird Callicott, "Animal Liberation," *Environmental Ethics* 2, 4, (1980); see also John Rodman, "Four Forms of Ecological Consciousness Reconsidered" in T. Attig and D. Scherer, eds., *Ethics and the Environment* (Englewood Cliffs, N.J.: Prentice-Hall, 1983).

5. Tom Regan, "The Nature and Possibility of an Environmental Ethic," *Environmental Ethics* 3 (1981), pp. 19–34.

Social Ecology Versus Deep Ecology

Murray Bookchin

BEYOND "ENVIRONMENTALISM"

The environmental movement has traveled a long way beyond those annual "Earth Day" festivals when millions of school kids were ritualistically mobilized to clean up streets and their parents were scolded by Arthur Godfrey, Barry Commoner, and Paul Ehrlich. The movement has gone beyond a naive belief that patchwork reforms and solemn vows by EPA bureaucrats will seriously arrest the insane pace at which we are tearing down the planet.

This shopworn "Earth Day" approach toward "engineering" nature so that we can ravage the Earth with minimal effects on ourselves—an approach that I called "environmentalism"—has shown signs of giving way to a more searching and radical mentality. Today, the new word in vogue is "ecology"—be it "deep ecology," "human ecology," "biocentric ecology," "anti-humanist ecology," or, to use a term uniquely rich in meaning, "*social* ecology."

Happily, the new relevance of the word "ecology" reveals a growing dissatisfaction with attempts to use our vast ecological problems for cheaply spectacular and politically manipulative ends. Our forests disappear due to mindless cutting and increasing acid rain; the ozone layer thins out from widespread use of fluorocarbons; toxic dumps multiply all over the planet; highly dangerous, often radioactive pollutants enter into our air, water, and food chains. These innumerable hazards threaten the integrity of life itself, raising far more basic issues than can be resolved by "Earth Day" cleanups and faint-hearted changes in environmental laws.

For good reason, more and more people are trying to go beyond the vapid "environmentalism" of the early 1970s and toward an *ecological* approach: one that is rooted in an ecological philosophy, ethics, sensibility, image of nature, and, ultimately, an ecological movement that will transform our domineering market society into a nonhierarchical cooperative one that will live in harmony with nature, because its members live in harmony with each other. They are beginning to sense that there is a tie-in between the way people deal with each other as social beings—men with women, old with young, rich with poor, white with people of color, first world with third, elites with "masses"—and the way they deal with nature.

The questions that now face us are: what do we really mean by an *ecological* approach? What is a *coherent* ecological philosophy, ethics, and movement? How can the answers to these questions and many others *fit together* so that they form a meaningful and creative whole? If we are not to repeat all the mistakes of the early seventies with their hoopla about "population control," their latent anti-feminism, elitism, arrogance, and ugly authoritarian tendencies, so we must honestly and seriously appraise the new tendencies that today go under the name of one or another form of "ecology."

TWO CONFLICTING TENDENCIES

Let us agree from the outset that the word "ecology" is no magic term that unlocks the real secret of our abuse of nature. It is a word that can be as easily abused, distorted, and tainted as words like "democracy" and "freedom." Nor does the word "ecology" put us all—whoever "we" may be—in the same boat against environmentalists who are simply trying to make a rotten society work by dressing it in green

Murray Bookchin, "Social Ecology Versus Deep Ecology," *Socialist Review* 88 (1988): 11–29. Reprinted with permission of the journal.

leaves and colorful flowers, while ignoring the deep-seated *roots* of our ecological problems.

It is time to face the fact that there are differences within the so-called "ecology movement" of the present time that are as serious as those between the "environmentalism" and "ecologism" of the early seventies. There are barely disguised racists, survivalists, macho Daniel Boones, and outright social reactionaries who use the word "ecology" to express their views, just as there are deeply concerned naturalists, communitarians, social radicals, and feminists who use the word "ecology" to express theirs.

The differences between these two tendencies in the so-called "ecology movement" consist not only in quarrels over theory, sensibility, and ethics. They have far reaching *practical* and *political* consequences on the way we view nature, "humanity," and ecology. Most significantly, they concern how we propose to *change* society and by what *means*.

The greatest differences that are emerging within the so-called "ecology movement" of our day are between a vague, formless, often self-contradictory ideology called "deep ecology" and a socially oriented body of ideas best termed "social ecology." Deep ecology has parachuted into our midst quite recently from the Sunbelt's bizarre mix of Hollywood and Disneyland, spiced with homilies from Taoism, Buddhism, spiritualism, reborn Christianity, and, in some cases, eco-fascism. Social ecology, on the other hand, draws its inspiration from such radical decentralist thinkers as Peter Kropotkin, William Morris, and Paul Goodman, among many others who have challenged society's vast hierarchical, sexist, class-ruled, statist, and militaristic apparatus.

Bluntly speaking, deep ecology, despite all its social rhetoric, has no real sense that our ecological problems have their roots in society and in social problems. It preaches a gospel of a kind of "original sin" that accuses a vague species called "humanity"—as though people of color were equatable with whites, women with men, the third world with the first, the poor with the rich, and the exploited with their exploiters. This vague, undifferentiated humanity is seen as an ugly "anthropocentric" thing—presumably a malignant product of natural

evolution—that is "overpopulating" the planet, "devouring" its resources, destroying its wildlife and the biosphere. It assumes that some vague domain called "nature" stands opposed to a constellation of non-natural things called "human beings," with their "technology," "minds," " society," and so on. Formulated largely by privileged white male academics, deep ecology has brought sincere naturalists like Paul Shepard into the same company with patently anti-humanist and macho mountain-men like David Foreman, who writes in *Earth First!*—a Tucson-based journal that styles itself as the voice of a wilderness-oriented movement of the same name—that "humanity" is a cancer in the world of life.

It is easy to forget that this same kind of crude eco-brutalism led Hitler to fashion theories of blood and soil that led to the transport of millions of people to murder camps like Auschwitz. The same eco-brutalism now reappears a half-century later among self-professed deep ecologists who believe that famines are nature's "population control" and immigration into the US should be restricted in order to preserve "our" ecological resources.

Simply Living, an Australian periodical, published this sort of eco-brutalism as part of a laudatory interview of David Foreman by Professor Bill Devall, co-author of *Deep Ecology,* the manifesto of the deep ecology movement. Foreman, who exuberantly expressed his commitment to deep ecology, frankly informs Devall that

> When I tell people how the worst thing we could do in Ethiopia is to give aid—the best thing would be to just let nature seek its own balance, to let the people there just starve—they think this is monstrous. . . . Likewise, letting the USA be an overflow valve for problems in Latin America is not solving a thing. It's just putting more pressure on the resources we have in the USA.

One could reasonably ask what it means for "nature to seek its own balance" in a part of the world where agribusiness, colonialism, and exploitation have ravaged a once culturally and ecologically stable area like East Africa. And who is this all-American "our" that owns the "resources we have in the USA"? Is it the ordinary people who are driven by sheer need to cut timber, mine ores, operate nuclear power plants? Or are they the giant corporations that are not only wrecking the good old USA, but have produced the main problems in Latin America that are sending Indian folk across the Rio Grande? As an ex-Washington lobbyist and political huckster, David Foreman need not be expected to answer these subtle questions in a radical way. But what is truly surprising is the reaction—more precisely, the *lack* of any reaction—which marked Professor Devall's behavior. Indeed, the interview was notable for his almost reverential introduction and description of Foreman.

WHAT IS "DEEP ECOLOGY"?

Deep ecology is enough of a "black hole" of half-digested and ill-formed ideas that a man like Foreman can easily express utterly vicious notions and still sound like a fiery pro-ecology radical. The very words "deep ecology" clue us into the fact that we are not dealing with a body of clear ideas, but with an ideological toxic dump. Does it make sense, for example, to counterpose "deep ecology" with "superficial ecology" as though the word "ecology" were applicable to *everything* that involves environmental issues? Does it not completely degrade the rich meaning of the word "ecology" to append words like "shallow" and "deep" to it? Arne Naess, the pontiff of deep ecology— who, together with George Sessions and Bill Devall, inflicted this vocabulary upon us—have taken a pregnant word—ecology— and stripped it of any inner meaning and integrity by designating the most pedestrian environmentalists as "ecologists," albeit "shallow" ones, in contrast to their notion of "deep."

This is not an example of mere wordplay. It tells us something about the mindset that exists among these "deep" thinkers. To parody the word "shallow" and "deep ecology" is to show not only the absurdity of this terminology but to reveal the superficiality of its inventors. In fact, this kind of absurdity

tells us more than we realize about the confusion Naess-Sessions-Devall, not to mention eco-brutalists like Foreman, have introduced into the current ecology movement. Indeed, this trio relies very heavily on the ease with which people forget the history of the ecology movement, the way in which the wheel is re-invented every few years by newly arrived individuals who, well-meaning as they may be, often accept a crude version of highly developed ideas that appeared earlier in a richer context and tradition of ideas. At worst, they shatter such contexts and traditions, picking out tasty pieces that become utterly distorted in a new, utterly alien framework. No regard is paid by such "deep thinkers" to the fact that *the new context in which an idea is placed may utterly change the meaning of the idea itself.* German "National Socialism " was militantly "anti-capitalist." But its "anti-capitalism" was placed in a strongly racist, imperialist, and seemingly "naturalist" context which extolled wilderness, a crude biologism, and anti-rationalism—features one finds in latent or explicit form in Sessions' and Devall's *Deep Ecology.*[1]

Neither Naess, Sessions, nor Devall have written a single line about decentralization, a nonhierarchical society, democracy, small-scale communities, local autonomy, mutual aid, communalism, and tolerance that was not already conceived in painstaking detail and brilliant contextualization by Peter Kropotkin a century ago. But what the boys from Ecotopia do is to totally recontextualize the framework of these ideas, bringing in personalities and notions that basically change their radical libertarian thrust. *Deep Ecology* mingles Woody Guthrie, a Communist Party centralist who no more believed in decentralization than Stalin, with Paul Goodman, an anarchist who would have been mortified to be placed in the same tradition with Guthrie. In philosophy, the book also intermingles Spinoza, a Jew in spirit if not in religious commitment, with Heidegger, a former member of the Nazi party in spirit as well as ideological affiliation—all in the name of a vague word called "process philosophy." Almost opportunistic in their use of catch-words and what Orwell called "double-speak," "process philosophy" makes it possible for Sessions-Devall to add Alfred North Whitehead to their list of ideological ancestors because he called his ideas "processual."

One could go on indefinitely describing this sloppy admixture of "ancestors," philosophical traditions, social pedigrees, and religions that often have nothing in common with each other and, properly conceived, are commonly in sharp opposition with each other. Thus, a reactionary like Thomas Malthus and the tradition he spawned is celebrated with the same enthusiasm in *Deep Ecology* as Henry Thoreau, a radical libertarian who fostered a highly humanistic tradition. Eclecticism would be too mild a word for this kind of hodge-podge, one that seems shrewdly calculated to embrace everyone under the rubric of deep ecology who is prepared to reduce ecology to a religion rather than a systematic and critical body of ideas. This kind of "ecological" thinking surfaces in an appendix to the Devall-Sessions book, called *Ecosophy T* by Arne Naess, who regales us with flow diagrams and corporate-type tables of organization that have more in common with logical positivist forms of exposition (Naess, in fact, was an acolyte of this school of thought for years) than anything that could be truly called organic philosophy.

If we look beyond the spiritual eco-babble and examine the *context* in which demands like decentralization, small-scale communities, local autonomy, mutual aid, communalism, and tolerance are placed, the blurred images that Sessions and Devall create come into clearer focus. These demands are not intrinsically ecological or emancipatory. Few societies were more decentralized than European feudalism, which was structured around small-scale communities, mutual aid, and the communal use of land. Local autonomy was highly prized, and autarchy formed the economic key to feudal communities. Yet few societies were more hierarchical. The manorial economy of the Middle Ages placed a high premium on autarchy or "self-sufficiency" and spirituality. Yet oppression was often intolerable and the great mass of people who belonged to that society lived in utter subjugation by their "betters" and the nobility.

If "nature worship," with its bouquet of wood sprites, animistic fetishes, fertility rites and other such ceremonies, paves the way to an ecological sensibility and society, then it would be hard to understand how ancient Egypt, with its animal deities and all-presiding goddesses, managed to become one of the most hierarchical and oppressive societies in the ancient world. The Nile River, which provided the "life-giving" waters of the valley, was used in a highly ecological manner. Yet the entire society was structured around the oppression of millions of serfs by opulent nobles, such that one wonders how notions of spirituality can be given priority over the need for a critical evaluation of social structures.

Even if one grants the need for a new sensibility and outlook—a point that has been made repeatedly in the literature of social ecology—one can look behind even this limited context of deep ecology to a still broader context. The love affair of deep ecology with Malthusian doctrines, a spirituality that emphasizes self-effacement, a flirtation with a *super*-naturalism that stands in flat contradiction to the refreshing naturalism that ecology has introduced into social theory, a crude positivism in the spirit of Naess—all work against a truly organic dialectic so needed to understand *development*. We shall see that all the bumper-sticker demands like decentralization, small-scale communities, local autonomy, mutual aid, communalism, tolerance, and even an avowed opposition to hierarchy, go awry when we place them in the larger context of anti-humanism and "biocentrism" that mark the authentic ideological infrastructure of deep ecology.

THE ART OF EVADING SOCIETY

The seeming ideological "tolerance" and pluralism which deep ecology celebrates has a sinister function of its own. It not only reduces richly nuanced ideas and conflicting traditions to their lowest common denominator; it legitimates extremely primitivistic and reactionary notions in the company of authentically radical contexts and traditions.

Deep ecology reduces people from social beings to a simple species—to zoological entities that are interchangeable with bears, bison, deer, or, for that matter, fruit flies and microbes. The fact that people can consciously change themselves and society, indeed enhance that natural world in a free ecological society, is dismissed as "humanism." Deep ecology essentially ignores the social nature of humanity and the social origins of the ecological crises.

This "zoologization" of human beings and of society yields sinister results. The role of capitalism with its competitive "grow or die" market economy—an economy that would devour the biosphere whether there were 10 billion people on the planet or 10 million—is simply vaporized into a vapid spiritualism. Taoist and Buddhist pieties replace the need for social and economic analysis, and self-indulgent encounter groups replace the need for political organization and action. Above all, deep ecologists explain the destruction of human beings in terms of the same "natural laws" that are said to govern the population vicissitudes of lemmings. The fact that major reductions of populations would not diminish levels of production and the destruction of the biosphere in a capitalist economy totally eludes Devall, Sessions, and their followers.

In failing to emphasize the unique characteristics of human societies and to give full due to the self-reflective role of human consciousness, deep ecologists essentially evade the *social* roots of the ecological crisis. Deep ecology contains no history of the emergence of society out of nature, a crucial development that brings social theory into organic contact with ecological theory. It presents no explanation of—indeed, it reveals no interest in—the emergence of hierarchy out of society, of classes out of hierarchy, of the state out of classes—in short, the highly graded social as well as ideological developments which are at the roots of the ecological problem.

Instead, we not only lose sight of the social differences that fragment "humanity" into a host of human beings—men and women, ethnic groups, oppressors and oppressed—we lose sight of the individual self in an unending flow of eco-babble that preaches the "realization of self-in-Self where the 'Self' stands for organic wholeness." More of the same cosmic eco-babble appears when we are informed that the "phrase 'one' includes not only men, an individual human, but all humans, grizzly bears, whole rain forest ecosystems, mountains and rivers, the tiniest microbes in the soil, and so on."

ON SELFHOOD AND VIRUSES

Such flippant abstractions of human individuality are extremely dangerous. Historically, a "Self" that absorbs all real existential selves has been used from time immemorial to absorb individual uniqueness and freedom into a supreme "Individual" who heads the state, churches of various sorts, adoring congregations, and spellbound constituencies. The purpose is the same, no matter how much such a "Self" is dressed up in ecological, naturalistic, and "biocentric" attributes. The Paleolithic shaman, in reindeer skins and horns, is the predecessor of the Pharaoh, the Buddha, and, in more recent times, of Hitler, Stalin, and Mussolini.

That the egotistical, greedy, and soloist bourgeois "self" has always been a repellent being goes without saying, and deep ecology as put forth by Devall and Sessions makes the most of it. But is there not a free, independently minded, ecologically concerned, idealistic self with a unique personality that can think of itself as different from "whales, grizzly bears, whole rain forest ecosystems (no less!), mountains and rivers, the tiniest microbes in the soil, and so on"? Is it not indispensable, in fact, for the individual self to disengage itself from a Pharonic "Self," discover its own capacities and uniqueness, and acquire a sense of personality, of self-control and self-direction—all traits indispensable for the achievement of *freedom?* Here, one can imagine Heidegger grimacing with satisfaction at the sight of this self-effacing and passive personality so yielding that it can easily be shaped, distorted, and manipulated by a new "ecological" state machinery with a supreme "Self" at its head. And this all in the name of a "biocentric equality" that is slowly reworked as it has been so often in history, into a social hierarchy. From Shaman to Monarch, from Priest or Priestess to Dictator, our warped social development has been marked by "nature worshippers" and their ritual Supreme Ones who produced unfinished individuals at best or deindividuated the "self-in-Self" at worst, often in the name of the "Great Connected Whole" (to use exactly the language of the Chinese ruling classes who kept their peasantry in abject servitude, as Leon E. Stover points out in his *The Cultural Ecology of Chinese Civilization*).

What makes this eco-babble especially dangerous today is that we are already living in a period of massive de-individuation. This is not because deep ecology or Taoism is making any serious in-roads into our own cultural ecology, but because the mass media, the commodity culture, and a market society are "reconnecting" us into an increasingly depersonalized "whole" whose essence is passivity and a chronic vulnerability to economic and political manipulation. It is not an excess of "selfhood" from which we are suffering, but rather the surrender of personality to the security and control of corporations, centralized government, and the military. If "selfhood" is identified with a grasping, "anthropocentric," and devouring personality, these traits are to be found not so much among ordinary people, who basically sense they have no control over their destinies, but among the giant corporations and state leaders who are not only plundering the planet, but also robbing from women, people of color, and the underprivileged. It is not deindividuation that the oppressed of the world require, but *re*individuation that will transform them into active agents in the task of remaking society and arresting the growing totalitarianism that threatens to homogenize us all into a Western version of the "Great Connected Whole."

We are also confronted with the delicious "and so on" that follows the "tiniest microbes in the soil" with which our deep ecologists identify the "Self." Taking their argument to its logical extreme, one might ask: why stop with the "tiniest microbes in the soil" and ignore the leprosy microbe, the viruses that give us smallpox, polio, and, more recently, AIDS? Are they, too, not part of "all organisms and entities

in the ecosphere . . . of the interrelated whole . . . equal in intrinsic worth . . . ," as Devall and Sessions remind us in their effluvium of eco-babble? Naess, Devall, and Sessions rescue themselves by introducing a number of highly debatable qualifiers:

> The slogan of "noninterference" does not imply that humans should not modify some ecosystems as do other species. Humans have modified the Earth and will probably continue to do so. At issue is the nature and extent of such interference.

One does not leave the muck of deep ecology without having mud all over one's feet. Exactly *who* is to decide the "nature" of human "interference" in nature and the "extent" to which it can be done? What are "some" of the ecosystems we can modify and which ones are not subject to human "interference"? Here, again, we encounter the key problem that deep ecology poses for serious, ecologically concerned people: the *social* bases of our ecological problems and the role of the human species in the evolutionary scheme of things.

Implicit in deep ecology is the notion that a "Humanity" exists that accurses the natural world; that individual selfhood must be transformed into a cosmic "Selfhood" that essentially transcends the person and his or her uniqueness. Even nature is not spared from a kind of static, prepositional logic that is cultivated by the logical positivists. "Nature," in deep ecology and David Foreman's interpretation of it, becomes a kind of scenic view, a spectacle to be admired around the campfire. It is not viewed as an *evolutionary* development that is cumulative and *includes* the human species.

The problems deep ecology and biocentricity raise have not gone unnoticed in the more thoughtful press in England. During a discussion of "biocentric ethics" in *The New Scientist 69* (1976), for example, Bernard Dixon observed that no "logical line can be drawn" between the conservation of whales, gentians, and flamingoes on the one hand and the extinction of pathogenic microbes like the smallpox virus. At which point David Ehrenfeld, in his *Arrogance of Humanism,*[2] work that is so selective and tendentious in its use of quotations that it should validly be renamed "The Arrogance of Ignorance"—cutely observes that the smallpox virus is "an endangered species." One wonders what to do about the AIDS virus if a vaccine or therapy should threaten its "survival"? Further, given the passion for perpetuating the "ecosystem" of every species, one wonders how smallpox and AIDS viruses should be preserved? In test tubes? Laboratory cultures? Or, to be truly "ecological" in their "native habitat," the human body? In which case, idealistic acolytes of deep ecology should be invited to offer their own bloodstreams in the interests of "biocentric equality." Certainly, "if nature should be permitted to take its course"—as Foreman advises for Ethiopians and Indian peasants—plagues, famines, suffering, wars, and perhaps even lethal asteroids of the kind that exterminated the great reptiles of the Mesozoic should not be kept from defacing the purity of "first nature" by the intervention of human ingenuity and—yes!—*technology*. With so much absurdity to unscramble, one can indeed get heady, almost dizzy, with a sense of polemical intoxication.

At root, the eclecticism which turns deep ecology into a goulash of notions and moods is insufferably reformist and surprisingly environmentalist—all its condemnations of "superficial ecology" aside. Are you, perhaps, a mild-mannered liberal? Then do not fear: Devall and Sessions give a patronizing nod to "reform legislation," "coalitions," "protests," the "women's movement" (this earns all of ten lines in their "Minority Tradition and Direct Action" essay), "working in the Christian tradition," "questioning technology" (a hammering remark, if there ever was one), "working in Green politics" (which faction, the "fundies" or the "realos"?). In short, everything can be expected in so "cosmic" a philosophy. Anything seems to pass through deep ecology's donut hole: anarchism at one extreme and eco-fascism at the other. Like the fast food emporiums that make up our culture, deep ecology is the fast food of quasi-radical environmentalists.

Despite its pretense of "radicality," deep ecology is more "New Age" and "Aquarian" than the environmentalist movements it denounces under those names. Indeed, the extent to which deep ecology accommodates itself to some of the worst features of the "dominant view" it professes to reject is seen with extraordinary clarity in one of its most fundamental and repeatedly asserted demands—namely, that the world's population must be drastically reduced, according to one of its devotees, to 500 million. If deep ecologists have even the faintest knowledge of the "population theorists" Devall and Sessions invoke with admiration—notably, Thomas Malthus, William Vogt, and Paul Ehrlich—then they would be obliged to add: by measures that are virtually eco-fascist. This specter clearly looms before us in Devall's and Sessions' sinister remark: ". . . the longer we wait [for population control], the more drastic will be the measures needed."

THE "DEEP" MALTHUSIANS

Devall and Sessions often write with smug assurance on issues they know virtually nothing about. This is most notably the case in the so-called "population debate," a debate that has raged for over two hundred years and more and involves explosive political and social issues that have pitted the most reactionary elements in English and American society against authentic radicals. In fact, the eco-babble which Devall and Sessions dump on us in only two paragraphs would require a full-sized volume of careful analysis to unravel.

Devall and Sessions hail Thomas Malthus (1766–1854) as a prophet whose warning "that human population growth would exponentially outstrip food production . . . was ignored by the rising tide of industrial/technological optimism." First of all, Thomas Malthus was not a prophet; he was an apologist for the misery that the Industrial Revolution was inflicting on the English peasantry and working classes. His utterly fallacious argument that population increases exponentially while food supplies increase arithmetically was not ignored by England's ruling classes; it was taken to heart and even incorporated into social Darwinism as an explanation of why oppression was a necessary feature of society and why the rich, the white imperialists, and the privileged were the "fittest" who were equipped to "survive—needless to say, at the expense of the impoverished many. Written and directed in great part as an attack upon the liberatory vision of William Godwin, Malthus' mean-spirited *Essay on the Principle of Population* tried to demonstrate that hunger, poverty, disease, and premature death are *inevitable* precisely because population and food supply increase at different rates. Hence war, famines, and plagues (Malthus later added "moral restraint") were necessary to keep population down—needless to say, among the "lower orders of society," whom he singles out as the chief offenders of his inexorable population "laws."[3] Malthus, in effect, became the ideologue par excellence for the land-grabbing English nobility in its effort to dispossess the peasantry of their traditional common lands and for the English capitalists to work children, women, and men to death in the newly emergent "industrial/technological" factory system.

Malthusianism contributed in great part to that meanness of spirit that Charles Dickens captured in his famous novels, *Oliver Twist* and *Hard Times*. The doctrine, its author, and its overstuffed wealthy beneficiaries were bitterly fought by the great English anarchist, William Godwin, the pioneering socialist, Robert Owen, and the emerging Chartist movement of English workers in the early 19th century. However, Malthusianism was naively picked up by Charles Darwin to explain his theory of "natural selection." It then became the bedrock theory for the new *social* Darwinism, so very much in vogue in the late nineteenth and early twentieth centuries, which saw society as a "jungle" in which only the "fit" (usually, the rich and white) could "survive" at the expense of the "unfit" (usually, the poor and people of color). Malthus, in effect, had provided an ideology that justified class domination, racism, the degradation of women, and, ultimately, British imperialism.

Malthusianism was not only revived in Hitler's Third Reich; it also reemerged in the late 1940s, following the discoveries of antibiotics to control infectious diseases. Riding on the tide of the new Pax Americana after World War II, William F. Vogt

and a whole bouquet of neo-Malthusians were to challenge the use of the new antibiotic discoveries to control disease and prevent death—as usual, mainly in Asia, Africa, and Latin America. Again, a new "population debate" erupted, with the Rockefeller interests and large corporate sharks aligning themselves with the neo-Malthusians, and caring people of every sort aligning themselves with third world theorists like Josua de Castro, who wrote damning, highly informed critiques of this new version of misanthropy.

Zero Population Growth fanatics in the early seventies literally polluted the environmental movement with demands for a government bureau to "control" population, advancing the infamous "triage" ethic, according to which various "underdeveloped" countries would be granted or refused aid on the basis of their compliance to population control measures. In *Food First*, Francis Moore Lappé and Joseph Collins have done a superb job in showing how hunger has its origins not in "natural" shortages of food or population growth, but in social and cultural dislocations. (It is notable that Devall and Sessions do *not* list this excellent book in their bibliography.) The book has to be read to understand the reactionary implications of deep ecology's demographic positions.

Demography is a highly ambiguous and ideologically charged social discipline that cannot be reduced to a mere numbers game in biological reproduction. Human beings are not fruit flies (the species which the neo-Malthusians love to cite). Their reproductive behavior is profoundly conditioned by cultural values, standards of living, social traditions, gender relations, religious beliefs, socio-political conflicts, and various sociopolitical expectations. Smash up a stable, precapitalist culture and throw its people off the land into city slums, and, due to demoralization, population may soar rather than decline. As Gandhi told the British, imperialism left India's wretched poor and homeless with little more in life than the immediate gratification provided by sex and an understandably numbed sense of personal, much less social, responsibility. Reduce women to mere reproductive factories and population rates will explode.

Conversely, provide people with decent lives, education, a sense of creative meaning in life, and, above all, expand the role of women in society—and population growth begins to stabilize and population rates even reverse their direction. Nothing more clearly reveals deep ecology's crude, often reactionary, and certainly superficial ideological framework—all its decentralist, antihierarchical, and "radical" rhetoric aside—than its suffocating "biological" treatment of the population issue and its inclusion of Malthus, Vogt, and Ehrlich in its firmament of prophets.

Not surprisingly, the *Earth First!* newsletter, whose editor professes to be an enthusiastic deep ecologist, carried an article titled "Population and AIDS" which advanced the obscene argument that AIDS is desirable as a means of population control. This was no spoof. It was earnestly argued and carefully reasoned in a Paleolithic sort of way. Not only will AIDS claim large numbers of lives, asserts the author (who hides under the pseudonym of "Miss Ann Thropy," a form of black humor that could also pass as an example of machomale arrogance), but it "may cause a breakdown in technology (read: human food supply) and its export which could also decrease human population." These people feed on human disasters, suffering, and misery, preferably in third world countries where AIDS is by far a more monstrous problem than elsewhere.

We have little reason to doubt that this mentality is perfectly consistent with the "more drastic . . . measures" Devall and Sessions believe we will have to explore. Nor is it inconsistent with Malthus and Vogt that we should make no effort to find a cure for this disease which may do so much to depopulate the world. "Biocentric democracy," I assume, should call for nothing less than a "hands-off" policy on the AIDS virus and perhaps equally lethal pathogens that appear in the human species.

WHAT IS SOCIAL ECOLOGY?

Social ecology is neither "deep," "tall," "fat," nor "thick." It is *social*. It does not fall back on incantations, sutras, flow diagrams or spiritual vagaries. It is avowedly *rational*. It does not try to regale metaphorical forms of spiritual mechanism and crude biologism with Taoist, Buddhist, Christian, or shamanistic ecobabble. It is a coherent form of *naturalism* that looks to *evolution* and the *biosphere,* not to deities in the sky or under the earth for quasi-religious and supernaturalistic explanations of natural and social phenomena.

Philosophically, social ecology stems from a solid organismic tradition in Western philosophy, beginning with Heraclitus, the near-evolutionary dialectic of Aristotle and Hegel, and the critical approach of the famous Frankfurt School—particularly its devastating critique of logical positivism (which surfaces in Naess repeatedly) and the primitivistic mysticism of Heidegger (which pops up all over the place in deep ecology's literature).

Socially, it is revolutionary, not merely "radical." It critically unmasks the entire evolution of hierarchy in all its forms, including neo-Malthusian elitism, the ecobrutalism of David Foreman, the antihumanism of David Ehrenfeld and "Miss Ann Thropy," and the latent racism, first-world arrogance, and Yuppie nihilism of postmodernistic spiritualism. It is noted in the profound eco-anarchistic analyses of Peter Kropotkin, the radical economic insights of Karl Marx, the emancipatory promise of the revolutionary Enlightenment as articulated by the great encyclopedist, Denis Diderot, the *Enrages* of the French Revolution, the revolutionary feminist ideals of Louise Michel and Emma Goldman, the communitarian visions of Paul Goodman and E. A. Gutkind, and the various eco-revolutionary manifestoes of the early 1960s.

Politically, it is *green*—radically green. It takes its stand with the left-wing tendencies in the German Greens and extra-parliamentary street movements of European cities; with the American radical ecofeminist movement; with the demands for a new politics based on citizens' initiatives, neighborhood assemblies, and New England's tradition of town-meetings; with nonaligned anti-imperialist movements at home and abroad; with the struggle by people of color for complete freedom from the domination of privileged whites and from the superpowers.

Morally, it is *humanistic* in the high Renaissance meaning of the term, not the degraded meaning of "humanism" that has been imparted to the world by David Foreman, David Ehrenfeld, and a salad of academic deep ecologists. Humanism from its inception has meant a shift in vision from the skies to the earth, from superstition to reason, from deities to people— who are no less products of natural evolution than grizzly bears and whales. Social ecology accepts neither a "biocentricity" that essentially denies or degrades the uniqueness of human beings, human subjectivity, rationality, aesthetic sensibility, and the ethical potentiality of humanity, nor an "anthropocentricity" that confers on the privileged few the right to plunder the world of life, including human life. Indeed, it opposes "centricity" of *any* kind as a new word for hierarchy and domination—be it that of nature by a mystical "Man" or the domination of people by an equally mystical "Nature." It firmly denies that nature is a static, scenic view which Mountain Men like a Foreman survey from a peak in Nevada or a picture window that spoiled yuppies view from their ticky-tacky country homes. To social ecology, nature *is* natural *evolution,* not a cosmic arrangement of beings frozen in a moment of eternity to be abjectly revered, adored, and worshipped like Gods and Goddesses in a realm of "*super*-nature." Natural evolution is nature in the very real sense that it is composed of atoms, molecules that have evolved into amino acids, proteins, unicellular organisms, genetic codes, invertebrates and vertebrates, amphibia, reptiles, mammals, primates, and human beings—all, in a cumulative thrust toward ever-greater complexity, ever-greater subjectivity, and finally, an ever greater capacity for conceptual thought, symbolic communication, and self-consciousness.

This marvel we call "Nature" has produced a marvel we call *Homo sapiens*—"thinking man"—and, more significantly for the development of society, "thinking woman," whose primeval domestic domain provided the arena for the origins of a caring society, human empathy, love, and idealistic commitment. The human species, in effect, is no less a product of natural evolution and differentiation than blue-green algae. To degrade the human species in the name of "anti-humanism," to deny people their uniqueness as thinking beings with an unprecedented gift for conceptual thought, is to deny the rich fecundity of natural evolution itself. To separate human beings and society from nature is to dualize and truncate nature itself, to diminish the meaning and thrust of natural evolution in the name of a "biocentricity" that spends more time disporting itself with mantras, deities, and supernature than with the realities of the biosphere and the role of society in ecological problems.

Accordingly, social ecology does not try to hide its critical and reconstructive thrust in metaphors. It calls "technological/industrial" society *capitalism*— a word which places the onus for our ecological problems on the *living* sources and *social* relationships that produce them, not on a cutesy "Third Wave" abstraction which buries these sources in technics, a technical "mentality," or perhaps the technicians who work on machines. It sees the domination of women not simply as a "spiritual" problem that can be resolved by rituals, incantations, and shamannesses, important as ritual may be in solidarizing women into a unique community of people, but in the long, highly graded, and subtly nuanced development of hierarchy, which long preceded the development of classes. Nor does it ignore class, ethnic differences, imperialism, and oppression by creating a grab-bag called "Humanity" that is placed in opposition to a mystified "Nature," divested of all development.

All of which brings us as social ecologists to an issue that seems to be totally alien to the crude concerns of deep ecology: natural evolution has conferred on human beings the capacity to form a "second" or cultural nature out of "first" or primeval nature. Natural evolution has not only provided humans with the *ability,* but also the *necessity* to be purposive interveners into "first nature," to consciously *change* "first nature" by means of a highly institutionalized form of community we call "society." It is not alien to natural evolution that a species called human beings have emerged over the billions of years who are capable of thinking in a sophisticated way. Nor is it alien for human beings to develop a highly sophisticated form of symbolic communication which a new kind of community—institutionalized, guided by thought rather than by instinct alone, and ever-changing—has emerged called "society."

Taken together, all of these human traits—intellectual, communicative, and social—have not only emerged from natural evolution and are inherently human; they can also be placed at the *service* of natural evolution to consciously increase biotic diversity, diminish suffering, foster the further evolution of new and ecologically valuable life-forms, reduce the impact of disastrous accidents or the harsh effects of mere change.

Whether this species, gifted by the creativity of natural evolution, can play the role of a nature rendered self-conscious or cut against the grain of natural evolution by simplifying the biosphere, polluting it, and undermining the cumulative results of organic evolution is above all a *social* problem. The primary question ecology faces today is whether an ecologically oriented society can be created out of the present anti-ecological one.

Unless there is a resolute attempt to fully anchor ecological dislocations in social dislocations; to challenge the vested corporate and political interests we should properly call *capitalism;* to analyze, explore, and attack hierarchy as a *reality,* not only as a sensibility; to recognize the material needs of the poor and of third world people; to function politically, and not simply as a religious cult; to give the human species and mind their due in natural evolution, rather than regard them as "cancers" in the biosphere; to examine economies as well as "souls," and freedom instead of scholastic arguments about the "rights" of pathogenic viruses—unless, in short, North American Greens and the ecology movement shift their focus toward a *social ecology* and let deep ecology sink into the pit it has created for us, the ecology movement will become another ugly wart on the skin of society.

What we must do, today, is return to *nature,* conceived in all its fecundity, richness of potentialities, and subjectivity—not to *super*nature with its shamans, priests, priestesses, and fanciful deities that are merely anthropomorphic extensions and distortions of the "Human" as all-embracing divinities. And what we must "enchant" is not only an abstract image of "Nature" *that often reflects our own systems of power, hierarchy, and domination—*but rather human beings, the human mind, the human spirit.

NOTES

1. Unless otherwise indicated, all future references and quotes come from Bill Devall and George Sessions, *Deep Ecology* (Layton, Utah: Gibbs M. Smith, 1985), a book which has essentially become the bible of the "movement" that bears its name.

2. David Ehrenfeld, *The Arrogance of Humanism* (New York: The Modern Library, 1978), pp. 207–211

3. Chapter five of his *Essay,* which, for all its "concern" over the misery of the "lower classes," inveighs against the poor laws and argues that the "pressures of distress on this part of the community is an evil so deeply seated that no human ingenuity can reach it." Thomas, Malthus, *On Population* (New York: The Modern Library), p. 34.

Why Do Species Matter?

Lilly-Marlene Russow

One seldom-noted consequence of most recent arguments for "animal rights" or against "speciesism" is their inability to provide a justification for differential treatment on the basis of species membership, even in cases of rare or endangered species. I defend the claim that arguments about the moral status of individual animals inadequately deal with this issue, and go on, with the help of several test cases, to reject three traditional analyses of our alleged obligation to protect endangered species. I conclude (a) that these traditional analyses fail, (b) that there is an important conceptual confusion in any attempt to ascribe value to a species, and (c) that our obligation must ultimately rest on the value—often aesthetic—of individual members of certain species.

INTRODUCTION

Consider the following extension of the standard sort of objection to treating animals differently just because they are not humans: the fact that a being is or is not a member of species *S* is not a morally relevant fact, and does not justify treating that being differently from members of other species. If so, we cannot treat a bird differently *just* because it is a California condor rather than a turkey vulture. The problem, then, becomes one of determining what special obligations, if any, a person might have toward California condors, and what might account for those obligations in a way that is generally consistent with the condemnation of speciesism. Since it will turn out that the solution I offer does not admit of a direct and tidy proof, what follows comprises three

sections which approach this issue from different directions. The resulting triangulation should serve as justification and motivation for the conclusion sketched in the final section.

SPECIES AND INDIVIDUALS

Much of the discussion in the general area of ethics and animals has dealt with the rights of animals, or obligations and duties toward individual animals. The first thing to note is that some, but not all, of the actions normally thought of as obligatory with respect to the protection of vanishing species can be recast as possible duties to individual members of that species. Thus, if it could be shown that we have a prima facie duty not to kill a sentient being, it would follow that it would be wrong, other things being equal, to kill a blue whale or a California condor. But it would be wrong for the same reason, and to the same degree, that it would be wrong to kill a turkey vulture or a pilot whale. Similarly, if it is wrong (something which I do not think can be shown) to deprive an individual animal of its natural habitat, it would be wrong, for the same reasons and to the same degree, to do that to a member of an endangered species. And so on. Thus, an appeal to our duties toward individual animals may provide some protection, but they do not justify the claim that we should treat members of a vanishing species with *more* care than members of other species.

More importantly, duties toward individual beings (or the rights of those individuals) will not always account for all the actions that people feel ob-

Lilly-Marlene Russow, "Why Do Species Matter?" *Environmental Ethics* 3 (1981): 101–12. Reprinted with permission of journal and author.

ligated to do for endangered species—e.g., bring into the world as many individuals of that species as possible, protect them from natural predation, or establish separate breeding colonies. In fact, the protection of a species might involve actions that are demonstrably contrary to the interests of some or all of the individual animals: this seems true in cases where we remove all the animals we can from their natural environment and raise them in zoos, or where we severely restrict the range of a species by hunting all those outside a certain area, as is done in Minnesota to protect the timber wolf. If such efforts are morally correct, our duties to preserve a species cannot be grounded in obligations that we have toward individual animals.

Nor will it be fruitful to treat our obligations to a species as duties toward, or as arising out of the rights of, a species thought of as some special superentity. It is simply not clear that we can make sense of talk about the interests of a species in the absence of beliefs, desires, purposeful action, etc.[1] Since having interests is generally accepted as at least a necessary condition for having rights,[2] and since many of the duties we have toward animals arise directly out of the animals' interests, arguments which show that animals have rights, or that we have duties towards them, will not apply to species. Since arguments which proceed from interests to rights or from interests to obligations make up a majority of the literature on ethics and animals, it is unlikely that these arguments will serve as a key to possible obligations toward species.

Having eliminated the possibility that our obligations toward species are somehow parallel to, or similar to, our obligation not to cause unwarranted pain to an animal, there seem to be only a few possibilities left. We may find that our duties toward species arise not out of the interests of the species, but are rooted in the general obligation to preserve things of value. Alternatively, our obligations to species may in fact be obligations to individuals (either members of the species or other individuals), but obligations that differ from the ones just discussed in that they are not determined simply by the interests of the individual.

SOME TEST CASES

If we are to find some intuitively acceptable foundation for claims about our obligations to protect species, we must start afresh. In order to get clear about what, precisely, we are looking for in this context, what obligations we might think we have toward species, what moral claims we are seeking a foundation for, I turn now to a description of some test cases. An examination of these cases illustrates why the object of our search is not something as straightforward as "Do whatever is possible or necessary to preserve the existence of the species"; a consideration of some of the differences between cases will guide our search for the nature of our obligations and the underlying reasons for those obligations.

Case 1. The snail darter is known to exist only in one part of one river. This stretch of river would be destroyed by the building of the Tellico dam. Defenders of the dam have successfully argued that the dam is nonetheless necessary for the economic development and well-being of the area's population. To my knowledge, no serious or large scale attempt has been made to breed large numbers of snail darters in captivity (for any reason other than research).

Case 2. The Pére David deer was first discovered by a Western naturalist in 1865, when Pére Armand David found herds of the deer in the Imperial Gardens in Peking: even at that time, they were only known to exist in captivity. Pére David brought several animals back to Europe, where they bred readily enough so that now there are healthy populations in several major zoos.[3] There is no reasonable hope of reintroducing the Pére David deer to its natural habitat; indeed, it is not even definitely known what its natural habitat was.

Case 3. The red wolf *(Canis rufus)* formerly ranged over the southeastern and south-central United States. As with most wolves, they were threatened, and their range curtailed, by trapping, hunting, and the destruction of habitat. However, a more immediate threat to the continued existence of the red wolf is that these changes extended the range of the more adaptable coyote, with whom the red wolf interbreeds very readily; as a result, there are very few "pure" red wolves left. An attempt has been made to capture some pure breeding stock and raise wolves on preserves.[4]

Case 4. The Baltimore oriole and the Bullock's oriole were long recognized and classified as two separate species of birds. As a result of extensive interbreeding between the two species in areas where their ranges overlapped, the American Ornithologists' Union recently declared that there were no longer two separate species; both ex-species are now called "northern orioles."

Case 5. The Appaloosa is a breed of horse with a distinctively spotted coat; the Lewis and Clark expedition discovered that the breed was associated with the Nez Percé Indians. When the Nez Percé tribe was defeated by the U.S. Cavalry in 1877 and forced to move, their horses were scattered and interbred with other horses. The distinctive coat pattern was almost lost; not until the middle of the twentieth century was a concerted effort made to gather together the few remaining specimens and reestablish the breed.

Case 6. Many strains of laboratory rats are bred specifically for a certain type of research. Once the need for a particular variety ceases—once the type of research is completed—the rats are usually killed, with the result that the variety becomes extinct.

Case 7. It is commonly known that several diseases such as sleeping sickness, malaria, and human encephalitis are caused by one variety of mosquito but not by others. Much of the disease control in these cases is aimed at exterminating the disease carrying insect; most people do not find it morally wrong to wipe out the whole species.

Case 8. Suppose that zebras were threatened solely because they were hunted for their distinctive striped coats. Suppose, too, that we could remove this threat by selectively breeding zebras that are not striped, that look exactly like mules, although they are still pure zebras. Have we preserved all that we ought to have preserved?

What does an examination of these test cases reveal? First, that our concept of what a species *is* is not at all unambiguous; at least in part, what counts as a species is a matter of current fashions in taxon-

omy. Furthermore, it seems that it is not the sheer diversity or number of species that matters: if that were what is valued, moral preference would be given to taxonomic schemes that separated individuals into a larger number of species, a suggestion which seems absurd. The case of the orioles suggests that the decision as to whether to call these things one species or two is not a moral issue at all.[5] Since we are not evidently concerned with the existence or diversity of species in *this* sense, there must be something more at issue than the simple question of whether we have today the same number of species represented as we had yesterday. Confusion sets in, however, when we try to specify another sense in which it is possible to speak of the "existence" of a species. This only serves to emphasize the basic murkiness of our intuitions about what the object of our concern really is.

This murkiness is further revealed by the fact that it is not at all obvious what we are trying to preserve in some of the test cases. Sometimes, as in the case of the Appaloosa or attempts to save a subspecies like the Arctic wolf or the Mexican wolf, it is not a whole species that is in question. But not all genetic subgroups are of interest—witness the case of the laboratory rat—and sometimes the preservation of the species at the cost of one of its externally obvious features (the stripes on a zebra) is not our only concern. This is not a minor puzzle which can be resolved by changing our question from "why do species matter?" to "why do species and/or subspecies matter?" It is rather a serious issue of what makes a group of animals "special" enough or "unique" enough to warrant concern. And of course, the test cases reveal that our intuitions are not always consistent: although the cases of the red wolf and the northern oriole are parallel in important respects, we are more uneasy about simply reclassifying the red wolf and allowing things to continue along their present path.

The final point to be established is that whatever moral weight is finally attached to the preservation of a species (or subspecies), it can be overridden. We apparently have no compunction about wiping out a species of mosquito if the benefits gained by such action are sufficiently important, although many people were unconvinced by similar arguments in favor of the Tellico dam.

The lesson to be drawn from this section can be stated in a somewhat simplistic form: it is not simply the case that we can solve our problems by arguing that there is some value attached to the mere existence of a species. Our final analysis must take account of various features or properties of certain kinds or groups of animals, and it has to recognize that our concern is with the continued existence of individuals that may or may not have some distinctive characteristics.

SOME TRADITIONAL ANSWERS

There are, of course, some standard replies to the question "Why do species matter?" or, more particularly, to the question "Why do we have at least a prima facie duty not to cause a species to become extinct, and in some cases, a duty to try actively to preserve species?" With some tolerance for borderline cases, these replies generally fall into three groups: (1) those that appeal to our role as "stewards" or "caretakers," (2) those that claim that species have some extrinsic value (I include in this group those that argue that the species is valuable as part of the ecosystem or as a link in the evolutionary scheme of things), and (3) those that appeal to some intrinsic or inherent value that is supposed to make a species worth preserving. In this section, with the help of the test cases just discussed, I indicate some serious flaws with each of these responses.

The first type of view has been put forward in the philosophical literature by Joel Feinberg, who states that our duty to preserve whole species may be more important than any rights had by individual animals.[6] He argues, first, that this duty does not arise from a right or claim that can properly be attributed to the species as a whole (his reasons are much the same as the ones I cited in section 2 of this paper), and second, while we have some duty to unborn generations that directs us to preserve species, that duty is much weaker than the actual duty we have to pre-

serve species. The fact that our actual duty extends beyond our duties to future generations is explained by the claim that we have duties of "stewardship" with respect to the world as a whole. Thus, Feinberg notes that his "inclination is to seek an explanation in terms of the requirements of our unique station as rational custodians of the planet we temporarily occupy."[7]

The main objection to this appeal to our role as stewards or caretakers is that it begs the question. The job of a custodian is to protect that which is deserving of protection, that which has some value or worth.[8] But the issue before us now is precisely *whether* species have value, and why. If we justify our obligations of stewardship by reference to the value of that which is cared for, we cannot also explain the value by pointing to the duties of stewardship.

The second type of argument is the one which establishes the value of a species by locating it in the "larger scheme of things." That is, one might try to argue that species matter because they contribute to, or form an essential part of, some other good. This line of defense has several variations.

The first version is completely anthropocentric: it is claimed that vanishing species are of concern to us because their difficulties serve as a warning that we have polluted or altered the environment in a way that is potentially dangerous or undesirable for us. Thus, the California condor whose eggshells are weakened due to the absorption of DDT indicates that something is wrong: presumably we are being affected in subtle ways by the absorption of DDT, and that is bad for us. Alternatively, diminishing numbers of game animals may signal overhunting which, if left unchecked, would leave the sportsman with fewer things to hunt. And, as we become more aware of the benefits that might be obtained from rare varieties of plants and animals (drugs, substitutes for other natural resources, tools for research), we may become reluctant to risk the disappearance of a species that might be of practical use to us in the future.

This line of argument does not carry us very far. In the case of a subspecies, most benefits could be derived from other varieties of the same species. More important, when faced with the loss of a unique variety or species, we may simply decide that, even taking into account the possibility of error, there is not enough reason to think that the species will ever be of use; we may take a calculated risk and decide that it is not worth it. Finally, the use of a species as a danger signal may apply to species whose decline is due to some subtle and unforeseen change in the environment, but will not justify concern for a species threatened by a known and forseen event like the building of a dam.

Other attempts to ascribe extrinsic value to a species do not limit themselves to potential human and practical goods. Thus, it is often argued that each species occupies a unique niche in a rich and complex, but delicately balanced, ecosystem. By destroying a single species, we upset the balance of the whole system. On the assumption that the system as a whole should be preserved, the value of a species is determined, at least in part, by its contribution to the whole.[9]

In assessing this argument, it is important to realize that such a justification (a) may lead to odd conclusions about some of the test cases, and (b) allows for changes which do not affect the system, or which result in the substitution of a richer, more complex system for one that is more primitive or less evolved. With regard to the first of these points, species that exist only in zoos would seem to have no special value. In terms of our test cases, the David deer does not exist as part of a system, but only in isolation. Similarly, the Appaloosa horse, a domesticated variety which is neither better suited nor worse than any other sort of horse, would not have any special value. In contrast, the whole cycle of mosquitoes, disease organisms adapted to these hosts, and other beings susceptible to those diseases is quite a complex and marvelous bit of systematic adaptation. Thus, it would seem to be wrong to wipe out the encephalitis-bearing mosquito.

With regard to the second point, we might consider changes effected by white settlers in previously isolated areas such as New Zealand and Australia. The introduction of new species has resulted in a whole new ecosystem, with many of the former indigenous species being replaced by introduced varieties. As long as the new system works, there seems to be no grounds for objections.

The third version of an appeal to extrinsic value is sometimes presented in Darwinian terms: species are important as links in the evolutionary chain. This will get us nowhere, however, because the extinction of one species, the replacement of one by another, is as much a part of evolution as is the development of a new species.

One should also consider a more general concern about all those versions of the argument which focus on the species' role in the natural order of things: all of these arguments presuppose that "the natural order of things" is, in itself, good. As William Blackstone pointed out, this is by no means obvious: "Unless one adheres dogmatically to a position of a 'reverence for all life,' the extinction of some species or forms of life may be seen as quite desirable. (This is parallel to the point often made by philosophers that not all 'customary' or 'natural' behavior is necessarily good)."[10] Unless we have some other way of ascribing value to a system, and to the animals which actually fulfill a certain function in that system (as opposed to possible replacements), the argument will not get off the ground.

Finally, then, the process of elimination leads us to the set of arguments which point to some *intrinsic value* that a species is supposed to have. The notion that species have an intrinsic value, if established, would allow us to defend much stronger claims about human obligations toward threatened species. Thus, if a species is intrinsically valuable, we should try to preserve it even when it no longer has a place in the natural ecosystem, or when it could be replaced by another species that would occupy the same niche. Most important, we should not ignore a species just because it serves no useful purpose.

Unsurprisingly, the stumbling block is what this intrinsic value might be grounded in. Without an explanation of that, we have no nonarbitrary way of deciding whether subspecies as well as species have intrinsic value or how much intrinsic value a species might have. The last question is meant to bring out issues that will arise in cases of conflict of interests: is the intrinsic value of a species of mosquito sufficient to outweigh the benefits to be gained by eradicating the means of spreading a disease like encephalitis? Is the intrinsic value of the snail darter sufficient to outweigh the economic hardship that might be alleviated by the construction of a dam? In short, to say that something has intrinsic value does not tell us *how much* value it has, nor does it allow us to make the sorts of judgments that are often called for in considering the fate of an endangered species.

The attempt to sidestep the difficulties raised by subspecies by broadening the ascription of value to include subspecies opens a whole Pandora's box. It would follow that any genetic variation within a species that results in distinctive characteristics would need separate protection. In the case of forms developed through selective breeding, it is not clear whether we have a situation analogous to natural subspecies, or whether no special value is attached to different breeds.

In order to speak to either of these issues, and in order to lend plausibility to the whole enterprise, it would seem necessary to consider first the justification for ascribing value to whichever groups have such value. If intrinsic value does not spring from anything, if it becomes merely another way of saying that we should protect species, we are going around in circles, without explaining anything.[11] Some further explanation is needed.

Some appeals to intrinsic value are grounded in the intuition that diversity itself is a virtue. If so, it would seem incumbent upon us to create new species wherever possible, even bizarre ones that would have no purpose other than to be different. Something other than diversity must therefore be valued.

The comparison that is often made between species and natural wonders, spectacular landscapes, or even works of art, suggest that species might have some aesthetic value. This seems to accord well with our naive intuitions, provided that *aesthetic value* is interpreted rather loosely; most of us believe that the world would be a poorer place for the loss of bald eagles in the same way that it would be poorer for the loss of the Grand Canyon or a great work of art. In all cases, the experience of seeing these things is an inherently worthwhile experience. And since diversity in some cases is a component in aesthetic appreciation, part of the previous intuition would be preserved. There is also room for degrees of selectivity and concern with superficial changes: the variety of rat that is allowed to become extinct may have no special aesthetic value, and a bird is neither more nor less aesthetically pleasing when we change its name.

There are some drawbacks to this line of argument: there are some species which, by no stretch of the imagination, are aesthetically significant. But aesthetic value can cover a surprising range of things: a tiger may be simply beautiful; a blue whale is awe-inspiring; a bird might be decorative; an Appaloosa is of interest because of its historical significance; and even a drab little plant may inspire admiration for the marvelous way it has been adapted to a special environment. Even so, there may be species such as the snail darter that simply have no aesthetic value. In these cases, lacking any alternative, we may be forced to the conclusion that such species are not worth preserving.

Seen from other angles, once again the appeal to aesthetic value of species is illuminating. Things that have an aesthetic value can be compared and ranked in some cases, and commitment of resources may be made accordingly. We believe that diminishing the aesthetic value of a thing for mere economic benefits is immoral, but that aesthetic value is not absolute—that the fact that something has aesthetic value may be overridden by the fact that harming that thing, or destroying it, may result in some greater good. That is, someone who agrees to destroy a piece of Greek statuary for personal gain would be condemned as having done something immoral, but someone who is faced with a choice between saving his children and saving a "priceless" painting would be said to have skewed values if he chose to save the painting. Applying these observations to species, we can see that an appeal to aesthetic value would justify putting more effort into the preservation of one species than the preservation of another; indeed, just as we think that the doodling of a would-be artist may have no merit at all, we may think that the accidental and unfortunate mutation of a species is not worth preserving. Following the analogy, allowing a species to become extinct for *mere* economic gain might be seen as immoral, while the possibility remains open that other (human?) goods might outweigh the goods achieved by the preservation of a species.

Although the appeal to aesthetic values has much to recommend it—even when we have taken account of the fact that it does not guarantee that all species matter—there seems to be a fundamental confusion that still affects the cogency of the whole argument and its application to the question of special obligations to endangered species, for if the value of a species is based on its aesthetic value, it is impossible to explain why an endangered species should be more valuable, or more worthy of preservation, than an unendangered species. The appeal to "rarity" will not help, if what we are talking about is species: each species is unique, no more or less rare than any other species: there is in each case one and only one species that we are talking about.[12]

This problem of application seems to arise because the object of aesthetic appreciation, and hence of aesthetic value, has been misidentified, for it is not the case that we perceive, admire, and appreciate a *species*—species construed either as a group or set of similar animals or as a name that we attach to certain kinds of animals in virtue of some classification scheme. What we value is the existence of individuals with certain characteristics. If this is correct, then the whole attempt to explain why species matter by arguing that *they* have aesthetic value needs to be redirected. This is what I try to do in the final section of this paper.

VALUING THE INDIVIDUAL

What I propose is that the intuition behind the argument from aesthetic value is correct, but misdirected. The reasons that were given for the value of a species

are, in fact, reasons for saying that an individual has value. We do not admire the grace and beauty of the species *Panthera tigris;* rather, we admire the grace and beauty of the individual Bengal tigers that we may encounter. What we value then is the existence of that individual and the existence (present or future) of individuals like that. The ways in which other individuals should be "like that" will depend on why we value that particular sort of individual: the stripes on a zebra do not matter if we value zebras primarily for the way they are adapted to a certain environment, their unique fitness for a certain sort of life. If, on the other hand, we value zebras because their stripes are aesthetically pleasing, the stripes do matter. Since our attitudes toward zebras probably include both of these features, it is not surprising to find that my hypothetical test case produces conflicting intuitions.

The shift of emphasis from species to individuals allows us to make sense of the stronger feelings we have about endangered species in two ways. First, the fact that there are very few members of a species—the fact that we rarely encounter one—itself increases the value of those encounters. I can see turkey vultures almost every day, and I can eat apples almost every day, but seeing a bald eagle or eating wild strawberries are experiences that are much less common, more delightful just for their rarity and unexpectedness. Even snail darters, which, if we encountered them every day would be drab and uninteresting, become more interesting just because we don't—or may not—see them every day. Second, part of our interest in an individual carries over to a desire that there be future opportunities to see these things again (just as when, upon finding a new and beautiful work of art, I will wish to go back and see it again). In the case of animals, unlike works of art, I know that this animal will not live forever, but that other animals like this one will have similar aesthetic value. Thus, because I value possible future encounters, I will also want to do what is needed to ensure the possibility of such encounters—i.e., make sure that enough presently existing individuals of this type will be able to reproduce and survive. This is rather like the duty that we have to support and contribute to museums, or to other efforts to preserve works of art.

To sum up, then: individual animals can have, to a greater or lesser degree, aesthetic value: they are valued for their simple beauty, for their awesomeness, for their intriguing adaptations, for their rarity, and for many other reasons. We have moral obligations to protect things of aesthetic value, and to ensure (in an odd sense) their continued existence; thus we have a duty to protect individual animals (the duty may be weaker or stronger depending on the value of the individual), and to ensure that there will continue to be animals of this sort (this duty will also be weaker or stronger, depending on value).

I began this paper by suggesting that our obligations to vanishing species might appear inconsistent with a general condemnation of speciesism. My proposal is not inconsistent: we value and protect animals because of their aesthetic value, not because they are members of a given species.

NOTES

1. Cf. Joel Feinberg, "The Rights of Animals and Future Generations," in *Philosophy and Environmental Crisis,* ed. William Blackstone (Athens: University of Georgia Press, 1974), pp. 55–57

2. There are some exceptions to this: for example, Tom Regan argues that some rights are grounded in the intrinsic value of a thing in "Do Animals Have a Right to Life?" in *Animal Rights and Human Obligations,* eds. Tom Regan and Peter Singer (Englewood Cliffs, N.J.: Prentice-Hall, 1975), pp. 198–203. These and similar cases will be dealt with by examining the proposed foundations of rights; thus, the claim that species have intrinsic value will be considered in section 3.

3. The deer in China were all killed during the Boxer rebellion; recently, several pairs were sent to Chinese zoos.

4. *Predator* 7, no. 2 (1980). Further complications occur in this case because a few scientists have tried to argue that all red wolves are the result of interbreeding between grey wolves (*Canis Lupus*) and coyotes (*C. latans*). For more information, see L. David Mech, *The Wolf* (Garden City, N.Y.: Natural History Press, 1970), pp. 22–25.

5. Sometimes there are moral questions about the practical consequences of such a move. The recent decision to combine two endangered species—the seaside sparrow and the dusky seaside sparrow—aggravates the difficulties faced by attempts to protect these birds.

6. Joel Feinberg, "Human Duties and Animal Rights," in *On the Fifth Day: Animal Rights and Human Ethics,* Richard Knowles Morris and Michael W. Fox, eds. (Washington: Acropolis Books, 1978), p. 67.

7. Feinberg, "Human Duties," p. 68

8. Cf. Feinberg's discussion of custodial duties in "The Rights of Animals and Future Generations," *Philosophy and Environmental Crisis,* pp. 49–50

9. A similar view has been defended by Tom Auxter, "The Right Not to Be Eaten," *Inquiry* 22 (1979): 221–230.

10. William Blackstone, "Ethics and Ecology," *Philosophy and Environmental Crisis,* p. 25.

11. This objection parallels Regan's attack on ungrounded appeals to the intrinsic value of human life as a way of trying to establish a human right to life. Cf. Thomas Regan, "Do Animals Have a Right to Life?" *Animal Rights and Human Obligations,* p. 199.

12. There is one further attempt that might be made to avoid this difficulty: one might argue that species do not increase in value due to scarcity, but that our duties to protect a valuable species involves more when the species is more in need of protection. This goes part of the way towards solving the problem, but does not yet capture our intuition that rarity does affect the value in some way.

Philosophical Problems for Environmentalism

Elliott Sober

INTRODUCTION

A number of philosophers have recognized that the environmental movement, whatever its practical political effectiveness, faces considerable theoretical difficulties in justification.[1] It has been recognized that traditional moral theories do not provide natural underpinnings for policy objectives and this has led some to skepticism about the claims of environmentalists, and others to the view that a revolutionary reassessment of ethical norms is needed. In this chapter, I will try to summarize the difficulties that confront a philosophical defense of environmentalism. I also will suggest a way of making sense of some environmental concerns that does not require the wholesale jettisoning of certain familiar moral judgments.

Preserving an endangered species or ecosystem poses no special conceptual problem when the instrumental value of that species or ecosystem is known. When we have reason to think that some natural object represents a resource to us, we obviously ought to take that fact into account in deciding what to do. A variety of potential uses may be under discussion, including food supply, medical applications, recreational use, and so on. As with any complex decision, it may be difficult even to agree on how to compare the competing values that may be involved. Willingness to pay in dollars is a familiar least common denominator, although it poses a number of problems. But here we have nothing that is specifically a problem for environmentalism.

The problem for environmentalism stems from the idea that species and ecosystems ought to be preserved for reasons additional to their known value as resources for human use. The feeling is that even when we cannot say what nutritional, medicinal, or recreational benefit the preservation provides, there still is a value in preservation. It is the search for a rationale for this feeling that constitutes the main conceptual problem for environmentalism.

The problem is especially difficult in view of the holistic (as opposed to individualistic) character of the things being assigned value. Put simply, what is special about environmentalism is that it values the preservation of species, communities, or ecosystems, rather than the individual organisms of which they are composed. "Animal liberationists" have urged that we should take the suffering of sentient animals into account in ethical deliberation.[2] Such beasts are not mere things to be used as cruelly as we like no matter how trivial the benefit we derive. But in "widening the ethical circle," we are simply including in the community more individual organisms whose costs and benefits we compare. Animal liberationists are extending an old and familiar ethical doctrine—namely, utilitarianism—to take account of the welfare of other individuals. Although the practical consequences of this point of view may be revolutionary, the theoretical perspective is not at all novel. If suffering is bad, then it is bad for any individual who suffers.[3] Animal liberationists merely remind us of the consequences of familiar principles.

But trees, mountains, and salt marshes do not suffer. They do not experience pleasure and pain, because, evidently, they do not have experiences at all. The same is true of species. Granted, individual organisms may have mental states; but the species—taken to be a population of organisms connected by certain sorts of interactions (preeminently, that of ex-

Elliott Sober, "Philosophical Problems for Environmentalism," in *The Preservation of Species*, ed. B. Norton (Princeton: Princeton University Press, 1986), 173–94. Copyright © 1986 by Princeton University Press, Princeton. Reprinted by permission of the publisher.

changing genetic material in reproduction)—does not. Or put more carefully, we might say that the only sense in which species have experiences is that their member organisms do: the attribution at the population level, if true, is true simply in virtue of its being true at the individual level. Here is a case where reductionism is correct.

So perhaps it is true in this reductive sense that some species experience pain. But the values that environmentalists attach to preserving species do not reduce to any value of preserving organisms. It is in this sense that environmentalists espouse a holistic value system. Environmentalists care about entities that by no stretch of the imagination have experiences (e.g., mountains). What is more, their position does not force them to care if individual organisms suffer pain, so long as the species is preserved. Steel traps may outrage an animal liberationist because of the suffering they inflict, but an environmentalist aiming just at the preservation of a balanced ecosystem might see here no cause for complaint. Similarly, environmentalists think that the distinction between wild and domesticated organisms is important, in that it is the preservation of "natural" (i.e., not created by the "artificial interference" of human beings) objects that matters, whereas animal liberationists see the main problem in terms of the suffering of any organism—domesticated or not. And finally, environmentalists and animal liberationists diverge on what might be called the $n + m$ question. If two species—say blue and sperm whales—have roughly comparable capacities for experiencing pain, an animal liberationist might tend to think of the preservation of a sperm whale as wholly on an ethical par with the preservation of a blue whale. The fact that one organism is part of an endangered species while the other is not does not make the rare individual more intrinsically important. But for an environmentalist, this holistic property—membership in an endangered species—makes all the difference in the world: a world with n sperm and m blue whales is far better than a world with $n + m$ sperm and 0 blue whales. Here we have a stark contrast between an ethic in which it is the life situation of individuals that matters, and an ethic in which the stability and

diversity of populations of individuals are what matter.[4]

Both animal liberationists and environmentalists wish to broaden our ethical horizons—to make us realize that it is not just human welfare that counts. But they do this in very different, often conflicting, ways. It is no accident that at the level of practical politics the two points of view increasingly find themselves at loggerheads. This practical conflict is the expression of a deep theoretical divide.

THE IGNORANCE ARGUMENT

"Although we might not now know what use a particular endangered species might be to us, allowing it to go extinct forever closes off the possibility of discovering and exploiting a future use." According to this point of view, our ignorance of value is turned into a reason for action. The scenario envisaged in this environmentalist argument is not without precedent; who could have guessed that penicillin would be good for something other than turning out cheese? But there is a fatal defect in such arguments, which we might summarize with the phrase *out of nothing, nothing comes:* rational decisions require assumptions about what is true and what is valuable (in decision-theoretic jargon, the inputs must be probabilities and utilities). If you are completely ignorant of values, then you are incapable of making a rational decision, either for or against preserving some species. The fact that you do not know the value of a species, by itself, cannot count as a reason for wanting one thing rather than another to happen to it.

And there are so many species. How many geese that lay golden eggs are there apt to be in that number? It is hard to assign probabilities and utilities precisely here, but an analogy will perhaps reveal the problem confronting this environmentalist argument. Most of us willingly fly on airplanes, when safer (but less convenient) alternative forms of transportation are available. Is this rational? Suppose it were argued that there is a small probability that the next flight you take will crash. This would be very bad for you. Is it not crazy for you to risk this, given that the only gain to you is that you can reduce your travel time by a few hours (by not going by train, say)? Those of us who not only fly, but congratulate ourselves for being rational in doing so, reject this argument. We are prepared to accept a small chance of a great disaster in return for the high probability of a rather modest benefit. If this is rational, no wonder that we might consistently be willing to allow a species to go extinct in order to build a hydroelectric plant.

That the argument from ignorance is no argument at all can be seen from another angle. If we literally do not know what consequences the extinction of this or that species may bring, then we should take seriously the possibility that the extinction may be beneficial as well as the possibility that it may be deleterious. It may sound deep to insist that we preserve endangered species precisely because we do not know why they are valuable. But ignorance on a scale like this cannot provide the basis for any rational action.

Rather than invoke some unspecified future benefit, an environmentalist may argue that the species in question plays a crucial role in stabilizing the ecosystem of which it is a part. This will undoubtedly be true for carefully chosen species and ecosystems, but one should not generalize this argument into a global claim to the effect that *every* species is crucial to a balanced ecosystem. Although ecologists used to agree that the complexity of an ecosystem stabilizes it, this hypothesis has been subject to a number of criticisms and qualifications, both from a theoretical and an empirical perspective.[5] And for certain kinds of species (those which occupy a rather small area and whose normal population is small) we can argue that extinction would probably not disrupt the community. However fragile the biosphere may be, the extreme view that everything is crucial is almost certainly not true.

But, of course, environmentalists are often concerned by the fact that extinctions are occurring now at a rate much higher than in earlier times. It is mass extinction that threatens the biosphere, they say, and this claim avoids the spurious assertion that communities are so fragile that even one extinction will

cause a crash. However, if the point is to avoid a mass extinction of species, how does this provide a rationale for preserving a species of the kind just described, of which we rationally believe that its passing will not destabilize the ecosystem? And, more generally, if mass extinction is known to be a danger to us, how does this translate into a value for preserving any particular species? Notice that we have now passed beyond the confines of the argument from ignorance; we are taking as a premise the idea that mass extinction would be a catastrophe (since it would destroy the ecosystem on which we depend). But how should that premise affect our valuing the California condor, the blue whale, or the snail darter?

THE SLIPPERY SLOPE ARGUMENT

Environmentalists sometimes find themselves asked to explain why each species matters so much to them, when there are, after all, so many. We may know of special reasons for valuing particular species, but how can we justify thinking that each and every species is important? "Each extinction impoverishes the biosphere" is often the answer given, but it really fails to resolve the issue. Granted, each extinction impoverishes, but it only impoverishes a little bit. So if it is the *wholesale* impoverishment of the biosphere that matters, one would apparently have to concede that each extinction matters a little, but only a little. But environmentalists may be loathe to concede this, for if they concede that each species matters only a little, they seem to be inviting the wholesale impoverishment that would be an unambiguous disaster. So they dig in their heels and insist that each species matters a lot. But to take this line, one must find some other rationale than the idea that mass extinction would be a great harm. Some of these alternative rationales we will examine later. For now, let us take a closer look at the train of thought involved here.

Slippery slopes are curious things: if you take even one step onto them, you inevitably slide all the way to the bottom. So if you want to avoid finding yourself at the bottom, you must avoid stepping onto them at all. To mix metaphors, stepping onto a slippery slope is to invite being nickeled and dimed to death.

Slippery slope arguments have played a powerful role in a number of recent ethical debates. One often hears people defend the legitimacy of abortions by arguing that since it is permissible to abort a single-celled fertilized egg, it must be permissible to abort a foetus of any age, since there is no place to draw the line from 0 to 9 months. Antiabortionists, on the other hand, sometimes argue in the other direction: since infanticide of newborns is not permissible, abortion at any earlier time is also not allowed, since there is no place to draw the line. Although these two arguments reach opposite conclusions about the permissibility of abortions, they agree on the following idea: since there is no principled place to draw the line on the continuum from newly fertilized egg to foetus gone to term, one must treat all these cases in the same way. Either abortion is always permitted or it never is, since there is no place to draw the line. Both sides run their favorite slippery slope arguments, but try to precipitate slides in opposite directions.

Starting with 10 million extant species, and valuing overall diversity, the environmentalist does not want to grant that each species matters only a little. For having granted this, commercial expansion and other causes will reduce the tally to 9,999,999. And then the argument is repeated, with each species valued only a little, and diversity declines another notch. And so we are well on our way to a considerably impoverished biosphere, a little at a time. Better to reject the starting premise—namely, that each species matters only a little—so that the slippery slope can be avoided.

Slippery slopes should hold no terror for environmentalists, because it is often a mistake to demand that a line be drawn. Let me illustrate by an example. What is the difference between being bald and not? Presumably, the difference concerns the number of hairs you have on your head. But what is the precise number of hairs marking the boundary between baldness and not being bald? There is no such number. Yet, it would be a fallacy to conclude that there is no difference between baldness and

hairiness. The fact that you cannot draw a line does not force you to say that the two alleged categories collapse into one. In the abortion case, this means that even if there is no precise point in foetal development that involves some discontinuous, qualitative change, one is still not obliged to think of newly fertilized eggs and foetuses gone to term as morally on a par. Since the biological differences are ones of degree, not kind, one may want to adopt the position that the moral differences are likewise matters of degree. This may lead to the view that a woman should have a better reason for having an abortion, the more developed her foetus is. Of course, this position does not logically follow from the idea that there is no place to draw the line; my point is just that differences in degree do not demolish the possibility of there being real moral differences.

In the environmental case, if one places a value on diversity, then each species becomes more valuable as the overall diversity declines. If we begin with 10 million species, each may matter little, but as extinctions continue, the remaining ones matter more and more. According to this outlook, a better and better reason would be demanded for allowing yet another species to go extinct. Perhaps certain sorts of economic development would justify the extinction of a species at one time. But granting this does not oblige one to conclude that the same sort of decision would have to be made further down the road. This means that one can value diversity without being obliged to take the somewhat exaggerated position that each species, no matter how many there are, is terribly precious in virtue of its contribution to that diversity.

Yet, one can understand that environmentalists might be reluctant to concede this point. They may fear that if one now allows that most species contribute only a little to overall diversity, one will set in motion a political process that cannot correct itself later. The worry is that even when the overall diversity has been drastically reduced, our ecological sensitivities will have been so coarsened that we will no longer be in a position to realize (or to implement policies fostering) the preciousness of what is left. This fear may be quite justified, but it is important to realize that it does not conflict with what was argued above. The political utility of making an argument should not be confused with the argument's soundness.

The fact that you are on a slippery slope, by itself, does not tell you whether you are near the beginning, in the middle, or at the end. If species diversity is a matter of degree, where do we currently find ourselves—on the verge of catastrophe, well on our way in that direction, or at some distance from a global crash? Environmentalists often urge that we are fast approaching a precipice; if we are, then the reduction in diversity that every succeeding extinction engenders should be all we need to justify species preservation.

Sometimes, however, environmentalists advance a kind of argument not predicated on the idea of fast approaching doom. The goal is to show that there is something wrong with allowing a species to go extinct (or with causing it to go extinct), even if overall diversity is not affected much. I now turn to one argument of this kind.

APPEALS TO WHAT IS NATURAL

I noted earlier that environmentalists and animal liberationists disagree over the significance of the distinction between wild and domesticated animals. Since both types of organisms can experience pain, animal liberationists will think of each as meriting ethical consideration. But environmentalists will typically not put wild and domesticated organisms on a par. Environmentalists typically are interested in preserving what is natural, be it a species living in the wild or a wilderness ecosystem. If a kind of domesticated chicken were threatened with extinction, I doubt that environmental groups would be up in arms. And if certain unique types of human environments—say urban slums in the United States—were "endangered," it is similarly unlikely that environmentalists would view this process as a deplorable impoverishment of the biosphere.

The environmentalist's lack of concern for humanly created organisms and environments may be practical rather than principled. It may be that at the level of values, no such bifurcation is legitimate, but

that from the point of view of practical political action, it makes sense to put one's energies into saving items that exist in the wild. This subject has not been discussed much in the literature, so it is hard to tell. But I sense that the distinction between wild and domesticated has a certain theoretical importance to many environmentalists. They perhaps think that the difference is that we created domesticated organisms which would otherwise not exist, and so are entitled to use them solely for our own interests. But we did not create wild organisms and environments, so it is the height of presumption to expropriate them for our benefit. A more fitting posture would be one of "stewardship": we have come on the scene and found a treasure not of our making. Given this, we ought to preserve this treasure in its natural state.

I do not wish to contest the appropriateness of "stewardship." It is the dichotomy between artificial (domesticated) and natural (wild) that strikes me as wrong-headed. I want to suggest that to the degree that "natural" means anything biologically, it means very little ethically. And, conversely, to the degree that "natural" is understood as a normative concept, it has very little to do with biology.

Environmentalists often express regret that we human beings find it so hard to remember that we are part of nature—one species among many others—rather than something standing outside of nature. I will not consider here whether this attitude is cause for complaint; the important point is that seeing us as part of nature rules out the environmentalist's use of the distinction between artificial-domesticated and natural-wild described above. *If we are part of nature, then everything we do is part of nature, and is natural in that primary sense.* When we domesticate organisms and bring them into a state of dependence on us, this is simply an example of one species exerting a selection pressure on another. If one calls this "unnatural," one might just as well say the same of parasitism or symbiosis (compare human domestication of animals and plants and "slave-making" in the social insects).

The concept of naturalness is subject to the same abuses as the concept of normalcy. *Normal* can mean *usual* or it can mean *desirable*. Although only the total pessimist will think that the two concepts are mutually exclusive, it is generally recognized that the mere fact that something is common does not by itself count as a reason for thinking that it is desirable. This distinction is quite familiar now in popular discussions of mental health, for example. Yet, when it comes to environmental issues, the concept of naturalness continues to live a double life. The destruction of wilderness areas by increased industrialization is bad because it is unnatural. And it is unnatural because it involves transforming a natural into an artificial habitat. Or one might hear that although extinction is a natural process, the kind of mass extinction currently being precipitated by our species is unprecedented, and so is unnatural. Environmentalists should look elsewhere for a defense of their policies, lest conservation simply become a variant of uncritical conservatism in which the axiom "Whatever is, is right" is modified to read "Whatever is (before human beings come on the scene), is right."

This conflation of the biological with the normative sense of "natural" sometimes comes to the fore when environmentalists attack animal liberationists for naive do-goodism. Callicott writes:

> . . . the value commitments of the humane movement seem at bottom to betray a world-denying or rather a life-loathing philosophy. The natural world as actually constituted is one in which one being lives at the expense of others. Each organism, in Darwin's metaphor, struggles to maintain its own organic integrity. . . . To live is to be anxious about life, to feel pain and pleasure in a fitting mixture, and sooner or later to die. That is the way the system works. *If nature as a whole is good, then pain and death are also good.* Environmental ethics in general require people to play fair in the natural system. The neo-Benthamites have in a sense taken the uncourageous approach. People have attempted to exempt themselves from the life death reciprocities of natural processes and from ecological limitations in the name of a prophylactic ethic of maximizing rewards (pleasure) and minimizing unwelcome information (pain). To be fair, the humane moralists seem to suggest that we should attempt to project the same values into the nonhuman animal world and to widen the charmed circle—no matter that it

would be biologically unrealistic to do so or biologically ruinous if, per impossible, such an environmental ethic were implemented.

> There is another approach. Rather than imposing our alienation from nature and natural processes and cycles of life on other animals, we human beings could reaffirm our participation in nature by accepting life as it is given without a sugar coating. . . .[6]

On the same page, Callicott quotes with approval Shepard's remark that "the humanitarian's projection onto nature of illegal murder and the rights of civilized people to safety not only misses the point but is exactly contrary to fundamental ecological reality: the structure of nature is a sequence of killings."[7]

Thinking that what is found in nature is beyond ethical defect has not always been popular. Darwin wrote:

> . . . That there is much suffering in the world no one disputes.

> Some have attempted to explain this in reference to man by imagining that it serves for his moral improvement. But the number of men in the world is as nothing compared with that of all other sentient beings, and these often suffer greatly without any moral improvement. A being so powerful and so full of knowledge as a God who could create the universe, is to our finite minds omnipotent and omniscient, and it revolts our understanding to suppose that his benevolence is not unbounded, for what advantage can there be in the sufferings of millions of the lower animals throughout almost endless time? This very old argument from the existence of suffering against the existence of an intelligent first cause seems to me a strong one; whereas, as just remarked, the presence of much suffering agrees well with the view that all organic beings have been developed through variation and natural selection.[8]

Darwin apparently viewed the quantity of pain found in nature as a melancholy and sobering consequence of the struggle for existence. But once we adopt the Panglossian attitude that this is the best of all possible worlds ("there is just the right amount of pain," etc.), a failure to identify what is natural with what is good can only seem "world-denying," "lifeloathing," "in a sense uncourageous," and "contrary to fundamental ecological reality."

Earlier in his essay, Callicott expresses distress that animal liberationists fail to draw a sharp distinction "between the very different plights (and rights) of wild and domestic animals."[9] Domestic animals are creations of man, he says. "They are living artifacts, but artifacts nevertheless. . . . There is thus something profoundly incoherent (and insensitive as well) in the complaint of some animal liberationists that the 'natural behavior' of chickens and bobby calves is cruelly frustrated on factory farms. It would make almost as much sense to speak of the natural behavior of tables and chairs."[10] Here again we see teleology playing a decisive role: wild organisms do not have the natural function of serving human ends, but domesticated animals do. Cheetahs in zoos are crimes against what is natural; veal calves in boxes are not.

The idea of "natural tendency" played a decisive role in pre-Darwinian biological thinking. Aristotle's entire science—both his physics and his biology—is articulated in terms of specifying the natural tendencies of kinds of objects and the interfering forces that can prevent an object from achieving its intended state. Heavy objects in the sublunar sphere have location at the center of the earth as their natural state; each tends to go there, but is prevented from doing so. Organisms likewise are conceptualized in terms of this natural state model:

> . . . [for] any living thing that has reached its normal development and which is unmutilated, and whose mode of generation is not spontaneous, the most natural act is the production of another like itself, an animal producing an animal, a plant a plant. . . .[11]

But many interfering forces are possible, and in fact the occurrence of "monsters" is anything but uncommon. According to Aristotle, mules (sterile hybrids) count as deviations from the natural state. In fact, females are monsters as well, since the natural tendency of sexual reproduction is for the offspring to perfectly resemble the father, who, according to Aristotle, provides the "genetic instructions" (to put the idea anachronistically) while the female provides only the matter.

What has happened to the natural state model in modern science? In physics, the idea of describing what a class of objects will do in the absence of "interference" lives on: Newton specified this "zero-force state" as rest or uniform motion, and in general relativity, this state is understood in terms of motion along geodesics. But one of the most profound achievements of Darwinian biology has been the jettisoning of this kind of model. It isn't just that Aristotle was wrong in his detailed claims about mules and women; the whole structure of the natural state model has been discarded. Population biology is not conceptualized in terms of positing some characteristic that all members of a species would have in common, were interfering forces absent. Variation is not thought of as a deflection from the natural state of uniformity. Rather, variation is taken to be a fundamental property in its own right. Nor, at the level of individual biology, does the natural state model find an application. Developmental theory is not articulated by specifying a natural tendency and a set of interfering forces. The main conceptual tool for describing the various developmental pathways open to a genotype is the norm of reaction. The norm of reaction of a genotype within a range of environments will describe what phenotype the genotype will produce in a given environment. Thus, the norm of reaction for a corn plant genotype might describe how its height is influenced by the amount of moisture in the soil. The norm of reaction is entirely silent on which phenotype is the "natural" one. The idea that a corn plant might have some "natural height," which can be, augmented or diminished by "interfering forces" is entirely alien to post-Darwinian biology.

The fact that the concepts of natural state and interfering force have lapsed from biological thought does not prevent environmentalists from inventing them anew. Perhaps these concepts can be provided with some sort of normative content; after all, the normative idea of "human rights" may make sense even if it is not a theoretical underpinning of any empirical science. But environmentalists should not assume that they can rely on some previously articulated scientific conception of "natural."

APPEALS TO NEEDS AND INTERESTS

The version of utilitarianism considered earlier (according to which something merits ethical consideration if it can experience pleasure and/or pain) leaves the environmentalist in the lurch. But there is an alternative to Bentham's hedonistic utilitarianism that has been thought by some to be a foundation for environmentalism. Preference utilitarianism says that an object's having interests, needs, or preferences gives it ethical, status. This doctrine is at the core of Stone's affirmative answer to the title question of his book *Should Trees Have Standing?*[12] "Natural objects can communicate their wants (needs) to us, and in ways that are not terribly ambiguous. . . . The lawn tells me that it wants water by a certain dryness of the blades and soil—immediately obvious to the touch—the appearance of bald spots, yellowing, and a lack of springiness after being walked on." And if plants can do this, presumably so can mountain ranges, and endangered species. Preference utilitarianism may thereby seem to grant intrinsic ethical importance to precisely the sorts of objects about which environmentalists have expressed concern.

The problems with this perspective have been detailed by Sagoff.[13] If one does not require of an object that it have a mind for it to have wants or needs, what is required for the possession of these ethically relevant properties? Suppose one says that an object needs something if it will cease to exist if it does not get it. Then species, plants, and mountain ranges have needs, but only in the sense that automobiles, garbage dumps, and buildings do too. If everything has needs, the advice to take needs into account in ethical deliberation is empty, unless it is supplemented by some technique for weighting and comparing the needs of different objects. A corporation will go bankrupt unless a highway is built. But the swamp will cease to exist if the highway is built. Perhaps one should take into account all relevant needs, but the question is how to do this in the event that needs conflict.

Although the concept of need can be provided with a permissive, all-inclusive definition, it is less easy to see how to do this with the concept of want. Why think that a mountain range "wants" to retain its unspoiled appearance, rather than house a new amusement park?[14] Needs are not at issue here, since in either case, the mountain continues to exist. One might be tempted to think that natural objects like mountains and species have "natural tendencies," and that the concept of want should be liberalized so as to mean that natural objects "want" to persist in their natural states. This Aristotelian view, as I argued in the previous section, simply makes no sense. Granted, a commercially undeveloped mountain will persist in this state, unless it is commercially developed. But it is equally true that a commercially untouched hill will become commercially developed, unless something causes this not to happen. I see no hope for extending, the concept of wants to the full range of objects valued by environmentalists.

The same problems emerge when we try to apply the concepts of needs and wants to species. A species may need various resources, in the sense that these are necessary for its continued existence. But what do species want? Do they want to remain stable in numbers, neither growing nor shrinking? Or since most species have gone extinct, perhaps what species really want is to go extinct, and it is human meddlesomeness that frustrates this natural tendency? Preference utilitarianism is no more likely than hedonistic utilitarianism to secure autonomous ethical status for endangered species.

Ehrenfeld describes a related distortion that has been inflicted on the diversity/stability hypothesis in theoretical ecology.[15] If it were true that increasing the diversity of an ecosystem causes it to be more stable, this might encourage the Aristotelian idea that ecosystems have a natural tendency to increase their diversity. The full realization of this tendency—the natural state that is the goal of ecosystems—is the "climax" or "mature" community. Extinction diminishes diversity, so it frustrates ecosystems from attaining their goal. Since the hypothesis that diversity causes stability is now considered controversial (to say the least), this line of thinking will not be very tempting. But even if the diversity/stability hypothesis were true, it would not permit the environmentalist to conclude that ecosystems have an interest in retaining their diversity.

Darwinism has not banished the idea that parts of the natural world are goal-directed systems, but has furnished this idea with a natural mechanism. We properly conceive of organisms (or genes, sometimes) as being in the business of maximizing their chances of survival and reproduction. We describe characteristics as adaptations—as devices that exist for the furtherance of these ends. Natural selection makes this perspective intelligible. But Darwinism is a profoundly individualistic doctrine. Darwinism rejects the idea that species, communities, and ecosystems have adaptations that exist for their own benefit. These higher-level entities are not conceptualized as goal-directed systems; what properties of organization they possess are viewed as artifacts of processes operating at lower levels of organization. An environmentalism based on the idea that the ecosystem is directed toward stability and diversity must find its foundation elsewhere.

GRANTING WHOLES AUTONOMOUS VALUE

A number of environmentalists have asserted that environmental values cannot be grounded in values based on regard for individual welfare. Aldo Leopold wrote in *A Sand County Almanac* that "a thing is right when it tends to preserve the integrity, stability, and beauty of the biotic community. It is wrong when it tends otherwise."[16] Callicott develops this idea at some length, and ascribes to ethical environmentalism the view that "the preciousness of individual deer, *as of any other specimen,* is inversely proportional to the population of the species."[17] In his *Desert Solitaire,* Edward Abbey notes that he would sooner shoot a man than a snake.[18] And Garrett Hardin asserts that human beings injured in wilderness areas ought not to be rescued: making great and spectacular efforts to save the life of an individual "makes sense only when there is a shortage of people. I have not lately heard that there is a shortage of people."[19] The point of view suggested by

these quotations is quite clear. It isn't that preserving the integrity of ecosystems has autonomous value, to be taken into account just as the quite distinct value of individual human welfare is. Rather, the idea is that the only value is the holistic one of maintaining ecological balance and diversity. Here we have a view that is just as monolithic as the most single-minded individualism; the difference is that the unit of value is thought to exist at a higher level of organization.

It is hard to know what to say to someone who would save a mosquito, just because it is rare, rather than a human being, if there were a choice. In ethics, as in any other subject, rationally persuading another person requires the existence of shared assumptions. If this monolithic environmentalist view is based on the notion that ecosystems have needs and interests, and that these take total precedence over the rights and interests of individual human beings, then the discussion of the previous sections is relevant. And even supposing that these higher-level entities have needs and wants, what reason is there to suppose that these matter and that the wants and needs of individuals matter not at all? But if this source of defense is jettisoned, and it is merely asserted that only ecosystems have value, with no substantive defense being offered, one must begin by requesting an argument: *why* is ecosystem stability and diversity the only value?

Some environmentalists have seen the individualist bias of utilitarianism as being harmful in ways additional to its impact on our perception of ecological values. Thus, Callicott writes:

On the level of social organization, the interests of society may not always coincide with the sum of the interests of its parts. Discipline, sacrifice, and individual restraint are often necessary in the social sphere to maintain social integrity as within the bodily organism. A society, indeed, is particularly vulnerable to disintegration when its members become preoccupied totally with their own particular interest, and ignore those distinct and independent interests of the community as a whole. One example, unfortunately, our own society, is altogether too close at hand to be examined with strict academic detachment. The United States seems to pursue uncritically a social policy of reductive utilitarianism, aimed at promoting the happiness of all its members severally. Each special interest accordingly clamors more loudly to be satisfied while the community as a whole becomes noticeably more and more infirm economically, environmentally, and politically.[20]

Callicott apparently sees the emergence of individualism and alienation from nature as two aspects of the same process. He values "the symbiotic relationship of Stone Age man to the natural environment" and regrets that "civilization has insulated and alienated us from the rigors and challenges of the natural environment. The hidden agenda of the humane ethic," he says, "is the imposition of the anti-natural prophylactic ethos of comfort and soft pleasure on an even wider scale. The land ethic, on the other hand, requires a shrinkage, if at all possible, of the domestic sphere; it rejoices in a recrudescence of the wilderness and a renaissance of tribal cultural experience."[21]

Callicott is right that "strict academic detachment" is difficult here. The reader will have to decide whether the United States currently suffers from too much or too little regard "for the happiness of all its members severally" and whether we should feel nostalgia or pity in contemplating what the Stone Age experience of nature was like.

THE DEMARCATION PROBLEM

Perhaps the most fundamental theoretical problem confronting an environmentalist who wishes to claim that species and ecosystems have autonomous value is what I will call the *problem of demarcation*. Every ethical theory must provide principles that describe which objects matter for their own sakes and which do not. Besides marking the boundary between these two classes by enumerating a set of ethically relevant properties, an ethical theory must say why the properties named, rather than others, are the ones that count. Thus, for example, hedonistic utilitarianism cites the capacity to experience pleasure and/or pain

as the decisive criterion; preference utilitarianism cites the having of preferences (or wants, or interests) as the decisive property. And a Kantian ethical theory will include an individual in the ethical community only if it is capable of rational reflection and autonomy. Not that justifying these various proposed solutions to the demarcation problem is easy; indeed, since this issue is so fundamental, it will be very difficult to justify one proposal as opposed to another. Still, a substantive ethical theory is obliged to try.

Environmentalists, wishing to avoid the allegedly distorting perspective of individualism, frequently want to claim autonomous value for wholes. This may take the form of a monolithic doctrine according to which the only thing that matters is the stability of the ecosystem. Or it may embody a pluralistic outlook according to which ecosystem stability and species preservation have an importance additional to the welfare of individual organisms. But an environmentalist theory shares with all ethical theories an interest in not saying that everything has autonomous value. The reason this position is proscribed is that it makes the adjudication of ethical conflict very difficult indeed. (In addition, it is radically implausible, but we can set that objection to one side.)

Environmentalists, as we have seen, may think of natural objects, like mountains, species, and ecosystems, as mattering for their own sake, but of artificial objects, like highway systems and domesticated animals, as having only instrumental value. If a mountain and a highway are both made of rock, it seems unlikely that the difference between them arises from the fact that mountains have wants, interests, and preferences, but highway systems do not. But perhaps the place to look for the relevant difference is not in their present physical composition, but in the historical fact of how each came into existence. Mountains were created by natural processes, whereas highways are humanly constructed. But once we realize that organisms construct their environments in nature, this contrast begins to cloud. Organisms do not passively reside in an environment whose properties are independently determined. Organisms transform their environments by physically interacting with them. An anthill is an artifact just as a highway is. Granted, a difference obtains at the level of whether conscious deliberation played a role, but can one take seriously the view that artifacts produced by conscious planning are thereby *less* valuable than ones that arise without the intervention of mentality.[22] As we have noted before, although environmentalists often accuse their critics of failing to think in a biologically realistic way, their use of the distinction between "natural" and "artificial" is just the sort of idea that stands in need of a more realistic biological perspective.

My suspicion is that the distinction between natural and artificial is not the crucial one. On the contrary, certain features of environmental concerns imply that natural objects are exactly on a par with certain artificial ones. Here the intended comparison is not between mountains and highways, but between mountains and works of art. My goal in what follows is not to sketch a substantive conception of what determines the value of objects in these two domains, but to motivate an analogy.

For both natural objects and works of art, our values extend beyond the concerns we have for experiencing pleasure. Most of us value seeing an original painting more than we value seeing a copy, even when we could not tell the difference. When we experience works of art, often what we value is not just the kinds of experiences we have, but, in addition, the connections we usually have with certain real objects. Routley and Routley have made an analogous point about valuing the wilderness experience: a "wilderness experience machine" that caused certain sorts of hallucinations would be no substitute for actually going into the wild.[23] Nor is this fact about our valuation limited to such aesthetic and environmentalist contexts. We love various people in our lives. If a molecule-for-molecule replica of a beloved person were created, you would not love that individual, but would continue to love the individual to whom you actually were historically related. Here again, our attachments are to objects and people as they really are, and not just to the experiences that they facilitate.

Another parallel between environmentalist concerns and aesthetic values concerns the issue of context. Although environmentalists often stress the importance of preserving endangered species, they would not be completely satisfied if an endangered species were preserved by putting a number of specimens in a zoo or in a humanly constructed preserve. What is taken to be important is preserving the species in its natural habitat. This leads to the more holistic position that preserving ecosystems, and not simply preserving certain member species, is of primary importance. Aesthetic concerns often lead in the same direction. It was not merely saving a fresco or an altar piece that motivated art historians after the most recent flood in Florence. Rather, they wanted to save these works of art in their original ("natural") settings. Not just the painting, but the church that housed it; not just the church, but the city itself. The idea of objects residing in a "fitting" environment plays a powerful role in both domains.

Environmentalism and aesthetics both see value in rarity. Of two whales, why should one be more worthy of aid than another, just because one belongs to an endangered species? Here we have the $n + m$ question mentioned in [the introduction to this selection]. As an ethical concern, rarity is difficult to understand. Perhaps this is because our ethical ideas concerning justice and equity (note the word) are saturated with individualism. But in the context of aesthetics, the concept of rarity is far from alien. A work of art may have enhanced value simply because there are very few other works by the same artist, or from the same historical period, or in the same style. It isn't that the price of the item may go up with rarity; I am talking about aesthetic value, not monetary worth. Viewed as valuable aesthetic objects, rare organisms may be valuable because they are rare.

A disanalogy may suggest itself. It may be objected that works of art are of instrumental value only, but that species and ecosystems have intrinsic value. Perhaps it is true, as claimed before, that our attachment to works of art, to nature, and to our loved ones extends beyond the experiences they allow us to have. But it may be argued that what is valuable in the aesthetic case is always the relation of a valuer to a valued object.[24] When we experience a work of art, the value is not simply in the experience, but in the composite fact that we and the work of art are related in certain ways. This immediately suggests that if there were no valuers in the world, nothing would have value, since such relational facts could no longer obtain. So, to adapt Routley and Routley's "last man argument," it would seem that if an ecological crisis precipitated a collapse of the world system, the last human being (whom we may assume for the purposes of this example to be the last valuer) could set about destroying all works of art, and there would be nothing wrong in this.[25] That is, if aesthetic objects are valuable only in so far as valuers can stand in certain relations to them, then when valuers disappear, so does the possibility of aesthetic value. This would deny, in one sense, that aesthetic objects are intrinsically valuable: it isn't they, in themselves, but rather the relational facts that they are part of, that are valuable.

In contrast, it has been claimed that the "last man" would be wrong to destroy natural objects such as mountains, salt marshes, and species. (So as to avoid confusing the issue by bringing in the welfare of individual organisms, Routley and Routley imagine that destruction and mass extinctions can be caused painlessly, so that there would be nothing wrong about this undertaking from the point of view of the nonhuman organisms involved.) If the last man ought to preserve these natural objects, then these objects appear to have a kind of autonomous value; their value would extend beyond their possible relations to valuers. If all this were true, we would have here a contrast between aesthetic and natural objects, one that implies that natural objects are more valuable than works of art.

Routley and Routley advance the last man argument as if it were decisive in showing that environmental objects such as mountains and salt marshes have autonomous value. I find the example more puzzling than decisive. But, in the present context, we do not have to decide whether Routley and Routley are right. We only have to decide whether this imagined situation brings out any relevant difference between aesthetic and environmental values. Were the last man to look up on a certain hillside, he would

see a striking rock formation next to the ruins of a Greek temple. Long ago the temple was built from some of the very rocks that still stud the slope. Both promontory and temple have a history, and both have been transformed by the biotic and the abiotic environments. I myself find it impossible to advise the last man that the peak matters more than the temple. I do not see a relevant difference. Environmentalists, if they hold that the solution to the problem of demarcation is to be found in the distinction between natural and artificial, will have to find such a distinction. But if environmental values are aesthetic, no difference need be discovered.

Environmentalists may be reluctant to classify their concern as aesthetic. Perhaps they will feel that aesthetic concerns are frivolous. Perhaps they will feel that the aesthetic regard for artifacts that has been made possible by culture is antithetical to a proper regard for wilderness. But such contrasts are illusory. Concern for environmental values does not require a stripping away of the perspective afforded by civilization; to value the wild, one does not have to "become wild" oneself (whatever that may mean). Rather, it is the material comforts of civilization that make possible a serious concern for both aesthetic and environmental values. These are concerns that can become pressing in developed nations in part because the populations of those countries now enjoy a certain substantial level of prosperity. It would be the height of condescension to expect a nation experiencing hunger and chronic disease to be inordinately concerned with the autonomous value of ecosystems or with creating and preserving works of art. Such values are not frivolous, but they can become important to us only after certain fundamental human needs are satisfied. Instead of radically jettisoning individualist ethics, environmentalists may find a more hospitable home for their values in a category of value that has existed all along.

NOTES

1. Mark Sagoff, "On Preserving the Natural Environment," *Yale Law Review* 84 (1974): 205–38; J. Baird Cal-

licott, "Animal Liberation: A Triangular Affair," *Environmental Ethics* 2 (1980): 311–38; and Bryan Norton, "Environmental Ethics and Nonhuman Rights," *Environmental Ethics* 4 (1982): 17–36.

2. Peter Singer, *Animal Liberation* (New York: Random House, 1975), has elaborated a position of this sort.

3. Occasionally, it has been argued that utilitarianism is not just *insufficient* to justify the principles of environmentalism, but is actually mistaken in holding that pain is intrinsically bad. Callicott writes: "I herewith declare in all soberness that I see nothing wrong with pain. It is a marvelous method, honed by the evolutionary process, of conveying important organic information. I think it was the late Alan Watts who somewhere remarks that upon being asked if he did not think there was too much pain in the world replied, 'No, I think there's just enough'" ("A Triangular Affair," p. 333). Setting to one side the remark attributed to Watts, I should point out that pain can be intrinsically bad and still have some good consequences. The point of calling pain intrinsically bad is to say that one essential aspect of experiencing it is negative.

4. A parallel with a quite different moral problem will perhaps make it clearer how the environmentalist's holism conflicts with some fundamental ethical ideas. When we consider the rights of individuals to receive compensation for harm, we generally expect that the individuals compensated must be one and the same as the individuals harmed. This expectation runs counter to the way an affirmative action program might be set up, if individuals were to receive compensation simply for being members of groups that have suffered certain kinds of discrimination, whether or not they themselves were victims of discrimination. I do not raise this example to suggest that a holistic conception according to which groups have entitlements is beyond consideration. Rather, my point is to exhibit a case in which a rather common ethical idea is individualistic rather than holistic.

5. David Ehrenfeld, "The Conservation of Non-Resources," *American Scientist* 64 (1976): 648–56. For a theoretical discussion see Robert M. May, *Stability and Complexity in Model Ecosystems* (Princeton: Princeton University Press, 1973).

6. Callicott, "A Triangular Affair," pp. 333–34 (my emphasis).

7. Paul Shepard, "Animal Rights and Human Rites," *North American Review* (Winter 1974): 35–41.

8. Charles Darwin, *The Autobiography of Charles Darwin* (London: Collins, 1876, 1958), p. 90.

9. Callicott, "A Triangular Affair," p. 330.

10. Callicott, "A Triangular Affair," p. 330.

11. Aristotle, *De Anima*, 415a26.

12. Christopher Stone, *Should Trees Have Standing?* (Los Altos, Calif.: William Kaufmann, 1972), p. 24.

13. Sagoff, "Natural Environment," pp. 220–24.

14. The example is Sagoff's, "Natural Environment," pp. 220–24.

15. Ehrenfeld, "The Conservation of Non-Resources," pp. 651–52.

16. Aldo Leopold, *A Sand County Almanac* (New York: Oxford University Press, 1949), pp. 224–25.

17. Callicott, "A Triangular Affair," p. 326 (emphasis mine).

18. Edward Abbey, *Desert Solitaire* (New York: Ballantine Books, 1968), p. 20.

19. Garrett Hardin, "The Economics of Wilderness," *Natural History* 78 (1969): 176.

20. Callicott, "A Triangular Affair," p. 323.

21. Callicott, "A Triangular Affair," p. 335.

22. Here we would have an inversion, not just a rejection, of a familiar Marxian doctrine—the labor theory of value.

23. Richard Routley and Val Routley, "Human Chauvinism and Environmental Ethics," *Environmental Philosophy, Monograph Series 2*, edited by D. S. Mannison, M. A. McRobbie, and R. Routley (Philosophy Department, Australian National University, 1980) p. 154.

24. Donald H. Regan, "Duties of Preservation," *The Preservation of Species*, ed. B. Norton (Princeton: Princeton University Press, 1986), pp. 195–220.

25. Routley and Routley, "Human Chauvinism," pp. 121–22.

Chapter 6
How Wild Does Nature Have to Be?

Questions for Reflection and Discussion

An Allegory

1. Several years ago, my sister visited me in Tucson. She lives in Canada, and the desert was completely new to her. I took her to the Sonoran Desert Museum just outside Tucson. At the museum is a cave, which I took her to see. As we descended into the cave, my sister marveled at how beautiful it was. After a few minutes, though, her eyes became accustomed to the dark. She took a closer look, and reached out to touch the wall. "It isn't real. It's concrete," she said softly.

Why was she disappointed? What difference does it make whether the cave is natural or artificial? What do you suppose Martin Krieger would say?

2. If you go to zoos, you have probably witnessed little kids ignoring the tigers and zebras and squealing with excitement about a ground squirrel running down the path beside them. The kids know that in some way, the ground squirrel is real in a way zoo animals are not. Somehow there is more meaning in the wild, in encounters with nature that have not been scripted for us by someone else. But what exactly is missing? What are the kids seeing in the squirrel that they do not see in caged tigers? What do you suppose Eric Katz would say?

What's Wrong with Plastic Trees?

Martin H. Krieger

A tree's a tree. How many more [redwoods] do you
need to look at? If you've seen one, you've seen
them all.

—Attributed to Ronald Reagan, then candidate for
governor of California.

A tree is a tree, and when you've seen one redwood,
given your general knowledge about trees, you have
a pretty good idea of the characteristics of a redwood.
Yet most people believe that when you've seen one,
you haven't seen them all. Why is this so? What implications does this have for public policy in a world
where resources are not scarce, but do have to be
manufactured; where choice is always present; and
where the competition for resources is becoming
clearer and keener? In this article, I attempt to explore some of these issues, while trying to understand the reasons that are given, or might be given,
for preserving certain natural environments.

THE ECOLOGY MOVEMENT

In the past few years, a movement concerned with
the preservation and careful use of the natural environment in this country has grown substantially. This
ecology movement, as I shall call it, is beginning to
have genuine power in governmental decision-
making and is becoming a link between certain government agencies and the publics to which they are
responsible. The ecology movement should be distinguished from related movements concerned with
the conservation and wise use of natural resources.
The latter, ascendant in the United States during the
first half of this century, were mostly concerned with
making sure that natural resources and environments
were used in a fashion that reflected their true worth
to man. This resulted in a utilitarian conception of

environments and in the adoption of means to partially preserve them—for example, cost-benefit
analysis and policies of multiple use on federal lands.

The ecology movement is not necessarily committed to such policies. Noting the spoliation of the
environment under the policies of the conservation
movement, the ecology movement demands much
greater concern about what is done to the environment, independently of how much it may cost. The
ecology movement seeks to have man's environment
valued in and of itself and thereby prevent its being
traded off for the other benefits it offers to man.

It seems likely that the ecology movement will
have to become more programmatic and responsive
to compromise as it moves into more responsible and
bureaucratic positions vis-à-vis governments and administrative agencies. As they now stand, the policies of the ecology movement may work against
resource-conserving strategies designed to lead to
the movement's desired ends in 20 or 30 years. Meier
has said:[1]

> The best hope, it seems now, is that the newly
> evolved ideologies will progress as social move-
> ments. A number of the major tenets of the belief
> system may then be expected to lose their central-
> ity and move to the periphery of collective atten-
> tion. Believers may thereupon only "satisfice" with
> respect to these principles; they are ready to con-
> sider compromises.

What is needed is an approach midway between
the preservationist and conservationist-utilitarian
policies. It is necessary to find ways of preserving
the opportunity for experiences in natural environments, while having, at the same time, some flexibility in the alternatives that the ecology movement
could advocate.

Martin H. Krieger, "What's Wrong with Plastic Trees?" *Science* 179 (1973): 446–55. Reprinted with permission of the American Association for the Advancement of Science.

A new approach is needed because of the success of economic arguments in the past. We are now more concerned about social equity and about finding arguments from economics for preserving "untouched" environments. Such environments have not been manipulated very much by mankind in the recent past (hundreds or thousands of years). Traditional resource economics has been concerned not as much with preservation as with deciding which intertemporal (the choice of alternative times at which one intervenes) use of natural resources over a period of years yields a maximum return to man, essentially independent of considerations of equity. If one believes that untouched environments are unlikely to have substitutes, then this economics is not very useful. In fact, a different orientation toward preservation has developed and is beginning to be applied in ways that will provide powerful arguments for preservation. At the same time, some ideas about how man experiences the environment are becoming better understood, and they suggest that the new economic approach will be in need of some modification, even if most of its assumptions are sound.

I first examine what is usually meant by natural environments and rarity; I will then examine some of the rationales for preservation. It is important to understand the character and the weak points of the usual arguments. I also suggest how our knowledge and sophistication about environments and our differential access to them are likely to lead to levers for policy changes that will effectively preserve the possibility of experiencing nature, yet offer alternatives in the management of natural resources.

One limitation of my analysis should be made clear. I have restricted my discussion to the nation-state, particularly to the United States. If it were possible to take a global view, then environmental questions would be best phrased in terms of the world's resources. If we want undisturbed natural areas, it might be best to develop some of them in other countries. But we do not live in a politically united world, and such a proposal is imperialistic at worst and unrealistic at best. Global questions about the environment need to be considered, but they must be considered in terms of controls that can exist. If we are concerned about preserving natural environments, it seems clear that, for the moment, we will most likely have to preserve them in our own country.

THE AMERICAN FALLS: KEEPING IT NATURAL

For the last few thousand years, Niagara Falls has been receding. Water going over the Falls insinuates itself into crevices of the rock, freezes and expands in winter, and thereby causes cracks in the formation. The formation itself is a problem in that the hard rock on the surface covers a softer substratum. This weakness results not only in small amounts of erosion or small rockfalls, but also in very substantial ones when the substratum gives way. About 350,000 cubic yards (1 cubic yard equals 0.77 cubic meter) of talus lie at the base of the American Falls.

The various hydroelectric projects that have been constructed during the years have also affected the amount of water that flows over the Falls. It is now possible to alter the flow of water over the American Falls by a factor of 2 and, consequently, to diminish that of the Horseshoe (Canadian) Falls by about 10%.

As a result of these forces, the quality of the Falls—its grandeur, its height, its smoothness of flow—changes over the millennia and the months.

There is nothing pernicious about the changes wrought by nature; the problem is that Americans' image of the Falls does not change. Our ideal of a waterfall, an ideal formed by experiences with small, local waterfalls that seem perfect and by images created by artists and photographers, is not about to change without some effort.

When one visits the Falls today, he sees rocks and debris at the base, too much or too little water going over the edge, and imperfections in the flow of water. These sights are not likely to make anyone feel that he is seeing or experiencing the genuine Niagara Falls. The consequent effects on tourism, a multimillion-dollar-per year industry, could be substantial.

At the instigation of local forces, the American Falls International Board has been formed under the auspices of the International Joint Commission of the United States and Canada. Some $5 to $6 million are being spent to investigate, by means of "dewatering" the Falls and building scale models, policies for intervention. That such efforts are commissioned suggests that we, as a nation, believe that it is proper and possible to do something about the future evolution of the Falls. A "Fallscape" committee, which is especially concerned with the visual quality of the Falls, has been formed. It suggests that three strategies, varying in degree of intervention, be considered.

(1) The Falls can be converted into a monument. By means of strengthening the structure of the Falls, it is possible to prevent rockfalls. Also, excess rock from the base can be removed. Such a strategy might cost tens of millions of dollars, a large part of this cost being for the removal of talus.

(2) The Falls could become an event. Some of the rocks at the base could be removed for convenience and esthetics, but the rockfalls themselves would not be hindered. Instead, instruments for predicting rockfalls could be installed. People might then come to the Falls at certain times, knowing that they would see an interesting and grand event, part of the cycle of nature, such as Old Faithful.

(3) The Falls might be treated as a show. The "director" could control the amount of water flowing over the Falls, the size of the pool below, and the amount of debris, thereby producing a variety of spectacles. Not only could there be *son et lumière,* but it could take place on an orchestrated physical mass.

Which of these is the most nearly natural environment? Current practice, exemplified by the National Park Service's administration of natural areas, might suggest that the second procedure be followed and that the Falls not be "perfected." But would that be the famous Niagara Falls, the place where Marilyn Monroe met her fate in the movie *Niagara?* The answer to this question lies in the ways in which efforts at preservation are presented to the public. If the public is seeking a symbolic Falls, then the Falls has to be returned to its former state. If the public wants to see a natural phenomenon at work, then the Falls should be allowed to fall.

Paradoxically, the phenomena that the public thinks of as "natural" often require great artifice in their creation. The natural phenomenon of the Falls today has been created to a great extent by hydroelectric projects over the years. Esthetic appreciation of the Falls has been conditioned by the rather mundane considerations of routes of tourist excursions and views from hotel windows, as well as the efforts of artists.

I think that we can provide a smooth flow of water over the Falls and at the same time not be completely insensitive to natural processes if we adopt a procedure like that described in the third proposal. Niagara Falls is not a virgin territory, the skyscrapers and motels will not disappear. Therefore, an aggressive attitude toward the Falls seems appropriate. This does not imply heavy-handedness in intervention (the first proposal), but a willingness to touch the "sacred" for esthetic as well as utilitarian purposes.

The effort to analyze this fairly straightforward policy question is not trivial. Other questions concerning preservation have fuzzier boundaries, less clear costs (direct and indirect), and much more complicated political considerations. For these reasons it seems worthwhile to examine some of the concepts I use in this discussion.

NATURAL ENVIRONMENTS

What is considered a natural environment depends on the particular culture and society defining it. It might be possible to create for our culture and society a single definition that is usable (that is, the definition would mean the same thing to many people), but this, of course, says nothing about the applicability of such a definition to other cultures. However,

I restrict my discussion to the development of the American idea of a natural environment.

The history of the idea of the wilderness is a good example of the development of one concept of natural environment. I follow Nash's discussion in the following.

A wilderness may be viewed as a state of mind, as an attitude toward a collection of trees, other plants, animals, and the land on which they all exist. The idea that a wilderness exists as a product of an intellectual movement is important. A wilderness is not discovered in the sense that some man from a civilization looked upon a piece of territory for the first time. It is the meanings that we attach to such a piece of territory that convert it to a wilderness.

The Romantic appreciation of nature, with its associated enthusiasm for the "strange, remote, solitary and mysterious," converted territory that was a threatening wildland into a desirable area capable of producing an invigorating spirit of wilderness. The appreciation of the wilderness in this form began in cities, for whose residents the wildland was a novelty. Because of the massive destruction of this territory for resources (primarily timber), city dwellers, whose livelihood did not depend on these resources and who were not familiar with the territory, called for the preservation of wildlands. At first, they did not try to keep the most easily accessible, and therefore most economically useful, lands from being exploited, but noted that Yellowstone and the Adirondacks were rare wonders and had no other utility. They did not think of these areas as wilderness, but as untouched lands. Eventually, a battle developed between conservationists and preservationists. The conservationists (Pinchot, for example) were concerned with the wise use of lands, with science and civilization and forestry; the preservationists (Muir, for example) based their argument on art and wilderness. This latter concept of wilderness is the significant one. The preservationists converted wildland into wilderness—a good that is indivisible and valuable in itself.

This capsule history suggests that the wilderness, as we think of it now, is the product of a political effort to give a special meaning to a biological system organized in a specific way. I suspect that this history is the appropriate model for the manner in which biological systems come to be designated as special.

But it might be said that natural environments can be defined in the way ecosystems are—in terms of complexity, energy and entropy flows, and so on. This is true, but only because of all the spadework that has gone into developing in the public a consensual picture of natural environments. What a society takes to be a natural environment is one.

Natural environments are likely to be named when there are unnatural environments and are likely to be noted only when they are outnumbered by these unnatural environments. The wildlands of the past, which were frightening, were plentiful and were not valued. The new wilderness, which is a source of revitalization, is rare and so valued that it needs to be preserved.

WHEN IS SOMETHING RARE?

Something is considered to be rare when there do not exist very many objects or events that are similar to it. It is clear that one object must be distinguishable from another in order to be declared rare, but the basis for this distinction is not clear.

One may take a realist's or an idealist's view of rarity. For the realist, an object is unique within a purview: given a certain boundary, there exists no other object like it. Certainly the Grand Canyon is unique within the United States. Perhaps Niagara Falls is also unique. But there are many other waterfalls throughout the world that are equally impressive, if not of identical dimensions.

For the idealist, a rare object is one that is archetypal: it is the most nearly typical of all the objects it represents, having the most nearly perfect form. We frequently preserve archetypal specimens in museums and botanical gardens. Natural areas often have these qualities.

A given object is not always rare. Rather, it is designated as rare at one time and may, at some other time, be considered common. How does this hap-

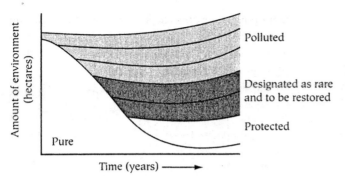

Figure 1. The Development of Rare Environments

pen? Objects become rare when a large number of people change their attitudes toward them. This may come about in a number of ways, but it is necessary that the object in question be noticed and singled out. Perhaps one individual discovers it, or perhaps it is common to everyone's experience. Someone must convince the public that the object is something special. The publicist must develop in others the ability to differentiate one object from among a large number of others, as well as to value the characteristic that makes the particular object different. If he convinces a group of people influential in the society, people who are able to affect a much larger group's beliefs, then he will have succeeded in his task. Thus it may be important that some form of snob appeal be created for the special object.

In order to create the differentiations and the differential valuations of characteristics, information and knowledge are crucial. A physical object can be transformed into an instrument of beauty, pleasure, or pride, thereby developing sufficient characteristics to be called rare, only by means of changing the knowledge we have of it and of its relation to the rest of the world. In this sense, knowledge serves an important function in the creation of rare environments, very much as knowledge in society serves an important function in designating what should be considered natural resources.

Advertising is one means of changing states of knowledge—nor does such advertising have to be wholly sponsored by commercial interests. Picture post cards, for example, are quite effective:[2]

. . . a large number of quiet beauty spots which in consequence of the excellence of their photographs had become tourist centres. . . .

The essential was to "establish" a picture, e.g., the Tower [of London] with barges in the foreground. People came to look for the barges and in the end wouldn't have the Tower without barges. Much of the public was very conservative and though such things as high-rise building and general facade-washing had made them [the postcard producers] rephotograph the whole of London recently, some people still insisted on the old sky-line, and grubby facades, and liked to believe certain new roads had never happened.

Similarly, the publicity given to prices paid at art auctions spurs the rise of these prices.

As a *result* of the social process of creating a rare object, the usual indicators of rarity become important. Economically, prices rise; physically, the locations of the rare objects become central, or at least highly significant spatially; and socially, rare objects and their possessors are associated with statuses that are valued and activities that are considered to be good.

ENVIRONMENTS CAN BE AND ARE CREATED

To recapitulate, objects are rare because men decide that they are and, through social action, convince others that they are. The rarity of an object is created through four mechanisms: designating the object as rare; differentiating it from other objects of the same species; establishing its significance; and determining its position in the context of society. The last two mechanisms are especially important, for the meaning that an environment has and its relation to other things in the society are crucial to its being considered rare. That a rare environment be irreproducible or of unchanging character is usually a necessary preliminary to our desire to preserve it. Technologies, which may involve physical processes or social organization and processes, determine how reproducible an object is, for we may make a copy of the original or we may transfer to another object the significance attached to the original. (Copying natural environments may be easier than copying artistic objects because the qualities of replicas and forgeries are not as well characterized in the case of the natural environment.) Insofar as we are incapable of doing either of these, we may desire to preserve the original environment.

In considering the clientele of rare environments, one finds that accessibility by means of transportation and communication is important. If there is no means of transportation to a rare environment then it is not likely that the public will care about that environment. An alternative to transportation is some form of communication, either verbal or pictorial, that simulates a feeling of being in the environment.

I am concerned here with the history of environments that, at first, are not considered unique. However, a similar argument could be applied to environments regarded as unique (for example, the Grand Canyon), provided they were classed with those environments most like them. Figure 1 should aid in the explanation that follows.

For example, suppose that a particular kind of environment is plentiful and that, over a period of time, frequent use causes it to become polluted. (Note that pollution need not refer just to our conventional concepts of dirtying the environment, but to a wide variety of uncleanliness and stigma as well.) Because there is a substantial amount of that environment available, man's use of it will, at first, have little ef-

fect on his perception of its rarity. As time goes on, however, someone will notice that there used to be a great deal more of that particular environment available. Suddenly, the once vast quantities of that environment begin to look less plentiful. The environment seems more special as it becomes distinguishable from the polluted environments around it. At that point, it is likely that there will be a movement to designate some fraction of the remaining environment as rare and in need of protection. There will also be a movement to restore those parts of the environment that have already been polluted. People will intervene to convert the polluted environment to a simulation of the original one.

REASONS FOR PRESERVATION

That something is rare does not imply that it must be preserved. The characteristics that distinguish it as rare must also be valued. Arguments in favor of preserving an object can be based on the fact that the object is a luxury, a necessity, or a merit.

We build temples or other monuments to our society (often by means of preservation) and believe that they represent important investments in social unity and coherence. If a forest symbolizes the frontier for a society and if that frontier is meaningful in the society's history, then there may be good reasons for preserving it. An object may also be preserved in order that it may be used in the future. Another reason, not often given but still true, for preserving things is that there is nothing else worth doing with them. For example, it may cost very little to preserve something that no one seems to have any particular reason for despoiling; therefore, we expend some small effort in trying to keep it untouched.

Natural environments are preserved for reasons of necessity also. Environments may provide ecological samples that will be useful to future generations. Recently, the long-lived bristlecone pine has helped to check radiocarbon dating and has thereby revised our knowledge of early Europe. It may be that the preservation of an environment is necessary for the preservation of an ecosystem and that our destruction of it will also destroy, as a product of a series of interactions, some highly valued aspects of our lives. Finally, it may be necessary to preserve environments in order that the economic development of the adjacent areas can proceed in a desired fashion.

Other reasons for preservation are based on merit: it may be felt by the society that it is good to preserve natural environments. It is good for people to be exposed to nature. Natural beauty is worth having, and the amenity resulting from preservation is important.

RARITY, UNIQUENESS, AND FORGERY: AN ARTISTIC INTERLUDE

The problems encountered in describing the qualities that make for "real" artistic experiences and genuine works of art are similar to those encountered in describing rare natural objects. The ideas of replica and forgery will serve to make the point.

Kubler[3] observes that, if one examines objects in a time sequence, he may decide that some are prime objects and the rest are replicas. Why should this be so? One may look at the properties of earlier objects and note that some of them serve as a source of later objects; however, since the future always has its sources in the present, any given object is a source. Therefore, one must distinguish important characteristics, perhaps arbitrarily, and say that they are seminal. Prime objects are the first to clearly and decisively exhibit important characteristics.

Why are there so few prime objects? By definition, prime objects exhibit characteristics in a clear and decisive way, and this must eliminate many other objects from the category; but why do artists not constantly create new objects, each so original that it would be prime? Not all artists are geniuses, it might be said. But this is just a restatement of the argument that most objects do not exhibit important characteristics in a clear, decisive manner. It might also be said that, if there are no followers, there will be no leaders, but this does not explain why some eras are filled with prime works and others are not.

Kubler suggests that invention, especially if too frequent, leads to chaos, which is frightening. Replication is calmer and leads only to dullness. Therefore, man would rather repair, replicate what he has done, than innovate and discard the past. We are, perhaps justifiably, afraid of what the prime objects of the future will be. We prefer natural environments to synthesized ones because we are familiar with techniques of managing the natural ones and know what the effects of such management are. Plastic trees are frightening.

What about those replicas of prime objects that are called forgeries? Something is a forgery if its provenance has been faked. Why should this bother us? If the forgery provides us with the same kind of experience we might have had with the original, except that we know it is a forgery, then we are snobbish to demand the original. But we do not like to be called snobs. Rather, we say that our opinion of the work, or the quality of our experience of it, depends on its context. History, social position, and ideology affect the way in which we experience the object. It may be concluded that our appreciation of something is only partly a product of the thing itself.

Art replicas and forgeries exist in an historical framework. So do the prime and genuine objects. And so do natural environments.

CRITERIA FOR PRESERVATION

Whatever argument one uses for preservation, there must be some criteria for deciding what to preserve. Given that something is rare and is believed to be worth preserving, rarity itself, as well as economic, ecological, or socio-historical reasons, can be used to justify preservation. I consider each of these here.

There are many economic reasons for planned intervention to achieve preservation, and I discuss two of them: one concerns the application of cost-benefit analysis to preservation; the other concerns the argument that present value should be determined by future benefits.

The work of Krutilla[4] is an ingenious application of economics; it rescues environments from current use by arguing for their future utility. The crux of the argument follows.

Nature is irreproducible compared to the materials it provides. There have been enough substitutions of natural materials to obviate the idea of a shortage of nature resources. It also seems likely that the value of nature and of experiences in nature will increase in the future, while the supply of natural environments will remain constant. Because it is comparatively easy to produce substitutes for the materials we get from natural environments, the cost of not exploiting an environment is small, compared to the cost of producing that environment. Finally, there is an option demand for environments: that is, there will be a demand, at a certain price, for that environment in the future. If a substantial fraction of the supply of the environment is destroyed now, it will be impossible to fill the demand in the future at a reasonable price. Therefore, we are willing to pay to preserve that option. The problem is not the intertemporal use of natural environments (as it is for natural resources), but the preservation of our options to use environments in the future, or at least the reduction of uncertainty about the availability of environments in the future.

Fisher[5] has applied optimal investment theory, including a possibility of restoring environments to a quasi-natural state, to the problem of preservation as formulated by Krutilla. Krutilla et al. have applied an analysis similar to Fisher's to the preservation of Hell's Canyon.[6]

Robinson[7] has criticized Krutilla's argument from the following perspectives: he suggests that the amenity valued so highly by Krutilla is not necessarily that valuable; that the experiences of nature are reproducible; that refraining from current use may be costly; and that the arguments for public intervention into such environments depend on the collective consumption aspects of these environments. That is, these environments benefit everyone, and, since people cannot be differentially charged for using them, the public must pay for these environments collectively, through government. It is well known that the users of rare environments tend to be that small fraction of the population who are better off socially and economically than the majority. How-

ever, a greater difficulty than any of these may be discerned.

It seems to me that the limitations of Krutilla's argument lie in his assumptions about how quickly spoiled environments can be restored (rate of reversion) and how great the supply of environments is. Krutilla et al. are sensitive to the possibility that the rate of reversion may well be amenable to technological intervention:[8]

> Perhaps more significant, however, is the need to investigate more fully the presumption of asymmetric implications of technological progress for the value of attributes of the natural environment when used as intermediate goods, compared with their retention as assets supplying final consumption services. Irreproducibility, it might be argued, is not synonymous with irreplaceability. If reasonably good substitutes can be found, by reliance on product development, the argument for the presumption of differential effects of technological progress is weakened; or if not weakened, the value which is selected [for the reversion rate] . . . would not remain unaffected.

The supply of natural environments is affected by technology in that it can manipulate both biological processes and information and significance. The advertising that created rare environments can also create plentiful substitutes. The supply of special environments can be increased dramatically by highlighting (in ways not uncommon to those of differentiating among groups of equivalent toothpastes) significant and rare parts of what are commonly thought to be uninteresting environments.

The accessibility of certain environments to population centers can be altered to create new rare environments. Also, environments that are especially rare, or are created to be especially rare, could be very far away, since people would be willing to pay more to see them. Thus it may be possible to satisfy a large variety of customers for rare environments. The following kind of situation might result.

(1) Those individuals who demand "truly" natural environments could be encouraged to fly to some isolated location where a national

park with such an environment is maintained; a substantial sum of money would be required of those who use such parks.

(2) For those who find a rare environment in state parks or perhaps in small national parks, such parks could be made more accessible and could be developed more. In this way, a greater number of people could use them and the fee for using them would be less than the fee for using isolated areas.

(3) Finally, for those who wish to have an environment that is just some trees, some woods, and some grass, there might be a very small park. Access would be very easy, and the rareness of such environments might well be enhanced beyond what is commonly thought possible by means of sophisticated methods of landscape gardening.

It seems to me that, as Krutilla suggests, the demand for rare environments is a learned one. It also seems likely that conscious public choice can manipulate this learning so that the environments which people learn to use and want reflect environments that are likely to be available at low cost. There is no lack of merit in natural environments, but this merit is not canonical.

THE VALUATION OF THE FUTURE

In any cost-benefit analysis that attempts to include future values, the rate at which the future is discounted is crucial to the analysis. (That is, a sum of money received today is worth more to us now than the same sum received in the future. To allow for this, one discounts, by a certain percent each year, these future payments.) Changes in discount rates can alter the feasibility of a given project. If different clientele's preferences for projects correspond to different discount rates at which these projects are feasible, then the choice of a particular discount rate would place the preferences of one group over another. Preservation yields benefits that come in the future. The rich have a low rate of discount compared to the poor (say, 5 percent as opposed to 10

or 20 percent) and would impute much higher present value to these future benefits than the poor would. Baumol suggests (though it is only a hunch) that:[9]

> . . . by and large, the future can be left to take care of itself. There is no need to lower artificially the social rate of discount in order to increase further the prospective wealth of future generations. . . . However, this does not mean that the future should in every respect be left at the mercy of the free market. . . . Investment in the preservation of such items then seems perfectly proper, but for this purpose the appropriate instrument would appear to be a set of selective subsidies rather than a low general discount rate that encourages indiscriminately all sorts of investment programs whether or not they are relevant.

Baumol is saying that the process of preserving environments may not always be fruitfully analyzed in terms of cost-benefit analyses; we are preserving things in very special cases, and each choice is not a utilitarian choice in any simple sense, but represents a balancing of all other costs to the society of having *no* preserved environments. Preservation often entails a gross change in policy, and utilitarian analyses cannot easily compare choices in which values may be drastically altered.

OTHER CRITERIA

We may decide to preserve things just because they are rare. In that case, we need to know which things are rarer than others. Leopold has tried to do this for a set of natural environments.[10] He listed a large number of attributes for each environment and then weighted each attribute as follows. For any single attribute, determine how many environments share that attribute and assign each of them a value of $1/N$ units, where N is the number of environments that share an attribute. Then add all the weights for the environments; the environment with the largest weight is the rarest. It is clear that, if an environment has attributes which are unique, it will get one unit of weight for each attribute and thus its total weight will just equal the number of attributes. If all of the environments are about the same, then each of them will have roughly the same weight, which will equal the number of attributes divided by the number of environments. The procedure is sensitive to how differentiated we wish to make our attributes and to the attributes we choose. It is straightforward and usable, as Leopold has shown.

It seems to me that there are two major difficulties in this approach. The first, and more important, is that the accessibility of environments to their clientele, which Leopold treats as one of his 34 attributes, needs to be further emphasized in deciding what to preserve. An environment that is quite rare but essentially inaccessible may not be as worthy of preservation as one that is fairly common but quite accessible. The other difficulty is that probably the quantity that should be used is the amount of information possessed by each environment—rather than taking $1/N$, one should take a function of its logarithm to the base 2.

An ecological argument is that environments which contribute to our stability and survival as an ecosystem should be preserved. It is quite difficult to define what survival means, however. If it means the continued existence of man in an environment quite similar to the one he lives in now, then survival is likely to become very difficult as we use part of our environment for the maintenance of life and as new technologies come to the fore. If survival means the maintenance of a healthy and rich culture, then ecology can only partially guide us in the choices, since technology has substantially changed the risk from catastrophe in the natural world. Our complex political and social organizations may serve to develop means for survival and stability sufficient to save man from the catastrophic tricks of his own technology.

If a taxonomy of environments were established, a few environments might stand out from all the rest. But what would be the criteria involved in such a taxonomy?

Another possibility is to search for relics of cultural, historical, and social significance to the nation. Such physical artifacts are preserved because the experiences they represent affect the nature of the present society. In this sense, forests are preserved to recall a frontier, and historic homes are preserved to recall the individuals who inhabited them. Of course the problem here is that there is no simple way of ordering the importance of relics and their referents. Perhaps a survey of a large number of people might enable one to assign priorities to these relics.

Finally, it might be suggested that preservation should only be used, or could sometimes be used, to serve the interests of social justice. Rather than preserving things for what they are or for the experiences they provide, we preserve them as monuments to people who deserve commemoration or as a means of redistributing wealth (when an environment is designated as rare, local values are affected). Rather than buy forests and preserve them, perhaps we should preserve slums and suitably reward their inhabitants.

All of these criteria are problematic. Whichever ones are chosen, priorities for intervention must still be developed.

PRIORITIES FOR PRESERVING THE ENVIRONMENT

Not every problem in environmental quality is urgent, nor does every undesirable condition that exists need to be improved. We need to classify environmental problems in order that we can choose from among the possible improvements.

(1) There are conditions about which we must do something soon or we will lose a special thing. These conditions pertain especially to rare environments, environments we wish to preserve for their special beauty or their uniqueness. We might allocate a fixed amount of money every year to such urgent problems. Niagara Falls might be one of these, and it might cost a fraction of a dollar per family to keep it in good repair. Wilderness and monument maintenance have direct costs of a few dollars per family per year.

(2) There are situations in which conditions are poor, but fairly stable. In such situations, it might be possible to handle the problem in 10 years without too much loss. However, the losses to society resulting from the delayed improvement of these facilities need to be carefully computed. For example, the eutrophied Lake Erie might be such a project. There, society loses fishing and recreational facilities. It might cost $100 per family, locally, to clean up the lake. Perhaps our environmental dollar should be spent elsewhere.

(3) There are also situations in which conditions are rapidly deteriorating and in which a small injection of environmental improvement and amelioration would cause dramatic changes in a trend. Smog control devices have probably raised the cost of driving by 2 or 3 percent, yet their contribution to the relative improvement of the environment in certain areas (for example, Los Angeles) has been substantial. Fifty dollars per car per year is the estimated current cost to the car owner.

(4) There may be situations in which large infusions of money are needed to stop a change. These problems are especially irksome. Perhaps the best response to them would be to change the system of production sufficiently that we can avoid such costs in the future. The costs of such change, one-time costs we hope, may be much smaller than the long-term costs of the problems themselves, although this need not be the case. The development of cleaner industrial processes is a case in point.

This is not an all-inclusive or especially inventive classification of problems, but I have devised it to suggest that many of the "urgent" problems are not so urgent.

Rare environments pose special problems and may require an approach different from that required by other environments. A poor nation is unlikely to destroy very much of its special environments. It lacks the technical and economic power to do so. It may certainly perform minor miracles of destruction through a series of small decisions or in single, major projects. These latter are often done with the aid of rich countries.

The industrialized, but not wealthy, nations have wreaked havoc with their environments in their efforts to gain some degree of wealth. It is interesting that they are willing to caution the poor nations against such a course, even though it may be a very rapid way of developing. At the U.N. Conference on the Environment this year, the poor nations indicated their awareness of these problems and their desire to develop without such havoc.

The rich nations can afford to have environments that are rare and consciously preserved. These environments are comparable to the temples of old, in that these environments will be relics of *our* time, yet this is no criterion for deciding how much should be spent on "temple building." The amount of money needed is only a small proportion of a rich country's wealth (as opposed to the cost of churches in medieval times).

Politically, the situation is complicated. There are many small groups in this country for whom certain environments are highly significant. The problem for each group is to somehow get its piece of turf, preferably uncut, unrenewed, or untouched. It seems likely that the ultimate determinant of which environments are preserved will be a process of political trade-off, in which some environments are preserved for some groups and other environments for others. Natural environments are likely to be viewed in a continuum with a large number of other environments that are especially valued by some subgroup of the society. In this sense, environmental issues will become continuous with a number of other special interests and will no longer be seen as a part of a "whole earth" movement. The power of the intellectuals, in the media, and even in union bureaucracies, with their upper middle class preferences for nature, suggests that special interest groups who are advocates for the poor and working classes will have to be wary of their own staffs.

Projects might be ranked in importance on the basis of the net benefits they provide a particular group.

Marglin has suggested a means by which income re-distribution could be explicitly included in cost-benefit calculations for environmental programs.[11] If one wishes to take efficiency into account, costs mi-nus benefits could be minimized with a constraint relating to income redistribution. This is not a sim-ple task, however, because pricing some commodi-ties at zero dollars, seemingly the best way of at-tempting a redistribution of income, may not be politically desirable or feasible. As Clawson and Knetsch have pointed out, we have to be sure that in making some prices low we do not make others pro-hibitively high and thereby deny the persons who are to benefit access to the low-priced goods.[12] In any case, Marglin shows that the degree to which income is redistributed will depend on how the same amount of money might have been spent in alternative ac-tivities (marginal opportunity cost). This parallels Kneese and Bower's view that the level of pollution we tolerate, or is "optimal," is that at which the mar-ginal benefits of increasing pollution are balanced by the marginal costs of abatement measures.[13]

In doing these cost-benefit calculations, one must consider the value of 10 years of clean lake (if we can clean up the lake now) versus 10 years of une-ducated man (if we wait 10 years for a manpower training program). According to Freeman:[14]

> . . . [the] equity characteristics of projects *within* broad classifications . . . will be roughly similar. If this surmise is correct, then the ranking of projects within these classes is not likely to be significantly affected by equity considerations. On the other hand, we would expect more marked differences in distribution patterns among classes of projects, e.g., rural recreation vs. urban air quality.

He goes on to point out that it is unlikely that such seemingly incommensurable kinds of projects will be compared with respect to equity. I suspect that it is still possible to affect specific groups in the de-sign of a given project; furthermore, equity can be taken into consideration more concretely at this level. Careful disaggregation, in measuring effects and benefits, will be needed to ensure that minorities are properly represented.

AN ETHICAL QUESTION

I still feel quite uncomfortable with what I have said here. I have tried to show that the utilitarian and ma-nipulative rationality inherited from the conserva-tionist movement and currently embodied in eco-nomic analyses and modes of argument can be helpful in deciding questions of preservation and rar-ity. By manipulating attitudes, we have levers for in-tervening into what is ordinarily considered fixed and uncontrollable. But to what end?

Our ability to manipulate preferences and values tends to lead to systems that make no sense. For ex-ample, an electrical utility encourages its customers to use more electricity, and the customers proceed to do so. As a result, there are power shortages. Simi-larly, if we allocate resources now in order to pre-serve environments for future generations, their pref-erences for environments may be altered by this action, and there may be larger shortages.

I also fear that my own proposals might get out of hand. My purpose in proposing interventions is not to preserve man's opportunity to experience na-ture, although this is important, but to promote so-cial justice. I believe that this concern should guide our attempts to manipulate, trade off, and control en-vironments. A summum bonum of preserving trees has no place in an ethic of social justice. If I took this ethic seriously, I could not argue the relative merits of schemes to manipulate environments. I would argue that the ecology movement is wrong and would not answer its question about what we are going to do about the earth—I would be worried about what we are going to do about men.

CONCLUSION

With some ingenuity, a transformation of our atti-tudes toward preservation of the environment will take place fairly soon. We will recognize the sym-bolic and social meanings of environments, not just their economic utility; we will emphasize their his-torical significance as well as the future generations that will use them.

At the same time, we must realize that there are things we may not want to trade at all, except in the sense of letting someone else have his share of the environment also. As environments become more differentiated, smaller areas will probably be given greater significance, and it may be possible for more groups to have a share.

It is likely that we shall want to apply our technology to the creation of artificial environments. It may be possible to create environments that are evocative of other environments in other times and places. It is possible that, by manipulating memory through the rewriting of history, environments will come to have new meaning. Finally, we may want to create proxy environments by means of substitution and simulation. In order to create substitutes, we must endow new objects with significance by means of advertising and by social practice. Sophistication about differentiation will become very important for appreciating the substitute environments. We may simulate the environment by means of photographs, recordings, models, and perhaps even manipulations in the brain. What we experience in natural environments may actually be more controllable than we imagine. Artificial prairies and wildernesses have been created, and there is no reason to believe that these artificial environments need be unsatisfactory for those who experience them.

Rare environments are relative, can be created, are dependent on our knowledge, and are a function of policy, not only tradition. It seems likely that economic arguments will not be sufficient to preserve environments or to suggest how we can create new ones. Rather, conscious choice about what matters, and then a financial and social investment in an effort to create significant experiences and environments will become a policy alternative available to us.

What's wrong with plastic trees? My guess is that there is very little wrong with them. Much more can be done with plastic trees and the like to give most people the feeling that they are experiencing nature. We will have to realize that the way in which we experience nature is conditioned by our society—which more and more is seen to be receptive to responsible interventions.

Bentham, the father of utilitarianism, was very concerned about the uses of the dead to the living and suggested:[15]

If a country gentleman have rows of trees leading to his dwelling, the auto-icons [embalmed bodies in an upright position] of his family might alternate with the trees: copal varnish would protect the face from the effects of rain—caoutchouc [rubber] the habiliments.

NOTES

1. R. Meier, *J. Amer. Inst. Plann.* **37**, 211, 1971.

2. A. Hamilton, *The Manchester Guardian* 4 September 1971, p. 3.

3. G. Kubler, *The Shape of Time* (New Haven, Conn.: Yale Univ. Press, 1962)

4. J. Krutilla, *Amer. Econ. Rev.* **57**, 777, 1967.

5. A. Fisher, "The optimum uses of natural areas." (Xeroxed, Brown Univ., Providence, R.I.)

6. J. V. Krutilla, C. M. Clechetti, A. M. Freeman III, C. S. Russell, in *Environmental Quality Analysis*, A. V. Kneese and B. T. Bowers, eds., (Baltimore: Johns Hopkins Press, 1972). See pp. 69–112.

7. W. Robinson, *Land Econ.* **45**, 453, 1969.

8. Krutilla et al., *Environmental Quality Analysis*, pp. 69–112.

9. W. Baumol, *Amer. Econ. Rev.* **58**, 788, 1968.

10. L. Leopold, *Nat. Hist.* **78**, (4), p. 36 October 1969; L. Leopold and M. O. Marchand, *Water Resour. Res.* **4**, 709, 1968.

11. S. A. Marglin, in *Design of Water-Resource Systems,* A. Maass, M. M. Hufschmidt, R. Dorfman, H. A. Thomas, Jr., S. A. Marglin, G. M. Fair, eds. Harvard Univ. Press, Cambridge, Mass., 1962 pp. 159–225; *Public Investment Criteria.* M.I.T. Press, Cambridge, Mass., 1967.

12. M. Clawson and J. Knetsch, *Economics of Outdoor Recreation.* Johns Hopkins Press, Baltimore, 1966.

13. A. Kneese and B. Bower, *Managing Water Quality: Economics, Technology and Institutions.* John Hopkins Press, Baltimore, 1968.

14. A. Freeman III, in *Environmental Quality Analysis.* Johns Hopkins Press, Baltimore, 972, pp. 243–278.

15. J. Bentham, Auto-Icon, or the Uses of the Dead to the Living in *Dictionary of National Biography*, L. Stephen and S. Lee, eds. Oxford: Oxford University Press, 1917, vol. 2, p. 268.

The Call of the Wild

Eric Katz

In this essay, I use encounters with the white-tailed deer of Fire Island to explore the "call of the wild"—the *attraction to value* that exists in a natural world outside of human control. Value exists in nature to the extent that it avoids modification by human technology. Technology "fixes" the natural world by improving it for human use or by restoring degraded ecosystems. Technology creates a "new world," an artifactual reality that is far removed from the "wildness" of nature. The technological "fix" of nature thus raises a moral issue: how is an artifact morally different from a natural and wild entity? Artifacts are human instruments; their value lies in their ability to meet human needs. Natural entities have no intrinsic functions; they were not created for any instrumental purpose. To attempt to manage natural entities is to deny their inherent autonomy: a form of domination. The moral claim of the wilderness is thus a claim against human technological domination. We have an obligation to struggle against this domination by preserving as much of the natural world as possible.

I

During the summer I live with my family on Fire Island, a barrier beach off the coast of Long Island. Most mornings, if I wake up early, I can look out my window and watch white-tailed deer munching their breakfast of flowers and leaves from the trees surrounding my house. The deer are rather tame; they have become accustomed to the transient human population that invades the island each summer. A few years ago, if they had heard me walking onto the deck, they would have jumped and run off into the thicker underbrush. Now, if they hear me, they might look up to see if I have a carrot; more likely

still, they will simply ignore me and continue foraging. My experiences with these deer are the closest encounters I have with what I like to call the "wild."

Using the adjective *wild* to describe these deer is obviously a distortion of terminology. These are animals that live in and around a fairly dense human community; they consume, much to the dismay of many residents, the cultivated gardens of flowers and vegetables; they seek handouts from passing humans—my daughters often feed them breadsticks and pretzels. Yet, seeing them is different than my experience with any other animal, surely different than seeing white-tailed deer in the zoo, on a petting farm, or in a nature documentary film on television. The mornings when I find them in my yard are something special. If I walk close to one, unaware, at night, my heart beats faster. These animals are my connection to "wild nature." Despite their acceptance of the human presence, they embody something untouched and beyond humanity. They are a deep and forceful *symbol* of the wild "other." The world—my world—would be a poorer place if they were not there.

In this essay, I explore this "call of the wild"—our *attraction to value* that exists in a natural world outside of human control. To understand this value, we must understand the relationship between technology and the natural world, the ways in which humanity attempts to "fix" and mold nature to suit human purposes. Thomas Birch has described this project as the "control of otherness,"[1] a form of domination that includes the control of nature and all such outsiders of human society. Here I bring together several ideas about the philosophy of technology and the nature of artifacts, and combine them with themes raised by Birch. I argue that value exists in nature to the extent it avoids the domination of hu-

Eric Katz, "The Call of the Wild," *Environmental Ethics* 14 (1992): 265–73. Reprinted with permission of the author and the journal.

man technological practice. Technology can satisfy human wants by creating the artifactual products we desire, but it cannot supply, replace, or restore the "wild."

II

One promise of the technological enterprise is the creation of "new worlds." This optimistic view of the ability of technology to improve the human condition is based on the belief that humanity has the power to alter the physical structure of the world. Consider the words of Emmanuel Mesthene:

> We . . . have enough . . . power actually at hand to create new possibilities almost at will. By massive physical changes deliberately induced, we can literally pry new alternatives out of nature. The ancient tyranny of matter has been broken, and we know it. . . . We can change it and shape it to suit our purposes.[2]

No longer limited by the physical necessities of the "given" natural world, our technological power enables us to create a new world of our dreams and desires. Nature can be controlled; its limitations overcome; humanity can achieve its highest potential. For Mesthene, "our technical prowess literally bursts with the promise of new freedom, enhanced human dignity, and unfettered aspiration."[3]

I admit to being mesmerized by the resonances of meaning in the concept of the "new world." The technological promise of a new dignity and freedom, a limitless opportunity, an unchained power, sounds suspiciously like the promise envisioned in the new political and social conditions of the New World of the European discovery, our homeland, the Americas. But the "new world" of the European discovery was not, in fact, a *new* world; indeed, it was a very *old* world, the world of a wild untamed nature, with a minimal human presence that was itself quite old. The freedom, dignity, and benefits of the new human population were achieved, to some degree, at

the expense of the older natural world. For the new world to be useful to humanity, it had to be developed and cultivated.[4] The New World had to cease being wild.[5]

The comparison between the taming of the American wilderness and the technological control of brute physical matter is disturbing. I do not believe that the technological control of nature is a desirable end of human activity. The control of nature is a dream, an illusion, a hallucination. It involves the replacement of the wild natural environment with a human artifactual environment. It creates a fundamental change in the value of the world. This change in value, in turn, forces a reexamination of the ethical relationship between humanity and the natural environment.

III

It is a commonplace to refer to the improvements of technology as a "technological fix." It is supposed that the advanced technology of the contemporary world can "fix" nature. The term *fix* is used here in two complementary ways: it implies either that something is broken or that it can be improved. Thus, the technological fix of nature means that natural processes can be "improved" to maximize human satisfaction and good; alternatively, damage to the environment can be repaired by the technological reconstruction of degraded ecological systems. Humans use nature to create benefits for humanity, and we can restore natural environments after they have been damaged by use. The only new aspect of this technological activity is its increased scope and power. The practical control of natural processes has increased to such an extent that we no longer acknowledge the impossibility of doing anything; nature can be improved and restored to any extent that we wish.

Both processes—the improvement-use and the restoration of nature—lead to serious questions about value and moral obligation. The idea that nature ought to be used (and improved, if necessary) for human benefit is the fundamental assumption of "resource environmentalism"—arguably the mainstream of the American conservation movement. Under this doctrine, environmental policies are designed to maximize human satisfactions or minimize human harms. The pollution of the atmosphere is a problem because of the health hazards to human beings. The extinction of a species is a problem because the extinct species may be useful to humans, or the resulting instability in the ecosystem may be harmful. The greenhouse effect is a problem because the changes in climate may have dramatic impacts on agriculture and coastal geography. With all environmental problems, the effects on humanity are the primary concern.[6]

These "human interest" resource arguments for environmental protection have been criticized by thinkers in several disciplines concerned with environmental philosophy and environmental ethics. A full inventory of the arguments against so-called "anthropocentric" environmental ethics is clearly beyond the scope of this discussion.[7] Here I focus on one particular implication of the anthropocentric resource view, i.e., the creation of an artificial world that more adequately meets the demands of human welfare. As Martin Krieger has written:

> Artificial prairies and wildernesses have been created, and there is no reason to believe that these artificial environments need be unsatisfactory for those who experience them. . . . What's wrong with plastic trees? My guess is that there is very little wrong with them. Much more can be done with plastic trees and the like to give most people the feeling that they are experiencing nature.[8]

Krieger thus argues for "responsible interventions" to manage, manipulate, and control natural environments for the promotion of human good. "A summum bonum of preserving trees has no place in an ethic of social justice."[9] Because human social justice, the production and distribution of human goods, is the primary policy goal, the manipulation of natural processes and the creation of artificial environments is an acceptable (and probably required) human activity.

Krieger's vision of a "user-friendly" plasticized human environment is chilling; it is not a world view that has many advocates. Nevertheless, the point of his argument is that a primary concern for the human uses of the natural environment leads inevitably to a policy of human intervention and manipulation in nature, and the subsequent creation of artificial environments. If humanity is planning to "fix" the natural environment, to use it and improve it to meet human needs, wants, and interests, the conclusion of the process is a technologically created "new" world of our own design. "Wild" nature will no longer exist, merely the controlled nature that offers pleasant experiences.

The restoration of nature, the policy of repairing damaged ecosystems and habitats, leads to similar results. The central issue is the *value* of the restored environments. If a restored environment is an adequate replacement for the previously existing natural environment, then humans can use, degrade, destroy, and replace natural entities and habitats with no moral consequences whatsoever. The value in the original natural entity does not require preservation.

The value of the restored environment, however, is questionable. Robert Elliot has argued that even a technologically perfect reproduction of a natural area is not equivalent to the original.[10] Elliot uses the analogy of an art forgery, in which even a perfect copy loses the value of the original artwork. What is missing in the forgery is the causal history of the original, the fact that a particular human artist created a specific work in a specific historical period. Although the copy may be as superficially pleasing as the original, the knowledge that it is not the work created by the artist distorts and disvalues our experience. Similarly, we value a natural area because of its "special kind of continuity with the past." This history, Eugene Hargrove argues, provides the authenticity of nature. He writes: "Nature is not simply a collection of natural objects; it is a process that progressively transforms those objects. . . . When we admire nature, we also admire that history."[11] Thus, a restored nature is a fake nature; it is an artificial human creation, not the product of a historical natural process.

The technological "fix" of repairing a damaged and degraded nature is an illusion and a falsehood; elsewhere, I have called it "the big lie."[12] As with all technology, the product of nature restoration is a human artifact, not the end result of a historically based natural process. Artifacts, of course, can have positive or negative value. However, what makes the value in the artifactually restored natural environment questionable is its ostensible claim to be the original.

Both forms of technological intervention in the natural world thus lead to the same result: the establishment of an artifactual world rather than a natural one. When our policy is to use nature to our best advantage, we end up with a series of so-called "responsible interventions" that manipulate natural processes to create the most pleasant human experiences possible. When our policy is to restore and repair a degraded natural environment, we end up with an unauthentic copy of the original. The technological "fix" of nature merely produces artifacts for the satisfaction of human interests.

IV

The issue of *value* now has a sharper focus. We can ask, "What is the value of artifacts and what are the moral obligations that derive from that value?" More precisely, "How is the value of the artifacts, and the derivative moral obligations, different from the value and moral obligations concerning 'wild' nature?" Framed in this manner, the answer to the problem is clear: artifacts differ from natural entities in their anthropocentric and instrumental origins. Artifacts are products of the larger human project of the domination of the natural world.

The concepts of function and purpose are central to an understanding of artifacts.[13] Artifacts, unlike natural objects, are created for a specific purpose. They are essentially anthropocentric instruments, tools or objects, that serve a function in human life. The existence of artifacts is centered on human life. It is impossible to imagine an artifact that is not de-

signed to meet a human purpose, for without a foreseen use the object would not have been created.

The anthropocentric instrumentality of artifacts is completely different from the essential characteristics of natural entities, species, and ecosystems. Living natural entities and systems of entities evolve to fill ecological niches in the biosphere; they are not designed to meet human needs or interests. Andrew Brennan thus argues that natural entities have no "intrinsic functions": they are not created for a particular purpose; they have no set manner of use. We may speak as if natural individuals (e.g., predators) have roles to play in ecosystemic wellbeing (the maintenance of optimum population levels), but this talk is either metaphorical or fallacious. No one created or designed the mountain lion as a regulator of the deer population.[14]

From a moral point of view, the difference between purposely designed artifacts and evolving natural entities is not generally problematic. The anthropocentric instrumentality of artifacts is not a serious moral concern, for most artifacts are designed for use in human social and cultural contexts. Nevertheless, the human intervention into "wild" nature is a different process entirely. Hargrove notes how human intervention alters the aesthetic evaluation of nature: "To attempt to manipulate nature, even for aesthetic reasons, alters nature adversely from an aesthetic standpoint. Historically, manipulation of nature, even to improve it, has been considered subjugation or domination."[15] This domination resulting from human intervention can be generalized beyond aesthetic valuations; it leads to more than just a loss of beauty. The management of nature results in the imposition of our anthropocentric purposes on areas that exist outside human society. We intervene in nature to create so-called natural objects and environments based on models of human desires, interests, and satisfactions. In doing so, we engage in the project of the human domination of nature: the reconstruction of the natural world in our own image, to suit our purposes.

Need we ask why domination is a moral issue? In the context of human social and political thought, domination is the evil that restricts, denies, or distorts individual (and social) freedom and autonomy. In the context of environmental philosophy, domination is the anthropocentric alteration of natural processes. The entities and systems that comprise nature are not permitted to be free, to pursue their own independent and unplanned course of development. Even Hargrove, who emphasizes the aesthetic value of nature, judges this loss of freedom the crucial evil of domination: it "reduces [nature's] ability to be creative."[16] Wherever it exists, in nature or in human culture, the process of domination attacks the preeminent value of self-realization.

Is the analysis of domination appropriate here? Does it make sense to say that we can deny the autonomy, the self-realization, of natural nonhuman entities? The central assumption of this analysis is that natural entities and systems have a value in their own right, a value that transcends the instrumentality of human concerns, projects, and interests. Nature is not merely the physical matter that is the *object* of technological practice and alteration; it is also a *subject,* with its own process and history of development independent of human intervention and activity. Nature thus has a value that can be subverted and destroyed by the process of human domination. In this way, human domination, alteration, and management are issues of moral concern.

V

But does the "wild" have a moral claim on humanity? The answer to this question determines the moral status of the human domination of nature. Does the wilderness, the world of nature untouched by the technological alteration of humanity, possess a moral value worth preserving? Is the creation of a technological "new world" morally harmful? Does it destroy the value of the original New World of the European discovery of American, the untamed and "wild" wilderness? How do we discern a method for answering these questions?

It is at this point that my thoughts return to my encounters with the white-tailed deer on Fire Island. They are not truly wild, for they are no longer afraid of the human presence on the island. They seem to realize that the summer residents are not hunters. These humans come with pretzels, not rifles. Nevertheless, there are some human residents who are deeply disturbed by the existence of the deer. The deer carry ticks that are part of the life cycle of Lyme disease. They eat the flowers and vegetables of well-tended gardens. They are unpredictable, and they can knock a person down. A considerable portion of the human community thus wants the deer hunted and removed from the island.

Just the thought of losing these deer disturbs me—and until recently I did not understand why. In my lucid rational moments, I realize that they are not "wild," that they have prospered on Fire Island due to an unnatural absence of predators; their population could be decreased with no appreciable harm to the herd or the remaining natural ecosystem of the barrier beach. Nevertheless, they are the vestiges of a truly wild natural community; they are reminders that the forces of domination and subjugation do not always succeed.

Birch describes the process of wilderness preservation as "incarceration" by "the technological imperium"—i.e., by the primary social-political force of the contemporary world.[17] The entire process of creating and maintaining wilderness reservations by human law is contradictory, for the wildness is destroyed by the power of the human-technological system:

> Wilderness reservations are not meant to be voids in the fabric of domination where "anarchy" is permitted, where nature is actually liberated. Not at all. The rule of law is presupposed as supreme. Just as wilderness reservations are created by law, so too they can be abolished by law. The threat of annihilation is always maintained.[18]

The domination of natural wildness is just one example of the system of power. "The whole point, purpose, and meaning of imperial power, and its most basic legitimation, is to give humans control over otherness."[19]

It is here that Birch sees the contradiction in the imperial technological domination of wild nature. "The wildness is still there, and it is still wild," and it maintains its own integrity.[20] The wildness, the otherness of nature, remains, I suggest, because the forces of the imperial power require its existence. If there is no "other" recognized as the victim of domination, then the power of the imperium is empty. There would be nothing upon which to exercise power. But maintaining the existence of the wild other, even in the diminished capacity of wilderness reservations managed by the government, lays the seeds for the subversion of the imperial domination of technology.

Birch thus recommends that we view wilderness, wherever it can be found, as a "sacred space" acting as "an implacable counterforce to the momentum of totalizing power." Wilderness appears anywhere: "old roadbeds, wild plots in suburban yards, flower boxes in urban windows, cracks in the pavement. . . ."[21] And it appears, in my life, in the presence of the white-tailed deer of Fire Island. My commitment to the preservation of the deer in my community is part of my resistance to the total domination of the technological world.

This resistance is based on yet a deeper moral commitment: the deer themselves are members of my moral and natural community. The deer and I are partners in the continuous struggle for the preservation of autonomy, freedom, and integrity. This shared partnership creates obligations on the part of humanity for the preservation and protection of the natural world. This is the *call of the wild*—the moral claim of the natural world.

We are all impressed by the power and breadth of human technological achievements. Why is it not possible to extend this power further, until we control and dominate the entire natural universe? This insidious dream of domination can only end by respecting freedom and self-determination, wherever it exists, and by recognizing the true extent of the moral community in the natural world.

NOTES

1. Thomas H. Birch, "The Incarceration of Wildness: Wilderness Areas as Prisons," *Environmental Ethics* 12 (1990): 18.

2. Emmanuel G. Mesthene, "Technology and Wisdom," *Philosophy and Technology: Readings in the Philosophical Problems of Technology,* ed. Carl Mitcham and Robert Mackey (New York: Free Press, 1983), p. 110.

3. Mesthenem, "Technology and Wisdom," p. 111.

4. One of the best examples of this attitude from a historical source contemporaneous with the period of European expansion is the discussion of property by John Locke, *Second Treatise on Government,* chap. 5, especially, secs. 40–43. Locke specifically mentions the lack of value in American land because of the absence of labor and cultivation.

5. For my purposes, it is irrelevant to raise the question, whether North America ever really was wild. It existed then, and now, as a *symbol* of nature uncontrolled by human civilization. Of course, it may have been altered and modified through fire and hunting by Native American populations. Such practices, however, do not change its *significance* as wild and untamed. First, the control of the natural world by Native Americans was definitely limited compared to the new European attempt of total cultivation. Second, the issue here is *not* the purity of the wild in frontier America, but rather the ethical significance of the Western belief that value only arises in nature with human intervention and modification. To discuss that issue, the New World of the Western discovery is useful, because it was relatively uncontrolled and uncultivated, i.e., wild.

6. There are sound political and motivational reasons for arguments that outline the threat to human interests caused by environmental degradation. These arguments have been the rallying cry of popular conservationists from Rachel Carson, *Silent Spring* (New York: Houghton Mifflin, 1962), to Barry Commoner, *The Closing Circle: Nature, Man, and Technology* (New York: Knopf, 1971), to Bill McKibben, *The End of Nature* (New York: Random House, 1989). My philosophical criticisms of these views do not diminish my respect for the positive social and political changes these works have inspired.

7. A complete listing of the relevant literature is impossible. One of the best early works is David Ehrenfeld, *The Arrogance of Humanism* (New York: Oxford University Press, 1978). Other major representative works of nonanthropocentric strands in environmental ethics are Holmes Rolston, III, *Environmental Ethics: Duties to and Values in the Natural World* (Philadelphia: Temple University Press, 1988), J. Baird Callicott, *In Defense of the Land Ethic* (Albany: SUNY Press, 1989), Paul Taylor, *Respect for Nature: A Theory of Environmental Ethics* (Princeton: Princeton University Press, 1986), Arne Naess, *Ecology, Community and Lifestyle,* trans. and ed. David

Rothenberg (Cambridge: Cambridge University Press, 1989). For a discussion of enlightened anthropocentric views, see Bryan G. Norton, *Why Preserve Natural Variety?* (Princeton: Princeton University Press, 1987), Eugene C. Hargrove, *The Foundations of Environmental Ethics* (Englewood Cliffs: Prentice Hall, 1989), and Mark Sagoff, *The Economy of the Earth: Philosophy, Law, and the Environment* (Cambridge: Cambridge University Press, 1988).

8. Martin H. Krieger, "What's Wrong with Plastic Trees?" *Science* 179 (1973): 453.

9. Krieger, "What's Wrong with Plastic Trees?" p. 453.

10. Robert Elliot, "Faking Nature," *Inquiry* 25 (1982): 81–93, specifically, p. 86.

11. Hargrove, *The Foundations of Environmental Ethics,* p. 195.

12. Eric Katz, "The Big Lie: Human Restoration of Nature," *Research in Philosophy and Technology,* 12 (1992): 231–41.

13. The argument of this section is based on Katz, "The Big Lie." For a further discussion, see Michael Losonsky, "The Nature of Artifacts," *Philosophy* 65 (1990): 81–88.

14. Andrew Brennan, "The Moral Standing of Natural Objects," *Environmental Ethics* 6 (1984): 41–44.

15. Hargrove, *The Foundations of Environmental Ethics,* p. 195.

16. Hargrove, *The Foundations.*

17. Birch, "The Incarceration of Wildness," p. 10.

18. Birch, "The Incarceration of Wildness," p. 10.

19. Birch, "The Incarceration of Wildness," p. 18.

20. Birch, "The Incarceration of Wildness," pp. 21–22.

21. Birch, "The Incarceration of Wildness," pp. 24–25.

Ecological Restoration and the Culture of Nature

Andrew Light

1. PRAGMATISM AND ECOLOGICAL RESTORATION

Many nonanthropocentrists in environmental ethics who have written about ecological restoration have been highly critical of it. Why? The argument goes something like this. If nature was dependent on human creation (as a restored landscape is) then it would have an irreconcilable anthropocentric (or anthropogenic) component. So, if restorations are human creations, so the arguments of the philosophical critics go, then they cannot ever count as the sort of thing that contains natural value, nonanthropocentrically conceived, since humans cannot create the sorts of things that contain that sort of value. At worst, restorations represent on this view the tyranny of humans over nature. Eric Katz has put it most emphatically in arguing that "the practice of ecological restoration can only represent a misguided faith in the hegemony and infallibility of the human power to control the natural world."[1]

I have long disagreed with claims like this one. My previous answer to such positions has been to simply set aside these kind of arguments and focus on other issues involving ecological restoration.[2] But I do not think it wise to ignore such views. In addition to the philosophical arguments which must be mustered to respond to such views, we should also consider whether the kind of environmental philosophy which produces such claims is really the best

Andrew Light, "Ecological Restoration and the Culture of Nature," in *Restoring Nature: Perspectives from the Social Sciences and Humanities,* ed. P. Gobster and B. Hall (Washington: Island Press, 2000). Revised for this volume. Reprinted with permission of the publisher.

context within which to assess practices like eco-logical restoration, a practice that surely seems to do more good than harm for the environment. I for one believe that environmental philosophers should be interested in more than simply describing the nonan-thropocentric value of nature: we should also be try-ing to appeal to the existing intuitions of the pubic so that they will better support more progressive en-vironmental polices. But since most nonanthro-pocentrists claim that most people are anthropocen-trists, those environmental ethicists interested in appealing to a wider audience must be open to mak-ing ethical claims about the value of nature in an-thropocentric terms, where possible, in order to get the public to go along with the ends of the environ-mental community.

I call the view that makes it plausible to appeal to human motivations in valuing nature, *environ-mental pragmatism*. By this I simply mean the recog-nition that a responsible and complete environmen-tal philosophy includes a public component with a clear policy emphasis.[3] It is certainly appropriate for philosophers to continue their search for a true and foundational nonanthropocentric description of the value of nature. But environmental philosophers would be remiss if they did not set aside that search at times and try to make other, perhaps more ap-pealing ethical arguments which may have an audi-ence in an anthropocentric public. Environmental pragmatism in my sense is agnostic concerning the existence of nonanthropocentric natural value. Those embracing this view can either continue to pursue such a theory or they can take a more traditional pragmatist stance denying the existence of such value.[4]

This approach modifies the philosophical contri-bution to questions about restoration ecology to pos-itive effect. For pragmatists, restoration makes sense because on the whole it results in many advantages over mere preservation of ecosystems that have been substantially damaged by humans. As we will see in the last section of this chapter, some of those ad-vantages have to do with the benefits of restoration to the human relationship with nature and not just benefits to nature itself. The philosopher may cer-

tainly have much to add to a full analysis of the rel-evant questions concerning the practice of ecologi-cal restoration. They may in fact be able to help to rethink the very normative ground of restoration as a public environmental practice. But first, how can we answer on philosophical grounds the sorts of crit-icisms offered of restoration by some nonanthro-pocentrists like Katz.

2. KATZ AGAINST RESTORATION

As Katz describes it, there are actually two separa-ble questions to put to advocates of restoration: (1) Do we have an obligation to try to restore damaged nature?, and (2) Do we have the ability to restore damaged nature? Katz argues quite forcefully that we do not have the ability to restore nature because what we actually create in ecological restorations are humanly produced artifacts and not nature, nonan-thropocentrically conceived. Based on this claim he assumes that the first question—whether we have an obligation to try to restore nature—is moot. Katz's logic is simple: we do not have an obligation to do what we can't in principle do.

But even if we were to grant Katz the argument that it is impossible to restore nature, in the sense that Katz understands nature, it might still be the case that we have moral obligations to *try* to restore na-ture. How could this be true? There are a number of reasons which I will raise below but for now con-sider that what we are really restoring with restora-tion is not necessarily nature itself, but some kind of relationship with nature (whether actually there in the restoration, adjacent to it, or as a more abstract idea). But before fully explicating this position we need to first better understand Katz's arguments.

There are five separable, but often overlapping, arguments in Katz's work on restoration against both the suggestion that we can restore nature and against the practice of trying to restore nature. They are listed below in order of how they arise in Katz's work, ac-companied with an example of supporting evidence from Katz's various papers on restoration.

KR1. The Duplicitous Argument

"I am outraged by the idea that a technologically created 'nature' will be passed off as reality."[5]

KR2. The Arrogance (or "Hubris") Argument

"The human presumption that we are capable of this technological fix demonstrates (once again) the arrogance with which humanity surveys the natural world."[6]

KR3. The Artifact Argument

"The re-created natural environment that is the end result of a restoration project is nothing more than an artifact created for human use."[7]

KR4. The Domination Argument

"The attempt to redesign, recreate and restore natural areas and objects is a radical intervention in natural processes. Although there is an obvious spectrum of possible restoration[s] . . . all of these projects involve the manipulation and domination of natural areas. All of these projects involve the creation of artifactual realities, the imposition of anthropocentric interests on the processes and objects of value. Nature is not permitted to be free, to pursue its own independent course of development."[8]

KR5. The Replacement Argument

"If a restored environment is an adequate replacement for the previously existing natural environment [which of course for Katz it can never be], then humans can use, degrade, destroy, and replace natural entities and habitats with no moral consequence whatsoever. The value in the original natural entity does not require preservation."[9]

Here, I will focus on KR4, the domination argument, which is perhaps the argument that comes up the most throughout all of Katz's restoration papers. I will argue that the rest of Katz's arguments can be conceded as long as KR4 can be independently answered.

KR1–3 and 5 can be ignored in rejecting Katz's position so long as we are prepared to concede for now one important premise to all of his arguments. This is Katz's ontological assumption (a claim concerning the nature or essence of a thing) that humans and nature can be meaningfully separated thus grounding the argument that restored nature is an artifact, a part of human culture, rather than a part of nature. As Katz has admitted in an as yet unpublished public forum on his work, he is a nature-culture dualist. If one rejects this overall ontological and metaphysical view about the separation of humans from nature then one may reject most of Katz's objections to restoration.

I will accept here, even though I disagree with it, the underlying assumption by Katz that restored nature does not reproduce nature, that is to say, it does not reproduce whatever value Katz wishes to attribute to nature. But even if I grant this point that restored nature is not really nature, KR4 is still false because it is arguably the case that restoration does not "dominate" nature in any coherent sense but often instead helps nature to be "free" of just the sort of domination that Katz is worried about. The reasoning here is straightforward enough. If I can show that restorations are valuable for nature, even if I concede that they do not recreate nature, then the various motivations for restoration will distinguish whether a restoration is duplicitous (KR1) or arrogant (KR2). If we restrict our discussion to what I call benevolent restorations (those intended to rectify a harm) rather than malevolent restorations (those intended to justify destruction of nature on the assumption that a restoration can always bring back the full natural value of a destroyed area), then we would not risk KR1 or 2 because in principle such restorations are not trying to fool anyone nor are they necessarily arrogant.[10]

A benevolent restoration, for example, would not risk KR1 or 2 because in principle it is not trying to fool anyone nor is it necessarily arrogant. Further, and more simply, conceding Katz's ontological claim about the distinction between nature and culture eliminates the significance of KR3—since we no longer care that what is created may or may not be an artifact—as well as KR5, since we have given up hope that a restoration could ever actually serve as a replacement for "real" nature. (Notice too that KR5 is only a problem if one wishes to defend malicious restorations which I doubt any environmentalist is willing to do.)

Now, back to the domination argument. KR4 is a claim that could hold even for a view that conceded Katz's nature-culture distinction. The reason for Katz would be that even a failed attempt to duplicate natural value—or create something akin to nature while conceding that in principle "real" nature can never be restored by humans—could still count as an instance of "domination" as Katz has described it. An *attempt* at restoration, on Katz's logic, would still prohibit nature from ever being able to pursue its own development. The reason is that for Katz, restoration is always a substitute for whatever would have occurred at a particular site absent human interference. The idea is that even if humans can produce a valuable landscape of some sort on a denuded acreage, this act of production is still an instance of domination over the alternative of a natural evolution of this same acreage even if a significant natural change would take ten times as long as the human induced change and would be arguably less valuable for the species making use of it. Still, there are a number of arguments that one can muster against KR4 (I will provide four) and still play largely within Katz's biggest and most contentious assumption about the ontological status of restored nature.

(1) We can imagine cases where nature cannot pursue its own interests (however one wishes to understand this sense of nature having interests) because of something we have done to it which must be rectified by restoration. For example, many instances of restoration are limited to bioactivation of soil which has become contaminated by one form or another of hazardous industrial waste. If restoration necessarily prohibits nature from being "free" as KR4 maintains, then how do we reconcile the relative freedom that bioactivation makes possible with this claim? Restoration need not determine exactly what grows in a certain place, but may in fact simply be the act of allowing nature to again pursue its own interests rather than shackling it to perpetual human-induced trauma. In many cases of restoration this point can be driven home further when we see how anthropogenically damaged land (or soil) can be uniquely put at risk of invasion by anthropogenically introduced exotic plants. South African ice plant, an exotic in Southern California which destroys the soil it is introduced on to, is highly opportunistic and can easily spread onto degraded land thus ensuring that native plants will not be able to reestablish themselves. I highlight here this contentious native-exotic distinction because I suspect that given Katz's strong nature-culture distinction he would necessarily have to prefer a landscape of native plants over a landscape of exotics where the existence of the exotics is a result of an act of human (cultural) interference in nature. If the original nature at such a site were never put at risk of invasion by exotics introduced by humans then we can be relatively sure that those exotics would not have made inroads onto the site. Allowing nature to pursue its own interests, given prior anthropogenic interference, thus involves at least as strong a claim to protect it from further anthropogenic risk through restoration practices as the case Katz makes for leaving it alone.

(2) Going back to a point made earlier, even if we do agree with Katz that restorations only produce artifacts, can't it still be the case that the harm we cause to nature requires us to engage in what we would have to term, following Katz, "attempted restorations"? It simply does not follow from the premise that something is more natural when it is relatively free of human interference that we should conclude that therefore we must always avoid interfering with nature. It is a classic premise of holism in environmental ethics (the theory that obligations to the non-human natural world are to whole ecosystems and not to individual entities, which makes it often opposed to the sort of views advocated by animal rights advocates) that some interference is warranted when we are the cause of an imbalance in nature: e.g., hunting of white-tailed deer is thought to be permissible under holism since humans have caused that species' population explosion. If such interventions as hunting are permissible as an aid to help to "rectify the balance of nature" then why are

there not comparable cases with the use of restoration as an aid for the "original," "real" nature? We can even imagine that such cases would be less controversial than holist defenses of hunting.

It turns out in fact that there are good cases where restoration, even if it results in the production of an artifact, does not lead to the domination described by Katz. Imagine the case where the restoration project is one which will restore a corridor between two wilderness preserves. If there is positive natural value in the two preserves that is threatened because wildlife is not allowed to move freely between them, then restoration projects which would restore a corridor (such as removing roads for example) would actually not only be morally permissible but possibly ethically required depending on one's views of the value of the nature in the preserves. This is not restoration as a "second best" to preservation, or a distraction away from preservation, it is restoration as an integral and critical part of the maintenance of natural value. So, even if we agree with Katz that humans cannot really restore nature, it does not follow that they ought not to engage in restoration projects which actually repair the damage caused by past domination rather than furthering that domination.

Given objections like the two discussed so far, it is important to try to get a better handle on exactly what sort of damage is caused by domination in the sense described by Katz. It turns out that the worst damage to nature for Katz is domination which prevents the "self-realization" of nature:

> The fundamental error is thus domination, the denial of freedom and autonomy. Anthropocentrism, the major concern of most environmental philosophers, is only one species of the more basic attack on the preeminent value of self-realization. From within the perspective of anthropocentrism, humanity believes it is justified in dominating and molding the nonhuman world to its own human purposes.[11]

Thus, the problem with restoration is that it restricts natural self-realization by forcing nature onto a path that we would find more appealing.

(3) With this clarification, we can then further object to Katz that his sense of restoration confuses restoration with mitigation, for example, the practice of creating new wetlands where none had existed before in order to make up for the loss of an original wetland elsewhere. The force of the charge of domination is that we mold nature to fit our "own human purposes." But with restoration as a practice the point of most scientific disputes over it is precisely that anything does not go. While there is always some variability in what can be restored at a particular site (what period after all do we restore to?), we cannot restore a landscape just any way we wish and still have a good restoration in scientific terms. We are also bound in the context of restoration, as was mentioned before, of restoring to some preexisting state even if we are unsure which particularly historical state we ought to restore to. If that is the case, then the broadly construed historical and scientific boundaries of restoration limit the purposes to which we can put a restoration. If Katz objects that when we restore a denuded bit of land we are at least making something that fits our need of having more attractive "natural" surroundings—an argument that Katz often makes—we can reply that because of the constraints that are on restoration, as opposed to mitigation, the fact that we find a restored landscape appealing is only contingently true. It can clearly be the case (and there are plenty of empirical examples) that what we must restore to is not the preferred landscape of most people. The Chicago Wilderness project (a joint endeavor of forty public and private agencies in Chicago to restore the forest preserves around the city, successfully restoring over 14,000 acres so far) was in fact in some trouble over exactly these kinds of worries. Many people see this project as involving the destruction of aesthetically pleasing forests in order to restore the original oak savannas (the kind of landscape which the project's organizers claim was in place there before the point of white settlement). But philosophically, because a restored landscape can never necessarily be tied only to our own desires (since our desires are not historically and scientifically determined in the same way as the parameters of a restoration) then those desires cannot

actually be the direct cause of any restriction on the self-realization of nature.

(4) Finally, we must wonder at this value of self-realization. Setting aside the inherent philosophical problems with understanding what this claim to self realization means in the case of nature, one has to wonder how we could know what natural self-realization would be in any particular case and why we would totally divorce a human role in helping to make it happen if we could discern it. In an analogous case involving two humans, we do not say that a human right to (or value of) self-realization is abrogated when a criminal who harms someone is forced to pay restitution. Even if the restitution is forced against the will of the victim, and even if the compensation in principle can never make up for the harm done, we would not say that somehow the victim's self-realization has been restricted by the act of restitution by the criminal. Again, there seems to be no clear argument here for why the moral obligation to try to restore has been diminished by Katz's arguments that we do not have the ability to really restore nature or pass off an artifact as nature.

3. RESTORING ENVIRONMENTAL PHILOSOPHY

If I am justified in setting aside the rest of Katz's arguments (KR 1–3 and 5) by accepting his claim that humans really cannot restore "real" nature, and if my objections to KR4 hold true, then what sort of conclusions could we draw about the role of philosophy in sorting out the normative issues involved in restoration? As it turns out, Katz gives us an insight in figuring out the next step.

After explaining the harm we do to nature in the domination we visit upon it through acts of restoration, Katz briefly assesses the harm that we do to ourselves through such actions:

> But a policy of domination transcends the anthropocentric subversion of natural processes. A policy of domination subverts both nature and human existence; it denies both the cultural and natural real-

ization of individual good, human and nonhuman. Liberation from all forms of domination is thus the chief goal of any ethical or political system.[12]

Though not very clearly explained by Katz, this intuition represents a crucial point for proceeding further. In addition to connecting environmental philosophy to larger projects of social liberation, Katz here opens the door to a consideration of the consequences of restoration on humans and human communities. As such, Katz allows an implicit assertion that there is a value involved in restoration that must be evaluated other than the value of the objects that are produced by restoration.

But the problem with drawing this conclusion is that this passage is also perhaps the most cryptic in all of Katz's work on restoration. What does Katz mean by this claim? How exactly does restoration deny the realization of an individual human, or cultural, good? This claim can only be made understandable by assuming that there is some kind of cultural value connected to nature which is risked through the act of domination, or otherwise causing harm to nature. But what is this value?

I think that the value that Katz is alluding to here, though which he never explores seriously, somehow describes the value of that part of human culture that is connected to external, non-human nature. This is not simply a suggestion that we humans are part of nature (for the implication here is that we cause a disvalue to ourselves and to nature by acting *on* nature in some way, thus confirming Katz's nature-culture distinction) but rather that we have a *relationship with* nature which exists on a moral as well as physical terrain in such a way that our actions toward nature can reciprocally harm us. If this is the view implicit in this claim then it is still consistent with much of the rest of Katz's larger views about the value of nature. We have a relationship with nature even if we are separable from it. Without fully explicating the content of that relationship it seems that Katz is right in assuming that somehow the way in which we act toward nature morally implicates us in a particular way. In the same sense, when we morally mistreat another human we not only harm them but harm ourselves (by diminishing our character, by implicating ourselves in evil, however you want to put it).

Now if this assumption is correct, and if there is anything to the arguments I have put forward so far that there can be some kind of positive value to our interaction with nature, then doing right by nature will have the same reciprocal effect of morally implicating us in a positive value as occurs when we do right by other persons. Perhaps Katz would agree. Where Katz would disagree is with the suggestion I would add to this that there is some part of many kinds of restoration (if not most kinds) that contain positive value. Aside from the other suggestions I have already made concerning the possible positive content of restoration, one can also consider that the relationship with nature that is implied in Katz's view has a moral content in itself that is not reducible to the value of fulfilling this relationship's concomitant obligations. The relationship between humans and nature imbues restoration with a positive value even if it cannot replicate natural value in its products. But understanding this point will require some explanation.

Consider that if I have a reciprocal relationship with another human (where I do right by them and they do right by me) then, to generalize Katz's account, there is a moral content to both of our actions which implicates each of us as persons. Each of us is a better person morally because of the way we interact with each other in the relationship. But the relationship itself, or rather just the fact of the existence of the relationship, also has a moral content of its own (or what we would call a "normative content," meaning that the relationship can be assessed as being in a better or worse state) which is independent of the fulfillment of any obligations. If this point of the possible separation between the value of a relationship and the value of the fulfillment of obligations does not follow intuitively, imagine the case where two people act according to duty toward each other without building a substantive normative relationship between them.

Consider the following example. I have a brother to whom I am not terribly close. While I always act

according to duty to him—I never knowingly do harm to him and I even extend special family obligations to him—I do not have a substantive relationship with him which in itself has a normative content. Thus, if I do not speak to him for a year, nothing is lost (indeed, neither of us feel a loss) because there is no relationship there to maintain or that requires maintenance for normative reasons. But if my brother needed a kidney transplant, I would give him my kidney unhesitatingly out of a sense of obligation—something I would not feel obliged to do for non-family members—even though I still do not feel intimately comfortable around him in the same way that I do with my closest friends. Our relationship as persons—that sense of intimate affection and care for another person that I have experienced with other people—has no positive value for me. (It isn't necessarily a disvalue, only it is a sense of indifference, a lack of closeness.) So, I can have interaction with another person, even interaction which involves substantial components of obligation and duty (and in Katz's terms I will never put myself in a position to dominate that other person) but still not have a relationship with them that involves any kind of positive value, or which has normative standards of maintenance.

I do not think that I have any obligation to have a relationship in this sense with my brother. I in fact do not, even though my mother would like it if I did. But if I did have a relationship with my brother in this sense then it would have a value above and beyond the moral interaction that I have with him now (the obligations that I have to him that can be iterated) that aids in a determination of our moral character.[13] If we had a relationship with normative content there would be a positive or negative value that could be assessed if I lost touch with my brother or ceased to care about his welfare. (I could very well claim that it would be better for me to have such a relationship with him, but this would require a further argument.)

Consider further that if I wanted to rectify or create anew a substantive normative relationship with my brother, like the relationship I have with several close friends, how would I do it? One thing that I could do would be to engage in activities with him. The same sorts of activities (let us call them "material interactions") that I do with my friends now. I might work with him to put up a fence, or help him plant his garden. I might begin to talk over my personal and professional problems with him. I might go on a long journey with him that demanded some kind of mutual reliance such as white water rafting or visiting a foreign city where neither of us spoke the native language. In short, though there are of course no guarantees, I could begin to have some kind of material relationship with him as a prelude to having some kind of substantive normative relationship with him. Many factors might mitigate the success of such a project. For one thing the distance between the two of us—he lives in our hometown of Atlanta and I live in New York City. So, if I was really serious about this project of building a relationship between us, that had value independent of the value of the fulfillment of our mutual obligations to each other which already exist, I'd have to come up with ways to bridge these interfering factors. Importantly though, I couldn't form a substantive normative relationship with him merely by respecting his right of self-realization and autonomy as a person; I would have to somehow become actively involved with him.

Now, when we compare the case of the estranged brother to that of nature, many parallels arise. We know that we can fulfill obligations to nature in terms of respecting its autonomy and self-realization as a subject (in Katz's terms) without ever forming a substantive normative relationship with it. Assuming also that there is a kind of relationship with nature possible on Katz's scheme (for this is in part what we harm when we dominate nature) it is fair to say that a relationship consisting in positive normative value with nature is compatible with Katz's overall view of the human-nature relationship. Because he says so little about what our positive relationship to nature could be, he is in no position to restrict it a priori. We also know that, as in the case of the estranged brother, we need some kind of material bridge to create a relationship with nature in order to see that relationship come about.

How to build that bridge? Suggesting ways to overcome the gap between humans and nature (without necessarily disvaluing it) seems in part to be the restored role of a pragmatist environmental philosophy in questions of ecological restoration. Certainly, as in the case of my brother, distance is a problem. Numerous environmental professionals have emphasized the importance of being in nature in order to care for nature. Also, acts of preservation are important in order for there to be nature to have a relationship with. But what about restoration? Can restoration help engender such a positive normative relationship with nature? It seems clear to me that it can. When we engage in acts of benevolent restoration we are bound *by* nature in the same sense that we are obligated to respect what it once was attempting to realize before we interfered with it. In Katz's terms, we are attempting to respect it as an autonomous subject. But we are also bound *to* nature in the act of restoring. In addition to the ample sociological and anthropological evidence on the positive value with nature that is engendered in benevolent restoration, we can say that restoration restores the human connection to nature by restoring that part of culture that has historically contained a connection to nature. While it would take further argument to prove, I believe that this is the kind of relationship that is a necessary condition for encouraging people to choose to preserve the natural system and landscapes around them rather than trade them off for short term monetary gains garnered by development. If I am in a normative relationship with the land around me (whether it is "real" nature or not) I am less likely to allow it to be harmed further.[14]

We can even look to Katz for help in completing this pragmatic task. We don't want restorations that try to pass themselves off as the real thing when they are really "fakes" (KR1), or are pursued through arrogance (KR2), nor are we interested in those that are offered as justifications for replacing or destroying nature (KR5). Nor would we want our human relationships to exhibit those properties either. But even given the legacy of inhuman treatment of each other, we know that it is possible to restore human relationships that do not resemble KR1, 2, or 5. There is however one possible worry to attend to in KR3, the artifact argument. While earlier I had said that the importance of KR3 is diminished by granting Katz's nature-culture distinction, there is a way that it can still cause us problems in grounding attempts at restoration in the positive value of strengthening the human-nature relationship.

Katz may object to my relationship argument that if we allow his claim that what has been restored is not really nature then what we are restoring is not a cultural relationship with nature but, in a sense, only extending the artifactual material culture of humans. At best, all we can have with restoration is a relationship with artifacts, not nature. Maybe he will allow that we improve relations with each other through cooperative acts of restoration, but this is not the same as a restoration of a relationship with nature itself.

But it should be clear by now that Katz would be mistaken to make such an objection for several reasons stemming in part from my earlier remarks. (1) Even if we admit that restored nature is an artifact and not real nature, restored nature can also serve as a conduit for real nature to free itself from the shackles we have previously placed upon it. Restoration can allow nature to engage in its own autonomous restitution. Of the different sorts of restoration projects which I have sketched above, many amount to aids to nature rather than creations of new nature.

(2) Even if restoration is the production of an artifact, these artifacts do bear a striking resemblance to the real thing. This is not to say that restorations can be good enough to fool us (KR1). Rather, it is simply to point out that an opportunity to interact with the flora and fauna of the sort most common in benevolent restorations will have the effect of increasing the bonds of care that people will have with non-restored nature. If a denuded and abandoned lot in the middle of an inner city ghetto is restored by local residents who have never been outside of their city, then it will give them a better appreciation of the fragility and complexity of the natural processes of nature itself should they encounter them. The fact that restorationists are engaged in a technological processes does not neces-

sarily mean that their practices do not serve the broader purpose of restoring a relationship with nature. Just as starting some form of mediated communication with my brother (like e-mail or regular phone calls) does not restore a fully healthy communicative relationship with him that could be found through face to face conversation, it still helps me to get used to the idea of some form of immediate and substantive communication.

And finally (3), if Katz persists in his worry that the act of restoration reifies domination by reaffirming our power over nature through the creation of artifacts, we can say that exactly the opposite is likely the case (at least in the case of benevolent restorations) where the goal is restoring the culture of nature if not nature itself. Restorationists get first hand (rather than anecdotal and textbook) exposure to the actual consequences of human domination of nature. A better understanding of the problems of bioactivating soil, for example, gives us a better idea of the complexity of the harm we have caused to natural processes. Knowing that harm can be empowering in a much healthier way than Katz seems willing to admit in that it can empower us to know more precisely why we should object to the kinds of activities that can cause that harm to nature in the first place[15]

It seems clear that benevolent restorations are valuable because they help us to restore our relationship with nature, by restoring what could be termed our culture of nature. This is true even if Katz is correct that restored nature has the ontological property of an artifact. Restoration is an obligation exercised in the interests of forming a positive community with nature, and thus is well within the boundaries of a constructive, pragmatic environmental philosophy.[16]

NOTES

1. Eric Katz, "The Problem of Ecological Restoration," *Environmental Ethics* 18 (1996), p. 222, my emphasis. See also "The Call of the Wild: The Struggle Against Domination and the Technological Fix of Nature," "The Big Lie:

Human Restoration of Nature," "Artifacts and Functions: A Note on the Value of Nature," and "Imperialism and Environmentalism." All of these papers are collected in Eric Katz, *Nature as Subject: Human Obligation and Natural Community* (Lanham, MD: Rowman & Littlefield Publishers, 1997). It is the versions of these papers as they appear in that volume that I have drawn on for this chapter.

2. See Andrew Light and Eric Higgs, "The Politics of Ecological Restoration," *Environmental Ethics* 18 (1996), pp. 227–247.

3. See for example, Andrew Light, "Environmental Pragmatism as Philosophy or Metaphilosophy," in A. Light & E. Katz (eds.), *Environmental Pragmatism* (London: Routledge, 1996), pp. 325–338; "Compatibilism in Political Ecology," in *Environmental Pragmatism,* op. cit., pp. 161–184; and "Callicott and Naess on Pluralism," *Inquiry* 39 (1996), pp. 273–94, as well as my chapter in the final section of this volume.

4. See for example, Kelly Parker, "Pragmatism and Environmental Thought," in *Environmental Pragmatism,* op. cit., pp. 21–37.

5. *Nature as Subject,* op. cit., p. 97. Originally in "The Big Lie" (as are KR2–KR4). KR1 is restated later in "The Call of the Wild": ". . . what makes value in the artifactually restored natural environment questionable is its ostensible claim to be the original." Ibid., p. 114.

6. Ibid., p. 97.

7. Ibid., p. 97. KR3 is most thoroughly elaborated later in "Artifacts and Functions."

8. Ibid., p. 105. The domination argument is repeated in "The Call of the Wild" (ibid., p. 115) with the addition of an imported quote from Eugene Hargrove: domination "reduces [nature's] ability to be creative." The argument is also repeated in "Artifacts and Functions" and further specified in "Imperialism and Environmentalism." As far as I can tell though, the argument for domination is not really expanded on in this last paper, except that imperialism is deemed wrong because it makes nature into an artifact (KR3).

9. Ibid., p. 113. Originally in "The Call of the Wild," and repeated in "Imperialism and Environmentalism." Ibid., p. 139.

10. Interestingly enough, the Society for Ecological Restoration, the primary organization that sets priorities and standards for restorations, specifically prohibits malicious restorations as its first policy recommendation to its membership.

11. Ibid., p. 105.

12. Ibid., p. 105.

13. On a broader scale, just as there can be a town full of decent, law abiding citizens, they may not constitute a moral community in any significant sense.

14. It is also the case that restoration will only be one out of a large collection of practices available for adaptive management. In a project to clean up an abandoned mine site, for example, we can imagine a case where restoring the site to a landscape that was there before would not be the best choice and that instead some other sustainable landscape which would help to preserve an endangered species now in the area would be more appropriate. I am indebted to Anne Chapman for pressing me to clarify this point.

15. Katz can legitimately respond here that there seems to be no unique reason why people couldn't get these kinds of experiences that generate a closer relationship with nature out of some other kinds of activities. Why couldn't we just use this sort of argument to encourage more acts of preservation, or simply walking though nature, etc. Such an objection would however miss a crucial point. Even if it can be proved that we can get these kinds of positive experiences with nature in forms other than acts of restoration (and I see no reason why we couldn't) this does not diminish the case being built here: that restoration does not necessarily result in the domination of nature. Arguably, moreover, our experiences as restorationists give us some of the kinds of understandings of the workings of natural processes required for aesthetic appreciation. (See Allen Carlson, "Nature, Aesthetic Appreciation, and Knowledge," *Journal of Aesthetics and Art Criticism* 53 (1995), pp. 393–400.) Importantly, this understanding is a transitive property: it not only gives us an ability to aesthetically appreciate the nature we are trying to restore, but also the nature we are not trying to restore. Restoration thus could provide a unique avenue into the aesthetic appreciation of all of nature, restored or not.

16. This paper is a shortened version of my "Ecological Restoration and the Culture of Nature: A Pragmatic Perspective," in *Restoring Nature: Perspectives from the Social Sciences and Humanities,* eds. Paul Gobster and Bruce Hall (Washington, D.C.: Island Press, 2000).

Chapter 7
Rethinking the Good Life

Questions for Reflection and Discussion

Voluntary Simplicity

1. Perhaps the most important lesson a student of environmental ethics could learn is how good the life of an environmentalist can be. People sometimes get the wrong idea about environmentalism: that an environmentalist is constantly on the lookout for things to feel guilty about, or for things to try to make other people feel guilty about: in short, I'm not okay, you're not okay.

But in *The Global Living Handbook,* Jim Merkel says, "We realize that we are not martyrs and we are not victims. If we ride our bikes to prove a point we will feel bitter. If we ride because we love getting exercise, hearing the birds, and watching the moon scribe the sky, then our life enters the realm of poetics. Let's face it: the corporations may be trying to dominate the planet, but they are not *making* us buy their cars and gas. We have a choice."[1]

How do you suppose your life would change if you were to become more environmentally conscious? In what ways would a more environmentally sound lifestyle represent a sacrifice on your part? What would you truly miss? Are there ways in which life might be *more* satisfying? If so, then why not start gently phasing them into your life? Why not today?

2. Tom Hill says the fundamental question is, what sort of person would destroy the natural environment? What is Hill's answer? Do you agree?

Why is that the question? Why does Hill not ask the seemingly simpler question, what is wrong with destroying the natural environment?

3. If we consumed less, would people in developing countries be better off? How so? Does our reason for consuming less stand or fall with whether importing less from developing countries would somehow improve their standard of living? Or is the main reason for living a simpler life closer to home, namely that a simpler life is a better life?

What does Milbrath say? What does Sagoff say?

4. Freya Mathews seems to say there is a sense in which environmental ethics is not "natural." (Environmental activists fail to live "within the framework of the given.") What

does she mean? Do you agree? If she is right, does that change how we ought to think about environmental ethics?

NOTES

1. Jim Merkel was once an electrical engineer. He made his living selling military technology. He gave it up, and for ten years has lived on five thousand dollars per year. For more on the Global Living Project, contact Jim Merkel and Erica Sherwood (www.netidea.com/~jmerkel/).

Ideals of Human Excellence and Preserving Natural Environments

Thomas E. Hill, Jr.

The moral significance of preserving natural environments is not entirely an issue of rights and social utility, for a person's attitude toward nature may be importantly connected with virtues or human excellences. The question is, "What sort of person would destroy the natural environment—or even see its value solely in cost/benefit terms?" The answer I suggest is that willingness to do so may well reveal the absence of traits which are a natural basis for a proper humility, self-acceptance, gratitude, and appreciation of the good in others.

I

A wealthy eccentric bought a house in a neighborhood I know. The house was surrounded by a beautiful display of grass, plants, and flowers, and it was shaded by a huge old avocado tree. But the grass required cutting, the flowers needed tending, and the man wanted more sun. So he cut the whole lot down and covered the yard with asphalt. After all it was his property and he was not fond of plants.

It was a small operation, but it reminded me of the strip mining of large sections of the Appalachians. In both cases, of course, there were reasons for the destruction, and property rights could be cited as justification. But I could not help but wonder, "What sort of person would do a thing like that?"

Many Californians had a similar reaction when a recent governor defended the leveling of ancient redwood groves, reportedly saying, "If you have seen one redwood, you have seen them all."

Incidents like these arouse the indignation of ardent environmentalists and leave even apolitical observers with some degree of moral discomfort. The reasons for these reactions are mostly obvious. Uprooting the natural environment robs both present and future generations of much potential use and enjoyment. Animals too depend on the environment; and even if one does not value animals for their own sakes, their potential utility for us is incalculable.

Thomas E. Hill, Jr., "Ideals of Human Excellence and Preserving Natural Environments," *Environmental Ethics* 5 (1983): 211–24. Reprinted with permission of the author and the journal.

Plants are needed, of course, to replenish the atmosphere quite aside from their aesthetic value. These reasons for hesitating to destroy forests and gardens are not only the most obvious ones, but also the most persuasive for practical purposes. But, one wonders, is there nothing more behind our discomfort? Are we concerned solely about the potential use and enjoyment of the forests, etc., for ourselves, later generations, and perhaps animals? Is there not something else which disturbs us when we witness the destruction or even listen to those who would defend it in terms of cost/benefit analysis?

Imagine that in each of our examples those who would destroy the environment argue elaborately that, even considering future generations of human beings and animals, there are benefits in "replacing" the natural environment which outweigh the negative utilities which environmentalists cite.[1] No doubt we could press the argument on the facts, trying to show that the destruction is shortsighted and that its defenders have underestimated its potential harm or ignored some pertinent rights or interests. But is this all we could say? Suppose we grant, for a moment, that the utility of destroying the redwoods, forests, and gardens is equal to their potential for use and enjoyment by nature lovers and animals. Suppose, further, that we even grant that the pertinent human rights and animal rights, if any, are evenly divided for and against destruction. Imagine that we also concede, for argument's sake, that the forests contain no potentially useful endangered species of animals and plants. Must we then conclude that there is no further cause for moral concern? Should we then feel morally indifferent when we see the natural environment uprooted?

II

Suppose we feel that the answer to these questions should be negative. Suppose, in other words, we feel that our moral discomfort when we confront the destroyers of nature is not fully explained by our belief that they have miscalculated the best use of natural resources or violated rights in exploiting them.

Suppose, in particular, we sense that part of the problem is that the natural environment is being viewed exclusively as a natural *resource*. What could be the ground of such a feeling? That is, what is there in our system of normative principles and values that could account for our remaining moral dissatisfaction?[2]

Some may be tempted to seek an explanation by appeal to the interests, or even the rights, of plants. After all, they may argue, we only gradually came to acknowledge the moral importance of all human beings, and it is even more recently that consciences have been aroused to give full weight to the welfare (and rights?) of animals. The next logical step, it may be argued, is to acknowledge a moral requirement to take into account the interests (and rights?) of plants. The problem with the strip miners, redwood cutters, and the like, on this view, is not just that they ignore the welfare and rights of people and animals; they also fail to give due weight to the survival and health of the plants themselves.

The temptation to make such a reply is understandable if one assumes that all moral questions are exclusively concerned with whether *acts* are right or wrong, and that this, in turn, is determined entirely by how the acts impinge on the rights and interests of those directly affected. On this assumption, if there is cause for moral concern, some right or interest has been neglected; and if the rights and interests of human beings and animals have already been taken into account, then there must be some other pertinent interests, for example, those of plants. A little reflection will show that the assumption is mistaken; but, in any case, the conclusion that plants have rights or morally relevant interests is surely untenable. We do speak of what is "good for" plants, and they can "thrive" and also be "killed." But this does not imply that they have "interests" in any morally relevant sense. Some people apparently believe that plants grow better if we talk to them, but the idea that the plants suffer and enjoy, desire and dislike, etc., is clearly outside the range of both common sense and scientific belief. The notion that the forests should be preserved to avoid *hurting* the trees or because they have a *right* to life is not part of a widely shared moral consciousness, and for good reason.[3]

Another way of trying to explain our moral discomfort is to appeal to certain religious beliefs. If one believes that all living things were created by a God who cares for them and entrusted us with the use of plants and animals only for limited purposes, then one has a reason to avoid careless destruction of the forests, etc., quite aside from their future utility. Again, if one believes that a divine force is immanent in all nature, then too one might have reason to care for more than sentient things. But such arguments require strong and controversial premises, and, I suspect, they will always have a restricted audience.

Early in this century, due largely to the influence of G. E. Moore, another point of view developed which some may find promising.[4] Moore introduced, or at least made popular, the idea that certain states of affairs are intrinsically valuable—not just valued, but valuable, and not necessarily because of their effects on sentient beings. Admittedly Moore came to believe that in fact the only intrinsically valuable things were conscious experiences of various sorts,[5] but this restriction was not inherent in the idea of intrinsic value. The intrinsic goodness of something, he thought, was an objective, nonrelational property of the thing, like its texture or color, but not a property perceivable by sense perception or detectable by scientific instruments. In theory at least, a single tree thriving alone in a universe without sentient beings, and even without God, could be intrinsically valuable. Since, according to Moore, our duty is to maximize intrinsic value, his theory could obviously be used to argue that we have reason not to destroy natural environments independently of how they affect human beings and animals. The survival of a forest might have worth beyond its worth *to* sentient beings.

This approach, like the religious one, may appeal to some but is infested with problems. There are, first, the familiar objections to intuitionism, on which the theory depends. Metaphysical and epistemological doubts about nonnatural, intuited properties are hard to suppress, and many have argued that the theory rests on a misunderstanding of the words *good, valuable,* and the like.[6] Second, even if we try to set aside these objections and think in Moore's terms, it is far from obvious that everyone would agree that the existence of forests, etc., is intrinsically valuable. The test, says Moore, is what we would say when we imagine a universe with just the thing in question, without any effects or accompaniments, and then we ask, "Would its existence be better than its nonexistence?" Be careful, Moore would remind us, not to construe this question as, "Would you *prefer* the existence of that universe to its nonexistence?" The question is, "Would its existence have the objective, nonrelational property, intrinsic goodness?"

Now even among those who have no worries about whether this really makes sense, we might well get a diversity of answers. Those prone to destroy natural environments will doubtless give one answer, and nature lovers will likely give another. When an issue is as controversial as the one at hand, intuition is a poor arbiter.

The problem, then, is this. We want to understand what underlies our moral uneasiness at the destruction of the redwoods, forests, etc., even apart from the loss of these as resources for human beings and animals. But I find no adequate answer by pursuing the questions, "Are rights or interests of plants neglected?" "What is God's will on the matter?" and "What is the intrinsic value of the existence of a tree or forest?" My suggestion, which is in fact the main point of this paper, is that we look at the problem from a different perspective. That is, let us turn for a while from the effort to find reasons why certain acts destructive of natural environments are morally wrong to the ancient task of articulating our ideals of human excellence. Rather than argue directly with destroyers of the environment who say, "Show me why what I am doing is *immoral*," I want to ask, "What sort of person would want to do what they propose?" The point is not to skirt the issue with an ad hominem, but to raise a different moral question, for even if there is no convincing way to show that the destructive acts are wrong (independently of human and animal use and enjoyment), we may find that the willingness to indulge in them reflects the absence of human traits that we admire and regard morally important.

This strategy of shifting questions may seem more promising if one reflects on certain analogous situations. Consider, for example, the Nazi who asks, in all seriousness, "Why is it wrong for me to make lampshades out of human skin—provided, of course, I did not myself kill the victims to get the skins?" We would react more with shock and disgust than with indignation, I suspect, because it is even more evident that the question reveals a defect in the questioner than that the proposed act is itself immoral. Sometimes we may not regard an act wrong at all though we see it as reflecting something objectionable about the person who does it. Imagine, for example, one who laughs spontaneously to himself when he reads a newspaper account of a plane crash that kills hundreds. Or, again, consider an obsequious grandson who, having waited for his grandmother's inheritance with mock devotion, then secretly spits on her grave when at last she dies. Spitting on the grave may have no adverse consequences and perhaps it violates no rights. The moral uneasiness which it arouses is explained more by our view of the agent than by any conviction that what he did was immoral. Had he hestiated and asked, "Why shouldn't I spit on her grave?" it seems more fitting to ask him to reflect on the sort of person he is than to try to offer reasons why he should refrain from spitting.

III

What sort of person, then, would cover his garden with asphalt, strip mine a wooded mountain, or level an irreplaceable redwood grove? Two sorts of answers, though initially appealing, must be ruled out. The first is that persons who would destroy the environment in these ways are either shortsighted, underestimating the harm they do, or else are too little concerned for the well-being of other people. Perhaps too they have insufficient regard for animal life. But these considerations have been set aside in order to refine the controversy. Another tempting re-

sponse might be that we count it a moral virtue, or at least a human ideal, to love nature. Those who value the environment only for its utility must not really love nature and so in this way fall short of an ideal. But such an answer is hardly satisfying in the present context, for what is at issue is *why* we feel moral discomfort at the activities of those who admittedly value nature only for its utility. That it is ideal to care for nonsentient nature beyond its possible use is really just another way of expressing the general point which is under controversy.

What is needed is some way of showing that this ideal is connected with other virtues, or human excellences, not in question. To do so is difficult and my suggestions, accordingly, will be tentative and subject to qualification. The main idea is that, though indifference to nonsentient nature does not *necessarily* reflect the absence of virtues, it often signals the absence of certain traits which we want to encourage because they are, in most cases, a natural basis for the development of certain virtues. It is often thought, for example, that those who would destroy the natural environment must lack a proper appreciation of their place in the natural order, and so must either be ignorant or have too little humility. Though I would argue that this is not necessarily so, I suggest that, given certain plausible empirical assumptions, their attitude may well be rooted in ignorance, a narrow perspective, inability to see things as important apart from themselves and the limited groups they associate with, or reluctance to accept themselves as natural beings. Overcoming these deficiencies will not guarantee a proper moral humility, but for most of us it is probably an important psychological preliminary. Later I suggest, more briefly, that indifference to nonsentient nature typically reveals absence of either aesthetic sensibility or a disposition to cherish what has enriched one's life and that these, though not themselves moral virtues, are a natural basis for appreciation of the good in others and gratitude.[7]

Consider first the suggestion that destroyers of the environment lack an appreciation of their place in the universe.[8] Their attention, it seems, must be focused on parochial matters, on what is, relatively speaking, close in space and time. They seem not to understand that we are a speck on the cosmic scene, a brief stage in the evolutionary process, only one among millions of species on Earth, and an episode in the course of human history. Of course, they know that there are stars, fossils, insects, and ancient ruins; but do they have any idea of the complexity of the processes that led to the natural world as we find it? Are they aware how much the forces at work within their own bodies are like those which govern all living things and even how much they have in common with inanimate bodies? Admittedly scientific knowledge is limited and no one can master it all; but could one who had a broad and deep understanding of his place in nature really be indifferent to the destruction of the natural environment?

This first suggestion, however, may well provoke a protest from a sophisticated anti-environmentalist.[9] "Perhaps *some* may be indifferent to nature from ignorance," the critic may object, "but *I* have studied astronomy, geology, biology, and biochemistry, and I still unashamedly regard the nonsentient environment as simply a resource for our use. It should not be wasted, of course, but what should be preserved is decidable by weighing longterm costs and benefits." "Besides," our critic may continue, "as philosophers you should know the old Humean formula, 'You cannot derive an *ought* from an *is*.' All the facts of biology, biochemistry, etc., do not entail that I ought to love nature or want to preserve it. What one understands is one thing; what one values is something else. Just as nature lovers are not necessarily scientists, those indifferent to nature are not necessarily ignorant."

Although the environmentalist may concede the critic's logical point, he may well argue that, as a matter of fact, increased understanding of nature tends to heighten people's concern for its preservation. If so, despite the objection, the suspicion that the destroyers of the environment lack deep understanding of nature is not, in most cases, unwarranted, but the argument need not rest here.

The environmentalist might amplify his original idea as follows: "When I said that the destroyers of nature do not appreciate their place in the universe,

I was not speaking of intellectual understanding alone, for, after all, a person can *know* a catalog of facts without ever putting them together and seeing vividly the whole picture which they form. To see oneself as just one part of nature is to look at oneself and the world from a certain perspective which is quite different from being able to recite detailed information from the natural sciences. What the destroyers of nature lack is this perspective, not particular information."

Again our critic may object, though only after making some concessions: "All right," he may say, "*some* who are indifferent to nature may lack the cosmic perspective of which you speak, but again there is no *necessary* connection between this failing, if it is one, and any particular evaluative attitude toward nature. In fact, different people respond quite differently when they move to a wider perspective. When *I* try to picture myself vividly as a brief, transitory episode in the course of nature, I simply get depressed. Far from inspiring me with a love of nature, the exercise makes me sad and hostile. You romantics think only of poets like Wordsworth and artists like Turner, but you should consider how differently Omar Khayyám responded when he took your wider perspective. His reaction, when looking at his life from a cosmic viewpoint, was 'Drink up, for tomorrow we die.' Others respond in an almost opposite manner with a joyless Stoic resignation, exemplified by the poet who pictures the wise man, at the height of personal triumph, being served a magnificent banquet, and then consummating his marriage to his beloved, all the while reminding himself, 'Even this shall pass away.' "[10] In sum, the critic may object, "Even if one should try to see oneself as one small transitory part of nature, doing so does not dictate any particular normative attitude. Some may come to love nature, but others are moved to live for the moment; some sink into sad resignation; others get depressed or angry. So indifference to nature is not necessarily a sign that a person fails to look at himself from the larger perspective."

The environmentalist might respond to this objection in several ways. He might, for example, argue that even though some people who see themselves as part of the natural order remain indifferent to nonsentient nature, this is not a common reaction. Typically, it may be argued, as we become more and more aware that we are parts of the larger whole we come to value the whole independently of its effect on ourselves. Thus, despite the possibilities the critic raises, indifference to nonsentient nature is still in most cases a sign that a person fails to see himself as part of the natural order.

If someone challenges the empirical assumption here, the environmentalist might develop the argument along a quite different line. The initial idea, he may remind us, was that those who would destroy the natural environment fail to *appreciate* their place in the natural order. "Appreciating one's place" is not simply an intellectual appreciation. It is also an attitude, reflecting what one values as well as what one knows. When we say, for example, that both the servile and the arrogant person fail to *appreciate* their place in a society of equals, we do not mean simply that they are ignorant of certain empirical facts, but rather that they have certain objectionable attitudes about their importance relative to other people. Similarly, to fail to appreciate one's place in nature is not merely to lack knowledge or breadth of perspective, but to take a certain attitude about what matters. A person who *understands* his place in nature but still views nonsentient nature merely as a resource takes the attitude that nothing is *important* but human beings and animals. Despite first appearances, he is not so much like the pre-Copernican astronomers who made the intellectual error of treating the Earth as the "center of the universe" when they made their calculations. He is more like the racist who, though well aware of other races, treats all races but his own as insignificant.

So construed, the argument appeals to the common idea that awareness of nature typically has, and should have, a humbling effect. The Alps, a storm at sea, the Grand Canyon, towering redwoods, and "the starry heavens above" move many a person to remark on the comparative insignificance of our daily concerns and even of our species, and this is generally taken to be a quite fitting response.[11] What seems to be missing, then, in those who understand nature but remain unmoved is a proper humility.[12]

Absence of proper humility is not the same as selfishness or egoism, for one can be devoted to self-interest while still viewing one's own pleasures and projects as trivial and unimportant.[13] And one can have an exaggerated view of one's own importance while grandly sacrificing for those one views as inferior. Nor is the lack of humility identical with belief that one has power and influence, for a person can be quite puffed up about himself while believing that the foolish world will never acknowledge him. The humility we miss seems not so much a belief about one's relative effectiveness and recognition as an attitude which measures the importance of things independently of their relation to oneself or to some narrow group with which one identifies. A paradigm of a person who lacks humility is the self-important emperor who grants status to his family because it is *his,* to his subordinates because *he* appointed them, and to his country because *he* chooses to glorify it. Less extreme but still lacking proper humility is the elitist who counts events significant solely in proportion to how they affect his class. The suspicion about those who would destroy the environment, then, is that what they count important is too narrowly confined insofar as it encompasses only what affects beings who, like us, are capable of feeling.

This idea that proper humility requires recognition of the importance of nonsentient nature is similar to the thought of those who charge meat eaters with "species-ism." In both cases it is felt that people too narrowly confine their concerns to the sorts of beings that are most like them. But, however intuitively appealing, the idea will surely arouse objections from our nonenvironmentalist critic. "Why," he will ask, "do you suppose that the sort of humility I *should* have requires me to acknowledge the importance of nonsentient nature aside from its utility? You cannot, by your own admission, argue that nonsentient nature *is* important, appealing to religious or intuitionist grounds. And simply to assert, without further argument, that an ideal humility requires us to view nonsentient nature as important for its own sake begs the question at issue. If proper humility is acknowledging the relative importance of things as one should, then to show that I must lack this you must first establish that one *should* acknowledge the importance of nonsentient nature."

Though some may wish to accept this challenge, there are other ways to pursue the connection between humility and response to nonsentient nature. For example, suppose we grant that proper humility requires only acknowledging a due status to sentient beings. We must admit, then, that it is logically possible for a person to be properly humble even though he viewed all nonsentient nature simply as a resource. But this logical possibility may be a psychological rarity. It may be that, given the sort of beings we are, we would never learn humility before persons without developing the general capacity to cherish, and regard important, many things for their own sakes. The major obstacle to humility before persons is self-importance, a tendency to measure the significance of everything by its relation to oneself and those with whom one identifies. The processes by which we overcome self-importance are doubtless many and complex, but it seems unlikely that they are exclusively concerned with how we relate to other people and animals. Learning humility requires learning to feel that something matters besides what will affect oneself and one's circle of associates. What leads a child to care about what happens to a lost hamster or a stray dog he will not see again is likely also to generate concern for a lost toy or a favorite tree where he used to live.[14] Learning to value things for their own sake, and to count what affects them important aside from their utility, is not the same as judging them to have some intuited objective property, but it is necessary to the development of humility and it seems likely to take place in experiences with nonsentient nature as well as with people and animals. If a person views all nonsentient nature merely as a resource, then it seems unlikely that he has developed the capacity needed to overcome self-importance.

IV

This last argument, unfortunately, has its limits. It presupposes an empirical connection between experiencing nature and overcoming self-importance, and

this may be challenged. Even if experiencing nature promotes humility before others, there may be other ways people can develop such humility in a world of concrete, glass, and plastic. If not, perhaps all that is needed is limited experience of nature in one's early, developing years; mature adults, having overcome youthful self-importance, may live well enough in artificial surroundings. More importantly, the argument does not fully capture the spirit of the intuition that an ideal person stands humbly before nature. That idea is not simply that experiencing nature tends to foster proper humility before other people; it is, in part, that natural surroundings encourage and are appropriate to an ideal sense of oneself as part of the natural world. Standing alone in the forest, after months in the city, is not merely good as a means of curbing one's arrogance before others; it reinforces and fittingly expresses one's acceptance of oneself as a natural being.

Previously we considered only one aspect of proper humility, namely, a sense of one's relative importance with respect to other human beings. Another aspect, I think, is a kind of *self-acceptance*. This involves acknowledging, in more than a merely intellectual way, that we are the sort of creatures that we are. Whether one is self-accepting is not so much a matter of how one attributes *importance* comparatively to oneself, other people, animals, plants, and other things as it is a matter of understanding, facing squarely, and responding appropriately to who and what one is, e.g., one's powers and limits, one's affinities with other beings and differences from them, one's unalterable nature and one's freedom to change. Self-acceptance is not merely intellectual awareness, for one can be intellectually aware that one is growing old and will eventually die while nevertheless behaving in a thousand foolish ways that reflect a refusal to acknowledge these facts. On the other hand, self-acceptance is not passive resignation, for refusal to pursue what one truly wants within one's limits is a failure to accept the freedom and power one has. Particular behaviors, like dying one's gray hair and dressing like those twenty years younger, do not *necessarily* imply lack of self-acceptance, for there could be reasons for acting in these ways other than the wish to hide from oneself what one really is. One fails to accept oneself when the patterns of behavior and emotion are rooted in a desire to disown and deny features of oneself, to pretend to oneself that they are not there. This is not to say that a self-accepting person makes no value judgments about himself, that he likes all facts about himself, wants equally to develop and display them; he can, and should feel remorse for his past misdeeds and strive to change his current vices. The point is that he does not disown them, pretend that they do not exist or are facts about something other than himself. Such pretense is incompatible with proper humility because it is seeing oneself as better than one is.

Self-acceptance of this sort has long been considered a human excellence, under various names, but what has it to do with preserving nature? There is, I think, the following connection. As human beings we are part of nature, living, growing, declining, and dying by natural laws similar to those governing other living beings; despite our awesomely distinctive human powers, we share many of the needs, limits, and liabilities of animals and plants. These facts are neither good nor bad in themselves, aside from personal preference and varying conventional values. To say this is to utter a truism which few will deny, but to accept these facts, as facts about oneself, is not so easy—or so common. Much of what naturalists deplore about our increasingly artificial world reflects, and encourages, a denial of these facts, an unwillingness to avow them with equanimity.

Like the Victorian lady who refuses to look at her own nude body, some would like to create a world of less transitory stuff, reminding us only of our intellectual and social nature, never calling to mind our affinities with "lower" living creatures. The "denial of death," to which psychiatrists call attention,[15] reveals an attitude incompatible with the sort of self-acceptance which philosophers, from the ancients to Spinoza and on, have admired as a human excellence. My suggestion is not merely that experiencing nature causally promotes such self-acceptance, but also that those who fully accept themselves as part of the natural world lack the common drive to disassociate themselves from nature by replacing

natural environments with artificial ones. A storm in the wilds helps us to appreciate our animal vulnerability, but, equally important, the reluctance to experience it may *reflect* an unwillingness to accept this aspect of ourselves. The person who is too ready to destroy the ancient redwoods may lack humility, not so much in the sense that he exaggerates his importance relative to others, but rather in the sense that he tries to avoid seeing himself as one among many natural creatures.

V

My suggestion so far has been that, though indifference to nonsentient nature is not itself a moral vice, it is likely to reflect either ignorance, a self-importance, or a lack of self-acceptance which we must overcome to have proper humility. A similar idea might be developed connecting attitudes toward nonsentient nature with other human excellences. For example, one might argue that indifference to nature reveals a lack of either an aesthetic sense or some of the natural roots of gratitude.

When we see a hillside that has been gutted by strip miners or the garden replaced by asphalt, our first reaction is probably, "How ugly!" The scenes assault our aesthetic sensibilities. We suspect that no one with a keen sense of beauty could have left such a sight. Admittedly not everything in nature strikes us as beautiful, or even aesthetically interesting, and sometimes a natural scene is replaced with a more impressive architectural masterpiece. But this is not usually the situation in the problem cases which environmentalists are most concerned about. More often beauty is replaced with ugliness.

At this point our critic may well object that, even if he does lack a sense of beauty, this is no moral vice. His cost/benefit calculations take into account the pleasure others may derive from seeing the forests, etc., and so why should he be faulted?

Some might reply that, despite contrary philosophical traditions, aesthetics and morality are not so distinct as commonly supposed. Appreciation of beauty, they may argue, is a human excellence which morally ideal persons should try to develop. But, setting aside this controversial position, there still may be cause for moral concern about those who have no aesthetic response to nature. Even if aesthetic sensibility is not itself a moral virtue, many of the capacities of mind and heart which it presupposes may be ones which are also needed for an appreciation of other people. Consider, for example, curiosity, a mind open to novelty, the ability to look at things from unfamiliar perspectives, empathetic imagination, interest in details, variety, and order, and emotional freedom from the immediate and the practical. All these, and more, seem necessary to aesthetic sensibility, but they are also traits which a person needs to be fully sensitive to people of all sorts. The point is not that a moral person must be able to distinguish beautiful from ugly people; the point is rather that unresponsiveness to what is beautiful, awesome, dainty, dumpy, and otherwise aesthetically interesting in nature probably reflects a lack of the openness of mind and spirit necessary to appreciate the best in human beings.

The anti-environmentalist, however, may refuse to accept the charge that he lacks aesthetic sensibility. If he claims to appreciate seventeenth-century miniature portraits, but to abhor natural wildernesses, he will hardly be convincing. Tastes vary, but aesthetic sense is not *that* selective. He may, instead, insist that he *does* appreciate natural beauty. He spends his vacations, let us suppose, hiking in the Sierras, photographing wildflowers, and so on. He might press his argument as follows: "I enjoy natural beauty as much as anyone, but I fail to see what this has to do with preserving the environment independently of human enjoyment and use. Nonsentient nature is a resource, but one of its best uses is to give us pleasure. I take this into account when I calculate the costs and benefits of preserving a park, planting a garden, and so on. But the problem you raised explicitly set aside the desire to preserve nature as a means to enjoyment. I say, let us enjoy nature fully while we can, but if all sentient beings were to die tomorrow, we might as well blow up all plant life as well. A redwood grove that no one can use or enjoy is utterly worthless."

The attitude expressed here, I suspect, is not a common one, but it represents a philosophical challenge. The beginnings of a reply may be found in the following. When a person takes joy in something, it is a common (and perhaps natural) response to come to cherish it. To cherish something is not simply to be happy with it at the moment, but to care for it for its own sake. This is not to say that one necessarily sees it as having feelings and so wants it to feel good; nor does it imply that one judges the thing to have Moore's intrinsic value. One simply wants the thing to survive and (when appropriate) to thrive, and not simply for its utility. We see this attitude repeatedly regarding mementos. They are not simply valued as a means to remind us of happy occasions; they come to be valued for their own sake. Thus, if someone really took joy in the natural environment, but was prepared to blow it up as soon as sentient life ended, he would lack this common human tendency to cherish what enriches our lives. While this response is not itself a moral virtue, it may be a natural basis of the virtue we call "gratitude." People who have no tendency to cherish things that give them pleasure may be poorly disposed to respond gratefully to persons who are good to them. Again the connection is not one of logical necessity, but it may nevertheless be important. A nonreligious person unable to "thank" anyone for the beauties of nature may nevertheless feel "grateful" in a sense; and I suspect that the person who feels no such "gratitude" toward nature is unlikely to show proper gratitude toward people.

Suppose these conjectures prove to be true. One may wonder what is the point of considering them. Is it to disparage all those who view nature merely as a resource? To do so, it seems, would be unfair, for, even if this attitude typically stems from deficiencies which affect one's attitudes toward sentient beings, there may be exceptions and we have not shown that their view of nonsentient nature is itself blameworthy. But when we set aside questions of blame and inquire what sorts of human traits we want to encourage, our reflections become relevant in a more positive way. The point is not to insinuate that all anti-environmentalists are defective, but to see that those who value such traits as humility, gratitude, and sensitivity to others have reason to promote the love of nature.

NOTES

1. When I use the expression "the natural environment," I have in mind the sort of examples with which I began. For some purposes it is important to distinguish cultivated gardens from forests, virgin forests from replenished ones, irreplaceable natural phenomena from the replaceable, and so on; but these distinctions, I think, do not affect my main points here. There is also a broad sense, as Hume and Mill noted, in which all that occurs, miracles aside, is "natural." In this sense, of course, strip mining is as natural as a beaver cutting trees for his dam, and, as parts of nature, we cannot destroy the "natural" environment but only alter it. As will be evident, I shall use *natural* in a narrower, more familiar sense.

2. This paper is intended as a preliminary discussion in *normative* ethical theory (as opposed to *metaethics*). The task, accordingly, is the limited, though still difficult, one of articulating the possible basis in our beliefs and values for certain particular moral judgments. Questions of ultimate justification are set aside. What makes the task difficult and challenging is not that conclusive proofs from the foundation of morality are attempted; it is rather that the particular judgments to be explained seem at first not to fall under the most familiar moral principles (e.g., utilitarianism, respect for rights).

3. I assume here that having a right presupposes having interests in a sense which in turn presupposes a capacity to desire, suffer, etc. Since my main concern lies in another direction, I do not argue the point, but merely note that some regard it as debatable. See, for example, W. Murray Hunt, "Are *Mere Things* Morally Considerable?" *Environmental Ethics* 2 (1980): 59–65; Kenneth E. Goodpaster, "On Stopping at Everything," *Environmental Ethics* 2 (1980): 288–294; Joel Feinberg, "The Rights of Animals and Unborn Generations," in William Blackstone, ed., *Philosophy and Environmental Crisis* (Athens: University of Georgia Press, 1974), pp. 43–68; Tom Regan, "Feinberg on What Sorts of Beings Can Have Rights," *Southern Journal of Philosophy* (1976): 485–498; Robert Elliot, "Regan on the Sort of Beings that Can Have Rights," *Southern Journal of Philosophy* (1978): 701–705;

Scott Lehmann, "Do Wildernesses Have Rights?" *Environmental Ethics* 2 (1981): 129–146.

4. G. E. Moore, *Principia Ethica* (Cambridge: Cambridge University Press, 1903); *Ethics* (London: H. Holt, 1912).

5. G. E. Moore, "Is Goodness a Quality?" *Philosophical Papers* (London: George Allen and Unwin, 1959), pp. 95–97.

6. See, for example, P. H. Nowell-Smith, *Ethics* (New York: Penguin Books, 1954).

7. The issues I raise here, though perhaps not the details of my remarks, are in line with Aristotle's view of moral philosophy, a view revitalized recently by Philippa Foot's *Virtue and Vice* (Berkeley: University of California Press, 1979), Alasdair McIntyre's *After Virtue* (Notre Dame: Notre Dame Press, 1981), and James Wallace's *Virtues and Vices* (Ithaca and London: Cornell University Press, 1978), and other works. For other reflections on relationships between character and natural environments, see John Rodman, "The Liberation of Nature," *Inquiry* (1976):83–131 and L. Reinhardt, "Some Gaps in Moral Space: Reflections on Forests and Feelings," in Mannison, McRobbie, and Routley, eds., *Environmental Philosophy* (Canberra: Australian National University Research School of Social Sciences, 1980).

8. Though for simplicity I focus upon those who do strip mining, etc., the argument is also applicable to those whose utilitarian calculations lead them to preserve the redwoods, mountains, etc., but who care for only sentient nature for its own sake. Similarly the phrase "indifferent to nature" is meant to encompass those who are indifferent *except* when considering its benefits to people and animals.

9. For convenience I use the labels *environmentalist* and *anti-environmentalist* (or *critic*) for the opposing sides in the rather special controversy I have raised. Thus, for example, my "environmentalist" not only favors conserving the forests, etc., but finds something objectionable in wanting to destroy them even aside from the costs to human beings and animals. My "anti-environmentalist" is not simply one who wants to destroy the environment; he is a person who has no qualms about doing so independent of the adverse effects on human beings and animals.

10. "Even this shall pass away," by Theodore Tildon, in *The Best Loved Poems of the American People,* ed. Hazel Felleman (Garden City, N.Y.: Doubleday & Co., 1936).

11. An exception, apparently, was Kant, who thought "the starry heavens" sublime and compared them with "the

moral law within," but did not for all that see our species as comparatively insignificant.

12. By "*proper* humility" I mean that sort and degree of humility that is a morally admirable character trait. How precisely to define this is, of course, a controversial matter; but the point for present purposes is just to set aside obsequiousness, false modesty, underestimation of one's abilities, and the like.

13. I take this point from some of Philippa Foot's remarks.

14. The causal history of this concern may well depend upon the object (tree, toy) having given the child pleasure, but this does not mean that the object is then valued only for further pleasure it may bring.

15. See, for example, Ernest Becker, *The Denial of Death* (New York: Free Press, 1973).

Redefining the Good Life in a Sustainable Society

Lester W. Milbrath

Everyone wants a good life. The criminal who steals, the gambler who hopes for a "killing," the monk who meditates, the scientist who searches, the shopper who buys and buys, the outdoorsman who hunts and fishes, the tycoon who grabs for power and wealth, the religious person who prays for salvation—all are seeking what they believe to be the good life. Obviously a good life can be defined in many ways. Economists, politicians, and advertisers assume that consuming goods leads to quality of life and constantly remind us that we should want prosperity. Does prosperity equate with a good life? Should we let them define for us what a good life is? Why not give some thought to redefining the good life and take charge of our own destiny?

The physical conditions in which we live our lives set some boundaries that must be observed as we proceed with our redefinition. To be sure, we can do a lot to redefine our physical conditions. We might move to another place, assuming that someone does not already occupy the place we want to take. Proffering lots of money may encourage the present occupant to allow us to take possession. Having lots of

power can allow us to take over by force in the way that we routinely seize habitat from wildlife. Our cleverness and technology have stretched many boundaries and opened up many possibilities. Some people believe we can proceed indefinitely to manipulate nature and extend its boundaries.

Ironically, our very success as a species has created unforeseen consequences that set new boundaries and force us to redefine what the good life is.

1. We have successfully extended human longevity by improving public health and by appropriating more and more of the biosphere to our purposes. We have unintentionally achieved a human population explosion which is ruining quality of life in many parts of the world. The planet's ecosphere and resource base may not tolerate even two more doublings of world population (to 20 billion). Either we thoughtfully limit our reproduction or nature will limit it for us by starvation and disease.

2. At the very time of our population explosion, we are achieving a drastic increase in throughput of materials in our economy. Not only does accelerat-

Lester W. Milbrath, "Redefining the Good Life in a Sustainable Society." *Environmental Values* 2 (1993): 261–69. Reprinted with permission of White Horse Press, Cambridge, U.K.

ing economic activity swiftly draw down our resource stocks (many of them nonrenewable) but it also creates so much waste that it is seriously injuring ecosystems and changing global geosphere/biosphere patterns. We are recklessly perturbing biospheric systems that are so complex that we cannot know the consequences of our actions. Swift and powerful changes in global climate patterns would devastate our economies, destroy many of our resource stocks, and bring death to billions of humans.

Even if some drastic technological breakthrough enabled humans to keep growing in population and economic activity, would we want to live in the world that continuing growth would create? Within a century there would be 20 billion or more people. To prosperously support that many people, most of the biosphere's productivity would have to be turned to human needs. Most of the wilderness would be gone and those species that escaped extinction would be confined to reserves. To prevent feverish economic activity from constantly changing geosphere/biosphere patterns, and to make life somewhat comfortable, our daily existence would be confined to artificial city environments where air, water, and material processing were all carefully controlled. With that many people, life would be made tolerable only by severely restricting personal freedom. Is that the kind of world you want? Would that be a good life? *By continuing to define progress and the good life as growth in material consumption, that is where we are headed.*

A key aspect of my argument, then, is that continuing growth in human population and material consumption is not desirable (we do not want to go there) and very likely not possible.

If growth is a false god, no longer deserving of our worship, our society must rethink what living a good life means. One fundamental mistake we must correct is our penchant for trying to define the good life in material quantities and express it in monetary terms. Quality in living is not a thing, it is a feeling; it is necessarily a matter of subjective experience. Recognizing its subjective character does not mean we cannot have a rational discourse about it. To ad-

vance that discourse, I offer a definition of quality of life that I worked out with a graduate seminar several years ago. It addresses quality of life as experienced by individuals.

Quality in living is experienced only by individuals and is *necessarily* subjective. Objective conditions may contribute to or detract from the experience of quality but human reactions to physical conditions are not automatic: the experience occurs only subjectively. Personal reports of experiences of quality are much better indicators of these subjective experiences than physical measures of physical conditions. (We should carefully distinguish environmental conditions that can be measured with objective indicators from the experience of quality that can only be measured with subjective indicators.)

Quality is not a constant state but a variable ranging from high quality to low quality. Persons usually experience some combination of high and low quality; they seldom experience only one extreme or the other.

Persons have high quality of life when they experience the following:

1. A sense of happiness but not simply a momentary happiness; rather a long-run sense of joy in living.
2. A sense of physical well-being; usually this means good health but the sense of physical well-being can be realized by persons having lost certain capacities.
3. A sense of completeness or fullness of life; a sense that one is on the way to achieving, or has achieved, what one aspires to become as a person.
4. A sense of zestful anticipation of life's unfolding drama, greeting each day with hope and confidence that living it will be good.

Persons have a low quality of life when they experience the following:

1. A sense of hopelessness and despair; mornings are greeted with fear and dread. A sense that

one is buffeted by fate and has lost control of one's life.

2. A sense of having failed to live up to one's image of oneself; that one's life has been a failure.

3. A sense of poor physical well-being; illness, injury, hunger, discomfort.

4. A pervading sense of unhappiness.

We should carefully distinguish quality of life judgements that are individual (personal) and subjective, from prescriptions for a good society. Individual experiences with the quality of this or that aspect of life do not translate directly into policy even though they are important informational inputs for policy makers. Ecosystem and social system values must be served in policy making as well as quality of life values.

We want a society and an environment that will allow people, as individuals, to work out their own quality of life. But there is a heavy responsibility on individuals to make the best of their situation and to take personal actions to achieve quality in living. We should be cautious about making the inference that a person living in what most people would assess as favourable conditions will experience high quality; or, conversely, that a person living in what most would assess as poor conditions will experience low quality. Yet, policy makers frequently make such inferences (when they report that per capita income has risen, or fallen, for example).

It is easy to recognize that a decent life requires minimal provision of food, shelter, and clothing, and that society bears an obligation to provide at least that minimum. In most developed countries those minima have been achieved for nearly everyone. But how do we decide what society should do to enhance quality of life beyond providing the minima? For example, we often hear the outcry of someone, or group, whose economic situation may be diminished in order to preserve some aspect of the ecosystem: they complain that they will starve if they cannot keep their job (and continue to injure the ecosystem). We need some clear thinking about values and what

it means to live a good life in order to arrive at appropriate policies.

Is it true, for example, that loggers in the Pacific Northwest of the USA will starve if they cannot continue to log old-growth forests on national forest lands (owned by all the people)? The central question is not whether people or spotted owls are more important; they are both important. No one is suggesting that people must die for spotted owls to live. The question, rather, is what values should have the greatest priority as such policies are made? I use this syllogism to clarify value priorities:

I can imagine a biocommunity thriving well without any human members but I cannot imagine human society thriving without a well-functioning biocommunity. Similarly, I can imagine human society functioning well without a given individual but I cannot imagine an individual thriving without a well-functioning biocommunity and a well-functioning human community. Therefore, individuals desiring quality of life must give top priority to protection and preservation of their biocommunity (their ecosystem). Second priority must go to preservation and protection of the good functioning of their social community. Only when people are careful to protect the viability of their two communities is it acceptable for individuals to pursue quality of life according to their own personal desires.

Being allowed to cut logs on national forests is a privilege granted by society and not a basic right that society is obliged to fulfil. As society decides whether or not to grant that privilege, it should give highest priority to protecting the integrity of the ecosphere. Societies that fail to keep that top priority firmly in mind will undercut their long-run sustainability. Leaders of contemporary societies constantly make this same basic error when they persistently press for economic growth.

It is clear we must find the good life in some other way than continuing to grow in material consumption. Finding a good life is more a search of our own minds than it is a search of a shopping mall.

NEW BUT OLD WAYS TO ENJOY LIFE WITH FEWER MATERIAL GOODS

The toy industry is now very big business. The inventiveness of designers using advanced technology has produced some fantastic creations. Children with a closet full of such toys can have stimulating and happy days (though a poor kid could envy a rich kid). But what did children do to enjoy life before they had the largess of affluent parents and the cleverness of the modern toy industry? While travelling recently in a developing country I watched some boys rolling an old auto tyre, guiding it with a stick; they seemed every bit as happy with their "toy" as the modern American child with a closet full of expensive toys.

The same question applies to adults. Thousands of generations of people enjoyed life with only a small fraction of our material goods. Were they less happy than we? We all have inner resources for meditation, conversation, loving, communion with nature, reading, writing, playing music, dancing, and engaging in sports. These talents may need to be developed further because our present society lures us to buy and consume, buy and be entertained, buy and be pampered. People who have given in to those inducements have become more bystanders than participants in life's unfolding drama.

Goods That Are Not Zero Sum

Economists characterize most goods exchanged in the market as "zero sum." Because I have it, you cannot have it—that is zero sum. Our conditioning toward material consumption inclines us to think of all enjoyment as zero sum. Actually, many of the most satisfying and fulfilling things in life are enhanced when shared.

You would think that everyone would know that love is good for people, that it is easy to give and to share, that fulfilment from loving is enhanced, not diminished by sharing. Leo Buscaglia is a well known professor, author and lecturer who colourfully and effectively conveys the message that love is good for people and society. Buscaglia's message is so popular because many people sense that our modern affluent society has somehow lost its understanding of the meaning of love. Ironically, Buscaglia reports numerous instances where persons reject his claims for the virtue of love. If some day our society turns away from trying to find fulfilment in material goods, we may, indeed, find much greater fulfilment in love. We should be actively learning from each other how best to love.

Some years ago I conducted a study of quality of life in the Niagara Frontier and discovered that the ways people sought fulfilment in life clustered into lifestyle patterns. As might be expected, some persons emphasized a consumer lifestyle; their greatest enjoyment came from buying and consuming. They were a minority, however.

Another lifestyle, favoured by many, emphasized fulfilment in interpersonal relations. These people loved to socialize with friends and relatives. Rewarding companionships with friends is not difficult to find and most of these people felt quite fulfilled. Most importantly, this lifestyle is not zero-sum, is not highly consuming of goods, does not waste scarce resources, and does not injure the environment. If we slowed down our frantic production pace, demanded less and consumed less, we would have more time for enjoying companionship; chances are, we also would enhance our quality of life.

Enjoyment of nature emerged as another lifestyle in our study; it is not consumed in the same way as restaurant meals, autos, or tickets to seats in a football stadium, and thus is not zero-sum. Normally, my enjoyment of nature does not detract from your enjoyment, but, nature can be overrun and destroyed by too many people. Having to contend with a crowded beach, or bumper-to-bumper traffic heading for a national park, or elbow-to-elbow fishing in a trout pool is not a fulfilling experience. Many U.S. National Parks have had to ration nature experiences by advance reservations, quotas, and admission tickets. They are so crowded in China that they have had to assign people to take holidays in nature on different days. The obvious demand for nature experiences makes it all the more important that nature be protected and, where necessary, restored to beauty.

Nature protection and beautification is a fulfilling activity that many people can join in, derive satisfaction from, and strengthen rather than diminish by their sharing. Urgent joint action also is needed to obtain and maintain such vital natural elements as clean air, water, and soils. Cutting back on consumption would help a lot, but collective political action to assure environmental protection also is imperative.

Learning is another pleasurable and fulfilling activity that is developed rather than diminished by sharing. Philosophical understanding, especially, is deepened by interpersonal discourse. Cultivation of the mind has been emphasized in many cultural traditions and surely would be an important activity to emphasize in a sustainable society. Deepening one's understanding requires time and periods of quiet contemplation; ironically, these are scarce goods that many frantically busy people today fervently wish they could have. If we slowed down, produced less, and consumed less, perhaps we could find more quiet times for learning and for deepening our understanding.

Enjoyment in creating, and appreciating literature, music, and art, similarly are not diminished if shared and should be emphasized in a sustainable society. Instead of life being bleak and cold when we are forced to slow down, it could be a flourishing period of creativity and learning.

> If we can understand how our possessions have failed us, we can more readily decrease our thralldom. Turning instead to a focus on the quality of our relations with others; on the clarity and intensity of our experiences; on intimacy, sensuality, aesthetic sensibility, and emotional freedom, we can see how a more ecologically sound society can be a more exciting and enjoyable one as well. (Wachtel 1983: 143)

Play is another pleasurable and fulfilling activity that typically consumes few resources and need not damage nature. I do not speak of energy consuming and nature destroying thrill contests such as off-road vehicle racing; they are incompatible with a good society. Nor do I speak of sporting events with large crowds of spectators; they should be seen as a branch of the entertainment industry. Rather, the sustainable society should emphasize widespread participation by nearly everyone in games that bring pleasure and are not wasteful or destructive; there certainly is sufficient variety to serve almost any taste. Games requiring vigorous activity not only pass the time pleasurably but also nurture good health.

Self governance also is non-zero-sum in the sense that everyone benefits when better laws are passed or when better community programs are undertaken. (Many elections are zero-sum when the winner takes all.) Self governance does require interest, concern, and time from people. Persons caught up in the rat race for money often claim that they are too busy to participate. However, if life were restructured to give less emphasis to getting rich and consuming, people could more likely see the relevance of their participation for a better life; furthermore, schedules would be more flexible, allowing people to take the time for political affairs—it could become a natural and expected aspect of everyday life.

Leisure?

So far I have not given specific attention to leisure, although I have strongly urged people to take time for personally fulfilling activities. Entrepreneurs in modern affluent society try to sell expensive goods and services to help people use their leisure "to the fullest"; that approach to leisure appropriately could be called an industry: it fits with our delusion that happiness must be bought. Most of the activities discussed above that people do to fulfil themselves might also be thought of as leisure but they do not make up an industry. People engage in such activities to enjoy their leisure but they consume few leisure goods. The sustainable society would have little need for a "leisure industry."

Voluntary Simplicity

Duane Elgin's (1981) book *Voluntary Simplicity: Toward a Way of Life That Is Outwardly Simple, Inwardly Rich* is a much deeper examination of philosophy, lifestyles, social forces, and revolutionary changes than one might expect from the title. His central thesis is that people voluntarily choose a life of simplicity because it is richer than modern consuming lifestyles. To live *voluntarily* means to live more deliberately, intentionally, purposefully, and to do so consciously. "We cannot be deliberate when we are distracted from our critical life circumstances. We cannot be purposeful when we are not being present. Therefore, crucial to acting in a voluntary manner is being aware of ourselves as we move through life." (Elgin 1981, p. 32)

He distinguishes "embedded consciousness" from "self-reflective consciousness." Embedded consciousness is our normal or waking consciousness so embedded within a stream of inner-fantasy dialogue that little attention can be paid to the moment-to-moment experiencing of ourselves. Self-reflective consciousness is a more advanced level of awareness in which we are continuously and consciously "tasting" our experience of ourselves. It is "marked by the progressive and balanced development of the ability to be simultaneously concentrated (with a precise and delicate attention to the details of life) and mindful (with a panoramic appreciation of the totality of life)" (Elgin 1981, p. 151).

Living more consciously has several enabling qualities:

1. Being more consciously attentive to our moment-to-moment experiences enhances our capacity to see things as they really are; thus, life will go more smoothly.
2. Living more consciously enables us to respond more quickly to subtle feedback that something is amiss, so that we can move with greater speed towards corrective action.
3. When we are conscious of our habitual patterns of thought and behaviour, we are less bound by them and can have greater choice in how we will respond.
4. Living more consciously promotes an ecological orientation toward all of life; we sense the subtle though profound connectedness of all life more directly.

These four enabling qualities are not trivial enhancements of human capacity; they are essential to our further evolution and to our survival.

> Our civilizational crisis has emerged in no small part from the gross disparity that exists between our relatively underdeveloped "inner faculties" and the extremely powerful external technologies now at our disposal. . . . Unless we expand our interior learning to match our technological learning, we are destined, I think, to act to the detriment of both ourselves and the rest of life on this planet. (Elgin 1981, p. 158)

> A greater degree of conscious simplicity is of crucial relevance for revitalizing our disintegrating civilizations. (Ibid., p. 125)

Self-reflective consciousness can open the door to a much larger journey in which our "self" is gradually but profoundly transformed. The inner and outer person gradually merge into one continuous flow of experience. Simone de Beauvoir said, "Life is occupied in both perpetuating itself and surpassing itself; if all it does is maintain itself, then living is only not dying."

To live with *simplicity* is not an ascetic but rather an aesthetic simplicity because it is consciously chosen; in doing so we unburden our lives to live more lightly, cleanly, and aerodynamically. Each person chooses a pattern or level of consumption to fit with grace and integrity into the practical art of daily living on this planet. We must learn the difference between those material circumstances that support our lives and those that constrict our lives. Conscious simplicity is not self-denying but life-affirming.

> Simplicity, then, should not be equated with poverty. Poverty is involuntary whereas simplicity is consciously chosen. Poverty is repressive, simplicity is liberating. Poverty generates a sense of helplessness, passivity, and despair; simplicity fosters personal empowerment, creativity, and a sense of ever present opportunity. Poverty is mean and degrading to the human spirit; simplicity has both

beauty and functional integrity that elevate our lives. Poverty is debilitating; simplicity is enabling. (Elgin 1981, p. 34)

Simplicity is not turning away from progress; it is crucial to progress. It should not be equated with isolation and withdrawal from the world; most who choose this way of life build a personal network of people who share a similar intention. It also should not be equated with living in a rural setting; it is a "make the most of wherever we are" movement. Voluntary simplicity would evolve both the material and the conscious aspects of life in balance with each other—allowing each aspect to infuse and inform the other.

We can get from where we are now to this new, yet old, way of defining the good life by assisting each other in our social learning. When it becomes obvious that material consumption does not lead to the good life, or that growth in material consumption is not possible, it will be somewhat easier for us to make this transformation to a new way of thinking. Life without material growth very likely will be better than the frantic chase after money and goods that now blights our lives and the ecosphere: it surely will be more sustainable.

CONCLUSION

Living a good life in a sustainable society could be a realization of the Greek concept of *Paideia*—the lifelong, transformation of our own person as an art form. It is ridiculous to characterize life with fewer material goods as "freezing in the dark," as some environmental critics have painted it. It would be a *very different* way of life: more contemplative, less frantic; more serene, less thrilling; valuing co-operation and love more, valuing competition and winning less; with more personal involvement, less being a spectator; more tuned to nature, less tuned to machines. Changes this sweeping may take several generations to come about. Many people have already begun the journey and their learning can help others find the way. Necessity may well hasten our relearning.

REFERENCES

Duane Elgin, *Voluntary Simplicity: Toward a Way of Life that is Outwardly Simple, Inwardly Rich* (New York: William Morrow, 1981).

Paul L. Wachtel, *The Poverty of Affluence* (New York: The Free Press, 1983).

Do We Consume Too Much?

Mark Sagoff

In 1994, when delegates from around the world gathered in Cairo for the International Conference on Population and Development, representatives from developing countries protested that a baby born in the United States will consume during its lifetime twenty times as much of the world's resources as an African or an Indian baby. The problem for the world's environment, they argued, is overconsumption in the North, not overpopulation in the South.

Mark Sagoff, "Do We Consume Too Much?" *Atlantic Monthly* 279, no. 6 (1997): 80–96. Reprinted with permission of the author.

Consumption in industrialized nations "has led to overexploitation of the resources of developing countries," a speaker from Kenya declared. A delegate from Antigua reproached the wealthiest 20 percent of the world's population for consuming 80 percent of the goods and services produced from the earth's resources.

Do we consume too much? To some, the answer is self-evident. If there is only so much food, timber, petroleum, and other material to go around, the more we consume, the less must be available for others. The global economy cannot grow indefinitely on a finite planet. As populations increase and economies expand, natural resources must be depleted; prices will rise, and humanity—especially the poor and future generations at all income levels—will suffer as a result.

Other reasons to suppose we consume too much are less often stated though also widely believed. Of these the simplest—a lesson we learn from our parents and from literature since the Old Testament—may be the best: although we must satisfy basic needs, a good life is not one devoted to amassing material possessions; what we own comes to own us, keeping us from fulfilling commitments that give meaning to life, such as those to family, friends, and faith. The appreciation of nature also deepens our lives. As we consume more, however, we are more likely to transform the natural world, so that less of it will remain for us to appreciate.

The reasons for protecting nature are often religious or moral. As the philosopher Ronald Dworkin points out, many Americans believe that we have an obligation to protect species which goes beyond our own well-being; we "think we should admire and protect them because they are important in themselves, and not just if or because we or others want or enjoy them."[1] In a recent survey Americans from various walks of life agreed by large majorities with the statement "Because God created the natural world, it is wrong to abuse it." The anthropologists who conducted this survey concluded that "divine creation is the closest concept American culture provides to express the sacredness of nature."[2]

During the nineteenth century, preservationists forthrightly gave ethical and spiritual reasons for protecting the natural world. John Muir condemned the "temple destroyers, devotees of ravaging commercialism" who "instead of lifting their eyes to the God of the mountains, lift them to the Almighty dollar."[3] This was not a call for better cost-benefit analysis: Muir described nature not as a commodity but as a companion. Nature is sacred, Muir held, whether or not resources are scarce.

Philosophers such as Emerson and Thoreau thought of nature as full of divinity. Walt Whitman celebrated a leaf of grass as no less than the journeywork of the stars: "After you have exhausted what there is in business, politics, conviviality, love, and so on," he wrote in *Specimen Days*, and "found that none of these finally satisfy, or permanently wear—what remains? Nature remains."[4] These philosophers thought of nature as a refuge from economic activity, not as a resource for it.

Today those who wish to protect the natural environment rarely offer ethical or spiritual reasons for the policies they favor. Instead they say we are running out of resources or causing the collapse of ecosystems on which we depend. Predictions of resource scarcity appear objective and scientific, whereas pronouncements that nature is sacred or that greed is bad appear judgmental or even embarrassing in a secular society. Prudential and economic arguments, moreover, have succeeded better than moral or spiritual ones in swaying public policy.

These prudential and economic arguments are not likely to succeed much longer. It is simply wrong to believe that nature sets physical limits to economic growth—that is, to prosperity and the production and consumption of goods and services on which it is based. The idea that increasing consumption will inevitably lead to depletion and scarcity, as plausible as it may seem, is mistaken both in principle and in fact. It is based on four misconceptions.

MISCONCEPTION NO. 1: WE ARE RUNNING OUT OF RAW MATERIALS

In the 1970s Paul Ehrlich, a biologist at Stanford University, predicted that global shortages would soon send prices for food, fresh water, energy, metals, paper, and other materials sharply higher. "It seems certain," Paul and Anne Ehrlich wrote in *The End of Affluence* (1974), "that energy shortages will be with us for the rest of the century, and that before 1985 mankind will enter a genuine age of scarcity in which many things besides energy will be in short supply." Crucial materials would be near depletion during the 1980s, Ehrlich predicted, pushing prices out of reach. "Starvation among people will be accompanied by starvation of industries for the materials they require."[5]

Things have not turned out as Ehrlich expected. In the early 1990s real prices for food overall fell.[6] Raw materials—including energy resources—are generally more abundant and less expensive today than they were twenty years ago. When Ehrlich wrote, economically recoverable world reserves of petroleum stood at 640 billion barrels.[7] Since that time reserves have *increased* by more than 50 percent, reaching more than 1,000 billion barrels in 1989.[8] They have held steady in spite of rising consumption. The pre tax real price of gasoline was lower during this decade than at any other time since 1947.[9] The World Energy Council announced in 1992 that "fears of imminent [resource] exhaustion that were widely held 20 years ago are now considered to have been unfounded."[10]

The World Resources Institute, in a 1994–1995 report, referred to "the frequently expressed concern that high levels of consumption will lead to resource depletion and to physical shortages that might limit growth or development opportunity." Examining the evidence, however, the institute said that "the world is not yet running out of most nonrenewable resources and is not likely to, at least in the next few decades." A 1988 report from the Office of Technology Assessment concluded, "The nation's future has probably never been less constrained by the cost of natural resources."

It is reasonable to expect that as raw materials become less expensive, they will be more rapidly depleted. This expectation is also mistaken. From 1980 to 1990, for example, while the prices of resource-based commodities declined (the price of rubber by 40 percent, cement by 40 percent, and coal by almost 50 percent), reserves of most raw materials increased. Economists offer three explanations.

First, with regard to subsoil resources, the world becomes ever more adept at discovering new reserves and exploiting old ones. Exploring for oil, for example, used to be a hit-or-miss proposition, resulting in a lot of dry holes. Today oil companies can use seismic waves to help them create precise computer images of the earth. New methods of extraction—for example, using bacteria to leach metals from low-grade ores—greatly increase resource recovery. Reserves of resources "are actually functions of technology," one analyst has written. "The more advanced the technology, the more reserves become known and recoverable."[11]

Second, plentiful resources can be used in place of those that become scarce. Analysts speak of an Age of Substitutability and point, for example, to nanotubes, tiny cylinders of carbon whose molecular structure forms fibers a hundred times as strong as steel, at one sixth the weight. As technologies that use more-abundant resources substitute for those needing less-abundant ones—for example, ceramics in place of tungsten, fiber optics in place of copper wire, aluminum cans in place of tin ones—the demand for and the price of the less-abundant resources decline.

One can easily find earlier instances of substitution. During the early nineteenth century whale oil was the preferred fuel for household illumination. A dwindling supply prompted innovations in the lighting industry, including the invention of gas and kerosene lamps and Edison's carbon-filament electric bulb.[12] Whale oil has substitutes, such as electricity and petroleum-based lubricants. Whales are irreplaceable.

Third, the more we learn about materials, the more efficiently we use them. The progress from candles to carbon-filament to tungsten incandescent lamps, for example, decreased the energy required for and the cost of a unit of household lighting by many times. Compact fluorescent lights are four times as efficient as today's incandescent bulbs and last ten to twenty times as long.[13] Comparable energy savings are available in other appliances: for example, refrigerators sold in 1993 were 23 percent more efficient than those sold in 1990 and 65 percent more efficient than those sold in 1980, saving consumers billions in electric bills.[14]

Amory Lovins, the director of the Rocky Mountain Institute, has described a new generation of ultralight automobiles that could deliver the safety and muscle of today's cars but with far better mileage—four times as much in prototypes and ten times as much in projected models.[15] Since in today's cars only 15 to 20 percent of the fuel's energy reaches the wheels (the rest is lost in the engine and the transmission), and since materials lighter and stronger than steel are available or on the way, no expert questions the feasibility of the high-mileage vehicles Lovins describes.

Computers and cameras are examples of consumer goods getting lighter and smaller as they get better. The game-maker Sega is marketing a handheld children's game, called Saturn, that has more computing power than the 1976 Cray supercomputer, which the United States tried to keep out of the hands of the Soviets. Improvements that extend the useful life of objects also save resources. Platinum spark plugs in today's cars last for 100,000 miles, as do "fill-for-life" transmission fluids. On average, cars bought in 1993 have a useful life more than 40 percent longer than those bought in 1970.[16]

As lighter materials replace heavier ones, the U.S. economy continues to shed weight. Our per capita consumption of raw materials such as forestry products and metals has, measured by weight, declined steadily over the past twenty years. A recent World Resources Institute study measured the "materials intensity" of our economy—that is, "the total material input and the hidden or indirect material flows, including deliberate landscape alterations" required for each dollar's worth of economic output. "The result shows a clearly declining pattern of materials intensity, supporting the conclusion that economic activity is growing somewhat more rapidly than natural resource use."[17] Of course, we should do better. The Organization for Economic Cooperation and Development, an association of the world's industrialized nations, has proposed that its members strive as a long-range goal to decrease their materials intensity by a factor of ten.

Communications also illustrates the trend toward lighter, smaller, less materials-intensive technology. Just as telegraph cables replaced frigates in transmitting messages across the Atlantic and carried more information faster, glass fibers and microwaves have replaced cables—each new technology using less materials but providing greater capacity for sending and receiving information. Areas not yet wired for telephones (in the former Soviet Union, for example) are expected to leapfrog directly into cellular communications. Robert Solow, a Nobel laureate in economics, says that if the future is like the past, "there will be prolonged and substantial reductions in natural-resource requirements per unit of real output." He asks, "Why shouldn't the productivity of most natural resources rise more or less steadily through time, like the productivity of labor?"[18]

MISCONCEPTION NO. 2: WE ARE RUNNING OUT OF FOOD AND TIMBER

The United Nations projects that the global population, currently 5.7 billion, will peak at about 10 billion in the next century and then stabilize or even decline.[19] Can the earth feed that many people? Even if food crops increase sufficiently, other renewable resources, including many fisheries and forests, are already under pressure. Should we expect fish stocks to collapse or forests to disappear?

The world already produces enough cereals and oilseeds to feed 10 billion people a vegetarian diet adequate in protein and calories. If, however, the idea is to feed 10 billion people not healthful vegetarian diets but the kind of meat-laden meals that Americans eat, the production of grains and oilseeds may have to triple—primarily to feed livestock.[20] Is anything like this kind of productivity in the cards?

Maybe. From 1961 to 1994 global production of food doubled. Global output of grain rose from about 630 million tons in 1950 to about 1.8 billion tons in 1992, largely as a result of greater yields.[21] Developing countries from 1974 to 1994 increased wheat yields per acre by almost 100 percent, corn yields by 72 percent, and rice yields by 52 percent.[22] "The generation of farmers on the land in 1950 was the first in history to double the production of food," the Worldwatch Institute has reported. "By 1984, they had outstripped population growth enough to raise per capita grain output an unprecedented 40 percent."[23] From a two-year period ending in 1981 to a two-year period ending in 1990 the real prices of basic foods fell 38 percent on world markets, according to a 1992 United Nations report. Prices for food have continually decreased since the end of the eighteenth century, when Thomas Malthus argued that rapid population growth must lead to mass starvation by exceeding the carrying capacity of the earth.

Farmers worldwide could double the acreage in production, but this should not be necessary. Better seeds, more irrigation, multi-cropping, and additional use of fertilizer could greatly increase agricultural yields in the developing world, which are now generally only half those in the industrialized countries. It is biologically possible to raise yields of rice to about seven tons per acre—about four times the current average in the developing world.[24] Super strains of cassava, a potato-like root crop eaten by millions of Africans, promise to increase yields tenfold. American farmers can also do better. In a good year, such as 1994, Iowa corn growers average about 3.5 tons per acre, but farmers more than double that yield in National Corn Growers Association competitions.

In drier parts of the world the scarcity of fresh water presents the greatest challenge to agriculture. But the problem is regional, not global. Fortunately, as Lester Brown, of the Worldwatch Institute, points out, "there are vast opportunities for increasing water efficiency" in arid regions, ranging from installing better water-delivery systems to planting drought-resistant crops.[25] He adds, "Scientists can help push back the physical frontiers of cropping by developing varieties that are more drought resistant, salt tolerant, and early maturing. The payoff on the first two could be particularly high."[26]

As if in response, Novartis Seeds has announced a program to develop water-efficient and salt-tolerant crops, including genetically engineered varieties of wheat. Researchers in Mexico have announced the development of drought-resistant corn

that can boost yields by a third. Biotechnologists are converting annual crops into perennial ones, eliminating the need for yearly planting. They also hope to enable cereal crops to fix their own nitrogen, as legumes do, minimizing the need for fertilizer (genetically engineered nitrogen-fixing bacteria have already been test-marketed to farmers). Commercial varieties of crops such as corn, tomatoes, and potatoes which have been genetically engineered to be resistant to pests and diseases have been approved for field testing in the United States; several are now being sold and planted.[27] A new breed of rice, 25 percent more productive than any currently in use, suggests that the Gene Revolution can take over where the Green Revolution left off.[28] Biotechnology, as the historian Paul Kennedy has written, introduces "an entirely new stage in humankind's attempts to produce more crops and plants."[29]

Biotechnology cannot, however, address the major causes of famine: poverty, trade barriers, corruption, mismanagement, ethnic antagonism, anarchy, war, and male-dominated societies that deprive women of food. Local land depletion, itself a consequence of poverty and institutional failure, is also a factor.[30] Those who are too poor to use sound farming practices are compelled to overexploit the resources on which they depend. As the economist Partha Dasgupta has written, "Population growth, poverty and degradation of local resources often fuel one another."[31] The amount of food in world trade is constrained less by the resource base than by the maldistribution of wealth.

Analysts who believe that the world is running out of resources often argue that famines occur not as a result of political or economic conditions but because there are "too many people." Unfortunately, as the economist Amartya Sen has pointed out, public officials who think in Malthusian terms assume that when absolute levels of food supplies are adequate, famine will not occur. This conviction diverts attention from the actual causes of famine, which has occurred in places where food output kept pace with population growth but people were too destitute to buy it.[32]

We would have run out of food long ago had we tried to supply ourselves entirely by hunting and gathering. Likewise, if we depend on nature's gifts, we will exhaust many of the world's important fisheries. Fortunately, we are learning to cultivate fish as we do other crops. Genetic engineers have designed fish for better flavor and color as well as for faster growth, improved disease resistance, and other traits. Two farmed species—silver carp and grass carp—already rank among the ten most-consumed fish worldwide.[33] A specially bred tilapia, known as the "aquatic chicken," takes six months to grow to a harvestable size of about one and a half pounds.[34]

Aquaculture produced more than 16 million tons of fish in 1993; capacity has expanded over the past decade at an annual rate of 10 percent by quantity and 14 percent by value. In 1993 fish farms produced 22 percent of all food fish consumed in the world and 90 percent of all oysters sold.[35] The World Bank reports that aquaculture could provide 40 percent of all fish consumed and more than half the value of fish harvested within the next fifteen years.

Salmon ranching and farming provide examples of the growing efficiency of aquacultural production. Norwegian salmon farms alone produce 400 million pounds a year. A biotech firm in Waltham, Massachusetts, has applied for government approval to commercialize salmon genetically engineered to grow four to six times as fast as their naturally occurring cousins. "There is so much salmon currently available that the supply exceeds demand, and prices to fishermen have fallen dramatically."[36]

For those who lament the decline of natural fisheries and the human communities that grew up with them, the successes of aquaculture may offer no consolation. In the Pacific Northwest, for example, overfishing in combination with dams and habitat destruction has reduced the wild salmon population by 80 percent. Wild salmon—but not their bioengineered aquacultural cousins—contribute to the cultural identity and sense of place of the Northwest. When wild salmon disappear, so will some of the region's history, character, and pride. What is true of wild salmon is also true of whales, dolphins, and other magnificent creatures—as they lose their economic importance, their aesthetic and moral worth becomes all the more evident. Economic considerations pull in one direction, moral considerations in the other. This conflict colors all our battles over the environment.

The transition from hunting and gathering to farming, which is changing the fishing industry, has taken place more slowly in forestry. Still there is no sign of a timber famine. In the United States forests now provide the largest harvests in history, and there is more forested U.S. area today than there was in 1920.[37] Bill McKibben has observed that the eastern United States, which loggers and farmers in the eighteenth and nineteenth centuries nearly denuded of trees, has become reforested during this century.[38] One reason is that farms reverted to woods. Another is that machinery replaced animals; each draft animal required two or three cleared acres for pasture.

Natural reforestation is likely to continue as biotechnology makes areas used for logging more productive. According to Roger Sedjo, a respected forestry expert, advances in tree farming, if implemented widely, would permit the world to meet its entire demand for industrial wood using just 200 million acres of plantations—an area equal to only five percent of current forest land. As less land is required for commercial tree production, more natural forests may be protected—as they should be, for aesthetic, ethical, and spiritual reasons.[39]

Often natural resources are so plentiful and therefore inexpensive that they undercut the necessary transition to technological alternatives. If the U.S. government did not protect wild forests from commercial exploitation, the timber industry would have little incentive to invest in tree plantations, where it can multiply yields by a factor of ten and take advantage of the results of genetic research. Only by investing in plantation silviculture can North American forestry fend off price competition from rapidly developing tree plantations in the Southern Hemisphere. Biotechnology-based silviculture can in the near future be expected to underprice "extractive" forestry worldwide. In this decade China will plant about 150 million acres of trees; India now plants four times the area it harvests commercially.[40]

The expansion of fish and tree farming confirms the belief held by Peter Drucker and other management experts that our economy depends far more on the progress of technology than on the exploitation of nature. Although raw materials will always be necessary, knowledge has become the essential factor in the production of goods and services. "Where there is effective management," Drucker has written, "that is, application of knowledge to knowledge, we can always obtain the other resources."[41] If we assume, along with Drucker and others, that resource scarcities do not exist or are easily averted, it is hard to see how economic theory, which after all concerns scarcity, provides the conceptual basis for valuing the environment. The reasons to preserve nature are ethical more often than they are economic.

MISCONCEPTION NO. 3: WE ARE RUNNING OUT OF ENERGY

Probably the most persistent worries about resource scarcity concern energy. "The supply of fuels and other natural resources is becoming the limiting factor constraining the rate of economic growth," a group of experts proclaimed in 1986. They predicted the exhaustion of domestic oil and gas supplies by 2020 and, within a few decades, "major energy shortages as well as food shortages in the world."[42]

Contrary to these expectations, no global shortages of hydrocarbon fuels are in sight. "One sees no immediate danger of 'running out' of energy in a global sense," writes John P. Holdren, a professor of environmental policy at Harvard University. According to Holdren, reserves of oil and natural gas will last seventy to a hundred years if exploited at 1990 rates. (This does not take into account huge deposits of oil shale, heavy oils, and gas from unconventional sources.) He concludes that "running out of energy resources in any global sense is not what the energy problem is all about."[43]

The global energy problem has less to do with depleting resources than with controlling pollutants. Scientists generally agree that gases, principally carbon dioxide, emitted in the combustion of hydrocarbon fuels can build up in and warm the atmosphere by trapping sunlight. Since carbon dioxide enhances photosynthetic activity, plants to some extent absorb the carbon dioxide we produce. In 1995 researchers reported in *Science* that vegetation in the Northern Hemisphere in 1992 and 1993 converted into trees and other plant tissue 3.5 billion tons of carbon—more than half the carbon produced by the burning of hydrocarbon fuels worldwide.[44]

However successful this and other feedback mechanisms may be in slowing the processes of global warming, a broad scientific consensus, reflected in a 1992 international treaty, has emerged for stabilizing and then decreasing emissions of carbon dioxide and other "greenhouse" gases. This goal is well within the technological reach of the United States and other industrialized countries.[45] Amory Lovins, among others, has described commercially available technologies that can "support present or greatly expanded worldwide economic activity while stabilizing global climate—and saving money." He observes that "even very large expansions in population and industrial activity need not be energy-constrained."[46]

Lovins and other environmentalists contend that pollution-free energy from largely untapped sources is available in amounts exceeding our needs. Geothermal energy—which makes use of heat from the earth's core—is theoretically accessible through drilling technology in the United States in amounts thousands of times as great as the amount of energy contained in domestic coal reserves. Tidal energy is also promising.[47] Analysts who study solar power generally agree with Lester Brown, of the Worldwatch Institute, that "technologies are ready to begin building a world energy system largely powered by solar resources."[48] In the future these and other renewable energy sources may be harnessed to the nation's system of storing and delivering electricity.

Joseph Romm and Charles Curtis have described advances in photovoltaic cells (which convert sunlight into electricity), fuel cells (which convert the hydrogen in fuels directly to electricity and heat, producing virtually no pollution), and wind power. According to these authors, genetically engineered organisms used to ferment organic matter could, with further research and development, bring down the costs of ethanol and other environmentally friendly "biofuels" to make them competitive with gasoline.[49]

Environmentalists who, like Amory Lovins, believe that our economy can grow and still reduce greenhouse gases emphasize not only that we should be able to move to renewable forms of energy but also that we can use fossil fuels more efficiently. Some improvements are already evident. In developed countries the energy intensity of production—the amount of fuel burned per dollar of economic output—has been decreasing by about two percent a year.[50]

From 1973 to 1986, for example, energy consumption in the United States remained virtually flat while economic production grew by almost 40 percent. Compared with Germany or Japan, this is a poor showing. The Japanese, who tax fuel more heavily than we do, use only half as much energy as the United States per unit of economic output. (Japanese environmental regulations are also generally stricter than ours; if anything, this has improved the competitiveness of Japanese industry.) The United States still wastes hundreds of billions of dollars annually in energy inefficiency. By becoming as energy-efficient as Japan, the United States could expand its economy and become more competitive internationally.

If so many opportunities exist for saving energy and curtailing pollution, why have we not seized them? One reason is that low fossil-fuel prices remove incentives for fuel efficiency and for converting to other energy sources. Another reason is that government subsidies for fossil fuels and nuclear energy amounted to many billions of dollars a year during the 1980s, whereas support for renewables dwindled to $114 million in 1989, a time when it had been proposed for near elimination.[51] "Lemon socialism," a vast array of subsidies and barriers to trade, protects politically favored technologies, however inefficient, dangerous, filthy, or obsolete. "At heart, the major obstacles standing in the way [of a renewable-energy economy] are not technical in nature," the energy consultant Michael Brower has written, "but concern the laws, regulations, incentives, public at-

titudes, and other factors that make up the energy market."[52]

In response to problems of climate change, the World Bank and other international organizations have recognized the importance of transferring advanced energy technologies to the developing world. Plainly, this will take a large investment of capital, particularly in education. Yet the "alternative for developing countries," according to José Goldemberg, a former Environment Minister of Brazil, "would be to remain at a dismally low level of development which . . . would aggravate the problems of sustainability."[53]

Technology transfer can hasten sound economic development worldwide. Many environmentalists, however, argue that economies cannot expand without exceeding the physical limits nature sets—for example, with respect to energy. These environmentalists, who regard increasing affluence as a principal cause of environmental degradation, call for economic retrenchment and retraction—a small economy for a small earth. With Paul Ehrlich, they reject "the hope that development can greatly increase the size of the economic pie and pull many more people out of poverty." This hope is "basically a humane idea," Ehrlich has written, "made insane by the constraints nature places on human activity."[54]

In developing countries, however, a no-growth economy "will deprive entire populations of access to better living conditions and lead to even more deforestation and land degradation," as Goldemberg warns.[55] Moreover, citizens of developed countries are likely to resist an energy policy that they associate with poverty, discomfort, sacrifice, and pain. Technological pessimism, then, may not be the best option for environmentalists. It is certainly not the only one.

MISCONCEPTION NO. 4: THE NORTH EXPLOITS THE SOUTH

William Reilly, when he served as administrator of the Environmental Protection Agency in the Bush Administration, encountered a persistent criticism at international meetings on the environment. "The problem for the world's environment is your consumption, not our population," delegates from the developing world told him. Some of these delegates later took Reilly aside. "The North buys too little from the South," they confided. "The real problem is too little demand for our exports."[56]

The delegates who told Reilly that the North consumes too little of what the South produces have a point. "With a few exceptions (notably petroleum)," a report from the World Resources Institute observes, "most of the natural resources consumed in the United States are from domestic sources."[57] Throughout the 1980s the United States and Canada were the world's leading exporters of raw materials.[58] The United States consistently leads the world in farm exports, running huge agricultural trade surpluses. The share of raw materials used in the North that it buys from the South stands at a thirty-year low and continues to decline; industrialized nations trade largely among themselves.[59] The World Resources Institute recently reported that "the United States is largely self sufficient in natural resources." Again, excepting petroleum, bauxite (from which aluminum is made), "and a few other industrial minerals, its material flows are almost entirely internal."[60]

Sugar provides an instructive example of how the North excludes—rather than exploits—the resources of the South. Since 1796 the United States has protected domestic sugar against imports. American sugar growers, in part as a reward for large contributions to political campaigns, have long enjoyed a system of quotas and prohibitive tariffs against foreign competition. American consumers paid about three times world prices for sugar in the 1980s, enriching a small cartel of U.S. growers. *Forbes* magazine has estimated that a single family, the Fanjuls, of Palm Beach, reaps more than $65 million a year as a result of quotas for sugar.[61]

The sugar industry in Florida, which is larger than that in any other state, makes even less sense environmentally than economically.[62] It depends on a publicly built system of canals, levees, and pumping stations. Fertilizer from the sugarcane fields chokes the Everglades. Sugar growers, under a special ex-

emption from labor laws, import Caribbean laborers to do the grueling and poorly paid work of cutting cane.

As the United States tightened sugar quotas (imports fell from 6.2 to 1.5 million tons annually from 1977 to 1987), the Dominican Republic and other nations with climates ideal for growing cane experienced political turmoil and economic collapse. Many farmers in Latin America, however, did well by switching from sugar to coca, which is processed into cocaine—perhaps the only high-value imported crop for which the United States is not developing a domestic substitute.[63]

Before the Second World War the United States bought 40 percent of its vegetable oils from developing countries. After the war the United States protected its oilseed markets—for example, by establishing price supports for soybeans. Today the United States is one of the world's leading exporters of oil and oilseeds, although it still imports palm and coconut oils to obtain laurate, an ingredient in soap, shampoo, and detergents. Even this form of "exploitation" will soon cease. In 1994 farmers in Georgia planted the first commercial acreage of a high-laurate canola, genetically engineered by Calgene, a biotechnology firm.

About 100,000 Kenyans make a living on small plots of land growing pyrethrum flowers, the source of a comparatively environmentally safe insecticide of which the United States has been the largest importer. The U.S. Department of Commerce, however, awarded $1.2 million to a biotechnology firm to engineer pyrethrum genetically. Industrial countries will soon be able to synthesize all the pyrethrum they need and undersell Kenyan farmers.[64]

An article in *Foreign Policy* in December of 1995 observed that the biotechnological innovations that create "substitutes for everything from vanilla to cocoa and coffee threaten to eliminate the livelihood of millions of Third World agricultural workers."[65] Vanilla cultured in laboratories costs a fifth as much as vanilla extracted from beans, and thus jeopardizes the livelihood of tens of thousands of vanilla farmers in Madagascar. In the past, farms produced agricultural commodities and factories processed them.

In the future, factories may "grow" as well as process many of the most valuable commodities—or the two functions will become one. As one plant scientist has said, "We have to stop thinking of these things as plant cells, and start thinking of them as new microorganisms, with all the potential that implies"—meaning, for instance, that the cells could be made to grow in commercially feasible quantities in laboratories, not fields.[66]

The North not only balks at buying sugar and other crops from developing countries; it also dumps its excess agricultural commodities, especially grain, on them. After the Second World War, American farmers, using price supports left over from the New Deal, produced vast wheat surpluses, which the United States exported at concessionary prices to Europe and then the Third World. These enormous transfers of cereals to the South, institutionalized during the 1950s and 1960s by U.S. food aid, continued during the 1970s and 1980s, as the United States and the European Community vied for markets, each outdoing the other in subsidizing agricultural exports.

Grain imports from the United States "created food dependence within two decades in countries which had been mostly self-sufficient in food at the end of World War II," the sociologist Harriet Friedman has written. Tropical countries soon matched the grain gluts of the North with their own surpluses of cocoa, coffee, tea, bananas, and other export commodities. Accordingly, prices for these commodities collapsed as early as 1970, catching developing nations in a scissors. As Friedman describes it, "One blade was food import dependency. The other blade was declining revenues for traditional exports of tropical crops."[67]

It might be better for the environment if the North exchanged the crops for which it is ecologically suited—wheat, for example—for crops easily grown in the South, such as coffee, cocoa, palm oil, and tea. Contrary to common belief, these tropical export crops—which grow on trees and bushes, providing canopy and continuous root structures to protect the soil—are less damaging to the soil than are traditional staples such as cereals and root crops.[68] Bet-

ter markets for tropical crops could help developing nations to employ their rural populations and to protect their natural resources. Allen Hammond, of the World Resources Institute, points out that "if poor nations cannot export anything else, they will export their misery—in the form of drugs, diseases, terrorism, migration, and environmental degradation."[69]

Peasants in less-developed nations often confront intractable poverty, an entrenched land-tenure system, and a lack of infrastructure; they have little access to markets, education, or employment. Many of the rural poor, according to the environmental consultant Norman Myers, "have no option but to overexploit environmental resource stocks in order to survive"—for example, by "increasingly encroaching onto tropical forests among other low-potential lands."[70] Myers observes that the principal agents of tropical deforestation are refugees from civil war and rural poverty, who are forced to eke out a living on marginal lands. According to Myers, slash-and-burn farming by displaced peasants accounts for far more deforestation than all commercial uses of forests combined. Most of the wood from trees harvested in tropical forests, that is, those not cleared for farms, is used locally for fuel. The likeliest path to protecting the rain forest is through economic development that enables peasants to farm efficiently, on land better suited to farming than to forest, and to purchase kerosene and other fuels.

These poorest of the poor, Myers has written, "are causing as much natural-resource depletion as the other three billion developing-world people put together." Peasants who try to scratch a living from a inhospitable environment, according to Myers, "are often the principal cause of deforestation, desertification, and soil erosion" as well as of the "mass extinction of species." These people "can be helped primarily by being brought into the mainstream of sustainable development, with all the basic needs benefits that would supply."[71]

Many have argued that economic activity, affluence, and growth automatically lead to resource depletion, environmental deterioration, and ecological collapse. Yet greater productivity and prosperity—which is what economists mean by growth—have become prerequisite for controlling urban pollution and protecting sensitive ecological systems such as rain forests. Otherwise, destitute people who are unable to acquire food and fuel will create pollution and destroy forests. Without economic growth, which also correlates with lower fertility, the environmental and population problems of the South will only get worse. For impoverished countries facing environmental disaster, economic growth may be the one thing that is sustainable.

WHAT IS WRONG WITH CONSUMPTION?

Any of us who attended college in the 1960s and 1970s took pride in how little we owned. We celebrated our freedom when we could fit all our possessions—mostly a stereo—into the back of a Beetle. Decades later, middle-aged and middle-class, many of us have accumulated an appalling amount of stuff. Piled high with gas grills, lawn mowers, excess furniture, bicycles, children's toys, garden implements, lumber, cinder blocks, ladders, lawn and leaf bags stuffed with memorabilia, and boxes yet to be unpacked from the last move, the two-car garages beside our suburban homes are too full to accommodate the family minivan. The quantity of resources, particularly energy, we waste and the quantity of trash we throw away (recycling somewhat eases our conscience) add to our consternation.

Even if predictions of resource depletion and ecological collapse are mistaken, it seems that they should be true, to punish us for our sins. We are distressed by the suffering of others, the erosion of the ties of community, family, and friendship, and the loss of the beauty and spontaneity of the natural world. These concerns reflect the most traditional and fundamental of American religious and cultural values.

Simple compassion instructs us to give to relieve the misery of others. There is a lot of misery worldwide to relieve. But as bad as the situation is, it is improving. In 1960 nearly 70 percent of the people in the world lived at or below the subsistence level.

Today less than a third do, and the number enjoying fairly satisfactory conditions (as measured by the United Nations Human Development Index) rose from 25 percent in 1960 to 60 percent in 1992.[72] Over the twenty-five years before 1992 average per capita consumption in developing countries increased 75 percent in real terms.[73] The pace of improvements is also increasing. In developing countries in that period, for example, power generation and the number of telephone lines per capita doubled, while the number of households with access to clean water grew by half.[74]

What is worsening is the discrepancy in income between the wealthy and the poor. Although world income measured in real terms has increased by 700 percent since the Second World War, the wealthiest people have absorbed most of the gains. Since 1960 the richest fifth of the world's people have seen their share of the world's income increase from 70 to 85 percent. Thus one fifth of the world's population possesses much more than four fifths of the world's wealth, while the share held by all others has correspondingly fallen; that of the world's poorest 20 percent has declined from 2.3 to 1.4 percent.[75]

Benjamin Barber described market forces that "mesmerize the world with fast music, fast computers, and fast food—with MTV, Macintosh, and McDonald's, pressing nations into one commercially homogeneous global network: one McWorld tied together by technology, ecology, communications, and commerce."[76] Affluent citizens of South Korea, Thailand, India, Brazil, Mexico, and many other rapidly developing nations have joined with Americans, Europeans, Japanese, and others to form an urban and cosmopolitan international society. Those who participate in this global network are less and less beholden to local customs and traditions. Meanwhile, ethnic, tribal, and other cultural groups that do not dissolve into McWorld often define themselves in opposition to it—fiercely asserting their ethnic, religious, and territorial identities.

The imposition of a market economy on traditional cultures in the name of development—for example, the insistence that everyone produce and consume more—can dissolve the ties to family, land, community, and place on which indigenous peoples traditionally rely for their security. Thus development projects intended to relieve the poverty of indigenous peoples may, by causing the loss of cultural identity, engender the very powerlessness they aim to remedy. Pope Paul VI, in the encyclical *Populorum Progressio* (1967), described the tragic dilemma confronting indigenous peoples: "either to preserve traditional beliefs and structures and reject social progress; or to embrace foreign technology and foreign culture, and reject ancestral traditions with their wealth of humanism."

The idea that everything is for sale and nothing is sacred—that all values are subjective—undercuts our own moral and cultural commitments, not just those of tribal and traditional communities. No one has written a better critique of the assault that commerce makes on the quality of our lives than Thoreau provides in *Walden*. The cost of a thing, according to Thoreau, is not what the market will bear but what the individual must bear because of it: it is "the amount of what I will call life which is required to be exchanged for it, immediately or in the long run."[77]

Many observers point out that as we work harder and consume more, we seem to enjoy our lives less. We are always in a rush—a "Saint Vitus' dance," as Thoreau called it. Idleness is suspect. Americans today spend less time with their families, neighbors, and friends than they did in the 1950s. Juliet B. Schor, an economist at Harvard University, argues that "Americans are literally working themselves to death."[78] A fancy car, video equipment, or a complex computer program can exact a painful cost in the form of maintenance, upgrading, and repair. We are possessed by our possessions; they are often harder to get rid of than to acquire.

That money does not make us happier, once our basic needs are met, is a commonplace overwhelmingly confirmed by sociological evidence. Paul Wachtel, who teaches social psychology at the City University of New York, has concluded that bigger incomes "do not yield an increase in feelings of satisfaction or well-being, at least for populations who are above a poverty or subsistence level."[79] This

cannot be explained simply by the fact that people have to work harder to earn more money: even those who hit jackpots in lotteries often report that their lives are not substantially happier as a result. Well-being depends upon health, membership in a community in which one feels secure, friends, faith, family, love, and virtues that money cannot buy. Robert Lane, a political scientist at Yale University, using the concepts of economics, has written, "If 'utility' has anything to do with happiness, above the poverty line the long-term marginal utility of money is almost zero."[80]

Economists in earlier times predicted that wealth would not matter to people once they attained a comfortable standard of living. "In ease of body and peace of mind, all the different ranks of life are nearly upon a level," wrote Adam Smith, the eighteenth-century English advocate of the free market.[81] In the 1930s the British economist John Maynard Keynes argued that after a period of great expansion further accumulation of wealth would no longer improve personal well-being.[82] Subsequent economists, however, found that even after much of the industrial world had attained the levels of wealth Keynes thought were sufficient, people still wanted more. From this they inferred that wants are insatiable.

Perhaps this is true. But the insatiability of wants and desires poses a difficulty for standard economic theory, which posits that humanity's single goal is to increase or maximize wealth. If wants increase as fast as income grows, what purpose can wealth serve?

Critics often attack standard economic theory on the ground that economic growth is "unsustainable." We are running out of resources, they say; we court ecological disaster. Whether or not growth is sustainable, there is little reason to think that once people attain a decent standard of living, continued growth is desirable. The economist Robert H. Nelson recently wrote in the journal *Ecological Economics* that it is no longer possible for most people to believe that economic progress will "solve all the problems of mankind, spiritual as well as material."[83] As long as the debate over sustainability is framed in terms of the physical limits to growth rather than the moral purpose of it, mainstream economic theory will have the better of the argument. If the debate were framed in moral or social terms, the result might well be otherwise.

MAKING A PLACE FOR NATURE

According to Thoreau, "a man's relation to Nature must come very near to a personal one."[84] For environmentalists in the tradition of Thoreau and John Muir, stewardship is a form of fellowship; although we must use nature, we do not value it primarily for the economic purposes it serves. We take our bearings from the natural world—our sense of time from its days and seasons, our sense of place from the character of a landscape and the particular plants and animals native to it. An intimacy with nature ends our isolation in the world. We know where we belong, and we can find the way home.

In defending old-growth forests, wetlands, or species, we make our best arguments when we think of nature chiefly in aesthetic and moral terms. Rather than having the courage of our moral and cultural convictions, however, we too often rely on economic arguments for protecting nature, in the process attributing to natural objects more instrumental value than they have. By claiming that a threatened species may harbor lifesaving drugs, for example, we impute to that species an economic value or a price much greater than it fetches in a market. When we make the prices come out right, we rescue economic theory but not necessarily the environment.

There is no credible argument, moreover, that all or even most of the species we are concerned to protect are essential to the functioning of the ecological systems on which we depend. (If whales went extinct, for example, the seas would not fill up with krill.) David Ehrenfeld, a biologist at Rutgers University, makes this point in relation to the vast ecological changes we have already survived. "Even a mighty dominant like the American chestnut," Ehrenfeld has written, "extending over half a continent, all but disappeared without bringing the eastern deciduous forest down with it." Ehrenfeld points out that the species most likely to be endangered are those the biosphere is least likely to miss. "Many of these species were never common or ecologically influential; by no stretch of the imagination can we make them out to be vital cogs in the ecological machine."[85]

Species may be profoundly important for cultural and spiritual reasons, however. Consider again the example of the wild salmon, whose habitat is being destroyed by hydroelectric dams along the Columbia River. Although this loss is unimportant to the economy overall (there is no shortage of salmon), it is of the greatest significance to the Amerindian tribes that have traditionally subsisted on wild salmon, and to the region as a whole. By viewing local flora and fauna as a sacred heritage—by recognizing their intrinsic value—we discover who we are rather than what we want. On moral and cultural grounds society might be justified in making great economic sacrifices—removing hydroelectric dams, for example—to protect remnant populations of the Snake River sockeye, even if, as critics complain, hundreds or thousands of dollars are spent for every fish that is saved.

Even those plants and animals that do not define places possess enormous intrinsic value and are worth preserving for their own sake. What gives these creatures value lies in their histories, wonderful in themselves, rather than in any use to which they can be put. The biologist E. O. Wilson elegantly takes up this theme: "Every kind of organism has reached this moment in time by threading one needle after another, throwing up brilliant artifices to survive and reproduce against nearly impossible odds."[86] Every plant or animal evokes not just sympathy but also reverence and wonder in those who know it.

In *Earth in the Balance,* Al Gore, then a senator, wrote, "We have become so successful at controlling nature that we have lost our connection to it." It is all too easy, Gore wrote, "to regard the earth as a collection of 'resources' having an intrinsic value no larger than their usefulness at the moment." The question before us is not whether we are going to run out of resources. It is whether economics is the appropriate context for thinking about environmental policy.

Even John Stuart Mill, one of the principal authors of utilitarian philosophy, recognized that the natural world has great intrinsic and not just instrumental value. More than a century ago, as England lost its last truly wild places, Mill condemned a world

> with nothing left to the spontaneous activity of nature; with every rood of land brought into cultivation, which is capable of growing food for human beings; every flowery waste or natural pasture ploughed up; all quadrupeds or birds which are not domesticated for man's use exterminated as his rivals for food, every hedgerow or superfluous tree rooted out, and scarcely a place left where a wild shrub or flower could grow without being eradicated as a weed in the name of improved agriculture.[87]

The world has the wealth and the resources to provide everyone the opportunity to live a decent life. We consume too much when market relationships displace the bonds of community, compassion, culture, and place. We consume too much when consumption becomes an end in itself and makes us lose affection and reverence for the natural world.

NOTES

First published in *The Atlantic Monthly*. The author gratefully acknowledges support under a grant from the Global Stewardship Initiative of the Pew Charitable Trusts to the Institute for Philosophy and Public Policy. The views expressed are those of the author not necessarily of any grant making agency.

1. Ronald Dworkin, *Life's Dominion* (New York: Vintage Books, 1994), p. 71–72; for an application of this principle to the endangered species issue, see pp. 76–77.

2. Willett Kempton, James S. Boster, and Jennifer A. Hartley, *Environmental Values in American Culture* (Cambridge, MA.: MIT Press, 1995), pp. 91, 92.

3. John Muir, *The Yosemite* (New York: Century Co., 1912), p. 256.

4. Walt Whitman, *Specimen Days* (Boston: David R. Godine, Publisher, 1971), p. 61.

5. Paul R. Ehrlich and Anne H. Ehrlich, *The End of Affluence* (New York: Ballantine Books, 1974), p. 33.

6. "Over the course of the twentieth century, according to a careful study conducted by the World Bank and published in 1988, the relative price of food grains dropped by over 40 percent." For this and other supporting evidence, see Nicholas Eberstadt, "Population, Food, and Income: Global Trends in the Twentieth Century." pp. 7–47 in Ronald Bailey, ed., *The True State of the Planet* (New York: The Free Press, for the Competitive Enterprise Institute, 1995), esp. pp. 28–29.

7. Paul and Anne Ehrlich give this estimate in *The End of Affluence,* p. 48.

8. The World Resources Institute, The United Nations Environment Programme, The United Nations Development Programme, and The World Bank, *World Resources 1996–97* (New York: Oxford University Press, 1996), p. 275 (observing that estimates of global petroleum reserves have increased by 43 percent between 1984 and 1994). Since 1989, "new discoveries, additions, and recisions have broadly matched the world's production, leaving total reserves basically unchanged."

9. Stephen Moore, "The Coming Age of Abundance," in Ronald Bailey, ed., *The True State of the Planet* (New York: Free Press, 1995), ch. 4, pp. 110–139; see p. 129.

10. The World Resources Institute, *World Resources 1994–95* (New York: Oxford University Press, 1994), p. 9 (quoting the *World Energy Council's 16th Survey of Energy Resources*).

11. Thomas H. Lee, "Advanced Fossil Fuel Systems and Beyond," in Jesse H. Ausubel and Hedy E. Sladovich, eds., *Technology and Environment* (Washington, DC: National Academy Press, 1989), pp. 114–136; quotation at p. 116.

12. See Jesse Ausubel, "The Liberation of the Environment," in Jesse Ausubel, ed., The Liberation of the Environment, *Daedalus* 125(3)(Summer 1996), pp. 1–19.

13. See Jesse Ausubel, "Can Technology Spare the Earth?" *American Scientist* 84 (March-April 1996): 16678; esp. pp. 164–170. For further information see, Solstice: Internet Information Service of the Center for Renewable Energy and Sustainable Technology, http://www.crest.org/.

14. See "Appliance Standards are Getting Results," *Energy Conservation News* 18, no. 2 (Sept. 1, 1995).

15. Amory Lovins, "Reinventing the Wheels," *The Atlantic Monthly* 275 (January, 1995).

16. See Warren Brown and Martha M. Hamilton, "Running On, and On, and On: Better Cars Are Changing

the Economics of Driving for Consumers and Firms," *The Washington Post,* March 9, 1997, p. H1.

17. See World Resources 1994–95, p. 15.

18. Robert M. Solow, "Is the End of the World at Hand?" in Andrew Weintraub, Eli Schwartz, and J. Richard Aronson, eds., *The Economic Growth Controversy* (White Plains, N.Y.: Institute of Arts and Sciences Press., 1973), p. 49.

19. See *World Resources* 1996–97, pp. 173–74.

20. See Paul Waggoner, *How Much Land Can 10 Billion People Spare for Nature? Task Force Report 121* (Ames, IA: Council for Agricultural Science and Technology, February, 1994), esp. Ch. 5. See also *World Resources* 1994–95, Ch. 6, esp. pp. 107–08.

21. See Lester R. Brown, Christopher Flavin, and Hal Kane, *Vital Signs* 1996 (New York: W.W. Norton, 1996), p. 25; see also Ronald Bailey, ed., *The True State of the Planet,* p. 409.

22. "Feeding a Hungrier World," The *Washington Post,* February 13, 1995, p. A3.

23. Lester Brown et al., *State of the World 1995* (New York: W.W. Norton), p. 7.

24. "Feeding a Hungrier World," The *Washington Post,* February 13, 1995, p. A3.

25. Lester R. Brown, Christopher Flavin, and Sandra Postel, *Saving the Planet* (New York: Norton, 199 1), p. 87.

26. Lester R. Brown, "The Grain Drain," *The Futurist* 23(4)(July-August 1989), pp. 17–18.

27. Robert Cooke, "Aw Shucks, This Here's Great Corn," *Newsday,* August 9 1994, p. 25; Rebecca Goldberg, "Novel Crops and Other Transgenics: How Green Are They?" in Ralph W. F. Hardy and Jane Baker Segelken, eds. *Agricultural Biotechnology: Novel Products and New Partnerships NABC Report 8* (Ithaca, NY: National Agricultural Biotechnology Council, 1996).

28. Royce Rensberger, "New 'Super Rice' Nearing Fruition," *Washington Post,* Oct. 24, 1994, p. A1.

29. Paul Kennedy, *Preparing for the Twenty-First Century* (New York: Vintage Books, 1993), p. 70.

30. World Bank, *World Development Report* 1992 (New York: Oxford University Press, 1992), esp. pp. 3033. The Bank states (p. 30): "Land-hungry farmers resort to cultivating unsuitable areas—steeply sloped, erosion-prone hillsides; semi-arid land where soil degradation is rapid; and tropical forests where crop yields on cleared fields frequently drop sharply after just a few years. . . . Poor families often lack the resources to avoid degrading their environment."

31. Partha S. Dasgupta, "Population, Poverty and the Local Environment." *Scientific American,* February 1995, p. 41.

32. Amartya Sen, *Resources, Values and Development* (Cambridge, MA: Harvard University Press, 1984), p. 524.

33. Lester Brown et al., *State of the World 1995* (New York: Norton, 1995), p. 30.

34. Christopher Dinsmore, "Tilapia Fish Farm, New in Suffolk, Aims Toward a Growing Market, *Virginian Pilot* (Norfolk), September 8, 1995, p. D2.

35. Lester Brown, Christopher Flavin, and Hal Kane, *Vital Signs* 1996 (New York: Norton 1996), p. 32.

36. Nancy Lord, "Born to be Wild," *Sierra,* November-December 1994, p. 63.

37. Roger A. SedJo, "Forest Resources: Resilient and Serviceable," in Kenneth Frederick and Roger SedJo, eds., *America's Renewable Resources* (Washington, DC: Resources for the Future, 199 1), pp. 81–120, esp. p. 110.

38. Bill McKibben, "An Explosion of Green," *The Atlantic Monthly* 275 (April, 1995): 61–83.

39. Roger A. SedJo, "Forests: Conflicting Signals," in Ronald Bailey, ed., *The True State of the Planet* (New York: Free Press, 1995), esp. p. 180.

40. World Resources Institute, *World Resources* 1994–95, pp. 79 and 134.

41. Peter Drucker, *Post Capitalist Society* (New York: Harper Business, 1993), p. 45.

42. John Gever, Robert Kaufmann, David Skole, Charles Vorosmarty, *Beyond Oil: The Threat to Food and Fuel in the Coming Decades* (a Project of Carrying Capacity, Inc.) (Cambridge, MA: Ballinger, 1986) pp. 9, xxix, and xxx.

43. John Holdren, "The Energy Predicament in Perspective" in Irving M. Mintzer, ed., *Confronting Climate Change: Risks, Implications and Responses* (New York: Cambridge University Press 1992), pp. 163–169; quotation at p. 165.

44. P. Ciais et al., "A Large Northern Hemisphere Terrestrial CO_2 Sink Indicated by the $^{13}C/^{12}C$ Ratio of Atmospheric CO_2." *Science* 269 (August 25, 1995), pp. 1098–1100.

45. For a discussion of the extent to which industrialized nations are developing non-carbon based sources of energy (thus moving to a hydrogen economy), see Nebcjsa Nakicenovic, "Freeing Energy from Carbon," in Jesse Ausubel, "The Liberation of the Environment," in Jesse Ausubel, ed., The Liberation of the Environment, *Daedalus* 125(3)(Summer 1996), pp. 95–112.

46. Amory B. Lovins, "Energy, People, and Industrialization," in Kingsley Davis and Nikhail S. Bernstam, eds., *Resources, Environment, and Population: Present Knowledge, Future Options* (New York: Oxford University Press, 1991): 95–124; quotation at p. 95. For further evidence and testimony to this effect, see Thomas B. Johnsson et al., eds., *Renewable Energy: Sources for Fuels and Electricity* (Washington, DC: Island Press, 1993).

47. For discussion of the promise of geothermal, tidal, and other alternative forms of energy, see Thomas B. Johnsson et al. eds., *Renewable Energy*; and see Michael Brower, *Cool Energy: Renewable Solutions to Environmental Problems* (Cambridge, MA: MIT Press, 1992); Robert H. Williams, "Powering the Future: Efficient Use and Renewable Supplies Are Key," *EPA Journal* 18(4), pp. 15–19.

48. Lester R. Brown, Christopher Flavin and Sandra Postel, *Saving the Planet,* p. 10.

49. Joseph J. Romm. and Charles B. Curtis, "Mideast Oil Forever?" *The Atlantic Monthly* 277 (April, 1996), pp. 57–74.

50. See A. Denny Ellerman, "Energy Policies, R&D, and Public Policy," in Davis Lewis Feldman, ed., *The Energy Crisis: Unresolved Issues and Enduring Legacies* (Baltimore: Johns Hopkins Press, 1996), esp. pp. 62–69.

51. Brower, *Cool Energy,* p. 22.

52. Brower, *Cool Energy,* p. 26.

53. Jose Goldemberg, "Energy Needs in developing Countries and Sustainability," *Science* 269, no. 5227 (25 August 1995), pp. 1058–59.

54. Paul R. Ehrlich and Anne H. Ehrlich, *The Population Explosion* (New York: Simon and Schuster 1990), p.269, n.29.

55. Goldemberg, "Energy Needs in Developing Countries," p. 1059.

56. In a phone interview, December 21, 1994, Mr. Reilly vouched for these remarks, noting that this incident happened more than once.

57. World Resources Institute, *World Resources* 1994–95, p. 16.

58. World Resources Institute, *World Resources* 1994–95, p. 291.

59. World Resources Institute, *World Resources* 1994–95, pp. 13–16.

60. Albert Adriannse et al., *Resource Flows,* p. 13.

61. Phyllis Berman and Alexandra Alger, "The Set-aside Charade," *Forbes,* March 13, 1995, p. 78.

62. See Keith Maskus, "Large Costs and Small Benefits of the American Sugar Programme," *World Economy* 12(1989): 85–104.

63. For an excellent account of the political costs of the sugar program internationally, see Anne O. Krueger, "The Political Economy of Controls: American Sugar," in Maurice Scott and Deepak Lal, eds., *Public Policy and Economic Development: Essays in Honor of Ian Little* (New York: Oxford University Press, 1990).

64. For this and other examples, see Kate de Selincourt, "Future Shock: Effects of Biotechnology on Developing Countries," *New Statesman & Society* 6(281)(December 3, 1993).

65. Robin Broad and John Cavanaugh, "Don't Neglect the Impoverished South's Developing Countries," *Foreign Policy,* December 22, 1995, pp. 18–27.

66. Quoted in Mary Ellen Curtin, "Harvesting Profitable Products from Plant Tissue Culture," *Bio/Technology* 1(1983): 657. See also, R. S. Chaleff, "Isolation of Agronomically Useful Mutants from Plant Cell Cultures," *Science* 219(1983): 676–82. ("With recognition of the similarities between cultured plant cells and microorganisms came the expectation that all the extraordinary feats of genetic experimentation accomplished with microbes would soon be realized with plants." Id. at 679. Chaleff enumerates the difficulties that must be resolved before this expectation may be fulfilled.)

67. Harriet Friedman, "The International Relations of Food: The Unfolding Crisis of National Regulation," in Barbara Harriss-White and Sir Raymond Hoffendberg, eds., *Food: Multidisciplinary Perspectives* (Oxford: Blackwell, 1994); at pp. 102–03.

68. Partha Dasgupta, Carl Folke, and Karl-Goren Maler, "The Environmental Resource Base of Human Welfare," *Population, Economic Development, and the Environment* (New York: Oxford University Press, 1994), p. 31.

69. Personal communication, April 2, 1997.

70. Norman Myers, "Population and Biodiversity" in Sir Francis Graham-Smith, ed., *Population: The Complex Reality* (Golden, CO: North American Press, 1994), pp. 117–136; quotation at p. 129.

71. Norman Myers, "The Question of Linkages in Environment and Development," *Bioscience* 43 (5) (May 1993), p. 306. See also, Norman Myers, "Population, Environment, Development," *Environmental Conservation* 20(3)(Autumn 1993), p. 205.

72. United Nations Development Programme (UNDP), *Human Development Report 1994* (New York: Oxford University Press, 1994), p. 2.

73. World Bank, *World Development Report: 1992* (New York: Oxford University Press, 1992), p. 29.

74. World Bank, *World Development Report: 1994* (New York: Oxford University Press, 1994), p. 1.

75. UNDP, *Human Development Report 1994*, esp. p. 35.

76. Benjamin R. Barber, "Jihad vs. McWorld," *The Atlantic Monthly* 269 (March, 1992), pp. 53–65; at p. 53.

77. Joseph Wood Krutch, *Thoreau: Walden and Other Writings* (New York: Bantam Books, 1965), p. 128.

78. Juliet B. Schor, *The Overworked American* (New York: Basic Books, 199 1), p. 11.

79. Paul Wachtel, "Consumption, Satisfaction and Self-Deception," paper presented at a conference on Consumption, Stewardship and the Good Life, University of Maryland, College Park, September 29–October 2, 1994, quotation at p. 5.

80. Robert E. Lane, "The Road Not Taken: Giving Friendship Priority Over Commodities," paper presented at a conference on Consumption, Global Stewardship and the Good Life, University of Maryland, College Park, MD, September 29–October 2, 1994; quotation at page 7.

81. Adam Smith, *The Theory of the Moral Sentiments,* D. D. Raphael and A. L. Macfie, eds., Oxford: Clarendon Press, 1976), Bk. IV, 1, 11, p. 185.

82. See John Maynard Keynes, "Economic Possibilities for Our Grandchildren" (1930), in Keynes, *Essays in Persuasion* (New York: Norton, 1963), pp. 366, 369–70, 372.

83. Robert H. Nelson, "In Memoriam: On the Death of the 'Market Mechanism,'" *Ecological Economics* 20(1997): 187–97; quotation at p. 188.

84. H. D. Thoreau, *The Journal of Henry David Thoreau,* vol. 10, ed. by Bradford Torrey and Francis H. Allen (Boston: Houghton Mifflin Company, 1949); quotation at page 252.

85. David Ehrenfeld, "Why Put a Value on Biodiversity?" in E. O. Wilson, ed., *Biodiversity* (Washington, DC: National Academy Press, 1988), pp. 212–216; quotation at p. 215.

86. Edward O. Wilson, *The Diversity of Life* (Cambridge, MA: Harvard University Press, 1992), p. 345.

87. John Stuart Mill, *Principles of Political Economy with Some of their Applications to Social Philosophy,* Book IV, chapter VI, Section 2 [1848] (Fairfield, NJ: Augustus M. Kelley Publishers, 1987), p. 750.

Letting the World Grow Old: An Ethos of Countermodernity

Freya Mathews

"Nature" is here understood, for environmental purposes, in terms of process rather than in terms of things: *nature* is whatever happens when we, or other agents with the capacity for abstract thought, let things be, let them unfold in their own way, run their own course. *Artifice,* in contrast, is understood as that which happens when such agents intentionally intervene to change the course of events for the sake of abstractly conceived ends of their own. From the viewpoint of this definition, the environmental ideal of "living with nature" or "returning to nature" implies an ethos of living within the framework of the given. Such an ethos seems conducive to the environmental goal of protecting the biosphere from the depredations of modern civilization, at any rate to the extent that it is arguable that, when all things are

Freya Mathews, "Letting the World Grow Old: An Ethos of Countermodernity," *Worldviews* 3 (1999), no. 2. Reprinted by permission of White Horse Press, Cambridge, U.K. Revised for this volume.

left to realize themselves in their own way, the life process on earth will in the long term be assured.[1] Modern civilization, on the other hand, rests on a deeply entrenched preference for artifice, for the abstractly imagined over the given, and the substitution of the possible—the planned, the "improved," the redesigned—for the actual.

LIVING WITH NATURE

The trap for environmentalists, in thinking about nature, has generally been to reify it, to conceive of it in terms of things rather than processes. When we think of it in this way, we understand it as consisting of all those things which are not the product of abstract human design: forests, swamps, mountains, oceans, etc. We then contrast nature with the human-made environment, consisting of cities, artefacts, technologies, etc. We make the same mistake in thinking about nature at the level of the self: the *natural* self is equated with the body, the instincts, intuitions, emotions etc., and this is contrasted with the civilized self, consisting of the controlled rational ego. The environmentalist's defence of nature is accordingly read as a project not only to save existing swamps, forests, etc., but to restore lost ones. Introspectively it is taken to imply a counter-cultural ethos of spontaneity, eros, intuitiveness and instinctuality. From the present point of view, this is a mistaken reading. To "return to nature" is not to restore a set of lost things or attributes, but rather to allow a certain process to begin anew. This is the process that takes over when we step back, when we cease intervening and making things over in accordance with our own abstract designs. Such a process can recommence anywhere, any time. It is not logically tied to those aspects of the world that we mistakenly reify as nature—the forests, swamps, instincts, bodily functions, etc.—but can start to unfold again in the midst of the most intensively urbanized and industrialized environments on earth and in the most controlled and civilized of persons.

In a world already urbanized, "returning to nature" means not tearing down the cities and factories, and planting woods and gardens in their stead.

Such action would merely perpetuate the cycle of making the world over in accordance with abstract designs—albeit in this case ecological designs—and would reinforce the mind-set involved in living against nature. Rather, "returning to nature" in an urbanized world means allowing this world to go its own way. It means letting the apartment blocks and warehouses and roads grow old. Yes, we shall have to maintain them, since we shall need to continue to use and inhabit them. Inhabitation will also call for adaptation and aesthetic enhancement. But this is compatible with a fundamental attitude of letting be, of acquiescence in the given, and of working within its terms of reference, rather than insisting upon further cycles of demolition and "redevelopment." Gradually such a world, left to grow old, rather than erased for the sake of something entirely new, will be absorbed into the larger process of life on earth. Concrete and bricks will become weathered and worn. Moss and ivy may take over the walls. Birds and insects may colonize overhangs and cavities within buildings. Green fingers will open up cracks in pavements. Bright surfaces will fade, acquiring natural patinas. Under the influence of gravity, the hard edges of modern architecture will soften, and imitate the moulded contours of landforms. Given time, everything is touched by the processes of life, and eventually taken over by them, to be fed into the cycle of decay and rebirth. Left to itself, the living world reclaims its own. Things which initially seemed discordant and out of place gradually fall into step with the rest of Creation. Old cars take their place beside old dogs and old trees; antiquity naturalizes even the most jarring of trash[2].

When the world is allowed to grow old, when things are retained, or left to unfold in their own way, then it is possible truly to *inhabit* places, to come to belong to them, in ways that are undreamt of in change-based societies. As years pass, and places retain their identities, they can, if we let them, come to be inscribed with our histories and the histories of our families and communities. They acquire meaning for us as our life experiences are woven into them. Here, on this road going down to the creek, where I walk my dog every week, is the house my great grandfather built. I have a faded photograph of it on lock-up day, sometime late in the 19th century. Around the corner is the store my grandfather ran, and over there is the park in which my parents walked, each evening, holding hands, for sixteen years. Here, alongside it, is the cemetery where I roamed in my gothic youth, looking for the grave of that same great grandfather, keeping trysts in the peppercorn groves, composing poems about roses. And it was along the tree-lined avenue at the edge of this cemetery that I pushed my baby son to creche. Layers and layers of significance accrete as our lives unfold amidst familiar spaces, significance that can for us never be reproduced in any other setting. The setting itself infiltrates our identity. This irreplaceable significance of our own place or places for us binds us to them. We become their natives.

This belonging is reinforced in another way when we let our world—whether urban or rural—grow old. For when the lay-out and structures and constellation of physical features that define a particular place are allowed to endure for a long time, then not only can it become interwoven with our individual and collective identity in a way that binds us to it, but, from a panpsychist point of view, *it* can come to know *us*. In time, and only in time, a place can, if we commit to it, come to accept us, open its arms to us, receive us—it agrees to be our place, attentive to us, attuned to us. We become its people. The land, or place, claims its own. It can never receive the casual or expedient sojourner or stranger in such familiar fashion. In this way too then, through time, and the reinhabitation of places that are allowed to be, we become native to our world.[3]

The self-realization of the biosphere—which is to say, the unfolding of nature on earth—involves a pattern of gradual but continuous change—a pattern of aging and decomposition followed by spontaneous reconstitution into new forms. This is what happens to things when we let them be. Artifice, as here understood, correspondingly consists in any regime of abrupt, wholesale change, change that involves the erasure of one environment, or order of things, and its replacement with an entirely new one. Such regimes generally come about only at the instigation of agents in the grip of abstract ideas or images which they are intent on actualizing irrespective of context—irrespective of what existed before and what surrounds the new "development." In this sense an old factory site, overlaid with grime and saturated with heavy metals, but in its cracks and neglected crannies also burgeoning with hardy and creative biological and social forms of life, is more natural than a town planner's lush park stocked with store-bought indigenous plants and subject to wholesale redesign or "redevelopment" at any time.

I should note here that by making the point that 'nature' in its deeper sense connotes not trees and grass and wildlife, but the processes which occur to any and all things when they are no longer subject to intentional control, I am by no means wanting to say that the conservation of trees and grass and wildlife—which is to say, environmentalism in its traditional form—becomes superfluous. Existing ecosystems should, like cities and selves, be allowed to unfold in their own way, free from undue human disturbance. Where such ecosystems have already been modified by the introduction of exotic species however, the present view entails that the new and old species should in principle—though there may be many countervailing considerations in practice—be left to sort it out. To respect nature in this connection does not imply that we should eradicate the exotics and restore the indigenous. It means that we should forego interventionist "management" and allow natural processes to reassert themselves. It may be deeply distressing to watch native plants and animals disappearing under the onslaught of aggressive invaders, and there may be many compassionate and practical reasons for attempting to temper this onslaught, but, to the extent that we opted out of the whole affair, we would at any rate have the satisfaction of knowing that what we were witnessing was in fact a return to nature. In this scenario it is likely that some of the original species would decline, and new ones would steal their niches, but as soon as competition had stabilized, speciation would begin again in situ, because we would no longer be intervening to reverse this trend.

A certain stepping back, then, is what is involved in 'returning to nature' in the outer world. At the level of self, making the transition from civilization to a more natural state is no more a matter of trying to reinstate an instinctual, free-and-easy, impulsive regime than returning the world to nature is a matter of restoring lost forests and swamps. To try to transform the tensed, guarded, rationally-minded self of civilized society in this way would only be to perpetuate the process of control—the process of making the self over to match a socially approved ideal. At deeper psychic, and perhaps somatic, levels, such an attempt, with the self-rejection it implies, would presumably only exacerbate the tension to which the self in question is subject. The way for a self-censoring self to "return to nature" is simply for it to stop altogether the business of attempting to make itself over in accordance with abstract ideals, and surrender instead to what it already is. When we give up being dissatisfied with ourselves, and reconcile ourselves to our "unnaturalness," our tedious uptightness, for instance, then, ironically, we start to relax anyway; as we stop forcing ourselves to follow the latest social prescriptions, our own instinctual conatus has a chance to make itself felt again. Gradually we become re-animated with our native will to self-realization.

The point I am making here, at the level of both self and world, is that it is never too late to return to nature. No matter how artificial our self or world has become, they can always, at any given moment, become subject again to natural processes, simply by our decision to call a halt to "development" and "progress" and "self improvement," and to allow things to remain as they are, to be retained rather than replaced. In saying this I am not of course intending to ban change altogether, but to insist that change should not disrupt the general unfolding of things. It should not raze the old and superimpose on the space that is left something unrelated to what preceded it. Change should carry us gently and smoothly into the future, respecting the cycles of creation, decay and regeneration. It should grow from within the shell of the given.

It might be objected at this point that the attitude of letting things be that I am recommending here is too passive to be of use to the environment movement, that in the end it amounts to little more than a laissez-faire acquiescence in the political status quo. To dispel this fear, let me explain in a little more detail how such an attitude would, if adopted by a significant proportion of the populace, in its quiet way thoroughly disable the present world-destroying order of capitalism, by systematically negating the following values on which that order rests.

Consumerism. When we embrace those things that are already at hand, we do not seek to replace them with new ones. Such embracing of the given is thus an antidote to the culture of disposability and conspicuous consumption fostered by capitalism. From the viewpoint of letting things be, we would be most pleased, not with our brightest and newest things, but with those that were our oldest and most well-worn, things which had long figured in our lives, and mingled their identity and destiny with ours. "Keeping up with the Joneses," if it applied at all in the letting-be scenario, would entail having fewer and older things than the Joneses. (Of course it would not apply, since in the new scenario we would not be measuring ourselves against the kind of social expectations personified by the Joneses.) Acquisitiveness, and hence consumerism, melt away in the face of an attitude of letting be.

Commodification. When we value things and places for the meaning that our own lives have invested in them, via our relationship with them, this removes them from the market place. They cannot be replaced by other things and places, even things and places of the same type, since the substitutes will not share our history nor hence be imbued with the same meaning for us. From this point of view, I could no more buy or sell things or places which had become part of the landscape of my life, part of my very identity, than I could buy or sell members of my family. Thus the pool of commodities is continually diminished.

Productivity. When we embrace the world as it is, and are no longer forever seeking to make it better, according to abstract (generally egocentric or anthropocentric) conceptions of the good, then greed is effectively abolished. We no longer crave bigger and better houses, cars, roads, cities, whatever. We are instead attached to what is already given. There is thus no call for ever-increasing productivity.

Progress. When people no longer believe that the world can always be improved, the slate wiped clean and a better world, a better society, inscribed on it, then the ideological rationalization for capitalism viz that it can continue to improve peoples' 'standard of living' indefinitely, collapses.

Efficiency. In late capitalism, efficiency—patently a notion pertaining to means—has acquired an almost fetishistic status. Tools (where this includes all kinds of techniques and procedures as well as implements and technologies) are valued not so much for what they do as for their efficiency, and they are retained only so long as their efficiency is perceived as maximal. When the attitude of letting be is assumed however, tools are valued not merely for their efficiency, but for their meaning. I may continue to use an old plough, or a leaky fountain pen, or a certain laborious method for making dough, simply because this is the plough, or pen, or method, that my mother or grandfather used. Efficiency may still be a consideration, but it will be only one factor determining the means I choose to achieve my ends.

Industry/business. These are the two definitive modalities of capitalism—industriousness and busyness—both connoting a certain kind of externally driven, externally focussed, hectic state of doing or acting. Those who are busy and industrious act on the world, they take initiatives and make things happen. When we assume the attitude of letting be however, we let the world do the doing, and we fit in with it. We favour "inaction,"[4] which is not passivity, but action which is effortless because emanating from our own conatus and meshed with the conatus of other beings rather than driven by external social expectations or ideologies.

Development. When we understand "development" in terms of the transformation and regeneration that eventually transpires when things are left to grow old, to unfold in their own way, then we will not tolerate the erasure of the given which is the precondition and prelude to "development" in the capitalist sense, i.e., the replacement of the given by the decontextualized abstractly imagined new.

Profit. If we do elect to let things be, it is on the assumption, as I explained earlier, that nature knows best—that nature, left to itself, conserves itself, does not exhaust itself, but rather replenishes itself, in ac-

cordance with the law of birth, decay and rebirth. To sustain itself in this way, nature returns *everything* to the life cycle, it recycles everything. There is no "surplus" in this system, and hence no accumulation. The law of return makes nonsense of the notion of "profit." "Profit" in one part of the system merely signals loss and depletion in another part.

Automation. For the capitalist, labour is merely a means to production; if automation provides a cheaper, more efficient means, it will be preferred. From the viewpoint of letting things be, human labour is, or can be, a vehicle for meaning. Things become significant to us partly as a result of our building, making, repairing or decorating them ourselves. How much more of a presence in our lives is a church—like the Russian Orthodox Church in my neighbourhood—which is built by the hands of the parishioners themselves, over a period of many years, than one which is contracted out to professional builders and erected "efficiently" in eight weeks. To "mix our labour" with things is, as Locke said, though with entirely different intent, to make them ours, in a sense analogous to that in which our family is ours. To make things ourselves, or to have them made by the hands of others, then, is in certain respects preferable, from the present point of view, to mechanization of the processes of production.

Property. When people honour the world as it is—honour its immanent telos, its capacity to unfold in its own way—they no longer seek to *own* the world, but rather to *belong* to it. They belong to their world by being faithful to the things it contains, keeping and tending them and letting the world manifest through them as they endure. The world expresses itself, reveals itself, through the changes it induces in these things, through the lichen on the walls, the cracks in the glaze, the slow, stooping, inevitable return to earth. By continually replacing things we never witness the way the world reclaims its own, so we miss out on knowing it, encountering it. Strangers to the world, we do not belong, we are anything but natives. We comport ourselves as invaders, conquerors, buying up the matter which means nothing to us, and trashing it when we are tired of it. We treat ourselves, our own bodies, in the same way, truculently professing to own them and reluctant to allow them to be reclaimed by the world, reluctant to see the world tenderly revealing itself to us through them, through the fading and crazywork and mute surrender of flesh to gravity. But of course, at the final call, the world claims us anyway, and we go, back into the earth, but no wiser, and a lot lonelier, strangers to the end.

To assume a panpsychist worldview, and to express this worldview via an attitude of letting be, is thus inevitably to extricate oneself, to a significant degree, from the ideological grid of capitalism. It is to begin to shift towards an entirely different form of praxis and of management of the material dimension of life—in other words, to an entirely different "economics," or way of ensuring the satisfaction of our material wants and needs. Since economics involves a certain engagement, on our part, with the world of matter, an economics with panpsychist presuppositions will obviously differ from an economics based on a mechanistic worldview. For when the material world is viewed as a subject, or as a manifold of subjects, then economics constitutes an opportunity for encounter: the ways in which we utilize matter must not conflict with, but enhance, our intersubjective engagement with it. An economics in accordance with the principle of letting be is an economics of the given, an economics which respects the world as it is, and finds metaphysical sufficiency in it.

THE POLITICS OF REINHABITATION

I have argued that when we assume the attitude of letting things be, we cease to be interested in consumerism and the pursuit of wealth and become defectors from capitalism. We become children of nature again, true natives, of our cities, of our world. When a significant proportion of the population adopts this attitude, the capitalist system, robbed of its consumers, would presumably wither away. But is such "inaction" enough? In a society in which this is not the majority position, a society dedicated to relentless progress and development, with the insatiable bulldozers and chainsaws and toxic spills that

this entails, can we stand by and "do nothing"? Wouldn't our attitude of letting things be merely abet the destruction in this scenario? Isn't *resistance* rather than acceptance the appropriate political response to a system which will not let things be?

I think there is indeed a place for resistance in the politics of letting be. The impulse to let things be, after all, springs from cherishing the given, embracing the world as it is. This commitment to the given is primarily a commitment to *things,* to concrete particulars and places. It implies a commitment to protect those things and places against arbitrary erasure undertaken for the sake of abstract ideals. We will thus defend the things and places to which we have pledged our loyalty, and we will do so, not in the name of an abstract ideology, but simply because a world which is allowed to grow old claims us as its own, and we shall spring to its defence as surely as natives have perennially sprung to the defence of their lands.

But how can we neo-natives, a tiny minority, conduct such defence against the forces of capitalism? Our defensive resources are no greater than those of a small country facing a large-scale foreign invasion. But just as civilian defence seems to be the principal strategy for small populations in this situation, so such a form of defence might provide a key to imagining resistance from the perspective of letting things be. Civilian defence, of course, involves bands of individuals from the occupied territories withdrawing to secret, often inaccessible, locations in the countryside or city, and, through sniping and ambush, making it impossible for the invaders to move freely through the occupied regions. By analogy, followers of the politics of letting be could block the expansionism of capitalist interests by *reinhabiting* places earmarked for the inevitable "development."

What does reinhabitation mean in this context? It signifies people acknowledging particular places as the inalienable landscape of their lives. Just as civilian defence requires of citizens that they get to know the lie of their own land intimately, so that they can live off it, and disappear into it when the heat is on, so the politics of reinhabitation requires of its followers that they explore and research their own homeplace or region thoroughly, discovering its secrets and substrata, checking titles offices and municipal and historical records, for instance, so that the offensives of planners and developers can be anticipated. It involves finding means of sustenance, on every level, within their own neighbourhood. To reinhabit place in this way is to enter into an indissoluble metaphysical relationship with it. And to acknowledge the metaphysical relation between people and places is to begin to resacralize those places, a resacralization which can be consummated and proclaimed in art and poetry, in festivals and ritual performances. Every place could eventually, in principle, be thus "sung up," and assume the status of a sacred site for some band of people, a site sacralized and immortalized in song, verse and dance.

To reinhabit the world in this way, ensuring that every place was unnegotiably, metaphysically home to someone, would provide a formidable obstacle to a system which has relied, for its justification, on its rendition of the entire world as, at a metaphysical level, a vast *terra nullius,* spiritually belonging to no-one, and hence up for grabs. If each place had its own true inhabitants, who could demonstrate its unique metaphysical significance for them, and who could not be bought out or "compensated," where would the developers go? The rules of the capitalist game no longer allow, at least explicitly, for bona fide natives simply to be shot, or forcibly removed. Their relationship to place has to be accommodated. So a politics of reinhabitation calls for us to find creative and forceful ways of both re-establishing and proclaiming ourselves as natives in the midst of the industrial and urban devastation of the world today. It also calls on us to recognize that global capitalism represents nothing short of an *invasion* of our world, and requires that we organize and comport ourselves with corresponding tenacity in our world's defence.

FROM MODERNITY TO COUNTERMODERNITY

From a panpsychist perspective, respect for nature, as we have seen, is not a matter of protecting only ecosystems, but *all* material things, from undue human disturbance, including things that do not usually arouse the concern of environmentalists, even non-anthropocentric environmentalists, such as deep ecologists. This view of nature, and what it is to live with rather than against it, implies an ethos that is far more encompassing than that of the traditional environment movement. It is an ethos as encompassing in fact as the ethos of modernity that it seeks to reverse. For the hallmark of modernity is radical change—in the form of development, control, management, design, intervention, progress, improvement, even salvation. (This is reflected in the very etymology of the word, "modern," which is derived from "mode," meaning "of the present," as in "a la mode," keeping up with the latest. Modernity is that period which can be characterized in terms of its commitment to the ever-emerging new, its dissatisfaction with the given, its radical discontinuity with the past and its dissociation from tradition.) The ethos of letting be challenges modernity head on, trusting as it does the innate wisdom of things, and eschewing as it does the definitive ambition of modernity, to remake the world in accordance with abstract ideas. From the present point of view, not only is environmentalism, even in its deep-ecological forms, missing the larger metaphysical picture in its approach to modernity; it is also itself deeply entangled or imbued with the modernist ethos in its understanding of its own mission; it needs to extricate its legitimate concern for nature from heroic modernist assumptions about its own world-changing, world-saving role.

I am suggesting that instead of perpetuating this profoundly modernist ethos of changing or saving the world, the environment movement could assume what I would venture to describe as a *counter*modern attitude of letting things be. We could step right outside the presuppositions of modernity, and dare *not* to try to make things better, at any rate if "making things better" is a rationalization for continually replacing one regime with another. When we say, "let's fix the world up—let's pull down these slummy old tenement blocks and build a brand new eco-permacultural-urban-village in their stead"—we are just as much in the grip of the old ethos of domination and control as the city fathers were. We are rejecting the given in favour of an abstract or imagined alternative of our own—we are refusing to "let things be"—and it is this hubristic mentality which is the motor of modern civilization and the source of the environmental crisis. In remaining in the grip of the old ethos, in nursing the desire to make things better, we are simply continuing to water the deeper modernist roots of the present predatory economic system.

An ethos which tries to avoid the pitfalls of this mentality will, of course, be an ethos of conservatism rather than radicalism. This conservatism has always been implicit in the environment movement, as plainly betokened by the fact that the term "conservation" is often regarded as synonymous with "environmentalism." However, such conservatism does not imply that the attitude of letting be is aligned with the political right. The political right has historically, of course, been conservative, that is, committed to the given, while the left has been opposed to the given, and committed to the abstract possible or ideal. The historical right however, though conservative, differed from the present position inasmuch as it was socially rather than ontologically motivated—it was at heart a defence of social, political and economic privilege, rather than a defence of the world for its own sake. In other words, the right insisted on the preservation of traditions and institutions because it was through these traditions and institutions that the upper classes retained their privileges. A degree of ontological conservatism—the conservation of architecture and landscapes, for instance—was implicit in this position, but this ontological conservatism was in reality a mere spin-off from a self-interested politics of oppression. The historical left rejected this politics of oppression, and demanded the overthrow—and ongoing readjustment—of the existing social order, in order to end the systematic privileging of the powerful few at the expense of the many. This revolutionary or radical politics however sustained an unremitting antagonism not only to traditions and institutions, but to the world that these traditions and institutions had built,

and this legacy has served, in the long run, to legitimate a rapacious contempt for the given in all its social and ontological forms, where this contempt is the hallmark of late capitalist modernity.

The attitude of letting things be, in contrast, is conservative out of genuine respect for the world, for the capacity of things to unfold in their own way. Its conservatism is ontologically rather than socially motivated, and it extends primarily to material things rather than to cultures, traditions and social institutions.[5] This attitude certainly does not spring from a desire to preserve the privileges of the few, as that of the historical right has done. Indeed, it tends, almost incidentally, towards a de facto form of nonhierarchism, inasmuch as it is antithetical to the accumulation of wealth, as I have explained above. It achieves this "equalizing" effect, however, without recourse to the radicalism, to the ethos of intervention and overthrow, of the historical left. So, without itself resorting to the ideality of morality, the ethos of letting be reconciles something of the custodial role of the right with something of the moral intent of the left. In this respect it is in fact the reverse image of the market-driven politics which is achieving hegemony in the industrialized world today, and which is also neither of the left nor the right. This latter politics—the new "economism"—combines the old rightwing investment in the perpetuation of minority privilege, and moral indifference to the suffering of the majority, with the old radicalism of the left, its dissatisfaction with the given, and its dedication to building ever new, ever more extravagant, worlds. In other words, "economism" has managed to combine the downsides of both the right and the left. In this unholy new regime, nothing is sacred, everything—every being, every object, every place, every institution, every element of culture and society, every relationship—is subject to obliteration or co-optation by a commerce that sustains fewer and fewer. The attitude of letting things be effectively inverts this nightmare and, by stepping outside the game of left and right altogether, inadvertently combines the essence of the upside of each of the old right and left.

The aim of such a conservative ethos then is not a brave new world, but an old world, a world unfolding naturally, redolent with meaning, beauty, and its own life and terms. The only way of achieving such a world, without engaging in further interventions, is, as I have explained, to let the present world grow old—to let the cities weather and fade, and the ivy creep up the walls.

That the ethos of letting be is *counter*- rather than *post*-modern is clear from the fact that its opposition to modernity is based not on the deconstruction of metaphysics, as postmodernism is, but on the substitution of some version of panpsychist metaphysics, broadly construed, for the materialist metaphysics of modernity. The project of modernity—of remaking the world according to our own abstract specifications—rests on the materialist assumption that matter is sheer externality, devoid of its own informing telos—putty for us to shape to our own designs. The relativist outlook of postmodernity presents no challenge to this view: by insisting on the entitlement of different cultures to live by their own metaphysical lights, postmodernists imply that there is no way the world is in itself, and to that extent they indirectly underwrite the message of modernity: the world has no informing meaning or purpose of its own. It follows from the meta-level assumptions of postmodernism then, just as it follows from the object-level assumptions of mechanism, that we can do with the world as we will. The present position overturns both these sets of assumptions, and thus puts an end to the project of modernity, by reintegrating human subjectivity and agency into the subjectivity and agency of a re-awakened world.

DISCOVERING THE TAO IN AUSTRALIA

The position that I have outlined in this paper is basically a Taoist one. Nature, according to my definition, is more or less equivalent to the Tao: it is the wise way the world unfolds when left to its own devices (Mathews 1996). The Taoism of Lao Tzu does not announce itself as panpsychist, but clearly a world animated by the Tao is one which is possessed of some intelligent inner principle, a principle that can be trusted to guide us into the deepest channels of life.

It is not my place to comment in detail here on the affinities between the broadly Taoist attitude of letting be and certain fundamental characteristics of Aboriginal thought. Suffice it to say that Aboriginal cultures evince a powerful engagement with the given that ensures their continuity with their own past but also their flexibility in the face of an almost unimaginable scale of externally imposed change. For while not *craving* the possible and the ideal, they exhibit a genius for accommodating the new once it has become actual. One of the flashpoints in the evolution of my own thinking occurred when a non-indigenous friend who had married into an Aboriginal family in the far north-west of Australia told me about an elder there who included *motorboats* in his Dreaming stories. Years later I happened to find myself living for a while in the very community to which the old man—by now deceased—had belonged, and I was enchanted by the way in which the people in this community refused nothing. They accepted—though they never craved—anything and everything that drifted their way, all the trappings and junk of modern civilization. But in the process of accepting this tawdry stuff, they also uncannily Aboriginalized it, so that it assumed an entirely different significance in the context of their community from its intended significance within the framework of a capitalist culture. Somehow, through this affectionate trust in the given, the everyday was rendered numinously spiritual, and the spiritual unpretentiously everyday.

Mary Graham has declared that one of the most taken-for-granted assumptions of Aboriginal thought is that spirit is real; another is that land is all there is (Graham 1992). That is to say, spirit has a status, in Aboriginal thought, as incontestable as that of energy and matter; and, since there is no heaven and hell, and since theories and ideas, however dazzling, are not real, land is ultimately the only thing that exists. If "land" is expanded to encompass the concrete given—all that is actual in a physical sense—then I think that the attitude of letting be follows from these twin premises: spirit animates the given rather than existing in the realm of the abstract, so we connect with spirit by engaging—and not unnecessarily interfering—with the given. By embracing the given even in its most adulterated forms, we reinhabit our own contemporary, mundane reality in the same kind of profound way that traditional Aboriginal peoples inhabited their reality, the still edenic land.

Aboriginal peoples learned to inhabit the real rather than escaping into the ideal by remaining attuned to the wisdom that this peaceful old land imparts to those who pay attention to it. I believe that my own early glimpses of this way of living came to me not in the first instance through explicit Aboriginal influences—though these influences later helped to bring it to consciousness—but through the opportunities for such attentiveness that were vouchsafed me as a child. Born into this intimately companionable land that has for so long been singing along, humming along, with its human inhabitants, non-Aboriginal Australians might also, if we collectively pause to feel the resonance of the endlessly poetic communiques that surround us, rediscover, in a contemporary context, some of the fundamental aspects of the Aboriginal relation to the world.

REFERENCES

Mary Graham, 1992, interviewed on *Aboriginal Perspectives,* Caroline Jones and Stephen Godley, ABC Religious Program.

Freya Mathews, "The Soul of Things," *Terra Nova* 1 (1996): 4, pp 55–64.

Freya Mathews, "Letting the World Grow Old: an Ethos of Countermodernity," *Worldviews* 3 (1999): 2.

Deborah Bird Rose, *Dingo Makes Us Human* (Cambridge: Cambridge University Press, 1992).

NOTES

1. This position is to a certain extent arguable from evolutionary premises, but it is more deeply tenable from a metaphysical position that I describe as broadly *panpsychist*, i.e., a position which imputes an underlying capacity for self-realization to material reality. It is the rejection of this kind of metaphysical position which, I argue, underlies the profoundly interventionist and instrumentalist ethos of modernity. For further discussion of this point, see the original version of this paper in *Worldviews* 3, 2, 1999, and a book, still in preparation, entitled *Reinhabiting Reality*.

2. I have observed a similar attitude to junk and rubbish in Aboriginal communities in Australia. Lots of litter and old machinery and cars and fridges and so on are left lying around in some of the remoter communities, apparently on the assumption that these things, like all others, have their place in the world, so there is no point in pretending that they do not exist by putting them out of sight. They will in time, again like everything else, be received back into the land, back into the cycles of life.

3. For a comparable account of the way the land claims its native sons and daughters in the Aboriginal world, see Deborah Bird Rose 1992.

4. I intend "inaction" here in the Taoist sense of the term.

5. There is a great deal more to be said than I can say here concerning the ultimate scope of the principle of letting be. On the face of it, the principle should apply only to concrete things, because its justification is that concrete things have their own informing principles of unfolding, principles that are clearly not possessed by ideas or abstract things. However, in social and cultural contexts, no clearcut division can be made between ideality and concreteness, since ideas inform the corporeality of human beings and their built environments. A more extended discussion of the scope of the principle of letting be is included in the book in preparation (entitled *Reinhabiting Reality*) from which this paper is extracted. For present purposes it will suffice to emphasize the ontological rather than the sociocultural scope of the principle.

Chapter 8
Ecofeminism in Theory and Practice

Questions for Reflection and Discussion

Dichotomies

Ecofeminism is one of the more controversial subfields in environmental ethics. Outside academia, though, there is no denying that a practical fusion is occurring between environmental ethics and women's liberation. It is not just an academic discussion. One of the most exciting recent developments in ecofeminism is that it is taking shape as a practical movement. As Rukmini Rao and Gita Sen explain, women in developing countries are seeing links between oppression of women and devastation of their natural environment, and realizing they can make changes. They are not powerless. This section is a transition from the more theoretical concerns of the first part of this book to the more policy-oriented concerns of the second part.

1. Different societies may come more or less close to overcoming their tendencies to oppress women and minorities. Different societies may come more or less close to developing sustainable relationships with their environment. It is fruitful to study the empirical connections between progress on these two fronts. For example, the education and emancipation of women in developing countries seems to go hand in hand with declining rates of population growth.

Karen Warren presents ecofeminism as the view that the oppression of women and the domination of nature do not merely *happen* to go hand in hand. Instead, there is a *conceptual* connection. How should we understand this? Is it a conceptual error to be a feminist without being an environmentalist, or vice versa? Most Western societies made dramatic progress over the past century toward improving the status of women. Is it *automatic* that these same societies also made dramatic progress toward developing a sustainable relationship with their natural environment? If not, what are the real connections between the domination/liberation of nature and the oppression/liberation of women?

2. Our ability to separate the world into logically complementary categories is one of the most natural and fruitful thought patterns we have. Ecofeminists, though, warn against

thinking in terms of dichotomies: male/female, oppressor/oppressed, and so on. But dichotomy thinking is not easy to transcend. For better or worse, it is natural to divide the world into those who are on our side and those who are not, and to see the latter category as consisting of people who are bad. Often enough, such thinking falls into the category of what we call *false* dichotomy.

Is dichotomy thinking all bad? When is it legitimate, and when not, to think in terms of dichotomies? Are all dichotomies false dichotomies? What does Karen Warren say?

Feminism and Ecofeminism

Kristen Hessler and Elizabeth Willott

In 1848, in Seneca Falls, New York, at a convention on women's rights, women's rights activist Elizabeth Cady Stanton proposed the radical idea that women should be given the right to vote. In her "Declaration of Sentiments" (modeled on the Declaration of Independence), Stanton declared: "Now, in view of this entire disenfranchisement of one-half the people of this country . . . and because women do feel themselves aggrieved, oppressed, and fraudulently deprived of their most sacred rights, we insist that they have immediate admission to all the rights and privileges which belong to them as citizens of the United States."[1] This convention is generally viewed as the official beginning of the women's rights movement in the United States. In 1920, after more than seventy years of feminist activism and lobbying against severe resistance from both men and women, women finally received the right to vote.

Liberal feminists believe the best way to combat women's oppression is to continue to seek equal rights for women, just as early American feminists sought the right to vote. This variant of feminism is based on the ideals of liberalism, the political ideology that emphasizes individual freedom—usually understood as individual rights—and the political equality of all citizens. Liberal feminism is a mod-

erate doctrine in the sense that, at least in liberal democracies, it does not advocate a social revolution for the sake of women's liberation. Instead, liberal feminists believe women's liberation consists in gaining equal status and rights for women within a liberal society.

Radical feminists, by contrast, see the domination of women by men as so basic that merely reforming the existing political or social structure will not eliminate women's oppression. Therefore, they advocate revolutionary social change for the sake of women's liberation. Many radical feminists argue that fundamental changes in our basic values are necessary for the liberation of women. They point out that women's lives traditionally have been private— concerned with the home and the family. In contrast, men have occupied the public realm, including most professions and government. Some radical feminists believe that, instead of seeking equality for women in the public realm, feminists should work to change our values so we ascribe positive value to the traditional roles of women.

Gains in women's status have not come easily. Women in the United States had to fight for the right to own property on the same terms as men. They had to fight to change laws that, as recently as the 1980s, made it impossible for a man to be charged with raping his wife.[2] Feminists are still working to improve representation of women in their governments, to end discrimination and sexual harassment in the workplace, to combat rape and domestic abuse, and to create arrangements for raising families so that women who choose to raise children are not disadvantaged in work.

Much progress has been made, not only in Western democracies, but much work still needs to be done. Asian women no longer have their feet mutilated. On the other hand, thousands of Asian women and girls each year are kidnapped or sold into forced prostitution or domestic slavery, often with the tacit permission of police.[3] In most countries, female genital mutilation[4] has been made illegal. On the other hand, it still occurs. In some countries, women are at risk of being killed by their families if even suspected of impermissible sexual conduct, and in some cases, the best protection the legal system can offer is to put a woman in jail, where her family cannot get to her. Some women have been in jail for years.[5]

In some countries, women have lost ground. In the mid-1990s, women in Afghanistan lost their right to work outside the home, attend university, and even to leave their houses without a male relative. They must wear clothing that covers them from head to foot; an ankle or wrist exposed can lead to a vicious public beating by members of the Department for the Propagation of Virtue and the Suppression of Vice. Prior to these decrees, women comprised 40 percent of the physicians in the capital city Kabul; in September 1997, not only were women forbidden to work as physicians in the hospitals, they were also banned as patients. Instead, a single, poorly equipped, clinic was to serve all 500,000 women who lived in the city. Because of international outcry, that has been rescinded—by May 1998, women are officially granted limited access to health care in all but military hospitals and some female health care providers were permitted to return to work.[6]

Feminist theory asks why and how women are oppressed. **Feminist activism** tries to do something about it: educating people about women's subordination and its causes, and teaching them how to resist in a constructive way. In feminism, as in other social movements, theory and activism usually work together; activism often is informed by theory, and theory often is a product of the systematic thinking of concerned and engaged activists.

Ecofeminism is short for "ecological feminism." Whether radical or liberal, ecofeminists share a belief that the oppression of women is in some way linked to the domination of nature. Ecofeminist theorists are still working on accounts of how these oppressions are linked. Some ecofeminists think men's psychology drives men to oppress both women and nature. Others argue that Western society has traditionally identified women with nature, and devalued both compared to men and culture.

Ecofeminism has prompted examination of several issues: Are attitudes toward women similar to attitudes toward nature? Can nature be oppressed in the same ways that people, specifically women, can be oppressed? What should we make of the fact that women have contributed to the disappearance of wilderness and other environmental damage? Are strategies designed to liberate women, but which ignore environmental degradation bound to fail in the long-term? Are strategies designed to preserve the environment, but which ignore the domination of women destined—or at least more likely—to fail? Do we need to care about both the domination of women and the environment, simultaneously, to achieve optimal results for either? Ecofeminist theorists continue to work on answers to such questions. Meanwhile, ecofeminist activists are working to protect our environment, as well as to combat the oppression of women.

NOTES

1. Elizabeth Cady Stanton, "Declaration of Sentiments," *Women's Rights Conventions: Seneca Falls and Rochester 1848* (New York: Arno and The New York Times, 1969), 7.

2. Diana H. Russell, *Rape in Marriage* [expanded and revised edition] (Bloomington: Indiana University Press, 1990), 21.

3. *Human Rights Watch Global Report on Women's Human Rights* (New York: Human Rights Watch, 1995), Ch. 4. Indeed, the police are sometimes customers at brothels where women are forced to work, or they capture women who escape and return them to the brothels.

4. Female genital mutilation refers to surgical removal of the clitoris. However, the "surgery" is sometimes performed without anesthetic and under highly unsterile conditions.

5. Douglas Jehl, "Arab Honor's Price: A Woman's Blood," *New York Times* (June 20, 1999), 1

6. Zohra Rasekh, Heidi M. Bauer, M. Michele Manos, and Vincent Iacopino, "Women's Health and Human

Rights in Afghanistan," *Journal of the American Medical Association* 280 (2000): 449–55. The situation for men is also horrific: men can be beaten if their beards are not long enough and for other spurious reasons. Also see U.S. Department of State. Bureau of Democracy, Human Rights, and Labor. *Country Reports on Human Rights Practices for 1999—Afghanistan* (U.S. Dept. of State, February 2000) http://www.usis.usemb.se/human/human1999/afghanis.html

The Power and the Promise of Ecological Feminism

Karen J. Warren

Ecological feminism is the position that there are important connections—historical, symbolic, theoretical—between the domination of women and the domination of nonhuman nature. I argue that because the conceptual connections between the dual dominations of women and nature are located in an oppressive patriarchal conceptual framework characterized by a logic of domination, (1) the logic of traditional feminism requires the expansion of feminism to include ecological feminism, and (2) ecological feminism provides a framework for developing a distinct feminist environmental ethic. I conclude that any feminist theory and any environmental ethic which fails to take seriously the interconnected domination of women and nature is simply inadequate.

INTRODUCTION

Ecological feminism (ecofeminism) has begun to receive a fair amount of attention lately as an alternative feminism and environmental ethic. Since Francoise d'Eaubonne introduced the term *ecofeminisme* in 1974 to bring attention to women's potential for bringing about an ecological revolution,[1] the term has been used in a variety of ways. As I use the term in this paper, ecological feminism is the position that there are important connections—historical, experiential, symbolic, theoretical—between the domination of women and the domination of nature, an understanding of which is crucial to both feminism and environmental ethics. I argue that the promise and power of ecological feminism is that *it provides a*

Karen J. Warren, "The Power and the Promise of Ecological Feminism," *Environmental Ethics* 12 (1990): 125–46. Reprinted with permission of the author and the journal.

distinctive framework both for reconceiving feminism and for developing an environmental ethic which takes seriously connections between the domination of women and the domination of nature. I do so by discussing the nature of a feminist ethic and the ways in which ecofeminism provides a feminist and environmental ethic. I conclude that any feminist theory *and* any environmental ethic which fails to take seriously the twin and interconnected dominations of women and nature is at best incomplete and at worst simply inadequate.

FEMINISM, ECOLOGICAL FEMINISM, AND CONCEPTUAL FRAMEWORKS

Whatever else it is, feminism is at least the movement to end sexist oppression. It involves the elimination of any and all factors that contribute to the continued and systematic domination or subordination of women. While feminists disagree about the nature of and solutions to the subordination of women, all feminists agree that sexist oppression exists, is wrong, and must be abolished.

A "feminist issue" is any issue that contributes in some way to understanding the oppression of women. Equal rights, comparable pay for comparable work, and food production are feminist issues wherever and whenever an understanding of them contributes to an understanding of the continued exploitation or subjugation of women. Carrying water and searching for firewood are feminist issues wherever and whenever women's primary responsibility for these tasks contributes to their lack of full participation in decision making, income producing, or high status positions engaged in by men. What counts as a feminist issue, then, depends largely on context, particularly the historical and material conditions of women's lives.

Environmental degradation and exploitation are feminist issues because an understanding of them contributes to an understanding of the oppression of women. In India, for example, both deforestation and reforestation through the introduction of a monocul-ture species tree (e.g., eucalyptus) intended for commercial production are feminist issues because the loss of indigenous forests and multiple species of trees has drastically affected rural Indian women's ability to maintain a subsistence household. Indigenous forests provide a variety of trees for food, fuel, fodder, household utensils, dyes, medicines, and income-generating uses, while monoculture-species forests do not.[2] Although I do not argue for this claim here, a look at the global impact of environmental degradation on women's lives suggests important respects in which environmental degradation is a feminist issue.

Feminist philosophers claim that some of the most important feminist issues are *conceptual* ones: these issues concern how one conceptualizes such mainstay philosophical notions as reason and rationality, ethics, and what it is to be human. Ecofeminists extend this feminist philosophical concern to nature. They argue that, ultimately, some of the most important connections between the domination of women and the domination of nature are conceptual. To see this, consider the nature of conceptual frameworks.

A *conceptual framework* is a set of *basic* beliefs, values, attitudes, and assumptions which shape and reflect how one views oneself and one's world. It is a socially constructed lens through which we perceive ourselves and others. It is affected by such factors as gender, race, class, age, affectional orientation, nationality, and religious background.

Some conceptual frameworks are oppressive. An *oppressive conceptual framework* is one that explains, justifies, and maintains relationships of domination and subordination. When an oppressive conceptual framework is *patriarchal,* it explains, justifies, and maintains the subordination of women by men.

I have argued elsewhere that there are three significant features of oppressive conceptual frameworks: (1) value-hierarchical thinking, i.e., "up-down" thinking which places higher value, status, or prestige on what is "up" rather than on what is "down"; (2) value dualisms, i.e., disjunctive pairs in which the disjuncts are seen as oppositional (rather than as complementary) and exclusive (rather than as inclusive), and which place higher value (status, prestige) on one disjunct rather than the other (e.g., dualisms which give higher value or status to that which has historically been identified as "mind," "reason," and "male" than to that which has historically been identified as "body," "emotion," and "female"); and (3) logic of domination, i.e., a structure of argumentation which leads to a justification of subordination.

The third feature of oppressive conceptual frameworks is the most significant. A logic of domination is not *just* a logical structure. It also involves a substantive value system, since an ethical premise is needed to permit or sanction the "just" subordination of that which is subordinate. This justification typically is given on grounds of some alleged characteristic (e.g., rationality) which the dominant (e.g., men) have and the subordinate (e.g., women) lack.

Contrary to what many feminists and ecofeminists have said or suggested, there maybe nothing *inherently* problematic about "hierarchical thinking" or even "value-hierarchical thinking" in contexts other than contexts of oppression. Hierarchical thinking is important in daily living for classifying data, comparing information, and organizing material. Taxonomies (e.g., plant taxonomies) and biological nomenclature seem to require *some* form of "hierarchical thinking." Even "value-hierarchical thinking" may be quite acceptable in certain contexts. (The same may be said of "value dualisms" in non-oppressive contexts). For example, suppose it is true that what is unique about humans is our conscious capacity to radically reshape our social environments (or "societies"), as Murray Bookchin suggests.[3] Then one could truthfully say that humans are better equipped to radically reshape their environments than are rocks or plants—a "value-hierarchical" way of speaking.

The problem is not simply *that* value-hierarchical thinking and value dualisms are used, but *the way* in which each has been used *in oppressive conceptual frameworks* to establish inferiority and to justify subordination.[4] It is the logic of domination, *coupled with* value-hierarchical thinking and value dualisms,

which "justifies" subordination. What is explanatorily basic, then, about the nature of oppressive conceptual frameworks is the logic of domination.

For ecofeminism, that a logic of domination is explanatorily basic is important for at least three reasons. First, without a logic of domination, a description of similarities and differences would be just that—a description of similarities and differences. Consider the claim, "Humans are different from plants and rocks in that humans can (and plants and rocks cannot) consciously and radically reshape the communities in which they live; humans are similar to plants and rocks in that they are both members of an ecological community." Even if humans are "better" than plants and rocks with respect to the conscious ability of humans to radically transform communities, one does not *thereby* get any *morally* relevant distinction between humans and nonhumans, or an argument for the domination of plants and rocks by humans. To get *those* conclusions one needs to add at least two powerful assumptions, viz. (A2) and (A4), in argument A below:

(A1) Humans do, and plants and rocks do not, have the capacity to consciously and radically change the community in which they live.

(A2) Whatever has the capacity to consciously and radically change the community in which it lives is morally superior to whatever lacks this capacity.

(A3) Thus, humans are morally superior to plants and rocks.

(A4) For any X and Y, if X is morally superior to Y, then X is morally justified in subordinating Y.

(A5) Thus, humans are morally justified in subordinating plants and rocks.

Without the two assumptions that *humans are morally superior* to (at least some) nonhumans, (A2), and that *superiority justifies subordination,* (A4), all one has is some difference between humans and some nonhumans. This is true *even if* that difference is given in terms of superiority. Thus, it is the logic of domination, (A4), which is the bottom line in ecofeminist discussions of oppression.

Second, ecofeminists argue that, at least in Western societies, the oppressive conceptual framework which sanctions the twin dominations of women and nature is a patriarchal one characterized by all three features of an oppressive conceptual framework. Many ecofeminists claim that, historically, within at least the dominant Western culture, a patriarchal conceptual framework has sanctioned the following argument B:

(B1) Women are identified with nature and the realm of the physical; men are identified with the "human" and the realm of the mental.

(B2) Whatever is identified with nature and the realm of the physical is inferior to ("below") whatever is identified with the "human" and the realm of the mental; or, conversely, the latter is superior to ("above") the former.

(B3) Thus, women are inferior to ("below") men; or, conversely, men are superior to ("above") women.

(B4) For any X and Y, if X is superior to Y, then X is justified in subordinating Y.

(B5) Thus, men are justified in subordinating women.

If sound, argument B establishes *patriarchy,* i.e., the conclusion given at (B5) that the systematic domination of women by men is justified. But according to ecofeminists, (B5) is justified by just those three features of an oppressive conceptual framework identified earlier: value-hierarchical thinking, the assumption at (B2); value dualisms, the assumed dualism of the mental and the physical at (B1) and the assumed inferiority of the physical vis-à-vis the mental at (B2); and a logic of domination, the assumption at (B4), the same as the previous premise (A4). Hence, according to ecofeminists, insofar as an oppressive patriarchal conceptual framework has functioned historically (within at least dominant Western culture) to sanction the twin dominations of women and nature (argument B), both argument B and the patriarchal conceptual framework, from whence it comes, ought to be rejected.

Of course, the preceding does not identify which premises of B are false. What is the status of premises (B1) and (B2)? Most, if not all, feminists claim that (B1), and many ecofeminists claim that (B2), have been assumed or asserted within the dominant Western philosophical and intellectual tradition. As such, these feminists assert, as a matter of historical fact, that the dominant Western philosophical tradition has assumed the truth of (B1) and (B2). Ecofeminists, however, either deny (B2) or do not affirm (B2). Furthermore, because some ecofeminists are anxious to deny any ahistorical identification of women with nature, some ecofeminists deny (B1) when (B1) is used to support anything other than a strictly historical claim about what has been asserted or assumed to be true within patriarchal culture—e.g., when (B1) is used to assert that women properly are identified with the realm of nature and the physical. Thus, from an ecofeminist perspective, (B1) and (B2) are properly viewed as problematic though historically sanctioned claims: they are problematic precisely because of the way they have functioned historically in a patriarchal conceptual framework and culture to sanction the dominations of women and nature.

What *all* ecofeminists agree about, then, is the way in which *the logic of domination* has functioned historically within patriarchy to sustain and justify the twin dominations of women and nature.[5] Since *all* feminists (and not just ecofeminists) oppose patriarchy, the conclusion given at (B5), all feminists (including ecofeminists) must oppose at least the logic of domination, premise (B4), on which argument B rests—whatever the truth-value status of (B1) and (B2) *outside of* a patriarchal context.

That *all* feminists must oppose the logic of domination shows the breadth and depth of the ecofeminist critique of B: it is a critique not only of the three assumptions on which this argument for the domination of women and nature rests, viz., the assumptions at (B1), (B2), and (B4); it is also a critique of patriarchal conceptual frameworks generally, i.e., of those oppressive conceptual frameworks which put men "up" and women "down," allege some way in which women are morally inferior to men, and use that alleged difference to justify the subordination of women by men. Therefore, ecofeminism is necessary to *any* feminist critique of patriarchy, and, hence, necessary to feminism (a point I discuss again later).

Third, ecofeminism clarifies why the logic of domination, and any conceptual framework which gives rise to it, must be abolished in order both to make possible a meaningful notion of difference which does not breed domination and to prevent feminism from becoming a "support" movement based primarily on shared experiences. In contemporary society, there is no one "woman's voice," no *woman* (or *human*) *simpliciter:* every woman (or human) is a woman (or human) of some race, class, age, affectional orientation, marital status, regional or national background, and so forth. Because there are no "monolithic experiences" that all women share, feminism must be a "solidarity movement" based on shared beliefs and interests rather than a "unity in sameness" movement based on shared experiences and shared victimization.[6] In the words of Maria Lugones, "Unity—not to be confused with solidarity—is understood as conceptually tied to domination."[7]

Ecofeminists insist that the sort of logic of domination used to justify the domination of humans by gender, racial or ethnic, or class status is also used to justify the domination of nature. Because eliminating a logic of domination is part of a feminist critique—whether a critique of patriarchy, white supremacist culture, or imperialism—ecofeminists insist that *naturism* is properly viewed as an integral part of any feminist solidarity movement to end sexist oppression and the logic of domination which conceptually grounds it.

ECOFEMINISM RECONCEIVES FEMINISM

The discussion so far has focused on some of the oppressive conceptual features of patriarchy. As I use the phrase, the "logic of traditional feminism" refers to the location of the conceptual roots of sexist op-

pression, at least in Western societies, in an oppressive patriarchal conceptual framework characterized by a logic of domination. Insofar as other systems of oppression (e.g., racism, classism, ageism, heterosexism) are also conceptually maintained by a logic of domination, appeal to the logic of traditional feminism ultimately locates the basic conceptual interconnections among *all* systems of oppression in the logic of domination. It thereby explains at a *conceptual* level why the eradication of sexist oppression requires the eradication of the other forms of oppression. It is by clarifying this conceptual connection between systems of oppression that a movement to end sexist oppression—traditionally the special turf of feminist theory and practice—leads to a reconceiving of feminism as *a movement to end all forms of oppression.*

Suppose one agrees that the logic of traditional feminism requires the expansion of feminism to include other social systems of domination (e.g., racism and classism). What warrants the inclusion of nature in these "social systems of domination"? Why must the logic of traditional feminism include the abolition of "naturism" (i.e., the domination or oppression of nonhuman nature) among the "isms" feminism must confront? The conceptual justification for expanding feminism to include ecofeminism is twofold. One basis has already been suggested: by showing that the conceptual connections between the dual dominations of women and nature are located in an oppressive and, at least in Western societies, patriarchal conceptual framework characterized by a logic of domination, ecofeminism explains how and why feminism, conceived as a movement to end sexist oppression, must be expanded and reconceived as also a movement to end naturism. This is made explicit by the following argument C:

(C1) Feminism is a movement to end sexism.
(C2) But sexism is conceptually linked with naturism (through an oppressive conceptual framework characterized by a logic of domination).
(C3) Thus, feminism is (also) a movement to end naturism.

Because, ultimately, these connections between sexism and naturism are conceptual—embedded in an oppressive conceptual framework—the logic of traditional feminism leads to the embrace of ecological feminism.

The other justification for reconceiving feminism to include ecofeminism has to do with the concepts of gender and nature. Just as conceptions of gender are socially constructed, so are conceptions of nature. Of course, the claim that women and nature are social constructions does not require anyone to deny that there are actual humans and actual trees, rivers, and plants. It simply implies that *how* women and nature are conceived is a matter of historical and social reality. These conceptions vary cross-culturally and by historical time period. As a result, any discussion of the "oppression or domination of nature" involves reference to historically specific forms of social domination of nonhuman nature by humans, just as discussion of the "domination of women" refers to historically specific forms of social domination of women by men. Although I do not argue for it here, an ecofeminist defense of the historical connections between the dominations of women and of nature, claims (B1) and (B2) in argument B, involves showing that within patriarchy the feminization of nature and the naturalization of women have been crucial to the historically successful subordinations of both.[8]

If ecofeminism promises to reconceive traditional feminism in ways which include naturism as a legitimate feminist issue, does ecofeminism also promise to reconceive environmental ethics in ways which are feminist? I think so. This is the subject of the remainder of the paper.

CLIMBING FROM ECOFEMINISM TO ENVIRONMENTAL ETHICS

Many feminists and some environmental ethicists have begun to explore the use of first-person narrative as a way of raising philosophically germane issues in ethics often lost or underplayed in mainstream philosophical ethics. Why is this so? What is it about narrative which makes it a significant resource for theory and practice in feminism and environmental ethics? Even if appeal to first-person narrative is a helpful literary device for describing ineffable experience or a legitimate social science methodology for documenting personal and social history, how is first-person narrative a valuable vehicle of argumentation for ethical decision making and theory building? One fruitful way to begin answering these questions is to ask them of a particular first-person narrative.

Consider the following first-person narrative about rock climbing:

For my very first rock climbing experience, I chose a somewhat private spot, away from other climbers and on-lookers. After studying "the chimney," I focused all my energy on making it to the top. I climbed with intense determination, using whatever strength and skills I had to accomplish this challenging feat. By midway I was exhausted and anxious. I couldn't see what to do next—where to put my hands or feet. Growing increasingly more weary as I clung somewhat desperately to the rock, I made a move. It didn't work. I fell. There I was, dangling midair above the rocky ground below, frightened but terribly relieved that the belay rope had held me. I knew I was safe. I took a look up at the climb that remained. I was determined to make it to the top. With renewed confidence and concentration, I finished the climb to the top.

On my second day of climbing, I rappelled down about 200 feet from the top of the Palisades at Lake Superior to just a few feet above the water level. I could see no one—not my belayer, not the other climbers, no one. I unhooked slowly from the rappel rope and took a deep cleansing breath. I looked all around me—really looked—and listened. I heard a cacophony of voices—birds, trickles of water on the rock before me, waves lapping against the rocks below. I closed my eyes and began to feel the rock with my hands—the cracks and crannies, the raised lichen and mosses, the almost imperceptible nubs that might provide a resting place for my fingers and toes when I began to climb. At that moment I was bathed in serenity. I began to talk to the rock in an almost inaudible, child-like way, as if the rock were my friend. I felt an overwhelming sense of gratitude for what it offered me—a chance to know myself and the rock differently, to appreciate unforeseen miracles like the tiny flowers growing in the even tinier cracks in the rock's surface, and to come to know a sense of *being in relationship* with the natural environment. It felt as if the rock and I were silent conversational partners in a longstanding friendship. I realized then that I had come to care about this cliff which was so different from me, so unmovable and invincible, independent and seemingly indifferent to my presence. I wanted to be with the rock as I climbed. Gone was the determination to conquer the rock, to forcefully impose my will on it; I wanted simply to work respectfully with the rock as I climbed. And as I climbed, that is what I felt. I felt myself *caring* for this rock and feeling thankful that climbing provided the opportunity for me to know it and myself in this new way.

There are at least four reasons why use of such a first-person narrative is important to feminism and environmental ethics. First, such a narrative gives voice to a felt sensitivity often lacking in traditional analytical ethical discourse, viz., a sensitivity to conceiving of oneself as fundamentally "in relationship with" others, including the nonhuman environment. It is a modality which *takes relationships themselves seriously*. It thereby stands in contrast to a strictly reductionist modality that takes relationships seriously only or primarily because of the nature of the *relators* or parties to those relationships (e.g., relators conceived as moral agents, right holders, interest carriers, or sentient beings). In the rock-climbing narrative above, it is the climber's relationship with the rock she climbs which takes on special significance—which is itself a locus of value—in addition to whatever moral status or moral considerability she or the rock or any other parties to the relationship may also have.

Second, such a first-person narrative gives expression to a variety of ethical attitudes and behaviors often overlooked or underplayed in mainstream Western ethics, e.g., the difference in attitudes and behaviors toward a rock when one is "making it to the top" and when one thinks of oneself as "friends

with" or "caring about" the rock one climbs.[9] These different attitudes and behaviors suggest an ethically germane contrast between two different types of relationship humans or climbers may have toward a rock: an imposed conqueror-type relationship, and an emergent caring-type relationship. This contrast grows out of, and is faithful to, felt, lived experience.

The difference between conquering and caring attitudes and behaviors in relation to the natural environment provides a third reason why the use of first-person narrative is important to feminism and environmental ethics: it provides a way of conceiving of ethics and ethical meaning as *emerging out of* particular situations moral agents find themselves in, rather than as being *imposed on* those situations (e.g., as a derivation or instantiation of some predetermined abstract principle or rule). This emergent feature of narrative centralizes the importance of *voice*. When a multiplicity of cross-cultural *voices* are centralized, narrative is able to give expression to a range of attitudes, values, beliefs, and behaviors which may be overlooked or silenced by imposed ethical meaning and theory. As a reflection of and on felt, lived experiences, the use of narrative in ethics provides a stance from which ethical discourse can be held accountable to the historical, material, and social realities in which moral subjects find themselves.

Lastly, and for our purposes perhaps most importantly, the use of narrative has argumentative significance. Jim Cheney calls attention to this feature of narrative when he claims, "To contextualize ethical deliberation is, in some sense, to provide a narrative or story, from which the solution to the ethical dilemma emerges as the fitting conclusion."[10] Narrative has argumentative force by suggesting *what counts* as an appropriate conclusion to an ethical situation. One ethical conclusion suggested by the climbing narrative is that what counts as a proper ethical attitude toward mountains and rocks is an attitude of respect and care (whatever that turns out to be or involve), not one of domination and conquest.

In an essay entitled "In and Out of Harm's Way: Arrogance and Love," feminist philosopher Marilyn Frye distinguishes between "arrogant" and "loving" perception as one way of getting at this difference in the ethical attitudes of care and conquest.[11] Frye writes:

> The loving eye is a contrary of the arrogant eye.
>
> The loving eye knows the independence of the other. It is the eye of a seer who knows that nature is indifferent. It is the eye of one who knows that to know the seen, one must consult something other than one's own will and interests and fears and imagination. One must look at the thing. One must look and listen and check and question.
>
> The loving eye is one that pays a certain sort of attention. This attention can require a discipline but *not* a self-denial. The discipline is one of self-knowledge, knowledge of the scope and boundary of the self. . . . In particular, it is a matter of being able to tell one's own interests from those of others and of knowing where one's self leaves off and another begins. . . .
>
> The loving eye does not make the object of perception into something edible, does not try to assimilate it, does not reduce it to the size of the seer's desire, fear and imagination, and hence does not have to simplify. It knows the complexity of the other as something which will forever present new things to be known. The science of the loving eye would favor The Complexity Theory of Truth [in contrast to The Simplicity Theory of Truth] and presuppose The Endless Interestingness of the Universe.[12]

According to Frye, the loving eye is not an invasive, coercive eye which annexes others to itself, but one which "knows the complexity of the other as something which will forever present new things to be known."

When one climbs a rock as a conqueror, one climbs with an arrogant eye. When one climbs with a loving eye, one constantly "must look and listen and check and question." One recognizes the rock as something very different, something perhaps totally indifferent to one's own presence, and finds in that difference joyous occasion for celebration. One knows "the boundary of the self," where the self—the "I," the climber—leaves off and the rock begins. There is no fusion of two into one, but a complement of two entities *acknowledged* as separate, different, independent, yet *in relationship;* they are in relationship *if only* because the loving eye is perceiving it, responding to it, noticing it, attending to it.

An ecofeminist perspective about both women and nature involves this shift in attitude from "arrogant perception" to "loving perception" of the non-human world. Arrogant perception of nonhumans by humans presupposes and maintains *sameness* in such a way that it expands the moral community to those beings who are thought to resemble (be like, similar to, or the same as) humans in some morally significant way. Any environmental movement or ethic based on arrogant perception builds a moral hierarchy of beings and assumes some common denominator of moral considerability in virtue of which like beings deserve similar treatment or moral consideration and unlike beings do not. Such environmental ethics are or generate a "unity in sameness." In contrast, "loving perception" presupposes and maintains *difference*—a distinction between the self and other, between human and at least some nonhumans—in such a way that perception of the other as other *is* an expression of love for one who/which is recognized at the outset as independent, dissimilar, different. As Maria Lugones says, in loving perception, "Love is seen not as fusion and erasure of difference but as incompatible with them."[13] "Unity in sameness" alone is an *erasure of difference.*

"Loving perception" of the nonhuman natural world is an attempt to understand what it means *for humans* to care about the nonhuman world, a world *acknowledged* as being independent, different, perhaps even indifferent to humans. Humans *are* different from rocks in important ways, even if they are also both members of some ecological community. A moral community based on loving perception of oneself *in relationship with* a rock, or with the natural environment as a whole, is one which acknowledges and respects difference, whatever "sameness" also exists.[14] The limits of loving perception are determined only by the limits of one's (e.g., a person's, a community's) ability to respond lovingly (or with appropriate care, trust, or friendship)—whether it is to other humans or to the non-human world and elements of it.[15]

If what I have said so far is correct, then there are very different ways to climb a mountain and *how* one climbs it and *how* one narrates the experience of climbing it matter ethically. If one climbs with "arrogant perception," with an attitude of "conquer and control," one keeps intact the very sorts of thinking that characterize a logic of domination and an oppressive conceptual framework. Since the oppressive conceptual framework which sanctions the domination of nature is a patriarchal one, one also thereby keeps intact, even if unwittingly, a patriarchal conceptual framework. Because the dismantling of patriarchal conceptual frameworks is a feminist issue, *how* one climbs a mountain and *how* one narrates— or tells the story—about the experience of climbing also are *feminist issues*. In this way, ecofeminism makes visible why, at a conceptual level, environmental ethics is a feminist issue. I turn now to a consideration of ecofeminism as a distinctively feminist and environmental ethic.

ECOFEMINISM AS A FEMINIST AND ENVIRONMENTAL ETHIC

A feminist ethic involves a twofold commitment to critique male bias in ethics wherever it occurs, and to develop ethics which are not male-biased. Sometimes this involves articulation of values (e.g., values of care, appropriate trust, kinship, friendship) often lost or underplayed in mainstream ethics.[16] Sometimes it involves engaging in theory building by pioneering in new directions or by revamping old theories in gender sensitive ways. What makes the critiques of old theories or conceptualizations of new ones "feminist" is that they emerge out of sex-gender analyses and reflect whatever those analyses reveal about gendered experience and gendered social reality.

As I conceive feminist ethics in the pre-feminist present, it rejects attempts to conceive of ethical theory in terms of necessary and sufficient conditions, because it assumes that there is no essence (in the sense of some transhistorical, universal, absolute abstraction) of feminist ethics. While attempts to formulate joint necessary and sufficient conditions of a feminist ethic are unfruitful, nonetheless, there are some necessary conditions, what I prefer to call "boundary conditions," of a feminist ethic. These boundary conditions clarify some of the minimal conditions of a feminist ethic without suggesting that feminist ethics has some ahistorical essence. They are like the boundaries of a quilt or collage. They delimit the territory of the piece without dictating what the interior, the design, the actual pattern of the piece looks like. Because the actual design of the quilt emerges from the multiplicity of voices of women in a cross-cultural context, the design will change over time. It is not something static.

What are some of the boundary conditions of a feminist ethic? First, nothing can become part of a feminist ethic—can be part of the quilt—that promotes sexism, racism, classism, or any other "isms" of social domination. Of course, people may disagree about what counts as a sexist act, racist attitude, classist behavior. What counts as sexism, racism, or classism may vary cross-culturally. Still, because a feminist ethic aims at eliminating sexism and sexist bias, and (as I have already shown) sexism is intimately connected in conceptualization and in practice to racism, classism, and naturism, a feminist ethic must be anti-sexist, anti-racist, anti-classist, anti-naturist and opposed to any "ism" which presupposes or advances a logic of domination.

Second, a feminist ethic is a *contextualist* ethic. A contextualist ethic is one which sees ethical discourse and practice as emerging from the voices of people located in different historical circumstances. A contextualist ethic is properly viewed as a *collage* or *mosaic*, a *tapestry* of voices that emerges out of felt experiences. Like any collage or mosaic, the point is not to have *one picture* based on a unity of voices, but a *pattern* which emerges out of the very different voices of people located in different circumstances. When a contextualist ethic is *feminist*, it gives central place to the voices of women.

Third, since a feminist ethic gives central significance to the diversity of women's voices, a feminist ethic must be structurally pluralistic rather than unitary or reductionistic. It rejects the assumption that there is "one voice" in terms of which ethical values, beliefs, attitudes, and conduct can be assessed.

Fourth, a feminist ethic reconceives ethical theory as theory in process which will change over time. Like all theory, a feminist ethic is based on some generalizations.[17] Nevertheless, the generalizations associated with it are themselves a pattern of voices within which the different voices emerging out of concrete and alternative descriptions of ethical situations have meaning. The coherence of a feminist theory so conceived is given within a historical and conceptual context, i.e., within a set of historical, socioeconomic circumstances (including circumstances of race, class, age, and affectional orientation) and within a set of basic beliefs, values, attitudes, and assumptions about the world.

Fifth, because a feminist ethic is contextualist, structurally pluralistic, and "in-process," one way to evaluate the claims of a feminist ethic is in terms of their *inclusiveness:* those claims (voices, patterns of voices) are morally and epistemologically favored (preferred, better, less partial, less biased) which are more inclusive of the felt experiences and perspectives of oppressed persons. The condition of inclusiveness requires and ensures that the diverse voices of women (as oppressed persons) will be given legitimacy in ethical theory building. It thereby helps to minimize empirical bias, e.g., bias rising from faulty or false generalizations based on stereotyping, too small a sample size, or a skewed sample. It does so by ensuring that any generalizations which are made about ethics and ethical decision making include—indeed cohere with—the patterned voices of women.[18]

Sixth, a feminist ethic makes no attempt to provide an "objective" point of view, since it assumes that in contemporary culture there really is no such point of view. As such, it does not claim to be "unbiased" in the sense of "value-neutral" or "objective." However, it does assume that whatever bias it has as an ethic centralizing the voices of oppressed persons is a *better bias*—"better" because it is more inclusive and therefore less partial—than those which exclude those voices.[19]

Seventh, a feminist ethic provides a central place for values typically unnoticed, underplayed, or misrepresented in traditional ethics, e.g., values of care, love, friendship, and appropriate trust.[20] Again, it need not do this at the exclusion of considerations of rights, rules, or utility. There may be many contexts in which talk of rights or of utility is useful or appropriate. For instance, in contracts or property relationships, talk of rights may be useful and appropriate. In deciding what is cost effective or advantageous to the most people, talk of utility may be useful and appropriate. In a feminist *qua* contextualist ethic, whether or not such talk is useful or appropriate depends on the context; *other values* (e.g., values of care, trust, friendship) are *not* viewed as reducible to or captured solely in terms of such talk.

Eighth, a feminist ethic also involves a reconception of what it is to be human and what it is for humans to engage in ethical decision making, since it rejects as either meaningless or currently untenable any gender-free or gender-neutral description of humans, ethics, and ethical decision making. It thereby rejects what Alison Jaggar calls "abstract individualism," i.e., the position that it is possible to identify a human essence or human nature that exists independently of any particular historical context.[21] Humans and human moral conduct are properly understood essentially (and not merely accidentally) in terms of networks or webs of historical and concrete relationships.

All the props are now in place for seeing how ecofeminism provides the framework for a distinctively feminist and environmental ethic. It is a feminism that critiques male bias wherever it occurs in ethics (including environmental ethics) and aims at providing an ethic (including an environmental ethic) which is not male biased—and it does so in a way that satisfies the preliminary boundary conditions of a feminist ethic.

First, ecofeminism is quintessentially anti-naturist. Its anti-naturism consists in the rejection of any way of thinking about or acting toward nonhuman nature that reflects a logic, values, or attitude of domination. Its anti-naturist, anti-sexist, anti-racist, anti-classist (and so forth, for all other "isms" of social domination) stance forms the outer boundary of the quilt: nothing gets on the quilt which is naturist, sexist, racist, classist, and so forth.

Second, ecofeminism is a contextualist ethic. It involves a shift *from* a conception of ethics as primarily a matter of rights, rules, or principles predetermined and applied in specific cases to entities viewed as competitors in the contest of moral standing, *to* a conception of ethics as growing out of what Jim Cheney calls "defining relationships," i.e., relationships conceived in some sense as defining who one is. As a contextualist ethic, it is not that rights, or rules, or principles are *not* relevant or important. Clearly they are in certain contexts and for certain purposes. It is just that what *makes* them relevant or important is that those to whom they apply are entities *in relationship with* others.

Ecofeminism also involves an ethical shift *from* granting moral consideration to nonhumans *exclusively* on the grounds of some similarity they share with humans (e.g., rationality, interests, moral agency, sentiency, rightholder status) *to* "a highly contextual account to see clearly what a human being is and what the nonhuman world might be, morally speaking, *for* human beings."[22] For an ecofeminist, *how* a moral agent is in relationship to another becomes of central significance, not simply *that* a moral agent is a moral agent or is bound by rights, duties, virtue, or utility to act in a certain way.

Third, ecofeminism is structurally pluralistic in that it presupposes and maintains difference—difference among humans as well as between humans and at least some elements of nonhuman nature. Thus, while ecofeminism denies the "nature/culture" split, it affirms that humans are both members of an ecological community (in some respects) and different from it (in other respects). Ecofeminism's attention to relationships and community is not, therefore, an erasure of difference but a respectful acknowledgment of it.

Fourth, ecofeminism reconceives theory as theory in process. It focuses on patterns of meaning which emerge, for instance, from the storytelling and first-person narratives of women (and others) who deplore the twin dominations of women and nature. The use of narrative is one way to ensure that the content of the ethic—the pattern of the quilt—may/will change over time, as the historical and material realities of women's lives change and as more is learned about women-nature connections and the destruction of the nonhuman world.

Fifth, ecofeminism is inclusivist. It emerges from the voices of women who experience the harmful domination of nature and the way that domination is tied to their domination as women. It emerges from listening to the voices of indigenous peoples such as Native Americans who have been dislocated from their land and have witnessed the attendant undermining of such values as appropriate reciprocity, sharing, and kinship that characterize traditional Indian culture. It emerges from listening to voices of those who, like Nathan Hare, critique traditional approaches to environmental ethics as white and bourgeois, and as failing to address issues of "black ecology" and the "ecology" of the inner city and urban spaces.[23] It also emerges out of the voices of Chipko women who see the destruction of "earth, soil, and water" as intimately connected with their own inability to survive economically.[24] With its emphasis on inclusivity and difference, ecofeminism provides a framework for recognizing that what counts as ecology and what counts as appropriate conduct toward both human and nonhuman environments is largely a matter of context.

Sixth, as a feminism, ecofeminism makes no attempt to provide an "objective" point of view. It is a social ecology. It recognizes the twin dominations of women and nature as social problems rooted both in very concrete, historical, socioeconomic circumstances and in oppressive patriarchal conceptual frameworks which maintain and sanction these circumstances.

Seventh, ecofeminism makes a central place for values of care, love, friendship, trust, and appropriate reciprocity—values that presuppose that our relationships to others are central to our understanding of who we are.[25] It thereby gives voice to the sensitivity that in climbing a mountain, one is doing something in relationship with an "other," an "other" whom one can come to care about and treat respectfully.

Lastly, an ecofeminist ethic involves a reconception of what it means to be human, and in what human ethical behavior consists. Ecofeminism denies abstract individualism. Humans are who we are in large part by virtue of the historical and social contexts and the relationships we are in, including our relationships with nonhuman nature. Relationships are not something extrinsic to who we are, not an "add on" feature of human nature; they play an essential role in shaping what it is to be human. Relationships of humans to the nonhuman environment are, in part, constitutive of what it is to be a human.

By making visible the interconnections among the dominations of women and nature, ecofeminism shows that both are feminist issues and that explicit acknowledgment of both is vital to any responsible environmental ethic. Feminism *must* embrace ecological feminism if it is to end the domination of women because the domination of women is tied conceptually and historically to the domination of nature.

A responsible environmental ethic also *must* embrace feminism. Otherwise, even the seemingly most revolutionary, liberational, and holistic ecological ethic will fail to take seriously the interconnected dominations of nature and women that are so much a part of the historical legacy and conceptual framework that sanctions the exploitation of nonhuman nature. Failure to make visible these interconnected, twin dominations results in an inaccurate account of how it is that nature has been and continues to be dominated and exploited and produces an environmental ethic that lacks the depth necessary to be truly *inclusive* of the realities of persons who at least in dominant Western culture have been intimately tied with that exploitation, viz., women. Whatever else can be said in favor of such holistic ethics, a failure to make visible ecofeminist insights into the common denominators of the twin oppressions of women and nature is to perpetuate, rather than overcome, the source of that oppression.

This last point deserves further attention. It may be objected that as long as the end result is "the same"—the development of an environmental ethic which does not emerge out of or reinforce an oppressive conceptual framework—it does not matter whether that ethic (or the ethic endorsed in getting there) is feminist or not. Hence, it simply is *not* the case that any adequate environmental ethic must be feminist. My argument, in contrast, has been that it *does* matter, and for three important reasons. First, there is the scholarly issue of accurately representing historical reality, and that, ecofeminists claim, requires acknowledging the historical feminization of nature and naturalization of women as part of the exploitation of nature. Second, I have shown that the conceptual connections between the domination of women and the domination of nature are located in an oppressive and, at least in Western societies, patriarchal conceptual framework characterized by a logic of domination. Thus, I have shown that failure to notice the nature of this connection leaves at best an incomplete, inaccurate, and partial account of what is required of a conceptually adequate environmental ethic. An ethic which *does not* acknowledge this is simply *not* the same as one that does, whatever else the similarities between them. Third, the claim that, in contemporary culture, one can have an adequate environmental ethic which is *not* feminist assumes that, in contemporary culture, the label *feminist* does not add anything crucial to the nature or description of environmental ethics. I have shown that at least in contemporary culture this is false, for the word *feminist* currently helps to clarify just *how* the domination of nature is conceptually linked to patriarchy and, hence, how the liberation of nature, is conceptually linked to the termination of patriarchy. Thus, because it has critical bite in contemporary culture, it serves as an important reminder that in contemporary sex-gendered, raced, classed, and naturist culture, an unlabeled position functions as a privileged and "unmarked" position. That is, without the addition of the word *feminist,* one presents environmental ethics as if it has no bias, including male-gender bias, which is just what ecofeminists deny: failure to notice the connections between the twin oppressions of women and nature *is* male-gender bias.

One of the goals of feminism is the eradication of all oppressive sex-gender (and related race, class, age, affectional preference) categories and the creation of a world in which *difference does not breed domination*—say, the world of 4001. If in 4001 an "adequate environmental ethic" is a "feminist environmental ethic," the word *feminist* may then be redundant and unnecessary. However, this is *not* 4001, and in terms of the current historical and conceptual reality the dominations of nature and of women are intimately connected. Failure to notice or make visible that connection in 1990 perpetuates the mistaken (and privileged) view that "environmental ethics" is *not* a feminist issue, and that *feminist* adds nothing to environmental ethics.

CONCLUSION

I have argued in this paper that ecofeminism provides a framework for a distinctively feminist and environmental ethic. Ecofeminism grows out of the felt and theorized about connections between the domination of women and the domination of nature. As a contextualist ethic, ecofeminism refocuses environmental ethics on what nature might mean, morally speaking, *for* humans, and on how the relational attitudes of humans to others—humans as well as nonhumans—sculpt both what it is to be human and the nature and ground of human responsibilities to the nonhuman environment. Part of what this refocusing does is to take seriously the voices of women and other oppressed persons in the construction of that ethic.

A Sioux elder once told me a story about his son. He sent his seven-year-old son to live with the child's grandparents on a Sioux reservation so that he could "learn the Indian ways." Part of what the grandparents taught the son was how to hunt and kill the four leggeds of the forest. As I heard the story, the boy was taught, "to shoot your four-legged brother in his hind area, slowing it down but not killing it. Then, take the four legged's head in your hands, and look

into his eyes. The eyes are where all the suffering is. Look into your brother's eyes and feel his pain. Then, take your knife and cut the four-legged under his chin, here, on his neck, so that he dies quickly. And as you do, ask your brother, the four-legged, for forgiveness for what you do. Offer also a prayer of thanks to your four-legged kin for offering his body to you just now, when you need food to eat and clothing to wear. And promise the four-legged that you will put yourself back into the earth when you die, to become nourishment for the earth, and for the sister flowers, and for the brother deer. It is appropriate that you should offer this blessing for the four-legged and, in due time, reciprocate in turn with your body in this way, as the four-legged gives life to you for your survival." As I reflect upon that story, I am struck by the power of the environmental ethic that grows out of and takes seriously narrative, context, and such values and relational attitudes as care, loving perception, and appropriate reciprocity, and doing what is appropriate in a given situation—however that notion of appropriateness eventually gets filled out. I am also struck by what one is able to see, once one begins to explore some of the historical and conceptual connections between the dominations of women and of nature. A *re-conceiving* and *re-visioning* of both feminism and environmental ethics, is, I think, the power and promise of ecofeminism.

NOTES

1. Francoise d'Eaubonne, *Le Feminisme ou la Mort* (Paris: Pierre Horay, 1974), pp. 213–52.

2. I discuss this in my paper, "Toward an Ecofeminist Ethic."

3. Murray Bookchin, "Social Ecology versus 'Deep Ecology,'" in *Green Perspectives: Newsletter of the Green Program Project,* no. 4–5 (Summer 1987): 9.

4. It may be that in contemporary Western society, which is so thoroughly structured by categories of gender, race, class, age, and affectional orientation, that there simply is no meaningful notion of "value-hierarchical thinking" which does not function in an oppressive context. For purposes of this paper, I leave that question open.

5. I make no attempt here to defend the historically sanctioned truth of these premises.

6. See, e.g., Bell Hooks, *Feminist Theory: From Margin to Center* (Boston: South End Press, 1984), pp. 51–52.

7. Maria Lugones, "Playfulness, 'World-Travelling,' and Loving Perception," *Hypatia* 2, no. 2 (Summer 1987): 3.

8. See, e.g., Gray, *Green Paradise Lost;* Griffin, *Women and Nature;* Merchant, *The Death of Nature;* and Ruether, *New Woman/New Earth.*

9. It is interesting to note that the image of being friends with the Earth is one which cytogeneticist Barbara McClintock uses when she describes the importance of having "a feeling for the organism," "listening to the material [in this case the corn plant]," in one's work as a scientist. See Evelyn Fox Keller, "Women, Science, and Popular Mythology," in *Machina Ex Dea: Feminist Perspectives on Technology,* ed. Joan Rothschild (New York: Pergamon Press, 1983), and Evelyn Fox Keller, *A Feeling For the Organism: The Life and Work of Barbara McClintock* (San Francisco: W. H. Freeman, 1983).

10. Cheney, "Eco-Feminism and Deep Ecology," 144.

11. Marilyn Frye, "In and Out of Harm's Way: Arrogance and Love," *The Politics of Reality* (Trumansburg, NY: The Crossing Press, 1983), pp. 66–72.

12. Ibid., pp. 75–76.

13. Maria Lugones, "Playfulness," p. 3.

14. Cheney makes a similar point in "Eco-Feminism and Deep Ecology," p. 140.

15. Ibid., p. 138.

16. This account of a feminist ethic draws on my paper "Toward an Ecofeminist Ethic."

17. Marilyn Frye makes this point in her illuminating paper, "The Possibility of Feminist Theory," read at the American Philosophical Association Central Division Meetings in Chicago, 29 April–1 May 1986. My discussion of feminist theory is inspired largely by that paper and by Kathryn Addelson's paper "Moral Revolution," in *Women and Values: Reading in Recent Feminist Philosophy,* ed. Marilyn Pearsall (Belmont, CA: Wadsworth Publishing Co., 1986), pp. 291–309.

18. Notice that the standard of inclusiveness does not exclude the voices of men. It is just that those voices must cohere with the voices of women.

19. For a more in-depth discussion of the notions of impartiality and bias, see my paper, "Critical Thinking and Feminism," *Informal Logic* 10, no. 1 (Winter 1988): 31–44.

20. The burgeoning literature on these values is noteworthy. See, e.g., Carol Gilligan, *In a Different Voice: Psychological Theories and Women's Development* (Cambridge: Harvard University Press, 1982); *Mapping the Moral Domain: A Contribution of Women's Thinking to Psychological Theory and Education,* ed. Carol Gilligan, Janie Victoria Ward, and Jill McLean Taylor, with Betty Bardige (Cambridge: Harvard University Press, 1988); Nel Noddings, *Caring: A Feminine Approach to Ethics and Moral Education* (Berkeley: University of California Press, 1984); Maria Lugones and Elizabeth V. Spelman, "Have We Got a Theory for You! Feminist Theory, Cultural Imperialism, and the Women's Voice," *Women's Studies International Forum* 6 (1983): 573–81; Maria Lugones, "Playfulness"; Annette C. Baier, "What Do Women Want in a Moral Theory?" *Nous* 19 (1985): 53–63.

21. Alison Jaggar, *Feminist Politics and Human Nature* (Totowa, NJ: Rowman and Allanheld, 1980), pp. 42–44.

22. Cheney, "Eco-Feminism and Deep Ecology," p. 144.

23. Nathan Hare, "Black Ecology," in *Environmental Ethics,* ed. K. S. Shrader-Frechette (Pacific Grove, CA: Boxwood Press, 1981), pp. 229–36.

24. For an ecofeminist discussion of the Chipko movement, see my "Toward an Ecofeminist Ethic," and Shiva's *Staying Alive.*

25. See Cheney, "Eco-Feminism and Deep Ecology," p. 122.

Women, Poverty, and Population: Issues for the Concerned Environmentalist

Gita Sen

INTRODUCTION

Differences in perceptions regarding the linkages between population and environment became particularly acute during the preparatory build-up to the UN Conference on Environment and Development, variously known as the Earth Summit and Rio 92. Disagreement between Southern and Northern countries on the extent of attention to be given to population received considerable publicity. At the non-governmental level too, the issue of population has been, of late, a subject of considerable debate among environmentalists (especially those from the North), feminists and population lobbyists.

The basis of these differences often appears baffling; the apparent lack of willingness to compromise, or to acknowledge the obvious merits of opposing views seem to indicate a lack of analytical rigor. The debate appears, to some at least, to be based on passionately held but ultimately ephemeral differences. I wish to argue that, although the positions taken in the policy debate have been exaggerated at times, some of the oppositions have deeper roots. They arise from conceptual and possibly paradigmatic differences rather than from disagreements regarding the "truth-value" of particular scientific propositions. These shape the protagonists' perceptions of problems, the analytical methods used, and the weights assigned to different linkages and relationships. In particular, varying views regarding development strategies, the linkages between poverty and population growth, and the role of gender relations in shaping those links color the positions taken in the debate.

This chapter is an attempt to examine the different perspectives on these issues held by environmental scientists and environmental activists[1] on the one hand, and women's health researchers and feminist activists on the other. Its motivation is twofold: first, to identify the positions taken by these two broad groupings within the larger discourses on development and on population; secondly to propose a possible basis for greater mutual understanding.[2]

GENDER IN THE POPULATION FIELD

In the history of population policy, women have been viewed typically in one of three ways. The narrowest of these is the view of women as the principal "targets" of family planning programs; of women's bodies as the site of reproduction, and therefore as the necessary locus of contraceptive technology, and reproductive manipulation. The early history of population programs is replete with examples of such views; but even more recently, the "objectification" of women's bodies as fit objects for reproductive re-engineering, independent of a recognition of women as social subjects, continues apace (Hubbard 1990).

A second view of women which gained currency after the Bucharest Population Conference in 1983 was women as potential decision-makers whose capabilities in managing childcare, children's health in particular, could be enhanced through greater education. Women began to be viewed as social subjects in this case, but the attention given to women's education has not spun off (in the population policy lit-

Gita Sen, "Women, Poverty, and Population: Issues for the Concerned Environmentalist," in *Feminist Perspectives on Sustainable Development,* ed. W. Harcourt (London: Zed, 1994), 216–25. Reprinted with permission of Society for International Development and the author.

erature) into a fuller consideration of the conditions under which the education of girls takes hold in a society, and therefore the extent to which education is embedded within a society, and therefore the extent to which education is embedded within larger social processes and structures. While this view represented a step away from objectification, women were still perceived as a means to a demographic end, with their own health and reproductive needs becoming thereby incidental to the process.

A third view which grew in the 1980s focused on maternal mortality as an important health justification for family planning. This view, which was at the core of the Safe Motherhood initiative, attempted to claim a health justification for family planning on the basis of rates of maternal mortality. In practice, the initiative has received relatively little funding or support.

CONCEPTUAL APPROACHES

Economic theories of fertility are closely associated with the "new" household economics. Premised on the belief that children are a source of both costs and benefits to their parents, such theories argue that parents determine their "optimum" number of children based on a balancing of costs and benefits at the margin. As a description of differences between societies where children are viewed as a source of both present and future streams of income vs. those where children are essentially a cost to parents (balanced by a measure of psychological satisfaction but not by a significant flow of money income), the theory has an appealing simplicity. It purports to explain why the former societies may be more pro-natalist than the latter. It also suggests that shifting children away from child labor (a source of parental income) towards schooling (a parental cost) might work to reduce fertility.

Such theories have been criticized on a number of grounds (Folbre 1988). The main criticism centers on the assumption that actual fertility is the result of choices made by a homogeneous household unit innocent of power and authority relations based on gender and age. Once such relations are acknowledged, and there is enough anthropological and historical evidence of their existence, the basis of decision-making within households has to be rethought in terms of differential short-term gains and losses for different members, as well as strategic choices by dominant members which will protect and ensure their continued dominance. For example, if the costs of child-raising increase, *ceteris paribus,* there may be little impact on fertility if the increased costs are largely borne by subordinate members of the household (such as younger women) who do not have much say in household decision-making.

Traditionally, in many societies the costs of high fertility in terms of women's health and work-burdens are rarely acknowledged as such, as long as the benefits in terms of access to a larger pool of subordinate children's labour or the social prestige inherent in being the father of many sons continue to accrue to men. Such authority relations are further cemented by ideologies which link woman's own personal status within the authoritarian household to her fertility. Newer game-theoretic models of household behavior (Sen 1987) provide more interesting and complex theories that take better account of the differential distribution of types of assets as well as gains and losses within the household. These have not thus far, however, generated adequate explanations of fertility outcomes.[3]

AGAINST THE STREAM: GENDER RELATIONS AND REPRODUCTIVE RIGHTS

Many of the influential approaches to theory and policy within the population field have been less than able or equipped to deal with the complexity and pervasiveness of gender relations in households and the economies and societies within which they function. Both feminist researchers and activists within women's health movements have been attempting to change the terms of the debate and to expand its scope. An important part of this challenge is the critique of population policy and of family-planning programs as being biased (in gender, class and race terms) in their basic objectives and in the methods that they predominantly use.

The definition of a social objective of population limitation[4] which does not recognize that there may be costs to limiting family size that are differential across social classes and income groups, has long been criticized.[5] In particular, such costs are likely to be less than transparent in non-democratic politics or even within democratic states where the costs are disproportionately visited on groups that are marginal on ethnic racial bases and therefore do not have sufficient voice.[6]

Population policy has also been criticized by some as being a substitute for rather than complementary to economic development strategies that are broad-based in their allocation of both benefits and costs. For example, if impoverished peasants were persuaded or coerced to limit family size on the premise that their poverty is a result of high fertility, independent of the possible causal impact of skewed land-holding patterns, commercialization processes, or unequal access to development resources, then it is questionable whether smaller families would make them more or less poor.

The critique becomes more complicated once the gender dimension is introduced. Critics of population policy on class grounds have sometimes been as gender blind as the policy itself. Having many children may be an economic imperative for a poor family in certain circumstances, but the costs of bearing and rearing children are still borne disproportionately by the women of the household. Gender concerns cannot be subsumed under a notion of homogeneous national or global concerns. For feminist critics of population policy, development strategies that otherwise ignore or exploit poor women, while making them the main target of population programs, are highly questionable. But they do not believe that the interests of poor women in the area of reproduction are identical to those of poor men.

In general terms, the feminist critique agrees with many other critics that population control cannot be made a surrogate for directly addressing the crisis of economic survival that many poor women face. Reducing population growth is not a sufficient condition for raising livelihoods or meeting basic needs.[7] In particular, the critique qualifies the argument that reducing fertility reduces the health risks of poor women and therefore meets an important basic need. This would be true provided the means used to reduce fertility did not themselves increase the health hazards that women face, or were considerably and knowably less than the risks of childbearing. If family-planning programs are to do this, critics argue, they will have to function differently in the future than they have in the past.

The most trenchant criticism questions the objectives (population control rather than, and often at the expense of, women's health and dignity), the strategies (family planning gaining dominance over primary and preventive health care in the budgets and priorities of ministries and departments), the methods (use of individual incentives and disincentives for both "target" populations and program personnel, targets and quotas for field personnel, overt coercion, the prevalence of "camps" and absence of medical care either beforehand or afterwards, inadequate monitoring of side-effects), and the birth-control methods (a narrow range of birth prevention methods, technology that has not been adequately tested for safety, or which has not passed regulatory controls in Northern countries) advocated and supplied through population programs. A now extensive debate around the "quality of care" has focused particularly on the implications of alternative program methods and birth-control techniques for the quality of family program services (Bruce 1989). More broad-ranging evaluations of population policy objectives and strategies have found them guilty of biases of class, race/ethnicity and gender (Hartmann 1987).

Viewed as a development strategy, the critics see population policies as usually falling within a class of strategies that are "top-down" in orientation, and largely unconcerned with (and often violating) the basic human rights needs of target populations. Even the developmentalist concern with improving child health and women's education has received little real support from population programs despite the extensive research and policy debate it has generated.

The critical perspective argues that ignoring co-requisites, such as economic and social justice and women's reproductive health and rights, also makes the overt target of population policies (a change in birth rates) difficult to achieve. Where birth rates do fall (or rise as the case may be) despite this, the achievement is often predicated on highly coercive methods, and is antithetical to women's health and human dignity. The women's health advocates argue for a different approach to population policy—one that makes women's health and other basic needs more central to policy and program focus, and by doing so increases human welfare, transforms oppressive gender relations, and reduces population growth rates (Germain and Ordway 1989).

Around the world there is a growing emergence of positive statements about what human rights in the area of reproduction might encompass (Petchesky and Weiner 1990). Many of these statements are culturally and contextually specific, but they usually share a common critique of existing population programs, and a common understanding of alternative principles. Many of them prioritize the perspective of poor women, although they recognize that the reproductive rights of all women in most societies are less than satisfactory. Their attempt to recast population policies and programs is also, therefore, a struggle to redefine development itself to be more responsive to the needs of the majority.

ENTER THE ENVIRONMENTALISTS

Environmentalist concern with population growth pre-dates the public debate sparked by the UN Conference on Environment and Development (UNCED). Probably some of the most influential early documents were the Club of Rome's *Limits to Growth* and Ehrlich and Ehrlich's *The Population Bomb* (Ehrlich 1969). The interest in global and local carrying capacity, vis-à-vis growing human population sizes and densities, stimulated the production of considerable literature, both scientific and popular. Unfortunately, the popular and activist literature has tended to ignore some of the important anthropological debates about carrying capacity, as well as

to disregard the inconclusiveness of empirical evidence linking environmental change to population growth.[8] It tends, furthermore, to treat the population-environment linkages as simple mathematical ones, linking numbers of people to their environments through technology.

But the argument of both developmentalists in the population field and women's health and rights advocates has been precisely that population is not just an issue of numbers, but of complex social relationships which govern birth, death and migration. People's interactions with their environments can be only partially captured by simple mathematical relationships which fail to take the distribution of resources, incomes and consumption into account; such mathematical relationships by themselves may therefore be inadequate as predictors of outcomes or as guides to policy.[9]

Furthermore, from a policy point of view, more precise modeling of population-environment interactions has not, thus far, provided much better guidance about appropriate population policy programs. Ignoring the wide disparities in the growth rates of consumption between rich and poor within developing countries and hence their relative environmental impacts, as well as the critiques of women's health advocates outlined in the previous sections, leads to single-minded policy prescriptions directed once more simply to increasing family-planning funding and effort. The leap from over-aggregated population-environmental relations to policy prescriptions favoring increased family planning becomes an implicit choice of politics, of a particular approach to population policy, to environmental policy, and to development. Because it glosses over so many fundamental issues of power, gender and class relations, and of distribution, and because it ignores the historical experience of population programs, it has come to be viewed by many as a retrograde step in the population-development discourse.

POPULATION ACTORS

The preceding discussion suggests that important actors in the population field are as follows.

First come those population specialists who traditionally have focused on the size and growth of populations, on age structures, migration and population composition. In general, they enter the development discourse primarily through their concern with what impact population growth might have on rates of economic growth. In addition, population projections are mapped onto planning needs in areas such as food production, energy, and other infrastructures, as well as health, education, and so on. These mappings can be said to belong to a class of simple mathematical planning models which usually ignore problems of distribution (based as they tend to be on per capita needs and availabilities), as well as the social and institutional aspects of making a plan actually work.

The second group are the developmentalists who focus less on the impact of demographic change, and more on the prerequisites of sustained decline in mortality and fertility rates. In particular they stress the importance of improving health and women's education. They thus represent a major revision of traditional population approaches, but all too often stop short of addressing the problem of sustainability or of livelihoods.

A third group, the fundamentalists, has become increasingly important in the population field during the 1980s, gaining political legitimacy through their links to mainstream political organizations. Their primary interest is not the size or growth of populations, but rather control over reproduction and a conservative concern to preserve traditional family structures and gender roles. The moral overtones of the U.S. abortion debate notwithstanding, their interest in procreation appears to derive largely from an opposition to changing gender relations in society.

The fourth group are the Northern environmentalists. At the risk of oversimplification, one might argue that many of these individuals and groups focus mainly on the links between economic growth and ecological sustainability on the one hand, and the size and growth of population on the other.

The fifth important group of actors are the women's health groups which have evolved either out of the feminist movement or out of other social movements or population organizations. Their understanding of the population problem is distinctive in that they define it as primarily a question of reproductive rights and reproductive health, in the context of livelihoods, basic needs and political participation. They often acknowledge that economic growth and ecological sustainability are concerns, but believe these ought to be viewed in the context of reproductive rights and health. In particular, many of them give priority to the needs and priorities of poor women in defining issues, problems and strategies.

Each of these sets of population actors has a view of the population question that is consistent with a particular view of development; as such they tend to overlap with particular sets of development actors, and find a niche within a particular set of development ideas. For example, population specialists are attracted to problems of economic growth, developmentalists to basic needs issues, and women's health activists to the problems of livelihoods, basic needs and political empowerment. Many Northern environmentalists, on the other hand, tend to view population through the lens of ecological sustainability, and this accounts for a considerable amount of the dissonance between their views and those of grassroots groups in the South.

TOWARDS MORE SYNERGY BETWEEN ENVIRONMENTALISTS AND FEMINISTS

Despite the dissonance provoked by the population-environment debate, there is much in common between feminists and environmentalists in their visions of society and in the methods they use. Both groups (or at least their more progressive wings) have a healthy critical stance towards ecologically profligate and inequitable patterns of economic growth, and have been attempting to change mainstream perceptions in this regard. Both use methods that rely on grassroots mobilization and participation, and are therefore sensitive to the importance of political openness and involvement. As such, both believe in the power of widespread knowledge and in the rights of people to be informed and to participate in decisions affecting their lives and those of nations and the planet. Indeed, there are many feminists within environmental movements (North and South) and environmentalists within feminist movements.

Greater mutual understanding on the population question can result from a greater recognition that the core problem is that of development within which population is inextricably meshed. Privileging the perspective of poor women can help ground this recognition in the realities of the lives and livelihoods of many within the South.

Economic growth and ecological sustainability must be such as to secure livelihoods, basic needs, political participation and women's reproductive rights, not work against them. Thus, environmental sustainability must be conceptualized so as to support and sustain livelihoods and basic needs, and not in ways that automatically counterpose "nature" against the survival needs of the most vulnerable. Where trade-offs among these different goals exist or are inevitable, the costs and burdens must not fall on the poorest and most vulnerable, and all people must have a voice in negotiating resolutions through open and genuinely participatory political processes. Furthermore, environmental strategies that enhance livelihoods and fulfill needs can probably help lay the basis for reduced rates of mortality and fertility.

Population and family-planning programs should be framed in the context of health and livelihood agendas, should give serious consideration to women's health advocates, and be supportive of women's reproductive health and rights. This has to be more than lip-service; it requires reorienting international assistance and national policy, reshaping programs and rethinking research questions and methodologies. Using the language of welfare, gender equity or health, while continuing advocacy for family planning as it is at present practiced will not meet the need.

Reproductive health strategies are likely to succeed in improving women's health and making it possible for them to make socially viable fertility decisions if they are set in the context of an overall supportive health and development agenda. Where general health and social development are poorly funded or given low priority, as has happened in the development agendas of many major development agencies and countries during the last decade, reproductive rights and health are unlikely to get the funding or attention they need. Reproductive health programs are also likely to be more efficacious when general health and development are served. A poor female agricultural wage-laborer, ill-nourished and anemic, is likely to respond better to reproductive health care if her nutritional status and overall health improve at the same time.

The mainstream Northern environmental movement needs to focus more sharply on gender relations and women's needs in framing its own strategies, as well as on the issues raised by minority groups. These issues (such as those raised by native peoples and African Americans in the U.S.) tend to link environmental issues with livelihoods and basic needs concerns in much the same way as do the people's organizations in the South.[10] Greater sensitivity to the one, therefore, might bring greater awareness of the other.

Wide discussion and acknowledgment of these principles could help to bridge some of the current gaps between feminists and environmentalists, and make it possible to build coalitions that can move both agendas forward.

REFERENCES

J. Bruce, "Fundamental Elements of the Quality of Care: A Simple Framework." The Population Council, Programmes Division Working Papers No. 1, May, 1989, New York.

J. Caldwell, and P. Caldwell "The Cultural Context of High Fertility in Sub-Saharan Africa," in *Population and Development Review*, 13 (1987):3, September, pp. 409–38.

P. Ehrlich, *The Population Bomb* (New York: Ballantine Books, 1969).

N. Folbre, "The Black Four of Hearts: Towards a New Paradigm, of Household Economics," in J. Bruce and D. Dwyer (eds.) *A Home Divided: Women and Income in the Third World* (Stanford: Stanford University Press, 1988).

A. Germain, and J. Ordway *Population Control and Women's Health: Balancing the Scales* (New York: International Women's Health Coalition, 1989).

B. Hartmann, *Reproductive Rights and Wrongs: The Global Politics of Population Control and Contraceptive Choice* (New York: Harper and Row, 1987).

R. Hubbard, *The Politics of Women's Biology* (New Brunswick: Rutgers University Press, 1990).

P. Little, "The Social Causes of Land Degradation in Dry Regions" (manuscript) (Binghamton: Institute of Development Anthropology, 1992).

M. Mamdani, *The Myth of Population Control* (New York: Monthly Review Press, 1974).

R. Petchesky and J. Weiner, *Global Feminist Perspectives on Reproductive Rights and Reproductive Health.* Report on the Special Sessions at the Fourth International Interdisciplinary Congress on Women (New York: Hunter College, 1990).

J. Scott, "Norplant: Its Impact on Poor Women and Women of Color" (Washington, DC: National Black Women's Health Project Public Policy/Education Office).

A. K. Sen, "Gender and Cooperative Conflicts." Discussion Paper No. 1342 (Cambridge: Harvard Institute of Economic Research, 1987).

R. P. Shaw, "Population Growth: Is It Ruining the Environment?" in *Populi,* 16 (1989):2, pp. 21–9.

NOTES

This chapter is based on a longer article written for a collaborative project of the International Social Sciences Association, the Social Science Research Council, and Development Alternatives with Women for A New Era (DAWN) on "Rethinking Population and the Environment." I am grateful for comments on an earlier draft by Carmen Barroso, David Bell, Lincoln Chen, Adrienne Germain and Jael Silliman. The usual disclaimers apply.

1. The dissonance addressed in this chapter is between mainstream environmentalists from the North and women's health researchers and activists from both North and South.

2. My own position is that of someone who has come to these debates from a background of working on issues of gender and development, and this chapter will perforce tilt heavily towards spelling out the positions taken from within the women's movements. I do not claim to be able to explicate how the mainstream of the environmental movement (especially in the North) has come to the particular definitions it has of "the population problem."

3. A different theoretical approach that takes better account of the shifts in patterns of inter-generational transfers, and therefore of age-based hierarchies, is contained in the work of Caldwell and Caldwell (1987).

4. Or, in the case of many parts of Europe, of population expansion through increased fertility.

5. For an influential early critique see Mamdani (1974).

6. See Scott (n.d.) for a look at Norplant use in the contemporary United States.

7. Even rapid fertility decline may sometimes be indicative of a strategy of desperation on the part of the poor who can no longer access the complementary resources needed to put children's labour to use.

8. Examples of the former are Little (1992), Blaikie (1985); of the latter, Shaw (1989) and UN (1992). The latter argues, for example, that "The failure to take fully into account the possible effects of other factors that might contribute to environmental degradation characterizes many analyses of population-environmental interrelationships at the national and global levels and thus limits their value in assessing the impact of demographic variables."

9. An example is the well known Ehrlich-Holden, identity, $I = PAT$, linking environmental impact (I) with population growth (P), growth in affluence/consumption per capita (A), and technological efficiency (T).

10. Personal discussion with V. Miller, co-founder of West Harlem Environmental Action in New York City.

Women Farmers of India's Deccan Plateau: Ecofeminists Challenge World Elites

V. Rukmini Rao

INTRODUCTION

This article describes the collective efforts of several thousand rural women and the staff of the Deccan Development Society. It is the story of economically and socially deprived women farmers living on the Deccan Plateau in Andhra Pradesh, a state in the south of India. The Deccan Plateau is one of the most ecologically sensitive regions in the country. It is a semi-arid desert with erratic rainfall and mostly poor quality soil. Government policies over the years have led to the deterioration of natural resources. Pricing policy, which favored rice and wheat production in the country, led to the near collapse of coarse grain production in the region, such as sorghum and pearl millet. The increasing costs of modern agricultural inputs also made it difficult for small and marginal farmers to continue production. As a result, large tracts of land now remain fallow in the drought-prone areas. The government has also encouraged the production of sugar cane by providing loans to dig bore-wells and setting up a sugar factory to process the cane. This has resulted in wealthy farmers over-utilizing ground water at the cost of poor farmers, whose shallow wells go dry. While 99% of the women farmers do not own their own land, through a number of initiatives they have established more control over agriculture, in the process conserving and enriching the soils.

SOCIO-ECONOMIC CONDITIONS OF DALIT[1] WOMEN

Dalit women and men belong to a number of sub-castes, which divide them.[2] Elite castes and classes in the village consider them "untouchable," which in effect means apartheid. Dalit women are not allowed to collect water from village hand pumps, and they cannot sit together with other communities. In public places they stand at a distance from upper castes because they are considered to be "polluting." They suffer from discrimination in the worst forms. At the same time the dalit communities do all the agricultural hard labor, such as ploughing, sowing, planting, weeding, and harvesting. They are exploited on a daily basis: they are paid extremely low wages, have little or no job security, and have no maternity or child care benefits.[3] In addition, women are at risk of sexual exploitation because they are poor and typically economically dependent on male landowners.[4] Dalit male farmers in the region own small plots of agricultural land on which they try to grow food for home consumption. Due to soil erosion and lack of access to irrigation and credit, their lands are kept fallow, resulting in poverty. Most men and women are in the grip of money-lenders who charge 60 to 120 percent annual interest on loans, often cheating farmers of their lands. Drought years leave the dalit community further in debt. While the government enacted legislation, which outlaws practices of untouchability, the practice of untouchability continues due to prevailing social customs imposed by upper castes and classes on the poor. Though the government has promoted affirmative action for the community with special quotas in educational institutions and jobs, the overall conditions remain grim. Literacy rates among dalit women are well below 10 percent, and 98 percent of the women work as daily wage workers without job security.

THE SUPPORT ORGANIZATION

The Deccan Development Society (DDS) was set up in 1983 by a group of professional men to help poor communities develop themselves. A few professional women have been in and out of senior management positions. The DDS has approximately 200 part time and full time staff, and 95 percent of the staff are local men and women. The DDS recognizes that the livelihoods of the rural poor can improve only when the environment in which they live is regenerated. Deprived people need organizational and financial support because they have been exploited for many generations. A number of European donors support the DDS. Also, the Government of India funds some of the DDS program. DDS believes that people have a right to a decent livelihood and government resources must be accessed to help them.

Initially, DDS attempted to organize men to take up development activities. DDS believed that because farmers owned some land, they could benefit if irrigation wells were provided along with electrical pumps to ensure irrigation. Because of frequent voltage fluctuations, however, the pumps were damaged, thus increasing a farmer's costs rather than improving his economy. In some cases farmers excavated wells and found there was too little ground water to be used. The wells went dry.

A second effort was to improve livestock. This also did not work for a number of reasons. The male groups were encouraged to start saving regularly to take up additional income-generating activities. The groups asked for large sums of matching grants to start small businesses. Groups of 15–20 women who start saving may be given financial support of INR Rs. 15,000 ($1 U.S. is approximately 43 Indian rupees [INR Rs]) in addition to their own savings to start very small businesses. The men expect to be given individual loans of Rs. 5,000 to Rs. 10,000 cach, and a group of 15 men would expect Rs. 1,50,000. The financial investment demanded by the men was much higher than the support DDS could provide.

Men's groups quickly fall apart for a number of reasons. Men have strong political identities, and groups break up during election periods when members canvas for and support rival candidates. In most villages men are sharply divided along political lines owing allegiance to local leaders in the different political parties. Leaders help their own supporters to access development projects and show undue favor regularly. Conflicts among groups are common. Also, men quarrel for leadership positions much more bitterly than women do. Dissatisfied men leave a group taking a small following with them, which ultimately can cause the collapse of the whole group.

While the men's groups failed, women came forward to set up local groups called Sangams. The DDS now works only with women because it recognizes that dalit women suffer from the triple burden of caste, class, and gender. Over the years, the organization has come to understand the situation of the rural poor and developed a strategy to work towards self-reliance. It works mainly with poor dalit women, although poor women from other castes are also included in the Sangam if they accept norms of equality and respect for each other, irrespective of caste. The groups are self-selected, and members belong to Christian, Hindu, and Islamic communities.

Women in the thrift groups have petty quarrels over a number of issues. If there are mistakes in bookkeeping and accounting the women quarrel, but usually such mistakes are easily sorted out. If the group fails in any collective task, individuals tend to blame each other, but after some loud quarreling during two or three meetings, everyone calms down and life returns to normal. In spite of differences, women are very keen to stay and work together because they can see clear benefits from working together. While some women also struggle to establish leadership, they are much more willing to accommodate each other. This may be partly due to the fact that women are overburdened by work outside and inside the home and are willing to allow others to take the burden of group management.

Over the past 15 years, more than 5,000 women have been organized into self-help groups who are on the path to sustainable development. The village of Edakulapalli illustrates the developments of the region.

THE STRUGGLE OF DALIT WOMEN IN EDAKULAPALLI VILLAGE

Financial Self-Help

A group of dalit women approached DDS in 1992, asking for assistance in starting a women's group. Forty-seven women from different sub-castes came together and started a savings program. Though the women were very poor and indebted, regular saving of a small amount of money helped the women create basic resources. Collectively, the fund creates space for action to improve consumption and take new economic initiatives. The individual members saved Rs. 5 every week (approximately U.S. $0.12).

A year after coming together, the group fell apart. The women developed strong differences among themselves. Male family members also created trouble for the group. To compound the problem, a DDS staff member who left the organization also created divisions. This is a common experience when the poor organize themselves. Upper caste and class men, men from the dalit community, male political leaders who feel threatened, and insensitive activists often cause the collapse of groups. However, two women leaders who had tasted the initial benefits of organization were determined to restart. They regrouped and started over with 36 members.

The group savings were strengthened by adding matching grants from donor funds. Over a seven-year period the group saved Rs. 1,24,915 (U.S. $2,905) as a revolving fund. This revolving fund was initially used to take loans for consumption of food grains, to buy clothes for women at Christmas, and for emergency relief in case of serious health problems. Since rural health care is practically inaccessible to most of the poor, immediate support to rush the sick to hospital is very important. Consumption loans to overcome the seasonal shortages of food at a low interest rate of 12 percent per annum (instead of 60 to 120 percent) help the women and their families maintain essential nutritional levels and prevent illnesses, which can ruin a family's economic stability and earning capacity. The core thrift and credit activities work as a safety net to members of the

Sangam. In addition, the women have accessed government funds to take up income generating activities. A group of 1,200 women who started organizing themselves at the same time now manage a revolving fund of Rs. 35,00,000 (U.S. $81,395).

Environment Regeneration

A major impact of the poor conditions of agriculture lands and small family holdings is that they are left fallow. Big landlords also cultivate only part of their holdings to grow sugar cane and other irrigated crops while leaving the rest fallow. This leads to (1) lack of employment; (2) lack of basic food since farm laborers are paid in kind when they harvest crops; (3) high rates of soil erosion; and eventually (4) forced migration of landless, small, and marginal farmers. The vulnerability of the poor leads to inhuman practices such as annual bondage of young boys (for a very small wage),[5] which prevents them from going to school. Young women belonging to poor families are considered fair game for sexual harassment,[6] so girls are married at the age of 10–12 years old because the families experience them as burdens. To overcome this deteriorating negative cycle, DDS has over the years worked out a program in collaboration with the women's groups. In Edakulapalli it took the following forms:

1. CREATE SUMMER EMPLOYMENT AND IMPROVE THE QUALITY OF LAND

Each summer, the women's groups identify agricultural land for development. Small plots of poor quality land are usually owned by men in their families. The women pick stones from fields, improve drainage, and build contour bunds to prevent soil erosion. These activities help to improve the productivity of the land and increase yields. Because the owners do not have the financial resources to take up the necessary activities, DDS provides a 50% subsidy to individual woman farmers. The whole group benefits because employment is created during the summer when no other employment is available to women. For example, in each village during the summer, DDS provides 10 women a loan of U.S. $23 each to improve their lands. A total of U.S. $230 is spent in the village to improve farmland. This creates 400 days of employment at existing wage rates. Each individual returns 50% of the loan during the following year to the thrift fund. The 400 days of employment created in the village is shared among the 20 members of the group. Each member gets 20 days of wage employment over a period of one or two months. With support to buy farm implements and bullocks for ploughing, small farmers who had never cultivated land turn into farmers who are able to grow food and to make an income.

2. LEASE THE LAND

Since land is the most productive resource in the region, the women form small groups and lease land. This provides employment, food, and also improves land quality because the farmers are encouraged to undertake organic agriculture. Group farming has given women access to this productive resource. As individuals they could not afford to farm and provide necessary inputs, but as a collective the women have gained recognition as farm managers and are not seen as only unskilled workers.

3. CONTROL THE SEED

Since seeds are the most critical input into agriculture, the women have collected a variety of seeds, which they lend to each other and other poor farmers. The traditional system of returning double the amount of borrowed seed has led to women creating their own seed banks.

COMMUNITY SEED BANKS

In India, as in most third world countries, a battle to control seeds rages between multinational companies such as Monsanto and Novartis and small farmers. The control over new seed varieties, including genetically modified seeds, coupled with intellectual property rights and the patent regime spells doom for small farmers. If they become dependent on seeds, fertilizers, and pesticides bought in the market, they will be pushed out of agriculture because they cannot afford the escalating costs.

Traditionally, people have survived drought and hardships in the region because of the rich biodiversity of food crops cultivated in the area. Elderly women and male farmers have identified more than 80 varieties of food crops that were grown locally. The DDS is working toward regaining the vast biodiversity of the region. Twenty-four women farmers in the village have taken the responsibility to identify different food crops grown in the area and replant them on their own lands. A community seed bank has been set up in the village. Throughout the region, women's groups have set up their own seed banks and reduced dependence on the market for seeds.

PROTECTING AND REGENERATING PRODUCTIVE RESOURCES

Because of rapid industrialization, poor farmers are tempted to sell their lands when prices escalate. Once they sell their lands, they are forced to migrate to nearby towns and live a life of destitution. Women in the Sangam prevented their men folk from selling away their barren land. Women in the Sangam do not have any legal rights to stop the men (their husbands) from selling their lands. However, as a group they have social power to influence men in the community. More important, women used their economic power to access loans to demonstrate to the men that barren lands could be made productive. The men were tempted to sell the land because it was barren and would fetch a high price if sold to an industry. The women are more conscious of the need to safeguard land, the main productive asset they own, and they work hard to make it productive. While wives cannot individually influence major decisions of their spouses, collectively they can strategize and influence community decisions. The women's Sangam has provided leadership: They negotiated a loan and subsidies from DDS to improve and develop 95 acres of their own land. With soil and moisture conservation efforts, barren land has been made productive. More than 20 varieties of cereals, pulses, oil seeds, spices, and vegetables have been grown on this land. The men have worked in the fields and supported the women.

ADDITIONAL INCOME-GENERATING ACTIVITIES

Since most farmers own only small plots of land and the climate conditions are harsh, the women need to secure their incomes through additional activities. Milk production and raising goats for meat production are lucrative. Women have also started selling vegetables and setting up village tea shops, which are managed by men in the family. The women use their revolving thrift fund to buy assets, create an income, and repay loans. Over a period of six to seven years, women's incomes have increased gradually. When the Sangam started functioning, a survey of the economic conditions of the members showed that all were indebted to money lenders. Many had pawned their lands for small amounts to raise money during emergencies such as ill health or consumption during drought years. Today only one member is still indebted and the group is planning a strategy to redeem her assets.

BASIC NEEDS VERSUS STRATEGIC NEEDS

One school of development thinking has emphasized the need to ensure women's basic needs are met. Another group insists that this is not enough. They emphasize the need to address issues of power relationships within society. If society is not gender balanced in terms of power, then economic gains made to meet basic needs can easily be lost.

In the efforts described above, it is clear that both basic needs and power relationships have to be addressed. For example, leasing of land by the women's group meets their basic need of ensuring incomes and food. At the same time, leasing of land has broken down class and caste barriers in the In-

dian village society. It is usually the large landowners who have land to lease out. Once the women's groups have the funds and the skills to take up collective farming, upper caste male landowners are coming to women and offering them leases. They come to the settlements where the dalits live, drink tea with the dalit women, request the women politely to lease the lands. This is a complete role reversal. Earlier, the landless dalit women would go begging for work from the landlord. She was usually kept standing outside the house, and when she was employed as a daily wage worker, she was told to come back a week later to collect her wages.

THE ETHIC OF CARE

In neighboring villages where wastelands were available, the women's groups have developed community forestry and woodlots. In some villages the women's group is growing traditional medicinal plants. Where extensive fallow land was available, the women have developed community grain banks. In their collective efforts, the women demonstrate a caring ethic. For example, paid employment is provided to elderly women, and child care facilities are set up to support young mothers. Intergenerational care is established as a norm. The women also show the same caring attitude to livestock. They regard livestock as more than mere production machines and consider the overall welfare of the animal. This consideration runs throughout their decision making. When asked why they prefer traditional varieties of sorghum, even though it has lower grain yield, their answer is: "What about our animals—the new dwarf variety means our animals will have little food. We need to feed our animals too!"

The dalit women are building on their traditional knowledge and wisdom to improve their environment. They combine traditional wisdom with modern practices such as Participatory Rural Appraisals (PRAs) to plan for medicinal plantations, watershed development, and crop planning. They also use PRA techniques to reduce conflicts. For example, wealth-ranking exercises, done publicly and collectively by the group, identify the most needy women as top priorities for receiving aid. They are assisted by staff from the organization to plan their activities.

The women have rejected use of chemical fertilizers and pesticides as harmful to the earth. They are experimenting with non-chemical approaches to pest management. To ensure long-term sustainability, they are working to establish regional federations and cooperatives which will produce and market traditional organic food.

FEMINISM IN PRACTICE

With success in improving their environment, women now have the confidence to tackle social problems. They intervene in domestic disputes and are able to influence local police and traditional leaders, leading to more gender-just decisions. Because the women's group supported the victim, for the first time in the area a rapist was punished in court.

Urban middle class feminists worked closely with women's groups to create awareness of the contribution women make to family incomes. During workshops the women could discuss among themselves the long hours of housework they contribute to ensure family well being. When the housework was assigned an economic value the women clearly understood that though they brought home lower cash income, they contribute more than men to the family. For example, collecting fuelwood, washing clothes, cooking, etc., all had economic value. Caste bias also increased women's workload. While upper caste women collect drinking water from a well in the centre of the village, dalit women may have to walk a longer distance if untouchability is practiced. Discussing such issues allowed women to work out some strategies for change. The most important understanding that emerged was the need for women to work collectively.

Through sharing experiences the women realize their individual worth and the potential of collective functioning to overcome gender discrimination. In collaboration with urban feminists, mainstream institutional norms for giving credit have been challenged and changed. The women as part of collectives are now able to access resources from institutions such as government development departments and banks. The working models set up by the women's groups have been adopted by government agencies.

QUESTIONS FOR THE FUTURE

Government policies in India, such as pricing policies that promote rice, wheat, and sugar cane production, have led to deterioration of natural resources. Often this deterioration has struck most harshly the poor, who are either landless or own marginal land. With globalization of agricultural marketing, many farmers have become dependent on relatively high-cost inputs like commercial seed, fertilizers, and pesticides. This has put or kept many poorer farmers in continual debt. The widespread cultural practice of discriminating against people on the basis of caste, class, and gender continues, despite official government legislation outlawing the practice. Again this has greater effects on the poor. Yet the poor have discovered local resources to work against these difficulties. With a little outside financial and organizational help, poor women have formed groups dedicated to norms of equality and respect for each other, irrespective of caste. They have established local seed banks, brought fallow land back into production, and promoted sustainable, organic agriculture. In accomplishing these, they have begun to incrementally acquire the power needed to change cultural norms that have held them down in society.

Women leaders in the area are very sensitive to issues of oppression and alert about their rights. Yet due to traditional gender values, most women still prefer sons and want them to inherit family property. At the same time a growing number of women question prevailing patriarchal ideology. Through years of hard work, the women have demonstrated an alternative to techno-industrial agriculture[7] and the potential for development without destroying nature. With the support of DDS the women have set up a local radio station and a media group of women videographers to propogate alternate values. Under what circumstances they succeed remains to be seen.

NOTES

1. "Dalit" is a self-proclaimed name for a group of people who are considered untouchable. They belong to 55 sub-castes in Andhra Pradesh. The word literally means "oppressed broken people."

2. Indian society is stratified into different caste groups. Traditionally the pure caste groups were Brahmins, Kshatriyas, Viashyas, and the Shudras. They represented the four basic occupations of society: priests, warriors, businessmen, and workers, respectively. Today, Indian caste society is extremely complex with many sub-castes. An individual is born into the caste of his parents and remains in that caste for life. The lowest castes are also usually the poorest, against whom untouchability is practiced. Now such groups identify themselves as dalit and there is a strong movement to assert the fundamental rights of men and women from these castes. Constitutionally and legally, discrimination on the basis of caste is strictly prohibited, and proof of discrimination can lead to long prison terms for offenders.

All dalits were a part of Hindu religion originally. After many dalit people were converted to Christianity, there was a newly emerging identity as dalit Christians. People who belong to the Christian community are not discriminated against because the constitution guarantees equality to members of all religious faiths. However, in rural communities, caste continues to be a primary source of identity; in spite of dalit community members embracing Christianity, there is no change in their social status. So, although many Hindu dalits became Christians, they still suffer caste discrimination as if they were dalits.

The caste system is enforced in rural India by caste leaders. While there is social harmony normally, conflicts arise over use of resources or if young people want to marry across caste groups, which is socially prohibited. The lowest caste groups live in separate parts of the village and are not allowed to use the common drinking water source. (In contrast, the word "class" is used to describe differences in wealth and access to productive resources and employment. Usually upper class people also belong to higher castes, but with rapid changes in the economy this is not always true. You can find very poor Brahmins and some rich dalit families in the cities.)

3. The main exploitation is the extremely low pay. In the Deccan area, the government has fixed a minimum wage of Rs. 32 per day (U.S. $0.77) for eight hours of work for male and female unskilled workers. In spite of this, women are usually paid only half the minimum wage and well below the wages of men. Though the official wage rate is revised regularly, real wages continue to be low. Women also work more than eight hours per day. There are no maternity benefits or child care facilities. Women workers may work for the same landlord for several years and not receive basic human entitlements.

4. When women go to work on farms, some farmers pressure or seduce women into sexual relationships. These are not based on mutuality since women are economically dependent on the farmers for their daily wages and livelihoods. The same farmers may be the main money lenders in the village, thus increasing the dependence of women, leading them to accept unwanted sexual advances.

5. When families are extremely poor and need loans to meet basic food needs or to deal with an emergency health problem, they pledge their sons to work with a landlord for a period of one year. A boy aged 8 to 12 years may be forced to work for one year to pay off a loan of U.S. $35 to $46. The boy will clean cowsheds, take the landlord's livestock out for grazing during the day, and is expected to do any housework assigned to him, such as sweeping the house. Some boys are expected to irrigate the farmer's fields during the day or night, although others are allowed to go home at the end of the day.

There are no fixed hours of employment. Some boys are given food by the landlord during the day. Others eat only a morning meal before leaving for work and then again upon returning home at night. Boys living in bondage are usually underweight and have no opportunity for schooling. Children may be bonded for four to five years with the same landlord or with different ones. Adult men may also enter bondage when the family faces a financial crisis. They are paid half the minimum wage for the year. Bondage is a sign of the desperate poverty in which a family is living.

6. Although some harassment consists "only" of making obscene remarks when girls or women are going by, or trying to touch the women physically, the situation can be much worse. Rape is a serious problem. Even when violence is not used, there is an element of coercion in most premarital sexual relationships involving dalit teenage girls because it is upper caste men who have premarital sexual relations with lower caste women. Since the women work as laborers in the fields of the upper caste families,

they are vulnerable to economic pressure. Upper caste families stand together when facing a problem, often ostracizing the poorer, lower caste families and refusing them wage employment if they file complaints with the police.

Rape is considered a serious offense, and there is a public discussion to strengthen the law to award the death penalty to rapists. However, the police and legal procedures have many loopholes, and rapists are very rarely punished. The women's movement in the country has been regularly protesting against rapists being allowed to go free.

7. "Techno-industrial agriculture" is characterized by excessive use of chemicals, dangerous pesticides, biotechnology, and over-production, which destroys natural resources, pollutes water, and degrades soil quality.

Part II

What Really Works?

Essays on Human Ecology

Chapter 9
Human Population

Questions for Reflection and Discussion

The Population Bomb

Paul Ehrlich started his book *The Population Bomb* with the words, "The battle to feed all of humanity is over. In the 1970's the world will undergo famines—hundreds of millions of people are going to starve to death in spite of any crash programs embarked upon now. At this late date nothing can prevent a substantial increase in the world death rate. . . ." Ehrlich, with many others, believed that the increasing world population would soon lead to devastation. Did that happen? If not, why not?

Ehrlich, like many others, believed that draconian measures were justified to control human population. He writes, "We can no longer afford merely to treat the symptoms of the cancer of population growth; the cancer itself must be cut out. Population control is the only answer." By population control, he doesn't mean handing out free condoms. In keeping with the cancer metaphor, he later writes, "The operation will demand many apparently brutal and heartless decisions. The pain may be intense. But the disease is so far advanced that only with radical surgery does the patient have a chance of survival." In light of what actually happened regarding world human population and food supply from 1970 through 2000, does Ehrlich's stance seem justified now? Why or why not?

How do we know how many people there are in the world? Who keeps track of such things as births and deaths? Key institutions include the United Nations, the U.S. Census Bureau, and the World Bank. All have extensive Web sites and regularly publish pamphlets and books. How reliable is their information?

Future Generations

Joel Feinberg

We have it in our power now to make the world a much less pleasant place for our descendants than the world we inherited from our ancestors. We can continue to proliferate in ever greater numbers, using up fertile soil at an even greater rate, dumping our wastes into rivers, lakes, and oceans, cutting down our forests, and polluting the atmosphere with noxious gases. All thoughtful people agree that we ought not to do these things. Most would say that we have a duty not to do these things, meaning not merely that conservation is morally required (as opposed to merely desirable) but also that it is something due our descendants, something to be done for their sakes. Surely we owe it to future generations to pass on a world that is not a used up garbage heap. Our remote descendants are not yet present to claim a livable world as their right, but there are plenty of proxies to speak now in their behalf. These spokesmen, far from being mere custodians, are genuine representatives of future interests.

Why then deny that the human beings of the future have rights which can be claimed against us now in their behalf? Some are inclined to deny them present rights out of a fear of falling into obscure metaphysics, by granting rights to remote and unidentifiable beings who are not yet even in existence. Our unborn great great-grandchildren are in some sense "potential" persons, but they are far more remotely potential, it may seem, than fetuses. This, however, is not the real difficulty. Unborn generations are more remotely potential than fetuses in one sense, but not in another. A much greater period of time with a far greater number of causally necessary and important events must pass before their potentiality can be actualized, it is true; but our collective posterity is just as certain to come into existence "in the normal course of events" as is any given fetus now in its mother's womb. In that sense the existence of the distant human future is no more remotely potential than that of a particular child already on its way.

The real difficulty is not that we doubt whether our descendants will ever be actual, but rather that we don't know who they will be. It is not their temporal remoteness that troubles us so much as their indeterminacy—their present facelessness and namelessness. Five centuries from now men and women will be living where we live now. Any given one of them will have an interest in living space, fertile soil, fresh air, and the like, but that arbitrarily selected one has no other qualities we can presently envision very clearly. We don't even know who his parents, grandparents, or great-grandparents are, or even whether he is related to us. Still, whoever these human beings may turn out to be, and whatever they might reasonably be expected to be like, they will have interests that we can affect, for better or worse, right now. That much we can and do know about them. The identity of the owners of these interests is now necessarily obscure, but the fact of their interest-ownership is crystal clear, and that is all that is necessary to certify the coherence of present talk about their rights. We can tell, sometimes, that shadowy forms in the spatial distance belong to human beings, though we know not who or how many they are; and this imposes a duty on us not to throw bombs, for example, in their direction. In like manner, the vagueness of the human future does not weaken its claim on us in light of the nearly certain knowledge that it will, after all, be human.

Doubts about the existence of a right to be born transfer neatly to the question of a similar right to come into existence ascribed to future generations. The rights that future generations certainly have against us are contingent rights: the interests they are sure to have when they come into being (assuming of course that they will come into being)

From: Joel Feinberg, "The Rights of Animals and Unborn Generations," in *Philosophy and Environmental Crisis,* ed. William Blackstone (Athens: University of Georgia Press, 1974), 43–68. Reprinted by permission of Jean Blackstone.

cry out for protection from invasions that can take place now. Yet there are no actual interests, presently existent, that future generations, presently nonexistent, have now. Hence, there is no actual interest that they have in simply coming into being, and I am at a loss to think of any other reason for claiming that they have a right to come into existence (though there may well be such a reason). Suppose then that all human beings at a given time voluntarily form a compact never again to produce children, thus leading within a few decades to the end of our species. This of course is a wildly improbable hypothetical example but a rather crucial one for the position I have been tentatively considering. And we can imagine, say, that the whole world is converted to a strange ascetic religion which absolutely requires sexual abstinence for everyone. Would this arrangement violate the rights of anyone? No one can complain on behalf of presently nonexistent future generations that their future interests which give them a contingent right of protection have been violated since they will never come into existence to be wronged. My inclination then is to conclude that the suicide of our species would be deplorable, lamentable, and a deeply moving tragedy, but that it would violate no one's rights. Indeed if, contrary to fact, all human beings could ever agree to such a thing, that very agreement would be a symptom of our species' biological unsuitability for survival anyway.

CONCLUSION

For several centuries now human beings have run roughshod over the lands of our planet, just as if the animals who do live there and the generations of humans who will live there had no claims on them whatever. Philosophers have not helped matters by arguing that animals and future generations are not the kinds of beings who can have rights now, that they don't presently qualify for membership, even "auxiliary membership," in our moral community. I have tried in this essay to dispel the conceptual confusions that make such conclusions possible. To acknowledge their rights is the very least we can do for members of endangered species (including our own). But that is something.

Population, Development, and the Environment
Clark Wolf

I. IS THERE A POPULATION PROBLEM?

Eighteen centuries ago, Tertullian wrote: "What most frequently meets our view and occasions complaint is our teeming population. Our numbers are burdensome to the world, which can hardly support us." People have expressed concerns about human population growth for thousands of years, but the existence of what we would now consider large human populations is quite a recent phenomenon: The human population of the earth did not reach the first billion until the early nineteenth century. Population did not reach two billion until the early twentieth century (between 1925 and 1935). The third, fourth, and fifth billions arrived around 1960, 1975, and 1990, respectively. The sixth billion arrived just before the turn of the millennium.

Shortly after the turn of the twenty-first century, estimates put the population of the earth just over 6 billion. But according to the UN and the U.S. Census Bureau, the rate of population growth in 2000 was approximately 1.26 percent per year. If that rate of growth were to remain stable, we would expect an additional billion people in about twelve years, and the population size would double in less than sixty years. But even though demographers predict that population size will continue to grow well into the twenty-first century, they also predict that the rate of growth will continue to decline over the next twenty years, and many now predict that world population may stabilize at some point in the mid–twenty-first century. There is less agreement, however, about what mechanism is likely to cause the rate of growth to decline, or about the population levels that may be achieved before population size stabilizes. Some have argued that human population is likely to keep growing until environmental destruction and consequent resource scarcity cause widespread famine, bringing the death rate high enough to compensate for the birth rate. Others more hopefully predict that fertility rates will fall as economic and human development increase the opportunity cost of fertility, and as people gain more autonomous control over their reproductive lives.

Those who are most concerned about human population growth often prescribe harsh medicine as a remedy. It is often argued that "we" in the developed North should close our borders to immigrants, promote reduced fertility by making international aid conditional on the imposition of harsh policies for population control, and above all promote the distribution of birth control. Still others argue that we should not consider population issues at all, and that it is racist or sexist or anti-humanist even to suggest that population growth is a problem. Such arguments are extreme, but they have a point: those who have argued that there are too many people are seldom willing to concede that they themselves might be among the excess. And those most concerned about population are often people who live in developed countries that already enjoy a high standard of living.

Those concerned that overpopulation will retard human development and lead to famine may be surprised when they look at the available data on population growth, resource availability, and development. Empirical evidence linking rapid population growth to slower development is limited, but the available evidence suggests that negative effects of population growth are quite small (NRC 1986, Birdsall 1994). And as Amartya Sen has conclusively shown, there is no reason to believe that population growth is a significant cause of famine. Sen argues that famines invariably have had political causes, and that there is no serious evidence that the rate of population growth is outrunning our ability to produce enough food to feed the earth's human population (Sen 1994b, p. 66). This concern, the centerpiece of Malthus's famous argument concerning the "Principles of Population," seems not to be a central concern of those who have done the very best and most comprehensive work on this issue (Sen 1996). Malthusian fear does persist in the work of more popular writers like Garret Hardin and Paul Ehrlich. But the first question that should arise in discussions about population growth is whether there really is a problem at all. If the problem is not food production or resource use, should we really be worried about the high rate of population growth?

This question should particularly concern us as we evaluate repressive population control measures that have been adopted in some parts of the developing world. For where they have been instituted, the human costs of these measures have been high. These costs have fallen disproportionately on women and girl-children, not merely because women are more likely than men to suffer sterilization or economic disadvantage as a result of such policies, but also because female infant mortality rates typically rise dramatically when repressive population policies are set in place. This is especially significant because infant mortality is already higher for females than males in every country in the world. We should be highly suspicious of policies that systematically disadvantage those who are already systematically disadvantaged worldwide.

In this article I will argue that there is indeed a population problem, and that it should be a major source of concern. I will argue that this concern is of sufficient weight that it justifies, in principle and often in practice, policy intervention aimed at reducing human fertility. But the problem of population is not the problem identified by contemporary Malthusians like Garrett Hardin, and the kind of intervention that is justifiable and appropriate bears no resemblance to the brutal policies recommended by Malthus or his contemporary allies. I begin by reviewing the outlines of a popular Malthusian argument.

II. THE MALTHUSIAN ARGUMENT AND ITS CRITICS

The core of the Malthusian worry is easy to articulate: If world resources are a finite pie, the more people there are to consume it, the smaller the share for each. Over time, population growth may leave insufficient resources for the much larger populations that will inhabit the earth in subsequent generations. Malthus argued that population size will increase geometrically, bounded only when starvation and deprivation render people too weak to procreate or to keep their children alive. This Malthusian view represents one extreme pole in current debates about human population. At the other extreme pole, critics like Julian Simon have leapt upon the assumption that resources are finite. Simon argues that people are themselves a resource—the more the better. The more people there are, argues Simon, the more goods will be produced, and the more we will all benefit from their added human energy, intelligence, and creativity. Simon goes on to urge that "doomsayers" have worried about population for centuries, but that human innovation has always been successful in responding to Malthusian concerns.

There is a kernel of truth in both of these extreme views. The growth of population over the twentieth century is dramatic and unprecedented, and many responsible demographers and economists worry about the likely consequences of this remarkable growth.

But surely there is something right in Simon's assertion that sometimes people themselves should be regarded as resources, not just as resource sinks. Still, recognition that people can be a resource must be qualified by recognition that people require resources and training before they can themselves become effective "resources," contributing to the lives of others. And fertility is usually highest in the poorest sector of the population where few children have access to the resources that would enable them to exercise their intelligence and creativity. Simon is also correct to point out that the earth and its physical resources are not simply a finite pie to be used up, since human innovation can extend resources and can make an enormous difference in the circumstances of people's lives. But technological innovation has brought serious costs as well as great benefits: technological innovation has facilitated the increasingly swift destruction of the earth's great ecosystems. A balanced examination of the "population problem" must give due weight to all of these observations, not a partisan subset.

III. POST-MALTHUSIAN POPULATION CONCERNS

One of the most important insights that contemporary economists have brought to discussions of population issues is that it is necessary to look at the microeconomics of individual fertility decisions. The innovation of recent work on the economics of fertility is analysis of individual economic incentives for fertility. This method of analysis represents fertility choices as economically rational decisions on the part of parents. Of course, fertility choices are not all rationally made: people often have children they would not rationally choose to have. But the degree to which such choices are rational is an important, if incomplete measure of the degree to which fertility is responsive to the influence of policy intervention.

Gary Becker and H. G. Lewis (1974) may be credited as among the first to develop this insight into a full theory. In their model, Becker and Lewis represent children as "consumer goods": human reproduction, they argue, is a way that parents satisfy their desire for children. So the fertility rate reflects the rate at which parents want to "consume" children in order to satisfy this desire. Becker and Lewis hypothesize that parents will "consume" children at efficient rates, balancing "quantity," the number of children they will have, against "quality," the amount of resources they will be able to provide for their children. They assume that children who are provided with more resources will be "better children," and will thus be more satisfying to their parents. On these assumptions, it is possible to show that rational parents will make optimal choices that will benefit children and parents alike.

But the Becker/Lewis model, in spite of its virtues, is fatally flawed, since a crucially important fertility motive is left out: in poor countries, children often constitute a primary means for security in old age. When such security is at risk and this motive is strong, parents may "consume children" in a more literal sense: they may improve their own welfare in ways that ultimately make their children much worse off. Under some circumstances, high fertility may reflect willingness to pass on the costs to the next generation, as a negative intergenerational externality. In poor families, high rates of fertility are typically associated with lower per capita investment in the well-being of children. This indicates another reason for regarding population as a problem for economic development: population growth may slow economic development by reducing per capita investment in "human capital" through health care, education, and basic resources. There is clear evidence that such investment can have positive effects on economic and human development (Rosenzweig and Scultz 1985; Birdsall 1994).

Even if all individual fertility decisions were fully rational, this would not guarantee that such decisions would be good. Sometimes lower fertility rates arc a public good for poor sectors of the population in developing countries, and defection from the participation aimed at the achievement of such goods may be an individually rational strategy. Nancy Birdsall has shown that it is possible to describe circum-

stances in which wages will decrease as population increases. "For individual landless or land-poor laborers it is [or may be] rational to have many children as a strategy for maximizing old-age income. When all pursue this strategy, however, wages are depressed, and both the parents' living standards and those of their children are reduced below their expectations. Hence, one poor family's decision to have children imposes costs on its peers; if all joined in a cartel and agreed to have fewer children, the group's income would increase" (Birdsall 1994, p. 177; Behrman and Birdsall 1988). The upshot is that there are describable circumstances in which lower rates of fertility would improve welfare, even though individuals have self-regarding reasons to maximize their own fertility. In such cases, declines in welfare are the result of rational reproductive choices. The "victims" who are worse off as a result are the generations of persons whose existence is the outcome of these rational choices, not the people who make the choices. Birdsall argues that these circumstances are actual in parts of the developing world—clearly they do not obtain in developed countries, where real wages have increased with population. But in areas where children still provide the primary means for old-age security, there is little reason to believe that the rationality of parents will be sufficient to guarantee that fertility choices will improve human welfare. Microeconomic models of fertility that fail to incorporate this insight will be seriously flawed.

IV. FERTILITY, HUMAN WELFARE, AND THE ENVIRONMENT

Before we can frame policies to address issues of population and fertility, we must clearly understand the relationships between population, fertility, development, and environmental protection. Some cconomists have recently argued that these four factors are correlative, and can feed on one another in a kind of downward spiral (Dasgupta et al. 1994). Others have emphasized the environmental damage that is frequently associated with high population density (Birdsall 1994; Dasgupta et al. 1994). Population growth may increase the rate and severity of environmental damage, leading to degradation of environmental resources at the local and national level, and contributing to problems of decreased biodiversity and possible global warming.

Another extremely serious concern is the burden that high fertility rates impose on women, for these burdens fall disproportionately on women. They include high mortality due to the stresses of pregnancy and childbirth as well as the labor involved in childcare (Dasgupta 1993, 1994b). In most developing countries, maternal mortality is the largest single cause of death among women in their reproductive years, and where fertility rates are high maternal mortality is also high. In some areas in sub-Saharan Africa, the maternal mortality rate may be as high as 1 in 50. Partha Dasgupta notes that in societies in which women have seven or more children during their reproductive years, the chance for each woman that she will not survive those years is about 1 in 6. "The reproductive cycle in this woman's life involves her playing Russian roulette" (Dasgupta 1994b, p. 157).

In addition to their disadvantages for women, it is possible that high fertility rates may also exacerbate poverty and social inequalities (Birdsall 1994; Dasgupta 1994b). One reason for this is that fertility rates are strongly linked to affluence and class differences: In northeast Brazil, the fertility rate of the poor has been as much as twice that of the wealthy. Unless the benefits of development are widely distributed so that the incentives of poor couples were changed, this trend would be expected to steadily increase social and economic inequality. It would also continue to increase poverty and deprivation in poor countries worldwide.

V. DEVELOPMENT, POVERTY, INEQUALITY, AND POPULATION

Where does this leave us? Development economists predicted that the trend should be toward less poverty and greater equality, not increased destitution and greater inequality. Simon Kuznetz hypothesized that initial income inequalities resulting from early stages of economic development should gradually level out as the benefits of economic prosperity are more broadly distributed. A corresponding hypothesis concerning population growth proposes that fertility rates in developing countries will initially spike upwards, but that they too should level off as the changes due to economic development cause couples to choose smaller families. This second hypothesis (sometimes called the "Notestein Transition Hypothesis") is based on the assumption that effective economic development will raise the opportunity costs of having children because children will be selected among a broader range of desirable alternatives. Simultaneously, the motive to have children as protection for old age security is supposed to fall as institutions provide alternate means for protection of well-being in old age.

But in some parts of the developing world, these optimistic economic hypotheses do not accurately describe the process of economic development. Although global fertility rates have declined in recent years, many poor regions have not experienced the social and economic benefits that were expected to reduce fertility. What has gone wrong? It can be argued that the failure of Kuznets' Hypothesis explains the failure of Notestein's Demographic Transition Hypothesis: fertility rates do not fall in the poor sectors of the population because the purported benefits of economic development are often not distributed widely within the population. Some forms of economic development may actually increase social inequalities instead of alleviating them, when a powerful minority manages to reap these benefits: for this reason, we should not be quick to identify economic development with human development.

What explains the local failure of Kuznets' hypothesis in some regions of the developing world? Perhaps Kuznets did not take into account the influence of local institutional barriers on persistent social inequalities. It is often in the interest of those who become wealthy in the early stages of the development process to do what they can to prevent the benefits of economic prosperity from being more widely distributed. In many cases, high profit margins and low production costs depend on the existence of a large and impoverished labor force. Furthermore, those who have an economic interest in perpetuating social and economic inequalities are the same people who have power over social institutions and can effectively put in place barriers that prevent or retard a broader distribution of development benefits. Thus in developing countries, wealthy elites are often adamantly opposed to development efforts that aim to improve general welfare. Ironically, Kuznets' optimistic economic hypothesis may be represented as an "iron law" of economics by just those people who have an interest in maintaining an impoverished and inegalitarian status quo (Todaro 1989, p. 166). When economic development does not bring the expected benefits for an impoverished majority, fertility and maternal mortality rates should not be expected to fall. This is just what we see when we look at persistently impoverished regions of the developing world.

VI. TWO MODELS OF DEVELOPMENT

Poverty and fertility are strongly linked: when people have few opportunities and are economically insecure, fertility rates are dramatically higher. Where people have more opportunities and more autonomous control over their lives, fertility rates decrease dramatically. Traditional programs for economic development in poor countries have often increased income inequality by providing benefits for the wealthy few, but in many places these programs have done little or nothing to improve the lives of the poor. Such programs are unlikely to reduce fertility because they do not effectively address the problem of poverty.

Such considerations suggest an alternative model for development efforts, quite different from the large-scale industrial strategy that has traditionally been favored by the World Bank and the International Monetary Fund. Large-scale development projects that import large industries into developing regions frequently do not effectively reduce in-

equality because the benefits simply do not "trickle down" to those who need them most. Further, such development is often highly destructive to traditional small-scale economies and ways of life and fails to replace them with similarly effective alternatives. Perhaps this model mistakenly conflates economic development with human development the two need not go together.

An alternative model for grass-roots development has recently arisen, represented by the Grameen Bank and the Bangladesh Rural Advancement Committee (BRAC) in Bangladesh, and the new "People's Banks" in Indonesia. These small-scale institutions make small loans (usually under $1,000) to individuals, and follow these loans with advice. These loans are made within small communities, and arrangements are made to ensure that community members have an interest in their neighbors' economic success: further loans within the community are sometimes contingent on prompt payment on previous loans. These small-scale grass-roots banks have been remarkably successful in helping people to create their own economic success, and the efforts of such grass-roots development begin immediately to address the needs of the poor. Consequently they are far more likely to be effective in changing the fertility incentives of those whose needs are most at risk.

VII. MODELS FOR POPULATION-SENSITIVE DEVELOPMENT POLICY

Efforts to control population have often been repressive and have had high social costs. Amartya Sen distinguishes between "Collaboration" and "Override" as alternative strategies for addressing the population problem. The former "involves voluntary choice," while the latter "overrides voluntarism through legal or economic coercion" (Sen 1994b, p. 63). China's aggressive effort to control population by imposing punitive sanctions on couples who exceed their quota of children is a prime example of a coercive strategy. Not only do such strategies penalize parents and their children, they are also likely to be less effective in the long run. When population policies are repressive, it is in each person's interest to attempt to skirt them and to avoid their effects and costs. But when population policies endeavor to provide people with incentives and opportunities, to raise the opportunity cost of having children, then low fertility may become individually rational.

Three kinds of collaborative measures for fertility reduction are most significant:

(i) Efforts to expand educational opportunities, and especially women's educational opportunities, have proven highly effective in reducing fertility. Such access not only improves women's employment prospects, but also results in later marriage and reproduction. When women have the opportunity to spend part of their reproductive years in school, each is likely to have fewer children overall. It is clear that restrictions on women's access to education in most parts of the world is an important contributing factor to high fertility rates.

(ii) Providing women with employment opportunities can have a similar effect: when women are prohibited from work, as they have been in Bangladesh for example, the opportunity costs of fertility are extremely low. When women's opportunities are expanded beyond the boundaries set by tradition and sexist oppression, these costs are considerably higher. Generally increased economic opportunity for both women and men will increase the opportunity cost of children, as Becker and Lewis (1974) showed. But because women have suffered radically diminished opportunities in every culture and every country in the world and they are still the primary caretakers for children worldwide, it is especially important to expand opportunities for women.

(iii) In developing countries, children often constitute the primary means of support for older people. Since such security is a prime incentive to have children, institutions that increase the economic security of the elderly remove an important but unfortunate motive to have children. As I argued earlier, the motive to have children to provide for one's old age is destructive in the sense that it passes costs on to the succeeding generation, whose interests may not be fully represented in fertility decisions. Evidence has shown that old-age pension and social security can indeed act as an economic "substitute" for children (Nugent and Gillaspy, 1983).

Many will regard these measures as too minimal or too indirect. But where they have been tried already they have proved remarkably effective—arguably far more effective than the harsh measures adopted in China, for example (Sen 1996). Collaborative responses to population problems are desirable not only because they are non-coercive and because they enhance welfare, but also because they are simply more effective and offer more enduring prospects for long term change. But most importantly, emphasizing these measures may help to move discussion of population toward a kind of practical consensus. Perhaps even those who disagree about the nature of the population problem can agree about what we should do.

REFERENCES

Gary Becker and H. G. Lewis, "Interaction Between the Quantity and Quality of Children," in *Economics and the Family*, ed. T.W. Schultz (Chicago: University of Chicago Press, 1974).

Jere R. Behrman and N. Birdsall, "The Reward for Good Timing: Cohort Effects and Earning Functions for Brazilian Males," *Review of Economics and Statistics* 70 (1988).

Nancy Birdsall, "Government, Population, and Poverty: A Win-Win Tale," in *Population, Economic Development, and the Environment,* ed. Kerstin Lindahl-Kiessling and Hans Landberg (New York: Oxford University Press, 1994).

Joel E. Cohen, *How Many People can the Earth Support?* (New York: W. W. Norton, 1995).

Partha Dasgupta, *An Inquiry into Well-Being and Destitution* (Oxford: Clarendon Press, 1993).

———, "Savings and Fertility: Ethical Issues," *Philosophy and Public Affairs* 23 (1994a): 99–127.

———, "The Population Problem," in *Population—The Complex Reality: A Report of the Population Summit of the World's Scientific Academies,* ed. Sir Francis Graham-Smith, F.R.S. (London: The Royal Society, 1994b).

Partha Dasgupta, Carl Folke, and Karl-Goran Maler, "The Environmental Resource Base and Human Welfare," in *Population, Economic Development, and the Environment,* ed. Kerstin Lindahl-Kiessling and Hans Landberg (New York: Oxford University Press, 1994).

Garret Hardin, *Living Within Limits* (New York: Oxford University Press, 1993).

Thomas Malthus, *An Essay on the Principle of Population* (New York: Cambridge University Press, 1992 [original 1797]).

NRC (National Research Council), *Population Growth and Economic Development: Policy Questions* (Washington DC: National Research Council, 1986).

J. Nugent and T. Gillaspy, "Old Age Pension and Fertility in Rural Areas of Less Developed Countries: Some Evidence from Mexico," *Economic Development & Cultural Change* 31 (1983).

M. R. Rosenzweig and T. P. Schultz, "Testing the Quantity-Quality Fertility Model: The Use of Twins as a Natural Experiment," *Econometrica* 48 (1985): 227–40.

Amartya Sen, "More Than a Million Women Are Missing," *NY Review of Books* 37 (1990):61–66.

————, "Population and Reasoned Agency: Food, Fertility, and Economic Development," in *Population, Economic Development, and the Environment,* ed. Kerstin Lindahl-Kiessling and Hans Landberg (New York: Oxford University Press, 1994a).

————, "Population: Delusion and Reality," *New York Review of Books* 41, no. 15 (September 22, 1994b):62–71.

————, "Legal Rights and Moral Rights," *Ratio Juris* 9, no. 2 (1996): 153–67.

J. L. Simon. *Population and Development in Poor Countries* (Princeton NJ: Princeton University Press, 1992).

————, *The Ultimate Resource 2* (Princeton NJ: Princeton University Press, 1996).

Michael P. Todaro, *Economic Development in the Third World,* 4th ed. (New York: Pittman Publishing Co., 1989).

Clark Wolf. "Population," in *The Blackwell Companion to Environmental Philosophy,* ed. Dale Jamieson (Cambridge: Blackwell Publishers, 2001), 362–76.

Recent Population Trends

Elizabeth Willott

In the 1800s, the Reverend Thomas Malthus, in his Essay on the Principles of Population as It Affects the Future Improvement of Society, discussed the implications of an exponentially growing population in a world of limited carrying capacity. The concern about population and the environment intensified in the 1960s.

In 1968, Paul Ehrlich published *The Population Bomb*. He began: "The battle to feed all of humanity is over. In the 1970s the world will undergo famines—hundreds of millions of people are going to starve to death in spite of any crash programs em-

barked upon now. At this late date nothing can prevent a substantial increase in the world death rate. . . ."[1]

Garrett Hardin's "Living on a Lifeboat," published in 1974, claimed that human population would increase to the point where some natural disaster or accident leads to a crisis causing many people to die; the population thereby gets reduced below the land's carrying capacity. Then the cycle starts again. He wrote: "In the absence of population control by a sovereign, sooner or later the population grows . . . and the cycle repeats."[2] In Hardin's view, giving

Elizabeth Willott, "Recent Population Trends," *Common Ground* 1 (2001). (http://commonground.umfk.maine.edu). Copyright © 2002 Elizabeth Willott and Oxford University Press.

food or other aid to overcome natural disasters merely exacerbates the population problem and subsequent environmental problems.

However, do the last 30 years agree with these claims? The massive food crises and increase in world death rate has not materialized. Instead, more people are better fed and live longer, and many countries that once had rapidly increasing populations now have fertility rates conducive to zero population growth or lower. For some developed countries, total population has decreased (though not by starvation). For some other countries, current population increases are due solely to immigration and to continued gains in longevity. In general, these changes resulted not from the effects of punitive laws (i.e., Hardin's sovereign), but rather from people, especially women, having more opportunities.

There are environmental and social demands arising from the unprecedented 6 billion humans living on this planet. There is reason for concern. However, the crisis models of Malthus, Ehrlich, and Hardin paint too grim a picture. By them, humans face an option of (a) horrific death by starvation or epidemics, or (b) draconian laws restricting human liberty in reproductive choice. Although the current situation is far from Utopian, even for the poorest countries in the throes of major AIDS epidemics, data support room for hope. Apparently, both Ehrlich and Hardin misjudged the cumulative effects of millions of individual men and women voluntarily controlling their sexual behavior and the number of babies they generate.

THE POPULATION EXPLOSION OF THE 1960s

What did Hardin and Ehrlich see, to write as they did? Death rates, particularly of children, dropped dramatically following World War II. Ehrlich attributes the drop in death rates to antibiotics, vaccines, and insecticides such as DDT (a synthetic insecticide developed in the 1940s and widely used to control disease-transmitting mosquitoes from 1945 through 1970).

While lowering death rates in the DCs (developing countries) was due in part to other factors, there is no question that "instant death control," exported by the DCs, has been responsible for the drastic lowering of death rates in the UDCs (under-developed countries). Medical science, with its efficient public health programs, has been able to depress the death rate with astonishing rapidity and at the same time drastically increase the birth rate; healthier people have more babies.[3]

He gives an example: DDT, introduced in 1946, resulted in Ceylon's death rate dropping from 22 per 1000 people to 10 per 1000 by 1955. "Victory over malaria, yellow fever, smallpox, cholera, and other infectious diseases has been responsible for similar plunges in death rate throughout most of the UDCs. In the decade 1940–1950 the death rate declined 46% in Puerto Rico, 43% in Formosa, and 23% in Jamaica. In a sample of 18 undeveloped areas, the average decline in death rate between 1945 and 1950 was 24%."[4]

Women were healthier and lived longer, so, on average, each woman gave birth to more children. More children survived. The result: In some countries children comprised over 40% of the population. By Hardin's view, giving those children food would result in an even bigger increase in population, since those children would bear at least as many children as their mothers had. However, that is not what happened, despite the doubling in world population between 1960 and 2000.

THE GROWING WORLD POPULATION

Consider the data in Table 1, also plotted in Figure 1. This is what Hardin and Ehrlich would have known. The rate of population increase looked out of control. Roughly one-quarter of the world population was undernourished.[6] How could people possibly increase food production and resources to feed and care for the rapidly increasing population? Understandably, many papers from this period are pessimistic.

Table 1. World Population (in Billions) from A.D. 1000 to A.D. 2000[5]

1000	1250	1500	1750	1900	1910	1920	1930	1940	1950	1960	1970	1980	1990	2000
0.31	0.40	0.50	0.79	1.65	1.75	1.86	2.07	2.30	2.52	3.02	3.70	4.44	5.27	6.06

What is the picture now? Adding the data to 2000 gives us Figure 2. At first glance, that doesn't appear to help. So why, in recent years, have the UN, the World Bank, and the U.S. Bureau of the Census predicted that world population will stabilize during the twenty-first or twenty-second century? A closer look at the data above, plus information about longevity and about fertility per woman, allows us to see some bases for their predictions.

Rate of Change of the World Population, 1900–2000

To get a crude idea of the rate of increase, we can subtract the population of 1900 from that of 1910. This gives the number of people added in that decade. Then divide that into the population at 1900 to get the rate of increase in that decade. We get $(1.75 - 1.65)/1.65 = 0.061$ as the increase rate *for the decade*. Multiply by 100 to get the percent. The data for each *decade* is given in Table 2. This crude treatment of the data suggests the rate of population increase reached a peak somewhere in the '60s and '70s and has declined since. A more refined analysis by the U.S. Bureau of the Census gave the peak to be 2.19% per year in 1962 and 1963.[7] So, in one sense Ehrlich was correct. The increase in the world's population would not continue as it had. However, he was wrong when he said it would be famines that lowered the increase. By his own account fewer than 10 million people per year died from malnutrition between 1970 and 1995.[8] Although this is still tragic for any individual caught in the situation, in absolute numbers, fewer people were undernourished in 1999 than in 1970. In 1970, roughly 900 million out of a population of 3.7 billion—1 in 4 people—were undernourished; in 1999, despite a population of 6 billion, roughly 800 million—or fewer than 1 in 7 people—were undernourished.[9] More famines affecting more people simply did not happen. Nor, until recently with AIDS, have other massive and tragic calamities struck, as Hardin claimed would happen. Few countries attempted directly and coercively to restrict fer-

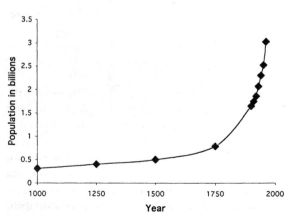

Figure 1.

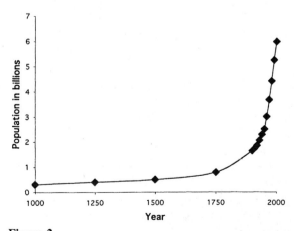

Figure 2.

Table 2. Rate of Change in World Population, 1900–2000

1900–1910	1910–1920	1920–1930	1930–1940	1940–1950	1950–1960	1960–1970	1970–1980	1980–1990	1990–2000
6.1	6.3	11.3	11.1	9.6	19.8	22.5	20.0	18.7	15.0

tility. Looking at the numbers, these attempts cannot account for the observed worldwide differences, although China's attempt probably made a large difference in China. Possibly the more coercive ventures in India and Bangladesh had partial success in slowing population growth, although some evidence suggests that because of people's distrust some attempts were actually counterproductive.

What Happened from 1960 to 2000

If we look again at the graph of total world population, but spread the data points from 1940–2000, we can compare the actual curve to the shape if the 1960 rate continued through 2000 (see Fig. 3). Actual population numbers are lower than numbers on the curve projected from 1960. This means the rate of increase of the world population has decreased relative to 1960, just as we found when we analyzed the numbers above.

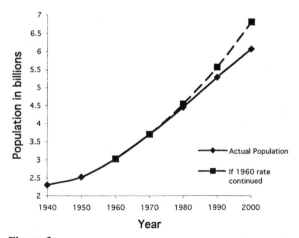

Figure 3.

People Live Longer

Expected life span at birth, worldwide, increased from 48 years in 1950 to 68 years in 1999. The longer people live, the more there will be of them at any time. Just this simple difference increased the world's population number by approximately 40% from 1950 to 2000. It accounts for 1 billion of the 3.5 billion people added to population numbers in that time.

Hardin and Ehrlich could see the effect of developed countries sending medicine and insecticides to developing countries—infant (babies to 1 year of age) and young child (1–5 years of age) mortality decreased dramatically. This trend continued. Worldwide, infant mortality was 148 per 1,000 live births in 1955; it was 59 in 1995.[10] Mortality for children under 5 years of age was 210 per 1,000 in 1955 and 78 per 1,000 in 1995. In absolute numbers that means, for 1955, 21 million children under 5 years old died worldwide; in 1995, despite there being *more* children under 5 years old, only 10 million died.[11] Worldwide, in 1980, less than 50% of children under 12 months were immunized against measles and diphtheria/polio/tetanus; by 1995, over 80% were immunized against these diseases.[12]

The Average Woman Bears Fewer Babies

With high child mortality rates in some areas of the world an individual woman might bear seven or eight children but only have two survive to adulthood.[13] With better hygiene and vaccinations reaching many of the poorest, fewer babies died and more reached reproductive age. This was a radical change, but there was another factor with a large impact. Beginning in the 1960's, more effective birth control technologies were developed, became more available;

and were accepted by more women. Hardin's food to population relation, i.e., extra food = extra babies, has not held.

Ehrlich, Hardin, and others in the 1960s and 1970s could not have predicted the widespread acceptance of the pill, the IUD, and other forms of birth control. They had no way of knowing that, almost worldwide, a woman on average would bear so many fewer babies than her mother had. Worldwide, the number of births per woman dropped from 5.0 in 1950 to 2.8 in 1999.[14,15] Data from some countries are not high quality—many poorer countries do not have effective data collection, and taking a census is not a regular event. However, data are sufficiently good to support a belief that major change has occurred.

Choosing to limit the number of children was initially seen in the more developed countries. When first noted, people cautioned against generalizing that the trend to limit fertility would spread to developing countries, partly because many of the more populated developing countries were nominally Catholic or had other traditions that, theoretically at least, worked against the acceptance of practicing birth control. To illustrate the trend, I am including UN Population Division data on fertility rates per woman, comparing data from the 1970s with the 1990s.[16] For brevity, only a few countries are included. Replacement fertility (i.e., the number of children a woman would bear, on average, that would sustain the population number) is 2.1 for countries in which infant and child mortality is minimal. By the mid-1970s some of the more developed countries were below replacement fertility. By the end of the 1990s, regardless of development status, nearly *all* countries show a drop in fertility rates (i.e., the number of babies per woman) since the 1970's.

In the Caribbean, the greatest change occurred in Puerto Rico, Trinidad/Tobago, Martinique, Barbados, Cuba, and the Bahamas, all of which went from between 3.2 and 3.7 children/woman in 1970 to less than 2.1 children/women by 1995. Haiti showed the least change, but still moved from 5.5 children/ woman in 1972–1977 to 5.0 children/woman in 1990–94 and down to 4.3 by 1999. The numbers in Tables 3 and 4 answer the question raised in the

Table 3. Central America: Fertility Rates per Woman

Most change			
Mexico	1971–1977	1990	1999
	6.2	3.4	2.7
El Salvador	1971	1990	1999
	6.2	3.7	3.1
Panama	1970	1990	1999
	5.0	3.0	2.6
Least change			
Guatemala	1973	1990	1999
	6.4	5.6	4.8

1970s: Despite the Pope's pronouncements, Catholics adopted birth control. Figures from Africa (Table 5) indicate that there, too, fertility per woman has dropped. The only African country in the U.N. *not* to show a decrease population between 1969 and 1990 was Togo. In 1970 it had a fertility rate of 6.6 children per woman and that was reported unchanged in 1983–1988. However, by 1999 the fertility rate in Togo was 5.9.[18] The trend is to reduced fertility rates; though all of these countries have fertility rates considerably above replacement level.

What about China and India, the two countries with the largest populations? China went from 6.0 children per woman in 1960 to 2.2 in 1990 and to 1.8 in 1999; India went from 6.2, to 3.8, to 3.0 in the same period.[19] Both these countries implemented extensive programs for birth control education and

Table 4. South America Fertility Rates per Woman

Most change			
Ecuador	1974	1990	1999
	5.5	3.8	3.0
Guyana	1970	1990	1999
	4.2	2.6	2.3
Peru	1973–1977	1990	1999
	5.6	3.7	2.9
Least change			
Paraguay	1974–1977	1990	1999
	5.0	4.7	4.1
Argentina	1970	1990	1999
	3.2	2.9	2.6

Table 5. Africa: Fertility Rates per Woman

Northern Africa			
Tunisia	1971	1990	1999
	6.0	3.6	2.5
Morocco	1974–1977	1990	1999
	6.9	3.8	2.9
Algeria	1977	1990	1999
	7.4	4.6	3.7
Western Africa			
Senegal	1973–1978	1990	2000
	7.1	6.3	5.4
Eastern Africa			
Kenya	1972–1977	1990	1999
	8.3	6.1	4.2
Uganda[17]	1969	1990	1999
	7.1	7.1	7.0
Rwanda	1977	1990	1999
	8.7	6.8	6.0
Southern Africa			
Botswana	1971	1990	1999
	6.5	5.1	4.2
Namibia	1977–1978	1990	1999
	6.0	5.4	4.8
South Africa	1970	1990	1999
	5.1	3.7	3.2
Zimbabwe	1968	1990	1999
	6.7	5.0	3.7
Zambia	1969	1990	1999
	7.4	6.2	5.4

in at least some cases engaged in coercive or otherwise ethically questionable interventions to reduce fertility. Was that intervention necessary? Countries that did not coercively intervene also show substantial decreases. For example, the same sources show Mexico's total fertility rate dropped from 6.2 in 1971–1977 to 2.7 in 1999. Some, and perhaps most of the drop in fertility rates in India and China could have resulted (and perhaps did result) simply from making birth control resources widely available and permitting and encouraging women and/or families to make their own decisions regarding contraception.

Where Are We Heading?

Any country that exceeds replacement level fertility will cause an increase in the world population un-less other countries have levels below replacement. As Hardin points out, slowing the increase only slows but does not solve the problem. There is a trend, virtually worldwide, toward decreased fertility, but will that ultimately result in a reduction of fertility to, or below, replacement level, globally? We really do not know. Just as, back in the 1960's, we could not know that so many women would practice birth control if given the option.

In 1998, the UN reported that 61 countries, accounting for 44% of the global population, had fertility rates below replacement levels.[20] These countries may still increase in population through immigration or if longevity continues to increase as it has for most countries of the world over the past 20 years.[21] Despite increases in longevity, the absolute number of people added globally per year decreased from a maximum of 87.4 million in 1989 to 77.6 million per year in 1999.[22] The UN projection[23] giving the earliest stabilization is for world population to peak around 8 billion between 2020 and 2050, then start to decline. We'll see. Their data allow us to see a dramatic change in fertility trends between 1955 and 2000. It is rash to project far into the future, although currently we appear to have decent grounds for guarded optimism concerning stabilization of world population.

Even when the year arrives when there is *no* increase in world population, problems will not be over. Individual countries may still have population growth that outstrips the ability to provide basic resources while suitably respecting the environment. Even those countries with stable populations may find they are exceeding the long-term carrying capacity of the environment. We may have a long way to go to reach sustainable living on this planet.

HIV/AIDS AND WORLD POPULATION

Lowering the birth rate is one way to lower population. Increasing the death rate is another. Massive famines did not increase the death rate in the 1970s, but AIDS has increased death rates markedly in several sub-Saharan countries. More than 95% of HIV-infected people live in developing countries; more than 95% of the deaths are likewise in those countries. Although significant for those countries and making it one of the key killers worldwide, AIDS killed only 2.8 million[24] out of an estimated total of 56 million deaths in 1999.[25] That number will increase in coming years as more HIV-infected people succumb. The UN reports: "Zimbabwe, which had relatively low adult death rates before the onslaught of AIDS, saw adult mortality among men nearly triple between 1988 and 1994. Among women the probability of dying between age 15 and 60 more than doubled over the same period."[26] Life expectancy has plummeted to 40 years.[27] In neighboring Botswana, children born between 2000–2010 have a calculated life expectancy of just over 40 years; if AIDS was not in the picture, their life expectancy would be about 70.[28]

In Botswana, HIV infects 36% of adults[29] and in Zimbabwe, around 25%.[30] The UN World Health Report for June 1998 writes of the Zimbabwe cities: "In Harare, 32% of pregnant women were already infected in 1995. In Beit Bridge, a major commercial farming center, HIV prevalence in pregnant women shot up from 32% in 1995 to 59% in 1996. Although infection levels in Zimbabwe's cities were slightly higher than in rural areas, the difference was not great.[31] South Africa, which had a rate of 13% in 1997, was 20% in 1999.[32] In some areas of South Africa the rate of infection of young women is staggering. The UN AIDS report for 2000 includes: "The rates among teenage girls and especially among women under 25 defy belief: in 7 of the 11 studies, more than one woman in five in her early 20s was infected with the virus; a large proportion of them will not live to see their 30th birthday. Close to 6 out of 10 women in this age group in the South African town of Carletonville tested positive for HIV."[33] Although obviously a crisis for Carletonville and similarly struck communities, HIV-AIDS is not likely to become a major world-wide killer.

Sub-Saharan Africa, however, clearly faces a crisis. AIDS typically kills adults in what normally would be their peak productive years. Instead of these people contributing net resources to the community, precious resources are diverted to caring for them, as noted in the UN AIDS epidemic report:[34] "In Zimbabwe, for instance, life insurance premiums quadrupled in just two years because of AIDS deaths. Some companies say that their health bills have doubled. Several report that AIDS costs absorb as much as one-fifth of company earnings. In Tanzania and Zambia, large companies have reported that AIDS illness and death cost more than their total profits for the year." The result is that there is greatly reduced opportunity for economic growth. The GNP (Gross National Product) annual growth rate for Zimbabwe from 1985 to 1995 was approximately −1%. They moved backwards economically. Their GNP per capita was about $540, clearly not sufficient to give people adequate health care under this crisis.

It is not clear what will happen in the next few years. On the one hand, we know severe suffering will continue, definitely continuing to cause social upheaval. On the other hand, there are some relative success stories. Uganda has a major HIV/AIDS problem. The problem was worse, but is lessening. A major educational campaign apparently made a difference. One research team, examining data from 1989 through 1998, found a decrease in new infections, dropping from an annual rate of new infections of 9.4 per 1,000 males to 2.4; and from 6.0 per 1,000 females to 4.0.[35] A spokesperson for the research group, Mbulaiteye, credits the drop to a delay in onset of initial sexual experience, increased condom use, and increased discussion about sex and HIV/AIDS. Another study found the HIV prevalence rate among 13–19-year-old women dropped dramatically from close to 4.5% down to 1.5% between 1989 and 1997.[36]

In September 1999, a test in Uganda showed the drug nevirapine effectively prevented transmission of HIV from mother to baby during birth.[37] The treatment was twice as effective and 70 times cheaper than the older accepted AZT protocol. The cost, $4 per patient, is no longer so prohibitive.

When HIV/AIDS first surfaced, Senegal initiated a major education campaign that included sex education in primary and secondary schools.[38] HIV infection rates have remained low—below 2% (contrast this with Zimbabwe's 25%). Condom use increased dramatically from approximately 5% use with non-regular partners in 1990 to 40–65% use in 1997.[39] (This is validated by condom distribution, which went from 800,000 in 1988 to over 7 million in 1997.)[40] Since abstinence and the use of condoms are the main means to combat HIV infection, and these are also excellent birth control methods, we would expect the birth rate to drop as a consequence of the epidemic. According to UN predictions, the number of births per Senegalese woman dropped from 6.3 in 1990 to 5.4 in 1999.[41]

Zambia, which was very hard hit by AIDS, also shows some signs of possible success. HIV prevalence rate among pregnant 15–19-year-old women visiting clinics in the capital, Lusaka, was 25–30% in 1993, but 10–16% in 1998. The change was due to fewer young men and women engaging in risky sexual behavior.[42]

Obstacles to dealing adequately with the AIDS epidemic include social restrictions: "In Zambia, for instance, people under 18 cannot choose to be tested for HIV without their parents' consent. Yet nearly half of young women have had sex by the time they are 16, and many teenagers are infected with HIV."[43] Other problems include the dilemma that a mother with HIV faces: She risks giving her baby HIV through breastfeeding, yet spending precious money on baby formula puts her baby at risk from diseases due to contaminated water. Also, the act of bottle feeding can be interpreted as a signal that she is HIV positive and can lead to her being ostracized from her community and possibly beaten to death—which does not help her infant, either. In recent years, the governments have started to tackle the stigma problem. In 1999, when in Zimbabwe, Zambia, and Botswana, I saw posters in many government buildings and banks showing a woman holding an infant and a bottle with the message: It's your choice.

THE FUTURE

What will the future bring? As in the 1960s, we don't know. We can predict that AIDS will continue to decimate the populations of some countries for at least the next decade. However, more and more it appears HIV/AIDS is not going to be the agent that reduces human population worldwide. If the anti-HIV drug nevirapine works as well as initial studies indicate and if women are provided the social and financial ability to safely formula-feed their infants then the transmission of HIV to infants can be greatly reduced. The epidemic seems under control in most parts of the world, and some hard-hit countries now seem to have passed the peak of new infections. Reports from several countries indicate people are changing their sexual behavior in ways that will reduce both AIDS transmission and fertility. If these reports bear true, then world population just might stabilize as the UN has predicted. This might happen without involving a major increase in death rate worldwide. (We can't avoid the increase already seen in some countries due to AIDS, but perhaps can prevent or ameliorate that increase in other countries.)

If the concern about human population is that humans need to live within the carrying capacity of the earth, then stabilization of the world's human population is only part of the solution. Presumably humans also have to use and generate resources in a sustainable manner. However, stabilization of the human population *is* one of the necessary parts to the solution—and the movement within the last 40 years toward that stabilization has been swift and astonishing. A major change has occurred. The major change seems to arise from millions and millions of women and men either (1) changing their own reproductive behavior, or (2) not following the behaviors of their parents. Ehrlich and Hardin envisioned a future with massive increases in death rates worldwide in the face of starvation or natural calamity, unless draconian regulations were imposed restricting personal freedom. Now, blessed with hindsight, we can see the changes the past 30 years have brought, and consider that a less tragic solution seems at least possible. We don't have to accept their vision as destiny.

NOTES

1. Paul R. Ehrlich, *The Population Bomb* (New York: Ballantine Books. 1968), Prologue.

2. Garrett Hardin, "Living on a Lifeboat," *BioScience* 24(1974): 561–68.

3. Ehrlich, *The Population Bomb,* 32.

4. Ehrlich, *The Population Bomb,* 33–34.

5. United Nations, Population Division, Department of Economic and Social Affairs, *1998 Revision of the World Population Estimates and Projections. World Population Growth from Year 0 to 2050,* http://www.popin.org/pop1998/4.htm. Similar data is available from the US Census Bureau.

6. UN, Food and Agriculture Organization, *The State of Food Insecurity in the World 1999,* http://www.FAO.org/FOCUS/E/SOFI/under-e.htm. See p. 6 of the pdf file: http://www.fao.org/NEWS/1999/img/SOFI99-E.PDF The FAO estimates that in 1970 roughly 900 million people were chronically undernourished. World population in 1970 was 3.7 billion.

7. U.S. Census Bureau, *International Data Base. Total Midyear Population for the World: 1950–2050,* May 2000, http://USCensusBureau.org/ipc/www.worldpop.html.

8. "In fact, some 250 million people, about as many as now live in the United States, have perished for lack of food since those words [in *The Population Bomb*] were written. Roughly 100 to 140 million of them died in the 1970s." P. Ehrlich and A. Ehrlich, *Betrayal of Science and Reason* (Island Press, Washington, DC: 1996), 75.

9. UN, FAO, *The State of Food Insecurity.* See p. 6 of http://www.fao.org/NEWS/1999/img/SOFI99-E.PDF.

10. UN, World Health Organization, *Fifty Facts from the World Health Report 1998,* http://www.who.int/whr/1998/factse.htm.

11. UN, World Health Organization, *Fifty Facts from the World Health Report 1998.*

12. World Bank, *World Development Indicators 1998 CD-ROM.* An 83% child immunization rate is given by World Bank, Also see World Bank. *World Development Indicators 2000. Health and Population. Disease prevention: coverage and quality.* Health Table 2.15. Access the pdf file via http://www.worldbank.org/data/databytopic/databytopic.html, then choose "Health and Population," "Disease prevention: coverage and quality Table 2.15."

13. Although no countries had child mortality rates of 80%, individual women often faced a grimmer situation than overall statistics indicate. The death rate for children in the poorest quintile is typically about twice that of the highest quintile (World Bank, *World Development Indicators 2000,* p 109). In Sierra Leone as late as 1978, the under-5 mortality rate was 335/1000 live births. Under those circumstances, *some* poor women would see the majority of their children die (World Bank, *World Development Indicators 1998,* Table 2.17 Mortality).

14. World Bank, *World Development Report 1999/2000. Selected World Development Indicators,* 243, http://www.worldbank.org/wdr/2000/fullreport.html.

15. UN, World Health Organization, *Fifty Facts from the World Health Report 1998.*

16. UN, Population Division, *World Fertility Patterns 1997,* UN pub. ST/ESA/SER.A/165 (1997), http://www.undp.org/popin/wdtrends/fer/bferraf.htm and UN. WHO, *World Health Report 2000. Annex Table 2: Basic Indicators for All Member States, Population Estimates,* 156–63, http://www.who.int/whr/2000/en/report.htm. The first of these references contrasts time periods in the 1970s with time periods in the 80s or 90s; the second compares 1990 with 1999.

17. Uganda has not conducted a population census since 1991. One was scheduled for August 2000. Some research indicates that fertility is dropping as people, particularly younger adults, change sexual behavior. See A. Kamali, L. M. Carpenter, J. A. G. Whitworth, R. Pool, A. Ruberantwari, and A. Ojwiya, "Seven-Year Trends in HIV-1 Infection Rates, and Changes in Sexual Behaviour, Among Adults in Rural Uganda," *AIDS* 14, no. 4, (2000) 427–34. Based on a sample survey of 1997, the World Bank revised Uganda's rate to 6.6. (World Bank, *World Development Report 1999/2000. Selected World Development Indicators,* 243, http://www.worldbank.org/wdr/2000/fullreport.html.)

18. UN, Population Division, *World Fertility Patterns 1997,* U.N. pub. ST/ESA/SER.A/165 (1997), http://www.undp.org/popin/wdtrends/fer/bferraf.htm and U.N., World Health Organization, *World Health Report 2000: Annex Table 2: Basic Indicators for All Member States: Population Estimates,* 156–63, http://www.who.int/whr/2000/en/report.htm.

19. UN, Population Division, *World Fertility Patterns 1997,* UN pub. ST/ESA/SER.A/165 (1997), http://www.undp.org/popin/wdtrends/fer/bferraf.htm and UN, World Health Organization, *World Health Report 2000: Annex Table 2: Basic Indicators for All Member States: Population Estimates,* 156–63, http://www.who.int/whr/2000/en/report.htm.

20. UN, Population Division, *1998 Revision of the World Population Estimates and Projections. Below-Replacement Fertility,* http://www.popin.org/pop1998/7.htm.

21. UN, World Health Organization. *Fifty Facts from the World Health Report 1998.*

22. U.S. Census Bureau, *International Data Base: Total Midyear Population for the World: 1950–2050,* May 2000, http://USCensusBureau.org/ipc/www.worldpop.html.

23. This projection is not based solely on decreased fertility per woman, but also includes changes in death rates.

24. U.N., World Health Organzation, *Report on the Global HIV/AIDS Epidemic June 2000,* Geneva. Joint United Nations Programme on HIV/AIDS (UNAIDS) (2000). See p. 6 of print version. The pdf file is called http://www.unaids.org/epidemic_update/report/Epi_report.pdf and is available at http://www.unaids.org/epidemic—update/report/index.html (Note: As of July 2000, page numbers and content differ in the html and the pdf versions of this report. The pdf version content is identical to the print version.)

25. U.N., World Health Organization, *World Health Report 2000: Annex Table 3: Deaths by Cause, Sex and Mortality Stratum in WHO Regions, Estimates for 1999,.* 164, http://www.who.int/whr/.

26. UN, UNAIDS, *Report on the Global HIV/AIDS Epidemic—June 1998.* Access the pdf file via: http://www.unaids.org/hivaidsinfo/statistics/june98/global_report/index.html. See p. 42. See also UN, UNAIDS, *AIDS Epidemic Update: December 1998.* Access the pdf file via: http://www.unaids.org/publications/documents/epidemiology/index.html. Also the UN, World Health Organization, *Fifty Facts from the World Health Report 1998,* 2, reported 52.2 million deaths worldwide in 1997: 2.3 million due to HIV/AIDS (i.e., roughly one in 23 deaths); 7.2 million deaths due to coronary heart disease, 3.3 million deaths due to cancer. Other leading causes of death included acute lower respiratory infections (3.7 million), tuberculosis (2.9 million), diaorrhea (2.5 million) and malaria (1.5–2.7 million).

27. U.N., *World Health Report 2000: Annex Table 2: Basic Indicators of All Member States.*

28. UN, UNAIDS, *AIDS Epidemic Update: December 1998,* p. 7.

29. UN, UNAIDS, *Report on the Global HIV/AIDS Epidemic—June 2000,* 9.

30. UN, UNAIDS, *AIDS Epidemic Update: December 1998,* 7.

31. UN, UNAIDS, *Report on the Global HIV/AIDS Epidemic—June 1998,* 11.

32. UN, UNAIDS, *Report on the Global HIV/AIDS Epidemic. June 2000,* 9.

33. UN, UNAIDS, *Report on the Global HIV/AIDS Epidemic. June 2000,* 11.

34. UN, UNAIDS, *AIDS Epidemic Update: December 1998,* 9

35. See E. J. Mundell, "Uganda First in Africa to Show Drop in New HIV Infections," July 13, 2000, Daily News, Yahoo, http://dailynews.yahoo.com/htx/nm/20000713/hl/uganda_hiv_1.html.

Also see UN, UNAIDS, *Report on the Global HIV/AIDS Epidemic—June 1998,* 12.

36. Kamali et al., *AIDS* 14 (2000): 427–34. This is also reported in UN, UNAIDS, *Report on the Global HIV/AIDS Epidemic—June 1998.*

37. *Nature Medicine* 5, no.9 (Sept. 1999): 963. Editorial.

38. UN, UNAIDS, *Report on the Global HIV/AIDS Epidemic—June 1998,* http://www.unaids.org/epidemic_update/report/. See p. 26 of full report, pdf version.

39. UN, UNAIDS, *AIDS Epidemic Update: December 1998,* 9.

40. UN, UNAIDS, *AIDS Epidemic Update: December 1998,* 9.

41. UN, World Health Organization, *World Health Report 2000: Annex Table 2: Basic Indicators for All Member States: Population Estimates,* 156–63, http://www.who.int/whr/2000/en/report.htm.

42. UN, UNAIDS, *Report on the Global HIV/AIDS Epidemic—June 1998,* 10–11 of pdf version.

43. UN, UNAIDS, *Report on the Global HIV/AIDS Epidemic—June 1998,* 33.

Chapter 10
What It Takes to Preserve Wilderness

Questions for Reflection and Discussion

South Africa

Kobus Krüger worked for eighteen years as a ranger in Kruger National Park, located along South Africa's eastern border with Mozambique. He often rescued orphaned animals. He once hand-reared an orphaned lion at his own expense. More than once, he tranquilized elephants in order to treat wounds they had suffered, occasionally tracking them long enough to do follow-up treatments. He has spent days and sometimes weeks in the bush, on his own, without supplies or fire or radio, risking his life to track down and stop poachers.

Kobus took us on a tour of the park. He was visibly upset one day when we hit a rabbit that darted in front of our car. He stopped the car and moved the rabbit off the road so that animals stopping to feed on it would not suffer the same fate. He was visibly delighted when we encountered sizable herds of healthy elephant and Cape Buffalo. We have never met a person who loves animals more than he does.

However, although Kruger Park is huge, it is not a self-sustaining ecosystem. To keep herds within the park's carrying capacity, the Park Service at one time culled a variety of large mammals. The current view is that this is unnecessary. Natural predators, starvation, and disease will suffice to control most animal populations. The one exception is the elephant.

Kobus was the last ranger in Kruger Park to be assigned the task of culling elephants. He shot them from a helicopter with an automatic rifle, killing as many as a dozen at a time in a matter of seconds (if all went well) with shots through the brain. At his elbow sat monitors from organizations such as the Society for the Prevention of Cruelty to Animals.

The SPCA did not stop the culling, but in 1995, public pressure did. There were 7,200 elephants at the time. As of 2001, there are at least 9,600, according to Kruger Park's senior scientist in charge of elephant management, Ian Whyte (see his article, this section). It is visibly apparent that the park is not producing enough food to sustain them indefinitely. Aari Schrieber, a Section Ranger (which means he is the chief ranger for a large section of the park), told us in 1999 that if the elephants were to disappear today, it would take twenty years for the land to recover from the damage the elephants have done since 1995.

The Park Service plans to move 1,100 elephants to Mozambique over the next four years. It will not be enough. If the population keeps growing at its present rate, there will be roughly 10,300 elephants left in Kruger Park when the relocation process is complete. (Meanwhile, it remains to be seen whether the relocated elephants will be slaughtered by poachers.) Barring a resumption of culling, the Park Service proposes to try to concentrate the elephants in an area constituting about half of the park. The elephants will strip that part of the park, but the Park Service will preserve biodiversity as best it can in the remainder. Is there a better alternative?

One way or another, thousands upon thousands of elephants have to go, and for most of them there is nowhere to go. We talked to a number of rangers. They all said it is only a matter of time before the culling begins anew. So, Kobus is waiting for the phone to ring—waiting for some friend to say it has started again and they need Kobus's help. The prospect horrifies him. What should he do?

For more on Kobus Krüger, see his wife's recent memoir on the often precarious and sometimes hilarious adventure of raising three daughters and assorted wild animals in Kruger Park's most remote wilderness: *The Wilderness Family,* by Kobie Krüger (New York: Ballantine, 2001).

Radical American Environmentalism and Wilderness Preservation: A Third World Critique

Ramachandra Guha

I present a Third World critique of the trend in American environmentalism known as deep ecology, analyzing each of deep ecology's central tenets: the distinction between anthropocentrism and biocentrism, the focus on wilderness preservation, the invocation of Eastern traditions, and the belief that it represents the most radical trend within environmentalism. I argue that the anthropocentrism/biocentrism distinction is of little use in understanding the dynamics of environmental degradation, that the implementation of the wilderness agenda is causing serious deprivation in the Third World, that the deep ecologist's interpretation of Eastern tradition is highly selective, and that in other cultural contexts (e.g., West Germany and India) radical environmentalism manifests itself quite differently, with a far greater emphasis on equity and the integration of ecological concerns with livelihood and work. I conclude that despite its claims to universality, deep ecology is firmly rooted in American environmental and cultural history and is inappropriate when applied to the Third World.

Even God dare not appear to the poor man except in the form of bread.

—*Mahatma Gandhi*

Ramachandra Guha, "Radical American Environmentalism and Wilderness Preservation: A Third World Critique," *Environmental Ethics,* 11 (1989): 71–83. Reprinted with permission of the author and the journal.

INTRODUCTION

The respected radical journalist Kirkpatrick Sale recently celebrated "the passion of a new and growing movement that has become disenchanted with the environmental establishment and has in recent years mounted a serious and sweeping attack on it—style, substance, systems, sensibilities and all."[1] The vision of those whom Sale calls the "New Ecologists"— and what I refer to in this article as deep ecology— is a compelling one. Decrying the narrowly economic goals of mainstream environmentalism, this new movement aims at nothing less than a philosophical and cultural revolution in human attitudes toward nature. In contrast to the conventional lobbying efforts of environmental professionals based in Washington, it proposes a militant defence of "Mother Earth," an unflinching opposition to human attacks on undisturbed wilderness. With their goals ranging from the spiritual to the political, the adherents of deep ecology span a wide spectrum of the American environmental movement. As Sale correctly notes, this emerging strand has in a matter of a few years made its presence felt in a number of fields: from academic philosophy (as in the journal *Environmental Ethics*) to popular environmentalism (for example, the group Earth First!).

In this article I develop a critique of deep ecology from the perspective of a sympathetic outsider. I critique deep ecology not as a general (or even a foot soldier) in the continuing struggle between the ghosts of Gifford Pinchot and John Muir over control of the U.S. environmental movement, but as an outsider to these battles. I speak admittedly as a partisan, but of the environmental movement in India, a country with an ecological diversity comparable to the U.S., but with a radically dissimilar cultural and social history.

My treatment of deep ecology is primarily historical and sociological, rather than philosophical, in nature. Specifically, I examine the cultural rootedness of a philosophy that likes to present itself in universalistic terms. I make two main arguments: first, that deep ecology is uniquely American, and despite superficial similarities in rhetorical style, the social and political goals of radical environmentalism in other cultural contexts (e.g., West Germany and India) are quite different; second, that the social consequences of putting deep ecology into practice on a worldwide basis (what its practitioners are aiming for) are very grave indeed.

THE TENETS OF DEEP ECOLOGY

While I am aware that the term *deep ecology* was coined by the Norwegian philosopher Arne Naess, this article refers specifically to the American variant.[2] Adherents of the deep ecological perspective in this country, while arguing intensely among themselves over its political and philosophical implications, share some fundamental premises about human-nature interactions. As I see it, the defining characteristics of deep ecology are fourfold:

First, deep ecology argues that the environmental movement must shift from an "anthropocentric" to a "biocentric" perspective. In many respects, an acceptance of the primacy of this distinction constitutes the litmus test of deep ecology. A considerable effort is expended by deep ecologists in showing that the dominant motif in Western philosophy has been anthropocentric—i.e., the belief that man and his works are the center of the universe—and conversely, in identifying those lonely thinkers (Leopold, Thoreau, Muir, Aldous Huxley, Santayana, etc.) who, in assigning man a more humble place in the natural order, anticipated deep ecological thinking. In the political realm, meanwhile, establishment environmentalism (shallow ecology) is chided for casting its arguments in human-centered terms. Preserving nature, the deep ecologists say, has an intrinsic worth quite apart from any benefits preservation may convey to future human generations. The anthropocentric-biocentric distinction is accepted as axiomatic by deep ecologists, it structures their discourse, and much of the present discussion remains mired within it.

The second characteristic of deep ecology is its focus on the preservation of unspoilt wilderness— and the restoration of degraded areas to a more pristine condition—to the relative (and sometimes absolute) neglect of other issues on the environmental agenda. I later identify the cultural roots and portentous consequences of this obsession with wilderness. For the moment, let me indicate three distinct sources from which it springs. Historically, it represents a playing out of the preservationist (read *radical*) and utilitarian (read *reformist*) dichotomy that has plagued American environmentalism since the turn of the century. Morally, it is an imperative that follows from the biocentric perspective; other species of plants and animals, and nature itself, have an intrinsic right to exist. And finally, the preservation of wilderness also turns on a scientific argument—viz., the value of biological diversity in stabilizing ecological regimes and in retaining a gene pool for future generations. Truly radical policy proposals have been put forward by deep ecologists on the basis of these arguments. The influential poet Gary Snyder, for example, would like to see a 90 percent reduction in human populations to allow a restoration of pristine environments, while others have argued forcefully that a large portion of the globe must be immediately cordoned off from human beings.[3]

Third, there is a widespread invocation of Eastern spiritual traditions as forerunners of deep ecology. Deep ecology, it is suggested, was practiced both by major religious traditions and at a more popular level by "primal" peoples in non-Western settings. This complements the search for an authentic lineage in Western thought. At one level, the task is to recover those dissenting voices within the Judeo-Christian tradition; at another, to suggest that religious traditions in other cultures are, in contrast, dominantly if not exclusively "biocentric" in their orientation. This coupling of (ancient) Eastern and (modern) ecological wisdom seemingly helps consolidate the claim that deep ecology is a philosophy of universal significance.

Fourth, deep ecologists, whatever their internal differences, share the belief that they are the "leading edge" of the environmental movement. As the polarity of the shallow/deep and anthropocentric/biocentric distinctions makes clear, they see themselves as the spiritual, philosophical, and political vanguard of American and world environmentalism.

TOWARD A CRITIQUE

Although I analyze each of these tenets independently, it is important to recognize, as deep ecologists are fond of remarking in reference to nature, the interconnectedness and unity of these individual themes.

(1) Insofar as it has begun to act as a check on man's arrogance and ecological hubris, the transition from an anthropocentric (human-centered) to a biocentric (humans as only one element in the ecosystem) view in both religious and scientific traditions is only to be welcomed.[4] What is unacceptable are the radical conclusions drawn by deep ecology, in particular, that intervention in nature should be guided primarily by the need to preserve biotic integrity rather than by the needs of humans. The latter for deep ecologists is anthropocentric, the former biocentric. This dichotomy is, however, of very little use in understanding the dynamics of environmental degradation. The two fundamental ecological problems facing the globe are (i) overconsumption by the industrialized world and by urban elites in the Third World and (ii) growing militarization, both in a short-term sense (i.e., ongoing regional wars) and in a long-term sense (i.e., the arms race and the prospect of nuclear annihilation). Neither of these problems has any tangible connection to the anthropocentric-biocentric distinction. Indeed, the agents of these processes would barely comprehend this philosophical dichotomy. The proximate causes of the ecologically wasteful characteristics of industrial society and of militarization are far more mundane: at an aggregate level, the dialectic of economic and political structures, and at a micro-level, the life style choices of individuals. These causes cannot be reduced, whatever the level of analysis, to a deeper anthropocentric attitude toward nature; on the contrary, by constituting a grave threat to human survival, the ecological degradation they cause does not even

serve the best interests of human beings! If my identification of the major dangers to the integrity of the natural world is correct, invoking the bogy of anthropocentrism is at best irrelevant and at worst a dangerous obfuscation.

(2) If the above dichotomy is irrelevant, the emphasis on wilderness is positively harmful when applied to the Third World. If in the U.S. the preservationist/utilitarian division is seen as mirroring the conflict between "people" and "interests," in countries such as India the situation is very nearly the reverse. Because India is a long settled and densely populated country in which agrarian populations have a finely balanced relationship with nature, the setting aside of wilderness areas has resulted in a direct transfer of resources from the poor to the rich. Thus, Project Tiger, a network of parks hailed by the international conservation community as an outstanding success, sharply posits the interests of the tiger against those of poor peasants living in and around the reserve. The designation of tiger reserves was made possible only by the physical displacement of existing villages and their inhabitants; their management requires the continuing exclusion of peasants and livestock. The initial impetus for setting up parks for the tiger and other large mammals such as the rhinoceros and elephant came from two social groups, first, a class of ex-hunters turned conservationists belonging mostly to the declining Indian feudal elite and second, representatives of international agencies, such as the World Wildlife Fund (WWF) and the International Union for the Conservation of Nature and Natural Resources (IUCN), seeking to transplant the American system of national parks onto Indian soil. In no case have the needs of the local population been taken into account, and as in many parts of Africa, the designated wildlands are managed primarily for the benefit of rich tourists. Until very recently, wildlands preservation has been identified with environmentalism by the state and the conservation elite; in consequence, environmental problems that impinge far more directly on the lives of the poor—e.g., fuel, fodder, water shortages, soil erosion, and air and water pollution—have not been adequately addressed.

Deep ecology provides, perhaps unwittingly, a justification for the continuation of such narrow and inequitable conservation practices under a newly acquired radical guise. Increasingly, the international conservation elite is using the philosophical, moral, and scientific arguments used by deep ecologists in advancing their wilderness crusade. A striking but by no means atypical example is the recent plea by a prominent American biologist for the takeover of large portions of the globe by the author and his scientific colleagues. Writing in a prestigious scientific forum, the *Annual Review of Ecology and Systematics,* Daniel Janzen argues that only biologists have the competence to decide how the tropical landscape should be used. As "the representatives of the natural world," biologists are "in charge of the future of tropical ecology," and only they have the expertise and mandate to "determine whether the tropical agroscape is to be populated only by humans, their mutualists, commensals, and parasites, or whether it will also contain some islands of the greater nature— the nature that spawned humans, yet has been vanquished by them." Janzen exhorts his colleagues to advance their territorial claims on the tropical world more forcefully, warning that the very existence of these areas is at stake: "if biologists want a tropics in which to biologize, they are going to have to buy it with care, energy, effort, strategy, tactics, time, and cash."[5]

This frankly imperialist manifesto highlights the multiple dangers of the preoccupation with wilderness preservation that is characteristic of deep ecology. As I have suggested, it seriously compounds the neglect by the American movement of far more pressing environmental problems within the Third World. But perhaps more importantly, and in a more insidious fashion, it also provides an impetus to the imperialist yearning of Western biologists and their financial sponsors, organizations such as the WWF and the IUCN. The wholesale transfer of a movement culturally rooted in American conservation history can only result in the social uprooting of human populations in other parts of the globe.

(3) I come now to the persistent invocation of Eastern philosophies as antecedent in point of time

but convergent in their structure with deep ecology. Complex and internally differentiated religious traditions—Hinduism, Buddhism, and Taoism—are lumped together as holding a view of nature believed to be quintessentially biocentric. Individual philosophers such as the Taoist Lao Tzu are identified as being forerunners of deep ecology. Even an intensely political, pragmatic, and Christian influenced thinker such as Gandhi has been accorded a wholly undeserved place in the deep ecological pantheon. Thus the Zen teacher Robert Aitken Roshi makes the strange claim that Gandhi's thought was not human-centered and that he practiced an embryonic form of deep ecology which is "traditionally Eastern and is found with differing emphasis in Hinduism, Taoism and in Theravada and Mahayana Buddhism."[6] Moving away from the realm of high philosophy and scriptural religion, deep ecologists make the further claim that at the level of material and spiritual practice "primal" peoples subordinated themselves to the integrity of the biotic universe they inhabited.

I have indicated that this appropriation of Eastern traditions is in part dictated by the need to construct an authentic lineage and in part a desire to present deep ecology as a universalistic philosophy. Indeed, in his substantial and quixotic biography of John Muir, Michael Cohen goes so far as to suggest that Muir was the "Taoist of the [American] West."[7] This reading of Eastern traditions is selective and does not bother to differentiate between alternate (and changing) religious and cultural traditions; as it stands, it does considerable violence to the historical record. Throughout most recorded history the characteristic form of human activity in the "East" has been a finely tuned but nonetheless conscious and dynamic manipulation of nature. Although mystics such as Lao Tzu did reflect on the spiritual essence of human relations with nature, it must be recognized that such ascetics and their reflections were supported by a society of cultivators whose relationship with nature was a far more *active* one. Many agricultural communities do have a sophisticated knowledge of the natural environment that may equal (and sometimes surpass) codified "scientific" knowledge; yet, the elaboration of such traditional ecological knowledge (in both material and spiritual contexts) can hardly be said to rest on a mystical affinity with nature of a deep ecological kind. Nor is such knowledge infallible; as the archaeological record powerfully suggests, modern Western man has no monopoly on ecological disasters.

In a brilliant article, the Chicago historian Ronald Inden points out that this romantic and essentially positive view of the East is a mirror image of the scientific and essentially pejorative view normally upheld by Western scholars of the Orient. In either case, the East constitutes the Other, a body wholly separate and alien from the West; it is defined by a uniquely spiritual and nonrational "essence," even if this essence is valorized quite differently by the two schools. Eastern man exhibits a spiritual dependence with respect to nature—on the one hand, this is symptomatic of his prescientific and backward self, on the other, of his ecological wisdom and deep ecological consciousness. Both views are monolithic, simplistic, and have the characteristic effect—intended in one case, perhaps unintended in the other—of denying agency and reason to the East and making it the privileged orbit of Western thinkers.

The two apparently opposed perspectives have then a common underlying structure of discourse in which the East merely serves as a vehicle for Western projections. Varying images of the East are raw material for political and cultural battles being played out in the West; they tell us far more about the Western commentator and his desires than about the "East." Inden's remarks apply not merely to Western scholarship on India, but to Orientalist constructions of China and Japan as well:

Although these two views appear to be strongly opposed, they often combine together. Both have a similar interest in sustaining the Otherness of India. The holders of the dominant view, best exemplified in the past in imperial administrative discourse (and today probably by that of "development economics"), would place a traditional, superstition-ridden India in a position of perpetual tutelage to a modern, rational West. The adherents of the romantic view, best exemplified academically in the discourses of Christian liberalism and analytic psychology, concede the realm of the public and impersonal to the positivist. Taking their succour not from governments and big business, but from a plethora of religious foundations and self-help institutes, and from allies in the "consciousness industry," not to mention the important industry of tourism, the romantics insist that India embodies a private realm of the imagination and the religious which modern, western man lacks but needs. They, therefore, like the positivists, but for just the opposite reason, have a vested interest in seeing that the Orientalist view of India as "spiritual," "mysterious," and "exotic" is perpetuated.[8]

(4) How radical, finally, are the deep ecologists? Notwithstanding their self-image and strident rhetoric (in which the label "shallow ecology" has an opprobrium similar to that reserved for "social democratic" by Marxist-Leninists), even within the American context their radicalism is limited and it manifests itself quite differently elsewhere.

To my mind deep ecology is best viewed as a radical trend within the wilderness preservation movement. Although advancing philosophical rather than aesthetic arguments and encouraging political militancy rather than negotiation, its practical emphasis—viz., preservation of unspoilt nature—is virtually identical. For the mainstream movement, the function of wilderness is to provide a temporary antidote to modern civilization. As a special institution within an industrialized society, the national park "provides an opportunity for respite, contrast, contemplation, and affirmation of values for those who live most of their lives in the workaday world."[9] Indeed, the rapid increase in visitations to the national parks in postwar America is a direct consequence of economic expansion. The emergence of a popular interest in wilderness sites, the historian Samuel Hays points out, was "not a throwback to the primitive, but an integral part of the modern standard of living as people sought to add new 'amenity' and 'aesthetic' goals and desires to their earlier preoccupation with necessities and conveniences."[10]

Here, the enjoyment of nature is an integral part of the consumer society. The private automobile (and the life style it has spawned) is in many respects the ultimate ecological villain, and an untouched wilderness the prototype of ecological harmony; yet, for most Americans it is perfectly consistent to drive a thousand miles to spend a holiday in a national park. They possess a vast, beautiful, and sparsely populated continent and are also able to draw upon the natural resources of large portions of the globe by virtue of their economic and political dominance. In consequence, America can simultaneously enjoy the material benefits of an expanding economy and the aesthetic benefits of unspoilt nature. The two poles of "wilderness" and "civilization" mutually coexist in an internally coherent whole, and philosophers of both poles are assigned a prominent place in this culture. Paradoxically as it may seem, it is no accident that Star Wars technology and deep ecology both find their fullest expression in that leading sector of Western civilization, California.

Deep ecology runs parallel to the consumer society without seriously questioning its ecological and socio-political basis. In its celebration of American wilderness, it also displays an uncomfortable convergence with the prevailing climate of nationalism in the American wilderness movement. For spokesmen such as the historian Roderick Nash, the national park system is America's distinctive cultural contribution to the world, reflective not merely of its economic but of its philosophical and ecological maturity as well. In what Walter Lippman called the American century, the "American invention of national parks" must be exported worldwide. Betraying an economic determinism that would make even a Marxist shudder, Nash believes that environmental preservation is a "full stomach" phenomenon that is confined to the rich, urban, and sophisticated. Nonetheless, he hopes that "the less developed nations may eventually evolve economically and intellectually to the point where nature preservation is more than a business."[11]

The error which Nash makes (and which deep ecology in some respects encourages) is to equate environmental protection with the protection of the wilderness. This is a distinctively American notion, borne out of a unique social and environmental history. The archetypal concerns of radical environmentalists in other cultural contexts are in fact quite different. The German Greens, for example, have elaborated a devastating critique of industrial society which turns on the acceptance of environmental limits to growth. Pointing to the intimate links between industrialization, militarization, and conquest, the Greens argue that economic growth in the West has historically rested on the economic and ecological exploitation of the Third World. Rudolf Bahro is characteristically blunt:

> The working class here [in the West] is the richest lower class in the world. And if I look at the problem from the point of view of the whole of humanity, not just from that of Europe, then I must say that the metropolitan working class is the worst exploiting class in history. . . . What made poverty bearable in eighteenth or nineteenth-century Europe was the prospect of escaping it through exploitation of the periphery. But this is no longer a possibility, and continued industrialism in the Third World will mean poverty for whole generations and hunger for millions.[12]

Here the roots of global ecological problems lie in the disproportionate share of resources consumed by the industrialized countries as a whole *and* the urban elite within the Third World. Since it is impossible to reproduce an industrial monoculture worldwide, the ecological movement in the West must begin by cleaning up its own act. The Greens advocate the creation of a "no growth" economy, to be achieved by scaling down current (and clearly unsustainable) consumption levels. This radical shift in consumption and production patterns requires the creation of alternate economic and political structures—smaller in scale and more amenable to social participation—but it rests equally on a shift in cultural values. The expansionist character of modern Western man will have to give way to an ethic of renunciation and self-limitation, in which spiritual and communal values play an increasing role in sustaining social life. This revolution in cultural values, however, has as its point of departure an understanding of environmental processes quite different from deep ecology.

Many elements of the Green program find a strong resonance in countries such as India, where a history of Western colonialism and industrial development has benefited only a tiny elite while exacting tremendous social and environmental costs. The ecological battles presently being fought in India have as their epicenter the conflict over nature between the subsistence and largely rural sector and the vastly more powerful commercial-industrial sector. Perhaps the most celebrated of these battles concerns the Chipko (Hug the Tree) movement, a peasant movement against deforestation in the Himalayan foothills. Chipko is only one of several movements that have sharply questioned the non sustainable demand being placed on the land and vegetative base by urban centers and industry. These include opposition to large dams by displaced peasants, the conflict between small artisan fishing and large-scale trawler fishing for export, the countrywide movements against commercial forest operations, and opposition to industrial pollution among downstream agricultural and fishing communities.

Two features distinguish these environmental movements from their Western counterparts. First, for the sections of society most critically affected by environmental degradation—poor and landless peasants, women, and tribals—it is a question of sheer survival, not of enhancing the quality of life. Second, and as a consequence, the environmental solutions they articulate deeply involve questions of equity as well as economic and political redistribution. Highlighting these differences, a leading Indian environmentalist stresses that "environmental protection per se is of least concern to most of these groups. Their main concern is about the use of the environment and who should benefit from it."[13] They seek to wrest control of nature away from the state and the industrial sector and place it in the hands of rural communities who live within that environment but are increasingly denied access to it. These communities have far more basic needs, their demands on the environment are far less intense, and they can draw upon a reservoir of cooperative social institutions and local ecological knowledge in managing the "commons"—forest, grasslands, and the waters—on a sustainable basis. If colonial and capitalist expansion has both accentuated social inequalities and signaled a precipitous fall in ecological wisdom, an alternate ecology must rest on an alternate society and polity as well.

This brief overview of German and Indian environmentalism has some major implications for deep ecology. Both German and Indian environmental traditions allow for a greater integration of ecological concerns with livelihood and work. They also place a greater emphasis on equity and social justice (both within individual countries and on a global scale) on the grounds that in the absence of social regeneration environmental regeneration has very little chance of succeeding. Finally, and perhaps most significantly, they have escaped the preoccupation with wilderness preservation so characteristic of American cultural and environmental history.

A HOMILY

In 1958, the economist J. K. Galbraith referred to overconsumption as the unasked question of the American conservation movement. There is a marked selectivity, he wrote, "in the conservationist's approach to materials consumption. If we are concerned about our great appetite for materials, it is plausible to seek to increase the supply, to decrease waste, to make better use of the stocks available, and to develop substitutes. But what of the appetite itself? Surely this is the ultimate source of the problem. If it continues its geometric course, will it not one day have to be restrained? Yet in the literature of the resource problem this is the forbidden question. Over it hangs a nearly total silence."[14]

The consumer economy and society have expanded tremendously in the three decades since Galbraith penned these words; yet his criticisms are nearly as valid today. I have said "nearly," for there are some hopeful signs. Within the environmental movement several dispersed groups are working to develop ecologically benign technologies and to encourage less wasteful life styles. Moreover, outside the self-defined boundaries of American environ-mentalism, opposition to the permanent war economy is being carried on by a peace movement that has a distinguished history and impeccable moral and political credentials.

It is precisely these (to my mind, most hopeful) components of the American social scene that are missing from deep ecology. In their widely noticed book, Bill Devall and George Sessions make no mention of militarization or the movements for peace, while activists whose practical focus is on developing ecologically responsible life styles (e.g., Wendell Berry) are derided as "falling short of deep ecological awareness."[15] A truly radical ecology in the American context ought to work toward a synthesis of the appropriate technology, alternate life style, and peace movements. By making the (largely spurious) anthropocentric-biocentric distinction central to the debate, deep ecologists may have appropriated the moral high ground, but they are at the same time doing a serious disservice to American and global environmentalism.[16]

NOTES

1. Kirkpatrick Sale, "The Forest for the Trees: Can Today's Environmentalists Tell the Difference," *Mother Jones* 11, no. 8 (November 1986): 26.

2. One of the major criticisms I make in this essay concerns deep ecology's lack of concern with inequalities *within* human society. In the article in which he coined the term *deep ecology,* Naess himself expresses concerns about inequalities between and within nations. However, his concern with social cleavages and their impact on resource utilization patterns and ecological destruction is not very visible in the later writings of deep ecologists. See Arne Naess, "The Shallow and the Deep, Long-Range Ecology Movement: A Summary, " *Inquiry* 16 (1973): 96 (I am grateful to Tom Birch for this reference).

3. Gary Snyder, quoted in Sale, "The Forest for the Trees," p. 32.

4. See, for example, Donald Worster, *Nature's Economy: The Roots of Ecology* (San Francisco: Sierra Club Books, 1977).

5. Daniel Janzen, "The Future of Tropical Ecology," *Annual Review of Ecology and Systematics* 17 (1986): 305–306; emphasis added.

6. Robert Aitken Roshi, "Gandhi, Dogen, and Deep Ecology," reprinted as appendix C in Bill Devall and George Sessions, *Deep Ecology: Living as if Nature Mattered* (Salt Lake City: Peregrine Smith Books, 1985).

7. Michael Cohen, *The Pathless Way* (Madison: University of Wisconsin Press, 1984), p. 120.

8. Ronald Inden, "Orientalist Constructions of India," *Modern Asian Studies* 20 (1986): 442. Inden draws inspiration from Edward Said's forceful polemic, *Orientalism* (New York: Basic Books, 1980). It must be noted, however, that there is a salient difference between Western perceptions of Middle Eastern and Far Eastern cultures respectively. Due perhaps to the long history of Christian conflict with Islam, Middle Eastern cultures (as Said documents) are consistently presented in pejorative terms. The juxtaposition of hostile and worshiping attitudes that Inden talks of applies only to Western attitudes toward Buddhist and Hindu societies.

9. Joseph Sax, *Mountains Without Handrails: Reflections on the National Parks* (Ann Arbor: University of Michigan Press, 1980), p. 42.

10. Samual Hayes, "From Conservation to Environment: Environmental Politics in the United States since World War Two," *Environmental Review* 6 (1982): 21. See also the same author's book entitled *Beauty, Health and Permanence: Environmental Politics in the United States, 1955–1985* (New York: Cambridge University Press, 1987).

11. Roderick Nash, *Wilderness and the American Mind,* 3rd ed. (New Haven: Yale University Press, 1982).

12. Rudolf Bahro, *From Red to Green* (London: Verso Books, 1984).

13. Anil Agarwal, "Human-Nature Interactions in a Third World Country," *The Environmentalist* 6, no. 3 (1986): 167.

14. John Kenneth Galbraith, "How Much Should a Country Consume?" in *Perspectives on Conservation,* ed. Henry Jarrett (Baltimore: Johns Hopkins Press, 1958), pp. 91–92.

15. Devall and Sessions, *Deep Ecology,* p. 122. For Wendell Berry's own assessment of deep ecology, see his "Amplications: Preserving Wildness," *Wilderness* 50 (Spring 1987): 39–40, 50–54.

16. In this sense, my critique of deep ecology, although that of an outsider, may facilitate the reassertion of those elements in the American environmental tradition for which there is a profound sympathy in other parts of the globe. A global perspective may also lead to a critical reassessment of figures such as Aldo Leopold and John Muir, the two patron saints of deep ecology. As Donald Worster has pointed out, the message of Muir (and, I would argue, of Leopold as well) makes sense only in an American context; he has very little to say to other cultures. See Worster's review of Stephen Fox's *John Muir and His Legacy,* in *Environmental Ethics* 5 (1983): 277–81.

Headaches and Heartaches: The Elephant Management Dilemma

Ian J. Whyte

The dilemmas of managing elephants in reserves are generally poorly understood. The different attitudes to basic management philosophies have led to many acrimonious debates and deep rifts have developed between some of the respective proponents. While those from the anti-culling lobby have condemned the killing of elephants, the non-interference policies are not without their own ethical dilemmas. It is not the purpose of this article to try to favor either one of these two points of view, but to try to set the situation in Kruger National Park against the background of other national parks in Africa. The intention is to get to the heart of the elephant dilemma so that readers themselves may understand the issues and have some empathy with elephant managers and the decisions with which they are faced.

Before the advent of firearms, the elephants of Africa were probably not greatly influenced by humans. But as firearms began to proliferate, and the ability to easily kill large elephants increased, the populations gradually started to decline. Initially this was due to the demand for ivory in Europe and Asia and because there was no control over the offtake. This situation persisted, and in spite of the establishment of reserves and national parks throughout Africa, many (if not most) elephants roamed outside of these parks and remained vulnerable. The numbers of elephants on the African continent in earlier times are not known, but by 1979 they had been reduced to an estimated 1.3 million. By this time the range states (countries which have elephant populations) north of Zimbabwe and Namibia were in the grip of a poaching epidemic that reduced the continental population to 609,000 by 1989.

Concern over this dramatic trend resulted in the banning by CITES (Convention on the International Trade in Endangered Species) of international trade in elephant products in 1989. Although one study four years later concluded that in most countries the ban had not halted the illegal offtake, it is widely believed that the ban had achieved much in reducing the poaching. The worst of the poaching was experienced in the countries to the north of the Zambezi and Cunene rivers. South of this, although increased poaching was experienced, this was not at a scale which significantly reduced elephant numbers. In Kruger the first case of elephant poaching was recorded in 1975. Since then the incidence has been sporadic except during the years 1981–1985 when a sharp increase in the incidence was experienced. During this time, 193 were shot. Active anti-poaching measures solved the problem to a large degree, and elephant poaching has occurred only sporadically since. In total only 285 are known to have been poached in the park's history. Populations in the

southern range states have continued to grow and by 1995 were estimated at 170,800, with the possibility that there could be as many as 228,000. This has had the result that northern range states generally favor the ban while southern countries do not. Wildlife departments could benefit enormously from the financial returns that the sale of elephant products could bring, and any form of elephant management in these countries is now impeded by financial constraints. So while the northern African range states welcome the ban as protection for their populations, most southern African range states are seeking ways of limiting theirs. But why limit elephant numbers? Why manage elephants at all? Why not just let them be?

THE PROBLEM

In many African countries today, elephant populations are confined to national parks and reserves. This is also true of most other wildlife species, both plant and animal. In South Africa nature reserves and national parks are conservation "islands" whose boundaries are hard-edged up against the activities of people. In these conservation islands, it is usually the wildlife manager's job to try to protect all of these species (maintenance of biodiversity), but some reserves have been proclaimed for the protection of particular species, and biodiversity may be less important. But there are some countries such as Kenya who can still claim that as much as 70 percent of their wildlife exists outside of national parks. Wildlife managers in these countries have their own set of problems, usually concerned with interactions between the human population and wild animals, and the dilemmas of conserving elephants in closed systems have not yet really become conservation priorities. Large parts of east Africa, particularly in Kenya and Tanzania, is Masai country, and the Masai were semi-nomadic pastoralists who traditionally had little interest in wildlife. They saw wild animals as "God's cattle," and their whole lives were centered around their own herds of cattle and goats. Competition with wildlife was confined to incidents where people or their livestock were killed or injured by animals, but by and large they could coexist in harmony. But this situation is changing slowly for two main reasons. Dramatic human population increases and hunger for land no longer affords people a nomadic lifestyle, or their herds free access to rangeland, and many are switching from pastoralism to agriculture. Agriculture is rarely tolerant of wild animals as crops planted by people are highly attractive to the larger herbivores. In the early 1990s the African Elephant Specialist Group considered human/elephant conflict to be the greatest current problem facing elephant conservation. These clashes will gradually force wild animals into sanctuaries. Secondly, college education of the Masai youth means that they have tasted the offerings of civilization and are no longer satisfied with the pastoralist's simple lifestyle. They want jobs, houses, and access to electricity and running water, and to the trappings of the modern world, none of which are compatible with pastoralism.

These two forces will probably ensure that the wildlife in these countries will also eventually occur only in reserves, and the problems of maintaining biodiversity in these reserves will be brought into sharper focus. As a general rule of thumb, the smaller the conservation "island," the greater the degree of management it will require, because some of the essential ecological processes will be missing. An example of this is that many small parks can not accommodate the larger predators, and in the absence of the population checks which these predators impose on prey populations, humans have to take over this role. But if the "island" is large enough (and the Kruger National Park is one of these), the vast majority of its component species and ecosystem processes will require no management at all. Throughout time, they have co-evolved to form a complex matrix of competition, interdependence, and above all, survival. This is the way it should be, and managers should interfere with these processes only when it is unavoidable.

In nature, nothing is static. Rainfall and temperature are the engines of ecological processes, and these are never constant. There are years when rainfall is abundant and others of drought. In most of Africa these conditions are cyclic, and there are periods of above average rainfall followed by periods below average. In Kruger, records show that rainfall cycles are of about twenty years in duration—ten dry years followed by ten wet ones, though it is usual to experience one or more dry years during the wet part of the cycle and vice-versa.

Different species respond differently to the prevailing conditions, some increasing during the wetter years, but some also favor the dry conditions, and their populations flourish during the drier parts of the cycle. In Kruger, wildebeest and zebra favor the drier years when the grass has been grazed and trampled to create more open conditions. These animals rely on their good eyesight to avoid predators, so when the grass becomes long and rank during the wetter years, lions have enough cover to get up close and make their kills more easily.

But most species prefer the wetter times and have developed ways of reducing the threat of predators in long grass. When food is abundant, buffalo congregate in large herds and the adult bulls are aggressive to predators and protective of the females and calves. But when droughts come, each buffalo must compete with the others for the meager grass that is available. Food shortages force them to split into smaller groups to allow more effective foraging. Being in a weakened physical condition, these small groups are much more vulnerable to lions. A single large herd of buffalo will find itself in only one lion pride's territory at any one time, but when a herd splits, more prides have access to the herd and individuals are in poorer physical condition, rendering them less able to defend themselves against these predators. Furthermore, water is in short supply. Lions wait at the water, and the buffalo, already weakened by dehydration, can be killed almost at will. Many cases have been recorded of lions making multiple buffalo kills during these times. It is a predator's instinct to kill, and each time the buffalo herd approaches the water, the lions kill another. During the severe droughts of 1992–1993, Kruger's buffalo population declined by more than 50 percent from nearly 30,000 to less than 15,000.

Kudu have other strategies for avoiding lions in long grass. They have excellent eyesight, smell, and hearing and live in small groups that forage silently. During droughts they lose condition and are forced to forage in habitats they would normally avoid. As with buffalo, they are forced to drink at the few remaining waterholes, where the lions are waiting. In most cases these population fluctuations are driven by the short-term (twenty-year) climatic cycles.

But elephants do not conform to this pattern. In today's imperfect world, Africa is no longer what it was before the advent of technological man, and the continent-wide ecological processes that used to operate can now no longer do so. Most of these processes are lost in the mists of time and can now only be speculated upon. The population cycles of elephants is one of these. Elephants had few natural enemies in those times, so how were their populations regulated? Of course, no population can continue to grow forever, as eventually they will exceed the resources upon which they are dependant. There must come a time when conditions are less favorable and the population will enter a phase of decline. Did elephant populations build up over centuries in local "events"—to the point that food became limiting—and then die out to a much lower level? Or did they move away when food became scarce? If so, where did they go? And what would have happened to the elephants already occupying the area to which they moved? Did disease play a role? Were primitive humans capable of limiting elephant numbers? These are all questions nobody can answer with certainty.

What is known is that elephants have the intellect and constitution to exploit a wider range of food resources than any other animal (except humans). When grass and browse are not available, they can eat twigs and branches or use their tusks to pry bark off trees, and even push trees over to reach the leaves in the canopy and to expose the roots. So natural limitation of elephant numbers will only begin to occur once even these resources have been depleted, at which time the environment will have been subjected to severe impacts. In this process, the question is what would have happened to the other species—both plant and animal—occupying these habitats?

Some may have even been eliminated locally. In the old Africa, this would not have been a problem as these species would likely have occurred elsewhere and recolonization could have taken place, even though it may have taken hundreds of years. In evolutionary time, this is nothing. Some species that could not adapt may have been pushed to extinction, but this is nature's way.

The old Africa is gone forever. No longer can species range far and wide, and no longer can most terrestrial life forms naturally recolonize areas where they have been extirpated, and so elephants, with their ability to drastically modify habitats, are a threat to many species within these reserves. A reserve like Kruger, which is large enough to allow minimum management of most species, is still too small to accommodate elephant population fluctuations without environmental damage. And thus, if the objective of a national park is the long-term conservation of all the indigenous biota occurring there, then something will ultimately have to be done to limit elephant numbers.

HISTORY OF THE KRUGER NATIONAL PARK ELEPHANT POPULATION

Elephant populations throughout Africa were decimated by the early hunters, whose writings were more concerned with the thrill of the hunt than of natural history. In the Lowveld areas of South Africa where Kruger is situated, all the elephants had been shot before the park was proclaimed in 1898. Nobody knows how abundant elephants were in this area, or how they utilized their range, but there is evidence from some sources that suggests that elephant numbers were never very high in the Kruger area, even before White hunters arrived with guns.

The San (Bushmen), whose characteristic rock paintings are still visible in rock shelters in both the southwestern and northern areas of the KNP, were associated with the latter part of the Late Stone Age between 7,000 B.C. and 300 A.D. Elephants must have occurred in the KNP area during this time as one of the paintings in a shelter along the Nwatindlopfu River shows a group of five of these animals. Of the 109 shelters containing rock art so far discovered in the KNP area, this is the only one featuring elephants. One other shelter with elephant paintings has been found in the area, some 30 kilometers to the west of the KNP.

It would be expected that a large, dramatic and dangerous animal like the elephant would feature prominently in Bushman folk lore. Elephants were a popular theme for paintings elsewhere in southern Africa because they provided a lot of meat and were associated with water and rain, which the Bushmen artists were keen to influence. Bushmen were capable of hunting elephants by "ham-stringing," as shown in a painting near Molteno in the eastern Cape. San art is believed to have been of considerable spiritual significance to the artists, depicting the experiences of shamans during states of altered consciousness induced by ritual dances. San art was not narrative of their lifestyles nor "menus" representative of their diet, and the incidence of different species in their art may not reflect those species' relative abundance. But elephants have been shown to be of special symbolic importance to San peoples elsewhere in South Africa. Human figures with trunks and even with heads of elephants have been painted. Given then that elephants were of considerable cultural significance to the San people, their relative scarcity in the rock art of the KNP and surrounding area may indicate that these animals were relatively rare during the San era.

There is also a lack of evidence of old elephant utilization of baobab trees. Elephants strip off the bark of these trees for food and scars on the trees persist for hundreds of years. One baobab in Kruger carries the inscription "BRISCOE 1890" carved in its bark. This carving, now 110 years old, is still as clearly visible as if it were carved only a year or two ago, and will probably persist for another 100 years or more. If elephants were utilizing baobabs 100 or even 200 years or more ago, it could be expected that the scars would still be clearly visible. Yet more than 50 percent of trees in the far north of the park show no sign of utilization by elephants. Baobabs outside the park show no signs of old elephant damage, but clearly show the impacts of earlier people who cut "panels" of bark from the trees for domestic use.

A third clue comes from the writings of early travelers to the area who made little mention of these animals. Francois de Cuiper and his party were the first to visit the area in 1752. His mission from Delagoa Bay (now Maputo in Mozambique) was to establish trade with the interior in gold, ivory, and copper. They saw few elephants and were informed by the indigenous people that if they wanted ivory and gold, they would have to go far to the north to the area now known as Zimbabwe. Copper could be obtained from the area that is now Phalaborwa. This last information has proved to be correct, so the information on ivory was probably also correct. Louis Trichardt, on his trek through Kruger in 1838, also made no mention of elephants in his diaries, though he mentioned an elephant hunt once they arrived in Lorenco Marques. Jo,o Albasini was the first white settler in the Kruger area. He arrived in Delagoa Bay in 1831 and established himself as a hunter and trader in Mozambique and the eastern Transvaal. He formed a company in Lorenco Marques whose objective was to hunt elephants and increase the trade in ivory. This lasted only six months, and he then established himself as a hunter and trader in the Phabeni area in the southern part of Kruger. After two years there he abandoned the store and moved to Ohrigstad. Though no records exist, the outcome of these ventures hint of an elephant population at too low a density to sustain viable hunting and trade. Of the later hunters who left any written record, it is perhaps significant that none who hunted elephants (e.g., Selous, Finaughty) did so in the KNP area, while those that did hunt there (Kirby, Glynn) did not shoot any elephants.

A final speculative clue may come from the floral and faunal diversity which still exists in the Kruger today. Over two thousand plant species have been recorded, some of which are known to be vulnerable to elephants. If there had been successive episodes of high densities of elephants over time, this complex diversity may have been much reduced.

Why elephant densities may have been low is not known, but one theory speculates that perhaps numbers could have been held in check by early humans. If densities were low, and humans had the means to kill elephant calves, say using poisoned arrows, they would not have to kill many to impose limits on their population growth. But however many elephants there may have been, they were killed by hunters, and by 1903 James Stevenson-Hamilton, the park's first warden, reported that there were no elephants to be found. They responded quickly to the new sanctuary, and by 1905 his staff had found evidence of their occurrence near the confluence of the Letaba and Olifants rivers, which is located roughly midway between the park's northern and southern boundaries. From there they gradually recolonized the whole park. Diaries of earlier rangers recorded the first sightings of elephants in new localities. The recolonization process to the northern and southern extremities of the park occurred at about the same rate. Recolonization northward to the Luvuvhu River took until 1945 (forty years to cover 290 kilometers), while the spread southward to the confluence of the Crocodile and Sigaas rivers was slightly slower, continuing until 1958 (fifty-three years to cover 280 kilometers).

Numbers increased steadily during this time, and concern over the evident impact the elephants were having was shown as early as 1942. In that year, a park ranger by the name of Steyn made the following tongue in cheek comment in his annual report: "With regard to the question of the control (culling) of elephants in certain areas where it may become necessary, the following idea has come to mind, i.e. to use a 10 or 12 ton armored car to remove them from any region. This will naturally only be possible after the present war and I leave the details to the imagination of the reader."

Early estimates of population size were made by park rangers based on their observations, but without modern aids like helicopters, these estimates were clearly severe underestimates. The concerns intensified until 1967, when the first comprehensive aerial census was conducted and the population estimate of 6,586 proved to be nearly three times larger

than the 1964 estimate of 2,374. The decision was then taken to limit the population to around 7,000, and culling was initiated.

This figure concurred with those of biologists working elsewhere in Africa at around that time. The elephant population density in Murchison Falls National Park in Uganda was five elephants per square mile, and it was felt that this considerably exceeded carrying capacity. In Tsavo National Park, Kenya, the early recommendation was that one per square mile was the right number (this recommendation was never implemented). The figure of 7,000 for Kruger, which has an area of 20,000 square kilometers (8,000 square miles), was just below this. This number gave an average area of 2.7 square kilometers per elephant. As this policy was implemented to prevent loss of biodiversity from Kruger's ecosystems, it was undoubtedly successful; no species are known to have been lost from the park.

So how was the Kruger elephant population managed so as to maintain the prescribed population of around 7,000? A unique technique was developed for the census of Kruger's elephant population, which is the most intensive and accurate census of elephants conducted anywhere in the world, though recent intensive fixed wing census techniques in Tsavo using multiple teams and GPS (global positioning system) technology probably give comparable results. The Kruger census is conducted annually during August and September to capitalize on the late dry season conditions. At this time of year the animals tend to congregate in the vicinity of watercourses and waterholes, and visibility is at its best because the trees have shed their leaves. A helicopter is preferred as it can fly at extremely low speeds and can hover as well. In large, loose aggregations of elephants, the pilot can maneuver the aircraft systematically from group to group at low altitude until all elephants have been counted. In contrast, fixed-wing aircraft are forced to maintain forward speed, which necessitates circling of the groups which is confusing to observers. Because of the helicopter's maneuverability, a flight pattern that follows the watercourses is flown. Kruger is particularly suitable for this as its undulating savanna terrain is drained by a well-spaced network of watercourses that are clearly visible from the air. The pilot begins by flying along one bank of a major watercourse, keeping close enough to it to allow careful scanning of this denser vegetation but yet far enough from it to allow adequate scanning of the ground as far as the watershed. He then turns up each tributary and subtributary, following it up one bank to its source and back down the other bank. In this way each drainage system is systematically covered before moving on to the next. The watercourses give the pilot visual cues as to where to fly, and systematic ground coverage thereafter is almost automatic. The census is conducted at an altitude of about 200 meters, depending on the terrain and visibility. The whole census is completed in eighteen days, about 130 hours of flying time. Research has shown that census totals have never exceeded the expected result by more than 7 percent. Once the census result is known, a committee (known as the Standing Committee for Wildlife Management, made up of the senior nature conservation staff of the Kruger) meets to decide on an appropriate culling quota to conform with the elephant management policy. This quota is then achieved either through capture and translocation to other conservation areas where they can be accommodated, or through culling.

But whereas the Kruger managers decided to limit elephant population growth, a laissez faire policy was adopted in east Africa. This policy's roots almost certainly originated from compassion for the elephants themselves. To sit quietly in the close proximity of a herd of elephants who are going quietly about their business is an emotional experience that cannot easily be described to anyone unfamiliar with these animals. Their sheer size alone induces a feeling of awe, and you will not have to sit for long before their intelligence, playfulness, compassion, and tolerance become evident. All of these attributes of elephants combine to instill in those lucky enough to have experienced them, a feeling of empathy that intensifies the longer that exposure to elephants lasts. These emotions are not comfortable bedfellows with the concepts of killing these wonderful animals. Elephants are also considered to be a "keystone species"—one upon which other species depend for their own survival. Elephants open up areas of thick woodland, affording habitats to species favoring those of a more open character. They also pass seeds through the gut to be deposited in seedbeds of fertile dung, assisting germination.

But to stand under the canopy of a massive old baobab tree (*Adansonia digitata*) and to ponder a little on the age of such old giants, is an emotional experience of a different kind, but one which in its own way is no less soul stirring than that which may be gained from elephants. It is perhaps also their size which makes the initial impression, but the aura of age is tangible. The age that these trees may attain is not known as the pithy wood shows none of the rings that allow the determination of age in other tree species. The "Briscoe" baobab is not a particularly large tree, suggesting that it is not one of the older ones, yet it was more than a hundred years ago since the carving was carried out. The tree can have changed little in the intervening 109 years, so some of the older ones must be many hundreds if not thousands of years old!

Baobabs are also a keystone species, and a little examination of some of these trees will reveal their significance in the environment. The convolutions in the trunks of these benevolent old giants form cracks and holes that provide shelter to many small animals and birds and offer ideal sites to rear their young. To some species, the presence of baobabs is critical—in Kruger the only known nesting sites of both the Batlike Spinetail (*Neafrapus boehmi*) and the Mottled Spinetail (*Telecanthura ussheri*) are in hollow baobabs. Without these trees, these birds would simply not occur in the area. Mosque Swallows (*Hirundo senegalensis*) and Cape Parrots (*Poicephalus robustus suahelicus*) also favor these trees for breeding, and any decline in the number of baobabs would have its effects on the populations of these birds also. Barn owls (*Tyto alba*) would occur at much lower densities if the nesting holes offered by baobabs were not available, and Whiteheaded Vultures (*Trigonoceps occipitalis*) favor baobabs for building their nests as well.

So, quite apart from their aesthetic appeal, both elephants and baobabs play important but different ecological roles—the elephant in its capacity to accelerate nutrient cycling and alter their environments, and the baobab because of its importance to many species of animals as a source of food and shelter. But elephants also feed on baobabs, stripping the bark off and even chipping away the pithy wood with their tusks. In extreme cases the trees may become so weakened that they eventually topple and die. Most tree species die when ring-barked, but baobabs have a remarkable capacity to regenerate bark. They are therefore resistant to utilization by elephants up to a point, but one of the major causes of mortality in baobabs is drought, particularly once they have had excessive amounts of bark removed by elephants, which probably accelerates moisture loss. Anyone visiting the northern parts of Kruger will not fail to notice that most baobabs have suffered considerable bark removal. During aerial censuses of the Kruger elephant population, dead baobabs are also recorded, and this has showed that over the past few years, more than 200 have died due to the combined effects of drought and elephants.

Baobabs are not the only plants which are vulnerable to utilization by elephants. The knobthorn (*Acacia nigrescens*) is another keystone species, as it is favored by a wide number of raptors and other birds for nesting. Wahlberg's (*Aquila wahlbergi*) and Tawny (*A. rapax*) eagles, Whitebacked vultures (*Gyps africanus*) and some of the small goshawks (*Accipiter species*) also favor the mature knobthorns, while quelea finches (*Quelea quelea*) and Wattled starlings (*Creatophora cinerea*) are communal breeders favoring stands of the stunted forms of this species. They breed in thousands (even millions) in these stands and are a staple food of migrant Steppe and Lesser Spotted eagles. Luckily, the knobthorn is a very common species, but few mature knobthorns in Kruger are free of some form of elephant utilization, and many have been ring-barked resulting in the death of the tree. Absence of knobthorns would have severe consequences for all of these species. Marula trees (*Sclerocarya birrea*) are often debarked or pushed over, and even the branches up to the

thickness of a man's forearm are eaten. The number of marulas has also declined over the years. Other plant species at risk are fever trees (*Acacia xanthophloea*), kiaat (*Pterocarpus angolensis*), and star chestnut (*Sterculia rogersii*). These are just a few of the species favored by elephants, but where elephant densities increase to the point where food availability becomes limiting on the elephant population, nearly all plant species are at some degree of risk. In some parks elsewhere in Africa, this has meant loss of species from systems with unlimited elephant populations.

In Amboseli National Park (Kenya), for example, an extremely high density of elephants (one elephant per 0.42 square kilometers) has led to a decline in the woodland in the park, resulting in the extirpation (local extinction) of both lesser kudu (*Tragelaphus imberbis*) and bushbuck (*Tragelaphus scriptus*). Other species favoring woodland, such as gerenuk (*Litocranius walleri*), giraffe (*Giraffa camelopardalis*), baboons (*Papio species*), and monkeys (*Cercopithicus species*), have also declined inside the park. In Tsavo National Park (Kenya), dense woodland was changed into open savanna, and baobabs are now very rare where they were once common.

The Tsavo story is an interesting one. The huge elephant herds that modified Tsavo's landscapes this way are now severely depleted—by poachers, not managers! Apart from being one of Africa's most famous national parks, it gained initial fame through the book *The Man-eaters of Tsavo*, "which tells the story of two lions which killed at least twenty-eight laborers and even held up the construction of the railway in 1898. J. H. Patterson, the author of this book, was a keen observer and he described the nature of the bush as "interminable nyika . . . the whole country covered in low stunted trees . . . the only clearing being the narrow track of the railway." Elephants are hardly mentioned in the book. In 1903, the writer/traveler Mienertzhagen found "very few" elephants in the thick Tsavo bush, but by 1970, this had changed and human developments outside had compressed the population into the park, an area roughly the same size as Kruger. Aerial surveys in that year estimated the population to stand at 45,000.

These elephants had a huge impact, and by 1974 a severe drought had reduced the population to 36,000. Nine thousand elephants had died, and at the same time, 4,000 black rhino also died of starvation. The carcasses of these animals offered an opportunity to local people and corrupt staff to establish an illegal trade in the horns and tusks. Once established, this trade turned to the poaching of live elephants and rhinos. By 1989, the Tsavo elephant population had been reduced to just 6,000. Thirty thousand elephants had been poached, and black rhinos had been all but extirpated. Tsavo today is an open savanna which has favored the grassland species, and the removal of the trees has had some other interesting consequences. Fountains have appeared where they were not known to occur before—the moisture which once was sucked up by the trees and transpired into the atmosphere now seeps into the drainage lines. These changes are perceived by some as benefits to the Tsavo ecosystem induced by high densities of elephants, and their role in this transformation has often been lauded. But an unanswered question remains—what would Tsavo look like today had the 30,000 elephants not been removed from the system by the poachers?

The poaching has now been contained and the most recent census of Tsavo's elephants in 1999 yielded a total of close to 8,000.

MANAGEMENT OPTIONS

Given this background, the obvious basic question about elephant management in any confined reserve is whether or not to limit elephant numbers. If the management authority decides that the maintenance of biodiversity is the objective, what options are available? In order to limit the population growth of any species (and cynically, this applies even to humans), there are only three possible options. These are translocation, contraception, culling, or a combination of these. Others such as hunting are just variations of one or more of these options. In Western society, non-lethal means of population limitation would clearly be preferable to the killing of ele-

phants, but there is a strong body of opinion in Africa which supports the sustainable use of wild animals (even elephants) to provide benefits to local people and communities. Who is right? Westerners who live far removed from the problems, or local people who often suffer terrible depredations from living close to elephants and see the killing of the animals as a desirable solution? For them, if the problem animals are removed, the meat becomes available and revenues can even be generated. In some areas such as in Zimbabwe, problem or excess animals are hunted by professional hunters in a scheme known as CAMPFIRE (Communal Areas Management Program For Indigenous Resources). These hunters pay for the privilege, and the money is given back to the people for community development projects.

If non-lethal means are to be employed, only two options are available—translocation or contraception. Translocation would usually be the first choice, as this has the additional advantage of establishing other elephant populations elsewhere, but in southern Africa today, the saturation point has almost been reached. Most conservation areas already have elephants, and their managers understand the consequences of too many elephants and do not wish to increase their populations any further. There is now hope, however, that a very large conservation area will be established on Kruger's eastern boundary in Mozambique. There are no elephants in this area, so it could provide a considerable opportunity to dispose of excess elephants.

There is a common perception that once the game-proof fence between Kruger and the proposed park has been removed, elephants will immediately move off into Mozambique, alleviating the need to limit the population in Kruger. But studies of elephant movement in Kruger have revealed that they show a remarkable degree of fidelity to their home ranges. These home ranges have an average size of about 1,200 square kilometers. Factors that may be expected to stimulate movements, such as rainfall in nearby areas and culling, have little effect on their movements. They may be induced to move to other parts of their home range, but they do not leave. This is certainly because these ranges are where they are most comfortable. The old matriarchs know the area well, for example, where the water is in dry season, where food availability may be best—information and experience that they have built up over their long lifetimes. They also have the ability to extract sufficient nutrition from the available vegetation even during severe droughts, so there is no real necessity to move.

The recolonization of Kruger after its proclamation was a slow process, and there is no reason to believe that the reverse process—the recolonization of Mozambique—will be any quicker. If the new park in Mozambique is to offer Kruger a non-lethal means of limiting its elephant numbers, it will probably have to be by translocation, not natural recolonization. But translocation is very expensive, and it should be remembered that translocations are still not the ideal solution. They provide temporary respite, but ultimately areas acquiring Kruger's excess elephants will be faced with exactly the same problems and dilemmas—the problems are merely transferred.

Contraception is the second non-lethal option. This is not yet a tool in the elephant management toolbox as it is still very much in the research phase. This research is being encouraged by South African National Parks with the hope that this may one day provide another practical option. Two methods have received attention so far, the first being through hormonal control using estrogens. This project has been terminated in Kruger on humane grounds, as there was strong evidence that the hormones were drastically affecting behavior of the vaccinated cows and attendant bulls. Females were induced into a state of "false estrus," and bulls were attempting to mate with them while they were not receptive. This led to harassment of the cows by the bulls to the point that they got separated from their families and even from their small calves. Three of the calves died during the research period. The other project achieves contraception through PZP (porcine zona pellucida) vaccination of adult elephant females. This vaccine is made from the ovaries of pigs, which are obtained from commercial slaughterhouses. The vaccine stimulates the animal's immune system to produce antibodies that bind to the outer membrane (zona pellu-

cida) of the elephant cow's egg cells and prevents penetration of sperm. This method has no behavioral consequences and is continuing. But in an area the size of Kruger with a population of 9,000 elephants, even this method will not provide the solution, for logistical reasons. Computer modeling has shown that to stabilize an elephant population, approximately 70 percent of all breeding females have to be under treatment at any one time. In Kruger this means between 3,000 and 4,000 females. These animals will require repeated dosages, which means that each will have to be individually radio-collared to enable location when the animal's booster shots become due. The expense would be astronomical, and there just are not that many radio frequencies available to us. However, there are some new developments that give hope for the future.

One negative consequence of limiting an elephant population through contraception would be a decline in the sizes of matriarchal (family) units. While young bulls leave the mothers at about fourteen years of age, young cows remain with their mothers for as long as the mother remains alive. The large extended family consists of the matriarch, her surviving daughters, and all their respective offspring. A cow may have as many as eight or ten calves in her life, of which half could be expected to be female. A family could thus comprise five or six adult females with calves of varying ages in a group size of around fifteen. This is an important social structure among savanna elephants in which young animals learn essential lessons in life, particularly with regard to birth, death, mating behavior, and rearing of young. If a contraception program aimed at stabilizing numbers in the population, each cow would theoretically only be allowed to have two offspring, one of which could be expected to be a male. The average group would thus consist of the old female, a single daughter, and possibly one or two calves. Given the social importance of the family, would this enforced change in elephant society be ethically acceptable to us?

Culling is currently the only remaining long-term alternative. Anaesthetic drugs would be ideal but they can not be used for such purposes, as the meat may subsequently not be used for human consumption. The leaving of such contaminated carcasses in the field for scavengers is therefore also questionable. The only drug that has been approved which allows for later human consumption of the meat is succinylcholine chloride (scoline), whose component compounds occur naturally in mammalian bodies. Scoline is a neuro/muscular blocking agent which paralyzes the animal by preventing the brain's impulses from reaching the muscles. This was used in Kruger to cull elephants in the past, as it had the clear advantage of obviating wounding and provided a far greater safety margin for staff and scientists attending such culls. However, research conducted in Kruger showed that the use of this drug on elephants was inhumane, as the heart muscle remained largely unaffected by the scoline. The locomotory muscles were the first to be affected, followed by those controlling breathing (the diaphragm). This meant that the animal was fully conscious but paralyzed and unable to breathe, and therefore died of suffocation if it could not be brain shot immediately after becoming recumbent. The use of scoline was then discontinued, and the current method is a sharpshooter using live ammunition from a helicopter at close range.

PREVIOUS AND CURRENT POLICIES

The policy of limiting the Kruger elephant population to a level around 7,000 was maintained until 1994, when it was challenged by an animal rights group. A decision was then taken to place a moratorium on culling until the policy had been reviewed. This review is now complete and the new policy awaits the final go-ahead. In the meantime, the population has increased to an estimated 9,150 at the last (1999) census.

This new policy focuses less on numbers of elephants than on the impacts that they are having. The park has been divided into six zones. The two in the northern and southwestern extremities have been designated as botanical reserves, which will be managed to limit elephant impacts on the rare or ecologically important plants to sustainable levels. These species include baobabs, star chestnut (*Sty-*

erculia rogersii), mopane (*Colophospermum mopane*) forest and sandveld communities in the north, and the species with affinities to higher rainfall such as kiaat (*Pterocarpus angolensis*), tree aloe (*Aloe bainsii*), and mountain syringa (*Kirkia wilmsii*) in the southwest. The rest of Kruger will be divided into four zones of roughly equal area. Two of these will be high elephant impact zones where no elephant population limitation will be practiced, and the other two will be low elephant impact zones. In these two zones elephant populations will be decreased through translocations and/or culling.

While the policy aims at reducing elephant impacts in these zones, it is stated that the priority will be to do so as far as is possible by non-lethal means. As many animals as there is a market for will be translocated, and should contraception become a feasible option, this will also be implemented. Where these options cannot be used, however, culling will have to be conducted. But will this work? Will the elephants respect the boundaries and stay in the designated zones? Some feel that they are smart enough to move from the low-impact zones to the safety of the high-impact zones. Others feel that once numbers build up and food becomes scarce, they will move out of the high-impact zones to where food is more readily available. The movement study has shown the high degree of fidelity that elephants have for their home ranges, so the boundaries of these zones were drawn up to roughly follow the boundaries of these ranges. Kruger managers are thus confident that the zoning will hold up under the strain of the different management options, but only time will tell.

The rationale behind this new policy is that in terms of biodiversity, it is expected that there will ultimately be negative consequences in habitats with elephant densities that are either too high or too low. As elephant densities increase, so will their impact, but also, as densities decline, habitats and biodiversity are expected to become impoverished through bush encroachment, declining rates of plant germination, etc. Programs monitoring many different aspects of biodiversity are being initiated in these zones to detect changes that may be related to changing elephant densities. These will include the monitoring of such aspects as trends in the numbers of mature trees and changes in the structure of communities of various life forms, such as plants, birds, frogs, reptiles, and small and large mammals. Many other aspects, such as rates of soil erosion, water quality, and vegetation cover, will also require monitoring. The complex interrelationship of elephants and fire on the woody vegetation (trees) needs to be carefully determined (changes induced by fire should not be confused with those by elephants). All of these will need to be repeated in all or most of the twelve different land types (major vegetation zones), as elephant impacts may differ between them.

For each of these aspects, limits to the amount of change that are considered acceptable will be set. These limits are known as "Thresholds of Potential Concern" or TPCs. For example, an 80-percent allowable change in the number of mature trees in a landscape may be set as a TPC. If and when the monitoring program detects that such an 80-percent change has occurred, the TPC is "evoked" and the authorities must become "officially concerned." The situation must be then considered in depth with all stakeholders present and all the data and evidence and information on the table. The outcome of this may be a decision either that an 80-percent change is not serious enough to warrant elephant management and that the TPC should be changed to 85 or 90 percent, or that the 80-percent TPC is valid and management should be implemented. These TPCs will be purposely set wide to accommodate a large degree of change that should take many years to trigger.

The two high- and two low-impact zones are to be interchangeable, and once TPCs have been triggered, the high-impact zones should become low-impact zones and vice versa, allowing heavily impacted areas a period of recovery. This will also induce high- and low-density cycles on the elephant population, which over the past thirty years has been held stable.

Other research will focus on the elephants themselves. The movement study will be particularly important as the policy will be successful only if high- and low-impact zones can in fact be maintained. If elephants move out of the high-impact zones, all that the new policy will achieve is the culling of excessive numbers of elephants in the low-impact zone and the hoped for high-impacted zone will never be achieved. Census and distribution information will be a major part of this. Differences in terms of population dynamics between these zones will also need to be monitored. It is suspected that fertility rates in elephants may decline as population densities increase. This information may yield invaluable insights on the future management of the population. Impacts of elephants on vegetation will also be monitored through computer analysis using image-processing techniques on aerial photos of Kruger's vegetation. Field studies of particular plant species have already started and will be maintained as elephant densities change under the new policy.

This new policy will not be a model that will work for every other national park that holds elephants. Ecosystems differ widely as do conservation priorities, and each should have its own rationale for the management of its populations, whether it be some form of limitation of numbers or one of non-interference. Much will be learned from the implementation of Kruger's policy, which should be of significant interest to all elephant managers.

SUMMING UP—THE DILEMMA

This brings us finally to the headaches and heartaches that are experienced by all managers of elephants. A decision has to be made before elephant damage occurs as to whether the area for which they are responsible will be managed as an elephant reserve or whether the maintenance of biodiversity will be the priority. The two approaches are mutually exclusive. The decision to manage as an elephant sanctuary is a valid one that should be taken out of respect for the elephants themselves. Elephants are wonderful animals with which most people easily empathize, and there should be areas where they can live out their lives free from the stresses of the various management options. Amboseli is probably a good case in point. The wonderful research that has been conducted there by Cynthia Moss and her colleagues has taught us most of what we know about the complexities of elephant behavior. There is still much to learn about long-term elephant cycles, and Amboseli may be the best place to study these. The Addo Elephant National Park in South Africa is another. This park was created as a sanctuary for the last remaining elephants in the Cape region, and this should probably always remain the conservation priority.

A decision not to limit growth of an elephant population has to be made consciously by the management authority, in full awareness of the consequences—they must be aware that, ultimately, other species will begin to disappear from the system due to overuse or habitat changes induced by elephants. In some cases this may even mean extinction. Also, when times of drought come (as they inevitably will in Africa), they must be prepared for the decrease in elephant population that will occur. These will be disturbing and emotional times.

But if the maintenance of biodiversity is the priority, something will have to be done (usually culling) to limit the numbers and densities of elephants before biodiversity is affected. This is also not an easy decision—the killing of elephants is never one that can or should be taken lightly. But here lies yet another moral dilemma. At what level should the population be held? To maintain a population at any particular level requires the removal from the population of a number of animals equal to the population's annual increase. The average increase in an elephant population has been calculated at a rate of 6.2 percent per year. To maintain a population at around 7,000 would require the annual removal of about 450 individuals. However, if managers should decided to allow the population to increase to a level around 20,000 and maintain it there, this would necessitate the removal of around 1,300 individuals per year! As we have seen, when such numbers are involved, the only option for the removal of most of them would be through culling. If we agonize over the morality and ethics of culling elephants, then the issue will be greatly compounded by having to cull a much larger number. Is it not better to keep a population small at the level where few animals need to be culled or better still, at a level where most excess animals could be translocated rather than culled?

There is no middle of the road on the issue of elephant management—a choice has to be made: to cull or not to cull? Choosing the latter (a valid choice depending on the conservation priority for the designated area) means there is no going back once extensive damage has occurred. When plant and/or animal species have been lost, it may (through the management of the elephant population) be able to maintain the remaining biodiversity, but the restoration of the system to its former richer state of biodiversity and function will scarcely be possible. The dilemma is in weighing the sacrifice of individual elephants against the sacrifice of species. Either way, the decision taken will always trouble the consciences of those involved in the process. You should not have cold feet if you enter the elephant management arena, and be prepared to be castigated for your opinions and your decisions whichever side of the debate they may lie.

If the decision were yours, what would you do?

At the Hand of Man: Peril and Hope for Africa's Wildlife

Raymond Bonner

In January 1989, as the international campaign to ban ivory trading was gaining momentum in the United States and Europe, the people in Nyaminyami, in northwestern Zimbabwe, were granted authority by the state to exercise dominion over the wildlife in their district. There were no front-page headlines, not even any news stories, but it was a critical step in a radical conservation program—one that will do more to save the elephant than the ban on ivory trading, and one that goes farther toward giving people the benefits of wildlife than anything being tried in Kenya or anywhere else on the continent. The people of Nyaminyami can cull impala herds, or sell concessions to hunt lions or elephants, or set up tourist joint ventures—and they get nearly all the financial returns, not just a small share. What enables them to do this is CAMPFIRE—the acronym used (mercifully) for the Communal Areas Management Programme for Indigenous Resources. The communal lands, which are akin to the Maasai group ranches in Kenya, make up about 40 percent of Zimbabwe's land area. During the colonial period, the communal lands were the tribal trust lands, where the colonialists told the blacks they had to live; not surprisingly, they are the poorest lands in the country. In many of the communal lands, as in much of rural Africa, wildlife is the only valuable resource.

Nyaminyami—it is pronounced "nee-ah-mee nee-ah-mee"—is rich in natural beauty. Its rolling hills are forested with thorn trees and stands of mopane, with its small, butterfly-shaped leaves; according to Shona legend, after God made all the animals, the butterflies complained to Him that they were being eaten by the birds, so He made the mopane tree, where the butterflies can hide. Nyaminyami also has a wealth of wildlife. During an hour's drive through the woods near Lake Kariba, a tourist encounters elephants at every turn. A hippo once ran across the path of my vehicle, then plunged into the lake, creating a huge wake, to the amusement of onlookers. On the cliff above the lake sits the Bumi Hills Safari Lodge; from the bar or rooms with sliding glass doors, guests can gaze down on elephants drinking from the lake as the sun sets. On another visit, I departed the lodge just before sunrise for a game drive and walk. Within minutes, the lanky guide directed his spotlight into the bushes and caught the soulful eyes of a dozen slumbering buffalo—massive beasts with thick flat horns. Farther on, in an open field, hundreds of buffalo were grazing, along with impala, kudu and zebra; warthogs scampered about, their long tails erect and whipping in the air. The guide shone his light at the base of a cliff a few hundred yards away and the glistening eyes of a leopard answered back; it quickly dashed off. Across the field in a copse were two lionesses, a mother and daughter. "Powerful lady," the guide commented with admiration as the mother got up and sauntered off; he had seen her mating several months before, and now two four-month-old cubs tottered toward our vehicle, stopping ten yards away. During the walk, we came upon a family of elephants. When they detected, our presence, they froze, and spread their ears wide. Deciding we were not a threat, they returned to cracking off tree limbs with their trunks as they ambled past the rocks where we were perched.

The "big five" on most safari-goers' checklist are elephants, lions, buffalo, leopards and rhino; most people leave disappointed, with the last two species the most elusive. I had just seen four of the five in a few hours, and though we did not come upon any rhino, our guide said that if we had gone into nearby

Raymond Bonner, *At the Hand of Man: Peril and Hope for Africa's Wildlife* (New York: Alfred A. Knopf, 1993), 253–78. Reprinted with permission of the author.

Matusadona National Park, we surely would have. There are forty rhino in Matusadona, and another twelve to sixteen rhino live in Nyaminyami outside the park; together that is more rhino than in any unfenced area of Kenya. The guide said that 90 percent of the guests at the lodge were people who had been to Kenya and now wanted a safari experience where there were not so many vans and people. He added that the owners of the Bumi Hills lodge had been talking about expanding from twenty-two rooms but that the staff had threatened to resign. "We don't want to become another Kenya," he said. To avoid that, he said, no more than two vehicles were out on a game drive at the same time, a welcome contrast to Kenya and even Tanzania's Ngorongoro, where minivans leave the lodges in convoys in the morning, again after lunch, and once more just before dusk. Tourists are enthralled by the wildlife in Nyaminyami, and sport fishermen angle for tiger fish in Lake Kariba—the record is nearly thirty pounds and fourteen-pounders are not unusual.

But nature's endowment has not meant much for the people of Nyaminyami, who are Shaangwa, a Shona-speaking tribe, and Tonga. Agriculturalists, the Tonga were living along the Zambezi River when David Livingstone explored it in the middle of the last century. The Zambezi's headwaters are in Angola, and 1,600 miles later they empty into the Indian Ocean off the coast of Mozambique. At one point, the waters plunge 600 feet, roaring and sending up a constant spray, forming Victoria Falls. In the 1950s, the British, in order to provide hydroelectric power for their colonies of Northern and Southern Rhodesia (today Zambia and Zimbabwe) and Nyasaland (Malawi), dammed the Zambezi at Kariba, 300 miles below Victoria Falls. As the waters rose, Lake Kariba was formed—the largest man-made lake in the world at the time; its length is comparable to the distance from New York to Washington—and the Tonga were forced off their lands. The name Nyaminyami comes from a mythological water snake that the Tonga believe lived in the Zambezi and during droughts came to help, curling itself on the bank of the river and allowing the people to cut nutritious meat from its body.

Nyaminyami could be just about any place in rural Africa. The people live in mud-and-wattle huts; they survive as subsistence farmers, coaxing maize, sorghum and a few vegetables out of soil that is shallow and sandy; there is little rainfall, less than thirty inches in the best years. The wildlife and the tsetse fly make their lives even more difficult.

One morning, Nyaminyami's executive officer, Simbarashe Hove, talked about CAMPFIRE and the people's attitude toward the wildlife. He was sitting in his office in Siakobvu, the district's administrative center, which consisted of a few cinder-block buildings, a police post, a health clinic and a general store. Hove's corner office had a cement floor and was sparsely furnished with a wooden desk and a high-back, vinyl-covered chair. It was a few weeks after the international ban on ivory trading had been imposed at Lausanne, and Hove said, "The decision was, let me put it bluntly, irresponsible. All these organizations, if they really wanted to come up with something, they should have talked with us. You know what this ban means to the local people? There will be too many elephants. The elephant population is growing. You don't need surveys, you can just see it. It means the people are exposed to more danger than they are now." Hove reached for a book in which he filed reports from villagers about damage by wild animals. Reading from one, he said that in the last growing season, elephants returning night after night to one man's plot had destroyed 264 bags of maize, 24 bags of groundnuts and 4 bales of cotton.

About this time, a district councillor, Wilson Nebiri, who is also a village chief, came in to talk to Hove about something, and when he realized the conversation was about the problems with wild animals, he mentioned that the previous night lions had killed twelve goats in hamlets in his constituency. A half hour or so later, a clerk brought in a note handwritten on a half-sheet of lined paper which had just arrived in Siakobvu. "Dear Chairman. Manyandu was nearly killed by an elephant and the women could not fetch water because of these elephants. There are two of them."

Also present in Hove's office was Elliot Nobula, the senior game officer for Nyaminyami, and after listening to Nebiri and reading the letter, he set off to investigate. He had already been at work since dawn, following up on last night's reports of wild animal attacks, much as a police officer coming on duty pursues the previous shift's crime reports. In Nobula's office, down the outside corridor from Hove's, the top of a low bookshelf was lined with animal skulls, and one wall was covered with a topographical map of the district. The map was overlaid with transparent plastic, and on the plastic were little dots, each one indicating where a wild animal had invaded someone's field—green for buffalo, blue for leopards and lions, red for elephants. In some places—near the lake and several small streams, most of which exist only in the rainy season—there were so many dots that they merged into a big mass. Most of the dots were red. In Mola, the largest of the four traditional chieftaincies in Nyaminyami, elephants and buffalo destroyed between six and seven tons of maize during the 1989 growing season.

After he left his office, Nobula's first stop was two miles down the dirt road, at a small hamlet where a man, his wives, their sons and their wives, and lots of children lived. Their huts were made of mud packed between a ribbing of rough posts, which was then covered with a thin layer of mud; the roofs were thatch, which extended over the sides of the hut to provide some shade. In this hamlet, as in most, there was a granary, a small circular structure raised off the ground, and a slated platform about four feet high where the women put their pots and pans to dry—a simple, and ancient, kitchen counter. Near a smoldering fire several women were sitting on the ground, sorting vegetables, some with tiny children held in slings on their backs. A brown dog limped about, an open wound on its rear left leg, the evidence that it had barely survived the swipe of a lion's paw the previous night.

Picking up faint paw marks, Nobula now tracked the lion's path through the hamlet and around the circular goat pen. Only one goat had been taken, but Nobula believed that it was probably the same lion—an adult male, he said—that had killed fourteen goats in a nearby hamlet two days earlier. "It is probably an old lion," Nobula remarked as he followed the tracks through the scrub before coming to a spot, two hundred yards from the huts, where the lion had stopped to feed on its catch. "He can't go around chasing impala, so he looks for a goat; goats are easy," Nobula explained. Before leaving the hamlet, Nobula assured the women that they would be compensated for the goats the lion had killed.

As part of its CAMPFIRE program, Nyaminyami set up its own wildlife department, which is called the Nyaminyami Wildlife Management Trust. One of the wildlife trust's first acts was to search for a warden. Twenty-five men applied, and after interviewing six of them, the trust, in 1989, chose Nobula, who was approaching thirty.

When he was fourteen, Nobula left school and went to work as a stock checker for a chemical company where his father was a security guard. He did not like the work. "I grew up in the communal lands and coming to town and sitting in a plant was boring," he says. "I didn't want to be confined. I wanted to be in the bush." He was also determined to get an education, and through correspondence courses, he earned his high school diploma; then he took a test and was admitted to Zimbabwe's national-parks college. After graduating, he worked as a game ranger in a wildlife reserve near Victoria Falls, and was then assigned to Chizarira National Park, which is just south of Nyaminyami. Within two years there, he advanced from ranger to acting warden. He had done well, but he left that promising future to work with CAMPFIRE in Nyaminyami. "This was a chance to work with the people in the communal lands," he explained. A quiet, but assured, lean six-footer, Nobula speaks Tonga, Shona, Xhosa and English, an invaluable skill in Zimbabwe's multilingual nation. As he goes from village to village, Nobula seems like a cross between a family doctor and a politician, soothingly talking to villagers about the importance of wildlife in order to enlist them in his cause to save it.

Leaving the hamlet where the lion had taken the goat, Nobula drove on the dirt road past fields of charred stumps and smoldering tree trunks. (To clear the land for cultivation, the men hack a notch in the base of a tree with a machete, and then prop the ends of burning logs against the notch; eventually, the fire burns through the base and the tree crashes.) In most of the fields there was a small log platform, perhaps ten feet off the ground, supported by not very sturdy poles. From this perch women and older children stand guard, throwing rocks or banging on pots to drive off animals, such as baboons, which forage for seeds, and even buffalo, which often stampede through a field. The men who had sent the letter about the elephant attack were lounging under a tree; nearby, women were doing daily chores—a typical picture of rural Africa, where the women do the heavy work, hauling firewood on their backs and water on their heads, and planting, weeding and harvesting.

The men, most of whom were barefoot, with mud caked on their cracked feet, described what had happened the previous evening. They had been drinking beer—a home brew made from sorghum—and communicating with their ancestors, they explained. About seven o'clock, the party broke up and Manyandu, the man referred to in the note to Hove, headed home. As he rounded a bend in the road, he saw the elephant, an adult bull, twenty yards away and ambling in his direction. Manyandu stopped, but the elephant continued moving toward him, and when it was only a few feet away, Manyandu, who is not sure of his age but looked to be in his fifties or sixties and has silver stubble on his chin, took off, running as fast as he could through a furrowed field. The elephant chased him. Reenacting the harrowing experience the next day, Manyandu pointed to two places where the elephant had scooped its tusks into the dirt to seize its prey; one time the dirt sprayed over Manyandu. He managed to reach a guard tower; the elephant gave up.

The elephant remained in the area, and the next morning it had frightened other villagers, about two hours before we arrived. This time, it had charged twenty-six-year-old Tobias Changwedera while he was clearing logs from his field. "They're just there, they're just there," Changwedera and the other men now said excitedly to Nobula, motioning toward the trees. They wanted Nobula to set out in pursuit of the elephants and kill them. Nobula takes every opportunity to explain to villagers about conservation, and he did so now. The wildlife belongs to them, he told the men. It is valuable, and if they look after it, it will benefit them and their children, he said.

The next day, Nobula drove to Mola, the commercial center of Nyaminyami; it consisted of four cement-wall general stores, painted in pastel colors and sparsely stocked with soap, pots, blankets, peanut butter, and a hodgepodge of sundries, most of which languish on the shelves for weeks because they are too expensive for the people of the district. At one hamlet, a mile or so from Mola, a small woman named Tenes Mutare told Nobula about a tragedy that had happened just a few weeks earlier.

One evening, after dinner, four small girls had gone into a field a hundred yards from their huts in order to go to the bathroom, Mrs. Mutare began. Moments later, the villagers heard screams and the girls came running back. But there were only three; Mrs. Mutare's seven year-old daughter was not with them. She had been seized by a lion. When Mrs. Mutare went to look, she found only her daughter's intestines, and farther away, pieces of her legs.

"If my husband had followed that lion and killed it, he'd be in jail now," Mrs. Mutare said, becoming increasingly agitated. Several other women expressed their anger to Nobula. Buffalo and elephants had destroyed their maize and sorghum, but the government did nothing, they said. When the people tried to protect themselves by killing the animals, they were put in jail. Or if a man shot an impala or a zebra in order to get meat for his family, he was arrested by the rangers and beaten. As far as these women were concerned the government's conservation laws and policies meant that wild animals were protected while people were persecuted and prosecuted. "That is the feeling we want to break through" Nobula remarked as he left the hamlet.

Nobula combines a concern for people with his commitment to conservation, an attitude far too rare among rangers, and on another occasion, he discussed his views of conservation and what he and CAMPFIRE hoped to accomplish. It was first light, and sitting in front of his "home"—a large tent, to which he had added a thatched porch—we could see in the distance the bright-orange meanderings of disconnected brush fires started by farmers to clear areas for cultivation. Nobula's rimless glasses were pushed down on the bridge of his nose, and he was wearing leaf-green shorts. "The concept of conservation is to conserve for the people of this country, but in actual effect it has been the visitors who have benefitted more," he said. "The people of the communal lands have been hunting for hundreds of years, so we have to educate them that the animals have a right to live and that they will be a benefit for the people. We have to educate them, not just arrest and beat them." In the past, national park rangers routinely beat poachers or suspected poachers, he explained. It has been the same throughout Africa.

Asked about the ivory ban, Nobula said, "It is not good for the people of Nyaminyami. Maybe they don't fully understand yet why it is important to conserve the elephant, but when they begin to see the economic value of the resource, we are very, very sure that eventually they'll understand. But the ban means they won't receive the economic benefits of the elephants; they won't have the meat and they will not be able to sell the skins and the ivory."

As another pot of coffee bubbled on the open fire, two men in yellow jumpsuits came through the trees, with tanks on their backs. They were spraying for tsetse fly. Nobula reacted with a few expletives, then said, "It is bad for the wildlife."

It might seem hard to imagine how anyone could be against eliminating the tsetse fly, but the tsetse fly is the wildlife conservationist's best friend. The reason is somewhat complex. To begin with, the tsetse fly transmits a disease that is fatal to cattle (the strain that causes sleeping sickness is virtually nonexistent in Africa today), so farmers stay away from areas with tsetse flies. Without humans and cattle, wildlife flourishes. Conversely, when the tsetse fly is eliminated, farmers move in. Then the battle with the wildlife begins because the farmers do not want zebra and giraffes competing with their grazing animals, elephants and buffalo destroying their crops, and lions killing their cattle.

The tsetse organism *Trypanosoma* is borne in the blood of wild animals, which share the woodlands and dense bush that the fly inhabits. Traditionally, Africans cleared small areas around their villages in order to get control of the tsetse fly. When the colonialists came to southern Africa, they had another approach to opening up tsetse-infested lands. They destroyed the game on a large scale. In the early 1930s, for instance, Southern Rhodesia adopted a tsetse fly eradication policy that resulted in the killing of 25,000 wild animals a year.

The Zimbabwe government still wants to eliminate the tsetse fly, because there is a shortage of good farming land, and also because the government wants ranchers to raise more cattle, primarily for export to the European Community. Once the tsetse is controlled, the people of Nyaminyami will have a choice: wildlife or cattle. It will probably be a fairly easy decision, as it would be for most Africans. In modern society, cows are private property; wildlife is not—you can't brand a kudu. You can go to the bank if you have cattle and borrow money; you can sell it. if the people of Nyaminyami have any doubt that their lives would be richer if they had cattle, they have only to look at their neighbors. The tsetse has been eliminated just outside Nyaminyami for several years, and in that area, where cattle are grazing, the homes are substantial—rectangular, with whitewashed bricks and glass in the windows, rather than squat mud-and-wattle structures.

Conservationists, of course, hope that the Nyaminyami villagers can be persuaded to choose wildlife over cattle, and they might if they can make money from wildlife as they do from cows. And that is the purpose of CAMPFIRE. "They have never had the opportunity to know the potential value, the full value, of wildlife," says Simon Metcalfe, who has worked with CAMPFIRE in Nyaminyami since its inception.

Along with Nobula, Metcalfe stands out as the person to be recognized for the success of CAMPFIRE in Nyaminyami. He was the catalyst for getting it started and remained as the advisor. And successful it has surely been, so much so that nearly every district in Zimbabwe where there is wildlife has instituted CAMPFIRE programs—Metcalfe became the national coordinator—and conservationists throughout Africa realize that CAMPFIRE is a model conservation program.

What is striking about Metcalfe is that he is not a professional conservationist or an ecologist. His work with wildlife is motivated by a desire to save humans. "I only came into this project because I wanted to try to do something for the needs of the people," he says, without an air of righteousness. An angular and intense man whose hair was beginning to grey and thin when he turned forty in 1991, Metcalfe is not a patrician by heritage, education or attitude. His father was an agricultural extension officer in the British colonial service who served in the Sudan before moving to Rhodesia in the 1950s. He didn't send his son away to England for schooling as so many whites did, and Simon graduated from the University of Rhodesia, with a degree in political science. That was in 1972, when the white Rhodesian government was drafting young men for its war against the black independence movement; Simon left the country rather than fight against a cause he sided with. He worked for the social services department in the London Borough of Lambeth.

As soon as Zimbabwe had achieved its independence, in 1980, Metcalfe returned and went to work in Nyaminyami for Save the Children, the non-profit humanitarian and development organization. At that time, malnutrition was so severe that most Nyaminyami children were physically and mentally retarded. Metcalfe remained with Save the Children until 1988, leaving only after he was approached by a local nonprofit development organization, Zimbabwe Trust, to help get CAMPFIRE started. After studying the CAMPFIRE policy, Metcalfe decided that it would be a way to increase the wealth and improve the nutrition of the people in Nyaminyami, and he signed on.

"Simon's brief for the first year was just to run around and talk to people," said Robert Monro, who as director of Zimbabwe Trust in Harare recruited Metcalfe. Metcalfe did precisely that, reluctantly leaving his wife, who managed a rock band, and two children behind in Harare, to spend long weeks in Nyaminyami sleeping on the ground and eating canned food heated over an open fire.

Zimbabwe Trust was founded by Monro and Keith Madders, young, liberal Rhodesians, who, like Metcalfe, lived in self-exile in England during the war, and returned after independence to help in their country's development. After establishing the trust, they came up with a creative way to raise an endowment. During the war for independence, when the international community imposed sanctions against the white Rhodesian government, one of the government's responses was to freeze the bank accounts of the foreign companies operating in Rhodesia. After independence, the new government offered these companies, most of which were British, bonds in the amount of their Zimbabwe accounts. Monro and Madders made them another offer: donate the money to this new trust, and take a tax deduction in Britain. They raised about $5 million, a considerable amount for a new charity, and Lady Soames, Winston Churchill's youngest daughter, became the trust's first president, a post she still holds.

The trust's approach to development differs from that of most humanitarian agencies and of institutionalized aid and development agencies such as the World Bank. "We establish right at the beginning the principle of business," says Monro. "This isn't aid." Aid has been ineffective at promoting development and alleviating poverty, he says—a criticism hard to dispute, looking at the billions of aid dollars that have been spent in Africa over the last quarter of a century and the plight of the people on the continent today. Most aid and development programs also tend to be "top-down"—planned by bureaucrats in Washington, London or from their offices in Third World capitals, too often without consulting the people the programs are intended to benefit. Finally, Monro noted, aid programs often create a dependency among the recipients; then, when the aid donors leave, as they invariably do, the people are worse off than they had been before.

The trust hopes to build institutions, such as the Nyaminyami Wildlife Management Trust, which will survive when the outside assistance is discontinued. In 1989, Zimbabwe Trust allocated $1.5 million over a five-year period to help Nyaminyami establish its wildlife management program; after that the trust expects the program to be self-sufficient. It almost certainly will be, because of CAMPFIRE.

Like many well-intentioned government projects in Africa, and throughout the developing world, CAMPFIRE languished for several years after the policy was announced in 1982, largely because the government did not allocate any money. Finally, in 1988, Zimbabwe Trust decided that CAMPFIRE fit with its own philosophy of development, and Monro approached his friend Metcalfe, offering him the equivalent of $25,000 a year (or less than half of what most of the Nairobi-based conservationists are paid).

Metcalfe is convinced that CAMPFIRE will make a radical difference in Nyaminyami. "From being one of the poorest areas in Zimbabwe, I predict that within a decade it could be one of the wealthiest," he said in 1990. He has calculated that by the mid-1990's, Nyaminyami will be earning $500,000 a year from wildlife, which is about $500,000 more than the district has now from all sources, except foreign aid.

Even before they recognize the full monetary value of their wildlife, however, the people of Nyaminyami have enjoyed a substantial nonmonetary benefit. Twice a year, beginning in 1989, the wildlife authorities have culled the impala herds and distributed the meat to the residents.

The impala is a graceful creature with a fawn coat, white stomach and black streaks on its white buttocks; the males have lyre-shaped horns. Shooting one, it seemed to me, would be as sickening as shooting Bambi. But the impala cull is integral to the success of CAMPFIRE in Nyaminyami—to the human and conservation aspects of it—and during my second visit to Nyaminyami, in September 1990, I warily asked to observe a cull.

The headquarters for the operation was on the edge of Lake Kariba, where, just after dark, the professional hunters and their assistants moved out, in a roofless Land Rover. A man in the back danced the beam of a powerful spotlight through the mopane thicket and tall grass. When the sparkle of eyes answered back, the professional hunters, one in the front and one in the back, began to shoot. With the first crack of rifle fire, impala leaped into the air, arching their backs, searching for the danger and alerting others. In a moment, some froze; others ran. An impala that was hit would often sprint for ten or twenty yards before falling forward on its knees, then rolling over dead. After the herd had scattered beyond rifle range, the hunters' assistants moved through the grass locating the dead and wounded; their ability to find the animals in the tall grass on an almost moonless night was astonishing. If an impala was still twitching, a man would slit its throat. Every effort was made to limit the suffering and above all not to leave a wounded impala for the hyenas and other predators. One young impala, only slightly wounded with the first shot, proved particularly difficult for the hunters to capture, always just out of reach of the rifle range or hidden by grass as it tried to escape. The hunters pursued that one impala for at least ten minutes without success; finally one of the hunters left the vehicle and stalked it on foot, into a thicket of trees, where he delivered the final blow.

It required two men to heave a carcass into the open back of the vehicle and when all of the kills had been located and loaded, the vehicle and spotlight would begin moving through the night again, until the hunters saw more twinkles. Throughout the night, loaded vehicles returned to the Lake Kariba site, where the impala were hung by their hind legs from hooks on a long rail. Their heads were severed—they were sold to a nearby crocodile farm—and then the heart, lungs, gut and other organs were removed. Then they were skinned. About four in the morning, a seven-ton truck full of impala carcasses began moving out to the first of thirteen distribution sites throughout Nyaminyami.

In Mola, one of the four Nyaminyami chieftaincies, men and women arrived early and waited patiently in order to buy some meat, which was distributed from the community center, a whitewashed circular building with a thatched roof. Black plastic sheets were spread on the floor and a scale hung from the rafters. Rangers from the Nyaminyami Wildlife Management Trust hacked up the carcasses, weighed the pieces and collected the money. The impala meat was sold for Z$1 a kilogram—well below the market price of Z$4. (Two Zimbabwe dollars equaled one United States dollar, roughly.) The bargain price was not charity, however; it covered the cost of each cull. One woman bought an entire carcass, another half of one. Outside, a woman with a baby swaddled on her back chopped carcasses into smaller pieces with an ax; the meat was then stuffed into bags and pails of all sizes, shapes, colors and materials, and carried away. In Negande, another of the Nyaminyami chieftaincies, a girl of about ten, barefoot and wearing a patterned dress, walked down the dirt road, two impala legs hanging out of the shallow wicker basket balanced on her head. Scenes like this were repeated throughout Nyaminyami.

At the lakeside culling center, Russell Taylor, a short, balding man with a clipboard, paced around like a football coach on the sidelines during a close game. An ecologist with WWF in Harare, he had previously spent eighteen years with Zimbabwe's wildlife department. He monitors every cull, requiring the hunters to fill out detailed forms: what time they started, how many kilometers they drove, how many impala they killed, how many rounds of ammunition they used. The data he collects will allow him to determine what impact the culls have on the impala population. Do they affect their breeding? Their migration patterns?

During a wide-ranging conversation, Taylor stressed that the hunters used 1.1 bullets per each impala killed. "If a Green says anything to me, I can show him it's humane," he said. He and others working with CAMPFIRE are sensitive to public reactions to the cull, and driving around with the hunters, it was easy to envision animal rights militants bring-

ing their sleeping bags and lying in the grass to prevent the operation.

"The animal rights people want to save individual animals. As a biologist, I want to save populations," Taylor said. His comment summarizes the critical distinction between the animal rights activists and more traditional conservationists; conservationists want to ensure the survival of species and ecosystems, and to do that requires management, such as culling elephant herds. Or as Taylor puts it, "To save populations in this world today, and especially in *this* world, means managing the populations." The world he is emphasizing is Africa. The reality of Africa is the expanding human populations, with the attendant pressures on land. "These land-use pressures and population pressures—that's what the people in the United States and Europe don't understand," Taylor said. Asked what he meant by "manage," Taylor was more graphic: "Populations may be conserved, but we may have to send a few to the wall to do it." It is that grim reality that Westerners find so hard to accept, and understandably. Culling is a brutal activity, and it seems inhumane. But is it not also brutal and inhumane to allow human beings to suffer from malnutrition amidst plenty? Metcalfe figures that the culls have doubled and maybe tripled the amount of meat protein for a Nyaminyami villager; the only other source is goats, and a family of eight to ten cannot afford to slaughter more than ten goats a year.

Culling the impala herds in Nyaminyami is an example of utilizing a resource for the benefit of impoverished people without jeopardizing the resource—that is, an example of the principle of sustainable utilization. Five hundred impala are killed in each cull; out of a total impala population of 15,000, this is a sustainable off-take. It was exactly the kind of program Sir Julian Huxley had in mind as a measure to save the African wildlife. One of the three articles he wrote for *The Observer* in 1960, the ones that led to the founding of WWF, was entitled "Cropping the Wild Protein." It began, "The wild lands of Africa and the wild life that they carry are a major asset, a natural resource waiting for proper utilisation." Noting that most Africans ate too little protein, he wrote, "Game-cropping . . . could become a major means for overcoming this dietary deficiency and putting the Africans on a proper plane of nutritional health." It could also be an antidote to poaching, he thought. "If extensive game-cropping schemes can be set up, whether the cropping is done by licensed local tribesmen, or Game Department staff, or selected white hunters or their clients on safari, this will go far to satisfy the Africans' legitimate meat-hunger, and to remove the financial and psychological incentives to poaching."

Huxley had the right ideas, but they were never put into practice because there were too few Western conservationists who cared about people, too few David Westerns, Garth Owen-Smiths, Simon Metcalfes. The major conservation organizations, such as WWF and AWF, paid little attention to the needs of people until the two organizations finally began to realize, in the mid-1980s, that they were not going to save the wildlife unless they did something for the people. And today, while both organizations believe in sustainable utilization, they do not have the courage of their convictions, fearing attacks from the animal rights activists, who in their championing of the rights of animals neglect the rights of people.

At the time of Nyaminyami's fourth cull, in September 1990, WWF was under siege because of its support for sustainable utilization. The attacks began in July 1990 with a segment about WWF on "The Cook Report," a popular British weekly television program similar to "60 Minutes" in America. Considered hard-hitting investigative journalism by its admirers, "The Cook Report" is criticized as assault journalism by others, who note Roger Cook's aggressive style of confronting people who do not wish to be interviewed. WWF's president, Prince Philip, and director general, Charles de Haes, tried to derail "The Cook Report" segment on WWF. Philip filed a complaint with the Independent Broadcasting Authority—which has a power to control the content of broadcasting that is unparalleled in the United States—charging that Cook had engaged in subterfuge to gain royal papers containing exchanges between Philip and de Haes, and that the report was biased and unfair. The complaint was rejected. Altogether WWF spent $350,000 to counter Cook's exposé, according to one WWF insider, but the efforts by WWF and Philip only succeeded in creating so much publicity that an estimated six million people watched the show, about a million more than the normal audience.

The program generated a barrage of stories in newspapers throughout the United Kingdom, and many carried sensational headlines: "WWF Accused of Aiding Slaughter in African Bush"—Dundee *Courier & Advertiser;* "Charity 'Encourages Wildlife Slaughter' "—*Western Daily Press;* "Philip's Fund Is Slammed"—*Sunday Mirror.*

Among the many charges Cook leveled against WWF, the one he seemed to consider the most serious was that the organization raised funds from the public to save animals while at the same time it was supporting utilization programs. He was right, of course, that WWF did this. But if conservation is the goal, WWF should have been praised, not damned. Cook, however, was displaying the same lack of understanding about, and emotional bias against, sustainable utilization that the general public has.

Inspired by "The Cook Report" and repeating many of the same criticisms, an article in *Newsweek International* said that WWF "makes no secret of its belief in the 'sustainable utilization' of wildlife," and added, "hunting, that is." In fact, hunting is only one form of sustainable utilization, but it is the one that arouses the most intense public emotion. Cook, too, equated sustainable utilization with hunting, and for the show he went on a hunting safari—with a hidden camera. He described it as "about the most distasteful assignment" he had ever undertaken. Standing before a kudu, an antelope with swept-back horns, he told viewers, "For five hundred dollars I could have killed this magnificent kudu. For a few dollars more, I could have shot an eland or a leopard. . . . I could even have killed an elephant." He went on, "The remarkable thing about this safari project here in Zimbabwe is that it's actively sponsored and supported by the very organization that you would think would be against it—the World Wide Fund for Nature."

He was right that WWF supported hunting and he was right that he would have been able to shoot an elephant. He was not interested, however, in probing further, in asking why WWF supported this activity and, more important, what it meant for conserving Zimbabwe's wildlife and particularly its elephants.

In a single sentence, he might have noted that Nyaminyami alone earned enough from hunting in 1989 to pay the costs of running its own conservation program. With the money, the district hired twelve game rangers, provided them with uniforms, rifles, shovels, tents and rations, and paid them the equivalent of $100 a month. It was one of the best-paid, best-equipped ranger units in Africa. On their daily patrols the rangers pick up snares that have been laid along the animal trails, and their presence deters would-be poachers of elephants and rhino.

For the people of Nyaminyami the most lucrative animal has been the elephant, because it is the animal that has attracted the hunters. The government-set trophy fee for an elephant was $3,750 in 1989. This amount didn't go into the central treasury, as hunting and park entrance fees generally do throughout Africa. Rather, under CAMPFIRE, nearly all of this amount went to Nyaminyami. In addition, Nyaminyami was paid a concession fee by the hunting company. . . .

To determine how much Nyaminyami had lost because of the ivory ban, Elliot Nobula, the warden, looked at a ledger that listed the elephants that had been shot because they were damaging people's fields and could not be chased away. Taking the total weight of the tusks of these elephants and the price of raw ivory during the preceding few years, he calculated that Nyaminyami lost Z$40,000 (roughly $20,000) during the first eight months of 1990. And that was just ivory from elephants that had to be shot. In addition, had it not been for the ban, Nyaminyami would have culled a few elephants and sold the ivory and skins. With advice from the professional conservationists at WWF in Harare, the Nyaminyami Wildlife Management Trust had determined that a sustainable off-take of elephants was

sixty-nine, or 3 percent of the elephant population. The sale of the ivory and skins from that off-take would have brought Z$250,000 to the poor community.

The advocates of a ban on ivory trading argued that the income from ivory sales was a small fraction of any African country's total exports—not more than 1 or 2 percent (1 percent of United States exports in 1989 amounted to $2.5 billion). While that may be so, the lost income looms much larger in an African village. The yearly earnings of a Nyaminyami household, which averages eight people, were less than Z$200 a year, according to Hove, the executive officer. He said that most of the families were so poor that they could not afford to send their children to secondary school, where the fee was only Z$40 and the total cost for a year, including books, clothes and shoes, was about Z$250. Nor could they buy the few goods that were for sale, unless they saved for many months. In the general store in Siakobvu, a blanket sold for Z$45.75; a small metal cooking pot, Z$13.75; a five-hundred-gram box of Cold Power Blue Strength ("Washes Out the Worst Dirt in Cold Water"), Z$4.75; men's shorts, Z$17.80. If Nyaminyami could have sold just the ivory from the problem elephants, and had then divided the proceeds among the households in Nyaminyami, it would have meant an increase of at least 25 percent in every family's income.

There is another way to look at the money that Nyaminyami lost because of the ban. In 1990 alone, it virtually equaled the amount of foreign aid the district received for development projects such as primary schools and nutrition programs. Not long after the ivory ban was imposed, I had a conversation with a senior World Bank official in Nairobi. He was a passionate advocate of the ban. I pointed out the economic impact of the ban on a place like Nyaminyami. He dismissed the argument, claiming it was always possible to find some small community that would be hurt by an international action; he went on to say that it was up to international organizations like the World Bank to make up those losses. Given all the needy development projects in the world, one would think the World Bank should be pleased to find a community that could raise its own funds instead of looking for handouts from the international community.

In September 1990, the Nyaminyami Wildlife Management Trust held one of its bimonthly board meetings. It took place in Siakobvu, in a room with a concrete floor and yellow walls; there was a green chalkboard in one corner, listing various committees and the members. The meeting began at 10:30 in the morning; by 2:30, it was so stifling hot it was a wonder anyone was still awake, and there had not been any breaks, nor would there be before the meeting ended at 5:00. Seated around the long tables, arranged in an open-ended rectangle, were fourteen people, including two chiefs, four councillors, Elliot Nobula, Simon Metcalfe and Simbarashe Hove, the executive officer. A variety of items was discussed, including hiring four senior game guards, and a proposed joint venture between the Wildlife Trust and a private company for fishing the Lake Kariba kapenta, a freshwater sardine. The company was offering to provide some of its catch to the local people and to share the profits from what it sold with the district; it was another illustration of the principles of CAMPFIRE at work. Toward the end of the meeting, Chief Msampakaruma said the traditional village chiefs would like some recognition, and he suggested that at each cull they be given the meat from one impala. The suggestion startled some board members, and Metcalfe reminded the board that this issue had come up before the first cull and that the board had decided the chiefs should be given no privileges—everything should be democratic. Hove pointed out that whenever an elephant was killed, whether because it was destroying crops or for ceremonial purposes, the chief was traditionally presented with the trunk and the meat from the side it fell on. After more discussion, it was decided that the four chiefs would each be given an impala, the first four shot. With a slight grin, Nobula noted that it would be impossible to determine which were the first impala shot. Chief Msampakaruma said any one would be satisfactory.

Most of the session was taken up by one issue: what to pay villagers for losses suffered because of the wildlife. Paying compensation is another example of the boldness of Nyaminyami's approach to wildlife management; like Kenya and Tanzania, and most other African governments, Zimbabwe does not compensate people for such damage. Everyone at the board meeting spoke on the subject—in Shona, Tonga or English and most more than once. The compensation schedule Nyaminyami had adopted provided payment of Z$20 for the loss of a goat and Z$20 for a kilogram bag of maize or sorghum. When elephants and buffalo trample through fields before the crops are harvested, it is impossible to know exactly how many bags are lost, however, so the Wildlife Trust had settled on an average yield as the basis for compensation.

"We've told people compensation is provided for, but they're not satisfied," Councillor Wilson Nebiri told the board. Many farmers argued that they were better farmers and their yields were above the average, and so the compensation schedule was not fair to them. Others complained that they were compensated for only three goats, when in fact the lions had killed five. "The people are saying it's no better than it was when National Parks was in charge, so let us go back to hunting."

Because of dissatisfaction with the compensation they were receiving, many people were losing faith in CAMPFIRE, Hove said sharply.

Nobula told the board about a man who was asking for Z$200 because elephants had knocked over his granary and eaten all the maize. He claimed to have lost the equivalent of ten bags of it. Nobula said he had spent two days investigating the claim but that he was simply unable to determine how much maize had, in fact, been in the granary. Some members of the board expressed concern that the chief game warden had to devote so much of his time to such a matter.

Another issue on the agenda was much more pleasant. The board had before it proposals from several companies to establish tourist facilities, and all were offering the district a share in the profits. Buffalo Safari and Zambezi Canoeing Lake Wilderness Safaris wanted to put up a game-viewing and fishing camp on Lake Kariba's Bumi Bay. The camp would have ten tents or thatched huts, flush toilets, hot and cold water, and a swimming pool. The company said it would invest Z$200,000, and it was asking for no capital investment by Nyaminyami. What Buffalo Safari wanted in exchange was a lease on the land, and the company offered to give Nyaminyami 10 percent of its after-tax profits. Another safari company, Kushanya Africa Safaris and Wilderness Trails, wanted to establish a luxury tented camp for a maximum of twenty-four guests, also on the edge of Lake Kariba. It would give Nyaminyami Wildlife Management Trust 5 percent of its gross, which it projected would reach Z$100,000 within a few years.

These proposals for tourist joint ventures were received and discussed at the board meeting with what might be described as giddiness, as if this wildlife cup just kept running over. And they were, of course, far beyond anything Leakey has promoted in Kenya as part of what he calls "bold" programs to bring tourist benefits to rural people. In Kenya, Leakey was giving villages a fraction of gate revenues. In Nyaminyami, the people were negotiating their own benefits and relationships with the tourist industry, and coming out a lot richer.

In the past, before CAMPFIRE came along, only a small portion of the income generated by wildlife in Zimbabwe was returned to the districts where the wildlife was found; and even then the return was indirect—in the form of, say, a school or a health clinic or the grading of a road. This is the pattern throughout Africa: wildlife proceeds generally go into the national treasury and are then more likely to be used for paving a road in a wealthy section of the capital than for extending electricity to a rural area.

In Zimbabwe, now that the district controls wildlife revenues, it is facing a new problem: how to distribute them. One of the principles of CAMPFIRE is that the benefits from wildlife ought to correlate as closely as possible with where the wildlife is. "He who bears the costs gets the benefits," Met-

calfe puts the theory. But it is not as simple as it sounds. Do the profits go to the district, the ward (which is a subdivision of the district), the village, or, getting down to the smallest unit, the family or household? The Nyaminyami Wildlife Management Trust decided to divide the 1989 profits among the district's twelve wards. With that, ward councils began thinking about what to do with the money. One considered building public latrines, another housing for teachers and nurses, and a lakeside ward talked about putting up a beer hall for thirsty, hard-drinking fishermen. The residents of Ward B in Negande held a public meeting to decide how to spend their share of the 1989 wildlife profits, which came to Z$16,500. Almost all of the ward's nine hundred adults showed up and the meeting lasted three hours.

The ward's councillor, Patrick Ngenya, a beefy man with muttonchop sideburns and a mustache, said nobody had suggested that the wildlife profits be divided among the families. One proposal was to build a general shop and warehouse, which would be stocked with grain, fertilizers, seeds, basic foodstuffs and agricultural implements, making all of these items more readily available and at lower prices than when they are hauled in by truck from Karoi, the nearest major commercial center, 120 miles distant. It would have been run like a cooperative.

But the cooperative wasn't built, because the women of Ward B said they wanted a grinding mill. The Zimbabwe government, which has done more to improve life for rural people than most African governments—CAMPFIRE is an example—has put up grinding mills around the country, where the women can take their corn and for a few cents have it ground by a machine, usually diesel-powered, since there is rarely electricity in rural areas. Most of the women of Negande Ward B, however, still had to walk a mile or more to the nearest mill. Their desire to build one closer to their village prevailed, and within a few months, the people had made four thousand bricks to house the mill. With future wildlife revenues, the villagers planned to build a footbridge across a stream that their children have to cross on their way to school.

I learned all this about Negande while sitting on the edge of a small field of bright green, knee-high maize stalks; it clashed with the dusty and parched brown surroundings and the mopane trees without leaves in September, the end of the dry winter months. What accounted for the vegetation was a small irrigation system put in by the government a few years ago. A shallow concrete culvert needed repair, and several women hauled plastic buckets filled with sand for mixing with cement. Other women, wearing patterned skirts and bright blouses, their hair tucked into bandannas, were bent over between the corn rows weeding with short-handled hoes. Thirty-nine families had plots in this twenty-two-acre field, and the women said that during the previous growing season, the average yield had been twelve bags of maize per family. Not all families had been so fortunate, however; some got only a bag or two, and a few got nothing. It was not because they were second-class farmers. It was because elephants had raided the field.

Asked if they would like to see all the elephants shot, the women answered with a quiet but unanimous "no." People from outside the country want the skins and tusks, one woman said. Elephants bring food and money, added another. They understood that the district will get the money from the elephants and then will use it to build schools and clinics. (It was clear that Elliot Nobula's efforts to educate the people about the benefits of wildlife have not been in vain.) Still, elephants in general are one matter, but specific elephants are another. The women were insistent that they wanted some elephants shot—any elephants that entered their fields. To guard against that happening, the Nyaminyami Wildlife Trust erected a fence around the field—ten strands of wire from ground level to about six feet, electrified by solar power. The women were clearly pleased about this.

About the same time that a CAMPFIRE program was launched in Nyaminyami, one was also begun in the district of Guruve, in northern Zimbabwe, along the border with Mozambique. Like Nyaminyami, Guruve is poor and undeveloped; there is too little rain

and the soil is sandy. But there is an abundance of wildlife, and it is potentially quite lucrative. Although there is no national park in Guruve and no international-quality facilities to attract tourists, sport hunters like the area, and Guruve is capitalizing on that. Indeed, rather than sell concessions to private safari operators, as Nyaminyami does, Guruve runs its own hunting safaris, which means, of course, that all the profits from hunting, not just a percentage of them, belong to the district. The Guruve council decided to distribute the hunting profits to the wards and in proportion to where the animals had been killed. Most of the hunting was in Masoka—five elephant bulls were shot there—and so it received Z$47,000 from the 1989 revenues.

This unexpected bonanza has had dramatic consequences. For one thing, the Masoka villagers were once intent on using most of their land for cattle, but now they say they can earn more from wildlife, so they plan to set aside the majority of their grazing land for the impala, zebra, buffalo and so on. But the effect of receiving money from wildlife has been more far-reaching.

As part of CAMPFIRE, the residents of Masoka elected a wildlife committee, and it was for this committee to determine how to spend the wildlife revenues. There were no objections when it decided that half of the first year's revenue should be invested in community projects—a school and a health clinic, fences around people's fields to keep the animals out, and salaries for more game guards. The remaining amount, the committee decided, should be divided among the households in the ward, probably the first time that money from wildlife has ever been paid directly to individuals anywhere in Africa. Here is where a controversy erupted and something remarkable occurred.

To distribute the money, the ward's politicians drew up a list containing the names of eighty-six men who were heads of households. At a community meeting, as each man's name was called, he came forward and was handed a paper bag containing the money. Each man received Z$200, which more than doubled most families' income. That was all good. But then several women stood up and complained.

Some of the young men who had received money had only very recently married, they said, and they had not really established a household. On the other hand, many of the women had been abandoned by their husbands and were running households with several children. Therefore, they were entitled to receive money, they said. They did not prevail—that time. But the process "let loose a new dynamic of female assertiveness," said Marshall Murphree, an advisor to the CAMPFIRE program in Guruve.

Murphree, who is CAMPFIRE's intellectual father, frequently recounts what happened at that meeting, and with great relish and enthusiasm. Born in Rhodesia of American missionaries, he received a Ph.D. in rural development from the London School of Economics in the early 1950s, and for many years he has been a professor of social sciences at the University of Zimbabwe in Harare and the director of the university's Centre for Applied Social Sciences. The Centre, along with WWF in Harare and Zimbabwe Trust, was critical to getting CAMPFIRE operational. But Murphree's association with wildlife conservation is not solely an academic one. Alone or with his youngest son, Michael, who is an ecologist in Zimbabwe's wildlife department, Murphree spends almost as much time in the bush as in his red-brick office. During a four-month sabbatical in 1990, Murphree traveled in Kenya, and one of the places he visited was Laikipia where the elephants are wreaking havoc on the shambas and fences have failed. "The whole Kenyan policy against consumptive utilization dooms those elephants," he says.

But for Murphree, as for Metcalfe, the ramifications of CAMPFIRE extend beyond conservation. In addition to giving a new awareness and assertiveness to women, Murphree says, CAMPFIRE is teaching the people something about involvement in decision-making. He explains that while the politicians in Masoka had drawn up a list of eighty-six households to receive money, in fact, there were only sixty-nine households in Masoka; the politicians, desirous of helping a few friends, had padded the list. Many people in the community were angry when they realized what had been done. In the future, Murphree said,

"they are going to make bloody sure that they are involved in drawing up that list." In other words, CAMPFIRE is developing grass-roots democracy. An individual who acquires the right to decide about the wildlife in his area and about how the money from that wildlife is spent might start asking how politicians in the capital spend public money; he might even want a say in electing the country's president. In Africa, these are radical concepts.

If Africa's wildlife is to be saved, it will not be with celebrity appeals, or more firearms for anti-poaching units, or ivory bans. It will require radical policies and changes in attitudes. Westerners who contribute to conservation organizations will have to understand and accept sustainable utilization. Conservation organizations will have to stand up for their conservation principles and not be intimidated by the fund-raisers. Tour operators, hotel owners and governments will have to be sure that local people get the lion's share of benefits from wildlife, and not the carcasses after they have been picked over by the vultures.

David Western says that if Kenya had adopted the Zimbabwe approach to wildlife utilization and allowed landowners, private and communal, to reap the benefits, the Kenya Wildlife Service "would have become financially self-sufficient fairly quickly." Because it has proceeded with such caution, the Kenyan government "is locked into dependence on aid," he says. Kenya, which is receiving more than $150 million from the international community for conservation, would need only a fraction of that, according to Western, if Kenyan landowners had an incentive to protect the wildlife.

If villagers living around a park make money from wildlife, they will protect not only the animals on their own land, but those inside the park as well, for when the animals wander from the park, landowners can utilize them. In effect, the park becomes the villagers' bank and the wild animals in the park their assets. This will provide a powerful incentive against poaching: people are not likely to rob their own bank, and will report those who do.

When Preservationism Doesn't Preserve

David Schmidtz

PRESERVATION AND CONSERVATION

Is it okay to chop down a Redwood so that you can take a picture of people dancing on the stump? Is it okay to shoot an elephant so that you can carve the tusks into fancy ivory chess pieces? Probably not. What exactly is wrong with such things, though? That is a tougher question, and there is a controversy in environmental ethics over how to answer it.

One approach is what we call conservationism. The idea is that elephants and Redwoods are a precious resource, too precious to waste on trifles. Scarce and precious resources should be conserved. They should be used wisely, taking into account costs and benefits for future generations as well as our own. Chopping down a Redwood so you can take pictures of people dancing on the stump is a waste: a waste of lumber or of a tourist attraction.

What if it is not a waste, though? What if the lumber is used efficiently and the tree stump dance floor itself becomes a major tourist attraction—a source of human happiness for generations to come? Wouldn't it still be wrong? Don't Redwoods somehow deserve more *respect* than that? Among people who do environmental ethics, conservationism has to some degree been supplanted by a second approach, which we call preservationism. Although we cannot avoid exploiting the natural world to some extent, preservationism's core idea is that nature has a moral status independent of its utility for humankind. There are some ecosystems that should simply be left alone to evolve according to their own lights, free of human use and human interference. The slogan for conservationism is "wise use." The slogan for preservationism is "let it be." According to preservation ethics, we should not think of wilderness as merely a resource. Wilderness commands reverence in a way mere resources do not.

One concern a preservationist might have about conservation ethics, then, is that it fails to make room for reverence. There are other, more contingent concerns as well. First, we ought to be skeptical about wise use policies regarding resources whose range of potential uses is largely unknown. "Wise use" of rain forests, for example, might not be very wise in the long term because there might be goods we do not know about yet that we unwittingly are squandering. Second, there might be other goods, like atmospheric oxygen, that rain forests would go on producing for us if we just left them alone. In that case, *using* a resource interferes with *benefiting* from it. Third, "wise use" of rain forests might be exposing us to diseases that otherwise would have stayed in the rain forests. There are species of mosquitoes that live only in the rain forest canopy. They feed only on monkeys that live in the canopy and they transmit diseases only to those monkeys. When you chop down the trees, though, those mosquitoes are suddenly on the forest floor where they have never been before. They and the organisms they carry suddenly are exposed to a population of six billion human beings. It would not be like them to let that much food go to waste.

So, there are reasons why people plausibly could say the wisest use of rain forests is virtually no use at all, at least for now. And when wise use is tantamount to no use at all, we have a situation where preservationism has won out on conservationism's own grounds. It is no surprise, then, that many (perhaps most) environmental ethicists today see conservationism as an ethic whose time has passed. My sympathies, too, lie mainly (although not exclusively) with preservationism.

David Schmidtz, "When Preservationism Doesn't Preserve," *Environmental Values*, 6 (1997): 327–39. Reprinted with permission of White Horse Press, Cambridge, U.K. Revised for this volume.

However, after reading Raymond Bonner's book on wildlife conservation in Africa, and after travelling to South Africa, Zimbabwe, Botswana, and Zambia to see as much as I could for myself, I have had to rethink the wisdom of preservationism, at least in the African context.[1] Bonner was in Africa on other business when he stumbled into an ugly debate over the legitimacy of the ivory trade. Was it a good idea to ban international trade in ivory products? I do not know. This paper's purpose is not to take sides in that debate but rather to do something more philosophical: to reflect on what Bonner's experience, and mine, reveals about the practical limitations of preservationist philosophy.

If you were writing a Hollywood movie script, you would have the bad guys being in favor of shooting elephants for ivory (at "sustainable levels" of course). The good guys would say elephants are a sacred world heritage and that it is a moral crime to be hacking their faces off and turning their tusks into trinkets. That is how you would be expected to write the script and that is just what Bonner expected to find. What he actually found was something quite different.

VIGILANTE PRESERVATIONISM

Guy Grant bought his ranch in Kenya in 1963. He had twenty-five zebra at the time. Today he has over a thousand. He once sold hunting rights to zebra, elephant, buffalo, and warthogs, which provided a third of his income. In any case, he needs to keep the zebra population down to have room to graze cattle. Sport hunting, however, was banned in 1977. He could not sell hunting licenses anymore, so he had to hunt zebra himself. He still made money selling meat and hides, but trade in wildlife products was banned in 1978, so he lost that income too. Now, because of the ban, he has to graze more cattle to make ends meet. And he still has to keep the zebra population down. Otherwise it will bankrupt him. The only change is that he cannot make money from the zebra. Think about what that means. Without income from zebra, Grant has to graze more cattle to make

the same money, which means he has less room for zebra, which means he has to shoot more zebra than otherwise would be necessary. *More zebra get shot* because of the ban on hunting them for sport.

The situation on Guy Grant's ranch is far from unique. For better or worse, Kenya had become one of Africa's most enlightened countries, at least in terms of paying lip service to preservationist ideals. Wildlife in general was protected by law. Even outside the national parks, hunting was tightly regulated. In particular, poaching elephants in Kenya was as illegal as dealing cocaine in Brooklyn. With similar results.

What do you do when your laws are treated with contempt? Naturally, you get tough on crime. That is what voters want. That is what lobbyists want. And that is what they got. In 1988, Kenya's president ordered that poachers be shot on sight. Forty-one suspected poachers were killed in the next eight months. No park rangers were killed. In Zimbabwe, with the same shoot-to-kill policy, one hundred and forty-five suspected poachers were killed between 1984 and 1991. Four rangers were killed in the same time frame.

The trouble is, when the score in favor of the game wardens is forty-one to zero in one country and one hundred and forty-five to four in another, it begins to seem absurd to think the alleged poachers are well-armed, war-hardened mercenaries, and indeed they were not. In fact, it was average rural peasants who were being shot. According to Richard Leakey, director of Kenya's wildlife department at the time, there were no more than a hundred hard-core poachers in Kenya and for the most part, their identities were known (Bonner 1993, p. 18).[2] Many of them were wildlife department rangers. By some accounts, over a third of the rhinos poached in the 1970s, when the population crashed from twenty thousand to under one thousand, were taken by members of the wildlife department itself (Bonner 1993, p. 134).[3] It occurs to me that if you are a game warden and some hard-luck farmer chasing a stray goat accidentally catches you sawing tusks off an elephant you have poached, it is awfully convenient to have, in effect, a legal right to shoot him. You have the carcass right there as proof that he was poaching. (You can claim he must have had a confederate who escaped with the tusks.) However we explain the statistics, though, the fact remains that the shoot-to-kill policy was an extreme response—a reactionary response—and it did not work. Lots of farmers were getting shot, yet all sides agree that poaching was escalating.

What else could you do? One suggestion: regulate trade in ivory. The Convention on International Trade in Endangered Species determined in 1977 that elephants were not yet an endangered species but would become so if the ivory trade were not brought under control. The Convention proposed that each exporting country establish self-imposed quotas on ivory exports, based on sustainable off-take— a level consistent with maintaining existing populations.

What happened? To give one example, in 1986, Somalia voluntarily limited its export quota to seventeen thousand tusks per year. The odd thing is that Somalia had only six thousand elephants to begin with. Where were all those tusks coming from? Probably Kenya, its neighbor to the southwest.

If *regulating* commerce in ivory does not work, how about *banning* it? The case against a ban is this: Elephant populations in many countries were not decreasing, and were in fact near carrying capacity. Ivory was an important source of revenue for conservation programs. In theory, at least, legal exports from countries like South Africa dampen demand for poached ivory from countries like Kenya where elephants are threatened. For better or worse, these considerations failed to carry the day. The World Wide Fund for Nature and the African Wildlife Foundation originally opposed a ban for the reasons just mentioned, but then changed their minds. Bonner suspects that the reason they changed their minds was that they could not afford to pass up the millions of dollars they stood to gain through highly publicized campaigns to ban ivory.[4]

Here is a different issue. Even if the ivory ban eliminated poaching entirely, the wildlife would still be disappearing (Bonner 1993, p. 212). In Theodore Roosevelt's time, Africa's human population was one hundred million. Now it is four hundred fifty million. As Bonner puts it, "People were once an island in a sea of wildlife. Now wildlife survives in parks that are islands in an ocean of people" (Bonner 1993, p. 8). Competition for water, disruption of migration routes, and farmers defending crops (and their families) against marauding wildlife will decimate wildlife with or without poaching. Clearly, the poaching has to stop, but in the long run, that will not be enough to save the elephants. Whether we like it or not, the elephants will not survive except by sharing the land with people, which means their long-term survival depends on whether the people of Africa can afford to share. Poaching is just one symptom of this larger problem.

THE LARGER PROBLEM

As Laura Westra tells us, "An Arab proverb says, Before the palm tree can be beautiful, our bellies must be full of dates. It is a truism, as indeed survival comes before aesthetic enjoyment. Unfortunately environmental concern is seen as aesthetic preference rather than urgently needed for survival . . ."[5] Accordingly, the view that environmental concern is a mere luxury is unjustified. However, there is a crucial complication: people like us, for whom short-term survival is not an issue, can afford to treat environmental concern as an urgent priority; people who can barely make ends meet from one day to the next cannot. That is true here, and it is true in Africa as well. Being able to think in terms of long-term survival is itself a luxury of a kind, and not one that everyone can afford. So, Westra has a point when she says it would be a mistake to view environmental issues as a luxury. At the same time, it also would be a mistake to ignore the fact that environmental concern falls by the wayside in a personal crunch. From an individual perspective, the survival of one's family comes first. Compared to that, environmental concern is indeed a luxury, and the rest of us do not have the luxury of ignoring that point.

Presumably, there are exceptions to this general rule. For example, Ramachandra Guha cringes at the depiction of environmental concern as a "full stomach" phenomenon and makes note of peasant movements against deforestation and industrial pollution in India.[6] Guha's point is well-taken, but it bears adding that, as Guha himself stresses, "environmental protection is of least concern to most of these groups. Their main concern is about the use of the environment and who should benefit from it."[7] Thus, even if our own attitude is one of deep and unconditional reverence for wilderness, we have to be aware that other people may have, in their own eyes, more pressing things to think about. If we really care about wilderness, we cannot just look at it through our own eyes. Part of our job is to help create the kind of society in which, for other people, from their perspectives, respecting wilderness is worth the cost. We can say preservation is morally right; therefore the Maasai tribes are morally obligated to preserve; therefore we should not have to bribe them to do what they are obligated to do. They should just do it. If we say that, though, we are kidding ourselves. Under such circumstances, David Western (current director of the Kenyan Wildlife Service) observes, "the African farmer's enmity toward elephants is as visceral as western mawkishness is passionate."[8]

Like us, the people of Africa care for their natural heritage when they can afford to do so, when rewards for doing so go to them and not just to others, and when they know how to do so. Some of them have been practicing wise use for a long time, killing wildlife when it threatens their families, hunting it for food, and for sport as well. When we try to impose our preservationist ideals on local villagers who have to live with wildlife, we risk starting a war between locals and wildlife, a war that both sides lose. The problem is that preservation ethics does not allow the local people to profit from wildlife, and not allowing people to profit from wildlife effectively pits people against wildlife, which is bad for wildlife as well as the local people. Kreuter and Simmons say that, because elephants "compete directly with humans for use of fertile land, we believe elephants will continue to be eliminated unless they provide . . . direct personal benefits to the people who incur the cost of co-existing with them. If the western preservationists do not respect the need for Africans

to benefit from their resources, they will one day stand justly accused of promoting rather than abating the demise of Africa's elephants."[9] Our own experiences and our conversations with a dozen people from five African countries suggests that Kreuter and Simmons are right, and that the hard choice in southern Africa is not so much between people and wildlife as between a pragmatic humanism that benefits both and an idealistic environmentalism that benefits neither. When it comes to African wildlife, preservation ethics runs into a problem. In a nutshell, preservationism does not preserve. It thereby fails by its own lights. We need alternatives. It turns out that there are many. Some are working.

WISE USE ALTERNATIVES

Namibia's Auxiliary Guard

In several countries, elephant numbers are increasing. Is it because of the ivory ban? That seems reasonable, but it does not explain why the numbers in some countries were increasing even before the ban. Nor does it explain why the numbers have increased only in some countries, not others. One variable that separates countries is their success in controlling poaching. (And successful countries seem to be those that see poaching as a symptom of more fundamental problems.) In contrast to Kenya, Namibia's Kaokoveld region, for example, is doing fairly well. In 1982, a conservation officer named Garth Owen-Smith diagnosed Namibia's problem as follows. Local villagers once had customs that effectively limited their own hunting activities to sustainable levels. Then foreign hunters started showing up in large numbers. It was a classic tragedy of the commons. Self-restraint seemed pointless, and villagers did not restrain themselves. They were helping to destroy wildlife and were destroying their own future in the process, and it was partly their fault. Somehow, the villagers had to reverse the deterioration of their own social norms, and they had to do something about trespassing poachers from outside. To western environmentalists, one obvious solution was to shoot the villagers (after all, they were poaching), but that had been tried elsewhere and Owen-Smith felt a different strategy was called for. Instead of shooting the villagers, he asked them for help.

He asked village headmen to assemble troops of auxiliary guards to act as neighborhood watch organizations. These watchdog organizations radically reduced poaching by outsiders, and also provided an institutional framework that made it easier to reassert community standards and re-establish norms of self-restraint. It was a simple idea, but it worked. Five years later, Owen-Smith went further. By then elephants, lions, and other animals were returning to the Kaokoveld, and with them came the tourists. The plan was to sell crafts to visitors who were coming through mainly to see wildlife and also to tax visitors for overnight stays within their territory. Both sources of income ultimately are tied to wildlife, so incentives to preserve are put in place (Bonner 1993, p. 33).

Does the program demean the animals? Perhaps, but we should keep in mind that we are not talking here about locking them up in zoos. Elephants have their value to the local people to the extent that they are wild and free and living in a natural setting. That is what the tourists (and hunters) are paying to see.

Revenue Sharing

To Westerners, the commercial value of tourism is a panacea (Bonner 1993, p. 218). Tourism could indeed help, but it depends on how the money is distributed. In Kenya, Richard Leakey announced in 1990 that twenty-five percent of entrance fees will go to local Maasai tribes (Bonner 1993, p. 222). Involving the Maasai is crucial, since eighty percent of Kenya's wildlife lives outside of its parks, and much of it is migratory. Thus, it is imperative that local farmers and herdsmen tolerate big animals coming and going, circulating among seasonal food and water supplies. And they were tolerant, after they started to get some of the money. In fact, the Maasai now use some of their share to hire their own wardens to track and protect animals outside the park—a remarkable change of attitude.

In Zambia, businesses that cater to the tourist industry take a percentage of their annual gross revenues and distribute it in equal shares amongst their entire staff. Accordingly, everyone you meet who is involved in the tourism industry, from janitors and dishwashers to maids and managers, directly profits from every dollar you spend, and thus is personally committed to making their business as attractive as possible to tourists. And since unspoiled land and especially wildlife is what draws the tourists, they have a personal interest in conservation as well.[10]

In Botswana, the Moremi Game Reserve was created in 1964—the first wildlife area to be set aside by tribal chiefs rather than by colonial powers. Licenses for doing business in the Reserve are allocated according to competitive bids. Winning bids receive a five year lease, renewable up to two times for a total of fifteen years maximum. From a European or North American perspective, it makes no sense at first, since it undercuts incentives to make long term investments in durable infrastructure. In Botswana, though, it may prove a brilliant solution to a vexing problem. Botswana needs foreign investment, but it does not want to find itself owned by white foreigners. So, under the current leasing arrangement, foreigners are investing and building infrastructure, but their buildings are flimsy shacks (with wooden rather than concrete foundations, for example). The roads are dirt trails built for Jeeps. In other words, investors are planning not to leave much behind when they leave, and as a result they seem to be building in a way that minimizes their environmental impact on the Reserve. Meanwhile, native Botswanan students (now about twenty years old) are being sent abroad to study tourism, management, ecology, and so on, returning home during the tourist season to work in the national parks as tour guides, assistant managers, and so on. Non-native entrepreneurs will help get Botswana's tourist industry going, and the hope is that, after they make a quick profit and a graceful exit, a generation of internationally trained and locally experienced Botswanans (who by that time will be about thirty-five years old) will be ready to take over.[11] We will see.

Tanzania's Bounty Hunters

In the Maswa Preserve, near Serengeti, Robin Hurt once led hunting safaris. Tanzania banned hunting in 1973, so Hurt went elsewhere. Tanzania legalized hunting again in 1984. Robin Hurt came back in 1985. During that twelve year moratorium on hunting, the wildlife virtually disappeared. Why? Because of poachers. Without licensed hunters to keep poachers in line, poachers ran amok.

But what is the difference between a poacher and a hunter? A hunter is just a poacher by another name, no? In fact, the difference is enormous. Hunters hunt with rifles. In Tanzania, poachers hunt with *snares*, and snares are a disaster for the wildlife (Bonner 1993, p. 236). The people of Makao, for example, were laying snares around water holes, or along time-worn paths to water holes, or they would cut new paths in the bushes and lay snares along those. Robin Hurt found twenty lion skulls in one snare line. He found snare lines that ran for two miles. More often than not, the animal caught is not what the poacher wants. Even if it is, vultures or hyenas often get to the animal before the poacher does. Snare-hunting is catastrophically wasteful from an ecological perspective, but from a poacher's perspective it is a lot easier than hunting with bow and arrow. The Makao switched to snares.[12]

When Hurt resumed operations in 1985, he began a casual anti-poaching effort, picking up snares as he went, in his spare time. Gradually realizing the magnitude of the problem, he concluded that the Makao had to be enlisted. How? Well, why not just pay them to turn in snares and poachers? Here, too, I would have worried about incentive problems. (If Hurt pays too much for the snares, won't people respond by making more snares?) Still, it was an idea worth trying. Hurt raised enough money to try it. It worked (Bonner 1993, p. 249).

Zimbabwe's Local Autonomy

There have been problems in Zimbabwe, as in other countries, with wildlife molesting villagers, to the point where villagers came to feel that government wildlife protection was persecuting people for the sake of the animals. And they were basically right. One major effect of the bans on commerce in wildlife was to prevent locals from making significant money. "It was clear that to the local people, the wildlife was simply a nuisance. Elephants and other large herbivores raided their meager crops and sometimes even trampled their huts, while lions and other large carnivores occasionally preyed on their domestic stock. The wild animals often moved into the communal lands from national parks and other protected areas, but because the locals saw no direct benefit from these areas, they saw no reason to protect this errant game."[13] Wildlife groups had failed to ask: What could make it *rational* for villagers to choose wildlife over cattle?

Today there is an answer. Shortly after Zimbabwe gained political independence in 1980, its Department of National Parks and Wildlife Management concluded that conventional agricultural practices were ecologically and economically unsound throughout much of Zimbabwe. (The soil is not right, and there is not enough water.) The best use of the land was as a reservoir for wildlife. The Department also realized that the problem would not be solved unless it were largely handed over to the local people. Over a period of years, the Department created the CAMPFIRE program. They surveyed community areas, assessed wildlife populations, and came to conclusions about what sort of numbers could be considered surplus game. They then gave local communities a nearly free hand in deciding what to do with the surplus.

Local communities were granted authority to cull herds, sell hunting permits, or set up tourist ventures, and since 1992 they have been allowed to keep eighty percent of the money. (The rest goes to wildlife management and rural district administration.) They put some of that money in a fund for compensating farmers when lions take their goats or elephants trample their crops, which defuses much of the resentment of wildlife. In some districts, rangers periodically hunt impala and sell meat to local villagers at a price that covers cost of the hunt, making villagers less dependent on cattle as a source of protein. The issue is not just money, but self-sufficiency. Decisions are made in the village square. In that setting, people have more knowledge, more understanding, more voice. There is less room for corruption. Decision-making is more efficient and more equitable.

David Holt-Biddle notes that for Tshikwarakwara, a village in southeastern Zimbabwe, "Poaching and illegal hunting were the order of the day, the general opinion being that these were just nuisance animals and the only people to benefit from them were the white hunters, usually from abroad." In the words of a local official, with the advent of CAMPFIRE, "the poaching and illegal hunting have stopped completely, because everyone in the community is a policeman now."[14]

A note of caution: there are programs in southern Africa that call themselves community-based but merely gesture at sharing revenue and at granting communities authority to set local policy. Such programs do not work.[15] Political corruption in Africa is deep and pervasive, and there is no magic cure for it. So far, though, CAMPFIRE seems to be working. "The foundation of community empowerment lies in devolution of management decisions to the local level. Just giving the communities economic resources from wildlife is not CAMPFIRE. In CAMPFIRE, the concept of community empowerment means actually giving the community the power to decide on the allocation of these resources."[16] As of 1994, there were twenty-two CAMPFIRE districts, comprising nearly half the country. As of 1999, when I was Zimbabwe, there were thirty-seven such districts, comprising well over half (and containing 56% of the country's population), and much of the land in those districts is reserved for wildlife. A pamphlet published by the CAMPFIRE Association says,

Today, the total land mass devoted to wildlife conservation is more than 33% whereas only 13% is officially designated as such in the form of Protected Areas. Most of these wildlands are being set aside by rural communities motivated by the actual or anticipated benefits from their midst—wilderness resources are paying their way to survival! In the immediate period before the introduction of CAMPFIRE, Protected Areas were in danger of becoming ecological islands, threatening the mainte-

nance of genetic and species diversity. CAMPFIRE has re-opened traditional migration routes of animals within the community, thus making a contribution to the preservation of biodiversity and the natural environment.[17]

In the village of Masoka, a revolution is taking place. In 1993, only a few years after launching their own local CAMPFIRE program, thirty-five percent of Masoka's household heads reported their primary employment to be a direct result of the program, mainly through safari camps.[18] Enough money is now coming in from hunting that villagers are turning their land over to wildlife rather than grazing cattle. This is crucial because the bigger threat to wildlife tends to be cattle, not hunting. Cattle crowds out wildlife. (Actually, pastoral herds are one problem; farms and ranches are another. Nomadic Maasai herdsmen compete with wildlife for space and water, but at least they do not cut off migration routes by erecting fences or otherwise defending their turf.)[19]

Villages (directly or through tour guides) sell elephant hunting licenses. Hunters currently pay as much as $30,000 for the privilege. It is a lot of money in a country where the per capita annual income is around $2,000. What about the morality of sport hunting? Is it something a sane person would do? Winston Churchill once shot a rhinoceros, but failed to kill it. The wounded rhino charged. The hunting party opened fire. The rhino kept coming into a hail of bullets, swerving aside at the last moment before more bullets finally brought it down. Churchill later wrote that, even in the midst of the charge, "There is time to reflect with some detachment that, after all, we it is who have forced the conflict by an unprovoked assault with murderous intent upon a peaceful herbivore; that if there is such a thing as right and wrong between man and beast—and who shall say there is not?—right is plainly on his side."[20]

I grew up on a farm, in a family of hunters, but I never joined in. I loved to shoot at targets, but I was never able to make sense of killing sentient beings for fun. Perhaps you feel the same way. And yet, we should hesitate before concluding that regular tourism is benign whereas hunting is destructive. Actually, tourism may do more damage than hunting relative to the money it brings in. Why? Mainly because, dollar for dollar, hunting does not need as much infrastructure as tourism does. Hunters in jeeps do not use precious water the way tourist hotels do, and do not demand wilderness-fragmenting highways the way tourist hotels do.

ANIMAL RIGHTS

I have been talking about selling hunting licenses as an alternative to grazing cattle that compete with wildlife for space. As things stand, though, it sometimes is necessary to cull elephant herds for straightforwardly ecological reasons—to preserve habitat, other animal species, and even the elephants themselves. In the Volcans National Park in Rwanda, a choice had to be made between elephants and gorillas. As the elephants deplete food sources in the park, they normally migrate, coming back only when the park has replenished itself. As human populations increase and human settlements surround the parks, though, elephants are forced to turn back into the parks, destroying habitat for everything else in the park as well as for themselves. To prevent that, Rwanda's two remaining elephant herds, about seventy animals each, were wiped out in 1973.[21]

Uganda also culled elephant herds for ecological reasons. Not Kenya. The elephant population in Kenya's Tsavo Park had reached forty thousand in the 1960s. "Some conservationists and wildlife officials wanted to cull three thousand elephants. Others argued that man should do nothing, that nature should be allowed to take its course" (Bonner 1993, p. 104). Preservationists prevailed, but during a subsequent drought, six to nine thousand elephants died of starvation, and they took several hundred rhinos with them.[22]

Today, the same thing is happening again, as we saw with our own eyes—especially in the Chobe and Moremi Game Reserves in Botswana and in Kruger National Park in South Africa. In many places, there are far too many elephants, and they are ruining the woodland. They are leaving both themselves and all the other wildlife without viable habitat. Mopalo

Setswantsho has been taking people on hiking and canoe trips into the Okavango Delta in the interior of Botswana since 1983 and has lived in the area all his life. I asked him whether there were fewer animals now. He answered that, on the contrary, there are more animals now, but the trees are disappearing.

Do we have the right to put a stop to it? Animal rights organizations say no. Their approach is individualistic rather than holistic. They focus on each and every animal rather than on larger questions about species or habitat. Their view is particularly salient in the case of elephants. When rangers cull elephants, they take out whole families in order to avoid leaving behind orphans and other remnants of shattered families. The horrible thing is that, under favorable conditions, elephants can hear the sound of a culling operation up to thirty kilometers away, and elephants are smart—smart enough to understand and share the terror of the ones being shot. Cynthia Moss, who has written fascinating and convincing books about what it is like to be an elephant, says elephants deserve something better than to be exterminated like rodents. She has a point.[23]

Lawrence Johnson, though, argues that there are times when "the interests of species are not adequately protected by a concern for individuals."[24] The individualistic animal rights position is powerful, given the nature of elephants, but it leaves us in a horrible quandary, for the price of absolute rights may be extinction. Nonetheless, elephants are not like zebra. They are not the kind of creature that we have a right to treat as mere means. Cynthia Moss (Bonner, 1993, p. 226) said she would rather see elephants go extinct than see individual animals murdered for sake of population control, and she is not alone. If elephants had a voice in the matter, perhaps they would thank Moss for her stand. Perhaps not.

PERSONAL AND INTERPERSONAL MORALITY

I asked what makes it wrong to cut down a Redwood in order to use the stump as a dance floor, or to shoot an elephant in order to use the tusks for ivory. Do we have an answer? We may have more than one. I say that partly because, in my view, morality is more than one thing. One part of morality ranges over the subject of personal aspiration—which goals we should spend our lives trying to achieve. Another part of morality ranges over the subject of interpersonal constraint—especially which socially or institutionally embedded constraints we ought to respect as we pursue our goals in a social setting. In those terms, then, I still believe in preservationism as part of a morality of personal aspiration. Committing ourselves to preservationist ideals—to reverence for nature and to a policy of "no use at all" at least in some contexts—is one way of giving ourselves something to live for.

I also believe a preservationist "no use at all" policy can work among people who share a commitment to preservationist ideals. What I mean by this is that when people accept the ideals behind a set of institutional constraints, and individually and collectively commit themselves to living within those constraints on behalf of those ideals, the institution has a decent chance of functioning in such a way as actually to further those ideals.

However, I have come to realize that preservationism often and predictably does not work in the context of a social arrangement in which the cost of upholding preservationist ideals has to be born by people who do not embrace those ideals. Even given that preservationism is acceptable as a personal ideal, it remains a bad idea to create institutions that depend upon people who do not share that ideal to take responsibility for realizing it. (Ramachandra Guha goes so far as to say our foisting preservationist ideals on third world countries is a form of cultural imperialism.)[25]

Some of our most beloved environmental heroes, Aldo Leopold, for example, were unrepentant hunters. They saw hunting as part of an environmentally benign overall pattern. But even if they were wrong, and even if their philosophy has no place within an enlightened morality of personal aspiration, it would be neither personally enlightened nor environmentally benign for us to interfere with hunting by other people if and when such hunting is the heart of a community's way of allowing people and wildlife to live together in some semblance of harmony.

NOTES

1. Raymond Bonner, *At the Hand of Man,* New York: Vintage (1993). Unless otherwise noted, page references in the text are to this book. Bonner's sources include interviews, memos, minutes of committee meetings, and newsletters. His reporting is consistent with my own experience and with other sources I have been able to check, except where otherwise noted.

2. Bonner's source is a publicly circulated report by Leakey to the U.S. State Department in 1989.

3. If it seems astonishing both that this could be true and that Leakey would publicly admit it, consider two things. First, there was pervasive corruption at the highest levels of government, allowing well-connected poachers to operate with impunity. Second, many rangers were paid less than a living wage, so it was need, not greed, that drove some of them to poach. Thus, Leakey sometimes had little choice but to put up with poaching within his own ranks. See also David Cumming and Raoul du Toit, "The African Elephant and Rhino Group Nyeri Meeting," *Pachyderm,* 11 (1989) pp. 4–6.

4. It is now about ten years since Bonner wrote, and in hindsight it seems clearer that the ivory ban did reduce poaching by depressing prices. Demand for ivory in the United States was almost completely choked off, not because border officials have the power to stop the influx of contraband but rather because ivory's main value is as a status symbol, and ivory today is too politically incorrect to be much of a status symbol, especially when it is illegal. Since sales of ivory have resumed (twenty tons each to Japan from Botswana, Zimbabwe, and Namibia), though, the rumor is that black market prices have begun to climb again. Perhaps it is because sixty tons is not very much, and the gesture at legalization may be doing more to increase demand than to increase supply.

5. Laura Westra, "The Principle of Integrity and *The Economy of the Earth,*" in W. Michael Hoffman, Robert Frederick, and Edward S. Petry, editors, *The Corporation, Ethics, and the Environment,* New York: Quorum Books (1990) p. 232.

6. Ramachandra Guha, "Radical American Environmentalism and Wilderness Preservation: A Third-World Critique," *Environmental Ethics,* 11 (1989) pp. 79–81.

7. p. 81. Guha here is quoting Anil Agarwal, "Human-Nature Interactions In a Third World Country," *The Environmentalist,* 6 (1986) p. 167.

8. David Western, "The Balance of Nature," *Wildlife Conservation,* (March/April, 1993) p. 52.

9. Urs P. Kreuter and Randy T. Simmons, "Who Owns the Elephants?" *Wildlife in the Marketplace,* edited by Terry Anderson and Peter J. Hill, Lanham: Rowman and Littlefield (1995) p. 161.

10. Source: Conversation (Livingstone, Zambia, July 28, 1999) with Phillip Roberts, a native of Zambia and proprieter of Wilderness Wheels Africa, a company that specializes in wildlife tours for customers in wheelchairs.

11. Source: Conversation (Moremi Game Reserve, Botswana, July 24 and 26, 1999) with Isrea Batlanang, a native of Botswana, assistant manager of Oddballs' Lodge in Moremi Game Reserve. Batlanang also is studying for a college degree in Tourism at Semmering University in Austria.

12. Even on private reserves, snare-poaching can be a problem. Khame Game Reserve in Zimbabwe is of moderate size, about ten thousand acres, and it employs five full-time rangers, which makes it reasonably well-policed compared to most national parks. Even so, when we visited the manager, Brianna Carne, she said they had caught a snare poacher on their property the previous week, and rangers had so far picked up ten snares, fearing they might yet find another two hundred.

13. David Holt-Biddle, "CAMPFIRE: An African Solution To An African Problem," *Africa Environment and Wildlife,* 2 (1994) 33–35, here p. 33.

14. An interview of Jacomea Nare, as reported in Holt-Biddle, p. 35.

15. Alexander N. Songorwa, "Community-Based Wildlife Management in Tanzania: Are the Communities Interested?" *World Development,* 27 (1999) 2061–79.

16. Gordin Edwin Matzke and Nontokozo Nabane, "Outcomes of a Community Controlled Wildlife Utilization Program in a Zambezi Valley Community," *Human Ecology,* 24 (1996) 65–85, here p. 73.

17. See http://www.campfire-zimbabwe.org or write campfir@id.co.zw for further information.

18. Matzke and Nabane, p. 80.

19. See Cynthia Moss, *Elephant Memories,* New York: William Morrow (1988) p. 209, 301.

20. Winston S. Churchill, *My African Journey,* London: Hodder and Stoughton (1908) p. 17.

21. J. C. Haigh, I. S. C. Parker, D. A. Parkinson, and A. L. Archer, "An Elephant Extermination," *Environmental Conservation,* 6 (1979) 305–10.

22. The figure of nine thousand is from Bonner. The figure of six thousand is from Daniel Botkin, *Discordant Harmonies: A New Ecology For the Twenty-First Century,* New York: Oxford University Press (1990) p. 18.

23. Moss, p. 317.

24. Lawrence E. Johnson, *A Morally Deep World,* New York: Cambridge University Press (1991) p. 173.

25. Guha, p. 55–56 in the original article.

Chapter 11

Sustainable Use and Institutional Structure

Questions for Reflection and Discussion

The Logic of the Commons

Sustainability is a central concept of environmental economics. Originally applied to the use of renewable resources such as forests and fish, the idea was to determine a maximum yield consistent with not depleting the stock. Current use is more vague and inclusive. People today take sustainability to be about meeting today's needs without compromising people's ability to meet needs in the future.

Here, in essence, is the problem. Suppose there is a plot of land. The land has a *carrying capacity,* which is the number of animals the land can sustain more or less indefinitely. Suppose the parcel's carrying capacity is 100 animals. The land is jointly owned by ten shepherds, each of whom owns ten animals for a total flock of 100 animals. The land is thus at its carrying capacity. As things stand, each animal is worth (let's say) one dollar to its owner, so that, at carrying capacity, 100 animals are worth $100. Crucially, although the ten shepherds treat their individual flocks as private property, they jointly treat the land as one large pasture, with no internal fences, so that each of their animals grazes freely.

10 shepherds × 10 animals each = 100 animals.
Individual flock's value = 10 animals × $1 = $10
Total flock's value = 100 animals × $1 = $100

Now suppose one shepherd adds an eleventh animal. We now have 101 animals altogether, and thus have exceeded the land's carrying capacity. There is not quite enough food per animal now; therefore they are a bit leaner, and the value per animal drops to 95 cents per head. At that rate, the total stock of 101 animals is now worth $95.95, which is $4.95 less than the total stock was worth before, when it was kept within the land's carrying capacity.

Total flock's value = 101 animals × 0.95 = $95.95

So, why would a shepherd add the extra animal, when it so clearly is a losing proposition? Here is why. At the original carrying capacity, the individual flocks of ten were worth $10. Having added one more sheep, the shepherd now has eleven and each is worth 95 cents. That works out to $10.45, which means that the individual shepherd actually made a profit of 45 cents by adding the extra animal, even though the value of the total stock went from $100 to $95.95.

$$\text{Individual flock's value} = 11 \text{ animals} \times 0.95 = \$10.45$$

What happened is this: Although the total cost to the group of adding the extra animal exceeded the total benefit, the individual shepherd receives 100 percent of the benefit while paying only 10 percent of the cost. The remaining 90 percent is paid by the other nine shepherds: because they own 90 percent of the animals, they suffer 90 percent of the loss involved in the falling price per head. Individual shepherds, though, see only individual costs and benefits, and act accordingly. The logic of the commons has begun its seemingly inevitable grind toward its tragic fate.

What can the shepherds do?

The Tragedy of the Commons

Garrett Hardin

At the end of a thoughtful article on the future of nuclear war, Wiesner and York concluded that: "Both sides in the arms race are . . . confronted by the dilemma of steadily increasing military power and steadily decreasing national security. It is our considered professional judgment that this dilemma has no technical solution. If the great powers continue to look for solutions in the area of science and technology only, the result will be to worsen the situation."[1]

I would like to focus your attention not on the subject of the article (national security in a nuclear world) but on the kind of conclusion they reached, namely that there is no technical solution to the problem. An implicit and almost universal assumption of discussions published in professional and semipopular scientific journals is that the problem under discussion has a technical solution. A technical solution may be defined as one that requires a change only in the techniques of the natural sciences, demanding little or nothing in the way of change in human values or ideas of morality.

In our day (though not in earlier times) technical solutions are always welcome. Because of previous failures in prophecy, it takes courage to assert that a desired technical solution is not possible. Wiesner and York exhibited this courage; publishing in a science journal, they insisted that the solution to the problem was not to be found in the natural sciences. They cautiously qualified their statement with the

Garrett Hardin, "The Tragedy of the Commons," *Science* 162 (1968): 1243–48. Copyright 1968. Reprinted with permission of the American Association for the Advancement of Science.

phrase, "It is our considered professional judgment. . . ." Whether they were right or not is not the concern of the present article. Rather, the concern here is with the important concept of a class of human problems which can be called "no technical solution problems," and, more specifically, with the identification and discussion of one of these.

It is easy to show that the class is not a null class. Recall the game of tick-tack-toe. Consider the problem, "How can I win the game of tick-tack-toe?" It is well known that I cannot, if I assume (in keeping with the conventions of game theory) that my opponent understands the game perfectly. Put another way, there is no "technical solution" to the problem. I can win only by giving a radical meaning to the word "win." I can hit my opponent over the head; or I can drug him; or I can falsify the records. Every way in which I "win" involves, in some sense, an abandonment of the game, as we intuitively understand it. (I can also, of course, openly abandon the game—refuse to play it. This is what most adults do.)

The class of "No technical solution problems" has members. My thesis is that the "population problem," as conventionally conceived, is a member of this class. How it is conventionally conceived needs some comment. It is fair to say that most people who anguish over the population problem are trying to find a way to avoid the evils of overpopulation without relinquishing any of the privileges they now enjoy. They think that farming the seas or developing new strains of wheat will solve the problem—technologically. I try to show here that the solution they seek cannot be found. The population problem cannot be solved in a technical way, any more than can the problem of winning the game of tick-tack-toe.

WHAT SHALL WE MAXIMIZE?

Population, as Malthus said, naturally tends to grow "geometrically," or, as we would now say, exponentially. In a finite world this means that the per capita share of the world's goods must steadily decrease. Is ours a finite world?

A fair defense can be put forward for the view that the world is infinite; or that we do not know that it is not. But, in terms of the practical problems that we must face in the next few generations with the foreseeable technology, it is clear that we will greatly increase human misery if we do not, during the immediate future, assume that the world available to the terrestrial human population is finite. "Space" is no escape.[2]

A finite world can support only a finite population; therefore, population growth must eventually equal zero. (The case of perpetual wide fluctuations above and below zero is a trivial variant that need not be discussed.) When this condition is met, what will be the situation of mankind? Specifically, can Bentham's goal of "the greatest good for the greatest number" be realized?

No—for two reasons, each sufficient by itself. The first is a theoretical one. It is not mathematically possible to maximize for two (or more) variables at the same time. This was clearly stated by von Neumann and Morgenstern,[3] but the principle is implicit in the theory of partial differential equations, dating back at least to D'Alembert (1717–1783).

The second reason springs directly from biological facts. To live, any organism must have a source of energy (for example, food). This energy is utilized for two purposes: mere maintenance and work. For man, maintenance of life requires about 1,600 kilocalories a day ("maintenance calories"). Anything that he does over and above merely staying alive will be defined as work, and is supported by "work calories" which he takes in. Work calories are used not only for what we call work in common speech; they are also required for all forms of enjoyment, from swimming and automobile racing to playing music and writing poetry. If our goal is to maximize population it is obvious what we must do: We must make the work calories per person approach as close to zero as possible. No gourmet meals, no vacations, no sports, no music, no literature, no art. . . . I think that everyone will grant, without argument or proof, that maximizing population does not maximize goods. Bentham's goal is impossible.

In reaching this conclusion I have made the usual assumption that it is the acquisition of energy that is the problem. The appearance of atomic energy has led some to question this assumption. However, given an infinite source of energy, population growth still produces an inescapable problem. The problem of the acquisition of energy is replaced by the problem of its dissipation, as J. H. Fremlin has so wittily shown.[4] The arithmetic signs in the analysis are, as it were, reversed; but Bentham's goal is still unobtainable.

The optimum population is, then, less than the maximum. The difficulty of defining the optimum is enormous; so far as I know, no one has seriously tackled this problem. Reaching an acceptable and stable solution will surely require more than one generation of hard analytical work—and much persuasion.

We want the maximum good per person; but what is good? To one person it is wilderness, to another it is ski lodges for thousands. To one it is estuaries to nourish ducks for hunters to shoot; to another it is factory land. Comparing one good with another is, we usually say, impossible because goods are incommensurable. Incommensurables cannot be compared.

Theoretically this may be true; but in real life incommensurables are commensurable. Only a criterion of judgment and a system of weighting are needed. In nature the criterion is survival. Is it better for a species to be small and hideable, or large and powerful? Natural selection commensurates the incommensurables. The compromise achieved depends on a natural weighting of the values of the variables.

Man must imitate this process. There is no doubt that in fact he already does, but unconsciously. It is when the hidden decisions are made explicit that the arguments begin. The problem for the years ahead is to work out an acceptable theory of weighting. Synergistic effects, nonlinear variation, and difficulties in discounting the future make the intellectual problem difficult, but not (in principle) insoluble.

Has any cultural group solved this practical problem at the present time, even on an intuitive level?

One simple fact proves that none has: there is no prosperous population in the world today that has, and has had for some time, a growth rate of zero. Any people that has intuitively identified its optimum point will soon reach it, after which its growth rate becomes and remains zero.

Of course, a positive growth rate might be taken as evidence that a population is below its optimum. However, by any reasonable standards, the most rapidly growing populations on earth today are (in general) the most miserable. This association (which need not be invariable) casts doubt on the optimistic assumption that the positive growth rate of a population is evidence that it has yet to reach its optimum.

We can make little progress in working toward optimum population size until we explicitly exorcize the spirit of Adam Smith in the field of practical demography. In economic affairs, *The Wealth of Nations* (1776) popularized the "invisible hand," the idea that an individual who "intends only his own gain," is, as it were, "led by an invisible hand to promote . . . the public interest."[5] Adam Smith did not assert that this was invariably true, and perhaps neither did any of his followers. But he contributed to a dominant tendency of thought that has ever since interfered with positive action based on rational analysis, namely, the tendency to assume that decisions reached individually will, in fact, be the best decisions for an entire society. If this assumption is correct it justifies the continuance of our present policy of laissez-faire in reproduction. If it is correct we can assume that men will control their individual fecundity so as to produce the optimum population. If the assumption is not correct, we need to reexamine our individual freedoms to see which ones are defensible.

TRAGEDY OF FREEDOM IN A COMMONS

The rebuttal to the invisible hand in population control is to be found in a scenario first sketched in a little-known pamphlet[6] in 1833 by a mathematical amateur named William Forster Lloyd (1794–1852).

We may well call it "the tragedy of the commons," using the word "tragedy" as the philosopher Whitehead used it:[7] "The essence of dramatic tragedy is not unhappiness. It resides in the solemnity of the remorseless working of things." He then goes on to say, "This inevitableness of destiny can only be illustrated in terms of human life by incidents which in fact involve unhappiness. For it is only by them that the futility of escape can be made evident in the drama."

The tragedy of the commons develops in this way. Picture a pasture open to all. It is to be expected that each herdsman will try to keep as many cattle as possible on the commons. Such an arrangement may work reasonably satisfactorily for centuries because tribal wars, poaching, and disease keep the numbers of both man and beast well below the carrying capacity of the land. Finally, however, comes the day of reckoning, that is, the day when the long-desired goal of social stability becomes a reality. At this point, the inherent logic of the commons remorselessly generates tragedy.

As a rational being, each herdsman seeks to maximize his gain. Explicitly or implicitly, more or less consciously, he asks, "What is the utility to me of adding one more animal to my herd?" This utility has one negative and one positive component.

1. The positive component is a function of the increment of one animal. Since the herdsman receives all the proceeds from the sale of the additional animal, the positive utility is nearly +1.
2. The negative component is a function of the additional overgrazing created by one or more animal. Since, however, the effects of overgrazing are shared by all the herdsmen, the negative utility for any particular decision-making herdsman is only a fraction of −1.

Adding together the component partial utilities, the rational herdsman concludes that the only sensible course for him to pursue is to add another animal to his herd. And another; and another. . . . But this is the conclusion reached by each and every rational herdsman sharing a commons. Therein is the tragedy. Each man is locked into a system that compels him to increase his herd without limit—in a world that is limited. Ruin is the destination toward which all men rush, each pursuing his own best interest in a society that believes in the freedom of the commons. Freedom in a commons brings ruin to all.

Some would say that this is a platitude. Would that it were! In a sense, it was learned thousands of years ago, but natural selection favors the forces of psychological denial. The individual benefits as an individual from his ability to deny the truth even though society as a whole, of which he is a part, suffers. Education can counteract the natural tendency to do the wrong thing, but the inexorable success of generations requires that the basis for this knowledge be constantly refreshed.

A simple incident that occurred a few years ago in Leominster, Massachusetts, shows how perishable the knowledge is. During the Christmas shopping season the parking meters downtown were covered with plastic bags that bore tags reading: "Do not open until after Christmas. Free parking courtesy of the mayor and city council." In other words, facing the prospect of an increased demand for already scarce space, the city fathers reinstituted the system of the commons. (Cynically, we suspect that they gained more votes than they lost by this retrogressive act.)

In an approximate way, the logic of the commons has been understood for a long time, perhaps since the discovery of agriculture or the invention of private property in real estate. But it is understood mostly only in special cases which are not sufficiently generalized. Even at this late date, cattlemen leasing national land on the western ranges demonstrate no more than an ambivalent understanding, in constantly pressuring federal authorities to increase the head count to the point where overgrazing produces erosion and weed dominance. Likewise, the oceans of the world continue to suffer from the survival of the philosophy of the commons. Maritime nations still respond automatically to the shibboleth of the "freedom of the seas." Professing to believe in the "inexhaustible resources of the oceans," they bring species after species of fish and whales closer to extinction.

The National Parks present another instance of the working out of the tragedy of the commons. At present they are open to all, without limit. The parks themselves are limited in extent—there is only one Yosemite Valley—whereas population seems to grow without limit. The values that visitors seek in the parks are steadily eroded. Plainly, we must soon cease to treat the parks as commons or they will be of no value to anyone.

What shall we do? We have several options. We might sell them off as private property. We might keep them as public property, but allocate the right to enter them. The allocation might be on the basis of wealth by the use of an auction system. It might be on the basis of merit, as defined by some agreed-upon standards. It might be by lottery. Or it might be on a first-come, first-served basis, administered to long queues. These, I think, are all the reasonable possibilities. They are all objectionable. But we must choose—or acquiesce in the destruction of the commons that we call our National Parks.

POLLUTION

In a reverse way, the tragedy of the commons reappears in problems of pollution. Here it is not a question of taking something out of the commons, but of putting something in—sewage, or chemical, radioactive, and heat wastes into water; noxious and dangerous fumes into the air; and distracting and unpleasant advertising signs into the line of sight. The calculations of utility are much the same as before. The rational man finds that his share of the cost of the wastes he discharges into the commons is less than the cost of purifying his wastes before releasing them. Since this is true for everyone, we are locked into a system of "fouling our own nest," so long as we behave only as independent, rational, free enterprisers.

The tragedy of the commons as a food basket is averted by private property, or something formally like it. But the air and waters surrounding us cannot readily be fenced, and so the tragedy of the commons as a cesspool must be prevented by different means, by coercive laws or taxing devices that make it cheaper for the polluter to treat his pollutants than to discharge them untreated. We have not progressed as far with the solution of this problem as we have with the first. Indeed, our particular concept of private property, which deters us from exhausting the positive resources of the earth, favors pollution. The owner of a factory on the bank of a stream—whose property extends to the middle of the stream—often has difficulty seeing why it is not his natural right to muddy the waters flowing past his door. The law, always behind the times, requires elaborate stitching and fitting to adapt it to this newly perceived aspect of the commons.

The pollution problem is a consequence of population. It did not much matter how a lonely American frontiersman disposed of his waste. "Flowing water purifies itself every 10 miles," my grandfather used to say, and the myth was near enough to the truth when he was a boy, for there were not too many people. But as population became denser, the natural chemical and biological recycling processes became overloaded, calling for a redefinition of property rights.

HOW TO LEGISLATE TEMPERANCE?

Analysis of the pollution problem as a function of population density uncovers a not generally recognized principle of morality, namely: *the morality of an act is a function of the state of the system at the time it is performed.*[8] Using the commons as a cesspool does not harm the general public under frontier conditions, because there is no public; the same behavior in a metropolis is unbearable. A hundred and fifty years ago a plainsman could kill an American bison, cut out only the tongue for his dinner, and discard the rest of the animal. He was not in any important sense being wasteful. Today, with only a few thousand bison left, we would be appalled at such behavior.

In passing, it is worth noting that the morality of an act cannot be determined from a photograph. One does not know whether a man killing an elephant or setting fire to the grassland is harming others until one knows the total system in which his act appears. "One picture is worth a thousand words" said an ancient Chinese proverb; but it may take 10,000 words to validate it. It is as tempting to ecologists as it is to reformers in general to try to persuade others by way of the photographic shortcut. But the essence of an argument cannot be photographed: it must be presented rationally—in words.

That morality is system-sensitive escaped the attention of most codifiers of ethics in the past. "Thou shalt not . . ." is the form of traditional ethical directives which make no allowance for particular circumstances. The laws of our society follow the pattern of ancient ethics, and therefore are poorly suited to governing a complex, crowded, changeable world. Our epicyclic solution is to augment statutory law with administrative law. Since it is practically impossible to spell out all the conditions under which it is safe to burn trash in the backyard or to run an automobile without smog-control, by law we delegate the details to bureaus. The result is administrative law, which is rightly feared for an ancient reason—*Quis custodiet ipsos custodes?*—"Who shall watch the watchers themselves?" John Adams said that we must have "a government of laws and not men." Bureau administrators, trying to evaluate the morality of acts in the total system, are singularly liable to corruption, producing a government by men, not laws.

Prohibition is easy to legislate (though not necessarily to enforce); but how do we legislate temperance? Experience indicates that it can be accomplished best through the mediation of administrative law. We limit possibilities unnecessarily if we suppose that the sentiment of *Quis custodiet* denies us the use of administrative law. We should rather retain the phrase as a perpetual reminder of fearful dangers we cannot avoid. The great challenge facing us now is to invent the corrective feedbacks that are needed to keep custodians honest. We must find ways to legitimate the needed authority of both the custodians and the corrective feedbacks.

FREEDOM TO BREED IS INTOLERABLE

The tragedy of the commons is involved in population problems in another way. In a world governed solely by the principle of "dog eat dog"—if indeed there ever was such a world—how many children a family had would not be a matter of public concern. Parents who bred too exuberantly would leave fewer descendants, not more, because they would be unable to care adequately for their children. David Lack and others have found that such a negative feedback demonstrably controls the fecundity of birds.[9] But men are not birds, and have not acted like them for millenniums, at least. If each human family were dependent only on its own resources; if the children of improvident parents starved to death; if, thus, overbreeding brought its own "punishment" to the germ line—*then* there would be no public interest in controlling the breeding of families. But our society is deeply committed to the welfare state, and hence is confronted with another aspect of the tragedy of the commons.

In a welfare state, how shall we deal with the family, the religion, the race, or the class (or indeed any distinguishable and cohesive group) that adopts overbreeding as a policy to secure its own aggrandizement? To couple the concept of freedom to breed with the belief that everyone born has an equal right to the commons is to lock the world into a tragic course of action.

Unfortunately this is just the course of action that is being pursued by the United Nations. In late 1967, some 30 nations agreed to the following:[10] "The Universal Declaration of Human Rights describes the family as the natural and fundamental unit of society. It follows that any choice and decision with regard to the size of the family must irrevocably rest with the family itself, and cannot be made by anyone else."

It is painful to have to deny categorically the validity of this right; denying it, one feels as uncomfortable as a resident of Salem, Massachusetts, who denied the reality of witches in the 17th century. At the present time, in liberal quarters, something like a taboo acts to inhibit criticism of the United Nations. There is a feeling that the United Nations is "our last and best hope," that we shouldn't find fault with it; we shouldn't play into the hands of the arch-conservatives. However, let us not forget what Robert Louis Stevenson said: "The truth that is suppressed by friends is the readiest weapon of the enemy." If we love the truth we must openly deny the validity of the Universal Declaration of Human Rights, even though it is promoted by the United Nations. We should also join with Kingsley Davis[11] in attempting to get Planned Parenthood–World Population to see the error of its ways in embracing the same tragic ideal.

CONSCIENCE IS SELF-ELIMINATING

It is a mistake to think that we can control the breeding of mankind in the long run by an appeal to conscience. Charles Galton Darwin made this point when he spoke on the centennial of the publication of his grandfather's great book. The argument is straightforward and Darwinian.

People vary. Confronted with appeals to limit breeding, some people will undoubtedly respond to the plea more than others. Those who have more children will produce a larger fraction of the next generation than those with more susceptible consciences. The difference will be accentuated, generation by generation.

In C. G. Darwin's words: "It may well be that it would take hundreds of generations for the progenitive instinct to develop in this way, but if it should do so, nature would have taken her revenge, and the variety *Homo contracipiens* would become extinct and would be replaced by the variety *Homo progenitivus*.[12]

The argument assumes that conscience or the desire for children (no matter which) is hereditary—but hereditary only in the most general formal sense. The result will be the same whether the attitude is transmitted through germ cells, or exosomatically, to use A. J. Lotka's term. (If one denies the latter possibility as well as the former, then what's the point of education?) The argument has here been stated in the context of the population problem, but it applies equally well to any instance in which society appeals to an individual exploiting a commons to restrain himself for the general good—by means of his conscience. To make such an appeal is to set up a selective system that works toward the elimination of conscience from the race.

PATHOGENIC EFFECTS OF CONSCIENCE

The long-term disadvantage of an appeal to conscience should be enough to condemn it; it has serious short-term disadvantages as well. If we ask a man who is exploiting a commons to desist "in the name of conscience," what are we saying to him? What does he hear?—not only at the moment but also in the wee small hours of the night when, half asleep, he remembers not merely the words we used but also the nonverbal communication cues we gave him unawares? Sooner or later, consciously or subconsciously, he senses that he has received two communications, and that they are contradictory: (i) (intended communication) "If you don't do as we ask, we will openly condemn you for not acting like a responsible citizen"; (ii) (the unintended communication) "If you *do* behave as we ask, we will secretly condemn you for a simpleton who can be shamed into standing aside while the rest of us exploit the commons."

Everyman then is caught in what Bateson has called a "double bind." Bateson and his co-workers have made a plausible case for viewing the double bind as an important causative factor in the genesis of schizophrenia.[13] The double bind may not always be so damaging, but it always endangers the mental health of anyone to whom it is applied. "A bad conscience," said Nietzsche, "is a kind of illness."

To conjure up a conscience in others is tempting to anyone who wishes to extend his control beyond the legal limits. Leaders at the highest level succumb to this temptation. Has any President during the past generation failed to call on labor unions to moderate voluntarily their demands for higher wages, or to steel companies to honor voluntary guidelines on prices? I can recall none. The rhetoric used on such occasions is designed to produce feelings of guilt in noncooperators.

For centuries it was assumed without proof that guilt was a valuable, perhaps even an indispensable, ingredient of the civilized life. Now, in this post-Freudian world, we doubt it. Paul Goodman speaks from the modern point of view when he says: "No good has ever come from feeling guilty, neither intelligence, policy, nor compassion. The guilty do not pay attention to the object but only to themselves, and not even to their own interests, which might make sense, but to their anxieties."[14]

One does not have to be a professional psychiatrist to see the consequences of anxiety. We in the Western world are just emerging from a dreadful two-centuries-long Dark Ages of Eros that was sustained partly by prohibition laws, but perhaps more effectively by the anxiety-generating mechanisms of education. Alex Comfort has told the story well in *The Anxiety Makers;*[15] it is not a pretty one.

Since proof is difficult, we may even concede that the results of anxiety may sometimes, from certain points of view, be desirable. The larger question we should ask is whether, as a matter of policy, we should ever encourage the use of a technique the tendency (if not the intention) of which is psychologically pathogenic. We hear much talk these days of responsible parenthood; the coupled words are incorporated into the titles of some organizations devoted to birth control. Some people have proposed massive propaganda campaigns to instill responsibility into the nation's (or the world's) breeders. But what is the meaning of the word responsibility in this context? Is it not merely a synonym for the word conscience? When we use the word responsibility in the absence of substantial sanctions are we not trying to browbeat a free man in a commons into acting against his own interest? Responsibility is a verbal counterfeit for a substantial quid pro quo. It is an attempt to get something for nothing.

If the word responsibility is to be used at all, I suggest that it be in the sense Charles Frankel uses it.[16] "Responsibility," says this philosopher, "is the product of definite social arrangements." Notice that Frankel calls for social arrangements—not propaganda.

MUTUAL COERCION MUTUALLY AGREED UPON

The social arrangements that produce responsibility are arrangements that create coercion, of some sort. Consider bank robbing. The man who takes money from a bank acts as if the bank were a commons. How do we prevent such action? Certainly not by trying to control his behavior solely by a verbal appeal to his sense of responsibility. Rather than rely on propaganda we follow Frankel's lead and insist that a bank is not a commons; we seek the definite social arrangements that will keep it from becoming a commons. That we thereby infringe on the freedom of would-be robbers we neither deny nor regret.

The morality of bank-robbing is particularly easy to understand because we accept complete prohibition of this activity. We are willing to say "Thou shalt not rob banks," without providing for exceptions. But temperance also can be created by coercion. Taxing is a good coercive device. To keep downtown shoppers temperate in their use of parking space we introduce parking meters for short periods, and traffic fines for longer ones. We need not actually forbid a citizen to park as long as he wants to; we need merely make it increasingly expensive for him to do so. Not prohibition, but carefully biased options are what we offer him. A Madison Avenue man might call this persuasion; I prefer the greater candor of the word coercion.

Coercion is a dirty word to most liberals now, but it need not forever be so. As with the four-letter words, its dirtiness can be cleansed away by exposure to light, by saying it over and over without apology or embarrassment. To many, the word coercion implies arbitrary decisions of distant and irresponsible bureaucrats; but this is not a necessary part of its meaning. The only kind of coercion I recommend is mutual coercion, mutually agreed upon by the majority of the people affected.

To say that we mutually agree to coercion is not to say that we are required to enjoy it, or even to pretend we enjoy it. Who enjoys taxes? We all grumble about them. But we accept compulsory taxes because we recognize that voluntary taxes would favor the conscienceless. We institute and (grumblingly) support taxes and other coercive devices to escape the horror of the commons.

An alternative to the commons need not be perfectly just to be preferable. With real estate and other material goods, the alternative we have chosen is the institution of private property coupled with legal inheritance. Is this system perfectly just? As a genetically trained biologist I deny that it is. It seems to me that, if there are to be differences in individual inheritance, legal possession should be perfectly correlated with biological inheritance—that those who are biologically more fit to be the custodians of property and power should legally inherit more. But genetic recombination continually makes a mockery of the doctrine of "like father, like son" implicit in our laws of legal inheritance. An idiot can inherit millions, and a trust fund can keep his estate intact. We must admit that our legal system of private property plus inheritance is unjust—but we put up with it because we are not convinced, at the moment, that anyone has invented a better system. The alternative of the commons is too horrifying to contemplate. Injustice is preferable to total ruin.

It is one of the peculiarities of the warfare between reform and the status quo that it is thoughtlessly governed by a double standard. Whenever a reform measure is proposed it is often defeated when its opponents triumphantly discover a flaw in it. As Kingsley Davis has pointed out,[17] worshippers of the status quo sometimes imply that no reform is possible without unanimous agreement, an implication contrary to historical fact. As nearly as I can make out, automatic rejection of proposed reforms is based on one of two unconscious assumptions: (i) that the status quo is perfect; or (ii) that the choice we face is between reform and no action; if the proposed reform is imperfect, we presumably should take no action at all, while we wait for a perfect proposal.

But we can never do nothing. That which we have done for thousands of years is also action. It also produces evils. Once we are aware that the status quo is action, we can then compare its discoverable advantages and disadvantages with the predicted advantages and disadvantages of the proposed reform, discounting as best we can for our lack of experience. On the basis of such a comparison, we can make a rational decision which will not involve the unworkable assumption that only perfect systems are tolerable.

RECOGNITION OF NECESSITY

Perhaps the simplest summary of this analysis of man's population problems is this: the commons, if justifiable at all, is justifiable only under conditions of low-population density. As the human population has increased, the commons has had to be abandoned in one aspect after another.

First we abandoned the commons in food gathering, enclosing farm land and restricting pastures and hunting and fishing areas. These restrictions are still not complete throughout the world.

Somewhat later we saw that the commons as a place for waste disposal would also have to be abandoned. Restrictions on the disposal of domestic sewage are widely accepted in the Western world; we are still struggling to close the commons to pollution by automobiles, factories, insecticide sprayers, fertilizing operations, and atomic energy installations. In a still more embryonic state is our recognition of the evils of the commons in matters of pleasure. There is almost no restriction on the propagation of sound waves in the public medium. The shopping public is assaulted with mindless music, without its consent. Our government is paying out billions of dollars to create supersonic transport which will disturb 50,000 people for every one person who is whisked from coast to coast 3 hours faster. Advertisers muddy the airwaves of radio and television and pollute the view of travelers. We are a long way from outlawing the commons in matters of pleasure. Is this because our Puritan inheritance makes us view pleasure as something of a sin, and pain (that is, the pollution of advertising) as the sign of virtue?

Every new enclosure of the commons involves the infringement of somebody's personal liberty. Infringements made in the distant past are accepted because no contemporary complains of a loss. It is the newly proposed infringements that we vigorously oppose; cries of "rights" and "freedom" fill the air.

But what does "freedom" mean? When men mutually agreed to pass laws against robbing, mankind became more free, not less so. Individuals locked into the logic of the commons are free only to bring on universal ruin; once they see the necessity of mutual coercion, they become free to pursue other goals. I believe it was Hegel who said, "Freedom is the recognition of necessity."

The most important aspect of necessity that we must now recognize is the necessity of abandoning the commons in breeding. No technical solution can rescue us from the misery of overpopulation. Freedom to breed will bring ruin to all. At the moment, to avoid hard decisions many of us are tempted to propagandize for conscience and responsible parenthood. The temptation must be resisted, because an appeal to independently acting consciences selects for the disappearance of all conscience in the long run, and an increase in anxiety in the short.

The only way we can preserve and nurture other and more precious freedoms is by relinquishing the freedom to breed, and that very soon. "Freedom is the recognition of necessity"—and it is the role of education to reveal to all the necessity of abandoning the freedom to breed. Only so, can we put an end to this aspect of the tragedy of the commons.

NOTES

1. J. B. Wiesner and H. F. York, *Sci. Amer.* 211 (No. 44), 27 (1964).

2. G. Hardin, *J. Hered.* 50, 68 (1959); S. von Hoernor, *Science* 137, 18 (1962).

3. J. von Neumann and O. Morgenstern, *Theory of Games and Economic Behavior* (Princeton, NJ: Princeton Univ. Press, 1947), p. 11.

4. J. H. Fremlin, *New Sci.* No. 415 (1964), p. 285.

5. A. Smith, *The Wealth of Nations* (New York: Modern Library, 1937), p. 423.

6. W. F. Lloyd, *Two Lectures on the Checks to Population* (Oxford, England: Oxford Univ. Press, 1833), reprinted (in part) in *Population, Evolution, and Birth Control,* G. Hardin, ed. (San Francisco: Freeman, 1964), p. 37.

7. A. N. Whitehead, *Science and the Modern World* (New York: Mentor, 1948), p. 17.

8. J. Fletcher, *Situation Ethics* (Philadelphia: Westminster, 1966).

9. D. Lack, *The Natural Regulation of Animal Numbers* (Oxford: Clarendon Press, 1954).

10. U Thant, *Int. Planned Parenthood News*, No. 168 (February 1968), p. 3.

11. K. Davis, *Science* 158, 730 (1967).

12. S. Tax, ed., *Evolution After Darwin* (Chicago: Univ. of Chicago Press, 1960), vol. 2, p. 469.

13. G. Bateson, D. D. Jackson, J. Haley, J. Weaklaad, *Behav. Sci.* 1, 251 (1956).

14. P. Goodman, *New York Rev. Books* 1968, 10 no. 8, 22 (23 May 1968).

15. A. Comfort, *The Anxiety Makers* (London: Nelson, 1967).

16. C. Frankel, *The Case for Modern Man* (New York: Harper, 1955), p. 203.

17. J. D. Roslansky, *Genetics and the Future of Man* (New York: Appleton-Century-Crofts, 1966), p. 177.

Approximate Optimality of Aboriginal Property Rights

Martin J Bailey

In contrast to the relatively rich literature, enlightened by many cases, on property rights in modern societies, the corresponding literature by economists on aboriginal societies is peremptory and uninformed by interdisciplinary studies. This relatively brief literature is enlightened by only a few case studies and concrete examples. Both the analysis and its credibility can be improved by more use of relevant data, covering a wider variety of cases. This article undertakes such an endeavor, using the observations of anthropologists of the diverse set of rights, customs, and practices of over fifty aboriginal peoples. The cases considered here include peoples who used their group territories for hunting and fishing; for gathering wild roots, fruit, vegetables, and invertebrates; and (sometimes) for primitive horticulture. Among the studied groups, one observes almost all conceivable structures of rights.

The study of aboriginals can make especially clear the advantages of one type of property rights over another because, in some cases, these people lived at the margin of subsistence. In more developed societies, departures from optimality mean lower living standards and lower growth rates—luxuries these societies can afford. By contrast, in societies near the margin of subsistence, with populations under Malthusian control, such departures had harsher effects, which one would expect to see reflected in the surviving societies. Unsound rights structures generally implied lower population size and, perhaps, the disappearance of the society. (Where the balance of advantage and disadvantage between alternative institutions was reasonably close, however, more than one could be found.) One therefore expects the data on aboriginals to provide relatively direct evidence on the structure of an op-

timal system of property rights under various circumstances. These circumstances generally include a small population when compared to a modern nation state, so that the enforcement of various behavioral norms through social pressure was much easier. For this and other, technological reasons, optimal rights structures in aboriginal societies could include more common property and group enterprises and fewer disjoint individual rights than are workable in developed societies.

The most widely cited works on this topic—by Demsetz and by Posner—fall short of doing justice to the richness of the data or the analytical issues involved.[1] Drawing on a cursory interpretation of the experience of a small group, Demsetz tells us that private property rights sprang up in response to the opportunity to trade with Europeans; his working postulate is that private rights are necessarily superior except where enforcement costs outweigh the advantages. Although his account of the rise of property rights among certain Northeastern American tribes is based on known facts, it is only a small part of the story. Posner countered with an explanation of why sometimes common property could be optimal for such peoples. This explanation is true but incomplete, both factually and analytically.

Looking at a larger set of cases, one discovers a striking set of regularities in aboriginal rights structures. Typically, the rights in each tribe vary among types of property; but in the case of land, the rights vary with the use or resources involved. Families often had private property in land (with clear boundaries) for one food resource but not another. As the norm, groups hunted across the entire tribal (or village) territory without regard to property lines that might exist for other purposes. Also the norm, pri-

Martin J. Bailey, "Approximate Optimality of Aboriginal Property Rights," *Journal of Law and Economics* 35 (1992): 183–97. Copyright 1992 by The University of Chicago. All rights reserved. Reprinted with permission of the Journal of Law and Economics.

vate property existed in food and other personal property as well as in land for horticultural use, where that use existed.[2]

PREMISES AND PRINCIPAL CONSIDERATIONS

I take as well established the Malthusian view of population, which implies that land tends to be scarce and valuable when viewed on a large-scale basis. If accessible land exists that can support more people than live there, then, given their customs and technology, the population grows and fills out the usable area until there is no longer surplus land available.[3] Therefore, the conventional arguments for the superiority of exclusive control over absolutely common property apply to land on the relevant, large scale. Social institutions reflect this elementary circumstance in accordance with the survival pressures mentioned above. Almost everywhere, each group lived on territory on which it had exclusive rights to hunt, fish, gather, or garden. Neighboring groups either accepted these territorial boundaries peaceably or fought. In either case, the boundaries were usually reasonably well defined at any given time, even if they were impermanent. (Of course, warfare sometimes created extensive tracts of unoccupied land that took more than a generation or two to fill out again. Moreover, habitual raiding and warfare forced land-use adjustments that reduced the land's carrying capacity indefinitely, yet the habit survived. These circumstances do not affect my analysis or main findings.) Indeed, this attribute of tribal territories is so commonplace that, although clearly implied in the writings of anthropologists and historians, it is often left unstated.[4] Groups of primitive peoples differed in this connection in the rights of households and individuals versus those of the tribe, district, village, or band. Either the people held and used the territory in common, or households and single persons held separate parcels, or, most often, some combination of the two existed. A similar state of affairs existed (and was observed) with respect to other types of property, such as food, shelter, and clothing.

Single parcels of land for households made sense if a parcel had a sufficiently reliable supply of food to provide a significant part of the household's subsistence in a season of scarcity and if there were no economies of scale to larger parcels used in common for food. Common property for the group made sense if either of these criteria failed to hold. In this connection, one can view a tribe's subsistence activity as an enterprise analogous to a firm. Under some circumstances, the minimum efficient size of the enterprise was the household, under other circumstances, it was a band of families or the tribe; there were economies of scale to the enterprise up to that size.

Moreover, the minimum efficient size of the enterprise could vary according to the specific hunting or gathering activity, and the allocation of rights could, and usually did, vary accordingly. For some activities, the households had their own parcels, whereas for other activities they acted communally over the group territory and disregarded the boundaries of individual parcels. There were also variations among groups in the type or degree of private property in the food itself once taken (within the group it might vary by the time of year or type of food resource). Some of the same general considerations that determined an advantage to common property in land could also work in favor of common property or rules of sharing in food.

THE EFFICIENT-SIZED ENTERPRISE

A single household could subsist on a fixed parcel if the relevant food resources were distributed in a relatively fixed, predictable manner over the tribal territory. In some cases, small game, fish, and so forth were distributed in fixed ways among the parcels so that one household's takings did not appreciably affect the resources available to other households. Further, there was no advantage to common or shared rights to the yields of different parcels because the variability of yield either was offsetting among the different resources within a parcel or, if not, was correlated among different parcels. Where these attributes held approximately true, the well-known incentive advantages of private property dominated, and one would expect to see separate household parcels. This conclusion applies with special force to horticulture. For garden plots, the advantages of a private property system seem especially clear.

By contrast, in many instances, either food resources could not be allocated efficiently through ownership of separate household parcels or their efficient taking required a group size larger than the household. These instances usually involved larger prey animals, such as large antelope or buffalo, but might also involve smaller prey or even seemingly nonmobile plant foods. Regarding either land or prey, the following attributes of the resource or technology favored common property over private property rights: (1) the low predictability of prey or plant location within the tribal territory; (2) the public-good aspect of information about the location of this kind of unpredictable food resource; (3) the high variance of the individual's success because of 1, 2, or other circumstances beyond the individual's control; (4) the superior productivity of group hunting techniques, such as driving prey into ambush or over a cliff; (5) the safety from large predators, especially when bringing home the product of a successful trip out. These attributes occurred in various combinations in the different groups. The first, second, and fourth were pertinent to the balance of advantage between common property and private property in land in different groups. The second, third, fourth, and fifth are pertinent to the corresponding balance in already taken food.

The first attribute—low predictability of location—was important for major food sources such as buffalo or other migratory animals. As a general rule, such animals appeared only in one season and were not the group's sole source of food. When they migrated into a tribe's territory, they were plentiful for a time but did not stay in or around any one location. Hunters could take them freely, subject to the limits of their technology and ability, until the animals left the territory. As Demsetz points out, "The value of establishing boundaries to private hunting territories is thus reduced by the relatively high cost of preventing the animals from moving to adjacent parcels."[5] Indeed, sometimes there was arguably no value at all in establishing such boundaries. In some cases, because of a group's primitive hunting technologies and their dependence on other food sources in winter (which limited expansion of their population), there was no appreciable depletion of the herds of migratory animals; that is, there was no appreciable negative externality of hunting. (The buffalo on the great plains is an obvious example.) Moreover, these circumstances in no way affected the balance between the incentive to hunt effectively or to shirk. This balance depended, instead, on property rights in the animals *after* a successful hunt, that is, on the response of custom to the balance of the other listed factors.

The second attribute—the public-good aspect of information—existed in those cases where the group could not easily locate a herd of migratory game or another food source. Coordinated searching and sharing the information gained would then produce better total results for the group than would an individual's solitary tracking or information. Where this attribute was not present, the balance of considerations often favored private ownership and nonsharing of the food. But sharing information and coordinating searches meant that all participants had a joint marginal product not solely attributable to the successful hunter. Accordingly, some method of sharing the food would provide incentives to more effective effort and tactics. Sharing would also promote individual specialization by comparative advantage: that is, the best trackers might not be those most skilled at closing for the kill. One would therefore expect a tendency to find effort-inducing sharing rules for these cases, taking due account of other circumstances.

The third attribute—the high variance of hunting or gathering success—sometimes implied a high risk of starvation. It also meant that the successful hunter or gatherer sometimes had more food than one household could consume before the food spoiled due to the lack of a technology for preserving it. Where the success of different households was random and uncorrelated, sharing would reduce appreciably the variance for the group; that is, common ownership or a practice of equivalent effect would reduce it.

The fourth attribute—the superior productivity of group hunting techniques—is logically similar to the second. As in that case, one would expect the results of the hunt to be shared. Whereas the second attribute would apply only to migratory animals or to plant foods that had to be searched out each year, group hunting was also productive for game such as rabbits, which were widely distributed and could be reliably found on each household's private land, if private land existed in the group. In that case, a group that otherwise respected separate household plots for other purposes might join in a group hunt and share the results.

The fifth attribute—safety from predators—was particularly relevant in Africa. Game taken in a successful hunt had to be carried back to the household or group camping place, a dangerous enterprise better performed by a group. As in the case of tracking information, a consideration of the incentives indicates the appropriateness of sharing the results of the hunt with those who cooperate in bringing it home.

SOME EXAMPLES

The most striking examples of aboriginal property rights are the cases of those tribes that have separate household parcels of land (private real estate) in winter but not in summer. The best-known cases are the Bushmen of the Kalahari desert in Africa and the Penobscot, Montagnais, Naskapi, and other nearby tribes living in the northeastern U.S. woodlands, Quebec, and western Labrador. In both these cases, food was relatively scarce in winter, and the best chances of survival were gained by solitary or familial hunting and gathering. Family property boundaries were well defined.

The Bushmen adjusted the family properties, which were not heritable, from year to year. They had no horticulture at any time of the year. Food location and scarcity in winter favored private prop-

erty. In the winter, game was relatively small, territorial rather than migratory, and distributed fairly evenly. They knew the distribution of plant foods at the beginning of winter, and they delimited the family parcels in such a way as to give every family a good chance of making it through the winter. As a matter of custom, households scrupulously respected each others' boundaries and rights to game.

In summer, food was generally more plentiful, and the Bushmen could efficiently indulge their preference for bringing their families together in bands. Larger, migratory game and any available water favored group cooperation. Sharing game-tracking information (and information about plants), coordinating hunting plans, and occasional group hunting, all involved a large minimum-efficient group size. There was a public-good aspect to maintaining waterholes and locating those that had recently received rain. If a single hunter took a large game animal, the tribe had no technology to preserve the meat; therefore, it would spoil unless shared. As noted above, bringing meat safely back to camp was a group enterprise. Although the successful hunter "owned" the meat, he was obligated to share it according to a set of customary rules that rewarded those who contributed. By contrast, plants gathered by each family belonged to that family alone.

The native tribes in northeastern North America shared this seasonal pattern of land use. The family parcels of land were comparatively permanent and generally heritable. Their concept of private property (including personal property such as food, canoes, and implements), however, was a more circumscribed case than with the Bushmen. In the value structure of these tribes, the problem of variable food supplies outweighed incentive effects, so sharing and rent-free lending were generally practiced. As is well known, the European fur trade led to a suspension of the sharing rules and thus, to strict respect for each family's property rights in furs, traps, and any other item of commercial use and purpose. (The sharing rules continued for subsistence food and for other items with no commercial use.)

Nevertheless, survival pressures fit the pattern described for the Bushmen of the Kalahari, so the seasonal cycle of separate family subsistence on their own parcels of land almost certainly existed before European contact. Local opportunities and circumstances varied, but, generally, the chances of survival were better for separate family groups on separate parcels of land than for larger groups. In summer, when food was more plentiful, there were opportunities for cooperative hunting and other group activities. The differences in property rights between these American Indians, on the one hand, and the Bushmen, on the other, illustrate the indeterminacy of institutions when the economic advantages of one institutional form are closely balanced with the advantages of another.[6] Survival pressures also led the Shoshone of Nevada to separate into individual family districts. In their case, periods of plenty or opportunities for group hunting usually occurred less than once a year, however, so the families would remain isolated for years at a time.

Examining the aboriginal peoples studied in this article, there is a rule for the hunters and gatherers that appears to be universally applicable: wherever the advantages of group searching and hunting are appreciable, they dominated every other consideration. In these cases, a lineage group, band, or village held common access, and the private property rights of "nuclear" families were irrelevant until the game was taken. Almost all American Indian tribes practiced group hunting over the entire tribal territory even if private property in land existed for other food sources.[7] Also, in those areas where game still existed at the time the African peoples were studied, most practiced some form of group hunting. Sometimes the right to hunt on specific land was held by large lineage groups and at other times by the king or chief for the entire tribe or district.

HORTICULTURE AND PROPERTY RIGHTS

As there was for hunting and gathering, there is a rule for horticulture and agriculture that appears to be universally applicable: wherever either appeared, each household or narrow kinship group had private property in the crop, which also meant, at least temporarily, in the land. This, in conjunction with the opposite tendency in the case of hunting rights, offers the clearest systematic confirmation of Demsetz's and Posner's conjectures that the structure of rights tends to respond to economic incentives.

In most observed cases of horticulture prior to European contact, the aboriginals did not maintain or improve soil fertility. In some cases, they used irrigation, but, if so, the irrigation works and allocation of water were community operations. Water rights varied from case to case, as they do in developed countries. These more advanced agricultural techniques could be thought of as analogous to group hunting. (In any case, it does not affect the following argument about heritability.) Because they lacked such techniques, these groups moved periodically or used lengthy periods of fallowing land to enrich the soil for further cultivation. In any case, with no way for the individual household to improve the land's fertility, a right to inherit or keep the land for long periods would have no economic consequence. By contrast, in those cases where an aboriginal people discovered fertilization, the right to inherit would provide a positive incentive to maintain the soil's fertility, so that heritability would serve the best interests of the tribe.

In all cases, the right to use a given plot for a full crop cycle, to own its produce, and to keep it for several cycles (if the family expended the labor to clear it) held obvious economic advantages. A family with exclusive rights to the crop (usufruct rights) will be more likely to effectively perform the efforts of clearing, preparing the ground, planting, harvesting, and guarding the plot (against birds, rodents, and other creatures that might damage it).

I should also note that aboriginal people's concepts of the family and of private rights sometimes differ from those in developed societies. For some, land rights belonged to individuals—including separate plots for the husband and wife in a "nuclear" family. In others, the rights belonged to that family as a whole. In still others, the rights belonged to an extended family that included a couple, their married sons or daughters, and their children. In a few cases, after the grandparents died, a group of brothers or sisters, together with their mates and children, jointly worked and owned the family property. In all of these cases, I refer to the rights as "private property." I refer to most other cases (such as rights held effectively in common by a band, village, or larger tribal group) as common, rather than private, property. I will also note below a case that is difficult to classify where land and personal property are owned by a large lineage group.

Several North American tribes domesticated food crops and also possessed some variant of either temporary or long-term property rights in land.[8] In some cases, they planted a "communal" field but then allotted it in family parcels. Iroquois women of a lineage group cooperated in cultivating each others' crops in areas where constant warfare favored staying in groups (although this did not occur elsewhere). The Ojibwa in eastern sub-Arctic Canada did not domesticate the wild rice they harvested, but they did possess private plots in the wild rice beds, where they invested in temporary improvements to increase their yields.

In two exceptional North American cases—the Penobscot of the northeast and the Natchez of the southeast—the tribes practiced horticulture but had little or no private rights to the crops. The Penobscot worked individual garden plots but had to share food on demand with anyone who "needed" it. The Natchez managed the entire crop cycle as a communal effort and shared the produce.

In Africa, private property was also generally the rule for horticultural land, although there existed a rich variety in the details and scope of the rights. Some groups still practiced strictly subsistence cultivation, but most began to grow cash crops during the time of these colonial observations. Apparently, groups that began growing cash crops under colonialism kept their property rules substantially unchanged.

The Suku in Zaire present a case that is difficult to classify. A Suku husband and wife kept their food and other personal property strictly separate. She prepared and provided him with produce from her garden for his own consumption, and he provided her with meat from the hunt; if he had a visitor, he could borrow her chickens and other food to offer a meal to the visitor but then had to repay it. A wife's surplus, however, stayed with her matriline: her uncles, mother, brothers, and, on demand, cousins. Thus, in this respect, her produce was common property. A wife's transfers to more senior members of her lineage group can be seen as a form of social security (in which her husband was also engaged with his lineage): a practice which they could be entitled to when they were older. All transfers to matrilineal kin were a strict obligation: they were viewed as preferable to permitting any property to fall into the hands of the husband's lineage in the event of divorce or death. These rules represent a partial exception to the general rule of private property in horticultural gardens and produce.[9]

Private property in land was found much less frequently among people without horticulture. Two notable instances—the Hupa of California and the northwest coast tribes—strongly emphasized private property and were relatively prosperous, as one would expect. They had family property rights in the superior fishing, hunting, and gathering sites and in personal property, which included slaves. The emphasis on family property, ostentation, and social standing probably reduced population pressure: food and artifacts were plentiful.[10]

A great diversity of household rights within group territories has been observed in aboriginal humans. It is similar to what is observed among birds and many other animals. It reflects the similar pressures that sometimes favor a separate territory for each mating pair and in other cases favor group territories. Another parallelism is that some of the variations in observed practices have no obvious relation to survival pressures; in apparently similar circumstances, different species sometimes resolve the issue differently.

CONCLUSION

This article broadly confirms the conjectures of Posner and Alchian and Demsetz that the structure of property rights will usually reflect economic advantage in those cases where the balance of advantage is clear. A nuanced and detailed picture emerges from the data, one that could scarcely be foreseen when reflecting on just one or two cases. Within each culture, not only do property rights vary among kinds of property, but, in the case of land, they vary according to the use, resources, or circumstances involved. Reinforcing Posner's discussion, I do not find that private property rights for individual families would always be advantageous were it not for the costs of creating and enforcing them. Instead, I find that economic advantage sometimes rested clearly and positively with group exploitation of its entire territory. It was not unusual for families to have private property in land with recognized boundaries for one food resource but not another. Indeed, almost all aboriginal peoples engaged in group hunting, fishing, or gathering in their common territory without regard to any individual household's property rights in the land for other purposes. This practice and the exclusiveness of group territories were the most widespread features of aboriginal property rights.

Private property in food and other personal property was the norm. There were occasional exceptions, usually where sharing provided social insurance against localized famine, that is, as a means of reducing variance to people who were understandably risk averse. In these and other cases, the risk of famine tipped the balance in favor of common property in land. Survival pressure, however, sometimes led families to separate and subsist on individual parcels of land, whether or not they viewed them as strictly private property.

Finally, the most important finding is that those people who engaged in horticulture or agriculture generally tended to have private property rights (either temporary or long term) in the use of land for a crop. These rights were, in some cases, heritable, and this attribute prevailed most reliably in those few groups that knew how to maintain and improve soil fertility. These findings provide food for thought about the probable interactions among the various influences in neolithic times that led to the emergence of property rights in our own and other societies.

NOTES

1. Harold Demsetz, Toward a Theory of Property Rights, *Am. Econ. Rev. Papers & Proc.* 347, p. 57 (1967); Richard A. Posner, A Theory of Primitive Society, with Special Reference to Law, *Law & Econ.* 1, p. 23 (1980). The occasional observations of anthropologists on these issues are of course better informed. See, for example, Ralph M. Linton, Land Tenure in Aboriginal America, in *The Changing Indian* (Oliver La Farge ed. 1943), p. 42, who made some of the points I make here.

2. One does find exceptions, notable though infrequent, to almost all these general findings.

3. This proposition appears to have been a subject of controversy among anthropologists because of anecdotal information and calculations of carrying capacity that suggest that hunter gatherers and those with shifting cultivation usually take up only a fraction of the land's apparent carrying capacity. The key to the matter is the carrying capacity in the leanest seasons of the leanest years in a long period, given the occupants' technology, warfare, and other cultural constraints. This key information has rarely been obtained.

4. For a clear statement of the general territorial rule, with examples, see William Allan, *The African Husbandman* 266 ff. (1965).

5. Demsetz, *supra* note 1.

6. John C. McManus, An Economic Analysis of Indian Behavior in the North American Fur Trade, *J. Econ. Hist.* 36, p. 32 (1974).

7. The recorded cases include the Pueblo tribes of the southwest, the Plateau tribes inland in the northwest, the California tribes, the tribes of the great basin, the tribes of the Great Plains, and the tribes of the southeast.

8. These included, among others, the Pueblos, the Mohave of the southwest, the Hidatsa and Mandan of the Great Plains, the eastern woodland tribes such as the Iroquois, and the Creek of the southeast.

9. Gray & Gulliver, *supra* note 15, at 84–85, 91–95, and 100–101.

10. For an economic analysis, see D. Bruce Johnsen, "The Formation and Protection of Property Rights among the Southern Kwakiutl Indians," *J. Legal Stud.* 41, p. 15 (1986).

Environmental Lessons

Carol Rose

Early in the modern history of environmentalism, James Krier and Edmund Ursin wrote a very useful book called *Pollution and Policy*.[1] Building on California's experience with air pollution control, the authors argued that environmental regulatory efforts involve a kind of learning process. That is, legislators operate by collective trial and error, enacting and then "exfoliating" one regulatory scheme after another, ideally using even the failures to learn more about the problems confronting them.

In these matters as in so many others, the country as a whole has followed California's lead, learning in fits and starts about environmental problems. But *what* have we learned in all the exfoliations since the first Earth Day? Readers . . . will no doubt observe that there are almost too many answers to that question; quite a number, however, fall into three major categories of problems. I call these, respectively the Information Problem, the Budget Problem, and the Priorities Problem. Regarding the first, we have special difficulties in simply finding out about environmental problems. As for the second, even when we do have information, we have additional difficulties in adopting a systematic, cost-effective approach to budgeting on environmental issues. And as for the third, even when we can budget for individual issues, we find still other impediments to comparing and ranking environmental issues—impediments that prevent us from addressing these issues in an orderly progression.

In the environmental area, learning, budgeting, and ranking are difficult tasks technically. But what is more daunting, as this Essay argues, is that some of the most promising approaches to the *technical* problems seem *socially* unattractive. All this should direct our attention to still another issue: We need to think about persuasion and rhetoric in dealing with environmental matters.

THE INFORMATION PROBLEM: SEEING THE ISSUES

One very useful intellectual device for discussing environmental issues has developed over the last generation: Social and economic thinkers have framed these issues as instances of the more generalized problem of the "commons." According to the now-conventional wisdom, the collective course should be to conserve or invest in common resources. Unfortunately, because of shared or open access, individuals cannot reap all the benefits of their own forbearance or investment, and hence may be motivated simply to grab before others do, sometimes with disastrous results. This motivation may affect even public-spirited individuals who fear that their personal restraint or contribution may go for naught, or worse, may only enrich the greedy and self-serving. This now-familiar tale can be told about the pollution of the oceans or the air mantle, the overhunting of wildlife stocks and underfunding of habitat, the pumping or poisoning of underground water sources—all cases where unowned or collective resources are subject to overuse and underinvestment.

Economics, of course, has an interest in such matters, as it does in all issues of scarce resources. Generally speaking, the greatest social well being should incorporate collective as well as individually owned goods. Even if one thinks that individual ownership generally enhances care for resources, one might call for "privatizing" the good things previously used or enjoyed in common, but it will not do to pretend that they were not good things in the first place.

The commons approach to environmental problems has thus assisted us in the simple first step of recognition: We can see that environmental problems really *are* problems, in the prosaic sense that overuse of environmental commons can decrease

Carol Rose, "Environmental Lessons," *Loyola of Los Angeles Law Review* 27 (1994): 1023–47. Reprinted courtesy of Loyola of Los Angeles Law Review.

overall social well-being. Despite the massive uncertainties about environmental questions, we have a good guess that auto exhaust fumes increase the chances of heart attacks; that acid rain kills trees and fish; that overforesting aggravates flooding; that fugitive refrigerant gases, floating high into the atmosphere, contribute to the irradiation and resulting damage to organic life in the oceans and on continents below.

If one looks only to the conventional theory of the commons, one can easily grow pessimistic about solving vast and multilayered ecological problems like these. But after a generation of concern with commons issues, we have also learned that whatever the difficulties in principle, people in practice sometimes do manage to cope with collective resources, so that the "inexorable" logic of commons does not always play out so inexorably after all.[2] Left to their own devices, people can figure out ways to preserve fishing grounds and wild animal stocks; they can organize and operate collective irrigation systems; and indeed as our own legislation suggests, they can make some inroads on the polluted commons in air and water, even if the successes have been costly and limited.

Unfortunately, however, we have also learned that despite our tentative grip on some large environmental problems, we really do not deal very well at all with vast numbers of others. The commons analysis suggests a reason why this is so, though the reason is only indirectly tied to the self-interest that supposedly induces people to trash the commons. The trouble is rather a derivative one: People have too few reasons even to *notice* commons problems.

Self-interest clearly does play a role here. For example, I easily observe how much more my new car costs because of the pollution control device that has been installed in it, but I am not likely to focus so sharply on my own and others' marginally improved chances of avoiding smog-induced respiratory ailments. Similarly, I quickly notice an increase in my electricity bill, but I have less pointed reason to contemplate how the utility's new pollution control expenditures may save trees and fish someplace far away. When we mix these weak informational motivations with the tremendous uncertainties of remote causation (Will carbon dioxide warm the oceans and threaten shorelands with inundation, or will additional clouds recool the surface?), the problem of simply *learning* about environmental problems seems overwhelming. This becomes increasingly so as we find ever remoter and ever vaster commons in the interactions of resources.[3]

In a sense, what we have learned about self-interest and the commons is not that people necessarily act selfishly in using common resources. Instead we have learned, among other things, that self-interest is a *signalling* or *attention-getting* device of great power. For instance, regardless of how you eventually act, when you are trying to decide whether to reroof your own or even a friend's or relative's house, you are apt to make at least a rough calculation of the costs and benefits and possible side effects. Unfortunately, environmental problems do not come packaged with any signalling systems as powerful as self-interest; quite aside from the enormous difficulties of collecting information scientifically about, say, airborne toxics, we often lack the motivational spur even to make the effort.

What, then, might focus human attention on common resource problems? Well, one thing is drama. But what makes things dramatic? I will return to this subject, but preliminarily, it seems that drama appears sometimes simply by accident, when events speak to what seem to be widely shared human emotions. On this point, some psychologists have noted that people exhibit a preference for status quo outcomes and a special aversion to losses.[4] Furthermore, some have identified a set of factors called "dread" that make a loss or change seem especially bad.[5] Among the factors of dread are the sense of large, remote, and sometimes suddenly erupting forces that cause large-scale havoc and lingering pain to some identifiable group of innocents. The accidental chemical leak at Bhopal is a textbook example of loss aversion compounded by dread factors. It was followed, as even nonpsychologists might have predicted, with its own rush of legislative responses.

When accidental events create such drama, they no doubt contribute to the herky-jerky character of our environmental legislation. But another way of creating drama is not so accidental: It is conscious *talk*. That is, speakers and actors can frame issues in ways that people will take notice; they implicitly recognize that people notice certain kinds of outcomes more readily than others. Environmentalists have certainly taken this cue, and often use disaster imagery in the furtherance of a variety of causes, just as they use appeals to so-called charismatic animals to dramatize conservation efforts. I do not believe that it is wise to be too critical of this kind of imagery. After all, it does call people's attention to important matters when ordinary self-interest might not. In any event, environmentalists are not the only ones to use talk; advertisers are in this business too, and appeal to environmental consumers with references to their own green-ness.

Aside from dramatic accidents and image making, what else catches people's attention? Psychological studies observe several revealing characteristics in the ways that people think about probabilities. Some psychologists use the terms "anchoring," "representativeness," or "availability" to describe aspects of people's tendency to guess probabilities as if the events in question were similar to other events, particularly those that are easily accessible in their own thought processes or prior experiences.[6] Along these lines, some environmental talk appeals to popularly accessible thought patterns, making issues " 'salient" by coupling them with already "available" ideas. The burgeoning discussion of environmental rights, such as animal rights or ecosystem rights, carries a familiar concept into unfamiliar territory, and thus lends a kind of mental mooring to the issues, especially in a culture like ours where rights talk bears considerable freight.[7]

Another referential coupling appears in the newly emerging topic of environmental racism, now discussed particularly in connection with the location of toxic or other wastes in low-income areas.[8] Although many of the specific issues have a familiar ring, since the siting of unwanted land uses in low income areas is a pattern with a long and shameful history, the language of environmental racism may

have helped to alert the residents of these areas that environmental problems are their problems too, and not just the musings of wealthy bird watchers. Moreover, this rhetorical coupling links environmental issues to our most serious historic social problems, thus highlighting for the wealthy bird watchers an underemphasized dimension of pollution.

I do not mean to suggest that these devices are complete antidotes to the Information Problem of environmental issues. Indeed, in responding to dramatic gestures or salient linkages, we could be embarking on just another set of herky-jerky routines, overlooking nuances of comparative advantage, or disguising from ourselves some causal factors that might be revealed by more patient inquiry. But one positive aspect of these appeals is that they may push the research—the information-seeking effort—in directions that would have been ignored otherwise. As I argue later in this Essay, all these rhetorical devices deserve very serious consideration.

Interestingly enough, our laws reflect a growing sophistication about the problem of motivating environmental information gathering. Environmental impact review for major federal projects was an early move in this direction. The federal law and related state laws operate by making a simple direct command to a project-proposing agency: Collect information! This begs other critical questions: Information about what? And, under what circumstances? In practice, of course, opponents of particular projects have used these statutes on occasion simply to delay offending projects, thus making them more costly and problematic.

In one sense, the impact-review statutes did recognize something important quite early in the modern environmental movement: They implicitly recognized that weak self-interest may result in only weak information. After all, why collect data on bird habitat when you do not have to pay for its loss? You might collect the data anyway, of course, but your shareholders or constituents generally will be just as happy if you do not, since this only adds to your costs. In short, there is no systematic motivation for you or others to collect data about inputs from or outputs to the unowned commons. The National Environmental Policy Act (NEPA) and its state clones were created in an effort, however clumsy, to counterbalance that lack of information-gathering motivation.

The command and control statutes of early environmental legislation can be seen as further steps in the legal quest to motivate information gathering. The explicit hope of technology-forcing legislation was not simply that it would reduce pollution, but also that it would induce industrialists to undertake research that would lead to more environmentally benign technology. One notable hope was that new types of automobile engines would result from legislation that punished the lack of best available technology, where the phrase included technology that *might* be ready in the middle-term future.

Critics have long berated technology forcing for its costs, inflexibility, and general futility, and have instead proposed a turn from the stick of mandatory technology to the carrot of economic incentives.[9] This has implications for information, because if environmental problems can be framed in ways that better jog self-interest, then knowledge will be jogged along with the economic incentives to improve.

The hopes for incentive approaches are particularly noticeable in two areas: "proto property" rights in pollution control and "shadow pricing" in cost-benefit analysis. A major experiment in proto property appears in the acid rain provisions of the 1990 Clean Air Act, which create a limited regime of tradeable emission rights. Such schemes should make each polluter regard its small measure of pollution as a bounded entitlement, and induce each one to figure out how to stay within the boundaries, or alternatively, bargain with others for some portion of their entitlements. As with more conventional forms of property, tradeable pollution entitlements should give entitlement holders and entitlement purchasers an interest in holding costs down. This, in turn, should provide an interest in finding cheap, effective pollution control methods that would presumably alleviate overall pollution.

This is not to imply that property approaches fully satisfy our pollution control needs; they too have garnered some hefty criticism. Proponents of entitlement schemes are often optimistic about administrative savings. But in fact, property regimes may be expensive, particularly where the entitlements are difficult to monitor and police, such as those involving air emissions.[10] It is no accident that most of the entitlement approaches to date have been applied to pollution from large, fixed, industrial sources. No one is seriously suggesting, for example, that automobile drivers receive individualized tradeable pollution entitlements, even though some crude surrogates have indeed been discussed, such as taxing gasoline or purchasing and destroying old, heavily polluting cars.

Quite aside from the administrative objections to entitlements regimes, however, some people sense that these stratagems carry a *moral* cost of very substantial dimensions. Property rights proponents sometimes seem to assume that only the *total* pollution matters, and are less attentive to local concentrations, even though ordinary people may be very sensitive to the equity of such "hotspots." More subtly, the older command and control approach required each polluter to do its very best to contain pollution—indeed, better than its best, insofar as best available pollution control technology included as-yet uninvented devices. The property rights approaches, on the other hand, seem subject to the complaint that polluters need not do their best at all—they can perpetrate a wrong if they simply purchase the right to do so. The moral message strikes some as repugnant and counterproductive, a point to which this Essay will return shortly.

In a different effort to enlist the self-interest of polluters, some economists have devised ways to derive shadow prices or "contingent values" to assess the nonmarket values of environmental resources—the value of their availability for future use, or for the pleasure that they convey by simply being there, for example. Shadow pricing appears in cost-benefit calculations at the regulatory stage, as well as in the ex post assessments of damage to natural resources in oil spills and other instances of unplanned pollution releases.

One of the attractions of shadow pricing is its hard quality, which makes environmental issues seem really to count for something—in a way, linking environmentalism to the market-oriented thought patterns so familiar in a larger commercial culture. Moreover, shadow pricing has the general advantage of quantification, insofar as shadow prices let people compare some environmental values to others, or compare environmental goods to more individualized ones. Perhaps most important, these assessments may jog the imagination, and may encourage people to pay attention to the otherwise ignored losses that they suffer from damage to common resources.

Unfortunately, shadow prices have some disadvantages too. One is precisely their seemingly hard numerical quality, which may mask their widely varying presuppositions. Moreover, these metaphoric "prices" sometimes seem rather bizarre to interview subjects, who may be either puzzled when asked how much they would pay to preserve a place they will never see, or aggravated at the implication that a price can be put on something too precious to be sold at all. Indeed, shadow prices have aroused furious denunciations even from very sophisticated commentators, notably Mark Sagoff, who has reacted with rage to what seem to be the commodifying premises of these studies, without perhaps noticing their attention-catching metaphoric usefulness.[11]

Thus our environmental legislation has clearly exfoliated a whole series of information-eliciting approaches to the general problem of learning about the environment. But upon reflection, it is quite daunting to realize that the very approaches that might be among the most promising—that is, those that enlist self-interest to motivate environmental information gathering and problem solving—seem to run into serious moral criticism precisely because they *do* enlist self-interest. Unfortunately, this serious rhetorical problem mirrors an equally serious rhetorical problem in the area of environmental budgeting.

THE BUDGET PROBLEM: MANAGING RISKS

If we think about environmental problems as variants on commons problems, it is pretty clear that not all commons problems are the same. Thomas Schelling pointed out several years ago that in some—but not all—of these problems, the slightest damage ruins the whole. In his example, the cutesy roadside sign "every litter bit hurts" is misleading. Instead, the *first* scrap offends the most in a pristine area, just as the first lawn mower disrupts a quiet Sunday morning, no matter how many others follow.[12] In such cases, there is an argument for all-or-nothing solutions: no snowmobiles in the park, no powerboats in the Boundary Waters Canoe Area, no trash fires in the backyard.

But pollution problems often have a different pattern, where many "litter bits" can occur before it matters. Just as your body readily manages small amounts of the same iodine that would poison you in larger volumes, so can many water bodies absorb a modicum of certain pollutants without any noticeable damage. Similarly, some wild animal stocks thrive even though, or perhaps because, they are subject to some predation. All-or-nothing approaches are unwarranted here; unrestrained exploitation would certainly decimate the common resource, but a total ban would neglect the regenerative qualities of the stock, or the absorptive and self-cleansing capacities of the medium.

There are many examples of resource stocks in which a few "litter bits" have no noticeably damaging effects. In a more complex variant, there are many other resource stocks where some activities *do* cause damage—but the damage costs are dwarfed by the costs of stopping. At least as of now, for example, most automobiles add to air pollution, and as a result of our long love affair with the car, we suffer noticeable health and aesthetic damage. On the other hand, forcing all cars to a screeching halt would be incredibly costly, both to the individuals who depend on them or just enjoy them, and to the larger industries that depend on their production and use. Pollution costs may be real, but control or forbearance costs are real too, and in vast numbers of environmental areas, a dominating task has been to weigh the one against the other. That is the first part of the budgeting problem: locating and providing for what has been called optimal pollution.[13]

Unfortunately, part-way solutions run counter to much of our legal tradition. All-or-nothing solutions pervade our tort law, or at least they did prior to modern ideas of comparative fault. Winner-take-all is the preference in American electoral law too. And all-or-nothing solutions, or slight variations on them, have dominated much of our environmental law as well, particularly in the early stages.

Indeed, it has taken some time to learn that all-or-nothing approaches can be quite awkward and costly. The first version of the Endangered Species Act permitted no disruption of species designated "endangered," and only after the Tellico Dam imbroglio was the Act modified to permit some post hoc reconsideration. Similarly, the Federal Water Pollution Control Act Amendments of 1972, having now evolved into the modern Clean Water Act (CWA), called for an end to the discharge of pollutants into the nation's waters by 1985, but this too has run into hitches. One example is the CWA's regulation of ocean disposal of various organic wastes. In some places, notably Hawaii, the surrounding waters are deep and vast; ocean disposal has genuine costs, but they are relatively minute in comparison to the cost of fully treating the sewage before discharge. Hawaiian officials have asked for and received many exemptions, but only after some considerable struggles—not only with the federal government, but also with the state's own irate citizens.

On the whole, the courts are not particularly friendly to these partial solutions. They have been hard on sewage spills in Hawaii, even when it has appeared that expensive treatment options might yield comparatively low returns. They have been equally unsympathetic to the EPA's own efforts to avoid what seem to be particularly high regulatory costs. For example, in *National Resources Defense Council v. Costle,* the court torpedoed the EPA's effort to exempt a variety of small feedlots from water pollution controls, giving short shrift to the ar-

gument that the small operations presented relatively high enforcement expenses. Similarly, in *Sierra Club v. Ruckelshaus,* the court required the EPA to issue regulations on radionuclide emissions. The court held that once the emissions were listed among toxic air pollutants, the EPA had an affirmative duty to regulate, and brushed aside the EPA's plea that it was impossible to regulate these intractable materials. In *Chemical Manufacturers Ass'n v. EPA,* a private party attempted to avoid regulation by presenting an explicit cost-calculation theory: Regulatory expenditures should only extend to the "knee-of-the-curve," the point at which additional and more thoroughgoing controls face steeply rising marginal costs. The argument fell on deaf ears.

In these and other judicial opinions, the courts often claim to be following the logic of Congress's legislation, and to a considerable degree they are. But some environmental laws suggest that regulators should not pursue pollutants on an all-out basis, but only somewhat beyond a margin where it seems to be worth the effort; much legislation requires not outright bans on dangerous substances, but only controls that assure "an adequate margin of safety." This language recognizes *some* limit on the effort to eradicate harmful materials, and hence embraces some partial solutions. To be sure, of course, this language cannot be read as a full commitment to optimizing, which would justify an earlier spending cutoff at that knee-of-the-curve where additional control expenditures rise rapidly without proportional benefits.

Critics like Barry Commoner argue that even the "margin of safety" route is misguided, and that we are wasting our time and resources when we adopt partial solutions. Better to abandon these unsuccessful halfway accommodations to problems, he argues, and to turn toward eliminating pollutants at the source.[14] On his prescription, we should reduce pollution not to some more or less acceptable level, but to zero.

Why have all-or-nothing solutions seemed so attractive, and half-a-loaf solutions so difficult to devise and defend? For one thing, people may have only a dim intuitive grasp of the benefits from partial measures. For another, these measures are likely to be organizationally and politically complex. Optimal pollution requires us to select allowable levels of pollution and determine the triggers for regulatory activity, all of which invite fervid lobbying—and even more so when the choices shift with experience and technological change. Thus, for example, it might make sense to permit more contact even with something as toxic as dioxin if we learn that this substance is not so dangerous as we once thought; or conversely, it may make sense to ratchet down the allowable amounts if new control technologies make restraint cheaper. Either way, we can predict that changes in permissible levels will generate innumerable headaches and resistance as well as figures and counterfigures from conflicting interests. By comparison, all-or-nothing approaches—let it go or ban it entirely—look attractively simple when intermediate choices face wrangles, as they always do on environmental questions, given the fuzziness of our information about them.

And of course, monitoring is apt to be easier with all-or-nothing approaches than with partial ones. Alcohol regulators reduce their policing costs by barring liquor sales to those under eighteen, even though many young people would doubtless drink prudently. A ban on a given pesticide may mean boarding up the manufacturing plant; but a rationed solution, or the requirement of particular application technologies, requires the monitoring of many more persons, locations, and activities. Small wonder, then, that commentators like Commoner despair of partial solutions and opt for banning instead of rationing.

But quite aside from these conventional problems of administrative feasibility, experience suggests that partial solutions raise substantial moral issues. At the most primitive level, the very materials of environmental degradation often strike us as repellent, revolting, and frightening. Oil slicks and sewage sludge seem loathsome in themselves. The common disgust at these contaminants impedes our coolly weighing the possibility of, say, simply closing the beaches a few times a year, rather than requiring better-built ships or demanding the installation of leakproof sewage treatment equipment, which would obviate these unpleasant events altogether. Is it cheaper to close the beaches occasionally? Arguably, yes; but this solution may be viscerally unacceptable.

At a considerably more sophisticated level is the ethical approach linked to a Kantian categorical imperative, according to which one should be able to universalize the moral principles upon which one acts. This certainly is not a prescription for partial solutions, whereby a little bit of a bad is accepted. Insofar as a Kantian ethic captures moral intuitions, it suggests that partial solutions may run into moral quagmires. As Commoner puts it, partial solutions allow the pollution perpetrators to set the baseline, and encourage meekness about a situation whose ill effects he says are likely to be felt most by the poor.[15]

Indeed, distributional issues may especially compound Kantian qualms when partial solutions take the form of tradeable, property-like entitlements. Not only are emission or effluent entitlements part-way approaches—since they contemplate some modicum of continuing pollution—but the entitlements themselves are unevenly distributed. Tradeable emission or effluent rights, however dear to the economic approach towards environmental budgeting, look rather like a dispensation from good behavior *sometimes,* enjoyed only by *some people,* namely those who pay for the privilege. Needless to say, Kantian or crypto-Kantian intuitions may find such solutions offensive.

Summing up the Budget Problem, then, when we compare the gains from environmental protections to their costs, it seems clear that we sometimes need some level of optimal pollution or optimal resource use. This is because at some marginal point, an extra measure of control will bring only diminishing returns in protection. Beyond this point, we waste resources by devoting more to pollution control.

But optimal pollution may be politically and administratively costly—a concern even for cost-benefit calculators. Perhaps more important, optimal pollution also may seem *morally* costly. Indeed, the very concept runs the risk of undermining the civility and mutual forbearance that quietly underlie so much of our practical environmental conservation. It is hard to see a little bit of pollution as the right thing to do. It is even harder to see it as the right thing for *some* people to do, simply because they can afford it. Moreover, regimes permitting such pollution-for-pay pose the threat of making citizens callous about polluting in general. Thus in the Budget Problem as in the Information Problem, moral objections seem strongest against just those approaches—the partial solutions and property-rights methods—that would otherwise appear to be particularly promising in environmental management. Unfortunately, the same depressing scenario appears when we try to prioritize risks.

THE PRIORITIES PROBLEM: RANKING THE ISSUES

I have used the Budget Problem as the label for a difficult, but relatively narrow, set of issues—that is, weighing the net benefits of some particular extractive or polluting activity, and balancing those against the benefits that we would enjoy if we alleviated the degradation of the same environmental resource. The Budget Problem, so defined, is about comparing particular resource risks to particular control costs.

An extended version of the Budget Problem is what I am calling the Priorities Problem, which raises budgetary concerns in a more global context. The Priorities Problem revolves about comparative risks: Should we turn first to Environmental Danger Number 1 (ED-1) or to Environmental Danger Number 2 (ED-2)? To answer that, we need to weigh the costs and benefits of controlling ED-1, at any given level, against the costs and benefits of controlling ED-2.

Looked at in this broader context, the Priorities Problem presumes that not all resources are equally valuable, not all risks are equally risky, and not all costs are equally costly. Moreover, even if ED-1 is our most serious risk at the outset, at some level of expenditure we would do better to shift our layouts to control ED-2; and similarly, later on, to ED-3 and so on. This, in very simplified form, is the idea that Richard Stewart has outlined as a "risk portfolio approach," where the goal is to achieve what military planners used to call "the Biggest Bang for the Buck"—the greatest level of risk protection, given

the budget available for the whole array of environmental risks that confront us.[16]

In view of the need to use our resources in the most prudent way, risk portfolio approaches seem to make obvious sense. This is something else we have learned over a generation of environmental law, and the lesson is reflected in the comparative risk approaches that now influence so much of the EPA's thinking. Indeed, a quite remarkable set of *New York Times* articles in the Spring of 1993 suggested that comparative risk approaches have seeped into the popular consciousness as well. Even Jane and John Doe now are starting to believe that we should concentrate on the big environmental issues first; if necessary even letting the little things ride for a while.

But a risk portfolio approach only magnifies the obstacles encountered in the Budget Problem, and adds a few besides. Most important is the question of assessing comparative costs and benefits. If these are difficult to calculate in the context of one single pollutant, they are exponentially more difficult where the control of each pollutant has to be weighed against the control of the other pollutants in the entire portfolio full of risks.

Then too, there are all the issues plaguing partial solutions. Comparative risk assessment drags in a whole portfolio full of these part-way solutions, and administrative and political obstacles are bound to multiply in this broad arena. Moreover, because comparative approaches pick and choose across a whole spectrum of risks, they may cluster the distribution of environmental burdens, and in so doing may raise particularly difficult equitable questions. That is, with a comparative risk approach, the issue is not simply that some air pollution controls may be halted before easing the discomfort of the most sensitive asthmatics. Rather, *all* the asthmatics' breathing problems might be disregarded, at least temporarily, while resources are concentrated instead on some other risk altogether, such as a waterborne pollutant linked to birth defects. The logic of comparative risk speaks clearly for dealing first with the most serious, most widespread, and most easily controlled harms; however, that logic creates "hotspots"—or rather, cold comfort for the asthmatics.

Once again, tradeable pollution entitlements seem especially vulnerable to such distributional complaints. For example, it has been suggested that toxins be ranked, and that control over more serious toxic materials might be exchanged for continued production of less toxic ones. That is, producers of ED-17 may continue to produce, if they clean up some portion of ED-3, on the theory that the expenditure on ED-3 will prevent more overall harm. But the nagging distributional question of these trades is obvious: What then happens to those populations particularly affected by the generally *less* damaging Environmental Danger Number 17?

Indeed, in principle, a risk portfolio approach should weigh the relative costs and benefits of *all* regulatory efforts; thus, in effect, we should be talking about an "Unhappiness Portfolio." In that sense, an *environmental* risk portfolio is itself a part-way approach writ large, since so-called environmental risks only constitute one slice of the array of risks existing in the world. Small wonder, then, that all the problems of partway solutions rise exponentially when risks are compared.

Perhaps it is not surprising, then, that comparative risk approaches have had faint resonance in the courts, where equitable considerations are never far in the background. I have already mentioned some instances in which the courts have disrupted partial solutions. Now, consider this hostility in the arena of comparative risks. If with respect to a single risk, an agency is forbidden from taking into account the marginally increasing costs of pursuing diminishing dangers, then by extension and a fortiori, it would seem that the same agency would be required to ignore the point that on average we would be better off if, after the control costs of ED-1 (say, smog precursors) started to rise very rapidly, the agency turned its attention instead to ED-2 (say, construction runoff), not to speak of ED-3 or ED-100.

Courts have a particular problem with such global approaches: As an institutional matter, they see problems one at a time. When judges say that the EPA has to go the regulatory whole hog once it has declared radionuclides a danger, they have no information about other potentially regulatable risks that

are claimants on the regulatory budget. Furthermore, even if they did have such information, they might not be able to predict whether the EPA would expend its budgetary savings on the next risk in line.

But of course it is hard for *anyone* to see risks in a global context. That too is one of the reasons for our herky-jerky legislation—our Love Canal legislation (CERCLA), our Bhopal legislation (EPCTRA), our Exxon Valdez legislation (Oil Pollution Act) and so on. The courts are not the only ones to see things one at a time. Indeed, the judicial decisions on environmental regulation only highlight a more widespread point about global approaches to risks: Once an evil is known, it becomes salient, and it crowds out other possibilities in the risk portfolio. Courts have their own rules for salience, but for the rest of us, the simple identification of a problem makes it more salient than other matters that remain undisclosed. It seems more important to follow through on controlling the known risk than the unknown, at least in part because we are often not comparing the known risk to anything else at all.

Hence the Priorities Problem—which is in a way only a globalized version of the Budget Problem—circles back around to the Information Problem, and to the difficulty of simply *noticing* environmental issues. Indeed, in a sense, the very notion of prioritizing risks suggests that we have already solved the Information Problem—that we already know the range of risks " 'out there," and which risks are more dangerous than others. Distressingly often, however, we do not have a firm grasp on that information at all, and even when we do in principle, the dramatic and already known things get noticed, the not-known and not-present risks remain beneath the surface, precluding any genuine comparison. The result, as the "loss aversion" psychologists point out, is that we may hate risks that threaten the things we now have, but are comparatively complacent about risks that threaten things we can only contemplate. Moreover, even when we are aware of comparative risks, the comparisons themselves do not carry much intuitive meaning, particularly in the context of very large or very small numbers. Who really grasps the difference between one-in-a-billion and one-in-a-trillion risk? What is a trillion, anyway? The psychologists suggest that while human beings can talk the talk, the numbers do not mean much.

Thus it may well be that a risk portfolio strategy is a useful approach to environmental regulation, but legal institutions do not easily take a synoptic and comparative view. Instead, particular and individual questions crowd out the big picture—and the most salient and dramatic questions have the biggest elbows.

And so, once again, one of our most promising approaches, a risk portfolio strategy, seems to face the greatest obstacles from the very intuitions we rely on to tell us what is important, appropriate, and normatively acceptable. Moreover, we have only a dim and quavering picture of what a risk portfolio would look like—but what we see looks administratively difficult and morally hard-hearted.

ENVIRONMENT AND RHETORIC

Are there ways out of these related dilemmas—that is, that the most promising efforts to learn about, and act upon, environmental risks seem to elicit only threadbare comprehension and stubborn normative resistance?

One response is to look to institutions. Bruce Ackerman and William Hassler have suggested that such problems are precisely why we need a kind of New Deal agency to manage environmental questions—an agency with wide latitude and with only light policing by Congress and the courts.[17] Such a superagency, the argument goes, is the only institutional chance we have to deal comprehensively with specific environmental questions on some basis other than sheer accident or theatricality.

Something akin to the superagency idea has been around for some time. William Ophuls, extrapolating from Garrett Hardin's work, gave an early and pessimistic assessment of such an agency by calling it a Hobbesian solution—a Leviathan in the form of an expert elite, necessitated by the general intractability of environmental issues to popular democratic choice.[18] Even with a Leviathan, of course,

one might question how well agency experts manage environmental problems. For one thing, they too seem prone to the errors of statistical judgment that plague the rest of us. For another, there is the question of accountability. Too much accountability makes the administrators simply second guess the elected branches, whatever the effects on the environment; too little accountability, if the dismal environmental example of the former Soviet bloc is any guide, makes them careless to the point of recklessness.

Indeed, a second response to this set of environmental dilemmas is simply pessimism. James Krier, for example, who among environmental scholars has taken an early and penetrating interest in the cognitive blocks to environmental understanding, often writes in a deep vein of melancholy.[19]

Nevertheless, our stock of intellectual traditions may have some supplies that we might well peruse more carefully. How does one engage the attention of persons who are otherwise uninterested? How does one change people's minds about the ways they should behave, individually or as members of larger communities? Accidental events can do these things, of course; but these matters are not always left to chance. Whole fields of study like theater, literature, art, and rhetoric, are devoted to such questions, even if these studies tend to be overlooked in much environmental scholarship.

It is quite astonishing to see how strongly environmentalism has been influenced by aesthetic presentations—even though the literature of environmental policy pays relatively little attention. Ansel Adams took photos; Aldo Leopold, Edward Abbey, and John Muir told stories and wrote essays. All these people have played a considerable hand in convincing others of the value and wonder of the unowned commons of our environment. In Germany, the novels of Karl May, a writer almost unknown in the United States, have had an immense effect in shaping that country's popular understandings of the American West. By the same token, there is a good reason why photography looms so large in the environmental journals, like *Sierra* or the *Audobon Magazine*. Sometimes, following in the tradition of Ansel

Adams, they use photographs of breathtaking beauty; sometimes they use pictures of heartbreaking despoliation. As was mentioned earlier, advertisers too are aware that aesthetic sensibilities have persuasive power; hence the vivid photography of "green advertising." Public broadcasting plays its part as well, with its extensive television narrations about animals and wild places.

With aesthetics and rhetoric in mind, we might reconsider the Information, Budget, and Priorities Problems, and think afresh whether a moral cloud need necessarily shadow some of the approaches that otherwise seem so promising. I argued earlier that property-rights approaches might be among the most promising with respect to the Information Problem, because property rights so often induce people to collect and weigh information carefully. Unfortunately, property has a long-standing image problem, suffering from a sometimes extraordinarily vivid association with the vices of greed and avarice.[20] Yet property also resonates to a much more positive rhetoric—that of thrift, care, and attention to the needs of potential trading partners in what Enlightenment thinkers called gentle commerce. Indeed the rhetoric of stewardship and trusteeship, so commonly used in environmental discussions, are derived from property arrangements. The stratagems of tradeable emission or effluent rights might well be more appealing if they were to draw on these latter traditions, and if they noted the association of property with the careful husbanding of resources, as well as responsibility to others. Some people worry that property-like devices permit the rich to perpetrate evils. But another way to think about this, as some economists already stress, is that those who use environmental resources must pay the costs, just as they must pay for privately held goods. After all, as environmentalists sometimes observe, the air and waters are property too—they belong to all of us—and property rhetoric can clarify that point.[21]

With respect to the Budget Problem, I argued that partial or moderating approaches are especially important, not only because it is wasteful to control environmental harms beyond the threshold at which they really *are* harms, but also because controls themselves tend to increase in expense as they move from alpha to omega. The commonly used phrase "optimal pollution" encapsulates a shorthand version of these ideas. But this phrase itself is a bit of a shocker, perhaps by design, given its mix of pollution with a word suggesting good. There are other possible phrases, however, that can imaginatively open up the important and essentially conservationist idea behind partial solutions. "Sustainable development," for example, implies not a hands-off approach but rather a moderate use of environmental resources that is compatible with their regeneration. Agriculture is a fountain of gentle language on the subject; "husbandry" and "shepherding" convey how resources may be used for a very long time, so long as they are used with attentiveness and care. Additionally, visual imagery sometimes flags these moderating aspects of part-way controls. Partial controls over resources often involve quotas, permitting the use of environmental resources up to some threshold. Several types of physical objects—a bridge, a beach, or a road—can metaphorically convey the idea that *some* use can be appropriate, so long as the use is kept within bounds.

As to the Priorities Problem, I argued that this set of issues loops back to the Information Problem. To compare risks in a risk portfolio, people need an intellectual grip on what can be compared. Just as important, people need a sense of what the comparisons actually mean when, for example, one-in-a-million and one-in-a-trillion risks do not seem that different—both just seem really, really *little*.

Here again is where rhetoric and aesthetics may help to expand our thinking. Consider "little." This is a word about physical size, and when we think of a little thing, our visual imagination is likely to be engaged. One way to get through the common intuitive gap about statistics is to use pictures creatively. Furthermore, the visual imagination can draw comparisons even without actual pictures. Most of us have encountered visual rhetorical devices many times. Take, for a recent example, the explanations telling us that if all the Defense Department's waste bullets and bombs were put in disposal trucks, the line would stretch from New York to St. Louis. Former Congressman Mike McCormack, who attempted to convey the relative sizes of large numbers (millions, billions, trillions), asked his audience to imagine beads covering spaces of varying dimensions, ranging from a jar to a committee room to the State of Ohio . . . .

Use of art, stories, and drama raise an obvious objection: the threat of manipulation. Pictures and stories do carry messages, sometimes in forms that are not easily noticeable and hence, not easily rebuttable. It has been observed lately, for example, that those glorious Ansel Adams photographs are empty of people, as if the indigenous peoples who once frequented Yosemite had simply melted into thin air, leaving behind an equally thin understanding of the human relationship to what we fondly call "natural" areas.

But the problem of manipulation, in a way, points even more toward learning about these forms of persuasion. If it is true that narrative, art, and drama can manipulate human beings, then we especially need to take these matters seriously. Otherwise, we could be pulled this way or that quite inadvertently, particularly given the difficulty that we have in wrapping our rational thinking around subjects as abstract and distant as environmental issues. Indeed, inattention to aesthetics and rhetoric then becomes an especially serious mistake. If we fail to pay attention, we may find our aesthetic responses to environmental events exploited by advertising ploys and political hucksterism, or buffeted by accidents and the accompanying journalistic attention—the new Bhopals or the next pair of stranded whales. Then too, we may find that hard-nosed rationalists ridicule ordinary responses, pointing out the hard costs and benefits of reacting to such events while neglecting to note that at least some of these responses might reflect rational patterns of value.

Thus, simply as citizens, we owe it to ourselves to try to understand, sort out, and educate such responses in a conscious and reflective fashion. . . .

Parenthetically, this may be an appropriate point to put in a word for science education as well. Some environmental literature shows a tendency to array humanistic concerns for justice, empathy, beauty, and holism on the one side and squinty-eyed, mechanistic, domineering modern science on the other. But whatever one's view of modern scientific method may be, it is important to bear in mind that knowledge of natural things often enhances one's passionate engagement in them. Otherwise, it would be difficult to understand such a pivotal environmental figure as Aldo Leopold, who was *both* a naturalist *and* a storyteller. Environmental issues call for considerable learning about the natural world, but learning also clearly has an aesthetic component: Knowing about things, on the whole, makes those things even more interesting, so that learning about the natural world can defy the usual declining demand curve and become a powerful spur to even further inquiry. . . .

Environmental issues present special difficulties of cognition and attention because of their remoteness, abstractness, and distance from the ordinary attention-getting features of self-interest. Those are not necessarily reasons for despair. Rather, they are reasons to think about thinking, and about communication, about moral and aesthetic responses, and about the relations of those responses to the cooperative actions that we need to deal with common resources. Those are the matters that, among others, make environmentalism an inquiry not only of great economic importance, but also of special intellectual excitement.

NOTES

1. James E. Krier and Edmund Ursin, *Pollution and Policy: A Case Essay on California and Federal Experience with Motor Vehicle Air Pollution 1940–1975* (1977).

2. See, e.g., Elinor Ostrom, *Governing the Commons: The Evolution of Institutions for Collective Action* 1990 (citing sources); *The Question of the Commons: the Culture and Ecology of Communal Resources* edited by Bon-

nie J. McCay and James M. Acheson, 198 (containing essays addressing theory of tragedy of commons); Carol Rose, "The Comedy of the Commons: Custom, Commerce, and Inherently Public Property," *University of Chicago Law Review* 53 (1986): 711.

3. See, e.g., Marlise Simons, "Winds Sweep African Soil to Feed Lands Far Away," *New York Times* Oct 29, 1992, at A1 (reporting that dust from Africa nourishes Atlantic biota and South American rain forest).

4. See Daniel Kahneman and Amos Tversky, "Prospect theory: An Analysis of Decision Under Risk" *Econometrica* 47 no. 263 (1979): 277–80.

5. See Paul Slovic, "Perception of Risk" *Science* 280 (1987): 236.

6. See Amos Tversky and Daniel Kahneman, "Judgment Under Uncertainty: Heuristics and Biases" *Science* 185 (1974) 1124. This literature is summarized in Roger G. Noll and James E. Krier, "Some implications of Cognitive Psychology for Risk Regulation," *Journal of Legal Studies,* 19 (1990): 747. See pp. 752–55.

7. See, e.g., Roderick Frazier Nash, *The Rights of Nature: A History of Environmental Ethics* (1989). For the import of rights rhetoric, see Carol M. Rose, "Environmental Faust Succumbs to Temptations of Economic Mephistopheles, or, Value by Any Other Name Is Preference" *Michigan Law Review* 87 (1989): 1631 (reviewing Mark Sagoff, *The Economy of the Earth* [1988]).

8. For a summary, see Robert W. Collins, "Environmental Equity: A Law and Planning Approach to Environmental Racism" *Virginia Environmental Law Journal* 11 (1992): 495.

9. See, e.g., Richard B. Stewart, "Controlling Environmental Risks through Economic Incentives" *Columbia Journal Environmental Law* 13 (1988) 153.

10. See Carol M. Rose, Rethinking Environmental Controls: Management Strategies for Common Resources, 1991 *Duke Law Journal* 1, 12–24. Even proponents recognize monitoring costs. See Robert W. Hahn and Gordon L. Hester, Marketable Permits: Lessons for Theory and Practice, *Ecology L.Q.* 16 (1989): 361. See pages 377–78.

11. Mark Sagoff, *The Economy of the Earth* (1988). See pages 83–92. But see Carol M. Rose, "Environmental Faust Succumbs to Temptations of Economic Mephistopheles, or, Value by Any Other Name Is Preference" *Michigan Law Review* 87 (1989): 1631 at 1645–1646.

12. Thomas C. Schelling, *Micromotives and Macrobehavior* (1978). See page 131.

13. See William J. Baumol and Wallace E. Oates, "The Use of Standards and Prices for Protection of the Environment," in *The Economics of Environment* (1971) 53, see p. 58 (eds. Peter Bohm and Allen V. Kneese).

14. Barry Commoner, "Failure of the Environmental Effort," *Environmental L. Rep.* (Envd. L. Inst.)18 (June 1988): 10. See p. 195.

15. Commoner, "Failure of the Environmental Effort," at pp. 10 and 198; Barry Commoner, *Making Peace with the Planet* (1990) pp. 42–43, 59–60.

16. Richard B. Stewart, "The Role of the Courts in Risk Management," 16 *Envtl. L. Rep.* (Envtl. L. Inst.) 16 (August 1986):10. See p. 208.

17. Bruce A. Ackerman and William T. Hassler, "Beyond the New Deal Coal and the Clean Air Act," *Yale Law Journal* 89 (1980): 1466.

18. William Ophuls, *Ecology and the Politics of Scarcity* (1977): 147–163.

19. See, e.g., James E. Krier, "The End of the World News," *Loyola (LA) Law Review* 27(1994): 851.

20. Medieval artists, for example, sometimes depicted avarice as an ape defecating money.

21. Older legal discussions were quite forthright about this, and talked of vindicating "public rights" in prohibiting private appropriations of such environmental resources as waterways. See, e.g., Harry N. Scheiber, "Public Rights and the Rule of Law in American Legal History," *California Law Review* 72(1984): 217. See pp. 222–224.

The Institution of Property

David Schmidtz

The evolution of property law is driven by an ongoing search for ways to internalize externalities: positive externalities associated with productive effort and negative externalities associated with misuse of commonly held resources. In theory, and sometimes in practice, costs are internalized over time. Increasingly, people pay for their own mistakes and misfortunes, and not for mistakes and misfortunes of others.

If all goes well, property law enables would-be producers to capture the benefits of productive effort. It also enables people to insulate themselves from negative externalities associated with activities around the neighborhood. Property law is not perfect. To minimize negative externalities that neighbors might otherwise impose on each other, people resort to nuisance and zoning laws. People turn to institutions like the Environmental Protection Agency for the same reasons they turn to central planners in other parts of the world; they think decentralized decision making is chaos, and that with chaos comes a burgeoning of negative externalities.

What is the reality? The reality is that decentralization may or may not be chaos. It depends on institutional structure. An open-access commons decentralizes decision making in one way; private property decentralizes it in another way, with systematically different results.

Philosophers speak of the ideal of society as a cooperative venture for mutual advantage. To be a cooperative venture for mutual advantage, though, society must first be a setting in which mutually advantageous interaction is possible. In the parlance of game theorists, society must be a positive sum game. What determines the extent to which society is a positive sum game? This essay explains how property institutions convert negative-sum or zero-sum games into positive-sum games, setting the stage for society's flourishing as a cooperative venture.

The term "property rights" is used to refer to a bundle of rights that could include rights to sell, lend, bequeath, and so on. In what follows, I use the phrase to refer primarily to the right of owners to exclude non-owners. Private owners have the right to exclude non-owners, but the right to exclude is a feature of property rights in general rather than the defining feature of private ownership in particular. The National Park Service claims a right to exclude. Communes claim a right to exclude nonmembers. This essay does not settle which kind or which mix of public and private property institutions is best. Instead, it asks how we could justify *any* institution that recognizes a right to exclude.

ORIGINAL APPROPRIATION: THE PROBLEM

The right to exclude presents a philosophical problem, though. Consider how full-blooded rights differ from mere liberties. If I am at liberty to plant a garden, that means my planting a garden is permitted. That leaves open the possibility of you being at liberty to interfere with my gardening as you see fit. Thus, mere liberties are not full-blooded rights. When I stake a claim to a piece of land, though, I claim to be changing other people's liberties—canceling them somehow—so that other people no longer are at liberty to use the land without my permission. To say I have a right to the land is to say I have a right to exclude.

Revised from David Schmidtz, "The Institution of Property," *Social Philosophy and Policy* 11 (1994): 42–62. Reprinted by permission of the Social Philosophy and Policy Foundation and Cambridge University Press.

From where could such rights have come? There must have been a time when no one had a right to exclude. Everyone had liberties regarding the land, but not rights. (Perhaps this does not seem obvious, but if no one owns the land, no one has a right to exclude. If no one has a right to exclude, everyone has liberties.) How, then, did we get from each person having a liberty to someone having an exclusive right to the land? What justifies original appropriation, that is, staking a claim to previously unowned resources?

To justify a claim to unowned land, people need not make as strong a case as would be needed to justify confiscating land already owned by someone else. Specifically, since there is no prior owner in original appropriation cases, there is no one from whom one can or needs to get consent. What, then, must a person do? Locke's idea seems to have been that any residual (perhaps need-based) communal claim to the land could be met if a person could appropriate it without prejudice to other people, in other words, if a person could leave "enough and as good" for others. This so-called Lockean Proviso can be interpreted in many ways, but an adequate interpretation will note that this is its point: to license claims that can be made without making other people worse off. In the language of modern environmental economics, we might read it as a call for sustainable use.

We also should consider whether the "others" who are to be left with enough and as good include not just people currently on the scene but latecomers as well, including people not yet born. John Sanders asks, "What possible argument could at the same time require that the present generation have scruples about leaving enough and as good for one another, while shrugging off such concern for future generations?" (Sanders 1987, p. 377). Most theorists accept the more demanding interpretation. It fits better with Locke's idea that the preservation of humankind (which includes future generations) is the ultimate criterion by which any use of resources is assessed. Aside from that, we have a more compelling defense of an appropriation (especially in environmental terms) when we can argue that there was enough left over not just for contemporaries but also for generations to come.

Of course, when we justify original appropriation, we do not in the process justify expropriation. Some say institutions that license expropriation make people better off; I think our histories of violent expropriation are ongoing tragedies for us all. Capitalist regimes have tainted histories. Communist regimes have tainted histories. Indigenous peoples have tainted histories. Europeans took land from native American tribes, and before that, those tribes took the same land from other tribes. We may regard those expropriations as the history of markets or governments or Christianity or tribalism or simply as the history of the human race. It makes little difference. This essay discusses the history of property institutions, not because their history can justify them, but rather because their history shows how some of them enable people to make themselves and the people around them better off without destroying their environment. Among such institutions are those that license original appropriation (and not expropriation).

ORIGINAL APPROPRIATION: A SOLUTION

Private property's philosophical critics often have claimed that justifying original appropriation is the key to justifying private property, frequently offering a version of Locke's Proviso as the standard of justification. Part of the Proviso's attraction for such critics was that it seemingly could not be met. Even today, philosophers generally conclude that the Proviso is, at least in the case of land appropriation, logically impossible to satisfy, and thus that (private) property in land cannot possibly be justified along Lockean lines.

The way Judith Thomson puts it, if "the first labor-mixer must literally leave as much and as good for others who come along later, then no one can come to own anything, for there are only finitely many things in the world so that every taking leaves less for others" (Thomson 1990, p. 330). To say the least, Thomson is not alone:

"We leave enough and as good for others only when what we take is not scarce" (Fried 1995, p. 230n).

"The Lockean Proviso, in the contemporary world of overpopulation and scarce resources, can almost never be met" (Held 1980, p. 6).

"Every acquisition worsens the lot of others—and worsens their lot in relevant ways" (Bogart 1985, p. 834).

"The condition that there be enough and as good left for others could not of course be literally satisfied by any system of private property rights" (Sartorius 1984, p. 210).

"If the 'enough and as good' clause were a necessary condition on appropriation, it would follow that, in these circumstances, the only legitimate course for the inhabitants would be death by starvation . . . since *no* appropriation would leave enough and as good in common for others" (Waldron 1976, p. 325).

And so on. If we take something out of the cookie jar, we *must* be leaving less for others. This appears self-evident. It has to be right.

Appropriation Is Not a Zero-Sum Game

But it is not right. First, it is by no means impossible—certainly not logically impossible—for a taking to leave as much for others. Surely we can at least imagine a logically possible world of magic cookie jars in which, every time you take out one cookie, more and better cookies take its place.

Second, the logically possible world I just imagined is the sort of world we actually live in. Philosophers writing about original appropriation tend to speak as if people who arrive first are luckier than those who come later. The truth is, first appropriators begin the process of resource creation; latecomers get most of the benefits. Consider America's first permanent English settlement, the Jamestown colony of 1607. (Or, if you prefer, imagine the lifestyles of people crossing the Bering Strait from Asia twelve thousand years ago.) Was their situation better than ours? How so? Was it that they never worried about being overcharged for car repairs?

They never awoke in the middle of the night to the sound of noisy refrigerators, leaky faucets, or flushing toilets? They never had to change a light bulb? They never agonized over the choice of long-distance telephone companies?

Philosophers are taught to say, in effect, that original appropriators got the good stuff for free. We have to pay for ugly leftovers. But in truth, original appropriation benefits latecomers far more than it benefits original appropriators. Original appropriation is a cornucopia of wealth, but mainly for latecomers. The people who got here first never dreamt of things we latecomers take for granted. The poorest among us have life expectancies exceeding theirs by several decades. This is not political theory. It is not economic rhetoric. It is fact.

Original appropriation diminishes the stock of what can be originally appropriated, at least in the case of land, but that is not the same thing as diminishing the stock of what can be owned.[1] On the contrary, in taking control of resources and thereby removing those particular resources from the stock of goods that can be acquired by originally appropriation, people typically generate massive increases in the stock of goods that can be acquired by trade. The lesson is that appropriation typically is not a zero-sum game. It normally is a positive sum game. As Locke himself stressed, it creates the possibility of mutual benefit on a massive scale. It creates the possibility of society as a cooperative venture.

The argument is not merely that enough is produced in appropriation's aftermath to compensate latecomers who lost out in the race to appropriate. The argument is that the bare fact of being an original appropriator is not the prize. The prize is prosperity, and latecomers win big, courtesy of those who got here first. If anyone had a right to be compensated, it would be the first appropriators.

The Commons Before Appropriation Is Not Zero-Sum Either

The second point is that the commons before appropriation is not a zero-sum game either. Typically it is a negative sum game. Let me tell two stories. The first comes from the coral reefs of the Philippine and Tongan Islands (Chesher 1985; Gomez, Alcala, and San Diego, 1981). People once fished those reefs with lures and traps, but have recently caught on to a technique called bleach-fishing, which involves dumping bleach into the reefs. Fish cannot breathe sodium hypochlorite. Suffocated, they float to the surface where they are easy to collect.[2]

The problem is, the coral itself is composed of living animals. The coral suffocates along with the fish, and the dead reef is no longer a viable habitat. (Another technique, blast-fishing, involves dynamiting the reefs. The concussion produces an easy harvest of stunned fish and dead coral.) You may say people ought to be more responsible. They ought to preserve the reefs for their children.

That would miss the point, which is that individual fishermen lack the option of saving the coral for their children. Individual fishermen obviously have the option of not destroying it themselves, but what happens if they elect not to destroy it? What they want is for the reef to be left for their children; what is actually happening is that the reef is left for the next blast-fisher down the line. If a fisherman wants to have anything at all to give his children, he must act quickly, destroying the reef and grabbing the fish himself. It does no good to tell fishermen to take responsibility. They are taking responsibility—for their children. Existing institutional arrangements do not empower them to take responsibility in a way that would save the reef.

Under the circumstances, they are at liberty to not destroy the reef themselves, but they are not at liberty to do what is necessary to save the reef for their children. To save the reef for their children, fishermen must have the power to restrict access to the reef. They must claim a right to exclude blast-fishers. Whether they stake that claim as individuals or as a group is secondary, so long as they actually succeed in restricting access. But one way or another, they must claim and effectively exercise a right to restrict access.

The second story comes from the Cayman Islands.[3] The Atlantic Green Turtle has long been prized as a source of meat and eggs. The turtles were a commonly held resource and were being harvested

in an unsustainable way. In 1968, when by some estimates there were as few as three to five thousand left in the wild, a group of entrepreneurs and concerned scientists created Cayman Turtle Farm and began raising and selling captive-bred sea turtles. In the wild, as few as one tenth of one percent of wild hatchlings survive to adulthood. Most are seized by predators before they can crawl from nest to sea. Cayman Farm, though, boosted the survival rate of captive-bred animals to well over fifty percent. At the peak of operations, they were rearing in excess of a hundred thousand turtles. They were releasing one percent of their hatchlings into the wild at the age of ten months, an age at which hatchlings had a decent chance of surviving to maturity.

In 1973, commerce in Atlantic Green Turtles was restricted by CITES (the Convention on International Trade in Endangered Species) and, in the United States, by the Fish and Wildlife Service, the Department of Commerce, and the Department of the Interior. Under the newly created Endangered Species Act, the U.S. classified the Atlantic Green Turtle as an endangered species, but Cayman Farm's business was unaffected, at first, because regulations pertaining to commerce in Atlantic Green Turtles exempted commerce in captive-bred animals. In 1978, however, the regulations were published in their final form, and although exemptions were granted for trade in captive-bred animals of other species, no exemption was made for trade in turtles. The company could no longer do business in the U.S. Even worse, the company no longer could ship its products through American ports, so it no longer had access via Miami to world markets. The Farm exists today only to serve the population of the Cayman Islands themselves.

What do these stories tell us? The first tells us we do not need to justify failing to preserve the commons in its pristine, original, unappropriated form, because preserving the commons in pristine original form is not an option. The commons is not a time capsule. Leaving our environment in the commons is not like putting our environment in a time capsule as a legacy for future generations. In some cases, putting resources in a time capsule might be a good idea. However, the second story reminds us: there are ways to take what we find in the commons and preserve it—to put it in a time capsule—but before we can put something in a time capsule, we have to appropriate it.[4]

Justifying the Game

Note a difference between justifying institutions that regulate appropriation and justifying particular acts of appropriation. Think of original appropriation as a game and of particular acts of appropriation as moves within the game. Even if the game is justified, a given move within the game may have nothing to recommend it. Indeed, we could say (for argument's sake) that any act of appropriation will seem arbitrary when viewed in isolation, and some will seem unconscionable. Even so, there can be compelling reasons to have an institutional framework that recognizes property claims on the basis of moves that would carry no weight in an institutional vacuum. Common law implicitly acknowledges morally weighty reasons for not requiring original appropriators to supply morally weighty reasons for their appropriations. Carol Rose (1985) argues that a rule of first possession, when the world is notified in an unambiguous way, induces discovery (and future productive activity) and minimizes disputes over discovered objects. Particular acts of appropriation are justified not because they carry moral weight but because they are permitted moves within a game that carries moral weight.

Needless to say, the cornucopia of wealth generated by the appropriation and subsequent mobilization of resources is not an unambiguous benefit. The commerce made possible by original appropriation creates pollution, and other negative externalities as well. (I will return to this point.) Further, there may be people who attach no value to the increases in life expectancy and other benefits that accompany the appropriation of resources for productive use. Some people may prefer a steady-state system that indefinitely supports their lifestyles as hunter-gatherers, untainted by the shoes and tents and safety matches of Western culture. If original appropriation forces such people to participate in a culture they want no part of, then from their viewpoint, the game does more harm than good.

Here are two things to keep in mind, though. First, as I said, the commons is not a time capsule. It does not preserve the status quo. For all kinds of reasons, quality of life could drop after appropriation. However, pressures that drive waves of people to appropriate are a lot more likely to compromise quality of life when those waves wash over an unregulated commons. In an unregulated commons, those who conserve pay the costs but do not get the benefits of conservation, while overusers get the benefits but do not pay the costs of overuse. Therefore, an unregulated commons is a prescription for overuse, not for conservation.

Second, the option of living the life of a hunter-gatherer has not entirely disappeared. It is not a comfortable life. It never was. But it remains an option. There are places in northern Canada and elsewhere where people can and do live that way. As a bonus, those who opt to live as hunter-gatherers retain the option of participating in western culture on a drop-in basis during medical emergencies, to trade for supplies, and so on. Obviously, someone might respond, "Even if the hunter-gatherer life is an option now, that option is disappearing as expanding populations equipped with advancing technologies claim the land for other purposes." Well, probably so. What does that prove? It proves that, in the world as it is, if hunter-gatherers want their children to have the option of living as hunter-gatherers, then they need to stake a claim to the territory on which they intend to preserve that option. They need to argue that they, as rightful owners, have a right to regulate access to it. If they want a steady-state civilization, they need to be aware that they will not find it in an unregulated commons. They need to argue that they have a right to exclude oil companies, for example, which would love to be able to treat northern Canada as an unregulated commons.

When someone says appropriation does not leave enough and as good for others, the reply should be "compared to what?" Compared to the commons as it was? As it is? As it will be? Often, in fact, leaving resources *in the commons* does not leave enough and as good for others. The Lockean Proviso, far from forbidding appropriation of resources from the commons, actually requires appropriation under conditions of scarcity. Moreover, the more scarce a resource is, the more urgently the Proviso requires that it be removed from the negative sum game that is the unregulated commons. Again, when the burden of common use exceeds the resource's ability to renew itself, the Proviso comes to require, not merely permit, people to appropriate and regulate access to the resource. Even in an unregulated commons, some fishermen will practice self-restraint, but something has to happen to incline the group to practice self-restraint in cases where it already has shown it has no such inclination in an unregulated commons.

Removing goods from the commons stimulates increases in the stock of what can be owned and limits losses that occur in tragic commons. Appropriation replaces a negative sum with a positive sum game. Therein lies a justification for social structures enshrining a right to remove resources from the unregulated commons: when resources become scarce, we need to remove them if we want them to be there for our children. Or anyone else's.

WHAT KIND OF PROPERTY INSTITUTION IS IMPLIED?

I have defended appropriation of, and subsequent regulation of access to, scarce resources as a way of preserving (and creating) resources for the future. When resources are abundant, the Lockean Proviso permits appropriation; when resources are scarce, the Proviso requires appropriation. It is possible to appropriate without prejudice to future generations. Indeed, when resources are scarce, it is leaving them in the commons that is prejudicial to future generations.

Private property enables people (and gives them an incentive) to take responsibility for conserving scarce resources. It preserves resources under a wide variety of circumstances. It is the preeminent vehicle for turning negative sum commons into positive sum property regimes. However, it is not the only way. Evidently, it is not always the best way, either.

Public property is ubiquitous, and it is not only rapacious governments and mad ideologues who create it. Sometimes it evolves spontaneously as a response to real problems, enabling people to remove a resource from an unregulated commons and collectively take responsibility for its management. The following sections discuss research by Martin Bailey, Harold Demsetz, Robert Ellickson, and Carol Rose, showing how various property institutions help to ensure that enough and as good is left for future generations.

The Unregulated Commons

An unregulated commons need not be a disaster. An unregulated commons will work well enough so long as the level of use remains within the land's carrying capacity. However, as use nears carrying capacity, there will be pressure to shift to a more exclusive regime. As an example of an unregulated commons evolving into something else as increasing traffic begins to exceed carrying capacity, consider Harold Demsetz's account of how property institutions evolved among indigenous tribes of the Labrador peninsula. As Demsetz tells the story, the region's people had, for generations, treated the land as an open-access commons. The human population was small. There was plenty to eat. Thus, the pattern of exploitation was within the land's carrying capacity. The resource maintained itself. In that situation, the Proviso, as interpreted above, was satisfied. Original appropriation would have been permissible, other things equal, but it was not required.

With the advent of the fur trade, though, the scale of hunting and trapping activity increased sharply. The population of game animals began to dwindle. The unregulated commons had worked for a while, but now the tribes were facing a classic tragedy. The benefits of exploiting the resource were internalized but the costs were not, and the arrangement was no longer viable. Clans began to mark out family plots. The game animals in question were small animals like beaver and otter that tend not to migrate from one plot to another. Thus, marking out plots of land effectively privatized small game as well as the land itself. In sum, the tribes converted the commons in nonmigratory fur-bearing game to family parcels when the fur trade began to spur a rising demand that exceeded the land's carrying capacity. When demand began to exceed carrying capacity, that was when the Proviso came not only to permit but to require original appropriation.

One other nuance of the privatization of fur-bearing game: although the fur was privatized, the meat was not. There was still plenty of meat to go around, so tribal law allowed trespass on another clan's land to hunt for meat. Trespassers could kill a beaver and take the meat, but had to leave the pelt displayed in a prominent place to signal that they had eaten and had respected the clan's right to the pelt. The new customs went to the heart of the matter, privatizing what had to be privatized, leaving intact liberties that people had always enjoyed with respect to other resources where unrestricted access had not yet become a problem.

The Communal Alternative[5]

We can contrast the unregulated or open-access commons with communes. A commune is a restricted-access commons. In a commune, property is owned by the group rather than by individual members. People as a group claim and exercise a right to exclude. Typically, communes draw a sharp distinction between members and nonmembers, and regulate access accordingly. Public property tends to restrict access by time of day or year. Some activities are permitted; others are prohibited.

Ellickson believes a broad campaign to abolish either private property or public and communal property would be ludicrous. Each kind of property serves social welfare in its own way. Likewise, every ownership regime has its own externality problems. Communal management leads to overconsumption and to shirking on maintenance and improvements, because people receive only a fraction of the value of their labor, and bear only a fraction of the costs of their consumption. To minimize these disincentives, a commune must intensively monitor people's production and consumption activities.

In practice, communal regimes can lead to indiscriminate dumping of wastes, ranging from piles of unwashed dishes to ecological disasters that threaten whole continents. Privately managed parcels also can lead to indiscriminate dumping of wastes and to various other uses that ignore spillover effects on neighbors. One advantage of private property is that owners can buy each other out and reshuffle their holdings in such a way as to minimize the extent to which their activities bother each other. But it does not always work out so nicely, and the reshuffling itself can be a waste. There are transaction costs. Thus, one plausible social goal would be to have a system that combines private and public property in a way that reduces the sum of transaction costs and the cost of externalities.

LOCAL VERSUS REMOTE EXTERNALITIES

Is it generally best to convert an unregulated commons to smaller private parcels or to manage it as a commune with power to exclude non-members? It depends on what kind of activities people tend to engage in. Ellickson separates activities into three categories: small (like cultivating a tomato plant), medium (like damming part of a river to create a pond for ducks), and large (like using an industrial smokestack to disperse noxious fumes). The distinction is not meant to be sharp. As one might expect, it is a matter of degree. It concerns the relative size of the area over which externalities are worth worrying about. The effects of small events are confined to one's own property. Medium events affect people in the immediate neighborhood. Their external effects are localized. Large events affect people who are more remote.

Ellickson says private regimes are clearly superior as methods for minimizing the costs of small and medium events. Small events are not much of a problem for private regimes. When land is parceled out, the effects of small events are internalized. Neighbors do not care much when we pick tomatoes on our own land; they care a great deal when we pick tomatoes on the communal plot. In the former case, we are minding our own business; in the latter, we are minding theirs.

In contrast, the effects of medium events tend to spill over onto one's neighbors, and thus can be a source of friction. Nevertheless, privatization has the advantage of limiting the number of people having to be consulted about how to deal with the externality, which reduces transaction costs. Instead of consulting the entire community of communal owners, each at liberty with respect to the affected area, one consults a handful of people who own parcels in the immediate area of the medium event. A further virtue of privatization is that disputes arising from medium events tend to be left in the hands of people in the immediate vicinity, who tend to have a better understanding of local conditions and thus are in a better position to devise resolutions without harmful unintended consequences. They are in a better position to foresee the costs and benefits of a medium event.

When it comes to large events, though, there is no easy way to say which mix of private and public property is best. Large events involve far-flung externalities among people who do not have face-to-face relationships. The difficulties in detecting such externalities, tracing them to their source, and holding people accountable for them are difficulties for any kind of property regime. It is no easy task to devise institutions that encourage pulp mills to take responsibility for their actions while simultaneously encouraging people downstream to take responsibility for their welfare, and thus to avoid being harmed by large-scale negative externalities. Ellickson says there is no general answer to the question of which regime best deals with them.

A large event will fall into one of two categories. Releasing toxic wastes into the atmosphere, for example, may violate existing legal rights or community norms. Or, such laws or norms may not yet be in place. Most of the problems arise when existing customs or laws fail to settle who (in effect) has the right of way. That is not a problem with parceling land per se but rather with the fact that key resources like air and waterways remain in a largely unregulated commons.

So, privatization exists in different degrees and takes different forms. Different forms have different incentive properties. Simply parceling out land or sea is not always enough to stabilize possession of re-sources that make land or sea valuable in the first place. Suppose, for example, that fish are known to migrate from one parcel to another. In that case, owners have an incentive to grab as many fish as they can whenever the school passes through their own territory. Thus, simply dividing fishing grounds into parcels may not be enough to put fishermen in a position collectively to avoid exceeding sustainable yields. It depends on the extent to which the sought-after fish migrate from one parcel to another, and on conventions that are continuously evolving to help neighbors deal with the inadequacy of their fences (or other ways of marking off territory). Clearly, then, not all forms of privatization are equally good at internalizing externalities. Privatization per se is not a panacea, and not all forms of privatization are equal. There are obvious difficulties with how private property regimes handle large events. The nature and extent of the difficulties depends on details. So, for purposes of comparison, Ellickson looked at how communal regimes handle large events.

JAMESTOWN AND OTHER COMMUNES

The Jamestown Colony is North America's first permanent English settlement. It begins in 1607 as a commune, sponsored by London-based Virginia Company. Land is held and managed collectively. The colony's charter guarantees to each settler an equal share of the collective product regardless of the amount of work personally contributed. Of the original group of one hundred and four settlers, two thirds die of starvation and disease before their first winter. New shiploads replenish the population, but the winter of 1609 cuts the population from five hundred to sixty. In 1611, visiting Governor Thomas Dale finds living skeletons bowling in the streets, waiting for someone else to plant the crops. Their main food source consists of wild animals such as turtles and raccoons, which settlers hunt and eat by dark of night before neighbors can demand equal shares. In 1614, Governor Dale has seen enough. He assigns three-acre plots to individual settlers, which reportedly increases productivity seven-fold. The colony converts the rest of its land holdings to private parcels in 1619.

Why go communal in the first place? Are there advantages to communal regimes? One advantage is obvious. Communal regimes can help people spread risks under conditions where risks are substantial and where alternative risk-spreading mechanisms, like insurance, are unavailable. But as communities build up capital reserves to the point where they can offer insurance, they tend to privatize, for insurance lets them secure a measure of risk-spreading without having to endure the externalities that afflict a communal regime.

A communal regime might also be an effective response to economies of scale in large scale public works that are crucial in getting a community started. To build a fort, man its walls, dig wells, and so on, a communal economy is an obvious choice as a way of mobilizing the teams of workers needed to execute these urgent tasks. But again, as these tasks are completed and community welfare increasingly comes to depend on small events, the communal regime gives way to private parcels. At Jamestown, Plymouth, the Amana colonies, and Salt Lake, formerly communal settlers "understandably would switch to private land tenure, the system that most cheaply induces individuals to undertake small and medium events that are socially useful" (Ellickson 1993, p. 1,342). (The legend of Salt Lake says the sudden improvement in the fortunes of once-starving Mormons occurred in 1848 when God sent sea gulls to save them from plagues of locusts, at the same time as they coincidentally were switching to private plots. Similarly, the Jamestown tragedy sometimes is attributed to harsh natural conditions, as if those conditions suddenly changed in 1614, multiplying productivity seven-fold while Governor Dale coincidentally was cutting the land into parcels.)

Of course, the tendency toward decentralized and individualized forms of management is only a (strong) tendency and, in any case, there are trade-offs. For example, what would be a small event on a larger parcel becomes a medium event under more crowded conditions. Loud music is an innocuous small event on a ranch but an irritating medium event

in an apartment complex. Changes in technology or population density affect the scope or incidence of externalities. The historical trend, though, is that as people become aware of and concerned about a medium or large event, they seek ways of reducing the extent to which the event's cost is externalized. Social evolution is partly a process of perceiving new externalities and devising institutions to internalize them.

Historically, the benefits of communal management have not been enough to keep communes together indefinitely. Perhaps the most enduring and successful communes in human memory are the agricultural settlements of the Hutterites, dating in Europe back to the sixteenth century. There are now around twenty-eight thousand people living in such communities. Hutterites believe in a fairly strict sharing of assets. They forbid the possession of radio or television sets, to give one example of how strictly they control contact with the outside world.

Ellickson says Hutterite communities have three special things going for them: 1. A population cap: when a settlement reaches a population of one hundred and twenty, a portion of the community must leave to start a new community. The cap helps them retain a close-knit society; 2. Communal dining and worship: people congregate several times a day, which facilitates a rapid exchange of information about individual behavior and a ready avenue for supplying feedback to those whose behavior deviates from the norm; 3. A ban on birth control: the average woman bears nine children, which more than offsets the trickle of emigration. We might add that Hutterite culture and education leave people ill-prepared to live in anything other than a Hutterite society, which surely accounts in part for the low emigration rate.

Ellickson discusses other examples of communal property regimes. But the most pervasive example of communal ownership in America, Ellickson says, is the family household. American suburbia consists of family communes nested within a network of open-access roadways. Family homes tacitly recognize limits to how far we can go in converting common holdings to individual parcels. Consider your living room. You could fully privatize, having one household member own it while others pay user fees. The fees could be used to pay family members or outside help to keep it clean. In some respects, it would be better that way. The average communal living room today, for example, is notably subject to overgrazing and shirking on maintenance. Yet we put up with it. No one charges user fees to household members. Seeing the living room degraded by communal use may be irritating, but it is better than treating it as one person's private domain.

Some institutions succeed while embodying a form of ownership that is essentially collective. History indicates, though, that members of successful communes internalize the rewards that come with that collective responsibility. In particular, they reserve the right to exclude nonmembers. A successful commune does not run itself as an open-access commons.

GOVERNANCE BY CUSTOM

Many commons (such as our living rooms) are regulated by custom rather than by government, so saying there is a role for common property and saying there is a role for government management of common property are two different things. As Ellickson notes, "Group ownership does not necessarily imply government ownership, of course. The sorry environmental records of federal land agencies and Communist regimes are a sharp reminder that governments are often particularly inept managers of large tracts." Carol Rose tells of how, in the nineteenth century, public property was thought to be owned by society at large. The idea of public property often was taken to imply no particular role for government beyond whatever enforcement role is implied by private property. Society's right to such property was held to precede and supersede any claim by government. Rose says, "Implicit in these older doctrines is the notion that, even if a property should be open to the public, it does not follow that public rights should necessarily vest in an active governmental manager" (Rose 1986, p. 720). Sometimes, rights

were understood to be held by an "unorganized public" rather than by a "governmentally organized public" (Rose 1986, p. 736).

Along the same lines, open-field agricultural practices of medieval times gave peasants exclusive cropping rights to scattered thin strips of arable land in each of the village fields. The strips were private only during the growing season, after which the land reverted to the commons for the duration of the grazing season. Thus, ownership of parcels was usufructuary in the sense that once the harvest was in, ownership reverted to the common herdsmen without negotiation or formal transfer. The farmer had an exclusive claim to the land only so long as he was using it for the purpose of bringing in a harvest. The scattering of strips was a means of diversification, reducing the risk of being ruined by small or medium events: small fires, pest infestations, etc. The post-harvest commons in grazing land exploited economies of scale in fencing and tending a herd.

According to Martin Bailey (this volume), the pattern observed by Rose and Ellickson also was common among aboriginal tribes. That is, tribes that practiced agriculture treated the land as private during the growing season, and often treated it as a commons after the crops were in. Hunter-gatherer societies did not practice agriculture, but they too tended to leave the land in the commons during the summer when game was plentiful. It was during the winter, when food was most scarce, that they privatized. The rule among hunter-gatherers is that where group hunting's advantages are considerable, that factor dominates (Bailey, this volume). But in the winter, small game is relatively more abundant, less migratory, and evenly spread. There was no "feast or famine" pattern of the sort one expects to see with big-game hunting. Rather, families tended to gather enough during the course of the day to get themselves through the day, day after day, with little to spare.

Even though this pattern corroborates my own general thesis, I confess to being a bit surprised. I might have predicted that it would be during the harshest part of the year that families would band together and throw everything into the common pot in order to pull through. Not so. It was when the land was nearest its carrying capacity that they recognized the imperative to privatize.

Customary use of medieval commons was hedged with restrictions limiting depletion of resources. Custom prohibited activities inconsistent with the land's ability to recover (Rose 1986, p. 743). In particular, the custom of "stinting" allowed the villagers to own livestock only in proportion to the relative size of their (growing season) land holdings. Governance by custom enabled people to avoid commons tragedies.[6]

Custom is a form of management unlike exclusive ownership by either individuals or governments. Custom is a self-managing system for according property rights (Rose 1986, p. 742). For example, custom governs the kind of rights-claims you establish by taking a place in line at a supermarket checkout counter. Rose believes common concerns often are best handled by decentralized, piecemeal, and self-managing customs that tend to arise as needed at the local level. So, to the previous section's conclusion that a successful commune does not run itself as an open-access commons, we can add that a successful commune does not entrust its governance to a distant bureaucracy.

THE HUTTERITE SECRET

I argued that the original appropriation of (and subsequent regulation of access to) scarce resources is justifiable as a mechanism for preserving opportunities for future generations. There are various means of exclusive control, though. Some internalize externalities better than others, and how well they do so depends on the context. My argument does not presume there is one form of exclusive control that uniquely serves this purpose. Which form is best depends on what kind of activities are most prevalent in a community at any given time. It also depends on the extent to which public ownership implies control by a distant bureaucracy rather than by local custom.

As mentioned earlier, I have heard people say Jamestown failed because it faced harsh natural conditions. But communal (and noncommunal) settlements typically face harsh natural conditions. James-

town had to deal with summer in Virginia. Hutterites dealt with winter on the Canadian prairie. It is revealing, not misleading, to compare Jamestown to settlements that faced harsher conditions more successfully. It also is fair to compare the two Jamestowns: the one before and the one immediately following Governor Dale's mandated privatization. What distinguished the first Jamestown from the second was not the harshness of its natural setting but rather the thoroughness with which it prevented people from internalizing externalities.

Sociologist Michael Hechter considers group solidarity to be a function of (a) the extent to which members depend on the group and (b) the extent to which the group can monitor and enforce compliance with expectations that members will contribute to the group rather than free ride upon it (Hechter 1983, p. 21). On this analysis, it is unsurprising that Hutterite communal society has been successful. Members are extremely dependent, for their upbringing leaves them unprepared to live in a non-Hutterite culture. Monitoring is intense. Feedback is immediate. But if that is the secret of Hutterite success, why did Jamestown fail? They too were extremely dependent on each other. They too had nowhere else to go. Monitoring was equally unproblematic. Everyone knew who was planting crops (no one) and who was bowling (everyone). What was the problem?

The problem lay in the guarantee embedded in the Jamestown colony's charter. Jamestown's charter entitled people to an equal share regardless of personal contribution, which is to say it took steps to ensure that individual workers would be maximally alienated from the fruits of their labors. The charter ensured that workers would think of their work as disappearing into an open-access commons.

Robert Goodin says, "Working within the constraints set by natural scarcity, the greatest practical obstacle to achieving as much justice as resources permit is, and always has been, the supposition that each of us should cultivate his own garden" (Goodin 1985, p. 1). However, Jamestown's charter did not suppose each of us should cultivate his own garden. It supposed the opposite. Colonists abided by the charter, and even while they suffered, people in other colonies were tending their own gardens, and thriving.

We should applaud institutions that encourage people to care for each other. But telling people they are required to tend someone else's garden rather than their own does not encourage people to care for each other. It does the opposite. It encourages spite. The people of Jamestown reached the point where they would rather die, bowling in the street, than tend the gardens of their free-riding neighbors, and die they did.

REFERENCES

Martin J. Bailey, "Approximate Optimality of Aboriginal Property Rights." *Journal of Law and Economics* 35 (1992): 183–98.

J. H. Bogart, "Lockean Provisos and State of Nature Theories." *Ethics* 95 (1985): 828–36.

R. Chesher, "Practical Problems in Coral Reef Utilization and Management: a Tongan Case Study." *Proceedings of the Fifth International Coral Reef Congress* 4 (1985): 213–24.

Harold Demsetz, "Toward a Theory of Property Rights." *American Economic Review* (Papers & Proceedings) 57 (1967): 347–59.

Robert C. Ellickson, "Property in Land." *Yale Law Journal* 102 (1993): 1315–1400.

Peggy Fosdick and Sam Fosdick, *Last Chance Lost?* (York, PA: Irvin S. Naylor Publishing, 1994)

Barbara Fried, "Wilt Chamberlain Revisited: Nozick's 'Justice in Transfer' and the Problem of Market-Based Distribution." *Philosophy and Public Affairs* 24 (1995): 226–45.

E. Gomez, A. Alcala, and A. San Diego. "Status of Philippine Coral Reefs—1981." *Proceedings of the Fourth International Coral Reef Symposium* 1 (1981): 275–85.

Robert E. Goodin, *Protecting the Vulnerable: Toward a Reanalysis of Our Social Responsibilities.* (Chicago: University of Chicago Press, 1985).

Michael Hechter, "A Theory of Group Solidarity." In Hechter, ed., *Microfoundations of Macrosociology* (Philadelphia: Temple University Press, 1983) pp. 16–57.

Virginia Held, "Introduction." In Held, ed., *Property, Profits, & Economic Justice* (Belmont: Wadsworth, 1980).

John Locke, *Second Treatise of Government,* ed. P.

Laslett. (Cambridge: Cambridge University Press, 1690 [reprinted 1960]).

J. Madeleine Nash, "Wrecking the Reefs." *Time* (September 30, 1996): 60–2.

Carol Rose, "Possession as the Origin of Property." *University of Chicago Law Review* 52 (1985) 73–88.

Carol Rose, "The Comedy of the Commons: Custom, Commerce, and Inherently Public Property." *University of Chicago Law Review* 53 (1986) 711–87.

John T. Sanders, "Justice and the Initial Acquisition of Private Property." *Harvard Journal of Law and Public Policy* 10 (1987) 367–99.

Rolf Sartorius, "Persons and Property." In Ray Frey, ed., *Utility and Rights* (Minneapolis: University of Minnesota Press, 1984)

Judith Jarvis Thomson, *The Realm of Rights* (Cambridge: Harvard University Press, 1990).

Jeremy Waldron, "Enough and As Good Left For Others." *Philosophical Quarterly* 29 (1976): 319–28.

NOTES

1. Is it fair for latecomers to be excluded from acquiring property by rules allowing original appropriation? Sanders (1987, p. 385) notes that latecomers "are *not* excluded from acquiring property by these rules. They are, instead, excluded from being the first to own what has not been owned previously. Is *that* unfair?"

2. Nash (1996) says fishermen currently pump 330,000 pounds of cyanide per year into Philippine reefs.

3. I thank Peggy Fosdick at the National Aquarium in Baltimore for correspondence and documents. See also Fosdick and Fosdick (1994).

4. A private non-profit organization, The Nature Conservancy, is pursuing such a strategy. Although not itself an original appropriator, it has acquired over a billion dollars' worth of land in an effort to preserve natural ecosystems. Note that this includes habitat for endangered species that have no market value.

5. This essay discusses Ellickson's article in some detail. While I take little credit for the ideas in the next few sections, any errors are presumably mine.

6. Of course, no one thinks governance by custom automatically solves commons problems. Custom works when local users can restrict outsider access and monitor insider behavior, but those conditions are not always met, and tragedies like those discussed earlier continue to occur.

Chapter 12

Poverty as an Environmental Problem

Questions for Reflection and Discussion

Zambia

Third-world poverty is an environmental issue because poverty forces people to think short-term. When people are desperate, even their own long-range survival becomes a secondary priority, while things like wildlife conservation are seen as a low priority at best, and as an excuse for ongoing colonial repression at worst.

However, there is only so much that foreign aid can do.

As I walked across the border from Zimbabwe into Zambia in July 1999, I saw a large sign warning that bringing second-hand clothing into Zimbabwe from Zambia is strictly prohibited. I wondered whether authorities were concerned that second-hand clothing might carry some form of plague.

Once across the border, I met Phillip Roberts, a construction worker who owned a Jeep, had some experience as a tour guide, was not otherwise working that day, and was willing to show me some of the country. I asked him about the sign. He said that if I wanted to understand what the sign meant, we needed to make a stop in the town of Livingstone, Zambia. We reached the town, and I heard its story.

A few years previously, there had been a drought. Relief agencies wanted to help. Sending money was a problem, though, because money often is used to buy guns, as in Somalia. Sending food was a problem. Food sent to India, improperly stored, had become a breeding ground for plague-carrying rats. When plague broke out, people who had flooded in from the countryside seeking the food fled back to their villages, taking plague with them. So the agencies wanted to lend aid in a form that at least would do no harm. They decided that what Zambia could use, and what would at least do no harm, was plane-loads of second-hand clothing.

Until then, Livingstone had been the hub of Zambia's textile industry. Cotton was grown, processed, and woven into cloth there. As was the case in North America as recently as a generation ago, consumers bought the cloth and did the sewing themselves. Livingstone cloth could not compete with factory-made clothing, though, especially free factory-made clothing. Livingstone's unemployment rate has hovered around 90 percent ever since. Finally, I understood: the plague was the clothing itself.[1]

The problem was not faulty execution by particular agencies, but something more fundamental: failing to appreciate that solutions to problems of developing countries ultimately lie in their own local economies. To be effective in the long term, foreign aid must assist local producers, not put them out of business.

If Holmes Rolston III is right, G-7 nations consume, and also produce, about 80 percent of the world's food while containing less than 20 percent of the world's population. What would happen if G-7 nations consumed, and produced, less? Would we be better off? Would Zambia? Under what circumstances?

NOTES

1. The Zambians did not know the exact point of the sign back at the Zimbabwe border. Zimbabwe may have been trying to nurture its own domestic textile industry, or trying to force Zimbabweans to go back to buying Zambian cloth, thereby helping to revive Livingstone's industry.

Living on a Lifeboat

Garret Hardin

Susanne Langer (1942) has shown it is probably impossible to approach an unsolved problem save through the door of metaphor. Later, attempting to meet the demands of rigor we may achieve some success in cleansing theory of metaphor, though our success is limited if we are unable to avoid using common language which is shot through and through with fossil metaphors. (I count no less than five in the preceding two sentences.)

Since metaphorical thinking is inescapable it is pointless merely to weep about our human limitations. We must learn to live with them, to understand them, and to control them. "All of us," said George Eliot in Middlemarch, "get our thoughts entangled in metaphors, and act fatally on the strength of them." To avoid unconscious suicide we are well advised to pit one metaphor against another. From the interplay of competitive metaphors, thoroughly developed, we may come closer to metaphor-free solutions to our problems.

No generation has viewed the problem of the survival of the human species as seriously as we have. Inevitably, we have entered this world of concern through the door of metaphor. Environmentalists have emphasized the image of the earth as a spaceship—Spaceship Earth. Kenneth Boulding (1966) is the principal architect of this metaphor. It is time, he says, that we replace the wasteful "cowboy economy" of the past with the frugal "spaceship economy" required for continued survival in the limited

Garrett Hardin, "Living on a Lifeboat," *BioScience* 24 (1974): 561–68. Reprinted with permission of Garrett Hardin, author, and BioScience, publisher.

world we now see ours to be. The metaphor is notably useful in justifying pollution control measures.

Unfortunately, the image of a spaceship is also used to promote measures that are suicidal. One of these is a generous immigration policy, which is only a particular instance of a class of policies that are in error because they lead to the tragedy of the commons (Hardin 1968). These suicidal policies are attractive because they mesh with what we unthinkably take to be the ideals of "the best people." What is missing in the idealistic view is an insistence that rights and responsibilities must go together. The "generous" attitude of all too many people results in asserting inalienable rights while ignoring or denying matching responsibilities.

For the metaphor of a spaceship to be correct the aggregate of people on board would have to be under unitary sovereign control (Ophuls 1974). A true ship always has a captain. It is conceivable that a ship could be run by a committee. But it could not possibly survive if its course were determined by bickering tribes that claimed rights without responsibilities.

What about Spaceship Earth? It certainly has no captain, and no executive committee. The United Nations is a toothless tiger, because the signatories of its charter wanted it that way. The spaceship metaphor is used only to justify spaceship demands on common resources without acknowledging corresponding spaceship responsibilities.

An understandable fear of decisive action leads people to embrace "incrementalism"—moving toward reform by tiny stages. As we shall see, this strategy is counterproductive in the area discussed here if it means accepting rights before responsibilities. Where human survival is at stake, the acceptance of responsibilities is a precondition to the acceptance of rights, if the two cannot be introduced simultaneously.

LIFEBOAT ETHICS

Before taking up certain substantive issues let us look at an alternative metaphor, that of a lifeboat. In developing some relevant examples the following nu-

merical values are assumed. Approximately two-thirds of the world is desperately poor, and only one-third is comparatively rich. The people in poor countries have an average per capita GNP (Gross National Product) of about $200 per year; the rich, of about $3,000. (For the United States it is nearly $5,000 per year.) Metaphorically, each rich nation amounts to a lifeboat full of comparatively rich people. The poor of the world are in other, much more crowded lifeboats. Continuously, so to speak, the poor fall out of their lifeboats and swim for a while in the water outside, hoping to be admitted to a rich lifeboat, or in some other way to benefit from the "goodies" on board. What should the passengers on a rich lifeboat do? This is the central problem of "the ethics of a lifeboat."

First we must acknowledge that each lifeboat is effectively limited in capacity. The land of every nation has a limited carrying capacity. The exact limit is a matter for argument, but the energy crunch is convincing more people every day that we have already exceeded the carrying capacity of the land. We have been living on "capital"—stored petroleum and coal—and soon we must live on income alone.

Let us look at only one lifeboat—ours. The ethical problem is the same for all, and is as follows. Here we sit, say 50 people in a lifeboat. To be generous, let us assume our boat has a capacity of 10 more, making 60. (This, however, is to violate the engineering principle of the "safety factor." A new plant disease or a bad change in the weather may decimate our population if we don't preserve some excess capacity as a safety factor.)

The 50 of us in the lifeboat see 100 others swimming in the water outside, asking for admission to the boat, or for handouts. How shall we respond to their calls? There are several possibilities.

One. We may be tempted to try to live by the Christian ideal of being "our brother's keeper," or by the Marxian ideal (Marx 1875) of "from each according to his abilities, to each according to his needs." Since the needs of all are the same, we take all the needy into our boat, making a total of 150 in a boat with a capacity of 60. The boat is swamped, and everyone drowns. Complete justice, complete catastrophe.

Two. Since the boat has an unused excess capacity of 10, we admit just 10 more to it. This has the disadvantage of getting rid of the safety factor, for which action we will sooner or later pay dearly. Moreover, *which* 10 do we let in? "First come, first served?" The best 10? The neediest 10? How do we *discriminate?* And what do we say to the 90 who are excluded?

Three. Admit no more to the boat and preserve the small safety factor. Survival of the people in the lifeboat is then possible (though we shall have to be on our guard against boarding parties).

The last solution is abhorrent to many people. It is unjust, they say. Let us grant that it is.

"I feel guilty about my good luck," say some. The reply to this is simple: *Get out and yield your place to others.* Such a selfless action might satisfy the conscience of those who are addicted to guilt but it would not change the ethics of the lifeboat. The needy person to whom a guilt-addict yields his place will not himself feel guilty about his sudden good luck. (If he did he would not climb aboard.) The net result of conscience-stricken people relinquishing their unjustly held positions is the elimination of their kind of conscience from the lifeboat. The lifeboat, as it were, purifies itself of guilt. The ethics of the lifeboat persist, unchanged by such momentary aberrations.

This then is the basic metaphor within which we must work out our solutions. Let us enrich the image step by step with substantive additions from the real world.

REPRODUCTION

The harsh characteristics of lifeboat ethics are heightened by reproduction, particularly by reproductive differences. The people inside the lifeboats of the wealthy nations are doubling in numbers every 87 years; those outside are doubling every 35 years, on the average. And the relative difference in prosperity is becoming greater.

Let us, for a while, think primarily of the U.S. lifeboat. As of 1973 the United States had a population of 210 million people, who were increasing by 0.8% per year, that is, doubling in number every 87 years.

Although the citizens of rich nations are outnumbered two to one by the poor, let us imagine an equal number of poor people outside our lifeboat—a mere 210 million poor people reproducing at a quite different rate. If we imagine these to be the combined populations of Colombia, Venezuela, Ecuador, Morocco, Thailand, Pakistan, and the Philippines, the average rate of increase of the people "outside" is 3.3% per year. The doubling time of this population is 21 years.

Suppose that all these countries, and the United States, agreed to live by the Marxian ideal, "to each according to his needs," the ideal of most Christians as well. Needs, of course, are determined by population size, which is affected by reproduction. Every nation regards its rate of reproduction as a sovereign right. If our lifeboat were big enough in the beginning it might be possible to live *for a while* by Christian-Marxian ideals. *Might.*

Initially, in the model given, the ratio of non-Americans to Americans would be one to one. But consider what the ratio would be 87 years later. By this time Americans would have doubled to a population of 420 million. The other group (doubling every 21 years) would now have swollen to 3,540 million. Each American would have more than eight people to share with. How could the lifeboat possibly keep afloat?

All this involves extrapolation of current trends into the future, and is consequently suspect. Trends may change. Granted: but the change will not necessarily be favorable. If—as seems likely—the rate of population increase falls faster in the ethnic group presently inside the lifeboat than it does among those now outside, the future will turn out to be even worse than mathematics predicts, and sharing will be even more suicidal.

RUIN IN THE COMMONS

The fundamental error of the sharing ethic is that it leads to the tragedy of the commons. Under a system of private property the man (or group of men) who own property recognize their responsibility to care for it, for if they don't they will eventually suffer. A farmer, for instance, if he is intelligent, will allow no more cattle in a pasture than its carrying capacity justifies. If he overloads the pasture, weeds take over, erosion sets in, and the owner loses in the long run.

But if a pasture is run as a commons open to all, the right of each to use it is not matched by an operational responsibility to take care of it. It is no use asking independent herdsmen in a commons to act responsibly, for they dare not. The considerate herdsman who refrains from overloading the commons suffers more than a selfish one who says his needs are greater. (As Leo Durocher says, "Nice guys finish last.") Christian-Marxian idealism is counterproductive. That it *sounds* nice is no excuse. With distribution systems, as with individual morality, good intentions are no substitute for good performance.

A social system is stable only if it is insensitive to errors. To the Christian-Marxian idealist a selfish person is a sort of "error." Prosperity in the system of the commons cannot survive errors. If *everyone* would only restrain himself, all would be well; but it takes *only one less than everyone* to ruin a system of voluntary restraint. In a crowded world of less than perfect human beings—and we will never know any other—mutual ruin is inevitable in the commons. This is the core of the tragedy of the commons.

One of the major tasks of education today is to create such an awareness of the dangers of the commons that people will be able to recognize its many varieties, however disguised. There is pollution of the air and water because these media are treated as commons. Further growth of population and growth in the per capita conversion of natural resources into pollutants require that the system of the commons be modified or abandoned in the disposal of "externalities."

The fish populations of the oceans are exploited as commons, and ruin lies ahead. No technological invention can prevent this fate: in fact, all improvements in the art of fishing merely hasten the day of complete ruin. Only the replacement of the system of the commons with a responsible system can save oceanic fisheries.

The management of western range lands, though nominally rational, is in fact (under the steady pressure of cattle ranchers) often merely a government-sanctioned system of the commons, drifting toward ultimate ruin for both the range lands and the residual enterprisers.

WORLD FOOD BANKS

In the international arena we have recently heard a proposal to create a new commons, namely an international depository of food reserves to which nations will contribute according to their abilities, and from which nations may draw according to their needs. Nobel laureate Norman Borlaug has lent the prestige of his name to this proposal.

A world food bank appeals powerfully to our humanitarian impulses. We remember John Donne's celebrated line, "Any man's death diminishes me." But before we rush out to see for whom the bell tolls let us recognize where the greatest political push for international granaries comes from, lest we be disillusioned later. Our experience with Public Law 480 clearly reveals the answer. This was the law that moved billions of dollars worth of U.S. grain to food-short, population-long countries during the past two decades. When P. L. 480 first came into being, a headline in the business magazine *Forbes* (Paddock and Paddock 1970) revealed the power behind it: "Feeding the World's Hungry Millions: How it will mean billions for U.S. business."

And indeed it did. In the years 1960 to 1970 a total of $7.9 billion was spent on the "Food for Peace" program as P. L. 480 was called. During the years 1948 to 1970 an additional $49.9 billion were extracted from American taxpayers to pay for other economic aid programs, some of which went for food and food-producing machinery. (This figure does *not* include military aid.) That P. L. 480 was a give-away program was concealed. Recipient countries went through the motions of paying for P. L. 480 food—with IOU's. In December 1973 the charade was brought to an end as far as India was concerned when the United States "forgave" India's $3.2 billion debt (Anonymous 1974). Public announcement of the cancellation of the debt was delayed for two months: one wonders why.

"Famine–1975!" (Paddock and Paddock 1967) is one of the few publications that points out the commercial roots of this humanitarian attempt. Though all U.S. taxpayers lost by P. L. 480, special interest groups gained handsomely. Farmers benefited because they were not asked to contribute the grain—it was bought from them by the taxpayers. Besides the direct benefit there was the indirect effect of increasing demand and thus raising prices of farm products generally. The manufacturers of farm machinery, fertilizers, and pesticides benefited by the farmers' extra efforts to grow more food. Grain elevators profited from storing the grain for varying lengths of time. Railroads made money hauling it to port, and shipping lines by carrying it overseas. Moreover, once the machinery for P. L. 480 was established an immense bureaucracy had a vested interest in its continuance regardless of its merits.

Very little was ever heard of these selfish interests when P. L. 480 was defended in public. The emphasis was always on its humanitarian effects. The combination of multiple and relatively silent selfish interests with highly vocal humanitarian apologists constitutes a powerful lobby for extracting money from taxpayers. Foreign aid has become a habit that can apparently survive in the absence of any known justification. A news commentator in a weekly magazine (Lansner 1974), after exhaustively going over all the conventional arguments for foreign aid—self-interest, social justice, political advantage, and charity—and concluding that none of the known arguments really held water, concluded: "So the search continues for some logically compelling reasons for giving aid . . ." In other words, *Act now, Justify later*—if ever. (Apparently a quarter of a century is too short a time to find the justification for expending several billion dollars yearly.)

The search for a rational justification can be short-circuited by interjecting the word "emergency." Borlaug uses this word. We need to look sharply at it. What is an "emergency?" It is surely something like an accident, which is correctly defined as *an event that is certain to happen, though with a low frequency* (Hardin 1972a). A well-run organization prepares for everything that is certain, including accidents and emergencies. It budgets for them. It saves for them. It expects them—and mature decision-makers do not waste time complaining about accidents when they occur.

What happens if some organizations budget for emergencies and others do not? If each organization is solely responsible for its own well-being, poorly managed ones will suffer. But they should be able to learn from experience. They have a chance to mend their ways and learn to budget for infrequent but certain emergencies. The weather, for instance, always varies and periodic crop failures are certain. A wise and competent government saves out of the production of the good years in anticipation of bad years that are sure to come. This is not a new idea. The Bible tells us that Joseph taught this policy to Pharaoh in Egypt more than 2,000 years ago. Yet it is literally true that the vast majority of the governments of the world today have no such policy. They lack either the wisdom or the competence, or both. Far more difficult than the transfer of wealth from one country to another is the transfer of wisdom between sovereign powers or between generations.

"But it isn't their fault! How can we blame the poor people who are caught in an emergency? Why must we punish them?" The concepts of blame and punishment are irrelevant. The question is, what are the operational consequences of establishing a world food bank? If it is open to every country every time a need develops, slovenly rulers will not be motivated to take Joseph's advice. Why should they? Others will bail them out whenever they are in trouble.

Some countries will make deposits in the world food bank and others will withdraw from it: there will be almost no overlap. Calling such a depository-transfer unit a "bank" is stretching the metaphor of *bank* beyond its elastic limits. The proposers, of course, never call attention to the metaphorical nature of the word they use.

THE RATCHET EFFECT

An "international food bank" is really, then, not a true bank but a disguised one-way transfer device for moving wealth from rich countries to poor. In the absence of such a bank, in a world inhabited by individually responsible sovereign nations, the population of each nation would repeatedly go through a cycle of the sort shown in Figure 1. P_2 is greater than P_1, either in absolute numbers or because a deterioration of the food supply has removed the safety factor and produced a dangerously low ratio of resources to population. P_2 may be said to represent a state of overpopulation, which becomes obvious upon the appearance of an "accident," e.g., a crop failure. If the "emergency" is not met by outside help, the population drops back to the "normal" level—the "carrying capacity" of the environment—or even below. In the absence of population control by a sovereign, sooner or later the population grows to P_2 again and the cycle repeats. The long-term population curve (Hardin 1966) is an irregularly fluctuating one, equilibrating more or less about the carrying capacity.

A demographic cycle of this sort obviously involves great suffering in the restrictive phase, but such a cycle is normal to any independent country with inadequate population control. The third century theologian Tertullian (Hardin 1969a) expressed what must have been the recognition of many wise men when he wrote: "The scourges of pestilence, famine, wars, and earthquakes have come to be regarded as a blessing to overcrowded nations, since they serve to prune away the luxuriant growth of the human race."

Only under a strong and farsighted sovereign—which theoretically could be the people themselves, democratically organized—can a population equilibrate at some set point below the carrying capacity, thus avoiding the pains normally caused by periodic and unavoidable disasters. For this happy state to be achieved it is necessary that those in power be able to contemplate with equanimity the "waste" of surplus food in times of bountiful harvests. It is essential that those in power resist the temptation to convert extra food into extra babies. On the public relations level it is necessary that the phrase "surplus food" be replaced by "safety factor."

But wise sovereigns seem not to exist in the poor world today. The most anguishing problems are created by poor countries that are governed by rulers insufficiently wise and powerful. If such countries can draw on a world food bank in times of "emergency," the population *cycle* of Figure 1 will be replaced by the population *escalator* of Figure 2. The input of food from a food bank acts as the pawl of a ratchet, preventing the population from retracing its steps to a lower level. Reproduction pushes the population upward, inputs from the world bank prevent its moving downward. Population size escalates, as does the absolute magnitude of "accidents" and "emergencies." The process is brought to an end only by the total collapse of the whole system, producing a catastrophe of scarcely imaginable proportions.

Such are the implications of the well-meant sharing of food in a world of irresponsible reproduction.

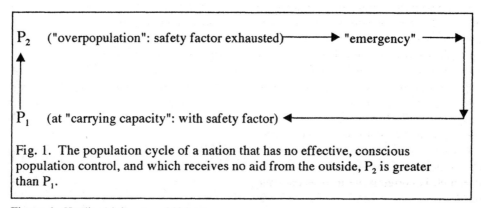

P_2 ("overpopulation": safety factor exhausted) ———▶ "emergency" ———▶

P_1 (at "carrying capacity": with safety factor) ◀———

Fig. 1. The population cycle of a nation that has no effective, conscious population control, and which receives no aid from the outside, P_2 is greater than P_1.

Figure 1. Hardin: Living on a Lifeboat.

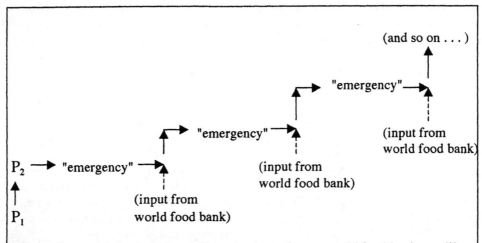

Fig. 2. The population escalator. Note that input from a world food bank acts like the pawl of a ratchet, preventing the normal population cycle shown in Figure 1 from being completed. P_{n+1} is greater than P_n, and the absolute magnitude of the "emergencies" escalates. Ultimately the entire system crashes. The crash is not shown, and few can imagine it.

Figure 2. Hardin: Living on a Lifeboat.

I think we need a new word for systems like this. The adjective "melioristic" is applied to systems that produce continual improvement; the English word is derived from the Latin *meliorare,* to become or make better. Parallel with this it would be useful to bring in the word *pejoristic* (from the Latin *pejorare,* to become or make worse). This word can be applied to those systems which, by their very nature, can be relied upon to make matters worse. A world food bank coupled with sovereign state irresponsibility in reproduction is an example of a pejoristic system.

This pejoristic system creates an unacknowledged commons. People have more motivation to draw from than to add to the common store. The license to make such withdrawals diminishes whatever motivation poor countries might otherwise have to control their populations. Under the guidance of this ratchet, wealth can be steadily moved in one direction only, from the slowly-breeding rich to the rapidly-breeding poor, the process finally coming to a halt only when all countries are equally and miserably poor.

All this is terribly obvious once we are acutely aware of the pervasiveness and danger of the commons. But many people still lack this awareness, and the euphoria of the "benign demographic transition" (Hardin 1973) interferes with the realistic appraisal of pejoristic mechanisms. As concerns public policy, the deductions drawn from the benign demographic transition are these:

1) If the per capita GNP rises the birth rate will fall; hence, the rate of population increase will fall, ultimately producing ZPG (Zero Population Growth).

2) The long-term trend all over the world (including the poor countries) is of a rising per capita GNP (for which no limit is seen.)

3) Therefore, all political interference in population matters is unnecessary; all we need to do is foster economic "development"—*note the metaphor*—and population problems will solve themselves.

Those who believe in the benign demographic transition dismiss the pejoristic mechanism of Figure 2 in the belief that each input of food from the world fosters development within a poor country thus resulting in a drop in the rate of population increase. Foreign aid has proceeded on this assumption for more than two decades. Unfortunately it has produced no indubitable instance of the asserted effect. It has, however, produced a library of excuses. The air is filled with plaintive calls for more massive foreign aid appropriations so that the hypothetical melioristic process can get started.

The doctrine of demographic laissez-faire implicit in the hypothesis of the benign demographic transition is immensely attractive. Unfortunately there is more evidence against the melioristic system than there is for it (Davis 1963). On the historical side there are many counter-examples. The rise in per capita GNP in France and Ireland during the past century has been accompanied by a rise in population growth. In the 20 years following the Second World War the same positive correlation was noted almost everywhere in the world. Never in world history before 1950 did the worldwide population growth reach 1% per annum. Now the average population growth is over 2% and shows no signs of slackening.

On the theoretical side, the denial of the pejoristic scheme of Figure 2 probably springs from the hidden acceptance of the "cowboy economy" that Boulding castigated. Those who recognize the limitations of a spaceship, if they are unable to achieve population control at a safe and comfortable level, accept the necessity of the corrective feedback of the population cycle shown in Figure 1. No one who knew in his bones that he was living on a true spaceship would countenance political support of the population escalator shown in Figure 2.

ECO-DESTRUCTION VIA THE GREEN REVOLUTION

The demoralizing effect of charity on the recipient has long been known. "Give a man a fish and he will eat for a day; teach him how to fish and he will eat for the rest of his days." So runs an ancient Chinese proverb. Acting on this advice the Rockefeller and Ford Foundations have financed a multipronged program for improving agriculture in the hungry nations. The result, known as the "Green Revolution," has been quite remarkable. "Miracle wheat" and "miracle rice" are splendid technological achievements in the realm of plant genetics.

Whether or not the Green Revolution can increase food production is doubtful (Harris 1972; Paddock 1970; Wilkes 1972), but in any event not particularly important. What is missing in this great and well-meaning humanitarian effort is a firm grasp of fundamentals. Considering the importance of the Rockefeller Foundation in this effort it is ironic that the late Alan Gregg, a much-respected vice president of the Foundation, strongly expressed his doubts of the wisdom of all attempts to increase food production some two decades ago. (This was before Borlaug's work—supported by Rockefeller—had resulted in the development of "miracle wheat.") Gregg (1955) likened the growth and spreading of humanity over the surface of the earth to the metastasis of cancer in the human body, wryly remarking that "Cancerous growths demand food; but, as far as I know, they have never been cured by getting it."

"Man does not live by bread alone"—the scriptural statement has a rich meaning even in the material realm. Every human being born constitutes a draft on all aspects of the environment—food, air, water, unspoiled scenery, occasional and optional solitude, beaches, contact with wild animals, fishing, hunting—the list is long and incompletely known. Food can, perhaps, be significantly increased: but what about clean beaches, unspoiled forests, and solitude? If we satisfy the need for food in a growing population we necessarily decrease the supply of other goods, and thereby increase the difficulty of equitably allocating scarce goods (Hardin 1969b, 1972b).

The present population of India is 600 million, and it is increasing by 15 million per year. The environmental load of this population is already great. The forests of India are only a small fraction of what they were three centuries ago. Soil erosion, floods, and the psychological costs of crowding are serious. Every one of the net 15 million lives added each year stresses the Indian environment more severely. *Every life saved this year in a poor country diminishes the quality of life for subsequent generations.*

Observant critics have shown how much harm we wealthy nations have already done to poor nations through our well-intentioned but misguided attempts to help them (Paddock and Paddock 1973). Particularly reprehensible is our failure to carry out post-audits of these attempts (Farvaar and Milton 1972). Thus we have shielded our tender consciences from knowledge of the harm we have done. Must we Americans continue to fail to monitor the consequences of our external "do-gooding"? If, for instance, we thoughtlessly make it possible for the present 600 million Indians to swell to 1,200 millions by the year 2001—as their present growth rate promises—will posterity in India thank *us* for facilitating an even greater destruction of *their* environment? Are good intentions ever a sufficient excuse for bad consequences?

IMMIGRATION CREATES A COMMONS

I come now to the final example of a commons in action, one for which the public is least prepared for rational discussion. The topic is at present enveloped by a great silence which reminds me of a comment made by Sherlock Holmes in A. Conan Doyle's story, "Silver Blaze." Inspector Gregory had asked, "Is there any point to which you would wish to draw my attention?" To this Holmes responded:

"To the curious incident of the dog in the night-time."

"The dog did nothing in the night-time," said the Inspector.

"That was the curious incident," remarked Sherlock Holmes.

By asking himself what would repress the normal barking instinct of a watchdog Holmes realized that it must be the dog's recognition of his master as the criminal trespasser. In a similar way we should ask ourselves what repression keeps us from discussing something as important as immigration?

It cannot be that immigration is numerically of no consequence. Our government acknowledges a *net* flow of 400,000 a year. Hard data are understandably lacking on the extent of illegal entries, but a not implausible figure is 600,000 per year (Buchanan 1973). The natural increase of the resident population is now about 1.7 million per year. This means that the yearly gain from immigration is at least 19%, and may be 37%, of the total increase. It is quite conceivable that educational campaigns like that of Zero Population Growth, Inc., coupled with adverse social and economic factors—inflation, housing shortage, depression, and loss of confidence in national leaders—may lower the fertility of American women to a point at which all of the yearly increase in population would be accounted for by immigration. Should we not at least ask if that is what we want? How curious it is that we so seldom discuss immigration these days!

Curious, but understandable—as one finds out the moment he publicly questions the wisdom of the status quo in immigration. He who does so is promptly charged with *isolationism, bigotry, prejudice, ethnocentrism, chauvinism,* and *selfishness.* These are hard accusations to bear. It is pleasanter to talk about other matters, leaving immigration policy to wallow in the cross-currents of special interests that take no account of the good of the whole—*or of the interests of posterity.*

We Americans have a bad conscience because of things we said in the past about immigrants. Two generations ago the popular press was rife with references to *Dagos, Wops, Pollacks, Japs, Chinks,* and *Krauts*—all pejorative terms which failed to acknowledge our indebtedness to Goya, Leonardo, Copernicus, Hiroshige, Confucius, and Bach. Because the implied inferiority of foreigners was *then* the justification for keeping them out, it is *now* thoughtlessly assumed that restrictive policies can only be based on the assumption of immigrant inferiority. *This is not so.*

Existing immigration laws exclude idiots and known criminals; future laws will almost certainly continue this policy. But should we also consider the quality of the average immigrant, as compared with the quality of the average resident? Perhaps we should, perhaps we shouldn't. (What is "quality" anyway?) But the quality issue is not our concern here.

From this point on, *it will be assumed that immigrants and native-born citizens are of exactly equal quality,* however quality may be defined. The focus is only on quantity. The conclusions reached depend on nothing else, so all charges of ethnocentrism are irrelevant.

World food banks move food to the people, thus facilitating the exhaustion of the environment of the poor. By contrast, unrestricted immigration moves people to the food, thus speeding up the destruction of the environment in rich countries. Why poor people should want to make this transfer is no mystery, but why should rich hosts encourage it? This transfer, like the reverse one, is supported by both selfish interests and humanitarian impulses.

The principal selfish interests in unimpeded immigration is easy to identify: it is the interest of the employers of cheap labor, particularly that needed for degrading jobs. We have been deceived about the forces of history by the lines of Emma Lazarus inscribed on the Statue of Liberty:

Give me your tired, your poor
Your huddled masses yearning to breathe free,
The wretched refuse of your teeming shore,
Send these, the homeless, tempest-tossed, to me:
I lift my lamp beside the golden door.

The image is one of an infinitely generous earth-mother, passively opening her arms to hordes of immigrants who come here on their own initiative. Such an image may have been adequate for the early days of colonization, but by the time these lines were written (1886) the force for immigration was largely manufactured inside our own borders by factory and mine owners who sought cheap labor not to be found among laborers already here. One group of foreigners after another was thus enticed into the United States to work at wretched jobs for wretched wages.

At present, it is largely the Mexicans who are being so exploited. It is particularly to the advantage of certain employers that there be many illegal immigrants. Illegal immigrant workers dare not complain about their working conditions for fear of being repatriated. Their presence reduces the bargaining power of all Mexican-American laborers. Cesar Chavez has repeatedly pleaded with congressional committees to close the doors to more Mexicans so that those here can negotiate effectively for higher wages and decent working conditions. Chavez understands the ethics of a lifeboat.

The interests of the employers of cheap labor are well served by the silence of the intelligentsia of the country. WASPs—White Anglo-Saxon Protestants—are particularly reluctant to call for a closing of the doors to immigration for fear of being called ethnocentric bigots. It was, therefore, an occasion of pure delight for this particular WASP to be present at a meeting when the points he would like to have made were made better by a non-WASP speaking to other non-WASPS. It was in Hawaii, and most of the people in the room were second-level Hawaiian officials of Japanese ancestry. All Hawaiians are keenly aware of the limits of their environment, and the speaker had asked how it might be practically and constitutionally possible to close the doors to more immigrants to the islands. (To Hawaiians, immigrants from the other 49 states are as much of a threat as those from other nations. There is only so much room in the islands, and the islanders know it. Sophistical arguments that imply otherwise do not impress them.)

Yet the Japanese-Americans of Hawaii have active ties with the land of their origin. This point was raised by a Japanese-American member of the audience who asked the Japanese-American speaker: "But how can we shut the doors now? We have many friends and relations in Japan that we'd like to bring to Hawaii some day so that they can enjoy this beautiful land."

The speaker smiled sympathetically and responded slowly: "Yes, but we have children now and someday we'll have grandchildren. We can bring more people here from Japan only by giving away some of the land that we hope to pass on to our grandchildren some day. What right do we have to do that?"

To be generous with one's own possessions is one thing; to be generous with posterity's is quite another. This, I think, is the point that must be gotten across to those who would, from a commendable love of distributive justice, institute a ruinous system of the commons, either in the form of a world food bank or that of unrestricted immigration. Since every speaker is a member of some ethnic group it is always possible to charge him with ethnocentrism. But even after purging an argument of ethnocentrism the rejection of the commons is still valid and necessary if we are to save at least some parts of the world from environmental ruin. Is it not desirable that at least some of the grandchildren of people now living should have a decent place in which to live?

THE ASYMMETRY OF DOOR-SHUTTING

We must now answer this telling point: "How can you justify slamming the door once you're inside? You say that immigrants should be kept out. But aren't we all immigrants, or the descendants of immigrants? Since we refuse to leave, must we not, as a matter of justice and symmetry, admit all others?"

It is literally true that we Americans of non-Indian ancestry are the descendants of thieves. Should we not, then, "give back" the land to the Indians; that is, give it to the now-living Americans of Indian ancestry? As an exercise in pure logic I see no way to reject this proposal. Yet I am unwilling to live by it; and I know no one who is. Our reluctance to embrace pure justice may spring from pure selfishness. On the other hand, it may arise from an unspoken recognition of consequences that have not yet been clearly spelled out.

Suppose, becoming intoxicated with pure justice, we "Anglos" should decide to turn our land over to the Indians. Since all our other wealth has also been derived from the land, we would have to give that to the Indians, too. Then what would we non-Indians do? Where would we go? There is no open land in the world on which men without capital can make their living (and not much unoccupied land on which men with capital can either). Where would 209 million putatively justice-loving, non-Indian, Americans go? Most of them—in the persons of their ancestors—came from Europe, but they wouldn't be welcomed back there. Anyway, Europeans have no better title to their land than we to ours. They also would have to give up their homes. (But to whom? And where would *they* go?)

Clearly, the concept of pure justice produces an infinite regress. The law long ago invented statutes of limitations to justify the rejection of pure justice, in the interest of preventing massive disorder. The law zealously defends property rights—but only *recent* property rights. It is as though the physical principle of exponential decay applies to property rights. Drawing a line in time may be unjust, but any other action is practically worse.

We are all the descendants of thieves, and the world's resources are inequitably distributed, but we must begin the journey to tomorrow from the point where we are today. We cannot remake the past. We cannot, without violent disorder and suffering, give land and resources back to the "original" owners—who are dead anyway.

We cannot safely divide the wealth equitably among all present peoples, so long as people reproduce at different rates, because to do so would guarantee that our grandchildren—everyone's grandchildren—would have only a ruined world to inhabit.

MUST EXCLUSION BE ABSOLUTE?

To show the logical structure of the immigration problem I have ignored many factors that would enter into real decisions made in a real world. No matter how convincing the logic may be it is probable that we would want, from time to time, to admit a few people from the outside to our lifeboat. Political refugees in particular are likely to cause us to make exceptions: We remember the Jewish refugees from Germany after 1933, and the Hungarian refugees after 1956. Moreover, the interests of national defense, broadly conceived, could justify admitting many men and women of unusual talents, whether refugees or not. (This raises the quality issue, which is not the subject of this essay.)

Such exceptions threaten to create runaway population growth inside the lifeboat, i.e., the receiving country. However, the threat can be neutralized by a population policy that includes immigration. An effective policy is one of flexible control.

Suppose, for example, that the nation has achieved a stable condition of ZPG, which (say) permits 1.5 million births yearly. We must suppose that an acceptable system of allocating birthrights to potential parents is in effect. Now suppose that an inhumane regime in some other part of the world creates a horde of refugees, and that there is a widespread desire to admit some to our country. At the same time, we do not want to sabotage our population control system. Clearly, the rational path to pursue is the following. If we decide to admit 100,000 refugees this year we should compensate for this by reducing the allocation of birthrights in the following year by a similar amount, that is downward to a total of 1.4 million. In that way we could achieve both humanitarian and population control goals. (And the refugees would have to accept the population controls of the society that admits them. It is not inconceivable that they might be given proportionately fewer rights than the native population.)

In a democracy, the admission of immigrants should properly be voted on. But by whom? It is not obvious. The usual rule of a democracy is votes for all. But it can be questioned whether a universal franchise is the most just one in a case of this sort. Whatever benefits there are in the admission of immigrants presumably accrue to everyone. But the costs would be seen as falling most heavily on potential parents, some of whom would have to postpone or forego having their (next) child because of the influx of immigrants. The double question *Who benefits? Who pays?* suggests that a restriction of the usual democratic franchise would be appropriate and just in this case. Would our particular quasi-democratic form of government be flexible enough to institute such a novelty? If not, the majority might, out of humanitarian motives, impose an unacceptable burden (the foregoing of parenthood) on a minority, thus producing political instability.

Plainly many new problems will arise when we consciously face the immigration question and seek rational answers. No workable answers can be found if we ignore population problems. And—if the argument of this essay is correct—so long as there is no true world government to control reproduction everywhere it is impossible to survive in dignity if we are to be guided by Spaceship ethics. Without a world government that is sovereign in reproductive matters, mankind lives, in fact, on a number of sovereign lifeboats. For the foreseeable future survival demands that we govern our actions by the ethics of a lifeboat. Posterity will be ill served if we do not.

REFERENCES

Anonymous, *Wall Street Journal,* February 19, 1974.

N. Borlaug, "Civilization's future: a call for international granaries." *Bull. At. Sci.* 29 (1973): 7–15.

K. Boulding, "The economics of the coming Spaceship earth." In H. Jarrett, ed., *Environmental Quality in a Growing Economy* (Baltimore: Johns Hopkins Press, 1966)

W. Buchanan, "Immigration statistics." *Equilibrium* 1 (1973): no. 3: 16–19.

K. Davis, "Population." *Scientific American* 209 (1963): no. 3, 62–71.

M.T. Farvar, and J. P. Milton, *The Careless Technology* (Garden City, N.Y.: Natural History Press, 1972).

A. Gregg, "A medical aspect of the population problem." *Science* 121 (1955) 681–682.

G. Hardin, Chap. 9. in *Biology: Its Principles and Implications,* 2nd ed. (San Francisco: Freeman, 1966).

G. Hardin (1968), "The tragedy of the commons." *Science* 162: 1243–1248.

G. Hardin (1969a), Page 18 in *Population, Evolution, and Birth Control,* 2nd ed. Freeman, San Francisco.

G. Hardin (1969b), "The economics of wilderness." *Nat Hist* 78(6): 20–27.

G. Hardin (1972a), Pages 81–82 in *Exploring New Ethics for Survival: The Voyage of the Spaceship Beagle.* Viking, N.Y.

G. Hardin (1972b), "Preserving quality on Spaceship Earth." *In* J. B. Trefethen, ed. *Translations of the Thirty-Seventh North American Wildlife and Natural Resources Conference* (Washington D.C.: Wildlife Management Institute, 1972) Washington D.C.

G. Hardin, Chap. 23 in *Stalking the Wild Taboo* (Los Altos, CA: Kaufmann, 1973).

M. Harris, "How green the revolution." *Nat Hist.* 81 (1972): no. 3, 28–30.

S. K. Langer, *Philosophy in a New Key* (Cambridge: Harvard University Press, 1942).

K. Lansner, "Should foreign aid begin at home?" *Newsweek,* February 11, 1974, p. 32.

K. Marx (1875), "Critique of the Gotha program." Page 388 in R. C. Tucker, ed., *The Marx-Engels Reader* (New York: Norton, 1972).

W. Ophuls, "The scarcity society." *Harpers* 248 (1974): no. 1487: 47–52.

W. C. Paddock, "How green is the green revolution?" *BioScience* 20 (1970): 897–902.

W. Paddock, and E. Paddock, *We Don't Know How* (Ames, IA: Iowa State University Press, 1973).

W. Paddock, and E. Paddock, *Famine-1975!* (Boston: Little, Brown, 1967).

H. G. Wilkes, "The green revolution." *Environment* 14 (1972): no. 8, 32–39.

Famine, Affluence, and Morality

Peter Singer

As I write this, in November 1971, people are dying in East Bengal from lack of food, shelter, and medical care. The suffering and death that are occurring there now are not inevitable, not unavoidable in any fatalistic sense of the term. Constant poverty, a cyclone, and a civil war have turned at least nine million people into destitute refugees; nevertheless, it is not beyond the capacity of the richer nations to give enough assistance to reduce any further suffering to very small proportions. The decisions and actions of human beings can prevent this kind of suffering. Unfortunately, human beings have not made the necessary decisions. At the individual level, people have, with very few exceptions, not responded to the situation in any significant way. Generally speaking, people have not given large sums to relief funds; they have not written to their parliamentary representatives demanding increased government assistance; they have not demonstrated in the streets, held symbolic fasts, or done anything else directed toward providing the refugees with the means to satisfy their essential needs. At the government level, no government has given the sort of massive aid that would enable the refugees to survive for more than a few days. Britain, for instance, has given rather more than most countries. It has, to date, given £14,750,000. For comparative purposes, Britain's share of the nonrecoverable development costs of the Anglo-French Concorde project is already in excess of £275,000,000, and on present estimates will reach £440,000,000. The implication is that the British government values a supersonic transport more than thirty times as highly as it values the lives of the nine million refugees. Australia is another country which, on a per capita basis, is well up in the "aid to Bengal" table. Australia's aid, however, amounts to less than one-twelfth of the cost of Sydney's new opera house. The total amount given, from all sources, now stands at about £65,000,000. The estimated cost of keeping the refugees alive for one year is

Peter Singer, "Famine, Affluence, and Morality," *Philosophy & Public Affairs* 1 (1972): 230–43. Copyright © 1972 by Princeton University Press. Reprinted with permission of the publisher.

£464,000,000. Most of the refugees have now been in the camps for more than six months. The World Bank has said that India needs a minimum of £300,000,000 in assistance from other countries before the end of the year. It seems obvious that assistance on this scale will not be forthcoming. India will be forced to choose between letting the refugees starve or diverting funds from her own development program, which will mean that more of her own people will starve in the future.[1]

These are the essential facts about the present situation in Bengal. So far as it concerns us here, there is nothing unique about this situation except its magnitude. The Bengal emergency is just the latest and most acute of a series of major emergencies in various parts of the world, arising both from natural and from man-made causes. There are also many parts of the world in which people die from malnutrition and lack of food independent of any special emergency. I take Bengal as my example only because it is the present concern, and because the size of the problem has ensured that it has been given adequate publicity. Neither individuals nor governments can claim to be unaware of what is happening there.

What are the moral implications of a situation like this? In what follows, I shall argue that the way people in relatively affluent countries react to a situation like that in Bengal cannot be justified; indeed, the whole way we look at moral issues—our moral conceptual scheme—needs to be altered, and with it, the way of life that has come to be taken for granted in our society.

In arguing for this conclusion I will not, of course, claim to be morally neutral. I shall, however, try to argue for the moral position that I take, so that anyone who accepts certain assumptions, to be made explicit, will, I hope, accept my conclusion.

I begin with the assumption that suffering and death from lack of food, shelter, and medical care are bad. I think most people will agree about this, although one may reach the same view by different routes. I shall not argue for this view. People can hold all sorts of eccentric positions, and perhaps from some of them it would not follow that death by starvation is in itself bad. It is difficult, perhaps impos-

sible, to refute such positions, and so for brevity I will henceforth take this assumption as accepted. Those who disagree need read no further.

My next point is this: if it is in our power to prevent something bad from happening, without thereby sacrificing anything of comparable moral importance, we ought, morally, to do it. By "without sacrificing anything of comparable moral importance" I mean without causing anything else comparably bad to happen, or doing something that is wrong in itself, or failing to promote some moral good, comparable in significance to the bad thing that we can prevent. This principle seems almost as uncontroversial as the last one. It requires us only to prevent what is bad, and not to promote what is good, and it requires this of us only when we can do it without sacrificing anything that is, from the moral point of view, comparably important. I could even, as far as the application of my argument to the Bengal emergency is concerned, qualify the point so as to make it: if it is in our power to prevent something very bad from happening, without thereby sacrificing anything morally significant, we ought, morally, to do it. An application of this principle would be as follows: if I am walking past a shallow pond and see a child drowning in it, I ought to wade in and pull the child out. This will mean getting my clothes muddy, but this is insignificant, while the death of the child would presumably be a very bad thing.

The uncontroversial appearance of the principle just stated is deceptive. If it were acted upon, even in its qualified form, our lives, our society, and our world would be fundamentally changed. For the principle takes, firstly, no account of proximity or distance. It makes no moral difference whether the person I can help is a neighbor's child ten yards from me or a Bengali whose name I shall never know, ten thousand miles away. Secondly, the principle makes no distinction between cases in which I am the only person who could possibly do anything and cases in which I am just one among millions in the same position.

I do not think I need to say much in defense of the refusal to take proximity and distance into account. The fact that a person is physically near to us, so that we have personal contact with him, may make it more likely that we *shall* assist him, but this does not show that we *ought* to help him rather than another who happens to be further away. If we accept any principle of impartiality, universalizability, equality, or whatever, we cannot discriminate against someone merely because he is far away from us (or we are far away from him). Admittedly, it is possible that we are in a better position to judge what needs to be done to help a person near to us than one far away, and perhaps also to provide the assistance we judge to be necessary. If this were the case, it would be a reason for helping those near to us first. This may once have been a justification for being more concerned with the poor in one's own town than with famine victims in India. Unfortunately for those who like to keep their moral responsibilities limited, instant communication and swift transportation have changed the situation. From the moral point of view, the development of the world into a "global village" has made an important, though still unrecognized, difference to our moral situation. Expert observers and supervisors, sent out by famine relief organizations or permanently stationed in famine-prone areas, can direct our aid to a refugee in Bengal almost as effectively as we could get it to someone in our own block. There would seem, therefore, to be no possible justification for discriminating on geographical grounds.

There may be a greater need to defend the second implication of my principle—that the fact that there are millions of other people in the same position, in respect to the Bengali refugees, as I am, does not make the situation significantly different from a situation in which I am the only person who can prevent something very bad from occurring. Again, of course, I admit that there is a psychological difference between the cases; one feels less guilty about doing nothing if one can point to others, similarly placed, who have also done nothing. Yet this can make no real difference to our moral obligations.[2] Should I consider that I am less obliged to pull the drowning child out of the pond if on looking around I see other people, no further away than I am, who have also noticed the child but are doing nothing?

One has only to ask this question to see the absurdity of the view that numbers lessen obligation. It is a view that is an ideal excuse for inactivity; unfortunately most of the major evils—poverty, overpopulation, pollution—are problems in which everyone is almost equally involved.

The view that numbers do make a difference can be made plausible if stated in this way: if everyone in circumstances like mine gave £5 to the Bengal Relief Fund, there would be enough to provide food, shelter, and medical care for the refugees; there is no reason why I should give more than anyone else in the same circumstances as I am; therefore I have no obligation to give more than £5. Each premise in this argument is true, and the argument looks sound. It may convince us, unless we notice that it is based on a hypothetical premise, although the conclusion is not stated hypothetically. The argument would be sound if the conclusion were: if everyone in circumstances like mine were to give £5, I would have no obligation to give more than £5. If the conclusion were so stated, however, it would be obvious that the argument has no bearing on a situation in which it is not the case that everyone else gives £5. This, of course, is the actual situation. It is more or less certain that not everyone in circumstances like mine will give £5. So there will not be enough to provide the needed food, shelter, and medical care. Therefore by giving more than £5 I will prevent more suffering than I would if I gave just £5.

It might be thought that this argument has an absurd consequence. Since the situation appears to be that very few people are likely to give substantial amounts, it follows that I and everyone else in similar circumstances ought to give as much as possible, that is, at least up to the point at which by giving more one would begin to cause serious suffering for oneself and one's dependents—perhaps even beyond this point to the point of marginal utility, at which by giving more one would cause oneself and one's dependents as much suffering as one would prevent in Bengal. If everyone does this, however, there will be more than can be used for the benefit of the refugees, and some of the sacrifice will have been unnecessary. Thus, if everyone does what he ought to do, the result will not be as good as it would be if everyone did a little less than he ought to do, or if only some do all that they ought to do.

The paradox here arises only if we assume that the actions in question—sending money to the relief funds—are performed more or less simultaneously, and are also unexpected. For if it is to be expected that everyone is going to contribute something, then clearly each is not obliged to give as much as he would have been obliged to had others not been giving too. And if everyone is not acting more or less simultaneously, then those giving later will know how much more is needed, and will have no obligation to give more than is necessary to reach this amount. To say this is not to deny the principle that people in the same circumstances have the same obligations, but to point out that the fact that others have given, or may be expected to give, is a relevant circumstance: those giving after it has become known that many others are giving and those giving before are not in the same circumstances. So the seemingly absurd consequence of the principle I have put forward can occur only if people are in error about the actual circumstances—that is, if they think they are giving even when others are not, but in fact they are giving when others are. The result of everyone doing what he really ought to do cannot be worse than the result of everyone doing less than he ought to do, although the result of everyone doing what he reasonably believes he ought to do could be.

If my argument so far has been sound, neither our distance from a preventable evil nor the number of other people who, in respect to that evil, are in the same situation as we are, lessens our obligation to mitigate or prevent that evil. I shall therefore take as established the principle I asserted earlier. As I have already said, I need to assert it only in its qualified form: if it is in our power to prevent something very bad from happening, without thereby sacrificing anything else morally significant, we ought, morally, to do it.

The outcome of this argument is that our traditional moral categories are upset. The traditional distinction between duty and charity cannot be drawn, or at least, not in the place we normally draw it. Giv-ing money to the Bengal Relief Fund is regarded as an act of charity in our society. The bodies which collect money are known as charities. These organizations see themselves in this way—if you send them a check, you will be thanked for your "generosity." Because giving money is regarded as an act of charity, it is not thought that there is anything wrong with not giving. The charitable man may be praised, but the man who is not charitable is not condemned. People do not feel in any way ashamed or guilty about spending money on new clothes or a new car instead of giving it to famine relief. (Indeed, the alternative does not occur to them.) This way of looking at the matter cannot be justified. When we buy new clothes not to keep ourselves warm but to look "well-dressed" we are not providing for any important need. We would not be sacrificing anything significant if we were to continue to wear our old clothes, and give the money to famine relief. By doing so, we would be preventing another person from starving. It follows from what I have said earlier that we ought to give money away, rather than spend it on clothes which we do not need to keep us warm. To do so is not charitable, or generous. Nor is it the kind of act which philosophers and theologians have called "supererogatory"—an act which it would be good to do, but not wrong not to do. On the contrary, we ought to give money away, and it is wrong not to do so.

I am not maintaining that there are no acts which are charitable, or that there are no acts which it would be good to do but not wrong not to do. It may be possible to redraw the distinction between duty and charity in some other place. All I am arguing here is that the present way of drawing the distinction, which makes it an act of charity for a man living at the level of affluence which most people in the "developed nations" enjoy to give money to save someone else from starvation, cannot be supported. It is beyond the scope of my argument to consider whether the distinction should be redrawn or abolished altogether. There would be many other possible ways of drawing the distinction—for instance, one might decide that it is good to make other people as happy as possible, but not wrong not to do so.

Despite the limited nature of the revision in our moral conceptual scheme which I am proposing, the revision would, given the extent of both affluence and famine in the world today, have radical implications. These implications may lead to further objections, distinct from those I have already considered. I shall discuss two of these.

One objection to the position I have taken might be simply that it is too drastic a revision of our moral scheme. People do not ordinarily judge in the way I have suggested they should. Most people reserve their moral condemnation for those who violate some moral norm, such as the norm against taking another person's property. They do not condemn those who indulge in luxury instead of giving to famine relief. But given that I did not set out to present a morally neutral description of the way people make moral judgments, the way people do in fact judge has nothing to do with the validity of my conclusion. My conclusion follows from the principle which I advanced earlier, and unless that principle is rejected, or the arguments shown to be unsound, I think the conclusion must stand, however strange it appears.

It might, nevertheless, be interesting to consider why our society, and most other societies, do judge differently from the way I have suggested they should. In a well-known article, J. O. Urmson suggests that the imperatives of duty, which tell us what we must do, as distinct from what it would be good to do but not wrong not to do, function so as to prohibit behavior that is intolerable if men are to live together in society.[3] This may explain the origin and continued existence of the present division between acts of duty and acts of charity. Moral attitudes are shaped by the needs of society, and no doubt society needs people who will observe the rules that make social existence tolerable. From the point of view of a particular society, it is essential to prevent violations of norms against killing, stealing, and so on. It is quite inessential, however, to help people outside one's own society.

If this is an explanation of our common distinction between duty and supererogation, however, it is not a justification of it. The moral point of view requires us to look beyond the interests of our own society. Previously, as I have already mentioned, this may hardly have been feasible, but it is quite feasible now. From the moral point of view, the prevention of the starvation of millions of people outside our society must be considered at least as pressing as the upholding of property norms within our society.

It has been argued by some writers, among them Sidgwick and Urmson, that we need to have a basic moral code which is not too far beyond the capacities of the ordinary man, for otherwise there will be a general breakdown of compliance with the moral code. Crudely stated, this argument suggests that if we tell people that they ought to refrain from murder and give everything they do not really need to famine relief, they will do neither, whereas if we tell them that they ought to refrain from murder and that it is good to give to famine relief but not wrong not to do so, they will at least refrain from murder. The issue here is: Where should we draw the line between conduct that is required and conduct that is good although not required, so as to get the best possible result? This would seem to be an empirical question, although a very difficult one. One objection to the Sidgwick-Urmson line of argument is that it takes insufficient account of the effect that moral standards can have on the decisions we make. Given a society in which a wealthy man who gives five percent of his income to famine relief is regarded as most generous, it is not surprising that a proposal that we all ought to give away half our incomes will be thought to be absurdly unrealistic. In a society which held that no man should have more than enough while others have less than they need, such a proposal might seem narrow-minded. What it is possible for a man to do and what he is likely to do are both, I think, very greatly influenced by what people around him are doing and expecting him to do. In any case, the possibility that by spreading the idea that we ought to be doing very much more than we are to relieve famine we shall bring about a general breakdown of moral behavior seems remote. If the stakes are an end to widespread starvation, it is worth the risk. Finally, it should be emphasized that these considerations are relevant only to the issue of what we should require from others, and not to what we ourselves ought to do.

The second objection to my attack on the present distinction between duty and charity is one which has from time to time been made against utilitarianism. It follows from some forms of utilitarian theory that we all ought, morally, to be working full time to increase the balance of happiness over misery. The position I have taken here would not lead to this conclusion in all circumstances, for if there were no bad occurrences that we could prevent without sacrificing something of comparable moral importance, my argument would have no application. Given the present conditions in many parts of the world, however, it does follow from my argument that we ought, morally, to be working full time to relieve great suffering of the sort that occurs as a result of famine or other disasters. Of course, mitigating circumstances can be adduced—for instance, that if we wear ourselves out through overwork, we shall be less effective than we would otherwise have been. Nevertheless, when all considerations of this sort have been taken into account, the conclusion remains: we ought to be preventing as much suffering as we can without sacrificing something else of comparable moral importance. This conclusion is one which we may be reluctant to face. I cannot see, though, why it should be regarded as a criticism of the position for which I have argued, rather than a criticism of our ordinary standards of behavior. Since most people are self-interested to some degree, very few of us are likely to do everything that we ought to do. It would, however, hardly be honest to take this as evidence that it is not the case that we ought to do it.

It may still be thought that my conclusions are so wildly out of line with what everyone else thinks and has always thought that there must be something wrong with the argument somewhere. In order to show that my conclusions, while certainly contrary to contemporary Western moral standards, would not have seemed so extraordinary at other times and in other places, I would like to quote a passage from a writer not normally thought of as a way-out radical, Thomas Aquinas.

Now, according to the natural order instituted by divine providence, material goods are provided for the satisfaction of human needs. Therefore the division and appropriation of property, which proceeds from human law, must not hinder the satisfaction of man's necessity from such goods. Equally, whatever a man has in superabundance is owed, of natural right, to the poor for their sustenance. So Ambrosius says, and it is also to be found in the *Decretum Gratiani:* "The bread which you withhold belongs to the hungry; the clothing you shut away, to the naked; and the money you bury in the earth is the redemption and freedom of the penniless."[4]

I now want to consider a number of points, more practical than philosophical, which are relevant to the application of the moral conclusion we have reached. These points challenge not the idea that we ought to be doing all we can to prevent starvation, but the idea that giving away a great deal of money is the best means to this end.

It is sometimes said that overseas aid should be a government responsibility, and that therefore one ought not to give to privately run charities. Giving privately, it is said, allows the government and the noncontributing members of society to escape their responsibilities.

This argument seems to assume that the more people there are who give to privately organized famine relief funds, the less likely it is that the government will take over full responsibility for such aid. This assumption is unsupported, and does not strike me as at all plausible. The opposite view—that if no one gives voluntarily, a government will assume that its citizens are uninterested in famine relief and would not wish to be forced into giving aid—seems more plausible. In any case, unless there were a definite probability that by refusing to give one would be helping to bring about massive government assistance, people who do refuse to make voluntary contributions are refusing to prevent a certain amount of suffering without being able to point to any tangible beneficial consequence of their refusal. So the onus of showing how their refusal will bring about government action is on those who refuse to give.

I do not, of course, want to dispute the contention that governments of affluent nations should be giving many times the amount of genuine, no-strings-attached aid that they are giving now. I agree, too, that giving privately is not enough, and that we ought to be campaigning actively for entirely new standards for both public and private contributions to famine relief. Indeed, I would sympathize with someone who thought that campaigning was more important than giving oneself, although I doubt whether preaching what one does not practice would be very effective. Unfortunately, for many people the idea that "it's the government's responsibility" is a reason for not giving which does not appear to entail any political action either.

Another, more serious reason for not giving to famine relief funds is that until there is effective population control, relieving famine merely postpones starvation. If we save the Bengal refugees now, others, perhaps the children of these refugees, will face starvation in a few years' time. In support of this, one may cite the now well-known facts about the population explosion and the relatively limited scope for expanded production.

This point, like the previous one, is an argument against relieving suffering that is happening now, because of a belief about what might happen in the future; it is unlike the previous point in that very good evidence can be adduced in support of this belief about the future. I will not go into the evidence here. I accept that the earth cannot support indefinitely a population rising at the present rate. This certainly poses a problem for anyone who thinks it important to prevent famine. Again, however, one could accept the argument without drawing the conclusion that it absolves one from any obligation to do anything to prevent famine. The conclusion that should be drawn is that the best means of preventing famine, in the long run, is population control. It would then follow from the position reached earlier that one ought to be doing all one can to promote population control (unless one held that all forms of population control were wrong in themselves, or would have significantly bad consequences). Since there are organizations working specifically for population control, one would then support them rather than more orthodox methods of preventing famine.

A third point raised by the conclusion reached earlier relates to the question of just how much we all ought to be giving away. One possibility, which has already been mentioned, is that we ought to give until we reach the level of marginal utility—that is, the level at which, by giving more, I would cause as much suffering to myself or my dependents as I would relieve by my gift. This would mean, of course, that one would reduce oneself to very near the material circumstances of a Bengali refugee. It will be recalled that earlier I put forward both a strong and a moderate version of the principle of preventing bad occurrences. The strong version, which required us to prevent bad things from happening unless in doing so we would be sacrificing something of comparable moral significance, does seem to require reducing ourselves to the level of marginal utility. I should also say that the strong version seems to me to be the correct one. I proposed the more moderate version—that we should prevent bad occurrences unless, to do so, we had to sacrifice something morally significant—only in order to show that even on this surely undeniable principle a great change in our way of life is required. On the more moderate principle, it may not follow that we ought to reduce ourselves to the level of marginal utility, for one might hold that to reduce oneself and one's family to this level is to cause something significantly bad to happen. Whether this is so I shall not discuss, since, as I have said, I can see no good reason for holding the moderate version of the principle rather than the strong version. Even if we accepted the principle only in its moderate form, however, it should be clear that we would have to give away enough to ensure that the consumer society, dependent as it is on people spending on trivia rather than giving to famine relief, would slow down and perhaps disappear entirely. There are several reasons why this would be desirable in itself. The value and necessity of economic growth are now being questioned not only by conservationists, but by economists as well.[5] There is no doubt, too, that the consumer society has had a distorting effect on the goals and purposes of its members. Yet looking at the matter purely from the point of view of overseas aid, there must be a limit to the extent to which we should deliberately slow down our economy; for it might be the case that if we gave away, say, forty percent of our Gross National Product, we would slow down the economy so much that in absolute terms we would be giving less than if we gave twenty-five percent of the much larger GNP that we would have if we limited our contribution to this smaller percentage.

I mention this only as an indication of the sort of factor that one would have to take into account in working out an ideal. Since Western societies generally consider one percent of the GNP an acceptable level for overseas aid, the matter is entirely academic. Nor does it affect the question of how much an individual should give in a society in which very few are giving substantial amounts.

It is sometimes said, though less often now than it used to be, that philosophers have no special role to play in public affairs, since most public issues depend primarily on an assessment of facts. On questions of fact, it is said, philosophers as such have no special expertise, and so it has been possible to engage in philosophy without committing oneself to any position on major public issues. No doubt there are some issues of social policy and foreign policy about which it can truly be said that a really expert assessment of the facts is required before taking sides or acting, but the issue of famine is surely not one of these. The facts about the existence of suffering are beyond dispute. Nor, I think, is it disputed that we can do something about it, either through orthodox methods of famine relief or through population control or both. This is therefore an issue on which philosophers are competent to take a position. The issue is one which faces everyone who has more money than he needs to support himself and his dependents, or who is in a position to take some sort of political action. These categories must include practically every teacher and student of philosophy in the universities of the Western world. If philosophy is to deal with matters that are relevant to both teachers and students, this is an issue that philosophers should discuss.

Discussion, though, is not enough. What is the point of relating philosophy to public (and personal)

affairs if we do not take our conclusions seriously? In this instance, taking our conclusion seriously means acting upon it. The philosopher will not find it any easier than anyone else to alter his attitudes and way of life to the extent that, if I am right, is involved in doing everything that we ought to be doing. At the very least, though, one can make a start. The philosopher who does so will have to sacrifice some of the benefits of the consumer society, but he can find compensation in the satisfaction of a way of life in which theory and practice, if not yet in harmony, are at least coming together.

NOTES

1. There was also a third possibility: that India would go to war to enable the refugees to return to their lands. Since I wrote this paper, India has taken this way out. The situation is no longer that described above, but this does not affect my argument, as the next paragraph indicates.

2. In view of the special sense philosophers often give to the term, I should say that I use "obligation" simply as the abstract noun derived from "ought," so that "I have an obligation to" means no more, and no less, than "I ought to." This usage is in accordance with the definition of "ought" given by the *Shorter Oxford English Dictionary:* "the general verb to express duty or obligation." I do not think any issue of substance hangs on the way the term is used; sentences in which I use "obligation" could all be rewritten, although somewhat clumsily, as sentences in which a clause containing "ought" replaces the term "obligation."

3. J. O. Urmson, "Saints and Heroes," in *Essays in Moral Philosophy,* ed. Abraham I. Melden (Seattle: University of Washington Press, 1958), p. 214. For a related but significantly different view see also Henry Sidgwick, *The Methods of Ethics,* 7th ed. (London: Dover Press, 1907), pp. 220–21, 492–93.

4. *Summa Theologica,* II-II, Question 66, Article 7, in *Aquinas, Selected Political Writings,* ed. A. P. d'Entreves, trans. J. G. Dawson (Oxford: Basil Blackwell, 1948), p. 171.

5. See, for instance, John Kenneth Galbraith, *The New Industrial State* (Boston: Houghton Mifflin, 1967); and E. J. Mishan, *The Costs of Economic Growth* (New York: Praeger, 1967).

Global Environment and International Inequality

Henry Shue

My aim is to establish that three commonsense principles of fairness, none of them dependent upon controversial philosophical theories of justice, give rise to the same conclusion about the allocation of the costs of protecting the environment.

Poor states and rich states have long dealt with each other primarily upon unequal terms. The imposition of unequal terms has been relatively easy for the rich states because they have rarely needed to ask for the voluntary cooperation of the less powerful poor states. Now the rich countries have realized that their own industrial activity has been destroying the ozone in the earth's atmosphere and has been making far and away the greatest contribution to global warming. They would like the poor states to avoid adopting the same form of industrialization by which they themselves became rich. It is increasingly clear that if poor states pursue their own economic development with the same disregard for the natural environment and the economic welfare of other states that rich states displayed in the past during their development, everyone will continue to suffer the effects of environmental destruction. Consequently, it is at least conceivable that rich states might now be willing to consider dealing cooperatively on equitable terms with poor states in a manner that gives due weight to both the economic development of poor states and the preservation of the natural environment.

If we are to have any hope of pursuing equitable cooperation, we must try to arrive at a consensus about what equity means. And we need to define equity, not as a vague abstraction, but concretely and specifically in the context of both development of the economy in poor states and preservation of the environment everywhere.

FUNDAMENTAL FAIRNESS AND ACCEPTABLE INEQUALITY

What diplomats and lawyers call equity incorporates important aspects of what ordinary people everywhere call fairness. The concept of fairness is neither Eastern nor Western, Northern nor Southern, but universal.[1] People everywhere understand what it means to ask whether an arrangement is fair or biased towards some parties over other parties. If you own the land but I supply the labour, or you own the seed but I own the ox, or you are old but I am young, or you are female but I am male, or you have an education and I do not, or you worked long and hard but I was lazy—in situation after situation it makes perfectly good sense to ask whether a particular division of something among two or more parties is fair to all the parties, in light of this or that difference between them. All people understand the question, even where they have been taught not to ask it. What would be fair? Or, as the lawyers and diplomats would put it, which arrangement would be equitable?

Naturally, it is also possible to ask other kinds of questions about the same arrangements. One can always ask economic questions, for instance, in addition to ethical questions concerning equity: would it increase total output if, say, women were paid less and men were paid more? Would it be more efficient? Sometimes the most efficient arrangement happens also to be fair to all parties, but often it is unfair. Then a choice has to be made between efficiency and fairness. Before it is possible to discuss such choices, however, we need to know the meaning of equity: what are the standards of equity and how do they matter?

Henry Shue, "Global Environment and International Inequality," *International Affairs* 75 (1999): 531–45. Reprinted with permission of the author and the publisher, The Royal Institute of International Affairs.

Complete egalitarianism—the belief that all good things ought to be shared equally among all people—can be a powerfully attractive view, and it is much more difficult to argue against than many of its opponents seem to think. I shall, nevertheless, assume here that complete egalitarianism is unacceptable. If it were the appropriate view to adopt, our inquiry into equity could end now. The answer to the question, "what is an equitable arrangement?" would always be the same: an equal distribution. Only equality would ever provide equity.

While I do assume that it may be equitable for some good things to be distributed unequally, I also assume that other things must be kept equal—most importantly, dignity and respect. It is part of the current international consensus that every person is entitled to equal dignity and equal respect. In traditional societies in both hemispheres, even the equality of dignity and respect was denied in theory as well as practice. Now, although principles of equality are still widely violated in practice, inequality of dignity and of respect have relatively few public advocates even among those who practice them. If it is equitable for some other human goods to be distributed unequally, but it is not equitable for dignity or respect to be unequal, the central questions become: "which inequalities in which other human goods are compatible with equal human dignity and equal human respect?" and "which inequalities in other goods ought to be eliminated, reduced or prevented from being increased?"

When one is beginning from an existing inequality, like the current inequality in wealth between North and South, three critical kinds of justification are: justifications of unequal burdens intended to reduce or eliminate the existing inequality by removing an unfair advantage of those at the top; justifications of unequal burdens intended to prevent the existing inequality from becoming worse through any infliction of an unfair additional disadvantage upon those at the bottom; and justifications of a guaranteed minimum intended to prevent the existing inequality from becoming worse through any infliction of an unfair additional disadvantage upon those at the bottom. The second justification for unequal bur-

dens and the justification for a guaranteed minimum are the same: two different mechanisms are being used to achieve fundamentally the same purpose. I shall look at these two forms of justification for unequal burdens and then at the justification for a guaranteed minimum.

UNEQUAL BURDENS

Greater Contribution to the Problem

All over the world parents teach their children to clean up their own mess. This simple rule makes good sense from the point of view of incentive: if one learns that one will not be allowed to get away with simply walking away from whatever messes one creates, one is given a strong negative incentive against making messes in the first place. Whoever makes the mess presumably does so in the process of pursuing some benefit—for a child, the benefit may simply be the pleasure of playing with the objects that constitute the mess. If one learns that whoever reaps the benefit of making the mess must also be the one who pays the cost of cleaning up the mess, one learns at the very least not to make messes with costs that are greater than their benefits.

Economists have glorified this simple rule as the "internalization of externalities." If the basis for the price of a product does not incorporate the costs of cleaning up the mess made in the process of producing the product, the costs are being externalized, that is, dumped upon other parties. Incorporating into the basis of the price of the product the costs that had been coercively socialized is called internalizing an externality.

At least as important as the consideration of incentives, however, is the consideration of fairness or equity. If whoever makes a mess receives the benefits and does not pay the costs, not only does he have no incentive to avoid making as many messes as he likes, but he is also unfair to whoever does pay the costs. He is inflicting costs upon other people, contrary to their interests and, presumably, without their consent. By making himself better off in ways that make others worse off, he is creating an expanding inequality.

Once such an inequality has been created unilaterally by someone's imposing costs upon other people, we are justified in reversing the inequality by imposing extra burdens upon the producer of the inequality. There are two separate points here. First, we are justified in assigning additional burdens to the party who has been inflicting costs upon us. Second, the minimum extent of the compensatory burden we are justified in assigning is enough to correct the inequality previously unilaterally imposed. The purpose of the extra burden is to restore an equality that was disrupted unilaterally and arbitrarily (or to reduce an inequality that was enlarged unilaterally and arbitrarily). In order to accomplish that purpose, the extra burden assigned must be at least equal to the unfair advantage previously taken. This yields us our first principle of equity:

> When a party has in the past taken an unfair advantage of others by imposing costs upon them without their consent, those who have been unilaterally put at a disadvantage are entitled to demand that in the future the offending party shoulder burdens that are unequal at least to the extent of the unfair advantage previously taken, in order to restore equality.[2]

In the area of development and the environment, the clearest cases that fall under this first principle of equity are the partial destruction of the ozone layer and the initiation of global warming by the process of industrialization that has enriched the North but not the South. Unilateral initiatives by the so-called developed countries (DCs) have made them rich, while leaving the less developed countries (LDCs) poor. In the process the industrial activities and accompanying lifestyles of the DCs have inflicted major global damage upon the earth's atmosphere. Both kinds of damage are harmful to those who did not benefit from Northern industrialization as well as to those who did. Those societies whose activities have damaged the atmosphere ought, according to the first principle of equity, to bear sufficiently unequal

burdens henceforth to correct the inequality that they have imposed. In this case, everyone is bearing costs—because the damage was universal—but the benefits have been overwhelmingly skewed towards those who have become rich in the process.

This principle of equity should be distinguished from the considerably weaker because entirely forward-looking—"polluter pays principle" (PPP), which requires only that all future costs of pollution (in production or consumption) be henceforth internalized into prices. Even the OECD formally adopted the PPP in 1974, to govern relations among rich states.[3]

Spokespeople for the rich countries make at least three kinds of counter-arguments to this first principle of equity. These are:

1. The LDCs have also benefited, it is said, from the enrichment of the DCs. Usually it is conceded that the industrial countries have benefited more than the non-industrialized. Yet it is maintained that, for example, medicines and technologies made possible by the lifestyles of the rich countries have also reached the poor countries, bringing benefits that the poor countries could not have produced as soon for themselves.

Quite a bit of breath and ink has been spent in arguments over how much LDCs have benefited from the technologies and other advances made by the DCs, compared to the benefits enjoyed by the DCs themselves. Yet this dispute does not need to be settled in order to decide questions of equity. Whatever benefits LDCs have received, they have mostly been charged for. No doubt some improvements have been widespread. Yet, except for a relative trickle of aid, all transfers have been charged to the recipients, who have in fact been left with an enormous burden of debt, much of it incurred precisely in the effort to purchase the good things produced by industrialization.

Overall, poor countries have been charged for any benefits that they have received by someone in the rich countries, evening that account. Much greater additional benefits have gone to the rich countries themselves, including a major contribution to the very process of their becoming so much richer than the poor countries. Meanwhile, the environmental damage caused by the process has been incurred by everyone. The rich countries have profited to the extent of the excess of the benefits gained by them over the costs incurred by everyone through environmental damage done by them, and ought in future to bear extra burdens in dealing with the damage they have done.

2. Whatever environmental damage has been done, it is said, was unintentional. Now we know all sorts of things about CFCs and the ozone layer, and about carbon dioxide and the greenhouse effect, that no one dreamed of when CFCs were created or when industrialization fed with fossil fuels began. People cannot be held responsible, it is maintained, for harmful effects that they could not have foreseen. The philosopher Immanuel Kant is often quoted in the West for having said, "Ought presupposes can"— it can be true that one ought to have done something only if one actually could have done it. Therefore, it is allegedly not fair to hold people responsible for effects they could not have avoided because the effects could not have been predicted.

This objection rests upon a confusion between punishment and responsibility. It is not fair to punish someone for producing effects that could not have been avoided, but it is common to hold people responsible for effects that were unforeseen and unavoidable.

We noted earlier that, in order to be justifiable, an inequality in something between two or more parties must be compatible with an equality of dignity and respect between the parties. If there were an inequality between two groups of people such that members of the first group could create problems and then expect members of the second group to deal with the problems, that inequality would be incompatible with equal respect and equal dignity. For the members of the second group would in fact be functioning as servants for the first group. If I said to you, "I broke it, but I want you to clean it up," then I would be your master and you would be my servant. If I thought that you should do my bidding, I could hardly respect you as my equal.

It is true, then, that the owners of many coal-burning factories could not possibly have known the bad effects of the carbon dioxide they were releasing into the atmosphere, and therefore could not possibly have intended to contribute to harming it. It would, therefore, be unfair to punish them—by, for example, demanding that they pay double or triple damages. It is not in the least unfair, however, simply to hold them responsible for the damage that they have in fact done. This naturally leads to the third objection.

3. Even if it is fair to hold a person responsible for damage done unintentionally, it will be said, it is not fair to hold the person responsible for damage he did not do himself. It would not be fair, for example, to hold a grandson responsible for damage done by his grandfather. Yet it is claimed this is exactly what is being done when the current generation is held responsible for carbon dioxide emissions produced in the nineteenth century. Perhaps Europeans living today are responsible for atmosphere-damaging gases emitted today, but it is not fair to hold people responsible for deeds done long before they were born.

This objection appeals to a reasonable principle, namely that one person ought not to be held responsible for what is done by another person who is completely unrelated. "Completely unrelated" is, however, a critical portion of the principle. To assume that the facts about the industrial North's contribution to global warming straightforwardly fall under this principle is to assume that they are considerably simpler than they actually are.

First, and undeniably, the industrial states' contributions to global warming have continued unabated long since it became impossible to plead ignorance. It would have been conceivable that as soon as evidence began to accumulate that industrial activity was having a dangerous environmental effect, the industrial states would have adopted a conservative or even cautious policy of cutting back greenhouse-gas emissions or at least slowing their rate of increase. For the most part this has not happened.

Second, today's generation in the industrial states is far from completely unrelated to the earlier generations going back all the way to the beginning of the Industrial Revolution. What is the difference between being born in 1975 in Belgium and being born in 1975 in Bangladesh? Clearly one of the most fundamental differences is that the Belgian infant is born into an industrial society and the Bangladeshi infant is not. Even the medical setting for the birth itself, not to mention the level of prenatal care available to the expectant mother, is almost certainly vastly more favourable for the Belgian than the Bangladeshi. Childhood nutrition, educational opportunities and life-long standards of living are likely to differ enormously because of the difference between an industrialized and a non-industrialized economy. In such respects current generations are, and future generations probably will be, continuing beneficiaries of earlier industrial activity.

Nothing is wrong with the principle invoked in the third objection. It is indeed not fair to hold someone responsible for what has been done by someone else. Yet that principle is largely irrelevant to the case at hand, because one generation of a rich industrial society is not unrelated to other generations past and future. All are participants in enduring economic structures. Benefits and costs, and rights and responsibilities, carry across generations.

We turn now to a second, quite different kind of justification of the same mechanism of assigning unequal burdens. This first justification has rested in part upon the unfairness of the existing inequality. The second justification neither assumes nor argues that the initial inequality is unfair.

Greater Ability to Pay

The second principle of equity is widely accepted as a requirement of simple fairness. It states:

> Among a number of parties, all of whom are bound to contribute to some common endeavour, the parties who have the most resources normally should contribute the most to the endeavour.

This principle of paying in accordance with ability to pay, if stated strictly, would specify what is often called a progressive rate of payment: insofar as a party's assets are greater, the rate at which the party should contribute to the enterprise in question also becomes greater. The progressivity can be strictly proportional—those with double the base amount of assets contribute at twice the rate at which those with the base amount contribute, those with triple the base amount of assets contribute at three times the rate at which those with the base amount contribute, and so on. More typically, the progressivity is not strictly proportional—the more a party has, the higher the rate at which it is expected to contribute, but the rate does not increase in strict proportion to increases in assets.

The general principle itself is sufficiently fundamental that it is not necessary, and perhaps not possible, to justify it by deriving it from considerations that are more fundamental still. Nevertheless, it is possible to explain its appeal to some extent more fully. The basic appeal of payment in accordance with ability to pay as a principle of fairness is easiest to see by contrast with a flat rate of contribution, that is, the same rate of contribution by every party irrespective of different parties' differing assets. At first thought, the same rate for everyone seems obviously the fairest imaginable arrangement. What could possibly be fairer, one is initially inclined to think, than absolutely equal treatment for everyone? Surely, it seems, if everyone pays an equal rate, everyone is treated the same and therefore fairly? This, however, is an exceedingly abstract approach, which pays no attention at all to the actual concrete circumstances of the contributing parties. In addition, it focuses exclusively upon the contribution process and ignores the position in which, as a result of the process, the parties end up. Contribution according to ability to pay is much more sensitive both to concrete circumstance and to final outcome.

Suppose that Party A has 90 units of something, Party B has 30 units, and Party C has 9 units. In order to accomplish their missions, it is proposed that everyone should contribute at a flat rate of one-third. This may seem fair in that everyone is treated equally: the same rate is applied to everyone, regardless of circumstances. When it is considered that

A's contribution will be 30 and B's will be 10, while C's will be only 3, the flat rate may appear more than fair to C who contributes only one-tenth as much as A does. However, suppose that these units represent $100 per year in income and that where C lives it is possible to survive on $750 per year but on no less. If C must contribute 3 units—$300—he will fall below the minimum for survival. While the flat rate of one-third would require A to contribute far more ($3,000) than C, and B to contribute considerably more ($1,000) than C, both A (with $6,000 left) and B (with $2,000 left) would remain safely above subsistence level. A and B can afford to contribute at the rate of one-third because they are left with more than enough while C is unable to contribute at that rate and survive.

While flat rates appear misleadingly fair in the abstract, they do so largely because they look at only the first part of the story and ignore how things turn out in the end. The great strength of progressive rates, by contrast, is that they tend to accommodate final outcomes and take account of whether the contributors can in fact afford their respective contributions.

A single objection is usually raised against progressive rates of contribution: disincentive effects. If those who have more are going to lose what they have at a greater rate than those who have less, the incentive to come to have more in the first place will, it is said, be much less than it would have been with a flat rate of contribution. Why should I take more risks, display more imagination, or expend more effort in order to gain more resources if the result will only be that, whenever something must be paid for, I will have to contribute not merely a larger absolute amount (which would happen even with a flat rate) but a larger percentage? I might as well not be productive if much of anything extra I produce will be taken away from me, leaving me little better off than those who produced far less.

Three points need to be noticed regarding this objection. First, of course, being fair and providing incentives are two different matters, and there is certainly no guarantee in the abstract that whatever arrangement would provide the greatest incentives would also be fair.

Second, concerns about incentives often arise when it is assumed that maximum production and limitless growth are the best goal. It is increasingly clear that many current forms of production and growth are unsustainable and that the last thing we should do is to give people self-interested reasons to consume as many resources as they can, even where the resources are consumed productively. These issues cannot be settled in the abstract either, but it is certainly an open question—and one that should be asked very seriously—whether in a particular situation it is desirable to stimulate people by means of incentives to maximum production. Sometimes it is desirable, and sometimes it is not. This is an issue about ends.

Third, there is a question about means. Assuming that it had been demonstrated that the best goal to have in a specific set of circumstances involved stimulating more production of something, one would then have to ask: how much incentive is needed to stimulate that much production? Those who are preoccupied with incentives often speculate groundlessly that unlimited incentives are virtually always required. Certainly it is true that it is generally necessary to provide some additional incentive in order to stimulate additional production. Some people are altruistic and are therefore sometimes willing to contribute more to the welfare of others even if they do not thereby improve their own welfare. It would be completely unrealistic, however, to try to operate an economy on the assumption that people generally would produce more irrespective of whether doing so was in their own interest—they need instead to be provided with some incentive. However, some incentive does not mean unlimited incentive.

It is certainly not necessary to offer unlimited incentives in order to stimulate (limited) additional production by some people (and not others). Whether people respond or not depends upon individual personalities and individual circumstances. It is a factual matter, not something to be decreed in the abstract, how much incentive is enough: for these people in these circumstances to produce this much more, how much incentive is enough? What is clearly mistaken is the frequent assumption that nothing less than the maximum incentive is ever enough.

In conclusion, insofar as the objection based on disincentive effects is intended to be a decisive refutation of the second principle of equity, the objection fails. It is not always a mistake to offer less than the maximum possible incentive, even when the goal of thereby increasing production has itself been justified. There is no evidence that anything less than the maximum is even generally a mistake. Psychological effects must be determined case by case.

On the other hand, the objection based on disincentive effects may be intended—much more modestly—simply as a warning that one of the possible costs of restraining inequalities by means of progressive rates of contribution, in the effort of being fair, may (or may not) be a reduction in incentive effects. As a caution rather than a (failed) refutation, the objection points to one sensible consideration that needs to be taken into account when specifying which variation upon the general second principle of equity is the best version to adopt in a specific case. One would have to consider how much greater the incentive effect would be if the rate of contribution were less progressive, in light of how unfair the results of a less progressive rate would be.

This conclusion that disincentive effects deserve to be considered, although they are not always decisive, partly explains why the second principle of equity is stated, not as an absolute, but as a general principle. It says: ". . . the parties who have the most resources *normally* should contribute the most . . ."— not always, but normally. One reason why the rate of contribution might not be progressive, or might not be as progressive as possible, is the potential disincentive effects of more progressive rates. It would need to be shown case by case that an important goal was served by having some incentive and that the goal in question would not be served by the weaker incentive compatible with a more progressive rate of contribution.

We have so far examined two quite different kinds of justifications of unequal burdens: to reduce or eliminate an existing inequality by removing an unfair advantage of those at the top and to prevent the existing inequality from becoming worse through any infliction of an unfair additional disadvantage upon those at the bottom. The first justification rests in part upon explaining why the initial inequality is unfair and ought to be removed or reduced. The second justification applies irrespective of whether the initial inequality is fair. Now we turn to a different mechanism that—much more directly—serves the second purpose of avoiding making those who are already the worst-off yet worse off.

GUARANTEED MINIMUM

We noted earlier that issues of equity or fairness can arise only if there is something that must be divided among different parties. The existence of the following circumstances can be taken as grounds for thinking that certain parties have a legitimate claim to some of the available resources: (a) the aggregate total of resources is sufficient for all parties to have more than enough; (b) some parties do in fact have more than enough, some of them much more than enough; and (c) other parties have less than enough. American philosopher Thomas Nagel has called such circumstances radical inequality.[4] Such an inequality is radical in part because the total of available resources is so great that there is no need to reduce the best-off people to anywhere near the minimum level in order to bring the worst-off people up to the minimum: the existing degree of inequality is utterly unnecessary and easily reduced, in light of the total resources already at hand. In other words, one could preserve considerable inequality—in order, for instance, to provide incentives, if incentives were needed for some important purpose—while arranging for those with less than enough to have at least enough.

Enough for what? The answer could of course be given in considerable detail, and some of the details would be controversial (and some, although not all, would vary across societies). The basic idea, however, is of enough for a decent chance for a reasonably healthy and active life of more or less normal length, barring tragic accidents and interventions.

"Enough" means the essentials for at least a bit more than mere physical survival—for at least a distinctively human, if modest, life. For example, having enough means owning not merely clothing adequate for substantial protection against the elements but clothing adequate in appearance to avoid embarrassment, by local standards, when being seen in public, as Adam Smith noted.

In a situation of radical inequality—a situation with the three features outlined above—fairness demands that those people with less than enough for a decent human life be provided with enough. This yields the third principle of equity, which states:

When some people have less than enough for a decent human life, other people have far more than enough, and the total resources available are so great that everyone could have at least enough without preventing some people from still retaining considerably more than others have, it is unfair not to guarantee everyone at least an adequate minimum.[5]

Clearly, provisions to guarantee an adequate minimum can be of many different kinds, and, concerning many of the choices, equity has little or nothing to say. The arrangements to provide the minimum can be local, regional, national, international or, more likely, some complex mixture of all, with secondary arrangements at one level providing a backstop for primary arrangements at another level.[6] Similarly, particular arrangements might assign initial responsibility for maintaining the minimum to families or other intimate groups, to larger voluntary associations like religious groups or to a state bureau. Consideration of equity might have no implications for many of the choices about arrangements, and some of the choices might vary among societies, provided the minimum was in fact guaranteed.

Children, it is worth emphasizing, are the main beneficiaries of this principle of equity. When a family drops below the minimum required to maintain all its members, the children are the most vulnerable. Even if the adults choose to allocate their own share of an insufficient supply to the children, it is still quite likely that the children will have less re-

sistance to disease and less resilience in general. And of course not all adults will sacrifice their own share to their children. Or, in quite a few cultures, adults will sacrifice on behalf of male children but not on behalf of female children. All in all, when essentials are scarce, the proportion of children dying is far greater than their proportion in the population, which in poorer countries is already high—in quite a few poor countries, more than half the population is under the age of 15.

One of the most common objections to this third principle of equity flows precisely from this point about the survival of children. It is what might be called the over-population objection. I consider this objection to be ethically outrageous and factually groundless, as explained elsewhere.[7]

The other most common objection is that while it may be only fair for each society to have a guaranteed minimum for its own members, it is not fair to expect members of one society to help to maintain a guarantee of a minimum for members of another society.[8] This objection sometimes rests on the assumption that state borders—national political boundaries—have so much moral significance that citizens of one state cannot be morally required, even by considerations of elemental fairness, to concern themselves with the welfare of citizens of a different political jurisdiction. A variation on this theme is the contention that across state political boundaries moral mandates can only be negative requirements not to harm and cannot be positive requirements to help. I am unconvinced that, in general, state political borders and national citizenship are markers of such extraordinary and over-riding moral significance. Whatever may be the case in general, this second objection is especially unpersuasive if raised on behalf of citizens of the industrialized wealthy states in the context of international cooperation to deal with environmental problems primarily caused by their own states and of greatest concern in the medium term to those states.

To help to maintain a guarantee of a minimum could mean either of two things: a weaker requirement (a) not to interfere with others' ability to maintain a minimum for themselves; or a stronger requirement (b) to provide assistance to others in maintaining a minimum for themselves. If everyone has a general obligation, even towards strangers in other states and societies, not to inflict harm on other persons, the weaker requirement would follow, provided only that interfering with people's ability to maintain a minimum for themselves counted as a serious harm, as it certainly would seem to. Accordingly, persons with no other bonds to each other would still be obliged not to hinder the others' efforts to provide a minimum for themselves.

One could not, for example, demand as one of the terms of an agreement that someone make sacrifices that would leave the person without necessities. This means that any agreement to cooperate made between people having more than enough and people not having enough cannot justifiably require those who start out without enough to make any sacrifices. Those who lack essentials will still have to agree to act cooperatively, if there is in fact to be cooperation, but they should not bear the costs of even their own cooperation. Because a demand that those lacking essentials should make a sacrifice would harm them, making such a demand is unfair.

That (a), the weaker requirement, holds, seems perfectly clear. When, if ever, would (b), the stronger requirement to provide assistance to others in maintaining a minimum for themselves, hold? Consider the case at hand. Wealthy states, which are wealthy in large part because they are operating industrial processes, ask the poor states, which are poor in large part because they have not industrialized, to cooperate in controlling the bad effects of these same industrial processes, like the destruction of atmospheric ozone and the creation of global warming. Assume that the citizens of the wealthy states have no general obligation, which holds prior to and independently of any agreement to work together on environmental problems, to contribute to the provision of a guaranteed minimum for the citizens of the poor states. The citizens of the poor states certainly have no general obligation, which holds prior to and independently of any agreement, to assist the wealthy states in dealing with the environmental problems that the wealthy states' own industrial processes are producing. It may ultimately be in the interest of the poor states to see ozone depletion and global warming stopped, but in the medium term the citizens of the poor states have far more urgent and serious problems—like lack of food, lack of clean water and lack of jobs to provide minimal support for themselves and their families. If the wealthy states say to the poor states, in effect, "our most urgent request of you is that you act in ways that will avoid worsening the ozone depletion and global warming that we have started," the poor states could reasonably respond, "our most urgent request of you is assistance in guaranteeing the fulfillment of the essential needs of our citizens."

In other words, if the wealthy have no general obligation to help the poor, the poor certainly have no general obligation to help the wealthy. If this assumed absence of general obligations means that matters are to be determined by national interest rather than international obligation, then surely the poor states are as fully at liberty to specify their own top priority as the wealthy states are. The poor states are under no general prior obligation to be helpful to the wealthy states in dealing with whatever happens to be the top priority of the wealthy states. This is all the more so as long as the wealthy states remain content to watch hundreds of thousands of children die each year in the poor states for lack of material necessities, which the total resources in the world could remedy many times over. If the wealthy states are content to allow radical inequalities to persist and worsen, it is difficult to see why the poor states should divert their attention from their own worst problems in order to help out with problems that for them are far less immediate and deadly. It is as if I am starving to death, and you want me to agree to stop searching for food and instead to help repair a leak in the roof of your house without your promising me any food. Why should I turn my attention away from my own more severe problem to your less severe one, when I have no guarantee that if I help you with your problem you will help me with mine? If any arrangement would ever be unfair, that one would.

Radical human inequalities cannot be tolerated and ought to be eliminated, irrespective of whether their elimination involves the movement of resources across national political boundaries: resources move across national boundaries all the time for all sorts of reasons. I have not argued here for this judgement about radical inequality, however.[9] The conclusion for which I have provided a rationale is even more compelling: when radical inequalities exist, it is unfair for people in states with far more than enough to expect people in states with less than enough to turn their attention away from their own problems in order to cooperate with the much better-off in solving their problems (and all the more unfair—in light of the first principle of equity—when the problems that concern the much better-off were created by the much better-off themselves in the very process of becoming as well off as they are). The least that those below the minimum can reasonably demand in reciprocity for their attention to the problems that concern the best-off is that their own most vital problems be attended to: that they be guaranteed means of fulfilling their minimum needs. Any lesser guarantee is too little to be fair, which is to say that any international agreement that attempts to leave radical inequality across national states untouched while asking effort from the worst-off to assist the best-off is grossly unfair.

OVERVIEW

I have emphasized that the reasons for the second and third principles of equity are fundamentally the same, namely, avoiding making those who are already the worst-off yet worse off. The second principle serves this end by requiring that when contributions must be made, they should be made more heavily by the better-off, irrespective of whether the existing inequality is justifiable. The third principle serves this end by requiring that no contributions be made by those below the minimum unless they are guaranteed ways to bring themselves up at least to the minimum, which assumes that radical inequalities are unjustified. Together, the second and third principles require that if any contributions to a common effort are to be expected of people whose minimum needs have not been guaranteed so far, guar-

antees must be provided; and the guarantees must be provided most heavily by the best-off.

The reason for the first principle was different from the reason for the second principle, in that the reason for the first rests on the assumption that an existing inequality is already unjustified. The reason for the third principle rests on the same assumption. The first and third principles apply, however, to inequalities that are, respectively, unjustified for different kinds of reasons. Inequalities to which the first principle applies are unjustified because of how they arose, namely some people have been benefiting unfairly by dumping the costs of their own advances upon other people. Inequalities to which the third principle applies are unjustified independently of how they arose and simply because they are radical, that is, so extreme in circumstances in which it would be very easy to make them less extreme.

What stands out is that in spite of the different content of these three principles of equity, and in spite of the different kinds of grounds upon which they rest, they all converge upon the same practical conclusion: whatever needs to be done by wealthy industrialized states or by poor non-industrialized states about global environmental problems like ozone destruction and global warming, the costs should initially be borne by the wealthy industrialized states.

NOTES

1. Or so I believe. I would be intensely interested in any evidence of a culture that seems to lack a concept of fairness, as distinguished from evidence about two cultures whose specific conceptions of fairness differ in some respects.

2. A preliminary presentation of these principles at New York University Law School has been helpfully commented upon in Thomas M. Franck, *Fairness in international law and institutions* (Oxford: Clarendon, 1997), pp. 390–91.

3. OECD Council, 14 November 1974C (1974), 223 (Paris: OECD).

4. See Thomas Nagel, "Poverty and food: why charity is not enough," in Peter G. Brown and Henry Shue, eds., *Food policy: the responsibility of the United States in the*

life and death choices (New York: Free Press, 1977), pp. 54–62. In an important recent and synthetic discussion Thomas W. Pogge has suggested adding two further features to the characterization of a radical inequality, as well as a different view about its moral status—see Thomas W. Pogge, "A global resources dividend," in David A. Crocker and Toby Linden, eds., *Ethics of consumption: the good life, justice and global stewardship,* in the series Philosophy and the global context (Lanham, MD, Oxford: Rowman & Littlefield, 1998), pp. 501–36. On radical inequality, see pp. 502–503.

5. This third principle of equity is closely related to what I called the argument from vital interests in Henry Shue, "The unavoidability of justice," in Andrew Hurrell and Benedict Kingsbury, eds., *The international politics of the environment* (Oxford: Oxford University Press, 1992.), pp. 373–97. It is the satisfaction of vital interests

that constitutes the minimum everyone needs to have guaranteed. In the formulation here the connection with limits on inequality is made explicit.

6. On the importance of backstop arrangements, or the allocation of default duties, see "Afterword" in Henry Shue, *Basic rights: subsistence, affluence, and US foreign policy,* 2nd ed (Princeton, NJ: Princeton University Press, 1996).

7. *Basic rights,* ch. 4.

8. This objection has recently been provided with a powerful and sophisticated Kantian formulation that deserves much more attention than space here allows—see Richard W. Miller, "Cosmopolitan respect and patriotic concern." *Philosophy & Public Affairs* 27: 3, Summer 1998, pp. 202–24.

9. And for the argument to the contrary see Miller, "Cosmopolitan respect and patriotic concern."

Feeding People Versus Saving Nature

Holmes Rolston III

When we must choose between feeding the hungry and conserving nature, people ought to come first. A bumper sticker reads: Hungry loggers eat spotted owls. That pinpoints an ethical issue, pure and simple, and often one where the humanist protagonist, taking high moral ground, intends to put the environmentalist on the defensive. You wouldn't let the Ethiopians starve to save some butterfly, would you?

"Human beings are at the centre of concerns for sustainable development." So the *Rio Declaration* begins. Once this was to be an *Earth Charter,* but the developing nations were more interested in getting the needs of their poor met. The developed nations are wealthy enough to be concerned about

saving nature. The developing nations want the anthropocentrism, loud and clear. These humans, they add, "are entitled to a healthy and productive life in harmony with nature," but there too they seem as concerned with their entitlements as with any care for nature.[1] Can we fault them for it?

We have to be circumspect. To isolate so simple a trade-off as hungry people versus nature is perhaps artificial. If too far abstracted from the complex circumstances of decision, we may not be facing any serious operational issue. When we have simplified the question, it may have become, minus its many qualifications, a different question. The gestalt configures the question, and the same question recon-

Holmes Rolston III, "Feeding People Versus Saving Nature," in *World Hunger & Morality,* 2nd ed., ed. W. Aiken and H. LaFollette (Upper Saddle River, NJ: Prentice-Hall, 1977), 248–67. Reprinted with permission of the author and Prentice-Hall.

figured can be different. So we must analyze the general matrix, and then confront the more particular people-versus-nature issue.

Humans win? Nature loses? After analysis, sometimes it turns out that humans are not really winning, if they are sacrificing the nature that is their life support system. Humans win by conserving nature—and these winners include the poor and the hungry. "In order to achieve sustainable development, environmental protection shall constitute an integral part of the development process and cannot be considered in isolation from it."[2] After all, food has to be produced by growing it in some reasonably healthy natural system, and the clean water that the poor need is also good for fauna and flora. Extractive reserves give people an incentive to conserve. Tourism can often benefit both the local poor and the wildlife, as well as tourists. One ought to seek win-win solutions wherever one can. Pragmatically, these are often the only kind likely to succeed.

Yet there are times when nature is sacrificed for human development; most development is of this kind. By no means all is warranted, but that which gets people fed seems basic and urgent. Then nature should lose and people win. Or are there times when at least some humans should lose and some nature should win? We are here interested in these latter occasions. Can we ever say that we should save nature rather than feed people?

FEED PEOPLE FIRST?
DO WE? OUGHT WE?

"Feed people first!" That has a ring of righteousness. The *Rio Declaration* insists, "All States and all people shall cooperate in the essential task of eradicating poverty as an indispensable requirement."[3] In the biblical parable of the great judgment, the righteous had ministered to the needy, and Jesus welcomes them to their reward." I was hungry and you gave me food, I was thirsty and you gave me drink." Those who refused to help are damned (Matthew 28:31–46). The vision of heaven is that "they shall hunger no more, neither thirst any more" (Revela-

tion 7:16), and Jesus teaches his disciples to pray that this will of God be done on earth, as it is in heaven. "Give us this day our daily bread" (Matthew 5:11). These are such basic values, if there is to be any ethics at all, surely food comes first.

Or does it? If giving others their daily bread were always the first concern, the Christians would never have built an organ or a sanctuary with a stained glass window, but rather always given all to the poor. There is also the biblical story of the woman who washed Jesus' feet with expensive ointment. When the disciples complained that it should have been sold and given to the poor, Jesus replied, "you always have the poor with you. She has done a beautiful thing" (Matthew 26:10–11). While the poor are a continuing concern, with whom Jesus demonstrated ample solidarity, there are other commendable values in human life, "beautiful things," in Jesus' phrase. The poor are always there, and if we did nothing else of value until there were no more poor, we would do nothing else of value at all.

Eradicating poverty is an indispensable requirement! Yes, but set these ideals beside the plain fact that we all daily prefer other values. Every time we buy a Christmas gift for a wife or husband, or go to a symphony concert, or give a college education to a child, or drive a late model car home, or turn on the air conditioner, we spend money that might have helped to eradicate poverty. We mostly choose to do things we value more than feeding the hungry.

An ethicist may reply, yes, that is the fact of the matter. But no normative ought follows from the description of this behavior. We ought not to behave so. But such widespread behavior, engaged in almost universally by persons who regard themselves as being ethical, including readers of this article, is strong evidence that we in fact not only have these norms but think we ought to have them. To be sure, we also think that charity is appropriate, and we censure those who are wholly insensitive to the plight of others. But we place decisions here on a scale of degree, and we do not feel guilty about all these other values we pursue, while yet some people somewhere on earth are starving.

If one were to advocate always feeding the hungry first, doing nothing else until no one in the world is hungry, this would paralyze civilization. People would not have invented writing, or smelted iron, or written music, or invented airplanes. Plato would not have written his dialogues, or Aquinas the *Summa Theologica;* Edison would not have discovered the electric light bulb or Einstein the theory of relativity. We both do and ought to devote ourselves to various worthy causes, while yet persons in our own communities and elsewhere go hungry.

A few of these activities redound subsequently to help the poor, but the possible feedback to alleviating poverty cannot be the sole justification of advancing these multiple cultural values. Let us remember this when we ask whether saving natural values might sometimes take precedence. Our moral systems in fact do not teach us to feed the poor first. The Ten Commandments do not say that; the Golden Rule does not; Kant did not say that; nor does the utilitarian greatest good for the greatest number imply that. Eradicating poverty may be indispensable but not always prior to all other cultural values. It may not always be prior to conserving natural values either.

CHOOSING FOR PEOPLE TO DIE

But food is absolutely vital. "Thou shalt not kill" is one of the commandments. Next to the evil of taking life is taking the sustenance for life. Is not saving nature, thereby preventing hunting, harvesting, or development by those who need the produce of that land to put food in their mouths, almost like killing? Surely one ought not to choose for someone else to die, an innocent who is only trying to eat; everyone has a right to life. To fence out the hungry is choosing that people will die. That can't be right.

Or can it? In broader social policy we make many decisions that cause people to die. When in 1988 we increased the national speed limit on rural Interstate highways from 55 to 65 miles per hour, we chose for 400 persons to die each year.[4] We decide against hiring more police, though if we did some murders

would be avoided. The city council spends that money on a new art museum, or to give the schoolteachers a raise. Congress decides not to pass a national health care program that would subsidize medical insurance for some now uninsured, who cannot otherwise afford it; and some such persons will, in result, fail to get timely medical care and die of preventable diseases.

We may decide to leave existing air pollution standards in place because it is expensive for industry to install new scrubbers, even though there is statistical evidence that a certain number of persons will contract diseases and die prematurely. All money budgeted for the National Endowment for the Humanities, and almost all that budgeted for the National Science Foundation, could be spent to prevent the deaths of babies that die from malnutrition. We do not know exactly who will die, but we know that some will; we often have reasonable estimates how many. The situation would be similar, should we choose to save nature rather than to feed people.

U.S. soldiers go abroad to stabilize an African nation, from which starving refugees are fleeing, and we feel good about it. All those unfortunate people cannot come here, but at least we can go there and help. All this masks, however, how we really choose to fight others rather than to feed them. The developed countries spend as much on military power in a year as the poorest two billion people on Earth earn in total income. The developed countries in 1990 provided 56 billion dollars in economic aid to the poorer countries but they also sold 36 billion dollars worth of arms to them. At a cost of less than half their military expenditures, the developing countries could provide a package of basic health care services and clinical care that would save 10 million lives a year. World military spending in 1992 exceeded 600 billion dollars. U.S. military spending accounted for nearly half this amount, yet in the United States one person in seven lives below the poverty line and over 37 million people lack any form of health care coverage.[5] These are choices that cause people to die, both abroad and at home.

But such spending, a moralist critic will object, is wrong. This only reports what people do decide, not what they ought to decide. Yes, but few are going to argue that we ought to spend nothing on military defense until all the poor are fed, clothed, and housed. We believe that many of the values achieved in the United States, which place us among the wealthier nations, are worth protecting, even while others starve. Europeans and others will give similar arguments. Say if you like that this only puts our self-interest over theirs, but in fact we all do act to protect what we value, even if this decision results in death for those beyond our borders. That seems to mean that a majority of citizens think such decisions are right.

Wealthy and poverty-stricken nations alike put up borders across which the poor are forbidden to pass. Rich nations will not let them in; their own governments will not let them out. We may have misgivings about this on both sides, but if we believe in immigration laws at all, we, on the richer side of the border, think that protecting our lifestyle counts more than their betterment, even if they just want to be better fed. If we let anyone who pleased enter the United States, and gave them free passage, hundreds of millions would come. Already 30 percent of our population growth is by immigration, legal and illegal. Sooner or later we must fence them out, or face the loss of prosperity that we value. We may not think this is always right, but when one faces the escalating numbers that would swamp the United States, it is hard not to conclude that it is sometimes right. Admitting refugees is humane, but it lets such persons flee their own national problems and does not contribute to any longterm solutions in the nations from which they emigrate. Meanwhile, people die as a result of such decisions.

Some of these choices address the question whether we ought to save nature if this causes people to die. Inside our U.S. boundaries, we have a welfare system, refusing to let anyone starve. Fortunately, we are wealthy enough to afford this as well as nature conservation. But if it came to this, we would think it wrong-headed to put animals (or art, or well-paid teachers) over starving people. Does that not show that, as domestic policy, we take care of our own? We feed people first—or at least second, after military defence. Yet we let foreigners die, when we are not willing to open our five hundred wilderness areas, nearly 100 million acres, to Cubans and Ethiopians.

HUNGER AND SOCIAL JUSTICE

The welfare concept introduces another possibility, that the wealthy should be taxed to feed the poor. We should do that first, rather than cut into much else that we treasure, possibly losing our wildlife, or wilderness areas, or giving up art, or underpaying the teachers. In fact, there is a way greatly to relieve this tragedy, could there be a just distribution of the goods of culture, now often so inequitably distributed. Few persons would need to go without enough if we could use the produce of the already domesticated landscape justly and charitably. It is better to try to fix this problem where it arises, within society, than to try to enlarge the sphere of society by the sacrifice of remnant natural values, by, say, opening up the wilderness areas to settlement. Indeed, the latter only postpones the problem.

Peoples in the South (a code word for the lesser developed countries, or the poor) complain about the overconsumption of peoples in the North (the industrial rich), often legitimately so. But Brazil has within its own boundaries the most skewed income distribution in the world. The U.S. ratio between personal income for the top 20 percent of people to the bottom 20 percent is 9 to 1; the ratio in Brazil is 26 to 1. Just one percent of Brazilians control 45 percent of the agricultural land. The biggest 20 landowners own more land between them than the 3.3 million smallest farmers. With the Amazon still largely undeveloped, there is already more arable land per person in Brazil than in the United States. Much land is held for speculation; 330 million hectares of farm land, an area larger than India, is lying idle. The top 10 percent of Brazilians spend 51 percent of the national income.[6] This anthropocentric inequity ought to be put "at the center of concern" when we decide about saving nature versus feeding people.

Save the Amazon! No! The howler monkeys and toucans may delight tourists, but we ought not save them if people need to eat. Such either-or choices mask how marginalized peoples are forced onto marginal lands; and those lands become easily stressed, both because the lands are by nature marginal for agriculture, range, and life support, and also because by human nature marginalized peoples find it difficult to plan for the long-range. They are caught up in meeting their immediate needs; their stress forces them to stress a fragile landscape.

Prime agricultural or residential lands can also be stressed to produce more, because there is a growing population to feed, or to grow an export crop, because there is an international debt to pay. Prime agricultural lands in southern Brazil, formerly used for growing food and worked by tenants who lived on these lands and ate their produce, as well as sent food into the cities, have been converted to growing coffee as an export crop, using mechanized farming, to help pay Brazil's massive debt, contracted by a military government since overthrown. Peoples forced off these lands were resettled in the Amazon basin, aided by development schemes fostered by the military government, resettled on lands really not suitable for agriculture. The integrity of the Amazon, to say nothing of the integrity of these peoples, is being sacrificed to cover for misguided loans. Meanwhile the wealthy in Brazil pay little or no income tax that might be used for such loan repayment.

The world is full enough of societies that have squandered their resources, inequitably distributed wealth, degraded their landscapes, and who will be tempted to jeopardize what natural values remain as an alternative to solving hard social problems. The decision about social welfare, poor people over nature, usually lies in the context of another decision, often a tacit one, to protect vested interests, wealthy people over poor people, wealthy people who have exploited nature already, ready to exploit anything they can. At this point in our logic, en route to any conclusion such as let-people-starve, we regularly reach an if-then, go-to decision point, where before we face the people-over-nature choice we have to reaffirm or let stand the wealthy-over-poor choice.

South Africa is seeking an ethic of ecojustice enabling five million privileged whites and twenty-nine million exploited blacks (as well as several million underprivileged "Coloureds") to live in harmony on their marvelously rich but often fragile landscape.[7] Whites earn nearly ten times the per capita income of blacks. White farmers, 50,000 of them, own 70 percent of farmland; 700,000 black farmers own 13 percent of the land (17% other). Black ownership of land was long severely restricted by law. Forced relocations of blacks and black birth rates have combined to give the homelands, small areas carved out within the South African nation, an extremely high-average population density. When ownership patterns in the homelands are combined with those in the rest of the nation, land ownership is as skewed as anywhere on Earth. Compounding the problem is that the black population is growing, and is already more than ten times what it was before the Europeans came.

The land health is poor. South African farmers lose twenty tons of topsoil to produce one ton of crops. Water resources are running out; the limited wetlands in an essentially arid nation are exploited for development; water is polluted by unregulated industry. Natal, one of the nation's greenest and most glorious areas, is especially troubled with polluted winds. Everywhere, herbicides float downwind with adverse human, vegetative, and wildlife effects on nontarget organisms.

With an abundance of coal, South Africa generates 60 percent of the electricity on the African continent, sold at some of the cheapest rates in the world, although less than a third of South Africans have electricity. The Eskom coal-burning power plants in the Transvaal are the worst offenders in air pollution, leaving the high veld as polluted as was Eastern Germany, also threatening an area producing 50 percent of South Africa's timber industry and 50 percent of the nation's high potential agricultural soils. As a result of all this, many blacks go poorly nourished; some, in weakened condition, catch diseases and die.

What is the solution? South Africa also has some of the finest wildlife conservation reserves in Africa.

Some are public; some are private. They are visited mostly by white tourists, often from abroad. One hears the cry that conserving elitist reserves, in which the wealthy enjoy watching lions and wildebeest, cannot be justified where poor blacks are starving. What South Africa needs is development, not conservation. In an industry-financed study, Brian Huntley, Roy Siegfried, and Clem Sunter conclude: "What is needed is a much larger cake, not a sudden change in the way it is cut."[8] One way to get a bigger cake would be to take over the lands presently held as wildlife reserves.

But more cake, just as unequally cut, is not the right solution in a nation that already stresses the carrying capacity of its landscape. Laissez-faire capitalists propose growth so that every one can become more prosperous, oblivious to the obvious fact that even the present South African relationship to the landscape is neither sustainable not healthy. They seem humane; they do not want anyone to starve. The rhetoric, and even the intent, is laudable. At the same time, they want growth because this will avoid redistribution of wealth. The result, under the rubric of feeding people versus saving nature, is in fact favoring the wealthy over the poor.

What is happening is that an unjust lack of sharing between whites and blacks is destroying the green. It would be foolish for all, even for white South Africans acting in their own self-interest, further to jeopardize environmental health, rather than to look first and resolutely to solving their social problems. It would not really be right, if South Africans were to open their magnificent wildlife reserves, seemingly in the interests of the poor, while the cake remains as inequitably divided as ever. Fortunately, many South Africans have realized the deeper imperative, and the recent historic election there, and efforts toward a new constitution, promise deep social changes. This, in turn, will make possible a more intelligent conservation of natural values.[9]

In the more fortunate nations, we may distribute wealth more equitably, perhaps through taxes or minimum wage laws, or by labor unions, or educational opportunities, and we do have in place the welfare

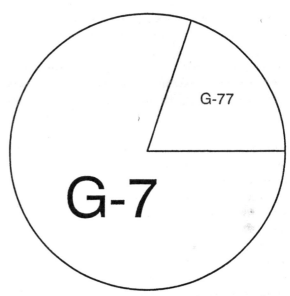

Figure 1. Proportionate Production and Consumption Among Nations

systems referred to earlier, refusing to let anyone starve. But lest we seem too righteous, we also recall that we have such policies only domestically. The international picture puts this in a different light. There are two major blocs, the G-7 nations (the Group of 7, the big nations of North America, Europe, and Japan, "the North"), and the G-77 nations, once 77 but now including some 128 lesser developed nations, often south of the industrial north. The G-7 nations hold about one fifth of the world's five billion persons, and they produce and consume about four fifths of all goods and services. The G-77 nations, with four fifths of the world's people, produce and consume one fifth. (See Figure 1.) For every person added to the population of the North, twenty are added in the South. For every dollar of economic growth per person in the South, 20 dollars accrue in the North.[10]

The distribution problem is complex. Earth's natural resources are unevenly distributed by nature. Diverse societies have often taken different directions of development; they have different governments, ideologies, and religions; they have made dif-

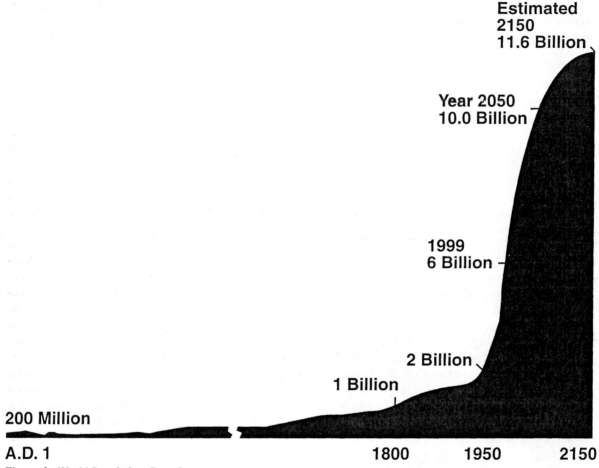

Figure 2. World Population Growth

ferent social choices, valued material prosperity differently. Typically, where there is agricultural and industrial development, people think of this as impressive achievement. Pies have to be produced before they can be divided, and who has produced this pie? Who deserves the pie? People ought to get what they earn. Fairness nowhere commands rewarding all parties equally; justice is giving each his or her due. We treat equals equally; we treat unequals equitably, and that typically means unequal treatment proportionately to merit. There is nothing evidently unfair in the pie diagram, not at least until we have inquired about earnings. Some distribution patterns reflect achievement. Not all of the asymmetrical distribution is a result of social injustice.

Meanwhile, it is difficult to look at a distribution chart and think that something is unfair. Is some of the richness on one side related to the poverty on the other? Regularly, the poor come off poorly when they bargain with the rich; and wealth that originates as impressive achievement can further accumulate through exploitation. Certainly many of the hungry people have worked just as hard as many of the rich.

Some will say that what the poorer nations need to do is to imitate the productive people. Unproductive people need to learn how to make more pies. Then they can feed themselves. Those in the G-7 nations who emphasize the earnings model tend to recommend to the G-77 nations that they produce more, often offering to help them produce by investments which can also be productive for the G-7 nations. Those in the G-77 nations do indeed wish to produce, but they also see the exploitation and realize that the problem is sharing as well as producing. Meanwhile the growth graphs caution us that producing can be as much part of the problem as part of the solution. One way to think of the circular pie chart is that this is planet Earth, and we do not have any way of producing a bigger planet. We could, though, feed more people by sacrificing more nature.

Meanwhile too, any such decisions take place inside this 1/5-gets-4/5ths, 4/5ths-gets-1/5 picture. So it is not just the Brazilians and the South Africans, but all of us in the United States, Europe, and Japan as well that have to face an if-then, go-to decision point, reaffirming and or letting stand the wealthy-over-poor division of the Earth's pie that we enjoy. This is what stings when we see the bumper sticker ethical injunction: "Live simply that others may simply live."

ESCALATING HUMAN POPULATIONS

Consider human population growth. (See Figure 2.) Not only have the numbers of persons grown, their expectations have grown, so that we must superimpose one exploding curve on top of another. A superficial reading of such a graph is that humans really start winning big in the twentieth century. There are lots of them, and they want, and many get, lots of things. If one is a moral humanist, this can seem a good thing. Wouldn't it be marvelous if all could get what they want, and none hunger and thirst any more?

But when we come to our senses, we realize that this kind of winning, if it keeps on escalating, is really losing. Humans will lose, and nature will be destroyed as well. Cultures have become consumptive, with ever-escalating insatiable desires, overlaid on ever-escalating population growth. Culture does not know how to say "Enough!" and that is not satisfactory. Starkly put, the growth of culture has become cancerous. That is hardly a metaphor, for a cancer is essentially an explosion of unregulated growth. Feeding people always seems humane, but, when we face up to what is really going on, by just feeding people, without attention to the larger social results, we could be feeding a kind of cancer.

One can say that where there is a hungry mouth, one should do what it takes to get food into it. But when there are two mouths there the next day, and four the day after that, and sixteen the day after that, one needs a more complex answer. The population of Egypt was less than 3 million for over five millennia, fluctuating between 1.5 to 2.5 million, even when Napoléon went there in the early 1800s. Today the population of Egypt is about 55 million. Egypt has to import more than half its food. The effects on nature, both on land health and on wildlife, have been adversely proportional.

If, in this picture, we look at individual persons, caught up in this uncontrolled growth, and if we try to save nature, some persons will go hungry. Surely, that is a bad thing. Would anyone want to say that such persons ought not to sacrifice nature, if needs be, to alleviate such harm as best they can? From their perspective, they are only doing what humans have always done, making a resourceful use of nature to meet their own needs. Isn't that a good thing anymore? Such persons are doomed, unless they can capture natural values.

But here we face a time-bound truth, in which too much of a good thing becomes a bad thing. We have to figure in where such persons are located on the population curve, and realize that a good thing when human numbers are manageable is no longer a good thing when such a person is really another cell of cancerous growth. That sounds cruel, and it is tragic, but it does not cease to be true for these reasons. For a couple to have two children may be a blessing; but the tenth child is a tragedy. When the child comes, one has to be as humane as possible, but one will only be making the best of a tragic situation, and if the tenth child is reared, and has ten children in turn, that will only multiply the tragedy. The quality of human lives deteriorates; the poor get poorer. Natural resources are further stressed; ecosystem health and integrity degenerate; and this compounds the losses again—a lose-lose situation. In a social system misfitted to its landscape, one's wins can only be temporary in a losing human ecology.

Even if there were an equitable distribution of wealth, human population cannot go on escalating without people becoming all equally poor. Of the 90 million new people who will come on board planet Earth this year, 85 million will appear in the Third World, the countries least able to support such population growth. At the same time, each North American will consume 200 times as much energy, and many other resources. The 5 million new people in the industrial countries will put as much strain on the environment as the 85 million new poor. There are three problems: overpopulation, overconsumption, and underdistribution. Sacrificing nature for development does not solve any of these problems, none at all. It only brings further loss. The poor, after a meal for a day or two, perhaps a decade or two, are soon hungry all over again, only now poorer still because their natural wealth is also gone.

To say that we ought always to feed the poor first commits a good-better-best fallacy. If a little is good, more must be better, most is best. If feeding some humans is good, feeding more is better. And more. And more! Feeding all of them is best? That sounds right. We can hardly bring ourselves to say that anyone ought to starve. But we reach a point of diminishing returns, when the goods put at threat lead us to wonder.

ENDANGERED NATURAL VALUES

Natural values are endangered at every scale: global, regional, and local, at levels of ecosystems, species, organisms, populations, fauna and flora, terrestrial and marine, charismatic megafauna down to mollusks and beetles. This is true in both developed and developing nations, though we have under discussion here places where poverty threatens biodiversity.

Humans now control 40 percent of the planet's land-based primary net productivity, that is, the basic plant growth that captures the energy on which everything else depends.[11] If the human population doubles again, the capture will rise to 60 to 80 percent, and little habitat will remain for natural forms of life that cannot be accommodated after we have put people first. Humans do not use the lands they have domesticated effectively. A World Bank study found that 35 percent of the Earth's land has now become degraded.[12] Daniel Hillel, in a soils study, concludes, "Present yields are extremely low in many of the developing countries, and as they can be boosted substantially and rapidly, there should be no need to reclaim new land and to encroach further upon natural habitats."[13]

Africa is a case in point, and Madagascar epitomizes Africa's future. Its fauna and flora evolved independently from the mainland continent; there are 30 primates, all lemurs; the reptiles and amphibians are 90 percent endemic, including two thirds of all the chameleons of the world; and plant species, of which 80 percent are endemic, including a thousand kinds of orchids. Humans came there about 1,500 years ago and lived with the fauna and flora more or less intact until this century. Now an escalating population of impoverished Malagasy people rely heavily on slash-and-burn agriculture, and the forest cover is one third of the original (27.6 million acres to 9.4 million acres), most of the loss occurring since 1950.[14] Madagascar is the most eroded nation on Earth, and little or none of the fauna and flora is safely conserved. Population is expanding at 3.2 percent a year; remaining forest is shrinking at 3 percent, almost all to provide for the expanding population. Are we to say that none ought to be conserved until after no person is hungry?

Tigers are sliding toward extinction. Populations have declined 95 percent in this century; the two main factors are loss of habitat and a ferocious black market in bones and other body parts used in traditional medicine and folklore in China, Taiwan, and

Korea, uses that are given no medical credence. Ranthambhore National Park in Rajasthan, India, is a tiger sanctuary; there were 40 tigers during the late 1980s, reduced in a few years by human pressures—illicit cattle grazing and poaching—to 20 to 25 tigers today. There are 200,000 Indians within three miles of the core of the park—more than double the population when the park was launched, 21 years ago. Most depend on wood from the 150 square miles of park to cook their food. They graze in and around the park some 150,000 head of scrawny cattle, buffalo, goats, and camels. The cattle impoverish habitat and carry diseases to the ungulates that are the tiger's prey base. In May 1993, a young tigress gave birth to four cubs; that month 316 babies were born in the villages surrounding the park.[15]

The tigers may be doomed, but ought they to be? Consider, for instance, that there are minimal reforestation efforts, or that cattle dung can be used for fuel with much greater efficiency than is being done, or that, in an experimental herd of jersey and holstein cattle there, the yield of milk increased ten times that of the gaunt, freeranging local cattle, and that a small group of dairy producers has increased milk production 1,000 percent in just 3 years. In some moods we may insist that people are more important than tigers. But in other moods these majestic animals seem the casualties of human inabilities to manage themselves and their resources intelligently, a tragic story that leaves us wondering whether the tigers should always lose and the people win.

WHEN NATURE COMES FIRST

Ought we to save nature if this results in people going hungry? In people dying? Regrettably, sometimes, the answer is yes. In 20 years Africa's black rhinoceros population declined from 65,000 to 2,500, a loss of 97 percent; the species faces imminent extinction. Again, as with the tigers, there has been loss of habitat caused by human population growth, an important and indirect cause; but the primary direct cause is poaching, this time for horns. People cannot eat horns; but they can buy food with the money from selling them. Zimbabwe has a hard-line shoot-to-kill policy for poachers, and over 150 poachers have been killed.[16]

So Zimbabweans do not always put people first; they are willing to kill some, and to let others to go hungry rather than sacrifice the rhino. If we always put people first, there will be no rhinos at all. Always too, we must guard against inhumanity, and take care, so far as we can, that poachers have other alternatives for overcoming their poverty. Still, if it comes to this, the Zimbabwean policy is right. Given the fact that rhinos have been so precipitously reduced, given that the Zimbabwean population is escalating (the average married woman there desires to have six children),[17] one ought to put the black rhino as a species first, even if this costs human lives.

But the poachers are doing something illegal. What about ordinary people, who are not breaking any laws? The sensitive moralist may object that, even when the multiple causal factors are known, and lamented, when it comes to dealing with individual persons caught up in these social forces, we should factor out overpopulation, overconsumption, and maldistribution, none of which are the fault of the particular persons who may wish to develop their lands. "I did not ask to be born; I am poor, not overconsuming; I am not the cause but rather the victim of the inequitable distribution of wealth." Surely there still remains for such an innocent person a right to use whatever natural resources one has available, as best one can, under the exigencies of one's particular life, set though this is in these unfortunate circumstances. "I only want enough to eat, is that not my right?"

Human rights must include, if anything at all, the right to subsistence. So even if particular persons are located at the wrong point on the global growth graph, even if they are willy-nilly part of a cancerous and consumptive society, even if there is some better social solution than the wrong one that is in fact happening, have they not a right that will override the conservation of natural value? Will it not just be a further wrong to them to deprive them of their right to what little they have? Can basic human rights ever be overridden by a society that wants to do better by conserving natural value?

This requires some weighing of the endangered natural values. Consider the tropical forests. There is more richness there than in other regions of the planet—half of all known species. In South America, for example, there are one fifth of the planet's species of terrestrial mammals (800 species); there are one third of the planet's flowering plants.[18] The peak of global plant diversity is in the three Andean countries of Columbia, Ecuador, and Peru, where over 40,000 species occur on just 2 percent of the world's land surface.[19] But population growth in South America has been as high as anywhere in the world,[20] and people are flowing into the forests, often crowded off other lands.

What about these hungry people? Consider first people who are not now there but might move there. This is not good agricultural soil, and such would-be settlers are likely to find only a short-term bargain, a long-term loss. Consider the people who already live there. If they are indigenous peoples, and wish to continue to live as they have already for hundreds and even thousands of years, there will be no threat to the forest. If they are cabaclos (of mixed European and native races), they can also continue the lifestyles known for hundreds of years, without serious destruction of the forests. Such peoples may continue the opportunities that they have long had. Nothing is taken away from them. They have been reasonably well fed, though often poor.

Can these peoples modernize? Can they multiply? Ought there to be a policy of feeding first all the children they bear, sacrificing nature as we must to accomplish this goal? Modern medicine and technology have enabled them to multiply, curing childhood diseases and providing better nutrition, even if these peoples often remain at thresholds of poverty. Do not such people have the right to develop? A first answer is that they do, but with the qualification that all rights are not absolute, some are weaker, some stronger, and the exercise of any right has to be balanced against values destroyed in the exercise of that right.

The qualification brings a second answer. If one concludes that the natural values at stake are quite high, and that the opportunities for development are low, because the envisioned development is inadvisable, then a possible answer is: No, there will be no development of these reserved areas, even if people there remain in the relative poverty of many centuries, or even if, with escalating populations, they become more poor. We are not always obligated to cover human mistakes with the sacrifice of natural values.

Again, one ought to be as humane as possible. Perhaps there can be development elsewhere, to which persons in the escalating population can be facilitated to move, if they wish. Indeed, this often happens, as such persons flee to the cities, though they often only encounter further poverty there, owing to the inequitable distribution of resources which we have lamented. If they remain in these areas of high biological diversity, they must stay under the traditional lifestyles of their present and past circumstances.

Does this violate human rights? Anywhere that there is legal zoning, persons are told what they may and may not do, in order to protect various social and natural values. Land ownership is limited ("imperfect," as lawyers term it) when the rights of use conflict with the rights of other persons. One's rights are constrained by the harm one does to others, and we legislate to enforce this (under what lawyers call "police power"). Environmental policy may and ought to regulate the harms that people do on the lands on which they live ("policing"), and it is perfectly appropriate to set aside conservation reserves to protect the cultural, ecological, scientific, economic, historical, aesthetic, religious, and other values people have at stake here, as well as for values that the fauna and flora have intrinsically in themselves. Indeed, unless there is such reserving of natural areas, counterbalancing the high pressures for development, there will be almost no conservation at all. Every person on Earth is told that he or she cannot develop some areas.

Persons are not told that they must starve, but they are told that they cannot save themselves from starving by sacrificing the nature set aside in reserves—not at least beyond the traditional kinds of uses that did leave the biodiversity on the landscape. If one is already residing in a location where development is constrained, this may seem unfair, and the invitation to move elsewhere a forced relocation. Relocation may be difficult proportionately to how vigorously the prevailing inequitable distribution of wealth is enforced elsewhere.

Human rights to development, even by those who are poor, though they are to be taken quite seriously, are not everywhere absolute, but have to be weighed against the other values at stake. An individual sees at a local scale; the farmer wants only to plant crops on the now forested land. But environmental ethics sees that the actions of individuals cumulate and produce larger scale changes that go on over the heads of these individuals. This ethic will regularly be constraining individuals in the interest of some larger ecological and social goods. That will regularly seem cruel, unfair to the individual caught in such constraints. This is the tragedy of the commons; individuals cannot see far enough ahead, under the pressures of the moment, to operate at intelligent ecological scales. Social policy must be set synoptically. This invokes both ecology and ethics, and blends them, if we are to respect life at all relevant scales.

These poor may not have so much a right to develop in any way they please, as a right to a more equitable distribution of the goods of the Earth that we, the wealthy, think we absolutely own.

Our traditional focus on individuals, and their rights, can blind us to how the mistakes (as well as the wisdom) of the parents can curse (and bless) the children, as the Ten Commandments put it, how "the iniquity of the fathers is visited upon the children to the third and fourth generation" (cf. Exodus 20.5). All this has a deeply tragic dimension, made worse by the coupling of human foibles with ecological realities. We have little reason to think that misguided compassion that puts food into every hungry mouth, be the consequences whatever they may, will relieve the tragedy. We also have no reason to think that the problem will be solved with-

out wise compassion, balancing a love for persons and a love for nature.

Ought we to feed people first, and save nature last? We never face so simple a question. The practical question is more complex.

> If persons widely demonstrate that they value many other worthwhile things over feeding the hungry (Christmas gifts, college educations, symphony concerts),
>
> and if developed countries, to protect what they value, post national boundaries across which the poor may not pass (immigration laws),
>
> and if there is unequal and unjust distribution of wealth, and if just redistribution to alleviate poverty is refused, and if charitable redistribution of justified unequal distribution of wealth is refused,
>
> and if one fifth of the world continues to consume four fifths of the production of goods and four fifths consumes one fifth,
>
> and if escalating birthrates continue so that there are no real gains in alleviating poverty, only larger numbers of poor in the next generation,
>
> and if low productivity on domesticated lands continues, and if the natural lands to be sacrificed are likely to be low in productivity,
>
> and if significant natural values are at stake, including extinctions of species,

then one ought not always to feed people first, but rather one ought sometimes to save nature.

Many of the "ands" in this conjunction can be replaced with "ors" and the statement will remain true, though we cannot say outside of particular contexts how many. The logic is not so much that of implication as of the weighing up of values and disvalues, natural and human, and of human rights and wrongs, past, present, and future.

Some will protest that this risks becoming misanthropic and morally callous. The Ten Commandments order us not to kill, and saving nature can never justify what amounts to killing people. Yes, but there is another kind of killing here, one not envisioned at Sinai, where humans are superkilling species. Extinction kills forms (*species*)—not just individuals; it kills collectively, not just distributively. Killing a natural kind is the death of birth, not just of an individual life. The historical lineage is stopped forever. Preceding the Ten Commandments is the Noah myth, when nature was primordially put at peril as great as the actual threat today. There, God seems more concerned about species than about the humans who had then gone so far astray. In the covenant re-established with humans on the promised Earth, the beasts are specifically included. "Keep them alive with you . . . according to their kinds" (Genesis 6.19–20). There is something ungodly about an ethic by which the late-coming *Homo sapiens* arrogantly regards the welfare of one's own species as absolute, with the welfare of all the other five million species sacrificed to that. The commandment not to kill is as old as Cain and Abel, but the most archaic commandment of all is the divine, "Let the earth bring forth" (Genesis 1). Stopping that genesis is the most destructive event possible, and we humans have no right to do that. Saving nature is not always morally naive; it can deepen our understanding of the human place in the scheme of things entire, and of our duties on this majestic home planet.

NOTES

1. *Rio Declaration on Environment and Development,* Principle I, UNCED document A/CONF. 151/26, vol. 1, pp. 15–25.

2. *Rio Declaration,* Principle 4.

3. *Rio Declaration,* Principle 5.

4. Insurance Institute for Highway Safety (Arlington, Virginia), *Status Report,* vol. 29 (no. 10, September 10, 1994):3

5. Ruth Leger Sivard, *World Military and Social Expenditures,* 15th ed., (Washington, DC: World Priorities, Inc., 1993).

6. Jonathan Power, 1992. "Despite Its Gifts, Brazil Is a Basket Case," *The Miami Herald,* June 22, p. 10A.

7. The empirical data below are in: Brian Huntley, Roy Siegfried, and Clem Sunter, *South African Environments into the 21st Century* (Cape Town: Human and Rousseau, Ltd, and Tafelberg Publishers Ltd., 1989); Rob Preston-Whyte and Graham House, eds., *Rotating the Cube: Environmental Strategies for the 1990s* (Durban: Department of Geographical and Environmental Sciences and Indicator Project South Africa, University of Natal, 1990); and Alan B. Durning, *Apartheid's Environmental Toll* (Washington, DC: Worldwatch Institute, 1990).

8. Huntley, Siegfried, and Sunter, p. 85.

9. Mamphela Ramphele, ed., *Restoring the Land: Environment and Change in Post-Apartheid South Africa* (London: Panos Publications, 1991).

10. The pie chart summarizes data in the *World Development Report 1991* (New York: Oxford University Press, 1991).

11. Peter M. Vitousek, Paul R. Ehrlich, Anne H. Ehrlich, and Pamela A. Matson, "Human Appropriation of the Products of Biosynthesis," *BioScience* 36(1986): 368–373.

12. Robert Goodland, "The Case That the World Has Reached Limits," pp. 3–22 in Robert Goodland, Herman E. Daly, and Salah El Serafy, eds., *Population, Technology, and Lifestyle* (Washington, DC: Island Press, 1992).

13. Daniel Hillel, *Out of the Earth* (New York: Free Press, Macmillan, 1991), p. 279.

14. E. O. Wilson, *The Diversity of Life* (Cambridge, MA: Harvard University Press, 1992), p. 267; Alison Jolly, *A World Like Our Own: Man and Nature in Madagascar* (New Haven: Yale University Press, 1980).

15. Geoffrey C. Ward, "The People and the Tiger," *Audubon* 96 (no. 4, July–August 1994): 62–69.

16. Joel Berger and Carol Cunningham, "Active Intervention and Conservation: Africa's Pachyderm Problem," *Science* 263(1994): 1241–1242.

17. John Bongaarts, "Population Policy Options in the Developing World," *Science* 263(1994): 771–776.

18. Michael A. Mares, "Conservation in South America: Problems, Consequences, and Solutions," *Science* 233(1986): 734–739.

19. Wilson, *The Diversity of Life,* p. 197.

20. Ansley J. Coale, "Recent Trends in Fertility in the Less Developed Countries," *Science* 221(1983): 828–832.

Natural Enemies: An Anatomy of Environmental Conflict

David Schmidtz

For those who live in modern cities, nature is a haven, a refuge from an urban jungle. The frustrations of the city make it easy to feel nostalgia for a simple life that never was: days spent hiking in the Grand Canyon, nights spent curled up by the fireplace after a hot shower and something nice from the refrigerator.

But nature is not a national park, as people who make their living in its midst are aware. My ancestors emigrated from Germany to North America in the 1850's, settling in Minnesota and Saskatchewan. Like most settlers, they had mixed feelings about nature.[1] Beautiful it may have been, but it was not the innocuous beauty that city dwellers find in art galleries. Nature was wild, literally. It could be kind. It could be indifferent. Or it could be an appalling enemy, a promise of hard life and sudden death. My mother lost a brother to diphtheria. A mile down the road, her uncle watched his whole family, a wife and three children, die of diphtheria in the space of three days. She grew up on a farm that got virtually no rain for a stretch of ten years.[2] She said, "You'd see black clouds boiling on the horizon. If you didn't know better you'd think the rain was finally coming. But it wasn't rain. When you got up in the morning everything would be covered by a carpet of dust. Or grasshoppers." For many of the world's people today, nature remains as it was for my ancestors—red in tooth and claw. It comes in the night to kill their children.[3] No hot shower. No refrigerator.

Western civilization has given me the luxury of being an environmentalist. I am insulated against nature, and this insulation gives me the luxury of no longer needing to see nature as a threat. Unfortunately, not everyone is so insulated, and thus not everyone is in a position to join me in treating wilderness preservation as an urgent priority. Therein lies a source of conflict, a kind of conflict that is bad for the environment and that we cannot resolve unless we understand that it is not like other kinds of conflict.

In the following sections, I describe three kinds of environmental conflict, concentrating on a subtle but crucial contrast between conflicting values and conflicting priorities.[4] I discuss what it takes to avoid, manage, and resolve these kinds of environmental conflict. I discuss the contingent connection between environmental conflict resolution and environmental justice. Finally, I argue that economics can help us understand how to resolve environmental conflict. While we need not (and should not) attempt to reduce all values to economic values, we do need to understand that there is a certain logic to the working of economic systems. To ignore the logic of human economy is to ignore the logic of human ecology and thus to ignore the logic of any ecology in which humans play a role. Anyone who truly cares about the environment would not do that.

THREE KINDS OF ENVIRONMENTAL CONFLICT

I will treat as basic a kind of conflict in which people simply find themselves in each other's way. I will refer to this as *conflict in use*. Conflict in use manifests itself in traffic jams, figuratively or literally. A pattern of overall use results in congestion, such that people trying to use a resource end up interfering with each other.[5] Conflict in use is resolved by institutions that literally or figuratively direct traffic, such as a system of property rights that lets

David Schmidtz, "Natural Enemies," *Environmental Ethics* 22 (2000): 379–408. Reprinted with permission of the author and the journal. Revised for this volume.

people know who has the right of way when their intentions put them on a collision course. Such institutions help people avoid, manage, and resolve conflict when they facilitate orderly use of a common resource, when they facilitate orderly removal of resources from the commons, and when they help people cope with *externalities,* including new externalities that emerge as property regimes evolve.[6] Property regimes can be a kind of public good if and when they solve commons problems and induce overall patterns of sustainable use.

Some environmental conflicts, though, cannot be addressed merely by settling on a system of property rights. In particular, some of our most serious conflicts concern what should be property in the first place. Thus, there is a second kind of conflict that ultimately is a matter of conflicting *values.* Should Maasai tribes be allowed to own and sell elephants as if elephants were pieces of property? One thing to be said on behalf of conferring such rights is that it would give the Maasai reason to protect elephants against poachers.[7] However, some would say turning elephants into a commodity is another way of destroying them. Even when it does not literally destroy the elephants, it still destroys what elephants stand for in the minds of those who cherish the idea of nature wild and free. This is not a conflict we can resolve by deciding who owns the resource. The parties disagree on whether anyone has the right to regard elephants as a resource in the first place.

Environmentalists sometimes distinguish between anthropocentric (i.e., human-centered) and biocentric (i.e., nature-centered) orientations toward nature. *Conservationists* care about nature in an anthropocentric way, saying nature should be used wisely. *Preservationists* care about nature in a biocentric way, saying that, although we (like any living creature) cannot avoid using nature, nature nevertheless has moral standing independent of its utility for humans.[8] A preservationist will say some ecosystems or species should be left to evolve according to their own lights, as free as possible from human interference. We should not think of wilderness as a mere resource. Wilderness commands reverence;

mere resources do not. We may call this clash a case of contested commodification. It exemplifies the second kind of conflict: conflict in values.

There is a third kind of environmental conflict: conflicting *priorities.* We misunderstand this kind of conflict if we see it simply as another case of conflicting values. The difference is that people's immediate goals can be incompatible even when their values are relevantly similar. International conservation groups raise money by pledging to fight for preservationist "no use at all" policies. Sometimes, though, farmers do not join in pursuing cosmopolitan environmentalist goals because they cannot *afford* to.

This kind of conflict could occur even among people who all feel precisely the same way about where elephants should rank in our hierarchy of values. To give a crude illustration, suppose we all agree that our children outrank elephants but elephants outrank chess sets carved out of ivory. Even so, we could come into conflict when North Americans denounce hunting elephants to acquire ivory for carving chess sets, while Africans defend the practice because ivory revenues are feeding their children. Although both sides have the same values, they do not face the same cost. For one person, no elephant hunting means no ivory chess sets; for another person, no elephant hunting means no children. Subsistence farmers for whom getting enough food is a day by day proposition can have priorities that differ from ours not because their values are different but precisely because their values are the same. Thus, there is a kind of conflict that originates not so much from a difference of values as from a difference in which values people can afford to pursue under their differing circumstances.

Moreover, there is an additional problem, a feature of real-world conflict that some preservationists fail to appreciate. In parts of Africa, the dilemma for subsistence farmers is this: if they cannot commodify elephants (by selling ivory, hunting licenses, or photo safaris), then they will have to push elephants out of the way to make room for livestock or crops. In the abstract, exploiting elephants seems obviously wrong, but it stops being obvious after spending time in rural Africa, and seeing that when rural people cannot exploit elephants in some fashion, their only alternative is to convert elephant habitat into farmland.

Whether we like it or not, elephants will not survive except by sharing the land with people, which means their long-term survival depends on whether people can afford to share. Realistically, at least in parts of Africa where this kind of conflict is extreme, threatened species will have to contribute to the local economy if they are to have any hope of survival. Thus, according to Brian Child, "wildlife will survive in Africa only where it can compete financially for space. The real threat to wildlife is poverty, not poaching."[9] With equal bluntness, Norman Myers says, "In emergent Africa, you either use wildlife or lose it. If it pays its own way, some of it will survive."[10] Kreuter and Simmons conclude that, because elephants "compete directly with humans for use of fertile land, we believe elephants will continue to be eliminated unless they provide . . . direct personal benefits to the people who incur the cost of coexisting with them."[11]

And please understand: co-existing with elephants is costly. We are not talking about animals one looks at through a pair of binoculars, at a safe distance, while on vacation at a national park. Elephants are an integral part, and a dangerous part, of everyday life. Although we knew this at an intellectual level, such knowledge left us unprepared when the time came to learn it from experience. In July of 1999, we arrived at Oddballs' Camp in Botswana's Okavanga Delta in an airplane just big enough for three passengers. (The wings of the plane were reinforced with duct tape.) The airstrip was dirt. As we landed, baboons and warthogs scattered before us. The person who was to meet us was late because, while walking to the airstrip from the camp, he had to detour around a herd of Cape Buffalo, reputedly among the most dangerous animals in the world. After a fifteen minute walk through the marsh, we arrived at the campground.

That night, we slept with the sound of baboons howling in the foreground and lions roaring in the background. We were woken around 4 A.M. by what sounded like trees being shaken by a gale-force wind. I got up and found myself standing in the open air, right next to a twelve-foot elephant. The elephant had been pressing its forehead against a lala palm, whipping the tree back and forth (thereby making sound that woke us up) in order to shake down the fruit higher up. Tiring of that, the elephant had torn the whole tree out of the ground and was taking an experimental munch at the roots. (The elephant knew I was there and it may have deliberately avoided letting the tree fall on us. Some elephants are considerate in that way. Some aren't.)

Elephants rarely sleep and spend about eighty percent of their lives eating, and there usually were a couple roaming the campground. It is important to grasp that these elephants were not pets. The camp did not adopt them. There was nothing domestic about them. There was nothing cute about them. They were magnificent by day and literally breathtaking by night. They were there because despite everyone's efforts to keep elephants out of camp, the bottom line is that if an elephant takes an interest in something inside camp, it is coming in and there is nothing anyone can do to stop it. Our experience makes for a great story and an unforgettable visit, but imagine spending your whole life that way, going to bed not knowing what will be left of your crop or garden or house or children when you get up in the morning. Do you suppose the children grow up loving animals?

Again, even people who embrace environmentalist values will act contrary to those values when they cannot afford to act in accordance with them. There are times when conflict is a matter of conflicting priorities.[12]

IDEALS, COMPROMISE, AND STEWARDSHIP

To some extent a philosopher's job is to say how the world ought to be in the grand scheme of things. It is an honorable job. But where environmental ethics is a study of ideals, environmental conflict resolution is the art of compromise in a world that is not a blank canvas. Conflict mediation typically involves trying to help negotiate win-win solutions.

Sometimes the negotiation is between people who would not both win in a more perfect world. Often, though, conflicts are not clashes between good and evil. When we try to stop people from burning the rain forest, the situation may be a conflict of *values* between us and evil condominium developers burning forests for the sheer thrill of raping the planet. However, it is as likely to be a conflict of *priorities* between us and displaced farmers who just want to feed their children. If we understood each other, we might have no quarrel whatsoever with each other's values, and might well have taken each other's side if circumstances had been different. We often have no reason at all to be trying to win by making our adversary lose.

In choosing our priorities, we sometimes need to be sensitive not only to our own values but to other people's as well, sometimes even when we *do not care* about other people's values. Why? Because we cannot *decide* that people will act according to our view of what is best for Gaia. People decide for themselves. We have to ask what their values are, what their priorities are, and what could lead people with such values and priorities to act in environmentally benign ways.

The most basic principle of conflict resolution is that mediators should try to get people to focus on their *interests,* not their *positions.*[13] In other words, it is better if negotiation does not turn into a contest of wills (drawing lines in the sand, as they say) but instead revolves around the actual problem, as defined by actual benefits that might be realized if negotiation leads to agreement.

Consider what this implies for the familiar idea that we are not owners of the land so much as stewards of it. If we see ourselves as stewards, then we see ourselves as obliged to care for the land on behalf of future generations. But if we are to take our stewardship role seriously, we need to understand that honest stewardship is a commitment to environmental interests, not environmentalist positions. Commitment to interests sometimes mandates compromise on positions. It sometimes requires negoti-

ation. Sometimes, what people call values are dressed-up positions that have little to do with any real interests. We make a huge mistake if we equate what is bad for our enemies (corporations, economists, ranchers, Western patriarchy, whatever) with what is good for the environment.

Mark Sagoff says government regulations have expressive and symbolic value. I agree that "regulation expresses what we believe, what we are, what we stand for as a nation."[14] Nevertheless, we need to be careful not to endorse a regulation merely because of what it symbolizes. If we want to make sure a law does not undermine a value in the course of symbolizing it, we must stop to ask what sort of behavior the law will induce when put in place.[15] Otherwise, when we glorify a regulation's symbolic value, we glorify the taking of environmentalist positions at the expense of environmental interests. We will be doing exactly what experience in the theory and practice of conflict resolution tells us to avoid.

My father was a farmer. When I was eight years old, a pair of red foxes built a den and raised a litter in our wheat field. I can remember watching Dad on his tractor in the late afternoon, giving the foxes a wide berth, and leaving that part of our field uncultivated that year. He protected the den because he could afford to (and even then, I admired him for it). If there had been a law prohibiting farming on land inhabited by foxes, analogous to laws that prohibit logging in forests inhabited by spotted owls, then Dad would have had to make sure his land was not inhabited by foxes. Which is to say, Dad probably would have killed them. Although he loved them, he would not have been able to afford to let them live.

A LESSON FOR ENVIRONMENTAL ETHICS

Environmental philosophers often talk about environmental justice, but almost never talk about environmental conflict resolution. This is unfortunate. From a mediator's perspective, progress requires negotiation and compromise. Moreover, achieving acceptable and stable compromise can be more important from an environmental perspective than getting it right in some idealized sense that abstracts from political realities. Where the world can go from here is constrained by the histories of stakeholders and by a plurality of values. Mediators deal with the situation as it is.

The practical relevance of environmental ethics depends on our ability to do likewise. We need to think about conflict, not merely about how the world ought to be in the grand scheme of things. If humanity were a decision-making entity, and if its component parts had no interests of their own, this entity might rationally decide to prune itself back, amputating overgrown parts for the sake of the whole, thereby leaving more room for wildlife. In Africa, though, and in the developing world more generally, if people manage to protect their land and wildlife, it will be because doing so is in their interest, not because doing so is in the interest of "the whole." If we fail to treat them as players with interests of their own, we will be our own worst enemies.

In formal terms, philosophy of law distinguishes between procedural and substantive justice. *Substantive* justice is, roughly, a property of outcomes. It is about people (or any entities with moral standing) receiving what they are due. *Procedural* justice is about following fair procedures: procedures intended to be impartial. When philosophers discuss environmental justice, they usually have one or another notion of substantive justice in mind. In large measure, though, conflict mediation tends to involve seeking justice in a procedural sense.

Perhaps mediators should and do seek to ground negotiations in principles of substantive justice as well. I am not a mediator and have no direct practical experience with institutions of conflict mediation, so it is hard for me to say. What I can say with confidence is that philosophers need to do their part to complete the circle. What I have in mind is that while mediators are trying to ground their practice in a sound theory, we could do our part by trying to ground our theories in the requirements of sound practice. If we say our philosophical principles ought to be put into practice, then we implicitly if not explicitly are warranting those principles as compatible with sound practice. However, if we make no effort to ground our theories in requirements of sound practice, then it would be fraudulent to recommend our theory to practitioners. In that case, if and when practitioners respond by ignoring us, they will be doing the right thing.[16]

ECONOMICS AS ECOLOGY

Conflict in priorities often is not only an environmental conflict. Often, perhaps typically, it is an economic conflict, too—a conflict rooted in differing economic circumstances—and it will not be resolved as an environmental conflict unless it also is resolved as an economic conflict.

Unfortunately, people who embrace ecological reasoning often reject that very reasoning as applied to human ecology. Environmentalists tend to be pretty far left of center, and they tend to think of economics as a tool of their enemies. It is not only ecofeminists and deep ecologists who tend to reject economics out of hand; even more mainstream philosophers such as Eugene Hargrove sometimes flatly reject what they call "the economic approach to nature preservation."[17] This attitude may sometimes be apt. I am an economist as well as a philosopher, but I too reject the economic approach insofar as "economic approach" refers to trying to reduce all values to economic values.[18]

However, rejecting economic value-reductionism and ignoring the real-world logic of economic systems are two different things. In cases of conflicting priorities, ignoring the economic approach to understanding the logic of human interaction is bad for the environment.[19] If in that sense we are not taking an economic approach, then we are not taking a genuinely ecological approach either. We need to pay attention to the logic of human ecology lest we stand rightly accused of not truly caring about ecology at all. Murray Bookchin offers what he calls "social" ecology as an alternative to "deep" ecology.[20] In Bookchin's terms, my point is that if we are serious about promoting deep ecology's values, then we must be equally serious in working with social ecology's logic.

Like economic reasoning, ecological reasoning is reasoning about equilibria and perturbations that keep systems from converging on equilibria. Like economic reasoning, ecological reasoning is reasoning about competition and unintended consequences, and the internal logic of systems, a logic that dictates how a system responds to attempts to manipulate it. Environmental activism and regulation do not automatically improve the environment. It is a truism in ecology, as in economics, that well-intentioned interventions do not necessarily translate into good results. Ecology (human and nonhuman) is complicated, our knowledge is limited, and environmentalists are themselves only human.

Intervention that works with the system's logic rather than against it can have good consequences. Even in a centrally planned economy, the shape taken by the economy mainly is a function not of the central plan but of how people respond to it, and people respond to central plans in ways that best serve their purposes, not the central planner's. Therefore, even a dictator is in no position simply to decide how things are going to go. Ecologists understand that this same point applies in their own discipline. They understand that an ecology's internal logic limits the directions in which it can be taken by would-be ecological engineers.

Within environmental philosophy, most of us have come around to something like Aldo Leopold's view of humans as plain citizens of the biotic community.[21] As Bryan Norton notes, the contrast between anthropocentrism and biocentrism obscures the fact that we increasingly need to be nature-centered to be properly human-centered; we need to focus on "saving the ecological systems that are the context of human cultural and economic activities."[22] If we do not tend to what is good for nature, we will not be tending to what is good for people either. As Gary Varner recently put it, on purely anthropocentric grounds we have reason to think biocentrically.[23]

I completely agree. What I wish to add is that the converse is also true: on purely biocentric grounds, we have reason to think anthropocentrically. We need to be human-centered to be properly nature-centered, for if we do not tend to what is good for people, we will not be tending to what is good for nature either. From a biocentric perspective, preservationists sometimes are not anthropocentric enough. They sometimes advocate policies and regulations with no concern for values and priorities that differ from their own. Even from a purely biocentric perspective, such slights are illegitimate. Policy makers who ignore human values and human priorities that differ from their own will, in effect, be committed to mismanaging the ecology of which those ignored values and priorities are an integral part.

Africans seem to understand this, and in some cases they have been able to structure their policies in ways that do not slight the priorities of rural people who pay the price of co-existing with the wildlife. They understand that rural people must also benefit from co-existing with wildlife if wildlife is to survive. For example, consider Zimbabwe's CAMPFIRE program (as discussed in "When Preservationism Doesn't Preserve," elsewhere in this collection). CAMPFIRE allows hunting. It does not treat animals as if they have rights. But in Zimbabwe, it is CAMPFIRE that protects the wildlife, not PETA.[24] It is CAMPFIRE that respects the priorities of the local people—that seems to understand the practical priority of what Murray Bookchin calls social ecology—and thus it is CAMPFIRE that offers some hope for the long-run survival of Zimbabwe's wildlife.

CONCLUSION

Those who embrace economic values and those who embrace preservationist values are not natural enemies. If we want other people's actions (or our own, for that matter) to be environmentally benign, then we will have to understand and work with human ecology. Environmentalists need to avoid thinking of economics as the enemy, because that antipathy interferes with understanding what it takes to resolve conflicting priorities in environmentally benign ways.

In cases of conflicting priorities, we need to think about people first, if we care about people, or even if we do not. If we care about wildlife, we need to accept that wildlife will survive to the extent that people who have to live with it are better off taking care of it. It is roughly that simple. Requiring subsistence farmers to cooperate in putting the interests of wildlife before (or even on a par with) their own is not a winning strategy for helping the wildlife. We need their cooperation, and the terms of cooperation will have to address not only our interest in preserving wildlife but also their interest in being able to live with it.

Wildlife will survive only if people can afford to share the land. If they cannot share, then they will not share, and the wildlife will die.

NOTES

1. I thank Don Scherer for his thoughts on how attitudes toward nature have changed over the centuries. See also Eugene C. Hargrove, "The Historical Foundations of American Environmental Attitudes," *Environmental Ethics* 1 (1979): 209–40.

2. I was the fifth of six children, and the first to be born into a house with running water and an indoor toilet. Before then, families like ours got through the summer on melted snow.

3. Malaria, for example, is transmitted by mosquitoes. As my ancestors were landing in New Orleans in the 1850's, malaria was widespread as far north as the Great Lakes. See Erwin H. Ackerknecht, *Malaria in the Upper Mississippi Valley, 1760–1900* (Baltimore: Johns Hopkins Press, 1945). Malaria remains endemic in many tropical and even temperate regions. When I visited Zambia recently, I met a young woman who told me that like everyone else in her village, she contracts malaria two or three times per year.

4. I will use the term "environmental conflict" to refer to conflict in which at least one party is voicing concerns about the environmental impact of the other party's projects.

5. A *commons tragedy* occurs if and when individually rational use of a common resource culminates in a pattern of collective overuse that exceeds the resource's capacity for self-renewal.

6. A resource use has an *external* cost when some of the activity's costs are born by people other than the user, without their consent. Air and water pollution are the standard examples.

7. Such schemes seem to have had that effect in places where they have been tried. For a number of cases studies describing the successes and failures of attempts to turn wildlife to the advantage of local economies in developing countries, thereby turning local economies to the advantage of wildlife, see *Natural Connections: Perspectives in Community-Based Conservation,* ed. David Western, R. Michael Wright, and Shirley C. Strum, Washington: Island Press (1994).

8. Some people equate preservationism with environmentalism. This paper uses "environmentalist" to refer equally to conservationists and preservationists. I agree with Bryan Norton that it is all too easy to exaggerate the distinction's practical importance. Norton notes that it is tempting to insist on reaching a verdict regarding which side is right, but Norton himself argues on behalf of an integrated approach to valuing nature, and a consensus-building approach in the policy arena. Indeed, most of us have both conservationist and preservationist sympathies. Our diverse values need not stop us from agreeing on what we realistically can accomplish. See Bryan Norton, *Toward Unity Among Environmentalists* (New York: Oxford University Press, 1991) pp. 12–13.

9. Brian Child, "The Elephant as a Natural Resource," *Wildlife Conservation* (March/April, 1993) p. 60.

10. Norman Myers, "A Farewell to Africa," *International Wildlife* 11 (1981) p. 36.

11. Urs P. Kreuter and Randy T. Simmons, "Who Owns the Elephants?" *Wildlife in the Marketplace,* ed. Terry Anderson and Peter J. Hill (Lanham: Rowman and Littlefield, 1995) p. 161.

12. Of course, the different kinds of conflict are not mutually exclusive. They can occur together.

13. Roger Fisher and William Ury, *Getting To Yes* (New York: Penguin Books, second edition, 1991).

14. Mark Sagoff, *The Economy of the Earth* (Cambridge: Cambridge University Press, 1988) p. 16.

15. In passing, we also need to accept that what we stand for as a nation differs from what any of us *want* to stand for as a nation. The things for which nations stand are a product of ongoing piecemeal compromise. We do well not to glorify the expressive value of such compromised ideals.

16. It would be far beyond the scope of this paper to defend a particular conception of substantive justice, but let me suggest what sort of conception could count as com-

pleting the circle. Consider the principle that people ought to take responsibility for environmental consequences of their own actions: not just legally relevant consequences as determined by some regulatory agency, but rather the real consequences, to the honest best of people's ability to ascertain them. In short, people ought to take responsibility for internalizing externalities. I believe such a principle is intuitively just. I also believe that promulgating this principle as a principle of justice could help mediators resolve real world conflicts in a principled way. (As far as I know, the connection between internalizing externalities and being substantively just has not been explored in the literature.)

17. Eugene C. Hargrove, *Foundations of Environmental Ethics* (Englewood Cliffs: Prentice-Hall, 1989) p. 210.

18. See Mark Sagoff, "At the Shrine of Our Lady of Fatima, or Why Political Questions Are Not All Economic," *Arizona Law Review* 23 (1981): 1283–98.

19. Of course, it can be bad for people too. Ramachandra Guha rails against those who assume that so long as they are "cutting edge radicals" they are ipso facto champions of the world's oppressed poor and thus are relieved of any responsibility for gathering real information concerning the effect their policy proposals would have on the world's oppressed poor. See "Radical American Environmentalism and Wilderness Preservation: A Third-World Critique," *Environmental Ethics* 11 (1989): 71–83.

20. Murray Bookchin, "Social Ecology versus Deep Ecology," *Socialist Review* 88 (1988): 11–29. Roughly, Bookchin's terms refer to our social environment as understood by social scientists versus our natural environment as understood by preservationist environmentalists.

21. Aldo Leopold, *A Sand County Almanac* (New York: Oxford University Press, 1966, first published in 1949) p. 240.

22. Bryan Norton, *Toward Unity,* p. 252.

23. Gary Varner, *In Nature's Interests?* (New York: Oxford University Press, 1998) p. 129.

24. PETA is an acronym for People for the Ethical Treatment of Animals.

Chapter 13
Vanishing Resources

Questions for Reflection and Discussion

Cities

1. Cities have acquired a bad reputation, ecologically speaking. Cities are where the pollution is, the reasoning seems to go, so if we get rid of the cities, won't we be getting rid of the pollution at the same time?

Environmentalists sometimes denigrate high-tech industries that are human-capital-intensive and correspondingly economical in their use of natural resources. Feeling nostalgia for the simple life we never had, we want to extol the virtues of living off the land in a low-tech, "natural" way, ignoring the fact that it takes a *lot* of land for a family to be able support itself that way, even at a bare subsistence level. Brazilian cities have been sending people back to the land—the Amazon rain forest, that is—and the migration back to the forest has been among the world's most infamous ecological disasters. In fact, given the size of the world's human population, what the forests need is high-tech, space-saving, energy-saving, high-rise cities. Above all, what the forests do not need is people going back to the land and using trees for firewood. Ironically, the focus on decentralization, small-scale development, and self-sufficiency ignores the fact that "urbanization can ease land pressures in the countryside, thus reducing rates of deforestation and desertification."[1]

First, what are the real alternatives to the status quo in which most of us live in familiar urban and suburban neighborhoods? Which alternatives would be worse, and which would be better, environmentally speaking? Second, what can you do, and what should you do, as individuals and as communities, to reduce your consumption of natural resources, to reduce your production of pollutants, and more generally to reduce your environmental impact? What would Jessica Woolliams say?

2. Are things getting better, or worse? Is there any general answer, or is the truth that some things are getting better while other things get worse? What do you suppose the various authors in this section would say? Which trends (regarding pollution, resource use, etc.) are the most encouraging? Which are the most worrisome?

NOTES

1. Martin Lewis, "Third World Development and Population," in *A Survey of Ecological Economics,* ed. Rajaram Krishnan, Jonathan M. Harris, and Neva R. Goodwin (Washington, D.C.: Island Press, 1995), 314–17, here 316.

Designing Cities and Buildings as if They Were Ethical Choices

Jessica Woolliams

The way we design and live in our cities and buildings has ethical implications. This article has two parts: the first argues that cities should be front and center in any environmental debate. The second argues that we as a society could design and live in our buildings in a way that would significantly lighten humanity's weight on the planet.

> The world's cities take up just 2 percent of the Earth's surface, yet account for roughly 78 percent of the carbon emissions from human activities, 76 percent of industrial wood use, and 60 percent of the water tapped for use by people.
> —*Molly O'Meara,* State of the World, *1999*

For over two and a half million years, humanity lived as a hunting and gathering society. For less than ten thousand years, humanity has been farming. It has only been since the Industrial Revolution in Europe, beginning in the early nineteenth century, that humanity has lived in an industrial society. One of the characteristics of this industrialized society is urbanization. In 1950, the United Kingdom became the first nation to have over 50 percent of their population living in urban areas. It was soon followed by a host of European nations, and North America and Japan were not far behind (O'Meara 1999). In the year 2000, for the first time in human history, over 50 percent of the human population lives in cities.

However, our collective understanding of humanity's impact on the planet has failed to catch up to our rapid urbanization. Humanity's understanding of their environmental impact is focused on the problems that we have created outside of cities. In 1993, 1,680 scientists from all over the world issued a "World Scientists' Warning to Humanity" concerning the environmental crisis. This comprehensive document outlined environmental problems in the areas of atmosphere, water resources, oceans, soil, forests, living species, and population. There was no talk of cities.

Recently, in what is being hailed as the most comprehensive study of global ecosystems to date, the World Bank, the UN Development Program, the UN Environment Program, and the World Resources Institute have come together to assess the health of the global ecosystem through the "Pilot Analysis of

Global Ecosystems" (UNDP 2000). The study is organized into ecological assessments of the following areas: forests, freshwater systems, coastal/marine habitats, grasslands, and agricultural lands. Cities receive a few sentences towards the end. It is as if humans, the animal with the largest impact on the planet, and cities, the locus of human activities, are not worth studying.[1]

This almost willful blindness toward the environmental impact of our cities is curious indeed. Cities have always been the loci of human consumption and waste, and now with over half of the world's people living in cities, cities are ever more the places where humanity consumes the natural resources of the planet and gives back wastes. Cities in the wealthy world, of course, are responsible for an even greater throughput of energy and materials, and a greater production of waste. While consumption is not the central environmental problem in itself, the way resources are consumed in cities presently ensures that consumption is inexorably linked with the associated problems of global warming, habitat destruction leading to species loss, fishery destruction, and damage to water systems. As Rees (1997) puts it: "Half the people and three-quarters of the world's environmental problems reside in cities, and rich cities, mainly in the developed North, impose by far the greater load on the ecosphere and global commons." The way humanity chooses to design and live in its cities will decide whether it can sustain life on this planet, so there are strong ethical reasons to change the way cities are built.

Cities have the potential to be part of the solution rather than part of the problem. Certainly there is no going back to the land. Going back to low density rural living would be the surest way to cause accelerated environmental destruction and habitat loss (Lewis 1992). Gathering people together in cities allows for efficient use of resources, thereby minimizing pollution and environmental harm. A built environment that is designed to be dense, low-energy, low-consumption, and waste-assimilative can play a vital role in restoring global ecological health (Walker and Rees 1997; Roseland 1998).

The way we build our cities has a profound impact on the emission of green house gases. A recent study by the David Suzuki Foundation found that in Canada emissions could be reduced by as much as 50 percent using standard technology. The largest portion of this reduction would come from retrofitting 80 percent of existing buildings, and all new ones, with better insulation and windows. The other major portion of the reduction would come from Canadians switching to hybrid gasoline-electric cars that use three times less gas than conventional cars. In most industrial nations, buildings and transportation have the biggest impact on the environment and on global climate change. Because transportation patterns are in many ways influenced by building patterns, the focus here shall be on the way we as a society design buildings.

BUILDINGS

What would it be like if developments produced more energy than they consumed? What if they increased habitat and biodiversity, produced food and clean water?

—*Amory Lovins,* Green Development, *1998*

The construction, renovation and operation of buildings worldwide devours more of the planet's resources than any other economic sector (ASMI 1999). Every year the buildings that we build and inhabit use as much as 40 percent of all of the raw materials and energy used on the planet (ASMI 1999). This means millions of tons of liquid and solid waste, toxic air pollution, and greenhouse gases. But what this means is that no other sector of the world economy has the potential to make such a large reduction in its impact on the environment. As architect Richard Rogers (1999) notes:

The principal objective currently facing humanity is to allow a continued growth in living standards world-wide within diminishing resources. Architects have an important part to play, as they influence up to 75% of total energy use (50% in buildings, 25% in transport).

At a time when the World Bank is warning that the wars of the next century will be waged over access to fresh water supply, North America and most "developed" nations are literally flushing their resources down the toilet. Canada has the unenviable position of having the second largest domestic water consumption in the world, second only to the U.S.A. This waste of water reflects our values about our natural world and the creatures with which we share it.

Our consumption of energy also reflects our environmental values. The use of energy is arguably more significant because it dictates the rate at which other resources are consumed, as well as having an impact on greenhouse gases. Energy use per capita in Canada is roughly 500 percent more than world average. Clearly one way to reduce Canada's morally and logically offensive overuse of resources and energy and its incredible production of waste and pollution is to green our built environment. Green building guidelines have a role to play.

A green building or "high performance" building has a lighter impact on the environment, and it also encourages its users to have a lighter impact on the environment. It usually addresses at least some of the following areas: energy, water, landscape, materials, waste, construction management, and indoor environmental quality.

A green building addresses some of the challenges of global climate change by using less carbon-based energy than a standard building. Large reductions can be made to conventional energy use by using the tried and true techniques of increased insulation, better windows, passive solar heating, daylighting, and natural cooling. Further reductions to carbon-based energy can be made by using more benign sources of energy, including solar water preheating, photovoltaic panels, wind power, geothermal heat exchange, local microhydro, or fuel cells. Encouraging walking, biking, and the use of public transit can make still further reductions. This can be done through locating the building close to pedestrian, bike, and transit routes and providing showers and secure lockers for cyclists.

A green building uses resources like water and materials with more care and creates less waste. Reductions in water use can start with installing water conserving fixtures, but can also include using biological waste water treatment systems for gray and blackwater; using waterless toilets or urinals; using composting toilets; or capturing on-site rainwater. It can also mean planting a landscape that is native and does not require watering. A green building should filter water pollution before it leaves site, recharge groundwater, preserve and encourage biodiversity, and use integrated pest management techniques. It should use materials that are not only durable but salvaged and salvageable, recycled and recyclable. It should make it easy for occupants to recycle and compost, reuse construction and demolition waste, and avoid air pollutants.

The goal with green buildings is to use only as much energy and resources and create only as much waste as can be sustained by the environment. But can we really build these buildings? Yes, there are many being built. The C. K. Choi Institute of Asian Research at the University of British Columbia, Canada, was awarded one of the "2000 Earth Day Top Ten" by the American Institute of Architects. It is over 50 percent below the standard energy consumption level, uses extensive daylighting and natural ventilation, and uses extensive reused and recycled materials. Its nine composting toilets and three urinals require no water. Gray water and rainwater are used for irrigation. The various water-saving devices save about 1,500 gallons of potable water every day (Cole 1996). This is enough water to serve the domestic needs of 1,500 Haitians, 9 Americans, or 12 Canadians for one day. Are these buildings affordable? Yes, they require the same or lower capital cost to build and they should incur significantly lower operating and maintenance costs (Hawken, Lovins, and Lovins 1999).

In the last ten years a growing number of guidelines and rating systems have arisen to assist in the building and rating of green buildings. The city of Austin, Texas, developed the first green building rating system in North America in 1991. The purpose of Austin's Green Building Program is to encourage building professionals (architects, builders, and developers) to use sustainable practices in their buildings and to encourage consumers to value sustainable buildings. The program involves training the industry, marketing green ideas to consumers, and certifying "Green Buildings" with a rating of between one and five stars. Points can be received for following various building practices and ensuring a certain level of environmental performance.

Austin beat a trail for others to follow. Today there are many guideline programs. These include the Green Builder Program of Colorado, developed in 1995, which was the first to be developed on a state-wide basis; Santa Monica's Green Building Design and Construction Guidelines; New York City's High Performance Building Guidelines; and the Commonwealth of Pennsylvania's Guidelines for Creating High-Performance Buildings, the latter three all developed in 1999.

Perhaps the most far-reaching "Green Building" rating system is the U.S. Green Building Council's Leadership in Energy and Environmental Design (LEED) Green Building Rating System, developed in 1997 and further developed in 2000. Seattle has adopted LEED as a standard for all of its city buildings. So has the U.S. Navy, whose policy requires all its buildings to be built to these criteria. The Navy's policy alone ensures that roughly $5 billion worth of construction—roughly one percent of all US construction—is built using the LEED standards. Many other cities and jurisdictions are also considering adopting the LEED Rating System.

The LEED system is designed for new and existing institutional, commercial, and high-rise residential buildings. Certification is given to buildings that meet certain non-negotiable prerequisites (like a minimum level of energy efficiency). The building designers may also choose among different options to receive a minimum number of credits. Like many other Green Building guideline systems, it was designed to be voluntary and driven by citizens' buying habits. There is much more work to be done on LEED to incorporate the overall urban form. There should also be a parallel standard for other building forms, like medium- and low-density residential, which are presently left out of the system. Like any standard, LEED will grow and change. However, it now stands as the first green building standard for the industry and consumers. Having an industry-wide standard should enable the power of the mar-

ket to be used to make more ethical decisions about our buildings and, ultimately, our cities. It is time for us as a society to start designing and living in our cities and buildings as if they were ethical choices, because that is what they are.

REFERENCES

Athena Sustainable Materials Institute (ASMI), 1999, Web site http://www.athenasmi.ca/.

Raymond J. Cole, "Green Buildings: In Transit to a Sustainable World," *Canadian Architect* 41, no. 7 (1996): 13–19.

Paul Hawken, Amory Lovins, and L. Hunter Lovins, *Natural Capitalism: Creating the Next Industrial Revolution* (New York: Little, Brown and Company, 1999).

Martin Lewis, "Introduction," in *Green Delusions—An Environmentalist Critique of Radical Environmentalism* (New York: Duke University Press, 1992).

Molly O'Meara, "Exploring a New Vision for Cities," in *State of the World* (New York: Worldwatch Institute, 1999).

William Rees, "Is 'Sustainable City' an Oxymoron?" *Local Environment* 2 (1997): 303–10.

Richard Rogers Partnership, "The Environment," Richard Rogers Partnership Web page, http://www.richardrogers.co.uk/, January 20, 1999.

Mark Roseland, *Towards Sustainable Communities: Resources for Citizens and Their Governments* (Gabriola Island B.C.: New Society Publishers, 1998).

United Nations Development Programme (UNDP); United Nations Environment Programme (UNEP); World Bank (WB); World Resources Institute (WRI), *A Guide to World Resources 2000–2001* (Washington, D.C.: World Resources Institute, 2000).

Lyle Walker and William Rees, "Urban Density and Ecological Footprints—An Analysis of Canadian Households," in *Eco-City Dimensions: Healthy Communities, Healthy Planet,* ed. Mark Roseland. (Gabriola Island, B.C.: New Society Publishers, 1997)

NOTES

1. This exclusion of cities is also seen in the behavior of environmental activists, who have traditionally been concerned with the environment that exists outside of cities. When Robert Hunter and Paul Watson established

Greenpeace in Vancouver in 1971, the first issue on the agenda was nuclear testing in the arctic. Soon after, there were demonstrations against sealing and whaling, then deforestation and destruction of land from oil drilling. Today, urban environmental activists are beginning to lobby for bike lanes and tougher clean air standards in cities. Greenpeace, for example, has taken a crucial role in guiding the development of what is now the world's largest solar community, containing 665 solar-powered homes at the Sydney 2000 Olympics.

Why the Good News Shouldn't Scare You

Gregg Easterbrook

In the autumn of 1992, I was struck by this headline in the *New York Times:* "Air Found Cleaner in U.S. Cities." The accompanying story said that in the past five years air quality had improved sufficiently that nearly half the cities once violating federal smog standards no longer did so.

I was also struck by how the *Times* treated the article—as a small box buried on page A24. I checked the nation's other important news organizations and learned that none had given the finding prominence. Surely any news that air quality was in decline would have received front-page attention. The treatment suggested that the world was somehow disappointed by an inappropriately encouraging discovery.

American air is getting cleaner. Can this be happening on the same planet from which most current environmental commentary emanates? Vice President Al Gore has described the U.S. environmental situation as "extremely grave—the worst crisis our country has ever faced." The worst: worse than the enslavement of African-Americans, worse than the persecution of Native Americans, worse than the Civil War, worse than the Depression, worse than World War II. George Mitchell, till 1994 the majority leader of the Senate, has declared that "we risk turning our world into a lifeless desert" through environmental abuse. Gaylord Nelson, who as a senator in 1970 originated Earth Day and who is now a lawyer for the Wilderness Society, said in 1990 that current environmental problems "are a greater threat to the Earth's life-sustaining systems than a nuclear war."

And can this be the same planet from which most contemporary environmental writing emanates? *Silent Spring,* published by Rachel Carson in 1962, foretold such a widespread biological wipeout that today robins should be extinct, no longer greeting the spring with song. Instead the robin is today one of the two or three most prolific birds in the United States. Paul Ehrlich's *The Population Bomb,* released in 1968, predicted that general crop failures would "certainly" result in mass starvation in the United States by the 1980s. Instead the leading American agricultural problem of that decade was oversupply. The same book found it "not inconceivable" that some ghastly plague triggered by pollution would flash-kill half a billion people. Instead life expectancies have steadily increased, even in the overcrowded Third World. *The Limits to Growth,* a saturnine 1972 volume acclaimed at the time by critics in the United States, projected that petroleum would be exhausted by the 1990s. Instead oil prices hover near postwar lows, reflecting ample supply.

The Sinking Ark, published in 1979 by the biologist Norman Myers, portrayed the vessel of nature as riddled with breaches and going under before our eyes, with thousands of species to become extinct during the 1980s. Instead there were at worst a handful of confirmed extinctions globally in that decade.

A *Blueprint for Survival,* a 1972 anthology that was a bestseller in the United Kingdom, decreed that environmental trends mean "the breakdown of society, and the irreversible disruption of the life support systems on this planet . . . are inevitable." *Green Rage,* a 1990 volume by Christopher Manes on "deep" ecology, spoke of humanity as engaged in a "lemming-like march into environmental oblivion." Other recent books and public-interest campaigns have proclaimed a mass "poisoning of America," general radiation calamities, catastrophic climate change, deadly drinking water, and exhaustion of the basic processes of life. Affairs are thought so unswervingly bleak that the writer Bill McKibben, in his much-discussed 1989 work *The End of Nature,* declared there is no need to wait for the worst. Nature has already ended: ultimately, irrevocably, horrendously.

Yet I look out my window and observe that the sky above the populous Washington, D.C., region where I live each year grows more blue. The sun not only continues to rise; it does so above a horizon that is progressively cleaner. Is everybody talking about the same world?

Let's contemplate smog for a moment. Findings like those described in the first paragraph hardly mean the battle against smog is over. But despite the impression given to the public by fashionably pessimistic commentary, underlying trends in air pollution were positive throughout the 1980s. In that decade ambient smog in the United States declined a composite 16 percent, even as economic output expanded and the number of automobiles increased rapidly. In the beginning of the 1980s there were about 600 air-quality-alert days each year in major cities. By the end of the 1980s there were about 300 such days annually. Air pollution from lead, by far the worst atmospheric poison, declined 89 percent during the 1980s; from carbon monoxide, also poi-

sonous, went down 31 percent; ambient levels of sulfur dioxide, the main precursor of acid rain, declined 27 percent; nitrogen dioxide, another smog cause, went down 12 percent; in no smog category did ambient levels rise. In sum, American air was much less dirty in 1990 than in 1980, not more dirty as commonly believed.

Environmental Protection Agency figures from the 1990s show the improvement trend accelerating. In 1992, the number of Americans living in counties that failed some aspect of air-quality standards was 54 million—too many, but down from the 86 million people who lived in dirty-air counties in 1991, and only half the 100 million who lived in dirty air in 1982. In 1992 13 major cities, including Detroit and Pittsburgh, met federal standards for smog reduction for the first time, while no new cities were added to the violations list.

In 1993 I wrote an article for *Newsweek* presenting in detail the argument that the air grows cleaner. Later Senator Frank Lautenberg of New Jersey, chair of an important environmental subcommittee, waved the article before EPA administrator Carol Browner during a Senate hearing and declared himself "outraged" that *Newsweek* had printed such words. Senator Lautenberg did not challenge any of the factual material in the article. He appeared upset simply that positive environmental information was being reported. The good news scared him.

The good news should not scare anyone, particularly lovers of nature. Consider that recent improvements in air quality came mainly during a decade of Republican presidents—prominently Ronald Reagan, who labored under the garbled impression that trees cause more air pollution than cars. If a significant aspect of the environment got better even under Reagan, it sounds like something important is going on.

Something important *is* going on here: a fundamental, far-reaching shift toward the positive in environmental events. . . .

[This] is not an attack on environmentalism. Ecological consciousness is a leading force for good in world affairs. Without the imperatives of modern environmentalism—without its three decades of unstinting pressure on government and industry—the Western world today might actually be in the kind of ecological difficulty conventional wisdom assumes it to be in. Instead, the Western world today is on the verge of the greatest ecological renewal that humankind has known; perhaps the greatest that the Earth has known. Environmentalists deserve the credit for this remarkable turn of events.

Yet our political and cultural institutions continue to read from a script of instant doomsday. Environmentalists, who are surely on the right side of history, are increasingly on the wrong side of the present, risking their credibility by proclaiming emergencies that do not exist. What some doctrinaire environmentalists wish were true for reasons of ideology has begun to obscure the view of what is actually true in "the laboratory of nature." It's time we began reading from a new script, one that reconciles the ideals of environmentalism with the observed facts of the natural world. Toward that end [I] will advance the following premises:[1]

- That in the Western world pollution will end within our lifetimes, with society almost painlessly adapting a zero-emissions philosophy.
- That several categories of pollution have *already* ended.
- That the environments of Western countries have been growing cleaner during the very period the public has come to believe they are growing more polluted.
- That First World industrial countries, considered the scourge of the global environment, are by most measures much cleaner than developing nations.
- That most feared environmental catastrophes, such as runaway global warming, are almost certain to be avoided.
- That far from becoming a new source of global discord, environmentalism, which binds nations to a common concern, will be the best thing that's ever happened to international relations.
- That nearly all technical trends are toward new devices and modes of production that are more efficient, use fewer resources, produce less waste, and cause less ecological disruption than technology of the past.
- That there exists no fundamental conflict between the artificial and the natural.
- That artificial forces which today harm nature can be converted into allies of nature in an incredibly short time by natural standards.
- Most important, that humankind, even a growing human population of many billions, can take a constructive place in the natural order.

None of these notions are now common currency. It is possible to find yourself hooted down for proposing them at some public forums. A few years ago at a speech at a Harvard Divinity School conference on environmental affairs I was hissed merely for saying "People are more important than plants and animals." What better barometer is there of how nonsensical doomsday thinking can become?

But that is a passing situation. In the near future the propositions stated above will be widely embraced by society and even by the intelligentsia. Collectively I call these views *ecorealism*.

Ecorealism will be the next wave of environmental thinking. The core principles of ecorealism are these: that logic, not sentiment, is the best tool for safeguarding nature; that accurate understanding of the actual state of the environment will serve the Earth better than expressions of panic; that in order to form a constructive alliance with nature, men and women must learn to think like nature.

The coming wave of ecorealism will enable people and governments to make rational distinctions between those environmental alarms that are genuine and those that are merely this week's fad. Once rational decision-making becomes the rule in environmental affairs, the pace of progress will accelerate.

Essential to the ecorealist awakening will be the understanding that in almost every ecological category, nature has for millions of centuries been generating worse problems than any created by people.

Consider, for example, that today U.S. factories, power plants, and vehicles emit about 19 million tons per year of sulfur dioxide, the chief cause of acid rain. That level is far too high. Yet in 1991, the Mount Pinatubo eruption in the Philippines emitted an estimated 30 million tons of sulfur dioxide in just a few hours. Less spectacular, ongoing natural processes such as volcanic outgassing and ocean chemistry put about 100 million tons of sulfur dioxide into the atmosphere annually.

That nature makes pollutants in no way excuses the industrial variety. The comparison simply points to an important aspect of the environment, understanding of which is absent from current debate: that nature has spent vast spans of time learning to cope with acid rain, greenhouse gases, climate change, deforestation, radiation, species loss, waste, and other problems we humans so quaintly believe ourselves hurling at the environment for the first time. This knowledge suggests that environmental mischief by women and men will harm the Earth much less than popular culture now assumes. It further suggests that if people have the sense to stop the pollution they make today, and clean up that which they made in the past, the environment will regenerate in an amazingly short time by nature's standards.

Environmental commentary is so fogbound in woe that few people realize measurable improvements have already been made in almost every area. In the United States air pollution, water pollution, ocean pollution, toxic discharges, acid rain emissions, soil loss, radiation exposure, species protection, and recycling are areas where the trend lines have been consistently positive for many years. Yet polls show that people believe the environment is getting worse. Some of this can be explained by the new dynamic of fashionable doomsaying. Today many environmentalists and authors compete to see who can stage the most theatrical display of despair; public officials who once denied that environmental problems exist attempt to compensate by exaggerating in the other direction; celebrities whose lifestyles hardly reflect an ethic of modest consumption pause at limousine doors to demand that SOMEBODY ELSE conserve.

A peculiar intellectual inversion has occurred in which good news about the environment is treated as something that ought to be hushed over, while bad news is viewed with relief. Suppose a satellite produced evidence that ozone depletion was all a data error: some elements of the environmental movement would be heartbroken. Vice President Gore has written, in *Earth in the Balance,* that journalists should downplay scientific findings of ecological improvement because good news may dilute the public sense of anxiety. Gore has even said that scientists who disagree with the doomsday premise are "unethical" and must be ignored.

To the ecorealist, fashionable pessimism about the environment could not be more wrong, if only because it denies the good done already. In some vexing policy areas such as crime or public education it is difficult to imagine where solutions reside. On environmental affairs I can promise you—and will show you—that public investments yield significant benefits within the lifetimes of the people who make the investment. The first round of environmental investments did not fail; they worked, which is a great reason to have more.

I consider this glorious if only because as a political liberal I long for examples of government action that serves the common good. The extraordinary success of modern environmental protection is such an example: perhaps the best instance of government-led social progress in our age.

For this reason I have trouble fathoming why guarded optimism about the environment is politically incorrect. I have no trouble imagining that this situation will change. In the coming ecorealist ethic we will all be environmental optimists, citing conservation and pollution prevention as that rare area where government action and public concern lead promptly to results beneficial to all. Someday even Vice President Gore will smile when he talks about the ecology. Perhaps not tomorrow. But soon.

Let's note here three things that ecorealism is not.

First, it is not a philosophy of don't worry, be happy. The ecorealist must acknowledge there exists a wide range of human actions careless, selfish, or destructive to the environment. The point of ecorealism is that this equation can change, and it is much closer to that moment of transformation than all but a few people realize.

Second, ecorealism is not an endorsement of the technological lifestyle. In the past many foolish projections have been made about the course of technical events: from the thinkers of the Enlightenment, who believed that the perfectibility of humanity was at hand, to those daffy 1950s *Popular Mechanics* articles about how we'd all be flying personal helicopters by now. The epitome of this genre was a popular 1842 book by a writer named J. A. Eltizer called *The Paradise Within Reach of All Men, By Power of Machinery.* The title of the volume says everything you need to know about it. Ecorealism does not posit that technology is anyone's benefactor. It's just not necessarily bad, as is now fashionably assumed. Technology is a tool, and as a tool such as a knife can be used either to cause mayhem or carve a walking stick, technology may be used wisely or foolishly. It is up to us to decide which it will be. . . .

Third and last in the inventory of what ecorealism is not, ecorealism has nothing to do with a minor fad called wise use. The phrase "wise use" once had a progressive meaning in environmental letters but in recent years has been expropriated by reactionary fundraisers. Today lovers of nature ought to have no use for wise use. The wise use crowd, for instance, is nearly psychasthenic in its opposition to the Endangered Species Act. The ecorealist ought to support strengthening of the act. . . .

One reason I propose ecorealism is to create a language in which environmental protection can be discussed without descending into the oratorical quicksand of instant doomsday on the left and bulldozer apologetics on the right. Ecorealism offers a guiding ideal for those who care about the integrity of nature yet hold no brief for the extreme positions on either side. People sharing those values—a group that I figure at about 90 percent of the American population—need a vocabulary and a platform for reasoned ecological debate. Ecorealism will provide it. Such debate will make environmental protection clearheaded and rational, and thus ultimately stronger still. . . .

There was a time when to cry alarm regarding environmental affairs was the daring position. Now, that's the safe position: People get upset when you say things may turn out fine. . . .

NOTES

1. Editors' note: For discussion of these claims, see *A Moment on the Earth,* from which this excerpt is taken.

The Doomslayer

Ed Regis

The environment is going to hell, and human life is doomed to only get worse, right? Wrong. Conventional wisdom, please meet Julian Simon, the Doomslayer.

This is the litany: Our resources are running out. The air is bad, the water worse. The planet's species are dying off—more exactly, we're killing them—at the staggering rate of 100,000 per year, a figure that

Ed Regis, "The Doomslayer," *Wired* 5, no. 2 (1997). Reprinted with permission of the author. Revised, with permission, for this volume.

works out to almost 2,000 species per week, 300 per day, 10 per hour, another dead species every six minutes. We're trashing the planet, washing away the topsoil, paving over our farmlands, systematically deforesting our wildernesses, decimating the biota, and ultimately killing ourselves.

The world is getting progressively poorer, and it's all because of population, or more precisely, *over*-population. There's a finite store of resources on our pale blue dot, spaceship Earth, our small and fragile tiny planet, and we're fast approaching its ultimate carrying capacity. The limits to growth are finally upon us, and we're living on borrowed time. The laws of population growth are inexorable. Unless we act decisively, the final result is written in stone: mass poverty, famine, starvation, and death.

Time is short, and we have to act *now*.

That's the standard and canonical litany. It's been drilled into our heads so far and so forcefully that to hear it yet once more is . . . well, it's almost reassuring. It's comforting, oddly consoling—at least we're face to face with the enemies: consumption, population, mindless growth. And we know the solution: cut back, contract, make do with less. "Live simply so that others may simply live."

There's just one problem with The Litany, just one slight little wee imperfection: every item in that dim and dreary recitation, each and every last claim, is false. Incorrect. At variance with the truth.

Not the way it is, folks.

Thus saith The Doomslayer, one Julian L. Simon, a neither shy nor retiring nor particularly mild-mannered professor of business administration at a middling eastern-seaboard state university. Simon paints a somewhat different picture of the human condition circa 1997.

"Our species is better off in just about every measurable material way," he says. "Just about every important long-run measure of human material welfare shows improvement over the decades and centuries, in the United States and the rest of the world. Raw materials—all of them—have become less scarce rather than more. The air in the US and in other rich countries is irrefutably safer to breathe. Water cleanliness has improved. The environment is increasingly

healthy, with every prospect that this trend will continue.

"Fear is rampant about rapid rates of species extinction," he continues, "but the fear has little or no basis. The highest rate of observed extinction, though certainly more have gone extinct unobserved, is one species per year . . . ."

(One species per year!)

". . . in contrast to the 40,000 per year that some ecologists have been forecasting for the year 2000.

"The scare that farmlands are blowing and washing away is a fraud upon the public. The aggregate data on the condition of farmland and the rate of erosion do not support the concern about soil erosion. The data suggest that the condition of cropland has been improving rather than worsening."

As for global deforestation, "the world is not being deforested; it is being reforested in general."

Still, there *is* one resource that the world does not have enough of, that's actually getting rarer, according to Julian Simon. That resource: people.

"People are becoming more scarce," he says, "even though there are more of us."

Hello?

Simon started off as a card-carrying antigrowth, antipopulation zealot. He'd been won over by the conventional reasoning; he regarded the central argument as absolutely persuasive. And indeed, if we rehearse it now, it sounds like a faultless proof, clear and compelling, even watertight.

The classical case against population growth was expressed in 1798 by Thomas Malthus, the British economist and country parson who wrote in *An Essay on the Principle of Population:* "Population, when unchecked, increases in a geometrical ratio. Subsistence increases only in an arithmetical ratio. A slight acquaintance with numbers will show the immensity of the first power in comparison of the second."

As a point of abstract mathematics, there is no way around the conclusion that a geometric progression, if carried on far enough, will eventually overtake an arithmetic progression, no matter what. If population increases geometrically while "subsistence," or food, increases arithmetically, then sooner or later the population will run out of food. End of story.

Or so it would appear, except for the following embarrassing fact:

"Population has never increased geometrically," says Simon. "It increases at all kinds of different rates historically, but however fast it increases, food increases at least as fast, if not faster. In other words, whatever the rate of population growth is, the food supply increases at an even faster rate."

These, he says, are the actual and empirical facts of the matter, information available to any inquirer. Simon first got a taste of those facts while studying the data amassed by the economic demographer Simon Kuznets (winner of the 1971 Nobel Prize in economics) and by economist Richard Easterlin, in the mid-1960s. Kuznets had followed population growth trends that went back 100 years and compared them against standard of living, while Easterlin analyzed the same data for selected countries since World War II. The studies showed that while population growth rates varied from country to country and from year to year, there was no general negative correlation with living standards. People did not become poorer as the population expanded; rather, as their numbers multiplied, they produced what they needed to support themselves, and they prospered.

The trends were the same for food supply. Rising population did *not* mean less food, just the opposite: instead of skyrocketing as predicted by the Malthusian theory, food prices, relative to wages, had *declined* historically. In the United States, for example, between 1800 and 1980, the price of wheat plummeted while the population grew from 5 million to 226 million. According to Malthus, all those people should have been long dead, the country reduced to a handful of fur trappers on the brink of starvation. In fact, there was a booming and flourishing populace, one that was better-fed, taller, healthier, more disease-free, with far less infant mortality and longer life expectancy than ever before in human history. Obesity, not starvation, was the major American food problem in 1980. Those were the facts.

Nor should they have come as any great surprise, once you gave the matter some thought. Plants and animals used for food constitute "populations" just as human beings do, and so they, too, ought to increase not arithmetically, as Malthus claimed, but geometrically. The food supply, in other words, ought to keep pace with human population growth, thereby leaving all of us well-fed, happy, and snug in our beds.

Which, Simon discovered, is exactly what has happened throughout history. So if you look at the facts—as opposed to spinning out theories—you find precisely the reverse of the situation described by Malthus. Just the opposite!

Simon acquired his habit of looking up the facts in early childhood, at the dinner table of the family home in Newark, New Jersey. He'd be in some argument with his father over the benefits of exercise, the price of butter, or the health value of air conditioning, and whether from ignorance, pigheadedness, or general perversity, his father would always take some outlandish, off-the-wall viewpoint, such as: "The price of butter is 8 cents a pound."

Julian: "No, it's not, it's 80 cents a pound. It's in the newspaper, take a look."

Father: "I don't have to look. I *know* it's 8 cents a pound."

Julian: "Do you want to bet? I'll *bet* you it's not 8 cents a pound."

His father would never take the bet, but Julian would go to the library anyway, look things up in books, and come back with a ream of facts and data. His father, however, couldn't care less.

"I clearly didn't like my father," says Simon.

It's an attitude that drives him crazy to this day—people who know in advance what the truth is, who don't need to avail themselves of any "facts." But Simon loves facts and figures, he loves tables, charts, graphs, information arranged in rows and columns. Tabulations, the slopes of curves, diagram pie charts, histograms—he's a regular Mr. Data.

Of course, since people don't particularly like to have their cherished beliefs contradicted by heaps of facts served up on a platter, Simon has never been

Mr. Popularity. He got fired from jobs in the navy because he hated the customary ass-kissing, sucking-up, and yessir requirements. Nor has he ever been much for schmoozing, glad-handing, or the latter-day manners of get-along, go-along.

"Socially I was always a bit marginal," he admits. "Also, there always lurked inside me some irreverence for authority and orthodoxy."

None of this held him back academically. He got a bachelor's in experimental psychology from Harvard, an MBA from the University of Chicago, and, two years later, in 1961, a PhD in business economics from the same school.

He was not one of those MBAs whose closest contact with the gritty business world was going down to the corner newsstand to purchase a copy of *The Wall Street Journal.* The year he got his doctorate he started and operated his own business, a mail-order firm that sold quality teas, coffees, and a book on how to make beer at home. The enterprise was successful enough, but not so much as the book he later wrote about it, *How to Start and Operate a Mail-Order Business* (McGraw-Hill, 1965), still in print and currently in its fifth edition.

He got married and had three kids and wound up, successively, as professor of advertising, of marketing, and of business administration and economics at the University of Illinois at Urbana-Champaign. Then in 1966 or so, he had his big idea about how to solve the airline overbooking problem. Anticipating no-shows, airlines routinely oversold their flights. But when more people showed up at the gate than the plane had seats, pandemonium ensued. *Well, why not pay people to get off the plane?* he wondered. *Offer them enough to make it attractive. It would be a voluntary system, and everyone would win.*

So in his practical, down-to-earth, this-is-only-reasonable fashion, he submitted his suggestion to the airlines. The idea was laughed at, mocked, and ridiculed as unrealistic and unworkable. An official at Pan American replied: "Of course, we instituted the procedure immediately, after having the instructions translated into 18 languages." Ha ha ha, thank you, and goodbye.

Eleven years later, in 1977, Simon hadn't given up on the scheme. He published it in *The Wall Street Journal,* in an op-ed piece titled "Wherein the Author Offers a Modest Proposal." And lo and behold, a year after that, when economist Alfred Kahn headed up the Civil Aeronautics Board, Simon's proposal was put into practice. It was a raging success from the start, remains so to this day, and anyone who's ever voluntarily offloaded themselves from a plane for cash or free miles owes a nod of thanks to Julian Simon.

Still, that was a mere flash in the pan, and Simon's overall impact on the world at large was rather less massive than he desired. He was not making a name for himself, not setting the world on fire.

But there were those who were—Paul Ehrlich, for example.

Ehrlich, a Stanford University entomologist who as a youth had seen his best butterfly hunting grounds churned under the real estate developer's plow, wrote the runaway best-seller *The Population Bomb.* Published in 1968, the book was solidly Malthusian.

"The battle to feed all of humanity is over," it began. "In the 1970s and 1980s hundreds of millions of people will starve to death in spite of any crash programs embarked upon now. At this late date nothing can prevent a substantial increase in the world death rate, although many lives could be saved through dramatic programs to 'stretch' the carrying capacity of the earth by increasing food production and providing for more equitable distribution of whatever food is available. But these programs will only provide a stay of execution unless they are accompanied by determined and successful efforts at population control." And so on, The Complete and Authoritative Litany, for the next 200 pages.

This late-breaking Malthusian outburst, strangely enough, did set the world on fire. The book sold 3 million copies, became the best-selling environmental tract of all time, and got the author on *The Tonight Show.*

At home in Illinois, Simon watched Ehrlich on the Johnny Carson show, and he went bananas. In fact, more bananas than he'd ever before gone in his life. Simon had by that time decided that the Malthusian stuff was the purest mythology, an invention out of whole cloth, a theory that was entirely controverted by every available empirical fact. And here was Paul Ehrlich on TV spreading his stardust all over the place and holding Johnny Carson in some kind of mystic thrall.

"It absolutely drove me out of my skull," he recalls. "Here was a guy reaching a vast audience, leading this juggernaut of environmentalist hysteria, and I felt utterly helpless. What could I do? Go talk to five people?"

As bad an experience as that was, matters immediately got worse. The next year, 1969, Ehrlich published an article called "Eco-Catastrophe!" in *Ramparts.* "Most of the people who are going to die in the greatest cataclysm in the history of man have already been born," it said. "By that time [1975] some experts feel that food shortages will have escalated the present level of world hunger and starvation into famines of unbelievable proportions."

Then, in 1974, Ehrlich and his wife, Anne Ehrlich, also a Stanford biologist, published a new book, *The End of Affluence,* in which they warned of a "nutritional disaster that seems likely to overtake humanity in the 1970s (or, at the latest, the 1980s). Due to a combination of ignorance, greed, and callousness, a situation has been created that could lead to a billion or more people starving to death. . . . Before 1985 mankind will enter a genuine age of scarcity" in which "the accessible supplies of many key minerals will be nearing depletion."

Julian Simon read this stuff, which he viewed as unalloyed and total nonsense. He brooded and fumed and stewed in his juices. He experienced what might be called a personal lull.

And then, finally, in 1980 he emerged from the cocoon. He'd gone into it as a humble professor of marketing and a passive spectator of global death sentence forecasts. But now, suddenly, he broke out into the light of day, he sprang forth onto the world stage, he started swinging his diamond-tipped sword—*thwick-thwack!*—as . . . The Doomslayer!

The rebirth occurred in the pages of *Science,* in an article titled "Resources, Population, Environ-ment: An Oversupply of False Bad News." It led with a summary that became a manifesto:

> False bad news about population growth, natural resources, and the environment is published widely in the face of contrary evidence. For example, the world supply of arable land has actually been increasing, the scarcity of natural resources including food and energy has been decreasing, and basic measures of U.S. environmental quality show positive trends. The aggregate data show no long-run negative effect of population growth upon standard of living. Models that embody forces omitted in the past, especially the influence of population size upon productivity increase, suggest a long-run positive effect of additional people.

Written in the form of Statement followed by Fact, every reigning doomsday dragon was neatly slashed in half, the severed beasts left flapping around on the ground like fish.

> Statement: The food situation in less-developed countries is worsening.
>
> Fact: Per capita (repeat: per capita!) food production has been increasing at roughly 1 percent yearly—25 percent during the last quarter century.
>
> Statement: Urban sprawl is paving over the United States, including, much "prime agricultural land" and recreational areas.
>
> Fact: All the land used for urban areas plus roadways totals less than 3 percent of the United States. . . . Each year 1.25 million acres are converted to efficient cropland by draining swamps and irrigating deserts. . . . A million acres yearly goes into additional wilderness recreation areas and wildlife refuges, and another 300,000 acres goes for reservoirs and flood control.

So on and so forth, fact piled upon fact, paragraph after paragraph, all of it buttressed by tables, charts, graphs, and diagrams, plus 42 footnotes, many of them containing additional data.

Letters to the editor poured into *Science* in an unseemly rush. A few of them expressed partial agreement, but the majority were heavily critical. Many of them repeated statutory items of The Litany—"human beings, like any other species, have the biological capacity to overrun the carrying capacity of their habitat"—and there were even some feeble attempts at humor: in extrapolating from past trends, said one writer, Simon is like "the person who leaped from a very tall building and on being asked how things were going as he passed the 20th floor replied, 'Fine, so far.'" (Simon's response: "I think the better story is about somebody who has a rope lifeline and falls off the 15th floor. Somewhere about 30 feet above the ground, she lets go of the rope. You ask her, 'Why did you let go of the rope?' And she answers, 'It was going to break anyway.' That's how many activists would like us to behave.")

Anne and Paul Ehrlich, along with two energy and natural resource experts, John Holdren and John Harte wrote their own letter to the editor. After charging Simon with various "errors about the economics of scarcity," they went on to make some new doomsday predictions: "If deforestation for agriculture proceeds on a large enough scale, the resulting pulse of carbon dioxide may combine with that from increasing fossil-fuel combustion to alter global climate in a way that undermines food production to an unprecedented degree." They also corrected one of Simon's data points having to do with electricity, which Simon claimed had gotten cheaper. "The fact is," they said, "that real electricity prices bottomed in 1971 and were already up 18 percent from that low point in 1972." An 18 percent increase where Simon said there'd been a decline!

"I was taken aback," said Simon in his published reply. "Holdren and Harte are energy scholars. I checked Fig. 1 and other sources but could see no sign of their 18 percent." So he placed a phone call to the coauthor of the report cited by Holdren, Harte, and the Ehrlichs. "He, too, was puzzled. Upon investigation, the 1971 number (80.2) proved to be a typographical error and should have been 93.3. So much for Holdren et alia's 'fact.'"

The battle lines now drawn, it was not long before Ehrlich and Simon met for a duel in the sun. The face-off occurred in the pages of *Social Science*

Quarterly, where Simon challenged Ehrlich to put his money where his mouth was. In response to Ehrlich's published claim that "If I were a gambler, I would take even money that England will not exist in the year 2000"—a proposition Simon regarded as too silly to bother with—Simon countered with "a public offer to stake US $10,000 . . . on my belief that the cost of non-government-controlled raw materials (including grain and oil) will not rise in the long run."

You could name your own terms: select any raw material you wanted—copper, tin, whatever—and select any date in the future, "any date more than a year away," and Simon would bet that the commodity's price on that date would be lower than what it was at the time of the wager.

"How about it, doomsayers and catastrophists? First come, first served."

In California, Paul Ehrlich stepped right up—and why not? He'd been repeating the Malthusian argument for years; he was sure that things were running out, that resources were getting scarcer—"nearing depletion," as he'd said—and therefore would have to become more expensive. A public wager would be the chance to demonstrate the shrewdness of his forecasts, draw attention to the catastrophic state of the world situation, and, not least, force this Julian Simon character to eat his words. So he jumped at the chance: "I and my colleagues, John P. Holdren (University of California, Berkeley) and John Harte (Lawrence Berkeley Laboratory), jointly accept Simon's astonishing offer before other greedy people jump in."

Ehrlich and his colleagues picked five metals that they thought would undergo big price rises: chromium, copper, nickel, tin, and tungsten. Then, on paper, they bought $200 worth of each, for a total bet of $1,000, using the prices on September 29, 1980, as an index. They designated September 29, 1990, 10 years hence, as the payoff date. If the inflation-adjusted prices of the various metals rose in the interim, Simon would pay Ehrlich the combined difference; if the prices fell, Ehrlich et alia would pay Simon.

Then they sat back and waited.

Between 1980 and 1990, the world's population grew by more than 800 million, the largest increase in one decade in all of history. But by September 1990, without a single exception, the price of each of Ehrlich's selected metals had fallen, and in some cases had dropped through the floor. Chrome, which had sold for $3.90 a pound in 1980, was down to $3.70 in 1990. Tin, which was $8.72 a pound in 1980, was down to $3.88 a decade later.

Which is how it came to pass that in October 1990, Paul Ehrlich mailed Julian Simon a check for $576.07.

A more perfect resolution of the Ehrlich-Simon debate could not be imagined. All of the former's grim predictions had been decisively overturned by events. Ehrlich was wrong about higher natural resource prices, about "famines of unbelievable proportions" occurring by 1975, about "hundreds of millions of people starving to death" in the 1970s and '80s, about the world "entering a genuine age of scarcity."

In 1990, for his having promoted "greater public understanding of environmental problems," Ehrlich received a MacArthur Foundation "genius" award. . . .

Simon always found it somewhat peculiar that neither the *Science* piece nor his public wager with Ehrlich nor anything else that he did, said, or wrote seemed to make much of a dent on the world at large. For some reason he could never comprehend, people were inclined to believe the very worst, about anything and everything; they were immune to contrary evidence just as if they'd been medically vaccinated against the force of fact. Furthermore, there seemed to be a bizarre reverse-Cassandra effect operating in the universe: whereas the mythical Cassandra spoke the awful truth and was not believed, these days "experts" spoke awful falsehoods, and they *were* believed. Repeatedly being wrong actually seemed to be an *advantage,* conferring some sort of puzzling magic glow upon the speaker.

There was Lester Brown, for example, founder and president of the Worldwatch Institute, who in 1981 wrote: "The period of global food security is over. As the demand for food continues to press against the supply, inevitably real food prices will rise. The question no longer seems to be whether they will rise but how much."

All during the 1980s, however, wheat and rice prices declined; in mid-decade, in fact, they reached all-time lows. But this made no difference, and in 1986, for his work on the "global economy and the natural resources and the systems that support it," Lester Brown, too, received a MacArthur Foundation "genius" award. . . .

In July 1996, at a public event sponsored by the World Future Society, Simon debated Hazel Henderson, a private researcher and author of *Building a Win-Win World* . . . Henderson, who was trying to make a case that government regulation was responsible for reduced air pollution, came armed with a graph showing a decline in pollution levels in London since the late 1950s. The slope of the line was clearly downward, illustrating, she said, the effect of London's Clean Air Act of 1956.

In his rebuttal period, Simon presented a graph of his own. Whenever he presents any data, his practice is to present the figures going all the way back to day one, to the start of record-keeping on the parameter in question. You have to focus on aggregate trends over the long term, he insists, not just pick and choose some little fleeting data chunks that seem to support your case. So his own chart of smoke levels in London stretched back into the 1800s, and the line from the 1920s on showed a constant and uniform downward slope. "If you look at *all* the data," he said, "you can't tell that there was a clean-air act at any point." . . .

Some of Simon's claims, however, are so far from received opinion as to be hard to take seriously—his view on species loss, for example, regarding which he asserts that "the highest rate of observed extinctions is one species per year."

That was hard to accept. Harvard biologist Edward O. Wilson, the guru of global species extinction, said in 1991: "Believe me, species become extinct. We're easily eliminating 100,000 a year." A year later, in his 1992 book *The Diversity of Life,* he had modified that figure somewhat, saying: "The number of species doomed each year is 27,000." Apparently, these numbers were a tiny bit slippery. Still, both of them were a far cry from Simon's "one species per year."

Simon, on the other hand, pointed out that the higher estimates did not come from observation, they came from *theory,* specifically from Wilson's own theory of "island biogeography" which correlates species extinction with tropical forest destruction. The theory's "species-area equation," supposedly, predicts that for each additional unit of forest destroyed, so many more species die out.

This was another mathematical argument, reminiscent of the one made long ago by Malthus, and it was exactly the type of Neat Mathematical Certainty that Julian Simon took so much joy in shooting big holes through, which is what he proceeded to do now. The problem with the theory, he wrote in a paper on species loss with Aaron Wildavsky, is that it is not borne out by the empirical facts.

"The only empirical observation we found is by Lugo for Puerto Rico, where 'human activity reduced the area of primary forests by 99 percent. . . . This massive forest conversion did not lead to a correspondingly massive species extinction.'" Simon quoted Lugo to the effect that "more land birds have been present on the Island in the 1980s (97 species) than were present in pre-Columbian times (60 species)."

Say again? The forest was 99 percent demolished, and the number of bird species actually *rose?*

Even for me, this was too much.

The International Institute of Tropical Forestry, part of the US Forest Service, is located in an overgrown gray stone building in San Juan's Botanical Gardens. Ariel E. Lugo, a slim, gray bearded man in a silver-green forest service uniform, is director.

He's also a world-class expert on tropical forests and species extinction. A native of Puerto Rico, Lugo was educated in San Juan through his master's degree, came to the mainland, got a PhD in plant ecology from the University of North Carolina at Chapel Hill, then taught botany for 10 years at the University of Florida. He spent two years at the Puerto Rico

Department of Natural Resources and two more years on Jimmy Carter's Council on Environmental Quality in Washington, DC. Finally, he went back to San Juan as director of the Institute, a position he's held for the last 17 years.

"I see myself as in the middle of the road," he says. "On the right of me is Julian Simon, who sees nothing wrong. You know, 'We're doing just fine.' I don't want you to put me at that extreme."

Still, Lugo is not what could be called a major supporter of Wilson's theory of island biogeography, or of the species-area equation that forms its mathematical centerpiece. The equation is simple enough: $S = CA^z$ where S is the number of species, A is the area, and C and z are constants for the type of species in question, its location, and other factors. The apparent certainty it embodies, however, is an illusion, according to Lugo.

"The first uncertainty is that we don't know how many species there are. The margin of error is enormous: depending on who you talk to there is anywhere between 5 million and 100 million species, but science has described only a million species. How can you predict how many species are lost if you don't know how many species you're dealing with?"

The second problem is that the equation was never intended to describe *extinctions* to begin with. "It was a device for explaining the number of species on islands," he says. Generally, the bigger the island, the more species it has, other things being equal. But even if cutting down an island's forests causes species to leave the area, that's not the same thing as making those species extinct. "The presence or absence of a species in a particular area is one thing, whereas wiping out the genome of that species is another thing altogether—wiping out the seed, wiping out the mechanisms for hibernation, wiping out its dispersal, wiping out the management of the species. That's a completely different biology.

"And what is the relationship between deforestation and species loss to begin with?" he asks. "Do we understand that? Do we know that when you deforest an acre, you lose x proportion of species, *to extinction?* Well, I'm afraid that nobody knows that.

There is not one study that can claim to have understood the relationship between deforestation and species lost *to extinction*.

"And so if you're an objective scientist," he says, "you cannot put a number to the rate of species lost. But I believe we're exaggerating the numbers.

"What's unstated in all this is that when you deforest, you go to zero, that you go to pavement. That's how I put it, that 'you go to pavement.' This is why people get mad at me, because at this point in my talks I show a slide of pavement, but the pavement has weeds growing through it. I can take you to places of abandoned roads in the rain forest that have *trees* growing out of them."

Trees sprouting from the asphalt! Birds perching on the branches, insects crawling, worms boring, bees buzzing, lizards walking, moss growing on the tree trunk!

"Look at the example of Puerto Rico," Lugo says. "This island has a documented deforestation rate of 90 percent, and it has a documented loss of primary forest of 97 to 98 percent. So here's an island that has lost in the past, in the *recent* past, up to the '50s— I was already born when the island was at the peak of deforestation—it's lost almost all of its forest.

"The first surprise is that there are more bird species here now than ever, in part due to the invasion of nonindigenous species. The second surprise is that much of the forest has grown back."

On Lugo's conference table is a book open to two photographs.

"Now, where I'm gonna send you today," he says, "is *here*."

He points to a road that winds through the western fringe of El Yunque, the Caribbean National Forest, the only tropical rain forest in the US national forest system. Picture One, an aerial photograph taken in 1951, shows the area on the west side of the road: clear-cut, mowed down, absolutely denuded of trees. It looks like stumps and dead grass. The east side of the road, by contrast, is deep, dark, and flush with vegetation, an untouched virgin rain forest.

Picture Two shows the same area 13 years later: from the aerial photograph, both sides of the road are identical.

"You can see that it recovered," says Lugo. "So, you take your car and you ride through these forests, and you tell me."

Puerto Rico Route 186 is not far away, about 30 minutes by traffic jam. The road is paved but unmarked, slightly more than a lane wide, just enough space for two cars to pass without the sound of impact. You drive toward the mountains, while clouds bunched above, isolated raindrops spattering the windshield, and in five or six minutes there's tropical forest on both sides. Tall ferns, flame trees, mahogany trees, humongous green leafy plants, plus massive clumps of bamboo—stalks that tower 20 or 30 feet overhead.

Julian Simon: The facts are fundamental.
Garrett Hardin: The facts are not fundamental. The theory is fundamental.

—from a 1982 debate with the
UC Santa Barbara biologist.

The doomslayer-doomsayer debate, Simon thinks, is an opposition between fact and bad theory, a case of empirical reality versus abstract principles that purport to define the way things work but don't.

"It's the difference," he says, "between a speculative analysis of what *must* happen versus my empirical analysis of what *has* happened over the long sweep of history."

The paradox is that those abstract principles and speculative analyses seem so very logical and believable, whereas the facts themselves, the story of what has happened, appear wholly illogical and impossible to explain. After all, people are fruitful and they multiply but the stores of raw materials in the earth's crust certainly don't, so how can it be possible that, as the world's population doubles, the price of raw materials is cut in half?

It makes no sense. Yet it has happened. So there must be an explanation.

And there is: resources, for the most part, don't grow on trees. People *produce* them, they *create* them, whether it be food, factories, machines, new technologies, or stockpiles of mined, refined, and purified raw materials.

"Resources come out of people's minds more than out of the ground or air," says Simon. "Minds matter economically as much as or more than hands or mouths. Human beings create more than they use, on average. It had to be so, or we would be an extinct species."

The defect of the Malthusian models, superficially plausible but invariably wrong, is that they leave the human mind out of the equation. "These models simply do not comprehend key elements of people—the imaginative and creative."

As for the future, "This is my long-run forecast in brief" says Simon. "The material conditions of life will continue to get better for most people, in most countries, most of the time, indefinitely.

Within a century or two, all nations and most of humanity will be at or above today's Western living standards.

"I also speculate, however, that many people will continue to *think and say* that the conditions of life are getting *worse*."

But you don't have to be one of those people, one of those forever Glum and Gloomy Gusses. All you've got to do is keep your mind on the facts.

The world is not coming to an end.

Things are not running out.

Time is not short.

So, smile!

Shout!

Enjoy the afternoon!

The Good News, in Perspective

Paul Ehrlich and Anne Ehrlich

American environmentalists are often accused of never being satisfied with the progress that has been made in environmental protection. Instead of applauding hard-won gains, they keep pointing out new or intensifying problems and calling for new policies or stricter laws and enforcement. On the other side, environmental critics have increasingly complained about the burdens of compliance with what they see as proliferating and troublesome environmental regulations—with little appreciation of the positive difference they have made in the quality and safety of American life.

Clearly, the United States has come a long way since the days when toxic chemicals were dumped indiscriminately, rivers burst into flames, and lakes were so polluted that fish couldn't survive. Even the most ardent opponents of environmental regulation would probably concede that our lives today are much safer, healthier, and more pleasant than they would be without America's efforts in environmental protection.[1]

Moreover, in the past decade or two, environmental consciousness has become well integrated into American life and business, in itself a remarkable and important social change. Hardly a day goes by without at least one environmental report in the newspapers or on television, and environmental studies programs proliferate in schools and colleges. Citizens willingly cooperate in curbside recycling programs despite some inconvenience, spend extra money for "organic foods," and buy "green" products such as compact fluorescent light bulbs and en-

Paul Ehrlich and Anne Ehrlich, "The Good News, In Perspective," in *Betrayal of Science and Reason* (Washington, D.C.: Island Press, 1996), 45–63. Reprinted with permission of Island Press.

ergy-efficient refrigerators. Not only have many businesses and industries risen to meet the demand for greener products and services, many have also been shifting to more environmentally responsible behavior than in the past. And the environmental movement has become a prominent element of the American social and political mainstream. In short, the United States has much to be proud of, with a record of environmental protection that ranks among the world's best.

Yet environmental protection is not just a matter of safeguarding the health of citizens; it includes a very broad range of issues beyond controlling pollution. But rather than deal with all these broad topics here, we focus first in this [article] on pollution abatement, which is both a major component of environmental policy in the United States and an area of good news that often goes unrecognized. . . .

Americans certainly can—and should—be proud of their success in reducing many kinds of pollution, especially pollution of air and water. The average number of days per urban area per year during which air quality was deemed "unhealthy" fell from nearly twenty in the early 1980s to about six in 1993.[2] Even Los Angeles, famous worldwide for its smog, is a salient success story—all the more so given its substantial population (and car population) growth in recent decades.[3]

The improved air quality reflects dramatic reductions over the past twenty-five years in emissions of some important pollutants that are produced when fossil fuels (coal, oil, and natural gas) are burned. Moreover, the efficiency of energy use has risen substantially, and emissions are lower when less fuel is used to produce the same goods and services. Water quality also has greatly improved in many important respects, especially the treatment of urban sewage and industrial effluents. And significant progress is being made in cleaning up thousands of places contaminated in the past with toxic wastes and protecting the public from current and future exposures to toxic substances.

But all this regulatory activity no doubt helped generate the recent backlash. No one seriously objected to curbing air or water pollution, which can readily be seen and smelled and can make people sick. And the public demanded action when pesticides and toxic waste sites were shown to be sources of illness, birth defects, and cancer. But regulation seems to have become increasingly intrusive, so new questions are being raised: How clean is clean? Haven't the costs exceeded the benefits of pollution abatement or cleanup measures? Isn't the Environmental Protection Agency too focused on "command-and-control" bureaucratic solutions, using too much stick and too little carrot? Such questions are clearly legitimate and appropriate, yet they imply that regulation has gone too far, that it is overly burdensome, too expensive, and unnecessary.

So why do environmentalists—to the great consternation of conservatives and wise-use proponents—keep pushing for tighter controls and new laws? There are two reasons for this persistence. First, environmental protection means much more than controlling pollution and disposing safely of wastes. More than anything, it means preserving the stability of natural processes and the ecosystem services that support civilization—concerns that have only recently appeared on the policy agenda. Only in the past few decades have environmental problems transcended national scales and become worldwide in scope; global warming, ozone depletion, acid precipitation, and the loss of biodiversity all were unsuspected or little known before 1970. Concern over these difficult global problems explains why so many scientists haven't been as forthcoming with "good news" as many people, especially brownlash advocates, claim they should be.

Second, just to stay in place, it is necessary to keep moving forward. As more and more people are added to the population, each consuming more and more resources and materials, they generate more and more waste and pollution. If, in the face of this constant escalation of consumption and waste, we don't keep ratcheting up environmental regulations, we'll slide backward as deterioration outpaces abatement. It's rather like trying to run up an escalator that is going down. This is why urban air quality continues to be a serious problem in many cities, with ozone alerts now commonly included in weather reports. In some cities, such as Dallas, it has gotten worse. And that's why water pollution is still troublesome—even more so in some ways because the remaining sources are numerous, diffuse, and not as easily controlled as when water pollution came mostly from sewage or factory discharge pipes.

SLIDING BACKWARD, STRUGGLING FORWARD

Automobile tailpipe emissions illustrate the running-up-the-down-escalator dilemma. Since 1970, when the first strong amendments to the national Clean Air Act were enacted, the U.S. population has grown by 31 percent—from 203 million to 266 million in 1996—while the number of vehicles (cars, trucks, and buses) grew a whopping 62 percent—from 120 million to almost 195 million. Moreover, since 1980, the average number of miles driven annually per vehicle has risen by about 20 percent.[4] In other words, not only are there more Americans buying more cars, they are also driving them longer distances.

With no change in cars and emissions, the result would have been a near doubling of pollution. But the average vehicle's fuel efficiency was improved by more than 60 percent (a figure that would have been even greater if gas-guzzling light trucks and recreational vehicles hadn't become so popular), so the total amount of fuel consumed each year by U.S. motor vehicles rose only about 42 percent.[5]

In addition, tailpipe emissions of particulates and carbon monoxide (CO) were substantially reduced. Perhaps the biggest success story was the 96 percent reduction in lead emissions made possible by removing lead from gasoline in the late 1970s.[6] But there has been little or no reduction in total emissions of some important pollutants such as nitrogen oxides, which in 1990 were some 7 percent higher than in 1970. And hundreds of other air pollutants still are not controlled at all. The bottom line is that progress was made, but not as much as might have been expected.

Meanwhile, hefty increases have occurred in emissions of some uncontrolled substances, particu-larly carbon dioxide, the leading culprit in global warming. Not surprisingly, since CO_2 emissions rise in tandem with fuel consumption, the U.S. transportation sector alone adds 40 percent more to the atmosphere now than it did in 1970. And, of course, the raising of highway speed limits in 1995 was a step backward for both fuel conservation and emissions control, to say nothing of public health.

Despite all the hurdles, American achievements in pollution control are very real and substantial, all the more so since the number of pollution-generating sources (of which motor vehicles are only a part) is so enormous. Energy use per capita in the United States is 25 to 60 percent higher than that of most other industrialized nations with comparable standards of living and five to 100 times higher than in developing nations. High per-capita energy use multiplied by a very large population (the third largest in the world) makes us the world's biggest consumer of energy.

Yet our urban air quality is as good or better than that of most other industrial nations and a lot better than that of cities in eastern Europe or the developing world.[7] Similar statements can be made for other aspects of environmental protection in the United States, such as reducing water pollution and dealing with hazardous substances. Indeed, our pollution-control and pollution-prevention technologies are among the best in the world and are increasingly in demand as export commodities.

THE BENEFITS AND COSTS OF CONTROLLING AIR POLLUTION

Following the passage of Clean Air Act amendments in 1970, and most recently, in 1990, the United States has significantly stemmed the flow of toxins into the air. Although estimates of the dollar value of controlling air pollution in the United States vary enormously, as do estimates of the costs, Americans clearly have gained enormous benefits, especially in the protection of health. The principal pollutants addressed by the Clean Air Act—carbon monoxide, hydrocarbons, particulates, oxides of nitrogen and sulfur, and the ozone formed by the action of sunlight on hydrocarbons and oxides of nitrogen—are precisely those that are most damaging to human health.[8] Controlling emissions of these substances saves many thousands of people from premature death every year. And billions of dollars are saved by reducing losses of productivity because of asthma, emphysema, bronchitis, and other respiratory diseases.

The benefits of eliminating lead from gasoline have ironically become clearer after the fact, spurring regulators to keep lowering tolerances. Improved technologies allowed detection of mental impairment in children caused by very low concentrations of lead from paint, plumbing, and other sources only after blood levels in the general population had declined far enough to make comparisons feasible.[9]

Important indirect benefits of controlling air pollutants, especially sulfur dioxide (a prime component of acid precipitation), also accrue to natural and agricultural ecosystems and to the built environment. Thus additional billions are saved through reduced losses of crop and forest productivity and reduced damage to buildings and materials.

Many of the easy reductions, accomplished with scrubbers, catalysts, and other pollution-control technologies, have already been achieved. But controls must be continually tightened to compensate for population growth and the accompanying increase in polluting activities. Unfortunately, as control is tightened, costs generally rise; capturing the last 5 percent of emissions of a pollutant from stacks or tailpipes may cost as much or more than removing the first 50 percent. So, although the problem can sometimes be sidestepped through process changes or substitution of materials that generate less pollution, abatement costs by and large have risen faster than pollution could be reduced.

As costs have climbed, resistance to increased pollution controls by some business and industry groups has also risen, contributing to the environmental backlash. Particularly hard hit have been small businesses in California—paint dealers, gas stations, and dry-cleaning establishments—which the state began regulating in 1990. Unlike large corporations, which are better positioned to absorb regulatory expenses, many of these small businesses can ill afford the costs and have been threatened with bankruptcy. Not surprisingly, their angry owners are a growing presence in the backlash.

Many conservative members of Congress are angry too and since early 1995 have made strenuous attempts to dismantle environmental regulations. They denounce what they consider wrongheaded laws that specify not only results but also methods for meeting standards. In some cases, their point is well taken. For instance, the 1977 amendments to the Clean Air Act required power plants to meet standards for sulfur dioxide emissions by technological means (that is, by installing scrubbers) rather than by switching to low-sulfur coal. To save a few thousand jobs for eastern coal miners, power companies had to spend roughly ten times the miners' collective incomes to install and operate scrubbers. Another cost-saving opportunity was lost when Congress refused to allow pollution trade-offs for carbon monoxide and nitrogen oxides between vehicles and stationary sources. During the 1980s, an estimated $2.4 billion per year could have been saved by imposing stiffer controls on stationary sources rather than on vehicles.[10]

Recent Congresses have adopted more cost-effective approaches to controlling air pollution. The 1990 Clean Air amendments initiated various forms of emissions trading, and others have been proposed by the Clinton administration. The 1990 law established a market for tradeable emissions allowances among power plants that will save the utility industry about $1 billion per year while reducing overall sulfur dioxide emissions by more than half by 2000.[11] The strength of the new law lies in its flexibility. Companies are given financial incentives to invest in whatever clean technologies are most cost-effective for themselves, whether that means switching to cleaner fuels, conserving energy, or buying emissions permits from other, more efficient companies. Meanwhile, total allowable emissions will be gradually cut throughout the 1990s, giving companies time to adjust cost-effectively. Shifting away from traditional command-and-control regulation creates a win-win situation: more efficient pollution control and less opposition from polluting industries.[12]

WATER QUALITY

Abatement of water pollution in the United States, like that of air pollution, has been largely a success story. It also is one of the longest running, with legislative origins that go back to the turn of the past century. Until the 1970s, most legislation addressed public health issues and included provisions for helping communities build water and sewage treatment plants. With passage of the Water Pollution Control Act in 1972 (later called the Clean Water Act), the federal government turned its attention to cleaning up the nation's waterways, which had become badly polluted from industrial effluents and inadequately treated sewage.

Although the Clean Water Act was vetoed by Republican president Richard Nixon, members of both parties overwhelmingly voted to override his veto, stirred by eloquent pleas from various members of Congress, including Senator Edmund Muskie of Maine:

> Can we afford clean water? Can we afford rivers and lakes and streams which continue to make life possible on this planet? Can we afford life itself? Those questions were never asked as we destroyed the waters of our Nation, and they deserve no answers as we finally move to restore and renew them. These questions answer themselves.[13]

The 1972 Clean Water Act gave the government power to set and enforce national standards and to regulate effluents of organic materials, suspended solids, bacteria, and some toxic substances. By the 1990s, most "point sources"—that is, readily identifiable, single-outlet sources such as sewage outlets and industrial discharge pipes—had been brought under control. Regulations and treatment of surface waters have considerably reduced eutrophication, a

process in which a water body first becomes over-enriched from sewage or fertilizer runoff, then falls victim to excessive bacterial growth and oxygen depletion. Massive fish kills linked to pesticide contamination also are largely a problem of the past. Even Lake Erie, declared "dead" from pollution and eutrophication in 1969, has come back to life, although the array of fish species available to fishers is not what it once was.

Overall, the quality of water in lakes and streams in the United States has improved or at least has not significantly deteriorated. This is no small achievement given the escalating growth of pollution-generating activities. Not only has the scale of such activities increased on all fronts—mining, industry, consumer use of polluting products, and chemical-based farming—but also the variety of harmful substances that can find their way into water bodies has proliferated, including thousands of chemical compounds previously unknown to nature. Indeed, some toxic chemical compounds and heavy metals in industrial effluents were not individually regulated until 1986.[14] Moreover, serious problems remain in estuaries such as San Francisco and Chesapeake Bays and Boston Harbor and in the Great Lakes. These water bodies have for decades been receiving accumulations of pollutants such as organic compounds that cause eutrophication, heavy metals, and long-lived toxic chemicals that are difficult to clean up. The latter substances often concentrate in food chains and have disruptive effects on aquatic ecosystems, including commercially valuable fish and shellfish populations, thus posing potential threats to human health.[15]

In the past quarter-century, by using increasingly sophisticated and stringent controls, Americans have managed in most cases to stay ahead of their capacity to generate pollution—but only just. Even as pollution from point sources has fallen, non-point sources (mainly runoff from farms, lawns, and city storm drains) have emerged as the dominant water pollution problem. Lacking identifiable discharge sites, non-point sources are much harder than factory or sewage outlets to regulate.

At the same time, toxic substances are turning up with ever greater frequency in groundwater, the source of drinking water for one of every two Americans. Once contaminated, groundwater is extremely difficult and costly to clean up.[16] The shift to no-till cultivation in the Midwest has done much to reduce soil erosion, but the price has been a widespread influx into aquifers of herbicides (needed to suppress weeds formerly destroyed by plowing). Even more worrisome has been the contamination of groundwater in many parts of the country with radioactive and toxic substances resulting from military activities and especially the nuclear weapons-making enterprise of the cold war.[17]

Even though Americans today take safe drinking water for granted, it is essential to guard against complacency. Even in recent years, frightening outbreaks of waterborne diseases have occurred.[18] The best known was an outbreak in 1993 of waterborne cryptosporidiosis in Milwaukee. Some 400,000 people got sick, and the lives of AIDS victims and other people with impaired immune systems were seriously threatened. Among contributing factors was a new strain of *Cryptosporidium* (a pathogenic protozoon) that was resistant to the chlorination used to treat Milwaukee's water.[19]

When activists opposed to further regulation of water pollution cite figures indicating that the costs of abatement (roughly $15 to $30 billion per year in the mid-1980s)[20] exceed the benefits, their calculations generally underestimate the value of clean water to society. Who can put a price on the social value of clean water? How much would Americans be willing to pay to avoid the loss of swimmable waters, clean beaches, edible catches, and placid blue lakes, to say nothing of potable tap water? How does one quantify the link between clean water and property values or recreational pursuits such as swimming, boating, fishing, and tourism? Such questions must be part of any regulatory discussion.

Abolishing or crippling water pollution-control legislation seems more likely to anger citizens than win their approval. Nevertheless, regulations could be made less onerous and costly without significantly reducing water quality. Permitting pollution trade-offs similar to those for air pollutants is one possibility.[21] Another approach, utilized in Germany, is to charge companies for their discharges, which provides a strong incentive to minimize them.

MANAGING TOXIC SUBSTANCES

Ever since the Love Canal scandal burst upon the scene in 1978, Americans have been aware of and outraged about toxic waste dumps and other sources of exposure to hazardous substances.[22] Love Canal was a national wake-up call; it soon proved to be just the tip of a very large iceberg. By the late 1980s, some 30,000 old and abandoned toxic waste sites in the United States had been listed by the Environmental Protection Agency (EPA) as needing to be cleaned up; other agencies estimated that as many as a half-million might exist. Thousands more sites were later found at various federal facilities, including military sites.[23] By 1995, the 1300 most dangerous sites had been assigned to the National Priorities List and were undergoing treatment.[24]

These old sites represent a legacy of nearly two hundred years of industrial activity during which wastes of all kinds were discarded in almost any convenient place, often with no record kept of their disposal. Spills and dumpings from factories, refineries, smelters, mines, metal and chemical works, town dumps, and even gas stations were left with no attempt to remove noxious residues. The public was blissfully unaware, and no one cared unless some toxic brew exploded. As in Love Canal, new housing or other facilities such as schools sometimes were built over an old site, thus exposing families and especially children (who generally are more vulnerable) to any lingering toxicity.[25] Indeed, the great majority of waste sites are in residential areas, and nearly all are within a mile of a well providing drinking water.[26]

With passage in 1976 of the Resource Recovery and Recycling Act (RCRA; known in the trade as "Rickra") and the Toxic Substances Control Act (TSCA or TOSCA), the federal government began regulating hazardous wastes. Industrial wastes—

amounting to well over 250 million metric tons generated every year in the 1980s—are now managed under license by independent companies, by the waste-producing industries, or by operators of industrial landfills.[27] TOSCA requires corporations to record their acquisition or creation, use, and disposal of potentially toxic materials. This information is filed with the EPA, which can ban or limit production of any substance found to pose an unreasonable risk. Thus currently produced, used, and discarded chemical substances—more than 60,000 chemicals by 1990—are carefully tracked from "cradle to grave."

A separate set of regulations covers pesticides: the Federal Insecticide, Fungicide, and Rodenticide Act (FIFRA). DDT and some other pesticides that posed threats to human health or the environment have been banned under FIFRA. Both TOSCA and FIFRA differ from other environmental laws in assigning the EPA responsibility to balance costs and benefits in its decisions.

Many uncertainties surround the risks from toxic substances, and these uncertainties cannot be entirely resolved by scientific testing before introduction. Such tests are required for new drugs, food additives, and pesticides but not for new chemicals entering the market under TOSCA, unless the EPA challenges their introduction. The toxic effects of many substances (cancers, developmental problems, or long-term environmental impacts), however, may appear only decades later. And, since the regulatory action is largely preventive, the damage a hazardous substance might cause remains unknown if it is never introduced.

The legacy of old waste sites, however, was not addressed by RCRA, TOSCA, or FIFRA. Galvanized by Love Canal and the rediscovery of thousands of other forgotten dump sites, Congress in 1980 passed the Comprehensive Environmental Response, Compensation, and Liability Act (CERCLA). Of all the laws regulating toxic substances, this one—widely, though not affectionately, known as Superfund—has aroused the most passionate opposition, serving as a lightning rod for anti-regulatory fervor. Polluters seemed to be clogging the

courts, channeling money into lawyers' pockets instead of into cleanup efforts. Many citizens concluded that the law was a failure; at the least, progress seems dishearteningly slow and incredibly expensive.[28] One estimate for the final bill over a thirty-year period (within a wide range of possibilities) was $750 billion.[29] And, of course, the public's irritation has been both promoted and exploited to considerable effect by the brownlash.

The purpose of Superfund was to make the original polluters pay for cleaning up their old toxic waste dumps. Unfortunately, many of the original polluters are no longer in business or cannot even be identified; often several parties are involved. This situation and the complexities of liability have led to a plethora of lawsuits among the guilty parties and their insurance companies.[30] The RAND Institute for Civil Justice found that 88 percent of insurance companies' Superfund-related costs in the late 1980s went to legal fees paid in largely successful efforts to avoid cleanup liability.[31]

Responding to the public's concerns, in 1986 Congress passed the Superfund Amendment and Re-authorization Act (SARA), which broadened the fund's tax base and eased the requirements of responsibility, thus (it was hoped) speeding up the process and lowering the angst. The EPA also became more flexible in negotiating with small companies or with larger firms whose involvement in the original site had been minimal. By the 1990s, many more cases were being privately settled and cleaned up without controversy.

Even without seemingly endless legal delays, the cleanup process is lengthy and expensive; assessing and ranking a site, designing remedial action, and carrying out the action can take a dozen years or more, especially when, as often happens, groundwater contamination is involved. In these cases, an ounce of prevention would be worth a ton of cure. Yet by 1989, nearly all of the original 30,000 Superfund sites had been assessed and ranked, and by 1993 some 150 of the nearly 1300 sites on the National Priority List (NPL) had been fully cleaned up.[32] Critics have called this a dismal record, but they neglect to mention other accomplishments. By

1993, long-term remediation was under way at more than half of the NPL sites, and planning for 200 more had begun. And preventive and remedial actions—removing leaking drums of wastes and contaminated debris, draining polluted ponds, and so on—had taken place at some 2600 other sites.

Moreover, the perception that most of Superfund's money has gone into lawyers' pockets is not accurate. The same RAND study that revealed the insurance companies' penchant for legal battles found that only 21 percent of the Superfund expenses paid by large industrial firms went for court costs, and only 11 percent of EPA's did.[33] The great bulk of funds from both sources went into cleanups.

Also passed in 1986 was the Emergency Planning and Community Right to Know Act (also known as SARA Title III), which requires manufacturers to report the types and amounts of chemicals they release to air, water, and land each year. The information is then published by the EPA in an annual report, the Toxics Release Inventory (TRI). Even though no regulation of the toxic compounds on the TRI list (more than 600 by 1996) is involved, the law had startling effects. Not only were people shocked by the huge volume of these materials being discharged into the environment, the disclosures motivated many industries to clean up their acts. No doubt, concern for corporate images was a big factor, but another seems to be a widespread belief among business-people that clean operations are better run, more efficient, and more competitive than dirty ones.[34]

The program's success is evident. Soon after TRI reports began to be required, the EPA saw a significant drop in reported emissions—all without any regulatory pressure or cumbersome rule making. Industries voluntarily made the changes for their own reasons and, evidently, considered them worth the investment.[35] Today, many corporations can boast of substantial reductions in their toxics output. For instance, the Monsanto Company's chemical division in 1995 reported a 90 percent reduction in its TRI emissions,[36] and the Procter & Gamble Company announced reductions of 75 percent in its U.S. operations.[37]

Many companies now adhere to the mantra of "reduce, reuse, and recycle," an integrated approach to waste management that minimizes waste at every stage of the industrial cycle rather than simply at the end of the pipe. Waste reduction strategies include materials substitution (finding less hazardous substances to use), packaging redesign (resulting in lighter weights and less need for raw materials), recycling of byproducts (materials once discarded are now reclaimed and either sold for profit or reused in the company), and improved emission controls. People involved in this new approach to industrial management refer to it as "industrial ecology" because of its similarities to the closed loop systems of natural ecosystems in which nutrients and organic matter are continuously recycled through the biosphere.

Even before emissions reporting was required, some companies recognized the link between economic and environmental benefits. Among the pioneers was the Minnesota Mining and Manufacturing Company (3M), which introduced its widely regarded Pollution Prevention Pays program in 1975.[38] The program led to the elimination of more than 1 billion pounds of polluting emissions for 3M factories and saved the company some $500 million.[39] Other companies have since jumped on the bandwagon, including Monsanto, E. I. du Pont de Nemours and Company,[40] the Dow Chemical Company, Xerox Corporation, and Procter & Gamble, earning greener reputations in the process.[41] Even the American Chemical Manufacturers Association, to its credit, has encouraged the trend toward cleaner industrial processes and production through its Responsible Care program.[42] Indeed, a whole new industry has arisen in response to the need for technologies to manage and detoxify toxic substances.

Thus the implementation of RCRA, TOSCA, and other toxics regulations has quietly revolutionized the way hazardous substances of all kinds are handled in the United States. Illegal midnight dumpings and other abuses that regularly made headlines in the 1970s are now essentially a thing of the past. Most major corporations have assumed much more responsible practices than those that led to the passage of RCRA and Superfund. Even so, Superfund and other toxics regulations remain exceedingly sore points for some members of the business community, inspiring many of Congress's recent efforts to extract the EPA's regulatory teeth. At least one congressman has even targeted the TRI reporting requirement for elimination as an unnecessary burden on business—a rule that costs practically nothing (except perhaps some embarrassment to businesses) and has led to substantial reductions in toxic emissions without any enforcement action at all!

PROVIDING PERSPECTIVE

The difficulty with assessing the real value of environmental regulation in the United States is that Americans haven't experienced the consequences that would have occurred without it. Some of the horrendous problems experienced in the past before environmental laws began protecting us have been forgotten or were never known by a generation of young people. Environmental protection has been swept along with myriad other factors that have made life materially better for most people today compared with several decades ago. Like credit cards, computers, jet airliners, and freeways, environmental protection is taken for granted.

Furthermore, most Americans don't realize how much of the progress made has been swallowed up by increased energy use and economic activity. For instance, without catalytic converters and increased fuel efficiency, the near doubling of miles traveled per year since 1970 would have doubled air pollution emissions from cars and trucks. This is why improvements in air and water quality seem scarcely noticeable, while the hassles and costs of compliance seem to have escalated to intolerable levels.

To see just how different American life would be without environmental laws, suppose one of the states opted out of federal regulation. For a realistic comparison, most industrial infrastructure, vehicles, homes and appliances, and water treatment facilities in the state would have to be state-of-the-art 1970. The inhabitants of the unlucky state no doubt would strenuously object to being made guinea pigs; Americans are not notably fond of smog or polluted water. Since the gains in energy efficiency since 1970 would be lost, there probably would be howls of

protest over the higher prices for many goods and services, especially electricity and fuel.

But these complaints might well be drowned out by the clamor over irritating air pollution and a substantial rise in incidence of lung ailments such as asthma, bronchitis, and emphysema—to say nothing of an increase in waterborne diseases and chemical hazards in drinking water. Farmers might also notice a drop in crop yields, while forests, rivers, and lakes would show signs of declining health and productivity.[43] Rising rates of cancer and birth defects might cause alarm, although pinning down the causes would be difficult. All this would, of course, carry economic costs. Meanwhile, polluting companies would be busy trying to convince the public that their activities had nothing to do with the problems and that people were certainly better off without burdensome regulation.

Anyone who still doubted the benefits of environmental regulation might benefit from a field trip to developing regions. Huge cities such as Mexico City, São Paulo, Jakarta, Bangkok, Beijing, Delhi, and Nairobi have horrific smog despite being located in countries with far less industry than the United States. Tens of thousands to millions of cars, trucks, and buses with no smog controls cram the streets; hundreds of uncontrolled factories, smelters, and power stations belch smoke and pollutants; and in some cities millions of open cooking fires foul the air. Third world rivers are often essentially open sewers spiked with pesticide cocktails. Many areas have yet to reach state-of-the-art-1970 U.S. pollution-control standards.

Equally enlightening might be a visit to industrialized regions of eastern Europe and former Soviet Union republics. Even though fairly strong pollution-control laws have long been on the books in those nations, they have seldom if ever been enforced. Nor was any effort made toward energy efficiency. The result, given a high level of industrial activity, has been horrendous pollution and a related severe decline in the population's health.[44]

During the 1970s, mortality rates in the Soviet Union stopped falling and began rising, and the government, presumably embarrassed, stopped publishing mortality statistics. The trend worsened after the

Soviet Union's breakup. Even though a faltering health care system and inadequate supplies of equipment and medicines have played a role, most medical authorities blame the public's exposure to various forms of pollution, from common air pollutants to pesticides, heavy metals, and radioactivity. By 1995, infant deaths from severe birth defects were five times as frequent in Russia as in other industrialized nations, presumably resulting from parental exposure to high levels of toxic and radioactive substances.[45]

Serious impacts have also been seen on agriculture, forests, and wildlife throughout the former Eastern Bloc. The tragedy of the Aral Sea region is relatively well known in the West, although not everyone realizes that pollution, especially by pesticides, was a major factor in the area's problems. The devastating effects of acid precipitation and industrial air pollutants on forests in Czechoslovakia, Poland, and parts of Russia are also familiar to environmentally conscious westerners, as is the aftermath of the Chernobyl disaster. But the widespread contamination of rivers and farmland, and its connection to declining health and reduced agricultural production, is not so well known. After the cold war ended, American companies sent representatives to forge partnerships and help former Soviets and eastern Europeans convert to capitalism, but the Americans often found the air, water, and soils too polluted to support the high-technology operations they were planning. Václav Havel, president of the Czech Republic, eloquently summarized the situation in his country: "The environmental desolation created by the Communist regimes is a warning for the whole of civilization today."[46]

NOTES

1. See, e.g., G. Easterbrook, *A Moment on the Earth: The Coming Age of Environmental Optimism* (New York: Viking, 1995).

2. U. S. Department of Energy, *Sustainable Energy Strategy (National Energy Policy Plan)* (Washington, D.C.: U.S. Government Printing Office, 1995).

3. J. Lents and W. Kelly, "Clearing the air in Los Angeles," *Scientific American*, October 1993, pp. 32–39.

4. *The American Almanac, Statistical Abstract of the United States, 1993–1994* (113th ed.) (Austin, TX: Reference Press, 1993).

5. *American Almanac;* C. Flavin and N. Lensson, *Power Surge* (New York: W. W. Norton, 1994).

6. Flavin and Lensson, 1994; P. Portney, Air pollution policy, chapter 3 in P. Portney (ed.), *Public Policies for Environmental Protection* (Washington, D.C.: Resources for the Future, 1990)

7. Portney, 1990; World Bank, *World Development Report 1992* (Washington, D.C.: World Bank, 1992).

8. P. Ehrlich, A. Ehrlich, and J. Holdren, *Ecoscience: Population, Resources, Environment* (San Francisco: W. H. Freeman, 1997). See chapter 10.

9. Edward Groth III, Consumers Union, personal communication, 26 November 1995.

10. Portney, 1990, pp. 75–76.

11. J. Alper, Protecting the environment with the power of the market, *Science* 260 (1993):1884–1885. By 1996, reductions reportedly were ahead of schedule.

12. Sen. T. Wirth and Sen. J. Heinz, 1988, Project 88: Harnessing market forces to protect our environment, unpublished. Washington, D.C.

13. R. Adler, J. Landman, and D. Cameron, 1993, *The Clean Water Act Twenty Years Later* (Washington, D.C.: Island Press, 1993), p. 2.

14. World Resources Institute, *The 1992 Information Please Environmental Almanac* (Boston: Houghton Mifflin, 1992).

15. T. Colborn, D. Dumanoski, and J. P. Myers, 1996, *Our Stolen Future* (New York: Dutton, 1996)

16. R. Patrick, E. Ford, and J. Quarles (eds.), *Groundwater Contamination in the United States* (2nd ed.) (Philadelphia: University of Pennsylvania Press, 1987)

17. S. Shulman, *The Threat at Home: Confronting the Toxic Legacy of the U.S. Military* (Boston: Beacon Press, 1992).

18. S. Terry, Drinking water comes to a boil, *New York Times* Magazine, 26 September (1993), pp. 42–45ff.

19. L. Garrett, *The Coming Plague: Newly Emerging Diseases in a World Out of Balance* (New York: Farrar, Straus, and Giroux, 1994), p. 430

20. Freeman, 1990.

21. In early 1996, the EPA announced that it was launching a program for trading permits for release of water pollutants (Pollution credits: EPA announces effluent

trading program, *Greenwire,* 5:182, no. 8, 31 January 1996).

22. R. Dower, 1990. Hazardous wastes, chapter 5 in Portney, Public Policies; J. Lewis, "Love Canal legacy—where are we now?," *EPA Journal,* July–August (1991), pp. 7–14; M. Russell, E. Colglazier, and B. Tonn, "The U.S. hazardous waste legacy," *Environment* 34 no. 6 (1992): 12–15, 34–39.

23. Shulman, 1992, appendix B.

24. T. Grumbly, Lessons from Superfund, *Environment* 37 no.3 (1995): 33–34.

25. Colborn, Dumanoski, and Myers, 1996; J. Harte, C. Holdren, R. Schneider, and C. Shirley, *Toxics A to Z: A Guide to Everyday Pollution Hazards* (Berkeley: University of California Press, 1991); National Research Council, *Pesticides in the Diets of Infants and Children* (Washington, D.C.: National Academy Press, 1993).

26. Grumbly, 1995.

27. Dower, 1990.

28. F. Cairncross, "Old horrors," *The Economist,* 29 May (1993): pp. 15–16 of a special section, *Environment Survey: Waste and Environment.*

29. Russell, Colglazier, and Tonn, 1992.

30. C. de Saillan, In praise of Superfund, *Environment* 35 no.8 (1993): 42–44.

31. Ibid.; J. Acton and L. Dixon, *Superfund and Transaction Costs: The Experiences of Insurers and Very Large Industrial Firms* (Santa Monica, CA: RAND Institute for Civil Justice, 1992)

32. Dower, 1990; de Saillan, 1993.

33. Acton and Dixon, 1992.

34. R. Gottlieb, *Reducing Toxics: A New Approach to Policy and Industrial Decisionmaking* (Washington, D.C.: Island Press, 1995); B. Allenby and D. Richards (eds.), *The Greening of Industrial Ecosystems* (National Academy of Engineering) (Washington, D.C.: National Academy Press, 1994)

35. K. Oldenburg and J. Hirschhorn, "Waste reduction: A new strategy to avoid pollution," *Environment* 29 no.2 (1987): 16–20, 39–45; U.S. Congress, Office of Technology Assessment, "Serious Reduction of Hazardous Waste," *OTA-ITE*-317 (Washington, D.C.: U.S. Government Printing Office, 1986); R. Frosch and N. Gallopoulos, "Strategies for manufacturing," *Scientific American,* September 1989, pp. 144–153. F. Cairncross, *Costing the Earth* (Boston: Harvard Business School Press, 1992).

36. Groth, 1995; C. Frankel, "Monsanto breaks the mold," *Tomorrow* 6 no. 3 (1996): 62–63.

37. *P&G 1995 Environmental Progress Report* (Cincinnati, OH: Procter & Gamble Company, 1995)

38. P. Sinsheimer and R. Gottlieb, "Pollution prevention voluntarism," chapter 12 in Gottlieb, 1995, pp. 389–420.

39. S. Schmidheiny, *Changing Course* (Cambridge, MA: Massachussets Institute of Technology Press, 1992).

40. Du Pont recently announced a goal of zero wastes, zero emissions (*Greenwire,* 5:185, 5 February 1996).

41. I. Amato, "The slow birth of green chemistry," *Science* 259 (1993): 1538–1541; E. Marshall, 1993, "Is environmental technology a key to a healthy economy?" *Science* 260 (1993): 1886–1888.

42. R. Frosch, "Industrial ecology: Adapting technology for a sustainable world," *Environment* 37 no. 10 (1995): 16–24, 34–37.

43. J. MacKenzie and M. El-Ashry, *Air Pollution's Toll on Forests and Crops* (New Haven, CT: Yale University Press, 1989).

44. M. Feshbach and A. Friendly, *Ecocide in the USSR* (New York: Basic Books, 1992).

45. M. Specter, "Plunging life expectancy puzzles Russia," *New York Times,* 8 August 1995.

46. Quoted in A. Lewis, "Marx and Gingrich," *New York Times,* 1 January 1996.

Chapter 14

Cost-Benefit Analysis and Environmental Policy

Questions for Reflection and Discussion

Optimal Pollution

William Baxter, in a notorious book called *People or Penguins: The Case For Optimal Pollution,* makes the quite reasonable point that if we could reduce pollution for free, then of course we'd want to reduce it all the way to zero. But reducing pollution is not free. Cleaner air is a good thing whose costs and benefits have to be weighed against costs and benefits of other good things in life. So Baxter proposes that the only rationally defensible course of action is: Recycle, clean up, and protect up to point where marginal benefit is offset by marginal cost. Then stop. The rational target therefore is not zero pollution but rather an optimal level of pollution.[1]

Is Baxter wrong? What would Steven Kelman or Andrew Brennan say? There is an unspoken agreement in environmental ethics to speak as if our ultimate goal is never again to defecate or exhale carbon dioxide or do any of the other things that affect the balance of nature. Would it be better to give up that pretense and join Baxter in approving of activities that pollute the environment whenever the benefit is worth the cost? Or is there a larger (perhaps symbolic) point in insisting that the ultimate goal is zero pollution, no matter what the cost? If so, then is there something wrong with the very idea of cost-benefit analysis? (In all circumstances, or only some?) Is insisting on a goal of zero pollution part of what we need to do to be able to experience nature as something more than a mere resource? What would Leonard and Zeckhauser say?

For any given pollutant, is the goal of zero pollution attainable? If so, how much should we be willing to sacrifice to achieve that goal? If not, should we be aiming at something other than zero pollution? What? Why?

NOTES

1. For discussion of the ethics of aiming at nonzero levels of air pollution, see Paul Steidlmeier, "The Morality of Pollution Permits," *Environmental Ethics*, 15 (1993): 133–50.

Cost-Benefit Analysis: An Ethical Critique

Steven Kelman

At the broadest and vaguest level, cost-benefit analysis may be regarded simply as systematic thinking about decision making. Who can oppose, economists sometimes ask, efforts to think in a systematic way about the consequences of different courses of action? The alternative, it would appear, is unexamined decision making. But defining cost-benefit analysis so simply leaves it with few implications for actual regulatory decision making. Presumably, therefore, those who urge regulators to make greater use of the technique have a more extensive prescription in mind. I assume here that their prescription includes the following views:

(1) There exists a strong presumption that an act should not be undertaken unless its benefits outweigh its costs.

(2) In order to determine whether benefits outweigh costs, it is desirable to attempt to express all benefits and costs in a common scale or denominator, so that they can be compared with each other, even when some benefits and costs are not traded on markets and hence have no established dollar values.

(3) Getting decision makers to make more use of cost-benefit techniques is important enough to warrant both the expense required to gather the data for improved cost-benefit estimation and the political efforts needed to give the activity higher priority compared to other activities, also valuable in and of themselves.

My focus is on cost-benefit analysis as applied to environmental, safety, and health regulation. In that context, I examine each of the above propositions from the perspective of formal ethical theory, that is, the study of what actions it is morally right to undertake. My conclusions are:

(1) In areas of environmental, safety, and health regulation, there may be many instances where a certain decision might be right even though its benefits do not outweigh its costs.

(2) There are good reasons to oppose efforts to put dollar values on non-marketed benefits and costs.

(3) Given the relative frequency of occasions in the areas of environmental, safety, and health regulation where one would not wish to use a benefits-outweigh-costs test as a decision rule, and given the reasons to oppose the monetizing of non-marketed benefits or costs that is a prerequisite for cost-benefit analysis, it is not justifiable to devote major resources to the generation of data for cost-benefit calculations or to undertake efforts to "spread the gospel" of cost-benefit analysis further.

How do we decide whether a given action is morally right or wrong and hence, assuming the desire to act morally, why it should be undertaken or refrained from? Like the Molière character who spoke prose without knowing it, economists who advocate use of cost-benefit analysis for public decisions are philosophers without knowing it: the answer given by cost benefit analysis, that actions should be undertaken so as to maximize net benefits, represents one of the classic answers given by moral philosophers—that given by utilitarians. To determine whether an action is right or wrong, utilitarians tote up all the positive consequences of the action in terms of human satisfaction. The act that maximizes attainment of satisfaction under the circumstances is the right act. That the economists' answer is also the answer of one school of philosophers should not be surprising. Early on, economics was a branch of moral philosophy, and only later did it become an independent discipline.

Steven Kelman, "Cost-Benefit Analysis: An Ethical Critique," *Regulation* 5 (1981): 74–82. Reprinted with permission of the publisher, American Enterprise Institute for Public Policy Research, and the author. Revised for this volume.

Before proceeding further, the subtlety of the utilitarian position should be noted. The positive and negative consequences of an act for satisfaction may go beyond the act's immediate consequences. A facile version of utilitarianism would give moral sanction to a lie, for instance, if the satisfaction of an individual attained by telling the lie was greater than the suffering imposed on the lie's victim. Few utilitarians would agree. Most of them would add to the list of negative consequences the effect of the one lie on the tendency of the person who lies to tell other lies, even in instances when the lying produced less satisfaction for him than dissatisfaction for others. They would also add the negative effects of the lie on the general level of social regard for truth-telling, which has many consequences for future utility. A further consequence may be added as well. It is sometimes said that we should include in a utilitarian calculation the feeling of dissatisfaction produced in the liar (and perhaps in others) because, by telling a lie, one has "done the wrong thing." Correspondingly, in this view, among the positive consequences to be weighed into a utilitarian calculation of truth-telling is satisfaction arising from "doing the right thing." This view rests on an error, however, because it *assumes* what it is the purpose of the calculation to *determine*—that telling the truth in the instance in question is indeed the right thing to do. Economists are likely to object to this point, arguing that no feeling ought "arbitrarily" to be excluded from a complete cost benefit calculation, including a feeling of dissatisfaction at doing the wrong thing. Indeed, the economists' cost-benefit calculations would, at least ideally, include such feelings. Note the difference between the economist's and the philosopher's cost-benefit calculations, however. The economist may choose to include feelings of dissatisfaction in his cost-benefit calculation, but what happens if somebody asks the economist, "Why is it right to evaluate an action on the basis of a cost-benefit test?" If an answer is to be given to that question (which does not normally preoccupy economists but which does concern both philosophers and the rest of us who need to be persuaded that cost-benefit analysis is right), then the circularity problem reemerges. And there is also another difficulty with counting feelings of dissatisfaction at doing the wrong thing in a cost-benefit calculation. It leads to the perverse result that under certain circumstances a lie, for example, might be morally right if the individual contemplating the lie felt no compunction about lying and morally wrong only if the individual felt such a compunction!

This error is revealing, however, because it begins to suggest a critique of utilitarianism. Utilitarianism is an important and powerful moral doctrine. But it is probably a minority position among contemporary moral philosophers. It is amazing that economists can proceed in unanimous endorsement of cost-benefit analysis as if unaware that their conceptual framework is highly controversial in the discipline from which it arose—moral philosophy.

Let us explore the critique of utilitarianism. The logical error discussed before appears to suggest that we have a notion of certain things being right or wrong that *predates* our calculation of costs and benefits. Imagine the case of an old man in Nazi Germany who is hostile to the regime. He is wondering whether he should speak out against Hitler. If he speaks out, he will lose his pension. And his action will have done nothing to increase the chances that the Nazi regime will be overthrown: he is regarded as somewhat eccentric by those around him, and nobody has ever consulted his views on political questions. Recall that one cannot add to the benefits of speaking out any satisfaction from doing "the right thing," because the purpose of the exercise is to determine whether speaking out *is* the right thing. How would the utilitarian calculation go? The benefits of the old man's speaking out would, as the example is presented, be nil, while the costs would be his loss of his pension. So the costs of the action would outweigh the benefits. By the utilitarians' cost-benefit calculation, it would be *morally wrong* for the man to speak out.

Another example: two very close friends are on an Arctic expedition together. One of them falls very sick in the snow and bitter cold, and sinks quickly before anything can be done to help him. As he is dying, he asks his friend one thing, "Please, make me a solemn promise that ten years from today you will come back to this spot and place a lighted candle here to remember me." The friend solemnly promises to do so, but does not tell a soul. Now, ten years later, the friend must decide whether to keep his promise. It would be inconvenient for him to make the long trip. Since he told nobody, his failure to go will not affect the general social faith in promise-keeping. And the incident was unique enough so that it is safe to assume that his failure to go will not encourage him to break other promises. Again, the costs of the act outweigh the benefits. A utilitarian would need to believe that it would be *morally wrong* to travel to the Arctic to light the candle.

A third example: a wave of thefts has hit a city and the police are having trouble finding any of the thieves. But they believe, correctly, that punishing someone for theft will have some deterrent effect and will decrease the number of crimes. Unable to arrest any actual perpetrator, the police chief and the prosecutor arrest a person whom they know to be innocent and, in cahoots with each other, fabricate a convincing case against him. The police chief and the prosecutor are about to retire, so the act has no effect on any future actions of theirs. The fabrication is perfectly executed, so nobody finds out about it. Is the *only* question involved in judging the act of framing the innocent man that of whether his suffering from conviction and imprisonment will be greater than the suffering avoided among potential crime victims when some crimes are deterred? A utilitarian would need to believe that it is *morally right to punish the innocent man* as long as it can be demonstrated that the suffering prevented outweighs his suffering.

And a final example: imagine two worlds, each containing the same sum total of happiness. In the first world, this total of happiness came about from a series of acts that included a number of lies and injustices (that is, the total consisted of the immediate gross sum of happiness created by certain acts, minus any long-term unhappiness occasioned by the lies and injustices). In the second world the same amount of happiness was produced by a different se-

ries of acts, none of which involved lies or injustices. Do we have any reason to prefer the one world to the other? A utilitarian would need to believe that the choice between the two worlds is a *matter of indifference.*

To those who believe that it would not be morally wrong for the old man to speak out in Nazi Germany or for the explorer to return to the Arctic to light a candle for his deceased friend, that it would not be morally right to convict the innocent man, or that the choice between the two worlds is not a matter of indifference—to those of us who believe these things, utilitarianism is insufficient as a moral view. We believe that some acts whose costs are greater than their benefits may be morally right and, contrariwise, some acts whose benefits are greater than their costs may be morally wrong.

This does not mean that the question whether benefits are greater than costs is morally irrelevant. Few would claim such. Indeed, for a broad range of individual and social decisions, whether an act's benefits outweigh its costs is a sufficient question to ask. But not for all such decisions. These may involve situations where certain duties—duties not to lie, break promises, or kill, for example—make an act wrong, even if it would result in an excess of benefits over costs. Or they may involve instances where people's rights are at stake. We would not permit rape even if it could be demonstrated that the rapist derived enormous happiness from his act, while the victim experienced only minor displeasure. We do not do cost-benefit analyses of freedom of speech or trial by jury. The Bill of Rights was not RARGed.[1] As the United Steelworkers noted in a comment on the Occupational Safety and Health Administration's economic analysis of its proposed rule to reduce worker exposure to carcinogenic coke-oven emissions, the Emancipation Proclamation was not subjected to an inflationary impact statement. The notion of human rights involves the idea that people may make certain claims to be allowed to act in certain ways or to be treated in certain ways, even if the sum of benefits achieved thereby does not outweigh the sum of costs. It is this view that underlies the statement that "workers have a right to a safe and healthy work place" and the expectation that OSHA's decisions will reflect that judgment.

In the most convincing versions of nonutilitarian ethics, various duties or rights are not absolute. But each has a prima facie moral validity so that, if duties or rights do not conflict, the morally right act is the act that reflects a duty or respects a right. If duties or rights do conflict, a moral judgment, based on conscious deliberation, must be made. Since one of the duties non-utilitarian philosophers enumerate is the duty of beneficence (the duty to maximize happiness), which in effect incorporates all of utilitarianism by reference, a nonutilitarian who is faced with conflicts between the results of cost-benefit analysis and nonutility-based considerations will need to undertake such deliberation. But in that deliberation, additional elements, which cannot be reduced to a question of whether benefits outweigh costs, have been introduced. Indeed, depending on the moral importance we attach to the right or duty involved, cost-benefit questions may, within wide ranges, become irrelevant to the outcome of the moral judgment.

In addition to questions involving duties and rights, there is a final sort of question where, in my view, the issue of whether benefits outweigh costs should not govern moral judgment. I noted earlier that, for the common run of questions facing individuals and societies, it is possible to begin and end our judgment simply by finding out if the benefits of the contemplated act outweigh the costs. This very fact means that one way to show the great importance, or value, attached to an area is to say that decisions involving the area should not be determined by cost-benefit calculations. This applies, I think, to the view many environmentalists have of decisions involving our natural environment. When officials are deciding what level of pollution will harm certain vulnerable people—such as asthmatics or the elderly—while not harming others, one issue involved may be the right of those people not to be sacrificed on the altar of somewhat higher living standards for the rest of us. But more broadly than this, many environmentalists fear that subjecting decisions about clean air or water to the cost-benefit tests that de-

termine the general run of decisions removes those matters from the realm of specially valued things.

In order for cost-benefit calculations to be performed the way they are supposed to be, all costs and benefits must be expressed in a common measure, typically dollars, including things not normally bought and sold on markets, and to which dollar prices are therefore not attached. The most dramatic example of such things is human life itself; but many of the other benefits achieved or preserved by environmental policy—such as peace and quiet, fresh-smelling air, swimmable rivers, spectacular vistas—are not traded on markets either.

Economists who do cost-benefit analysis regard the quest after dollar values for nonmarket things as a difficult challenge—but one to be met with relish. They have tried to develop methods for imputing a person's "willingness to pay" for such things, their approach generally involving a search for bundled goods that *are* traded on markets and that vary as to whether they include a feature that is, *by itself,* not marketed. Thus, fresh air is not marketed, but houses in different parts of Los Angeles that are similar except for the degree of smog are. Peace and quiet is not marketed, but similar houses inside and outside airport flight paths are. The risk of death is not marketed, but similar jobs that have different levels of risk are. Economists have produced many often ingenious efforts to impute dollar prices to nonmarketed things by observing the premiums accorded homes in clean air areas over similar homes in dirty areas or the premiums paid for risky jobs over similar nonrisky jobs.

These ingenious efforts are subject to criticism on a number of technical grounds. It may be difficult to control for all the dimensions of quality other than the presence or absence of the non-marketed thing. More important, in a world where people have different preferences and are subject to different constraints as they make their choices, the dollar value imputed to the non-market things that most people would wish to avoid will be lower than otherwise, because people with unusually weak aversion to those things or unusually strong constraints on their choices will be willing to take the bundled good in question at less of a discount than the average person. Thus, to use the property value discount of homes near airports as a measure of people's willingness to pay for quiet means to accept as a proxy for the rest of us the behavior of those least sensitive to noise, of airport employees (who value the convenience of a near-airport location) or of others who are susceptible to an agent's assurances that "it's not so bad." To use the wage premiums accorded hazardous work as a measure of the value of life means to accept as proxies for the rest of us the choices of people who do not have many choices or who are exceptional riskseekers.

A second problem is that the attempts of economists to measure people's willingness to pay for nonmarketed things assume that there is no difference between the price a person would require for *giving up* something to which he has a preexisting right and the price he would pay to *gain* something to which he enjoys no right. Thus, the analysis assumes no difference between how much a homeowner would need to be paid in order to give up an unobstructed mountain view that he already enjoys and how much he would be willing to pay to get an obstruction moved once it is already in place. Available evidence suggests that most people would insist on being paid far more to assent to a worsening of their situation than they would be willing to pay to improve their situation. The difference arises from such factors as being accustomed to and psychologically attached to that which one believes one enjoys by right. But this creates a circularity problem for any attempt to use cost-benefit analysis to determine *whether* to assign to, say, the homeowner the right to an unobstructed mountain view. For willingness to pay will be different depending on whether the right is assigned initially or not. The value judgment about whether to assign the right must thus be made first. (In order to set an upper bound on the value of the benefit, one might hypothetically assign the right to the person and determine how much he would need to be paid to give it up.)

Third, the efforts of economists to impute willingess to pay invariably involve bundled goods exchanged in *private* transactions. Those who use figures garnered from such analysis to provide guidance for *public* decisions assume no difference between how people value certain things in private individual transactions and how they would wish those same things to be valued in public collective decisions. In making such assumptions, economists insidiously slip into their analysis an important and controversial value judgment, growing naturally out of the highly individualistic microeconomic tradition—namely, the view that there should be no difference between private behavior and the behavior we display in public social life. An alternative view—one that enjoys, I would suggest, wide resonance among citizens—would be that public, social decisions provide an opportunity to give certain things a higher valuation than we choose, for one reason or another, to give them in our private activities.

Thus, opponents of stricter regulation of health risks often argue that we show by our daily risk-taking behavior that we do not value life infinitely, and therefore our public decisions should not reflect the high value of life that proponents of strict regulation propose. However, an alternative view is equally plausible. Precisely because we fail, for whatever reasons, to give life-saving the value in everyday personal decisions that we in some general terms believe we should give it, we may wish our social decisions to provide us the occasion to display the reverence for life that we espouse but do not always show. By this view, people do not have fixed unambiguous "preferences" to which they give expression through private activities and which therefore should be given expression in public decisions. Rather, they may have what they themselves regard as "higher" and "lower" preferences. The latter may come to the fore in private decisions, but people may want the former to come to the fore in public decisions. They may sometimes display racial prejudice, but support antidiscrimination laws. They may buy a certain product after seeing a seductive ad, but be skeptical enough of advertising to want the government to keep a close eye on it. In such cases, the use of private behavior to impute the values that should be entered for public decisions, as is done by using willingness to pay in private transactions, commits grievous offense against a view of the behavior of the citizen that is deeply engrained in our democratic tradition. It is a view that denudes politics of any independent role in society, reducing it to a mechanistic, mimicking recalculation based on private behavior.

Finally, one may oppose the effort to place prices on a non-market thing and hence in effect incorporate it into the market system out of a fear that the very act of doing so will reduce the thing's perceived value. To place a price on the benefit may, in other words, reduce the value of that benefit. Cost-benefit analysis thus may be like the thermometer that, when placed in a liquid to be measured, itself changes the liquid's temperature.

Examples of the perceived cheapening of a thing's value by the very act of buying and selling it abound in everyday life and language. The disgust that accompanies the idea of buying and selling human beings is based on the sense that this would dramatically diminish human worth. Epithets such as "he prostituted himself," applied as linguistic analogies to people who have sold something, reflect the view that certain things should not be sold because doing so diminishes their value. Praise that is bought is worth little, even to the person buying it. A true anecdote is told of an economist who retired to another university community and complained that he was having difficulty making friends. The laconic response of a critical colleague—"If you want a friend why don't you buy yourself one"—illustrates in a pithy way the intuition that, for some things, the very act of placing a price on them reduces their perceived value.

The first reason that pricing something decreases its perceived value is that, in many circumstances, non-market exchange is associated with the production of certain values not associated with market exchange. These may include spontaneity and various other feelings that come from personal relationships. If a good becomes less associated with the production of positively valued feelings because of market exchange, the perceived value of the good declines to the extent that those feelings are valued. This can be seen clearly in instances where a thing may be transferred both by market and by non-market mechanisms. The willingness to pay for sex bought from a prostitute is less than the perceived value of the sex consummating love. (Imagine the reaction if a practitioner of cost-benefit analysis computed the benefits of sex based on the price of prostitute services.)

Furthermore, if one values in a general sense the existence of a non-market sector because of its connection with the production of certain valued feelings, then one ascribes added value to any non-marketed good simply as a repository of values represented by the nonmarket sector one wishes to preserve. This seems certainly to be the case for things in nature, such as pristine streams or undisturbed forests: for many people who value them, part of their value comes from their position as repositories of values the non-market sector represents.

The second way in which placing a market price on a thing decreases its perceived value is by removing the possibility of proclaiming that the thing is "not for sale," since things on the market by definition are for sale. The very statement that something is not for sale affirms, enhances, and protects a thing's value in a number of ways. To begin with, the statement is a way of showing that a thing is valued for its own sake. Furthermore, to say that something cannot be transferred in that way places it in the exceptional category—which requires the person interested in obtaining that thing to be able to offer something else that is exceptional, rather than allowing him the easier alternative of obtaining the thing for money that could have been obtained in an infinity of ways. This enhances its value. If I am willing to say "You're a really kind person" to whoever pays me to do so, my praise loses the value that attaches to it from being exchangeable only for an act of kindness.

In addition, if we have already decided we value something highly, one way of stamping it with a cachet affirming its high value is to announce that it is "not for sale." Such an announcement does more, however, than just reflect a preexisting high valuation. It signals a thing's distinctive value to others and helps us persuade them to value the thing more highly than they otherwise might. It also expresses our resolution to safeguard that distinctive value. To state that something is not for sale is thus also a source of value for that thing, since if a thing's value is easy to affirm or protect, it will be worth more than an otherwise similar thing without such attributes.

If we proclaim that something is not for sale, we make a once-and-for-all judgment of its special value. When something is priced, the issue of its perceived value is constantly coming up, as a standing invitation to reconsider that original judgment. Were people constantly faced with questions such as "how much money could get you to give up your freedom of speech?" or "how much would you sell your vote for if you could?", the perceived value of the freedom to speak or the right to vote would soon become devastated as, in moments of weakness, people started saying "maybe it's not worth *so much* after all." Better not to be faced with the constant questioning in the first place. Something similar did in fact occur when the slogan "better red than dead" was launched by some pacifists during the Cold War. Critics pointed out that the very posing of this stark choice—in effect, "would you *really* be willing to give up your life in exchange for not living under communism?"—reduced the value people attached to freedom and thus diminished resistance to attacks on freedom.

Finally, of some things valued very highly it is stated that they are "priceless" or that they have "infinite value." Such expressions are reserved for a subset of things not for sale, such as life or health. Economists tend to scoff at talk of pricelessness. For them, saying that something is priceless is to state a willingness to trade off an infinite quantity of all other goods for one unit of the priceless good, a situation that empirically appears highly unlikely. For most people, however, the word priceless is pregnant with meaning. Its value-affirming and value-protecting functions cannot be bestowed on expressions that merely denote a determinate, albeit high, valuation. John Kennedy in his inaugural address proclaimed that the nation was ready to "pay any price

[and] bear any burden . . . to assure the survival and the success of liberty." Had he said instead that we were willing to "pay a high price" or "bear a large burden" for liberty, the statement would have rung hollow.

An objection that advocates of cost-benefit analysis might well make to the preceding argument should be considered. I noted earlier that, in cases where various non-utility-based duties or rights conflict with the maximization of utility, it is necessary to make a deliberative judgment about what act is finally right. I also argued earlier that the search for commensurability might not always be a desirable one, that the attempt to go beyond expressing benefits in terms of (say) lives saved and costs in terms of dollars is not something devoutly to be wished.

In situations involving things that are not expressed in a common measure, advocates of cost-benefit analysis argue that people making judgments "in effect" perform cost-benefit calculations anyway. If government regulators promulgate a regulation that saves 100 lives at a cost of $1 billion, they are "in effect" valuing a life at (a minimum of) $10 million, whether or not they say that they are willing to place a dollar value on a human life. Since, in this view, cost-benefit analysis "in effect" is inevitable, it might as well be made specific.

This argument misconstrues the real difference in the reasoning processes involved. In cost-benefit analysis, equivalencies are established *in advance* as one of the raw materials for the calculation. One determines costs and benefits, one determines equivalencies (to be able to put various costs and benefits into a common measure), and then one sets to toting things up—waiting, as it were, with bated breath for the results of the calculation to come out. The outcome is determined by the arithmetic; if the outcome is a close call or if one is not good at long division, one does not know how it will turn out until the calculation is finished. In the kind of deliberative judgment that is performed without a common measure, no establishment of equivalencies occurs in advance. Equivalencies are not aids to the decision process. In fact, the decision maker might not even be aware of what the "in effect" equivalencies were, at least before they are revealed to him afterwards by some-one pointing out what he had "in effect" done. The decision maker would see himself as simply having made a deliberative judgment; the "in effect" equivalency number did not play a causal role in the decision but at most merely reflects it. Given this, the argument against making the process explicit is the one discussed earlier in the discussion of problems with putting specific quantified values on things that are not normally quantified—that the very act of doing so may serve to reduce the value of those things.

My own judgment is that modest efforts to assess levels of benefits and costs are justified, although I do not believe that government agencies ought to sponsor efforts to put dollar prices on non-market things. I also do not believe that the cry for more cost-benefit analysis in regulation is, on the whole, justified. If regulatory officials were so insensitive

about regulatory costs that they did not provide acceptable raw material for deliberative judgments (even if not of a strictly cost-benefit nature), my conclusion might be different. But a good deal of research into costs and benefits already occurs— actually, far more in the U.S. regulatory process than in that of any other industrial society. The danger now would seem to come more from the other side.

NOTES

1. Editor's note: RARG stands for "Regulatory Analysis Review Group," which was a group set up during the Ford Administration to do cost-benefit analyses of regulatory proposals. In Washington circles at the time, it was common to speak of a proposal as having been "RARGed."

Cost-Benefit Analysis Defended

Herman B. Leonard and Richard J. Zeckhauser

Cost-benefit analysis, particularly as applied to public decisions involving risks to life and health, has not been notably popular. A number of setbacks— Three Mile Island is perhaps the most memorable— have called into question the reliability of analytic approaches to risk issues. We believe that the current low reputation of cost-benefit analysis is unjustified, and that a close examination of the objections most frequently raised against the method will show that it deserves wider public support.

Society does not and indeed could not require the explicit consent of every affected individual in order to implement public decisions that impose costs or

risks. The transactions costs of assembling unanimous consent would be prohibitive, leading to paralysis in the status quo. Moreover, any system that required unanimous consent would create incentives for individuals to misrepresent their beliefs so as to secure compensation or to prevent the imposition of relatively small costs on them even if the benefits to others might be great.

If actual individual consent is an impractically strong standard to require of centralized decisions, how should such decisions be made? Our test for a proposed public decision is whether the net benefits of the action are positive. The same criterion is fre-

Herman B. Leonard and Richard J. Zeckhauser, "Cost-Benefit Analysis Defended," *Report from the Institute for Philosophy and Public Policy* 3, no. 3 (Summer 1983). Reprinted with permission of the publisher, Institute for Philosophy and Public Policy, and the authors.

quently phrased: Will those favored by the decision gain enough that they would have a net benefit even if they fully compensated those hurt by the decision? Applying this criterion to all possible actions, we discover that the chosen alternative should be the one for which benefits most exceed costs. We believe that the benefit-cost criterion is a useful way of defining "hypothetical consent" for centralized decisions affecting individuals with widely divergent interests: hypothetically, if compensation could be paid, all would agree to the decision offering the highest net benefits. We turn now to objections commonly raised against this approach.

COMPENSATION AND HYPOTHETICAL CONSENT

An immediate problem with the pure cost-benefit criterion is that it does not require the actual payment of compensation to those on whom a given decision imposes net costs. Our standard for public decision-making does not require that losers be compensated, but only that they *could* be if a perfect system of transfers existed. But unless those harmed by a decision are *actually* compensated, they will get little solace from the fact that someone is reaping a surplus in which they could have shared.

To this we make two replies. First, it is typically infeasible to design a compensation system that ensures that all individuals will be net winners. The transactions costs involved in such a system would often be so high as to make the project as a whole a net loss. But it may not even be desirable to construct full compensation systems, since losers will generally have an incentive under such systems to overstate their anticipated losses in order to secure greater compensation.

Second, the problem of compensation is probably smaller in practice than in principle. Society tends to compensate large losses where possible or to avoid imposing large losses when adequate compensation is not practical. Moreover, compensation is sometimes overpaid; having made allowances *ex ante* for imposing risks, society still chooses sometimes to

pay additional compensation *ex post* to those who actually suffer losses.

Libertarians raise one additional argument about the ethical basis of a system that does not require full compensation to losers. They argue that a public decision process that imposes uncompensated losses constitutes an illegal taking of property by the state and should not be tolerated. This objection, however strongly grounded ethically, would lead to an untenable position for society by unduly constraining public decisions to rest with the status quo.

ATTENTION TO DISTRIBUTION

Two distinct types of distributional issue are relevant in cost-benefit analysis. First, we can be concerned about the losers in a particular decision, whoever they may be. Second, we can be concerned with the transfers between income classes (or other defined groups) engendered by a given project. If costs are imposed differentially on groups that are generally disadvantaged, should the decision criterion include special consideration of their interests? This question is closely intertwined with the issue of compensation, because it is often alleged that the uncompensated costs of projects evaluated by cost-benefit criteria frequently fall on those who are disadvantaged to start with.

These objections have little to do with cost-benefit analysis as a method. We see no reason why any widely agreed upon notion of equity, or weighting of different individuals' interests, cannot in principle be built into the cost-benefit decision framework. It is merely a matter of defining carefully what is meant by a benefit or a cost. If, in society's view, benefits (or costs) to some individuals are more valuable (costly) than those to others, this can be reflected in the construction of the decision criterion.

But although distribution concerns could be systematically included in cost-benefit analyses, it is not always—or even generally—a good idea to do so. Taxes and direct expenditures represent a far more efficient means of effecting redistribution than virtually any other public program; we would strongly prefer to rely on one consistent comprehensive tax and expenditure package for redistribution than on attempts to redistribute within every project.

First, if distributional issues are considered everywhere, they will probably not be adequately, carefully, and correctly treated anywhere. Many critics of cost-benefit analysis believe that project-based distributional analysis would create a net addition to society's total redistributive effort; we suggest that is likely, instead, to be only an inefficient substitution.

Second, treating distributional concerns within each project can only lead to transfers within the group affected by a project, often only a small subset of the community. For example, unisex rating of auto insurance redistributes only among drivers. Cross-subsidization of medical costs affects only those who need medical services. Why should not the larger society share the burden of redistribution?

Third, the view that distributional considerations should be treated project-by-project reflects a presumption that on average they do not balance out—that is, that some groups systematically lose more often than others. If it were found that some groups were severely and systematically disadvantaged by the application of cost-benefit analyses that ignore distributional concerns, we would favor redressing the balance. We do not believe this is generally the case.

that cannot be traded off to obtain other gains. Nor can we carry out a cost-benefit analysis to decide which values should be included and which treated separately—this decision will always have to be made in some other manner.

These considerations do not invalidate cost-benefit analysis, but merely illustrate that more is at stake than just dollar measures of costs and benefits. We would, however, make two observations. First, we must be very careful that only genuinely important and relevant social values be permitted to outweigh the findings of an analysis. Second, social values that frequently stand in the way of important efficiency gains have a way of breaking down and being replaced over time, so that in the long run society manages to accommodate itself to some form of cost-benefit criterion. If nuclear power were 1000 times more dangerous for its employees but 10 times less expensive than it is, we might feel that ethical considerations were respected and the national interest well served if we had rotating cadres of nuclear power employees serving short terms in high-risk positions, much as members of the armed services do. In like fashion, we have fire-fighters risk their lives; universal sprinkler systems would be less dangerous, but more costly. Such policies reflect an accommodation to the costs as a recognition of the benefits.

SENSITIVE SOCIAL VALUES

Cost-benefit analysis, it is frequently alleged, does a disservice to society because it cannot treat important social values with appropriate sensitivity. We believe that this view does a disservice to society by unduly constraining the use of a reasonable and helpful method for organizing the debate about public decisions. We are not claiming that every important social value can be represented effectively within the confines of cost-benefit analysis. Some values will never fit in a cost-benefit framework and will have to be treated as "additional considerations" in coming to a final decision. Some, such as the inviolability of human life, may simply be binding constraints

MEASURABILITY

Another objection frequently raised against cost-benefit analysis is that some costs and benefits tend to be ignored because they are much more difficult to measure than others. The long-term environmental impacts of large projects are frequently cited as an example. Cost-benefit analysis is charged with being systematically biased toward consideration of the quantifiable aspects of decisions.

This is unquestionably true: cost-benefit analysis is *designed* as a method of quantification, so it surely is better able to deal with more quantifiable aspects of the issues it confronts. But this limitation is in itself ethically neutral unless it can be shown that the quantifiable considerations systematically push decisions in a particular direction. Its detractors must show that the errors of cost-benefit analysis are systematically unjust or inefficient—for example, that it frequently helps the rich at the expense of the poor, or despoils the environment to the benefit of industry, or vice versa. We have not seen any carefully researched evidence to support such assertions.

We take some comfort in the fact that cost-benefit analysis is sometimes accused of being biased toward development projects and sometimes of being biased against them. Cost-benefit analyses have foiled conservation efforts in national forests—perhaps they systematically weight the future too little. But they have also squelched clearly silly projects designed to bring "economic development" to Alaska—and the developers argued that the analysis gave insufficient weight to the "unquantifiable," value of future industrialization.

In our experience, cost-benefit analysis is often a tool of the "outs"—those not currently in control of the political process. Those who have the political power to back the projects they support often have little need of analyses. By contrast, analysis can be an effective tool for those who are otherwise not strongly empowered politically.

ANALYZING RISKS

Even those who accept the ethical propriety of cost-benefit analysis of decisions involving transfers of money or other tangible economic costs and benefits sometimes feel that the principles do not extend to analyzing decisions involving the imposition of risks. We believe that such applications constitute a *particularly* important area in which cost-benefit analysis can be of value. The very difficulties of reaching appropriate decisions where risks are involved make it all the more vital to employ the soundest methods available, both ethically and practically.

Historically, cost-benefit analysis has been applied widely to the imposition and regulation of risks, in particular to risks of health loss or bodily harm.

The cost-benefit approach is particularly valuable here, for several reasons. Few health risks can be exchanged on a voluntary basis. Their magnitude is difficult to measure. Even if they could be accurately measured, individuals have difficulty interpreting probabilities or gauging how they would feel should the harm eventuate. Compounding these problems of valuation are difficulties in contract, since risks are rarely conveyed singly between one individual and another.

The problem of risks conveyed in the absence of contractual approval has been addressed for centuries through the law of torts, which is designed to provide compensation after a harm has been received. If only a low-probability risk is involved, it it often efficient to wait to see whether a harm occurs, for in the overwhelming majority of circumstances transactions costs will be avoided. This approach also limits debate over the magnitude of a potential harm that has not yet eventuated. The creator of the risk has the incentive to gauge accurately, for he is the one who must pay if harm does occur.

While in principle it provides efficient results, the torts approach encounters at least four difficulties when applied to many of the risks that are encountered in a modern technological society. The option of declaring bankruptcy allows the responsible party to avoid paying and so to impose risks that it should not impose. Causality is often difficult to assign for misfortunes that may have alternative or multiple (and synergistically related) causes. Did the individual contract lung cancer from air pollution or from his own smoking, or both? Furthermore, the traditional torts requirement that individuals be made whole cannot be met in many instances (death, loss of a limb). Finally, paying compensation after the fact may also produce inappropriate incentives, and hence be inefficient. Workers who can be more or less careful around dangerous machinery, for example, are likely to be more careful if they will not be compensated for losing an appendage.

Our normal market and legal system tends to break down when substantial health risks are imposed on a relatively large population. These are, therefore, precisely the situations in which the cost-benefit approach is and should be called into play. Cost-benefit analysis is typically used in just those situations where our normal risk decision processes run into difficulty. We should therefore not expect it to lead to outcomes that are as satisfactory as those that evolve when ordinary market and private contractual trade are employed. But we should be able to expect better outcomes than we would achieve by muddling through unsystematically.

We have defended cost-benefit analysis as the most practical of ethically defensible methods and the most ethical of practically usable methods for conducting public decision-making. It cannot substitute for—nor can it adequately encompass, analyze, or consider—the sensitive application of social values. Thus it cannot be made the final arbiter of public decisions. But it does add a useful structure to public debate, and it does enable us to quantify some of the quantifiable aspects of public decisions. Our defense parallels Winston Churchill's argument for democracy: it is not perfect, but it is better than the alternatives.

Moral Pluralism and the Environment

Andrew Brennan

Cost-benefit analysis makes the assumption that everything from consumer goods to endangered species may in principle be given a value by which its worth can be compared with that of anything else, even though the actual measurement of such value may be difficult in practice. The assumption is shown to fail, even in simple cases, and the analysis to be incapable of taking into account the transformative value of new experiences. Several kinds of value are identified, by no means all commensurable with one another—a situation with which both economics and contemporary ethical theory must come to terms. A radical moral pluralism is recommended as in no way incompatible with the requirements of rationality, which allows that the business of living decently involves many kinds of principles and various sorts of responsibilities. In environmental ethics, pluralism offers the hope of reconciling various rival theories, even if none of them is universally applicable.

WHAT IS WRONG WITH COST-BENEFIT ANALYSIS?

It is normal for writers to make extravagant claims for their disciplines. Perhaps there is no discipline at present of which this is more true than economics. In environmental discussions, the economist often takes the part of the sensible, rational being, the person who wants to be objective, and base judgments

Andrew Brennan, "Moral Pluralism and the Environment," *Environmental Values* 1 (1992): 15–33. Reprinted with permission of White Horse Press, Cambridge U.K.

on solid fact. Yet the appeal to economic rationality is highly dangerous—some would say immoral.

Let us start by thinking about a case where economic rationality may make some sense. Suppose we want to reduce the carbon and sulfur pollution associated with a range of industries. Is there any sensible way we can allocate a level of taxation on these pollutants which will be fair? Let us further suppose that part of our idea of what is fair involves being able to justify the proposed level of tax to the industries which produce the pollution.

We can approach this problem by considering first of all just how much damage is caused by the pollution and how to put a monetary value on it. Thus for the pollutants mentioned, we can look at effects on health, in terms of treatment costs for patients with respiratory disease directly due to the pollution. We can consider the cost of repairing damaged buildings, the losses suffered by forestry and the loss of agricultural production. All of these costs can be put in monetary terms (more or less), and give us a measure of the costs associated with air pollution. Put another way, the same figures indicate the scale of benefits that could be achieved by restriction of such pollution.

Now it is not a simple matter to fix the appropriate level of sulfur and carbon taxes in the light of the above information. But we can make sense of the idea that quantifiable costs are associated with pollution and quantifiable benefits are to be gained from controlling it. However, economists typically want to count in other effects of air pollution apart from the ones just mentioned. Consider, for example, the loss of pleasure due to impaired viewing conditions. If air pollution is bad enough in an area with a tourist industry, then there may well be loss of tourist revenue to count in with the other losses. But what of the people who already live or work in the area? Would they not also count in the economic equation? Even if their health is not directly affected, are they not suffering other losses of amenity?

In trying to count in the losses of this last sort, economists usually resort to a technique known as "contingent valuation" or "shadow pricing." But this technique is not without problems. How, for example, can we put a price on reduction of visibility in everyday life? Some American economists from the University of Wyoming tried to do this. They showed a number of people photographs of their surroundings in which air quality was better and worse. They then asked how much the subjects would be willing to pay in addition to their normal electricity bills to preserve a particular level of visibility rather than the next lower one.[1]

This attempt to elicit willingness-to-pay is regularly used by economists. In another study, economists managed to put values on grizzly bears and bighorn sheep by quizzing hunters about how much they were willing to pay to maintain sufficient stocks of these animals.[2] But, as Mark Sagoff points out in a critique of such studies, they are often undermined by the large number of people who refuse cooperation. Thus, instead of agreeing on some level of payment to ensure better visibility, many of those questioned simply refused to play the economists' game. They would either refuse to make bids, or they would lodge protest bids which were in excess of any sums they could actually afford to pay. In cases where subjects are asked about levels of compensation for some loss or disbenefit, protest bids—as Sagoff points out—sometimes include a demand for infinite compensation.

The existence of protest bids is uncomfortable for the economist. But the fact that some people show discomfort about the whole exercise of contingent valuation is itself interesting. For what the exercise is supposed to reveal is something about preferences. We are all consumers of various goods and services, and in making consumer choices we reveal, so it is thought, our preferences. It seems logical, then, to try to find out what our preferences about visibility are, just as it is worthwhile to find out what our preferences are on hospital treatment, the color of toothpaste or whatever. The moral that Sagoff draws, however, is rather different. For he argues that the existence of protest bids in the contingent valuation experiments reveals that the issues involved are not simply ones about preferences.

ENVIRONMENTAL POLICY AND ITS FOUNDATIONS

Sagoff's general strategy is to argue that matters of public policy involve values as well as preferences. He has a general objection to economic analysis on the grounds that it pretends there is no difference between matters of preference and matters of value. However, I want to consider whether economic analysis can even get to grips with preferences themselves. It turns out, if I am correct, that the economist's claim to rationality is a feature of a wider view about rationality which is quite false. But the falsity of that wider view has important consequences for ethics as well as economics.[3]

It is widely recognized in human communities that not all preferences are of equal weight. If my preference is to make money by stealing, or by murdering those who are wealthy, then the laws of every society will be against me. Passing laws against murder and stealing is one way a community can protect itself against citizens who might otherwise develop unworthy preferences. From the point of view of the law-abiding individual, illegal acts do not find a place on that person's preference-map.

Economists have long recognized that the preferences of individuals are hard to map. For example, as Mark Sagoff has pointed out, a person may rationally bribe a judge on one occasion (in order to save their driving license) yet later help to vote the judge out of office (because the same person disapproves of corruption in the law). One way of explaining this behavior is to suppose that in the role of *consumer* I operate with quite different preferences from those I have in the role of *citizen*. In taking this approach, Sagoff develops arguments originally put forward by other writers (see Tullock 1967; Sen 1977; and Sagoff 1988). If Sagoff and these other writers are correct, then there is no single order in which all my preferences can be placed, for there is no single role which embraces all my roles. It would then follow that there is no single preference-map which can be ascribed to me. Yet it is a feature of standard neoclassical economic theory that all of us do possess a single set of ordered preferences.

I would be inclined to go further than Sagoff and argue that even within a single social role, I lack an ordered preference set. Consider, for example, our behavior concerning books or music. Do I prefer Schumann's *Études Symphoniques* to Chopin's *Préludes?* I have no answer to give to this question, not because I am indifferent between the Schumann and the Chopin but because each has its own strengths. The Chopin is more pianistic, while Schumann's work makes, so to speak, an orchestra out of the piano. Sometimes I would rather listen to the Schumann, and other times to the Chopin. But such an observation shows nothing about the possibility of placing the two works in a single map of ordered preferences. The difficulty here is noteworthy, for we might have expected two standard works from the romantic piano repertoire to be commensurable in many ways.

One way of explaining this difficulty about preferences is by resort to the idea of *value*. In the case of music, we might say that different pieces have different mixes of values. The aesthetics of music will thus not be simple. Even in comparing two romantic composers of the piano, like Chopin and Schumann, we will encounter complexes of value which make rankings difficult, if not impossible. Now, a simple story about preferences, let us suppose, is that we try to accord the higher preference to the item of greater value. According to this story, the acquisition of musical taste is in part the process of learning to prefer music of greater value to music of lesser value. But if values are themselves mixed, and fail to condense into a single order, there is no single set of values for our preferences to latch on to.[4]

KINDS OF VALUE

If we lay the question of mixed values aside for a moment, we can try to make sense of ordering our preferences in a different way. If we can distinguish a number of kinds of value, then perhaps we can try to ground our preferences in the different values that things have. When we try to defend our *considered* preferences, we can do so perhaps by pointing to the different sources for these preferences in the things valued.

Theorists of environmental policy and ethics usually distinguish three kinds of values. First, there is a major distinction between *intrinsic* and *instrumental* value. Something is of intrinsic value if it has value in its own right, or for its own sake. Education, for example, is often held up as an example of something of intrinsic value, as is the study of music, literature, the sciences and the visual arts. By contrast, something is of instrumental value when its existence is necessary for the preservation or realization of some other value. A good violin is of instrumental value because without it we could not appreciate certain kinds of fine music. A forest is of instrumental value if it yields timber for building and paper making. Notice that the forest may also be of value in its own right: the categories of instrumental and intrinsic value are not exclusive.

Bryan Norton has pointed out that there is a class of instrumentally valuable goods which stand in a peculiar relation to our preferences (see Norton 1987). For they are things which do not simply satisfy our considered felt preferences. Rather, they provide an occasion for examining and sometimes revising these preferences themselves. In this way, they contrast with what might be called "demand values." The latter are characteristic of things which either have a use for us, or which may conceivably yield a use for us in future. Norton contrasts demand values of this sort with non-demand values. See the following table:

The items we buy at the market or in the shops are typical examples of what have a use value. To argue that rainforest species should be preserved on the grounds that they may one day yield useful medicines is to claim that such species have an option value for us.

But some people would like rainforest species to be preserved independent of any future industrial or pharmaceutical value we might find for them. What they are recognizing, then, is value in the existence of such wild places. Now to recognize such existence values, we do not need to argue that rainforests have value in their own right. Rather, it may be that the existence of rainforest species is instrumentally valuable, in that without them other things of value would be lost.[5]

Finally, the category of transformative value represents a further instrumental type of value that something may possess. Norton gives the example of a teenager who is forced, by circumstances beyond her control, to go to a classical music concert. Until then, we are to suppose that she was keen on popular music and had no time for other musical forms. Surprisingly, the classical concert appeals to her; she subsequently develops an interest in Mozart and starts collecting classical music. Attending the concert has transformed her considered preferences. We can thus classify the three forms of value in general as follows:

Now a very difficult problem is posed by the existence of transformative value, at least as far as the economist is concerned. For if we try to put a price on transformative value, we shall fail. The impact of transformative values on people's preferences is completely unpredictable, and the degree of impact (when it occurs) will vary massively from person to person. However good cost-benefit analysis is when

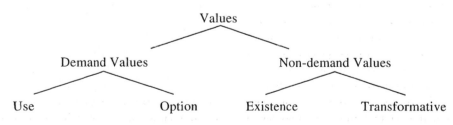

Figure 1.

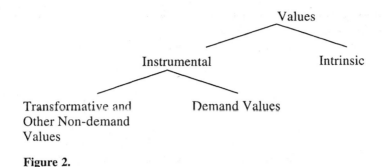

Figure 2.

dealing with demand values, it is bound to leave out transformative value. If we now agree with Norton that natural things and systems themselves possess transformative values, then it will follow immediately that they cannot be priced by the standard techniques of economics.

Norton's results are very much what we might expect. It would be foolish to think that an economic technique which has important application in the field of pollution control can be extended to all environmental policy areas. Yet this is precisely what is attempted by those economists who aim to include all values in their calculations. They are pursuing a phantom; for however hard they try, there will be values which forever elude them.

These thoughts about value also provide the answer to an earlier problem. Recall the suggestion that we might try to make our preferences line up, so to speak, with the order of values in the things around us. If there is no single order of values, then we cannot look for help here in constructing our preferences. We saw already that musical compositions may display mixes of different values, as do novels, paintings, scientific treatises and natural objects. These various values, we can now see, break down further according to whether they are intrinsic, instrumental or transformative. But since some of these forms of value will forever elude quantification, it would be folly to try to set up a single order of values, or of corresponding preferences. Much though economics may like to present itself as a rational discipline, commitment to a single order of values and of preferences would be quite the opposite of rationality.

PLURALISM DEFENDED

The suggestions I have just made may seem to give grounds for pessimism. How can we approach issues of public policy in medical ethics, allocation of scarce resources and environmental protection in the absence of shared, objective standards by means of which to judge between different values and different sets of preferences? Unfortunately, it will do no good to turn for help to ethics rather than economics. For ethical theory, as understood by the majority of contemporary moral philosophers, parallels economics in its attempt to reduce complexities about value to simple principles and single measures. Even people who are sympathetic to what I have argued so far may prefer to stick with the methods of cost-benefit analysis, and try to extend these to all forms of environmental impact assessment. The alternative looks like muddling through in an impressionistic, irrational way.

It is important not to underestimate the power of the conception of rationality that is built into the fear just mentioned. That conception is central to economics, and to standard moral philosophy.6 Bernard Williams has described it in the following terms:

> [There is] an assumption about rationality, to the effect that two considerations cannot be rationally weighed against each other unless there is a common consideration in terms of which they can be compared. This assumption is at once very powerful and utterly baseless . . . The drive toward a rationalistic conception of rationality comes . . . from social features of the modern world. . . . (Williams 1985, p. 16–17)

Williams goes on to explain that the social features to which he is referring impose on *personal* deliberations a model drawn from a particular understanding of public rationality. According to that model, every decision must be based on grounds which can be laid out by appeal to certain general principles which are comparable with each other.

I think it is clear both that the phenomenon exists and that it exerts a peculiarly compelling force on us. If we want to regard ourselves as operating in *principled* ways, we expect that our behavior falls under certain principles, even if we are not terribly good at articulating them clearly. Likewise, if there are regularities in natural processes and systems, we hope that our sciences at least approximate to some of these, even if we can never be entirely sure that we have hit upon the ultimately *true* theory. It is a short step from these thoughts to the idea that the sciences are ultimately concerned with one kind of object or event in terms of which everything else can be explained. This is what has motivated atomism in its various guises over the years. It is also one of the motives in the positivists' search for a unified science. Likewise, economic theory—as we have seen—orders values according to one monetary weighting and orders our preferences in a corresponding way. Finally, moral philosophy often purports to deal with just one kind of state of affairs in terms of which the good or the right is defined. For example, in utilitarianism all morally relevant states will be compared in terms of overall pleasure (or in terms of some other single measure of utility).

Once these ideas are out in the open, it is easy to see why Williams regards the shared notions as baseless. Few modern scientists would want to make the objectivity of science depend on there being a single set of objects (or events), and a single theory of them, which explains everything.[7] And once we are free from the lures of economic theory we recognize that economic considerations are different from, and not commensurate with, moral or aesthetic ones. So the attempt to reduce all science to a common coin, like the attempt to reduce all values to monetary ones, looks doomed.

But we could agree to what has just been said while still defending monism in morality itself. We could argue that there will be just one set of principles concerning just one form of value that provides ultimate government for our actions. But why should we want to do so? It cannot be to defend notions of objectivity and impartiality. For, once we give up the monistic model of rationality, we recognize that there is nothing whimsical, or unreasonable, in deciding on one issue to be swayed by economic considerations, while on another to follow aesthetic ones. If we use statistical mechanics for studying the behavior of gases, this by no means determines the theory to be used in studying the ecology of a salt marsh. Nor is there anything irrational about preferring Schumann one day and Chopin the next. For, as we have seen, within the aesthetic sphere there are mixes of values and mixes of preferences. If we have really shaken off the rationalistic picture of rationality, then it is not a lapse of rationality that there is no higher set of comprehensive considerations under which all aesthetic considerations fall, let alone both aesthetic and economic ones. Still less would we want to reduce the aesthetic to the economic.

If we can be objective and rational in adjudicating the competing claims of aesthetics and economics, then we can be equally objective and rational, within the moral enterprise itself, when faced with competing claims. That we come to moral decisions does not mean, then, that we must somehow have reduced all the competing claims to a common measure, or have seen them as failing under some single hierarchy of principles. *Moral pluralism*—to give a name to the position opposed to monism—allows that the business of living decently involves many kinds of principles and various sorts of responsibilities. It recognizes that our feelings and responses to situations are drawn from many sources and cannot be simplified without distortion. Moreover, it maintains that the absence of any clear principles we can articulate for a given case is no evidence of the absence of moral significance. Once we have succeeded in resisting the lure of the rationalistic conception of rationality, it is hard to see why moral monism should commend itself over a pluralist perspective.

It remains true that a pluralist perspective will not be easy to use. If many different sets of values are in play when environmental issues are being discussed, the role of the policy-maker becomes much more complicated. But life is complicated, and we will not make progress in tackling the grave difficulties we face unless we learn to avoid shallow thinking and simple solutions. Although Sagoff has expressed the hope that democratic communities are well placed for establishing procedures by which we can start to give weight to the many complexities of environmental problems, it remains to be seen whether his optimism is justified.

ENVIRONMENTAL ETHICS

I conclude with a brief survey of the main underlying theories of environmental ethics and with a suggestion about how we should think about the challenge they pose to conventional ethical theory. There are two main approaches: ethics that are human-based (anthropocentric) and those that are non-anthropocentric. The human-based ethics focus on human beings not only as the actors in morality, but also as the proper subjects of morality too. Now some human beings value natural things and processes in their own right. An anthropocentric ethic can take account of this, since it regards human interests as the only ethically significant ones. Likewise, an anthropocentric ethic can make sense of preserving buildings, paintings or other artifacts for the benefit of those humans who enjoy or study them.

But over the last twenty years or so, environmental ethics has been largely occupied with exploring an alternative, non-anthropocentric approach to morality. According to this approach, things apart from human agents might be proper subjects of moral concern. Those theories that are *biocentric* claim that at least some other living things are possessors of value in their own right. But other accounts of moral value suggest that the possession of life is not itself morally significant. For these last theorists, there can be ethical (and aesthetic) value in a lake, a landscape or a mountain range, even though none of these things is itself alive.

The range of non-anthropocentric theories has posed something of a problem for moral philosophy as it is usually conceived. Contrasted with the conventional treatment of human beings as both moral agents and moral subjects, the new theories have forced reflection on the moral, legal and aesthetic standing of many kinds of non-human beings. These include artifacts (such as paintings, buildings and corporations), living and non-living natural objects, and also systems and processes (see Figure 3).

We can map the various kinds of non-anthropocentric value theory by noting that some of them are very much individually-based, while others are holistic in the sense that they attribute intrinsic value to aggregates of individuals. Under the impact of writers like the Scot John Muir and the American preservationist, Aldo Leopold, several more recent theorists have argued that whole communities, ecosystems and even the land itself are complexes which deserve respectful treatment (see Muir 1988; Leopold 1949; Rolston 1988). Of course, the distinction between an individual and an aggregate is not clear-cut, but it is possible to make a rough and ready distinction between holistic and individualistic theories (see Table 1).

These positions are by no means exclusive. For example, Holmes Rolston has argued that there is moral value in individual lives, in species, and in ecosystems. Other theorists, Paul Taylor for one, have adopted a resolutely individualistic, life-centered ethic, while those who follow Arne Naess's thoughts about deep ecology generally support the view that living things are knots in a larger web of value (see Taylor 1984 and Naess 1973).

What is striking about all the non-anthropocentric value positions is that they challenge centuries of orthodox philosophical theory. The fact that things other than human beings have a place in our moral thinking in their own right is something on which all the major theories of morality—whether rights-based, utilitarian, or virtue-based—have been largely silent.[8] Environmental ethics thus differs from other areas of applied philosophy, in that it does not call for the extension of existing value categories and moral analysis. Rather, it challenges the standard cat-

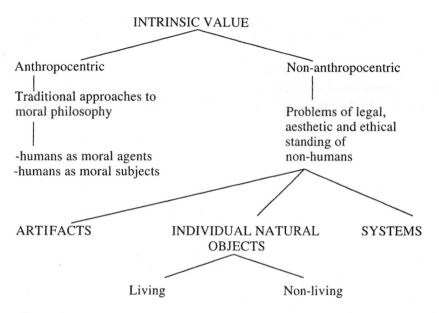

Figure 3.

egories and analyses themselves. Environmental ethics does not call for expanding the circle of beings recognized as having feelings, for example, or capable of feeling pain. In this way it contrasts with the position of those who argue for the extension of moral consideration to non-human animals (see Callicott 1980). Rather, some environmental thinkers have posed the question of why feelings should be so important to morality. Forests, lakes and rocky crests have no feelings, nor have they, as far as we know, any other interests we can take into account. But that fact alone does not mean that they have to be left out of the moral reckoning.

Many workers in the field would disagree strongly with what has just been suggested. For some of them, the heart of our environmental concerns lies precisely in a kind of extended individual benevolence. Writers like Stephen Clark defend vegetarianism and the elimination of animal experimentation on the grounds that present human practices do wrong to other animals (Clark 1977). It is perhaps natural to extend this concern, as Clark does himself. If animals can be wronged, then perhaps so can plants, forests, lakes and rocky crests. Tom Regan, to take another notable example, holds that non-human animals have what he calls "inherent value" through being subjects of a life. Such value does not come in degrees: if rabbits have it at all, they have it equally with us. For Regan, our duties towards other animals, and their rights, are founded on this inherent value. For the environment, Regan articulates an ethic of general non-intervention in nature, based on the inherent value of all natural objects. These examples could be multiplied.

Without in any way wishing to challenge the moral sincerity of the writers just mentioned, I would like to propose that theirs is not a route worth following. I have given detailed reasons elsewhere for thinking that species, natural systems and landscapes

Table 1. Non-Anthropocentric Value

	Holistic	Individualistic
Biocentric	*Deep Ecology*	*Animal Rights*
	Gaia	*Respect for Trees*
Non-biocentric	*Systemic Value*	*Artworks*
		Rocky crests

cannot plausibly be regarded as having interests of any sort, nor do they have modes of flourishing, nor can we make sense of the claim that they have directions of development.[9] I will not repeat these arguments now but instead I would like to suggest a partial explanation for why so many writers have taken the route, however ill-advised it is to do so. They have, I conjecture, simply followed tradition. The recent tradition of moral philosophy has regarded the interests of the parties concerned as central to their role in the moral enterprise. For the utilitarian, the morally relevant parties in any situation are those whose pleasures or pains will be affected by what is done in that situation. A standard prescription for the agent is that he or she should act so as to ensure that pains are minimized or pleasures maximized. For the contract theorist, the moral community consists of a group of beings with interests, and principles of morality and justice are devised so that these interests are respected without special regard to status or special position. Rights theorists who are not contractarians normally have in mind a moral community of items who can be represented in their own right, and thus as possessors of interests.[10]

In the face of this near-unanimity on the features of the moral community, we are faced with a real problem if we try to introduce considerations on behalf of items that lack interests in the sense of having no primary goods, no projects, no directions of development, no possibilities of pleasure, pain or other utility and no other features in terms of which they can be represented in their own right in moral debate. How could such items possibly have a moral claim on us? In desperation, heroic efforts are sometimes made to try to establish that trees, rocks, landscapes, and even natural systems have interests. A great deal of nonsense has been written in the attempt to characterize ecosystems as having possibilities of flourishing, directions of development or ways of being more or less healthy. Moreover, the need to introduce considerations about preserving trees, species and landscapes into debates on public policy has seemingly added urgency to the underlying philosophical project. Even though the works of philosophers have little direct bearing on public pol-

icy, it is not helpful to our reflections on these matters to find no room for valued environmental features in our ethical deliberations.

PROSPECTS FOR A "NEW ETHIC"

There has been a tendency in recent years for concerned people to suggest that what we need is a new ethic to moderate our dealings with nature. If my diagnosis of the challenge posed by environmental ethics is correct, we can begin to see why this is so. The conventional model for moral deliberations has been built on the understanding that the moral community is constituted of a number of individuals each with their own interests. Extending that community from humans first to other animals and ultimately to ecosystems has seemed to be an attractive option. But even early in the process there were symptoms that something was amiss. The claim by some animal liberationists that the world would be a better place if there were no predators and no parasites is entirely in keeping with the utilitarian arguments in favor of changing our modes of treating animals. Yet such a claim is anathema to many environmental philosophers. Over the last fifteen years, the animal rights and environmental philosophy camps have showed ever wider divisions, despite some attempts to heal the rift. The rift itself signifies a tension in the way the extension of individual benevolence has been perceived. Finally, attempts like Regan's to suggest that we should adopt an ethic of non-intervention in nature seem to constitute a reductio of the whole project of extending the circle of benevolence (Regan 1981). Such non-intervention has never been an option for humans, any more than it has been an option for other living species.

In the face of the challenge to find a new ethic, what can moral philosophy do? And, more urgently, what can the philosopher say to those who are concerned to frame environmentally sensitive policy and regulations? If we follow the monistic tradition and the rationalistic conception of rationality, we may perhaps look to interests or some other single feature to fund the value of trees, rocks, ecosystems, bacteria, dogs and people. Such a feature would be one in terms of which natural things and systems could gain entry to policy debates and be recognized as having standing in their own right. I now think there is probably no such feature.[11] But even if such a feature could be found, it is hard to believe that we could develop any plausible ranking of the relative value of all the things which possess it. Alternatively we can give up the rationalistic conception of rationality and the associated monistic point of view. We can start to think in terms of a plurality of values, and an associated plurality of principles. More radically, we will recognize that not all matters of morality can even be thought of in terms of principles, rules, contracts and the rest of the apparatus of conventional moral theory.[12]

To make clear just what is at stake here, notice that there are several kinds of pluralism. Liberal democracies are supposed to admit that there are competing conceptions of the good, and an associated plurality of values, held by their citizens. What might be called *moral liberalism* would be the ethical equivalent of this political position. It would accept that different people might bring different ethical perspectives to bear on an individual case (noting that in some cases the different perspectives would agree on what counts as the *right* course of action). This is *not* the kind of pluralism that I am advocating here. By contrast, in the present paper, moral pluralism is meant as a philosophical, not a moral, thesis. In its philosophical sense, we can still distinguish a number of forms for pluralism to take. I will look at two different forms, noting that the first form itself permits of several varieties.

The first kind of moral pluralism recognizes the possibility that *different considerations apply in different cases*. This somewhat ambiguous notion of pluralism has been at the center of attention in recent discussions of moral pluralism in environmental ethics.[13] It is surprising that any controversy at all has been aroused by this idea. Take three simple cases. Consider, first, the proper response to an injured animal. If it is badly injured and in obvious pain, the most humane course might be to kill it speedily. By contrast, there are circumstances in which it is decent to preserve the life of a human being who is suffering extreme pain. Third, trees, as far as we know, are not sentient beings at all, yet it may be proper to take steps to preserve a tree or trees by actions which cause pain to a sentient being (for example, when a vandal is forcibly restrained). What the first form of pluralism suggests is that no one set of considerations provides the rationale for these three cases, let alone for the multitude of others that face us daily. Yet what is involved in treating different cases differently? Someone who holds only a single, structured theory of ethics with a single standard of right and wrong might well count considerations involving human interests and welfare differently from those affecting other animals and plants. Although the considerations are not the same, this kind of pluralist would hold that—at a suitably abstract level—the principles are always the same.

As pointed out already, this version of pluralism has several varieties. Perhaps a more interesting variant is associated with the thought that principles drawn from one kind of understanding of ethics may apply in one case, while those drawn from a separate understanding apply in another. For example, maybe we could approach issues of public policy from a utilitarian point of view, yet be committed to some quite different point of view in our dealings with friends and relatives. Even if I think about public policy in terms of the balance of benefits or happiness over disbenefits, when fulfilling a promise to a friend, it may never occur to me to consider whether greater good overall might be achieved by breaking the promise and doing something else instead. Notice two points that arise from this example. First, the discrepancy between utilitarianism on public policy and some quite different approach to private morality does not indicate inconsistency on the part of the thinker or moral agent. Second, even if I do think about public policy in ways different from the way I think about obligations to my friends, it is not clear that the conventional distinctions of standard moral theories are best for describing such a difference.

More generally, it seems extremely simplistic to try to characterize our thinking about issues of public policy in terms of any one theory of ethics. For we are caught up in a number of very different considerations as soon as we try to give detailed attention to whether, for example, a leisure development should take place on farmland recently set aside from arable use. In such cases, we typically think of impacts on local employment, the many different interests and needs of those living in nearby towns and villages, effects on local ecosystems and biological communities—both physical and chemical—as well as aesthetic issues. Then there are notions we have about the sense of place shared by inhabitants of an area, and to what extent any proposed development will fit in with a continuing narrative history that can be given for that place. To reduce all these considerations to ones of utility, duty or beauty may be, in its own way, just as simplistic as the attempt to reduce all values to monetary ones.

These ideas give rise, finally, to a second development of the concept of moral pluralism. According to this, any particular situation in which we face a decision, or have to act, is complex. Its complexity could be described in terms of the idea of mixed values introduced earlier. Alternatively, it can be claimed that there is no single activity of valuing involved in assessing any situation. Pluralism of the second sort maintains that there is no single theoretical lens which provides a privileged set of concepts, principles and structure in terms of which a situation is to be viewed. Furthermore, complexity is a feature of the situations that arise in public debate and also in the most private of moral deliberations. This second kind of pluralism seems to me more interesting than the first sort, although related to it. As opposed to the claim that different cases call for different treatment, this new form recognizes that one and the same case can properly be viewed in many different ways.

There is a way into the thesis that the ethical enterprise is pluralistic in this second way which draws on the first, less controversial form of pluralism. Suppose, for the sake of argument, that the simplistic philosophical models have some merit. I think about public policy as a utilitarian, let us imagine, but I think about duties to my friends in terms of their moral claims on me as Kantian ends-in-themselves.

By contrast, I cultivate a caring and responsible attitude to my local environment by way of a conception of worthwhile human living in nature which does not reduce either to utilitarianism or Kantianism. I do not, for a moment, intend that any of these descriptions does more than caricature the moral situation of an agent. But if we accept the caricature for the moment notice how the switch of perspective from one case to the next can reveal something we may overlook when we concentrate on a single case viewed through a single lens. This is that the various perspectives brought to bear on the several cases can be brought to bear—to some degree—on the individual case as well. If each case can be viewed from more than one perspective, then the business of being morally engaged with the world around us involves a multiplicity of perspectives and a value complexity which is ignored in the standard, reductionist accounts found in textbooks. That a certain perspective tends to dominate in a particular kind of case does not mean that the others are inapplicable to it. Moral pluralism as a philosophically interesting thesis is the claim that valuing things is pluralistic in just this way.[14]

It is the second form of moral pluralism which is not only interesting, but which urgently requires exploration. By adopting the pluralist stance, we not only start to do justice to the complexity of real situations, but we also can start to look for ways by which environmental ethics can be linked up with other modes of valuing and ways of responding to our surroundings. Utilitarianism and its rivals need not be abandoned, but can be considered as partial accounts of the moral life. There is scope, for example, for developing notions such as attention, humility and selflessness in our dealings with nature as part of the story of what makes a worthwhile human life. These notions should not be thought of as *the truth* about morality—any more than utilitarianism is. Rather, they provide greater depth in characterizing our situation.[15] Abandoning reductive monism about values and valuing makes even more sense once the force of moral pluralism in this latest form is recognized.

If we accept moral pluralism as a philosophical position, the project of environmental ethics can be seen in a new light. The challenge of non-anthropocentric ethics to the western, human-centered tradition need not be described as an attempt to supplant one set of principles (ones regarding human welfare, or human virtues or whatever) with some new overarching set that embrace not only *human* concerns but also the interests, whatever they are, of other natural things. Instead, exploring non-anthropocentric ethics is to be seen as adding further sophistication to our moral discourse and helping us understand a further dimension to our lived experience. Seen in this way, environmental ethics is less a competitor for a certain moral position, but an investigation of a more sophisticated turn that moral philosophy has taken. Embarking upon it is a partial recognition of the complexity of our moral situation. Note, once more, that the complexity in question is intrinsic to the business of being moral. Moral pluralism is a philosophical, not a moral, thesis.

To say this may seem not to help the policymaker, for it involves admitting that we face a challenge to which philosophy has not so far found a solution. None the less, it provides at least some negative advice. We can caution against the use of reductionist methods, and the trap of thinking that policy decisions can always be reduced to some common, comprehensive weighting. Environmental ethics can provide an antidote to theories which encourage the idea that our moral situation is a simple one. So it can be an antidote to a tradition of systematic, but simplistic, theorizing. When we turn our attention to the challenge within philosophy itself, it will hardly be surprising if we find that many of our philosophical concepts do not quite fit us for meeting the challenge of moral pluralism. But this is certainly not the first time that efforts have to be made to see just which of our concepts are adequate to map newly encountered terrain. Indeed, it remains to be seen to what extent a developed ethics of the environment will fit in with the complex of other theories, intuitions and feelings we have about value. But this exploration is not something for rationality to avoid, but one which an appropriate sense of imagination and discovery should commend to us.

REFERENCES

Andrew Brennan, "Ecological Theory and Value in Nature," *Philosophical Inquiry* 8 (1986): 66–95.

Andrew Brennan, *Thinking About Nature* (London: Routledge, 1988).

Andrew Brennan, "The Moral Standing of Natural Objects," *Environmental Ethics* 6 (1984): 35–56.

J. Baird Callicott, "Animal Liberation: A Triangular Affair," *Environmental Ethics* 2 (1980): 311–38.

J. Baird Callicott, "The Case Against Moral Pluralism," *Environmental Ethics* 12 (1990).

Stephen Clark, *The Moral Status of Animals* (Oxford: Clarendon Press, 1977).

Joel Feinberg, "The Rights of Animals and Unborn Generations," in *Philosophy and Environmental Crisis,* edited by W. T. Blackstone (Athens: University of Georgia Press, 1974) pp. 43–68.

M. Friedman, "Carnap's *Aufbau* Reconsidered," *Nous* 21 (1987): 521–45.

Aldo Leopold, *A Sand County Almanac* (Oxford: Oxford University Press, 1949).

Maurice Mandelbaum, *History, Man and Reason* (Baltimore: Johns Hopkins Press, 1971)

John Muir, *My First Summer in the Sierra* (Edinburgh: Cationgate Publishing, 1988).

Iris Murdoch, *The Sovereignty of Good* (London: Routledge and Kegan Paul, 1970)

Arne Naess, "The Shallow and the Deep, Long-Range Ecology Movement: A Summary," *Inquiry* 16 (1973): 95–100.

Bryan Norton, *Why Preserve Natural Variety?* (Princeton University Press, 1987).

Martha Nussbaum, *The Fragility of Goodness* (Cambridge University Press, 1986).

D. Pearce, A. Markandya, and E. Barbier, *Blueprint for a Green Economy* (London: Earthscan, 1989).

J. Raz, and J. Griffin, "Mixing Values," *Proceedings of the Aristotelian Society,* supplementary volume 65 (1991): 83–118.

Tom Regan, "The Nature and Possibility of an Environmental Ethic," *Environmental Ethics* 3 (1981): 19–34.

Holmes Rolston III, *Environmental Ethics* (Philadelphia: Temple University Press, 1988).

Robert D. Rowe, R. C. D'Arge, and D. Brookshire, "An Experiment on the Economic Value of Visibility," *Journal of Environmental Economics and Management* 7 (1980): 1–19.

Mark Sagoff, *The Economy of the Earth* (Cambridge University Press, 1988).

Amartya K. Sen, "Rational Fools: A Critique of the Behavioral Foundations of Economic Theory," *Philosophy and Public Affairs* 6 (1977): 317–44.

Christopher D. Stone, *Earth and Other Ethics* (New York: Harper and Row, 1987)

Christopher D. Stone, "Moral Pluralism and the Course of Environmental Ethics," *Environmental Ethics* 10 (1988): 139–54.

Paul Taylor, *Respect for Nature* (Princeton University Press, 1984).

Gordon Tullock, *Toward a Mathematics of Politics* (Ann Arbor: University of Michigan Press, 1967).

Karen Warren, "Feminism and Ecology: Making Connections," *Environmental Ethics* 9 (1987): 3–21.

Bernard Williams, *Ethics and the Limits of Philosophy* (London: Fontana, 1985).

NOTES

1. See Rowe, D'Arge and Brookshire, 1980. This study is described and commented on in chapter 4 of Sagoff, 1988.

2. For references to this and other studies, see Pearce, Markandya and Barbier, 1989, chapter 3.

3. That economists do lay claim to rationality is shown by statements like the following: "By trying to value environmental services we are forced into a rational decision-making frame of mind. Quite simply, we are forced to think about the gains and losses, the benefits and costs of what we do. If nothing else, economic valuation has made a great advance in that respect." (Pearce, Markandya and Barbier 1989, p. 81).

4. See the recent discussion in Raz and Griffin 1991. A sensitive treatment of value pluralism is found in Nussbaum 1986. Clearly, in a brief attack on common assumptions about preferences, I am unable to give detailed attention to all the possible kinds of orderings for preferences. The difficulties suggested here arise well before the stage at which it would be necessary to investigate different orders for individual preferences.

5. There is a dispute about whether existence values are to be considered as a kind of demand value (given that people clearly indicate preferences regarding the existence of things remote from them and which do not impinge in a direct way on their lives). I am not intending to take sides on this issue in the present paper.

6. It is also to be found elsewhere, I would argue, particularly in the positivists' conception of a *unified science,* and particularly in Rudolf Carnap's early work on scientific objectivity. Mandelbaum points to the influence of the economist Emmanuel Hermann on Carnap's thinking (Mandelbaum 1971).

7. At the height of his Vienna Circle involvement, Carnap put forward a view of science which related its unity to just the conception of objectivity which I think is implausible. Michael Friedman has pointed out that Carnap's view of how concepts are to be discriminated from one another is deeply linked with the idea that all concepts are part of a single interconnected system. Such a single organization can only be possible if, in Carnap's own words, "there is only one object domain and each scientific statement is about the objects in this domain." See Friedman 1987.

8. An important exception to this claim is the work of Iris Murdoch, which, although focusing on the virtues of attention and care, does not rule out the importance of what she calls the "sheer alien otherness" of non-humans (Murdoch 1970). I also ignore dissenting voices within the western tradition itself, such as Heidegger's.

9. See Brennan 1986, and further discussion in Brennan 1988.

10. One standard statement of the link between interests, rights and the capacity to be represented is given in Feinberg 1974

11. Although if there is such a feature it would have to be something like the lack of function characteristic of natural objects—see Brennan 1984, and Brennan 1988, chapter 13, paragraphs 13.2–13.3.

12. Feminist and other critiques of conventional moral philosophy have made this point repeatedly. Although the status of feminism as an epistemological and metaphysical position is unclear, I am happy to be aligned with feminists in their objection to how the project of morality has been followed in post-Renaissance western philosophy. For a useful overview of ecological feminism, see Warren, 1987.

13. This is the conception of pluralism which seems to be attacked in Callicott 1990. Callicott's principal target is Stone 1988 (and Stone 1987).

14. Christopher Stone uses an analogy with the multiplicity of maps which can be produced for a single territory. See Stone 1987, chapter 5.

15. In an interesting, but so far unpublished essay, Tom Birch has tried to develop an account of meaningful attention which would fund our valuation not only of other living things, but also of rocks and lakes. Many of the remarks in Murdoch's *Sovereignty of Good* seem to merit exploration in an environmental context.

A Place for Cost-Benefit Analysis

David Schmidtz

What next? We are forever making decisions. Typically, when unsure, we weigh pros and cons. Occasionally, we make the weighing explicit, listing pros and cons and assigning numerical weights. What could be wrong with that? In fact, things sometimes go terribly wrong. This paper considers what cost-benefit analysis can do, and also what it cannot.

WHAT IS CBA, AND WHAT IS IT FOR?

Here is an example of how things go wrong. Ontario Hydro is a Canadian government-owned utility company (a Crown Corporation, on a par with Canada Post). Ten years ago, Ontario Hydro was expecting to become a hugely profitable provider of electricity to consumers all over the continent. At that time, Ontario circulated a report explaining how it planned to meet projected demand. Of interest to us is the report's admission that, "The analysis conducted in the development of the Demand/Supply Plans includes those costs which are borne directly by Hydro. It is these costs which can properly be included in Hydro's rates. Costs and benefits for the Ontario community, beyond these direct costs, are not factored into the cost comparisons." Why not? Because "even if desirable, these costs are difficult to estimate in monetary terms given the diffuse nature of the impacts and wide variety of effects." The costs that Ontario Hydro proposed to take into account "include the social and environmental costs incurred by Hydro but do not include social and environmental costs external to Hydro. This reflects normal business practice. In Hydro's judgment, including additional costs and benefits on an equitable basis would be impracticable."[1]

It is amazing that people would defend such a patently unethical stance by describing it as "normal business practice." Sadly, though, appealing to "normal business practice" is itself normal business practice, and Ontario Hydro is not especially guilty in that regard. Indeed, it is notable that Ontario Hydro was not duplicitous, since it did, after all, express its policy bluntly and publicly. Those who wrote the report evidently had no idea that what they were saying was wrong.

Environmentalists have their own "normal business practices," though, and it is too easy to condemn organizations like Ontario Hydro without thinking things through. Many critics of cost-benefit analysis (henceforth CBA) seem driven by a gut feeling that CBA is heartless. They think that, in denouncing CBA, they are taking a stand against heartlessness. This is unfortunate. The fact is, weighing a proposal's costs and benefits does not make you a bad person. What makes you a bad person is *ignoring* costs—the costs you impose on others.

The problem with Ontario Hydro arose, not when Ontario Hydro took costs and benefits into account, but rather when it decided *not* to do so. The problem in general terms is a problem of *external* costs. External costs are costs that decision makers ignore, leaving them to be paid by someone else. Ontario Hydro makes a decision that has certain costs. Some of the costs will fall not on Ontario Hydro but on innocent bystanders; following normal business practice, Ontario Hydro seems to say, "That's not our problem."

Decision makers naturally are tempted to ignore external costs. It is only human. Almost everyone does the same sort of thing in one context or another. Every time you leave an empty popcorn box in a theater rather than dispose of it properly, you are doing the same sort of thing as the person who dumps industrial waste in the river rather than dispose of it properly. Every time you drive a car, you are risking other people's lives, and you probably have never

David Schmidtz, "A Place for Cost-Benefit Analysis," *Philosophical Issues* 11 (2001): 148–71. Reprinted with permission of the author and Blackwell Publishers Inc.

wasted a minute feeling guilty about it. (And just like you, industrial polluters defend themselves by saying, "But everybody does it!") It is not only bad people who ignore the costs they impose on others. Part of the problem is simple laziness, when we think no one is watching. Another part of the problem is the normal human desire to conform, even when "normal practice" is unconscionable.

IS CBA ANTI-ENVIRONMENTALIST?

CBA comes in many variations, and there are many that no ethicist would defend. Needless to say, no ethicist would defend conventional CBA, that is, CBA in the narrowly focused way that Ontario Hydro used it at the end of the 1980s. All sides agree: there can be no general justification for foisting external costs on innocent bystanders. Any controversy concerns whether there exists some other form of CBA that can, in general, be justified.

Those with expertise in accounting are trained to draw fine-grained distinctions between different variations on the basic theme of conventional CBA. Full Cost Accounting, for example, refers to an attempt to carry out CBA in such a way as to take *all* known costs, external as well as internal, into account.[2] From here on, except where otherwise noted, when I speak of CBA, I will be referring to cost-benefit analysis with Full Cost Accounting. As E. J. Mishan's influential text defines it, "in cost-benefit analysis we are concerned with the economy as a whole, with the welfare of a defined society, and not any smaller part of it."[3]

Understood in this way, CBA is not merely an accounting method. It is a commitment to take responsibility for the consequences of one's actions. That is why, historically, environmentalists were among the most vocal *advocates* of CBA as a vehicle for making industries and governments answerable for the full cost of their decisions. It can work. Indeed, there has been an interesting further development in the case of Ontario Hydro. Perhaps having learned something about environmental ethics, Ontario Hydro changed its stance in 1993

and now trumpets its use of Full Cost Accounting methods.[4]

Under what general circumstances, then, should we want policy makers to employ CBA? Two answers come to mind: first, when one group pays the cost of a piece of legislation while another group gets the benefit; second, and more generally, whenever decision makers have an incentive not to take full costs into account. Where benefits of political decisions are concentrated while costs are dispersed, special interest groups can push through favorable policies even when costs to the population at large outweigh benefits.[5] To contain the proliferation of such unconscionable policies, we might require that policies be justified by the lights of a proper CBA. Requiring decision makers to provide a CBA, which is then made available for public scrutiny, is one way of trying to teach decision makers to take environmental costs into account. We do not want upstream people ignoring costs they foist on downstream people.[6] We want social and cultural and legal arrangements that encourage people to be aware of the full environmental cost, and also the full human cost, of what they do.

The most fundamental argument in favor of CBA has to do with CBA's role as a means of introducing accountability into decisions that affect whole communities. Think about it. If a business pollutes, would it be wrong to insist that the business should be paying the true full cost of its operation? As a mechanism for holding decision makers publicly accountable for external costs, CBA has the potential to constrain activities that are not worthwhile when external costs are taken into account. Accordingly, the National Policy Act of 1969 required CBA of all environment-related federal projects. To that extent, CBA is a friend of the environment. Or at least, it seemed that way at one time.

The tables seemingly have been turning, though. Throughout the 1970s, the Council on Wage and Price Stability and the Office of Management and Budget pressured the Environmental Protection Agency to pay more attention to the costs of complying with standards the EPA was trying to impose on industry. Finally, in 1981, President Reagan issued an Executive Order requiring government agencies to justify new regulations by submitting a formal CBA (of which an environmental impact statement would be only one part) to the Office of Management and Budget. Why? Why force agencies to perform CBA of their regulatory proposals? The point, very generally, was to force agencies to take into account costs they otherwise would have preferred to ignore. The Reagan administration reputedly felt some regulations were being pushed through by environmental zealots who did not care what their proposals cost in human terms. Accordingly, the Executive Order mandating CBA was perceived as having an anti-environmental thrust. Perhaps partly because of that bit of recent history, current environmentalist opinion remains, on the whole, anti-CBA. The following sections consider some of the main reasons (some cogent, some not) for distrusting CBA.

IS CBA ANTHROPOCENTRIC?

Is it only the interests of human persons that can be taken into account in a CBA? If so, then isn't CBA essentially anthropocentric? The answer is no. CBA as construed here is partly an accounting procedure, and partly a way of organizing public debate. In no way is it a substitute for philosophical debate. Animal liberationists who think full costs must (by definition?) include pain suffered by animals, for example, must argue for that point in philosophical debate with those who think otherwise. If CBA presupposed one or the other position, thereby pre-empting philosophical debate, that would be a flaw.

DOES CBA PRESUPPOSE UTILITARIAN MORAL THEORY?

Utilitarian moral theory holds roughly that X is right if and only if X maximizes utility, where maximizing utility is a matter of producing the best possible balance of benefits over costs. It may seem obvious that CBA presupposes the truth of utilitarian moral theory. In fact, it does not. CBA is a way of organizing a public forum expressing respect for persons: persons present at the meeting and other persons as well, on whose behalf those present can speak (citizens of faraway countries, future generations, etc.). For that matter, those present at the forum will speak not only on behalf of other persons but on behalf of whatever they care about: animals, trees, canyons, historic sites, and so on.

The forum therefore is defensible on utilitarian grounds, but it does not depend on utilitarian moral theory, for this sort of CBA could and probably should be advocated by deontologists.[7] A conventional CBA that ignored external costs would be endorsed neither by deontologists nor utilitarians, but CBA with Full Cost Accounting, defended in a public forum, could be endorsed by either.[8]

DOES CBA TELL US TO SACRIFICE THE ONE FOR THE SAKE OF THE MANY?

We can imagine advocates of CBA jumping to the conclusion that policies are justified whenever benefits exceed costs. That would be a mistake. We need to be more circumspect than that. When benefits exceed costs, the conclusion should be that the policy has passed one crucial test and therefore further discussion is warranted. On the other hand, when a proposal *fails* the test of CBA, when costs exceed benefits, the implication is more decisive, namely that further discussion is not warranted. If enacting a certain proposal would help some people and hurt others, then showing that winners are gaining more than losers are losing counts for something, but it is not decisive. One must then argue that the gain is so great for some people that it justifies imposing a loss on other people. In contrast, to show that losers are losing more than winners are gaining should pretty much end the conversation. Failing CBA is a fairly reliable test of when something is wrong.[9] Passing CBA, however, is not a reliable test of when something is right.

Consider the following case.[10]

HOSPITAL: Five patients lie on operating tables about to die for lack of suitable organ donors. A UPS delivery person just walked into the office. She is a suitable organ donor for all five patients. If you kidnap her and harvest her organs, you will be saving five and killing one.

Suppose we perform CBA in that case, and it yields the conclusion that, well, five is more than one. Would that imply that taking the delivery person's life is permissible? Required, even? No. Of course, we could quibble about how the calculation works out, but that would miss the fundamental point, which is that when we are talking about killing people, costs and benefits are not the only issue. CBA offers us guidance when our objective is to promote the best possible balance of costs and benefits, but not all situations call on us to maximize what is valuable. Promoting value is not always the best way of respecting it. There are times when morality calls on us not to maximize value but simply to respect it.

I argued that CBA does not presume the truth of utilitarian moral theory. Now it may seem that what I call CBA presumes that utilitarian moral theory is false! On the contrary, even from a broadly utilitarian perspective, we do not want ordinary citizens to have a license to kill whenever they think they can do a lot of good in the process. Some institutions have their utility precisely by *prohibiting* decisions based on utilitarian calculation. Hospitals, for example, cannot serve their purpose if they are a menace to innocent bystanders. Hospitals cannot serve their purpose unless people can trust hospitals to treat people as rights-bearers. Respecting people's rights is part of what helps make it safe to visit hospitals. And making it safe to visit the hospital is a prerequisite of hospitals functioning properly. Accordingly, we cannot justify cutting up one patient to save five simply by saying five is more than one. Sometimes, numbers do not count. It is good policy to forbid killing, requiring ordinary citizens to respect human rights, period.

Therefore, there are limits to the legitimate scope of CBA, and must be, even from a utilitarian perspective. Consider the case of *Peeveyhouse vs. Garland Coal*.[11] Having completed a strip-mining operation on the Peeveyhouse property, Garland Coal refused to honor its contractual promise to restore the land to its original condition. The restored land would have been worth only $300 and it would have cost $29,000 to restore it. Still, Peeveyhouse wanted the land restored and Garland Coal had promised to do it.

Incredibly, the Oklahoma court awarded Peeveyhouse only the $300, judging that Garland Coal could not be held financially liable for a restoration when such restoration would not be cost-effective. The Court's verdict generally is regarded as utterly mistaken, though, and one way of understanding the mistake is to see it as a case of failing to understand the limits of CBA's legitimate scope. We live in a society where hospitals cannot take organs without consent. We live in a society where Garland Coal normally would have to honor its contract with Peeveyhouse. Thus, we know where we stand. We need not be perpetually preparing to prove before a tribunal that strip-mining our land or harvesting our internal organs without consent is not cost-effective. Instead, we have a right simply to say no. In giving us moral space that we govern by right, our laws limit the energy we have to waste: trying to influence public regulators, fighting to keep what belongs to us, fighting to gain what belongs to others. In treating us as rights-bearers, our laws enable us simply to decline proposals that would benefit others at our expense.

Crucially, our being able to say no teaches people to search for ways of making progress that benefit everyone. CBA in its simplest form allows some to be sacrificed for the sake of the greater good of others, and therefore CBA in its simplest form is morally problematic. In contrast, CBA as a framework for public discussion, in a regime that treats people as rights-bearers, creates at least some pressure to craft proposals that promise benefits for all.

Again, part of the message to take away from these discussions is that the proper purpose of CBA is not to show when a taking is permissible. If we see CBA as indicating when takings are permissible, we will have a problem, because breaking contracts, or taking things from people (including their lives) whenever the benefit is worth the cost is not a way of respecting people. But if we treat CBA as a *constraint* on takings, ruling out inefficient takings without licensing efficient takings, then it is not disrespectful.

Therefore, it would be a mistake to see CBA as an *alternative* to treating people as ends in themselves. On the contrary, when CBA is working properly, and in particular when treated not as a seal of approval for good proposals but rather as a means of filtering out bad proposals, CBA becomes a way of preventing people from treating each other as mere means. The point is to stop people from foisting the costs of their policies on innocent people without consent. In other words, requiring people to offer an accounting of the true costs and benefits of their operations is a way of holding them publicly accountable for failing to treat fellow citizens as ends in themselves. CBA will not filter out every proposal that ought to be filtered out, but it will help to filter out many of the most flagrantly disrespectful proposals, and that is its proper purpose.

MUST CBA TREAT ALL VALUES AS MERE COMMODITIES?

As Mark Sagoff nicely expresses the point, "There are some who believe on principle that worker safety and environmental quality ought to be protected only insofar as the benefits of protection balance the costs. On the other hand, people argue—also on principle—that neither worker safety nor environmental quality should be treated as a commodity to be traded at the margin for other commodities, but rather each should be valued for its own sake."[12] The second argument, though, presents a false dichotomy. CBA is perfectly compatible with the idea that worker safety and environmental quality ought to be valued for their own sake.

To see why, imagine a certain recycling process is risky to the workers involved. The process improves environmental quality, but inevitably workers risk getting their hands caught in the machines, and so on. Notice: although we treat both environmental quality and worker safety as ends in themselves, we still have to weigh the operation's costs and benefits. Is recycling's environmental benefit worth the risk? It is a good question, and we would be missing the point if we tried to answer it by saying environmental quality is valued for its own sake.

Nor must we imagine cases of different values (worker safety and environmental quality) coming into conflict. The need for CBA can arise even when environmental quality is the sole value at stake. For example, suppose the recycling process in question saves paper (and therefore trees), but saving trees comes at a cost of all the water and electricity used in the process; gasoline is used by trucks that collect the paper from recycling bins, and so on. Therefore, the very recycling process that reduces pollution and natural resource consumption in some respects also increases pollution and natural resource consumption in other respects. In this case, our reason to do CBA is precisely that we care about environmental quality. (If maintaining a politically correct environmentalist appearance were our only concern, we would not worry about it.)

Again, it would be beside the point to talk about environmental quality being valued for its own sake. In a nutshell, we sometimes find ourselves in situations of conflicting values, where the values at stake are really important. Critics of CBA sometimes seem to say, when values at stake are really important, that is when we should *not* think hard about the costs and benefits of resolving the conflict in one way rather than another. They seem to have things backwards.

Sagoff asserts, "It is the characteristic of cost-benefit analysis that it treats all value judgments other than those made on its behalf as nothing but statements of preference, attitude, or emotion."[13] There are several things going on in this passage. I will mention three. First, the words "other than those made on its behalf" are a jest at the pseudo-scientific posturing of radical subjectivists, and the jest is on target. Second, Sagoff is insinuating that it is a mistake simply to assume that all values are reducible to costs and benefits, and here too, Sagoff is on target. On the one hand, it is an economist's job to go as far as possible in treating values as preferences, and within economics narrowly construed, the reductionist bias serves a purpose. On the other hand, when we look at values in more philosophical terms, we cannot treat all values as mere preferences, as if attaching value to honesty were on a par with attaching value to chocolate. Accordingly, there is a problem with jumping from economic to philosophical discussions without stopping to remind ourselves that what is taken for granted in one kind of discussion cannot be taken for granted in the other.

The third thing Sagoff is saying is that CBA characteristically treats all values as mere preferences. Now, if Sagoff means to say CBA *typically* does so, he may be right. But if Sagoff were saying CBA *necessarily* does so, he would be mistaken. CBA is about weighing costs and benefits. It does not presume everything is either a cost or a benefit. We have to decide which values can be treated as mere preferences, costs, or benefits, and which have to be treated separately, as falling outside the scope of CBA. CBA itself does not make that decision for us. It is true by definition that to care about X is to have a preference regarding X, but we can care about X without thinking X is merely a preference. CBA assumes nothing about the nature of values, other than that they sometimes come into conflict and that no matter what we do, we will in effect be trading them off against each other. It does not assume trading off values is unproblematic; it assumes only that we sometimes have no choice.

"Recycling" is a politically correct word, to be sure, but does that mean we should support any operation that uses the word in its title, even if the operation is environmentally catastrophic? Or should we instead stop to think about the operation's costs and benefits? Contra Sagoff, if we stop to think, that does not mean we are treating environmental quality as a mere "preference, attitude, or emotion." Stopping to think can be a way of showing respect.

CAN CBA HANDLE QUALITATIVE VALUES?

Steven Kelman says CBA presupposes the desirability of being able to express all values as dollar values. However, as Kelman correctly notes, converting values to dollars can be a problem. It can distort the true nature of the values at stake. On the other hand, it would be a mistake to think CBA *requires* us to represent every value as a dollar value. For example, Kelman and Sagoff surely would agree that if we care about Atlantic Green Turtles and do a CBA of alternative ways of protecting them, nothing in that process even suggests we have reduced the value of turtles to dollars.

We can do CBA with respect to different values; we can accept conflicts of value that prevent definitive answers. Kelman is right that something is gained when we genuinely and fairly can reduce all values to dollar values, because if we can do that, then there will be a "bottom line." We can simply tally up values, and it will be clear what CBA recommends. Often, though, trying to force the process to yield an unambiguously numerical bottom line would be to chase a mirage. If the art museum is about to close and I have one last chance to see either my beloved Vermeer or my beloved Seurat, but there is no time to see both, then I must make a choice. The interesting point is that, even when I know precisely what the costs and benefits will be of seeing the Vermeer versus seeing the Seurat, that does not entail that there will be an unambiguous bottom line. Normally, people do not attach numbers to their values. You never hear people saying, "Well, according to my calculations, the Vermeer experience is seven percent more valuable than the Seurat experience, so clearly Vermeer is the way to go." Nor do we hear, "Although I'm more in the mood for Seurat, the rational choice is the Vermeer, since appraisers say the Vermeer is worth more money." The latter thought would be irrelevant when the values at issue concern my own appreciation of the paintings' intrinsic merits as paintings rather than the paintings' value as instruments for raising cash. In cases like that, the bottom line will be qualitative rather than quantitative. No matter how accurately I appraise the intrinsic merits of the paintings, my appraisals will still be qualitative.

An object's *intrinsic* value is the value it has in and of itself, beyond any value it has as a means to further ends. Note that an object's having intrinsic value does not imply that the object is priceless. There is such a thing as limited intrinsic value. A painting can have an intrinsic value that is real without being infinite, or even particularly large. The value I would get from selling it is its instrumental value to me. The value it has to me in and of itself, simply because it is a beautiful painting, is its intrinsic value to me.[14] Both values are real, but one is instrumental and the other is intrinsic. Neither is necessarily large.

A related point: it would be better if Kelman had not said, "selling a thing for money demonstrates that it was valued only instrumentally."[15] Suppose I sell a painting. The money I receive from the sale is the painting's instrumental value to me, but does my decision to sell imply that the painting had no intrinsic value? No. Suppose I love the painting, but I need to raise a large sum of money to save my life, so I sell the painting. What this implies is not that the painting has zero intrinsic value but rather that the instrumental value of selling it outweighs the intrinsic value of keeping it, in that circumstance.

More generally, we sometimes put dollar values on things even when their value to us is essentially different from the value of dollars. Incommensurability of different values is not generally an insurmountable obstacle to CBA. Still, there often is no point in trying to convert a qualitative balancing into something that *looks* like a precise quantitative calculation and thus *looks* scientific but in fact remains the same qualitative balancing, only now its qualitative nature is disguised by the attaching of made-up numbers.

Policy decisions can be like that. We can make up numbers when assessing the value of a public library we could build on land that otherwise will remain a public park. Maybe the numbers will mean something, maybe not. More often, even when we

can accurately predict a policy's true costs and benefits, that does not entail that there will be any bottom line from which we simply read off what to do. When competing values cannot be reduced to a common measure without distortion, that makes it harder to know the bottom line. It may even mean there is no unitary bottom line to be known. Sometimes the bottom line is simply that one precious and irreplaceable thing is gained while another precious and irreplaceable thing is lost. Even so, that does not mean there is a problem with the very idea of taking costs and benefits into account. It just means we should not assume too much about what kind of bottom line we can expect to see.[16]

Ontario Hydro (since its reorganization), and the City of Vancouver Planning Department, to name two examples, say that in striving to provide a Full Cost Accounting, they try not to ignore vague non-monetized costs, even though in practice such sensitivity means their bottom line will reflect not (or not only) numerical inputs so much as their version of informed common sense.[17] Consider an analogy. A computer program can play chess by algorithm. Human chess players cannot. Human chess players need creativity, experience, alertness to unintended consequences, and other skills and virtues that are not algorithmic. People who formulate policy need similar skills and virtues, and interpersonal skills as well. Employing CBA cannot change that.

SOME THINGS ARE PRICELESS. SO WHAT?

Critics of CBA think they capture the moral high ground when they say some things are beyond price. They miss the point. Even if Atlantic Green Turtles are a priceless world heritage, we still have to decide how to save them. We still need to look at costs and benefits of trying to protect them in one way rather than another, for two reasons. First, we need to know whether a certain approach will be effective, given available resources. Dollar for dollar, an effective way of protecting them is better than an ineffective way. Second, we need to know whether the cost of saving them involves sacrificing something else we consider equally priceless.

If baby Jessica has fallen into an abandoned well in Midland, Texas and it will cost nine million dollars to rescue her, is it worth the cost? It seems somehow wrong even to ask the question; after all, it is only money. But it is not wrong. If it would cost nine million dollars to save Jessica's life, what would the nine million dollars otherwise have purchased? Could it have been sent to Africa where it might have saved nine thousand lives? Consider an even more expensive case. If a public utility company in Pennsylvania (in the wake of a frivolous lawsuit blaming its high-voltage power lines for a child's leukemia) calculates that burying its power lines underground will cost two billion dollars, in the process maybe preventing one or two deaths from leukemia, is it only money? If the two billion dollars could have been sent to Africa where it might have saved two million lives, is it obvious we should *not* stop to think about it?

Critics like to say not all values are economic values. They are right, but no values whatsoever are purely economic values in that sense. Even money itself is never only money. In a small town in Texas in 1987, a lot of money was spent to save a baby's life—money that took several lifetimes to produce. It was not only money. It did after all save a baby's life. It also gave a community a chance to show the world what it stands for. These are not trivial things. Neither are many of the other things on which nine million dollars could have been spent.

There are things so valuable to us that we think of them as beyond price. Some economists might disagree, but it is, after all, a fact. What does this fact imply? When we have no choice but to make tradeoffs, should we ignore items we consider priceless, or should we take them into account?[18] The hard fact is, priceless values sometimes come into conflict. When that happens, and when we try rationally to weigh our options, we are in effect putting a price on that which is priceless. In that case, CBA is not the problem. It is a response to the problem. The world has handed us a painful choice, and trying ra-

tionally to weigh our options is our way of trying to cope with it.

Note in passing that although critics often speak of incommensurable values, incommensurability is not quite the issue, strictly speaking. Consider the central dilemma of the novel, *Sophie's Choice*.[19] Sophie's two children are about to be executed by a concentration camp commander. The commander says he will kill both children unless Sophie picks one to be killed, in which case the commander will spare the other one. Now, to Sophie, both children are beyond price. She does not value one more than the other. In some sense, she values each of them more than anything. Nevertheless, she does in the end pick one for execution, thereby saving the other one's life. The point is, although her values were incommensurate, she was still able to rank them in a situation where failing to rank them would have meant losing both. The values were incommensu*rate,* but not incommensur*able.* To Sophie, both children were beyond price, but when forced to put a price on them, she could.

Of course, the decision broke her heart. As the sadistic commander foresaw, the process of ranking her previously incommensurate values was psychologically devastating. At some level, commensuration is *always* possible, but there are times when something (our innocence, perhaps) is lost in the process of making values commensurate. Perhaps that explains why some critics want to reject CBA; they see it as a mechanism for ranking values that should not be ranked. Unfortunately, although we can hope people like Sophie will never need to rank their children and can instead go on thinking of each child as having infinite value, and although we can wish we never had to choose between worker safety and environmental quality, or between different aspects of environmental quality, the real world sometimes requires tradeoffs.

DOES CBA WORK?

When individuals engage in CBA, they typically are asking themselves how much they should be willing to pay. That is an obvious and legitimate question because they are, after all, constrained by their budget. In contrast, legislators ask themselves how much they are willing to make *other* people pay, and that is a problem. In that case, paying has become an external cost, and it is no surprise if legislators seem rather cavalier about how much they are making other people pay. I said earlier that if the analysis shows that losers are losing more than winners are gaining, that should pretty much end the conversation. Unfortunately, in the real world, the conversation does not always stop there. When a program's benefits are concentrated within influential constituencies, legislators conceal how costly the program is to taxpayers at large. Similarly, owners of dogs that bark all night ignore the costs they impose on neighbors. Again, it is not because people are evil. They are only human. Situations where we are not fully accountable—where we have the option of not paying the full cost of our decisions—tend not to bring out the best in us. CBA with Full Cost Accounting is one way of trying to introduce accountability.

In theory, then, CBA is a way of organizing agenda for public debates that respect all persons, and valuable nonpersons, too. How does it work in practice? An effective resolution to hold decision makers and policy makers accountable for all costs would, in theory, make for a cleaner, safer, more prosperous society. The prospect of a public accounting can make corporations and governments rethink what they owe to the environment, and in Ontario Hydro's case, it seems to have done exactly that. Still, there is much corruption in the world and nothing like CBA will ever put an end to it. As with any other accounting method, the quality of the output typically will be only as good as the quality of the inputs. The valuations we supply as inputs drive the results, so how to avoid biased valuations? Biased inputs generate biased outputs. CBA, then, has the potential to be a smokescreen for the real action that takes place before numbers get added.

Can anything guarantee that the process of CBA will not itself be subject to the same political piracy that CBA was supposed to limit? Probably not. As I said earlier, the verdict in *Peeveyhouse* generally is regarded as mistaken. What I did not mention is that, as Andrew Morriss notes, "Shortly after the *Peeveyhouse* decision, a corruption investigation uncovered more than thirty years of routine bribery of several of the court's members."[20] CBA per se does not correct for corrupted inputs. Neither does CBA stop people from applying CBA to cases in which CBA has no legitimate role. However, if the process is public, with affected parties having a chance to protest when their interests are ignored, public scrutiny will have some tendency to correct for biased inputs. It also will encourage planners to supply inputs that can survive scrutiny in the first place. If the process is public, people can step forward to scrutinize not only valuations, but also the list of options, suggesting possibilities that planners may have concealed or overlooked.

Even if we know the costs and benefits of any particular factor, that does not guarantee that we have considered everything. In the real world, we must acknowledge that for any actual calculation we perform, there could be some cost or benefit or risk we have overlooked. What can we do to avoid overlooking what in retrospect will become painfully obvious? Although it is no guarantee, the best thing I can think of is to open the process to public scrutiny.

Kelman says CBA presumes we should spare no cost in enabling policy makers to make decisions in accordance with CBA. Kelman is right to be critical of such a presumption, for CBA is itself an activity with costs and benefits. The activity of analyzing costs and benefits is not always warranted on cost-benefit grounds. It can be a waste of time. Therefore, CBA on its own grounds ought to be able to recognize that there is a limit to CBA's legitimate scope. Decisions have to be made about what options are worth considering in cost-benefit terms. When we bring people together to scrutinize a proposal, we risk starting a fight over how to distribute costs and benefits. We take people who otherwise might peacefully mind their own business, and we teach them to think of each other as political adversaries. Not all problems can be solved by community policy. Often enough, neighbors are perfectly capable of quietly working things out among themselves, and often enough it is best simply to let them.

MUST CBA MEASURE VALUATIONS IN TERMS OF WILLINGNESS TO PAY?

Suppose we want to assess the costs and benefits of building a library on land that otherwise would remain a public park. How are we supposed to measure costs and benefits? Must we look into people's souls to see how much they really want the library? What alternative do we have? What if we asked people how much they are willing to pay to have the library, and compared that to what they say they are willing to pay to keep the park? Would that be a reasonable way of ascertaining how much they care?

CBA often is depicted as requiring us to measure a good's value by asking how much people would pay for it. Such a requirement is indeed problematic. One problem: willingness to pay is a function not only of perceived values but also of resources available for bidding on those values. Poorer people show up as less willing to pay even if, in some other sense, they value the good as much.

Is there anything we could do to make it legitimate to use willingness to pay as a surrogate for value in some other sense? Perhaps. Part of the problem, to judge from the literature, is that surveys designed to measure willingness to pay do not in fact take willingness to pay seriously. What they ask subjects to declare is not willingness to pay but *hypothetical* willingness to pay. The idea is, we justify building a waste treatment plant in a poorer neighborhood when we *judge* that poorer people would not pay as much as richer people would to have the plant built elsewhere. Critics call this environmental racism (because minorities tend to live in poorer neighborhoods). Whatever we call it, it looks preposterous.

Is there an alternative that would be more respectful of neighborhoods that provide the most likely building sites? Suppose we initially choose the site by random lottery, and suppose that by luck of the draw, Beverly Hills is selected as the site of the new waste treatment plant. Suppose we then ask Beverly Hills's rich residents what they are willing to pay to site the plant elsewhere. Suppose they say they jointly would pay ten million dollars to locate the plant elsewhere. Suppose we then announce that the people of Beverly Hills are actually, not just hypothetically, offering ten million to any neighborhood willing to make room for a waste treatment facility that otherwise will be built in Beverly Hills. Suppose one of the poorer neighborhoods votes to accept the bid. Would that be more respectful? Or instead, suppose no one accepts the Beverly Hills offer, and therefore the plant is built in Beverly Hills. Is there anything wrong with richer residents moving out, selling their houses to poorer people willing to live near the plant in order to live in better houses than they otherwise could afford? If siting a waste treatment plant drives down property values so that poorer people can afford to live in Beverly Hills, while rich people take their money elsewhere, is that a problem?

Note that even a random lottery will produce nonrandom results. No matter where the waste treatment facility is built, people who can afford to move away from waste treatment plants tend to be richer than the people who cannot. Home buyers who move in, accepting the nuisance in order to have a nicer house at a lower price, will tend to be poorer than buyers who opt to pay higher prices to live farther from the nuisance. One thing will never change: waste treatment facilities will tend to be found in poorer neighborhoods. Not even putting them all in Beverly Hills could ever change that.

Oddly, activists in effect are agitating for plants to be sited as far as possible from people who work in them, since siting waste treatment facilities within walking distance of the homes of people who might want the jobs they provide is classified as environmental racism. Perhaps the question of how far people have to commute is not important; normally, though, environmentalists urge us to pay more attention to such issues. In any case, if a waste treatment plant must be in a populated area, neighbors will be affected. Someone will have to pay, and no accounting tool is to blame for that.

Critics presume the process of siting waste treatment facilities will *not* be conducted in a respectful manner. They presume politicians will site waste treatment facilities not in response to actual negotiations with communities but rather in response to calculations about what will minimize adverse effects on campaign contributions and ultimately on reelection bids. The critics may be right.[21] If that is how it actually works, then politicians are asking the wrong question, morally speaking. In that case, no accounting method can yield the right answer. Under those circumstances, the point of subjecting the decision to public scrutiny is to lead (possibly racist) politicians not to recalculate answers so much as to start asking the right questions.

MUST FUTURE GENERATIONS BE DISCOUNTED?

In financial markets, a dollar acquired today is worth more than a dollar we will acquire in a year. The dollar acquired today can be put to work immediately. At worst, it can be put in the bank, and thus be worth perhaps $1.05 in a year. Therefore, if you ask me how much I would pay today to be given a dollar a year from now, I certainly would not pay as much as a dollar. I would pay something less, perhaps about ninety-five cents. Properly valued, then, the future dollar sells at a discount. Therefore, there is nothing irrational about borrowing against the future to get a profitable project off the ground, even though the cost of borrowing a thousand dollars now will be more than a thousand dollars later.

But here is the catch. There is nothing wrong with taking out a loan, so long as we *pay it back*. But there is something obviously wrong with taking out a loan we have no intention of repaying. In other words, discounting is one thing when the cost of raising capital is internalized; it is something else when we borrow against *someone else's* future rather than our own. We have no right to discount the price that *others* will have to pay for our projects. We have no right to discount externalities. *Redistributive* discounting is objectionable: morally, economically, and sometimes ecologically as well.

Some critics worry about the moral status of the discounting they think CBA presupposes. Thus, Peter Wenz says, "Absurdities arise when the current worth of future human lives is discounted, as CBA requires of all values that will be realized only in the future."[22] As an example of such an absurdity, Wenz goes on to calculate that at a five percent discount rate, "a human life today is worth four human lives that will not be realized for 28.8 years, eight lives that are 43.2 years in the future, and so on."[23] Obviously, Wenz is right: that would be absurd.[24] So, why think CBA requires that life's value, or any other value, be discounted? Some economists say it does not, and few (none that I know) would discount the value of lives in the way Wenz says they must.[25] There are economists who go so far as to claim a proper analysis requires that values *not* be discounted.[26] In any case, if we undertake a CBA, we must decide whether to introduce a discount rate. CBA will not make the decision for us. We also must decide whether to discount all considerations or only some. For example, we must decide whether to discount a life in the same way we discount the financial cost of *saving* a life (say, by building safer highways). To philosophers, the decision appears clear-cut: human lives are not commodities, although things we use to save lives typically are.

The thing about affluent people, and the reason why environmentalists are correct (not merely politically correct) to worry about poverty, is that affluent people can afford to be more future-oriented, that is, to operate with lower discount rates. The task, then, is two-fold: first, to teach people to see their future as depending on resources they are in a position to preserve, conserve, or degrade, and, second, to put them in a position where they can afford to be future-oriented.

CONCLUSIONS

What can you do with a CBA? You can draw conclusions like this: "We conducted CBA, taking the following costs and benefits into account. The proposal before us appears to pass inspection by the lights of such analysis. We therefore recommend further discussion. Or where the proposal does not pass inspection, where the losers would lose more than the winners would gain, we recommend that the proposal be rejected. In either case, we could be wrong. First, there may be costs or benefits we have not anticipated. Second, even known costs and benefits are often impossible to quantify precisely; therefore, our numbers must be viewed with caution. Third, when used in support of a given proposal, CBA need not be decisive, for there are other grounds upon which policies can be prohibited, favorable CBA notwithstanding. Nevertheless, until someone either identifies additional costs or benefits for us to consider, or else informs us that the proposal violates a treaty (for example) that created rights and obligations that render costs and benefits moot, all we can do is go with our best understanding of the information before us. Barring new information, proceeding in accordance with the result of this CBA appears to be the best we can do."

I talked about doing CBA with Full Cost Accounting, but no mechanical procedure can be guaranteed to take all costs into account. For any mechanical procedure we devise, there will be situations where that procedure overlooks something important. This is not a reason to reject the very idea of CBA, though. Rather, it is a reason to be wary of the desire to make decisions in a mechanical way. We cannot wait for someone to devise the perfect procedure, guaranteed to give everything its proper weight. Whatever procedures we devise for making decisions as individuals or as a community, we need to exercise judgment. At some point we draw the line, make a decision, and get on with our lives, realizing that any real-world decision procedure inevitably will be of limited value. It will not be perfect. It never will be beyond question.

CBA with Full Cost Accounting is only one form of CBA. Many other forms of CBA are indefensible, and no ethicist would defend them. We do well not to conflate different forms of CBA, though, and we do well not to demonize the general idea of weighing costs and benefits. CBA is an important response to a real problem. However, it is not magic. There is a limit to what it can do. CBA is a way of organizing information. It can be a forum for eliciting further information. It can be a forum for correcting biased information. It can be a forum for giving affected parties a voice in community decision making, thereby leading to better understanding of, and greater acceptance of, the tradeoffs involved in running a community. CBA can be all of these good things, but it is not necessarily so. CBA can constrain a system's tendency to invite abuse, such as the environmental racism just discussed, but CBA is prone to the same abuse that infects the system as a whole. It is no panacea. It is an antidote to abuse that is itself subject to abuse.

CBA is not inherently biased, but if inputs are biased, then so will be the outputs, generally speaking. However, although the method does not inherently correct for biased inputs, if the process is conducted publicly, so that people can publicly challenge suppliers of biased inputs, there will be some tendency for the process to correct for biased inputs as well. We can hope there will be adequate opportunity for those with minority viewpoints to challenge mainstream biases, but we cannot guarantee it. The most we can say is that CBA done in public view helps to give democracies a fighting chance to operate as democracies are supposed to operate.

NOTES

1. Demand/Supply Report of the Ontario Hydro Commission, as quoted in Michael McDonald, J. T. Stevenson, and Wesley Craig, *Finding a Balance of Values: An Ethical Assessment of Ontario Hydro's Demand/Supply Plan*, Report to Aboriginal Research Coalition of Ontario (1992) pp. 33–34.

2. In speaking to different people, I find that the terms are not quite standardized. What I have in mind when I speak of Full Cost Accounting is what some people call Multiple Accounts Analysis or Life Cycle Analysis. They might reserve the term "Full Cost Accounting" to refer to a kind of CBA that considers all costs, but only in terms of their impact on current stakeholders. Whatever term we use, though, suffice it to say I have in mind a kind of CBA that does not deliberately ignore any cost whatever, including costs imposed on future generations.

3. E. J. Mishan, *Elements of Cost-Benefit Analysis,* 2nd ed. (London: George Allen & Unwin, 1976) p. 11.

4. I do not know whether Ontario Hydro's change of heart was partly in response to the 1992 *Ethical Assessment* of McDonald, Stevenson, and Craig, cited above.

5. And if everyone belongs to one interest group or another, that does not mean we all break even in the final accounting. It is as if a hundred of us sat in a circle, and the government went round the circle collecting a penny from each, then favoring one of us with a fifty cent windfall. After repeating the process a hundred times, we are each a dollar poorer, fifty cents richer, and happy. So David Friedman describes the game in *The Machinery of Freedom* (LaSalle: Open Court Publishing, 1989).

6. This is the illuminating central metaphor used by Don Scherer in *Upstream/Downstream: Issues in Environmental Ethics,* edited by Donald Scherer (Philadelphia: Temple University Press, 1990).

7. In modern moral theory, deontology often is thought of as the main theoretical alternative to utilitarianism. Generally and roughly, deontology is the theory that X is right if and only if X expresses respect for all persons as ends in themselves, and treats no one as a mere means.

8. Kristin Shrader-Frechette offers different arguments for a similar conclusion in "A Defense of Risk-Cost-Benefit Analysis," *Environmental Ethics: Readings In Theory and Application,* edited by Louis Pojman, 2nd ed., (Belmont: Wadsworth, 1998) 507–14.

9. Steven Kelman argues that there are cases in which an action is right even though its costs exceed its benefits. Kelman has in mind actions that involve keeping a promise or speaking out against injustice, cases in which there is something wrong with the very idea of asking about costs and benefits. In such cases, the balance of costs and benefits normally is not decisive because we should not have been asking about costs and benefits in the first place. All of that is compatible with my claim that, in cases where costs and benefits *should* be taken into account, deter-

mining that the losers are losing more than the winners are gaining should be considered a conversation stopper.

10. For a classic discussion of this case, see Judith Jarvis Thomson, "Killing, Letting Die, and the Trolley Problem," *Monist* 59 (1976) 204–17.

11. For a discussion of what the case shows about relative merits of statutory versus common law, see Andrew Morriss, "Lessons for Environmental Law from the American Codification Debate," *The Common Law and the Environment,* edited by Roger Meiners and Andrew Morriss (Lanham: Rowman & Littlefield, 2000) 130–57, here p. 144.

12. Mark Sagoff, "At the Shrine of Our Lady of Fatima, or Why Political Questions Are Not All Economic," *Arizona Law Review* 23 (1981) 1283–98, here 1288–89.

13. Sagoff, p. 1290–91.

14. There is also a debate over whether there is a kind of intrinsic value that does not presuppose the existence of a valuer. We often speak of persons as having a value as ends in themselves, independently of any value attributed to them by other valuers. The questions is whether trees, for example, also can in this sense be ends in themselves. The purpose of the "Last Man Argument" in environmental ethics is to set the stage for discussion of this latter question.

15. Editors' note: Kelman authorized us to delete this phrase from the version of the paper to be reprinted in this volume.

16. See also Charles Lindblom, "The Science of Muddling Through," *Foundations of Administrative Law,* edited by Peter Schuck (New York: Oxford University Press, 1994) 104–10.

17. "Full Cost Accounting For Decision Making At Ontario Hydro: A Case Study," prepared by ICF Incorporated for the Environmental Protection Agency; "Visions, Tools, and Targets: Environmentally Sustainable Development Guidelines For Southeast False Creek," prepared by Sheltair Inc. For the City of Vancouver, 1998.

18. Hargrove notes that quantitative analysis may be inappropriate when dealing with intrinsic values. See Eugene C. Hargrove, *Foundations of Environmental Ethics* (Denton: Environmental Ethics Books, 1989) p. 211. Fair enough, but quantitative analysis often is inappropriate with purely instrumental values too. Not all instrumental values are reducible to monetary values. For example, seat belts are of purely instrumental value, yet when the car hits the ditch and begins to roll over, no amount of money would be a reasonable substitute for having our seat belts fastened.

19. William Styron, *Sophie's Choice* (New York: Random House, 1979).

20. Morriss, p. 144.

21. See Robert Bullard, *Dumping In Dixie: Race, Class, and Environmental Quality* (Boulder: Westview Press, 1990).

22. Peter Wenz, "Democracy and Environmental Change," *Ethics and Environmental Responsibility,* edited by Nigel Dower (Aldershot: Avebury, 1989) 91–109, here p. 100.

23. Wenz, p. 100.

24. Actually, it looks economically problematic as well. If we suppose a zero inflation rate, then a dollar in the future is not worth less than a dollar today. It is worth exactly one dollar. That does not change when we introduce the possibility of earning interest. The possibility of interest means only that it is better to get the dollar earlier because we then can earn additional interest. If lives are like dollars in that respect, then the implication is not that a life later is worth less than a life now. Rather, the implication is very roughly that, just as it would be better to have an extra year's interest, it would be better to have an extra year of life. (That is, if I were going to be given a second life, and if I knew my second life would end in the year 2150, I would pay to have that life begin in 2110 rather than 2130. For analogous reasons, the dollar that began to collect interest in 2110 rather than 2130 would sell at a premium.)

25. For a typically circumspect discussion, see J. E. Stiglitz, "The Rate of Discount for Benefit-Cost Analysis and the Theory of the Second Best," *Cost-Benefit Analysis,* edited by Richard Layard and Stephen Glaister (Cambridge: Cambridge University Press, 1994) 116–59.

26. See Tyler Cowen, "Consequentialism Implies a Zero Rate of Discount," in Peter Laslett and James Fishkin, editors, *Philosophy, Politics, and Society,* sixth series (New Haven: Yale University Press, 1992) 162–168.

Chapter 15

Environmentalism in Practice

Questions for Reflection and Discussion

The Ethics of Confrontation

1. Can you recall episodes in your own life in which you have faced a dilemma like Norton's, where the "aggregationist" approach would prove too little, while the moral approach would prove too much?

Norton's tale of sand dollar "strip mining" is a case in which the story's villain is an innocent little girl. How often is that the case? How often are polluters and overconsumers simply innocent people who mean no harm? Does that affect how (or whether) we ought to confront them? What would Andrew Light say?

2. Many people would argue that it is morally wrong for the crew of the *Sea Shepherd* to be destroying fishing boats. Others would disagree. Can such disagreements be settled? If not, where does that leave us? What should be done?

Are the Japanese fishermen in Watson's story as innocent as the little girl in Norton's story? How do you suppose the fishermen felt about having their boats destroyed? How would you feel if the *Sea Shepherd* crew singled you out, making an example of you by destroying your car to stop you from using it to pollute the atmosphere?

The Environmentalists' Dilemma: Dollars and Sand Dollars

Bryan G. Norton

The poignancy of the dilemma facing advocates of environmental protection was dramatized for me in an encounter with a little girl. It was a sleepy, summer-beach Saturday and I was walking on a sandbar just off my favorite remnant of unspoiled beach on the north tip of Longboat Key, Florida. The little girl clambered up the ledge onto the sandbar, trying not to lose a dozen fresh sand dollars she cradled against her pushed-out and Danskinned stomach. I guessed she was about eight.

Thirty yards away, in knee-deep water, her mother and older sister were strip mining sand dollars—they walked back and forth through the colony, systematically scuffing their feet just under the soft sand on the bottom of the lagoon and bending over to retrieve each disk as it was dislodged. Their treasure was held until collected by the eight-year-old transporter, whose feet were too small to serve as plowshares. Gathering the sand dollars at the point of excavation, she relayed them to the sand bar where a considerable pile was accumulating near the family's beached powerboat.

Many months earlier, I had noted how the fickle current through Longboat Inlet had begun to dump sand in a large crescent spit out into the Gulf of Mexico, forming a waist-deep lagoon. Next came a profusion of shore birds and the colony of sand dollars that multiplied in the protected water, and then came the little girl and her family in their powerboat.

I was startled by the level of industrial organization; even the little girl executed her task with square-jawed efficiency. I engaged her as she emerged onto the sand bar. "You know, they're alive," I said.

"We can put 'em in Clorox at home and they'll turn white."

I asked whether they needed so many. She said, "My Momma makes em outta things."

I persisted: "How many does she need to make things?"

"We can get a nickel apiece for the extras at the craft store. " I sighed and walked away. Our brief conversation had ended in ideological impasse.

But I was troubled. How could my indignation be stilled so simply? Must the environmental conscience always give way to economic arguments? As I wandered off, I analyzed the short and unsatisfactory debate. I had begun by expressing my concern for life, for the several hundred green discs drying in the afternoon sun. Yet I'd have felt silly saying, "Put them back, they have a right to live." I'd have felt silly because I don't think it's immoral for little girls to take a few sand dollars from the beach, any more than I had been immoral when I had red snapper for lunch that same day. I felt ill-equipped to make my point, about which I had little doubt, that the little girl should put most of the sand dollars back. If I admitted that sand dollars are just resources, like chunks of coal, salable in an available market, I could not at the same time argue that the little girl should put most of them back. Once sand dollars are economic resources, their value is counted in nickels. Therefore, I could not express my indignation in the language of economic aggregation.

Nor could I precisely express it in the language of rights of sand dollars, especially not if that language is given its accepted meaning in the tradition of John Locke and Thomas Jefferson. I did not find

Bryan G. Norton, *Toward Unity Among Environmentalists* (New York: Oxford University Press, 1991), 3–13. Used by permission of Oxford University Press, Inc. Editors' note: To avoid confusion, where Norton refers in the original to "this book," we have inserted the book's title.

it self-evident that all sand dollars are created equal with little girls. Imagine instead that I had encountered the little girl with a half-dozen sand dollars submerged in seawater in her bucket and she had said, "We're going to cut up a couple and put the rest in our saltwater aquarium and watch 'em." If I appeal to the rights of sand dollars as individuals (or, even somewhat more weakly, to the intrinsic value of individual sand dollars), I would have to object to this purely instrumental use of sand dollars in a rudimentary science lesson.

I faced the environmentalists' dilemma;[1] it was a dilemma, not because I did not know what I wanted the little girl to do, but because I could not coherently explain why she should put most of them back. If I chose the language of economic aggregation, I would have to say she could take as many as she could use, up to the sustainable yield of the population. On this approach, more is better—the value of sand dollars is their market value, and I could not use this language to express the moral indignation I felt at the family's strip mining sand dollars and hauling them away in their powerboat. To apply, on the other hand, the language of moralism, I would have to decry the treatment of sand dollars as mere resources; I would have to insist that the little girl put all of them back. Neither language could express my indignation and my common sense feeling that, while it was not wrong for the little girl to take a few sand dollars, she should put most of them back—the aggregationist approach to valuing sand dollars would prove too little, and the moral approach would prove too much.

Consider again the altered scenario in which the little girl takes a half dozen home in her bucket to be cut up or imprisoned in an aquarium. Suppose the little girl takes them home, and they are, predictably, dead in a week, but that the little girl attains an interest in biology, eventually becoming a marine biologist who works to protect echinoids. If sand dollars had myths and legends, the sacrificed sand dollars might be worshiped as saviors of their kind. And to the little girl, also, they would then have been far more valuable than nickels. It is this sense of respect for sand dollars as living creatures, worth more

than mere nickels but less than little, round people, that I could not express in either the strict language of moralism or in the language of simple economic aggregationism. I knew I wanted to get the little girl to put most of them back, and to respect the remaining ones as living creatures from whom we might learn something worthwhile; I was torn between two inadequate languages for expressing the value of sand dollars. In this sense, the environmentalists' dilemma is primarily a dilemma in values, conceptualizations, and worldviews more than a dilemma regarding actions and policies. It affects mainly how environmentalists explain and justify their policies, and only occasionally and tangentially does it affect those policies themselves.

My conversation on the beach represents, in microcosm, a larger dilemma facing environmentalists. I know that this practical and industrious family would not be moved by speeches for sand dollar liberation, however eloquent. That argument had been cut short, rendered irrelevant by the little girl's utilitarian reply. Sand dollars are by no means an endangered species, so that line of argument wasn't applicable.

Once I'd given up my moral high ground and asked only whether they needed so many, I'd conceded the utilitarian value of sand dollars. If a few are useful as commodities, surely more are correspondingly so. Of course I could have given her the conservationist line, that she should take only the sustainable yield of the colony. But I didn't have the faintest idea how to do a population model to show the little girl that she'd exceeded permissible levels of exploitation and, even if I could have, it wouldn't have satisfied me. I wanted to say more. So I fell silent, stymied.

As in my conversation with the little girl, environmentalists often begin by implying that there is something morally wrong in the systematic exploitation of nature, something that cannot be fully expressed in the language of scientific resource management and maximum sustainable yields. When the heat is on, however, they retreat to the solid ground of economic arguments, as I did when I tried the "How-many-do-you-need?" routine.

Environmentalists face two crises, one external and one internal. Against outsiders, they must continually defend their hard-won successes and urge new reforms against advocates of commercial interests who insist that environmental legislation ought never to disrupt "economic efficiency." Examples abound. The Reagan Administration set out, almost immediately after taking office, to invalidate all regulations, environmental and otherwise, that could not be shown, through a benefit-cost analysis, to promote economic efficiency. After decades of trying, environmentalists intent upon saving the Chesapeake Bay from progressive deterioration of water quality caused by industrial dumping and run-off from farmers' fields and subdivision yards achieved a regional plan for protecting the bay. Now they are fighting innumerable battles on a local level as development interests in individual communities pressure local governments to implement the plan by fleshing it out with maximally lenient local land-use plans.

While these external challenges command the attention of environmentalists, a theoretical crisis, in language and worldviews, causes paralysis and miscommunication within the movement: There has emerged within the movement no single, coherent consensus regarding positive values, no widely shared vision of a future and better world in which human populations live in harmony with the natural world they inhabit.

The environmentalists' dilemma, which is primarily a dilemma in ultimate values, results in inarticulation when environmentalists discuss, explain, and justify their policies. To the extent that utilitarian and more preservationist approaches are seen as exclusive choices—as opposed rather than complementary values—it follows that I must choose between two inadequate languages to express my indignation. Neither the language of biocentric moralism nor the language of utilitarianism was adequate to explain and justify my view that the little girl should put most of the sand dollars back.

Historically, it has been useful to speak of two divisions of the environmental movement, "conservationists" and "preservationists," because some environmentalists have faced this dilemma squarely and

have opted for one horn of it or the other. Most conservationists see natural ecosystems and other species as resources and are concerned mainly with the wise use of them. Finding its philosophical roots in the ideas of Gifford Pinchot, first official forester of the United States, this group judges all questions according to the criterion of the greatest good for the greatest number in the long run. The members of this faction, who are often trained as professional resource managers, have usually exerted their influence through control of governmental agencies such as the Forest Service and the Bureau of Reclamation. These environmentalists apparently diverge from the value system of their more commercially concerned opponents in industry only in insisting that costs and benefits of development and exploitative projects be computed over longer frames of time. Conservationism, or wise-use environmentalism, emphasizes avoidance of waste in the present pursuit of economic well-being. Thus, while natural ecosystems and other species are resources to be used wisely, they are very definitely to be used for human purposes. Pinchot once said, "The first great fact about conservation is that it stands for development. . . . [Its] first principle is the use of the natural resources now existing on this continent for the benefit of the people who live here now."[2]

Conservationists, especially those who are trained in resource management and those who work in government resource agencies, have generally applied concepts and a value system that tend toward economic reductionism, which interprets values as individual preferences expressed in free markets. The value of a sand dollar, on this view, is what someone is willing to pay for it. This reductionistic approach has led to a long-standing collaboration of conservationists with economists and to a tendency to pose questions in quantified terms in which information on resource use and its consequences can be aggregated and presented in dollar terms.

Opposed to this group is another, often called "preservationists," which is committed to protecting large areas of the landscape from alteration. This faction derives its spirit and mandate from John Muir, who was the first president of the Sierra Club (in

1892). Muir saw his quest to preserve nature as a moral one. He rejected or reinterpreted the Christian views of monotheism and the Judeo-Christian idea that nature exists for the sake of humans, arguing that the dogma "that the world was made especially for the uses of men" was the fundamental error of the age, and that "Every animal, plant, and crystal controverts it in the plainest terms." Muir railed against human arrogance that judges nature only according to human values:

> How narrow we selfish, conceited creatures are in our sympathies! how blind to the rights of our fellow mortals! Though alligators, snakes, etc., naturally repel us, they are not mysterious evils. They . . . are part of God's family, unfallen, undepraved, and cared for with the same species of tenderness and love as is bestowed on angels in heaven or saints on earth.[3]

Initially, Pinchot, Muir, and their disparate groups of followers worked together in opposition to the timber barons and other wasteful exploiters of natural resources. Both of these leaders, especially Pinchot, can today be thanked for creating the immense National Forest system. But Muir and Pinchot quarreled over grazing in the national forest preserves, and opposed each other bitterly over the plan to dam Hetch Hetchy, a beautiful canyon in Yosemite National Park. Pinchot allied himself with the developers: "As to my attitude regarding the proposed use of Hetch Hetchy by the city of San Francisco . . . I am fully persuaded that . . . the injury . . . [caused] by substituting a lake for the present swampy floor of the valley . . . is altogether unimportant compared with the benefits to be derived from its use as a reservoir."[4]

Muir stated the case for preservation: "These temple destroyers, devotees of ravaging commercialism, seem to have a perfect contempt for Nature, and instead of lifting their eyes to the God of the mountains, lift them to the Almighty Dollar."[5] "Dam Hetch Hetchy! As well dam for watertanks the people's cathedrals and churches, for no holier temple has ever been consecrated by the heart of man."[6] Muir's pantheism implied that humans exist as part of a great spiritual whole. We worship that whole, the creator and sustainer of us all (which Muir identified with nature itself), he thought, by preserving and studying the most spectacular and beautiful areas as shrines. But Muir's heretical theological reasoning was never made explicit in his public writings. Indeed, he was referred to as a "man of God" by his contemporaries, and he appealed effectively to the powerful tradition in American protestantism, traceable to Jonathan Edwards, that saw nature as God's messenger to humans.

With scientifically trained professional conservationists lined up against Muir over Hetch Hetchy, he appealed to the public. In reviewing the revised edition of Muir's Our National Parks in 1909, the *New York Times* declared: "It is the sentimentalist like Mr. Muir who will rouse the people rather than the materialist."[7] And rouse them he did. Against all odds, Muir and his band of amateur preservationists held up the Hetch Hetchy Project for more than a decade. But when Woodrow Wilson took office and swung his weight in favor of the dam, the bill was forced through Congress by a narrow margin. The despondent Muir died shortly thereafter.[8] But his flaming rhetoric had created a powerful force of *moralism* in American environmentalism. That force has, from time to time, come to the fore as a political power, as when the Sierra Club, under the radicalized leadership of David Brower in the 1950s, succeeded in quashing a proposed dam in Dinosaur National Monument.

When I asked environmentalists what they thought was meant by the terms "conservationist" and "preservationist" today, most of them said the terms were meaningless or that the old terms have deteriorated into pejoratives, with "preservationist" being an epithet for someone who wants to "lock up" resources, and "conservationist" referring to a person who has demonstrated too great a willingness to compromise with economic interests. Since there seems to be a real question whether these terms are meaningful and useful today, I will use them sparingly and usually in historical contexts.

For the purposes of this book [*Toward Unity*], however, I think it best to question the continuing usefulness of categorizing environmentalists as two exclusive groups. Here, Economic Aggregators and Moralists will mainly appear as ideal arguers. They are idealized spokespersons who have "bought into" one worldview or the other. A worldview will be considered as a constellation of concepts, values, and axioms that shape the world its proponents encounter. We can count on idealized spokespersons to give the best account they can, with their respective worldviews, of any given situation. It is best to think of Aggregators and Moralists in this way, as idealized arguers, because we can then leave open the question of whether most environmentalists, in their day-to-day activities, exclusively employ one or the other of these worldviews. Using this ploy, we can allow real individuals to be the spokespersons for Aggregators or Moralists in specific situations, without presupposing that environmentalists are always and permanently arrayed in two exclusive camps.

Muir's and Pinchot's respective successors in the modern environmental movement have more recently cooperated by maintaining an uneasy coalition. In general the environmental movement achieves its greatest unity when confronted with a sustained attack on environmental policies and programs, such as the one mounted by the President and his Secretary of the Interior James Watt in the early years of the Reagan presidency. The divergent elements also unify to defend specific resources and natural areas against threats of environmental degradation. In spite of these broad agreements on policy, however, the environmental movement still faces a dilemma: There has emerged within the movement no shared, positive understanding of the human relationship to the natural world; consequently, environmentalists lack a consensually accepted set of ideals and values. They therefore ricochet back and forth between two apparently exclusive worldviews and sets of value assumptions.

The choice between the legacies of Muir and Pinchot also presents itself to the environmentalist as a political dilemma: To follow Muir and grant rights to rattlesnakes is to embrace a radical ideal, one that appeals deeply to a small but committed minority that rejects the thoroughgoing anthropocentrism of our Judeo-Christian tradition. This ideal, which elevates all nature to moral standing, calls into question the very idea motivating the American faith in Adam Smith's invisible hand, the idea that the path of economic development should be guided by a free market. Since nature has no dollars to spend, its voice cannot be heard in a marketplace; on any easily intelligible theory of the rights of rattlesnakes, these rights will limit the free choices of industrialists and consumers to buy and sell, to exploit and make profits. Embracing rights for rattlesnakes therefore damns the environmentalists, at least until there are fundamental changes in the value system of mainstream American society, to appealing to a very small audience of quacks and cranks, who are out of step with the economic values of our period of history.

But to follow Pinchot, to forget Muir's impassioned moral rhetoric, reduces environmentalists to a role as one more interest group, fighting for clean air, for clean water, for protection of the National Parks. These activities appear, politically, as no more than spirited support for strongly felt preferences. Clean air must be "balanced" against jobs and economic growth, and if consumers want clean air, they must be willing to pay for it in forgone jobs and dividends. On this side of the dilemma, environmentalists have lots of company. Everywhere there are interest groups shouting to protect their piece of a limited economic pie, and environmentalists are in danger of being entirely drowned out in the frantic melee, as everyone from profiteers to moral zealots attempts to focus governmental resources on social problems both real and imagined.

The environmentalists' dilemma, then, manifests itself in a number of ways. Among those who have opted for one or the other horn of the dilemma, it manifests itself in factionalism and distrust of those perceived to have joined the other camp. Other environmentalists remain uncommitted and uneasily embody both factions as internal personae. The resulting theoretical schizophrenia can paralyze us with inarticulation and humble us in a debate with an eight-year-old in the sand dollar business.

The dilemma is especially evident in accounts of, and commentaries on, the progress of environmentalism. Historians, social scientists, and philosophers who have discussed the movement have been quick to see dichotomies and polarities. For example, the historian Stephen Fox emphasizes that Pinchot derived his strength from professionals, scientific forest managers and bureaucrats who made their living in exploiting or regulating resource use, while Muir drew upon the enthusiasm of amateurs motivated by an almost-religious zeal for the preservation of nature. Political scientist Lester Milbrath notes that environmentalism is a value-oriented reform movement but insists that "we must make a distinction between environmentalists who wish to retain the present socio-economic-political system and those who wish to drastically change it."[9] Philosophers who have discussed environmental values have concentrated almost exclusively on the dichotomy between anthropocentric (human-related) values and biocentric (nature-oriented) values.[10]

While these dichotomies do not all draw precisely the same distinction, they emphasize the polarization of environmentalists and suggest that the polarization derives from essential differences regarding values. For better or worse, these diverse but related dichotomies were given a generic characterization by Arne Naess when he distinguished a "shallow" from a "deep" ecology movement.[11] Naess's categories generally serve to characterize clusters of individuals who largely fit the Pinchot/conservationist mold and the Muir/preservationist mold, respectively. We must leave it an open question whether this dichotomy corresponds directly to our separation of Moralists and Aggregators. When pressed for an essential difference marking this generic distinction, Naess and his followers emphasize that shallow ecologists retain the anthropocentric view that the natural world exists as resources for the use of humans, while deep ecologists adopt the biocentric view that nature, as well as man, has intrinsic value and that it should be preserved for its own sake.

While Naess's provocative and tendentious characterization of conservationists as "shallow" environmentalists represents an extreme example, it is generally true that academic and social commentary on the environmental movement has accepted and even reinforced the dilemma and the deep polarities it evokes. Historical and sociological accounts that emphasize the different training and backgrounds of conservationists and preservationists, as well as philosophical analyses that concentrate on the dichotomy between anthropocentric and biocentric value systems, conspire to reinforce these polarities. This emphasis on deep underlying differences in values forces us to wonder whether the environmental movement is a "movement" after all. If the individuals and groups often referred to as "environmentalists" embrace no common values, then why assume that the environmental movement has a true and lasting identity? If left unchallenged, these suspicions undermine the task at hand—to understand a movement. Presumably, it is a movement toward something. To emphasize only the disparity of visions pursued by the various contributing factions is, in effect, to deny that environmentalism is a movement at all.

The purpose of *Toward Unity* is to challenge the suggestion that environmentalists hold no common ground, and the associated suggestion that environmentalists represent at best a shifting coalition of interest groups. That suggestion is implicit in the persistent emphasis, among historians and commentators, on the competing worldviews and value frameworks that constitute the vocabularies in which environmentalists argue their political case. According to the thesis of *Toward Unity,* those who see only chaos and confusion, internal disputes and dissensions, and those who deny that environmentalism is a unified social movement, are looking in the wrong place for the unity of environmentalism. Environmentalists, I am admitting at the outset, have not accepted a common and shared worldview, and those who look for unity in the explanations and rhetoric of environmentalists will be disappointed.

I will pursue a different strategy and look first for the common ground, the shared policy goals and objectives that might characterize the unity of environmentalists. To support this strategy, I will employ a useful, if somewhat arbitrarily drawn, distinction between values and objectives. An objective will be understood as some concrete goal such as a change in policy or the designation of a particular area as a wilderness preserve. Values will be understood more abstractly as the basis for an estimation of worth, which can serve as a justification and explanation for more concrete objectives. Thus two environmentalists might work together to achieve the objective of prohibiting strip mining in a wilderness area, while justifying their activities by appeal to quite different values. One of them might, for example, value the wilderness area as sacred, while the other wishes to perpetuate its recreational value for the use of the community. Differences in value may, therefore, lead to shifting coalitions regarding objectives; once strip mining is effectively prohibited, supporters of recreational values may find themselves allied with the local Chamber of Commerce in supporting a larger parking lot for access to the wilderness, while their former ally opposes both, insisting that ease of access will cheapen and degrade the sacred place.

Providing environmentalists can usually agree on what to do, a diversity of value concerns need not debilitate the movement. Indeed, freedom to appeal to a variety of value systems may ultimately prove the greatest strength of the movement, allowing environmentalists to appeal to the broadest spectrum of American voters.[12] Nevertheless, it is tempting to assume that one side or the other in the debate between Moralists and Aggregators is correct, and that there are some facts or theoretical arguments that will decisively vindicate one worldview or the other as expressing the correct vision to guide environmental policy. Most philosophers who have written on environmental ethics adopt this assumption, and have therefore debated the truth of "nonanthropocentrism," the view that nonhuman elements of nature have value independent of human values. Scientists, on the other hand, adopt the same assumption that we must choose between moralism and aggregationism, and expect that more scientific data and more sophisticated theories will determine what our approach should be.

The most important consequence of [my] policy-oriented approach, and the rough distinction we have drawn between policies and the ideas that justify them, is that we will not miss examples where environmentalists pursue a policy by consensus in the policy arena, even while discussing and supporting these policies in quite different frameworks of concepts and values.[13] Another consequence of the approach is to hold open, throughout the inquiry, the possibility of a pluralistic integration of environmental values rather than an all-or-nothing decision between the Aggregators and the Moralists. It may be possible, given this approach, to escape the excruciating dilemma and construct an integrated approach to valuing the natural world.

NOTES

1. Cf. David Ehrenfeld, "The Conservationist's Dilemma," in *The Arrogance of Humanism* (New York: Oxford University Press, 1978). I have modified Ehrenfeld's terminology because, in the historical sections of this book, it has been helpful to use the term "conservationist" more narrowly, to represent only one faction of the early environmental movement.

2. Gifford Pinchot, *Breaking New Ground* (Washington, D.C.: Island Press, 1987; originally published 1947), p. 261.

3. John Muir, *A Thousand-Mile Walk to the Gulf* (Boston: Houghton Mifflin, 1981; originally published 1916), pp. 98–99.

4. Roderick Nash, *Wilderness and the American Mind,* 3rd ed. (New Haven: Yale University Press, 1982), p. 161.

5. Ibid., p. 161.

6. Ibid., p. 168.

7. Stephen Fox, *John Muir and His Legacy* (Boston: Little, Brown, 1981), p. 121.

8. Ibid., pp. 145–46.

9. Lester W. Milbrath, *Environmentalists: Vanguard for a New Society* (Albany: State University of New York Press, 1984), p. 72.

10. Bryan G. Norton, "Conservation and Preservation: A Conceptual Rehabilitation, " *Environmental Ethics* 8 (1986): 195–220.

11. Arne Naess, "The Shallow and the Deep, Long-Range Ecology Movement. A Summary," *Inquiry* 16 (1973): 95–100.

12. See Peter Borelli, "Environmentalism at a Crossroads," *Amicus,* Summer (1987): 34.

13. One might call this general approach "philosophical pragmatism," although I hope that the analysis presented here will be of interest to readers who reject pragmatism as a philosophical theory and also to those who care little about philosophical theory at all.

Fragile Freedoms

Bryan G. Norton

Back to the beach, one more time: When I saw the little girl with so many sand dollars, I was struck speechless because the languages readily available to an environmentalist were inadequate. Once it is admitted that sand dollars can be exchanged for nickels, the language of economic aggregation encourages the application of a maximization criterion. On that language, the little girl's utilitarian logic was unassailable: More is better. But the traditional language of morality, developed and honed over centuries and millennia to articulate rules for interpersonal behavior among human individuals, was equally inadequate: An extension of the language of individual rights and interests to apply to this interspecific situation would encourage a total prohibition on exploitation—and thus would deny the obvious fact that humans must sometimes exploit elements of nature in order to live and enjoy.

Our search for a way between the horns of the environmentalists' dilemma has led to an emphasis on the *context* of human actions. The family's strip-mining operation, on this view, is wrong primarily because it was inappropriate to its context. The exploitative activity turned the beach into the first stage of a trinket factory; building sandcastles and learning about nature had lost out to an economic perspective. That little remnant of beach was saved for little girls, but for little girls to learn to love and respect their natural context, not for them to learn to exploit its products.

I wish now that I had used the incident as an opportunity (with her parents' consent, of course) to teach the little girl some ecology and natural history. I'll bet I could have interested her in the way that sand dollars make a living. I could turn over a sand dollar so that the little girl could see and feel the kneading of the hundreds of little sucker-feet by which sand dollars pull themselves through the sand

while passing some of the particles through their bodies, digesting diatoms from the particles as they pass through and are then flushed out.

I'll bet the little girl would have been fascinated to see that the sand dollar has a pentagonal structure analogous to our head, arms, and legs, but that the sand dollar's nervous system is undifferentiated. Therefore the behavioral repertoire of sand dollars is far more limited than our own. Sand dollars' life in predator-rich lagoons encouraged them to invest in external armour rather than mobility.

This approach, turning the beach into a natural laboratory rather than a trinket factory, is in keeping with the environmentalists' long-standing commitment to the educability of the American public. They believe that if enough people adopt the ecological viewpoint, their approach to environmental policy will win out and their common-denominator goals will be achieved. The natural history approach to the situation on the beach is, in other words, to follow Thoreau, Muir, and Leopold in putting faith in the power of observation and experience to transform worldviews. Here, it is possible to say, is the single greatest failure of the environmental movement. While groups have been quite successful in educating their own members through slick membership magazines, they have made less headway in educating the general population. For example, few schools teach conservation in any systematic way, and most science texts do no more than mention conservation in passing.

But I should not, as part of my lesson, insist that the little girl value the sand dollars *in their own right.* That would be like taking the little girl to a symphony concert and trying to teach her to value one note or to an art museum and trying to teach her to value one brush stroke. We must value nature from our point of view *in a total context,* which includes

Bryan G. Norton, *Toward Unity Among Environmentalists* (New York: Oxford University Press, 1991), 244–55. Used by permission of Oxford University Press, Inc. Editors' note: To avoid confusion, where Norton refers in the original to "this book," we have inserted the book's title.

our cultural history and our natural history. Nature must be valued, from the ecological-evolutionary viewpoint of environmentalists, in its full contemporary complexity and in its largest temporal dynamic.

And this crucial lesson of our dependence on the larger systems of nature can be learned from sand dollars—for sand dollars, just like humans, act within an ecological context. The success of their activities depends on a relatively stable context to which they have adapted. The freedom and creativity of sand dollars is a *constrained* freedom, freedom to adapt to a limiting context. We differ from sand dollars in having a repertoire of behaviors almost infinitely more complex than theirs. But our freedom and creativity is no less than theirs a constrained freedom.

The freedom to collect sand dollars, to catch rockfish and bluefish, and to propel ourselves about the countryside by burning petroleum are all fragile freedoms. They are freedoms that depend on the relatively stable environmental context in which they have evolved. If I could, then, have used the incident on the beach to teach the little girl that sand dollars embody an ancient wisdom from which we can learn, and also to illustrate for her the way in which our activities—just like the activities of sand dollars—are possible, and gain meaning and value, only in a larger context, I would have progressed a good way toward the goal of getting the little girl to put most of the sand dollars back. The strip-mining activities of the family were not wrong in the absolute terms of interpersonal morality; they were inappropriate on a beach set aside for relaxation and enjoyment of nature.

The family's reaction, upon finding sand dollars in the lagoon, was to treat them as an economic resource. But the power boat gave me a clue that they did not really need the nickels, and the little girl's dogged efforts convinced me that she was the loser on the beach. Trips to the beach should be explorations of a larger world than the limited sphere of economic activity in which the little girl will no doubt spend most of the rest of her life. Like Muir and Leopold I should have emphasized the ecstatic

aspect of observation and natural history studies. I could have avoided the environmentalists' dilemma by encouraging the little girl to see the world through a lens larger than a cash register. Then, she might have killed some sand dollars to study them, but she would still have *respected* sand dollars as living things with a story to tell. I hope she would also have realized, then, that sand dollars are more valuable alive than dead.

Moralists among environmental ethicists have erred in looking for a value in living things that is *independent* of human valuing. They have therefore forgotten a most elementary point about valuing anything. Valuing always occurs from the viewpoint of a conscious valuer. Since I doubt that sand dollars are conscious, I doubt they are loci of value-expression. To recognize that only the humans are valuing agents at the beach, however, need not enforce the conclusion that the sand dollar will be valued only from the narrow perspective of human economics. If the little girl can learn to value sand dollars in a larger perspective, an ecological context in which sand dollars are fellow travelers in a huge, creative adventure, she will have taken the first tentative steps toward thinking like a lagoon.

Charter captains see restrictions on the taking of bluefish as unjustified infringements of their freedoms. That, as Leopold recognized, represents a failure of *perception,* not value. The captains, used to apparently unlimited bounty from nature, are unable to think like the bay. Environmentalism will succeed if it educates the public so that all citizens are capable of seeing environmental problems at the interface of two systems—the slow-changing systems of nature that change in ecological and evolutionary time and the relatively fast-changing systems of human economics. To the extent that individual freedoms to take bluefish or rockfish depend on the complex, usually slow-changing, systems of nature, they are fragile freedoms. They depend upon, and gain meaning and value within the larger, natural context in which they are pursued.

Does the fragility of freedoms to use nature entail onerous restrictions? Have we, after all, arrived at the depressing conclusion that the future—if environmentalists are correct in seeing the world contextually—will be one of increasing constraints on individual freedoms? Will we, in a world of growing populations and increasing scarcity, be driven to ever more oppressive restrictions on individual freedoms?

I think not. This depressing conclusion follows only if we accept the contextualist worldview incompletely. It is not arrogant to value things from one's own conscious perspective, and to that extent a degree of anthropocentrism is a foregone conclusion. The hard questions will concern which actual activities will be discouraged or limited, and in those arguments environmentalists, anthropocentrists, and ecocentrists alike will support a broadly scientific, ecological, and contextual viewpoint. Most values, from the ecological perspective, depend on saving the ecological systems that are the context of human cultural and economic activities.

Most environmental ethicists have, to date, assumed that we must, to escape arrogance, posit value as independent of human valuing or human valuers. This value has proven to offer little guidance in action and has raised innumerable and intractable questions in the metaphysics of morals. The moral premise of this book is that there exist limits on human treatment of nature—thereby rejecting the implication that humans may do anything they please to their natural context—while leaving the original idea of anthropocentrism—that all value will be perceived from the viewpoint of conscious beings—intact.

To accept the contextualist viewpoint encouraged by an ecological worldview is to recognize that the creative force is outside us. We do not create either energy or biomass—we are derivative beings, who value and choose within a complicated system to which we adapt. Even as we learn more and more about the cunning and creativity of nature, we learn simultaneously that we are finite beings who are free only in the sense that we are free to react creatively and differentially to ever-changing situations outside us, a system that extends beyond our bodies in both time and space.

As Muir and the ecological thinkers who succeeded him emphasized our role as a part of a larger whole, they did not *introduce* the idea that our freedoms are fragile—that idea is clearly implied in the story of the fall from grace and the expulsion from the Garden of Eden. Freedom has always been understood as occurring within constraints. The new idea that must guide environmental ethics is not that our freedoms are limited, but that an important element of those limits exists in nature itself, not in the commandments of a disembodied God or the rights of our fellow humans. The rules governing our treatment of nature are guided neither by the authority of God nor by a priori, precultural moral norms such as rights of natural objects. Environmentalists have been forced to recognize that we must struggle to articulate limits on acceptable behavior by learning more and more about how we affect, and are affected by, our environmental context. The land ethic is nothing more than the latter half of our culture's search for a good life in a good environment. Ecology, the transformative science, prefers an organic metaphor; environmentalists believe that the organic analogy of nature as creative—which is illustrated throughout natural history studies—provides a better metaphor for understanding our adaptive role in larger environments.

In this sense, environmentalists must reject the arrogance involved in the suggestion that humans can do as they please with regard to nature. They must also admit that the creativity of nature is the Great Mystery. If we destroy without understanding, we commit the greatest arrogance, for it is understanding the sweep of millennia, the ability of nature to create more and more elaborate life forms from the deaths of countless individuals, that will ultimately explain our own existence, our correct place. The search for the self-moved mover has only since Darwin become a question in biology. But it was the prophetic Muir who recognized most clearly that science and theology would eventually merge once again as they did in Genesis I. The linchpin of the modern environmental movement is the belief that the study of nature has this ecstatic aspect; the ability to inspire wonder at our "partness" and at the whole of which we are a part is simply the ability to inspire a shift to a new perspective in which nature is an object of contemplation, not exploitation. If that change were to occur, environmentalists believe, there would be more support for contextually sensitive policies.

But still we are left with the disturbing question: How onerous must the restrictions be on future human activities? The answer to this question, I think, must be "It depends." It depends on how we conceive those restrictions. If we, as at present, conceive nature as a machine capable of producing unlimited amounts of a small number of economically useful items, we will view nature and our opportunities statically. If charter captains, who once could offer their clients unlimited catches of bluefish, insist on that freedom indefinitely, they will destroy that freedom. Bluefish catches will eventually be limited by rules and regulations or by natural declines in bluefish stocks. The outlook for human freedom from this static viewpoint looks bleak.

But consider an analogy. Whaling is in the process of fading away as an economically feasible activity. Whale stocks are so depleted that the search becomes ever more expensive. Technology has found substitutes for all but the most esoteric uses of whale oil. Environmentalists therefore insist that whaling is no longer an appropriate activity, even if there are governments that will prop up the dying industry with economic subsidies. If environmentalists and others succeed in the desperate effort to save populations of the great whales, however, there will be a whole new, nonconsumptive, and dynamic industry, whale watching, that will take its place. Children of future generations will pay, it can be assumed, to watch a great whale swim playfully under their boat and breach a few yards away. The fragile freedom to kill whales will be replaced with a more secure freedom, a freedom consonant with the life history of these great, but not reproductively prolific, creatures.

And this suggests the proper answer to charter boat captains who are justifiably wary of catch restrictions given the present attitudes of charter renters. The charter captains have an obligation to educate as well as profit from their customers. The whale-watching case suggests how salable a natural spectacle is. Participation in a bluefish run should be reward enough—and it would be if fishermen carried away information and understanding as well as a couple of bluefish. Charter captains should teach themselves some marine ecology and pass it on as a part of their explanations of why, next year, we're going to release all bluefish but three per fisherman. This is the proper response to a demand for bluefish that cannot be met indefinitely: educate the public and have them pay for it as part of the skills of a competent charter captain. If charter captains will not educate their fishermen, who will?

The writer Annie Dillard expresses a sense of awe, a dogged persistence in seeing and wondering at it all. Nowhere is this sense of wonder—which was, after all, what was missing from the little girl's afternoon at the beach—stronger than in her graphic description of nature's profligacy, a chapter called "Fecundity," in *Pilgrim at Tinker Creek*. She describes aphids, which lay a million eggs to achieve a few adults.[1]

Dillard is saying something very profound, and it holds the key to being content with fragile freedoms. The recognition that our freedoms are fragile is, in a sense, no more than an admission of our own finitude. That, by way of bad news, is nothing new. But Dillard's illustration of the incredible, virtually infinite creativity of nature is the good news. Our freedom and creativity may appear limited when looked at from a conservative viewpoint that insists on pressing fragile freedoms, such as the freedom to take bluefish, rockfish, or whales to their limit. But the same insight should encourage us to recognize that we have the ability to learn, through science, the limitations of populations of rockfish and whales to reproduce, and to encourage alternative, more adaptive human behaviors before an element of nature's productive fabric is destroyed.

And here we see the potentially true nobility of the human species. Unlike the other forces of nature, which react unconsciously to their surroundings, mainly through the weeding out of unfit individuals, we are conscious beings who can adapt consciously to our changing environment. If we can progress beyond the environmentalists' dilemma, which encourages us to understand and value nature either in the limited context of human economics or in the limited context of human ethics, and value nature from *our* point of view, but in its full and glorious context, there is yet hope for the human species.

Conservation biology must now move rapidly to propose a positive criterion of ecological health for natural systems, a criterion that places value neither on simply exploiting the atomistic elements of nature nor on isolating nature and separating human activities from it. But conservationists should not propose their criterion imperiously; they should work with nature interpreters in parks, on television, and in books to involve the public in the search for a land ethic. It should be a positive criterion for the ecological health of systems that recognizes that some human activities are compatible with the ongoing health of the energy pyramid, and others will positively enhance it. The good news for us and future generations of humans is that we, as conscious

beings with scientific tools, can occupy a synoptic viewpoint from which we can understand, and protect, the incredible creativity of nature. Our success will depend on how quickly we develop such a positive criterion and how quickly this criterion can become a basis for private actions and public policies. And that, of course, will depend on how successful environmentalists are in encouraging contextual thinking and educating the public in the ecological, systematic viewpoint on nature. It is the firm commitment to the dynamic aspect of human valuing—its reactivity to changing situations—that marks the ecological/evolutionary perspective: humans must understand and value from a realistic perspective by recognizing their role in the larger ecological context.

NOTES

1. Annie Dillard, *Pilgrim at Tinker Creek* (New York: Harper and Row, 1974), p. 175.

Therapeutic Nihilism and Environmental Management

Eugene C. Hargrove

In 1965, Ian Douglas-Hamilton went to Lake Manyara in Tanzania to study the effect of elephants on *Acacia tortilis* woodland in a national park. The elephants were destroying the forest by stripping the bark off of the trees. These trees were important because they were used by lions to sleep in, and the lions were the most famous tourist attraction in the park. Douglas-Hamilton was supposed to determine a management solution to this problem. There were two main alternatives based on two contradictory interpretations of what was happening in the park. One group of managers argued that protection of Manyara's elephants had created an overpopulation problem, with the result that the elephants were destroying their environment. According to the other group, the destruction of the acacia thorn woodlands was not damage but rather habitat modification that occurred cyclically. As the trees were destroyed in one area, new woodlands developed elsewhere, allowing the cycle of destruction and new growth to continue indefinitely. If the first account of the elephant-tree relationship was correct, large numbers of elephants probably had to be culled (killed) to reduce the herd to save the ecological system and the trees for the lions. If the second was correct, the elephants' activities could be disregarded, and no action of any kind was required.[1]

Douglas-Hamilton found what he called a "unique" scientific solution: He recommended, first of all, that farmland be purchased to serve as a corridor to a nearby forest, so that the elephants could spread their damage among more trees over a larger area, thereby reducing the impact on the most endangered trees in the park. Second, since his research revealed that the lions really liked to climb only seventeen trees in the park, he advocated giving them special protection by wrapping their trunks with wire, thereby preventing the elephants from stripping the bark but still allowing lions easy access when they wanted to sleep in them. This solution was unique because it solved the problem in terms of both theories. If there was a population problem, it was taken care of by increasing the number of the trees available to the elephants. At the same time, by not interfering with the elephants, it still allowed the system to continue through its natural cycles. The only unnatural intrusion was the wire on the seventeen trees used by the lions.[2]

When Douglas-Hamilton proposed his solution, it was quickly accepted. As he put it:

> No one opposed this idea and indeed everybody at the seminar seemed relieved that there might be an alternative to decimating the Manyara elephants by shooting, and that the loss of the *Acacia tortilis* woodlands could be accepted with equanimity.[3]

The reason for the quick acceptance of this solution was partly because no one wanted to kill elephants and partly because it did not require a resolution of the conflict of the two opposing accounts of the situation, but primarily it was because everyone involved wanted a management approach in which the managers intervened in the ecology of the park as little as possible. This was an occupational preference more than a personal preference: Like most ecologists, environmentalists, and environmental managers, they preferred a management approach that advocated doing nothing whenever feasible.

This preference, and its implications for environmental management and environmental ethics, is the subject of this chapter. Although the preference was not popularly accepted at the time Douglas-Hamilton made his study in Manyara, a few years later it was elevated to the status of a law of ecology in Barry Commoner's book, *The Closing Circle*. According to Commoner, the third law of ecology is "Nature knows best." Stated baldly, this law means that "any major man-made change in a natural system is likely to be *detrimental* to that system." In terms of this law, doing nothing is better than doing something, because any action will most likely have bad consequences whether it succeeds in solving the initial problem or not.[4]

Since the promulgation of Commoner's law, this preference has gained broad public acceptance even among people who do not support environmental attitudes and ideology. Peter Singer, for example, who is very critical of environmentalists in his book *Animal Liberation,* nevertheless, accepts the approach as the best one for dealing with wildlife. As he puts it:

> Judging by our past record, any attempt to change ecological systems on a large scale is going to do far more harm than good. For this, reason, if for no other, it is true to say that except in a very few and limited cases, we cannot and should not try to police nature.[5]

Although the general public's knowledge and approval of this managerial approach can probably be traced back to Commoner's book, the approach was already well known to environmental professionals and environmentalists not only at Lake Manyara but throughout North America and elsewhere around the world. It is, for example, implicit in many of Aldo Leopold's essays in *Sand County Almanac* and *Round River*. It is perhaps most explicit in the essay "Round River," where Leopold writes:

The outstanding scientific discovery of the twentieth century is not television, or radio, but rather the complexity of the land organism. Only those who know the most about it can appreciate how little is known about it. The last word in ignorance is the man who says of an animal or plant: "What good is it?" If the land mechanism as a whole is good, then every part is good, whether we understand it or not. If the biota, in the course of aeons, has built something we like but do not understand, then who but a fool would discard seemingly useless parts? To keep every cog and wheel is the first precaution of intelligent tinkering.[6]

Picking up on the same theme in his more famous essay, "The Land Ethic," Leopold goes on to assert that although ordinary citizens believe that scientists know how nature works, "the scientist is equally sure that he does not. He knows that the biotic mechanism is so complex that its workings may never be fully understood."[7] Manipulations or alterations in ecological systems may, Leopold argues, often have unforeseen and devastating consequences. According to Leopold, the cutting of the cane fields of Kentucky might have adversely altered the course of the settlement of the United States, if the cane had been replaced not by bluegrass but by "some worthless sedge, shrub, or weed."[8]

In recent years, this let-it-be approach has come to be interpreted as the official policy of the National Park Service, in part because of the influence of a study of the park service's game management programs, conducted by a committee of ecologists, chaired by Starker Leopold, Aldo Leopold's son.[9] Although the Leopold report advocates active, rather than passive, management of national parks, the authors admit in the report itself that "in essence, we are calling for a set of ecological skills unknown in this country today."[10] In this context, the resource management policy evolved into "the application of ecological management techniques to neutralize the unnatural influences of man, thus permitting the natural environment to be maintained essentially by nature."[11] According to Alston Chase, the policy became official in 1978 when the following statement was added to the National Park Service's *Management Policies:* "The concept of perpetuation of a natural environment or ecosystem, as compared with the protection of individual features or species, is a distinguishing aspect."[12] In terms of this policy, for example, the elk herd in Yellowstone was to be kept under control not by culling as before but by allowing the herd to fall into ecological balance with the rest of the surrounding natural system.

In part, the policy is a common sense approach based on our limited scientific ability to understand and manipulate natural areas, but it is also something more. Most fundamentally, it represents a kind of scientific pessimism that is virtually the mirror image of the scientific and technological optimism that pervades the physical sciences and engineering. Whereas scientists and technologists generally assume that it is only a matter of time before this or that problem will be solved through additional research or technological innovation, many environmentalists and environmental managers have come to assume that scientific answers to most of their problems may never be found. The consequences of these two attitudes are strikingly different. In accordance with scientific and technological optimism, one forges ahead, confident that later discoveries and techniques will solve the problems created by current actions—later on, but before they become too bad. In accordance with environmental pessimism, however, one tries to do as little as possible, feeling that there will be large numbers of bad consequences from any active manipulation that either cannot be solved at all or will in practice be too costly to deal with adequately. Essentially, from this perspective, the cure is considered to be worse than the disease.

Alston Chase uses various terms and phrases to identify and describe this environmental management approach in his book, *Playing God in Yellowstone:* "natural regulation," "noninterference with wildlife," "ecosystems management," and "self-regulation." While these tags serve as adequate identification in scientific and management contexts, at least one other term is more appropriate in historical and philosophical contexts: *therapeutic nihilism,* a term frequently used by the Viennese medical community in the nineteenth century.

TRADITIONAL THERAPEUTIC NIHILISM

Nihilism was originally the name for an anarchical and revolutionary political movement in Russia in the early nineteenth century that held that existing social, political, and economic systems had to be destroyed before new institutions could be established. The term quickly spread throughout Europe, but in doing so it lost its political meaning, finding a home instead in intellectual debates about atheism, moral skepticism, and the meaninglessness of life. In the twentieth century, it has also been connected with controversy about the limits and foundations of knowledge. *Webster's New World Dictionary* defines it as "the denial of the existence of any basis for knowledge or truth"; "the general rejection of customary beliefs in morality, religion, etc.," and "the belief that there is no meaning or purpose in existence."

Therapeutic nihilism is closely associated with the establishment of modern medical practice in the nineteenth century in Austria. William Johnston traces its origin back to a Dutch physician in the eighteenth century, Hermann Boerhave, who advocated the "slow accumulation of observations" aimed at discrediting "quack practices," and to Gerhard van Swieten, a student of Boerhave, who founded the Vienna Medical Faculty in 1745 and put Boerhave's teachings into practice as standard procedure. Followers of van Swieten, for example, "revived Hippocrates' doctrine of the healing power of nature in order to diminish the frequency of blood letting." One early name for this new approach was *passive therapy;* another was *expectant therapy.* Doctors who practiced this kind of therapy usually did little or nothing for their patients except wait for nature to cure them.[13]

This new approach was especially useful in helping doctors move beyond folk medicine into modern medical practice. In particular, it revealed the ineffectiveness of most traditional cures. In a wide range of cases, doctors were able to show that patients who were passively treated were as likely to recover as those subjected to most traditional remedies. This advance in medical knowledge, however, did have some unpleasant consequences. In its extreme form, as therapeutic nihilism, as Johnston notes, it "encouraged neglect of patients and indifference to human life."[14] Gradually the focus shifted from treatment to diagnosis, from prescribing remedies to analyzing illness, and with this shift came an increase in unnecessary human suffering. Since medicine given to patients to reduce their suffering also distorted symptoms that were important to the patients' diagnoses, doctors stopped prescribing medication to relieve pain. By 1850, cherry brandy was the only painkiller used in the General Hospital in Vienna.

Lack of success in finding cures was generally taken as support for therapeutic nihilism: It encouraged doctors to believe that there really were no cures for most health problems and that it was useless to look for any. The most famous example of this self-fulfilling skepticism was the problem of childbed fever. In Vienna in the 1840s, it was very dangerous to have a baby delivered in the hospital, for the mortality rate was inversely proportional to the degree of professional care given. There were two divisions in the General Hospital, the First Maternity Division, administered by the doctors of the Medical Faculty, and the Second Maternity Division, administered by midwives. In 1846, some 20 to 30 percent of the women admitted each month to the first division died of childbed fever, for a total of 451 women for the year. In contrast, the chance of dying from the disease was five times less for a woman if she received treatment from a midwife in the second division, and the lowest mortality rate was among women who had their babies on the street on the way to the hospital. The obvious conclusion reached by doctors and patients alike was that it was safest not to go to the hospital at all, a conclusion completely in keeping with the spirit of therapeutic nihilism.[15]

The influence of therapeutic nihilism on the treatment of childbed fever was so inhibitive that doctors paid no attention when Ignaz Semmelweis, the head of the first division, discovered that most of the deaths could be avoided if doctors disinfected their hands after dissecting cadavers and before examining their patients.[16] Incredibly, because he was considered to be devoting excessive attention to the problem, Semmelweis was actually demoted one year later and eventually forced to leave the hospital. His discovery, moreover, continued to be ignored by the medical community. Upon his departure, the death rates for childbed fever in the first division, which had been sharply reduced, returned to normal. Semmelweis' discovery was not universally recognized, and hospital practice appropriately altered, until fourteen years later, when his emotionally charged, but carefully documented book on the subject was published.[17]

Although Carl Hempel cites Semmelweis' research on childbed fever as a model for scientific inquiry,[18] his contemporaries, quite to the contrary, did not perceive his work as being scientific at all. In accordance with the dictates of therapeutic nihilism, a doctor was not supposed to treat a patient for an illness until the cause of the illness was properly identified. This Semmelweis was unable to do. The general medical wisdom at that time was that childbed fever was "an unknown epidemic influence of an atmospheric-cosmic-telluric nature," and Semmelweis' speculation that it was blood poisoning caused by "putrid animal matter" was not considered a theoretical improvement.[19] If Semmelweis could have identified hemolytic streptococcus as the cause of childbed fever, he probably would not have had much trouble convincing doctors to practice the hygienic procedures he recommended. He was not, however, in a position to do so, since the very existence of bacteria and viruses was in those days still unknown.

Although it is tempting to treat therapeutic nihilism as a misstep in the development of modern medicine, that would be a mistake, for therapeutic nihilism is in fact alive and well today both in medical research and medical practice. A computer search of medical journals, for example, would reveal frequent use of the term in research papers on almost every aspect of medicine (a preliminary search I made of *Excerpta Medica* turned up twenty-nine citations).[20] In theory, doctors today, if confronted with an unknown disease, would, in accordance with therapeutic nihilism, study the disease and as much as possible avoid medication that might distort symptoms.

All in all, therapeutic nihilism deserves neither wholehearted praise nor denunciation. There are both pluses and minuses to be considered. It cannot be denied that the practice of therapeutic nihilism has been beneficial in the past and will continue to be so in the future. The benefits, however, are usually long-term—to future patients, not to current ones. The first victims of a newly identified disease are able to benefit only if doing nothing really does allow their recovery. When this is not the case, the patients serve simply as objects of scientific study, a step toward the theoretical understanding of a medical condition, not its cure. Moreover, they serve in a dehumanizing way when analysis takes precedence over treatment and to the degree that medication that might ease their suffering is withheld in order to avoid distorting symptoms and to aid in the collection of valuable medical information. To be sure, this approach is often the most efficient way in which to study a medical problem. It is not, however, always the most efficient way to find a cure or to treat terminally ill patients humanely, for, as Semmelweis clearly demonstrated with childbed fever, it is possible in some cases to find a cure without the theoretical understanding therapeutic nihilism calls for.

THERAPEUTIC NIHILISM AND MODERN SCIENCE

As the nineteenth century progressed, therapeutic nihilism began to have a significant intellectual impact outside medicine. Johnston notes its importance in the thought of Karl Kraus and Albert Ehrenstein in literature, Richard Wahle and Ludwig Wittgenstein in philosophy, Carl Menger and Ludwig von Mises in economics, and Otto Weininger in psychology. Even in politics, the stagnation caused by the long reign of Kaiser Franz Joseph I was eventually deemed preferable to any conceivable political change. Although Johnston argues that Freud's contribution to psychology was a rejection of therapeutic nihilism (favoring compassion for patients), his methods were similar enough that an English-language version of therapeutic nihilism, *therapeutic positivism,* was sometimes characterized as a kind of psychoanalysis. It is largely because therapeutic nihilism can be given a positivistic look, thereby transforming it into something that is compatible with early twentieth-century philosophy of science, that the position has some plausibility as a scientific approach to environmental management.[21]

Positivism is a philosophical position that originated in the early nineteenth century in the writings of Henri, Comte de Saint-Simon, and of Auguste Comte, according to which scientific knowledge is treated as the only legitimate kind of knowledge possible. This view was rigorously developed and defended as "logical positivism" in the early twentieth century by a group of philosophers of science in Vienna, collectively known as the Vienna Circle, and was spread to various English-speaking countries around the world in the 1930s when the members of the group left Austria just before World War II. Because the connotations of nihilism and positivism are so very different, the idea that therapeutic nihilism could surface in positivism may at first seem almost counterintuitive. However, the positivists differed dramatically from nihilists only in claiming that objective, scientifically verifiable knowledge was possible. When it came to subjects such as ethics and religion, the conclusions they reached were as negative and as skeptical as those of the nihilists, if not more so: Ethical, aesthetic, and religious statements were declared meaningless because they are not scientifically verifiable; ultimately they were treated as nothing more than nonsensical outpourings of emotion.[22]

Although the first logical positivists did not themselves officially embrace therapeutic nihilism, as Viennese they were undoubtedly familiar with the position, and their recommendations concerning the treatment of nonscientific issues—to ignore them—was a straightforward application of therapeutic nihilism in an academic and scientific, rather than a medical, context. They were, moreover, heavily influenced by the early writings of Ludwig Wittgen-

stein, another philosopher from Vienna, whose work, both early and late, shows the mark of therapeutic nihilism. Because Wittgenstein's work remained oriented toward therapeutic nihilism even after he rejected and broke free from logical positivism, his writings are one of the best applications of the general position in twentieth-century philosophy. While the later Wittgenstein and his students are most appropriately classified as ordinary language philosophers, they had the distinction of being labeled therapeutic positivists in a critical article in *Mind* in 1946.[23]

As the positivists interpreted Wittgenstein's writings, especially his early work, his basic position was an excellent model for their own scientific approach. According to this interpretation, the study of philosophy, ethics, aesthetics, and religion should be disregarded in favor of scientific research on the grounds that our inability to verify hypotheses scientifically in these nonscientific fields of inquiry makes such inquiry pointless activity that contributes nothing to our pursuit of knowledge and indeed frequently inhibits it by treating nonsense as if it is in some way meaningful.

On the surface, this interpretation is supported by most of Wittgenstein's writings throughout his philosophical career. The influence of therapeutic nihilism on Wittgenstein's philosophy is most obvious in his characterizations of philosophy and philosophical method in his book *Philosophical Investigations.* Here he openly declares that "the philosopher's treatment of a question is like the treatment of an illness."[24] The treatment as such is not really a cure but rather a demonstration that there is nothing to cure. One is supposed to study a philosophical problem until it becomes clear that the problem does not really exist: "The clarity that we are aiming at is indeed *complete* clarity. But this simply means that philosophical problems should *completely* disappear." The therapeutic result is an end to a kind of psychological torment brought on by the contemplation of philosophical puzzles: "The real discovery is one that makes me capable of stopping doing philosophy when I want to—the one that gives philosophy peace, so that it is no longer tormented by questions which bring *itself* in question."[25]

For Wittgenstein, philosophical problems are intellectual confusions resulting from attempts to say what cannot be said in language, to thrust against and try to go beyond the limits of language. As he put it in his first book, *Tractatus Logico-Philosophicus,* what can be said is subject to scientific investigation and what cannot be said is mystical (nonscientific) and must be passed over in silence:

> We feel that even when all possible scientific questions have been answered, the problems of life remain completely untouched. Of course there are then no questions left, and this itself is the answer.
> The solution of the problem of life is seen in the vanishing of the problem.[26]

This approach to philosophy is nihilistic to the degree that it rejects the idea that it is possible to find solutions to philosophical problems; it is positivistic in that it accepts the view that scientific problems can be solved through rational and scientific inquiry.

The *Tractatus* was intended as a reductio ad absurdum proof that traditional philosophical inquiry is impossible. Knowing that not everyone would accept his proof, Wittgenstein offered an alternative method—"the correct method"—at the end of the *Tractatus* that would allow doubters to verify his conclusions independently. In accordance with this method, one is supposed to say

> ₙothing except what can be said—i.e. propositions of natural science—i.e. something that has nothing to do with philosophy—and then, whenever someone else wanted to say something metaphysical, to demonstrate to him that he had failed to give a meaning to certain signs in his propositions.

This method is the one used by Wittgenstein in all of his later writings. Its purpose is to quiet the urge to go beyond the limits of language.

In the *Investigations,* Wittgenstein compares thrusting against the limits of language with banging one's head against a wall: "The results of phi-

losophy are the uncovering of one or another piece of plain nonsense and of bumps that the understanding has got by running its head against the limits of language."[27] There are at least two sources for this remark. First, it is a paraphrase of an aphorism by Karl Kraus that recommends the inactivity of traditional therapeutic nihilism: "If I cannot get further, this is because I have banged my head against the wall of language. Then with my head bleeding, I withdraw."[28] Second, it is supported by Wittgenstein's own experiences as documented in a series of notebooks that he kept in preparation for the writing of the *Tractatus*. Here we find him actually thrusting against the limits of language trying to define ethical terms and eventually concluding that such definitions are impossible because they exceed the limits of language.[29] Because of such documentation in Wittgenstein's writings and lectures, it is easy to characterize him as a very straightforward traditional therapeutic nihilist. As it turns out, however, his actual position is much more complicated and includes elements that essentially turn therapeutic nihilism on its head.

One early indication that Wittgenstein's interpretation of his own writings is incompatible with the positivists' understanding of them is a letter written to Ludwig von Ficker about the *Tractatus* in which he states that the things that we cannot speak about are more important than the things that we can:

> My work consists of two parts: the one presented here plus all that I have not written. And it is precisely this second part that is the important one. My book draws limits to the sphere of the ethical from the inside as it were. . . . In short, . . . I have managed in my book to put everything firmly into place by being silent about it.[30]

Commenting on this passage, Paul Engelmann, a Viennese friend of Wittgenstein, distinguishes the positivistic interpretation of Wittgenstein's writings from his own views as follows:

> A whole generation of disciples was able to take Wittgenstein for a positivist because he has some-

thing of enormous importance in common with the positivists: he draws the line between what we can speak about and what we must be silent about just as they do. The difference is only that they have nothing to be silent about. Positivism holds—and this is its essence—that what we can speak about is all that matters in life. *Whereas Wittgenstein passionately believes that all that really matters in human life is precisely what, in his view, we must be silent about.* When he nevertheless takes immense pains to delimit the unimportant, it is not the coastline of that island which he is bent on surveying with such meticulous accuracy, but the boundary of the ocean.[31]

Seen in this way, the difference between Wittgenstein and his positivistic followers becomes a matter of value. While they hold that only scientifically verifiable statements are worthy of attention, Wittgenstein holds that they are less important than the unverifiable ones, which are frequently worth investigating whether or not any positive epistemic result is achieved.

Although Wittgenstein's initial experiences thrusting against the limits of language were in accordance with the traditional model for therapeutic nihilism—that is, he himself stopped trying to go beyond the limits of language—by the early 1930s at the latest, and probably much earlier, he concluded that there is a natural tendency in human beings to try to solve philosophical problems and that such activity is beneficial whether it is successful or not. He stresses this point, for example, at the end of his "Lecture on Ethics":

This running against the walls of our cage is perfectly, absolutely hopeless. Ethics so far as it springs from the desire to say something about the ultimate meaning of life, the absolute good, the absolute valuable, can be no science. But it is a document of a tendency in the human mind which I personally cannot help respecting deeply and I would not for my life ridicule it.[32]

As this passage makes clear, the major change in Wittgenstein's attitude toward therapeutic nihilism between the early and late periods was his gradual realization that his method of dissolving philosophical problems had therapeutic value. In the *Tractatus,* as mentioned, after describing his alternative method, Wittgenstein goes on to suggest that the people who want philosophical answers will not find the method "satisfying." By the time he had returned to England to begin his second period of philosophical work, however, he had changed his mind completely. G. E. Moore, who attended Wittgenstein's lectures in the 1930s, records this change in his notes on those classes, specifically with regard to the alternative method of the *Tractatus,* which was then being put into action:

He did not expressly try to tell us what the "new method" which had been found was. But he gave some hints as to its nature. He said . . . that we had to follow a certain instinct which leads us to ask certain questions, though we don't even know what these questions mean; that our asking them results from "a vague uneasiness," like that which leads children to ask "Why?"; and that this uneasiness can only be cured "either by showing that a particular question is not permitted, or by answering it."[33]

Wittgenstein's reevaluation and approval of the thrusts against the limits of language dramatically transformed his therapeutic positivism into something very different from the therapeutic nihilism upon which it was initially based. For medical therapeutic nihilists, it was a complete waste of a doctor's time to thrust against the limits of medical knowledge—to attempt to cure patients when the theoretical knowledge of a disease was still unknown. The therapy was supposed to come from doing nothing, letting nature take its course. In philosophy, likewise, it could be said that the logical positivists followed their Viennese medical counterparts in rejecting investigations that were not aimed at uncovering scientific knowledge in accordance with standard scientific methods. Wittgenstein, however, was not so much interested in uncovering scientific knowledge as in clearly defining the limits to scientific knowledge, and for him what lay outside those limits was more interesting than what was within. The therapy, moreover, came from trying to thrust against the limits of philosophical, religious, and ethical knowledge, whether one succeeded or failed, and despite the likely prospect that failure would be the final result.

This shift of emphasis from concern about the value of the product of the therapeutic activity to the value of the activity itself, regardless of its consequences, reveals an unexpected valuational flexibility in therapeutic nihilism that will haunt its application in environmental affairs. Although a direct application of therapeutic nihilism, following the positivistic model, would discourage environmental manipulation on the grounds that the results are nearly always damaging, it is nevertheless possible, taking an approach analogous to Wittgenstein's approach in philosophy, to conclude that environmental manipulation is good for its own sake or in terms of various nonenvironmental consequences—for example, the expansion of the economy or the humanizing or civilizing of the world[34]—and argue that these goods override concern about environmental damage.

THE ORIGINS OF ENVIRONMENTAL THERAPEUTIC NIHILISM

Unlike Wittgenstein's therapeutic positivism, which arose directly out of medical therapeutic nihilism, environmental therapeutic nihilism seems to be historically independent of it. In particular, there is no evidence that those who have supported the position drew any inspiration from therapeutic nihilism of any kind or even knew what it was. Thus the first step in examining the environmental variant is to take a look at the reasons that environmentalists give for holding their version of the general position.

Since Barry Commoner's third law of ecology, "Nature knows best," is the official and most popular formulation of environmental therapeutic nihilism, one might suppose that it would be the starting point for any analysis of the position. In fact, however, Commoner provides very little support for the law: He tries to explain it, but he does not make any attempt to justify it; he does not even provide an anecdotal account of how he came to hold the

view. Although he provides examples, they are not ecological examples.

The purpose of Commoner's explanation is to provide "a properly defined context" for his claim that "any major man-made change in a natural system is likely to be *detrimental* to that system." He proceeds by analogy with an example about a watch. He argues that random thrusts into the works of the watch are more likely to damage the watch than to make it work better because the watch is a finely tuned mechanism with a great deal of research and development behind it. From here he moves on to random changes in an organism induced by X-radiation. The living organism, he maintains, is also more likely to be damaged than benefited because of the biological research and development that it has acquired through evolution. Based on these two examples, Commoner goes on to suggest by analogy that random interference in the organization of natural systems will result in damage in the same way.

There are a number of problems with Commoner's exposition. First, there are the analogies themselves. Since the rationalist world view of nature as a machine is often cited as one of the most fundamental causes of the environmental crisis in this century, it is odd that Commoner immediately turns to a mechanistic example to defend his ecological principle. Even his shift from a machine to an organism falls short, since ecosystems are usually treated as communities of organisms, not as superorganisms. These analogies, moreover, work only if the organization of an ecosystem really is as rigidly structured as that of a watch or an organism, and it is very doubtful that this is the case. Random changes in the watch and the organism are usually damaging because these entities are able to function well only within very limited mechanical or biological parameters. The organization of an ecosystem, by contrast, is obviously more loosely structured than a watch or an organism and does not have comparable functions and purposes built into it. Losing a species to extinction in an ecosystem, for example, is usually not anything like losing the mainspring in a watch or a vital organ in an animal. The ecosystem does not break down or die; it simply changes, taking on different "functions" and "purposes." Described in this way, it is hard to assess whether particular changes constitute damage. Usually, depending on various contexts and perspectives, such changes are damaging to some parts of the system but not to the whole.

In short, Commoner's examples fail to take into account the resilience of the ecological system, which, unlike a watch or an organism, can avoid destruction by changing its structure. In this respect, an ecosystem is more analogous to an economic system, for example, a market system, than to a machine. Virtually any change in such a system has innumerable good and bad consequences. A drop in the price of oil, for example, may devastate some parts of the system, such as oil-producing companies that have trouble continuing to provide oil at the reduced price, while dramatically improving other parts of the system, such as oil-using companies that do a booming business selling cheaper products. Even the near or complete destruction of a commercial or industrial activity does not necessarily have any long-term impact on the market system, since other related activities may produce a new surge of growth, in some cases bolstering the same activities that they very nearly destroyed. The appearance of new products such as television and videocassette players that initially hurt the motion picture industry has over the long term provided it with new commercial opportunities. Similarly, the loss of particular species in an ecosystem may have negligible impact if other species are waiting in the wings—as, for example, when coyotes replace wolves—and may even benefit some species that might otherwise have been lost—for example, from wolf predation, but not from coyote predation. In this context, the claim that any change is likely to be detrimental is, on the one hand, a trivial truth, since in principle all change is likely to produce damage of some kind, and, on the other hand, a serious falsehood, if it fails to note that the same change is also just as likely to produce benefits.

Finally, there is the problem of Commoner's emphasis on randomness. While it is reasonable to assume that random pokes at a mechanism will damage the watch, it does not follow that skilled pokes by a watch repairman will have a similar effect. Likewise, although random doses of radiation are bad for an organism, carefully administered doses by a doctor for medical purposes often benefit the organism. Thus Commoner's analogies suggest only that any *random* man-made change in a natural system is likely to be detrimental, not that *any* man-made change most likely will be. To justify his law, or even to explain it adequately, Commoner needs to demonstrate that ecological adjustments to ecosystems, comparable to competent watch repair service or to good medical treatment, are impossible.

Traditional therapeutic nihilism is supported by a belief that there are definite limits to medical knowledge. Therapeutic positivism is supported likewise by a belief that traditional philosophical problems are puzzles that can never be solved. In neither case, however, is this belief based on a proof that the limits can never be overcome. Rather, a kind of pessimism is generated by the experience of many people who fail to go beyond those limits. As Johnston has noted, poor results in surgery and other fields of medicine in Vienna gave strong support to a general feeling that further research was futile. In therapeutic positivism, Wittgenstein's failure in his attempts to define certain ethical terms, together with his studies of Kierkegaard and other philosophers, had a similar effect on him. Although Commoner provides us with no comparable accounts in ecology, personal or otherwise, it seems safe to assume that his ecological principle must be based on experiences of this kind, which, while not constituting a final proof, provide psychologically convincing evidence. Furthermore, given the widespread acceptance of environmental therapeutic nihilism, it is reasonable to assume that many other people have had such experiences as well.

Susan Flader skillfully documents one such case in her intellectual biography of Aldo Leopold, *Thinking like a Mountain*.[35] Much of Leopold's life was devoted to uncovering ecological management principles that would allow the manipulation of ecosystems for the benefit of human beings, most specifically for the benefit of those who wished to hunt deer. His early work in the U.S. Forest Service was directed toward finding ways to increase the uses of national forests by maximizing the size of deer herds in those forests for recreational hunting. Leopold's studies culminated in his book *Game Management,* in which he provided what he thought were the principles necessary to "substitute a new and objective equilibrium for any natural one which civilization might have destroyed."[36] Leopold argued that he had identified a series of factors that could be manipulated independently of one another to maintain ecosystem stability and to provide products like deer for recreational consumption. These factors are hunting, predation, starvation, disease parasites, accidents, food supply, water supply, coverts, and special factors. Leopold believed at that time that these factors could be manipulated with great subtlety. For example, on one occasion, in order to avoid a doe season on the Gila, he suggested to Frank Pooler that "concentrating the predatory animal work on coyotes and letting the lions alone for awhile might be a better remedy."[37] According to Leopold, such manipulation represented the domination of nature by civilization. As he put it in his book "Civilization is, in its essence, the will to interpret and govern [the fundamental behavior of all aggregations of living things]."[38]

Leopold's book was published the same year that he made the transition from game manager to teacher, accepting a newly created chair of game management at the University of Wisconsin. Within three years, he denounced the management techniques that he had so carefully developed and embraced instead environmental therapeutic nihilism. This major change in his view of game management was the result not so much of any particular scientific experimentation as of his reflections on the consequences, out in the field, of the kind of manipulation he had encouraged.

As Flader presents it, Leopold was primarily influenced by deer irruptions on the Kaibab plateau, north of the Grand Canyon, and especially in a game refuge called Black Canyon that Leopold had been instrumental in establishing.[39] The Black Canyon refuge was supposed to be a breeding ground for deer where they would be free of both predators and

hunters. In theory, the overflow from the refuge was supposed to supply greatly increased numbers of deer for recreational hunting around the perimeter of the refuge. In practice, the deer, free from hunting and predation, increased as expected but remained in the refuge, destroying the carrying capacity of the land. In the end, the result was less deer rather than more, and a severely damaged ecosystem as far as deer farming was concerned. During the same period, a similar disaster occurred on the Kaibab plateau for the same reasons: The deer population increased from four thousand in 1904 to one hundred thousand in 1924, followed by massive depletion in the herd through starvation in the next few years and a drop in the carrying capacity below the 1904 level.[40]

Although Leopold was very much aware of the problems with deer in Black Canyon and on the Kaibab plateau when he was writing *Game Management,* he did not at that time view them as problems that his general management approach could not overcome. Indeed, he cited them "as illustrations of the effectiveness of management."[41] It was not until Leopold was busy with another excess deer problem, this time in Wisconsin, that he finally began to rethink his factor manipulation management approach. According to Flader, what finally changed Leopold's mind was a trip to Dauerwald in Germany in 1935, where a policy to maximize forest growth and deer populations had been in force for centuries, followed by a trip to Chihuahua in Mexico the following year, where no management policies had been undertaken and the land was in a reasonably natural condition.[42] In Dauerwald, Leopold saw that efforts to maximize both deer and forest were mutually contradictory, since maximized forest growth created conditions in which there was no undergrowth for the deer to eat: Food had to be grown on farms and brought in. In Chihuahua, in contrast, he found stable natural conditions in which deer, wolves, and forest were coexisting, seemingly in harmony, and without the deer irruptions that were now occurring with some regularity north of the border. These observations, Flader argues, convinced Leopold that active manipulation of the environment, with the goal of maximizing particular elements, could lead only to the artificial conditions he had found in Germany. To avoid this outcome, Leopold began reformulating his management approach to retain and rely on the ecological harmony he had found in Mexico—that is, he turned to natural regulation.

Although theoretically Leopold could have embraced natural regulation without radically changing his mind about his factor management approach, and perhaps thereby avoiding environmental therapeutic nihilism, this was not the case. Leopold had, in fact, already clearly rejected factor manipulation months before his trip to Mexico in a lecture given at Beloit College in 1936 called "Means and Ends in Wildlife Management." At the outset, Leopold takes back his earlier claim that game management—now wildlife management—can "substitute a new and objective equilibrium for any natural one that civilization might have destroyed." He writes:

> Agriculture has assumed that by the indefinite pyramiding of new "controls" an artificial plant-animal community can be substituted for the natural one. There are many omens that this assumption may be false. Pests and troubles in need of control seem to be piling up even faster than new science and new dollars for control work.

Because of these problems, Leopold continues, "Wildlife management . . . has already admitted its inability to replace natural equilibria with artificial ones, and its unwillingness to do so even if it could." According to Leopold, wildlife management is not only unable to synthesize wildlife environment but is not even able to "isolate variables in research." In turn, this "inability of isolating variables leads the game manager to place dependence on observation in the wild." While these observations can suggest "items which are susceptible [to] experimental verification," "the unnatural simplicity of his controlled tests forces [the wildlife manager] to be suspicious of even the most carefully verified results." Few such conclusions, Leopold adds, "stay put for a long period."[43]

Leopold's loss of confidence in the reductionist method as a foundation for ecological manipulation, together with his realization in Chihuahua that ecosystems, if left alone, can be expected to remain reasonably stable, except for some cyclic change, seem to be the primary sources of the environmental therapeutic nihilism that surfaces in "Round River" and "The Land Ethic." Leopold's path is similar to the one Wittgenstein took when he encountered seemingly insurmountable difficulties trying to define ethical and metaphysical terms. The failure of all attempts to solve particular ecological problems—for example, deer irruptions—provided Leopold with psychologically convincing evidence that such problems probably cannot be solved, a conclusion straightforwardly in the tradition of medical therapeutic nihilism. Thwarted in his efforts to maintain ecosystem stability through active manipulation, Leopold opted for passive therapy, placing his faith in self-regulation as the best basis for what he came to call land or ecosystemic health. Like his medical counterparts in Vienna, he decided to rely on the healing powers of nature, concluding that doing nothing is better than doing something, since the former permits self-healing while the latter produces random and unpredictable damage to the system as a whole.

This version of therapeutic nihilism, although most prominently aligned with the traditional medical position, not only has some features in common with therapeutic positivism but also has some special features of its own. First, just as Wittgenstein did not try to discourage the utterly hopeless thrusts of others against the limits of language, Leopold does not try to discourage continuing research into factor manipulation. In a closing section of "Means and Ends," Leopold discusses cycles, which he characterizes as "a problem defying the experimental method." Although he makes it clear that he considers the problems in this area unsolvable, he nevertheless provides practical advice, suggesting that it may be possible to split the problems into smaller parts, which might be testable on domesticated animals, and notes, with a hint of optimism, that "a virgin field awaits the investigator who is able to do the splitting."[44] Even though Wittgenstein thought that no one really could go beyond the limits of language, he did feel that it was possible that someone trying to do so might achieve positive results. A successful effort, however, would not constitute a thrust beyond the limits but a clarification of the limits in an area where they had been too narrowly understood. Similarly, in Leopold's therapeutic nihilism, the solution of a difficult problem in ecology can alternately be taken as a clarification of the limits of ecological knowledge rather than as an indication that those limits can be or have been broken. In this context, ecological research is still worth doing, not for its own sake, as in Wittgenstein's therapeutic positivism, but because of the scattered positive results it might bring from time to time.

Second, a unique valuational feature separates Leopold's therapeutic nihilism from the two versions already discussed. Leopold spent most of his life trying to identify the principles that would allow us to dominate nature—to substitute an artificial equilibrium for a natural one. When problems with his factor approach convinced him that such artificial equilibria could not be maintained, the result was a transformation not simply in his method but also in his values. In "Means and Ends," when Leopold writes that wildlife management "has already admitted its inability to replace natural equilibria with artificial ones," he adds that it has also admitted "its unwillingness to do so even if it could." Throughout the lecture, wild things are treated as aesthetically valuable objects on the model of art objects:

> The value of wild things is in part a scarcity value, like that of gold. It is also in part an artistic value, like that of a painting. The final arbiter of both is that elusive entity known as "good taste." There is though the residual difference: a painting might conceivably be recreated, but an extinct species never.

This change in value is a step beyond that of Wittgenstein's therapeutic positivism, in which the activity of thrusting against the limits of language is valued for its own sake and without regard to its success or failure. Leopold has gone on to admire the intractable object of his study—the natural ecosystem—a shift analogous in traditional therapeutic nihilism to doctors coming to admire the diseases they are trying to cure. It is a transvaluation of values that highlights the central problem of environmental therapeutic nihilism: its relationship to nature preservation.

ENVIRONMENTAL THERAPEUTIC NIHILISM AND NATURE PRESERVATION

In assessing the importance of therapeutic nihilism in nature preservation arguments, we need to look at two very different kinds of things: first, the relationship of therapeutic nihilism to environmental values, and second, the long-term viability of therapeutic nihilism as an ecosystem management approach.

In some important ways, therapeutic nihilism may not promote appropriate environmental values at all. First, it seems likely that environmental therapeutic nihilism has contributed to a peculiar kind of callousness toward wild animals. just as the seeming inability to help patients in the nineteenth century hardened most doctors and encouraged neglect and indifference to human life and suffering, our seeming inability to manipulate ecosystems beneficially appears to have fostered a similar indifference to the suffering of animal life in natural settings. The perpetuation of such an attitude not only runs counter to our basic moral sentiments but may also be counterproductive in terms of environmental management. Letting a buffalo freeze to death in a river in winter certainly conflicts with our moral intuitions, and it is hard to believe that an occasional rescue will have any serious environmental, ecological, or evolutionary consequences. Even when large numbers of animals are involved, assisting them may in many cases produce less damage than leaving them to their fate. For example, it probably would have been better to have treated the sheep in Yellowstone for pinkeye than to have watched most of the animals die from accidents caused by blindness. Similarly, Jane Goodall's decision to inoculate the chimpanzees she was studying against polio was probably less damaging than her decision to set up a banana feeding station.[45]

Second, therapeutic nihilism may sometimes allow environmental managers to avoid confronting their environmental values altogether. There is, of course, a strong tendency among scientists to defend their positions exclusively in terms of scientific research whenever possible: to argue in terms of facts rather than values. Douglas-Hamilton, for example, brings this point up specifically in connection with the problem of the elephants and the trees. He had not been at work very long, he writes, before he concluded that "scientifically there was no objective reason either for or against shooting the elephants that were doing the damage" and that the fate of the elephants had to depend on nonscientific factors:

> Here was an issue that could only be decided in relation to aesthetic, economic or political considerations. In ecological terms the Seronera tree damage was insignificant. The very desire to preserve the animals was a subjective statement of faith in the animals' intrinsic worth. It was a feeling possessed by most of the scientists there, who regarded the wildebeest migration with the same awe that others feel for the Mona Lisa, but they would not admit this sentiment into their arguments because it could not be backed up by facts; the right and wrong of aesthetics being imponderables not open to scientific analysis.[46]

Of the three factors listed, Douglas-Hamilton was most concerned about the first. He wanted to place great emphasis on the aesthetic worth of elephants, their intrinsic worth, which he equated with the value of art objects. Nevertheless, he was reluctant to do so because "this sentiment . . . could not be backed up by facts" and is "not open to scientific analysis." As a result, the aesthetic factor, which he considered so important, did not enter into his study and his conclusions, since it was not scientific, and he instead opted for a "unique" scientific solution that among all the possible alternatives was most compatible with therapeutic nihilism, doing almost nothing.

Since these considerations suggest that there is often no positive, straightforward connection between therapeutic nihilism and environmental values, it is probably best to say that while a management approach based on therapeutic nihilism cannot in general be depended on to promote environmental values, it at least establishes a scientific context in which they can persist without direct challenge. By contrast, much less can be said for the factor manipulation approach to management, since anyone who practices it must consciously act so as to destroy or replace natural environmental values on a regular basis. Leopold's own flirtation with the factor manipulation approach illustrates this point fairly well: His early preference for natural environmental values was suppressed during the time he actively sought to manipulate natural systems and reappeared in full only when he lost confidence in the approach and turned to therapeutic nihilism. Although Leopold was throughout his life well aware of and very appreciative of the aesthetic value of nature, his Pinchotian training at the Yale Forestry School, which stressed the instrumental use of nature for human purposes, was not entirely consistent with this value perspective. To become enthusiastically involved in factor manipulation of the environment, Leopold needed to resolve the tension between these two perspectives, and he did so by concluding that natural systems in civilized countries had already been so disrupted that the original natural environmental values no longer existed. As Leopold puts it in the first chapter of *Game Management:*

> A state of undisturbed nature is, of course, no longer found in countries facing the necessity of game management; civilization has upset every factor of productivity for better or worse. Game management proposes to substitute a new and objective equilibrium for any natural one which civilization may have destroyed.[47]

The replacement of the natural but disturbed equilibrium with an artificial one meant at the same time the replacement of natural values with a set of humanly imposed artificial ones. Once this intellectual hurdle was overcome, Leopold was able to look on the management of natural systems as nothing more than a special kind of landscape gardening. In the chapter "Game Management and Aesthetics" in *Game Management,* for example, he argues that the conservation of game and nongame animals (such as songbirds) alike requires nothing more than the identification of the habitats required and their construction by artificial means: "Environments can, by judicious use of those tools employed in gardening or landscaping or farming, be built to order with the assurance of attracting the desired bird.[48] This reluctant acceptance of artificial systems and artificial values persisted until Leopold finally came to realize that the factor manipulation approach did not work after all and that permitting natural systems to regulate themselves was the best he and other environmental managers could do, given the state of ecological science.

Within this context, nevertheless, there may still be some ways in which therapeutic nihilism positively influences our environmental values, especially instrumental values. That environmental therapeutic nihilism enhances our awareness of the importance of the instrumental value of natural systems seems fairly obvious. Leopold makes this point quite clearly in the passage from "Round River" quoted earlier in which he concludes, "To keep every cog and wheel is the first precaution of intelligent tinkering." At the end of Commoner's discussion of therapeutic nihilism, he also seems to take the same position, suggesting that following his principle, "Nature knows best," is basically a matter of "prudence" or "caution," an admonition to be careful when we are not sure what our man-made changes will do to the environment.[49] Just what therapeutic nihilism has to do with intrinsic value, however, is far less obvious. There are several possibilities. First, it may be that the relationship of therapeutic nihilism to the preservation of natural systems for their own sake is merely a pragmatic one. They are connected because the support therapeutic nihilism happens to provide to arguments for maintaining natural systems instrumentally can be extended uncritically and informally to include intrinsic value positions, but

not because intrinsic value arguments in any way follow in deductive sense from the basic principles of environmental therapeutic nihilism. Second, as suggested by Leopold's "Land Ethic," it is also possible that our ignorance about underlying causal interrelationships in nature may force us to rely intuitively on aesthetic properties of ecosystems as "second-best" indicators of ecosystemic health, in much the same way that rosy cheeks and a twinkle in the eye might suggest health in a human. Leopold's remark in "The Land Ethic," "A thing is right when it tends to preserve the integrity, stability, and beauty of the biotic community," suggests such an approach. Although these values are unscientific, they remain useful, since the alternative to using them may be to use nothing at all. In this context, however, the value orientation ultimately remains instrumental in spirit and in deed.

Regardless of what Leopold narrowly and historically might have had in mind in writing "The Land Ethic," it is still possible to draw a positive connection between therapeutic nihilism and the preservation of natural values independent of their instrumental value to humans. Mark Sagoff, for example, has identified two medical analogies in which concern for the promotion of certain moral values frequently overrides the desire for the efficient and effective treatment of human patients. The first is an analogy between ecology and medicine. According to Sagoff, doctors can prescribe medication either to help maintain normal good health or, for example, in the case of an athlete, "to change the normal healthy functioning of a person's body to allow that person to do abnormal or extraordinary things."[50] In the context of ecosystemic health, nature preservationists want the former, conservationists and related commercial interests want the latter. In going from the first to the second, certain values are lost because, once the transition is made, the human or the ecosystem ceases to function naturally. If it is discovered that the athlete's victory was due to special drugs, it alters our admiration for his or her achievement. Likewise, when we discover that an ecosystem is being maintained artificially to maximize the production of certain animals or plants, our appreciation of and admiration for the system are frequently diminished in a similar way. Although we may on some occasions find values to admire in such an ecosystem, they will not be the values of a natural system but values introduced technologically by humans. Regardless of what has been conserved, what the nature preservationists want to preserve has been lost.

A similar loss of value also occurs in the second analogy, in which the factor manipulation and ecosystem management approaches are compared to behavioral and therapeutic psychology. As Sagoff points out, although the behavioral approach is usually very effective and the therapeutic approach rarely works at all, nearly everyone nonetheless prefers the therapeutic approach over the behavioral, since the therapeutic approach respects the autonomy of the individual and various associated values, for example, freedom and dignity, whereas the behavioral approach does not. For many people, there is a similar contrast between the factor manipulation and therapeutic approaches in environmental management. Once the manipulation begins, the system is transformed into a living machine controlled and dominated by humans for exclusively human purposes: It is enslaved; it is no longer wild and free; and the values that we respect and admire in nature are destroyed.

Although these analogies clearly demonstrate that therapeutic nihilism can promote appropriate noninstrumental values *in theory,* we still need to consider carefully whether we can depend on such associations to arise and flourish *in practice* and whether such value promotion counterbalances other negative aspects of the general therapeutic approach. A number of problems frequently arise when we turn to practical application. First, doing nothing may be as unnatural as doing something. If, as Chase argues, the American wilderness was consciously managed by the Indians, it probably cannot remain in the condition in which whites originally found it without continued management.[51] Second, it may not really be possible to do nothing. It is very difficult for a doctor to deny medication to a patient even when he or she knows that it probably will not help. Moreover, when humans can af-

fect the outcome, it is often hard to say that choosing not to intercede is simply doing nothing. As Sartre once put it in another context, choosing to do nothing is still choosing to do something: to let the current state of affairs reach its final conclusion unhindered.[52] Third, it is easy to drift into factor manipulation while trying to follow an approach based on therapeutic nihilism, for example, when a manager decides to counter outside influences so as otherwise to allow the unfolding of natural history within the protected area. Once this kind of factor manipulation begins in the name of therapeutic nihilism, there is the very real possibility that the values being protected will be lost by trying to protect them. Since it can be difficult or even impossible to distinguish between natural and humanly induced change, managers may either unconsciously or consciously (through pressure from the general public) try to freeze the natural area in its current state or return it to an earlier state, as a museum piece, thereby bringing its natural history to an end and unwittingly destroying the very thing that the therapeutic approach was supposed to protect.

The problem of creeping factor manipulation in a therapeutic context, moreover, highlights what is probably the single most serious difficulty with therapeutic nihilism as a preservationist strategy, for the aim of the mainstream argument for this approach is not to preserve values but to avoid damage through the employment of ineffective or inept ecological technology. This is especially clear when one considers alternative interpretations of Commoner's "Nature knows best" principle. There are really two interpretations with very different consequences: (1) that we ought to be careful until we have developed appropriate techniques to manipulate the environment without random damage occurring and (2) that we ought to be careful permanently because it will never be possible to develop the appropriate techniques needed to manipulate the environment without random damage occurring. If it is true that we will never develop the ability to manipulate nature as Leopold originally intended in his factor approach, environmental therapeutic nihilism is a strong foundation for nature preservation arguments. There is, however, a great danger here, for it is a strong foundation only as long as there is good reason to believe that the second interpretation is true. If it ever turns out that ecological engineering on a substantial scale is feasible, nature preservation arguments and environmental ethics in general, to the degree that they depend on environmental therapeutic nihilism, will be based on false premises. For this reason, it is probably best pragmatically to guard against this possibility by separating intrinsic value arguments from therapeutic nihilism and interpreting Commoner's principle as a temporary precaution to be followed until such time, if ever, that ecological engineering becomes a practical reality.

Humans have most successfully manipulated nature by applying principles from the physical sciences, for example, in making steel, plastic, gasoline, and the like. No comparable degree of manipulative ability has as yet been developed in the environmental or natural history sciences. Although it is sometimes suggested that complete technological mastery of the environment might be possible if environmental science could somehow be reduced to physics and chemistry, it is important to recognize that these sciences are based on a reductionist method that may be only partially appropriate to environmental science, thereby making this possibility very unlikely. Everything depends on whether environmental factors can in fact, and not just in theory, be isolated and manipulated independently. David Kitts argues that geology, in particular, is fundamentally different as a science from physics and chemistry: that unlike the physical sciences, which focus on the discovery of universal laws that work in isolation, geology is historically oriented, that is, primarily concerned with the generation of singular historical statements that aid us in reconstructing the history of the Earth. As a result, Kitts contends, geology is more concerned with explanation than prediction, and the methods used to produce geological explanation have little use in formulating predictions about future events.[53] Can geology and other environmental sciences become adequately future-oriented? It is probably not possible for the therapeutic nihilist to prove in advance that the en-

vironmental sciences will not develop the ability to make the precise predictions needed for factor manipulation of the environment any more than it is possible for the technological optimist to prove that he will always be able to find solutions to the various problems that his new technologies generate. If factor manipulation can be done successfully, humans will almost certainly figure out how to do it. If it cannot, it will remain an intriguing possibility as long as Western science and technology continue to be practiced.

Even if successful, nondisruptive factor manipulation technology is never developed, there is still a serious problem with any association of therapeutic nihilism in the strong sense with nature preservation arguments. While there might not be much danger of these arguments being factually undermined in terms of a therapeutic nihilism that demands full theoretical understanding before factor manipulation begins, one of the lessons of Semmelweis' discovery is that rules of thumb can be found and applied whether theoretical underpinnings exist or not. Thus it is always possible, whether or not an ecological technology ever materializes, that procedures for maximizing particular elements of ecosystems without excessive damage might be found that work well even though we do not know why they do. If such procedures are discovered, the argument that in general we cannot manipulate ecosystems without random damage will be overridden by the fact that we can in such and such cases, and environmentalists will be forced to defend their positions on the basis of their value preferences alone without the aid of arguments about the limits of ecological knowledge.

As I noted earlier, scientists, environmentalists, and policymakers are naturally reluctant to defend their positions in terms of value considerations, and therapeutic nihilism, at this time, at least, provides everyone with an easy way to stick to the facts. Instead of arguing that we ought not to do this or that because it conflicts with the kinds of environmental values we want to promote individually or as a society, they can argue that we ought not to do it because we cannot, because it is not scientifically or technologically possible. What we end up with, then, is a counter to the technological *ought* (if we can, we ought to) by a technological *ought not* (if we cannot, we should not), an argument that is effective only as long as it is factually true.

In summary, for the time being, environmental therapeutic nihilism as precaution or prudence continues to be a pragmatically useful foundation for nature preservation. However, whether it will continue to be in the future depends on whether breakthroughs in ecology occur, and the prospects for such breakthroughs are better than most environmentalists might imagine. Environmental therapeutic nihilism is really an outgrowth of historical developments in ecology and environmental management, and although it is still widely held by most environmentalists and many applied ecologists working in environmental management, it no longer represents the attitudes prevalent among contemporary ecologists, most of whom now believe that it is possible to make accurate recommendations for action in many circumstances, including deer herds. While the improvements in the ability to make ecological predictions since Leopold's time are not a revolutionary leap forward, they are substantial and can be expected to translate into greatly improved expertise at the applied level in the near future. If these improvements continue, with or without a major breakthrough, therapeutic nihilism will almost certainly become indefensible as a mainstream preservationist position: As in medicine today, it will then become an approach that is relevant and useful only in cases in which an appropriate technical solution is not yet available.

The vulnerability of therapeutic nihilism to future developments in ecology puts environmentalists in an unusual and unpleasant position. They must either actively root against advances in ecology or look for better preservationist arguments. Because the science of ecology has played such an important role in the development of modern environmental attitudes, the first alternative would certainly be a sad and probably also a self-defeating course of action. Although the second alternative may seem equally unappealing, the prospects may be good, if environmentalists are willing to bring their values to the surface and turn them into ethical and aesthetic arguments in defense of nature.

NOTES

1. Iain and Oria Douglas-Hamilton, *Among the Elephants* (New York: Viking Press, 1975), pp. 31–33, 74–75.

2. Ibid., pp. 259–263.

3. Ibid., p. 263.

4. Barry Commoner, *The Closing Circle: Nature, Man, and Technology* (New York: Knopf, 1971), p. 41.

5. Peter Singer, *Animal Liberation: A New Ethics for Our Treatment of Animals* (New York: Avon Books, 1975), pp. 238–239.

6. Aldo Leopold, "Round River," in *A Sand County Almanac: With Essays on Conservation from Round River* (New York: Ballantine Books, 1970), p. 190.

7. Leopold, "The Land Ethic," ibid., pp. 240–241.

8. Ibid.

9. See A. S. Leopold et al., "Wildlife Management in the National Parks," in National Park Service, *Compilation of the Administrative Policies for the National Parks and National Monuments of Scientific Significance* (Natural Area Category), rev. ed. (Washington, D.C.: U.S. Government Printing Office, 1970), pp. 99–112.

10. Ibid., p. 106.

11. A. S. Leopold et al., "Resource Management Policy," in *Compilation of Administrative Policies*, p. 17.

12. Alston Chase, *Playing God in Yellowstone: The Destruction of America's First National Park* (Boston: Atlantic Monthly Press, 1986), p. 42. Quotation from National Park Service, Management Policies (Washington, D.C.: U.S. Government Printing Office, 1978), p. iv.

13. William M. Johnston, *The Austrian Mind: An Intellectual and Social History, 1848–1938* (Berkeley: University of California Press, 1972), pp. 71, 223–224.

14. Ibid., p. 71.

15. Ibid., p. 226; for a fuller account of this problem, see Paul de Kruif, *Men against Death* (Orlando, Fla.: Harcourt Brace Jovanovich, 1932), pp. 35–58.

16. For a philosophical discussion of Semmelweis' discovery, see Carl G. Hempel, *Philosophy of Natural Science* (Englewood Cliffs, N.J.: Prentice-Hall, 1966), pp. 3–8.

17. Johnston, *Austrian Mind*, p. 226; de Kruif, *Men against Death*, pp. 49–50.

18. Hempel, *Philosophy of Natural Science*, p. 3.

19. De Kruif, *Men against Death*, pp. 39, 54.

20. Therapeutic nihilism is frequently discussed in connection with health care in the elderly, psychiatry, deafness, breast cancer, liver disease, the common cold, and other problems. In most cases, authors analyze a particular health issue and argue that there are now good reasons why therapeutic nihilism is no longer justified. See, for example, Carl Eisdorfer, "Therapeutic Nihilism and Other Rationalizations for Avoiding the Issues in Health Care," *Geriatrics* 31 (1976), no. 1: 35–42. In some cases, nearly all medical practice is depicted as therapeutic nihilism. See, for example, Paul Starr, "The Politics of Therapeutic Nihilism," *Hastings Center Report* 6 (1976), no. 5: 24–30.

21. Johnston, *Austrian Mind,* pp. 71, 223, 228–229; Norman Malcolm, *Ludwig Wittgenstein: A Memoir* (London: Oxford University Press, 1958), p. 56.

22. See Alfred Jules Ayer, "Critique of Ethics and Theology," in *Language, Truth, and Logic* (New York: Dover Publications, 1952), pp. 102–120.

23. See B. A. Farrell, "An Appraisal of Therapeutic Positivism," *Mind* 55 (1946): 25–48, 133–150.

24. Ludwig Wittgenstein, *Philosophical Investigations,* trans. G. E. M. Anscombe, 3d ed. (New York: Macmillan, 1958), par. 255.

25. Ibid., par. 133.

26. Ludwig Wittgenstein, *Tractatus Logico-Philosophicus,* trans. D. F. Pears and B. F. McGuinness (London: Routledge & Kegan Paul, 1961), par. 6.52–6.52 1.

27. Wittgenstein, *Philosophical Investigations,* par. 119.

28. Quoted in Eric Heller, "Wittgenstein: Unphilosophical Notes," in *Ludwig Wittgenstein: The Man and His Philosophy,* ed. K. T. Fann (New York: Dell, 1967), p. 101, n. 28.

29. Ludwig Wittgenstein, *Notebooks,* 1914–1916, ed. G. H. von Wright and G. E. M. *Anscombe* (New York: Harper & Row, 1961), pp. 78–79e.

30. Quoted in Paul Engelmann, *Letters from Ludwig Wittgenstein, with Memoir,* trans. L. Furtmuller (Oxford: Basil Blackwell, 1967), pp. 143–144.

31. Ibid., p. 97; emphasis in original.

32. Ludwig Wittgenstein, "Wittgenstein's Lecture on Ethics," *Philosophical Review* 74 (1965): 11–12.

33. G. E. Moore, "Wittgenstein's Lectures in 1930–33," *Mind* 64 (1955): 26–27.

34. Both views are strongly held by John Passmore in *Man's Responsibility for Nature.*

35. Susan L. Flader, *Thinking like a Mountain: Aldo Leopold and the Evolution of an Ecological Attitude toward Deer, Wolves, and Forests* (Columbia: University of Missouri Press, 1974).

36. Aldo Leopold, *Game Management* (New York: Scribner, 1933), p. 26.

37. Flader, *Thinking like a Mountain,* p. 93.

38. Leopold, *Game Management,* p. 45.

39. Flader, *Thinking like a Mountain,* pp. 76–121.

40. Ibid., pp. 84–85. Although Flader's account of the Kaibab remains a historically accurate account of the situation as Leopold perceived it, the idea that the irruptions there were caused by the removal of predators has been challenged by Graeme Caughley in his paper "Eruption of Ungulate Populations with Emphasis on Himalayan Thar in New Zealand," *Ecology* 51 (1970): 53–56.

41. Flader, *Thinking like a Mountain,* p. 120.

42. Ibid., pp. 139–150.

43. Aldo Leopold, "Means and Ends in Wild Life Management," holograph, LP 6–16, *Leopold Papers,* University of Wisconsin Archives, Madison; lecture delivered at Beloit College on May 5, 1936.

44. Ibid.

45. Chase, *Playing God,* pp. 81–82; Jane van Lawick-Goodall, *In the Shadow of Man* (Boston: Houghton Mifflin, 1971), ch. 8, 17.

46. Douglas-Hamilton, *Among the Elephants,* pp. 75–76.

47. Leopold, *Game Management,* p. 26.

48. Ibid., p. 405.

49. Commoner, *Closing Circle,* p. 45.

50. Mark Sagoff, "Fact and Value in Ecological Science," *Environmental Ethics* 7 (1985): 112–113.

51. Chase, *Playing God,* ch. 9.

52. Jean-Paul Sartre, *Existentialism and the Human Emotions* (New York: Philosophical Library, 1957), p. 41.

53. David B. Kitts, *The Structure of Geology* (Dallas: Southern Methodist University Press, 1977), ch. 1–2.

Mad Cowboy: The Cattle Rancher Who Won't Eat Meat

Howard F. Lyman with Glen Merzer

My great-grandfather owned and operated a mid-sized organic dairy farm outside of Great Falls, Montana. My grandfather took the farm over from him, and my father took it over from my grandfather. I knew from the time I was knee-high to a grasshopper that someday that farm would belong to me and my brother.

When I was three or four years old, my mother used to wake me up at dawn and bring me to the cow barn, in order, I suppose, to have someone to talk to as she milked the cows. From the time I was five, I was doing real chores around the farm. Often I worked under the wing of my brother, Dick, who was a year older and a lot bigger. When he wasn't beating me up, he was telling me what to do. It was my job to feed the calves buttermilk, and since we didn't have buckets with nipples in those days, I used my hands. Every weekend I'd have to clean the calf barn of manure; in the winter it froze and that could make the work particularly unpleasant. I still remember a time when I was about seven, working in the fields late on a frigid afternoon. I allowed myself to cry a few tears, and my father told me, "You might as well grit your teeth, because cryin's only going to slow you down, and we're not quittin' till we're finished." It was a lesson I burned into my heart.

At eight or nine I began milking cows and branding calves. At ten I learned how to castrate calves. At harvest time, I'd work long past dark cutting the grain. I'd rake hay and stack it, and I learned to drive a tractor and a team of horses. I worked every day of the year but two: July Fourth and Christmas. On those days all I had to do was feed the animals—and that took just a few hours, so I looked forward to those holidays with great patriotism and Christian feeling, respectively.

At the end of his sophomore year in high school, Dick was diagnosed with Hodgkin's disease. In those days, the disease was always fatal. We didn't talk about it much in my family, but it was a quiet fact around which much of our lives revolved. From that point on, Dick always did exactly what he wanted to do, and nobody questioned him. He loved the woods more than anything, and he'd go hunting and fishing at the drop of a hat. I stayed behind and did more than my share of the farmwork.

My confidence in my farming future stood behind the disastrous academic record I achieved in high school. I excelled in football, but I didn't do much else well. When I somehow managed to graduate, I was delighted to be back on the farm I loved. But when my father, nervous about the prospect of my someday taking over the 540-acre spread, prevailed upon me to look seriously at all the business aspects of actually running a farm, I realized how ill-equipped I was. I decided to do what any self-respecting red-blooded American boy does who's partied and daydreamed his way through twelve years of school without learning a damn thing: I went to college.

At Montana State University I wasn't about to repeat the mistake I had made in high school. This time, I paid attention and did my homework. I took courses at the College of Agriculture. The late Fifties and early Sixties was an exciting time to be launching into agricultural studies. We learned to spurn the old-fashioned, inefficient methods of farming—the organic methods of my father, grandfather, and great-grandfather. There was not one course offered in organic agriculture. In its place, a bold new age of chemically enhanced agriculture was dawning. We learned the most up-to-date methods of using pesticides and herbicides, hormones and antibiotics. My professors, all chemists and academicians, were so good at what they did, I figured, they didn't even have to get their hands dirty. I bought it all, hook, line, and sinker.

When I came home after college and a stint in the Army, my brother was dying. My father was getting older and, burdened with more than he could handle, he needed me to run the farm. I studied the farm's books, and I suddenly understood something that had simply never occurred to me before. We were poor. My old man was barely making ends meet. I told him that if I was going to take over this operation, I sure as hell wasn't going to keep running it on a hand-to-mouth basis as an organic dairy farm. I was going to deficit-finance, expand, and employ all the brand-new chemical farming techniques I'd learned about in college.

My father had no choice. He handed over the farm. But as he shook my hand on the deal, he had a few short words for me.

He told me I was wrong.

Crop rotation was the first principle of the old-fashioned organic method of dairy farming employed by my father, grandfather, and great-grandfather. A field that was used to grow alfalfa one year got planted with, say, wheat the next, and corn the following year. Farmers paid particular attention to nitrogen-fixing crops, like beans or clover or alfalfa, which pulled nitrogen out of the air and put it into the soil, thus naturally fertilizing it. The second principle was leaving fields fallow, usually at least once every few years. Doing so restored moisture in the soil, made weeding simple, and let the micro-organisms and earthworms in the soil go to work regenerating it. The third principle was best expressed in the old farmer's saying: "When you raise an animal on grass, take half and leave half." In other words, don't let cattle overgraze. By leaving roughly half the grass alive in the grazing field, the grass would come back each year and its roots would hold the soil and protect it from erosion.

Finally, farming organically meant working with Nature, not against it. Organic agriculture is predicated on doing things in Nature's time frame. Crops are harvested when they're ripe, and fields are cut into small sections so that each crop can be picked at its peak condition.

Those of us who had been schooled in the ways of the Green Revolution were going to bury these quaint old ways just as electricity had buried the kerosene lamp. I found beauty in the almost mathematical precision of the new chemical agriculture. I would take a hollow tube, three feet long and maybe an inch in diameter, and press it into the ground to obtain a soil sample. By bringing this sample to a soil testing lab, I could determine which of the three basic soil nutrients—nitrogen, phosphorus, and potassium—were needed in the soil, at what depths and in what percentages. I'd spread the fields with a customized mixture of fertilizer, and it would seep down into the soil like a time-released medicine.

Fertilizing this way worked like a dream, especially after I'd had a few years to fiddle around and discover the best mixtures. I found that by loading the soil with about 100 pounds per acre of "33-0-0" in the spring, and then "rotating" that with an equivalent amount of "16-20-0" in the fall, I was doubling the yields per acre of all our crops. And I didn't have to waste any acreage by leaving it fallow.

I handled the problem of weeds with something called 2-4 D, a chemical weed-control product. I just sprayed it throughout the farm, covering five or six hundred acres a day. If a little was good, more was better. Before long I was looking for new and more powerful concoctions of 2-4 D. Then I began using an excellent variety of herbicide called 2-4-5 T. In Vietnam they called it Agent Orange.

Once I had the extra crop yield, of course, I was faced with the problem of what to do with it. Except occasionally for wheat, none of the crops I was raising fetched much of a price on the market. They were more useful as livestock feed, but it was more feed than I needed for the fifty head of cattle I then had. You didn't have to be a brain surgeon to come up with the solution: Buy more cattle.

Around 1970, after I acquired more cattle than I could possibly allow to graze on my fields, I simply put them in confinement and converted a grazing operation into a feedlot. I corralled the animals in roofless pens, 100 or 200 in each, with a trough for feed on one side of the pen. And I embraced the fundamental challenge of the feedlot operator, to make the cattle grow as big and fat as possible, as quickly as possible. I learned how to alter my cattle's natural dietary habits. Whereas my father and grandfather raised cattle almost completely on grass and roughage, I now cut out their grazing rights and fed them only roughage, grain, and protein concentrates. Gradually I increased the percentage of grain until they were 90[%] grain-fed. This made their meat extremely fatty and gave it the nice white flecks you see in the better cuts of beef in your grocery stores.

This diet also, unfortunately, upsets the cow's natural digestive system, which was designed for grass, not grain. As a consequence, many of my animals suffered vaginal and rectal prolapses—organs that belonged on the inside of the cow fell out. It was too expensive to call a vet every time this happened, so I spent countless hours stuffing twenty-five pounds of cow back inside the animal and then sewing the wound, the whole force of a six-hundred-pound heifer straining against me. I have been out of cattle farming for fifteen years now, and I will go back to it the day I wake up with a burning desire to perform another bovine rectal prolapse operation.

While I was expanding my feedlot operation, I would acquire cattle at auction. I might get a hundred head at a single auction, from maybe twenty different sources. Unfortunately, with so many animals from different origins concentrated close together, disease became my worst enemy. When I shifted from a grazing operation to a feedlot, the health problems of my herd rose dramatically.

It was a constant battle: Economics Versus Nature. If you don't catch a cow during the first few days it's symptomatic, there's about a fifty percent chance it'll die on you. If even five percent of your cattle die, there's no way you'll ever make a profit. Unfortunately, cattle in confinement develop more diseases than you can vaccinate against. In an enclosed space such as a cattle pen, even those afflicted cattle that successfully respond to a vaccination can pass the germ to other cattle in the process of shedding the disease. So, like most feedlot operators, I learned to put antibiotics in the cattle's feed. It would have been too time-consuming to try to target only the sick cattle with the antibiotic-enhanced feed; it was much easier and more logical to simply put the antibiotics in the feed of all the cattle. Here again, like all other feedlot operators, I was outsmarted by Nature, which endowed the bacteria causing these diseases with the capacity to mutate and gain immunity to any antibiotic science can develop. I found myself changing antibiotics in the feed every thirty days or so, and they were becoming less and less effective.

Sometimes the drugs I used to inoculate cattle were later determined to be dangerous to human health and were banned. But the government always seemed to be sufficiently cooperative with agribusiness to make sure that the stockpiles of the suspect drug inventoried by the drug companies were sold before the ban went into effect. Once the banned drugs were in farmers' hands, they were used until exhausted.

After bovine diseases, flies constitute the greatest hazard to feedlot operations. With every cow in a pen producing twenty-five pounds of manure in a day, the flies can get so thick that they actually threaten a cow's ability to breathe. Trying to do something about the flies persecuting them, cows sometimes kick up so much dust that they can contract what is called dust pneumonia. But the great promise of chemical agriculture is that every problem represents merely another challenge to science, and the scientific fix for the fly problem was insecticide. Early in the morning, I would fill up a fly fogger with insecticide and spray great clouds of it over the whole operation. It would, of course, fall into the feed and the water of the cattle, as well as on the trees and the grass and the crops. In addition, I treated the animals for grubs—the wormlike larvae of certain insects—by covering their backs with insecticides that were absorbed through the skin in order to kill the fly eggs. Naturally, I had neither the time nor the inclination to think about the possibility of this deadly chemical passing through the hide into the tissues that would become somebody's dinner; nor did I for a moment consider my own hide.

To make cattle grow faster, I didn't restrict myself to merely forcing upon them an unnatural diet of grain. Like most cattle farmers today, I used growth hormones similar to the steroids that misguided muscle-builders use at significant risk to their own health. From the early Sixties to the late Seventies, the hormone I used most frequently was diethylstilbestrol, or DES. I used it not only to stimulate growth but also to cause abortions in pregnant heifers. (After all, the added weight of a fetus would have been wasted, since it wasn't going to become hamburger.) During the years that I used the hormone, the debate raged over whether or not it could be carcinogenic to humans. Finally, in the late Seventies, the government banned the use of DES, but since it was so cheap and effective, many feedlot operators bought up as much product as possible for use after it was no longer available for sale. I regret to say I was one of them. When my DES ran out, about two years after the ban went into effect, I continued to use a whole bunch of new and improved growth hormones. In those days, I never met a chemical I didn't like.

Most Americans don't have any idea how well the Department of Agriculture protects the grower at the expense of the consumer. When a chemical is banned from use, a farmer or livestock operator who has the chemical in stock has a choice: either to lose money by disposing of the product, or to use it and take the risk of getting caught breaking the law. How severe is that risk? Well, if you use a banned product in your cattle feed, you have to face the prospect that the government is going to inspect one out of every 250,000 carcasses. They will test this carcass not for all banned substances, but just for a small fraction of them. And even if they detect some residue of a banned substance, and even if they're able to trace the carcass to the ranch that produced it, the guilty rancher is likely at most to receive a stern letter with a strongly worded warning. I never met a rancher who suffered in any way from break-

ing any regulation meant to protect the safety of our meat. The whole procedure is, in short, a charade.

I didn't lose too much sleep over breaking the rules. I had bigger worries.

Even though I had increased crop yields dramatically, even though I could now grow a heifer to 1,100 pounds in just 15 months instead of the 30 months it used to take, even though I had bought or leased many of my neighbors farms and increased my acreage fortyfold, it was getting harder and harder to make ends meet. The chemicals themselves were expensive, and every year I had to use more chemical fertilizer and more antibiotics to get the same result as the year before. And the cattle continued to get sick and sometimes die in spite of my best efforts.

I was working 18-hour days, and feeling less and less secure financially. I had dug myself into a chemical pit so deep I didn't have time to do anything except keep digging. Only my wife, Willow Jeane, would occasionally comment to me: "Are you sure we're going in the right direction?" She would note that the trees were starting to die, and that in spite of the herbicides, the weed problem seemed to be getting worse. And she wasn't at all pleased the day I came in with so much herbicide on my clothing that my mere presence killed off the houseplants.

I used to have lunch once a week in Great Falls with a group of about 15 Montana feedlot operators. We figured that by sharing our experiences we could help each other find the right technological solution for every problem we encountered. We didn't question the underlying theology of our revolution: a magic chemical bullet would cure any problem we ran into. We stuck by that theology in spite of the mounting evidence that every bullet caused more problems.

Of those 15 feedlot operators who were in business 15 years ago, I believe just one may still be in business today.

Our challenge had been to defeat Nature. And we found that we could do it. But only by destroying the land, and with it, ourselves.

As long as I've known Willow Jeane, I've seen terror in her eyes only once. It was on a snowy winter's night in 1979. I was lying in a hospital bed, facing an emergency operation for a tumor that had been found that same day on my spine. Willow Jeane's first husband had died of cancer when he was 28, and the prospect of widowhood once more was a bit much even for her. I was damned sure I was going to survive, but my trusted friend and surgeon, Alex, had told that if the tumor was inside the cord, there was less than one chance in a million I'd walk again. As long as I could move my feet, the operation could wait until morning, which was the earliest he could get there because of the blizzard.

I stayed up all night, moving my feet and thinking. I was thinking about what counted and what didn't.

Having 10,000 acres and 7,000 head of cattle didn't count. Having 30 trucks and 20 tractors and seven combines didn't count. Having a $5 million-a-year agribusiness didn't count.

My family counted, and the land counted.

For some reason, I kept thinking about the soil—the magnetic feel of cool, dark, loamy, worm-laden soil in my hands. I'd grown up with my hands in that soil, and I'd always liked the feeling so much, I rarely troubled to wash them. I thought about how rich the soil had looked when I was a kid. It didn't look like that anymore. Now it crumbled in my hands. It was thin as sand. There were no more worms in it. After all the tons of herbicides and pesticides and chemical fertilizer I'd poured into it, the soil looked more like asbestos. The trees on and around the farm were dying. The birds were gone. The farm was no longer a living, breathing thing; it was an increasingly precarious chemical equation. I made up my mind then and there that no matter what the outcome of my operation, I'd dedicate the rest of my life to restoring the land to what it had been when I'd had the good fortune to be born to it.

At the crack of dawn, I was wheeled into surgery. I awoke in the intensive care unit, propped up on my side. The first thing I did was to look down at my feet. With effort, I was able to slide down the bed so that they could reach the metal bars at the end. I felt the metal. It was cold to the touch. It was the most euphoric sensation I've ever known in my life.

When Alex came to check on me, he explained that, after cutting the bone off the outside of my spinal column, he had discovered the tumor not only inside the cord but also extended beneath it. His only option was to pick a nerve, cut the nerve, and hope the tumor was attached to it like a fish on a line. Alex picked one, cut it, and I escaped paralysis with a one-in-a-million operation.

I kept my promise to the land. I organized a group of chemically disillusioned fellow farmers to develop environmentally sound ways to control weeds—our biggest problem—and we came up with plenty of solutions. That work drew me into politics, and I found myself running for Congress on a platform of clean air, clean water and clean food. I might well have won if the bank hadn't unexpectedly foreclosed on my farm in the middle of a very public campaign. I sold our land to Hutterites, whose way of life seemed compatible with organic farming methods. Then I went to Washington after all, as a lobbyist for the National Farmers Union, and, among other things, worked to help pass the National Organic Standards Act of 1990. President Bush signed the bill into law that year. Eight years later, the standards still have not been agreed upon, and the law has yet to be put into effect.

After my tumor operation, I had started studying everything I could get hold of about the relationship between livestock, farming and the environment. One summer day in Washington in 1990, I was sitting with my feet up on my desk, looking out at the Potomac. I started thinking about all the issues, personal and political, that were concerning me. I was feeling a growing sense of cynicism about my work, and about the chances to effect change through legislation. I knew that most of the bureaucratic subsidies I was fighting for went to the raising of feed crops, not human food. I'd read a whole host of depressing statistics about the loss of rain forests throughout the world, and I knew that a large part of that rain forest loss came about in order to clear land for cattle grazing. I'd read, too, that livestock outnumber humans on the planet by five to one. I'd learned that about 50% of our water usage in this country is dedicated to livestock production, and that our natural aquifers were being depleted at an alarming rate. I'd learned that we were losing topsoil at a rate of one inch every sixteen years, and that much of that loss of topsoil was related to cattle grazing and to the chemically intensive methods that factory farmers were using (and that I had once used). I'd seen rivers polluted from the waste of cattle and pigs and chickens, and seen birds disappear from the skies over fields sprayed with herbicides that were meant to facilitate the growth of crops used to feed those animals. I'd put many thousands of head of cattle into confinement and seen how they suffered from unnatural conditions. I knew that while a billion people went to sleep hungry, the overfed part of the world was busy feeding sixteen pounds of grain to cattle in order to make one pound of beef. I'd seen countless friends suffer from heart disease. I'd seen the cancer rate in America increase dramatically. My own health was hardly exemplary: I weighed 350 pounds, my cholesterol topped 300, my blood pressure was off the charts, and I was getting nosebleeds.

Suddenly the circle came together for me. We were, as a civilization, making one big mistake. This mistake was killing us as individuals just as it was destroying our land and our forests and our rivers.

We were eating animals, and it wasn't working. If those animals had set out to take their revenge on us, they couldn't have done a better job.

And I became, right then and there, something I never dreamed I'd become: a vegetarian.

Within a year of eating no meat, my health problems all started to go away. Not only did I feel better physically, but I felt better knowing that there was one answer to many of the different ills afflicting both ourselves and our environment.

Everything revolves around the fork.

We must ask ourselves as a culture whether we want to embrace the change that must come or resist it. I would love to see organic farming replace chemical agriculture. I would love to know that I've wandered into my nation's heartland by the sweet smell of grain and not the forbidding smell of excrement. I can no longer fathom what there is to be afraid of except the status quo.

While writing my book I returned to Montana. At the largest commercial supermarket in Great Falls, I could hardly believe my eyes. Soy milk and rice milk on the shelves. Soy hot dogs, veggie burgers, tofu, seitan. It's not hard anymore to be a vegetarian in America. If it can be done in Great Falls, it can be done anywhere.

Tora! Tora! Tora!

Paul Watson

On December 7, 1941, the Imperial Japanese First Naval Air fleet launched a surprise attack against the US Naval base at Pearl Harbor on the Hawaiian island of Oahu.

As the Japanese planes swooped in low, their wing commander gave his orders. The Japanese words "Tora, Tora, Tora" crackled through the cockpits of the torpedo bombers.

"Attack, attack, attack." Such was the battle cry of a people who had mastered the martial strategies of Asia. The attack was swift, surprising, ruthless, and effective.

Paul Watson, "Tora! Tora! Tora!" *Earth Ethics*, ed. J. Sterba (Englewood Cliffs: Prentice Hall, 1995), 341–46. Reprinted with permission of the author.

As an ecological strategist, I have faced the Japanese as adversaries on numerous occasions. For this reason, I have studied Japanese martial strategy, especially the classic work entitled *A Book of Five Rings* written by Miyamoto Musashi in 1648. Musashi advocated the "twofold way of pen and sword," which I interpret to mean that one's actions must be both effective and educational.

In March 1982, the Sea Shepherd Conservation Society successfully negotiated a halt to the slaughter of dolphins at Iki Island in Japan. Contributing to this success was our ability to quote Musashi and talk to the Japanese fishermen in a language they could understand—the language of no compromise confrontation.

During our discussion, a fisherman asked me, "What is of more value, the life of a dolphin or the life of a human?"

I answered that, in my opinion, the life of a dolphin was equal in value to the life of a human.

The fisherman then asked, "If a Japanese fisherman and a dolphin were both caught in a net and you could save the life of one, which would you save?"

All the fishermen in the room smirked. They had me pegged a liberal and felt confident that I would say that I would save the fisherman, thus making a mockery of my declaration that humans and dolphins are equal.

I looked about the room and smiled. "I did not come to Japan to save fishermen; I came here to save dolphins."

They were surprised but not shocked by my answer. All the fishermen treated me with respect thereafter.

Why? Because the Japanese understand duty and responsibility. Saving dolphins was both my chosen duty and my responsibility.

Sea Shepherd had already established a reputation in Japan as the "Samurai protector of whales." This came in an editorial that appeared in the Tokyo daily *Asahi Shimbun* in July 1979, a few days after we rammed and disabled the Japanese owned pirate whaler, the *Sierra,* off the coast of Portugal.

That incident ended the career of the most notorious outlaw whaler. In February of 1980, we had

the *Sierra* sunk in Lisbon harbor. A few months later, in April, our agents sank two outlaw Spanish registered whalers, the *Isba I* and the *Isba II,* in Vigo Harbor in northern Spain.

We then gave attention to two other Japanese pirate whalers, the *Susan* and the *Theresa.* Given the controversy of the *Sierra,* and the fact that the *Susan* and the *Theresa* were owned by the same Japanese interests, the South Africans, who had just publicly denounced whaling did not want the stigma of harboring illegal whaling ships. The South African Navy confiscated and sank the *Susan* and *Theresa* for target practise after we publicly appealed to them to do so, in 1980.

The last of the Atlantic pirate whalers, the *Astrid* was shut down after I sent an agent to the Spanish Canary Islands with a reward offer of $25,000 US to any person who would sink her. The owners saw the writing on the wall and voluntarily retired the whaler.

Because of these actions many have labeled us pirates ourselves. Yet we have never been convicted of a criminal charge nor have we ever caused injury or death to a human. Nor have we attempted to avoid charges. On the contrary, we have always invited our enemies to continue the fight, in the courts. Most times they have refused and the few times that they complied, they lost.

Vigilante buccaneers we may well be but we are policing the seas where no policing authority exists. We are protecting whales, dolphins, seals, birds, and fish by enforcing existing regulations, treaties and laws that heretofore have had no enforcement.

In November 1986, when two Sea Shepherd agents, Rod Coronado and David Howitt, attacked the Icelandic whaling industry, they were enforcing the law. The International Whaling Commission (IWC) had banned commercial whaling, yet Iceland continued to whale without a permit. We did not wish to debate the issue of legality with the Icelanders. We acted instead. Coronado and Howitt destroyed the whaling station and scuttled half the Icelandic whaling fleet.

Iceland refused to press charges. I traveled to Reykjavik to insist that they press charges. They refused and deported me without a hearing. The only legal case to result from the incident is my suit against Iceland for illegal deportation.

In March of 1983, the crew of the *Sea Shepherd II* were arrested under the Canadian Seal Protection Regulations, an Orwellian set of rules which actually protected the sealing industry. The only way to challenge these unjust rules was to break them. We did and at the same time we chased the sealing fleet out of the nursery grounds of the Harp Seals. We beat the charges and in the process helped the Supreme Court of Canada in its decision to dismiss the Seal Protection Act as unconstitutional.

In the years since, we have intervened against the Danish Faeroese fishermen in the North Atlantic to save the Pilot Whales they kill for sport. We have shut down seal hunts in Scotland, England and Ireland. We have confronted Central American tuna seiners off the coast of Costa Rica in an effort to rescue dolphins.

In 1987, we launched our first campaign to expose drift net operations in the North Pacific. Our ship the *Divine Wind* voyaged along the Aleutian chain documenting the damage of the drift nets and ghost nets (abandoned nets). We helped convince Canada to abandon plans to build a drift net industry.

For new supporters who do not know what drift nets are, I will briefly explain. Drift nets are to the Pacific Ocean what clear-cuts are to the Amazon Rainforest or the Pacific Northwest Temperate Rainforest. Drift netting is strip-mine fishing.

From May until late October, some 1800 ships each set a net measuring from 10 to 40 miles in length! These monofilament nylon gill nets drift freely upon the surface of the sea, hanging like curtains of death to a depth of 26 or 34 feet. Each night, the combined fleet sets between 28,000 and 35,000 miles of nets. The nets radiate across the breadth of the North Pacific like fences marking off property. The nets are efficient. Few squid and fish escape the perilous clutches of the nylon. Whales and dolphins, seals and sea lions, sea turtles, and sea birds are routinely entangled. The death is an agonizing ordeal of strangulation and suffocation.

Drift nets take an annual incidental kill of more than one million sea birds and a quarter of a million marine mammals each year, plus hundreds of millions of tons of fish and squid. A few short years ago, the North Pacific fairly teemed with dolphins, turtles, fur seals, sea lions, dozens of species of birds and uncountable schools of fish. Today it is a biological wasteland.

The Japanese say their nets are taking fewer incidental kills now than a few years ago. This is true, but the reason the kills are down is simply that there are now fewer animals to kill.

For many years, governments and environmental groups have talked about the problem. Nobody actually did anything about it. Sick of talk, the Sea Shepherd Conservation Society decided to take action.

The *Sea Shepherd II* moved to Seattle, Washington, in September 1989 to prepare for an expedition to intercept the Japanese North Pacific drift net fleet. We set our departure date for June 1990. Overhauls and refitting were completed by May to meet the targeted date.

We were unable to leave Seattle. One of our crew was a paid infiltrator working, we believe, for the Japanese fishing industry. He successfully sabotaged our engine by pouring crushed glass into our oil, destroying our turbo-charger, and destroying electrical motors. Although we discovered the damage and identified the saboteur, we faced extensive repairs.

The saboteur fled to Britain. We asked Scotland Yard to track him down and investigate the incident. However, the damage was done and we were hardly in a position to cry foul. After all, we had already been responsible for destroying six whaling ships ourselves. The enemy had succeeded in striking a blow—it was as simple as that. We were down, but not for long.

We immediately set to work to repair the damage. Thanks to an appeal to Sea Shepherd Society members, funds were raised to purchase a replacement turbocharger.

The *Sea Shepherd II* was prepared for departure again on August 5. We left Seattle and stopped briefly in Port Angeles on the Olympic Peninsula.

Port Angeles resident and Sea Shepherd veteran David Howitt stopped by to visit us. He could not bring himself to leave. The ship departed with David on board. He had left his job and an understanding wife on the spur of the moment. We needed him and he knew it and that was reason enough to return to the eco-battles. He took the position of 1st Engineer.

It was with confidence that I took the helm of our ship and headed out the Strait of Juan de Fuca for the open Pacific beyond. I had a good crew, including many veterans.

Myra Finkelstein was 2nd Engineer. A graduate zoologist, Myra had worked for weeks in the bowels of the engine room to repair the damage to the engine. She was a veteran of the 1987 drift net campaign and the 1989 tuna dolphin campaign. In addition she had been a leader of the Friends of the Wolf campaign in northern British Columbia where she had parachuted into the frigid and remote wilderness to interfere with a government sponsored wolf kill.

Sea Shepherd Director Peter Brown was on board with the camera gear to document the voyage. Peter was also helmsman and my deputy coordinator for the expedition.

Marc Gaede, who had sailed with us a year ago on the campaign off the coast of Costa Rica, returned as our photographer. Trevor Van Der Gulik, my nephew, a lad of only 15 from Toronto, Canada, became—by virtue of his skills—our 3rd Engineer. Trevor had helped to deliver the *Sea Shepherd* from Holland to Florida in 1989.

Also sailing with us this summer was Robert Hunter. Bob and I had both been founders of Greenpeace and he had been the first President of the Greenpeace Foundation. Bob had been the dynamic force behind the organization and ultimate success of Greenpeace. Like myself, he had been forced out of Greenpeace by the marauding bureaucrats who in the late 1970s ousted the original activists and replaced us with fundraisers and public relations people.

With Bob on board, I felt a little of the old spirit which got us moving in the early 70s. We had no doubts: we would find the drift net fleets.

Five days out to sea, we saw a military ship on the horizon, moving rapidly toward us. We identified her as a large Soviet frigate. The frigate hailed us and asked us what we were about. I replied that we were searching for the Japanese drift net fleet and asked if they had seen any Japanese fishing vessels.

The Russians said they thought the Japanese were a few days to the west. Then, surprisingly, the Soviet officer, who spoke impeccable English, said, "Good luck, it is a noble cause that you follow. We are with you in spirit."

Eco-glasnost? Only a few years ago we battled the Russian whalers. In 1975 Bob Hunter and I had survived a Russian harpoon fired over our heads by a Soviet whaler we had confronted. In 1981, we had invaded Siberia to capture evidence on illegal whaling by the Russians. We had narrowly escaped capture. Now, here we were being hailed by the Soviets with a statement of support. We have indeed made progress.

In fact, the Soviets were allies in more than just words. On 29 May 1990, the Russians had seized a fleet of North Korean fishing boats with drift nets in Soviet waters. Japan was diplomatically embarrassed when it was discovered that the 140 supposedly North Korean fishermen in Soviet custody were in fact Japanese.

On the eighth day out from Seattle, I put the *Sea Shepherd II* on a course of due west and decided not to correct the drift. I felt that the drift would take us to the outlaws. Slowly we began to drift north on the course line. Forty-eight hours later, my intuition proved itself right. The sea herself had taken us directly to a drift net fleet.

At 2030 Hours on August 12, we sailed into the midst of six Japanese drift netters. The fleet had just completed laying their nets—more than 200 miles of net in the water. The Japanese ships were each about 200 feet long, equal in size to our own.

As we approached, the Japanese fishermen warned us off, angrily telling us to avoid their nets. Our ship is a large 657 ton North Atlantic trawler with an ice strengthened bow and a fully enclosed protected prop. We were able to cruise harmlessly over the lines of floating nets. We made close runs on the vessels to inspect them closely.

With darkness rapidly closing in, we decided to wait until morning before taking action against the ships. The Japanese vessels had shut down for the night. They drifted quietly. We waited out the night with them.

An hour before dawn they began to move. We moved with them. For three hours, we filmed the hauling in of mile after mile of net from the vessel *Shunyo Maru #8*. We watched the catch of two-foot-long squids being hauled into the boat along with incidental kills of sharks, sea birds and dolphins. The catching of the sea birds violated the Convention for the Protection of Migratory Birds, a treaty signed between the US and Japan in March 1972. The nets impact more than 22 species of birds, 13 of which are protected by the treaty. It was to enforce this treaty that our ship and crew had made this voyage.

The fishing boats were brilliantly illuminated and the work on the deck could be adequately filmed. As the power blocks pulled in the nets, the bodies of squid, fish and birds fell from the nets to the deck or back into the sea.

We had the evidence we needed. We had seen the bodies of protected species in the net. For the next step we needed more light. It was painful to continue watching but it was imperative that we wait for dawn and the light we needed to properly film events.

At 0540 Hours, there was enough light. We prepared the deck and the engine room for confrontation. We positioned our cameramen and photographers. I took the wheel. We brought the engine up to full power and charged across the swells toward the *Shunyo Maru #8* whose crew were still hauling in nets. Our objective was to destroy the net retrieval gear. To do so, we had to hit her on an angle on her port mid-side.

We sounded a blast on our horn to warn the Japanese crew that we were coming in. I piloted the *Sea Shepherd II* into position. We struck where intended. The ships ground their hulls together in a fountain of sparks amidst a screeching cacophony of tearing and crushing steel. The net was severed, the power blocks smashed. We broke away as the Japanese stood dumbfounded on their decks.

One fisherman, however, hurtled his knife at photographer Marc Gaede. The knife missed Marc and hit the sea. The same fisherman grabbed a second knife and sent it flying at cameraman Peter Brown. Peter's camera followed it as it came toward the lens. It fell at Peter's feet.

As we pulled away, I looked with satisfaction on the damage we had inflicted. One ship down for the season. On board our own ship, a damage control party reported back that we had suffered minimal injury. The Japanese ships were no match for our ice-strengthened steel reinforced hull.

We immediately targeted a second ship, the *Ryoun Maru #6*. The Japanese were attempting to cut a large shark out of the net. Looking up, they saw us bearing down at full speed upon them. Eyes wide, they ran toward the far deck.

We struck where intended. Again to the roaring crescendo of tortured metal, the power blocks and gear were crushed; the deck and gunnels buckled. The net was severed.

We broke off and immediately set out for the third ship. By now, the Japanese realized what was happening. The first and second ships had been successfully Pearl Harbored. The third was not to be surprised. As we approached, she dropped her net and fled. We pursued.

We then turned and targeted a fourth ship. She also fled, dropping her net in panic. We stopped and pulled up alongside the radio beacon marking the abandoned net. We confiscated the beacon. We then grappled the net, secured a ton of weight to one end and dropped it, sending the killer net to the bottom, two miles beneath us. We watched the cork line drop beneath the surface, the floats disappearing in lines radiating out from our ship toward the horizon.

On the bottom the net would be rendered harmless. Small benthic creatures would literally cement it to the ocean floor over a short period of time.

We cleaned up the remaining nets and then returned to the chase. For the next twenty hours, we chased the six ships completely out of the fishing area.

The next morning, we could look at what we had achieved with pleasure. Two ships completely disabled from further fishing, a million dollars' worth of net sunk and destroyed and all six ships prevented from continued fishing and running scared.

We had delivered our message to the Japanese fishing industry. Our tactics had been both effective and educational. Effective in that we directly saved lives by shutting down a fleet, and educational in that we informed the Japanese fishing industry that their greed will no longer be tolerated.

Our ship was only slightly damaged. Most importantly, there were no injuries on any of the ships involved.

I turned the bow of our ship southward to Honolulu to deliver the documentation to the media and to begin again the tedious task of fundraising which will allow us to mount further attacks against these mindless thugs slaughtering our oceans.

As we headed south, we stopped repeatedly to retrieve drifting remnants of nets. In one we found 54 rotting fish. In another a large dead mahi-mahi. In another a dead albatross. These "ghost nets" present an additional problem for life in the sea. Each day the large fleets lose an average of six miles of net. At present an estimated 10,000 plus miles of ghost nets are floating the seas. These non-biodegradable nets kill millions of fish and sea creatures each year. Decaying fish attract more fish and birds . . . a vicious cycle of death and waste.

Arriving in Honolulu, we berthed at pier eleven ironically just in front of two fishery patrol vessels, one from Japan, the other from Taiwan. The crew of each scowled at us.

We were prepared for the Japanese to attempt to lay charges against us or failing that to publicly denounce us. Instead, they refused to even recognize that an incident took place.

We contacted the Japanese Consulate and declared that we had attacked their ships and had destroyed Japanese property. We informed the Consulate that we were ready to contest charges, be they in the International Court at the Hague or in Tokyo itself. The Consulate told us he had no idea of what we were talking about.

The Japanese realize they have nothing to gain by taking us to court and much to lose. Which means that we must return to the oceans and must escalate the battle.

The Taiwanese drift netters are beginning to move into the Caribbean Sea. We must head them off. We must continue to confront the Japanese fleets, and we must take on the Koreans.

Each net we sink will cost the industry a million dollars. Each vessel we damage will buy time for the sea animals. Each confrontation we mount will embarrass the drift net industry.

This summer, we won a battle. However, the war to end high seas drift netting continues.

The Japanese, Taiwanese, and Korean drift net fleets can be driven from the oceans. We need only the will, the courage, and the financial support to do so.

The Missing Shade of Green

Kate Rawles

According to *The Collins Paperback English Dictionary,* an activist is someone who takes direct action to achieve a political or social goal. Philosophy, on the other hand, "is the academic discipline concerned with making explicit the nature and significance of beliefs, and investigating the intelligibility of concepts by means of rational arguments." These definitions coincide rather neatly with those offered by many from outside academia (and some from inside)—the consensus here being that while activists get on and do something, philosophers just think. In this paper, I am particularly concerned with activists who get on and do something about animals or the environment and philosophers who take these as the focus of their thoughts. I suppose paradigmatic, if slightly caricatured, cases might be Paul Watson and the crew of *Sea Shepherd* releasing dolphins from drift nets and a philosopher in an office thinking about the concept of nature.

There is, of course, something not quite right about a straight contrast between thinking and doing. Thinking *is* doing; it is, in some sense, an activity. Here, the kind of activity to be contrasted with thinking is the kind that has, and intends to have, a direct effect on the world. But deciding what will qualify as a desirable effect clearly requires some thought. "She acted blindly" presumably means she acted without thinking, and blind or mindless action isn't what we are after when we talk of activism. So thinkers and activists will not be cleanly separated.

Nevertheless, a person could be described as an environmental philosopher without having any intentions to "save the world." And Paul Watson does not have a philosophy degree—and seems to get along pretty well without it. So one question concerns the extent to which philosophical thought does, or can, bear constructively upon activism. In the early part of this paper I want to explore the suggestion that philosophy can contribute to activism (1) by motivating it, in the sense of encouraging people to take action on various issues; (2) by guiding it, in the sense of helping to ensure that the actions taken are thoughtful or skillful ones; (3) by offering reasoned and systematic justification for action and hence helping to legitimize it.

Presumably we are interested in activism because we want to see changes made or prevented from occurring in the world. So a broader question might be that of the extent to which philosophy does or can contribute to such change, whether directly through activism or indirectly, by other means. I will consider two suggestions: first, that philosophy can contribute to constructive change by facilitating dialogue between opposing sides; second that philosophy may help by changing people's perceptions of the world.

I start, then, by singing philosophy's praises, albeit tentatively. In the second part of the paper I will exercise various reservations about the usefulness of philosophy in this context. For example, I suggest that it may paralyze action rather than galvanize it, and that its potential efficacy is limited when set in an academic context.

PHILOSOPHY AND ACTIVISM

In this paper, I take various things for granted. First, that species extinction, climate change, pollution, widespread hunger, persecution of humans and nonhumans, and many other things are really happening. Second, that it would be better if they were not. Third, that activism which contributes to constructive change (which may of course sometimes mean conservation) is important and valuable. Any of these claims taken singularly might be disputed. For ex-

Kate Rawles, "The Missing Shade of Green," in *Environmental Philosophy and Environmental Activism,* ed. D. Marieta and L. Embree (Lanham, MD: Rowman & Littlefield, 1995), 149–67. Reprinted with permission of the publisher.

ample, there is much well-known contention about whether global warming is a genuine threat, and not everyone will agree with my position vis-à-vis the treatment of animals. But what concerns me here is the general claim that, on the environmental front, things could be better. This does not seem particularly contentious.

Perhaps I should also say that I am a philosopher, in the sense that I teach and study philosophy, and also in the sense that it is a subject I am attached to for reasons other than its potential effect upon the world's environmental problems. But if I had to prioritize my concerns, then trying to contribute something to the resolution of these problems would come first. A question which runs throughout this paper, then, is whether working as a philosopher in an academic department is really a viable way of helping to change things out there in the world. This question is for me a vivid and often troublesome one.

Does Philosophy Motivate Activism?

Can philosophy prompt people to take action on particular issues? (I'm not talking about the whole of philosophy. It would be a strange thesis that mathematical logic led to environmental activism.) My own interest in environmental issues developed out of an involvement with animal rights issues and this was initially sparked off by a philosophy book, Peter Singer's *Animal Liberation*.[1] Here, then, is an initial suggestion; philosophers write books and articles and (sometimes!) people read them. Philosophers also take courses. If Singer's lectures are as powerful as his book I would guess that many of his students have changed their eating habits.

An objection to this might be that it is not the philosophy in Singer's book that motivates action as much as the facts. In addition to the famous argument condemning speciesism, *Animal Liberation* contains several chapters that give vivid information about intensive agriculture, slaughterhouses, and the less salubrious aspects of medical research. The facts are in many cases so horrific that they seem to make any argument redundant. Surely in this kind of context, just knowing what goes on is sufficient to lead

to the judgment that it is wrong, and that it should stop. To claim that it is philosophy which is motivating activism here is to give philosophy credit where it is not due.

In my own case I do not think I can say to what extent I was swayed specifically by the argument against speciesism and to what extent by the information. I certainly found the information very distressing, and I also felt very angry that until then I had no idea that the animals I ate lived such unnecessarily miserable lives. This lack of knowledge resulted in my being a party to something I deeply objected to. Moreover, it turned out that this was just the beginning of the trail. I did not know about all sorts of practices that I certainly did not wish to condone once I did know about them. I now think that this was not (just) ignorance on my part; rather that what might be called the Western lifestyle has implications for other animals, other people, and the environment that are often both very negative and well concealed. If this is correct, then the sort of information deficit I uncovered will be pretty common, and giving people access to this information will be an important task.

An objection here might be that I am not on the payroll as a philosopher in order to act as a consciousness raiser! Well, yes and no. It is hard to discuss ethical issues in our treatment of animals without knowing what this treatment is. Similar points can obviously be made in the context of environmental or developmental issues. Raising awareness of environmental problems may not be the primary goal of, say, an applied ethics course, but it may well be a welcome and inevitable side effect. To return to the argument, we might agree that the facts are powerful but add that the arguments are embedded in the facts. It seems rather unjust to say that it was not really the philosophy in the philosophy book that influenced me.

The suggestion that facts alone will motivate action, that we only need the information about intensive farming or environmental degradation to be convinced that it ought to be stopped, can in any case be challenged. The facts "by themselves" will sometimes motivate, but often they will not. A suggested explanation of this might amount to a stronger claim, namely, that we don't really have "facts by themselves" nor are we motivated by such things. Rather, it might be said that we receive—and select—information through a filter of beliefs, values, and assumptions that we may or may not be aware of, and that will affect how we respond to the information in question. A simplified example: learning about environmental degradation will not trouble me if I believe that the environment is only important insofar as humans need it, and I am reassured that this degradation does not constitute a threat to something which humans need.

What philosophy can do in this context is, of course, to draw attention to these values and assumptions and subject them to a critical scrutiny. This might lead to activism first by viewing the facts in a new way and, second, by leading to a change in values.

Identifying beliefs and assumptions, and starting to look at them critically, can create a space between those beliefs and the person who holds them; it can lift the assumptions off the person so that the facts can sneak in underneath. Whatever, in the end, is made of the argument against speciesism, just thinking about it can startle someone away from the "oh, it's just a chicken" response for long enough to let information about intensive farming appear in a new light. I witnessed a particularly striking example of this taking place in a student of Professor Bernie Rollins at Colorado State who, after debating the moral status of animals in Bernie's philosophy class, went, on his own initiative, to all the local slaughterhouses. As a result of this, he became a vegetarian and campaigned for better conditions for the animals still being eaten by others. What makes this a particularly striking case is that Geoff was a cowboy from a ranching community. The attitude toward animals he had been brought up with was extremely different from the one he eventually endorsed. It might be added that very many people in Europe and North America are brought up with the belief that nonhuman animals are vastly inferior to human ones and that the environment is essentially a resource for people. So this may be a particularly vivid example

but it will not necessarily be a particularly unusual one.

It might be said, then, that philosophy can open the way for the facts to get in, and that this may prompt action. But I also suggested that it may be misleading to talk about facts motivating single-handedly. It was a suspension of his society-inherited beliefs and attitudes about animals that prompted Geoff to discover for himself what happens at slaughterhouses and this suspension also allowed the information to really hit home. But presumably this would not have developed into a systematic and long-term campaign unless his original beliefs about the moral status of animals had also changed.

But to what extent can philosophical thought lead to a change in values and moral beliefs? As a philosopher, am I entitled to throw my weight behind one set of moral beliefs rather than another? Clearly, there is a great deal that could be said on this topic alone. Here I will do no more than sketch the beginnings of a response.

I take it that we are thoroughly imbued with values and attitudes and that many of these come from our background in various ways. We are influenced in this respect by our parents, school, religion, and society in a broader sense. I take it that the sort of independence of thought or integrity that results from identifying and examining these values and assumptions is something of value in its own right, and that philosophy, insofar as it leaves people better able to decide for themselves what to think, is a liberating discipline, which enhances people's autonomy. But what is the relationship between this and environmental activism? Is there any guarantee or even likelihood that critical reflection will lead to the endorsement of "green" values, say, rather than some other set? No doubt if we are brainwashed it is not in a green direction. So removing the brainwashing is a start. But does philosophy have the means to take us further than this?

The suggestion is that it is the role of philosophy to present the correct facts—"thick" facts—and that this will lead to specific values and appropriate action is one I will take up in the next section. First, I want to consider the objection that as a philosopher one's function is not to take sides, but simply to encourage critical debate by laying out the arguments. In *Moral Literacy* Colin McGinn writes, "If you finish this book with a totally opposite set of beliefs to mine, but with an enhanced capacity to articulate and justify your moral position, I will be happy."[2] So do I have to be happy when a slave-owning, mahogany-exporting chicken farmer emerges from my course on environmental ethics better able to justify her position?

I do not think so. The claim that I do rests on the supposition that all moral positions can be equally well justified. But my position on intensive chicken farming includes the conviction that the arguments against it are stronger than the arguments for it. So the student who concludes that it is acceptable either has a different idea about the relative strength of the arguments and ought to be able to persuade me of it—or she has missed something. What arguments deserve from philosophers is impartial rather than equal treatment. The conclusion of the argument should not automatically influence my assessment of it but I am not expected to consider all arguments to be equally valid. Hence, I am not expected to consider all conclusions to be equally correct. Indeed, McGinn himself hints at this in his book's subtitle—*How to Do the Right Thing*—that rather suggests the view that there is a right thing and that thinking clearly can put you in touch with it.

As a philosopher, then, it seems that I am at least entitled to indicate where I think the stronger arguments lead. Of course, this leaves open the question of whether careful and critical reflection has any tendency to lead to environmentally friendly conclusions. It may turn out that the stronger arguments lead to Thatcherite materialism. I believe that this is unlikely, but have to admit that I would be hard pressed to offer good grounds for this conviction.

Philosophy as Legitimizing Activism

I have suggested that philosophy may prompt people to take action on various issues by raising awareness of these issues, by encouraging people to take a critical look at their beliefs and values, and by offering support for sets of values which will have implications for action and ways of living. The next question I want to raise is that of whether and how philosophical skills are of value to those who are already activists.

One suggestion is that the ability to offer reasoned and systematic justification for any particular action can help to legitimize it in the eyes of other people. For example, to return to Paul Watson, a recent documentary showed pictures of whales being harpooned and gutted on boat decks awash with blood. It then showed Watson and the *Sea Shepherd* sabotaging whaling ships. The viewers' inevitable sympathies for the saboteurs were abruptly suspended by the suggestion that for Watson to tell the Norwegian people they ought not to kill whales, because of their intelligence and rarity, is comparable to an Asian Indian enjoining North Americans not to kill cows in virtue of their status as sacred animals.[3] The program did not offer Watson's response. But a convincing response was clearly called for, and this would have involved a careful analysis of the claims showing, perhaps, why the analogy is not a good one. The point is obvious: activists are often called upon to justify their actions, and to do this convincingly presumably requires a certain amount of philosophical skill.

This particular issue has recently acquired an even more complex twist to it. "Sustainable development," this year's apple-pie and motherhood buzzword for all things undeniably good, has been invoked on the side of the whalers, against environmentalists, by none other than Gro Harlem Brundtland.[4] To unravel this issue, Paul Watson may need a philosophy degree after all.

Philosophy as Guiding Activism

Clearly, activists need to think about what they are doing, and why. This is not just so that they can offer reasoned and convincing defenses of their actions if challenged—but also because mindless or confused activism can be useless or even harmful. In this context, philosophy may be able to guide activism by helping to ensure that actions taken are thoughtful or skillful ones, and by helping to define the problem and what might count as a solution to it. Indeed, it is hard to see how constructive activism is possible without some thought about what counts as change for the better—and this sort of thought is philosophical. The point might be illustrated by a cartoon I once saw on a notice-board at the Glasgow vet school—which showed a member of the Animal Liberation Front exclaiming "don't worry, mate, we'll soon get you out of there," as he took a crow-bar to a tortoise.

A more complex version of the tortoise case would be the development of Third World countries. The assumption that development can be equated with an increase in GNP and that the questions to be asked about development are purely technical ones, i.e., how to achieve such increase, has caused and continues to cause much social and environmental mayhem. The normative questions inherent in development—what are and ought to be its goals, aims, and acceptable means—are still urgently in need of debate. Development activists, for example, are busy building the Narmada Dam, in western India, as a monument to progress, while local people who have not been consulted and who certainly will not benefit from it have said they will drown when the monsoon arrives rather than leave their villages.[5] "Don't worry, mate, we will help you develop" may be a most threatening cry.

PHILOSOPHY AS INDIRECT ACTIVISM

Philosophy, then, can help in the skillful direction of activism. Indeed, it can be argued that constructive activism is not possible without a certain amount of reflection on what constitutes valuable change or conservation.

A rather different suggestion is that philosophy may sometimes be indirect activism. For example, philosophy may be able to provide the means by which dialogue can be generated between opposing sides, or within an institution that normally manifests a particular attitude. A case of the latter with which I am familiar is veterinary colleges. My ex-perience of "teaching ethics" at a Scottish vet school is really a case of promoting discussion about the moral status of animals within an institution that typically—and perhaps surprisingly—endorses the view that animals are essentially resources, albeit ones which should, within certain limits, be treated humanely. Where these limits are to be drawn is a contentious subject badly in need of discussion given that many vets will be effectively employed by the agricultural industry.

The use of animals in medical research is a case that has led to deep polarization. Often, those who oppose such research are written off as lunatics while those who condone it are condemned as sadists. Verbal warfare and physical intimidation has led to much defensiveness and retraction on the part of the medical establishment. But this does not lead to change. Here, dialogue is activism and a philosopher is well placed to promote this by identifying the assumptions that each party is making, the common ground they may share, and so on.

Philosophy and Worldviews

The suggestion that I want to look at in slightly more detail, however, is that philosophy constitutes activism insofar as it changes worldviews.

To return to the ALF activist taking a crowbar to the tortoise, it might be objected, again, that what he lacks is not philosophical aptitude but certain facts about the nature of tortoises. Now suppose the picture were of an antitortoise activist, deliberately crushing the tortoise with the crowbar. What is interesting is that one might be tempted to say much the same thing; that this person cannot really know what it is like to be a tortoise. If she did know, for example, how much pain and fear tortoises experience when their shells are battered then, other things being equal, she would not be doing it.

This takes us back to the idea that facts influence action. The notion this time is that if one really knows about the way animals and the environment are, a certain sort of response to them will naturally follow. I want to briefly explore this idea with reference to Hume and Callicott.

Hume says "we cannot form to ourselves a just idea of the taste of a pineapple, without having actually tasted it."[6] Certainly, one problem in discussing issues having to do with our treatment of animals is, to bend Hume more than a little, that people form ideas of animals without ever having had impressions of them. People who have had little contact with animals can say the oddest things about them, for example, that "they are not really conscious of what they are doing"; "their behavior is all instinctive, they don't learn anything"; "animals don't have feelings." Moral beliefs about animals may thus be based on a false picture of what animals are actually like, for these beliefs are built on ideas and ideas depend on impressions. For Hume the only exception to this might arise were someone to be presented with a color chart in which tones of blue are graded from light to dark; with one tone missing. In this case, Hume thought, it might be possible to have an idea of that particular color of blue without ever having had the impression of it. "The missing shade of blue" is, however, a case which Hume thought to be "so particular and singular that it is scarce worth our observing, and so does not merit that for it alone we should alter our general maxim."[7]

I take it, then, that we can't get a good idea of the natural world by extrapolating from a series of impressions of streets with fewer and fewer houses on. Rather, we need, let's say, to experience it and to have some ecological understanding of it. Without this, we may reach ethical conclusions about the natural world which are based on a false picture of what it is. This seems uncontroversial.

I am less sure about variations on the claim that experience and/or understanding of animals or the environment is a sufficient condition for believing that, and acting as if, animals and the environment have a high moral status. Deep Ecologists, for example, may suggest that recognition of the intrinsic value and moral standing of the natural world will follow from certain sorts of experience of it. The position of J. Baird Callicott, as I understand it, is that a good ecological and evolutionary understanding of animals and the environment will engender a positive moral attitude toward them or, to put it another way, that the claim that animals and the environment are morally irrelevant is underpinned by "facts" which are "false." Replace the false facts with true ones and anthropocentrism will be replaced by an attitude of benevolence and respect toward the nonhuman world.

I would not want to dispute that changing the general way in which we perceive animals and the environment is important. In *Man and the Natural World* Keith Thomas writes, "as for cattle and sheep, Henry More in 1653 was convinced that they had only been given life in the first place so as to keep their meat fresh 'till we shall have need to eat them.'"[8] In *Last Chance to See* Douglas Adams writes, "The giant tortoises were eaten to extinction because the early sailors regarded them much as we regard canned food. They just picked them off the beach and put them in their ship's hold as ballast, and then, if they felt hungry they'd go down to the hold, pull one up, kill it and eat it."[9] If Paul Watson is to become redundant, our attitude to marine and other creatures must become such that drift-netting is no longer considered to be an acceptable practice. This will involve seeing such creatures as something other than substitutes for canned food.

What troubles me is that on Callicott's view all normative disputes are in the end reducible to disputes about facts, albeit what he refers to as "thick facts." His position implies that, as long as someone is not a psychopath, if she genuinely understands and accepts that from an evolutionary perspective animals are kin and from an ecological perspective the land is a community, she will agree that she has strong moral obligations toward land and animals and will treat them accordingly. What the tortoise aggressor and the general anthropocentrist need is fact-therapy.

But what if the fact-therapy fails? Is it true that, other things being equal, a person would not attack a tortoise, if she really knew what tortoises are like? I think it is quite possible to imagine various nonpsychopathic anthropocentrists stubbornly maintaining their anthropocentrism in the face of such fact-therapy, assenting to the evolutionary and ecological perspectives on animals and the environment, but insisting nevertheless that they have moral obligations only toward humans. In this case an argument is needed, to show why anthropocentrists ought to feel morally inclined to treat the environment better than they in fact do. And such an argument will not be forthcoming from a Humean theory. To put it another way, the sort of changed worldview required will include irreducibly normative components.

Another reservation concerns the possibility of the fact-therapy operating in the wrong direction. I spent some months working on a farm and left disliking chickens intensely. This was because I came to see that these creatures, which I had until then rather liked, are typically mean, stupid, aggressive, and greedy. In this case, my positive sentiments toward chickens were based on a false picture of them, which, when corrected, drained my compassion and respect entirely. However, I would argue, presumably against the Humean, that such a response to chickens is no basis for treating them badly.

These problems, then, are to do with the kind of view which says, first, that a human being's informed and uncorrupted response to animals and the environment is a positive one; and second, that this positive response forms the basis of our ethical obligations. The first is a claim that I would like to believe, but about which I am skeptical. The second is worrying because it may leave one defenseless against those who fail to respond positively despite being well-informed, as well as vulnerable to the claim that well-informed negative responses sanction bad treatment. All these issues have clear practical implications, relating, for example, to the viability of Callicott's and the Deep Ecologists' program for change, and to any suggestion that exposing people to animals or the environment will necessarily help to produce a positive orientation toward them.

A third problem relates to the claim that changed worldviews will necessarily be accompanied by changed action. Again, I think that there are many reservations to be expressed about such a claim, some of which have been famously explored by Byron Earhart in "The Ideal of Nature in Japanese Religion and Its Possible Significance for Environmental Concerns."[10] Here, however, I will only say that I think that alleged links between worldviews and action merit cautious treatment and that the issue would be worth returning to.

To conclude this section, if it is true that changing people's world views results in better treatment of animals and the environment, the philosophers who change people's worldviews will surely qualify as activists. While I would agree that an alternative to the canned food view of animals—and the resource view of the environment in general—is a necessary component of change, I am not convinced that this will be achieved by fact-therapy alone. Moreover, even if one's conception of the world, or worldview, is changed, I am not sure that this will guarantee changed action. In this context, then, we might conclude that philosophers are necessary but not sufficient.

RESERVATIONS

I have suggested that philosophy may motivate, legitimize, and guide activism; that it may help to create dialogue effective in bringing about desirable change; and that it may help to alter our perceptions of animals and the environment—in some cases at least, a necessary if not sufficient condition of treating them better. If this is correct, the claim that while activists do something, philosophers just think, needs to be revised.

What follows, however, are various reservations about the extent to which philosophy either does or can contribute to desirable change. Some of these reservations are to do with philosophy as a skill or subject and some are to do with philosophy as it is practiced in contemporary academic institutions—though these are of course connected.

An obvious preliminary is that there is no necessary connection between particular environmental philosophers and environmental activism. An environmental philosopher may have little to do with the great outdoors but commute to work and spend all day in her study; she may discuss the concept of the environment at a very abstract level so that students who are already actively inclined find the course interesting from a philosophical point of view but irrelevant to their activism. Moreover, just as, according to the introduction of a popular *Dictionary of Philosophy,* there is no logical contradiction involved in being an immoral moral philosopher, an environmental philosopher could without contradiction live an extremely ungreen lifestyle, refusing to recycle, driving a sports car, deliberately eating chemically saturated vegetables, taking airplanes to conferences, and so on. However, even if we are concerned exclusively with environmental philosophers who are concerned about environmental issues, there may be ways in which the philosophy proves to be more of a hindrance than a help.

Philosophy as a Skill or Subject

Philosophy has a way of retreating away from the question it is trying to answer. Take the issue of the relationship between environmental philosophy and environmental activism. If one tackles this as a philosopher, it is very difficult not to ask: what, exactly, is activism? What is action? How do thinking and acting relate? What did Aristotle have to say about this? It is also difficult not to feel that these questions all have to be resolved before one can attempt to answer the initial question. A. A. Milne perhaps captures the essence of this in the poem "The Old Sailor," which begins,

> *There once was a sailor my grandfather knew*
> *Who had so many things which he wanted to do*
> *That, whenever he thought it was time to begin,*
> *He couldn't because of the state he was in.*[11]

A related problem is that it seems part of the internal logic of the subject to become increasingly focused on fine-grained questions. It is very difficult to stay with a big, broad problem like the one under discussion. To get on with it requires giving rather cavalier treatment to concepts like "nature" and "environment," batting them about as if there were no conceptual questions to be asked. But a more conventionally philosophical approach might never get beyond the question, what do we mean by "the environment"?

Such an approach will not necessarily lead to action, for action is often motivated by simplifying the issues, rather than by revealing their complexities. Consider what Allison Pearson of *The Independent* has to say about John Pilger's documentary *Return to Year Zero:* "Shawcross' film [also about Cambodia] was fine journalism but it was Pilger's that made you angry. After his last one, 18,000 viewers wrote to Margaret Thatcher about Cambodia. That's what he does best, *choosing to find truths where there is uncertainty*" (my emphasis).[12] It is this, she suggests, that motivates. On the other hand, one might say that philosophers choose to find uncertainty. This is a feature of philosophy that is actually extremely attractive. A philosophical gaze turned upon concepts so familiar they are hardly noticed not only brings them vividly back into focus but may reveal them as troublesome or illusory. What is nature? What is wilderness? What is it that nature conservationists are supposed to be conserving? And of course a philosopher's film about Cambodia might be in some sense more honest than Pilger's, and this might be a reason for thinking it preferable. But whatever merits this aspect of philosophy has, they probably do not include inspiring action. Telling the truth, the whole truth and nothing but the very, very complicated truth is likely to paralyze action rather than galvanize it.

Philosophy in Context

These problems may all be exacerbated by the academic context within which much philosophical thinking takes place. Here, one's remit is not to think about this problem until it is no longer useful to do so. Rather one often ends up following the problem wherever it goes and for the sake of the problem rather than for the light it may be able to shed on external issues. Consider the question of the metaphysical status of value in nature. The question is of interest in its own right. But from the perspective of improving states of affairs in the world, the complex and convoluted trail one embarks upon in order to try to answer it seems, after a certain point, to become quite unrelated to the starting point. If philosophy is to contribute to change, it needs a constant pulling back to the question, how does this help?—so that philosophy runs in its own direction and is then returned, runs on again, and so on.

In an academic context, however, it is relatively easy just to run with the problem. The question how does this help may be lost, or may not even be asked. Moreover, it might be suggested that many academic journals actually require complexity beyond what is useful as a condition of publication and that, in general, to ask how helpful a given project is may be considered a sort of betrayal of the academic endeavor. Clearly there is more to be said on what counts as "helpful," and I am not suggesting that philosophy should be exclusively concerned with being "helpful," whatever this turns out to mean. But neither, surely, should philosophy amount to no more than a clever and beautiful game or, to use Kingsley Amis's wonderful phrase, a discipline concerned merely with "shining a pseudo-light on a nonproblem."[13]

The feeling that philosophers must continuously struggle to resist strong undercurrents which pull toward increasingly abstract and remote shores might be less frustrating if contemporary environmental problems were less serious or less immediate. But this is not the case. The monsoon that may end the lives of many Indian villagers if the construction of the Narmada Dam continues will arrive in June, and ours is the last decade which will have the chance to prevent complete destruction of the world's rain forests. In these and many other cases we do not have time to solve all the philosophical problems before we act—nor would this be necessary. We do not need to know the precise status of value in nature, nor exactly what is meant by nature, before we can conclude that rain forests should not be destroyed at the rate of a football field per minute. Philosophy and activism, then, can seem to operate within quite different time frames and this can lead one to become impatient with philosophy, or even to feel dragged

under by it. On the other hand, activists can also become trapped, both in their own institutions and in the present moment, a problem which philosophical thought may help to redress. Some sort of dynamic equilibrium between philosophical thought and practical issues seems to be called for. At the moment, however, at least within British philosophy departments, the process is often lopsidedly biased toward the theoretical and the abstract.

Moreover, even if attention were focused on keeping philosophy useful, philosophers may be handicapped by the fact that, in the main, they have little to do with activists. Nor will they necessarily have a great knowledge of biology, ecology, or animals. Philosophers may be weak on both facts and experience, and this may be an obstacle to successfully relating their work to particular problems in the field. The response that this is up to individuals to remedy is too glib. The amount of published material is doubling exponentially every seven years, but no one supposes that the amount of time available for reading is increasing at the same rate.[14] Staying on top of the literature in any particular area is a genuine problem, and current academic arrangements regarding teaching and administrative loads hardly lend themselves to taking on an additional clutch of new subjects.

Finally, an obvious point is that philosophers' audiences are actually rather small. Few philosophical books, even in the environmental sphere, are bestsellers while the audience for academic journals is even more restricted. On the other hand, writing for "popular" journals that do have a wider readership is not encouraged by current research rating systems.

Mary Midgley in *Wisdom, Information and Wonder* offers a critique of academic pursuits in general.[15] This critique, I think, is a revealing one, and it may be helpful to consider environmental philosophy in this broader context.

Midgley argues that one result of the massive increase in information I have already referred to is increasing specialization. We have more knowledge, so each individual has a smaller percentage of it. But, she says, if a thousand individuals each know a thousandth of something and nobody knows it in its entirety, we do not really have knowledge at all. Knowledge involves understanding and this involves knowledge of the whole, not just of specialized bits.

Clearly, each individual cannot master details of all subjects. Rather, "what is needed," according to Midgley, "is that all should have in their minds a general background map of the whole range of knowledge as a context for their own specialty, and should integrate this wider vision with their practical and emotional attitude to life. They should be able to place their own small area on the map of the world and to move outside it freely when they need to."[16] If this is not the case, when we talk about accumulating knowledge, we are simply talking about storing information, holding onto it like inert property or "handing it on like a dead fish to students."[17] This cannot be our ideal of knowledge, nor what we really think knowledge is for.

The question of the purpose of knowledge is one Midgley thinks we urgently need to ask. She writes, "the question is not a demand for a simple, hedonistic pay-off at a given moment. The gratification it looks for may be something much wider, slower, vaster, and more pervasive. But it still does have to touch down somewhere in the sentient lives of those who seek it."[18] The way in which it should touch down is in relation to the question of how we are to live. Thus, while bits of knowledge only make sense in relation to all knowledge, knowledge as a whole gains its meaning and value from the role it plays in helping us live well. Knowledge correctly understood, then, is an aspect of wisdom: "an understanding of life as a whole, and a sense of what really matters in it."[19]

What Midgley fears is that academia tends to pursue knowledge in the sense of a passive store of specialized bits of information. For this reason, academic knowledge can become irrelevant (and of course the word "academic" is sometimes used in a derogatory manner to mean precisely this). Moreover, given this notion of knowledge, it makes perfect sense to contrast knowledge with action, thinking with doing.

But if knowledge is taken to be an active process aiming at wisdom, both the contrast and the criticism are undermined.

Thus Midgley rebukes Marx for implying, in his famous "The philosophers have only interpreted the world in various ways; the point is to change it,"[20] that we need to change the world *rather* than understand it. Proper understanding, she says, is a necessary condition of proper change. But understanding is different from information storing, and understanding is not always going on in academic institutions for the reasons sketched above.

If Midgley's analysis is correct, one problem with environmental philosophy is that the academic endeavor in general has become increasingly specialized and dislocated, in such a way that its pursuits have become increasingly pointless and unhelpful. This is a radical claim and seems to suggest the need for a radical restructuring of universities in response to it. If this were undertaken, part of the very purpose of environmental philosophy would presumably be to explicitly address the question "how ought we to live" in relation to the environment. This would certainly help to counteract some of the problems of relevance discussed earlier—though it would not amount to an alternative to activism. Understanding may be active, but it is not necessarily the same sort of thing as that prescribed by activists. We might conclude that the best philosophy and the best activism complement each other, and that neither is capable of achieving desirable change single-handedly. However, in the context of academic institutions, we are not always witnessing the best philosophy, and the helpfulness of philosophy may thus be compromised.

This last suggestion can be put in another way. Suppose you wanted to encourage the development of wise and effective activists. Would you do it by sending them to study environmental philosophy in a university philosophy department? Probably not. A better choice might be a multidisciplinary course involving not just separate modules of ecology, biology, politics, and policy in addition to philosophy but these and other subjects taught so that the connections between the subjects are also revealed. In addition, the course might include active contact with animals and the environment, and it would combine activism with philosophy not just in the sense of bringing activists and philosophers together in the same room—but also by encouraging these skills in the same person. This course—let us call it 301, Applied World Saving—would certainly raise awareness and understanding of environmental problems. But it would also seek to facilitate a translation of this into effective action in both immediate and long-term ways.

Would this be the kind of course that could be legitimately held within an academic institution? I suppose that how this is answered will depend partly on whether you agree with Midgley and on how far you think the "Midgley reforms" would take you. I don't think anyone would suppose that academic life should be entirely taken over with this kind of course. But I would argue that there has to be a legitimate space for such a course within it. On our planet currently we have extremely complex and pressing environmental problems and also institutions containing collections of highly intelligent people. It seems simply perverse for the one not to address the other.

CONCLUSION

I want to conclude by returning to the activists releasing dolphins from drift nets. I have said that philosophy, however well conceived and practiced, will never amount to a replacement for this kind of immediate action. But not everyone agrees that such direct action should take place and drift-netting as a practice still continues. There is a need for activism to be legitimized and for the practice of drift-netting to cease. For this to happen, critical reflection and debate about our ethical relationship to the rest of the natural world is called for, and this surely indicates a key role for philosophy. Working to change the canned food attitude to animals will not free those dolphins stuck in drift nets right now. But endlessly cutting drift nets is not a long-term solution either.

Moreover, we do not want mindless activism nor do we want our horizons in terms of time and imagination to be limited to the horizons of those working in the present on compelling issues. Activists may be trapped and limited by their institutions as much as philosophers.

I would argue, then, that philosophy is both crucial to and a component of activism and that thinking and acting are both essential components of long- and short-term constructive change. However, philosophy also has the potential to be quite unhelpful or even obstructive, and these tendencies in the subject may be exacerbated by the academic institutions within which much philosophizing takes place. Keeping philosophy useful requires, I think, deliberate effort, and this in a direction that may be counter to the general academic flow. Moreover, specialization within universities can result in philosophy and philosophers becoming increasingly abstract and out of touch. The missing shade of green in academic institutions may be the one that deliberately sets itself to address contemporary environmental problems, in an interdisciplinary way.

I want to end, however, with something of a qualification to the above. The most effective green activists might be produced by some form of relentless media campaign and I left quite open the question of whether there are any necessary links between independence of thought and greenness of values. I am just not sure what I think about this. But a large part of my commitment to philosophy in any case derives from the belief that the sort of greenness that may be evoked by assaulting people with new age music, the smell of pine cones, and stirring rhetoric, so that everyone emerges with firm resolve and inanely beatific smiles is just as offensive as the advertisement-induced conviction that success in life is defined by the make of your running shoes. Philosophy, I maintain, is an antidote effective against both complaints. But it may leave us with an ongoing tension between the desire to encourage the resolution of environmental problems as rapidly and effectively as possible and the desire to foster and promote integrity, autonomy, and independence of thought.

NOTES

1. Peter Singer, *Animal Liberation* (London: Thorsons, 1976).

2. Colin McGinn, *Moral Literacy or How to Do the Right Thing* (London: Duckworth, 1992), p. 16.

3. "Defenders of the Wild," Channel 4 Television (April, 1993).

4. John Vidal, "Weeping and Whaling," *The Guardian,* May 7 1993.

5. Reported, for example, in *The Guardian,* April 1993.

6. David Hume, *A Treatise of Human Nature* (London: Collins Fontana, 1962), p. 48.

7. Hume, *A Treatise,* p. 50.

8. Keith Thomas, *Man and the Natural World* (London: Penguin, 1983), p. 20.

9. Douglas Adams, *Last Chance to See* (Pan, 1991), p. 193.

10. Byron Earhart, "The Idea of Nature in Japanese Religion and Its Possible Significance for Environmental Concerns," *Contemporary Religions in Japan,* 11.1:26.

11. A. A. Milne, *Now We Are Six* (London: Methuen, 1927), p. 36.

12. Allison Pearson, "Not on a Level Filming Field," *The Guardian,* April 25 1993.

13. Kingsley Amis, *Lucky Jim* (New York: Penguin, 1993).

14. Mary Midgley, *Wisdom, Information and Wonder* (London: Routledge, 1989), p. 6.

15. Midgley, *Wisdom.*

16. Midgley, *Wisdom,* p. 8.

17. Midgley, *Wisdom,* p. 8.

18. Midgley, *Wisdom,* p. 17.

19. Midgley, *Wisdom,* p. 13.

20. Karl Marx, "Theses on Feuerbach," in *Karl Marx: Selected Writings,* ed. David McLellan (Oxford: Oxford University Press, 1977), p. 158.

Environmental Philosophy Is Environmental Activism: The Most Radical and Effective Kind

J. Baird Callicott

Here is one picture of philosophy. It goes on in an ivory tower pursued by cloistered academics who endlessly dispute the contemporary equivalents of questions like "how many angels can dance on the head of a pin?" It is far removed from the "real world," even when philosophers spin theories about what is "real." (In the real world, everyone knows what's real, without needing philosophers to inform or misinform them.) Here is another picture of philosophy. Socrates is hauled into court and sentenced to death—not for anything he might have done, such as sell state secrets to the Lacedaimonians or assassinate Kleon—but for questioning religious ideas and moral ideals, thus bringing about the precipitous transformation of Athenian society. In the first picture, philosophy seems socially irrelevant. In the second, it seems to be the most potent force of social change imaginable.

There does seem to be a lot of ivory tower philosophy—a kind of new scholasticism—going on today in academe. But only future historians will be in a position to judge whether it will prove to

J. Baird Callicott, "Environmental Philosophy Is Environmental Activism: The Most Radical and Effective Kind," in *Environmental Philosophy and Environmental Activism,* ed. D. Marieta and L. Embree (Lanham, MD: Rowman & Littlefield, 1995), 19–35. Reprinted with permission of the publisher.

have actually been socially transformative. But let's grant, for the sake of argument, that the test of time will prove that what seems to be irrelevant ivory tower philosophy is indeed just that. The post-sixties "applied" movement in late twentieth-century philosophy has been an attempt, on the part of many academic philosophers, to descend from the ivory tower and directly engage real-world issues. The advent of business ethics, biomedical ethics, animal welfare ethics, engineering ethics, and environmental ethics illustrates two points. First, that many young academic philosophers then believed that business-as-usual analytic philosophy, phenomenology, philosophy of science, and the like are, as many nonphilosophers suspect, socially irrelevant; and second, that an attempt was deliberately made to reorient philosophy so as to apply its rich heritage of theory and powerful methods of argument to illuminate and help solve real-world problems.

The "pure" philosophers, as if to confirm the suspicion that their preoccupations are ivory tower irrelevancies, have responded with contempt. Applied philosophy is scorned as not "real" (that is, genuine) philosophy and as merely yeoman's (and yeowoman's) work, appropriating the creative ideas of the true, the pure, the real philosophers and mechanically applying them to current social "issues." Applied work is perhaps suitable for academic philosophers toiling in bush-league undergraduate departments, but not for those holding prestigious chairs in major-league research departments.

Since environmental philosophy came into being in such circumstance—in deliberate reaction to what was perceived as the reigning neoscholasticism and in a deliberate attempt to help society deal with real-world problems—it is surprising to find some people now suggesting that environmental philosophy is itself an ivory tower preoccupation of little practical moment. Though the people I have in mind occupy positions in philosophy departments and publish papers in philosophy journals, I hesitate to call them philosophers, since they seem to think that philosophy, even environmental philosophy, is worse than an irrelevancy, it's a subterfuge.

One such environmental antiphilosopher is Kenneth Sayre. He writes,

In no case does the reasoning of an ethical theorist actually cause a norm to be socially instituted or cause a norm once in force to lose that status. Whether a moral norm is actually in effect within a given community depends not at all on ethical theorizing. . . . If norms encouraging conservation and proscribing pollution were actually in force in industrial society, it would not be the result of ethical theory; and the fact that currently they are not in force is not alleviated by any amount of adroit ethical reasoning.[1]

Sayre's understanding of ethical theory is very narrow and formal. No doubt there is a kernel of truth in his claim, if by "ethical theory" we refer to some arid inferential exercise in which a philosopher deduces that (4) action X should be proscribed, since (3) X is wrong, because (2) X has the property A and (1) all actions that have A are wrong. The alternatives to ethical theorizing, so conceived, that Sayre suggests would seem to dissolve environmental ethics into various social sciences, much as sociobiology would absorb the social sciences into biology. "Environmental ethics," he writes, "should join forces with anthropology, economics, and other areas of social science in hopes of generating a basis for empirical information about how moral norms actually operate."[2]

For Sayre "moral norms" seem just to exist in splendid isolation from the larger cognitive culture. Sayre's example of a norm that is socially "in place" is honesty. An example of an environmental ethical norm that is not in place is recycling. Sayre seems to think that eventually people may just up and adopt the recycling norm, and a new breed of environmental ethicists transformed into sociologists, social psychologists, and economists can empirically describe the mysterious process by which such a norm shift will have occurred, if it does. Or empirically examining how new norms, such as antislavery, came to be adopted in the recent past, environmental ethicists can help socially engineer new environmental norms, such as recycling, in the near future.

One thing Sayre is sure of is that no amount of theorizing is going to induce most people to believe that recycling is simply the right thing to do in the same way that most people believe that honesty is simply the best policy.

Doubtless he is right if environmental ethical theory conforms to Sayre's caricature. But such formal reasoning is not what actually goes on in theoretical environmental philosophy. Environmental philosophers, rather, are attempting to articulate a new worldview and a new conception of what it means to be a human being, distilled from the theory of evolution, the new physics, ecology, and other natural sciences. On this basis, we might suggest how people ought to relate to the natural environment, but there is rather little deducing of specific rules of conduct. People come to believe that old norms (such as stone adulterers and burn witches) should be abandoned, and new ones adopted (such as abolish slavery and feed the hungry) only when their most fundamental ideas about themselves and their world undergo radical change. Much of the theoretical work in environmental ethics is devoted to articulating and thus helping to effect such a radical change in outlook. The specific ethical norms of environmental conduct remain for the most part only implicit—a project postponed to the future or something left for ecologically informed people to work out for themselves.

Bryan Norton, another environmental antiphilosopher, thinks that theoretical environmental ethics is not only an irrelevant subterfuge, but that it is also downright pernicious. Environmental ethicists arguing with one another about whether nature has intrinsic as well as instrumental value and about whether intrinsic value is objective or subjective divide environmentalists into deep and shallow camps. While these two camps spend precious time and energy criticizing one another, their common enemy, the hydra-headed forces of environmental destruction, remains unopposed by a united and resolute counterforce. But according to Norton a long and wide anthropocentrism "converges" on the same environmental policies—the preservation of biological diversity, for, example—as nonanthropocentrism.

Hence the intellectual differences between anthropocentrists and nonanthropocentrists, deep ecologists and reform environmentalists are, practically speaking, otiose. Environmental philosophers, in Norton's view, should therefore cease spinning nonanthropocentric theories of the intrinsic value of nature and, as Norton himself does, concentrate instead on refining environmental policy. Norton opts for anthropocentrism because it is the more conservative alternative. Most people are anthropocentrists to begin with, and when the instrumental value of a whole and healthy environment to both present and future generations of humans is fully accounted, anthropocentrism, he believes, is sufficient to support the environmental policy agenda.[3]

Norton's "convergence hypothesis," however, is dead wrong. If all environmental values are anthropocentric and instrumental, then they have to compete head-to-head with the economic values derived from converting rain forests to lumber and pulp, savannahs to cattle pasture, and so on. Environmentalists, in other words, must show that preserving biological diversity is of greater instrumental value to present and future generations than lucrative timber extraction, agricultural conversion, hydroelectric empoundment, mining, and so on. For this simple reason, a persuasive philosophical case for the intrinsic value of nonhuman natural entities and nature as a whole would make a huge practical difference. Warwick Fox explains why. Granting an entity intrinsic value would not imply "that it cannot be interfered with *under any circumstances*."[4] Believing, as we do, that human beings are intrinsically valuable does not imply that human beings ought never be uprooted, imprisoned, put at grave risk, or even deliberately killed. Intrinsically valuable human beings may—ethically may—be made to suffer these and other insults with sufficient justification. Therefore, Fox points out,

the mere fact that moral agents must be able to justify their actions in regard to their treatment of entities that are intrinsically valuable means that recognizing the intrinsic value of the nonhuman world has a dramatic effect upon the framework of environmental debate and decision-making. If the non-human world is only considered to be instrumentally valuable then people are permitted to use and otherwise interfere with any aspect of it for whatever reasons they wish (i.e., no justification is required). If anyone objects to such interference then, within this framework of reference, the onus is clearly on the person who objects to justify why it is more useful to humans to leave that aspect of the nonhuman world alone. If, however, the nonhuman world is considered to be intrinsically valuable then the onus shifts to the person who wants to interfere with it to justify why they should be allowed to do so: anyone who wants to interfere with any entity that is intrinsically valuable is morally obliged to be able to offer a sufficient justification for their actions. Thus recognizing the intrinsic value of the nonhuman world shifts the onus of justification from the person who wants to protect the nonhuman world to the person who wants to interfere with it—and that, in itself, represents a fundamental shift in the terms of environmental debate and decision-making.[5]

Just as Sayre seems to think of moral norms as hanging alone in an intellectual void, so Norton seems to think of environmental policies in the same way. We environmentalists just happen to have a policy agenda—saving endangered species, preserving biodiversity in all its forms, lowering CO_2 emissions, etc. To rationalize these policies—to sell them to the electorate and their representatives—is the intellectual task, if there is any. (Much of Norton's research for his book, *Unity Among Environmentalists,* consisted of interviewing the Washington based lobbyists for "big ten" environmental groups. Such cynicism may be characteristic of lobbyists who are hired to pitch a policy, but starting with a policy and looking for persuasive reasons to support it is not how sincere environmentalists outside the Beltway actually think.) People just don't adopt a policy like they decide which color is their favorite. They adopt it for what seems to them to be good reasons. Reasons come first, policies second, not the other way around.

Most people, of course, do not turn to philosophers for something to believe—as if they didn't at all know what to think and philosophers can and

should tell them. Rather, philosophers such as Thoreau, Muir, Leopold, and Rolston give voice to the otherwise inchoate and articulate thoughts and feelings in our changing cultural Zeitgeist. A maximally stretched anthropocentrism may, as Norton argues, rationalize the environmental policy agenda, but anthropocentrism may no longer ring true. That is, the claim that all and only human beings have intrinsic value may not be consistent with a more general evolutionary and ecological worldview. I should think that contemporary environmental philosophers would want to give voice and form to the still small but growing movement that supports environmental policies for the right reasons—which, as Fox points out, also happen to be the strongest reasons.

Granted, we may not have the leisure to wait for a majority to come over to a new worldview and a new nonanthropocentric, holistic environmental ethic. We environmentalists have to reach people where they are, intellectually speaking, right now. So we might persuade Jews, Christians, and Muslims to support the environmental policy agenda by appeal to such concepts as God, creation, and stewardship; we might persuade humanists by appeal to collective enlightened human self-interest; and so on. But that is no argument for insisting, as Norton seems to do, that environmental philosophers should stop exploring the real reasons why we ought to value other forms of life, ecosystems, and the biosphere as a whole.

The eventual institutionalization of a new holistic, nonanthropocentric environmental ethic will make as much practical difference in the environmental arena as the institutionalization of the intrinsic value of all human beings has made in the social arena. As recently as a century and a half ago, it was permissible to own human beings. With the eventual institutionalization of Enlightenment ethics—persuasively articulated by Hobbes, Locke, Bentham, and Kant, among others—slavery was abolished in Western civilization. Of course, a case could have been made to slaveowners and an indifferent public that slavery was economically backward and more trouble than it was worth. But that would not have gotten at the powerful moral truth that for one human being to own another is wrong. With the eventual institutionalization of a holistic, nonanthropocentric environmental ethic—today persuasively articulated by Aldo Leopold, Arne Naess, Holmes Rolston, and Val Plumwood, among others—the wanton destruction of the nonhuman world will, hopefully, come to be regarded as equally unconscionable.

Anthony Weston seems to believe that systematic environmental philosophy is premature. In an article entitled "Before Environmental Ethics," he suggests that it is much too early in the sea change of values that is presently taking place to try to articulate and systematize a new environmental ethic. We should let these new environmental values ferment and bubble up organically. Instead of theorizing, philosophers should help to create "quiet zones" or "ecosteries" (an analogy with medieval monasteries) where people can "reinhabit" the land; and, through "enabling practice," unpredictable but ultimately appropriate environmental values will "emerge."[6]

Specifically criticizing my case against moral pluralism, Weston writes,

> The flaw in this argument, I believe, is that it greatly overrates the role of metaphysical views in shaping and justifying values. . . . Values and their larger explanatory contexts evolve together . . . . At least sometimes we may even rearrange our metaphysics to suit our values. Inconsistent metaphysics, anyway, are just the price we sometimes pay for keeping all our essential values in play. . . .[7]

Weston apparently agrees with Ralph Waldo Emerson that "consistency is the hobgoblin of little minds."[8] It is, I rather suppose, the very foundation of critical judgment. Certainly the intellectual virtue of selfconsistency or noncontradiction has enjoyed a long tenure of solid support in the Western tradition. Is Socrates the little mind and Euthyphro the great one when Socrates rejects Euthyphro's account of piety because it is self-contradictory? I'm sure that Euthyphro would also have gladly agreed with Emerson. To abandon consistency as a criterion of what one permits oneself to believe is to abandon the examined life, personally, and Western civilization, culturally.

For Sayre, norms seem independent from a supporting matrix of ideas; for Norton, policies seem to be equally free-floating, and for Weston, values are much less embedded in and dependent upon a worldview than I suggest they are.

To think as I do, that ideas shape our values, that moral norms depend upon a cognitive context, and that policies reflect a worldview, may seem like a typical intellectual and more especially philosophical myopia. Only intellectuals and more especially philosophers live in a world of ideas, concern themselves with self-consistency, and ask questions like, Given that this is the kind of world we live in and this is the kind of being we are, how should we relate to the world and to one another? As Sayre ingenuously remarks,

> most people treat the relevant actions as [prescribed or] proscribed simply because they have been taught to do so by their parents or teachers, but for no reason amounting to a rationally perceived cause. Although various members of contemporary American society, for instance, may be aware that lying often causes distress, the reason lying is actually proscribed (to the extent that it is) has more to do with the fact that responsible persons have learned to abide by that norm as they take their place in mature society.[9]

Of course Sayre is right. Most people acquire their moral norms through a process of socialization. When children are chastised for, say, telling a lie, most parents probably answer "because I told you so," when their children ask why lying is proscribed. Most people acquire their most basic values—"family values" as they were called in the 1992 presidential campaign—in the same way. I guess that's why we call them family values, they're instilled by the process of primary socialization, without the benefit of ethical theory or moral philosophy. And for most people, new values, such as an acute concern for the pain and suffering of animals or for endangered species, just seem spontaneously to bubble up in consciousness.

Still, I think, though most people may not be at all aware of it, that every day of our lives—from our tenderest years to our old age—we live, move, and have our being in an ambient intellectual ether. That ordinary people interpret their experience by means of a conceptual framework, quite unbeknownst to them, may not be evident to us when we are reflecting on our own culture, because we too may take the prevailing worldview for granted. We routinely mistake for reality itself an elaborate cognitive superstructure imposed upon phenomenal consciousness. But students of another and very different culture are keenly aware that ordinary people in that culture unconsciously filter sensory and affective experience through a conceptual framework. Because that framework—and thus that culture's "reality"—is often so strikingly different from his or her own, the inquiring outsider cannot help but notice it.

For example, anthropologist A. Irving Hallowell, a student of woodland American Indian peoples, writes,

> Human beings in whatever culture are provided with cognitive orientation in a cosmos; there is "order" and "reason" rather than chaos. There are basic premises and principles implied, even if these do not happen to be consciously formulated and articulated by the people themselves. We are confronted with the philosophical implications of their thought, the nature of the world of being as they conceive it. If we pursue the problem deeply enough we come face to face with a relatively unexplored territory—ethnometaphysics.[10]

We live today in a culture undergoing a profound paradigm shift. Like the anthropologist confronting the strange cognitive orientation of people in another, very foreign culture, we are also keenly aware that our compatriots have a worldview—whether they know it or not—because the waxing new set of ideas uncomfortably coexists with the waning old set. Students of another culture are also keenly aware how intimately linked to a more general conceptual framework are its norms, values, ethics, and morality. For example, anthropologist Clifford Geertz writes,

In recent anthropological discussion the moral and aesthetic aspects of a given culture, the evaluative elements, have been summed up in the term "ethos," while the cognitive, existential aspects have been designated by the term "world view." A people's ethos is the tone, character, and quality of their life, its moral and aesthetic style and mode; it is the underlying attitude toward themselves and their world that life reflects. Their world view is the picture of the way things in sheer actuality are, their concept of nature, of self, of society. It contains their most comprehensive ideas of order.[11]

But Geertz goes on to draw attention to the fact that although ethos and worldview may be distinguished for purposes of analysis, in the living context of culture, they are thoroughly blended together. "The powerfully coercive 'ought' is felt to grow out of the comprehensive, factual 'is,'" he says, and by his choice of language indicates sensitivity to the academic philosophical controversy dating from Hume, often mislabeled, "the Naturalistic Fallacy." "The tendency to synthesize world view and ethos at some level, if not logically necessary, is at least empirically coercive; if it is not philosophically justified, it is at least pragmatically universal."[12]

Although anthropologist Paul Radin wrote an influential work entitled *Primitive Man as Philosopher,* the consensus of anthropological opinion seems to be that the prevailing worldview in most nonliterate cultures, like Topsy, just grew, just evolved, without significant input from native philosophers. Nonliterate cultural worldviews, in other words, seem not to have been self-consciously created by an intellectual elite, by a cadre of speculative shamans, who think them up and disseminate them to everyone else. And indeed, if we imagine the process of worldview and ethos genesis like that, it is just as implausible to suppose that the prevailing literate Western worldview is a product of philosophical excogitation.

Weston correctly points out that the prevailing modern "ethic of persons" and the intimately associated concept of "rights" gradually evolved in Western civilization. Material cultural forces, such as the printing press and the availability of the Bible in vernacular languages, helped to create persons and their rights. Weston asks us to "Imagine the extraordinary self-preoccupation created by having to choose for the first time between rival versions of the same revelation, with not only one's eternal soul in the balance, but often one's earthly life as well. Only against such a background of practice did it become possible to begin to experience oneself as an individual, separate from others, beholden to inner voices and 'one's own values,' 'giving direction to one's life' oneself . . . and bearing the responsibility for one's choices."[13]

On the other hand, there can be little doubt that past philosophers have left an indelible stamp on the prevailing Western worldview. Notice how Weston assumes that the early modern protoperson is a dualist, concerned with his or her "eternal soul" as well as with his or her "earthly life." Right down to the present, most moderns take it for granted that their "physical" bodies are inhabited by an independently existing psychic substance. Keeping up with my general reading in the field, for example, I came across the following sentence in the *Journal of Philosophy:* "Friends, of course, inhabit separate bodies."[14] Friends usually inhabit separate houses and often inhabit separate bioregions, but do they *inhabit* separate bodies? "Of course" they do, the author avers. He can be so sure only because he uncritically accepts the popular view that persons are psychic substances; and while sojourning in "this world" they inhabit bodies. Aren't nearly all contemporary Christian children taught to recite the following prayer at bedtime?: "Now I lay me down to sleep, I pray the Lord my soul to keep; if I should die before I wake, I pray the Lord my soul to take."

Such a prayer would make no sense to Buddhists who hold the doctrine of anatman or no-self and hope not for eternal spiritual life, but extinction—liberation from samsara—if they should die before they wake. The Hebrew Bible has practically nothing to say about the soul or about what doubtless to Moses would have seemed the paradoxical, indeed, the apparently self-contradictory idea of life after death. Could Moses, by the way, even comprehend the verbally simple proposition that "Friends inhabit separate bodies"? "Tents, do you mean?" Moses might

quizzically reply, "I thought I heard you say 'bodies.'"

The concept of the soul was introduced into Western thought by Pythagoras. It was developed and enriched by Plato. This essentially Greek philosophical notion—that one's true self is an independently existing immortal soul temporarily residing in an alien earthy body—became a cornerstone of the Hellenistic hybrid religion, Christianity. And with the eventual triumph of that religion in the West, the concept of the soul became a key element of the prevailing Western worldview.

Another characteristic feature of the prevailing Western worldview is mechanism, the view that the physical world is ultimately composed of externally related inert material particles which are assembled into various macroscopic aggregates, that all events in the physical world are causally determined, and that all causal relations are ultimately mechanical, the direct transfer of kinetic energy from one material mass to another.

Proof that mechanism is a fundamental feature of the prevailing Western worldview is the fervent faith placed by most people in modern medicine, the great prestige of medical doctors, and the proportion of the gross national product of the United States and other industrialized nations spent on health care. When people's health or in some cases their very lives are on the line, their actions betray their beliefs. And in such circumstances most people turn unquestioningly to the medical establishment. But modern medicine is almost a caricature of mechanism. The whole human being is reduced to a body which is objectified and discussed—by the doctor with the body's resident soul—in impersonal terms. Diagnosis consists of identifying the broken part and a cure is effected either by means of surgery, a mechanical procedure par excellence, or by prescribing chemical medicines, which work mechanically at the molecular level of organization.

But who could say that this fundamental element of the prevailing Western worldview was not the creation of philosophers? Leucippus and Democritus invented the concept of the atomic particle and, I would argue, the complementary concept of homogenous, isotropic physical space. Geometry, the analysis of space so conceived, was begun by Pythagoras, advanced in the Academy of Plato, and systematized by Euclid. In the seventeenth century, Galileo, Descartes, and Newton synthesized the Democritean ontology and Euclidean geometry to create the mechanical natural philosophy. Engineers applied the concepts that Newton so powerfully and persuasively articulated to create an array of machines—weaving machines, sewing machines, steam engines, automobiles, airplanes, rockets, etc. Recall Weston's cogent argument that the advent of the printing press helped to create the ethics of persons. But the printing press itself was an early embodiment of the mechanical intellectual motif. (In this connection it is revealing to remember that when Aristotle discusses atomism he uses the letters of the alphabet to illustrate how the atoms differ from one another).[15] Look around you at this thoroughly mechanized environment. It didn't just happen. It isn't just the result of an inevitable process of blind technical evolution. It is, rather, the direct legacy of Western natural philosophy going all the way back to the Presocratics. As Ludwig von Bertalanffy perceptively comments,

> The *Weltanschauung,* the view of life and the world, of the man in the street—the chap who repairs your car or sells you an insurance policy—is a product of Lucretius Carus, Newton, Locke, Darwin, Adam Smith, Ricardo, Freud, and Watson—even though you may safely bet that the high school or even the university graduate has never heard of most of them or knows of Freud only through the Dear Abby column of his newspaper.[16]

If Western philosophy played a major role in the creation of the prevailing dualistic-mechanistic Western worldview, then Western philosophy would seem to have a major role to play in deconstructing it and reconstructing a new ecological-organic worldview. (By "philosophy" I mean "philosophy" in the old-fashioned sense of the word inclusive of theory in the natural and social sciences, as well as in history and the humanities, generally, not just philosophy as practiced by today's narrowly specialized professional philosophers. In this sense, Albert Einstein, Niels Bohr, and Werner Heisenberg are philosophers as are Aldo Leopold, Rachel Carson, and Eugene Odum.)

In my opinion, the seminal paper in environmental ethics is "The Historical Roots of Our Ecologic Crisis" by Lynn White Jr. His brassy and cavalier critique of Christianity as the ultimate cause of our contemporary environmental malaise overshadows a more general (and more credible) subtext in that essay. Four or five times he reiterates the claim that what we do depends upon what we think and thus that if we are to effect any lasting changes in behavior, we must first effect fundamental changes in our worldview: "What shall we do?" he asks, about our environmental crisis. "No one yet knows. Unless we think about fundamentals, our specific measures may produce new backlashes more serious than those they are designed to remedy."[17] Is he right about this? Sure. For example, the Green Revolution and Eucalyptus afforestation programs, couched in the modern industrial paradigm, have proved to be socially and environmentally disastrous in recipient countries.[18] Certainly they created "new backlashes more serious than those they were designed to remedy." In the next paragraph, White adds, "The issue is whether a democratized world can survive its own implications. Presumably we cannot unless we rethink our axioms."[19]

Toward the middle of his infamous essay, White returns to this subtext:

> What people do about their ecology [that is, how people treat their natural environments] depends on what they think about themselves in relation to things around them. Human ecology is deeply conditioned by beliefs about our nature and destiny— that is, by religion. To Western eyes this is very evident in, say, India or Ceylon [that is, Sri Lanka]. It is equally true of ourselves and of our medieval ancestors.[20]

And in his peroration White writes,

> What we do about ecology [that is, what we do about environmental problems] depends on our ideas of the man-nature relationship. More science and more technology are not going to get us out of the present ecologic crisis until we find a new religion or rethink our old one.[21]

White, of course, rejects the first alternative, finding a new religion, and opts for the second, rethinking our old ones, Judaism, Christianity, and Islam. Finally, in his penultimate sentence, he writes, "We must rethink and refeel our nature and destiny."[22]

The agenda for a future environmental philosophy thus was set. First, we identify and criticize our inherited beliefs about the nature of nature, human nature, and the relationship between the two. White himself initiated this stage with a critique of those most evident biblical ideas of nature, "man," and the man-nature relationship. Other environmental philosophers, I among them, went on to identify and criticize the more insidious intellectual legacy of Western natural and moral philosophy going back to the Greeks. Second, we try to articulate a new natural philosophy and moral philosophy distilled from contemporary science. We try, in other words, to articulate an evolutionary-ecological worldview and an associated environmental ethic.

This two-phase program of environmental philosophy has been gaining momentum for the past two decades. In that amount of time—which is really not very much time to bring off a cultural revolution comparable to the shift from the medieval to the modern world—how effective has environmental philosophy been? In so short a time, the rethinking of our old religion that White called for is virtually a fait accompli. The stewardship interpretation of the God-"man"-nature relationship set out in Genesis is now semiofficial religious doctrine among "people of the Book"—Jews, Catholics, Protestants, even Muslims.[23] Such an interpretation and its dissemination would not have come about, or at least it would not have come about so soon, had White's despotic interpretation not provoked it. The currently institutionalized Judeo-Christian-Islamic stewardship environmental ethic was a dialectical reaction to White's critique. It has now trickled down into the synagogues and churches, and may be on its way into the mosques. Children learning about God's creation and our responsibility to care for it and pass it on intact to future generations may never hear White's name, or the names of John Black, James Barr, Robert Gordis, Jonathan Helfand, Francis

Schaeffer, Albert Fritsch, Thomas Berry, Wendell Berry, Matthew Fox, Iqtidar Zaidi, and the other Jewish, Christian, and Islamic theologians whom White provoked, but what they are being taught—and as a result of that teaching how in the future they may try to be good stewards of God's creation—owes a lot to Lynn White and those whom he challenged to reconceive Judeo-Christian-Islamic attitudes and values toward nature.

But if you think I'm impossibly biased—a philosopher affirming the power of ideas and defending the practical efficacy of philosophy—then perhaps you can trust Dave Foreman, environmental activist extraordinaire, to provide a candid assessment of the role that environmental philosophy has played in shaping the contemporary environmental movement. Remember that it was Foreman who wrote, "Let our actions set the finer points of our philosophy."[24] And in a 1983 debate with Eugene C. Hargrove about the wisdom of monkeywrenching, it was Foreman who dismissed environmental philosophers in the following terms: "Too often, philosophers are rendered impotent by their inability to act without analyzing everything to absurd detail. To act, to trust your instincts, to go with the flow of natural forces, is an underlying philosophy. Talk is cheap. Action is dear."[25]

Eight years later, Foreman changed his tune. In "The New Conservation Movement," Foreman identified four forces that are shaping the conservation movement of the 1990s. They are, and I quote, first "academic philosophy," second, "conservation biology," third, "independent local groups," and fourth, "Earth First!" That's right, "academic philosophy" heads the list. This is some of what Foreman has to say about it:

> During the 1970s, philosophy professors in Europe, North America, and Australia started looking at environmental ethics as a worthy focus for discussion and exploration. . . . By 1980, enough interest had coalesced for an academic journal called *Environmental Ethics* to appear. . . . An international network of specialists in environmental ethics developed, leading to one of the more vigorous debates

in modern philosophy. At first, little of this big blow in the ivory towers drew the notice of working conservationists, but by the end of the '80s, few conservation group staff members or volunteer activists were unaware of the Deep Ecology–Shallow Environmentalism distinction or of the general discussion about ethics and ecology. At the heart of the discussion was the question of whether other species possessed intrinsic value or had value solely because of their use to humans. Ginger Rogers to this Fred Astaire was the question what, if any, ethical obligations humans had to nature or other species.[26]

And part of the way that Earth First!—last but not least on Foreman's list—helped to shape the new conservation movement was by bringing "the discussion of biocentric philosophy—Deep Ecology—out of dusty academic journals."[27]

Clearly Foreman understands the power of ideas. Of course, we philosophers do not simply create new environmental ideas and ideals ex nihilo. Rather, we try to articulate and refine those that the intellectual dialectic of the culture has ripened. To employ a Socratic metaphor, we philosophers are the midwives assisting the birth of new cultural notions and associated norms. In so doing we help to change our culture's worldview and ethos. Therefore, since all human actions are carried out and find their meaning and significance in a cultural ambience of ideas, we speculative environmental philosophers are inescapably environmental activists.

All environmentalists should be activists, but activism can take a variety of forms. The way that environmental philosophers can be the most effective environmental activists is by doing environmental philosophy. Of course, not everyone can be or wants or needs to be an environmental philosopher. Those who are not can undertake direct environmental action in other ways. My point is that environmental philosophers should not feel compelled to stop thinking, talking, and writing about environmental ethics, and go do something about it instead—because talk is cheap and action is dear. In thinking, talking, and writing about environmental ethics, environmental philosophers already have their shoulders to the wheel, helping to reconfigure the pre-vailing cultural worldview and thus helping to push general practice in the direction of environmental responsibility.

NOTES

1. Kenneth M. Sayre, "An Alternative View of Environmental Ethics," *Environmental Ethics* 13 (1991): 200.

2. Sayre, "An Alternative View of Environmental Ethics," 195.

3. Bryan Norton, *Toward Unity Among Environmentalists* (New York: Oxford University Press, 1991).

4. Warwick Fox, "New Philosophical Directions in Environmental Decision-Making," unpublished manuscript, 18, emphasis added.

5. Fox, "New Philosophical Directions in Environmental Decision-Making," 18–19, emphasis in original.

6. Anthony Weston, "Before Environmental Ethics," *Environmental Ethics* 14 (1992): 321–38.

7. Anthony Weston, "On Callicott's Case Against Moral Pluralism," *Environmental Ethics* 13 (1991): 284.

8. Ralph Waldo Emerson, "Self-Reliance," in *The Collected Works of Ralph Waldo Emerson, Volume 2, Essays: First Series,* ed. Alfred R. Ferguson et. al. (Cambridge: Harvard University-Belknap Press, 1971), 33.

9. Sayre, "An Alternative View of Environmental Ethics," 205.

10. A. Irving Hallowell, "Ojibwa Ontology, Behavior and World View," in *Culture in History,* ed. Stanley Diamond (New York: Columbia University Press, 1960), 20.

11. Clifford Geertz, *The Interpretation of Cultures* (New York: Basic Books, 1973), 126–127.

12. Geertz, *The Interpretation of Cultures,* 127.

13. Weston, "Before Environmental Ethics," 331, emphasis added.

14. Michael J. Meyer, "Rights between Friends," *Journal of Philosophy* 89 (1992): 476.

15. Aristotle, *Metaphysica,* 985b17.

16. Ludwig von Bertalanffy, *Robots, Men, and Minds* (New York: Brazillier, 1967).

17. Lynn White Jr., "The Historical Roots of Our Ecologic Crisis," in *Ecology and Religion in History,* ed. David Spring and Eileen Spring (New York: Harper Torchbooks, 1974), 18, emphasis added

18. See Ramachandra Guha, *The Unquiet Woods: Ecological Change and Peasant Resistance in the Himalaya* (Berkeley: University of California Press, 1990) and Van-

dana Shiva, *The Violence of the Green Revolution: Third World Agriculture, Ecology, and Politics* (London: Zed Books, 1991).

19. White, "The Historical Roots," 19.

20. White, "The Historical Roots," 23.

21. White, "The Historical Roots," 28.

22. White, "The Historical Roots," 31.

23. See David Ehrenfeld and Philip J. Bently, "Judaism and the Practice of Stewardship," *Judaism: A Quarterly Journal of Jewish Life and Thought* 34 (1985); Anonymous, *Strangers and Guests: Toward Community in the Heartland* (Demoines, Iowa: Heartland Project, 1980); Anonymous, *The Land: God's Giving, Our Caring* (Minneapolis, Minn.: Augsburg Publishing House, 1982); Abou Bakr Ahmed Ba Kader, Abdul Latif Tawfik El Shirazy Al Sabbagh, Mohamed Al Sayyed Al Glenid, and Mouel Yousef Samarri Izzidien, *Islamic Principles for the Conservation of the Natural Environment* (Gland, Switzerland: IUCN, 1983).

24. Dave Foreman, "More on Earth First! and the Monkey Wrench Gang," *Environmental Ethics* 5 (1993): 95.

25. Foreman, "More on Earth First!", 95.

26. Dave Foreman, "The New Conservation Movement," *Wild Earth* 1 (Summer 1991): 8.

27. Foreman, "The New Conservation Movement," p. 10.

Taking Environmental Ethics Public

Andrew Light

At present, environmental ethics, especially in North America, is dominated by a concern with abstract questions of value theory, primarily, though not exclusively, focused on the issue of whether nature has "intrinsic value," or more generally noninstrumental value, understood in a nonanthropocentric scheme of valuing. Such work, as the introduction to this volume suggests, not only makes environmental ethics a form of normative ethics, but also creates a body of metaethical work which challenges the traditional assumptions of normative ethics. If nature has such noninstrumental value, then a wide range of duties, obligations, and rights may obtain in our treatment of it.

While this goal in the field is philosophically sound it has tended to engender two unfortunate results: (1) the focus on the value of nature itself has largely excluded discussion of the beneficial ways in which arguments for environmental protection can be based on human interests, and relatedly (2) the focus on somewhat abstract concepts of value theory has pushed environmental ethics away from discussion of which arguments morally motivate people to embrace more supportive environmental views. As such, those agents of change who will effect efforts at environmental protection, namely humans, have been oddly left out of discussions about the moral value of nature. As a result, environmental ethics has become more abstract and less able to contribute to cross-disciplinary discussions with other environmental professionals on the resolution of environmental problems, especially those professionals who also have an interest in human welfare.

In recent years a critique of this predominant trend in environmental ethics has emerged from within the pragmatist tradition in American philosophy.[1] The force of this critique is driven by the intuition that environmental philosophy cannot afford to be quiescent about the public reception of ethical arguments over the value of nature. The original motivations of environmental philosophers for turning their philosophical insights to the environment support such a position. Environmental philosophy evolved out of a concern about the state of the growing environmental crisis, and a conviction that a philosophical contribution could be made to the resolution of this crisis. But if environmental philosophers spend all of their time debating non-human–centered forms of value theory they will arguably never get very far in making such a contribution. For example, to continue to ignore human motivations for the act of valuing nature causes many in the field to overlook the fact that most people find it very difficult to extend moral consideration to plants and animals on the grounds that these entities possess some form of intrinsic, inherent, or otherwise conceived nonanthropocentric value. It is even more difficult for people to recognize that nonhumans could have rights. Claims about the value of nature as such do not appear to resonate with the ordinary moral intuitions of most people who, after all, spend most of their lives thinking of value, moral obligations, and rights in exclusively human terms. Indeed, while most environmental philosophers begin their work with the assumption that most people think of value in human-centered terms (a problem that has been decried since the very early days of the field), few have considered the problem of how a non-human–centered approach to valuing nature can ever appeal to such human intuitions. The particular version of the pragmatist critique of environmental ethics that I have endorsed recognizes that we need to rethink the utility of anthropocentric arguments in environmental moral and political theory, not necessarily because the traditional nonanthropocentric arguments in the field are false, but because they hamper attempts to contribute to the public discussion of environmental problems, in terms familiar to the public.

If the pragmatist critique is taken seriously, then environmental ethics (and perhaps environmental philosophy more broadly) necessarily encompasses both a traditional philosophical task involving an in-

vestigation into the value of nature, and a second public task involving the articulation of arguments that will be morally motivating concerning environmental protection. This article will briefly overview the case for a demarcation of these tasks and make a claim about their relative importance in relation to each other in the context of my methodological form of environmental pragmatism. The set of arguments I will suggest here answer the call by Willott and Schmidtz at the end of their introduction to this volume to consider not only which values in the environment matter, but also to "figure out what really works." I take this to mean that we should not only worry about how to apply a new scheme of valuing nature, but also consider testing our schemes of valuing nature on the grounds of whether they could ever be convincing to a critical mass of other humans.

1. WHO IS ENVIRONMENTAL PHILOSOPHY FOR?

An open question that I believe still plagues most environmental philosophers is what our discipline is actually for, and consequently, who our audience is. Willott and Schmidtz suggest that environmental ethics is not like other fields of applied ethics—such as medical or business ethics—because it is not tied to a particular profession. Not coincidentally, I believe, environmental ethics has evolved largely as a conversation that occurs mostly among philosophers, directed primarily toward other environmental philosophers and our students (as most traditional philosophical subfields are usually directed), often untethered by the burdens of everyday environmental disputes. But given the history of the field, one would think that the ambitions would be greater.

As has been demonstrated in this collection, environmental ethics got off the ground in the early 1970s through the work of thinkers as diverse as Arne Naess, Val Plumwood, Holmes Rolston III, Peter Singer, and Richard Sylvan, who all seemed concerned with how philosophers could make some sort of contribution to the actual resolution of environmental problems, not simply contribute new ideas on nature to theories of value. While it is certainly true that a contribution to value theory could help to resolve environmental problems, the worry is that such discussions usually have little impact beyond those who actually participate in the development of such theories.

But if environmental philosophy is for an audience other than philosophers, who is it for? There are a number of candidates. Realizing this other potential, however, requires reevaluating Willott and Schmidtz's suggestion with respect to the relative difference of environmental ethics from other applied fields. While surely they are correct that environmental ethics is not tied to a profession, there certainly are professions, and other kinds of human activity, concerned with the environment that the field could be in a position to assist. Environmental philosophy might also serve as (1) a guide for environmental activists searching for ethical justifications for activities in defense of other animals and ecosystems, (2) an applied ethic for natural resource managers, (3) a general tool for policy makers, helping them to shape more responsible environmental policies, or, beyond this still further, (4) be directed at the public at large, attempting to expand their notions of moral obligations beyond the traditional confines of anthropocentric moral concerns.

For reasons that I will save until later, my usual answer to the question of who environmental philosophy is for is "all of the above," though I think that environmental philosophers should focus their energies more on category (3) policy makers and (4) the general public. While it is undeniable that the work of environmental philosophers on topics like value theory could be helpful for all of these audiences, these contributions have, by and large, not been delivered in a manner that is very useful since the theories are often unconnected to how humans actually think about environmental questions. But I think environmental ethicists, perhaps more so than other applied ethicists, should pay closer attention to the issue of whether their work is useful to the public and policy makers.

My rationale goes something like this: if the original reason for philosophers starting this field in the first place was principally to make a philosophical contribution to the resolution of environmental problems (consistent with the flurry of activity in the early 1970s around environmental concerns), then the continuation (indeed, the urgency) of those problems demands that philosophers do all that they can to actually help change present policies and attitudes now involving environmental problems rather than restrict their work to the traditional task of theory building. If we philosophers only end up talking to each other then we have failed as environmental professionals. But if we can somehow help to convince policy makers to form better policies—or, more accurately, come up with reasons to morally ground better environmental policies—and aid in making the case to the public at large to support these policies for ethical reasons, then we will have made a contribution to the resolution of environmental problems similar to the sorts of contributions made by other environmental professionals, though constituted through our particular talents as philosophers. This goal of moving closer to other environmental professionals is also very important.

At present, the focus in environmental philosophy on the search for a description of the nonanthropocentric value of nature also separates it from other forms of environmental inquiry. Most other environmental professionals look at environmental problems in a human context rather than trying to define an abstract sense of natural value outside of the human appreciation or interaction with nature. Fields such as environmental sociology and environmental health, for example, are concerned not with the environment per se but the environment as the location of human community. This is not to say that these fields reduce the value of nature to a crude resource instrumentalism. It is to say instead that they realize that a discussion of nature outside of the human context impedes our ability to discuss ways in which anthropogenic impacts on nature can be understood and ameliorated. If environmental philosophers continue to pursue their work as a contribution to value theory only, they cut themselves off from the rest of the environmental community, which seeks to provide practical solutions to environmental problems, solutions that it is almost trite these days to suggest—must be interdisciplinary. Further, if environmental philosophers define the terms of their work in language radically different from that of other environmental professionals, then they will quickly find themselves operating in isolation, unable to make a contribution to the interdisciplinary discussion of environmental issues.

Now, one may fairly wonder how environmental philosophers can make a contribution to something other than value theory. After all, what else are they trained to do as philosophers? My claim is that if philosophers could help to articulate moral foundations for environmental policies in a way that is translatable to the general public, they will have made a contribution to the resolution of environmental problems commensurate with their talents and in a fashion compatible with the work of other environmental professionals. But making such a contribution may require doing environmental philosophy in some different ways. At a minimum it requires a more public philosophy, as the American pragmatist philosopher John Dewey envisioned, though one specifically more focused on making the kind of arguments that resonate with the moral intuitions that most people carry around with them on an everyday basis. A public environmental philosophy would not rest with a mere description of the value of nature (even a description that justified a secure foundation for something as strong as a claim for the rights of nature). A public environmental philosophy would further question whether the description of the value of nature it provided could possibly cause human agents to change their moral attitudes about nature, taking into account the overwhelming ethical anthropocentrism of most humans.[2] As such, a public environmental philosophy would have to either embrace an enlightened anthropocentrism about natural value or endorse a pluralism which admitted the possibility, indeed the necessity, of sometimes describing natural value in human-centered terms rather than always through nonanthropocentric conceptions of natural value.

In a strong sense, this suggestion is consistent with Willott and Schmidtz's claim in the introduction that "doing environmental ethics without pertinent facts is . . . unethical." Willott and Schmidtz no doubt have in mind the idea of doing environmental ethics without recourse to facts about nature. Here I am suggesting that another pertinent set of facts to take into account is how humans think about nature.[3] And whether we like it or not, most humans think about nature in human-centered terms.

In a survey by Ben Minteer and Robert Manning about the sources of positive attitudes toward environmental protection in Vermont, respondents overwhelmingly indicated that the reason why they most thought the environment should be protected is because they think that we have positive obligations to protect nature for *human* future generations.[4] More exhaustive surveys of American attitudes toward environmental protection have also found such results. In the preparatory work for their landmark study of American environmental attitudes in the U.S., Willett Kempton and his colleagues found that obligations to future generations was so powerfully intuitive a reason for most people to favor environmental protection that they would volunteer this view before they were asked. In a series of interviews that helped determine the focus of their questions for the survey, the authors remarked:

> We found that our informants' descendants loom large in their thinking about environmental issues. Although our initial set of questions never asked about children, seventeen of the twenty lay informants themselves brought up children or future generations as a justification for environmental protection. Such a high proportion of respondents mentioning the same topic is unusual in answering an open-ended question. In fact, concern for the future of children and descendants emerged as one of the strongest values in the interviews.[5]

The larger survey conducted by Kempton, which included questions about obligations to the future, confirmed these findings. Any philosophical views that would extend such intuitions of necessity have to start with anthropocentric premises.

But does my suggestion that we begin to make arguments closer to anthropocentric, everyday, moral intuitions mean that environmental philosophers must give up their pursuit of a theory of nonanthropocentric natural value in order to make their philosophy more publicly useful? I don't think so. It only requires that philosophers be willing to rearticulate their philosophical views about the value of nature in terms that will morally motivate policy makers and the general public even when they have come to their views about the value of nature through a nonanthropocentric approach. A public environmental philosophy requires a certain skill at translation, and a tolerance for pluralism in moral theory—that is to say, it requires philosophers to accept that there will be more than one way to express the value of a given natural object or environmental practice and some of those ways may be anthropocentric, such as the value of preserving nature out of obligations to human future generations.[6]

I call this view "methodological environmental pragmatism." As I will explain in more detail, by this term I do not mean an application of the traditional writings of the American pragmatists—Dewey, William James, Charles Sanders Pierce, etc.—to environmental problems. Instead, I mean that environmental philosophy of any variety ought to be pursued within the context of a recognition that a responsible and complete environmental philosophy includes a public component with a clear policy emphasis. It is perfectly fine for philosophers to continue their search for a true and foundational nonanthropocentric description of the value of nature. But we are remiss if we do not set aside that search at times and try to make other, perhaps more pedestrian ethical arguments in a public context which may have an audience with an anthropocentric public. Environmental pragmatism, as I see it, is, properly speaking, a methodology permitting environmental philosophers to consistently endorse a pluralism allowing for one kind of philosophical task inside the philosophy community—searching for the "real" value of nature, though this is not a task that all environmental philosophers have to take up—and another task outside of that community—articulating a value to nature that resonates with the public. Environmental pragmatism in my sense is agnostic concerning the existence of nonanthropocentric natural value or the relative superiority of one form of natural value verses another. Those embracing this view can either continue to pursue nonanthropocentric theories or they can take a more traditional pragmatist stance denying the existence of such value.[7]

A more traditional pragmatist would be more inclined to engage in the debates over intrinsic value mentioned in the introduction to this volume. Such theorists would argue, for instance, that the question of whether a redwood has intrinsic value is answered by the pragmatist claim that nothing has value apart from the act of human valuing of a thing. But if environmental pragmatism in my sense is truly concerned with making environmental philosophy relevant to the actual public discussion and resolution of environmental problems, then it cannot afford to serve as a launching pad for yet another round of metaethical debates in environmental ethics. To insist that all environmental philosophers give up their nonanthropocentric commitments in favor of a Deweyian naturalism, for example, would be an invitation to plunge further into debates that can only be resolved (if ever) through a long and protracted discussion of the metaphysical relationship between humans, nature, and the act of valuing. As such, I believe that the principle task for an environmental pragmatism is not to philosophically obviate the metaethical and metaphysical foundations of current trends in environmental ethics, but rather to impress upon environmental philosophers the need to take up the largely empirical question of what morally motivates humans to change their attitude, behaviors, and policy preferences toward those more supportive of long-term environmental sustainability.

But my discussion so far has been exceedingly general. If we are to justify a shift in focus in environmental philosophy at least partly toward a public task, then how will this shift be justified in philosophical terms? What are its parameters, and what are the acceptable limits of this philosophical project so that it will remain a philosophical project and not just a project in rhetoric or communication studies? What is the relationship between the traditional task in environmental ethics of finding a moral foundation for valuing nature, often in nonanthropocentric terms, and the public task of appealing to anthropocentric intuitions? I cannot fully justify my methodological pragmatism in the space provided here, so for now will simply sketch out how such a form of public philosophy might work.

2. TWO TASKS, TWO COMMUNITIES

It should be clear by now that endorsing a methodological environmental pragmatism requires an acceptance of some form of anthropocentrism in environmental ethics, if only because we have sound empirical evidence that humans think about the value of nature in human terms and pragmatists insist that we must pay attention to how humans think about the value of nature. Indeed, as I said above, it is a common presupposition among committed nonanthropocentrists that the proposition that humans are anthropocentrists is true, though regrettable. There are many problems involved in the wholesale rejection of anthropocentrism by most environmental philosophers. While I cannot adequately explain my reservations to this rejection, for now I hope the reader will accept the premise that not expressing reasons for environmental priorities in human terms seriously hinders our ability to communicate a moral basis for better environmental policies to the public. Both anthropocentric and nonanthropocentric claims should be open to us.

But of course we cannot simply pick and choose our application of philosophical conceptions of value willy-nilly, without some reason for our choices. We must have reasons that support appeals to human-centered moral motivations without endorsing crass versions of anthropocentrism (and a concomitant rejection of nonanthropocentrism). How then can a methodologically pragmatic anthropocentrism be made palatable even to those who doubt that anthropocentrism is an adequate basis for an environmental ethic?

As suggested before, for a variety of reasons, environmental ethics has evolved over the course of the last thirty years as a fairly abstract philosophical activity. Certainly the reasons for why the field has evolved primarily as a branch of value theory are understandable. Like other areas of applied ethics, environmental ethicists have long sought intellectual credibility as a branch of philosophy, or, in other words, as part of the larger philosophical community. While some may disagree, environmental ethics has done a good job of situating itself as part of that community (and I will use "community" in what follows in a very ill defined and general sense) while remaining quite distinctive, especially given its emphasis on nonanthropocentric theories of value.

But we are also part of another community as well, namely the environmental community. And while the connection has never been clear, the field continues to be part of at least an ongoing conversation about environmental issues, if not an outright intentional community of environmentalists. The necessity of engaging in a policy, or at least problem-oriented environmental ethics, is driven by the particular exigencies of the environmental community and the problems that it orients itself around. The drive to create a public environmental philosophy is thus not only motivated by a desire to actively participate in the resolution of environmental problems, but to hold up our philosophical end, as it were, among the community of environmentalists.

But how should environmental ethicists serve the environmental community? The answer for the pragmatist begins in a recognition that if philosophy is to serve a larger community then it must allow the interests of the community to help to determine the philosophical problems that the theorist addresses.[8] This does not mean that the pragmatic philosopher necessarily finds all the problems that a given community is concerned with as the problems for her own work. Nor does it mean that she assumes her conclusions before analyzing a problem like a hired legal counsel who doesn't inquire as to the guilt or innocence of his client. It only means that a fair description of the work of pragmatic philosophers is to investigate the problems of interest to their community and then articulate the policy recommendations of the community on these problems to those outside of their community, that is, to the public at large.

Knowing how to forge this connection with a larger community and understanding its relationship to more traditional philosophical projects is a tricky, but not insurmountable problem. To begin with, we can take Bryan Norton's convergence hypothesis as a plausible point of departure. First expressed in Norton's *Toward Unity among Environmentalists* (excerpted earlier in this section of this book), and then later explicated in a series of papers and defenses of the view, the convergence hypothesis is an empirical claim about the likely overlap between environmentalists of different orientations. After spending some time studying the various demands of different environmental organizations, from radicals to liberals, Norton came to the conclusion that there was more that was agreed upon between anthropocentrists and nonanthropocentrists than many people had assumed. The convergence hypothesis encapsulates this overlap inside a practical framework:

> Provided anthropocentrists consider the full breadth of human values as they unfold into the indefinite future, and provided nonanthropocentrists endorse a consistent and coherent version of the view that nature has intrinsic value, all sides may be able to endorse a common policy direction.[9]

Norton's convergence hypothesis has been often misunderstood as an overly optimistic claim. Commentators have lined up to provide Norton with examples of where anthropocentrists and nonanthropocentrists disagree. But this is to miss the point of the suggestion: empirically, there is much agreement among a wide variety of environmentalists concerning what they want to achieve. Assuming that this claim holds up under empirical scrutiny—and so far it has—we can begin to build an agenda for a public environmental philosophy on top of this claim and orient it around two clear tasks for environmental philosophers: (1) to help express the environmental community's position on some environmental problem to those outside the community who may not even see the problem as a problem and (2) to attempt to influence the views within the environmental community of a problem of interest to that community. But more detail is needed.

Task 1. The first task of a methodologically pragmatist environmental philosophy is its public task. Here, following the convergence hypothesis, the role of environmental philosophers is to take those issues that the environmental community agrees upon, for whatever reasons, and communicate these issues to the larger public. These issues will be the relatively easy ones that most environmental philosophers, if not all, also already endorse. But our role here is not just rhetorical, it is necessarily philosophical. The goal is to come up with ethical grounds upon which environmental policies can be justified. Not just any grounds, however, but those grounds which will motivate the broader public to act on or assent to the passage of environmental policies even if they do not count themselves as environmentalists. The successful pursuit of this task requires environmental philosophers to endorse, at least publicly, a robust and consistent pluralism that allows for both anthropocentric and nonanthropocentric arguments, and attention to research in moral psychology on what reasons morally motivate people to actually change their lifestyle or behavior. Since many people are motivated by anthropocentric reasons, environmental pragmatists engaged in task 1 will of necessity have to endorse anthropocentrism in a public policy–oriented context. I call this form of anthropocentrism a "strategic anthropocentrism" which operates according to the following rule of thumb: (1) Always first pursue the anthropocentric justification for the environmental policy in order to persuade a broader array of people to embrace the view, because (2) anthropocentric justifications can most plausibly speak to people's ordinary moral intuitions more persuasively than nonanthropocentric justifications. But just as the convergence hypothesis is empirical, so is the endorsement of strategic anthropocentrism. If it turns out to be the case that the best social science research on why people act on environmental policies in general, or even on a particular issue, tells us that a nonanthropocentric justification will better provide a warrant for action, then a strategic anthropocentrism must give way to a strategic nonanthropocentrism.

No doubt many will object to describing task 1 as philosophical at all. Is this not simply rhetoric driven by an unreasoned and careless endorsement of substantial policy goals? But I believe this objection fails. What is being asked of philosophers here is not an endorsement of ends that they do not agree with, but rather the pursuit of a reasonable project of engaging the public on the moral grounds of better environmental policies, which surely any environmental philosopher would see as a worthy goal. An environmental philosopher at work at task 1 cannot offer just any reason for endorsing a given environmental policy, but must stick to the traditional criteria of what counts as a good philosophical argument, such as coherence, consistency and adequacy.

A philosopher engaging in this task must also not stray from other expected ethical norms. If a methodological pragmatist were an atheist, and was called by a Christian church group to speak at a Sunday service on the importance of voting on a referendum expanding a local forest preserve, the pragmatist could not say, "Jesus sent me here today to tell you to vote for this bill," because she thought it would be more convincing to the congregation. What she could do is come to the congregation with an awareness of how seriously they took the Christian Bible and argue that there is an ethic of stewardship in the Old Testament that would encourage a favorable view on the forest preserve bill. Sincerity is also clearly an issue. No one endorsing this methodology would be required to say things that they felt very strongly were false, simply to convey a reason to support a policy agreed on by the larger environmental community. But a philosopher endorsing this view would still have a warrant to articulate a multiplicity of arguments for a converged upon policy which presumably would go beyond those reasons that she firmly stood against.

Task 2. Because the environmental community does not always agree on its priorities, our second task is the traditional one of searching for better philosophical foundations for environmental values. As Norton says, "The convergence hypothesis does not, of course, claim that the interests of humans and interests of other species *never* diverge, only that

they *usually* converge."[10] When environmentalists are at an impasse about how to proceed, environmental ethicists must go back into the more private philosophical task of discerning the best assessment of the truth about whatever aspect of environmental value is at issue. The pluralism in public argumentation warranted in task 1 is then not granted when convergence does not exist. We could call task 2 "environmental first philosophy." Such a project is more in line with traditional philosophical practices in the field as they have been engaged in for the last thirty years. And while there is no guarantee that such a project will ever achieve a resolution between anthropocentrists and nonanthropocentrists on any given issue, it is, at first gloss, the only recourse of philosophers who are committed to trying to respond to the problems of the environmental community. Here, the environmental ethicist is acting more as a member of the philosophical community, though they are still responding to the needs of the environmental community.

It is important to note however that the relation of task 1 to task 2 is not necessarily linear: it isn't as if pragmatist philosophers can only turn to task 2 after task 1. We must always instead engage in both tasks simultaneously. Even when the environmental community agrees on its ends it is appropriate for philosophers to continually think about the foundations of environmental value and push on the converged ends to make sure that they can stand up to critical scrutiny. As we learn more about how the environment works, and consequently how we affect it, we will need to continually revise our understanding of what counts as right action in relation to the environment. Pointing out the separable importance of task 1 from task 2 is simply a way of reminding us that if we only engage in task 2 then we are not fulfilling our full potential as philosophers taking part in the environmental community. It is also a reminder that those more interested in the value theory debates of task 2 ought not to continually put up roadblocks for those doing the more public work of environmental philosophy.

This last comment further opens the discussion of the relationship between task 1 and task 2, which surely deserves more treatment than I can provide here. For example, what if someone comes to the conclusion that they have discerned the exclusive truth of the matter about how we are to value nature and that truth can only be expressed in terms of a nonanthropocentric ascription of the value of nature? If ever such a view was discerned, and if it were persuasive over all competitors, then I would assume that it could serve as the basis for a strong set of obligations, policies, even laws which could stand above and beyond the predilections of human preferences (and I am certainly open to the claim that a body of law acknowledging something like the rights of nature would be the most stable foundation for environmental protection). But assuming the view did not have such force—and I am skeptical that a nonanthropocentric view could ever get such agreement on a description of the value of nature—then our best recourse will be some kind of pluralism (task 1) aimed at making arguments that morally motivate people embedded within the regulating context of a methodological pragmatism. This view can justify articulating reasons for an end, even when we think that the end will most properly be justified for other reasons, while still working within the context of a consistent and coherent philosophical practice.

One thing more for now. Are the tasks of the environmental philosopher exhausted by these two tasks as they have been described so far? I don't think so. For one thing, a fair question could be: who counts as the environmental community to which the pragmatist environmental philosopher should respond in gauging the relative propriety of task 1 or task 2 at any given time? This is a serious problem for this view. There seems to be no fair way of discerning who counts as an environmentalist. At best, it seems that all we can fairly say at present is that someone counts as an environmentalist if they claim to be an environmentalist. (Other options for segregating "real" environmentalists seem implausible. What policy, for example, must someone endorse in order to claim that they are an environmentalist?) But this will be an unsatisfactory answer. Is there no way to exclude the "wise use" movement, which cloaks anti-environmental policies in the language of envi-

ronmentalism? This is a particularly important question for my view where the environmental ethicist's first task is driven by those policies that the environmental community comes to converge upon. How can there be convergence in a community when anti-environmentalists count as environmentalists?

This worry has lead me to further develop the terrain covered by task 2. Even though the convergence hypothesis is a nice starting point for describing the appropriate work of environmental philosophers, it need not drive the end of all philosophical inquiry or set up rigid marching orders for philosophical work. As philosophers, we ought not only to wait on convergence and then go about our public work, we should also help to fashion the converged ends of the environmental community. Specifically, environmental ethicists can help to fashion ends by working on the problem of what we might call "environmental intuitions." Before the disputes that may divide the environmental community begin, or maybe because of the ones that already have divided the community, we need an account of what counts as an environmental intuition, or a fair starting place for an environmental claim, as a way of getting to a narrower description of who counts as an environmentalist. "Environmentalists" could be defined as those who begin their arguments with such intuitions even though the specific arguments made by any given environmentalist could differ from those made by others.

The details of such an account will need to be more clearly laid out, but at minimum we can imagine that this account of intuitions would have to be one that assumes the inherent revisability of intuitions as well as articulates a relationship between environmental intuitions and environmental science as mediated through experience and experimentation. The more we know about nature, the more able we are to assess whatever nonanthropocentrists would imagine are nature's "interests," and whatever anthropocentrists would imagine are our interests in relationship to nature. For example, the horrific Yellowstone fires of several years ago settled the debate among environmentalists over the merits of fire suppression in wilderness areas. We now understand much more about fire and its role in ecosystems and know that excessive suppression actually hinders rather than helps preservation efforts by creating surplus brush matter that can fuel a fire. Any environmentalist today who maintains support for a policy of fire suppression—perhaps because they think the purpose of national parks is to preserve some bit of wilderness as an unchangeable aesthetic ideal—does so only through a willful ignorance of the best that experience and science have to offer on this issue. Legitimate environmental intuitions then must at minimum be sensitive to the received views of environmental science, as those views change over time. The challenge will be figuring out what other criteria we ought to use to describe such intuitions.

Let me close with a slogan. As a philosopher interested in the revival of a public philosophy, I'm rather fond of slogans. To date, if environmental philosophers thought that they were serving any interests, they would best be described as the interests of nature. Some, such as the deep ecologists, have been explicit about this, others have been less so. If we can conceive of environmentalism in general as being interested in two broad concerns, namely the preservation of the nature still around and the restoration of that which has been degraded by anthropogenic causes, then environmental philosophers, even when they are engaged in pedestrian and traditional debates in value theory, have been concerned primarily with the preservation and restoration of nature for nature's sake.

But the pragmatist environmental ethicist asks that we complicate this neat picture a bit and broaden the overall scope of environmental philosophy to include other interests as well. These are not the interests of those who want to destroy the environment through crude discussions of the utility of natural resources (criticized through task 2), but those who, as humans, want to work for long term environmental sustainability for a variety of reasons (promoted through task 1). So rather than thinking about environmental philosophy as being in the service of the preservation and restoration of nature itself, we should think about environmental ethics as working toward (and here's the slogan) the preservation and restoration of a human "culture of nature." Surely no progress on environmental issues, from any quarter, can succeed without the flourishing of that culture.

NOTES

1. The term "environmental pragmatism" was first used in *Environmental Pragmatism,* ed. Andrew Light and Eric Katz (London: Routledge Press, 1996), to refer to a broad range of approaches to environmental ethics, capturing under one label the similarities between the work of figures like Norton, Anthony Weston, and more historically oriented theorists like Kelly Parker, Sandra Rosenthal, and Larry Hickman. See "Environmental Ethics and Environmental Pragmatism as Contested Terrain," in *Environmental Pragmatism,* op. cit., 1–18. For a more recent summary of the development of this loosely amalgamated "school" in environmental philosophy, see Ben A. Minteer, "No Experience Necessary?: Foundationalism and the Retreat from Culture in Environmental Ethics," *Environmental Values* 7, no. 3 (August 1998): 333–48. As we will see below, I think there are at least two identifiable strains of environmental pragmatism whose compatibility is yet to be proven. This is why I hesitate to call the collection of this work a "school" of thought in the proper sense.

2. In addition to the claims that most environmental ethicists have made decrying the anthropocentrism prevalent in contemporary human societies and forms of thought that point to this palpable hurdle, Anthony Weston has argued that committed nonanthropocentrists have failed to adequately describe what a nonanthropocentric culture would possibly look like. Weston takes this failure to be indicative of the need to relax the severe denigration of anthropocentrism in the field. See Weston, "Before Environmental Ethics," in *Environmental Pragmatism,* op. cit., 139–60.

3. Several essays in the second half of this volume do discuss what it would mean to treat humans as more integral parts of the nature rather than leaving them out of these discussions entirely. Also, on the importance of evaluating proposed environmental regulations by asking whether people can afford to obey them, see David Schmidtz's paper, "Natural Enemies: An Anatomy of Environmental Conflict," *Environmental Ethics* 22, no. 4 (2000): 397–408, reprinted in this volume.

4. Ben Minteer and Robert Manning, "Pragmatism in Environmental Ethics: Democracy, Pluralism, and the Management of Nature," *Environmental Ethics* 21, no. 2 (1999): 191–207.

5. Willett Kempton et. al., *Environmental Values in American Culture* (Cambridge, MA: Massachussets Institute of Technology, 1997), 95.

6. For a longer justification of my approach to pluralism in environmental ethics, as connected to policy concerns, see my "Callicott and Naess on Pluralism," *Inquiry* 39, no. 2 (June 1996): 273–94.

7. See for example Kelly Parker, "Pragmatism and Environmental Thought," in *Environmental Pragmatism,* op. cit., 21–37, and Anthony Weston, "Before Environmental Ethics," op. cit.

8. While developed independently of each other, some readers will no doubt see a similarity between my focus on taking seriously the interests of the environmental community and Avner de-Shalit's similar endorsement of what he calls "public reflective equilibrium" for environmental ethics. See de-Shalit's *The Environment Between Theory and Practice* (Oxford: Oxford University Press, 2000).

9. Bryan Norton, "Convergence and Contextualism," *Environmental Ethics* 19, no.1 (1997). See p. 87.

10. Bryan Norton, "Convergence and Contextualism," *Environmental Ethics* 19, no. 1 (1997). See p. 100.